The Strat-Tutor Courseware for Students

ACCOMPANYING THIS TEXTBOOK is a Windows-based software package consisting of (1) 11 chapter self-tests and 2 practice hour exams you can complete and have computer-graded to gauge your understanding of the text material, (2) study questions for each of the 36 cases, and (3) case preparation exercises for 15 of the cases that walk you through the needed analysis, tutor you in appropriate use of the concepts and tools, and provide number-crunching assistance. The 15 cases for which there are case preparation exercises are indicated by an asterisk in the Table of Contents (and also wherever the Strat-Tutor logo appears on the first page of a case).

Strat-Tutor can be used on any PC equipped with Windows 95/98 or Windows NT and loaded with Microsoft Word; however, Microsoft Excel is required (in addition to Microsoft Word) for portions of those case exercises involving number-crunching. You'll have all you need if the PC you use has Office 97 or 2000 (either the Professional Edition or the Small Business Edition).

- **Obtaining Access to Strat-Tutor.** The software can be downloaded free from the Web site for the textbook (www.mhhe.com/thompson) provided you first obtain the required user-name and password from your instructor.
- **Using the Software.** The needed instructions for downloading the files and getting started are on the Web site. The remaining instructions are either provided directly on the screen as needed or else are readily evident (assuming you are familiar with Windows and Microsoft Word). To get the most benefit from Strat-Tutor, you should do the chapter self-tests promptly after reading each chapter to measure how well you really understand the material (without a solid grasp of the concepts and tools of strategic analysis, you will struggle when it comes time to tackle the assigned cases). The practice exams can be taken as part of your preparation for the tests on the chapter material given by your instructor. You should use the study questions as a guide of what to think about and what to analyze in preparing the assigned cases. You'll find the case preparation exercises valuable in learning how to "think strategically" about a company's situation, applying the tools and concepts covered in the 11 chapters, and arriving at sound recommendations about what actions management should take to improve the company's performance.

STRATEGIC MANAGEMENT
Concepts and Cases

balanced scorecard is not mentioned

Arthur A. Thompson, Jr.
A. J. Strickland III

Both of the University of Alabama

Eleventh Edition

Boston   Burr Ridge, IL   Dubuque, IA   Madison, WI   New York   San Francisco   St. Louis
Bangkok   Bogotá   Carácas   Lisbon   London   Madrid
Mexico City   Milan   New Delhi   Seoul   Singapore   Sydney   Taipei   Toronto

To Hasseline and Kitty

Irwin/McGraw-Hill

*A Division of The **McGraw-Hill** Companies*

STRATEGIC MANAGEMENT: CONCEPTS AND CASES

1 2 3 4 5 6 7 8 9 0 DOW/DOW 9 3 2 1 0 9

ISBN 0-07-303714-1

Vice president/Editor-in-chief: *Michael W. Junior*
Publisher: *Craig S. Beytien*
Senior sponsoring editor: *John E. Biernat*
Senior developmental editor: *Laura Hurst Spell*
Marketing manager: *Ellen Cleary*
Senior project manager: *Mary Conzachi*
Production supervisor: *Scott M. Hamilton*
Designer: *Michael Warrell*
Senior photo research coordinator: *Keri Johnson*
Supplement coordinator: *Becky Szura*
Compositor: *GAC Shepard Poorman Communications*
Typeface: *10.5/12 Times Roman*
Printer: *R. R. Donnelley & Sons Company*

Library of Congress Cataloging-in-Publication Data

Thompson, Arthur A. (date)
   Strategic management : concepts and cases / Arthur A. Thompson, Jr.,
A. J. Strickland, III.
     p. cm.
   ISBN 0-07-303714-1
   Available with this edition is the software product Strat-Tutor, a
computer-assisted, interactive study guide, accessible free at the publisher's
web site for the book: http://www.mhhe.com/thompson. Strat-Tutor consists
of a series of self-tests and study questions/case preparation guides for the
36 cases discussed. Computers equipped with Windows 3.1x, Windows 95/98,
or Windows NT required.
   Other materials available: an upgraded version of the software, The
Business Strategy Game; a companion volume, Readings in strategic
management; an instructor's package including test bank, transparencies, etc.
   Includes index.
   1. Strategic planning. 2. Strategic planning—Case studies. I. Strickland,
A. J. (Alonzo J.) II. Title.
HD30.28.T53   1999
658.4'012—dc21   98-50674

http://www.mhhe.com

PREFACE

This 11th edition, coming on the heels of the milestone 10th edition published last year, represents a continuing response to the market's unrelenting appetite for freshly researched cases of top-notch quality. While the pace of new developments in the literature of strategic management doesn't warrant an ultrashort *text* revision cycle, keeping users supplied with a stream of the latest and best cases satisfies a legitimate and growing market need. With so many business schools offering the strategic management course every term, the case collection in any one edition wears out after a few terms—we've all experienced the speed with which case files sprout and circulate. Moreover, fast-changing industry and company circumstances can prematurely render an otherwise good case obsolete. Growing interest among adopters for fresh cases, together with an expanding supply of first-rate cases being written annually, has again prompted us to institute a short *case* revision cycle and provide a second collection of 36 cases to choose from. Only the classic two-page Robin Hood case in carried over from the 10th edition; the remaining 35 cases are all different from those in the 10th edition. Aside from the new cases, however, the content of the 11th edition matches that of the 10th edition; the 11 chapters of text material remain untouched except for minor editing.

If you are a user of the 10th edition, shifting to the 11th edition merits consideration (1) as soon as you deem it's time to incorporate a new case collection in your course offering or (2) if you are intrigued with the pedagogical possibilities of having your students utilize the Strat-TUTOR chapter self-tests and case preparation exercises, which they can now access free at the publisher's Web site for the text (www.mhhe.com/thompson). If you haven't been an adopter of the 10th edition, we suggest first exploring this 11th edition and looking into the value that full-scale use of the Strat-TUTOR courseware can add to students' understanding of the concepts and tools of analysis. There's also a newly published upgraded edition of *The Business Strategy Game* (version 6.0) for use with either the 10th or 11th edition.

THE CASE COLLECTION IN THE 11TH EDITION

The 36 cases in this edition include 29 new cases not appearing in any of our previous editions, 5 thoroughly updated and revised cases appearing in the 9th edition, one carryover case from the 9th edition, and one carryover case from the 10th edition. To highlight the close linkage between the cases and strategic management concepts, we have grouped the cases under five chapter-related and topical headings. In the Section A grouping are four cases spotlighting the role and tasks of the manager as chief strategy-maker and chief strategy-implementer; these cases—Starbucks Corporation,

"Chainsaw Al" Dunlap and Sunbeam Corporation, Caribbean Internet Café, and KUVO Radio—provide convincing demonstration of why the discussions in Chapters 1 and 2 are relevant to a company's long-term market success. Section B contains 15 cases whose central issues deal with analyzing industry and competitive situations and crafting business-level strategy; these cases call upon students to apply the text material in Chapters 3 through 6. In Section C are four cases involving strategy assessments and strategy-making in diversified companies that make nice follow-ons to the coverage of Chapters 7 and 8. There are 10 cases in Section D, all revolving around the managerial challenges of implementing strategy and giving students an opportunity to apply the concepts presented in Chapters 9, 10, and 11. Section E contains three cases highlighting the links between strategy, ethics, and social responsibility.

The case lineup in this 11th edition, as in prior editions, reflects our steadfast preference for cases that feature interesting products and companies and that are capable of sparking both student interest and lively classroom discussions. At least 24 of the cases involve high-profile companies, products, or people that students will have heard of, know about from personal experience, or can easily identify with. The Dell Computer Corporation, Acer in Canada, Brøderbund Software Inc., and Competition in the Electronic Brokerage Industry cases will provide students with insight into the special demands of competing in "high velocity" industry environments where technological advances are an everyday event, product life cycles are short, and competitive maneuvering among rivals comes fast and furious. At least 19 of the cases involve situations where company resources and competitive capabilities play as much a role in the strategy-making, strategy-implementing scheme of things as industry and competitive conditions. Indeed, we made a special effort to ensure that the cases selected for this edition demonstrated the relevance of the resource-based view of the firm.

Scattered throughout the lineup are 10 cases concerning non-U.S. companies, globally competitive industries, and/or cross-cultural situations; these cases, in conjunction with the globalized content of the text chapters, provide ample material for linking the study of strategic management tightly to the ongoing globalization of the world economy—in proper keeping with AACSB standards. You'll also find three cases on nonprofit organizations, three cases where the central figures are women (plus one where the central issue is reverse sex discrimination), 10 cases dealing with the strategic problems of family-owned or relatively small entrepreneurial businesses, and 19 cases involving public companies about which students can do further research in the library or on the Internet. Six of the cases (Starbucks Corporation, "Chainsaw Al" Dunlap and Sunbeam Corporation, Competition in the Video Game Industry, Outback Steakhouse Goes International, Herb Kelleher and Southwest Airlines, and Stew Leonard's Dairy) have videotape segments that either are available from the publisher or can be ordered from other sources.

The case researchers whose work appears in this edition have done an absolutely first-class job of preparing cases that contain valuable teaching points, that illustrate the important kinds of strategic challenges managers face, and that allow students to apply the tools of strategic analysis. We believe you will find the 11th edition's collection of 36 cases exceptionally appealing, eminently teachable, and very suitable for drilling students in the use of the concepts and analytical treatments in Chapters 1 through 11. It is an unusually attractive and stimulating case lineup from beginning to end.

Company Web Site Addresses and Use of the Internet   Following Chapter 11 and prior to Case 1, we have once again included "A Guide to Case Analysis," which gives students positive direction in what case method pedagogy is all about and offers suggestions for approaching case analysis. The guide incorporates a section on how to use the Internet and various on-line services to (1) do further research on an industry or company, (2) obtain a company's latest financial results, and (3) get updates on what has happened since the case was written. The amount of information available on the Internet is exploding at a rapid-fire pace. We think students will find our list of information-laden Web sites and the accompanying suggestions on how to use the various search engines a time-saving and valuable asset in running down the information they are interested in. And to further facilitate student use of the Internet, we have included company Web site addresses at appropriate locations in the cases themselves.

CONTENT FEATURES OF THE TEXT CHAPTERS

Tenth and eleventh editions are milestones in the evolution of a textbook. For potential adopters they signal effective pedagogy and sustained market acceptance, but for authors they impose a responsibility to reflect on how the presentation can be recast in ways that add disciplinary coherence and that move the subject matter to a new plateau of clarity and understanding. We've tried to live up to this responsibility, endeavoring to include in the 11 chapters of text a teaching/learning package that squarely targets what every student needs to know about crafting, implementing, and executing business strategies.

New concepts, analytical tools, and methods of managing continue to surface at rates that mandate important edition-to-edition changes in content and emphasis. One of the most important new developments in the strategy literature concerns advances in the conceptual underpinning and articulation of the resource-based view of the firm. While SWOT analysis and evaluation of core competencies have always pointed to the importance of careful internal strength–weakness assessment in crafting strategy, recent contributions to the literature make it clear that there's much more to the resource-based view of the firm than is implied in a simple weighing of company strengths, weaknesses, opportunities, and threats. We have made a concerted attempt *throughout* the 11 text chapters to drive home the strategy-making, strategy-implementing relevance of strengthening a company's resource complement and upgrading its competencies and competitive capabilities to match market realities and create competitive advantage. The 10th and 11th editions give balanced treatment to the thesis that a company's strategy must be matched *both* to its external market circumstances and to its resources and competitive capabilities. Hence, you'll find the resource-based view of the firm prominently integrated into the coverage of crafting business strategy (Chapters 2 and 4) and crafting diversification strategies (Chapters 7 and 8). You'll also find that Chapters 9 and 10 have a strong resource-based perspective as concerns the role of building and nurturing core competencies, competitive capabilities, and organizational resources in implementing and executing strategy.

In addition to the exceptionally thorough resource-based orientation, we've incorporated important new material on cooperative strategies, collaborative alliances, and competing in "high-velocity" market environments where the pace of change (from whatever source) places special demands on a company to adapt its strategy and its resource capabilities to rapidly unfolding events. Once again, there's front-to-back coverage of global issues in strategic management, prominent treatment of ethical and social responsibility issues, and margin notes in every chapter that highlight basic concepts, strategic management principles, and kernels of wisdom. Extensive rewriting to sharpen the presentations in every chapter has allowed us to include the new material and still cover everything in less than 350 pages—something that readers and adopters ought to welcome, given the jam-packed content of the course.

Specific Chapter Modifications and Content Improvements

While the overall chapter organization parallels prior editions, we've made a number of noteworthy adjustments in chapter content and topical emphasis:

- Chapters 1 and 2 contain fresh presentations on the importance of a clear, motivating strategic vision, stretch objectives, and rapid adaptation of strategy to newly unfolding market conditions and customer expectations. We continue to place strong emphasis on how and why a company's strategy emerges from (*a*) the deliberate and purposeful actions of management and (*b*) as-needed reactions to unanticipated developments and fresh competitive pressures. The material in Chapter 1 underscores even more strongly that a company's strategic plan is a collection of strategies devised by different managers at different levels in the organizational hierarchy and builds a case for why all managers are on a company's strategy-making, strategy-implementing team. The worldwide organizational shift to empowered employees and managers makes it imperative for company personnel to be "students of the business" and skilled users of the concepts and tools of strategic management.

- Chapter 4 now incorporates a full-blown discussion of all the concepts and analytical tools required to understand why a company's strategy must be well matched to its internal resources and competitive capabilities. The roles of core competencies and organizational resources and capabilities in creating customer value and helping build competitive advantage have been given *center stage* in the discussions of company resource strengths and weaknesses. SWOT analysis has been recast as a tool for assessing a company's resource strengths and resource weaknesses. There are new sections on determining the competitive value of specific company resources and assets and on selecting the competencies and capabilities having the biggest competitive advantage potential. The now standard tools of value-chain analysis, strategic cost analysis, benchmarking, and competitive strength assessments, however, continue to have a prominent role in the methodology of evaluating a company's situation—they are an essential part of understanding a company's relative cost position and competitive standing vis-à-vis rivals.

- Together, the material in Chapter 3 (Industry and Competitive Analysis) and Chapter 4 (Evaluating Company Resources and Competitive Capabilities) creates the understanding for why managers must carefully match company strategy both to industry and competitive conditions and to company resources and capabilities. The role of Chapter 3 is to set forth the now familiar analytical tools and concepts of industry and competitive analysis and demonstrate the importance of tailoring strategy to fit the circumstances of a company's industry and competitive environment. The role of Chapter 4 is to establish the equal importance of doing solid company situation analysis as a basis for matching strategy to organizational resources, competencies, and competitive capabilities.

- Chapter 5 contains a major new section on using cooperative strategies to build competitive advantage. Chapter 6 features a new section on competing in industry situations characterized by rapid-fire technological change, short product life-cycles, frequent moves by competitors, and/or rapidly evolving customer requirements and expectations. It also includes more extensive discussions of strategic alliances to enhance a company's competitiveness in both high-velocity and global markets.

- We continue to believe that global competition and global strategy issues are best dealt with by integrating the relevant discussions into each chapter rather than partitioning the treatment off in a separate chapter. The globalization of each chapter, a prominent feature of the two previous editions, is carried over and strengthened in this edition, plus we've added more illustration capsules to highlight the strategies of non-U.S. companies.

- We have recast our analytical treatment of corporate diversification strategies in Chapters 7 and 8, eliminating much of the attention formerly given to drawing business portfolio matrices and instead putting the analytical emphasis on (1) assessing industry attractiveness, (2) evaluating the company's competitive strength in each of its lines of business, (3) appraising the degree of strategic fits among a diversified company's different businesses, and (4) appraising the degree of *resource fit* among the different businesses. You'll find a very strong resource-based view of the firm in the recommended methodology for evaluating the pros and cons of a company's diversification strategy. Chapter 8 continues to incorporate analytical use of the industry attractiveness/business strength portfolio matrix because of its conceptual soundness and practical relevance, but we have abandoned coverage of the flawed growth-share matrix and the little-used life-cycle matrix.

- The three-chapter module (Chapters 9–11) on strategy implementation features a solid, compelling conceptual framework structured around (1) building the resource strengths and organizational capabilities needed to execute the strategy in competent fashion; (2) developing budgets to steer ample resources into those value-chain activities critical to strategic success; (3) establishing strategically appropriate policies and procedures; (4) instituting the best practices and mechanisms for continuous improvement; (5) installing information, communication, and operating systems that enable company personnel to carry out their strategic roles successfully day in and day out; (6) tying rewards and incentives tightly to the achievement of performance objectives and good strategy execution; (7) creating a strategy-supportive work environment and corporate culture; and (8) exerting the internal leadership needed to drive implementation forward and to keep improving on how the strategy is being executed.

- The eight-task framework for understanding the managerial components of strategy implementation and execution is explained in the first section of Chapter 9. The remainder of Chapter 9 focuses on building an organization with the competencies, capabilities, and resource strengths needed for successful strategy execution. You'll find welcome coverage of what it takes for an organization to build and enhance its competencies and capabilities, develop the dominating depth in competence-related activities needed for competitive advantage, and forge arrangements to achieve the necessary degree of collaboration and cooperation both among internal departments and with outside resource providers. There is much-expanded treatment of the task of building resource strengths through collaborative alliances and partnerships. We've continued the coverage initiated in the last two editions concerning the pros and cons of outsourcing noncritical activities, downsizing and delayering hierarchical structures, employee empowerment, reengineering core business processes, and the use of cross-functional and self-contained work teams. The result is a powerful treatment of building resource capabilities and structuring organizational activities that ties together and makes strategic sense out of all the revolutionary organizational changes sweeping through today's corporations. So far, the efforts of companies across the world to organize the work effort around teams, reengineer core business processes, compete on organizational capabilities (as much as on differentiated product attributes), and install leaner, flatter organization structures are proving to be durable, fundamental additions to the conventional wisdom about how to manage and valuable approaches for improving the caliber of strategy execution.

- As before, Chapter 10 surveys the role of strategy-supportive budgets, policies, reward structures, and internal support systems and explains why the benchmarking of best practices, total quality management, reengineering, and continuous improvement programs are important managerial tools for enhancing organizational competencies in executing strategy. Chapter 11 continues to deal with creating a strategy-supportive corporate culture and exercising the internal leadership needed to drive implementation forward. There's coverage of strong versus weak cultures, low-performance and unhealthy cultures, adaptive cultures, and the sustained leadership commitment it takes to change a company with a problem culture, plus sections on ethics management and what managers can do to improve the caliber of strategy execution.
- There are 17 new or revised Illustration Capsules.

The use of margin notes to highlight basic concepts, major conclusions, and "core" truths was well received in earlier editions and remains a visible feature of this edition. The margin notes serve to distill the subject matter into concise principles, bring the discussion into sharper focus for readers, and point them to what is important.

Diligent attention has been paid to putting life into the explanations and to improving clarity and writing style. We've tried to take dead aim on creating a text presentation that is crisply written, clear and convincing, interesting to read, comfortably mainstream, and as close to the frontiers of theory and practice as a basic textbook should be.

The Strat-Tutor Software Supplement for Students

Available with the 11th edition is a third generation software product called Strat-Tutor that is, in effect, a full-fledged, computer-assisted, interactive study guide for the whole text. Students can access the Strat-Tutor software free at the publisher's Web site for the book www.mhhe.com/thompson. It consists of two main sections:

- A series of self-tests that students can use to measure their comprehension, chapter by chapter, of the material presented in the text.
- Study questions for each of the 36 cases in the 11th edition, plus a set of custom-designed case preparation guides for 15 of the cases that lead students through the needed analysis, provide number-crunching assistance, and tutor students in use of the concepts and tools presented in the chapters.

The Self-Testing Feature   The test section of Strat-Tutor contains (1) a 25-question self-test for each text chapter, (2) a 50-question self-exam covering the material in Chapters 1–6, and (3) a 50-question self-exam covering the material in Chapters 7–11. The 11 chapter tests consist of an assortment of true–false, fill-in-the-blank, and challenging multiple-answer questions that cover the text presentation rather thoroughly. These tests were deliberately made demanding (given their "open-book" nature) so as to require careful reading and good comprehension of the material. When the student completes each test, Strat-TUTOR automatically grades the answers, provides a test score, points the test score in the student's personal "grade book," indicates the questions with wrong answers, and directs students to the text pages where the correct answers can be found. Questions incorrectly answered can be attempted as many times as needed to arrive at the right answer. In addition, we created conventional (single-answer) multiple-choice tests covering Chapters 1–6 (50 questions) that students can use to prepare for in-class exams given by the instructor.

Used properly and in conjunction with each other, we think these tests will provide students with a welcome and effective way to gauge their readiness for the course instructor's own examinations on the 11 chapters. *None of the questions on Strat-TUTOR correspond to those on the instructor's test bank.*

The Study Questions and Case Preparation Guides   We've all experienced poor and uneven student preparation of cases for class discussion. Sometimes it's because of inadequate effort, but more often it is because of confusion over exactly what analysis to do and/or inexperience in using the tools of strategic analysis to arrive at solid recommendations. To give students some direction in what to think about in preparing a case for class, Strat-TUTOR provides study questions for all 36 cases in the 11th edition. To help them learn how to use the concepts and analytical tools properly, there's an interactive guide (not a solution) for use in preparing 15 of the cases. Each study guide has been *tailored* to fit the specific issues/problems and analytical requirements posed by the case. We have scrupulously avoided creating one generic study guide because cases in strategic management cut across a broad range of issues and problems and entail diverse analytical requirements (strategy analysis in single-business situations is fundamentally different from strategy analysis of diversified companies; cases where the spotlight is on developing a strategy are fundamentally different from cases where the main issues revolve around strategy implementation and execution).

The Strat-TUTOR case preparation guides provide:

- *Study questions* to trigger the process of thinking strategically and to point students toward the analysis needed to arrive at sound recommendations.

- *A series of interactive screens that coach students in the use the whatever analytical tools are appropriate*—whether it be five-forces analysis, strategic group mapping, identification of key success factors, SWOT analysis, value-chain analysis, competitive strength assessments, construction of business portfolio matrixes, industry attractiveness assessments, strategic fit matchups, or internal organization analysis.

- *Follow-on questions* to prod students to think clearly about what conclusions flow from their analysis.

- *Calculations* of financial ratios, compound average growth rates, common-size income statements and balance sheets, and any other statistics useful in evaluating industry data, company financial statements, and company operating performance.

- *What-iffing capability* that allows students to readily develop projections of company financial performance (when such projections are germane to the case).

- *Reminders* of strategy principles and generic strategic options to help students arrive at a set of pragmatic action recommendations.

- *Printouts* of the work done (to serve as notes students can use in the class discussion).

The interactive design of the case preparation guides keeps the ball squarely in the student's court to do the analysis, to decide what story the numbers tell about a company's situation and performance, and to think through the options to arrive at recommendations. Strat-TUTOR is thus not a crutch or "answer file" for the cases; rather, *it is a vehicle for using the PC to tutor students in strategic thinking and helping them learn to correctly apply the tools and concepts of strategic management.* We've endeavored to design the case preparation guides to coach students in how to think strategically about business problems/issues, to drill them in the methods of strategic analysis, and to promote sound business judgment. You can be assured that the case notes students develop with the aid of Strat-TUTOR will represent their work, not ours.

To decide whether Strat-TUTOR makes sense as a requirement or recommended option in your course, we suggest going to the Web site for the text (www.mhhe.com/ thompson), reviewing one or two of the chapter tests and case preparation guides, and perusing their contents to get a feel for the caliber of the software and its fit with your instructional approach. Strat-TUTOR utilizes a Windows format (familiar to most students) and is very user-friendly; the software must be used on computers equipped with Windows 3.1x, Windows 95/98, or Windows NT.

The Business Strategy Game Option

There's an upgraded version of *The Business Strategy Game* to accompany this 11th edition. The new sixth-edition is the product of valuable feedback and suggestions from users, some new ideas on our part, and reworked programming—and represents an ongoing effort to continuously improve the simulation. This latest version incorporates a revised executive compensation option, the use of Eurodollars instead of German marks, modest enhancements in the Player's Manual, and an assortment of programming refinements that makes it a welcome improvement over the version introduced in 1998.

What Sets This Simulation Apart   *The Business Strategy Game* has five features that make it an uncommonly effective teaching–learning aid for strategic management courses: (1) *the product and the industry*—producing and marketing athletic footwear is a business that students can readily identify with and understand; (2) *the global industry environment*—students gain up-close exposure to what global competition is like and the kinds of strategic issues that managers in global industries have to address; (3) *the realistic quality of the simulation exercise*—we've designed the simulation to be as faithful as possible to real-world markets, competitive conditions, and revenue-cost-profit relationships; (4) *the wide degree of strategic freedom students have in managing their companies*—we've gone to great lengths to make the game free of bias as concerns one strategy versus another; and (5) *the five-year planning and decision-making capability it incorporates as an integral part of the exercise of running a company.* These features, wrapped together as a package, provide an exciting and valuable bridge between concept and practice, the classroom and real-life management, and reading conventional wisdom about management and learning-by-doing. You'll find opportunity after opportunity to use examples and happenings in *The Business Strategy Game* to connect to your lectures on the text chapters.

The Value a Simulation Adds   Our own experiences with simulation games, along with hours of discussions with users, have convinced us that simulation games are the *sin-*

gle best exercise available for helping students understand how the functional pieces of a business fit together and giving them an integrated, capstone experience. First and foremost, the exercise of running a simulated company over a number of decision periods helps develop students' business judgment. Simulation games provide a live case situation where events unfold and circumstances change as the game progresses. Their special hook is an ability to get students personally involved in the subject matter. *The Business Strategy Game* is very typical in this respect. In plotting their competitive strategies each decision period, students learn about risk-taking. They have to respond to changing market conditions, react to the moves of competitors, and choose among alternative courses of action. They get valuable practice in reading the signs of industry change, spotting market opportunities, evaluating threats to their company's competitive position, weighting the trade-offs between profits now and profits later, and assessing the long-term consequences of short-term decisions. They chart a long-term direction, set strategic and financial objectives, and try out different strategies in pursuit of competitive advantage. They become active strategic thinkers, planners, analysts, and decision-makers. And by having to live with the decisions they make, they experience what it means to be accountable for decisions and responsible for achieving satisfactory results. All this serves to drill students in responsible decision-making and improve their business acumen and managerial judgment.

Second, students learn an enormous amount from working with the numbers, exploring options, and trying to unite production, marketing, finance, and human resource decisions into a coherent strategy. They begin to see ways to apply knowledge from prior courses and figure out what really makes a business tick. The effect is to help students integrate a lot of material, look at decisions from the standpoint of the company as a whole, and see the importance of thinking strategically about a company's competitive position and future prospects. Since a simulation game is, by its very nature, a hands-on exercise, the lessons learned are forcefully planted in students' minds—the impact is far more lasting than what is remembered from lectures. Third, students' entrepreneurial instincts blossom as they get caught up in the competitive spirit of the game. The resulting entertainment value helps maintain an unusually high level of student motivation and emotional involvement in the course throughout the term.

About the Simulation   We designed *The Business Strategy Game* around athletic footwear because producing and marketing athletic footwear is a business students can readily understand and because the athletic footwear market displays the characteristics of many globally competitive industries—fast growth followed by market maturity, worldwide use of the product, competition among companies from several continents, production located in low-wage locations, and a marketplace where a variety of competitive approaches and business strategies can coexist. The simulation allows companies to manufacture and sell their brands in North America, Europe, and Asia; plus there's the option to compete for supplying private-label footwear to North American chain retailers. Competition is head-to-head—each team of students must match their strategic wits against the other company teams. Companies can focus their branded marketing efforts on one geographic market or two or all three or they can deemphasize branded sales and specialize in private-label production (an attractive strategy for low-cost producers). They can establish a one-country production base or they can manufacture in all three of the geographic markets. Low-cost leadership, differentiation strategies, best-cost producer strategies, and focus strategies are all visible competitive options. Companies can position their products in the low end of the market, the high end, or stick close to the middle on price, quality, and service; they can have a wide or narrow product line, small or big dealer networks, extensive or limited advertising. Company market shares are based on how each company's competitive effort stacks up against the efforts of rivals. Demand conditions, tariffs, and wage rates vary from geographic area to geographic area. Raw materials used in footwear production are purchased in a worldwide commodity market at prices that move up or down in response to supply–demand conditions. If a company's sales volume is unexpectedly low, management has the option to liquidate excess inventories at deep discount prices.

The company that students manage has plants to operate, a workforce to compensate, distribution expenses and inventories to control, capital expenditure decisions to make, marketing and sales campaigns to wage, sales forecasts to consider, and ups and downs in exchange rates, interest rates, and the stock market to take into account. Students must weave functional decisions in production, distribution, marketing, finance, and human resources into a cohesive action plan. They have to react to changing market and competitive conditions, initiate moves to try to build competitive advantage, and decide how to defend against aggressive actions by competitors. And they must endeavor to maximize shareholder wealth via increased dividend payments and stock price appreciation. Each team of students is challenged to use their entrepreneurial and strategic skills to become the next Nike or Reebok and ride the wave of growth to the top of the worldwide athletic footwear industry. The whole exercise is representative of a real-world competitive market where companies try to outcompete and outperform rivals—things are every bit as realistic and true to actual business practice as we could make them.

There are built-in planning and analysis features that allow students to (1) craft a five-year strategic plan, (2) gauge the long-range financial impact of current decisions, (3) do the number-crunching to make informed short-run versus long-run trade-offs, (4) assess the revenue-cost-profit consequences to alternative strategic actions, and (5) build different strategy scenarios. Calculations at the bottom of each decision screen provide instantly updated projections of sales revenues, profits, return on equity, cash flow, and other key outcomes as each decision entry is made. The sensitivity of financial and operating outcomes to different decision entries is easily observed on the screen and on detailed printouts of projections. With the speed of today's personal computers, the relevant number-crunching is done in a split second. The game is designed throughout to lead students toward making decisions based on "My analysis shows . . ." and away from the quicksand of making decisions based on "I think," "It sounds good," "Maybe, it will work out," and other such seat-of-the pants approaches.

The Business Strategy Game is programmed to work on any PC capable of running Windows 3.1x, Windows 95/98, or Windows NT, and it is suitable for both senior-level and MBA courses. The game accommodates a wide variety of computer setups (as concerns microprocessors, monitors, and printers) and runs quite nicely on a network.

Features of the New Version   This latest version is evolutionary, not revolutionary—the changes are minor compared to transformations undertaken in prior editions. We've shifted from the use of German marks to Eurodollars to reflect the monetary changes under way throughout much of Europe, and we've substantially improved the stock bonus element of the executive compensation option. In addition, we've instituted an assortment of behind-the-scenes programming changes to eliminate various bugs and quirks. As you would expect, we have retained the array of new features and improvements introduced in the two previous versions: the demand forecasting feature, the inventory liquidation option, the celebrity endorsements feature, the optional executive compensation feature, the extensive on-screen decision support calculations and what-iffing capability, the much-improved five-year strategic plan format, and the added scoring flexibility.

As before, instructors have numerous ways to heighten competition and keep things lively as the game progresses. There are options to raise or lower interest rates, alter certain costs up or down, and issue special news flashes announcing new tariff levels, materials cost changes, shipping difficulties, or other new considerations to stir the pot a bit and keep business conditions dynamic. And the built-in scoreboard of company performance keeps students constantly informed about where the company stands and how well they are doing. Rapid advances in PC technology continue to cut processing times—it should take no more than 45 minutes for you or a student assistant to process the results on an older PC and well under 30 minutes on a PC with a Pentium 166 or faster chip.

A separate Instructor's Manual for *The Business Strategy Game* describes how to integrate the simulation exercise into your course, provides pointers on how to administer the game, and contains step-by-step processing instructions. Should you encounter technical difficulties or have questions, the New Media department at Irwin/McGraw-Hill can provide quick assistance via a toll-free number (1-800-331-5094). There's also a special publisher's Web site for the game at www.mhhe.com/bsg where you can obtain the latest information and software upgrades (after obtaining a user name and password at 1-800-331-5094).

The Readings Book Option

For instructors who want to incorporate samples of the strategic management literature into the course, a companion *Readings in Strategic Management* containing 43 selections is available. Thirty-four of the 43 readings are new to this latest edition. All 43 selections are quite readable and are suitable for seniors and MBA students. Most of the selections are articles reprinted from leading journals; they add in-depth treatment to important topic areas covered in the text and put readers at the cutting edge of academic thinking and research on the subject. Some of the articles are drawn from practitioner sources and stress how particular tools and concepts relate directly to actual companies and managerial practices.

To make the close linkage between the selected readings and the 11 chapters of text material readily apparent to students, we have grouped the readings into five categories. Six articles examine the role of the manager as chief strategist and chief strategy-implementer and expand on the topics covered in Chapters 1 and 2. Eleven articles concern strategic analysis and strategy formation at the business-unit level and add more range and depth to the material presented in Chapters 3 through 6. There are five articles dealing with strategy in diversified companies that are very appropriate for use with Chapters 7 and 8. Seventeen of the readings relate to various aspects of strategy implementation and execution, making them suitable complements for the material in Chapters 9, 10, and 11. Four of the articles focus on strategy, values, and ethics.

In tandem, the readings package provides an effective, efficient vehicle for reinforcing and expanding the text–case approach. It is an exceptionally solid lineup of recently published articles.

The 11th Edition Instructor's Package

A full complement of instructional aids is available to assist adopters in using the 11th edition successfully. The two-volume *Instructor's Manual* contains suggestions for using the text materials, various approaches to course design and course organization, a sample syllabus, alternative course outlines, a thoroughly revised and expanded set of 940 multiple-choice and essay questions, and a comprehensive teaching note for each case. There is a computerized test bank for generating examinations, a set of color transparencies depicting the figures and tables in the 11 text chapters, and PowerPoint presentation software containing a full set of color visuals for classrooms equipped with computer screen projection capability. The PowerPoint disks can also be used to make black-and-white overheads in the event you utilize an overhead projector to support your lectures. The PowerPoint package includes over 500 visuals that thoroughly cover the material presented in the 11 chapters, thus providing plenty to select from in creating support for your classroom lectures (we deliberately created enough visuals for each chapter to give you an ample number of choices in putting together a presentation that fits both your preferences and time constraints). To help instructors enrich and vary the pace of class discussions of cases, there are video supplements for use with the Starbucks Corporation, "Chainsaw Al" Dunlap and Sunbeam Corporation, Competition in the Video Game Industry, Outback Steakhouse Goes International, Herb Kelleher and Southwest Airlines, and Stew Leonard's Dairy cases.

In concert, the textbook, the three companion supplements, and the comprehensive instructor's package provide a complete, integrated lineup of teaching materials. The package gives you exceptional latitude in course design, allows you to capitalize on the latest computer-assisted instructional techniques, arms you with an assortment of visual aids, and offers rich pedagogical options for keeping the nature of student assignments varied and interesting. We've endeavored to equip you with all the text materials and complementary resources you need to create and deliver a course that is very much in keeping with contemporary strategic management issues and that wins enthusiastic student approval.

Acknowledgments

We have benefited from the help of many people during the evolution of this book. Students, adopters, and reviewers have generously supplied an untold number of insightful comments and helpful suggestions. Our intellectual debt to those academics, writers, and practicing managers who have blazed new trails in the strategy field will be obvious to any reader familiar with the literature of strategic management.

We are particularly indebted to the case researchers whose casewriting efforts appear herein and to the companies whose cooperation made the cases possible. To each one goes a very special thank-you. The importance of timely, carefully researched cases cannot be overestimated in contributing to a substantive study of strategic management issues and practices. From a research standpoint, cases in strategic management are invaluable in exposing the generic kinds of strategic issues that companies face, in forming hypotheses about strategic behavior, and in drawing experienced-based generalizations about the practice of strategic management. Pedagogically, cases about strategic management give students essential practice in diagnosing and evaluating strategic situations, in learning to use the tools and concepts of strategy analysis, in sorting through various strategic options, in crafting strategic action plans, and in figuring out successful ways to implement and execute the chosen strategy. Without a continuing stream of fresh, well-researched, and well-conceived cases, the discipline of strategic management would quickly fall into disrepair, losing much of its energy and excitement. There's no question, therefore, that first-class case research constitutes a valuable scholarly contribution.

The following focus-group panelists provided insightful suggestions and advice regarding ways to make the 11th edition better:

Steve Barndt, Pacific Lutheran University
J. Michael Geringer, California Polytechnic University
Mingfang Li, California State University-Northridge
Richard W. Stackman, University of Washington-Tacoma
Stephen Tallman, Cranfield School of Management
Gerardo R. Ungson, University of Oregon

We are also indebted to David Aviel, Maria A. Corso, David Flynn, J. Le Jankovich, Eveann Lovero, Vince Luchsinger, James Boulgarides, Betty Die Daniel F. Jennings, Daivd Kuhn, Kathryn Martell, Wilbur Mouton, Bobby Vau Tuck Bounds, Lee Burk, Ralph Catalanello, William Crittenden, Stan Mendenh John Moore, Will Mulvaney, Sandra Richard, Ralph Roberts, Thomas Turk, Gor VonStroh, Fred Zimmerman, S. A. Billion, Charles Byles, Gerald L. Geisler, R Knotts, Joseph Rosenstein, James B. Thurman, Ivan Able, W. Harvey Hegarty, Ro Evered, Charles B. Saunders, Rhae M. Swisher, Claude I. Shell, R. Thomas Le Michael C. White, Dennis Callahan, R. Duane Ireland, William E. Burr II, C. Millard, Richard Mann, Kurt Christensen, Neil W. Jacobs, Louis W. Fry, D. Robl Wood, George J. Gore, and William R. Soukup. These reviewers were of considerab help in directing our efforts at various stages in the evolution of the text.

Naturally, as custom properly dictates, we are responsible for any errors of fact, d ficiencies in coverage or presentation, and oversights that remain. As always, we valu your recommendations and thoughts about the book. Your comments regarding cove age and contents will be most welcome, as will your calling our attention to specifi errors. Please fax us at (205) 348-6695, e-mail us at athompso@cba.ua.edu, or write u at P.O. Box 870225, Department of Management and Marketing, The University of Al abama, Tuscaloosa, Alabama 35487-0225.

Arthur A. Thompso
A. J. Stricklan

Steve Barndt, Pacific Lutheran University

J. Michael Geringer, California Polytechnic University

Mingfang Li, California State University-Northridge

Richard W. Stackman, University of Washington-Tacoma

Stephen Tallman, Cranfield School of Management

Gerardo R. Ungson, University of Oregon

We are also indebted to David Aviel, Maria A. Corso, David Flynn, J. Leslie Jankovich, Eveann Lovero, Vince Luchsinger, James Boulgarides, Betty Diener, Daniel F. Jennings, Daivd Kuhn, Kathryn Martell, Wilbur Mouton, Bobby Vaught, Tuck Bounds, Lee Burk, Ralph Catalanello, William Crittenden, Stan Mendenhall, John Moore, Will Mulvaney, Sandra Richard, Ralph Roberts, Thomas Turk, Gordon VonStroh, Fred Zimmerman, S. A. Billion, Charles Byles, Gerald L. Geisler, Rose Knotts, Joseph Rosenstein, James B. Thurman, Ivan Able, W. Harvey Hegarty, Roger Evered, Charles B. Saunders, Rhae M. Swisher, Claude I. Shell, R. Thomas Lenz, Michael C. White, Dennis Callahan, R. Duane Ireland, William E. Burr II, C. W. Millard, Richard Mann, Kurt Christensen, Neil W. Jacobs, Louis W. Fry, D. Robley Wood, George J. Gore, and William R. Soukup. These reviewers were of considerable help in directing our efforts at various stages in the evolution of the text.

Naturally, as custom properly dictates, we are responsible for any errors of fact, deficiencies in coverage or presentation, and oversights that remain. As always, we value your recommendations and thoughts about the book. Your comments regarding coverage and contents will be most welcome, as will your calling our attention to specific errors. Please fax us at (205) 348-6695, e-mail us at athompso@cba.ua.edu, or write us at P.O. Box 870225, Department of Management and Marketing, The University of Alabama, Tuscaloosa, Alabama 35487-0225.

Arthur A. Thompson
A. J. Strickland

long-term direction, develops competitively effective strategic moves and business approaches, and implements what needs to be done internally to produce good day-in/day-out strategy execution. Indeed, *good strategy and good strategy execution are the most trustworthy signs of good management.* Managers don't deserve a gold star for designing a potentially brilliant strategy, but failing to put the organizational means in place to carry it out in high-caliber fashion—weak implementation and execution—undermines the strategy's potential and paves the way for shortfalls in customer satisfaction and company performance. Competent execution of a mediocre strategy scarcely merits enthusiastic applause for management's efforts either. To truly qualify as excellently managed, a company must exhibit excellent execution of an excellent strategy. Otherwise, any claim of talented management is suspect.

> *Competent execution of a well-conceived strategy is not only a proven recipe for organizational success, but also the best test of managerial excellence.*

Granted, good strategy combined with good strategy execution doesn't *guarantee* that a company will avoid periods of so-so or even subpar performance. Sometimes it takes several years for management's strategy-making/strategy-implementing efforts to show good results. Sometimes blue-chip organizations with showcase practices and reputable managers have performance problems because of surprisingly abrupt shifts in market conditions or internal miscues. But neither the "we need more time" reason nor the bad luck of unforeseeable events excuses mediocre performance year after year. It is the responsibility of a company's management team to adjust to unexpectedly tough conditions by undertaking strategic defenses and business approaches that can overcome adversity. Indeed, the essence of good strategy making is to build a market position strong enough and an organization capable enough to produce successful performance despite unforeseeable events, potent competition, and internal difficulties. The rationale for using the twin standards of good strategy making and good strategy execution to determine whether a company is well managed is therefore compelling: The better conceived a company's strategy and the more competently it is executed, the more likely the company will be a solid performer and a competitive success in the marketplace.

THE FIVE TASKS OF STRATEGIC MANAGEMENT

The strategy-making, strategy-implementing process consists of five interrelated managerial tasks:

1. *Forming a strategic vision of what the company's future business makeup will be and where the organization is headed*—so as to provide long-term direction, delineate what kind of enterprise the company is trying to become, and infuse the organization with a sense of purposeful action.
2. *Setting objectives*—converting the strategic vision into specific performance outcomes for the company to achieve.
3. *Crafting a strategy to achieve the desired outcomes.*
4. *Implementing and executing the chosen strategy efficiently and effectively.*
5. *Evaluating performance and initiating corrective adjustments in vision, long-term direction, objectives, strategy, or implementation in light of actual experience, changing conditions, new ideas, and new opportunities.*

Figure 1.1 displays this process. Together, these five components define what we mean by the term *strategic management.* Let's examine this five-task framework in enough detail to set the stage for all that follows in the forthcoming chapters.

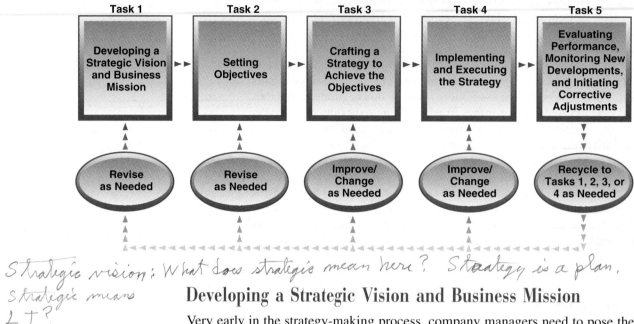

[Handwritten notes in left margin: Strategic vision: What does strategic mean here? Strategy is a plan. Strategic means LT? 1–3. 4a. IV Pearce apparently = current (4 LT) desired kind of org. as on p. 5 T.]

Developing a Strategic Vision and Business Mission

Very early in the strategy-making process, company managers need to pose the issue of "What is our vision for the company—where should the company be headed, what kind of enterprise are we trying to build, what should the company's future business makeup be?" Drawing a carefully reasoned conclusion about what the company's long-term direction should be pushes managers to take a hard look at the company's present business and form a clearer sense of whether and how it needs to change over the next 5 to 10 years. Management's views about "where we plan to go from here—what businesses we want to be in, what customer needs we want to satisfy, what capabilities we're going to develop" charts a course for the organization to pursue and creates organizational purpose and identity.

What a company is currently seeking to do for its customers is often termed the company's *mission*. A mission statement is useful for putting the spotlight on what business a company is presently in and the customer needs it is presently endeavoring to serve. But just clearly setting forth what a company is doing today doesn't speak to the company's future or incorporate a sense of needed change and long-term direction. There is an even greater managerial imperative to consider what the company will have to do to meet its customers' needs tomorrow and whether and how the company's business makeup will have to evolve for the company to grow and prosper. Thus, managers are obligated to look beyond the present business mission and think strategically about the impact of new technologies on the horizon, changing customer needs and expectations, the emergence of new market and competitive conditions, and so on. They have to make some fundamental choices about where they want to take the company and form a vision of the kind of enterprise they believe the company needs to become. In other words, management's concept of the *present* company mission has to be supplemented with a concept of the company's *future* business makeup, product line, and customer base. The faster a company's business environment is changing, the more that coasting along with the status quo is an invitation to disaster and the greater the managerial imperative to consider what the enterprise's future strategic path should be in light of changing conditions and emerging market opportunities.

Management's view of the kind of company it is trying to create and the kind of business position it wants to stake out in the years to come constitutes a *strategic vision* for the company. In the event a company's mission statement not only sets forth a clear definition of the present business but also indicates where the company is headed and what its business will become in the years ahead, then the concepts of company mission (or mission statement) and strategic vision merge into one and the same—in other words, a strategic vision and a future-oriented business mission amount to essentially the same thing. In practice, actual company mission statements tend to exhibit more concern with "what our business is now" than with "what our business will be later," so the conceptual distinction between company mission and strategic vision is relevant. Forming a strategic vision of a company's future is a prerequisite to effective strategic leadership. A manager cannot succeed as an organization leader or a strategy maker without first having drawn some soundly reasoned conclusions about where the enterprise needs to head, the changes in business makeup that are called for, and the organizational capabilities it will take to meet future customer needs and compete successfully. With a clear, well-conceived strategic vision, a manager has a beacon to truly guide managerial decision making, a course for the organization to follow, and a basis for shaping the organization's strategy and operating policies.

A strategic vision is a roadmap of a company's future—the direction it is headed, the business position it intends to stake out, and the capabilities it plans to develop.

Some examples of company mission and vision statements are presented in Illustration Capsule 1.

Setting Objectives

The purpose of setting objectives is to convert managerial statements of strategic vision and business mission into specific performance targets, something the organization's progress can be measured by. Successful managers set company performance targets that require stretch and disciplined effort. The challenge of trying to achieve bold, aggressive performance targets pushes an organization to be more inventive, to exhibit some urgency in improving both its financial performance and its business position, and to be more intentional and focused in its actions. Setting objectives that require real organizational stretch helps build a firewall against complacent coasting and low-grade improvements in organizational performance. As Mitchell Leibovitz, CEO of Pep Boys–Manny, Moe, and Jack, puts it, "If you want to have ho-hum results, have ho-hum objectives."

Objective setting is required of *all* managers. Every unit in a company needs concrete, measurable performance targets that contribute meaningfully toward achieving company objectives. When companywide objectives are broken down into specific targets for each organizational unit and lower-level managers are held accountable for achieving them, a results-oriented climate builds throughout the enterprise. There's little if any internal confusion over what to accomplish. The ideal situation is a team effort where each organizational unit strives to produce results in its area of responsibility that contribute to the achievement of the company's performance targets and strategic vision.

Objectives are yardsticks for tracking an organization's performance and progress.

From a companywide perspective, two very distinct types of performance yardsticks are required: those relating to *financial performance* and those relating to

ILLUSTRATION CAPSULE 1   Examples Of Company Mission and Vision Statements

McDonald's Corporation

McDonald's vision is to dominate the global foodservice industry. Global dominance means setting the performance standard for customer satisfaction while increasing market share and profitability through our Convenience, Value, and Execution Strategies.

Otis Elevator

Our mission is to provide any customer a means of moving people and things up, down, and sideways over short distances with higher reliability than any similar enterprise in the world.

Microsoft Corporation

One vision drives everything we do: A computer on every desk and in every home using great software as an empowering tool.

Avis Rent-a-Car

Our business is renting cars. Our mission is total customer satisfaction.

The Body Shop

We aim to achieve commercial success by meeting our customers' needs through the provision of high quality, good value products with exceptional service and relevant information which enables customers to make informed and responsible choices.

American Red Cross

The mission of the American Red Cross is to improve the quality of human life; to enhance self-reliance and concern for others; and to help people avoid, prepare for, and cope with emergencies.

Eastman Kodak

To be the world's best in chemical and electronic imaging.

Ritz-Carlton Hotels

The Ritz-Carlton Hotel is a place where the genuine care and comfort of our guests is our highest mission.

We pledge to provide the finest personal service and facilities for our guests who will always enjoy a warm, relaxed yet refined ambience.

The Ritz-Carlton experience enlivens the senses, instills well-being, and fulfills even the unexpressed wishes and needs of our guests.

Intel

Intel supplies the computing industry with chips, boards, systems, and software. Intel's products are used as "building blocks" to create advanced computing systems for PC users. Intel's mission is to be the preeminent building block supplier to the new computing industry worldwide.

Compaq Computer

To be the leading supplier of PCs and PC servers in all customer segments.

Long John Silver's

To be America's best quick service restaurant chain. We will provide each guest great tasting, healthful, reasonably priced fish, seafood, and chicken in a fast, friendly manner on every visit.

Bristol-Myers Squibb

The mission of Bristol-Myers Squibb is to extend and enhance human life by providing the highest quality health and personal care products. We intend to be the preeminent global diversified health and personal care company.

strategic performance. Achieving acceptable financial results is crucial. Without adequate profitability, a company's pursuit of its vision, as well as its long-term health and ultimate survival, is jeopardized. Neither shareowners nor lenders will continue to sink additional monies into an enterprise that can't deliver satisfactory financial results. Even so, the achievement of satisfactory financial performance, by itself, is not enough. Attention also has to be paid to a company's strategic well-being—its competitiveness and overall long-term business position. Unless a company's performance reflects improving competitive strength and a stronger long-term market position, its progress is less than inspiring and its ability to continue delivering good financial performance is suspect.

The need for both good financial performance and good strategic performance calls for management to set financial objectives and strategic objectives. *Financial objectives* signal commitment to such outcomes as earnings growth, an acceptable return on investment (or economic value added—EVA), dividend growth, stock price appreciation (or market value added—MVA), good cash flow, and creditworthiness.[1] *Strategic objectives*, in contrast, direct efforts toward such outcomes as winning additional market share, overtaking key competitors on product quality or customer service or product innovation, achieving lower overall costs than rivals, boosting the company's reputation with customers, winning a stronger foothold in international markets, exercising technological leadership, gaining a sustainable competitive advantage, and capturing attractive growth opportunities. Strategic objectives serve notice that management not only intends to deliver good financial performance but also intends to improve the organization's competitive strength and long-range business prospects.

Both financial and strategic objectives ought to be time-based—that is, involve both near-term and longer-term performance targets. Short-range objectives focus organizational attention on the need for immediate performance improvements and outcomes. Long-range objectives serve the valuable purpose of prompting managers to consider what to do *now* to put the company in position to perform well over the longer term. As a rule, when trade-offs have to be made between achieving long-run objectives and achieving short-run objectives, long-run objectives should take precedence. Rarely does a company prosper from repeated management actions that put better short-term performance ahead of better long-run performance.

Examples of the kinds of strategic and financial objectives companies set are shown in Illustration Capsule 2.

Crafting a Strategy

A company's strategy represents management's answers to such gut business issues as whether to concentrate on a single business or build a diversified group of businesses, whether to cater to a broad range of customers or focus on a particular market niche, whether to develop a wide or narrow product line, whether to pursue a competitive advantage based on low cost or product superiority or unique organiza-

---

[1]Economic value added (EVA) is profit over and above the company's cost of debt and equity capital. More specifically, it is defined as operating profit less income taxes less the cost of debt less an allowance for the cost of equity capital. For example, if a company has operating profits of $200 million, pays taxes of $75 million, pays interest expenses of $25 million, has shareholders' equity of $400 million with an estimated equity cost of 15 percent (which translates into an equity cost of capital of $60 million), then the company's EVA is $200 million minus $75 million minus $25 million minus $60 million, or $40 million. The EVA of $40 million can be interpreted to mean that the company's management has generated profits well in excess of the benchmark 15 percent equity cost needed to justify or support the shareholder investment of $400 million—all of which represents wealth created for the owners above what they could expect from making investment of comparable risk elsewhere. Such companies as Coca-Cola, AT&T, and Briggs & Stratton use EVA as a measure of their profit performance.

Market value added (MVA) is defined as the amount by which the total value of the company has appreciated above the dollar amount actually invested in the company by shareholders. MVA is equal to a company's current stock price times the number of shares outstanding less shareholders' equity investment; it represents the value that management has added to shareholders' wealth in running the business. For example, if a company's stock price is $50, there are 1,000,000 shares outstanding, and shareholders' equity investment is $40 million, then MVA is $10 million ($50 million in market value of existing shares minus $40 million in equity investment); in other words, management has taken the shareholders' investment of $40 million in the company and leveraged it into a current company value of $50 million, creating an additional $10 million in shareholder value. If shareholder value is to be maximized, management must select a strategy and long-term direction that maximizes the market value of the company's common stock. In recent years, MVA and EVA have gained widespread acceptance as valid measures of a company's financial performance.

ILLUSTRATION CAPSULE 2   Strategic And Financial Objectives Of Well-Known Corporations

Banc One Corporation
To be one of the top three banking companies in terms of market share in all significant markets we serve.

Domino's Pizza
To safely deliver a hot, quality pizza in 30 minutes or less at a fair price and a reasonable profit.

Ford Motor Company
To satisfy our customers by providing quality cars and trucks, developing new products, reducing the time it takes to bring new vehicles to market, improving the efficiency of all our plants and processes, and building on our teamwork with employees, unions, dealers, and suppliers.

Exxon
To provide shareholders a secure investment with a superior return.

Alcan Aluminum
To be the lowest-cost producer of aluminum and to outperform the average return on equity of the Standard and Poor's industrial stock index.

General Electric
To become the most competitive enterprise in the world by being number one or number two in market share in every business the company is in. To achieve an average of 10 inventory turns and a corporate operating profit margin of 16% by 1998.

Bristol-Myers Squibb
To focus globally on those businesses in health and personal care where we can be number one or number two through delivering superior value to the customer.

Atlas Corporation
To become a low-cost, medium-size gold producer, producing in excess of 125,000 ounces of gold a year and building gold reserves of 1,500,000 ounces.

3M
To achieve annual growth in earnings per share of 10% or better, on average; a return on stockholders' equity of 20-25%; a return on capital employed of 27% or better; and have at least 30% of sales come from products introduced in the past four years.

> *An organization's strategy consists of the actions and business approaches management employs to achieve the targeted organizational performance.*

tional capabilities, how to respond to changing buyer preferences, how big a geographic market to try to cover, how to react to new market and competitive conditions, and how to grow the enterprise over the long-term. A strategy thus reflects managerial choices among alternatives and signals organizational commitment to particular products, markets, competitive approaches, and ways of operating the enterprise.

Crafting a winning strategy needs to be a top-priority managerial task in every organization. To begin with, there is a compelling need for managers to be proactive in shaping *how* the company's business will be conducted. It is management's responsibility to exert strategic leadership and commit the enterprise to going about its business in one fashion rather than another. Without a strategy, managers have no prescription for doing business, no roadmap to competitive advantage, no game plan for pleasing customers or achieving objectives. Such a lack is a surefire ticket for organizational drift, competitive mediocrity, and lackluster performance. Moreover, there is an equally compelling need to mold the business decisions and competitive actions taken across various parts of the company into a coordinated, compatible *pattern*. A company's activities necessarily involve the efforts and decisions of many divisions, departments, managers, and employees. All the actions and initiatives being taken in such areas as production, marketing, customer service, human resources, information systems, R&D, and finance need to be mutually supportive if a *companywide* game plan that makes good business sense is to emerge. Absent a company strategy, managers have no framework for weaving many different decisions into a cohesive whole and no overarching business rationale that unites departmental operations into a team effort.

FIGURE 1.2   A Company's Actual Strategy Is Partly Planned and Partly Reactive to Changing Circumstances

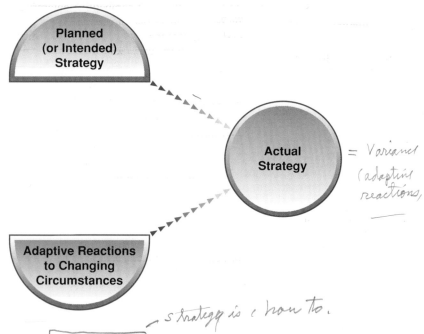

= Variance (adaptive reactions)

— strategy is (how to.

Strategy making brings into play the critical managerial issue of *how* to achieve the targeted results in light of the organization's situation and prospects. Objectives are the "ends," and strategy is the "means" of achieving them. The hows of a company's strategy are typically a blend of (1) deliberate and purposeful actions and (2) as-needed reactions to unanticipated developments and fresh competitive pressures.[2] As illustrated in Figure 1.2, strategy is more than what managers have carefully plotted out in advance and *intend* to do as part of some grand strategic plan. New circumstances always emerge, whether important technological developments, rivals' successful new product introductions, newly enacted government regulations and policies, widening consumer interest in different kinds of performance features, or whatever. Future business conditions are sufficiently uncertain that managers cannot plan every strategic action in advance and pursue a preplanned or *intended strategy* without any need for alteration. Company strategies end up, therefore, being a composite of planned actions and business approaches (intended strategy) and as-needed reactions to unforeseen conditions ("unplanned" or "adaptive" strategy responses). Consequently, *strategy is best looked upon as being a combination of planned actions and on-the-spot adaptive reactions to freshly developing industry and competitive events.* The strategy-making task involves developing a game plan, or intended strategy, and then adapting it as events unfold. A company's actual strategy is something managers must shape and reshape as events transpire outside and inside the company. It is normal, therefore, for a company's actual strategy to differ from management's

Strategy is both proactive (intended) and reactive (adaptive).

[2]Henry Mintzberg and J. A. Waters, "Of Strategies, Deliberate and Emergent," *Strategic Management Journal*, 6 (1985), pp.257–72.

planned strategy as new strategy features are added and others subtracted to react and adapt to changing conditions.

What Does a Company's Strategy Consist Of?

Company strategies concern *how:* how to grow the business, how to satisfy customers, how to outcompete rivals, how to respond to changing market conditions, how to manage each functional piece of the business and develop needed organizational capabilities, how to achieve strategic and financial objectives. The hows of strategy tend to be company-specific, customized to a company's own situation and performance objectives. In the business world, companies have a wide degree of strategic freedom. They can diversify broadly or narrowly, into related or unrelated industries, via acquisition, joint venture, strategic alliances, or internal start-up. Even when a company elects to concentrate on a single business, prevailing market conditions usually offer enough strategy-making latitude that close competitors can easily avoid carbon-copy strategies—some pursue low-cost leadership, others stress particular attributes of their product or service, and still others concentrate on developing unique capabilities to meet the special needs and preferences of narrow buyer segments. Some compete only locally or regionally, others compete nationally, and others compete globally. Hence, descriptions of the content of company strategy necessarily have to cut broadly across many aspects of the business to be complete.

Company strategies are partly visible and partly hidden to outside view.

Figure 1.3 depicts the kinds of actions and approaches that reflect a company's overall strategy. Because many are visible to outside observers, most of a company's strategy can be deduced from its actions and public pronouncements. Yet, there's an unrevealed portion of strategy outsiders can only speculate about—the actions and moves company managers are considering. Managers often, for good reason, choose not to reveal certain elements of their strategy until the time is right.

To get a better understanding of the content of company strategies, see the overview of McDonald's strategy in Illustration Capsule 3 on page 12.

Strategy and Entrepreneurship.   Crafting strategy is an exercise in entrepreneurship and *outside-in* strategic thinking. The challenge is for company managers to keep their strategies closely matched to such *outside drivers* as changing buyer preferences, the latest actions of rivals, new technological capabilities, the emergence of attractive market opportunities, and newly appearing business conditions. Company strategies can't end up being well matched to the company's present and future environment unless managers exhibit first-rate entrepreneurship in studying market trends, listening to customers, enhancing the company's competitiveness, and steering company activities in whatever new directions are dictated by market conditions and customer preferences. Good strategy making is therefore inseparable from good business entrepreneurship. One cannot exist without the other.

Strategy-making is fundamentally a market-driven and customer-driven entrepreneurial activity—venturesomeness, business creativity, an eye for spotting emerging market opportunities, keen observation of customer needs, and an appetite for risk-taking are inherent to the task of crafting company strategies.

A company encounters two dangers when its managers fail to exercise strategy-making entrepreneurship. One is a stale strategy. The faster a company's business environment is changing, the more critical it becomes for its managers to be good entrepreneurs in diagnosing shifting conditions and instituting whatever strategic adjustments are indicated. Coasting along with a status quo strategy tends to be riskier than making modifications. Managers with weak entrepreneurial skills are usually risk-averse and disinclined to embark on a different strategic course so long as they believe the present strategy can produce acceptable results for a while

FIGURE 1.3 Understanding a Company's Strategy—What to Look For

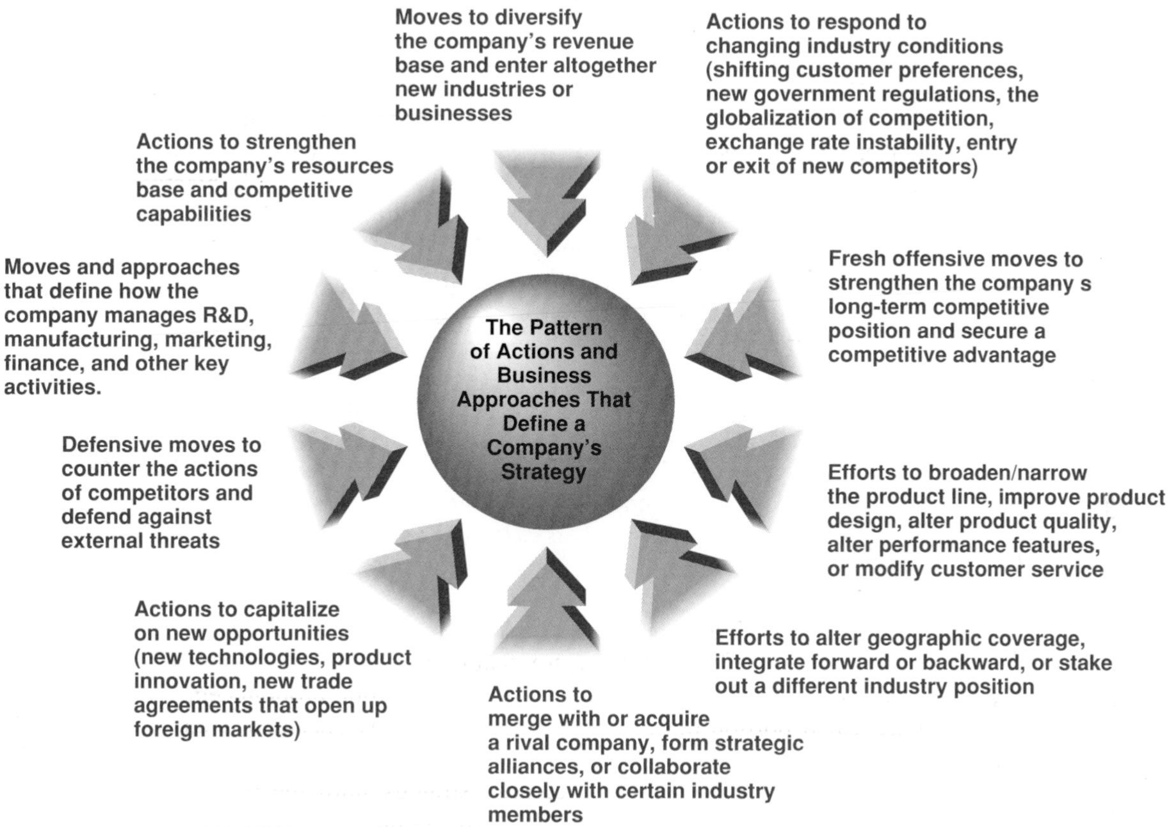

Moves to diversify
the company's revenue
base and enter altogether
new industries or
businesses

Actions to respond to
changing industry conditions
(shifting customer preferences,
new government regulations, the
globalization of competition,
exchange rate instability, entry
or exit of new competitors)

Actions to strengthen
the company's resources
base and competitive
capabilities

Moves and approaches
that define how the
company manages R&D,
manufacturing, marketing,
finance, and other key
activities.

**The Pattern
of Actions and
Business
Approaches That
Define a
Company's
Strategy**

Fresh offensive moves to
strengthen the company s
long-term competitive
position and secure a
competitive advantage

Defensive moves to
counter the actions
of competitors and
defend against
external threats

Efforts to broaden/narrow
the product line, improve product
design, alter product quality,
alter performance features,
or modify customer service

Actions to capitalize
on new opportunities
(new technologies, product
innovation, new trade
agreements that open up
foreign markets)

Actions to
merge with or acquire
a rival company, form strategic
alliances, or collaborate
closely with certain industry
members

Efforts to alter geographic coverage,
integrate forward or backward, or stake
out a different industry position

longer. They are prone to misread market trends and put too little weight on subtle shifts in customers' needs and behavior. Often, they either dismiss the signs of impending developments as unimportant ("we don't think it will really affect us") or else move so slowly in taking actions that the company is habitually late in responding to market change. There's pervasive resistance to bold strategic change, a wariness of deviating very far from the company's tried-and-true business approaches unless absolutely forced to. Strategies that grow increasingly out of touch with market and customer realities weaken a company's competitiveness and performance.

The second danger of failing to exercise strategy-making entrepreneurship is inside-out strategic thinking. Managers with deficient entrepreneurial skills or an entrepreneurially cautious nature usually focus most of their time and energy inwardly—on solving internal problems, improving organizational processes and procedures, and taking care of daily administrative chores. The strategic actions they do decide to initiate tend to be heavily dictated by inside considerations—what is philosophically comfortable, what is acceptable to various internal political coalitions, and what is safe, both organizationally and career-wise. Often, outside considerations end up being compromised to accommodate internal considerations, resulting in strategies that are as much a reflection of inwardly focused strategic thinking as of the need to respond to changing external market and customer conditions. Inside-out strategies, while not disconnected from external developments, nearly always fall short of being truly market-driven and customer-driven,

Good strategy making is more outside-in than inside-out.

ILLUSTRATION CAPSULE 3   A Strategy Example: McDonald's

In 1997 McDonald's was the leading food service retailer in the global consumer marketplace, with a strong brand name and systemwide restaurant sales approaching $35 billion. Two-thirds of its 22,000-plus restaurants were franchised to nearly 5,000 owner/operators around the world. Sales had grown an average of 6 percent in the United States and 20 percent outside the United States over the past 10 years. McDonald's food quality specifications, equipment technology, marketing and training programs, operating systems, site selection techniques, and supply systems were considered industry standards throughout the world. The company's strategic priorities were continued growth, providing exceptional customer care, remaining an efficient and quality producer, offering high value and good-tasting products, and effectively marketing McDonald's brand on a global scale. McDonald's strategy had eight core elements:

Growth Strategy

- Penetrate the market not currently served by adding 2,500 restaurants annually (an average of 8 per day), some company-owned and some franchised, with about two-thirds outside the United States. Establish a leading market position in foreign countries ahead of competitors.
- Promote more frequent customer visits via the addition of attractive menu items, low-price specials, Extra Value Meals, and children's play areas.

Franchising Strategy

- Grant franchises only to highly motivated, talented entrepreneurs with integrity and business experience and train them to become active, on-premise owners of McDonald's (no franchises were granted to corporations, partnerships, or passive investors).

Store Location and Construction Strategy

- Locate restaurants on sites offering convenience to customers and profitable growth potential. The company's research indicated that 70 percent of all decisions to eat at McDonald's were made on the spur of the moment, so its goal was to pick locations that were as convenient as possible for customers to visit. In the United States, the company supplemented its traditional suburban and urban locations with satellite outlets in food courts, airports, hospitals, universities, large shopping establishments (Wal-Mart, The Home Depot), and service stations; outside the United States, the strategy was to establish an initial presence in center cities, then open freestanding units with drive-thrus outside center cities.
- Reduce site costs and building costs by using standardized, cost-efficient store designs and by consolidating purchases of equipment and materials via a global sourcing system.
- Make sure restaurants are attractive and pleasing inside and out and, where feasible, provide drive-thru service and play areas for children.

Product Line Strategy

- Offer a limited menu.
- Improve the taste appeal of the items offered (especially sandwich selections).
- Expand product offerings into new categories of fast food (chicken, Mexican, pizza, adult-oriented sandwiches, and so on) and include more items for health-conscious customers.
- Do extensive testing to ensure consistent high quality and ample customer appeal before rolling out new menu items systemwide.

once again setting the stage for weakened competitiveness, impaired ability to exercise industry leadership, and underperformance.

How boldly managers embrace new strategic opportunities, how much they emphasize outinnovating the competition, and how often they champion actions to improve organizational performance are good barometers of their entrepreneurial spirit. Entrepreneurial strategy-makers are inclined to be first-movers, responding quickly and opportunistically to new developments. They are willing to take prudent risks and initiate trailblazing strategies. In contrast, reluctant entrepreneurs are risk-averse; they tend to be late-movers, hopeful about their chances of soon catching up and alert to how they can avoid whatever "mistakes" they believe first-movers have

Store Operations

- Enforce stringent standards regarding food quality, store and equipment cleanliness, restaurant operating procedures, and friendly, courteous counter service.
- Develop new equipment and production systems that improve the ability to serve hotter, better-tasting food, faster and with greater accuracy.

Sales Promotion, Marketing, and Merchandising

- Enhance the McDonald's image of quality, service, cleanliness, and value globally via heavy media advertising and in-store merchandise promotions funded with fees tied to a percent of sales revenues at each restaurant.
- Use Ronald McDonald to create greater brand awareness among children and the Mc prefix to reinforce the connection of menu items and McDonald's.
- Project an attitude of happiness and interest in children.

Human Resources and Training

- Offer wage rates that are equitable and nondiscriminatory in every location; teach job skills; reward both individual and team performance; create career opportunities; have flexible work hours for student employees.

- Hire restaurant crews with good work habits and courteous attitudes and train them to act in ways that will impress customers; promote promising employees quickly.
- Provide proper training on delivering customer satisfaction and running a fast-food business to franchisees, restaurant managers, and assistant managers. (Instructors at Hamburger University campuses in Illinois, Germany, England, Australia, and Japan annually train over 5,000 students in 22 languages.)

Social Responsibility and Community Citizenship

- Take an active community role—support local charities and community projects; help create a neighborhood spirit; promote educational excellence.
- Sponsor Ronald McDonald Houses (at year-end 1995, there were 168 houses in 12 countries providing a home-away-from-home for families of seriously ill children receiving treatment at nearby hospitals).
- Promote workforce diversity, voluntary affirmative action, and minority-owned franchises (over 25% of McDonald's franchisees were females and minorities).
- Adopt and encourage environmentally friendly practices.
- Provide nutritional information on McDonald's products to customers.

Source: Company annual reports.

made. They prefer incremental strategic change over bold and sweeping strategic moves.

In strategy-making, all managers, not just senior executives, must take prudent risks and exercise entrepreneurship. Entrepreneurship is involved when a district customer service manager, as part of a company's commitment to better customer service, crafts a strategy to speed the response time on service calls by 25 percent and commits $15,000 to equip all service trucks with mobile telephones. Entrepreneurship is involved when a warehousing manager contributes to a company's strategic emphasis on total quality by figuring out how to reduce the error frequency on filling customer orders from one error every 100 orders to one error every 100,000. A sales manager exercises strategic entrepreneurship by deciding to run a special promotion and cut sales prices by 5 percent to wrest market share away from rivals. A manufacturing manager exercises strategic entrepreneurship in deciding, as part of a companywide emphasis on greater cost competitiveness, to source an important component from a lower-priced South Korean supplier instead of making it in-house. Company strategies can't be truly market- and customer-driven unless the strategy-related activities of managers all across the company have an outside-in entrepreneurial character aimed at boosting customer satisfaction and achieving sustainable competitive advantage.

Why Company Strategies Evolve   Frequent fine-tuning and tweaking of a company's strategy, first in one department or functional area and then in another, are quite normal. On occasion, quantum changes in strategy are called for—when a competitor makes a dramatic move, when technological breakthroughs occur, or when crisis strikes and managers are forced to make radical strategy alterations very quickly. Because strategic moves and new action approaches are ongoing across the business, an organization's strategy forms over a period of time and then reforms as the number of changes begin to mount. Current strategy is typically a blend of holdover approaches, fresh actions and reactions, and potential moves in the planning stage. Except for crisis situations (where many strategic moves are often made quickly to produce a substantially new strategy almost overnight) and new company start-ups (where strategy exists mostly in the form of plans and intended actions), it is common for key elements of a company's strategy to emerge piece by piece as events transpire and the enterprise seeks to improve its position and performance.

A company's strategy is dynamic, forming in bits and pieces and then reforming as managers see avenues for improvement or a need to adapt business approaches to changing conditions.

Rarely is a company's strategy so well crafted and durable that it can go unaltered for long. Even the best-laid business plans must be adapted to shifting market conditions, altered customer needs and preferences, the strategic maneuvering of rival firms, the experience of what is working and what isn't, emerging opportunities and threats, unforeseen events, and fresh thinking about how to improve the strategy. This is why strategy-making is an ongoing process and why a manager must reevaluate strategy regularly, refining and recasting it as needed.

However, when managers decide to change strategy so fast and so fundamentally that their business game plan undergoes major overhaul every year, they are almost certainly guilty of poor entrepreneurship, faulty situation analysis, and inept "strategizing." Quantum changes in strategy may well be needed occasionally, especially in crisis situations or during unusually rapid periods of industry change, but they cannot be made on a regular basis without creating a zigzag market wake, generating undue confusion among customers and employees, and undermining performance. Well-crafted strategies normally have a life of at least several years, requiring only minor tweaking to keep them in tune with changing circumstances.

Strategy and Strategic Plans   Developing a strategic vision and mission, establishing objectives, and deciding on a strategy are basic direction-setting tasks. They map out where the organization is headed, its short-range and long-range performance targets, and the competitive moves and internal action approaches to be used in achieving the targeted results. Together, they constitute a *strategic plan*. In some companies, especially those committed to regular strategy reviews and the development of explicit strategic plans, a document describing the company's strategic plan is circulated to managers and employees (although parts of the plan may be omitted or expressed in general terms if they are too sensitive to reveal before they are actually undertaken). In other companies, the strategic plan is not put in writing for widespread distribution but rather exists in the form of oral understandings and commitments among managers about where to head, what to accomplish, and how to proceed.

Organizational objectives are the part of the strategic plan most often spelled out explicitly and communicated to managers and employees. Some companies spell out key elements of their strategic plans in the company's annual report to shareholders or in statements provided to the business media, while others deliberately refrain from candid public discussion of their strategies for reasons of competitive sensitivity.

However, strategic plans seldom anticipate all the strategically relevant events that will transpire in upcoming months and years. Unforeseen events, unexpected opportunities or threats, plus the constant bubbling up of new proposals encourage managers to modify planned actions and forge "unplanned" reactions. Postponing the recrafting of strategy until it's time to work on next year's strategic plan is both foolish and unnecessary. Managers who confine their strategizing to the company's regularly scheduled planning cycle (when they can't avoid turning something in) have a wrongheaded concept of what their strategy-making responsibilities are. Once-a-year strategizing under "have-to" conditions is not a prescription for managerial success.

Implementing and Executing the Strategy

The managerial task of implementing and executing the chosen strategy entails assessing what it will take to make the strategy work and to reach the targeted performance on schedule—the managerial skill here is being good at figuring out what must be done to put the strategy in place, execute it proficiently, and produce good results. Managing the process of implementing and executing strategy is primarily a hands-on, close-to-the-scene administrative task that includes the following principal aspects:

- Building an organization capable of carrying out the strategy successfully.
- Developing budgets that steer resources into those internal activities critical to strategic success.
- Establishing strategy-supportive policies and operating procedures.
- Motivating people in ways that induce them to pursue the target objectives energetically and, if need be, modifying their duties and job behavior to better fit the requirements of successful strategy execution.
- Tying the reward structure to the achievement of targeted results.
- Creating a company culture and work climate conducive to successful strategy implementation and execution.
- Installing information, communication, and operating systems that enable company personnel to carry out their strategic roles effectively day in and day out.
- Instituting best practices and programs for continuous improvement.
- Exerting the internal leadership needed to drive implementation forward and to keep improving on how the strategy is being executed.

The strategy implementer's aim must be to create strong "fits" between the way things are done internally to try to execute the strategy and what it will take for the strategy to succeed. The stronger the methods of implementation fit the strategy's requirements, the better the execution and the better the odds that performance targets will be achieved. The most important fits are between strategy and organizational capabilities, between strategy and the reward structure, between strategy and internal support systems, and between strategy and the organization's culture (the latter emerges from the values and beliefs shared by organizational members, the company's approach to people management, and ingrained behaviors, work practices, and ways of thinking). Fitting the ways the organization does things internally to what is needed for strategic success helps unite the organization behind the accomplishment of strategy.

The strategy-implementing task is easily the most complicated and time-consuming part of strategic management. It cuts across virtually all facets of managing and must be initiated from many points inside the organization. The strategy-implementer's agenda for action emerges from careful assessment of what the organization must do differently and better to carry out the strategic plan proficiently. Each manager has to think through the answer to "What has to be done in my area to carry out my piece of the strategic plan, and how can I best get it done?" How much internal change is needed to put the strategy into place depends on the degree of strategic change, how far internal practices and competencies deviate from what the strategy requires, and how well strategy and organizational culture already match. As needed changes and actions are identified, management must see that all the details of implementation are attended to and apply enough pressure on the organization to convert objectives into results. Depending on the amount of internal change involved, full implementation can take several months to several years.

Strategy implementation is fundamentally an action-oriented, make-it-happen activity— developing competencies and capabilities, budgeting, policy making, motivating, culture building, and leading are all part of the process.

Evaluating Performance, Monitoring New Developments, and Initiating Corrective Adjustments

It is always incumbent on management to evaluate the organization's performance and progress. It is management's duty to stay on top of the company's situation, deciding whether things are going well internally, and monitoring outside developments closely. Subpar performance or too little progress, as well as important new external circumstances, call for corrective actions and adjustments. Long-term direction may need to be altered, the business redefined, and management's vision of the organization's future course narrowed or broadened or radically revised. Performance targets may need raising or lowering in light of past experience and future prospects. Strategy may need to be modified because of shifts in long-term direction, because new objectives have been set, because some elements are not working well, or because of shifting market conditions and customer preferences.

A company's vision, objectives, strategy, and approach to implementation are never final; evaluating performance, monitoring changes in the surrounding environment, and making adjustments are normal and necessary parts of the strategic management process.

Likewise, one or more aspects of implementation and execution may not be going as well as intended. Budget revisions, policy changes, reorganization, personnel changes, revamped activities and work processes, culture-changing efforts, and revised compensation practices are typical managerial actions that may have to be taken to hasten implementation or improve strategy execution. *Proficient strategy execution is always the product of much organizational learning.* It is achieved unevenly—coming quickly in some areas and proving nettlesome in others. Progress reviews, ongoing searches for ways to continuously improve, and corrective adjustments are thus normal.

WHY STRATEGIC MANAGEMENT IS A PROCESS, NOT AN EVENT

The march of external and internal events guarantees that a company's vision, objectives, strategy, and implementation approaches will have to be revisited, reconsidered, and eventually revised. This is why the task of evaluating performance and initiating corrective adjustments is both the end and the beginning of the strategic management *cycle*. Evaluating and adjusting means that prior strategy-related decisions and actions are subject to modification as conditions in the surrounding environment change and ideas for improvement emerge. The choice of whether to continue or change the company's vision, objectives, strategy, and implementation approaches always presents itself. Strategic management is thus an ongoing, never-ending *process*, not a start-stop event that once done can be safely put aside for a while. Managers have everpresent responsibility for detecting when new developments require a strategic response and when they don't. It is their job to track progress, spot problems early, monitor the winds of market and customer change, and initiate adjustments.

Characteristics of the Process

Although forming a strategic vision, setting objectives, crafting a strategy, implementing and executing the strategic plan, and evaluating performance portray what strategic management involves, actually performing these five tasks is not so cleanly divided into separate, neatly sequenced compartments. There is much interplay and recycling among the five tasks, as shown in Figure 1.1. For example, considering what strategic actions to take raises issues about whether and how the strategy can be satisfactorily implemented. Deciding on a company mission and vision shades into setting objectives (both involve directional priorities). Objective setting entails considering current performance, the strategy options available to improve performance, and what the organization can really achieve when pushed and challenged. Deciding on a strategy is entangled with decisions about long-term direction and whether objectives have been set in all the key financial and strategic areas. Clearly, the direction-setting tasks of developing a mission, setting objectives, and crafting strategy need to be integrated and done as a package, not individually.

> *Strategic management is a process; the boundaries between the five tasks are conceptual, not fences that prevent some or all of them being done together.*

Second, the five strategic management tasks are not done in isolation from a manager's other duties and responsibilities—administering day-to-day operations, dealing with crises, going to meetings, reviewing information, handling people problems, and taking on special assignments and civic duties. Thus, while the job of managing strategy is the most important managerial function insofar as organizational success or failure is concerned, it isn't all managers must do or be concerned about.

Third, crafting and implementing strategy make erratic demands on a manager's time. Change does not happen in an orderly or predictable way. Events can build quickly or gradually; they can emerge singly or in rapid-fire succession; and their implications for strategic change can be easy or hard to diagnose. Hence the task of reviewing and adjusting the strategic game plan can take up big chunks of management time in some months and little time in other months. As a practical matter, there is as much skill in knowing *when* to institute strategic changes as there is in knowing what to do.

Last, the big day-in, day-out time-consuming aspect of strategic management involves trying to get the best strategy-supportive performance out of every individual and trying to perfect the current strategy by refining its content and execution. Managers usually spend most of their efforts improving bits and pieces of the current strategy rather than developing and instituting radical changes. Excessive changes in strategy can be disruptive to employees and confusing to customers, and they are usually unnecessary. Most of the time, there's more to be gained from improving execution of the present strategy. Persistence in making a sound strategy work better is often the key to managing the strategy to success.

WHO PERFORMS THE FIVE TASKS OF STRATEGIC MANAGEMENT?

An organization's chief executive officer, as captain of the ship, is the most visible and important strategy manager. The title of CEO carries with it the mantles of chief direction setter, chief objective setter, chief strategy maker, and chief strategy implementer for the total enterprise. Ultimate responsibility for *leading* the tasks of formulating and implementing a strategic plan for the whole organization rests with the CEO, even though other senior managers normally have significant *leadership* roles also. What the CEO views as strategically important usually is reflected in the company's strategy, and the CEO customarily puts a personal stamp of approval on big strategic decisions and actions.

Vice presidents for production, marketing, finance, human resources, and other key departments have important strategy-making and strategy-implementing responsibilities as well. Normally, the production VP has a lead role in developing the company's production strategy; the marketing VP oversees the marketing strategy effort; the financial VP is in charge of devising an appropriate financial strategy; and so on. Usually, senior managers below the CEO are also involved in proposing key elements of the overall company strategy and developing major new strategic initiatives, working closely with the CEO to hammer out a consensus and coordinate various aspects of the strategy more effectively. Only in the smallest, owner-managed companies is the strategy-making, strategy-implementing task small enough for a single manager to handle.

But managerial positions with strategy-making and strategy-implementing responsibility are by no means restricted to CEOs, vice presidents, and owner-entrepreneurs. Every major organizational unit in a company—business unit, division, staff plant, support group, or district office—normally has a leading or supporting role in the company's strategic game plan. And the manager in charge of that organizational unit, with guidance from superiors, usually ends up doing some or most of the strategy making for the unit and deciding how to implement whatever strategic choices are made. While managers farther down in the managerial hierarchy obviously have a narrower, more specific strategy-making/strategy-implementing role than managers closer to the top, *every manager is a strategy maker and strategy implementer for the area he/she supervises.*

Every company manager has a strategy-making, strategy-implementing role—it is flawed thinking to view strategic management as solely a senior executive responsibility.

One of the primary reasons why middle- and lower-echelon managers are part of the strategy-making/strategy-implementing team is that the more geographically scattered and diversified an organization's operations are, the more unwieldy it becomes for senior executives at the company's headquarters to craft and implement all the necessary actions and programs. Managers in the corporate office seldom know enough about the situation in every geographic area and operating unit to direct every move made in the field. It is common practice for top-level managers to grant some strategy-making responsibility to managerial subordinates who head the organizational subunits where specific strategic results must be achieved. Delegating a strategy-making role to on-the-scene managers charged with implementing whatever strategic moves are made in their areas fixes accountability for strategic success or failure. When the managers who implement the strategy are also its architects, it is hard for them to shift blame or make excuses if they don't achieve the target results. And, having participated in developing the strategy they are trying to implement and execute, they are likely to have strong buy-in and support for the strategy, an essential condition for effective strategy execution.

In diversified companies where the strategies of several different businesses have to be managed, there are usually four distinct levels of strategy managers:

- The chief executive officer and other senior corporate-level executives who have primary responsibility and personal authority for big strategic decisions affecting the total enterprise and the collection of individual businesses the enterprise has diversified into.

- Managers who have profit-and-loss responsibility for one specific business unit and who are delegated a major leadership role in formulating and implementing strategy for that unit.

- Functional area heads and department heads within a given business unit who have direct authority over a major piece of the business (manufacturing, marketing and sales, finance, R&D, personnel) and whose role it is to support the business unit's overall strategy with strategic actions in their own areas.

- Managers of major operating units (plants, sales districts, local offices) who have on-the-scene responsibility for developing the details of strategic efforts in their areas and for implementing and executing their piece of the overall strategic plan at the grassroots level.

Single-business enterprises need no more than three of these levels (a business-level strategy manager, functional-area strategy managers, and operating-level strategy managers). In a large single-business company, the team of strategy managers consists of the chief executive, who functions as chief strategist with final authority over both strategy and its implementation; the vice presidents and department heads in charge of key activities (R&D, production, marketing, finance, human resources, and so on); plus as many operating-unit managers of the various plants, sales offices, distribution centers, and staff support departments as it takes to handle the company's scope of operations. Proprietorships, partnerships, and owner-managed enterprises, however, typically have only one or two strategy managers since in small-scale enterprises the whole strategy-making/strategy-implementing function can be handled by just a few key people.

Managerial jobs involving strategy formulation and implementation abound in not-for-profit organizations as well. In federal and state government, heads of local, district, and regional offices function as strategy managers in their efforts to respond to the needs and situations of the areas they serve (a district manager in Portland may need a slightly different strategy than a district manager in Orlando). In municipal government, the heads of various departments (fire, police, water and sewer, parks and recreation, health, and so on) are strategy managers because they have line authority for the operations of their departments and thus can influence departmental objectives, the formation of a strategy to achieve these objectives, and how the strategy is implemented.

Managerial jobs with strategy-making/strategy-implementing roles are thus the norm rather than the exception.[3] The job of crafting and implementing strategy touches virtually every managerial job in one way or another, at one time or another. Strategic management is basic to the task of managing; it is not something just top-level managers deal with.

Is Strategy-Making an Individual Responsibility or a Group Task?

Many companies today are involving teams of managers and key employees in strategy-making exercises, partly because many strategic issues cut across traditional functional and departmental lines, partly to tap into the ideas and problem-solving skills of people with different backgrounds, expertise, and perspectives, and partly to give a greater number of people an ownership stake in the strategy that emerges and win their wholehearted commitment to implementation. Frequently, these teams include line and staff managers from different disciplines and departmental units, a few handpicked junior staffers known for their ability to think creatively, and near-retirement veterans noted for being keen observers, telling it like it is, and giving sage advice. And it is not uncommon for these teams to involve customers and suppliers in assessing the future market situation and deliberating the various strategy options. One of the biggest causes of flawed strategy is insufficient focus on what customers really need and want; another is not seeing the company as part of a wider environment and recognizing the value of reaching out and collaborating closely with key suppliers and customers (and maybe even select competitors) to gain competitive advantage.[4]

Electronic Data Systems recently conducted a yearlong strategy review involving 2,500 of its 55,000 employees that was coordinated by a core of 150 managers and staffers from all over the world.[5] J.M. Smucker, a maker of jams and jellies, formed a team of 140 employees (7 percent of its 2,000-person workforce) who spent 25 percent of their time over a six-month period to seek ways to rejuvenate the company's growth; the team, which solicited input from all employees, came up with 12 initiatives to double the company's revenues over the next five years. Nokia Group, a Finland-based telecommunications company, involved 250 employees in a recent strategy review of how different communications technologies were converging, how this would impact the company's business, and what strategic responses were needed.

Broad participation in a company's strategy-creating exercises is usually a strong plus.

Involving teams of people to dissect complex situations and find market-driven, customer-driven solutions is becoming increasingly necessary in many businesses. Not only are many strategic issues too big or too complex for a single manager to handle but they often are cross-functional and cross-departmental in nature, requiring the contributions of many disciplinary experts and the collaboration of managers from different parts of the organization to decide upon sound strategic actions. The notion that an organization's strategists are at the top and its doers are in the ranks below needs to be cast aside; very often, key pieces of strategy

---

[3]The strategy-making, strategy-implementing roles of middle managers are thoroughly discussed and documented in Steven W. Floyd and Bill Wooldridge, *The Strategic Middle Manager* (San Francisco: Jossey-Bass Publishers, 1996), Chapters 2 and 3.

[4]See James F. Moore, *The Death of Competition* (New York: HarperBusiness, 1996), Chapter 3.

[5]"Strategic Planning," *Business Week*, August 26, 1996, pp. 51–52.

originate in the middle and lower ranks of the organization, with senior managers endorsing what emerges from below and providing the resources necessary for implementation.

Is There a Role for Full-Time Strategic Planners?

If senior and middle managers have the lead roles in strategy making and strategy implementing in their areas of responsibility, supplemented by multidisciplinary strategy teams and broad employee participation in some circumstances, is there any need for full-time strategic planners or staffers with expertise in strategic analysis? The answer is perhaps in a few companies, but even then a planning staff's role and tasks should consist chiefly of helping to gather and organize information that strategy makers decide they need, providing administrative support to line managers in revising their strategic plans, and coordinating the process of higher-level executive review and approval of the strategic plans developed for all the various parts of the company. A strategic planning staff can help line managers and strategy teams crystallize the strategic issues that ought to be addressed; in addition, they can provide data, conduct studies of industry and competitive conditions as requested by the strategy makers, and develop assessments of the company's strategic performance. But strategic planners should not make strategic decisions, prepare strategic plans (for someone else to implement), or make strategic action recommendations that usurp the strategy-making responsibilities of line managers or self-directed work teams in charge of operating units or particular activities.

Sometimes
1 - 3

When strategic planners are asked to go beyond providing staff assistance and actually prepare a strategic plan for management's consideration, any of four adverse consequences may occur. One, weak managers will gladly turn tough strategic problems over to strategic planners to do their strategic thinking for them—a questionable outcome because it deludes managers into thinking they shouldn't be held responsible for crafting a strategy for their own organizational unit or for acting on strategic issues related to their areas of responsibility.

Two, planners, however expert they may be in strategic analysis and writing snappy reports, can't know as much about all the ins and outs of the situation as on-the-scene managers who are responsible for staying on top of things in their assigned area on a daily basis. This puts planning staffers at a severe disadvantage in devising sound action recommendations and taking into account the practical difficulties of implementing what they recommend.

Three, giving planners responsibility for strategy making and line managers responsibility for implementation makes it hard to fix accountability for poor results. Planners can place the blame for poor results on weak implementation; line managers can claim the problem rests with bad strategy.

Four, when line managers see no urgency in or have no ownership stake in the strategic agenda proposed by the planning staff, there's a big risk they will give it lip service, perhaps make a few token implementation efforts, and then let most of the planners' recommendations die through inaction. Handing the strategy-making function off to a strategic planning staff runs the risk that line managers and senior executives will not see the urgency or necessity of following through on what is proposed. Skepticism or disagreement over planners' recommendations breeds inaction. Absent strong concurrence with the actions recommended by planners, their work is likely to fall through the cracks—and strategic planning exercises come to be seen

Strategic Management Principle

Strategy making is a job for line managers, not a staff of planners—the doers should be the strategy makers.

as an unproductive bureaucratic activity. Such outcomes raise the chances that a company will drift along with no strong top-down strategic direction and with fragmented, uncoordinated strategic decisions. The hard truth is that strategy making is not a staff function.

All four consequences are unacceptable. Strategizing efforts get a bum rap as ineffective, line managers don't develop the skills or the discipline to think strategically about the business, and the company encounters much bigger risk of a strategy-making vacuum. On the other hand, when people are expected to be the chief strategy makers and strategy implementers for the areas they head, their own strategy and implementation efforts end up being put to the test. They quickly see the necessity of having a workable strategic plan (their annual performance reviews and perhaps even their future careers with the organization are at risk if their strategies prove unsound and they fail to achieve the target results!). When responsibility for crafting strategy is lodged with the same people charged with implementing strategy, there's no question who is accountable for results. Furthermore, pushing authority for crafting and implementing the strategy down to the people closest to the action puts decision making in the hands of those who *should* know best what to do. Broad participation gives more organizational members experience in thinking strategically about the business and in crafting and implementing strategies. People who consistently prove incapable of crafting and implementing good strategies and achieving target results have to be moved to less responsible positions.

The Strategic Role of the Board of Directors

Since lead responsibility for crafting and implementing strategy falls to key managers, the chief strategic role of an organization's board of directors is to exercise oversight and see that the five tasks of strategic management are done in a manner that benefits shareholders (in the case of investor-owned enterprises) or stakeholders (in the case of not-for-profit organizations). Recent increases in the number of stockholder lawsuits and the escalating costs of liability insurance for directors and officers have underscored that corporate board members do indeed bear ultimate responsibility for the strategic actions taken. Moreover, holders of large blocks of shares (mutual funds and pension funds), regulatory authorities, and the financial press are all calling for board members, especially outside directors, to be more active in their oversight of company strategy.

It is standard procedure for executives to brief board members on important strategic moves and to submit the company's strategic plans to the board for official approval. But directors rarely can or should play a direct, hands-on role in formulating or implementing strategy. Most outside directors lack industry-specific experience; their company-specific knowledge is limited (especially if they are relatively new board members). Boards of directors typically meet once a month (or less) for six to eight hours. Board members can scarcely be expected to have detailed command of all the strategic issues or know the ins and outs of the various strategic options. They can hardly be expected to come up with compelling strategy proposals of their own to debate against those put forward by management. Such a hands-on role is unnecessary for good oversight. The immediate task of directors is to be *supportive critics*, exercising their own independent judgment about whether proposals have been adequately analyzed and whether proposed strategic actions

Strategic Management Principle

A board of directors' role in the strategic management process is to critically appraise and ultimately approve strategic action plans but rarely, if ever, to develop the details.

appear to have greater promise than available alternatives.[6] If executive management is bringing well-supported strategy proposals to the board, there's little reason for board members to aggressively challenge and try to pick apart everything put before them—asking perceptive and incisive questions is usually sufficient to test whether the case for the proposals is compelling and to exercise vigilant oversight. However, if the company is experiencing gradual erosion of profits and market share, and certainly when there is a precipitous collapse in profitability, board members have a duty to be proactive, expressing their concerns about the validity of the strategy, initiating debate about the company's strategic path, having one-on-one discussions with key executives and other board members, and perhaps directly intervening as a group to alter both the strategy and the company's executive leadership.

The real hands-on role of directors is to evaluate the caliber of senior executives' strategy-making and strategy-implementing skills. The board is always responsible for determining whether the current CEO is doing a good job of strategic management (as a basis for awarding salary increases and bonuses and deciding on retention or removal). In recent years, at Apple Computer, General Motors, IBM, American Express, Kmart, W.R. Grace, and Compaq Computer, company directors concluded that top executives were not adapting their company's strategy fast enough and fully enough to the changes sweeping their markets. They pressured the CEOs to resign, and installed new leadership to provide the impetus for strategic renewal. Boards must also exercise due diligence in evaluating the strategic leadership skills of other senior executives in line to succeed the CEO. When the incumbent CEO retires, the board must elect a successor, either going with an insider (frequently nominated by the retiring CEO) or deciding that an outsider is needed to perhaps radically change the company's strategic course.

Hence, the strategic role of the board of directors is twofold: (1) to continuously audit the validity of a company's long-term direction and strategy, typically giving top executives free rein but always monitoring, offering constructive critiques, and standing ready to intervene if circumstances require, and (2) to evaluate the strategic leadership skills of the CEO and other insiders in line to succeed the incumbent CEO, proactively making personnel changes whenever the organization's performance is deemed not to be as good as it should be. Board oversight and vigilance is therefore very much in play in the strategy arena.

THE BENEFITS OF A "STRATEGIC APPROACH" TO MANAGING

The message of this book is that doing a good job of managing inherently requires good strategic thinking and good strategic management. Today's managers have to think strategically about their company's position and about the impact of changing conditions. They have to monitor the external situation closely enough to know when to institute strategy changes. They have to know the business well enough to know what kinds of strategic changes to initiate. Simply said, the fundamentals of strategic

---

[6]For a good discussion of the role of the board of directors in overseeing the strategy-making, strategy-implementing process, see Gordon Donaldson, "A New Tool for Boards: The Strategic Audit," *Harvard Business Review* 73, no.4 (July–August 1995), pp. 99–107.

management need to drive the whole approach to managing organizations. The chief executive officer of one successful company put it well when he said:

> In the main, our competitors are acquainted with the same fundamental concepts and techniques and approaches that we follow, and they are as free to pursue them as we are. More often than not, the difference between their level of success and ours lies in the relative thoroughness and self-discipline with which we and they develop and execute our strategies for the future.

The advantages of first-rate strategic thinking and conscious strategy management (as opposed to freewheeling improvisation, gut feel, and hoping for luck) include (1) providing better guidance to the entire organization on the crucial point of "what it is we are trying to do and to achieve"; (2) making managers more alert to the winds of change, new opportunities, and threatening developments; (3) providing managers with a rationale for evaluating competing budget requests for investment capital and new staff—a rationale that argues strongly for steering resources into strategy-supportive, results-producing areas; (4) helping to unify the numerous strategy-related decisions by managers across the organization; and (5) creating a more proactive management posture and counteracting tendencies for decisions to be reactive and defensive.

The advantage of being proactive is that trailblazing strategies can be the key to better long-term performance. Business history shows that high-performing enterprises often initiate and lead, not just react and defend. They launch strategic offensives to outinnovate and outmaneuver rivals and secure sustainable competitive advantage, then use their market edge to achieve superior financial performance. Aggressive pursuit of a creative, opportunistic strategy can propel a firm into a leadership position, paving the way for its products/services to become the industry standard. High-achieving enterprises are nearly always the product of astute, proactive management, rather than the result of lucky breaks or a long run of good fortune.

TERMS TO REMEMBER

In the chapters to come, we'll be referring to *mission, vision, objectives, strategy, strategic plan,* and other terms common to the language of strategy again and again. In practice, these terms generate a lot of confusion—managers, consultants, and academics often use them imprecisely and sometimes interchangeably. No single, common vocabulary exists. To cut down on the confusion and promote precise meaning, we're going to incorporate the following definitions throughout our presentation.

Strategic vision—a view of an organization's future direction and business makeup; a guiding concept for what the organization is trying to do and to become.

Organization mission—management's customized answer to the question "What is our business and what are we trying to accomplish on behalf of our customers?" A mission statement broadly outlines the organization's activities and present business makeup. Whereas the focus of a strategic vision is on a company's future, the focus of a company's mission *tends* to be on the present. (If the statement of mission speaks as much to the future path the organization intends to follow as to the present organizational purpose, then the mission statement incorporates the strategic vision and there's no *separate* managerial need for a vision.)

Financial objectives—the targets management has established for the organization's financial performance.

Strategic objectives—the targets management has established for strengthening the organization's overall business position and competitive vitality.

Long-range objectives—the results to be achieved either within the next three to five years or else on an ongoing basis year after year.

Short-range objectives—the organization's near-term performance targets; the amount of short-term improvement signals how fast management is trying to achieve the long-range objectives.

Strategy—the pattern of actions and business approaches managers employ to please customers, build an attractive market position, and achieve organizational objectives; a company's actual strategy is partly planned and partly reactive to changing circumstances.

Strategic plan—a statement outlining an organization's mission and future direction, near-term and long-term performance targets, and strategy.

Strategy formulation—the entire direction-setting management function of conceptualizing an organization's mission, setting performance objectives, and crafting a strategy. The end product of strategy formulation is a strategic plan.

Strategy implementation—the full range of managerial activities associated with putting the chosen strategy into place, supervising its pursuit, and achieving the targeted results.

On the following pages, we will probe the strategy-related tasks of managers and the methods of strategic analysis much more intensively. When you get to the end of the book, we think you will see that two factors separate the best-managed organizations from the rest: (1) superior strategy making and entrepreneurship, and (2) competent implementation and execution of the chosen strategy. There's no escaping the fact that the quality of managerial strategy making and strategy implementing has a significant impact on organization performance. A company that lacks clear-cut direction, has vague or undemanding objectives, has a muddled or flawed strategy, or can't seem to execute its strategy competently is a company whose performance is probably suffering, whose business is at long-term risk, and whose management is lacking. In short, the better conceived a company's strategy and the more proficient its execution, the greater the chances the company will be a leading performer in its markets and truly deserve a reputation for talented management.

SUGGESTED READINGS

Andrews, Kenneth R. *The Concept of Corporate Strategy*, 3rd ed. Homewood, Ill.: Richard D. Irwin, 1987, chap. 1.

Collins, James C., and Jerry I. Porras. "Building Your Company's Vision." *Harvard Business Review* 74, no.5 (September–October 1996), pp. 65–77.

Farkas, Charles M., and Suzy Wetlaufer. "The Ways Chief Executive Officers Lead," *Harvard Business Review* 74 no. 3 (May–June 1996), pp. 110–22.

Hamel, Gary. "Strategy as Revolution," *Harvard Business Review* 74 no. 4 (July–August 1996), pp. 69–82.

Lipton, Mark. "Demystifying the Development of an Organizational Vision." *Sloan Management Review* (Summer 1996), pp. 83–92.

Mintzberg, Henry. "Rethinking Strategic Planning: Pitfalls and Fallacies." *Long Range Planning* 27, no. 3 (1994), pp. 12–19.

————."Rethinking Strategic Planning: New Roles for Planners." *Long Range Planning* 27, no. 3 (1994), pp. 22–29.

————. "Crafting Strategy." *Harvard Business Review* 65, no. 4 (July–August 1987), pp. 66–75.

Porter, Michael E. "What Is Strategy?" *Harvard Business Review* 74, no. 6 (November–December 1996), pp. 61–78.

Yip, George S. *Total Global Strategy: Managing for Worldwide Competitive Advantage.* Englewood Cliffs, N.J.: Prentice-Hall, 1992, chap. 1.

THE THREE STRATEGY-MAKING TASKS

Lt Planning

Developing a Strategic Vision, Setting Objectives, and Crafting a Strategy

2

I n this chapter, we take a more in-depth look at the three strategy-making tasks: developing a strategic vision and business mission, setting performance objectives, and crafting a strategy to produce the desired results. We also examine the kinds of strategic decisions made at each management level, the major determinants of a company's strategy, and four frequently used managerial approaches to forming a strategic plan.

DEVELOPING A STRATEGIC VISION AND MISSION: THE FIRST DIRECTION-SETTING TASK——————

Early on, a company's senior management has to look to the future and address the issue of "where do we go from here— what customer needs and buyer segments do we need to be concentrating on, what should the company's business makeup be 5 to 10 years down the road?" Management's views and conclusions about the organization's future course, the customer focus it should have, the market position it should try to occupy, and the business activities to be pursued constitute a *strategic vision* for the company. A strategic vision indicates management's aspirations for the organization, providing a panoramic view of "what businesses we want to be in, where we are headed, and the kind of company we are trying to create." It spells out a direction and describes the destination.

The last thing IBM needs right now is a vision. (July 1993) What IBM needs most right now is a vision. (March 1996)

> **Louis V. Gerstner, Jr**
> *CEO, IBM Corporation*

How can you lead if you don't know where you are going?

> **George Newman**
> *The Conference Board*

Management's job is not to see the company as it is . . . but as it can become.

> **John W. Teets**
> *CEO, Greyhound Corporation*

A strategy is a commitment to undertake one set of actions rather than another.

> **Sharon M. Oster**
> *Professor, Yale University*

ILLUSTRATION CAPSULE 4   Delta Airlines' Strategic Vision

In late 1993, Ronald W. Allen, Delta's chief executive officer, described the company's vision and business mission in the following way:

> . . . we want Delta to be the **Worldwide Airline of Choice**.
>
> Worldwide, because we are and intend to remain an innovative, aggressive, ethical, and successful competitor that offers access to the world at the highest standards of customer service. We will continue to look for opportunities to extend our reach through new routes and creative global alliances.
>
> Airline, because we intend to stay in the business we know best—air transportation and related ser-

vices. We won't stray from our roots. We believe in the long-term prospects for profitable growth in the airline industry, and we will continue to focus time, attention, and investment on enhancing our place in that business environment.

> Of Choice, because we value the loyalty of our customers, employees, and investors. For passengers and shippers, we will continue to provide the best service and value. For our personnel, we will continue to offer an ever more challenging, rewarding, and result-oriented workplace that recognizes and appreciates their contributions. For our shareholders, we will earn a consistent, superior financial return.

Source: *Sky Magazine*, December 1993, p. 10.

Why Have a Mission or Strategic Vision?

A clear and entrepreneurially astute strategic vision is a prerequisite to effective strategic leadership. A manager cannot function effectively as either leader or strategy maker without a future-oriented concept of the business—what customer needs to work toward satisfying, what business activities to pursue, and what kind of long-term market position to build vis-à-vis competitors. Forming a strategic vision is thus not a wordsmithing exercise to create a catchy company slogan; rather, it is an exercise in thinking strategically about a company's future, forming a viable concept of the company's future business, and putting the company on a strategic path that management is deeply committed to. It is an exercise in coming up with a coherent and powerful picture of what the company's business can and should be 5 or 10 years hence. When management's strategic vision conveys something substantive about what business position it intends for the company to stake out and what course the company is going to follow, then the vision is truly capable of *guiding* managerial decision making, *shaping* the company's strategy, and *impacting* how the company is run. Such outcomes have *real managerial value*. Illustration Capsule 4 presents Delta Airlines' strategic vision.

Effective strategy making begins with a concept of what the organization should and should not do and a vision of where the organization needs to be headed.

Dream?

Strategic Visions Chart a Company's Future   The term *strategic vision* is inherently more future oriented than the oft-used terms *business purpose* or *mission statement*. The statements of mission or business purpose that most companies include in their annual reports tend to deal more with the present ("What is our business?") than with the organization's aspirations and long-term direction (where we are headed, what new things we intend to pursue, what we want our business makeup to be in 5 to 10 years, what kind of company we are trying to become, and what sort of long-term market position we aspire to achieve). However, a here-and-now-oriented purpose/mission statement highlighting the boundaries of the company's current business is a logical vantage point from which to look down the road, decide what the enterprise's future business makeup and customer focus need to be, and chart a strategic path for the company to take. As a rule, strategic visions should have a time horizon of a decade or more.

Strategic Visions Are Company-Specific, Not Generic   Strategic visions and company mission statements ought to be highly personalized—unique to the organization for which they were developed. There's nothing unusual about companies in the same industry pursuing significantly, even radically, different strategic paths. For example, the current mission and future direction of a globally active New York bank like Citicorp has little in common with that of a locally owned hometown bank even though both are in the banking industry. IBM, with its mainframe computer business, its line-up of personal computers, and its software and services business, is not on the same long-term strategic course as Compaq Computer (which concentrates on PCs and servers), even though both are leaders in the personal computer industry. *The whole idea behind developing a strategic vision/mission statement is to set an organization apart from others in its industry and give it its own special identity, business emphasis, and path for development.*

Generically worded statements, couched in everything-and-everybody language that could apply just as well to many companies and lines of business, are not managerially useful—they paint no mental picture of where the company is destined and offer no guidance to managers in deciding which business activities to pursue and not to pursue, what strategies make the best sense, or how to operate the company. Nor do they communicate useful information about a company's long-term direction and future business makeup to employees and investors. Ambiguous or vaguely worded mission/vision statements may have some public relations value, but they don't help managers manage. *The best vision statements are worded in a manner that clarifies the direction in which an organization needs to move.*

Visionless companies are unsure what business position they are trying to stake out.

The Mission or Vision Is Not to Make a Profit   Sometimes companies couch their business purpose or mission in terms of making a profit. This is misguided—profit is more correctly an *objective* and a *result* of what the company does. The desire to make a profit says nothing about the business arena in which profits are to be sought. Missions or visions based on making a profit are incapable of distinguishing one type of profit-seeking enterprise from another—the business and long-term direction of Sears are plainly different from the business and long-term direction of Toyota, even though both endeavor to earn a profit. A company that says its mission/business purpose/strategic vision is to make a profit begs the question "What will we do to make a profit?" To understand a company's business and future direction, we must know management's answer to "make a profit doing what and for whom?"

The Elements of a Strategic Vision   There are three distinct pieces to the task of forming a strategic vision of a company's business future:

- Defining what business the company is *presently* in.
- Deciding on a *long-term* strategic course for the company to pursue.
- Communicating the vision in ways that are clear, exciting, and inspiring.

Defining a Company's Present Business

Coming up with a strategically insightful definition of what business an organization is presently in is not as simple as it might seem. Is IBM in the computer business (a product-oriented definition) or the information and data-processing business (a customer service or customer needs type of definition) or the advanced electronics business (a technology-based definition)? Is America Online in the computer services business, the information business, the business of connecting people to the Internet, the on-line content business, or the entertainment business? Is AT&T in the long-distance business or the telephone business or the telecommunications business? Is Coca-Cola in the soft-drink business (in which case management's strategic attention can be concentrated on outselling and outcompeting Pepsi, 7UP, Dr Pepper, Canada Dry, and Schweppes) or is it in the beverage business (in which case management also needs to think strategically about positioning Coca-Cola products to compete against other fruit juices, ready-to-drink teas, bottled water, sports drinks, milk, and coffee)? Whether to take a soft-drink perspective or a beverage perspective is not a trivial question for Coca-Cola management—only partly because Coca-Cola is also the parent of Minute Maid and Hi-C juice products. With a beverage industry vision as opposed to a soft-drink focus, Coca-Cola management can better zero in on how to convince young adults to get their morning caffeine fix by drinking Coca-Cola instead of coffee.

A company's business is defined by what needs it is trying to satisfy, by which customer groups it is targeting, and by the technologies it will use and the functions it will perform in serving the target market.

Incorporating What, Who, and How Into the Business Definition   To arrive at a strategically revealing business definition, three elements need to be incorporated:[1]

1. Customer needs, or *what* is being satisfied.
2. Customer groups, or *who* is being satisfied.
3. The technologies used and functions performed—*how* customers' needs are satisfied.

Defining a business in terms of what to satisfy, who to satisfy, and how the organization will go about producing the satisfaction produces a comprehensive definition of what a company does and what business it is in. Just knowing what products or services a firm provides is never enough. Products or services per se are not important to customers; a product or service becomes a business when it satisfies a need or want. Without the need or want there is no business. Customer groups are relevant because they indicate the market to be served—the geographic domain to be covered and the types of buyers the firm is going after.

Technology and functions performed are important because they indicate *how* the company will satisfy the customers' needs and how much of the industry's production-distribution chain its activities will span. For instance, a firm's business can be *fully integrated*, extending across the entire range of industry activities that must be performed to get a product or service in the hands of end users. Major international oil companies like Exxon, Mobil, BP, Royal Dutch Shell, and Chevron lease drilling sites, drill wells, pump oil, transport crude oil in their own ships and pipelines to their own refineries, and sell gasoline and other refined products through their own networks of branded distributors and service station outlets. Their operations cover all stages of the industry's entire production-distribution chain.

Other firms stake out *partially integrated* positions, participating only in selected stages of the industry. Goodyear, for instance, both manufactures tires and operates a chain of company-owned retail tire stores, but it has not integrated backward into

---

[1]Derek F. Abell, *Defining the Business: The Starting Point of Strategic Planning* (Englewood Cliffs, N.J.: Prentice-Hall, 1980), p. 169.

rubber plantations and other tire-making components. General Motors, the world's most integrated manufacturer of cars and trucks, makes between 60 and 70 percent of the parts and components used in assembling GM vehicles. But GM is moving to outsource a greater fraction of its parts and systems components, and it relies totally on a network of independent, franchised dealers to handle sales and service functions. Still other firms are *specialized*, concentrating on just one stage of an industry's total production-distribution chain. Wal-Mart, Home Depot, Toys-R-Us, Lands' End, and The Limited are essentially one-stage firms. Their operations focus on the retail end of the production-distribution chain; they don't manufacture the items they sell. Delta Airlines is a one-stage enterprise; it doesn't manufacture the airplanes it flies, and it doesn't operate the airports where it lands. Delta has made a conscious decision to limit its business activities to moving travelers from one location to another via commercial jet aircraft.

An example of a company that does a pretty good job of covering the three bases of what, who, and how is Russell Corporation, the largest U. S. manufacturer of athletic uniforms:

> Russell Corporation is a vertically integrated international designer, manufacturer, and marketer of athletic uniforms, activewear, better knit shirts, leisure apparel, licensed sports apparel, sports and casual socks, and a comprehensive line of lightweight, yarn-dyed woven fabrics. The Company's manufacturing operations include the entire process of converting raw fibers into finished apparel and fabrics. Products are marketed to sporting goods dealers, department and specialty stores, mass merchandisers, golf pro shops, college bookstores, screen printers, distributors, mail-order houses, and other apparel manufacturers.

The concepts that McDonald's uses to define its business are a limited menu, good-tasting fast-food products of consistent quality, fast and accurate service, value pricing, exceptional customer care, convenient locations, and global market coverage. McDonald's business mission is built around "serving a limited menu of hot, tasty food quickly in a clean, friendly restaurant for a good value" to a broad base of fast-food customers worldwide (McDonald's serves approximately 30 million customers daily at 20,000-plus restaurants in over 90 countries).

Trying to identify needs served, target market, and functions performed in a single, snappy sentence is a challenge, and many firms' business definitions/mission statements fail to illuminate all three bases explicitly. The business definitions of some companies are thus better than others in terms of how they cut to the chase of what the enterprise is really about and the strategic position it is trying to stake out.[2]

A Broad or Narrow Business Definition?

Merck, one of the world's foremost pharmaceutical companies, has defined its business broadly as "providing society with

---

[2]For a more extensive discussion of the challenges of developing a well-conceived vision, as well as some in-depth examples, see James C. Collins and Jerry I. Porras, "Building Your Company's Vision," *Harvard Business Review* 74, no.5 (September–October 1996), pp. 65–77; Robert A. Burgelman and Andrew S. Grove, "Strategic Dissonance," *California Management Review* 38, no. 2 (Winter 1996), pp. 8–25; and Ron McTavish, "One More Time: What Business Are You In?" *Long Range Planning* 28, no. 2 (April 1995), pp. 49–60. For a discussion of some of the alternative ways a company can position itself in the marketplace, see Michael E. Porter, "What Is Strategy," *Harvard Business Review* 74, no. 6 (November–December 1996), pp. 65–67. Porter argues that the three basic strategic positions are based on (a) the range of customer needs to be served, (b) the variety of products to be offered (anywhere along the spectrum of one to many), and (c) the means by which customers are accessed—the terms Porter uses are needs-based positioning, variety-based positioning, and access-based positioning. For an empirical study of executive success in formulating and implementing a company vision and the difficulties encountered, see Laurie Larwood, Cecilia M. Falbe, Mark Kriger, and Paul Miesing, "Structure and Meaning of Organizational Vision," *Academy of Management Journal*, 38, no. 3 (June 1995), pp. 740–69.

superior products and services—innovations and solutions that satisfy customer needs and improve the quality of life." Such broad language, however, offers no practical strategic guidance. With such a definition Merck could pursue limitless strategic paths—developing innovative computer software, producing and marketing uniquely satisfying snack foods, manufacturing very appealing sports utility vehicles, or providing tax preparation services—businesses well outside its capabilities and actual intent. Trying to go in several business directions at once may be tempting and even fashionable, but it risks lack of business focus and dilution of effort. Few businesses fail because they are clearly focused on one market opportunity; many do badly because they try to pursue too many things at once.

To have managerial value, strategic visions, business definitions, and mission statements must be narrow enough to pin down the company's real arena of business interest. Consider the following definitions based on broad-narrow scope:

Broad Definition	Narrow Definition
• Beverages	• Soft drinks
• Children's products	• Toys
• Furniture	• Wrought-iron lawn furniture
• Global mail delivery	• Overnight package delivery
• Travel and tourism	• Ship cruises in the Caribbean

Broad-narrow definitions are relative to a company's business focus and intent, however. Being in "the furniture business" is probably too broad a concept for a company intent on being the largest manufacturer of wrought-iron lawn furniture in North America. On the other hand, toys has proved too narrow a scope for a growth-oriented company like Toys-R-Us, which, with its desire to capitalize on the potential of providing parents with more of what their children need, has ventured beyond toys and opened Kids-R-Us stores containing a wide selection of children's apparel and Books-R-Us stores specializing in children's books and reading programs. The U.S. Postal Service operates with a broad definition, providing global mail-delivery services to all types of senders. Federal Express, however, operates with a narrow business definition based on handling overnight package delivery for customers who have unplanned emergencies and tight deadlines.

Diversified companies have broader missions and business definitions than single-business enterprises.

Diversified firms, understandably, employ more sweeping business definitions than single-business enterprises. For example, Times Mirror Corp. describes itself broadly as a media and information company (which covers a lot of ground) but then goes on to pin down its business arenas in fairly explicit terms:

> Times Mirror is a media and information company principally engaged in newspaper publishing; book, magazine and other publishing; and cable and broadcast television.

Mission Statements for Functional Departments   There's also a place for mission statements for key functions (R&D, marketing, finance) and support units (human resources, training, information systems). Every department can benefit from a consensus statement spelling out its contribution to the company mission, its principal role and activities, and the direction it needs to be moving. Functional and departmental managers who think through and debate with subordinates and higher-

---

ILLUSTRATION CAPSULE 5   Intel's Bold Decision to Radically Alter Its Strategic Vision

Sometimes there's an order-of-magnitude change in a company's environment that dramatically alters its future prospects and mandates radical revision of its direction and strategic course—Intel's Chairman Andrew Grove calls such occasions "strategic inflection points." Grove and Intel encountered such an inflection point in the mid-1980s. At the time, memory chips were Intel's principal business, and Japanese manufacturers, intent on dominating the memory chip business, were cutting their prices 10 percent below the prices charged by Intel and other U.S. memory chip manufacturers; each time U.S. companies matched the Japanese price cuts, the Japanese manufacturers responded with another 10 percent price cut. Intel's management explored a number of strategic options to cope with the aggressive pricing of its Japanese rivals—building a giant memory chip factory to overcome the cost advantage of Japanese producers, investing in R&D to come up with a more advanced memory chip, and retreating to niche markets for memory chips that were not of interest to the Japanese. Grove concluded that none of these options offered much promise and that the best long-term solution was to abandon the memory chip business even though it accounted for 70 percent of Intel's revenue.

Grove then proceeded to commit Intel's full energies to the business of developing ever more powerful microprocessors for personal computers (Intel had invented microprocessors in the early 1970s but had recently been concentrating on memory chips because of strong competition and excess capacity in the market for microprocessors).

Grove's bold decision to withdraw from memory chips, absorb a $173 million write-off in 1986, and go all out in microprocessors produced a new strategic vision for Intel—becoming the preeminent supplier of microprocessors to the personal computing industry, making the PC the central appliance in the workplace and the home, and being the undisputed leader in driving PC technology forward. Grove's vision for Intel and the strategic course he subsequently charted has produced spectacular results. Today, 85 percent of the PCs have "Intel inside," and Intel was one of the five most profitable U.S. companies in 1996, earning after-tax profits of $5.2 billion on revenues of $20.8 billion.

---

ups what their unit needs to focus on and do have a clearer view of how to lead the unit. Three examples from actual companies indicate how a functional mission statement puts the spotlight on a unit's organizational *role* and *scope*:

- The mission of the human resources department is to contribute to organizational success by developing effective leaders, creating high-performance teams, and maximizing the potential of individuals.
- The mission of the corporate claims department is to minimize the overall cost of liability, workers compensation, and property damage claims through competitive cost containment techniques and loss prevention and control programs.
- The mission of corporate security is to provide services for the protection of corporate personnel and assets through preventive measures and investigations.

Deciding on a Long-Term Strategic Vision for the Company

Coming to grips with what a company's business can and should be 5 or 10 years down the road is something of a daunting task. It requires rational analysis of what the company should be doing to get ready for the changes coming in its present business and to capitalize on newly developing market opportunities. It also requires good entrepreneurial instincts, creativity, and an intuitive sense of what the company is capable of when pushed and challenged. Management's strategic vision ought to be realistic about the market, competitive, technological, economic, regulatory, and societal conditions the company is likely to encounter, and it ought to be realistic about the company's resources and capabilities. A strategic vision is not supposed to be a pipe dream or a fantasy about the company's future. Indeed, it has got to be compelling enough to shape the company's actions and energize its strategy.

The entrepreneurial challenge in developing a strategic vision is to think creatively about how to prepare a company for the future.

Often, the driving consideration is how best to position the enterprise to be successful in light of emerging developments and changes on the horizon. Alertness to the winds of change lessens the chances of the company becoming trapped in a stagnant or declining business or letting attractive new growth opportunities slip away because of inaction. Good entrepreneurs and strategists have a sharp eye for shifting customer wants and needs, new technological developments, openings to enter attractive foreign markets, and other important signs of growing or shrinking business opportunity. They attend quickly to users' problems and complaints with the industry's current products and services. They listen intently when a customer says, "If only . . . " Such clues and information tidbits stimulate them to think creatively and strategically about ways to break new ground. Appraising new customer-market-technology opportunities ultimately leads to entrepreneurial judgments about which fork in the road to take and what kind of strategic position to stake out in the marketplace. It is the strategy maker's job to evaluate the risks and prospects of alternative paths and make direction-setting decisions to position the enterprise for success in the years ahead. *A well-chosen vision and long-term business mission prepare a company for the future.*

Many successful organizations need to change direction not to survive but to maintain their success.

Communicating the Strategic Vision

How to communicate the strategic vision down the line to lower-level managers and employees is almost as important as the strategic soundness of the organization's business concept and long-term direction. One-way communication is seldom adequate, however; conversations with employees that allow for give-and-take discussion work best. People have a need to believe that the company's management knows where it's trying to take the company, where the company's markets are headed, and what changes lie ahead. When management can paint a picture of the company's future path in words that inspire employees and arouse a committed organizational effort, then the strategic vision serves as a powerful motivational tool—the simple, clear, lofty mission of the International Red Cross is a good example: "to serve the most vulnerable." Bland language, platitudes, and dull motherhood-and-apple-pie-style verbiage must be scrupulously avoided—they can be a turn-off rather than a turn-on. Managers need to communicate the vision in words that induce employee buy-in, build pride, and create a strong sense of organizational purpose. People are proud to be associated with a company pursuing a worthwhile strategic course and trying to be the world's best at something competitively significant and beneficial to customers. Hence, expressing the strategic vision in engaging language that reaches out and grabs people, that creates a vivid image in their heads, and that provokes emotion and excitement has enormous motivational value; it lifts thoughts above and beyond the daily routine of the business.

A well-articulated strategic vision creates enthusiasm for the future course management has charted and poses a challenge that inspires and engages members of the organization.

Having an exciting business cause energizes the company's strategy, brings the workforce together, galvanizes people to act, stimulates extra effort, and gets people to live the business instead of just coming to work.[3] In organizations with a just-revised vision and long-term direction, it is particularly important for executives to provide a compelling rationale for the new strategic path and why the company must

---

[3]Tom Peters, *Thriving on Chaos* (New York: Harper & Row, Perennial Library Edition, 1988), pp. 486–87; and Andrall E. Pearson, "Corporate Redemption and The Seven Deadly Sins," *Harvard Business Review* 70, no. 3 (May–June 1992), pp. 66–68.

ILLUSTRATION CAPSULE 6   NovaCare's Business Mission and Vision

NovaCare is a health care company specializing in providing patient rehabilitation services on a contract basis to nursing homes. Rehabilitation therapy is a $12 billion industry, of which 35 percent is provided contractually. In 1996 NovaCare was an $800 million company with 17,000 employees at 2,300 sites in 43 states. The company stated its business mission and vision as follows:

NovaCare is people committed to making a difference . . . enhancing the future of all patients . . . breaking new ground in our professions . . . achieving excellence . . . advancing human capability . . . changing the world in which we live.

We lead the way with our enthusiasm, optimism, patience, drive, and commitment.

We work together to enhance the quality of our patients' lives by reshaping lost abilities and teaching new skills. We heighten expectations for the patient and family. We rebuild hope, confidence, self-respect, and a desire to continue.

We apply our clinical expertise to benefit our patients through creative and progressive techniques. Our ethical and performance standards require us to expend every effort to achieve the best possible results.

Our customers are national and local health care providers who share our goal of enhancing the patients' quality of life. In each community, our customers consider us a partner in providing the best possible care. Our reputation is based on our responsiveness, high standards, and effective systems of quality assurance. Our relationship is open and proactive.

We are advocates of our professions and patients through active participation in the professional, regulatory, educational, and research communities at national, state, and local levels.

Our approach to health care fulfills our responsibility to provide investors with a high rate of return through consistent growth and profitability.

Our people are our most valuable asset. We are committed to the personal, professional, and career development of each individual employee. We are proud of what we do and dedicated to our Company. We foster teamwork and create an environment conducive to productive communication among all disciplines.

NovaCare is a company of people in pursuit of this Vision.

Source: Company annual report and website.

begin to stake out a different future business position. Unless people understand how a company's business environment is changing and why a new course is being charted, a new vision and long-term business mission does little to win employees' commitment and wholehearted cooperation. Employee failure to understand or accept the need for redirecting organizational efforts often produces resistance to change and makes it harder to move the organization down a newly chosen path. Hence, explaining and justifying the new strategic vision in persuasive terms that everyone can understand and agree with is a necessary step in getting the organization redirected and ready to move along the new course.

Well-worded vision statements give employees a larger sense of purpose—so that they see themselves as "building a cathedral" rather than "laying stones."

The best-worded mission statements and visions of a company's future are simple and easy to grasp; they convey unmistakable meaning, generate enthusiasm for the firm's future course, and elicit personal effort and dedication from everyone in the organization. They have to be presented and then repeated over and over as a worthy organizational challenge, one capable of benefiting customers in a valuable and meaningful way—indeed, it is crucial that the mission/vision stress the payoff for customers, not the payoff for stockholders. It goes without saying that the company intends to profit shareholders from its efforts to provide real value to its customers. A crisp, clear, often-repeated, inspiring strategic vision has the power to turn heads in the intended direction and begin a new organizational march. When this occurs, the first step in organizational direction-setting is successfully completed. Illustration Capsule 6 is a good example of an inspiration-oriented company vision and mission.

A well-conceived, well-worded strategic vision/mission statement has real managerial value: (1) it crystallizes senior executives' own views about the firm's long-term direction and future business makeup; (2) it reduces the risk of visionless management and rudderless decision making; (3) it conveys an organizational purpose that arouses employee buy-in and commitment and that motivates employees to go all out and contribute to making the vision a reality; (4) it provides a beacon lower-level managers can use to form departmental missions, set departmental objectives, and craft functional and departmental strategies that are in sync with the company's direction and strategy; and (5) it helps an organization prepare for the future.

ESTABLISHING OBJECTIVES: THE SECOND DIRECTION-SETTING TASK

Setting objectives converts the strategic vision and directional course into specific performance targets. Objectives represent a managerial commitment to achieving specific outcomes and results. They are a call for action and for results.

Objectives represent a managerial commitment to achieving specific performance targets within a specific time frame.

Unless an organization's long-term direction and business mission are translated into specific performance targets and managers are pressured to show progress in reaching these targets, vision and mission statements are likely to end up as nice words, window dressing, and unrealized dreams of accomplishment. The experiences of countless companies and managers teach that *companies whose managers set objectives for each key result area and then press forward with actions aimed directly at achieving these performance outcomes typically outperform companies whose managers exhibit good intentions, try hard, and hope for the best.*

For objectives to function as yardsticks of organizational performance and progress, they must be stated in *quantifiable* or measurable terms and they must contain a *deadline for achievement.* They have to spell out *how much* of *what kind* of performance *by when.* This means avoiding generalities like "maximize profits," "reduce costs," "become more efficient," or "increase sales," which specify neither how much or when. As Bill Hewlett, cofounder of Hewlett-Packard, once observed, "You cannot manage what you cannot measure . . . And what gets measured gets done."[4] Spelling out organization objectives in measurable terms and then holding managers accountable for reaching their assigned targets within a specified time frame (1) substitutes purposeful strategic decision making for aimless actions and confusion over what to accomplish and (2) provides a set of benchmarks for judging the organization's performance and progress.

What Kinds of Objectives to Set

Objectives are needed for each *key result* managers deem important to success.[5] Two types of key result areas stand out: those relating to *financial performance*

---

[4]As quoted in Charles H. House and Raymond L. Price, "The Return Map: Tracking Product Teams," *Harvard Business Review* 60, no. 1 (January–February 1991), p. 93.

[5]The literature of management is filled with references to *goals* and *objectives.* These terms are used in a variety of ways, many of them conflicting. Some writers use the term goals to refer to the long-run outcomes an organization seeks to achieve and the term objectives to refer to immediate, short-run performance targets. Some writers reverse the usage, referring to objectives as the desired long-run results and goals as the desired short-run results. Others use the terms interchangeably. And still others use the term goals to refer to broad organizationwide performance targets and the term objectives to designate specific

and those relating to *strategic performance*. Achieving acceptable financial performance is a must; otherwise the organization's financial standing can alarm creditors and shareholders, impair its ability to fund needed initiatives, and perhaps even put its very survival at risk. Achieving acceptable strategic performance is essential to sustaining and improving the company's long-term market position and competitiveness. Representative kinds of financial and strategic performance objectives are listed below:

Strategic Management Principle

Every company needs both strategic objectives and financial objectives.

LT competitive position

Financial Objectives	Strategic Objectives
• Growth in revenues	• A bigger market share
• Growth in earnings	• Quicker design-to-market times than rivals
• Higher dividends	• Higher product quality than rivals
• Wider profit margins	• Lower costs relative to key competitors
• Higher returns on invested capital	• Broader or more attractive product line than rivals
• Attractive economic value added (EVA) performance[6]	• A stronger reputation with customers than rivals
• Strong bond and credit ratings	• Superior customer service
• Bigger cash flows	• Recognition as a leader in technology and/or product innovation
• A rising stock price	• Wider geographic coverage than rivals
• Attractive and sustainable increases in market value added (MVA)[7]	• Higher levels of customer satisfaction than rivals
• Recognition as a "blue chip" company	
• A more diversified revenue base	
• Stable earnings during periods of recession	

Illustration Capsule 7 presents the strategic and financial objectives of four well-known enterprises.

---

targets set by operating divisions and functional departments to support achievement of overall company performance targets. In our view, little is gained from semantic distinctions between goals and objectives. The important thing is to recognize that the results an enterprise seeks to attain vary as to both organizational scope and time frame. Nearly always, organizations need to have companywide performance targets and division/department performance targets for both the near-term and long-term. It is inconsequential which targets are called goals and which objectives. To avoid a semantic jungle, we use the single term *objectives* to refer to the performance targets and results an organization seeks to attain. We use the adjectives *long-range* (or long-run) and *short-range* (or short-run) to identify the relevant time frame, and we try to describe objectives in words that indicate their intended scope and level in the organization.

[6]Economic value added (EVA) is profit over and above the company's weighted average after-tax cost of capital; specifically, it is defined as operating profit less income taxes less the weighted average cost of capital. Such companies as Coca-Cola, AT&T, Briggs & Stratton, and Eli Lilly use EVA as a measure of the profit performance. For more details on EVA, consult footnote 1 in Chapter 1.

[7]Market value added (MVA) is defined as the amount by which the total value of the company has appreciated above the dollar amount actually invested in the company by shareholders. MVA is equal to a company's current stock price times the number of shares outstanding less shareholders' equity investment; it represents the value that management has added to shareholders' wealth in running the business. If shareholder value is to be maximized, management must select a strategy and long-term direction that maximizes the market value of the company's common stock.

ILLUSTRATION CAPSULE 7   Examples Of Corporate Objectives: McDonald's, 3M Corp., Anheuser-Busch, and McCormick & Company

McDonald's

- To achieve 100 percent total customer satisfaction . . . everyday . . . in every restaurant . . . for every customer.

Anheuser-Busch

- To make all of our companies leaders in their industries in quality while exceeding customer expectations.
- To achieve a 50% share of the U.S. beer market.
- To establish and maintain a dominant leadership position in the international beer market.
- To provide all our employees with challenging and rewarding work, satisfying working conditions, and opportunities for personal development, advancement, and competitive compensation.
- To provide our shareholders with superior returns by achieving double-digit annual earnings per share growth, increasing dividends consistent with earnings growth, repurchasing shares when the opportunity is right, pursuing profitable international beer expansions, and generating quality earnings and cash flow returns.

3M Corporation

- 30 percent of the company's annual sales must come from products fewer than four years old.

McCormick & Company

- To achieve a 20 percent return on equity.
- To achieve a net sales growth rate of 10 percent per year.
- To maintain an average earnings per share growth rate of 15 percent per year.
- To maintain total debt-to-total capital at 40 percent or less.
- To pay out 25 percent to 35 percent of net income in dividends.
- To make selective acquisitions which complement our current businesses and can enhance our overall returns.
- To dispose of those parts of our business which do not or cannot generate adequate returns or do not fit our business strategy.

Source: Company annual reports.

LT competitive position

Strategic Objectives versus Financial Objectives: Which Take Precedence?   Even though an enterprise places high priority on achieving both financial and strategic objectives, what if situations arise where a trade-off has to be made? Should a company under pressure to pay down its debt elect to kill or postpone investments in strategic moves that hold promise for strengthening the enterprise's future business and competitive position? Should a company under pressure to boost near-term profits cut back R&D programs that could help it achieve a competitive advantage over key rivals in the years ahead? The pressures on managers to opt for better near-term financial performance and to sacrifice or cut back on strategic initiatives aimed at building a stronger competitive position become especially pronounced when (1) an enterprise is struggling financially, (2) the resource commitments for strategically beneficial moves will materially detract from the bottom line for several years, and (3) the proposed strategic moves are risky and have an uncertain competitive or bottom-line payoff.

> *Strategic objectives need to be competitor-focused, often aiming at unseating a rival considered to be the industry's best in a particular category.*

Yet, there are dangers in management's succumbing time and again to the lure of immediate gains in profitability when it means paring or forgoing strategic moves that would build a stronger business position. A company that consistently passes up opportunities to strengthen its long-term competitive position in order to realize better near-term financial gains risks diluting its competitiveness, losing momentum in its markets, and impairing its ability to stave off market challenges from ambitious rivals. The business landscape is littered with ex-market leaders who put more emphasis on boosting next quarter's profit than strengthening long-term market position. The danger of trading off long-term gains in market position for near-term gains in bottom-line performance is greatest when a profit-conscious market leader has competitors who invest relentlessly in gaining market share, striving to become big and strong enough to outcompete the leader in a head-to-head market battle. One need look no further than Japanese companies' patient and persistent strategic efforts to gain market ground on their more profit-centered American and European rivals to appreciate the pitfall of letting short-term financial objectives dominate. The surest path to protecting and sustaining a company's profitability quarter after quarter and year after year is for its managers to pursue strategic actions that strengthen the company's competitiveness and business position.

> **Strategic Management Principle**
>
> *Building a stronger long-term competitive position benefits shareholders more lastingly than improving short-term profitability.*

The Concept of Strategic Intent

A company's strategic objectives are important for another reason—they indicate *strategic intent* to stake out a particular business position.[8] The strategic intent of a large company may be industry leadership on a national or global scale. The strategic intent of a small company may be to dominate a market niche. The strategic intent of an up-and-coming enterprise may be to overtake the market leaders. The strategic intent of a technologically innovative company may be to pioneer a promising discovery and create a whole new vista of products that change the way people work and live—as many entrepreneurial companies are now trying to do with the Internet.

> **Basic Concept**
>
> *A company exhibits strategic intent when it relentlessly pursues an ambitious strategic objective and concentrates its competitive actions and energies on achieving that objective.*

   The time horizon underlying a company's strategic intent is *long term*. Ambitious companies almost invariably begin with strategic intents that are out of proportion to their immediate capabilities and market positions. But they set aggressive long-term strategic objectives and pursue them relentlessly, sometimes even obsessively, over a 10- to 20-year period. In the 1960s, Komatsu, Japan's leading earthmoving equipment company, was less than one-third the size of Caterpillar, had little market presence outside Japan, and depended on its small bulldozers for most of its revenue. But Komatsu's strategic intent was to eventually "encircle Caterpillar" with a broader product line and then compete globally against Caterpillar. By the late 1980s, Komatsu was the industry's second-ranking company, with a strong sales presence in North America, Europe, and Asia plus a product line that included industrial robots and semiconductors as well as a broad selection of earthmoving equipment.

   Often, a company's strategic intent takes on a heroic character, serving as a rallying cry for managers and employees alike to go all out and do their very best. Canon's strategic intent in copying equipment was to "Beat Xerox." Komatsu's motivating battle cry was "Beat Caterpillar." When Yamaha overtook Honda in the motorcycle

---

[8]The concept of strategic intent is described in more detail in Gary Hamel and C. K. Pralahad, "Strategic Intent," *Harvard Business Review* 89, no. 3 (May–June 1989), pp. 63–76; this section draws upon their pioneering discussion. See, also, Michael A. Hitt, Beverly B. Tyler, Camilla Hardee, and Daewoo Park, "Understanding Strategic Intent in the Global Marketplace," *Academy of Management Executive*, 9, no. 2 (May 1995), pp. 12–19. For a discussion of the different ways that companies can position themselves in the marketplace, see Michael E. Porter, "What Is Strategy?" *Harvard Business Review* 74, no. 6 (November–December 1996), pp. 65–67.

market, Honda responded with "Yamaha wo tsubusu" ("We will crush, squash, slaughter Yamaha"). The strategic intent of the U.S. government's Apollo space program was to land a person on the moon ahead of the Soviet Union. Throughout the 1980s, Wal-Mart's strategic intent was to "overtake Sears" as the largest U.S. retailer (a feat accomplished in 1991). Netscape's running battle with Microsoft over whose Internet browser software will reign supreme prompted employees to hang "Beat Microsoft" banners in Netscape's offices. In such instances, strategic intent signals a deep-seated commitment to winning—unseating the industry leader or remaining the industry leader (and becoming more dominant in the process) or otherwise beating long odds to gain a significantly stronger business position. Small, capably managed enterprises determined to achieve ambitious strategic objectives exceeding their present reach and resources often prove to be more formidable competitors than larger, cash-rich companies with modest strategic intents.

The Need for Long-Range and Short-Range Objectives

Objective setting should result in both long-range and short-range performance targets. Absent an impending crisis or pressing reason to bolster a company's long-term position and future performance, managers are prone to focus on the near term and place a higher priority on what has to be done to hit this year's numbers. The trouble with giving too high a priority to short-term objectives, of course, is the potential for managers to neglect actions aimed at enhancing a company's long-term business position and sustaining its capacity to generate good results over the long term. Setting bold, long-range performance targets and then putting pressure on managers to show progress in achieving them helps balance the priorities between better near-term results and actions calculated to ensure the company's competitiveness and financial performance down the road. A strong commitment to achieving long-range objectives forces managers to begin taking actions *now* to reach desired performance levels *later.* (A company that has an objective of doubling its sales within five years can't wait until the third or fourth year of its five-year strategic plan to begin growing its sales and customer base!)

By spelling out the near-term results to be achieved, short-range objectives indicate the *speed* at which management wants the organization to progress as well as the *level of performance* being aimed for over the next two or three periods. Short-range objectives can be identical to long-range objectives anytime an organization is already performing at the targeted long-term level. For instance, if a company has an ongoing objective of 15 percent profit growth every year and is currently achieving this objective, then the company's long-range and short-range profit objectives coincide. The most important situation where short-range objectives differ from long-range objectives occurs when managers are trying to elevate organizational performance and cannot reach the long-range/ongoing target in just one year. Short-range objectives then serve as stairsteps or milestones.

How Much Stretch Should Objectives Entail?

As a starter, objectives should be set high enough to produce outcomes at least incrementally better than current performance. But incremental improvements are not necessarily sufficient, especially if current performance levels are subpar. At a minimum, a company's financial objectives must aim high enough to generate the resources to execute the chosen strategy proficiently. But an "enough-to-get-by" mentality is not the way to approach objective setting. Arriving at an appropriate set of performance targets requires considering what performance is possible in light of external conditions, what performance other comparably situated companies are achieving, what performance it will take to please shareholders, what performance is required for long-term competitive success, and what performance the organization is capable of achieving when pushed. Ideally, objectives ought to serve as a managerial tool for truly *stretching an organization to reach its full potential;* this means setting them high enough to be *challenging*—to energize the organization and its strategy.

Company performance targets should require organizational stretch.

However, there is a school of thought that objectives should be set boldly and aggressively high—above levels that many organizational members would consider "realistic." The idea here is that *more* organizational creativity and energy is unleashed when stretch objectives call for achieving performance levels well beyond the reach of the enterprise's immediate resources and capabilities. One of the most avid practitioners of setting bold, audacious objectives and challenging the organization to go all out to achieve them is General Electric, arguably the world's best-managed corporation. Jack Welch, GE's CEO, believes in setting stretch targets that seem "impossible" and then challenging the organization to go after them. Throughout the 1960s, 1970s, and 1980s, GE's operating margins hovered around 10 percent and its sales-to-inventory ratio averaged about five turns per year. In 1991, Welch set stretch targets for 1995 of at least a 16 percent operating margin and 10 inventory turns. Welch's letter to the shareholders in the company's 1995 annual report said:

> 1995 has come and gone, and despite a heroic effort by our 220,000 employees, we fell short on both measures, achieving a 14.4 percent operating margin and almost seven turns. But in stretching for these "impossible" targets, we learned to do things faster than we would have going after "doable" goals, and we have enough confidence now to set new stretch targets of at least 16 percent operating margin and more than 10 turns by 1998.

GE's philosophy is that setting very aggressive stretch targets pushes the organization to move beyond being only as good as what is deemed doable to being as good as it possibly can be. GE's management believes challenging the company to achieve the impossible improves the quality of the organization's effort, promotes a can-do spirit, and builds self-confidence. Hence, a case can be made that objectives ought to be set at levels *above* what is doable with a little extra effort; there's merit in setting stretch targets that require something approaching a heroic degree of organizational effort.

Objectives Are Needed at All Organizational Levels

For strategic thinking and strategy-driven decision making to permeate organization behavior, performance targets must be established not only for the organization as a whole but also for each of the organization's separate businesses, product lines, functional areas, and departments. Only when each unit's strategic and financial objectives support achievement of the company's strategic and financial objectives is the objective-setting process sufficiently complete to conclude that each part of the organization knows its strategic role and that the various organizational units are on board in helping the whole organization move down the chosen strategic path.

The Need for Top-Down Objective-Setting   To appreciate why a company's objective-setting process needs to be more top-down than bottom-up, consider the following example. Suppose the senior executives of a diversified corporation establish a corporate profit objective of $5 million for next year. Suppose further, after discussion between corporate management and the general managers of the firm's five different businesses, each business is given a stretch profit objective of $1 million by year-end (i.e., if the five business divisions contribute $1 million each in profit, the corporation can reach its $5 million profit objective). A concrete result has thus been agreed on and translated into measurable action commitments at two levels in the managerial hierarchy. Next, suppose the general manager of business unit X, after some analysis and discussion with functional area managers, concludes that reaching the $1 million profit objective will require selling 100,000 units at an average price of $50 and producing them at an average cost of $40 (a $10 profit margin times 100,000 units equals $1 million profit). Consequently, the general manager and the manufacturing manager settle on a production objective of 100,000 units at a unit cost of $40; and the general manager and the marketing manager agree on a sales objective of 100,000 units and a target selling price of $50. In turn, the marketing manager breaks the sales objective of 100,000 units into unit sales targets for each sales territory, each item in the product line, and each salesperson. It is logical for organizationwide objectives and strategy to be established first so they can *guide* objective setting and strategy making at lower levels. Top-down objective setting and strategizing steer lower-level units toward objectives and strategies that take their cues from those of the total enterprise.

> **Strategic Management Principle**
>
> *Objective setting needs to be more of a top-down than a bottom-up process in order to guide lower-level managers and organizational units toward outcomes that support the achievement of overall business and company objectives.*

A top-down process of setting companywide performance targets first and then insisting that the financial and strategic performance targets established for business units, divisions, functional departments, and operating units be directly connected to the achievement of company objectives has two powerful advantages. One, it helps produce *cohesion* among the objectives and strategies of different parts of the organization. Two, it helps *unify internal efforts* to move the company along the chosen strategic course. If top management, in the interest of involving a broad spectrum of organizational members, allows objective setting to start at the bottom levels of an organization without the benefit of companywide performance targets as a guide, then lower-level organizational units have no basis for connecting their performance targets to the company's. Letting organizationwide objectives be the product of whatever priorities and targets bubble up from below simply leaves too much room for the objectives and strategies of lower-level organizational units to be uncoordinated with each other and lacking in what makes good business sense for the company as a whole. Bottom-up objective setting, with little or no guidance from above, nearly always signals an absence of strategic leadership on the part of senior executives.

CRAFTING A STRATEGY: THE THIRD DIRECTION-SETTING TASK

Organizations need strategies to guide *how* to achieve objectives and *how* to pursue the organization's business mission and strategic vision. Strategy making is all about *how*—how to achieve performance targets, how to outcompete rivals, how to achieve sustainable competitive advantage, how to strengthen the enterprise's long-term business position, how to make management's strategic vision for the company a reality. A strategy is needed for the company as a whole, for each business the company is in, and for each functional piece of each business—R&D, purchasing, production, sales and marketing, finance, customer service, information systems, and so on. An organization's overall strategy emerges from the *pattern of actions already initiated and the plans managers have for fresh moves*. In forming a strategy out of the many feasible options, a manager acts as a forger of responses to market change, a seeker of new opportunities, and a synthesizer of the different moves and approaches taken at various times in various parts of the organization.[9]

The strategy-making spotlight, however, needs to be kept trained on the important facets of management's game plan for running the enterprise—those actions that determine what market position the company is trying to stake out and that underpin whether the company will succeed. Low-priority issues (whether to increase the advertising budget, raise the dividend, locate a new plant in country X or country Y) and routine managerial housekeeping (whether to own or lease company vehicles, how to reduce sales force turnover) are not basic to the strategy, even though they must be dealt with. Strategy is inherently action-oriented; it concerns what to do and when to do it. Unless there is action, unless something happens, unless somebody does something, strategic thinking and planning simply go to waste and, in the end, amount to nothing.

An organization's strategy evolves over time. The future is too unknowable for management to plan a company's strategy in advance and encounter no reason for changing one piece or another as time passes. Reacting and responding to unpredictable happenings in the surrounding environment is a normal and necessary part of the strategy-making process. There is always something new to react to and some new strategic window opening up—whether from new competitive developments, budding trends in buyer needs and expectations, unexpected increases or decreases in costs, mergers and acquisitions among major industry players, new regulations, the raising or lowering of trade barriers, or countless other events that make it desirable to alter first one then another aspect of the present strategy.[10] This is why the task of crafting strategy is never ending. And it is why a company's actual strategy turns out to be a blend of managerial plans and intentions and as-needed reactions to fresh developments.

While most of the time a company's strategy evolves incrementally, there are occasions when a company can function as an industry revolutionary by creating a rule-breaking strategy that redefines the industry and how it operates. A strategy can challenge fundamental conventions by reconceiving a product or service (like creating a single-use, disposable camera or a digital camera), redefining the marketplace (the growing potential for electronic commerce on the Internet is allowing companies to market their products anywhere at any time rather than being restricted to making their products available at particular locations during normal shopping times), or redrawing industry boundaries (consumers can now get their credit cards from Shell Oil or General Motors, or have their checking account at Charles Schwab, or get a home mortgage from Merrill Lynch, or get a family-style meal for takeout at the Boston Market or the supermarket).[11]

Basic Concept

An organization's strategy deals with the game plan for moving the company into an attractive business position and building a sustainable competitive advantage.

A company's actual strategy usually turns out to be both more and less than the planned strategy as new strategy features are added and others are deleted in response to newly emerging conditions.

---

[9]Henry Mintzberg, "The Strategy Concept II: Another Look at Why Organizations Need Strategies," *California Management Review* 30, no. 1 (Fall 1987), pp. 25–32.

[10]Henry Mintzberg and J. A. Waters, "Of Strategies, Deliberate and Emergent," *Strategic Management Journal*, 6 (1985), pp.257–72.

[11]For an in-depth discussion of revolutionary strategies, see Gary Hamel, "Strategy as Revolution," *Harvard Business Review* 74, no. 4 (July–August 1996), pp. 69–82.

The Strategy-Making Pyramid

As we emphasized in the opening chapter, strategy making is not just a task for senior executives. In large enterprises, decisions about what business approaches to take and what new moves to initiate involve senior executives in the corporate office, heads of business units and product divisions, the heads of major functional areas within a business or division (manufacturing, marketing and sales, finance, human resources, and the like), plant managers, product managers, district and regional sales managers, and lower-level supervisors. In diversified enterprises, strategies are initiated at four distinct organization levels. There's a strategy for the company and all of its businesses as a whole (*corporate strategy*). There's a strategy for each separate business the company has diversified into (*business strategy*). Then there is a strategy for each specific functional unit within a business (*functional strategy*)—each business usually has a production strategy, a marketing strategy, a finance strategy, and so on. And, finally, there are still narrower strategies for basic operating units—plants, sales districts and regions, and departments within functional areas (*operating strategy*). Figure 2.1 shows the strategy-making pyramids for a diversified company and a single-business company. In single-business enterprises, there are only three levels of strategy (business strategy, functional strategy, and operating strategy) unless diversification into other businesses becomes an active consideration. Table 2.1 highlights the kinds of strategic actions that distinguish each of the four strategy-making levels.

Corporate Strategy

Corporate strategy is the overall managerial game plan for a diversified company. *Corporate strategy extends companywide—an umbrella over all a diversified company's businesses. It consists of the moves made to establish business positions* in different industries and the approaches used to manage the company's group of businesses. Figure 2.2 depicts the core elements that identify a diversified company's corporate strategy. Crafting corporate strategy for a diversified company involves four kinds of initiatives:

Basic Concept

Corporate strategy *concerns how a diversified company intends to establish business positions in different industries and the actions and approaches employed to improve the performance of the group of businesses the company has diversified into.*

---

1. *Making the moves to establish positions in different businesses and achieve diversification.* In a diversified company, a key piece of corporate strategy is how many and what kinds of businesses the company should be in—specifically, what industries should the company participate in and whether to enter the industries by starting a new business or acquiring another company (an established leader, an up-and-coming company, or a troubled company with turnaround potential). This piece of corporate strategy establishes whether diversification is based narrowly in a few industries or broadly in many industries and whether the different businesses will be related or unrelated.

2. *Initiating actions to boost the combined performance of the businesses the firm has diversified into.* As positions are created in the chosen industries, corporate strategy making concentrates on ways to strengthen the long-term competitive positions and profitabilities of the businesses the firm has invested in. Corporate parents can help their business subsidiaries be more successful by financing additional capacity and efficiency improvements, by supplying missing skills and managerial know-how, by acquiring another company in the same industry and merging the two operations into a stronger business, and/or by acquiring new businesses that strongly complement existing businesses. Management's overall strategy for improving companywide performance usually involves pursuing rapid-growth strategies in the most

FIGURE 2.1   The Strategy-Making Pyramid

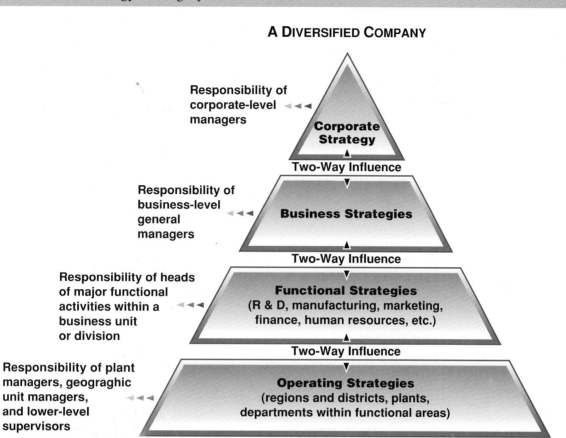

TABLE 2.1   How the Strategy-Making Task Tends to Be Shared

Strategy Level	Lead Responsibility	Primary Strategy-Making Concerns at Each Managerial Level
• Corporate strategy	• CEO, other key executives (decisions are typically reviewed/approved by boards of directors)	• Building and managing a high-performing portfolio of business units (making acquisitions, strengthening existing business positions, divesting businesses that no longer fit into management's plans) • Capturing the synergy among related business units and turning it into competitive advantage • Establishing investment priorities and steering corporate resources into businesses with the most attractive opportunities • Reviewing/revising/unifying the major strategic approaches and moves proposed by business-unit managers
• Business strategies	• General manager/head of business unit (decisions are typically reviewed/approved by a senior executive or a board of directors)	• Devising moves and approaches to compete successfully and to secure a competitive advantage • Forming responses to changing external conditions • Uniting the strategic initiatives of key functional departments • Taking action to address company-specific issues and operating problems
• Functional strategies	• Functional managers (decisions are typically reviewed/approved by business-unit head)	• Crafting moves and approaches to support business strategy and to achieve functional/departmental performance objectives • Reviewing/revising/unifying strategy-related moves and approaches proposed by lower-level managers
• Operating strategies	• Field-unit heads/lower-level managers within functional areas (decisions are reviewed/approved by functional area head/department head)	• Crafting still narrower and more specific approaches/moves aimed at supporting functional and business strategies and at achieving operating-unit objectives

promising businesses, keeping the other core businesses healthy, initiating turnaround efforts in weak-performing businesses with potential, and divesting businesses that are no longer attractive or that don't fit into management's long-range plans.

3. *Pursuing ways to capture the synergy among related business units and turn it into competitive advantage.* When a company diversifies into businesses with related technologies, similar operating characteristics, common distribution channels or customers, or some other synergistic relationship, it gains competitive advantage potential not open to a company that diversifies into totally unrelated businesses. Related diversification presents opportunities to transfer skills, share expertise or facilities, and leverage a common brand name, thereby reducing overall costs, strengthening the competitive-

FIGURE 2.2   Identifying the Corporate Strategy of a Diversified Company

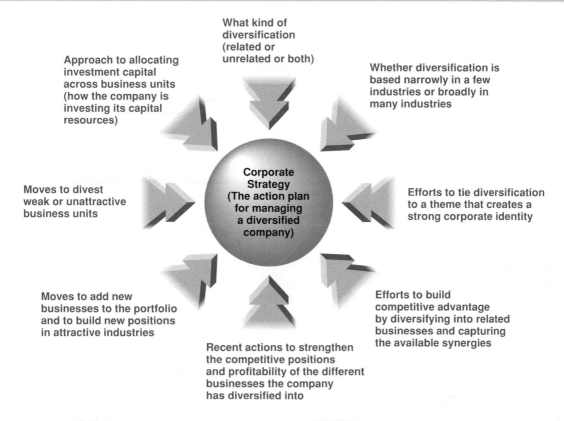

ness of some of the company's products, or enhancing the capabilities of particular business units—any of which can represent a significant source of competitive advantage and provide a basis for greater overall corporate profitability.

4. *Establishing investment priorities and steering corporate resources into the most attractive business units.* A diversified company's different businesses are usually not equally attractive from the standpoint of investing additional funds. This facet of corporate strategy making involves channeling resources into areas where earnings potentials are higher and away from areas where they are lower. Corporate strategy may include divesting business units that are chronically poor performers or those in an increasingly unattractive industry. Divestiture frees up unproductive investments for redeployment to promising business units or for financing attractive new acquisitions.

Corporate strategy is crafted at the highest levels of management. Senior corporate executives normally have lead responsibility for devising corporate strategy and for choosing among whatever recommended actions bubble up from lower-level managers. Key business-unit heads may also be influential, especially in strategic decisions affecting the businesses they head. Major strategic decisions are usually reviewed and approved by the company's board of directors.

Business Strategy

The term *business strategy* (or business-level strategy) refers to the managerial game plan for a single business. It is mirrored in the pattern of approaches and moves crafted by management to produce successful performance in *one specific*

FIGURE 2.3   Identifying Strategy for a Single-Business Company

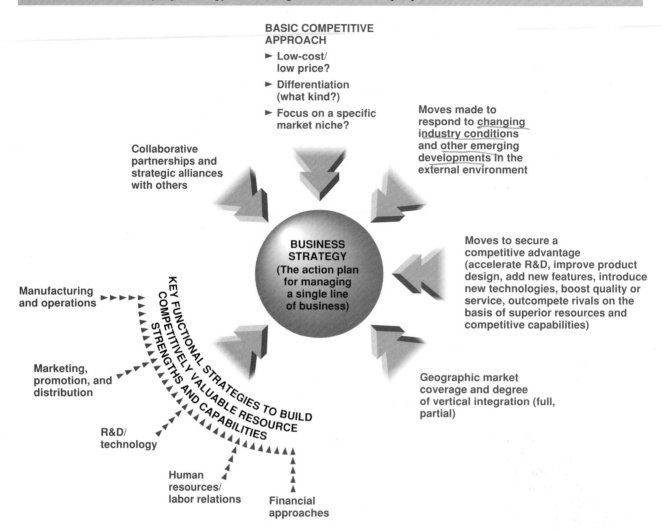

BASIC COMPETITIVE
APPROACH
► Low-cost/
  low price?
► Differentiation
  (what kind?)
► Focus on a specific
  market niche?

Collaborative
partnerships and
strategic alliances
with others

Moves made to
respond to changing
industry conditions
and other emerging
developments in the
external environment

BUSINESS
STRATEGY
(The action plan
for managing
a single line
of business)

Moves to secure a
competitive advantage
(accelerate R&D, improve product
design, add new features, introduce
new technologies, boost quality or
service, outcompete rivals on the
basis of superior resources and
competitive capabilities)

Manufacturing
and operations

KEY FUNCTIONAL STRATEGIES TO BUILD
COMPETITIVELY VALUABLE RESOURCE
STRENGTHS AND CAPABILITIES

Marketing,
promotion, and
distribution

Geographic market
coverage and degree
of vertical integration (full,
partial)

R&D/
technology

Human
resources/
labor relations

Financial
approaches

Basic Concept

Business strategy *concerns the actions and the approaches crafted by management to produce successful performance in one specific line of business; the central business strategy issue is* <u>how</u> *to build a stronger long-term competitive position.*

line of business. The core elements of business strategy are illustrated in Figure 2.3. For a stand-alone single-business company, corporate strategy and business strategy are one and the same since there is only one business to form a strategy for. The distinction between corporate strategy and business strategy is relevant only for diversified firms.

The central thrust of business strategy is how to build and strengthen the company's long-term competitive position in the marketplace. Toward this end, business strategy is concerned principally with (1) forming responses to changes under way in the industry, the economy at large, the regulatory and political arena, and other relevant areas, (2) crafting competitive moves and market approaches that can lead to sustainable competitive advantage, (3) building competitively valuable competencies and capabilities, (4) uniting the strategic initiatives of functional departments, and (5) addressing specific strategic issues facing the company's business.

Clearly, business strategy encompasses whatever moves and new approaches managers deem prudent in light of market forces, economic trends and developments, buyer needs and demographics, new legislation and regulatory requirements, and other such broad external factors. *A good strategy is well-matched to the external situation;* as the external environment changes in significant ways, then adjustments in strategy are made on an as-needed basis. Whether a company's response to external change is quick or slow tends to be a function of how long events must unfold before managers can assess their implications and how much longer it then takes to form a strategic response. Some external changes, of course, require little or no response, while others call for significant strategy alterations. On occasion, external factors change in ways that pose a formidable strategic hurdle—for example, cigarette manufacturers face a tough challenge holding their own against mounting efforts to combat smoking.

What separates a powerful business strategy from a weak one is the strategist's ability *to forge a series of moves and approaches capable of producing sustainable competitive advantage.* With a competitive advantage, a company has good prospects for above-average profitability and success in the industry. Without competitive advantage, a company risks being outcompeted by stronger rivals and locked into mediocre performance. Crafting a business strategy that yields sustainable competitive advantage has three facets: (1) deciding what product/service attributes (lower costs and prices, a better product, a wider product line, superior customer service, emphasis on a particular market niche) offer the best chance to win a competitive edge; (2) developing skills, expertise, and competitive capabilities that set the company apart from rivals; and (3) trying to insulate the business as much as possible from the effects of competition.

A business strategy is powerful if it produces a sizable and sustainable competitive advantage; it is weak if it results in competitive disadvantage.

A company's strategy for competing is typically both offensive and defensive— some actions are aggressive and amount to direct challenges to competitors' market positions; others aim at countering competitive pressures and the actions of rivals. Three of the most frequently used competitive approaches are (1) striving to be the industry's low-cost producer (thereby aiming for a cost-based competitive advantage over rivals); (2) pursuing differentiation based on such advantages as quality, performance, service, styling, technological superiority, or unusually good value; and (3) focusing on a narrow market niche and winning a competitive edge by doing a better job than rivals of serving the special needs and tastes of niche members.

Internally, business strategy involves taking actions to develop the capabilities and resource strengths needed to achieve competitive advantage. Successful business strategies usually aim at building strong competencies and competitive capabilities in one or more activities crucial to strategic success and then using them as a basis for winning a competitive edge over rivals. A *distinctive competence* is something a firm does especially well in comparison to rival companies. It thus represents a source of competitive strength. Distinctive competencies can relate to R&D, mastery of a technological process, manufacturing capability, sales and distribution, customer service, or anything else that is a competitively important aspect of creating, producing, or marketing the company's product or service. *A distinctive competence is a basis for competitive advantage because it represents expertise or capability that rivals don't have and cannot readily match.*

Having superior internal resource strengths and competitive capabilities is an important way to outcompete rivals.

On a broader internal front, business strategy must also aim at uniting strategic initiatives in the various functional areas of business (purchasing, production, R&D, finance, human resources, sales and marketing, distribution, and customer service). Strategic actions are needed in each functional area to *support* the company's competitive approach and overall business strategy. Strategic unity and coordination across the various functional areas add power to the business strategy.

Business strategy also extends to action plans for addressing any special strategy-related issues unique to the company's competitive position and internal situation (such as whether to add new capacity, replace an obsolete plant, increase R&D funding for a promising technology, reduce burdensome interest expenses, form strategic alliances and collaborative partnerships, or build competitively valuable competencies and capabilities). Such custom tailoring of strategy to fit a company's specific situation is one of the reasons why companies in the same industry employ different business strategies.

Lead responsibility for business strategy falls in the lap of the manager in charge of the business. Even if the business head does not personally wield a heavy hand in the business strategy-making process, preferring to delegate much of the task to others, he or she is still accountable for the strategy and the results it produces. The business head, as chief strategist for the business, has at least two other responsibilities. The first is seeing that supporting strategies in each of the major functional areas of the business are well conceived and consistent with each other. The second is getting major strategic moves approved by higher authority (the board of directors and/or corporate-level officers) if needed and keeping them informed of important new developments, deviations from plan, and potential strategy revisions. In diversified companies, business-unit heads may have the additional obligation of making sure business-level objectives and strategy conform to corporate-level objectives and strategy themes.

Functional Strategy

The term *functional strategy* refers to the managerial game plan for a particular functional activity, business process, or key department within a business. A company's marketing strategy, for example, represents the managerial game plan for running the marketing part of the business. A company's new product development strategy represents the managerial game plan for keeping the company's product lineup fresh and in tune with what buyers are looking for. A company needs a functional strategy for every competitively relevant business activity and organizational unit—for R&D, production, marketing, customer service, distribution, finance, human resources, information technology, and so on. Functional strategies, while narrower in scope than business strategies, add relevant detail to the overall business game plan by setting forth the actions, approaches, and practices to be employed in managing a particular functional department or business process or key activity. They aim at establishing or strengthening specific competencies and competitive capabilities calculated to enhance the company's market position and standing with its customers. The primary role of a functional strategy is to *support* the company's overall business strategy and competitive approach. Well-executed functional strategies give the enterprise competitively valuable competencies, capabilities, and resource strengths. A related role is to create a managerial roadmap for achieving the functional area's objectives and mission. Thus, functional strategy in the production/manufacturing area represents the game plan for *how* manufacturing activities will be managed to support business strategy and achieve the manufacturing department's objectives and mission. Functional strategy in the finance area consists of *how* financial activities will be managed in supporting business strategy and achieving the finance department's objectives and mission.

Lead responsibility for conceiving strategies for each of the various important business functions and processes is normally delegated to the respective functional

Basic Concept

Functional strategy *concerns the managerial game plan for running a major functional activity or process within a business—R&D, production, marketing, customer service, distribution, finance, human resources, and so on; a business needs as many functional strategies as it has strategy-critical activities.*

department heads and activity managers unless the business-unit head decides to exert a strong influence. In crafting strategy, the manager of a particular business function or activity ideally works closely with key subordinates and touches base with the managers of other functions/processes and the business head often. If functional or activity managers plot strategy independent of each other or the business head, they open the door for uncoordinated or conflicting strategies. Compatible, collaborative, mutually reinforcing functional strategies are essential for the overall business strategy to have maximum impact. Plainly, a business's marketing strategy, production strategy, finance strategy, customer service strategy, new product development strategy, and human resources strategy should be in sync rather than serving their own narrower purposes. Coordination and consistency among the various functional and process/activity strategies are best accomplished during the deliberation stage. If inconsistent functional strategies are sent up the line for final approval, it is up to the business head to spot the conflicts and get them resolved.

Operating Strategy

Operating strategies concern the even narrower strategic initiatives and approaches for managing key operating units (plants, sales districts, distribution centers) and for handling daily operating tasks with strategic significance (advertising campaigns, materials purchasing, inventory control, maintenance, shipping). Operating strategies, while of limited scope, add further detail and completeness to functional strategies and to the overall business plan. Lead responsibility for operating strategies is usually delegated to frontline managers, subject to review and approval by higher-ranking managers.

Even though operating strategy is at the bottom of the strategy-making pyramid, its importance should not be downplayed. For example, a major plant that fails in its strategy to achieve production volume, unit cost, and quality targets can undercut the achievement of company sales and profit objectives and wreak havoc with the whole company's strategic efforts to build a quality image with customers. One cannot reliably judge the strategic importance of a given action by the organizational or managerial level where it is initiated.

Frontline managers are part of an organization's strategy-making team because many operating units have strategy-critical performance targets and need to have strategic action plans in place to achieve them. A regional manager needs a strategy customized to the region's particular situation and objectives. A plant manager needs a strategy for accomplishing the plant's objectives, carrying out the plant's part of the company's overall manufacturing game plan, and dealing with any strategy-related problems that exist at the plant. A company's advertising manager needs a strategy for getting maximum audience exposure and sales impact from the ad budget. The following two examples illustrate how operating strategy supports higher-level strategies:

- A company with a low-price, high-volume business strategy and a need to achieve low manufacturing costs launches a companywide effort to boost worker productivity by 10 percent. To contribute to the productivity-boosting objective: (1) the manager of employee recruiting develops a strategy for interviewing and testing job applicants that is thorough enough to weed out all but the most highly motivated, best-qualified candidates; (2) the manager of information systems devises a way to use office technology to boost the productivity of office workers; (3) the employee compensation manager

Basic Concept

Operating strategies concern how to manage frontline organizational units within a business (plants, sales districts, distribution centers) and how to perform strategically significant operating tasks (materials purchasing, inventory control, maintenance, shipping, advertising campaigns).

devises a creative incentive plan to reward increased output by manufacturing employees; and (4) the purchasing manager launches a program to obtain new efficiency-increasing tools and equipment in quicker, less costly fashion.

- A distributor of plumbing equipment emphasizes quick delivery and accurate order-filling as keystones of its customer service approach. To support this strategy, the warehouse manager (1) develops an inventory stocking strategy that allows 99.9 percent of all orders to be completely filled without back-ordering any item and (2) institutes a warehouse staffing strategy that allows any order to be shipped within 24 hours.

Uniting the Strategy-Making Effort

The previous discussion underscores that *a company's strategic plan is a collection of strategies* devised by different managers at different levels in the organizational hierarchy. The larger the enterprise, the more points of strategic initiative it has. Management's direction-setting effort is not complete until the separate layers of strategy are unified into a coherent, supportive pattern. Ideally the pieces and layers of strategy should fit together like the pieces of a picture puzzle. Unified objectives and strategies don't emerge from an undirected process where managers set objectives and craft strategies independently. Indeed, functional and operating-level managers have a duty to work in harmony to set grassroots performance targets and invent frontline strategic actions that will help achieve business objectives and increase the power of business strategy.

Objectives and strategies that are unified from top to bottom of the organizational hierarchy require a team effort.

Harmonizing objectives and strategies piece by piece and level by level can be tedious and frustrating, requiring numerous consultations and meetings, periodic strategy review and approval processes, the experience of trial and error, and months (sometimes years) of consensus building and collaborative effort. The politics of gaining strategic consensus and the battle of trying to keep all managers and departments focused on what's best for the total enterprise (as opposed to what's best for their departments or careers) are often big obstacles in unifying the layers of objectives and strategies and producing the desired degree of cooperation and collaboration.[12] Broad consensus is particularly difficult when there is ample room for opposing views and disagreement. Managerial discussions about an organization's mission and vision, long-term direction, objectives, and strategies often provoke heated debate and strong differences of opinion.

Consistency between business strategy and functional/operating strategies comes from the collaborative efforts of functional and operating-level managers to set performance targets and invent strategic actions in their respective areas of responsibility that contribute directly to achieving business objectives and improving the execution of business strategy.

Figure 2.4 portrays the networking of objectives and strategies through the managerial hierarchy. The two-way arrows indicate that there are simultaneous bottom-up and top-down influences on missions, objectives, and strategies at each level. Furthermore, there are two-way influences across the related businesses of a diversified company and across the related processes, functions, and operating activities within a business. These vertical and horizontal linkages, if man-

---

[12]Functional managers are sometimes more interested in doing what is best for their own areas, building their own empires, and consolidating their personal power and organizational influence than they are in cooperating with other functional managers to unify behind the overall business strategy. As a result, it's easy for functional area support strategies to conflict, thereby forcing the business-level general manager to spend time and energy refereeing functional strategy conflicts and building support for a more unified approach.

FIGURE 2.4 The Networking of Strategic Visions, Missions, Objectives, and Strategies in the Strategy-Making Pyramid

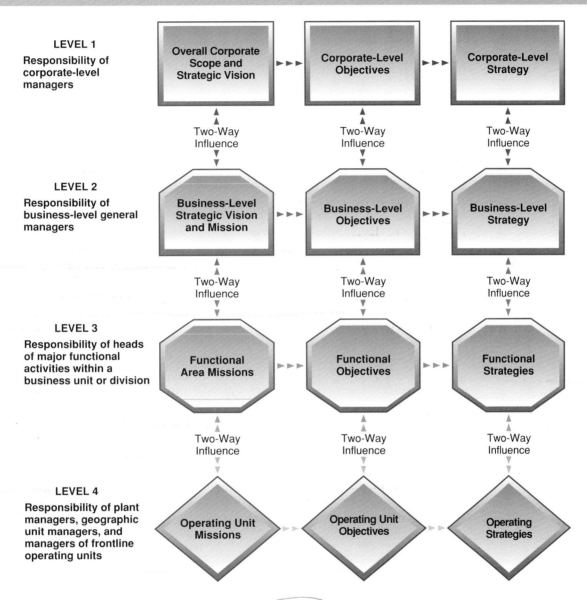

aged in a way that promotes coordination, can help unify the direction-setting and strategy-making activities of many managers into a mutually reinforcing pattern. The tighter that coordination is enforced, the tighter the linkages in the missions, objectives, and strategies of the various organizational units. Tight linkages safeguard against organizational units straying from the company's charted strategic course.

As a practical matter, however, corporate and business strategic visions, objectives, and strategies need to be clearly outlined and communicated down the line before much progress can be made in direction setting and strategy making at the functional and operating levels. Direction and guidance need to flow from the corporate level to the business level and from the business level to functional and grassroots operating levels. The strategic disarray that occurs in an organization when senior managers don't exercise strong top-down direction setting and strategic leadership is akin to what would happen to a football team's offensive performance if the quarterback decided not to call a play for the team, but instead let each player pick whatever play he thought would work best at his respective position. In business, as in sports, all the strategy makers in a company are on the same team. They are obligated to perform their strategy-making tasks in a manner that benefits the whole company, not in a manner that suits personal or departmental interests. A company's strategy is at full power only when its many pieces are united. This means that the strategizing process has to proceed more from the top down than from the bottom up. Lower-level managers cannot do good strategy making without understanding the company's long-term direction and higher-level strategies.

THE FACTORS THAT SHAPE A COMPANY'S STRATEGY

Many situational considerations enter into crafting strategy. Figure 2.5 depicts the primary factors that shape a company's strategic approaches. The interplay of these factors and the influence that each has on the strategy-making process vary from situation to situation. Very few strategic choices are made in the same context—even in the same industry, situational factors differ enough from company to company that the strategies of rivals turn out to be quite distinguishable from one another rather than imitative. This is why carefully sizing up all the various situational factors, both external and internal, is the starting point in crafting strategy.

Societal, Political, Regulatory, and Citizenship Considerations

What an enterprise can and cannot do strategywise is always constrained by what is legal, by what complies with government policies and regulatory requirements, and by what is in accord with societal expectations and the standards of good community citizenship. Outside pressures also come from other sources—special-interest groups,

Societal, political, regulatory, and citizenship factors limit the strategic actions a company can or should take.

the glare of investigative reporting, a fear of unwanted political action, and the stigma of negative opinion. Societal concerns over health and nutrition, alcohol and drug abuse, environmental pollution, sexual harassment, corporate downsizing, and the impact of plant closings on local communities have caused many companies to temper or revise aspects of their strategies. American concerns over jobs lost to foreign imports and political debate over how to cure the chronic U.S. trade deficit are driving forces in the strategic decisions of Japanese and European companies to locate plants in the United States. Heightened consumer awareness about the hazards of saturated fat and cholesterol have driven most food products companies to phase out high-fat ingredients and substitute low-fat ingredients, despite the extra costs.

Factoring in societal values and priorities, community concerns, and the potential for onerous legislation and regulatory requirements is a regular part of external situation analysis at more and more companies. Intense public pressure and adverse media coverage make such a practice prudent. The task of making an organization's strategy socially responsible means (1) conducting organizational activities within the bounds of what is considered to be in the general public interest; (2) responding positively to emerging societal priorities and expectations; (3) demonstrating a willingness to take action ahead of regulatory confrontation; (4) balancing stockholder interests against the larger interests of society as a whole; and (5) being a good citizen in the community.

FIGURE 2.5 Factors Shaping the Choice of Company Strategy

STRATEGY-SHAPING FACTORS EXTERNAL TO THE COMPANY

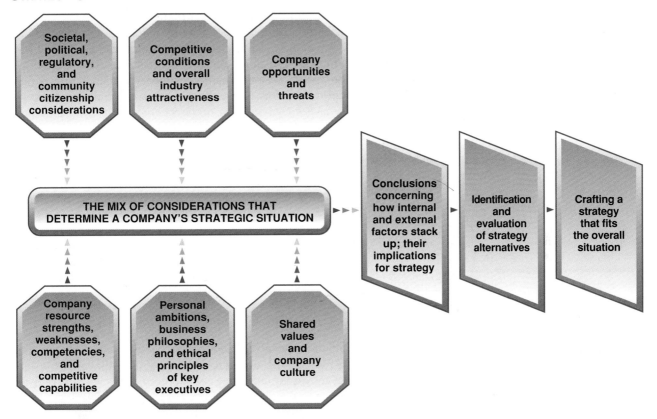

STRATEGY-SHAPING FACTORS INTERNAL TO THE COMPANY

Corporate social responsibility is showing up in company mission statements. John Hancock, for example, concludes its mission statement with the following sentence:

> In pursuit of this mission, we will strive to exemplify the highest standards of business ethics and personal integrity; and shall recognize our corporate obligation to the social and economic well-being of our community.

At Union Electric, a St. Louis-based utility company, the following statement is official corporate policy:

> As a private enterprise entrusted with an essential public service, we recognize our civic responsibility in the communities we serve. We shall strive to advance the growth and welfare of these communities and shall participate in civic activities which fulfill that goal—for we believe this is both good citizenship and good business.

Competitive Conditions and Overall Industry Attractiveness

An industry's competitive conditions and overall attractiveness are big strategy-determining factors. A company's strategy has to be tailored to the nature and mix of competitive factors in play—price, product quality, performance features, service, warranties, and so on. When competitive conditions intensify significantly, a company must respond with strategic actions to protect its position. Competitive weakness on the part of one or more rivals may signal the need for a strategic offensive.

Furthermore, fresh moves on the part of rival companies, changes in the industry's price-cost-profit economics, shifting buyer needs and expectations, and new technological developments often alter the requirements for competitive success and mandate reconsideration of strategy. The industry environment, as it exists now and is expected to exist later, thus has a direct bearing on a company's best competitive strategy option and where it should concentrate its efforts. *A company's strategy can't produce real market success unless it is well-matched to the industry and competitive situation.* When a firm concludes its industry environment has grown unattractive and it is better off investing company resources elsewhere, it may begin a strategy of disinvestment and eventual abandonment. A strategist, therefore, has to be a student of industry and competitive conditions.

Strategic Management Principle

A company's strategy should be tailored to fit industry and competitive conditions.

The Company's Market Opportunities and External Threats

The particular business opportunities open to a company and the threatening external developments that it faces are key influences on strategy. Both point to the need for strategic action. A company's strategy needs to be deliberately aimed at capturing its best growth opportunities, especially the ones that hold the most promise for building sustainable competitive advantage and enhancing profitability. Likewise, strategy should be geared to providing a defense against external threats to the company's well-being and future performance. For strategy to be successful, it has to be well matched to market opportunities and threatening external developments; this usually means crafting offensive moves to capitalize on the company's most promising market opportunities and crafting defensive moves to protect the company's competitive position and long-term profitability.

Strategic Management Principle

A well-conceived strategy aims at capturing a company's best growth opportunities and defending against external threats to its well-being and future performance.

Company Resource Strengths, Competencies, and Competitive Capabilities

One of the most pivotal strategy-shaping internal considerations is whether a company has or can acquire the resources, competencies, and capabilities needed to execute a strategy proficiently. An organization's resources, competencies, and competitive capabilities are important strategy-making considerations because of (1) the competitive strengths they provide in capitalizing on a particular opportunity, (2) the competitive edge they may give a firm in the marketplace, and (3) the potential they have for becoming a cornerstone of strategy. The best path to competitive advantage is found where a firm has competitively valuable resources and competencies, where rivals do not have matching or offsetting resources and competencies, and where rivals can't develop comparable capabilities except at high cost and/or over an extended period of time.

Even if an organization has no outstanding competencies and capabilities (and many do not), managers still must tailor strategy to fit the enterprise's particular resources and capabilities. It is foolish to develop a strategic plan that cannot be executed with the resources and capabilities a

---

Strategic Management Principle

A company's strategy ought to be grounded in its resource strengths and in what it is good at doing (its competencies and competitive capabilities); likewise, it is perilous to craft a strategy whose success is dependent on resources and capabilities that a company lacks.

firm is able to assemble. In short, *strategy must be well-matched to a company's resource strengths and weaknesses and to its competitive capabilities.* Experience shows that winning strategies aim squarely at capitalizing on a company's resource strengths and neutralizing its resource deficiencies and skills gaps. An organization's resource strengths make some strategies and market opportunities attractive to pursue; likewise, its resource deficiencies, its gaps in important skills and know-how, and the weaknesses in its present competitive market position make the pursuit of certain strategies or opportunities risky (or even out of the question). Consequently, what resources, competencies, and capabilities a company has and how competitively valuable they are is a very relevant strategy-making consideration.

The Personal Ambitions, Business Philosophies, and Ethical Beliefs of Managers

Managers do not dispassionately assess what strategic course to steer. Their choices are often influenced by their own vision of how to compete and how to position the enterprise and by what image and standing they want the company to have. Both casual observation and formal studies indicate that managers' ambitions, values, business philosophies, attitudes toward risk, and ethical beliefs have important influences on strategy.[13] Sometimes the influence of a manager's personal values, experiences, and emotions is conscious and deliberate; at other times it may be unconscious. As one expert noted in explaining the relevance of personal factors to strategy, "People have to have their hearts in it."[14]

> *The personal ambitions, business philosophies, and ethical beliefs of managers are usually stamped on the strategies they craft.*

Several examples of how business philosophies and personal values enter into strategy making are particularly noteworthy. Ben Cohen and Jerry Greenfield, cofounders and major stockholders in Ben and Jerry's Homemade Ice Cream, have consistently insisted that the company's strategy be supportive of social causes of their choosing and incorporate a strong social mission. Japanese managers are strong proponents of strategies that take a long-term view and that aim at building market share and competitive position. In contrast, some U.S. and European executives have drawn criticism for overemphasizing short-term profits at the expense of long-term competitive positioning because of pressures to meet investors' quarterly and annual earnings expectations. Japanese companies also display a quite different philosophy regarding the role of suppliers. Their preferred supplier strategy is to enter into long-term partnership arrangements with key suppliers because they believe that working closely with the same supplier year after year improves the quality and reliability of component parts, facilitates just-in-time delivery, and reduces inventory carrying costs. In U.S. and European companies, the traditional strategic approach has been to play suppliers off against one another, doing business on a short-term basis with whoever offers the best price and promises acceptable quality.

---

[13]The role of personal values, individual ambitions, and managerial philosophies in strategy making has long been recognized and documented. The classic sources are William D. Guth and Renato Tagiuri, "Personal Values and Corporate Strategy," *Harvard Business Review* 43, no. 5 (September–October 1965), pp. 123–32; Kenneth R. Andrews, *The Concept of Corporate Strategy*, 3rd ed. (Homewood, Ill.: Richard D. Irwin, 1987), chap. 4; and Richard F. Vancil, "Strategy Formulation in Complex Organizations," *Sloan Management Review* 17, no. 2 (Winter 1986), pp. 4–5.

[14]Andrews, *The Concept of Corporate Strategy*, p. 63.

Attitudes toward risk also have a big influence on strategy. Risk-avoiders are inclined toward "conservative" strategies that minimize downside risk, have a quick payback, and produce sure short-term profits. Risk-takers lean more toward opportunistic strategies where visionary moves can produce a big payoff over the long term. Risk-takers prefer innovation to imitation and bold strategic offensives to defensive moves to protect the status quo.

Managerial values also shape the ethical quality of a firm's strategy. Managers with strong ethical convictions take pains to see that their companies observe a strict code of ethics in all aspects of the business. They expressly forbid such practices as accepting or giving kickbacks, badmouthing rivals' products, and buying political influence with political contributions. Instances where a company's strategic actions run afoul of high ethical standards include charging excessive interest rates on credit card balances, employing bait-and-switch sales tactics, continuing to market products suspected of having safety problems, and using ingredients that are known health hazards.

The Influence of Shared Values and Company Culture on Strategy

An organization's policies, practices, traditions, philosophical beliefs, and ways of doing things combine to create a distinctive culture. Typically, the stronger a company's culture the more that culture is likely to shape the strategic actions it decides to employ, sometimes even dominating the choice of strategic moves. This is because culture-related values and beliefs are so embedded in management's strategic thinking and actions that they condition how the enterprise responds to external events. Such firms have a culture-driven bias about how to handle strategic issues and what kinds of strategic moves it will consider or reject. Strong cultural influences partly account for why companies gain reputations for such strategic traits as leadership in technological advance and product innovation, dedication to superior craftsmanship, a proclivity for financial wheeling and dealing, a desire to grow rapidly by acquiring other companies, having a strong people orientation and being a good company to work for, or unusual emphasis on customer service and total customer satisfaction.

A company's values and culture can dominate the kinds of strategic moves it considers or rejects.

In recent years, more companies have articulated the core beliefs and values underlying their business approaches. One company expressed its core beliefs and values like this:

> We are market-driven. We believe that functional excellence, combined with teamwork across functions and profit centers, is essential to achieving superb execution. We believe that people are central to everything we will accomplish. We believe that honesty, integrity, and fairness should be the cornerstone of our relationships with consumers, customers, suppliers, stockholders, and employees.

Wal-Mart's founder, Sam Walton, was a fervent believer in frugality, hard work, constant improvement, dedication to customers, and genuine care for employees. The company's commitment to these values is deeply ingrained in its strategy of low prices, good values, friendly service, productivity through the intelligent use of technology, and hard-nosed bargaining with suppliers.[15] At Hewlett-Packard, the

---

[15]Sam Walton with John Huey, *Sam Walton: Made in America* (New York: Doubleday, 1992); and John P. Kotter and James L. Heskett, *Corporate Culture and Performance* (New York: Free Press, 1992), pp. 17 and 36.

company's basic values, known internally as "the HP Way," include sharing the company's success with employees, showing trust and respect for employees, providing customers with products and services of the greatest value, being genuinely interested in providing customers with effective solutions to their problems, making profit a high stockholder priority, avoiding the use of long-term debt to finance growth, individual initiative and creativity, teamwork, and being a good corporate citizen.[16] At both Wal-Mart and Hewlett-Packard, the value systems are deeply ingrained and widely shared by managers and employees. Whenever this happens, values and beliefs are more than an expression of nice platitudes; they become a way of life within the company and they mold company strategy.[17]

LINKING STRATEGY WITH ETHICS

Strategy ought to be ethical. It should involve rightful actions, not wrongful ones; otherwise it won't pass the test of moral scrutiny. This means more than conforming to what is legal. Ethical and moral standards go beyond the prohibitions of law and the language of "thou shalt not" to the issues of *duty* and the language of "should do and should not do." Ethics concerns human duty and the principles on which this duty rests.[18]

Every strategic action a company takes should be ethical.

Every business has an ethical duty to each of five constituencies: owners/shareholders, employees, customers, suppliers, and the community at large. Each of these constituencies affects the organization and is affected by it. Each is a stakeholder in the enterprise, with certain expectations as to what the enterprise should do and how it should do it.[19] Owners/shareholders, for instance, rightly expect a return on their investment. Even though investors may individually differ in their preferences for profits now versus profits later, their tolerances for greater risk, and their enthusiasm for exercising social responsibility, business executives have a moral duty to pursue profitable management of the owners' investment.

A company's duty to employees arises out of respect for the worth and dignity of individuals who devote their energies to the business and who depend on the business for their economic well-being. Principled strategy making requires that employee-related decisions be made equitably and compassionately, with concern for due process and for the impact that strategic change has on employees' lives. At best, the chosen strategy should promote employee interests as concerns compensation, career opportunities, job security, and overall working conditions. At worst, the chosen strategy should not disadvantage employees. Even in crisis situations where adverse employee impact cannot be avoided, businesses have an ethical duty to minimize whatever hardships have to be imposed in the form of workforce reductions, plant closings, job transfers, relocations, retraining, and loss of income.

A company has ethical duties to owners, employees, customers, suppliers, the communities where it operates, and the public at large.

The duty to the customer arises out of expectations that attend the purchase of a good or service. Inadequate appreciation of this duty led to product liability laws and a host of regulatory agencies to protect consumers. All kinds of strategy-related

---

[16]Kotter and Heskett, *Corporate Culture and Performance*, pp. 60–61.

[17]For another example of the impact of values and beliefs, see Richard T. Pascale, "Perspectives on Strategy: The Real Story behind Honda's Success," in Glenn Carroll and David Vogel, *Strategy and Organization: A West Coast Perspective* (Marshfield, Mass.: Pitman Publishing, 1984), p. 60.

[18]Harry Downs, "Business Ethics: The Stewardship of Power," working paper provided to the authors.

[19]Ibid.

ethical issues still abound, however. Should a seller voluntarily inform consumers that its product contains ingredients that, though officially approved for use, are suspected of having potentially harmful effects? Is it ethical for the makers of alcoholic beverages to sponsor college events, given that many college students are under 21? Is it ethical for cigarette manufacturers to advertise at all (even though it is legal)? Is it ethical for manufacturers to stonewall efforts to recall products they suspect have faulty parts or defective designs? Is it ethical for supermarkets and department store retailers to lure customers with highly advertised "loss-leader" prices on a few select items, but then put high markups on popular or essential items?

A company's ethical duty to its suppliers arises out of the market relationship that exists between them. They are both partners and adversaries. They are partners in the sense that the quality of suppliers' parts affects the quality of a firm's own product. They are adversaries in the sense that the supplier wants the highest price and profit it can get while the buyer wants a cheaper price, better quality, and speedier service. A company confronts several ethical issues in its supplier relationships. Is it ethical to purchase goods from foreign suppliers who employ child labor and/or pay substandard wages and/or have sweatshop working conditions in their facilities? Is it ethical to threaten to cease doing business with a supplier unless the supplier agrees not to do business with key competitors? Is it ethical to reveal one supplier's price quote to a rival supplier? Is it ethical to accept gifts from suppliers? Is it ethical to pay a supplier in cash? Is it ethical *not* to give present suppliers advance warning of the intent to discontinue using what they have supplied and to switch to components supplied by other enterprises?

A company's ethical duty to the community at large stems from its status as a citizen of the community and as an institution of society. Communities and society are reasonable in expecting businesses to be good citizens—to pay their fair share of taxes for fire and police protection, waste removal, streets and highways, and so on, and to exercise care in the impact their activities have on the environment, on society, and on the communities in which they operate. For example, is it ethical for a liquor firm to advertise its products on TV at times when these ads are likely to be seen by children and people under the age of 21? Is it ethical for liquor firms to even advertise on TV at any time? Some years ago, an oil company was found to have spent $2 million on environmental conservation and $4 million advertising its virtue and good deeds—actions that seem deliberately manipulative and calculated to mislead. A company's community citizenship is ultimately demonstrated by whether it refrains from acting in a manner contrary to the well-being of society and by the degree to which it supports community activities, encourages employees to participate in community activities, handles the health and safety aspects of its operations, accepts responsibility for overcoming environmental pollution, relates to regulatory bodies and employee unions, and exhibits high ethical standards.

Carrying Out Ethical Responsibilities   Management, not constituent groups, is responsible for managing the enterprise. Thus, it is management's perceptions of its ethical duties and of constituents' claims that drive whether and how strategy is linked to ethical behavior. Ideally, managers weigh strategic decisions from each constituent's point of view and, where conflicts arise, strike a rational, objective, and equitable balance among the interests of all five constituencies. If any of the five constituencies conclude that management is not doing its duty, they have their own avenues for recourse. Concerned investors can protest at the annual shareholders' meeting, appeal to the board of directors, or sell their stock. Concerned employees can unionize and

---

ILLUSTRATION CAPSULE 8   Harris Corporation's Commitments to Its Stakeholders

Harris Corporation is a major supplier of information, communication, and semiconductor products, systems, and services to commercial and governmental customers throughout the world. The company utilizes advanced technologies to provide innovative and cost-effective solutions for processing and communicating data, voice, text, and video information. The company had sales of $3.6 billion in 1996, and it employs nearly 23,000 people. In a recent annual report, the company set forth its commitment to satisfying the expectations of its stakeholders:

Customers—For customers, our objective is to achieve ever-increasing levels of satisfaction by providing quality products and services with distinctive benefits on a timely and continuing basis worldwide. Our relationships with customers will be forthright and ethical, and will be conducted in a manner to build trust and confidence.

Shareholders—For shareholders, the owners of our company, our objective is to achieve sustained growth in earnings-per-share. The resulting stock-price appreciation combined with dividends should provide our shareholders with a total return on investment that is competitive with similar investment opportunities.

Employees—The people of Harris are our company's most valuable asset, and our objective is for every em-

ployee to be personally involved in and share the success of the business. The company is committed to providing an environment that encourages all employees to make full use of their creativity and unique talents; to providing equitable compensation, good working conditions, and the opportunity for personal development and growth which is limited only by individual ability and desire.

Suppliers—Suppliers are a vital part of our resources. Our objective is to develop and maintain mutually beneficial partnerships with suppliers who share our commitment to achieving increasing levels of customer satisfaction through continuing improvements in quality, service, timeliness, and cost. Our relationships with suppliers will be sincere, ethical, and will embrace the highest principles of purchasing practice.

Communities—Our objective is to be a responsible corporate citizen. This includes support of appropriate civic, educational, and business activities, respect for the environment, and the encouragement of Harris employees to practice good citizenship and support community programs. Our greatest contribution to our communities is to be successful so that we can maintain stable employment and create new jobs.

Source: 1988 Annual Report.

---

bargain collectively, or they can seek employment elsewhere. Customers can switch to competitors. Suppliers can find other buyers or pursue other market alternatives. The community and society can do anything from staging protest marches and urging boycotts to stimulating political and governmental action.[20]

A management that truly cares about business ethics and corporate social responsibility is proactive rather than reactive in linking strategic action and ethics. It steers away from ethically or morally questionable business opportunities (for example, in late 1996, Anheuser-Busch announced it would no longer run its beer commercials on MTV). It won't do business with suppliers that engage in activities the company does not condone. It produces products that are safe for its customers to use. It operates a workplace environment that is safe for employees. It recruits and hires employees whose values and behavior match the company's principles and ethical standards. It acts to reduce any environmental pollution it causes. It cares about how it does business and whether its actions reflect integrity and high ethical standards. Illustration Capsule 8 describes Harris Corporation's ethical commitments to its stakeholders.

---

[20]Ibid.

Tests of a Winning Strategy

What are the criteria for weeding out candidate strategies? How can a manager judge which strategic option is best for the company? What are the standards for determining whether a strategy is successful or not? Three tests can be used to evaluate the merits of one strategy over another and to gauge how good a strategy is:

1. *The Goodness of Fit Test*—A good strategy is tailored to fit the company's internal and external situation—without tight situational fit, there's real question whether a strategy appropriately matches the requirements for market success.

2. *The Competitive Advantage Test*—A good strategy leads to sustainable competitive advantage. The bigger the competitive edge that a strategy helps build, the more powerful and effective it is.

3. *The Performance Test*—A good strategy boosts company performance. Two kinds of performance improvements are the most telling of a strategy's caliber: gains in profitability and gains in the company's competitive strength and long-term market position.

Strategic options that clearly come up short on one or more of these tests are candidates to be dropped from further consideration. The strategic option that best meets all three tests can be regarded as the best or most attractive strategic alternative. Once a strategic commitment is made and enough time elapses to see results, these same tests can be used to determine whether the chosen strategy qualifies as a winning strategy. The more a strategy fits the situation, builds sustainable competitive advantage, and boosts company performance, the more it qualifies as a winner.

> **Strategic Management Principle**
>
> *A winning strategy must fit the enterprise's situation, build sustainable competitive advantage, and improve company performance.*

There are, of course, some additional criteria for judging the merits of a particular strategy: completeness and coverage of all the bases, internal consistency among all the pieces of strategy, clarity, the degree of risk involved, and flexibility. These criteria are useful supplements and certainly ought to be looked at, but they can in no way replace the three tests posed above.

APPROACHES TO PERFORMING THE STRATEGY-MAKING TASK

Companies and managers go about the task of developing strategic plans differently. In small, owner-managed companies, strategy making usually occurs informally, emerging from the experiences, personal observations and assessments, verbal exchanges and debates, and entrepreneurial judgments of a few key people at the top—with perhaps some data gathering and number-crunching analysis involved. Often, the resulting strategy exists mainly in the entrepreneur's own mind and in oral understandings with key subordinates, but is not reduced to writing and laid out in a formal document called a strategic plan.

Large companies, however, tend to develop their strategic plans more formally (occasionally using prescribed procedures, forms, and timetables) and in deeper detail. There is often considerable data gathering, situational analysis, and intense study of particular issues, involving the broad participation of managers at many organizational levels and numerous meetings to probe, question, sort things out, and hammer out the pieces of the strategy. The larger and more diverse an enterprise, the more managers feel it is better to have a structured process with timetables, studies and debate, and written plans that receive official approval from up the line.

Along with variations in the organizational process of formulating strategy are variations in how managers personally participate in analyzing the company's situation and deliberating what strategy to pursue. The four basic strategy-making styles managers use are:[21]

The Master Strategist Approach Some managers take on the role of chief strategist and chief entrepreneur, singlehandedly exercising *strong* influence over assessments of the situation, over the strategy alternatives that are explored, and over the details of strategy. This does not mean that the manager personally does all the work; it means that the manager personally becomes the chief architect of strategy and wields a proactive hand in shaping some or all of the major pieces of strategy. Master strategists act as strategy commanders and have a big ownership stake in the chosen strategy.

The Delegate-It-to-Others Approach Here the manager in charge delegates pieces and maybe all of the strategy-making task to others, perhaps a group of trusted subordinates, a cross-functional task force, or self-directed work teams with authority over a particular process or function. The manager then personally stays in touch with how the strategy deliberations are progressing, offers guidance when appropriate, smiles or frowns as trial balloon recommendations are informally run by him/her for reaction, and reserves final approval until the strategy proposals are formally presented, considered, modified (if needed), and deemed ready for implementation. While strategy delegators may leave little of their own imprint on individual pieces of the strategy proposals presented for approval, they often must still play an integrative role in bringing the separate strategy elements devised by others into harmony and in fleshing out any pieces not delegated. They also must bear ultimate responsibility for the caliber of the strategy-making efforts of subordinates, so their confidence in the business judgments of those to whom strategy-making tasks are delegated must be well placed. This strategy-making style allows for broad participation and input from many managers and areas, plus it gives managers some flexibility in picking and choosing from the smorgasbord of strategic ideas that bubble up from below. The big weakness of delegation is that its success depends heavily on the business judgments and strategy-making skills of those to whom the strategy-making tasks are delegated—for instance, the strategizing efforts of subordinates may prove too short-run oriented and reactive, dealing more with how to address today's problems than with positioning the enterprise and adapting its resources to capture tomorrow's opportunities. Subordinates may not have either the clout or the inclination to tackle changing major components of the present strategy.[22] A second weakness of chartering a group of subordinates to develop strategy is that it sends the wrong signal: Strategy development isn't important enough to warrant a big claim on the boss's personal time and attention. Moreover, a manager can end up too detached from the process to

---

[21]This discussion is based on David R. Brodwin and L. J. Bourgeois, "Five Steps to Strategic Action," in Glenn Carroll and David Vogel, *Strategy and Organization: A West Coast Perspective* (Marshfield, Mass.: Pitman Publishing, 1984), pp. 168–78.

[22]For a case in point of where the needed strategy changes were too big for a chartered group of subordinates to address, see Thomas M. Hout and John C. Carter, "Getting It Done: New Roles for Senior Executives," *Harvard Business Review* 73 no. 6 (November–December 1995), pp. 140–44.

exercise strategic leadership if the group's deliberations bog down in disagreement or go astray, either of which set the stage for rudderless direction setting and/or ill-conceived strategy.

The Collaborative Approach   This is a middle approach whereby the manager enlists the help of key peers and subordinates in hammering out a consensus strategy. The strategy that emerges is the joint product of all concerned, with the collaborative effort usually being personally led by the manager in charge. The collaborative approach is well suited to situations where strategic issues cut across traditional functional and departmental lines, where there's a need to tap into the ideas and problem-solving skills of people with different backgrounds, expertise, and perspectives, and where it makes sense to give as many people as feasible a participative role in shaping the strategy that emerges and help win their wholehearted commitment to implementation. Involving teams of people to dissect complex situations and find market-driven, customer-driven solutions is becoming increasingly necessary in many businesses. Not only are many strategic issues too far-reaching or too involved for a single manager to handle but they often are cross-functional and cross-departmental in nature, thus requiring the contributions of many disciplinary experts and the collaboration of managers from different parts of the organization to decide upon sound strategic actions. A valuable strength of this strategy-making style is that the group of people charged with crafting the strategy can easily include the very people who will also be charged with implementing it. Giving people an influential stake in crafting the strategy they must later help implement is not only motivational but also means they can be held accountable for putting the strategy into place and making it work—the oft-used excuse of "It wasn't my idea to do this" won't fly.

The Champion Approach   In this style, the manager is interested neither in a big personal stake in the details of strategy nor in the time-consuming task of leading others through participative brainstorming or a collaborative "group wisdom" exercise. Rather, the idea is to encourage individuals and teams to develop, champion, and implement sound strategies on their own initiative. Here important pieces of company strategy originate with the "doers" and the "fast-trackers." Executives serve as judges, evaluating the strategy proposals needing their approval. This approach works well in large diversified corporations where the CEO cannot personally orchestrate strategy making in each of many business divisions. For headquarters executives to capitalize on having people in the enterprise who can see strategic opportunities that they cannot, they must delegate the initiative for strategy making to managers at the business-unit level. Corporate executives may well articulate general strategic themes as organizationwide guidelines for strategic thinking, but the key to good strategy making is stimulating and rewarding new strategic initiatives conceived by a champion who believes in the opportunity and badly wants the blessing to go after it. With this approach, the total strategy ends up being the sum of the championed initiatives that get approved.

These four basic managerial approaches to forming a strategy illuminate several aspects about how companies arrive at a planned strategy. When the manager in charge personally functions as the chief architect of strategy, the choice of what strategic course to steer is a product of his/her own vision about how to position the enterprise and of the manager's ambitions, values, business philosophies, and entrepreneurial judgment about what moves to make next. Highly centralized strategy making works fine when the manager in charge has a powerful, insightful vision of where to head and how to get there. The primary weakness of the master strategist approach is that the caliber of the strategy depends so heavily on one person's strategy-making skills and entrepreneurial acumen. It also breaks down in large enterprises where many strategic initiatives are needed and the strategy-making task is too complex for one person to handle alone.

Of the four basic approaches managers can use in crafting strategy, none is inherently superior—each has strengths and weaknesses and each is workable in the "right" situation.

On the other hand, the group approach to strategy making has its risks too. Sometimes, the strategy that emerges from group consensus is a middle-of-the-road compromise, void of bold, creative initiative. Other times, it represents political consensus, with the outcome shaped by influential subordinates, by powerful functional departments, or by majority coalitions that have a common interest in promoting their particular version of what the strategy ought to be. Politics and the exercise of power are most likely to come into play in situations where there is no strong consensus on what strategy to adopt; this opens the door for a political solution to emerge. The collaborative approach is conducive to political strategic choices as well, since powerful departments and individuals have ample opportunity to try to build a consensus for their favored strategic approach. The big weakness of a delegate-it-to-others approach is the potential lack of sufficient top-down direction and strategic leadership.

The strength of the champion approach is also its weakness. The value of championing is that it encourages people at lower organizational levels to be alert for profitable market opportunities, to propose innovative strategies to capture them, and to take on responsibility for new business ventures. Individuals with attractive strategic proposals are given the latitude and resources to try them out, thus helping renew an organization's capacity for innovation and growth. On the other hand, a series of championed actions, because they spring from many places in the organization and can fly off in many directions, are not likely to form a coherent pattern or result in a clear strategic direction for the company as a whole without some strong top-down leadership. With championing, the chief executive has to work at ensuring that what is championed adds power to the overall organization strategy; otherwise, strategic initiatives may be launched in directions that have no integrating links or overarching rationale. Another weakness of the championing approach is that top executives will be more intent on protecting their reputations for prudence than on supporting sometimes revolutionary strategies, in which case innovative ideas can be doused by corporate orthodoxy.[23] It is usually painful and laborious for a lowly employee to champion an out-of-the-ordinary idea up the chain of command.

All four styles of handling the strategy-making task thus have strengths and weaknesses. All four can succeed or fail depending on whether they are used in the right circumstances, on how well the approach is managed, and on the strategy-making skills and judgments of the individuals involved.

KEY POINTS

Management's direction-setting task involves charting a company's future strategic path, setting objectives, and forming a strategy. Early on in the direction-setting process, managers need to address the question of "What is our business and what will it be?" Management's views and conclusions about the organization's future

---

[23]See Hamel, "Strategy as Revolution," pp. 80–81.

course, the market position it should try to occupy, and the business activities to be pursued constitute a *strategic vision* for the company. A strategic vision indicates management's aspirations for the organization, providing a panoramic view of "what businesses we want to be in, where we are headed, and the kind of company we are trying to create." It spells out a direction and describes the destination. Effective visions are clear, challenging, and inspiring; they prepare a firm for the future, and they make sense in the marketplace. A well-conceived, well-said mission/vision statement serves as a beacon of long-term direction, helps channel organizational efforts along the path management has committed to following, builds a strong sense of organizational identity, and creates employee buy-in.

The second direction-setting step is to establish *strategic* and *financial* objectives for the organization to achieve. Objectives convert the business mission and strategic vision into specific performance targets. The agreed-on objectives need to spell out precisely how much by when, and they need to require a significant amount of organizational stretch. Objectives are needed at all organizational levels.

The third direction-setting step entails forming strategies to achieve the objectives set in each area of the organization. A corporate strategy is needed to achieve corporate-level objectives; business strategies are needed to achieve business-unit performance objectives; functional strategies are needed to achieve the performance targets set for each functional department; and operating-level strategies are needed to achieve the objectives set in each operating and geographic unit. In effect, an organization's strategic plan is a collection of unified and interlocking strategies. As shown in Table 2.1, different strategic issues are addressed at each level of managerial strategy making. Typically, the strategy-making task is more top-down than bottom-up. Lower-level strategies should support and complement higher-level strategy and contribute to the achievement of higher-level, companywide objectives.

Strategy is shaped by both outside and inside considerations. The major external considerations are societal, political, regulatory, and community factors; competitive conditions and overall industry attractiveness; and the company's market opportunities and threats. The primary internal considerations are company strengths, weaknesses, and competitive capabilities; managers' personal ambitions, philosophies, and ethics; and the company's culture and shared values. A good strategy must be well matched to all these situational considerations. In addition, a good strategy must lead to sustainable competitive advantage and improved company performance.

There are essentially four basic ways to manage the strategy formation process in an organization: the master strategist approach where the manager in charge personally functions as the chief architect of strategy, the delegate-it-to-others approach, the collaborative approach, and the champion approach. All four have strengths and weaknesses. All four can succeed or fail depending on how well the approach is managed and depending on the strategy-making skills and judgments of the individuals involved.

SUGGESTED READINGS

Campbell, Andrew, and Laura Nash. *A Sense of Mission: Defining Direction for the Large Corporation.* Reading, Mass.: Addison-Wesley, 1993.

Collins, James C. and Jerry I. Porras. " Building Your Company's Vision." *Harvard Business Review* 74, no.5 (September–October 1996), pp. 65–77.

Drucker, Peter. "The Theory of the Business." *Harvard Business Review* 72, no. 5 (September–October 1994), pp. 95–104.

Hamel, Gary, and C. K. Prahalad. "Strategic Intent." *Harvard Business Review* 67, no. 3 (May–June 1989), pp. 63–76.

———. "Strategy as Stretch and Leverage." *Harvard Business Review* 71, no. 2 (March–April 1993), pp. 75–84.

Hamel, Gary. "Strategy as Revolution," *Harvard Business Review* 74 no. 4 (July–August 1996), pp. 69–82.

Hammer, Michael, and James Champy. *Reengineering the Corporation*. New York: HarperBusiness, 1993, chap. 9.

Ireland, R. Duane, and Michael A. Hitt. "Mission Statements: Importance, Challenge, and Recommendations for Development." *Business Horizons* (May–June 1992), pp. 34–42.

Kahaner, Larry. "What You Can Learn from Your Competitors' Mission Statements." *Competitive Intelligence Review* 6 no. 4 (Winter 1995), pp. 35–40.

Lipton, Mark. "Demystifying the Development of an Organizational Vision." *Sloan Management Review* (Summer 1996), pp. 83–92.

McTavish, Ron. "One More Time: What Business Are You In?" *Long Range Planning* 28, no. 2 (April 1995), pp. 49–60.

Mintzberg, Henry. "Crafting Strategy." *Harvard Business Review* 65, no. 4 (July–August 1987), pp. 66–77.

Porter, Michael E. "What Is Strategy?" *Harvard Business Review* 74, no. 6 (November–December 1996), pp. 61–78.

Wilson, Ian. "Realizing the Power of Strategic Vision." *Long Range Planning* 25, no.5 (1992), pp. 18–28.

3 INDUSTRY AND COMPETITIVE ANALYSIS

Crafting strategy is an analysis-driven exercise, not a task where managers can get by with opinions, good instincts, and creative thinking. Judgments about what strategy to pursue need to flow directly from solid analysis of a company's external environment and internal situation. The two biggest considerations are (1) industry and competitive conditions (these are the heart of a single-business company's "external environment") and (2) a company's competitive capabilities, resources, internal strengths and weaknesses, and market position.

Figure 3.1 illustrates what is involved in sizing up a company's situation and deciding on a strategy. The analytical sequence is from strategic appraisal of the company's external and internal situation to identification of issues to evaluation of alternatives to choice of strategy. Accurate diagnosis of the company's situation is necessary managerial preparation for deciding on a sound long-term direction, setting appropriate objectives, and crafting a winning strategy. Without perceptive understanding of the strategic aspects of a company's macro- and microenvironments, the chances are greatly increased that managers will concoct a strategic game plan that doesn't fit the situation well, that holds little prospect for building competitive advantage, and that is unlikely to boost company performance.

This chapter examines the techniques of *industry and competitive analysis*, the term commonly used to refer to assessing the strategically relevant aspects of a company's macroenvironment or *business ecosystem*. In the next chapter, we'll cover the methods of *company situation analysis* and see how to appraise the strategy-shaping aspects of a firm's immediate *microenvironment*.

> Analysis is the critical starting point of strategic thinking.
>
> **Kenichi Ohmae**
>
> Awareness of the environment is not a special project to be undertaken only when warning of change becomes deafening . . . .
>
> **Kenneth R. Andrews**
>
> Nothing focuses the mind better than the constant sight of a competitor who wants to wipe you off the map.
>
> **Wayne Calloway**
> *Former CEO, PepsiCo*

THE METHODS OF INDUSTRY AND COMPETITIVE ANALYSIS

Industries differ widely in their economic characteristics, competitive situations, and future profit prospects. The economic and competitive character of the trucking industry bears little resemblance to that of discount retailing. The economic and competitive traits of the fast-food business have little in common with those of providing Internet-related products or services. The cable-TV business is shaped by industry and competitive conditions radically different from those in the soft-drink business.

FIGURE 3.1 How Strategic Thinking and Strategic Analysis Lead to Good Strategic Choices

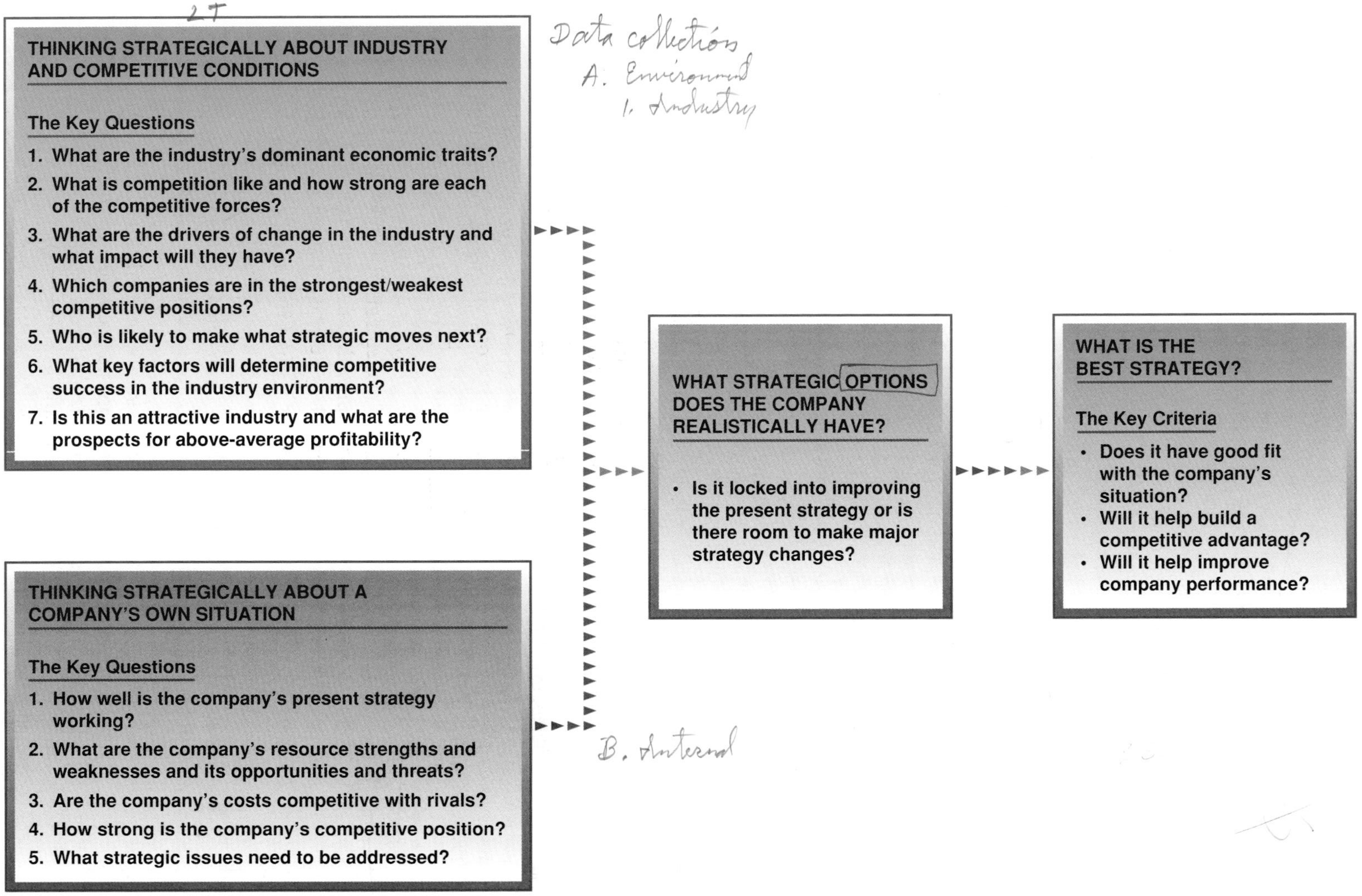

Handwritten annotations:

2 +

Data collection
A. Environment
1. Industry

B. Internal

THINKING STRATEGICALLY ABOUT INDUSTRY AND COMPETITIVE CONDITIONS

The Key Questions

1. What are the industry's dominant economic traits?
2. What is competition like and how strong are each of the competitive forces?
3. What are the drivers of change in the industry and what impact will they have?
4. Which companies are in the strongest/weakest competitive positions?
5. Who is likely to make what strategic moves next?
6. What key factors will determine competitive success in the industry environment?
7. Is this an attractive industry and what are the prospects for above-average profitability?

THINKING STRATEGICALLY ABOUT A COMPANY'S OWN SITUATION

The Key Questions

1. How well is the company's present strategy working?
2. What are the company's resource strengths and weaknesses and its opportunities and threats?
3. Are the company's costs competitive with rivals?
4. How strong is the company's competitive position?
5. What strategic issues need to be addressed?

WHAT STRATEGIC OPTIONS DOES THE COMPANY REALISTICALLY HAVE?

• Is it locked into improving the present strategy or is there room to make major strategy changes?

WHAT IS THE BEST STRATEGY?

The Key Criteria

• Does it have good fit with the company's situation?
• Will it help build a competitive advantage?
• Will it help improve company performance?

The economic character of industries varies according to a number of factors: the overall size and market growth rate, the pace of technological change, the geographic boundaries of the market (which can extend from local to worldwide), the number and sizes of buyers and sellers, whether sellers' products are virtually identical or highly differentiated, the extent to which costs are affected by economies of scale, and the types of distribution channels used to access buyers. Competitive forces can be moderate in one industry and fierce, even cutthroat, in another. Moreover, industries differ widely in the degree of competitive emphasis put on price, product quality, performance features, service, advertising and promotion, and new product innovation. In some industries, price competition dominates the marketplace while in others the competitive emphasis is centered on quality or product performance or customer service or brand image/reputation. In other industries, the challenge is for companies to work cooperatively with suppliers, customers, and maybe even select competitors to create the next round of product innovations and open up a whole new vista of market opportunities (as we are witnessing in computer technology and telecommunications).

Managers are not prepared to decide on a long-term direction or a strategy until they have a keen understanding of the company's strategic situation—the exact nature of the industry and competitive conditions it faces and how these conditions match up with its resources and capabilities.

An industry's economic traits and competitive conditions and how they are expected to change determine whether its future profit prospects will be poor, average, or excellent. Industry and competitive conditions differ so much that leading companies in unattractive industries can find it hard to earn respectable profits, while even weak companies in attractive industries can turn in good performances.

Industry and competitive analysis uses a tool kit of concepts and techniques to get a clear fix on key industry traits, the intensity of competition, the drivers of industry change, the market positions and strategies of rival companies, the keys to competitive success, and the industry's future profit outlook. This tool kit provides a way of thinking strategically about any industry and drawing conclusions about whether the industry represents an attractive investment for company funds. It entails examining a company's business in the context of a much wider environment. Industry and competitive analysis aims at developing probing, insightful answers to seven questions:

1. What are the industry's dominant economic features?
2. What competitive forces are at work in the industry and how strong are they?
3. What are the drivers of change in the industry and what impact will they have?
4. Which companies are in the strongest/weakest competitive positions?
5. Who's likely to make what competitive moves next?
6. What key factors will determine competitive success or failure?
7. How attractive is the industry in terms of its prospects for above-average profitability?

The answers to these questions build understanding of a firm's surrounding environment and, collectively, form the basis for matching its strategy to changing industry conditions and competitive realities.

Question 1: What Are the Industry's Dominant Economic Features?

Because industries differ significantly in their character and structure, industry and competitive analysis begins with an overview of the industry's dominant economic features. As a working definition, we use the word *industry* to mean a group of firms whose products have so many of the same attributes that they compete for the same buyers. The factors to consider in profiling an industry's economic traits are fairly standard:

- Market size.
- Scope of competitive rivalry (local, regional, national, international, or global).
- Market growth rate and where the industry is in the growth cycle (early development, rapid growth and takeoff, early maturity, mature, saturated and stagnant, declining).
- Number of rivals and their relative sizes—is the industry fragmented with many small companies or concentrated and dominated by a few large companies?
- The number of buyers and their relative sizes.
- The prevalence of backward and forward integration.
- The types of distribution channels used to access buyers.
- The pace of technological change in both production process innovation and new product introductions.
- Whether the product(s)/service(s) of rival firms are highly differentiated, weakly differentiated, or essentially identical.
- Whether companies can realize economies of scale in purchasing, manufacturing, transportation, marketing, or advertising.
- Whether certain industry activities are characterized by strong learning and experience effects such that unit costs decline as *cumulative* output (and thus the experience of "learning by doing") grows.
- Whether high rates of capacity utilization are crucial to achieving low-cost production efficiency.
- Resource requirements and the ease of entry and exit.
- Whether industry profitability is above/below par. *How is par determined?*

Table 3.1 provides a sample profile of the economic character of the sulfuric acid industry.

An industry's economic features are important because of the implications they have for strategy. For example, in capital-intensive industries where investment in a single plant can run several hundred million dollars, a firm can spread the burden of high fixed costs by pursuing a strategy that promotes high utilization of fixed assets and generates more revenue per dollar of fixed-asset investment. Thus commercial airlines try to boost the revenue productivity of their multimillion-dollar jets by cutting ground time at airport gates (to get in more flights per day with the same plane) and by using multi-tiered price discounts to fill up otherwise empty seats. In industries characterized by one product advance after another, companies must spend enough time and money on R&D to keep their technical prowess and innovative capability abreast of competitors—a strategy of continuous product innovation becomes a condition of survival.

An industry's economic features help frame the window of strategic approaches a company can pursue.

In industries like semiconductors, strong *learning/experience* effects in manufacturing cause unit costs to decline about 20 percent each time *cumulative* production volume doubles. With a 20 percent experience curve effect, if the first

TABLE 3.1   A Sample Profile of the Dominant Economic Characteristics of the Sulfuric Acid Industry

Market Size: $400–$500 million annual revenues; 4 million tons total volume.

Scope of Competitive Rivalry: Primarily regional; producers rarely sell outside a 250-mile radius of plant due to high cost of shipping long distances.

Market Growth Rate: 2–3 percent annually.

Stage in Life Cycle: Mature.

Number of Companies in Industry: About 30 companies with 110 plant locations and capacity of 4.5 million tons. Market shares range from a low of 3 percent to a high of 21 percent.

Customers: About 2,000 buyers; most are industrial chemical firms.

Degree of Vertical Integration: Mixed; 5 of the 10 largest companies are integrated backward into mining operations and also forward in that sister industrial chemical divisions buy over 50 percent of the output of their plants; all other companies are engaged solely in the production of sulfuric acid.

Ease of Entry/Exit: Moderate entry barriers exist in the form of capital requirements to construct a new plant of minimum efficient size (cost equals $10 million) and ability to build a customer base inside a 250-mile radius of plant.

Technology/Innovation: Production technology is standard and changes have been slow; biggest changes are occurring in products—1–2 newly formulated specialty chemicals products are being introduced annually, accounting for nearly all of industry growth.

Product Characteristics: Highly standardized; the brands of different producers are essentially identical (buyers perceive little real difference from seller to seller).

Scale Economies: Moderate; all companies have virtually equal manufacturing costs but scale economies exist in shipping in multiple carloads to same customer and in purchasing large quantities of raw materials.

Learning and Experience Effects: Not a factor in this industry.

Capacity Utilization: Manufacturing efficiency is highest between 90–100 percent of rated capacity; below 90 percent utilization, unit costs run significantly higher.

Industry Profitability: Subpar to average; the commodity nature of the industry's product results in intense price-cutting when demand slackens, but prices firm up during periods of strong demand. Profits track the strength of demand for the industry's products.

Basic Concept

When strong economies of learning and experience result in declining unit costs as cumulative production volume builds, a strategy to become the largest-volume manufacturer can yield the competitive advantage of being the industry's lowest-cost producer.

1 million chips cost $100 each, by a production volume of 2 million the unit cost would be $80 (80 percent of $100), by a production volume of 4 million the unit would be $64 (80 percent of $80), and so on. When an industry is characterized by sizable economies of experience in its manufacturing operations, a company that first initiates production of a new-style product and develops a successful strategy to capture the largest market share gains sustainable competitive advantage as the low-cost producer.[1] The bigger the experience-curve effect, the bigger the cost advantage of the company with the largest *cumulative* production volume, as shown in Figure 3.2.

Table 3.2 presents some additional examples of how an industry's economic traits are relevant to managerial strategy making.

---

[1]There are a large number of studies of the size of the cost reductions associated with experience; the median cost reduction associated with a doubling of cumulative production volume is approximately 15 percent, but there is a wide variation from industry to industry. For a good discussion of the economies of experience and learning, see Pankaj Ghemawat, "Building Strategy on the Experience Curve," *Harvard Business Review* 64, no. 2 (March–April 1985), pp. 143–49.

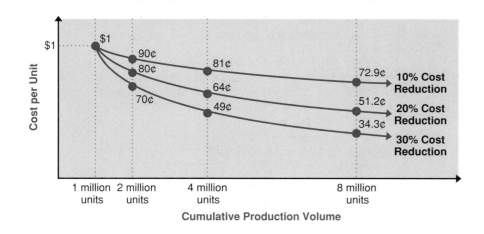

FIGURE 3.2 Comparison of Experience Curve Effects for 10 Percent, 20 Percent, and 30 Percent Cost Reductions for Each Doubling of Cumulative Production Volume

Question 2: What Is Competition Like and How Strong Are Each of the Competitive Forces?

An important part of industry and competitive analysis is to delve into the industry's competitive process to discover the main sources of competitive pressure and how strong each competitive force is. This analytical step is essential because managers cannot devise a successful strategy without understanding the industry's competitive character.

The Five-Forces Model of Competition   Even though competitive pressures in various industries are never precisely the same, the competitive process works similarly enough to use a common analytical framework in gauging the nature and intensity of competitive forces. As Professor Michael Porter of the Harvard Business School has convincingly demonstrated, *the state of competition in an industry is a composite of five competitive forces:*[2]

1. The rivalry among competing sellers in the industry.
2. The market attempts of companies in other industries to win customers over to their own *substitute* products.
3. The potential entry of new competitors.
4. The bargaining power and leverage suppliers of inputs can exercise.
5. The bargaining power and leverage exercisable by buyers of the product.

Porter's *five-forces model*, as depicted in Figure 3.3, is a powerful tool for systematically diagnosing the chief competitive pressures in a market and assessing how

---

[2]For a thoroughgoing treatment of the five-forces model by its originator, see Michael E. Porter, *Competitive Strategy: Techniques for Analyzing Industries and Competitors* (New York: Free Press, 1980), chapter 1.

TABLE 3.2   Examples of the Strategic Importance of an Industry's Key Economic Features

Economic Feature	Strategic Importance
• Market size	• Small markets don't tend to attract big/new competitors; large markets often draw the interest of companies looking to acquire competitors with established positions in attractive industries.
• Market growth rate	• Fast growth breeds new entry; growth slowdowns spawn increased rivalry and a shake-out of weak competitors.
• Capacity surpluses or shortages	• Surpluses push prices and profit margins down; shortages pull them up.
• Industry profitability	• High-profit industries attract new entrants; depressed conditions encourage exit.
• Entry/exit barriers	• High barriers protect positions and profits of existing firms; low barriers make existing firms vulnerable to entry.
• Product is a big-ticket item for buyers	• More buyers will shop for lowest price.
• Standardized products	• Buyers have more power because it is easier to switch from seller to seller.
• Rapid technological change	• Raises risk factor; investments in technology facilities/equipment may become obsolete before they wear out.
• Capital requirements	• Big requirements make investment decisions critical; timing becomes important; creates a barrier to entry and exit.
• Vertical integration	• Raises capital requirements; often creates competitive differences and cost differences among fully versus partially versus nonintegrated firms.
• Economies of scale	• Increases volume and market share needed to be cost competitive.
• Rapid product innovation	• Shortens product life cycle; increases risk because of opportunities for leapfrogging.

strong and important each one is. Not only is it the most widely used technique of competition analysis, but it is also relatively easy to understand and apply.

The Rivalry among Competing Sellers   The strongest of the five competitive forces is *usually* the jockeying for position and buyer favor that goes on among rival firms. In some industries, rivalry is centered around price competition—sometimes resulting in prices below the level of unit costs and forcing losses on most rivals. In other industries, price competition is minimal and rivalry is focused on such factors as performance features, new product innovation, quality and durability, warranties, after-the-sale service, and brand image.

Competitive jockeying among rivals heats up when one or more competitors sees an opportunity to better meet customer needs or is under pressure to improve its performance. *The intensity of rivalry among competing sellers is a function of how vigorously they employ such tactics as lower prices, snazzier features, expanded customer services, longer warranties, special promotions, and new product introductions.* Rivalry can range from friendly to cutthroat, depending on how frequently and how aggressively companies undertake fresh moves that threaten rivals' profitability. Ordinarily, industry rivals are clever at adding new wrinkles to their product offer-

FIGURE 3.3   The Five-Forces Model of Competition: A Key Analytical Tool

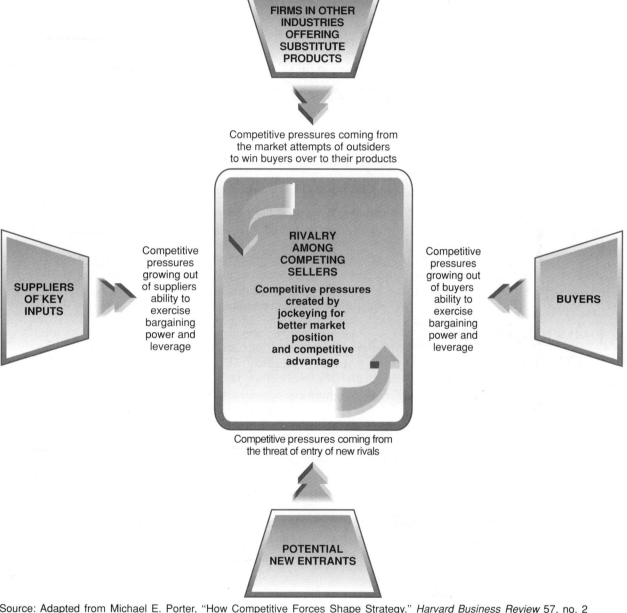

Source: Adapted from Michael E. Porter, "How Competitive Forces Shape Strategy," *Harvard Business Review* 57, no. 2 (March–April 1979), pp. 137–45.

ings that enhance buyer appeal, and they persist in trying to exploit weaknesses in each other's market approaches.

Whether rivalry is lukewarm or heated, every company has to craft a successful strategy for competing—ideally, one that *produces a competitive edge over rivals* and strengthens its position with buyers. The big complication in most industries is that *the success of any one firm's strategy hinges partly on what offensive and defensive maneuvers its rivals employ and the resources rivals are willing and able to put behind their strategic efforts.* The "best" strategy for one firm in its maneuvering for competitive advantage depends, in other words, on the competitive capabilities and strategies of rival companies. Thus, whenever one firm makes a strategic move, its rivals often retaliate with offensive or defensive countermoves. This pattern of action and reaction makes competitive rivalry a "war-games" type of contest conducted according to the rules of fair competition. Indeed, from a strategy-making perspective, *competitive markets are economic battlefields*, with the ebb and flow of the competitive battle varying with the latest strategic moves of the players. In practice, the market outcome is almost always shaped by the strategies of the leading players.

Principle of Competitive Markets

Competitive jockeying among rival firms is a dynamic, ever-changing process as firms initiate new offensive and defensive moves and emphasis swings from one blend of competitive weapons and tactics to another.

Not only do competitive contests among rival sellers assume different intensities but the kinds of competitive pressures that emerge from cross-company rivalry also vary over time. The relative emphasis that rival companies put on price, quality, performance features, customer service, warranties, advertising, dealer networks, new product innovation, and so on shifts as they try different tactics to catch buyers' attention and as competitors launch fresh offensive and defensive maneuvers. Rivalry is thus dynamic; the current competitive scene is ever-changing as companies act and react, sometimes in rapid-fire order and sometimes methodically, and as they swing from one mix of competitive tactics to another.

Regardless of the industry, several common factors seem to influence the tempo of rivalry among competing sellers:[3]

1. *Rivalry intensifies as the number of competitors increases and as competitors become more equal in size and capability*. Up to a point, the greater the number of competitors, the greater the probability of fresh, creative strategic initiatives. In addition, when rivals are more equal in size and capability, they can usually compete on a fairly even footing, making it harder for one or two firms to "win" the competitive battle and dominate the market.

2. *Rivalry is usually stronger when demand for the product is growing slowly*. In a rapidly expanding market, there tends to be enough business for everybody to grow. Indeed, it may take all of a firm's financial and competitive resources just to keep up with buyer demand, much less steal rivals' customers. But when growth slows or when market demand drops unexpectedly, expansion-minded firms and/or firms with excess capacity often cut prices and deploy other sales-increasing tactics, thereby igniting a battle for market share that can result in a shakeout of the weak and less efficient firms. The industry then consolidates into a smaller, but individually stronger, number of sellers.

3. *Rivalry is more intense when industry conditions tempt competitors to use price cuts or other competitive weapons to boost unit volume*. Whenever fixed costs account for a large fraction of total cost, unit costs tend to be lowest at or near full capacity since fixed costs can be spread over more units of production. Unused capacity imposes a significant cost-increasing penalty because there are fewer units

---

[3]These indicators of what to look for in evaluating the intensity of intercompany rivalry are based on Porter, *Competitive Strategy*, pp. 17–21.

carrying the fixed cost burden. In such cases, if market demand weakens and capacity utilization begins to fall off, the pressure of rising unit costs often pushes rival firms into secret price concessions, special discounts, rebates, and other sales-increasing tactics, thus heightening rivalry. Likewise, when a product is perishable, seasonal, or costly to hold in inventory, competitive pressures build when one or more firms decide to dump excess supplies on the market.

4. *Rivalry is stronger when customers' costs to switch brands are low.* The lower the costs of switching, the easier it is for rival sellers to raid one another's customers. High switching costs, however, give sellers a more protected customer base and work against the efforts of rivals to promote brand-switching.

5. *Rivalry is stronger when one or more competitors is dissatisfied with its market position and launches moves to bolster its standing at the expense of rivals.* Firms that are losing ground or in financial trouble often react aggressively by introducing new products, boosting advertising, discounting prices, acquiring smaller rivals to strengthen their capabilities, and so on. Such actions can trigger a new round of maneuvering and a more hotly contested battle for market share.

6. *Rivalry increases in proportion to the size of the payoff from a successful strategic move.* The more rewarding an opportunity, the more likely some firm will aggressively pursue a strategy to capture it. The size of the payoff varies partly with the speed of retaliation. When competitors respond slowly (or not at all), the initiator of a fresh competitive strategy can reap benefits in the intervening period and perhaps gain an advantage that is not easily surmounted. The greater the benefits of moving first, the more likely some competitor will accept the risk and try it.

7. *Rivalry tends to be more vigorous when it costs more to get out of a business than to stay in and compete.* The higher the exit barriers, the stronger the incentive for existing rivals to remain and compete as best they can, even though they may be earning low profits or even incurring losses.

8. *Rivalry becomes more volatile and unpredictable the more diverse competitors are in terms of their visions, strategic intents, objectives, strategies, resources, and countries of origin.* A diverse group of sellers often contains one or more mavericks willing to rock the boat with unconventional moves and market approaches, thus generating a livelier and less predictable environment. Attempts by cross-border rivals to gain stronger footholds in each other's domestic markets boosts the intensity of rivalry, especially when foreign rivals have lower costs or very attractive products.

9. *Rivalry increases when strong companies outside the industry acquire weak firms in the industry and launch aggressive, well-funded moves to transform their newly acquired competitors into major market contenders.* A concerted effort to turn a weak rival into a market leader nearly always entails launching well-financed strategic initiatives to dramatically improve the competitor's product offering, excite buyer interest, and win a much bigger market share. If these actions are successful, they put pressure on rivals to counter with fresh moves of their own.

Two facets of competitive rivalry stand out: (1) the launch of a powerful competitive strategy by one company intensifies the pressures on the remaining companies and (2) the character of rivalry is shaped partly by the strategies of the leading players and partly by the vigor with which industry rivals use competitive weapons to try to outmaneuver one another. In sizing up the competitive pressures created by rivalry among existing competitors, the strategist's job is to identify the current weapons and tactics of competitive rivalry, to stay on top of which tactics are most and least successful, to understand the "rules" that industry rivals play by, and to decide whether and why rivalry is likely to increase or diminish in strength.

Judgments about how much pressure cross-company rivalry is going to put on profitability is the key to concluding whether and why the rivalry among existing sellers is fierce, strong, moderate, or attractively weak. Competitive rivalry is considered intense when the actions of competitors are driving down industry profits, moderate when most companies can earn acceptable profits, and weak when most companies in the industry can earn above-average returns on investment. Chronic outbreaks of cutthroat competition among rival sellers make an industry brutally competitive.

The Competitive Force of Potential Entry   New entrants to a market bring new production capacity, the desire to establish a secure place in the market, and sometimes substantial resources.[4] Just how serious the competitive threat of entry is in a particular market depends on two classes of factors: *barriers to entry* and the *expected reaction of incumbent firms to new entry*. A barrier to entry exists whenever it is hard for a newcomer to break into the market and/or economic factors put a potential entrant at a disadvantage. There are several types of entry barriers:[5]

1. *Economies of scale*—Scale economies deter entry because they force potential competitors either to enter on a large-scale basis (a costly and perhaps risky move) or to accept a cost disadvantage (and lower profitability). Trying to overcome scale economies by entering on a large-scale basis at the outset can result in long-term overcapacity problems for the new entrant (until sales volume builds up), and it can so threaten the market shares of existing firms that they retaliate aggressively (with price cuts, increased advertising and sales promotion, and similar blocking actions). Either way, a potential entrant is discouraged by the prospect of lower profits. Entrants may encounter scale-related barriers not just in production, but in advertising, marketing and distribution, financing, after-sale customer service, raw materials purchasing, and R&D as well.

2. *Inability to gain access to technology and specialized know-how*—Many industries require technological capability and skills not readily available to a newcomer. Key patents can effectively bar entry as can lack of technically skilled personnel and an inability to execute complicated manufacturing techniques. Existing firms often carefully guard know-how that gives them an edge. Unless new entrants can gain access to such proprietary knowledge, they will lack the capability to compete on a level playing field.

3. *The existence of learning and experience curve effects*—When lower unit costs are partly or mostly a result of experience in producing the product and other learning curve benefits, new entrants face a cost disadvantage competing against firms with more know-how.

4. *Brand preferences and customer loyalty*—Buyers are often attached to established brands. Japanese consumers, for example, are fiercely loyal to Japanese brands of motor vehicles, electronics products, cameras, and film. European consumers have traditionally been loyal to European brands of major household appliances. High brand loyalty means that a potential entrant must build a network of distributors and

---

[4]Michael E. Porter, "How Competitive Forces Shape Strategy," *Harvard Business Review* 57, no. 2 (March–April 1979), p. 138.
[5]Porter, *Competitive Strategy*, pp. 7–17.

dealers, then be prepared to spend enough money on advertising and sales promotion to overcome customer loyalties and build its own clientele. Establishing brand recognition and building customer loyalty can be a slow and costly process. In addition, if it is difficult or costly for a customer to switch to a new brand, a new entrant must persuade buyers that its brand is worth the costs. To overcome the switching-cost barrier, new entrants may have to offer buyers a discounted price or an extra margin of quality or service. All this can mean lower profit margins for new entrants—something that increases the risk to start-up companies dependent on sizable, early profits.

5. *Resource requirements*—The larger the total dollar investment and other resource requirements needed to enter the market successfully, the more limited the pool of potential entrants. The most obvious capital requirements are associated with manufacturing plant and equipment, distribution facilities, working capital to finance inventories and customer credit, introductory advertising and sales promotion to establish a clientele, and cash reserves to cover start-up losses. Other resource barriers include access to technology, specialized expertise and know-how, and R&D requirements, labor force requirements, and customer service requirements.

6. *Cost disadvantages independent of size*—Existing firms may have cost advantages not available to potential entrants. These advantages can include access to the best and cheapest raw materials, patents and proprietary technology, the benefits of learning and experience curve effects, existing plants built and equipped years earlier at lower costs, favorable locations, and lower borrowing costs.

7. *Access to distribution channels*—In the case of consumer goods, a potential entrant may face the barrier of gaining access to consumers. Wholesale distributors may be reluctant to take on a product that lacks buyer recognition. A network of retail dealers may have to be set up from scratch. Retailers have to be convinced to give a new brand display space and a trial period. The more existing producers tie up distribution channels, the tougher entry will be. To overcome this barrier, potential entrants may have to "buy" distribution access by offering better margins to dealers and distributors or by giving advertising allowances and other incentives. As a consequence, a potential entrant's profits may be squeezed unless and until its product gains enough acceptance that distributors and retailers want to carry it.

8. *Regulatory policies*—Government agencies can limit or even bar entry by requiring licenses and permits. Regulated industries like cable TV, telecommunications, electric and gas utilities, radio and television broadcasting, liquor retailing, and railroads feature government-controlled entry. In international markets, host governments commonly limit foreign entry and must approve all foreign investment applications. Stringent safety regulations and environmental pollution standards are entry barriers because they raise entry costs.

9. *Tariffs and international trade restrictions*—National governments commonly use tariffs and trade restrictions (antidumping rules, local content requirements, and quotas) to raise entry barriers for foreign firms. In 1996, due to tariffs imposed by the South Korean government, a Ford Taurus cost South Korean car buyers over $40,000. The government of India requires that 90 percent of the parts and components used in Indian truck assembly plants be made in India. And to protect European chipmakers from low-cost Asian competition, European governments instituted a rigid formula for calculating floor prices for computer memory chips.

Whether an industry's entry barriers ought to be considered high or low depends on the resources and competencies possessed by the pool of potential entrants. Entry barriers are usually steeper for new start-up enterprises than for companies in other industries or for current industry participants looking to enter new geographic markets. Indeed, the most likely entrants into a geographic market are often enterprises looking to expand their market reach. A company already well established in one geographic market may have the resources, competencies, and competitive capabilities to hurdle the barriers of entering an attractive new geographic market. In evaluating the potential threat of entry, one must look at (1) how formidable the entry barriers are for each type of potential entrant—new start-up enterprises, candidate companies in other industries, and current industry participants aiming to enter additional geographic markets and (2) how attractive the profit prospects are for new entrants. High profits act as a magnet to potential entrants, motivating them to commit the resources needed to hurdle entry barriers.[6]

Even if a potential entrant has or can acquire the needed competencies and resources to attempt entry, it still faces the issue of how existing firms will react.[7]

Principle of Competitive Markets

The threat of entry is stronger when entry barriers are low, when there's a sizable pool of entry candidates, when incumbent firms are unable or unwilling to vigorously contest a newcomer's efforts to gain a market foothold, and when a newcomer can expect to earn attractive profits.

Will they offer only passive resistance, or will they aggressively defend their market positions using price cuts, increased advertising, new product improvements, and whatever else will give a new entrant (as well as other rivals) a hard time? A potential entrant can have second thoughts when financially strong incumbent firms send clear signals that they will stoutly defend their market positions against newcomers. It may also turn away when incumbent firms can leverage distributors and customers to retain their business.

The best test of whether potential entry is a strong or weak competitive force is to ask if the industry's growth and profit prospects are attractive enough to induce additional entry. When the answer is no, potential entry is a weak competitive force. When the answer is yes and there are entry candidates with enough expertise and resources, then potential entry adds to competitive pressures in the marketplace. The stronger the threat of entry, the more that incumbent firms are driven to fortify their positions against newcomers.

One additional point: The threat of entry changes as the industry's prospects grow brighter or dimmer and as entry barriers rise or fall. For example, the expiration of a key patent can greatly increase the threat of entry. A technological discovery can create an economy of scale advantage where none existed before. New actions by incumbent firms to increase advertising, strengthen distributor-dealer relations, step up R&D, or improve product quality can raise the roadblocks to entry. In international markets, entry barriers for foreign-based firms fall as tariffs are lowered, as domestic wholesalers and dealers seek out lower-cost foreign-made goods, and as domestic buyers become more willing to purchase foreign brands.

Competitive Pressures from Substitute Products   Firms in one industry are, quite often, in close competition with firms in another industry because their products are good substitutes. The producers of eyeglasses compete with the makers of contact lenses. The producers of wood stoves compete with such substitutes as kerosene heaters and

---

[6]When profits are sufficiently attractive, entry barriers fail to deter entry; at most, they limit the pool of candidate entrants to enterprises with the requisite competencies and resources and with the creativity to fashion a strategy for competing with incumbent firms. George S. Yip, "Gateways to Entry," *Harvard Business Review* 60, no. 5 (September–October 1982), pp. 85–93.

[7]Porter, "How Competitive Forces Shape Strategy," p. 140, and Porter, *Competitive Strategy*, pp. 14–15.

portable electric heaters. The sugar industry competes with companies that produce artificial sweeteners and high-fructose corn syrup. The producers of glass bottles and jars confront strong competition from manufacturers of plastic containers, paper-board cartons, and metal cans. Aspirin manufacturers compete against the makers of substitute types of pain relievers. Newspapers compete with television in providing news (television has taken over as the preferred source of late-breaking news) and with Internet sources in providing sports results, stock quotes, and job opportunities. Just how strong the competitive pressures are from substitute products depends on three factors: (1) whether attractively priced substitutes are available, (2) how satisfactory the substitutes are in terms of quality, performance, and other relevant attributes, and (3) the ease with which buyers can switch to substitutes.

Readily available and attractively priced substitutes create competitive pressure by placing a ceiling on the prices an industry can charge for its product without giving customers an incentive to switch to substitutes and risking sales erosion.[8] This price ceiling, at the same time, puts a lid on the profits that industry members can earn unless they find ways to cut costs. When substitutes are cheaper than an industry's product, industry members come under heavy competitive pressure to reduce their prices and find ways to absorb the price cuts with cost reductions.

The availability of substitutes inevitably invites customers to compare quality and performance as well as price. For example, ski boat manufacturers are facing strong competition from jet skis because water sports enthusiasts are finding that jet skis have exciting performance features that make them satisfying substitutes. The users of glass bottles and jars constantly weigh the performance trade-offs with plastic containers, paper cartons, and metal cans. Competition from substitute products pushes industry participants to heighten efforts to convince customers their product has superior attributes.

> **Principle of Competitive Markets**
>
> *The competitive threat posed by substitute products is strong when substitutes are readily available and attractively priced, buyers believe substitutes have comparable or better features, and buyers' switching costs are low.*

Another determinant of the strength of competition from substitutes is how difficult or costly it is for the industry's customers to switch to a substitute.[9] Typical switching costs include the extra price premium if any, the costs of additional equipment that may be required, the time and cost in testing the substitute's quality and reliability, the costs of severing old supplier relationships and establishing new ones, payments for technical help in making the changeover, and employee retraining costs. If switching costs are high, sellers of substitutes must offer a major cost or performance benefit in order to entice the industry's customers away. When switching costs are low, it's much easier for sellers of substitutes to convince buyers to change over to their products.

As a rule, then, the lower the price of substitutes, the higher their quality and performance, and the lower the user's switching costs, the more intense the competitive pressures posed by substitute products. Good indicators of the competitive strength of substitute products are the rate at which their sales and profits are growing, the market inroads they are making, and their plans for expanding production capacity.

The Power of Suppliers   Whether the suppliers to an industry are a weak or strong competitive force depends on market conditions in the supplier industry and the

---

[8]Porter, "How Competitive Forces Shape Strategy," p. 142, and Porter, *Competitive Strategy*, pp. 23–24.
[9]Porter, *Competitive Strategy*, p. 10.

significance of the item they supply.[10] Supplier-related competitive pressures tend to be minimal whenever the items supplied are standard commodities available on the open market from a large number of suppliers with ample capability. Then it is simple to obtain whatever is needed from a list of capable suppliers, perhaps dividing purchases among several to promote competition for orders. In such cases, suppliers have market power only when supplies become tight and users are so eager to secure what they need that they agree to terms more favorable to suppliers. Suppliers are also relegated to a weak bargaining position whenever there are good substitute inputs and switching is neither costly nor difficult. For example, soft-drink bottlers can check the bargaining power of aluminum can suppliers on price or delivery by using more plastic containers and glass bottles.

Suppliers also tend to have less leverage to bargain over price and other terms of sale when the industry they are supplying is a *major* customer. In such cases, the well-being of suppliers is closely tied to the well-being of their major customers. Suppliers then have a big incentive to protect and enhance their customers' competitiveness via reasonable prices, exceptional quality, and ongoing advances in the technology and performance of the items supplied.

On the other hand, when the item accounts for a sizable fraction of the costs of an industry's product, is crucial to the industry's production process, and/or significantly affects the quality of the industry's product, suppliers have great influence on the competitive process. This is particularly true when a few large companies control most of the available supplies and have pricing leverage. Likewise, a supplier (or group of suppliers) has bargaining leverage the more difficult or costly it is for users to switch to alternate suppliers. Big suppliers with good reputations and growing demand for their output are harder to wring concessions from than struggling suppliers striving to broaden their customer base or more fully utilize their production capacity.

Principle of Competitive Markets

The suppliers to a group of rival firms are a strong competitive force whenever they have sufficient bargaining power to put certain rivals at a competitive disadvantage based on the prices they can command, the quality and performance of the items they supply, or the reliability of their deliveries.

Suppliers are also more powerful when they can supply a component more cheaply than industry members can make it themselves. For instance, most producers of outdoor power equipment (lawnmowers, rotary tillers, snowblowers, and so on) find it cheaper to source small engines from outside manufacturers rather than make their own because the quantity they need is too little to justify the investment, master the process, and capture scale economies. Specialists in small-engine manufacture, by supplying many kinds of engines to the whole power equipment industry, obtain a big enough sales volume to fully realize scale economies, become proficient in all the manufacturing techniques, and keep costs low. Small-engine suppliers, then, are in a position to price the item below what it would cost the user to self-manufacture but far enough above their own costs to generate an attractive profit margin. In such situations, the bargaining position of suppliers is strong *until* the volume of parts a user needs becomes large enough for the user to justify backward integration into self-manufacture of the component. The more credible the threat of backward integration into the suppliers' business becomes, the more leverage users have in negotiating favorable terms with suppliers.

There are a couple of other instances in which the relationship between industry members and suppliers is a competitive force. One is when suppliers, for one reason

---

[10]Ibid., pp. 27–28.

or another, cannot provide items of high or consistent quality. For example, if a manufacturer's suppliers provide components that have a high defect rate or that fail prematurely, they can so increase the warranty and defective goods costs of the manufacturer that its profits, reputation, and competitive position are seriously impaired. A second is when one or more industry members form close working relationships with key suppliers in an attempt to secure lower prices, better quality or more innovative components, just-in-time deliveries, and reduced inventory and logistics costs; such benefits can translate into competitive advantage for industry members who do the best job of managing their relationships with key suppliers.

The Power of Buyers   Just as with suppliers, the competitive strength of buyers can range from strong to weak. Buyers have substantial bargaining leverage in a number of situations.[11] The most obvious is when buyers are large and purchase much of the industry's output. Typically, purchasing in large quantities gives a buyer enough leverage to obtain price concessions and other favorable terms. Retailers often have negotiating leverage in purchasing products because of manufacturers' need for broad retail exposure and favorable shelf space. Retailers may stock one or even several brands but rarely all available brands, so competition among sellers for the business of popular or high-volume retailers gives such retailers significant bargaining leverage. In the United States and Britain, supermarket chains have sufficient leverage to require food products manufacturers to make lump-sum payments to gain shelf space for new products. Motor vehicle manufacturers have significant bargaining power in negotiating to buy original-equipment tires not only because they buy in large quantities but also because tire makers believe they gain an advantage in supplying replacement tires to vehicle owners if their tire brand is original equipment on the vehicle. "Prestige" buyers have a degree of clout in negotiating with sellers because a seller's reputation is enhanced by having prestige buyers on its customer list.

> **Principle of Competitive Markets**
>
> *Buyers are a strong competitive force when they are able to exercise bargaining leverage over price, quality, service, or other terms of sale.*

Even if buyers do not purchase in large quantities or offer a seller important market exposure or prestige, they may still have some degree of bargaining leverage in the following circumstances:

- *If buyers' costs of switching to competing brands or substitutes are relatively low*—Anytime buyers have the flexibility to fill their needs by switching brands or sourcing from several sellers, they gain added negotiating room with sellers. When sellers' products are virtually identical, it is relatively easy for buyers to switch from seller to seller at little or no cost. However, if sellers' products are strongly differentiated, buyers may be less able to switch without sizable changeover costs.
- *If the number of buyers is small*—The smaller the number of buyers, the less easy is it for sellers to find alternatives when a customer is lost. The prospect of losing a customer often makes a seller more willing to grant concessions of one kind or another.
- *If buyers are well informed about sellers' products, prices, and costs*—The more information buyers have, the better bargaining position they are in.
- *If buyers pose a credible threat of backward integrating into the business of sellers*—Retailers gain bargaining power by stocking and promoting their

---

[11]Ibid., pp. 24–27.

own private-label brands alongside manufacturers' name brands. Companies like Campbell's soup, Anheuser-Busch, Coors, and Heinz have integrated backward into metal can manufacturing to gain bargaining power in buying cans from otherwise powerful metal can manufacturers.

- *If buyers have discretion in whether they purchase the product*—The buying power of personal computer manufacturers in purchasing from Intel and Microsoft is greatly muted by the critical importance of Intel chips and Microsoft software in making personal computers attractive to PC users. Or, if consumers are unhappy with the sticker prices of new motor vehicles, they can delay purchase or buy a used vehicle instead.

One last point: all buyers of an industry's product are not likely to have equal degrees of bargaining power with sellers, and some may be less sensitive than others to price, quality, or service. For example, apparel manufacturers confront significant customer power when selling to retail chains like Wal-Mart or Sears, but they can command much better prices selling to small owner-managed apparel boutiques. Independent tire retailers have less bargaining power in purchasing replacement tires than do motor vehicle manufacturers in purchasing original-equipment tires and they are also less quality sensitive—motor vehicle manufacturers are very particular about tire quality and tire performance because of the effects on vehicle performance.

Strategic Implications of the Five Competitive Forces   The five-forces model thoroughly exposes what competition is like in a given market—the strength of each of the five competitive forces, the nature of the competitive pressures comprising each force, and the overall structure of competition. As a rule, the stronger the collective impact of competitive forces, the lower the combined profitability of participant firms. The most brutally competitive situation occurs when the five forces create market conditions tough enough to impose prolonged subpar profitability or even losses on most or all firms. The structure of an industry is clearly "unattractive" from a profit-making standpoint if rivalry among sellers is very strong, low entry barriers are allowing new rivals to gain a market foothold, competition from substitutes is strong, and both suppliers and customers are able to exercise considerable bargaining leverage.

A company's competitive strategy is increasingly effective the more it provides good defenses against the five competitive forces, alters competitive pressures in the company's favor, and helps create sustainable competitive advantage.

On the other hand, when competitive forces are not strong, the structure of the industry is "favorable" or "attractive" from the standpoint of earning superior profits. The "ideal" environment from a profit-making perspective is where both suppliers and customers are in weak bargaining positions, there are no good substitutes, entry barriers are relatively high, and rivalry among present sellers is only moderate. However, even when some of the five competitive forces are strong, an industry can be attractive to those firms whose market position and strategy provide a good enough defense against competitive pressures to preserve their ability to earn above-average profits.

To contend successfully against competitive forces, managers must craft strategies that (1) insulate the firm as much as possible from the five competitive forces, (2) influence competitive pressures to change in directions that favor the company, and (3) build a strong, secure position of advantage. Managers cannot expect to develop winning competitive strategies without first identifying what competitive pressures exist, gauging the relative strength of each, and gaining a deep and profound understanding of the industry's whole competitive structure. The five-forces model is a powerful tool for gaining this understanding. Anything less leaves strategy makers short of the competitive insights needed to craft a successful competitive strategy.

Question 3: What Are the Drivers of Change in the Industry and What Impact Will They Have?

An industry's economic features and competitive structure say a lot about the character of industry and competitive conditions but very little about how the industry environment may be changing. All industries are characterized by trends and new developments that gradually or speedily produce changes important enough to require a strategic response from participating firms. The popular hypothesis about industries going through evolutionary phases or life-cycle stages helps explain industry change but is still incomplete.[12] The life-cycle stages are strongly keyed to changes in the overall industry growth rate (which is why such terms as rapid growth, early maturity, saturation, and decline are used to describe the stages). Yet *there are more causes of industry change than an industry's position on the growth curve.*

Industry conditions change because important forces are driving industry participants (competitors, customers, or suppliers) to alter their actions; the driving forces in an industry are the major underlying causes of changing industry and competitive conditions.

The Concept of Driving Forces   While it is important to judge what growth stage an industry is in, there's more value in identifying the factors causing fundamental industry and competitive adjustments. Industry and competitive conditions change *because forces are in motion that create incentives or pressures for change.*[13] The most dominant forces are called driving forces because they have the biggest influence on what kinds of changes will take place in the industry's structure and environment. Driving forces analysis has two steps: identifying what the driving forces are and assessing the impact they will have on the industry.

The Most Common Driving Forces   Many events can affect an industry powerfully enough to qualify as driving forces. Some are one of a kind, but most fall into one of several basic categories.[14]

- *Changes in the long-term industry growth rate*—Shifts in industry growth up or down are a force for industry change because they affect the balance between industry supply and buyer demand, entry and exit, and how hard it will be for a firm to capture additional sales. An upsurge in long-term demand attracts new entrants to the market and encourages established firms to invest in additional capacity. A shrinking market can cause some companies to exit the industry and induce those remaining to close their least efficient plants and retrench.

- *Changes in who buys the product and how they use it*—Shifts in buyer demographics and new ways of using the product can alter the state of competition by forcing adjustments in customer service offerings (credit, technical assistance, maintenance and repair), opening the way to market the industry's product through a different mix of dealers and retail outlets, prompting producers to broaden/narrow their product lines, bringing

---

[12]For more extended discussion of the problems with the life-cycle hypothesis, see Porter, *Competitive Strategy*, pp. 157–62.

[13]Porter, *Competitive Strategy*, p. 162.

[14]What follows draws on the discussion in Porter, *Competitive Strategy*, pp. 164–83.

different sales and promotion approaches into play. Mushrooming popularity of the Internet at home and at work is creating new opportunities for electronic shopping, on-line brokerage services, e-mail services, bulletin board services, data services, and Internet-provider services. The changing demographics generated by longer life expectancies are creating growth markets for residential golf resorts, retirement planning services, mutual funds, and health care.

- *Product innovation*—Product innovation can shake up the structure of competition by broadening an industry's customer base, rejuvenating industry growth, and widening the degree of product differentiation among rival sellers. Successful new product introductions strengthen the market position of the innovating companies, usually at the expense of companies who stick with their old products or are slow to follow with their own versions of the new product. Industries where product innovation has been a key driving force include copying equipment, cameras and photographic equipment, golf clubs, electronic video games, toys, prescription drugs, frozen foods, personal computers, and personal computer software.

- *Technological change*—Advances in technology can dramatically alter an industry's landscape, making it possible to produce new and/or better products at lower cost and opening up whole industry frontiers. Technological developments can also produce significant changes in capital requirements, minimum efficient plant sizes, vertical integration benefits, and learning or experience curve effects. For instance, the pace of technological developments in electronic commerce via the Internet is fast changing the way business is conducted in many industries (stock trading, software sales and distribution, and mail-order retailing, to name a few) and is ushering in "the Information Age."

- *Marketing innovation*—When firms are successful in introducing new ways to market their products, they can spark a burst of buyer interest, widen industry demand, increase product differentiation, and/or lower unit costs—any or all of which can alter the competitive positions of rival firms and force strategy revisions. The Internet is becoming the vehicle for all kinds of marketing innovations.

- *Entry or exit of major firms*—The entry of one or more foreign companies into a market once dominated by domestic firms nearly always shakes up competitive conditions. Likewise, when an established domestic firm from another industry attempts entry either by acquisition or by launching its own start-up venture, it usually applies its skills and resources in some innovative fashion that pushes competition in new directions. Entry by a major firm often produces a "new ball game" with new key players and new rules for competing. Similarly, exit of a major firm changes the competitive structure by reducing the number of market leaders (perhaps increasing the dominance of the leaders who remain) and causing a rush to capture the exiting firm's customers.

- *Diffusion of technical know-how*—As knowledge about how to perform an activity or execute a manufacturing technology spreads, any technically based competitive advantage held by firms originally possessing this know-how erodes. The diffusion of such know-how can occur through scientific journals, trade publications, on-site plant tours, word-of-mouth among suppliers and customers, and the hiring away of knowledgeable employees. It can also occur when the possessors of technological know-how license others to use it for a royalty fee or team up with a company interested in turning the technology into a new business venture. Quite often, technological know-how can be acquired by simply buying a company that has the wanted skills, patents, or manufacturing capabilities. In recent years technology transfer across national boundaries has emerged as one of the most important driving forces in globalizing markets and competition. As companies in more countries gain access to technical know-how, they upgrade their manufacturing capabilities in a long-term effort to compete head-on against established companies. Examples include automobiles, tires, consumer electronics, telecommunications, and computers.

- *Increasing globalization of the industry*—Industries move toward globalization for any of several reasons. One or more nationally prominent firms may launch aggressive long-term strategies to win a globally dominant market position. Demand for the industry's product may pop up in more and more countries. Trade barriers may drop. Technology transfer may open the door for more companies in more countries to enter the industry arena on a major scale. Significant labor cost differences among countries may create a strong reason to locate plants for labor-intensive products in low-wage countries (wages in China, Taiwan, Singapore, Mexico, and Brazil, for example, are about one-fourth those in the United States, Germany, and Japan). Firms with world-scale volumes as opposed to national-scale volumes may gain important cost economies. Multinational companies with the ability to transfer their production, marketing, and management know-how from country to country at very low cost can sometimes gain a significant competitive advantage over domestic-only competitors. As a consequence, global competition usually shifts the pattern of competition among an industry's key players, favoring some and hurting others. Such occurrences make globalization a driving force in industries (1) where scale economies are so large that rival companies need to market their product in many country markets to gain enough volume to drive unit costs down, (2) where low-cost production is a critical consideration (making it imperative to locate plant facilities in countries where the lowest costs can be achieved), (3) where one or more growth-oriented companies are pushing hard to gain a significant competitive position in as many attractive country markets as they can, and (4) based on natural resources (supplies of crude oil, copper, and cotton, for example, are geographically scattered all over the globe).

- *Changes in cost and efficiency*—Widening or shrinking differences in the costs and efficiency among key competitors tends to dramatically alter the state of competition. The low-cost economics of e-mail and faxing has put mounting competitive pressure on the relatively inefficient and high-cost operations of the U.S. Postal Service—sending a one-page fax is cheaper and far quicker than sending a first-class letter. In the electric power industry, sharply lower costs to generate electricity at newly constructed combined-cycle generating plants has put older coal-fired and gas-fired plants under the gun to lower their production costs to remain competitive; moreover, solar power and windpower companies have been forced to aggressively pursue technological breakthroughs to get the costs down far enough to survive against the much-improved cost and efficiency of combined-cycle plants.

• *Emerging buyer preferences for differentiated products instead of a commodity product (or for a more standardized product instead of strongly differentiated products)*—Sometimes growing numbers of buyers decide that a standard "one-size-fits-all" product at a budget price is a better bargain than premium-priced brands with lots of snappy features and personalized services. Such a development tends to shift patronage away from sellers of more expensive differentiated products to sellers of cheaper look-alike products and to create a market characterized by strong price competition. Pronounced shifts toward greater product standardization can so dominate a market that rival producers are limited to driving costs out of the business and remaining price competitive. On the other hand, a shift away from standardized products occurs when sellers are able to win a bigger and more loyal buyer following by introducing new features, making style changes, offering options and accessories, and creating image differences with advertising and packaging. Then the driver of change is the contest among rivals to cleverly outdifferentiate one another. Competition evolves differently depending on whether the market forces are increasing or decreasing the emphasis on product differentiation.

• *Regulatory influences and government policy changes*—Regulatory and governmental actions can often force significant changes in industry practices and strategic approaches. Deregulation has been a potent procompetitive force in the airline, banking, natural gas, telecommunications, and electric utility industries. Governmental efforts to reform Medicare and health insurance have become potent driving forces in the health care industry. In international markets, host governments can drive competitive changes by opening up their domestic markets to foreign participation or closing them off to protect domestic companies.

• *Changing societal concerns, attitudes, and lifestyles*—Emerging social issues and changing attitudes and lifestyles can instigate industry change. Growing antismoking sentiment has emerged as the major driver of change in the tobacco industry. Consumer concerns about salt, sugar, chemical additives, saturated fat, cholesterol, and nutritional value have forced food producers to revamp food-processing techniques, redirect R&D efforts into the use of healthier ingredients, and compete in coming up with healthy, good-tasting products. Safety concerns have transformed products with safety features into a competitive asset in the automobile, toy, and outdoor power equipment industries, to mention a few. Increased interest in physical fitness has spawned whole new industries in exercise equipment, mountain biking, outdoor apparel, sports gyms and recreation centers, vitamin and nutrition supplements, and medically supervised diet programs. Social concerns about air and water pollution have forced industries to add expenses for controlling pollution into their cost structures. Shifting societal concerns, attitudes, and lifestyles usually favor those players that respond quicker and more creatively with products targeted to the new trends and conditions.

• *Reductions in uncertainty and business risk*—A young, emerging industry is typically characterized by an unproven cost structure and uncertainty over potential market size, how much time and money will be needed to surmount technological problems, and what distribution channels to emphasize. Emerging industries tend to attract only risk-taking entrepreneurial companies. Over time, however, if the industry's pioneers succeed and uncertainty about the product's viability fades, more conservative firms are usually enticed to enter the market. Often, these later entrants are larger, financially strong firms looking to invest in attractive growth industries. Lower business risks and less industry uncertainty also affect competition in international markets. In the early stages of a company's entry into foreign markets, conservatism prevails and firms limit their downside exposure by using less risky strategies like exporting, licensing, and joint ventures to accomplish entry. Then, as experience accumulates and perceived risk levels decline, companies move more boldly, constructing plants and making acquisitions to build strong competitive positions in each country market and beginning to link the strategies in each country to create a global strategy.

The many different *potential driving forces* explain why it is too simplistic to view industry change only in terms of the growth stages model and why a full understanding of the *causes* underlying the emergence of new competitive conditions is a fundamental part of industry analysis.

> *The task of driving forces analysis is to separate the major causes of industry change from the minor ones; usually no more than three or four factors qualify as driving forces.*

However, while many forces of change may be at work in a given industry, no more than three or four are likely to qualify as *driving* forces in the sense that they will act as *the major determinants* of why and how the industry is changing. Thus, strategic analysts must resist the temptation to label everything they see changing as driving forces; the analytical task is to evaluate the forces of industry and competitive change carefully enough to separate major factors from minor ones.

The Link between Driving Forces and Strategy   Sound analysis of an industry's driving forces is a prerequisite to sound strategy making. Without keen awareness of what external factors will produce the biggest potential changes in the company's business over the next one to three years, managers are ill prepared to craft a strategy tightly matched to emerging conditions. Similarly, if managers are uncertain about the implications of each driving force or if their views are incomplete or off-base, it's difficult for them to craft a strategy that is responsive to the driving forces and their consequences for the industry. So driving forces analysis is not something to take lightly; it has practical strategy-making value and is basic to the task of thinking about where the business is headed and how to prepare for the changes.

> *Managers can use environmental scanning to spot budding trends and clues of change that could develop into new driving forces.*

Environmental Scanning Techniques   One way to try to detect future driving forces early on is to systematically monitor the environment for new straws in the wind. *Environmental scanning* involves studying and interpreting the sweep of social, political, economic, ecological, and technological events in an effort to spot budding trends and conditions that could become driving forces. Environmental scanning involves time frames well beyond the next one to three years—for example, it could involve judgments about the demand for energy in the year 2010, what kinds of household appliances and computerized electronic controls will be in the "house of the future," how people will communicate over long distances 10 years from now, or what will happen to the income levels and purchasing habits of retired people in the 21st century if average life expectancies continue to increase. Environmental scanning thus attempts to spot first-of-a-kind happenings and new ideas and approaches that are catching on and to extrapolate their implications 5 to 20 years into the future. *The purpose and value of environmental scanning is to raise the consciousness of managers about potential developments that could have an important impact on industry conditions and pose new opportunities or threats.*

Environmental scanning can be accomplished by monitoring and studying current events, constructing scenarios, and employing the Delphi method (a technique for finding consensus among a group of knowledgeable experts). Environmental scanning methods are highly qualitative and subjective. The appeal of environmental scanning, notwithstanding its speculative nature, is that it helps managers lengthen their planning horizon, translate vague inklings of future opportunities or threats into clearer strategic issues (for which they can begin to develop strategic answers), and think strategically about future developments in the surrounding environment.[15] Companies that undertake formal environmental scanning include General Electric, AT&T, Coca-Cola, Ford, General Motors, Du Pont, and Shell Oil.

Question 4: Which Companies Are in the Strongest/Weakest Positions?

The next step in examining the industry's competitive structure is to study the market positions of rival companies. One technique for revealing the competitive positions of industry participants is *strategic group mapping*.[16] This analytical tool is a bridge between looking at the industry as a whole and considering the standing of each firm separately. It is most useful when an industry has so many competitors that it is not practical to examine each one in depth.

Strategic group mapping is a technique for displaying the competitive positions that rival firms occupy in the industry.

Using Strategic Group Maps to Assess the Competitive Positions of Rival Firms   A strategic group consists of those rival firms with similar competitive approaches and positions in the market.[17] Companies in the same strategic group can resemble one another in any of several ways: They may have comparable product line breadth, be vertically integrated to much the same degree, offer buyers similar services and technical assistance, use essentially the same product attributes to appeal to similar types of buyers, emphasize the same distribution channels, depend on identical technological approaches, and/or sell in the same price/quality range. An industry contains only one strategic group when all sellers pursue essentially identical strategies and have comparable market positions. At the other extreme, there are as many strategic groups as there are competitors when each rival pursues a distinct competitive approach and occupies a substantially different competitive position in the marketplace.

Strategic group analysis helps pinpoint a firm's closest competitors.

---

[15]For further discussion of the nature and use of environmental scanning, see Roy Amara and Andrew J. Lipinski, *Business Planning for an Uncertain Future: Scenarios and Strategies* (New York: Pergamon Press, 1983); Harold E. Klein and Robert U. Linneman, "Environmental Assessment: An International Study of Corporate Practice," *Journal of Business Strategy* 5, no. 1 (Summer 1984), pp. 55–75; and Arnoldo C. Hax and Nicolas S. Majluf, *The Strategy Concept and Process* (Englewood Cliffs, N.J.: Prentice-Hall, 1991), chapters 5 and 8.

[16]Porter, *Competitive Strategy,* Chapter 7.

[17]Ibid., pp. 129–30.

The procedure for constructing a strategic group map and deciding which firms belong in which strategic group is straightforward:

- Identify the characteristics that differentiate firms in the industry—typical variables are price/quality range (high, medium, low), geographic coverage (local, regional, national, global), degree of vertical integration (none, partial, full), product line breadth (wide, narrow), use of distribution channels (one, some, all), and degree of service offered (no-frills, limited, full service).

- Plot the firms on a two-variable map using pairs of these differentiating characteristics.

- Assign firms that fall in about the same strategy space to the same strategic group.

- Draw circles around each strategic group, making the circles proportional to the size of the group's respective share of total industry sales revenues.

This produces a two-dimensional *strategic group map* such as the one for the retail jewelry industry portrayed in Illustration Capsule 9.

Several guidelines need to be observed in mapping the positions of strategic groups in the industry's overall strategy space.[18] First, the two variables selected as axes for the map should *not* be highly correlated; if they are, the circles on the map will fall along a diagonal and strategy makers will learn nothing more about the relative positions of competitors than they would by considering just one of the variables. For instance, if companies with broad product lines use multiple distribution channels while companies with narrow lines use a single distribution channel, then looking at broad versus narrow product lines reveals just as much about who is positioned where as looking at single versus multiple distribution channels—one of the variables is redundant. Second, the variables chosen as axes for the map should expose big differences in how rivals position themselves to compete. This, of course, means analysts must identify the characteristics that differentiate rival firms and use these differences as variables for the axes and as the basis for deciding which firm belongs in which strategic group. Third, the variables used as axes don't have to be either quantitative or continuous; rather, they can be discrete variables or defined in terms of distinct classes and combinations. Fourth, drawing the sizes of the circles on the map proportional to the combined sales of the firms in each strategic group allows the map to reflect the relative sizes of each strategic group. Fifth, if more than two good competitive variables can be used as axes for the map, several maps can be drawn to give different exposures to the competitive positioning relationships present in the industry's structure. Because there is not necessarily one best map for portraying how competing firms are positioned in the market, it is advisable to experiment with different pairs of competitive variables.

What Can Be Learned from Strategic Group Maps   One thing to look for is whether *industry driving forces and competitive pressures favor some strategic groups and hurt others.*[19] Firms in adversely affected strategic groups may try to shift to a more favorably situated group; how hard such a move is depends on whether entry barriers into the target strategic group are high or low. Attempts by rival firms to enter a new strategic group nearly always increase competition. If certain firms are known to be trying to

[18]Ibid., pp. 152–54.

[19]Ibid., pp. 130, 132–38, and 154–55.

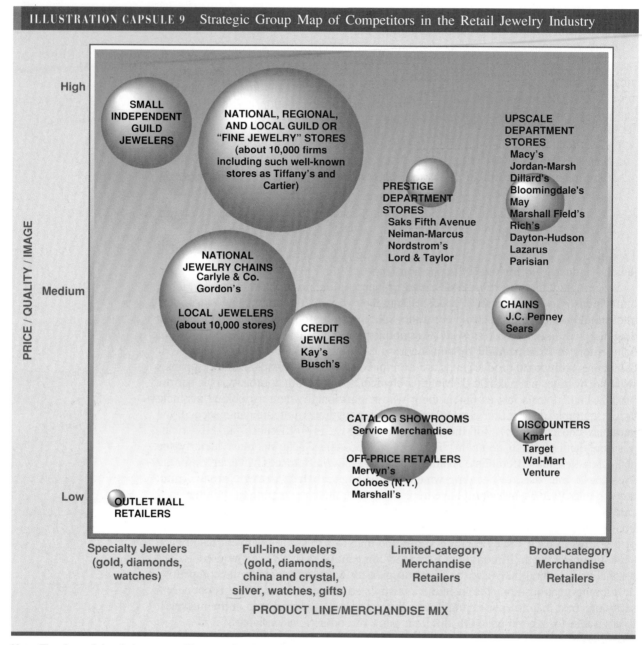

ILLUSTRATION CAPSULE 9   Strategic Group Map of Competitors in the Retail Jewelry Industry

Note: The sizes of the circles are roughly proportional to the market shares of each group of competitors.

change their positions on the map, then attaching arrows to the circles showing the targeted direction helps clarify the picture of competitive jockeying among rivals.

Another consideration is whether *the profit potential of different strategic groups varies due to the competitive strengths and weaknesses in each group's market position.* Differences in profitability can occur because of differing degrees of bargaining leverage with suppliers or customers, differing degrees of exposure to competition from substitute products outside the industry, differing degrees of competitive rivalry within strategic groups, and differing growth rates for the principal buyer segments served by each group. Driving forces and competitive forces do not affect each strategic group evenly.

Generally speaking, *the closer strategic groups are to each other on the map*, the stronger competitive rivalry among member firms tends to be. Although firms in the same strategic group are the closest rivals, the next closest rivals are in the immediately adjacent groups.[20] Often, firms in strategic groups that are far apart on the map hardly compete at all. For instance, Tiffany's and Wal-Mart both sell gold and silver jewelry, but the prices and perceived qualities of their products are much too different to generate any real competition between them. For the same reason, Timex is not a meaningful competitive rival of Rolex, and Subaru is not a close competitor of Lincoln or Mercedes-Benz.

Some strategic groups are usually more favorably positioned than other strategic groups.

Question 5: What Strategic Moves Are Rivals Likely to Make Next?

Unless a company pays attention to what competitors are doing, it ends up flying blind. A company can't expect to outmaneuver its rivals without monitoring their actions, understanding their strategies, and anticipating what moves they are likely to make next. As in sports, scouting the opposition is essential. The strategies rivals are using and the actions they are likely to take next have direct bearing on a company's own best strategic moves—whether it needs to defend against specific actions taken by rivals or whether rivals' moves provide an opening for a new offensive thrust.

Successful strategists take great pains in scouting competitors—understanding their strategies, watching their actions, sizing up their strengths and weaknesses, and trying to anticipate what moves they will make next.

Understanding Competitors' Strategies   The best source of information about a competitor's strategy comes from examining what it is doing and what its management is saying about the company's plans (Figure 2.3 indicates what to look for in identifying a company's business strategy). Additional insights can be gotten by considering the rival's geographic market arena, strategic intent, market share objective, competitive position on the industry's strategic group map, willingness to take risks, basic competitive strategy approach, and whether the competitor's recent moves are mostly offensive or defensive.[21] Good sources for such information include the company's annual report and 10-K filings, recent speeches by its managers, the reports of securities analysts, articles in the business media, company press releases, information searches on the Internet, rivals' exhibits at international trade shows, visits to the company's Web site, and talking with a rival's customers, suppliers, and former employees. Many companies have a competitive intelligence unit that gathers information on rivals and makes it available on the company's intranet.

P. 48

It is advantageous to know more about your competitors than they know about you.

---

[20]Strategic groups act as good reference points for firms' strategies and for predicting future strategies and the evolution of an industry's competitive structure. See Avi Fiegenbaum and Howard Thomas, ''Strategic Groups as Reference Groups: Theory, Modeling and Empirical Examination of Industry and Competitive Strategy,'' *Strategic Management Journal* 16 (1995), pp. 461–76. For a study of how strategic group analysis helps identify the variables that lead to sustainable competitive advantage, see S. Ade Olusoga, Michael P. Mokwa, and Charles H. Noble, ''Strategic Groups, Mobility Barriers, and Competitive Advantage,'' *Journal of Business Research* 33 (1995), pp. 153–64.

[21]For a discussion of legal ways of gathering competitive intelligence on rival companies, see Larry Kahaner, *Competitive Intelligence* (New York: Simon & Schuster, 1996).

1-4

Gathering competitive intelligence on rivals can sometimes tread the fine line between honest inquiry and illegal behavior, subterfuge, and unethical conduct, however. For example, calling rivals to get information about prices, the dates of new product introductions, or wage and salary levels is legal, but misrepresenting one's company affiliation is unethical. Pumping rivals' representatives at trade shows is ethical only if one wears an accurate name tag like everyone else. In an effort to learn more about a competitor's strategic plans, Avon in 1991 was able to secure discarded materials about its biggest rival, Mary Kay Cosmetics, by having its personnel search through the garbage dumpsters outside MKC's headquarters.[22] When MKC officials learned of the action and sued, Avon claimed it did nothing illegal (a 1988 Supreme Court case ruled that trash left on public property—in this case, a sidewalk—was anyone's for the taking). Avon even produced a videotape of its removal of the trash at the MKC site. Avon won—but the legality of Avon's action does not mean that what it did was ethical.

Table 3.3 provides an easy-to-apply classification scheme for profiling the objectives and strategies of rival companies. Such profiles, along with a strategic group map, provide a working diagnosis of the strategies and recent moves of rivals and are readily supplemented by whatever additional information is available about each competitor.

Evaluating Who the Industry's Major Players Are Going to Be   It's usually obvious who the *current* major contenders are, but these same firms are not necessarily positioned most strongly for the future. Some may be losing ground or be ill equipped to compete in the future. Smaller companies may be moving into contention and poised for an offensive against larger but vulnerable rivals. Long-standing contenders for market leadership sometimes slide quickly down the industry's ranks; others end up being acquired. Today's industry leaders don't automatically become tomorrow's.

> *The company that consistently has more and better information about its competitors is better positioned to prevail, other things being equal.*

Whether a competitor is favorably or unfavorably positioned to gain market ground depends on why there is potential for it to do better or worse. Usually, how securely a company holds its present market share is a function of its vulnerability to driving forces and competitive pressures, whether it has a competitive advantage or disadvantage, and whether it is the likely target of offensive attack from other industry participants. Pinpointing which rivals are poised to gain market position and which seem destined to lose market share helps a strategist anticipate what kinds of moves they are likely to make next.

Predicting Competitors' Next Moves   This is the hardest yet most useful part of competitor analysis. Good clues about what moves a specific company may make next come from studying its strategic intent, monitoring how well it is faring in the marketplace, and determining how much pressure it is under to improve its financial performance. The likelihood of a company continuing with its present strategy usually depends on how well it is doing and its prospects for continued success with its current strategy. Content rivals are likely to continue their present strategy with only minor fine-tuning. Ailing rivals can be performing so poorly that fresh strategic moves, either offensive or defensive, are virtually certain. Aggressive rivals with ambitious strategic intent are strong candidates for pursuing emerging market opportunities and exploiting weaker rivals.

Since managers generally operate from assumptions about the industry's future and beliefs about their own firm's situation, insights into the strategic thinking of

---

[22]Kahaner, *Competitive Intelligence*, pp. 84–85.

TABLE 3.3   Categorizing the Objectives and Strategies of Competitors

Competitive Scope	Strategic Intent	Market Share Objective	Competitive Position/Situation	Strategic Posture	Competitive Strategy
• Local • Regional • National • Multicountry • Global	• Be the dominant leader • Overtake the present industry leader • Be among the industry leaders (top 5) • Move into the top 10 • Move up a notch or two in the industry rankings • Overtake a particular rival (not necessarily the leader) • Maintain position • Just survive	• Aggressive expansion via both acquisition and internal growth • Expansion via internal growth (boost market share at the expense of rival firms) • Expansion via acquisition • Hold on to present share (by growing at a rate equal to the industry average) • Give up share if necessary to achieve short-term profit objectives (stress profitability, not volume)	• Getting stronger; on the move • Well-entrenched; able to maintain its present position • Stuck in the middle of the pack • Going after a different market position (trying to move from a weaker to a stronger position) • Struggling; losing ground • Retrenching to a position that can be defended	• Mostly offensive • Mostly defensive • A combination of offense and defense • Aggressive risk-taker • Conservative follower	• Striving for low cost leadership • Mostly focusing on a market niche —High end —Low end —Geographic —Buyers with special needs —Other • Pursuing differentiation based on —Quality —Service —Technological superiority —Breadth of product line —Image and reputation —More value for the money —Other attributes

Note: Since a focus strategy can be aimed at any of several market niches and a differentiation strategy can be keyed to any of several attributes, it is best to be explicit about what kind of focus strategy or differentiation strategy a given firm is pursuing. All focusers do not pursue the same market niche, and all differentiators do not pursue the same differentiating attributes.

rival company managers can be gleaned from their public pronouncements about where the industry is headed and what it will take to be successful, what they are saying about their firm's situation, information from the grapevine about what they are doing, and their past actions and leadership styles. Another thing to consider is whether a rival has the flexibility to make major strategic changes or whether it is locked into pursuing its same basic strategy with minor adjustments.

Managers who fail to study competitors closely risk being blindsided by "surprise" actions on the part of rivals.

To succeed in predicting a competitor's next moves, one has to have a good feel for the rival's situation, how its managers think, and what its options are. Doing the necessary detective work can be tedious and time-consuming since the information comes in bits and pieces from many sources. But scouting competitors well enough to anticipate their next moves allows managers to prepare effective countermoves (perhaps even beat a rival to the punch!).

Question 6: What Are the Key Factors for Competitive Success?

An industry's *key success factors* (KSFs) are those things that most affect the ability of industry members to prosper in the marketplace—the particular strategy elements, product attributes, resources, competencies, competitive capabilities, and business outcomes that spell the difference between profit and loss. *Key success factors concern what every industry member must be competent at doing or concentrate on achieving in order to be competitively and financially successful.* KSFs are so important that all firms in the industry must pay them close attention—they are the *prerequisites* for industry success. The answers to three questions help identify an industry's key success factors:

An industry's key success factors concern the product attributes, competencies, competitive capabilities, and market achievements with the greatest direct bearing on company profitability.

- On what basis do customers choose between the competing brands of sellers?
- What must a seller do to be competitively successful—what resources and competitive capabilities does it need?
- What does it take for sellers to achieve a sustainable competitive advantage?

In the beer industry, the KSFs are full utilization of brewing capacity (to keep manufacturing costs low), a strong network of wholesale distributors (to gain access to as many retail outlets as possible), and clever advertising (to induce beer drinkers to buy a particular brand). In apparel manufacturing, the KSFs are appealing designs and color combinations (to create buyer interest) and low-cost manufacturing efficiency (to permit attractive retail pricing and ample profit margins). In tin and aluminum cans, because the cost of shipping empty cans is substantial, one of the keys is having plants located close to end-use customers so that the plant's output can be marketed within economical shipping distances (regional market share is far more crucial than national share). Table 3.4 provides a shopping list of the most common types of key success factors.

Determining the industry's key success factors is a top priority. At the very least, managers need to understand the industry situation well enough to know what is more important to competitive success and what is less important. They need to know what kinds of resources are valuable. Misdiagnosing the industry factors critical to long-term competitive success greatly raises the risk of a misdirected strategy—one that overemphasizes less important competitive targets and under-emphasizes more important competitive capabilities. On the other hand, a company with perceptive understanding of industry KSFs can gain sustainable competitive advantage by training its strategy on industry KSFs and devoting its energies to being better than rivals on one or more of these factors. Indeed, *key success factors represent golden opportunities for competitive advantage*—companies that stand out on a particular KSF enjoy a stronger market position for their efforts. Hence using one or more of the industry's KSFs as *cornerstones* for the company's strategy and trying to gain sustainable competitive advantage by excelling at one particular KSF is a fruitful approach.[23]

Strategic Management Principle

A sound strategy incorporates efforts to be competent on all industry key success factors and to excel on at least one factor.

Key success factors vary from industry to industry and even from time to time within the same industry as driving forces and competitive conditions change. Only rarely does an industry have more than three or four key success factors at any one time. And even among these three or four, one or two usually outrank the others in importance. Managers, therefore, have to resist the temptation to include factors that

---

[23]Some experts dispute the strategy-making value of key success factors. Professor Ghemawat claims that the "whole idea of identifying a success factor and then chasing it seems to have something in common with the ill-considered medieval hunt for the *philosopher's stone*, a substance which would transmute everything it touched into gold." Pankaj Ghemawat, *Commitment: The Dynamic of Strategy* (New York: Free Press, 1991), p.11.

TABLE 3.4   Common Types of Key Success Factors

Technology-Related KSFs

Scientific research expertise (important in such fields as pharmaceuticals, medicine, space exploration, other "high-tech" industries)

Technical capability to make innovative improvements in production processes

Product innovation capability

Expertise in a given technology

Capability to use the Internet to disseminate information, take orders, deliver products or services

Manufacturing-Related KSFs

Low-cost production efficiency (achieve scale economies, capture experience curve effects)

Quality of manufacture (fewer defects, less need for repairs)

High utilization of fixed assets (important in capital intensive/high fixed-cost industries)

Low-cost plant locations

Access to adequate supplies of skilled labor

High labor productivity (important for items with high labor content)

Low-cost product design and engineering (reduces manufacturing costs)

Flexibility to manufacture a range of models and sizes/take care of custom orders

Distribution-Related KSFs

A strong network of wholesale distributors/dealers (or electronic distribution capability via the Internet)

Gaining ample space on retailer shelves

Having company-owned retail outlets

Low distribution costs

Fast delivery

Marketing-Related KSFs

Fast, accurate technical assistance

Courteous customer service

Accurate filling of buyer orders (few back orders or mistakes)

Breadth of product line and product selection

Merchandising skills

Attractive styling/packaging

Customer guarantees and warranties (important in mail-order retailing, big-ticket purchases, new product introductions)

Clever advertising

Skills-Related KSFs

Superior workforce talent (important in professional services like accounting and investment banking)

Quality control know-how

Design expertise (important in fashion and apparel industries and often one of the keys to low-cost manufacture)

Expertise in a particular technology

An ability to develop innovative products and product improvements

An ability to get newly conceived products past the R&D phase and out into the market very quickly

Organizational Capability

Superior information systems (important in airline travel, car rental, credit card, and lodging industries)

Ability to respond quickly to shifting market conditions (streamlined decision making, short lead times to bring new products to market)

Superior ability to employ the Internet and other aspects of electronic commerce to conduct business

More experience and managerial know-how

Other Types of KSFs

Favorable image/reputation with buyers

Overall low cost (not just in manufacturing)

Convenient locations (important in many retailing businesses)

Pleasant, courteous employees in all customer contact positions

Access to financial capital (important in newly emerging industries with high degrees of business risk and in capital-intensive industries)

Patent protection

have only minor importance on their list of key success factors—the purpose of identifying KSFs is to make judgments about what things are more important and what things are less important. To compile a list of every factor that matters even a little bit defeats the purpose of concentrating management attention on the truly critical factors.

Question 7: Is the Industry Attractive and What Are Its Prospects for Above-Average Profitability?

The final step of industry and competitive analysis is to use the answers to the previous six questions to draw conclusions about the relative attractiveness or unattractiveness of the industry, both near term and long term. Important factors for company managers to consider include:

- The industry's growth potential.
- Whether competition currently permits adequate profitability and whether competitive forces will become stronger or weaker.
- Whether industry profitability will be favorably or unfavorably impacted by the prevailing driving forces.
- The company's competitive position in the industry and whether its position is likely to grow stronger or weaker (being a well-entrenched leader or strongly positioned contender in an otherwise lackluster industry can still produce good profitability; on the other hand, having to fight an uphill battle against much stronger rivals can make an otherwise attractive industry unattractive).
- The company's potential to capitalize on the vulnerabilities of weaker rivals (perhaps converting an unattractive *industry* situation into a potentially rewarding *company* opportunity).
- Whether the company is insulated from, or able to defend against, the factors that make the industry unattractive.
- How well the company's competitive capabilities match the industry's key success factors.
- The degrees of risk and uncertainty in the industry's future.
- The severity of problems/issues confronting the industry as a whole.
- Whether continued participation in this industry adds to the firm's ability to be successful in other industries in which it may have interests.

As a general proposition, *if an industry's overall profit prospects are above average, the industry can be considered attractive*. If its profit prospects are below average, it is unattractive. However, it is a mistake to think of industries as being attractive or unattractive *to all industry participants and all potential entrants*. Attractiveness is relative, not absolute, and conclusions one way or the other are in the eye of the beholder—industry attractiveness *always* has to be appraised from the standpoint of a particular company. Industries unattractive to outsiders may be attractive to insiders. Industry environments unattractive to weak competitors may be attractive to strong competitors. Companies on the outside may look at an industry's environment and conclude that it is an unattractive business for them to get into; they may see more profitable opportunities elsewhere, given their particular resources and competencies. But a favorably positioned company already in the industry may survey the very

A company that is uniquely well situated in an otherwise unattractive industry can, under certain circumstances, still earn unusually good profits.

same business environment and conclude that the industry is attractive because it has the resources and competitive capabilities to take sales and market share away from weaker rivals, build a strong leadership position, and earn good profits.

An assessment that the industry is fundamentally attractive suggests that current industry participants employ strategies that strengthen their long-term competitive positions in the business, expanding sales efforts and investing in additional facilities and capabilities as needed. If the industry and competitive situation is relatively unattractive, more successful industry participants may choose to invest cautiously, look for ways to protect their long-term competitiveness and profitability, and perhaps acquire smaller firms if the price is right; over the longer term, strong companies may consider diversification into more attractive businesses. Weak companies in unattractive industries may consider merging with a rival to bolster market share and profitability or, alternatively, begin looking outside the industry for attractive diversification opportunities.

ACTUALLY DOING AN INDUSTRY AND COMPETITIVE ANALYSIS

Table 3.5 provides a *format* for presenting the pertinent findings and conclusions of industry and competitive analysis. It embraces all seven questions discussed above and leads would-be analysts to do the strategic thinking and evaluation needed to draw conclusions about the state of the industry and competitive environment.

Two things should be kept in mind in doing industry and competitive analysis. One, the task of analyzing a company's external situation is not a mechanical, formula-like exercise in which facts and data are plugged in and definitive conclusions come pouring out. Strategic analysis always leaves room for differences of opinion about how all the factors add up and what future industry and competitive conditions will be like. There can be several appealing scenarios about how an industry will evolve, how attractive it will be, and how good the profit outlook is. However, while no methodology can guarantee a conclusive diagnosis, it doesn't make sense to shortcut strategic analysis and rely on opinion and casual observation. Managers become better strategists when they know what analytical questions to pose, have the skills to read clues about which way the winds of industry and competitive change are blowing, and can use situation analysis techniques to find answers and identify strategic issues. This is why we concentrated on suggesting the right questions to ask, explaining concepts and analytical approaches, and indicating the kinds of things to look for.

Two, sweeping industry and competitive analyses need to be done every one to three years; in the interim, managers are obliged to continually update and reexamine their thinking as events unfold. There's no substitute for being a good student of industry and competitive conditions and staying on the cutting edge of what's happening in the industry. Anything else leaves a manager unprepared to initiate shrewd and timely strategic adjustments.

Thinking strategically about a company's external situation involves probing for answers to the following seven questions:

KEY POINTS

1. *What are the industry's dominant economic traits?* Industries differ significantly on such factors as market size and growth rate, the geographic scope of competitive

TABLE 3.5   Sample Form for an Industry and Competitive Analysis Summary

1. **Dominant Economic Characteristics of the Industry Environment** (market size and growth rate, geographic scope, number and sizes of buyers and sellers, pace of technological change and innovation, scale economies, experience curve effects, capital requirements, and so on)

2. **Competition Analysis**
   - Rivalry among competing sellers (a strong, moderate, or weak force/weapons of competition)

   - Threat of potential entry (a strong, moderate, or weak force/assessment of entry barriers)

   - Competition from substitutes (a strong, moderate, or weak force/why)

   - Power of suppliers (a strong, moderate, or weak force/why)

   - Power of customers (a strong, moderate, or weak force/why)

3. **Driving Forces**

4. **Competitive Position of Major Companies/Strategic Groups**
   - Favorably positioned/why

   - Unfavorably positioned/why

5. **Competitor Analysis**
   - Strategic approaches/predicted moves of key competitors

   - Whom to watch and why

6. **Key Success Factors**

7. **Industry Prospects and Overall Attractiveness**
   - Factors making the industry attractive

   - Factors making the industry unattractive

   - Special industry issues/problems

   - Profit outlook (favorable/unfavorable)

rivalry, the number and relative sizes of both buyers and sellers, ease of entry and exit, whether sellers are vertically integrated, how fast basic technology is changing, the extent of scale economies and experience curve effects, whether the products of rival sellers are standardized or differentiated, and overall profitability. An industry's economic characteristics are important because of the implications they have for crafting strategy.

2. *What is competition like and how strong are each of the five competitive forces?* The strength of competition is a composite of five forces: the rivalry among competing sellers, the presence of attractive substitutes, the potential for new entry, the leverage major suppliers have, and the bargaining power of customers. The task of competition analysis is to understand the competitive pressures associated with each force, determine whether these pressures add up to a strong or weak competitive force in the marketplace, and then think strategically about what sort of competitive strategy, given the "rules" of competition in the industry, the company will need to employ to (a) insulate the firm as much as possible from the five competitive forces, (b) influence the industry's competitive rules in the company's favor, and (c) gain a competitive edge.

3. *What are the drivers of change in the industry and what impact will they have?* Industry and competitive conditions change because forces are in motion that create incentives or pressures for change. The most common driving forces are changes in the long-term industry growth rate, changes in buyer composition, product innovation, entry or exit of major firms, globalization, changes in cost and efficiency, changing buyer preferences for standardized versus differentiated products or services, regulatory influences and government policy changes, changing societal and lifestyle factors, and reductions in uncertainty and business risk. Sound analysis of driving forces and their implications for the industry is a prerequisite to sound strategy making.

4. *Which companies are in the strongest/weakest competitive positions?* Strategic group mapping is a valuable, if not necessary, tool for understanding the similarities, differences, strengths, and weaknesses inherent in the market positions of rival companies. Rivals in the same or nearby strategic group(s) are close competitors whereas companies in distant strategic groups usually pose little or no immediate threat.

5. *What strategic moves are rivals likely to make next?* This analytical step involves identifying competitors' strategies, deciding which rivals are likely to be strong contenders and which weak contenders, evaluating their competitive options, and predicting what moves they are likely to make next. Scouting competitors well enough to anticipate their actions helps prepare effective countermoves (perhaps even beat a rival to the punch) and allows managers to take rivals' probable actions into account in designing their own company's best course of action. Managers who fail to study competitors closely risk being blindsided by "surprise" actions on the part of rivals. A company can't expect to outmaneuver its rivals without monitoring their actions and anticipating what moves they may make next.

6. *What key factors will determine competitive success or failure?* Key success factors are the particular strategy elements, product attributes, competitive capabilities, and business outcomes that spell the difference between profit and loss and, ultimately, between competitive success or failure. KSFs point to the things all firms in an industry must be competent at doing or must concentrate on achieving in order to be competitively and financially successful—they are the *prerequisites* for good performance in the industry. Frequently, a company can gain sustainable competitive advantage by training its strategy on industry KSFs and devoting its energies to being distinctively better than rivals at succeeding on these factors. Companies that only dimly perceive what factors are truly crucial to long-term competitive success are less likely to have winning strategies.

7. *Is the industry attractive and what are its prospects for above-average profitability?* The answer to this question is a major driver of company strategy. An assessment that the industry and competitive environment is fundamentally attractive typically suggests employing a strategy calculated to build a stronger competitive position in the business, expanding sales efforts, and investing in additional facilities and capabilities as needed. If the industry is relatively unattractive, outsiders considering entry may decide against it and look elsewhere for opportunities, weak companies in the industry may merge with or be acquired by a rival, and strong companies may restrict further investments and employ cost-reduction strategies and/or product innovation strategies to boost long-term competitiveness and protect their profitability. On occasion, an industry that is unattractive overall is still very attractive to a favorably situated company with the skills and resources to take business away from weaker rivals.

Good industry and competitive analysis is a prerequisite to good strategy making. A competently done industry and competitive analysis provides the understanding of a company's macroenvironment needed for shrewdly matching strategy to the company's external situation.

SUGGESTED READINGS

D'Aveni, Richard A. *Hypercompetition*. New York: Free Press, 1994, chaps. 5 and 6.

Ghemawat, Pankaj. "Building Strategy on the Experience Curve." *Harvard Business Review* 64, no. 2 (March–April 1985), pp. 143–49.

Kahaner, Larry. "What You Can Learn from Your Competitors' Mission Statements." *Competitive Intelligence Review* 6 no. 4 (Winter 1995), pp. 35–40.

Langley, Ann. "Between 'Paralysis by Analysis' and 'Extinction by Instinct.'" *Sloan Management Review* (Spring 1995), pp. 63–75.

Linneman, Robert E., and Harold E. Klein. "Using Scenarios in Strategic Decision Making." *Business Horizons* 28, no. 1 (January–February 1985), pp. 64–74.

Porter, Michael E. "How Competitive Forces Shape Strategy." *Harvard Business Review* 57, no. 2 (March–April 1979), pp. 137–45.

_____. *Competitive Strategy: Techniques for Analyzing Industries and Competitors*. New York: Free Press, 1980, chap. 1.

_____. *Competitive Advantage*. New York: Free Press, 1985, chap. 2.

Yip, George S. *Total Global Strategy: Managing for Worldwide Competitive Advantage*. Englewood Cliffs, N.J.: Prentice-Hall, 1992, chap. 10.

Zahra, Shaker A., and Sherry S. Chaples. "Blind Spots in Competitive Analysis." *Academy of Management Executive* 7, no. 2 (May 1993), pp. 7–28.

EVALUATING COMPANY RESOURCES AND COMPETITIVE CAPABILITIES

4

In the previous chapter we described how to use the tools of industry and competitive analysis to assess a company's external situation. In this chapter we discuss the techniques of evaluating a company's resource capabilities, relative cost position, and competitive strength versus rivals. Company situation analysis prepares the groundwork for matching the company's strategy *both* to its external market circumstances and to its internal resources and competitive capabilities. The spotlight of company situation analysis is trained on five questions:

1. How well is the company's present strategy working?
2. What are the company's resource strengths and weaknesses and its external opportunities and threats?
3. Are the company's prices and costs competitive?
4. How strong is the company's competitive position relative to its rivals?
5. What strategic issues does the company face?

To explore these questions, four new analytical techniques will be introduced: SWOT analysis, value chain analysis, strategic cost analysis, and competitive strength assessment. These techniques are basic strategic management tools because they expose the company's resource strengths and deficiencies, its best market opportunities, the outside threats to its future profitability, and its competitive standing relative to rivals. Insightful company situation analysis is a precondition for identifying the strategic issues that management needs to address and for tailoring strategy to company resources and competitive capabilities as well as to industry and competitive conditions.

Organizations succeed in a competitive marketplace over the long run because they can do certain things their customers value better than can their competitors.

Robert Hayes, Gary Pisano, and David Upton

The greatest mistake managers make when evaluating their resources is failing to assess them relative to competitors'.

David J. Collis and Cynthia A. Montgomery

Only firms who are able to continually build new strategic assets faster and cheaper than their competitors will earn superior returns over the long term.

C. C. Markides and P. J. Williamson

QUESTION 1: HOW WELL IS THE PRESENT STRATEGY WORKING?

In evaluating how well a company's present strategy is working, a manager has to start with what the strategy is (see Figure 2.3 in Chapter 2 to refresh your recollection of the key components of business strategy). The first thing to pin down is the company's competitive approach—whether it is (1) striving to be a low-cost leader or stressing ways to differentiate its product offering and (2) concentrating its efforts on serving a broad spectrum of customers or a narrow market niche. Another strategy-defining consideration is the firm's competitive scope within the industry—how many stages of the industry's production-distribution chain it operates in (one, several, or all), what its geographic market coverage is, and the size and makeup of its customer base. The company's functional strategies in production, marketing, finance, human resources, information technology, new product innovation, and so on further characterize company strategy. In addition, the company may have initiated some recent strategic moves (for instance, a price cut, newly designed styles and models, stepped-up advertising, entry into a new geographic area, or merger with a competitor) that are integral to its strategy and that aim at securing an improved competitive position and, optimally, a competitive advantage. The strategy being pursued can be further nailed down by probing the logic behind each competitive move and functional approach.

While there's merit in evaluating the strategy from a qualitative standpoint (its completeness, internal consistency, rationale, and suitability to the situation), the best quantitative evidence of how well a company's strategy is working comes from study-ing the company's recent strategic and financial performance and seeing what story the numbers tell about the results the strategy is producing. The two best empirical indicators of whether a company's strategy is working well are (1) whether the company is achieving its stated financial and strategic objec-tives and (2) whether it is an above-average industry performer. Persistent shortfalls in meeting company performance targets and weak performance relative to rivals are reliable warning signs that the company suffers from either a malfunctioning strategy or less-than-competent strategy execution (or both). Sometimes company objectives are not explicit enough (especially to company outsiders) to benchmark actual performance against, but it is nearly always feasible to evaluate the performance of a company's strategy by looking at:

The stronger a company's financial performance and market position, the more likely it has a well-conceived, well-executed strategy.

- Whether the firm's market share ranking in the industry is rising, stable, or declining.
- Whether the firm's profit margins are increasing or decreasing and how large they are relative to rival firms' margins.
- Trends in the firm's net profits, return on investment, and economic value added and how these compare to the same trends in profitability for other companies in the industry.
- Whether the company's overall financial strength and credit rating is improving or on the decline.
- Trends in the company's stock price and whether the company's strategy is resulting in satisfactory gains in shareholder value (relative to the MVA gains of other companies in the industry).
- Whether the firm's sales are growing faster or slower than the market as a whole.

- The firm's image and reputation with its customers.
- Whether the company is regarded as a leader in technology, product innovation, product quality, customer service, or other relevant factor on which buyers base their choice of brands.

The stronger a company's current overall performance, the less likely the need for radical changes in strategy. The weaker a company's financial performance and market standing, the more its current strategy must be questioned. Weak performance is almost always a sign of weak strategy or weak execution or both.

QUESTION 2: WHAT ARE THE COMPANY'S RESOURCE STRENGTHS AND WEAKNESSES AND ITS EXTERNAL OPPORTUNITIES AND THREATS?

Sizing up a firm's resource strengths and weaknesses and its external opportunities and threats, commonly known as *SWOT analysis*, provides a good overview of whether a firm's business position is fundamentally healthy or unhealthy. SWOT analysis is grounded in the basic principle that *strategy-making efforts must aim at producing a good fit between a company's resource capability and its external situation*. A clear view of a company's resource capabilities and deficiencies, its market opportunities, and the external threats to the company's future well-being is essential. Otherwise, the task of conceiving a strategy becomes a chancy proposition indeed.

Identifying Company Strengths and Resource Capabilities

A *strength* is something a company is good at doing or a characteristic that gives it enhanced competitiveness. A strength can take any of several forms:

- *A skill or important expertise*—low-cost manufacturing know-how, technological know-how, a proven track record in defect-free manufacture, expertise in providing consistently good customer service, skills in developing innovative products, excellent mass merchandising skills, or unique advertising and promotional know-how.
- *Valuable physical assets*—state-of-the-art plants and equipment, attractive real estate locations, worldwide distribution facilities, natural resource deposits, or cash on hand.
- *Valuable human assets*—an experienced and capable workforce, talented employees in key areas, motivated employees, managerial know-how, or the collective learning and know-how embedded in the organization and built up over time.
- *Valuable organizational assets*—proven quality control systems, proprietary technology, key patents, mineral rights, a base of loyal customers, a strong balance sheet and credit rating, a company intranet for accessing and exchanging information both internally and with suppliers and key customers, computer-assisted design and manufacturing systems, systems for conducting business on the World Wide Web, or e-mail addresses for many or most of the company's customers.
- *Valuable intangible assets*—brand-name image, company reputation, buyer goodwill, a high degree of employee loyalty, or a positive work climate and organization culture.

- *Competitive capabilities*—short development times in bringing new products to market, build-to-order manufacturing capability, a strong dealer network, strong partnerships with key suppliers, an R&D organization with the ability to keep the company's pipeline full of innovative new products, organizational agility in responding to shifting market conditions and emerging opportunities, or state-of-the-art systems for doing business via the Internet.

- *An achievement or attribute that puts the company in a position of market advantage*—low overall costs, market share leadership, having a better product, wider product selection, stronger name recognition, or better customer service.

- *Alliances or cooperative ventures*—partnerships with others having expertise or capabilities that enhance the company's own competitiveness.

Company strengths thus have diverse origins. Sometimes they relate to fairly specific skills and expertise (like know-how in researching consumer tastes and buying habits or training customer contact employees to be cordial and helpful) and sometimes they flow from different resources teaming together to create a competitive capability (like continuous product innovation—which tends to result from a combination of knowledge of consumer needs, technological know-how, R&D, product design and engineering, cost-effective manufacturing, and market testing). The regularity with which employees from different parts of the organization pool their knowledge and expertise, their skills in exploiting and building upon the organization's physical and intangible assets, and the effectiveness with which they collaborate can create competitive capabilities not otherwise achievable by a single department or organizational unit.

Basic Concept

A company is positioned to succeed if it has a good complement of resources at its command.

Taken together, a company's strengths—its skills and expertise, its collection of assets, its competitive capabilities, and its market achievements—determine the complement of *resources* with which it competes. These resources, in conjunction with industry and competitive conditions, are big drivers in how well the company will be able to perform in a dynamic competitive marketplace.[1]

Identifying Company Weaknesses and Resource Deficiencies

A *weakness* is something a company lacks or does poorly (in comparison to others) or a condition that puts it at a disadvantage. A company's internal weaknesses can relate to (a) deficiencies in competitively important skills or expertise, (b) a lack of competitively important physical, human, organizational, or intangible assets, or (c) missing or weak competitive capabilities in key areas. *Internal weaknesses are thus shortcomings in a company's complement of resources.* A weakness may or may not make a company competitively vulnerable, depending on how much the weakness matters in the market-

---

[1]In the past decade, there's been considerable research into the role a company's resources and competitive capabilities play in crafting strategy and in determining company profitability. The findings and conclusions have coalesced into what is called the resource-based view of the firm. Among the most insightful articles are Birger Wernerfelt, "A Resource-Based View of the Firm," *Strategic Management Journal*, September–October 1984, pp. 171–80; Jay Barney, "Firm Resources and Sustained Competitive Advantage," *Journal of Management*, 17, no. 1, 1991, pp. 99–120; Margaret A. Peteraf, "The Cornerstones of Competitive Advantage: A Resource-Based View," *Strategic Management Journal*, March 1993, pp. 179–91; Birger Wernerfelt, "The Resource-Based View of the Firm: Ten Years After," *Strategic Management Journal*, 16 (1995), pp. 171–74 and Jay B. Barney, "Looking Inside for Competitive Advantage," *Academy of Management Executive* 9, no. 4 (November 1995), pp. 49–61.

TABLE 4.1   SWOT Analysis—What to Look for in Sizing Up a Company's Strengths, Weaknesses, Opportunities, and Threats

Potential Resource Strengths and Competitive Capabilities

- A powerful strategy supported by good skills and expertise in key areas
- A strong financial condition; ample financial resources to grow the business
- Strong brand-name image/company reputation
- A widely recognized market leader and an attractive customer base
- Ability to take advantage of economies of scale and/or learning and experience curve effects
- Proprietary technology/superior technological skills/important patents
- Cost advantages
- Strong advertising and promotion
- Product innovation skills
- Proven skills in improving production processes
- A reputation for good customer service
- Better product quality relative to rivals
- Wide geographic coverage and distribution capability
- Alliances/joint ventures with other firms

Potential Company Opportunities

- Serving additional customer groups or expanding into new geographic markets or product segments
- Expanding the company's product line to meet a broader range of customer needs
- Transferring company skills or technological know-how to new products or businesses
- Integrating forward or backward
- Falling trade barriers in attractive foreign markets
- Openings to take market share away from rival firms
- Ability to grow rapidly because of strong increases in market demand
- Acquisition of rival firms
- Alliances or joint ventures that expand the firm's market coverage and competitive capability
- Openings to exploit emerging new technologies
- Market openings to extend the company's brand name or reputation to new geographic areas

Potential Resource Weaknesses and Competitive Deficiencies

- No clear strategic direction
- Obsolete facilities
- A weak balance sheet; burdened with too much debt
- Higher overall unit costs relative to key competitors
- Missing some key skills or competencies/lack of management depth
- Subpar profitability because . . .
- Plagued with internal operating problems
- Falling behind in R&D
- Too narrow a product line relative to rivals
- Weak brand image or reputation
- Weaker dealer or distribution network than key rivals
- Subpar marketing skills relative to rivals
- Short on financial resources to fund promising strategic initiatives
- Lots of underutilized plant capacity
- Behind on product quality

Potential External Threats to a Company's Well-Being

- Likely entry of potent new competitors
- Loss of sales to substitute products
- Slowdowns in market growth
- Adverse shifts in foreign exchange rates and trade policies of foreign governments
- Costly new regulatory requirements
- Vulnerability to recession and business cycle
- Growing bargaining power of customers or suppliers
- A shift in buyer needs and tastes away from the industry's product
- Adverse demographic changes
- Vulnerability to industry driving forces

place and whether it can be overcome by the resources and strengths in the company's possession.

Table 4.1 indicates the kinds of factors to be considered in determining a company's resource strengths and weaknesses. Sizing up a company's resource capabilities and deficiencies is akin to constructing *a strategic balance sheet* where resource strengths represent *competitive assets* and resource weaknesses represent *competitive liabilities*. Obviously, the ideal condition is for the company's strengths/competitive assets to outweigh its weaknesses/competitive liabilities by an ample margin—50-50 balance is definitely not the desired condition!

Basic Concept

A company's resource strengths represent competitive assets; its resource weaknesses represent competitive liabilities.

Once managers identify a company's resource strengths and weaknesses, the two compilations need to be carefully evaluated for their competitive and strategy-making implications. Some strengths are more *competitively important* than others because they matter more in forming a powerful strategy, in contributing to a strong market position, and in determining profitability. Likewise, some weaknesses can prove fatal if not remedied, while others are inconsequential, easily corrected, or offset by company strengths. A company's resource weaknesses suggest a need to review its resource base: What existing resource deficiencies need to be remedied? Does the company have important resource gaps that need to be filled? What needs to be done to augment the company's future resource base?

Identifying Company Competencies and Capabilities

Core Competencies: A Valuable Company Resource   One of the most valuable resources a company has is the ability to perform a competitively relevant activity very well. A competitively important internal activity that a company performs better than other competitively important internal activities is termed a *core competence*.

> **Basic Concept**
>
> *A core competence is something a company does well relative to other internal activities; a distinctive competence is something a company does well relative to competitors.*

What distinguishes a *core* competence from a competence is that a *core* competence is *central* to a company's competitiveness and profitability rather than peripheral. A core competence can relate to demonstrated expertise in performing an activity, to a company's scope and depth of technological know-how, or to a *combination* of specific skills that result in a competitively valuable capability. Frequently, a core competence is the product of effective collaboration among different parts of the organization, of individual resources teaming together. Typically, *core competencies reside in a company's people, not in its assets on the balance sheet.* They tend to be grounded in skills, knowledge, and capabilities.

In practice, companies exhibit many different types of core competencies: skills in manufacturing a high-quality product, know-how in creating and operating a system for filling customer orders accurately and swiftly, fast development of new products, the capability to provide good after-sale service, skills in selecting good retail locations, innovativeness in developing popular product features, skills in merchandising and product display, expertise in an important technology, a well-conceived methodology for researching customer needs and tastes and spotting new market trends, skills in working with customers on new applications and uses of the product, and expertise in integrating multiple technologies to create whole families of new products.

Plainly, *a core competence gives a company competitive capability* and thus qualifies as a genuine company strength and resource. A company may have more than one core competence, but rare is the company that can legitimately claim more than several.

> **Strategic Management Principle**
>
> *A distinctive competence empowers a company to build competitive advantage.*

Distinctive Competencies: A Competitively Superior Company Resource   Whether a company's core competence represents a *distinctive* competence depends on how good the competence is relative to what competitors are capable of—is it a competitively superior competence or just an internal company competence? *A distinctive competence is a competitively important activity that a company performs well in comparison to its competitors.*[2] Most every com-

---

[2]For a fuller discussion of the core competence concept, see C. K. Prahalad and Gary Hamel, "The Core Competence of the Corporation," *Harvard Business Review* 68, no. 3 (May–June 1990), pp. 79–93.

pany does one competitively important activity *enough better than other activities* that it can claim its best-performed activity as a core competence. But an internal assessment of what a company does best doesn't translate into a distinctive competence unless the company performs that activity in a *competitively superior* fashion. For instance, most all retailers believe they have core competencies in product selection and in-store merchandising, but many retailers who build strategies on these competencies run into trouble because they encounter rivals whose competencies in these areas are better. Consequently, *a core competence becomes a basis for competitive advantage only when it is a distinctive competence.*

Sharp Corporation's distinctive competence in flat-panel display technology has enabled it to dominate the worldwide market for liquid-crystal-displays (LCDs). The distinctive competencies of Toyota, Honda, and Nissan in low-cost, high-quality manufacturing and in short design-to-market cycles for new models have proven to be considerable competitive advantages in the global market for motor vehicles. Intel's distinctive competence in rapidly developing new generations of ever more powerful semiconductor chips for personal computers has given the company a dominating position in the personal computer industry. Motorola's distinctive competence in virtually defect-free manufacture (six-sigma quality—an error rate of about one per million) has contributed significantly to the company's world leadership in cellular telephone equipment. Rubbermaid's distinctive competence in developing innovative rubber and plastics products for household and commercial use has made it the clear leader in its industry.

The importance of a distinctive competence to strategy making rests with (1) the competitively valuable capability it gives a company, (2) its potential for being a cornerstone of strategy, and (3) the competitive edge it can potentially produce in the marketplace. It is always easier to build competitive advantage when a firm has a distinctive competence in performing activities important to market success, when rival companies do not have offsetting competencies, and when it is costly and time-consuming for rivals to imitate the competence. A distinctive competence is thus an especially valuable competitive asset, with potential to be the mainspring of a company's success—unless it is trumped by more powerful resources of rivals.

Determining the Competitive Value of a Company Resource   No two companies are alike in their resources. They don't have the same skill sets, assets (physical, human, organizational, and intangible), competitive capabilities, and market achievements— a condition that results in different companies having different resource strengths and weaknesses. *Differences in company resources are an important reason why some companies are more profitable and more competitively successful than others.* A company's success is more certain when it has appropriate and ample resources with which to compete, and especially when it has a valuable strength, asset, capability, or achievement with the potential to produce competitive advantage.

For a particular company resource—whether it be a distinctive competence, an asset (physical, human, organizational, or intangible), an achievement, or a competitive capability—to qualify as the basis for sustainable competitive advantage, it must pass four tests of competitive value:[3]

[3]See David J. Collis and Cynthia A. Montgomery, "Competing on Resources: Strategy in the 1990s," *Harvard Business Review* 73, no. 4 (July–August 1995), pp. 120–23.

1. *Is the resource hard to copy?* The more difficult and more expensive it is to imitate a resource, the greater its potential competitive value. Hard-to-copy resources limit competition, making any profit stream they are able to generate more sustainable. Resources can be difficult to copy because of their uniqueness (a fantastic real estate location, patent protection), because they must be built over time in ways that are difficult to accelerate (a brand name, mastery of a technology), and because they carry big capital requirements (a new cost-effective plant to manufacture semiconductor chips can cost $1 to $2 billion).

2. *How long does the resource last?* The longer a resource lasts, the greater its value. Some resources lose their value quickly because of the rapid speeds with which technologies or industry conditions are moving. The value of FedEx's resources to provide overnight package delivery is rapidly being undercut by fax machines and electronic mail. The value of the programming know-how underlying Netscape's software for browsing the Internet is a rapidly depreciating asset because of the lightning speed with which Internet technology is advancing.

3. *Is the resource really competitively superior?* Companies have to guard against pridefully believing that their core competences are distinctive competences or that their brand name is more powerful than those of rivals. Who can really say whether Coca-Cola's consumer marketing skills are better than Pepsi-Cola's or whether Mercedes-Benz's brand name is more powerful than BMW's or Lexus's?

4. *Can the resource be trumped by the different resources/capabilities of rivals?* Many commercial airlines (American Airlines, Delta Airlines, United Airlines, Singapore Airlines) have succeeded because of their resources and capabilities in offering safe, convenient, reliable air transportation services and in providing an array of amenities to passengers. However, Southwest Airlines has been more consistently profitable by building the capabilities to provide safe, reliable, fewer frills services at radically lower fares. Intel's and Microsoft's resources have trumped those of IBM in personal computers—IBM's long-standing industry experience and prestigious brand name has faded as a dominating factor in choosing what PC to buy; whether a PC has the "Intel inside" sticker and the ability to run the latest Windows programs have become bigger buying considerations than the brand name on the PC.

The vast majority of companies are not well endowed with competitively valuable resources, much less with competitively superior resources capable of passing the above four tests with flying colors. Most businesses have a mixed bag of strengths/assets/competencies/capabilities—one or two quite valuable, some good, many satisfactory to mediocre. Only a few companies, usually industry leaders or future leaders, possess a superior resource of great competitive value. Furthermore, nearly all companies have competitive liabilities: internal weaknesses, a lack of assets, missing expertise or capabilities, or resource deficiencies.

Strategic Management Principle

Successful strategists seek to capitalize on what a company does best—its expertise, resource strengths, and strongest competitive capabilities.

Even if a company doesn't possess a competitively superior resource, the potential for competitive advantage is not lost. *Sometimes a company derives significant competitive vitality, even competitive advantage, from a collection of good to adequate resources that, in combination, have competitive power.* Toshiba's laptop computers are the market share leader—an indicator that Toshiba is good at something. Yet, Toshiba's laptops are not demonstrably faster than rivals' laptops, nor do they have superior performance features than rival brands (bigger screens, more memory, longer battery power, a better pointing device, and so on), nor does Toshiba provide clearly superior technical support services. And Toshiba laptops are definitely not cheaper, model for model, than comparable brands. But while Toshiba laptops do not consistently rank first in performance ratings or have low-price appeal, Toshiba's competitive superiority springs from a *combination* of "good" resource strengths and capabilities—its strategic partnerships with suppliers of laptop components, its efficient assembly capability, its design expertise, its skills in choosing quality components, its creation of a wide selection of models, the attractive mix of built-in performance features found in each model when balanced against price, the much-better-than-average reliability of its laptops (based on buyer ratings), and its very good technical support services (based on buyer ratings). The verdict from the marketplace is that Toshiba laptops are better, *all things considered*, than rival brands.

From a strategy-making perspective, a company's resource strengths are significant because they can form the cornerstones of strategy and the basis for creating competitive advantage. If a company doesn't have ample resources and competitive capabilities around which to craft an attractive strategy, managers need to take decisive remedial action to upgrade existing organizational resources and capabilities and add others. At the same time, managers have to look toward correcting competitive weaknesses that make the company vulnerable, hold down profitability, or disqualify it from pursuing an attractive opportunity. The strategy-making principle here is simple: *A company's strategy should be tailored to fit its resource capabilities—taking both strengths and weaknesses into account.* It is foolhardy to pursue a strategic plan that can be undermined by company weaknesses or that cannot be competently executed. As a rule, managers should build their strategies around exploiting and leveraging company capabilities—*its most valuable resources*—and avoid strategies that place heavy demands on areas where the company is weakest or has unproven ability. Companies fortunate enough to have a distinctive competence or other competitively superior resource must be wise in realizing that its value will be eroded by time and competition.[4] So attention to building a strong resource base for the future and to maintaining the competitive superiority of an existing distinctive competence are ever-present requirements.

Selecting the Competencies and Capabilities to Concentrate On   Enterprises succeed over time because they can do certain things that their customers value better than their rivals. The essence of astute strategy making is selecting the competencies and capabilities to concentrate on and to underpin the strategy. Sometimes the company already has competitively valuable competencies and capabilities in place and sometimes it has to be proactive in developing and building new competencies and capabilities to complement and strengthen its existing resource base. Sometimes the desired competencies and capabilities need to be developed internally, and sometimes it is best to outsource them by working with key suppliers and forming strategic alliances.

Identifying a Company's Market Opportunities

Market opportunity is a big factor in shaping a company's strategy. Indeed, managers can't properly tailor strategy to the company's situation without first identifying each company opportunity, appraising the growth and profit potential each one holds, and

---

[4]Collis and Montgomery, "Competing on Resources: Strategy in the 1990s," p. 124.

ILLUSTRATION CAPSULE 10   TCI's Retreat to a Vision and Strategy in Line with Its Resources and Market Opportunities

In early 1997, Tele-Communications Inc., the biggest cable TV provider in the United States with 14 million subscribers, announced that its much heralded vision of transforming itself into an information superhighway and multimedia powerhouse providing cable television, telephone, Internet access, and an array of futuristic data and telecommunications services to all customers in its cable franchise territories was too sweeping, overhyped, and infeasible for the company to pursue profitably within the announced time frame. John Malone, the company's CEO and widely regarded as one of the most astute and influential visionaries of how new information superhighway technologies could transform the world of media and communications, said:

> We were just chasing too many rabbits at the same time. The company got overly ambitious about the things it could do simultaneously.
>
> If you read our annual report last year, you'd think we're one-third data, one-third telephone and one-third video entertainment, instead of 100 percent video entertainment and two experiments. Right now, we've got zero revenue from residential telephone service, diminishing revenue from high-speed Internet, and $6 billion in revenue from video entertainment.
>
> My job is to prick the bubble. Let's get real.

For years, Malone and TCI had been touting the potential of deploying newly discovered telecommunications technologies over the company's existing cable connections to deliver a dazzling array of information and telecommunications products and services in head-on competition against the telephone companies. The first generation of expanded services was to be rolled out in 1996 and 1997 via a new digital-cable box installed on residential TVs that would access 500 channels, provide on-screen viewer guides, and deliver better sound and picture quality. However, the manufacturer of the boxes encountered problems and was able to produce only

small quantities. Meanwhile, aggressive investment in new technological infrastructure ($1.6 billion in 1996) to deliver the expanded array of products/services put a strain on TCI's cash flow and prompted bond-rating agencies to put the company on their watch lists for possible credit rating downgrade. TCI's stock price went nowhere in a strong stock market. Plus the new Telecommunications Act enacted into law in 1996 created a swirl of strategic maneuvers by local and long-distance telephone companies to position themselves to compete nationwide in both the telephone business and in information superhighway products and services, a development that meant cable operators suddenly confronted a whole new set of larger, resource-rich competitors.

TCI's new, narrower vision was to focus more on the cable TV business (under attack from alternative providers utilizing satellite dish technology as well as from the fiber optic wire capability being installed by telephone companies) and to push the vision of information superhighway and multimedia provider farther out into the future, conditional upon clearer technological opportunities to profit from investments to modify the existing cable system and provide a wider array of products and services. The retrenched strategy involved slower rollout of the new digital cable box (to give the supplier time to ramp up production and work out quality bugs), continued market testing of telephone service, curtailed investment in two-way communications capabilities until the company's debt levels were reduced and cash flows were stronger, and until it was clear that the new technologies would be both cost-effective and competitive against the fiberoptic and wireless technologies being installed by rivals. TCI also decided to spin off some of the company's businesses into independent companies (Liberty Media's programming assets, a satellite operation, international operations, and telephone operations) and put some life back into the company's languishing stock price.

Source: Based on information in "Malone Says TCI Push Into Phones, Internet Isn't Working for Now," *The Wall Street Journal*, January 2, 1997, pp. A1 and A3.

crafting strategic initiatives to capture the most promising of the company's market opportunities. Depending on industry conditions, a company's opportunities can be plentiful or scarce and can range from wildly attractive (an absolute "must" to pursue) to marginally interesting (low on the company's list of strategic priorities). Table 4.1 presents a checklist of things to be alert for in identifying a company's market opportunities.

In appraising a company's market opportunities and ranking their attractiveness, managers have to guard against viewing every *industry* opportunity as a *company* opportunity. Not every company in an industry is equipped with the resources to pursue each opportunity that exists—some companies have more capabilities to go after particular opportunities than others, and a few companies may be hopelessly outclassed in trying to contend for a piece of the action. Wise strategists are alert to when a company's resource strengths and weaknesses make it better suited to pursuing some market opportunities than others. Wise strategists are also alert to opportunities that don't match especially well with existing resources, but still offer attractive growth potential if the company aggressively moves to develop or acquire the missing resource capabilities. *The market opportunities most relevant to a company are those that offer important avenues for profitable growth, those where a company has the most potential for competitive advantage, and those that match up well with the financial and organizational resource capabilities which the company already possesses or can acquire.*

> **Strategic Management Principle**
>
> *A company is well-advised to pass on a particular market opportunity unless it has or can build the resource capabilities to capture it.*

Identifying the Threats to a Company's Future Profitability

Often, certain factors in a company's external environment pose *threats* to its profitability and market standing: the emergence of cheaper technologies, rivals' introduction of new or better products, the entry of lower-cost foreign competitors into a company's market stronghold, new regulations that are more burdensome to a company than to its competitors, vulnerability to a rise in interest rates, the potential of a hostile takeover, unfavorable demographic shifts, adverse changes in foreign exchange rates, political upheaval in a foreign country where the company has facilities, and the like. External threats may pose no more than a moderate degree of adversity (all companies confront some threatening elements in the course of doing business) or they may be so imposing as to make a company's situation and outlook quite tenuous. Management's job is to identify the threats to the company's future well-being and evaluate what strategic actions can be taken to neutralize or lessen their impact.

Table 4.1 presents a list of potential threats to a company's future profitability and market position. Opportunities and threats point to the need for strategic action. Tailoring strategy to a company's situation entails (1) pursuing market opportunities well suited to the company's resource capabilities and (2) building a resource base that helps defend against external threats to the company's business.

> **Strategic Management Principle**
>
> *Successful strategists aim at capturing a company's best growth opportunities and creating defenses against external threats to its competitive position and future performance.*

SWOT analysis is therefore more than an exercise in making four lists. The important part of SWOT analysis involves *evaluating* a company's strengths, weaknesses, opportunities, and threats and *drawing conclusions* about (1) how best to deploy the company's resources in light of the company's internal and external situation and (2) how to build the company's future resource base. SWOT analysis isn't complete until several questions about the company's resource base are answered: What adjustments in the company's resource base are needed to respond to emerging industry and competitive conditions? Are there resource gaps that need to be filled? In what ways does the company need to strengthen its resource base? What actions are needed to build the company's future resource base? Which opportunities should be given top priority in allocating resources?

QUESTION 3: ARE THE COMPANY'S PRICES AND COSTS COMPETITIVE?

Assessing whether a company's costs are competitive with those of its close rivals is a necessary and crucial part of company situation analysis.

Company managers are often stunned when a competitor cuts price to "unbelievably low" levels or when a new market entrant comes on strong with a very low price. The competitor may not, however, be "dumping," buying market share, or waging a desperate move to gain sales; it may simply have substantially lower costs. *One of the most telling signs of whether a company's business position is strong or precarious is whether its prices and costs are competitive with industry rivals.* Price-cost comparisons are especially critical in a commodity-product industry where the value provided to buyers is the same from seller to seller, price competition is typically the ruling market force, and lower-cost companies have the upper hand. But even in industries where products are differentiated and competition centers around the different attributes of competing brands as much as around price, rival companies have to keep their costs *in line* and make sure that any added costs they incur create added buyer value and don't result in prices that customers consider "out-of-line."

Competitors usually don't incur the same costs in supplying their products to end users. The cost disparities can range from tiny to competitively significant and can stem from any of several factors:

- Differences in the prices paid for raw materials, components parts, energy, and other items purchased from suppliers.

- Differences in basic technology and the age of plants and equipment. (Because rival companies usually invest in plants and key pieces of equipment at different times, their facilities have somewhat different technological efficiencies and different fixed costs (depreciation, maintenance, property taxes, and insurance. Older facilities are typically less efficient, but if they were less expensive to construct or were acquired at bargain prices, they *may* still be reasonably cost competitive with modern facilities.)

- Differences in production costs from rival to rival due to different plant efficiencies, different learning and experience curve effects, different wage rates, different productivity levels, and the like.

- Differences in marketing costs, sales and promotion expenditures, advertising expenses, warehouse distribution costs, and administrative costs.

- Differences in inbound transportation costs and outbound shipping costs.

- Differences in forward channel distribution costs (the costs and markups of distributors, wholesalers, and retailers associated with getting the product from the point of manufacture into the hands of end users).

Principle of Competitive Markets

The higher a company's costs are above those of close rivals, the more competitively vulnerable it becomes.

- Differences in rival firms' exposure to the effects of inflation, changes in foreign exchange rates, and tax rates (a frequent occurrence in global industries where competitors have operations in different nations with different economic conditions and governmental taxation policies).

For a company to be competitively successful, its costs must be in line with those of close rivals. While some cost disparity is justified so long as the products or services of closely competing companies are sufficiently differentiated, a high-cost firm's market position becomes increasingly vulnerable the more its costs exceed those of close rivals.

Strategic Cost Analysis and Value Chains

Competitors must be ever alert to how their costs compare with rivals'. While every firm engages in *internal* cost analysis to stay on top of what its own costs are and how they might be changing, *strategic* cost analysis goes a step further to explore how costs compare against rivals. *Strategic cost analysis focuses on a firm's cost position relative to its rivals'.*

Every company's business consists of a *collection of activities* undertaken in the course of designing, producing, marketing, delivering, and supporting its product or service. Each of these activities give rise to costs. The combined costs of all these various activities define the company's internal cost structure. Further, the cost of each activity contributes to whether the company's overall cost position relative to rivals is favorable or unfavorable. The task of strategic cost analysis is to compare a company's costs *activity by activity* against the costs of key rivals and to learn which internal activities are a source of cost advantage or disadvantage. A company's relative cost position is a function of how the overall costs of the activities it performs in conducting its business compare to the overall costs of the activities performed by rivals.

Basic Concept

Strategic cost analysis involves comparing how a company's unit costs stack up against the unit costs of key competitors activity by activity, *thereby pinpointing which internal activities are a source of cost advantage or disadvantage.*

The Concept of a Company Value Chain The primary analytical tool of strategic cost analysis is a *value chain* identifying the separate activities, functions, and business processes performed in designing, producing, marketing, delivering, and supporting a product or service.[5] The chain starts with raw materials supply and continues on through parts and components production, manufacturing and assembly, wholesale distribution, and retailing to the ultimate end user of the product or service.

A *company's value chain* shows the linked set of activities and functions it performs internally (see Figure 4.1). The value chain includes a profit margin because a markup over the cost of performing the firm's value-creating activities is customarily part of the price (or total cost) borne by buyers—creating value that exceeds the cost of doing so is a fundamental objective of business. Disaggregating a company's operations into strategically relevant activities and business processes exposes the major elements of the company's cost structure. Each activity in the value chain incurs costs and ties up assets; assigning the company's operating costs and assets to each individual activity in the chain provides cost estimates for each activity. Quite often, there are linkages between activities such that the way one activity is performed can spill over to affect the costs of performing other activities (for instance, Japanese VCR producers were able to reduce prices from $1,300 in 1977 to under $300 in 1984 by spotting the impact of an early step in the value chain, product design, on a later step, production, and deciding to drastically reduce the number of parts).[6]

Basic Concept

A company's value chain identifies the primary activities that create value for customers and the related support activities.

Why the Value Chains of Rival Companies Often Differ A company's value chain and the manner in which it performs each activity reflect the evolution of its own

---

[5]Value chains and strategic cost analysis are described at greater length in Michael E. Porter, *Competitive Advantage* (New York: Free Press, 1985), chapters 2 and 3; Robin Cooper and Robert S. Kaplan, "Measure Costs Right: Make the Right Decisions," *Harvard Business Review* 66, no. 5 (September–October, 1988), pp. 96–103; and John K. Shank and Vijay Govindarajan, *Strategic Cost Management* (New York: Free Press, 1993), especially chapters 2–6 and 10.

[6]M. Hegert and D. Morris, "Accounting Data for Value Chain Analysis," *Strategic Management Journal* 10 (1989), p. 183.

FIGURE 4.1   Representative Company Value Chain

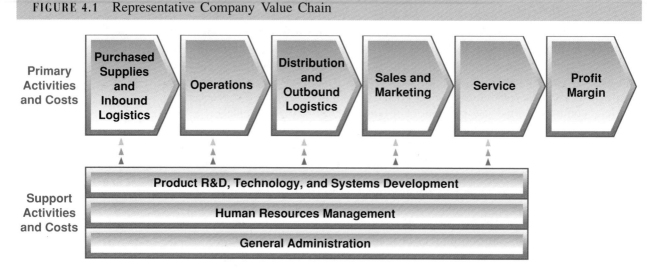

Primary Activities

- **Purchased Supplies and Inbound Logistics**—Activities, costs, and assets associated with purchasing fuel, energy, raw materials, parts components, merchandise, and consumable items from vendors; receiving, storing, and disseminating inputs from suppliers; inspection; and inventory management.
- **Operations**—Activities, costs, and assets associated with converting inputs into final product form (production, assembly, packaging, equipment maintenance, facilities, operations, quality assurance, environmental protection).
- **Distribution and Outbound Logistics**—Activities, costs, and assets dealing with physically distributing the product to buyers (finished goods warehousing, order processing, order picking and packing, shipping, delivery vehicle operations, establishing and maintaining a network of dealers and distributors).
- **Sales and Marketing**—Activities, costs, and assets related to sales force efforts, advertising and promotion, market research and planning, and dealer/distributor support.
- **Service**—Activities, costs, and assets associated with providing assistance to buyers, such as installation, spare parts delivery, maintenance and repair, technical assistance, buyer inquiries, and complaints.

Support Activities

- **Research, Technology, and Systems Development**—Activities, costs, and assets relating to product R&D, process R&D, process design improvement, equipment design, computer software development, telecommunications systems, computer-assisted design and engineering, new database capabilities, and development of computerized support systems.
- **Human Resources Management**—Activities, costs, and assets associated with the recruitment, hiring, training, development, and compensation of all types of personnel; labor relations activities; development of knowledge-based skills and core competencies.
- **General Administration**—Activities, costs, and assets relating to general management, accounting and finance, legal and regulatory affairs, safety and security, management information systems, forming strategic alliances and collaborating with strategic partners, and other "overhead" functions.

Source: Adapted from Michael E. Porter, *Competitive Advantage* (New York: The Free Press, 1985), pp. 37–43.

business and internal operations, its strategy, the approaches it is using to execute its strategy, and the underlying economics of the activities themselves.[7] Consequently, it is normal for the value chains of rival companies to differ, perhaps substantially—a

---

[7]Porter, *Competitive Advantage*, p. 36.

condition that complicates the task of assessing rivals' relative cost positions. For instance, competing companies may differ in their degrees of vertical integration. Comparing the value chain for a fully integrated rival against a partially integrated rival requires adjusting for differences in scope of activities performed—clearly the *internal* costs for a manufacturer that makes all of its own parts and components will be greater than the *internal* costs of a producer that buys the needed parts and components from outside suppliers and only performs assembly operations.

Likewise, there is legitimate reason to expect value chain and cost differences between a company that is pursuing a low-cost/low-price strategy and a rival positioned at the high-end of the market with a prestige quality product that possesses a wealth of features. In the case of the low-cost firm, the costs of certain activities along the company's value chain should indeed be relatively low whereas the high-end firm may understandably be spending relatively more to perform those activities that create the added quality and extra features.

Moreover, cost and price differences among rival companies can have their origins in activities performed by suppliers or by forward channel allies involved in getting the product to end users. Suppliers or forward channel allies may have excessively high cost structures or profit margins that jeopardize a company's cost competitiveness even though its costs for internally performed activities are competitive. For example, when determining Michelin's cost competitiveness vis-à-vis Goodyear and Bridgestone in supplying replacement tires to vehicle owners, one has to look at more than whether Michelin's tire manufacturing costs are above or below Goodyear's and Bridgestone's. If a buyer has to pay $400 for a set of Michelin tires and only $350 for comparable sets of Goodyear or Bridgestone tires, Michelin's $50 price disadvantage in the replacement tire marketplace can stem not only from higher manufacturing costs (reflecting, *perhaps*, the added costs of Michelin's strategic efforts to build a better quality tire with more performance features) but also from (1) differences in what the three tire makers pay their suppliers for materials and tire-making components and (2) differences in the operating efficiencies, costs, and markups of Michelin's wholesale distributors and retail dealers versus those of Goodyear and Bridgestone. Thus, determining whether a company's prices and costs are competitive from an end user's standpoint requires looking at the activities and costs of competitively relevant suppliers and forward allies, as well as the costs of internally performed activities.

A company's cost competitiveness depends not only on the costs of internally performed activities (its own value chain) but also on costs in the value chains of its suppliers and forward channel allies.

The Value Chain System for an Entire Industry   As the tire industry example makes clear, a company's value chain is embedded in a larger system of activities that includes the value chains of its upstream suppliers and downstream customers or allies engaged in getting its product/service to end users.[8] Accurately assessing a company's competitiveness in end-use markets requires that company managers understand the entire value chain system for delivering a product or service to end-users, not just the company's own value chain. At the very least, this means considering the value chains of suppliers and forward channel allies (if any)—as shown in Figure 4.2. Suppliers' value chains are relevant because suppliers perform activities and incur costs in creating and delivering the purchased inputs used in a company's own value chain; the cost and quality of these inputs influence a company's own cost and/or differentiation capabilities. Anything a company can do to reduce its suppliers' costs or improve suppliers'

[8]Porter, *Competitive Advantage*, p. 34.

FIGURE 4.2   The Value Chain System

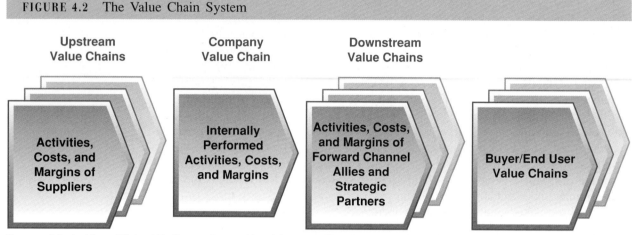

Source: Adapted from Michael E. Porter, *Competitive Advantage* (New York: The Free Press, 1985), p. 35.

effectiveness can enhance its own competitiveness—a powerful reason for working collaboratively or partnering with suppliers. Forward channel value chains are relevant because (1) the costs and margins of downstream companies are part of the price the ultimate end user pays and (2) the activities performed by forward channel allies affect the end user's satisfaction. There are powerful reasons for a company to work closely with forward channel allies to revise or reinvent their value chains in ways that enhance their mutual competitiveness. Furthermore, a company may be able to improve its competitiveness by undertaking activities that beneficially impact *both* its own value chain and its customers' value chains. For instance, some aluminum can producers constructed plants next to beer breweries and delivered cans on overhead conveyors directly to brewers' can-filling lines. This resulted in significant savings in production scheduling, shipping, and inventory costs for both container producers and breweries.[9] The lesson here is that a company's relative cost position and overall competitiveness is linked to the entire industry value chain system and to customers' value chains as well.

Although the value chains in Figures 4.1 and 4.2 are representative, the activity makeup of the chains and the relative importance of the activities within them vary by industry and by company position. Value chains for products differ from value chains for services. The major value chain elements for the pulp and paper industry (timber farming, logging, pulp mills, papermaking, printing, and publishing) differ from the major chain elements for the home appliance industry (parts and components manufacture, assembly, wholesale distribution, retail sales). The value chain for the soft-drink industry (processing of basic ingredients, syrup manufacture, bottling and can filling, wholesale distribution, retailing) differs from the makeup of the chain for the computer software industry (programming, disk loading, marketing, distribution). A producer of bathroom and kitchen faucets depends heavily on the activities of wholesale distributors and building supply retailers in winning sales to homebuilders and do-it-yourselfers. A wholesaler's most important activities and costs deal with purchased goods, inbound logistics, and outbound logistics. A hotel's most important activities and costs are in operations—check-in and check-out, maintenance and housekeeping, dining and room service, conventions and meetings, and

---

[9]Hegert and Morris, "Accounting Data for Value Chain Analysis," p. 180.

accounting. A global public accounting firm's most important activities and costs revolve around customer service and human resources management (recruiting and training a highly competent professional staff). Outbound logistics is a crucial activity at Domino's Pizza but comparatively insignificant at Blockbuster. Sales and marketing are dominant activities at Nike but only minor activities at electric and gas utilities. Consequently, generic value chains like those in Figures 4.1 and 4.2 are illustrative, not absolute, and may have to be adapted to fit a particular company's circumstances.

Developing the Data for Strategic Cost Analysis   Once the major value chain elements are identified, the next step in strategic cost analysis involves breaking down a firm's departmental cost accounting data into the costs of performing specific activities.[10] The appropriate degree of disaggregation depends on the economics of the activities and how valuable it is to develop cross-company cost comparisons for narrowly defined activities as opposed to broadly defined activities. A good guideline is to develop separate cost estimates for activities having different economics and for activities representing a significant or growing proportion of cost.[11]

Traditional accounting identifies costs according to broad categories of expenses—wages and salaries, employee benefits, supplies, travel, depreciation, R&D, and other fixed charges. *Activity-based costing* entails defining expense categories based on the specific activities being performed and then assigning costs to the appropriate activity responsible for creating the cost. An example is shown in Table 4.2.[12] Perhaps 10 percent of the companies that have explored the feasibility of activity-based costing have adopted this accounting approach. To fully understand the costs of activities all along the industry value chain, cost estimates for activities performed in suppliers' and customers' value chains also have to be developed.

To benchmark the firm's cost position against rivals, costs for the same activities for each rival must be estimated—an advanced art in competitive intelligence. But despite the tediousness of developing cost estimates activity by activity and the imprecision of some of the estimates for rivals, the payoff in exposing the costs of particular internal tasks and functions and the company's cost competitiveness makes activity-based costing a valuable strategic analysis tool.[13] Illustration Capsule 11 shows a simplified value chain comparison for two prominent brewers of beer—Anheuser-Busch (the U.S. industry leader) and Adolph Coors (the third-ranking U.S. brewer).

The most important application of value chain analysis is to expose how a particular firm's cost position compares with its rivals'. What is needed is competitor versus competitor cost estimates for supplying a product or service to a well-defined customer group or market segment. The size of a company's cost advantage/disadvantage can vary from item to item in the product line, from customer group to customer group (if different distribution channels are used), and from geographic market to geographic market (if cost factors vary across geographic regions).

---

[10]For discussions of the accounting challenges in calculating the costs of value chain activities, see Shank and Govindarajan, *Strategic Cost Management*, pp. 62–72 and chapter 5, and Hegert and Morris, "Accounting Data for Value Chain Analysis," pp. 175–88.

[11]Porter, *Competitive Advantage*, p. 45.

[12]For a discussion of activity-based cost accounting, see Cooper and Kaplan, "Measure Costs Right: Make the Right Decisions," pp. 96–103; Shank and Govindarajan, *Strategic Cost Management*, Chapter 11; and Joseph A. Ness and Thomas G. Cucuzza, "Tapping the Full Potential of ABC," *Harvard Business Review* 73 no. 4 (July–August 1995), pp. 130–38.

[13]Shank and Govindarajan, *Strategic Cost Management,* p. 62.

TABLE 4.2   The Difference between Traditional Cost Accounting and Activity-Based Cost Accounting

Traditional Cost Accounting Categories in Departmental Budget		Cost of Performing Specific Departmental Activities Using Activity-Based Cost Accounting	
Wages and salaries	$350,000	Evaluate supplier capabilities	$135,750
Employee benefits	115,000	Process purchase orders	82,100
Supplies	6,500	Expedite supplier deliveries	23,500
Travel	2,400	Expedite internal processing	15,840
Depreciation	17,000	Check quality of items purchased	94,300
Other fixed charges	124,000	Check incoming deliveries against purchase orders	48,450
Miscellaneous operating expenses	25,250	Resolve problems	110,000
		Internal administration	130,210
	$640,150		$640,150

Source: Adapted from information in Terence P. Paré, "A New Tool for Managing Costs," *Fortune*, June 14, 1993, pp. 124–29.

Benchmarking the Costs of Key Activities

Many companies today are benchmarking the costs of performing a given activity against competitors' costs (and/or against the costs of a noncompetitor in another industry that efficiently and effectively performs much the same activity or business process). Benchmarking focuses on cross-company comparisons of how well basic functions and processes in the value chain are performed—how materials are purchased, how suppliers are paid, how inventories are managed, how employees are trained, how payrolls are processed, how fast the company can get new products to market, how the quality control function is performed, how customer orders are filled and shipped, and how maintenance is performed.[14] *The objectives of benchmarking are to understand the best practices in performing an activity, to learn how lower costs are actually achieved, and to take action to improve a company's cost competitiveness whenever benchmarking reveals that the costs of performing an activity are out of line with those of other companies.*

Benchmarking the performance of company activities against rivals and other best-practice companies provides hard evidence of a company's cost competitiveness.

In 1979, Xerox became an early pioneer in the use of benchmarking when Japanese manufacturers began selling midsize copiers in the United States for $9,600 each—less than Xerox's production costs.[15] Although Xerox management suspected its Japanese competitors were dumping, it sent a team of line managers to Japan, including the head of manufacturing, to study competitors' business processes and costs. Fortunately, Xerox's joint venture partner in Japan, Fuji-Xerox, knew the competitors well. The team found that Xerox's costs were excessive due to gross

---

[14]For more details, see Gregory H. Watson, *Strategic Benchmarking: How to Rate Your Company's Performance Against the World's Best* (New York: John Wiley, 1993) and Robert C. Camp, *Benchmarking: The Search for Industry Best Practices That Lead to Superior Performance* (Milwaukee: ASQC Quality Press, 1989). See also Alexandra Biesada, "Strategic Benchmarking," *Financial World*, September 29, 1992, pp. 30–38.

[15]Jeremy Main, "How to Steal the Best Ideas Around," *Fortune*, October 19, 1992, pp. 102–3.

ILLUSTRATION CAPSULE 11 Value Chains for Anheuser-Busch and Adolph Coors Beers

In the table below are average cost estimates for the combined brands of beer produced by Anheuser-Busch and Coors. The example shows raw material costs, other manufacturing costs, and forward channel distribution costs. The data are for 1982.

	Estimated Average Cost Breakdown for Combined Anheuser-Busch Brands		Estimated Average Cost Breakdown for Combined Adolph Coors Brands	
Value Chain Activities and Costs	Per 6-Pack of 12-oz. Cans	Per Barrel Equivalent	Per 6-Pack of 12-oz Cans	Per Barrel Equivalent
1. Manufacturing costs:				
Direct production costs:				
Raw material ingredients	$0.1384	$ 7.63	$0.1082	$ 5.96
Direct labor	0.1557	8.58	0.1257	6.93
Salaries for nonunionized personnel	0.0800	4.41	0.0568	3.13
Packaging	0.5055	27.86	0.4663	25.70
Depreciation on plant and equipment	0.0410	2.26	0.0826	4.55
Subtotal	0.9206	50.74	0.8396	46.27
Other expenses:				
Advertising	0.0477	2.63	0.0338	1.86
Other marketing costs and general administrative expenses	0.1096	6.04	0.1989	10.96
Interest	0.0147	0.81	0.0033	0.18
Research and development	0.0277	1.53	0.0195	1.07
Total manufacturing costs	$1.1203	$ 61.75	$1.0951	$ 60.34
2. Manufacturer's operating profit	0.1424	7.85	0.0709	3.91
3. Net selling price	1.2627	69.60	1.1660	64.25
4. Plus federal and state excise taxes paid by brewer	0.1873	10.32	0.1782	9.82
5. Gross manufacturer's selling price to distributor/wholesaler	1.4500	79.92	1.3442	74.07
6. Average margin over manufacturer's cost	0.5500	30.31	0.5158	28.43
7. Average wholesale price charged to retailer (inclusive of taxes in item 4 above but exclusive of other taxes)	$ 2.00	$110.23	$ 1.86	$102.50
8. Plus other assorted state and local taxes levied on wholesale and retail sales (this varies from locality to locality)	0.60		0.60	
9. Average 20% retail markup over wholesale cost	0.40		0.38	
10. Average price to consumer at retail	$ 3.00		$ 2.84	

Note: The difference in the average cost structures for Anheuser-Busch and Adolph Coors is, to a substantial extent, due to A-B's higher proportion of super-premium beer sales. A-B's super-premium brand, Michelob, was the best-seller in its category and somewhat more costly to brew than premium and popular-priced beers.

Source: Compiled by Tom McLean, Elsa Wischkaemper, and Arthur A. Thompson, Jr., from a wide variety of documents and field interviews.

ILLUSTRATION CAPSULE 12   Ford Motor Company's Benchmarking of Its Accounts Payable Activity

In the 1980s Ford's North American accounts payable department employed more than 500 people. Clerks spent the majority of their time straightening out the relatively few situations where three documents—the purchase order issued by the purchasing department, the receiving document prepared by clerks at the receiving dock, and the invoice sent by the vendor/supplier to accounts payable—did not match. Sometimes resolving the discrepancies took weeks of time and the efforts of many people. Ford managers believed that by using computers to automate some functions performed manually, head count could be reduced to 400. Before proceeding, Ford managers decided to visit Mazda—a company in which Ford had recently acquired a 25 percent ownership interest. To their astonishment, Mazda handled its accounts payable function with only five people. Following Mazda's lead, Ford benchmarkers created an invoiceless system where payments to suppliers were triggered automatically when the goods were received. The reengineered system allowed Ford to reduce its accounts payable staff to under 200, a lot more than Mazda but much better than would have resulted without benchmarking the accounts payable activity.

Sources: Michael Hammer and James Champy, *Reengineering the Corporation* (New York: HarperBusiness, 1993), pp. 39–43, and Jeremy Main, "How to Steal the Best Ideas Around," *Fortune*, October 19, 1992, p. 106.

inefficiencies in its manufacturing processes and business practices; the study proved instrumental in Xerox's efforts to become cost competitive and prompted Xerox to embark on a long-term program to benchmark 67 of its key work processes against companies identified as having the "best practices" in performing these processes. Xerox quickly decided not to restrict its benchmarking efforts to its office equipment rivals but to extend them to any company regarded as "world class" in performing an activity relevant to Xerox's business. Illustration Capsule 12 describes one of Ford Motor's benchmarking experiences.

Sometimes cost benchmarking can be accomplished by collecting information from published reports, trade groups, and industry research firms and by talking to knowledgeable industry analysts, customers, and suppliers (customers, suppliers, and joint-venture partners often make willing benchmarking allies). Usually, though, benchmarking requires field trips to the facilities of competing or noncompeting companies to observe how things are done, ask questions, compare practices and processes, and perhaps exchange data on productivity, staffing levels, time requirements, and other cost components. However, benchmarking involves competitively sensitive information about how lower costs are achieved, and close rivals can't be expected to be completely open, even if they agree to host facilities tours and answer questions. But the explosive interest of companies in benchmarking costs and identifying best practices has prompted consulting organizations (for example, Andersen Consulting, A. T. Kearney, Best Practices Benchmarking & Consulting, and Towers Perrin) and several newly formed councils and associations (the International Benchmarking Clearinghouse and the Strategic Planning Institute's Council on Benchmarking) to gather benchmarking data, do benchmarking studies, and distribute information about best practices and the costs of performing activities to clients/members without identifying the sources. The ethical dimension of benchmarking is discussed in Illustration Capsule 13. Over 80 percent of *Fortune* 500 companies now engage in some form of benchmarking.

Benchmarking is a manager's best tool for determining whether the company is performing particular functions and activities efficiently, whether its costs are in line with competitors, and which activities and processes need to be improved. It is a way

---

ILLUSTRATION CAPSULE 13   Benchmarking and Ethical Conduct

Because actions between benchmarking partners can involve competitively sensitive data and discussions, conceivably raising questions about possible restraint of trade or improper business conduct, the SPI Council on Benchmarking and The International Benchmarking Clearinghouse urge all individuals and organizations involved in benchmarking to abide by a code of conduct grounded in ethical business behavior. The code is based on the following principles and guidelines:

- In benchmarking with competitors, establish specific ground rules up front, e.g., "We don't want to talk about those things that will give either of us a competitive advantage; rather, we want to see where we both can mutually improve or gain benefit." Do not discuss costs with competitors if costs are an element of pricing.
- Do not ask competitors for sensitive data or cause the benchmarking partner to feel that sensitive data must be provided to keep the process going. Be prepared to provide the same level of information that you request. Do not share proprietary information without prior approval from the proper authorities of both parties.

- Use an ethical third party to assemble and blind competitive data, with inputs from legal counsel, for direct competitor comparisons.
- Consult with legal counsel if any information gathering procedure is in doubt, e.g., before contacting a direct competitor.
- Any information obtained from a benchmarking partner should be treated as internal, privileged information. Any external use must have the partner's permission.
- Do not:
  - Disparage a competitor's business or operations to a third party.
  - Attempt to limit competition or gain business through the benchmarking relationship.
  - Misrepresent oneself as working for another employer.
- Demonstrate commitment to the efficiency and effectiveness of the process by being adequately prepared at each step, particularly at initial contact. Be professional, honest, and courteous. Adhere to the agenda—maintain focus on benchmarking issues.

Sources: The SPI Council on Benchmarking, The International Benchmarking Clearinghouse, and conference presentation of AT&T Benchmarking Group, Des Moines, Iowa, October 1993.

---

of learning which companies are best at performing certain activities and functions and then imitating—or, better still, improving on—their techniques. Toyota managers got their idea for just-in-time inventory deliveries by studying how U.S. supermarkets replenished their shelves. Southwest Airlines reduced the turnaround time of its aircraft at each scheduled stop by studying pit crews on the auto racing circuit.

Strategic Options for Achieving Cost Competitiveness

Value chain analysis and benchmarking can reveal a great deal about a firm's cost competitiveness. One of the fundamental insights of strategic cost analysis is that a company's competitiveness depends on how well it manages its value chain relative to how well competitors manage theirs.[16] Examining the makeup of a company's own value chain and comparing it to rivals' indicates who has how much of a cost advantage/disadvantage and which cost components are responsible. Such information is vital in crafting strategies to eliminate a cost disadvantage or create a cost advantage.

---

[16]Shank and Govindarajan, *Strategic Cost Management*, p. 50.

Looking again at Figure 4.2, observe that important differences in the costs of competing firms can occur in three main areas: in the suppliers' part of the industry value chain, in a company's own activity segments, or in the forward channel portion of the industry chain. If a firm's lack of cost competitiveness lies either in the backward (upstream) or forward (downstream) sections of the value chain, then reestablishing cost competitiveness may have to extend beyond the firm's own in-house operations. When a firm's cost disadvantage stems from the costs of items purchased from suppliers (the upstream end of the industry chain), company managers can take any of several strategic steps:[17]

Strategic actions to eliminate a cost disadvantage need to be linked to the location in the value chain where the cost differences originate.

- Negotiate more favorable prices with suppliers.
- Work with suppliers to help them achieve lower costs.
- Integrate backward to gain control over the costs of purchased items.
- Try to use lower-priced substitute inputs.
- Do a better job of managing the linkages between suppliers' value chains and the company's own chain; for example, close coordination between a company and its suppliers can permit just-in-time deliveries that lower a company's inventory and internal logistics costs and that may also allow its suppliers to economize on their warehousing, shipping, and production scheduling costs—a win-win outcome for both (instead of a zero-sum game where a company's gains match supplier concessions).[18]
- Try to make up the difference by cutting costs elsewhere in the chain.

A company's strategic options for eliminating cost disadvantages in the forward end of the value chain system include:[19]

- Pushing distributors and other forward channel allies to reduce their markups.
- Working closely with forward channel allies/customers to identify win-win opportunities to reduce costs. A chocolate manufacturer learned that by shipping its bulk chocolate in liquid form in tank cars instead of 10-pound molded bars, it saved its candy bar manufacturing customers the cost of unpacking and melting, and it eliminated its own costs of molding bars and packing them.
- Changing to a more economical distribution strategy, including forward integration.
- Trying to make up the difference by cutting costs earlier in the cost chain.

When the source of a firm's cost disadvantage is internal, managers can use any of nine strategic approaches to restore cost parity:[20]

---

[17]Porter, *Competitive Advantage*, chapter 3.

[18]In recent years, most companies have moved aggressively to collaborate with and partner with key suppliers to implement better supply chain management, often achieving cost savings of 5 to 25 percent. For a discussion of how to develop a cost-saving supply chain strategy, see Shashank Kulkarni, "Purchasing: A Supply-side Strategy," *Journal of Business Strategy* 17, no. 5 (September–October 1996), pp. 17–20.

[19]Porter, *Competitive Advantage*, Chapter 3.

[20]Ibid.

1. Streamline the operation of high-cost activities.

2. Reengineer business processes and work practices (to boost employee productivity, improve the efficiency of key activities, increase the utilization of company assets, and otherwise do a better job of managing the cost drivers).

3. Eliminate some cost-producing activities altogether by revamping the value chain system (for example, shifting to a radically different technological approach or maybe bypassing the value chains of forward channel allies and marketing directly to end users).

4. Relocate high-cost activities to geographic areas where they can be performed more cheaply.

5. See if certain activities can be outsourced from vendors or performed by contractors more cheaply than they can be done internally.

6. Invest in cost-saving technological improvements (automation, robotics, flexible manufacturing techniques, computerized controls).

7. Innovate around the troublesome cost components as new investments are made in plant and equipment.

8. Simplify the product design so that it can be manufactured more economically.

9. Make up the internal cost disadvantage through savings in the backward and forward portions of the value chain system.

From Value Chain Activities to Competitive Capabilities to Competitive Advantage

How well a company manages its value chain activities is a key to building valuable competencies and capabilities and leveraging them into sustainable competitive advantage. With rare exceptions, a firm's products or services are not a basis for sustainable competitive advantage—it is too easy for a resourceful company to clone, improve on, or find a substitute for them.[21] Rather, a company's competitive edge is usually grounded in its skills, know-how, and capabilities relative to those of its rivals and, more specifically, in the scope and depth of its ability to perform competitively crucial activities along the value chain better than rivals.

Developing the capability to perform competitively crucial value chain activities better than rivals is a dependable source of competitive advantage.

Competitively valuable competencies and capabilities emerge from a company's experience, learned skills, organizational routines and operating practices, and focused efforts in performing one or more related value chain components—they are not simply a consequence of the company's collection of resources. FedEx has purposefully built and integrated its resources to create the internal capabilities for providing customers with guaranteed overnight delivery services. McDonald's ability to turn out virtually identical-quality hamburgers at some 20,000-plus outlets around the world reflects impressive capability to replicate its operating systems at many locations through detailed rules and procedures and intensive training of franchise operators and outlet managers. Merck and Glaxo, two of the world's most competitively capable pharmaceutical companies, built their strategic

[21]James Brian Quinn, *Intelligent Enterprise* (New York: Free Press, 1993), p. 54.

positions around expert performance of a few key activities: extensive R&D to achieve first discovery of new drugs, a carefully constructed approach to patenting, skill in gaining rapid and thorough clinical clearance from regulatory bodies, and unusually strong distribution and sales force capabilities.[22]

Creating valuable competitive capabilities typically involves integrating the knowledge and skills of individual employees, leveraging the economies of learning and experience, effectively coordinating related value chain activities, making trade-offs between efficiency and flexibility, and exerting efforts to gain dominating expertise over rivals in one or more value chain activities critical to customer satisfaction and market success. Valuable capabilities enhance a company's competitiveness. The strategy-making lesson here is that sustainable competitive advantage can flow from concentrating company resources and talent on one or more competitively sensitive value chain activities; competitive advantage results from developing distinctive capabilities to serve customers—capabilities that buyers value highly and that company rivals don't have and are unable or unwilling to match.

QUESTION 4: HOW STRONG IS THE COMPANY'S COMPETITIVE POSITION?

Using the tools of value chains, strategic cost analysis, and benchmarking to determine a company's cost competitiveness is necessary but not sufficient. A broader assessment needs to be made of a company's competitive position and competitive strength. Particular issues that merit examination include (1) whether the firm's market position can be expected to improve or deteriorate if the present strategy is continued (allowing for fine-tuning), (2) how the firm ranks *relative to key rivals* on each industry key success factor and each relevant measure of competitive strength and resource capability, (3) whether the firm enjoys a competitive advantage over key rivals or is currently at a disadvantage, and (4) the firm's ability to defend its market position in light of industry driving forces, competitive pressures, and the anticipated moves of rivals.

Systematic assessment of whether a company's overall competitive position is strong or weak relative to close rivals is an essential step in company situation analysis.

Table 4.3 lists some indicators of whether a firm's competitive position is improving or slipping. But company managers need to do more than just identify the areas of competitive improvement or slippage. They have to judge whether the company has a net competitive advantage or disadvantage vis-á-vis key competitors and whether the company's market position and performance can be expected to improve or deteriorate under the current strategy.

Managers can begin the task of evaluating the company's competitive strength by using benchmarking techniques to compare the company against industry rivals not just on cost but also on such important measures as product quality, customer service, customer satisfaction, financial strength, technological skills, product cycle time (how quickly new products can be taken from idea to design to market), and the possession of competitively important resources and capabilities. It is not enough to benchmark the costs of activities and identify best practices; a company should benchmark itself against competitors on all strategically and competitively important aspects of its business.

---

[22]Quinn, *Intelligent Enterprise*, p. 34.

TABLE 4.3 The Signs of Strength and Weakness in a Company's Competitive Position

Signs of Competitive Strength	Signs of Competitive Weakness
• Important resource strengths, core competencies, and competitive capabilities	• Confronted with competitive disadvantages
• A distinctive competence in a competitively important value chain activity	• Losing ground to rival firms
• Strong market share (or a leading market share)	• Below-average growth in revenues
• A pace-setting or distinctive strategy	• Short on financial resources
• Growing customer base and customer loyalty	• A slipping reputation with customers
• Above-average market visibility	• Trailing in product development and product innovation capability
• In a favorably situated strategic group	• In a strategic group destined to lose ground
• Well positioned in attractive market segments	• Weak in areas where there is the most market potential
• Strongly differentiated products	• A higher-cost producer
• Cost advantages	• Too small to be a major factor in the marketplace
• Above-average profit margins	• Not in good position to deal with emerging threats
• Above-average technological and innovational capability	• Weak product quality
• A creative, entrepreneurially alert management	• Lacking skills, resources, and competitive capabilities in key area
• In position to capitalize on emerging market opportunities	• Weaker distribution capability than rivals

Competitive Strength Assessments

The most telling way to determine how strongly a company holds its competitive position is to quantitatively assess whether the company is stronger or weaker than close rivals on each of the industry's key success factors and on each pertinent indicator of competitive capability and potential competitive advantage. Much of the information for competitive strength assessment comes from prior analytical steps. Industry and competitive analysis reveals the key success factors and competitive determinants that separate industry winners from losers. Competitor analysis and benchmarking data provide information for judging the strengths and capabilities of key rivals.

Step one is to make a list of the industry's key success factors and most telling determinants of competitive advantage or disadvantage (6 to 10 measures usually suffice). Step two is to rate the firm and its key rivals on each strength indicator. Rating scales from 1 to 10 are best to use, although ratings of stronger (+), weaker (−), and about equal (=) may be appropriate when information is scanty and assigning numerical scores conveys false precision. Step three is to sum the individual strength overall ratings to get an measure of competitive strength for each competitor. Step four is to draw conclusions about the size and extent of the company's net competitive advantage or disadvantage and to take specific note of those strength measures where the company is strongest and weakest.

High competitive strength ratings signal a strong competitive position and possession of competitive advantage; low ratings signal a weak position and competitive disadvantage.

Table 4.4 provides two examples of competitive strength assessment. The first one employs an *unweighted rating scale*. With unweighted ratings each key success factor/competitive strength measure is assumed to be *equally important* (a rather dubious assumption). Whichever company has the highest strength rating on a given measure has an implied edge on that factor; the size of its edge is mirrored in the margin of difference between its rating and the ratings assigned to rivals. Summing a company's strength ratings on all the

TABLE 4.4   Illustrations of Unweighted and Weighted Competitive Strength Assessments

A. Sample of an Unweighted Competitive Strength Assessment

Rating scale: 1 = Very weak; 10 = Very strong

Key Success Factor/Strength Measure	ABC Co.	Rival 1	Rival 2	Rival 3	Rival 4
Quality/product performance	8	5	10	1	6
Reputation/image	8	7	10	1	6
Manufacturing capability	2	10	4	5	1
Technological skills	10	1	7	3	8
Dealer network/distribution capability	9	4	10	5	1
New product innovation capability	9	4	10	5	1
Financial resources	5	10	7	3	1
Relative cost position	5	10	3	1	4
Customer service capabilities	5	7	10	1	4
Unweighted overall strength rating	61	58	71	25	32

B. Sample of a Weighted Competitive Strength Assessment

Rating scale: 1 = Very weak; 10 = Very strong

Key Success Factor/Strength Measure	Weight	ABC Co.	Rival 1	Rival 2	Rival 3	Rival 4
Quality/product performance	0.10	8/0.80	5/0.50	10/1.00	1/0.10	6/0.60
Reputation/image	0.10	8/0.80	7/0.70	10/1.00	1/0.10	6/0.60
Manufacturing capability	0.10	2/0.20	10/1.00	4/0.40	5/0.50	1/0.10
Technological skills	0.05	10/0.50	1/0.05	7/0.35	3/0.15	8/0.40
Dealer network/distribution capability	0.05	9/0.45	4/0.20	10/0.50	5/0.25	1/0.05
New product innovation capability	0.05	9/0.45	4/0.20	10/0.50	5/0.25	1/0.05
Financial resources	0.10	5/0.50	10/1.00	7/0.70	3/0.30	1/0.10
Relative cost position	0.35	5/1.75	10/3.50	3/1.05	1/0.35	4/1.40
Customer service capabilities	0.15	5/0.75	7/1.05	10/1.50	1/0.15	4/1.60
Sum of weights	1.00					
Weighted overall strength rating		6.20	8.20	7.00	2.15	4.90

A weighted competitive strength analysis is conceptually stronger than an unweighted analysis because of the inherent weakness in assuming that all the strength measures are equally important.

measures produces an overall strength rating. The higher a company's overall strength rating, the stronger its competitive position. The bigger the margin of difference between a company's overall rating and the scores of lower-rated rivals, the greater its implied net competitive advantage. Thus, ABC's total score of 61 (see the top half of Table 4.4) signals a greater net competitive advantage over Rival 4 (with a score of 32) than over Rival 1 (with a score of 58).

However, it is better methodology to use a weighted rating system because the different measures of competitive strength are unlikely to be equally important. In a commodity-product industry, for instance, having low unit costs relative to rivals is nearly always the most important determinant of competitive strength. But in an industry with strong product differentiation the most significant measures of competitive strength may be brand awareness, amount of advertising, reputation for quality, and distribution capability. In a *weighted rating system* each measure of competitive strength is assigned a weight based on its perceived importance in shaping competitive success. The largest weight could be as high as .75 (maybe even higher) when one particular competitive variable is overwhelmingly decisive or as low as .20 when two or three strength measures are more important than the rest. Lesser competitive strength indicators can carry weights of .05 or .10. No matter whether the differences between the weights are big or little, *the sum of the weights must add up to 1.0.*

Weighted strength ratings are calculated by deciding how a company stacks up on each strength measure (using the 1 to 10 rating scale) and multiplying the assigned rating by the assigned weight (a rating score of 4 times a weight of .20 gives a weighted rating of .80). Again, the company with the highest rating on a given measure has an implied competitive edge on that measure, with the size of its edge reflected in the difference between its rating and rivals' ratings. The weight attached to the measure indicates how important the edge is. Summing a company's weighted strength ratings for all the measures yields an overall strength rating. Comparisons of the weighted overall strength scores indicate which competitors are in the strongest and weakest competitive positions and who has how big a net competitive advantage over whom.

The bottom half of Table 4.4 shows a sample competitive strength assessment for ABC Company using a weighted rating system. Note that the unweighted and weighted rating schemes produce a different ordering of the companies. In the weighted system, ABC Company dropped from second to third in strength, and Rival 1 jumped from third into first because of its high strength ratings on the two most important factors. Weighting the importance of the strength measures can thus make a significant difference in the outcome of the assessment.

Competitive strength assessments provide useful conclusions about a company's competitive situation. The ratings show how a company compares against rivals, factor by factor or capability by capability. Moreover, the overall competitive strength scores indicate whether the company is at a net competitive advantage or disadvantage against each rival. The firm with the largest overall competitive strength rating can be said to have a net competitive advantage over each rival.

Knowing where a company is competitively strong and where it is weak is essential in crafting a strategy to strengthen its long-term competitive position. As a general rule, a company should try to convert its competitive strengths into sustainable competitive advantage and take strategic actions to protect against its competitive weaknesses. At the same time, competitive strength ratings point to which rival companies may be vulnerable to competitive attack and the areas where they are weakest. When a company has important competitive strengths in areas where one or more rivals are weak, it makes sense to consider offensive moves to exploit their competitive weaknesses.

Competitive strengths and competitive advantages enable a company to improve its long-term market position.

QUESTION 5: WHAT STRATEGIC ISSUES DOES THE COMPANY FACE?

The final analytical task is to zero in on the issues management needs to address in forming an effective strategic action plan. Here, managers need to draw upon

Identifying and thoroughly understanding the strategic issues a company faces is a prerequisite to effective strategy-making.

all the prior analysis, put the company's overall situation into perspective, and get a lock on exactly where they need to focus their strategic attention. This step should not be taken lightly. Without a precise fix on what the issues are, managers are not prepared to start crafting a strategy—a good strategy must offer a plan for dealing with all the strategic issues that need to be addressed.

To pinpoint issues for the company's strategic action agenda, managers ought to consider the following:

- Does the present strategy offer attractive defenses against the five competitive forces—particularly those that are expected to intensify in strength?
- Should the present strategy be adjusted to better respond to the driving forces at work in the industry?
- Is the present strategy closely matched to the industry's *future* key success factors?
- Does the present strategy adequately capitalize on the company's resource strengths?
- Which of the company's opportunities merit top priority? Which should be given lowest priority? Which are best suited to the company's resource strengths and capabilities?
- What does the company need to do to correct its resource weaknesses and to protect against external threats?
- To what extent is the company vulnerable to the competitive efforts of one or more rivals and what can be done to reduce this vulnerability?
- Does the company possess competitive advantage or must it work to offset competitive disadvantage?
- Where are the strong spots and weak spots in the present strategy?
- Are additional actions needed to improve the company's cost position, capitalize on emerging opportunities, and strengthen the company's competitive position?

The answers to these questions point to whether the company can continue the same basic strategy with minor adjustments or whether major overhaul is called for.

The better matched a company's strategy is to its external environment and to its resource strengths and capabilities, the less need there is to contemplate big shifts in strategy. On the other hand, when the present strategy is not well-suited for the road ahead, managers need to give top priority to the task of crafting a better strategy.

Table 4.5 provides a format for doing company situation analysis. It incorporates the concepts and analytical techniques discussed in this chapter and provides a way of reporting the results of company situation analysis in a systematic, concise manner.

KEY POINTS

There are five key questions to consider in performing company situation analysis:

1. *How well is the present strategy working?* This involves evaluating the strategy from both a qualitative standpoint (completeness, internal consistency, rationale, and suitability to the situation) and a quantitative standpoint (the strategic and financial

TABLE 4.5   Company Situation Analysis

1. Strategic Performance Indicators

Performance Indicator	19__	19__	20__	20__	20__
Market share					
Sales growth					
Net profit margin					
Return on equity investment					
Other?					

2. Internal Resource Strengths and Competitive Capabilities

Internal Weaknesses and Resource Deficiencies

External Opportunities

External Threats to the Company's Well-Being

3. Competitive Strength Assessment

Rating scale: 1 = Very weak; 10 = Very strong

Key Success Factor/ Competitive Strength Measure	Weight	Firm A	Firm B	Firm C	Firm D	Firm E
Quality/product performance						
Reputation/image						
Manufacturing capability						
Technological skills and know-how						
Dealer network/distribution capability						
New product innovation capability						
Financial resources						
Relative cost position						
Customer service capability						
Other?						
Overall strength rating						

4. Conclusions Concerning Competitive Position

(Improving/slipping? Competitive advantages/disadvantages?)

5. Major Strategic Issues the Company Must Address

results the strategy is producing). The stronger a company's current overall performance, the less likely the need for radical strategy changes. The weaker a company's performance and/or the faster the changes in its external situation (which can be gleaned from industry and competitive analysis), the more its current strategy must be questioned.

2. *What are the company's resource strengths and weaknesses and its external opportunities and threats?* A SWOT analysis provides an overview of a firm's situation and is an essential component of crafting a strategy tightly matched to the company's situation. A company's resource strengths, competencies, and competitive capabilities are important because they are the most logical and appealing building blocks for strategy; resource weaknesses are important because they may represent vulnerabilities that need correction. External opportunities and threats come into play because a good strategy necessarily aims at capturing a company's most attractive opportunities and at defending against threats to its well-being.

3. *Are the company's prices and costs competitive?* One telling sign of whether a company's situation is strong or precarious is whether its prices and costs are competitive with industry rivals. Strategic cost analysis and value chain analysis are essential tools in benchmarking a company's prices and costs against rivals, determining whether the company is performing particular functions and activities cost effectively, learning whether its costs are in line with competitors, and deciding which internal activities and business processes need to be scrutinized for improvement. Value chain analysis teaches that how competently a company manages its value chain activities relative to rivals is a key to building valuable competencies and competitive capabilities and then leveraging them into sustainable competitive advantage.

4. *How strong is the company's competitive position?* The key appraisals here involve whether the company's position is likely to improve or deteriorate if the present strategy is continued, how the company matches up against key rivals on industry KSFs and other chief determinants of competitive success, and whether and why the company has a competitive advantage or disadvantage. Quantitative competitive strength assessments, using the methodology presented in Table 4.4, indicate where a company is competitively strong and weak and provide insight into the company's ability to defend or enhance its market position. As a rule a company's competitive strategy should be built around its competitive strengths and should aim at shoring up areas where it is competitively vulnerable. Also, the areas where company strengths match up against competitor weaknesses represent the best potential for new offensive initiatives.

5. *What strategic issues does the company face?* The purpose of this analytical step is to develop a complete strategy-making agenda using the results of both company situation analysis and industry and competitive analysis. The emphasis here is on drawing conclusions about the strengths and weaknesses of a company's strategy and framing the issues that strategy makers need to consider.

Good company situation analysis, like good industry and competitive analysis, is crucial to good strategy making. A competently done evaluation of a company's resources and competencies exposes strong and weak elements in the present strategy, points to important company capabilities and vulnerabilities, and indicates the company's ability to protect or improve its competitive position in light of driving forces, competitive pressures, and the competitive strength of rivals. Managers need such understanding to craft a strategy that fits the company's situation well.

Collis, David J., and Cynthia A. Montgomery. "Competing on Resources: Strategy in the 1990s." *Harvard Business Review* 73 no. 4 (July–August 1995), pp. 118–28.

Fahey, Liam, and H. Kurt Christensen. "Building Distinctive Competencies into Competitive Advantages." Reprinted in Liam Fahey, *The Strategic Planning Management Reader*. Englewood Cliffs, N.J.: Prentice-Hall, 1989, pp. 113–18.

Prahalad, C. K., and Gary Hamel. "The Core Competence of the Corporation." *Harvard Business Review* 90, no. 3 (May–June 1990), pp. 79–93.

Shank, John K., and Vijay Govindarajan. *Strategic Cost Management: The New Tool for Competitive Advantage*. New York: Free Press, 1993.

Stalk, George, Philip Evans, and Lawrence E. Shulman. "Competing on Capabilities: The New Rules of Corporate Strategy." *Harvard Business Review* 70, no. 2 (March–April 1992), pp. 57–69.

Watson, Gregory H. *Strategic Benchmarking: How to Rate Your Company's Performance Against the World's Best*. New York: John Wiley & Sons, 1993.

SUGGESTED READINGS

5 STRATEGY AND COMPETITIVE ADVANTAGE

Successful business strategy is about actively shaping the game you play, not just playing the game you find.

Adam M. Brandenburger and Barry J. Nalebuff

The essence of strategy lies in creating tomorrow's competitive advantages faster than competitors mimic the ones you possess today.

Gary Hamel and C. K. Prahalad

Competitive strategy is about being different. It means deliberately choosing to perform activities differently or to perform different activities than rivals to deliver a unique mix of value.

Michael E. Porter

Strategies for taking the hill won't necessarily hold it.

Amar Bhide

Winning business strategies are grounded in sustainable competitive advantage. A company has *competitive advantage* whenever it has an edge over rivals in attracting customers and defending against competitive forces. There are many routes to competitive advantage: developing a product that becomes the industry standard, manufacturing the best-made product on the market, delivering superior customer service, achieving lower costs than rivals, having a more convenient geographic location, developing proprietary technology, incorporating features and styling with more buyer appeal, having the capability to bring new products to market faster than rivals, having greater technological expertise than rivals, developing unique competencies in customized mass production techniques, doing a better job of supply chain management than rivals, building a better-known brand name and reputation, and providing buyers more value for the money (a combination of good quality, good service, and acceptable price). *Investing aggressively in creating sustainable competitive advantage is a company's single most dependable contributor to above-average profitability.*

To succeed in building a competitive advantage, a company's strategy must aim at providing buyers with what they perceive as superior value—a good product at a lower price or a better product that is worth paying more for. This translates into performing value chain activities differently than rivals and building competencies and resource capabilities that are not readily matched.

This chapter focuses on how a company can achieve or defend a competitive advantage.[1] We begin by describing the basic types of competitive strategies in some depth. Next are sections examining the pros and cons of a vertical integration strategy and the merits of cooperative strategies. There are also major sections surveying the use of offensive moves to build competitive advantage and the use of defensive moves to protect it. In the concluding section we look at the competitive importance of timing strategic moves—when it is advantageous to be a first-mover and when it is better to be a fast-follower or late-mover.

---

[1]The definitive work on this subject is Michael E. Porter, *Competitive Advantage* (New York: Free Press, 1985). The treatment in this chapter draws heavily on Porter's pioneering contribution.

THE FIVE GENERIC COMPETITIVE STRATEGIES

A company's competitive strategy consists of its business approaches and initiatives to attract customers and fulfill their expectations, to withstand competitive pressures, and to strengthen its market position.[2] The competitive aim, quite simply, is to do a significantly better job of providing what buyers are looking for, enabling the company to earn a competitive advantage and outcompete rivals. The core of a company's competitive strategy consists of its internal initiatives to deliver superior value to customers. But it also includes offensive and defensive moves to counter the maneuvering of key rivals, actions to shift resources around to improve the firm's long-term competitive capabilities and market position, and tactical efforts to respond to whatever market conditions prevail at the moment.

The objective of competitive strategy is to knock the socks off rival companies by doing a significantly better job of providing what buyers are looking for.

Companies the world over are imaginative in conceiving strategies to win customer favor, outcompete rivals, and secure a market edge. Because a company's strategic initiatives and market maneuvers are usually tailor-made to fit its specific situation and industry environment, there are countless variations in the strategies that companies employ—strictly speaking, there are as many competitive strategies as there are competitors. However, when one strips away the details to get at the real substance the biggest and most important differences among competitive strategies boil down to (1) whether a company's market target is broad or narrow and (2) whether it is pursuing a competitive advantage linked to low costs or product differentiation. Five distinct approaches stand out:[3]

1. *A low-cost leadership strategy*—Appealing to a broad spectrum of customers based on being the overall low-cost provider of a product or service.

2. *A broad differentiation strategy*—Seeking to differentiate the company's product offering from rivals' in ways that will appeal to a broad spectrum of buyers.

3. *A best-cost provider strategy*—Giving customers more value for the money by combining an emphasis on low cost with an emphasis on upscale differentiation; the target is to have the best (lowest) costs and prices relative to producers of products with comparable quality and features.

4. *A focused or market niche strategy based on lower cost*—Concentrating on a narrow buyer segment and outcompeting rivals by serving niche members at a lower cost than rivals.

5. *A focused or market niche strategy based on differentiation*—Concentrating on a narrow buyer segment and outcompeting rivals by offering niche members a customized product or service that meets their tastes and requirements better than rivals' offerings.

Each of these five generic competitive approaches stakes out a different market position—as shown in Figure 5–1. Each involves distinctively different approaches to competing and operating the business. The listing in Table 5–1 highlights the

---

[2]Competitive strategy has a narrower scope than business strategy. Competitive strategy deals exclusively with management's action plan for competing successfully and providing superior value to customers. Business strategy not only concerns how to compete but also how management intends to address the full range of strategic issues confronting the business.

[3]The classification scheme is an adaptation of one presented in Michael E. Porter, *Competitive Strategy: Techniques for Analyzing Industries and Competitors* (New York: Free Press, 1980), chapter 2 and especially pp. 35–39 and 44–46.

FIGURE 5-1   The Five Generic Competitive Strategies

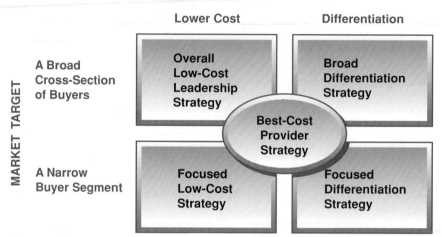

Source: Adapted from Michael E. Porter, *Competitive Strategy* (New York: Free Press, 1980), pp. 35–40.

contrasting features of these generic competitive strategies (for simplicity, the two strains of focused strategies are combined under one heading since they differ fundamentally on only one feature—the basis of competitive advantage).

Low-Cost Provider Strategies

Striving to be the industry's overall low-cost provider is a powerful competitive approach in markets where many buyers are price sensitive. The aim is to operate the business in a highly cost-effective manner and open up a sustainable cost advantage over rivals. A low-cost provider's strategic target is *low cost relative to competitors*, not the absolutely lowest possible cost. In pursuing low-cost leadership, managers must take care to include features and services that buyers consider essential—a product that is too spartan and frills-free weakens rather than strengthens competitiveness. Furthermore, it matters greatly whether the company achieves its cost advantage in ways difficult for rivals to copy or match. The value of a cost advantage depends on its sustainability. If rivals find it relatively easy and/or inexpensive to imitate the leader's low-cost methods, then the low-cost leader's advantage is too short-lived to yield a valuable edge.

A low-cost leader's basis for competitive advantage is lower overall costs than competitors. Successful low-cost leaders are exceptionally good at finding ways to drive costs out of their businesses.

A low-cost leader has two options for achieving superior profit performance. Option one is to use the lower-cost edge to underprice competitors and attract price-sensitive buyers in great enough numbers to increase total profits.[4] Option two is to

---

[4]The trick to profitably underpricing rivals is either to keep the size of the price cut smaller than the size of the firm's cost advantage (thus reaping the benefits of both a bigger profit margin per unit sold and the added profits on incremental sales) or to generate enough added volume to increase total profits despite thinner profit margins (larger volume can make up for smaller margins provided the price reductions bring in enough extra sales).

TABLE 5-1   Distinctive Features of the Generic Competitive Strategies

Type of Feature	Low-Cost Leadership	Broad Differentiation	Best-Cost Provider	Focused Low-Cost and Focused Differentiation
Strategic target	• A broad cross-section of the market.	• A broad cross-section of the market.	• Value-conscious buyers.	• A narrow market niche where buyer needs and preferences are distinctively different from the rest of the market.
Basis of competitive advantage	• Lower costs than competitors	• An ability to offer buyers something different from competitors.	• Give customers more value for the money	• Lower cost in serving the niche (focused low cost) *or* an ability to offer niche buyers something customized to their requirements and tastes (focused differentiation).
Product line	• A good basic product with few frills (acceptable quality and limited selection).	• Many product variations, wide selection, strong emphasis on the chosen differentiating features.	• Good-to-excellent attributes, several-to-many upscale features.	• Customized to fit the specialized needs of the target segment
Production emphasis	• A continuous search for cost reduction without sacrificing acceptable quality and essential features.	• Invent ways to create value for buyers; strive for product superiority.	• Incorporate upscale features and attributes at low cost.	• Tailor-made for the niche.
Marketing emphasis	• Try to make a virtue out of product features that lead to low cost.	• Build in whatever features buyers are willing to pay for. • Charge a premium price to cover the extra costs of differentiating features.	• Underprice rival brands with comparable features	• Communicate the focuser's unique ability to satisfy the buyer's specialized requirements
Sustaining the strategy	• Economical prices/ good value. • All elements of strategy aim at contributing to a sustainable cost advantage—the key is to manage costs down, year after year, in every area of the business.	• Communicate the points of difference in credible ways. • Stress constant improvement and innovation to stay ahead of imitative competitors. • Concentrate on a few key differentiating features; tout them to create a reputation and brand image.	• Unique expertise in managing costs down and product/ service caliber up simultaneously.	• Remain totally dedicated to serving the niche better than other competitors; don't blunt the firm's image and efforts by entering segments with substantially different buyer requirements or adding other product categories to widen market appeal.

refrain from price-cutting altogether, be content with the present market share, and use the lower-cost edge to earn a higher profit margin on each unit sold, thereby raising the firm's total profits and overall return on investment.

Illustration Capsule 14 describes ACX Technologies' strategy for gaining low-cost leadership in aluminum cans.

Opening Up a Cost Advantage   To achieve a cost advantage, a firm's cumulative costs across its value chain must be lower than competitors' cumulative costs. There are two ways to accomplish this:[5]

- Do a better job than rivals of performing internal value chain activities efficiently and of managing the factors that drive the costs of value chain activities.
- Revamp the firm's value chain to permit some cost-producing activities to be bypassed altogether.

Let's look at each of the two avenues.

Controlling the Cost Drivers   A firm's cost position is the result of the behavior of costs in each activity in its total value chain. Any of nine different cost drivers can come into play in determining a company's costs in a particular value chain activity:[6]

1. *Economies or diseconomies of scale.* The costs of a particular value chain activity are often subject to economies or diseconomies of scale. Economies of scale arise whenever activities can be performed more cheaply at larger volumes than smaller volumes and from the ability to spread out certain costs like R & D and advertising over a greater sales volume. Astute management of those activities subject to scale economies or diseconomies can be a major source of cost savings. For example, manufacturing economies can usually be achieved by simplifying the product line, by scheduling longer production runs for fewer models, and by using common parts and components in different models. In global industries, making separate products for each country market instead of selling a standard product worldwide tends to boost unit costs because of lost time in model changeover, shorter production runs, and inability to reach the most economic scale of production for each country model. Scale economies or diseconomies also arise in how a company manages its sales and marketing activities. A geographically organized sales force can realize economies as regional sales volume grows because a salesperson can write larger orders at each sales call and/or because of reduced travel time between calls; on the other hand, a sales force organized by product line can encounter travel-related diseconomies if salespersons have to spend travel time calling on distantly spaced customers. Boosting local or regional market share can lower sales and marketing costs per unit, whereas opting for a bigger national share by entering new regions can create scale diseconomies unless and until market penetration reaches efficient proportions.

2. *Learning and experience curve effects.* The cost of performing an activity can decline over time due to economies of experience and learning. Experience-based cost savings can come from much more than just personnel learning how to perform their tasks more efficiently and the debugging of new technologies. Other valuable

---

[5]Michael E. Porter, *Competitive Advantage* (New York: Free Press, 1985), p. 97.
[6]The list and explanations are condensed from Porter, *Competitive Advantage*, pp. 70–107.

ILLUSTRATION CAPSULE 14   ACX Technologies' Strategy to Become a Low-Cost Producer of Aluminum Cans

ACX Technologies began as an idea of William Coors, CEO of Adolph Coors beer company, to recycle more used aluminum cans back into new cans. Typical aluminum can-making operations involved producing thick aluminum slabs from a smelter using bauxite ore combined with as much as 50 percent scrap aluminum, including used aluminum beverage cans; the slabs of aluminum ingot were fed into a rolling mill to achieve the required thickness. Cans were then formed by stamping pieces of thin aluminum sheet into a seamless can with the top open for filling.

Coors's idea was to produce aluminum-can sheet from 95 percent recycled cans. He began by purchasing rights to technology that his company had helped develop in Europe; the technology used lower-cost electric arc furnaces to melt aluminum scrap directly, short-cutting the smelter process, which required heavy capital investment and big production volumes to be competitive. Coors then built a plant in Colorado that could grind and melt used cans and pour hot aluminum through a continuous caster to make aluminum sheet suitable for the tops and tabs of beverage cans. It took seven years to develop alloys with the desired attributes and to fine-tune the process—Coors originally believed it could be done in less than two years.

In mid-1991 Coors announced it would build a new $200 million mill in Texas to make sheet aluminum for the body of the can—the product with the most exacting specifications but also the number one end use for aluminum in the United States. Production was expected to begin by mid-1992, but problems and delays soon pushed the start-up date into fall 1993. The new plant's low-cost advantages stemmed from several factors:

- Lower capital investment.
- Use of 95 percent recycled aluminum cans as feedstock—reducing raw material costs in producing aluminum sheet by 10 to 15.
- Lower electricity requirements—electric arc technology used only about one-fifth of the electricity of bauxite-smelter technology.
- Comparatively low electric rates at the Texas location.

- Reduced labor costs as compared to bauxite-smelter technology.

Overall, production costs were expected to be anywhere from 20 to 35 percent below the costs of aluminum can producers using traditionally produced aluminum sheet, depending on the prevailing market prices for aluminum ingot and scrap aluminum. In addition, the mill had greater flexibility than traditional producers to vary its alloy mixes to meet different customer specifications.

Meanwhile, in December 1992 during construction of the Texas plant, Coors decided to spin off all aluminum can operations (along with a paper-packaging operation making patented polyethylene cartons with high-quality metallic graphics—packaging for Cascade boxes and Lever 2000 soapbars are examples; a ceramics unit making materials for high-tech applications; and several developmental businesses) into a new publicly owned company called ACX Technologies. The new company had 1992 revenues of $570 million, about 28 percent of which were sales to Coors. The breakdown of revenues in 1992 was aluminum for cans 17 percent, graphics packaging 37 percent, ceramics materials 32 percent, and developmental businesses 14 percent (including corn wet milling, biotechnology, defense electronics, and biodegradable polymers).

In summer 1993, the Texas plant was in start-up and can makers began testing the quality of its aluminum sheet. Coors was the first to qualify ACX's output for use; at year-end 1993 four other can users were testing the suitability of the plant's output for their products. ACX expected the plant to ship close to 50 million pounds of aluminum by year-end 1993 and 100 million pounds or more in 1994 as new customers placed orders. Analysts believed that ACX, given its cost advantage, could grow its annual volume to 1.0 to 1.5 billion pounds in 10 years as it perfected the process and gained acceptance for the quality of its output.

The company's new shares were issued at $10.75 in December 1992 when it went public. In the first 20 days of trading the price climbed to $21.75. Later in 1993, shares traded as high as $46. In May 1994 they were trading in the mid-$30s.

Sources: Based on information published by The Robinson-Humphrey Company and on Marc Charlier, "ACX Strives to Become Aluminum's Low-Cost Producer," *The Wall Street Journal*, September 29, 1993, p. B2.

sources of learning/experience economies include seeing ways to improve plant layout and work flows, to modify product designs to enhance manufacturing efficiency, to redesign machinery and equipment to gain increased operating speed, and to tailor parts and components in ways that streamline assembly. Learning can also reduce the cost of constructing and operating new retail outlets, new plants, or new distribution facilities. Plus there are learning benefits from getting samples of a rival's products and having design engineers study how they are made, benchmarking company activities against the performance of similar activities in other companies, and interviewing suppliers, consultants, and ex-employees of rival firms to tap into their wisdom. Learning tends to vary with the amount of management attention devoted to capturing the benefits of experience of both the firm and outsiders. Astute managers make a conscious effort not only to capture learning benefits but also to keep the benefits proprietary by building or modifying production equipment in-house, endeavoring to retain knowledgeable employees (to reduce the risk of them going to work for rivals firms), limiting the dissemination of cost-saving information through employee publications that can fall into rivals' hands, and enforcing strict nondisclosure provisions in employment contracts.

a.

3. *The cost of key resource inputs.* The cost of performing value chain activities depends in part on what a firm has to pay for key resource inputs. All competitors do not incur the same costs for items purchased from suppliers or for resources used in performing value chain activities. How well a company manages the costs of acquiring inputs is often a big driver of costs. Input costs are a function of three factors:

Labor price

- *Union versus nonunion labor*—Avoiding the use of union labor is often a key to low-cost manufacturing, not just to escape paying high wages (because such prominent low-cost manufacturers as Nucor and Cooper Tire are noted for their incentive compensation systems that allow their nonunion workforces to earn more than their unionized counterparts at rival companies) but rather to escape union work rules that stifle productivity.

Pur. large volumes

- *Bargaining power vis-à-vis suppliers*—Many large enterprises (Wal-Mart, Home Depot, the world's major motor vehicle producers) have used their bargaining clout in purchasing large volumes to wrangle good prices on their purchases from suppliers. Differences in buying power among industry rivals can be an important source of cost advantage or disadvantage.

Geo. location

- *Locational variables*—Locations differ in their prevailing wage levels, tax rates, energy costs, inbound and outbound shipping and freight costs, and so on. Opportunities may exist for reducing costs by relocating plants, field offices, warehousing, or headquarters operations.

4. *Linkages with other activities in the company or industry value chain.* When the cost of one activity is affected by how other activities are performed, costs can be reduced by making sure that linked activities are performed in cooperative and coordinated fashion. For example, when a company's quality control costs or materials inventory costs are linked to the activities of suppliers, costs can be saved by working cooperatively with key suppliers on the design of parts and components, quality-assurance procedures, just-in-time delivery, and integrated materials supply.

Supply chain mgt.

Cross-funct. teams

The costs of new product development can often be reduced by having cross-functional task forces (perhaps including representatives of suppliers and key customers) jointly work on R&D, product design, manufacturing plans, and market launch. Linkages with forward channels tend to center on location of warehouses, materials handling, outbound shipping, and packaging (nail manufacturers, for example, learned that nails delivered in prepackaged 1-pound, 5-pound, and 10-pound assortments instead of 100-pound bulk cartons could reduce a hardware dealer's labor costs in filling individual customer orders). The lesson here is that effective coordination of linked activities holds potential for cost reduction.

   5. *Sharing opportunities with other organizational or business units within the enterprise.* Different product lines or business units within an enterprise can often share the same order processing and customer billing systems, use a common sales force to call on customers, share the same warehouse and distribution facilities, or rely upon a common customer service and technical support team. Such combining of like activities and the sharing of resources across sister units can create significant cost savings. Cost sharing can help achieve scale economies, shorten the learning curve in mastering a new technology, and/or promote fuller capacity utilization. Furthermore, the know-how gained in one division or geographic unit can be used to help lower costs in another; sharing know-how across organizational lines has significant cost-saving potential when the activities are similar and know-how is readily transferred from one unit to another.

   6. *The benefits of vertical integration versus outsourcing.* Partially or fully integrating into the activities of either suppliers or forward channel allies can allow an enterprise to detour suppliers or buyers with bargaining power. Vertical integration forward or backward also has potential if merging or tightly coordinating adjacent activities in the industry value chain offers significant cost savings. On the other hand, it is sometimes cheaper to outsource certain functions and activities to outside specialists who by virtue of their expertise and volume, can perform the activity/function more cheaply.

   7. *Timing considerations associated with first-mover advantages and disadvantages.* Sometimes the first major brand in the market is able to establish and maintain its brand name at a lower cost than later brand arrivals—being a first-mover turns out to be cheaper than being a late-mover. On other occasions, such as when technology is developing fast, late purchasers can benefit from waiting to install second- or third-generation equipment that is both cheaper and more efficient; first-generation users often incur added costs associated with debugging and learning how to use an immature and unperfected technology. Likewise, companies that follow rather than lead new product development efforts sometimes avoid many of the costs that pioneers incur in performing pathbreaking R&D and opening up new markets.

   8. *The percentage of capacity utilization.* Capacity utilization is a big cost driver for value chain activities that have substantial fixed costs associated with them. Higher rates of capacity utilization allow depreciation and other fixed costs to be spread over a larger unit volume, thereby lowering fixed costs per unit. The more capital-intensive the business and/or the higher the percentage of fixed costs as a percentage of total costs, the more important this cost driver becomes because there's such a stiff unit-cost penalty for underutilizing existing capacity. In such cases, finding ways to operate close to full capacity on a year-round basis can be an important source of cost advantage.[7]

---

[7]A firm can improve its capacity utilization by *(a)* serving a mix of accounts with peak volumes spread throughout the year, *(b)* finding off-season uses for its products, *(c)* serving private-label customers that can intermittently use the excess capacity, *(d)* selecting buyers with stable demands or demands that are counter to the normal peak/valley cycle, *(e)* letting competitors serve the buyer segments whose demands fluctuate the most, and *(f)* sharing capacity with sister units having a different seasonal production pattern (producing snowmobiles for the winter season and jet skis for summer water sports).

9. *Strategic choices and operating decisions.* A company's costs can be driven up or down by a fairly wide assortment of managerial decisions:

- Increasing/decreasing the number of products or varieties offered.
- Adding/cutting the services provided to buyers.
- Incorporating more/fewer performance and quality features into the product.
- Paying higher/lower wages and fringes to employees relative to rivals and firms in other industries.
- Increasing/decreasing the number of different forward channels used in distributing the firm's product.
- Lengthening/shortening delivery times to customers.
- Putting more/less emphasis than rivals on the use of incentive compensation to motivate employees and boost worker productivity.
- Raising/lowering the specifications for purchased materials.

Managers intent on achieving low-cost leader status have to develop sophisticated understanding of how the above nine factors drive the costs of each activity in the value chain. Then they not only have to use their knowledge to reduce costs for every activity where cost savings can be identified but they have to do so with enough ingenuity and commitment that the company ends up with a sustainable cost advantage over rivals.

Outperforming rivals in controlling the factors that drive costs is a very demanding managerial exercise.

Revamping the Makeup of the Value Chain   Dramatic cost advantages can emerge from finding innovative ways to restructure processes and tasks, cut out frills, and provide the basics more economically. The primary ways companies can achieve a cost advantage by reconfiguring their value chains include:

- Simplifying product design (utilizing computer-assisted design techniques, reducing the number of parts, standardizing parts and components across models and styles, shifting to an easy-to-manufacture product design).
- Stripping away the extras and offering only a basic, no-frills product or service, thereby cutting out activities and costs of multiple features and options.
- Shifting to a simpler, less capital-intensive, or more streamlined or flexible technological process (computer-assisted design and manufacture, flexible manufacturing systems that accommodate both low-cost efficiency and product customization).
- Finding ways to bypass the use of high-cost raw materials or component parts.

- Using direct-to-end-user sales and marketing approaches that cut out the often large costs and margins of wholesalers and retailers (costs and margins in the wholesale-retail portions of the value chain often represent 50 percent of the price paid by final consumers).
- Relocating facilities closer to suppliers, customers, or both to curtail inbound and outbound costs.
- Dropping the "something-for-everyone" approach and focusing on a limited product/service to meet a special, but important, need of the target buyer, thereby eliminating activities and costs of numerous product versions.

- Reengineering core business processes to consolidate work steps and cut out low-value-added activities (many low-cost providers are adept at learning how to operate with exceptionally small corporate staffs and corporate overheads).

- Using electronic communications technologies to eliminate paperwork (paperless invoice systems and electronic funds transfer), reduce printing and copying costs, speed communications via e-mail, curtail travel costs via teleconferencing, distribute information via company intranets, and establish relationships with customers using Websites and Web pages—companies the world over are using such technologies to restructure how they do business. Ford Motor has aggressively adopted videoconferencing and computer-assisted design and manufacturing technologies—its new "global car" (marketed as the Contour in North America) was developed by a team of designers at Ford locations around the world who used an on-line computer network to share ideas, create the actual designs, integrate the designs for the various parts and components (the chassis, engine, transmission, body. and instrumentation), and build and test prototypes via computer simulations. The Internet is fast becoming an attractive channel for retailing new software products (downloading new software directly from the Internet eliminates the costs of producing and packaging disks, then shipping and distributing them through wholesale and retail channels).

Companies can sometimes achieve dramatic cost advantages from creating altogether new value chain systems or from restructuring existing value chains and slicing out cost-producing activities that produce little customer value. For example, both Hallmark and American Greetings are marketing CD-ROM software that allows customers to select or design a card electronically, type in the recipient's name and address, and click on an "order" icon; computer technicians at the company take over from there—printing and mailing the card to arrive via regular mail or e-mail on the appropriate date. Card senders can pick out all the cards they want to send for an entire year at a single time if they wish and get a confirmation from the company that the appropriate card has been sent on its way. Such electronic value chains can radically alter how greeting cards are designed, produced, distributed, sold, and delivered.

Dell Computer has proved a pioneer in revamping the value chain in manufacturing and marketing PCs. Whereas most PC makers produce their models in volume and sell them through independent dealers and distributors, Dell markets directly to consumers, building its PCs as customers order them and shipping them to customers within a few days of receiving the order. Dell's value chain approach has proved cost effective in coping with the PC industry's blink-of-an-eye product life cycle (new models equipped with faster chips and new features appear every few months). Dell's build-to-order strategy enables it to avoid misjudging buyer demand for its various models and being saddled with fast-obsoleting components and finished goods inventories; its sell-direct strategy slices dealer/distributor costs and margins out of the value chain (although some of these savings are offset by the cost of Dell's direct marketing and customer support activities—functions that would otherwise be performed by dealers and distributors). In 1996, Dell's shipments of PCs grew 58 percent compared to growth of 30 percent for industry leader Compaq Computer and of 15 percent for the industry as a whole. In a number of industries, efforts are under way to restructure the value chain to remove the inefficiencies and costs of getting goods and services from the producer to the end users. Illustration Capsule 15 provides additional examples of the cost advantages of value chain restructuring.

ILLUSTRATION CAPSULE 15   Winning A Cost Advantage via Value Chain Restructuring: Iowa Beef Packers, FedEx, Southwest Airlines, and the Internet Entrepreneurs

Iowa Beef Packers, FedEx, and Southwest Airlines have been able to win strong competitive positions by restructuring the traditional value chains in their industries.

In beef packing, the traditional cost chain involved raising cattle on scattered farms and ranches, shipping them live to labor-intensive, unionized slaughtering plants, and then transporting whole sides of beef to grocery retailers whose butcher departments cut them into smaller pieces and packaged them for sale to grocery shoppers. Iowa Beef Packers revamped the traditional chain with a radically different strategy—large automated plants employing nonunion labor were built near economically transportable supplies of cattle, and the meat was partially butchered at the processing plant into smaller high-yield cuts (sometimes sealed in plastic casing ready for purchase), boxed, and shipped to retailers. IBP's inbound cattle transportation expenses, traditionally a major cost item, were cut significantly by avoiding the weight losses that occurred when live animals were shipped long distances; major outbound shipping cost savings were achieved by not having to ship whole sides of beef with their high waste factor. Iowa Beef's strategy was so successful that it became the largest U.S. meatpacker, surpassing the former industry leaders, Swift, Wilson, and Armour.

FedEx innovatively redefined the value chain for rapid delivery of small parcels. Traditional firms like Emery and Airborne Express operated by collecting freight packages of varying sizes, shipping them to their destination points via air freight and commercial airlines, and then delivering them to the addressee. Federal Express opted to focus only on the market for overnight delivery of small packages and documents. These were collected at local drop points during the late afternoon hours and flown on company-owned planes during early evening hours to a central hub in Memphis where from 11 P.M. to 3 A.M. each night all parcels were sorted, then reloaded on company planes, and flown during the early morning hours to their destination points, where they were delivered the next morning by company personnel using company trucks. The cost structure achieved by FedEx is low enough to permit it to guarantee overnight delivery of a small parcel anywhere in the United States for a price as low as $13.

Southwest Airlines has tailored its value chain to deliver low-cost, convenient service to passengers. It has mastered fast turnarounds at the gates (about 15 minutes versus 45 minutes for rivals); because the short turnarounds allow the planes to fly more hours per day, Southwest can schedule more flights per day with fewer aircraft. Southwest does not offer inflight meals, assigned seating, baggage transfer to connecting airlines, or first-class seating and service, thereby eliminating all the cost-producing activities associated with these features. Automated ticketing at its airport ticket counters and gates encourages customers to bypass travel agents (allowing Southwest to avoid paying commissions and to avoid the costs of maintaining an elaborate on-line computerized reservation system readily available to every travel agent) and also reduces the need for so many agents. Southwest's full-service rivals have higher costs because they must perform all the activities associated with providing meal service, assigned seating, premium classes of service, interline baggage checking, and computerized reservation systems.

Internet entrepreneurs are currently leading a revolution to revamp the value chains for providing traditional mail services, for providing all sorts of information to businesses and households, for conducting meetings via cameras and computers while the attendees sit at their desks in their offices, for providing long-distance telephone services via the Internet, for shopping for goods and services, for trading stocks, and on and on. They are employing "virtual value chains" and exploiting the new economics of doing business in the market*space* of the World Wide Web and commercial on-line services. Web pages are fast becoming retail showrooms and a new retail channel where business can sometimes be transacted faster, better, and less expensively than in the physical world of the marketplace. The shift to E-mail, faxing, and electronic funds transfer (which utilize digital or virtual value chains) is undermining the business of the U.S. Postal Service (which estimates that 25 percent of its revenues are at risk).

Source: Based in part on information in Michael E. Porter, *Competitive Advantage* (New York: Free Press, 1985), p. 109 and Jeffrey F. Rayport and John J. Sviokla, "Exploiting the Virtual Value Chain," *Harvard Business Review* 73, no. 6 (November–December 1995), pp. 75–85.

The Keys to Success in Achieving Low-Cost Leadership   Managers intent on pursuing a low-cost-provider strategy have to scrutinize each cost-creating activity and determine what drives its cost. Then they have to use their knowledge about the cost drivers to manage the costs of each activity downward. They have to be proactive in restructuring the value chain, reengineering business processes, and eliminating non-essential work steps—some companies have been able to reduce the costs of reengineered activities by 30 to 70 percent, compared to the 5 to 10 percent possible with creative tinkering and adjusting.

Successful low-cost providers usually achieve their cost advantages by exhaustively pursuing cost savings throughout the value chain. All avenues for reducing costs are explored and no area of potential is overlooked—the success of Japanese manufacturers is largely due to their persistent search for continuous cost reductions across all aspects of their operations. Normally, low-cost producers have cost-conscious corporate cultures featuring broad employee participation in cost-control efforts, ongoing efforts to benchmark costs against best-in-class performers of an activity, intensive scrutiny of operating expenses and budget requests, programs to promote continuous cost improvement, limited perks and frills for executives, and adequate, but not lavish, facilities.

But while low-cost providers are champions of frugality, they are usually aggressive in investing in resources and capabilities that promise to drive costs out of the business. Wal-Mart, for example, employs state-of-the-art technology throughout its operations—its distribution facilities are an automated showcase, it uses on-line computer systems to order goods from suppliers and manage inventories, its stores are equipped with cutting-edge sales-tracking and check-out systems, and it operates a private satellite-communications system that daily sends point-of-sale data to 4,000 vendors.

Companies that employ low-cost leadership strategies include Lincoln Electric in arc-welding equipment, Briggs and Stratton in small gasoline engines, BIC in ball-point pens, Black & Decker in power tools, Stride Rite in footwear, Beaird-Poulan in chain saws, Ford in heavy-duty trucks, General Electric in major home appliances, Toys-R-Us in discount retailing, and Southwest Airlines in commercial airline travel.

The Competitive Defenses of Low-Cost Leadership   Being the low-cost provider in an industry provides some attractive defenses against the five competitive forces.

- In meeting the challenges of *rival competitors*, the low-cost company is in the best position to compete on the basis of price, to use the appeal of lower price to grab sales (and market share) from rivals, to remain profitable in the face of strong price competition, and to survive price wars and earn above-average profits (based on bigger profit margins or greater sales volume). Low cost is a powerful defense in markets where many buyers are price sensitive and price competition thrives.

- In defending against the power of *buyers*, low costs provide a company with partial profit-margin protection, since powerful customers are rarely able to bargain price down past the survival level of the next most cost-efficient seller.

- In countering the bargaining leverage of *suppliers*, the low-cost producer is more insulated than competitors from powerful suppliers if the primary source of its cost advantage is greater internal efficiency. (A low-cost provider whose cost advantage stems from being able to buy components at favorable prices from outside suppliers could be vulnerable to the actions of powerful suppliers.)

- As concerns *potential entrants*, the low-cost leader can use price-cutting to make it harder for a new rival to win customers; the pricing power of the low-cost provider acts as a barrier for new entrants.
- In competing against *substitutes*, a low-cost leader is better positioned to use low price as a defense against companies trying to gain market inroads with a substitute product or service.

A low-cost leader is in the strongest position to win the business of price-sensitive buyers, set the floor on market price, and still earn a profit.

A low-cost company's ability to set the industry's price floor and still earn a profit erects protective barriers around its market position. Anytime price competition becomes a major market force, less efficient rivals get squeezed the most. Firms in a low-cost position relative to rivals have a competitive edge in profitably selling to price-sensitive buyers.

When a Low-Cost Provider Strategy Works Best   A competitive strategy predicated on low-cost leadership is particularly powerful when

1. Price competition among rival sellers is especially vigorous.
2. The industry's product is essentially standardized or a commodity readily available from a host of sellers (a condition that allows buyers to shop for the best price).
3. There are few ways to achieve product differentiation that have value to buyers (put another way, the differences between brands do not matter much to buyers), thereby making buyers very sensitive to price differences.

In markets where rivals compete mainly on price, low cost relative to competitors is the only competitive advantage that matters.

4. Most buyers use the product in the same ways—with common user requirements, a standardized product can satisfy the needs of buyers. In this case low selling price, not features or quality, becomes the dominant factor in causing buyers to choose one seller's product over another's.
5. Buyers incur low switching costs in changing from one seller to another, thus giving them the flexibility to switch readily to lower-priced sellers having equally good products.
6. Buyers are large and have significant power to bargain down prices.

As a rule, the more price sensitive buyers are and the more inclined they are to base their purchasing decisions on which seller offers the best price, the more appealing a low-cost strategy becomes.

The Pitfalls of a Low-Cost Provider Strategy   Perhaps the biggest pitfall of a low-cost provider strategy, however, is getting carried away with overly aggressively price-cutting and ending up with lower, rather than higher, profitability. A low-cost/low-price advantage results in superior profitability only if (1) prices are cut by less than the size of the cost advantage or (2) the added gains in unit sales are large enough to bring in a bigger total profit despite lower margins per unit sold—a company with a 5 percent cost advantage cannot cut prices 20 percent, end up with a volume gain of only 10 percent, and still expect to earn higher profits!

A second big pitfall is not emphasizing avenues of cost advantage that can be kept proprietary or that relegate rivals to playing catch-up. The value of a cost advantage depends on its sustainability. Sustainability, in turn, hinges on whether the company achieves its cost advantage in ways difficult for rivals to copy or match.

A third pitfall is becoming too fixated on cost reduction. Low cost cannot be pursued so zealously that a firm's offering ends up being too spartan and frills-free to generate buyer appeal. Furthermore, a company driving zealously to push its costs down has to guard against misreading or ignoring subtle but significant market swings—like growing buyer interest in added features or service, declining buyer sensitivity to price, or new developments that start to alter how buyers use the product. A low-cost zealot risks getting left behind if buyers begin to opt for enhanced quality, innovative performance features, faster service, and other differentiating features.

A low-cost provider's product offering must always contain enough attributes to be attractive to prospective buyers.

Even if these mistakes are avoided, a low-cost competitive approach still carries risk. Technological breakthroughs can open up cost reductions for rivals that nullify a low-cost leader's past investments and hard-won gains in efficiency. Heavy investments in cost reduction can lock a firm into both its present technology and present strategy, leaving it vulnerable to new technologies and to growing customer interest in something other than a cheaper price.

Differentiation Strategies

Differentiation strategies are an attractive competitive approach when buyer preferences are too diverse to be fully satisfied by a standardized product or when buyer requirements are too diverse to be fully satisfied by sellers with identical capabilities. To be successful with a differentiation strategy, a company has to study buyers' needs and behavior carefully to learn what they consider important, what they think has value, and what they are willing to pay for. Then the company has to either incorporate selected buyer-desired attributes that set its offering visibly and distinctively apart from rivals or else develop *unique* capabilities to serve buyer requirements. Competitive advantage results once a sufficient number of buyers become strongly attached to the differentiated attributes, features, or capabilities. The stronger the buyer appeal of the differentiated offering, the more that customers *bond* with the company and the stronger the resulting competitive advantage.

The essence of a differentiation strategy is to be unique in ways that are valuable to customers and that can be sustained.

Successful differentiation allows a firm to

- Command a premium price for its product, and/or
- Increase unit sales (because additional buyers are won over by the differentiating features), and/or
- Gain buyer loyalty to its brand (because some buyers are strongly attracted to the differentiating features and bond with the company and its products).

Differentiation enhances profitability whenever the extra price the product commands outweighs the added costs of achieving the differentiation. Company differentiation strategies fail when buyers don't value the brand's uniqueness enough to buy it instead of rivals' brands and/or when a company's approach to differentiation is easily copied or matched by its rivals.

Types of Differentiation Themes   Companies can pursue differentiation from many angles: a unique taste (Dr Pepper and Listerine), a host of features (America Online), reliable service (FedEx in overnight package delivery), spare parts availability (Caterpillar guarantees 48-hour spare parts delivery to any customer anywhere in the

. vs. low c) low price.

world or else the part is furnished free), more for the money (McDonald's and Wal-Mart), engineering design and performance (Mercedes in automobiles), prestige and

---
Easy-to-copy differentiating features cannot produce sustainable competitive advantage.

---

distinctiveness (Rolex in watches), product reliability (Johnson & Johnson in baby products), quality manufacture (Karastan in carpets and Honda in automobiles), technological leadership (3M Corporation in bonding and coating products), a full range of services (Merrill Lynch), a complete line of products (Campbell's soups), and top-of-the-line image and reputation (Gucci, Ralph Lauren, and Chanel in fashions and accessories, Ritz-Carlton in hotels, and Mont Blanc and Cross in writing instruments).

The most appealing approaches to differentiation are those that are hard or expensive for rivals to duplicate. Indeed, resourceful competitors can, in time, clone almost any product or feature or attribute—if American Airlines creates a program for frequent fliers, so can Delta; if Ford offers a 30,000-mile bumper-to-bumper warranty on its new cars, so can Chrysler and Nissan. This is why *sustainable* differentiation usually has to be linked to unique internal skills, core competencies, and capabilities. When a company has competencies and capabilities that competitors cannot readily match and when its expertise can be used to perform activities in the value chain where differentiation potential exists, then it has a strong basis for sustainable differentiation. As a rule, differentiation yields a longer-lasting and more profitable competitive edge when it is based on new product innovation, technical superiority, product quality and reliability, and comprehensive customer service. Such attributes are widely perceived by buyers as having value; moreover, the competencies and competitive capabilities required to produce them tend to be tougher for rivals to copy or overcome profitably.

Where Along the Value Chain to Create the Differentiating Attributes   Differentiation is not something hatched in marketing and advertising departments, nor is it limited to the catchalls of quality and service. Differentiation is about understanding what the customer values, about where along the value chain to create the differentiating attributes, and about what resources and capabilities are needed to produce brand uniqueness. Differentiation possibilities exist in virtually every activity along an industry's value chain, most commonly in:

1. *Purchasing and procurement activities* that ultimately spill over to affect the performance or quality of the company's end product. (McDonald's gets high ratings on its french fries partly because it has very strict specifications on the potatoes purchased from suppliers.)

2. *Product R&D activities* that aim at improved product designs and performance features, expanded end uses and applications, shorter lead times in developing new models, more frequent first-on-the-market victories, wider product variety, added user safety, greater recycling capability, or enhanced environmental protection.

3. *Production R&D and technology-related activities* that permit custom-order manufacture at an efficient cost, make production methods more environmentally safe, or improve product quality, reliability, and appearance. (Vehicle manufacturers have developed flexible manufacturing systems that allow different models to be made on the same assembly line and to equip models with different options as they come down the assembly line.)

4. *Manufacturing activities* that reduce product defects, prevent premature product failure, extend product life, allow better warranty coverages, improve

economy of use, result in more end-user convenience, or enhance product appearance. (The quality edge enjoyed by Japanese automakers stems partly from their distinctive competence in performing assembly-line activities.)

5. *Outbound logistics and distribution activities* that allow for faster delivery, more accurate order filling, and fewer warehouse and on-the-shelf stockouts.

6. *Marketing, sales, and customer service activities* that can result in superior technical assistance to buyers, faster maintenance and repair services, more and better product information, more and better training materials for end users, better credit terms, quicker order processing, more frequent sales calls, or greater customer convenience.

Managers need to fully understand the value-creating differentiation options and the activities that drive uniqueness to devise a sound differentiation strategy and evaluate various differentiation approaches.[8]

Achieving a Differentiation-Based Competitive Advantage The cornerstone of a successful differentiation strategy is creating buyer value in ways unmatched by rivals. There are four differentiation-based approaches to creating buyer value. One is to incorporate product attributes and user features that lower the buyer's overall costs of using the company's product—Illustration Capsule 16 lists options for making a company's product more economical. A second approach is to incorporate features that raise the performance a buyer gets out of the product—Illustration Capsule 17 contains differentiation avenues that enhance product performance and buyer value.

> *A differentiator's basis for competitive advantage is either a product/service offering whose attributes differ significantly from the offerings of rivals or a set of capabilities for delivering customer value that are unmatched by rivals.*

A third approach is to incorporate features that enhance buyer satisfaction in noneconomic or intangible ways. Goodyear's new Aquatread tire design appeals to safety-conscious motorists wary of slick roads in rainy weather. Wal-Mart's campaign to feature products "Made in America" appeals to customers concerned about the loss of American jobs to foreign manufacturers. Rolls-Royce, Tiffany's, and Gucci have competitive advantages linked to buyer desires for status, image, prestige, upscale fashion, superior craftsmanship, and the finer things in life. L. L. Bean makes its mail-order customers feel secure in their purchases by providing an unconditional guarantee with no time limit: "All of our products are guaranteed to give 100 percent satisfaction in every way. Return anything purchased from us at anytime if it proves otherwise. We will replace it, refund your purchase price, or credit your credit card, as you wish."

A fourth approach is to compete on the basis of capabilities—to deliver value to customers via competitive capabilities that rivals don't have or can't afford to match.[9] *The strategy-making challenge is selecting which differentiating capabilities to develop.* Successful capabilities-driven differentiation begins with a deep understanding of what customers need and ends with building organizational capabilities to satisfy these needs better than rivals. The Japanese auto manufacturers have the capability to bring new models to market faster than American and European automakers, thereby allowing them to satisfy changing consumer preferences for one

---

[8]Porter, *Competitive Advantage*, p. 124.

[9]For a more detailed discussion, see George Stalk, Philip Evans, and Lawrence E. Schulman, "Competing on Capabilities: The New Rules of Corporate Strategy," *Harvard Business Review* 70, no.2 (March–April 1992), pp. 57–69.

ILLUSTRATION CAPSULE 16 Differentiating Features That Lower Buyer Costs

A company doesn't have to resort to price cuts to make it cheaper for a buyer to use its product. An alternative is to incorporate features and attributes into the company's product/service package that

- Reduce the buyer's scrap and raw materials waste. Example of differentiating feature: cut-to-size components.

- Lower the buyer's labor costs (less time, less training, lower skill requirements). Examples of differentiating features: snap-on assembly features, modular replacement of worn-out components.

- Cut the buyer's downtime or idle time. Examples of differentiating features: greater product reliability, ready spare parts availability, or less frequent maintenance requirements.

- Reduce the buyer's inventory costs. Example of differentiating feature: just-in-time delivery.

- Reduce the buyer's pollution control costs or waste disposal costs. Example of differentiating feature: scrap pickup for use in recycling.

- Reduce the buyer's procurement and order-processing costs. Example of differentiating feature: computerized on-line ordering and billing procedures.

- Lower the buyer's maintenance and repair costs. Example of differentiating feature: superior product reliability.

- Lower the buyer's installation, delivery, or financing costs. Example of differentiating feature: 90-day payment same as cash.

- Reduce the buyer's need for other inputs (energy, safety equipment, security personnel, inspection personnel, other tools and machinery). Example of differentiating feature: fuel-efficient power equipment.

- Raise the trade-in value of used models.

- Lower the buyer's replacement or repair costs if the product unexpectedly fails later. Example of differentiating feature: longer warranty coverage.

- Lower the buyer's need for technical personnel. Example of differentiating feature: free technical support and assistance.

- Boost the efficiency of the buyer's production process. Examples of differentiating features: faster processing speeds, better interface with ancillary equipment.

Source: Adapted from Michael E. Porter, *Competitive Advantage* (New York: Free Press, 1985), pp. 135–37.

---

vehicle style versus another. CNN has the capability to cover breaking news stories faster and more completely than the major networks. Microsoft, with its three PC operating systems (DOS, Windows 95, and Windows NT), its large project teams of highly talented and antibureaucratic programmers who thrive on developing complex products and systems, and its marketing savvy and know-how, has greater capabilities to design, create, distribute, advertise, and sell an array of software products for PC applications than any of its rivals. Microsoft's capabilities are especially suited to fast-paced markets with short product life cycles and competition centered around evolving product features.

Real Value, Perceived Value, and Signals of Value Buyers seldom pay for value they don't perceive, no matter how real the unique extras may be.[10] Thus the price premium that a differentiation strategy commands reflects *the value actually delivered* to the buyer and *the value perceived* by the buyer (even if not actually delivered). Actual and perceived value can differ whenever buyers have trouble assessing what their experience with the product will be. Incomplete knowledge on the part of buyers often causes them to judge value based on such *signals* as price (where price

---

[10]This discussion draws from Porter, *Competitive Advantage*, pp. 138–42. Porter's insights here are particularly important to formulating differentiating strategies because they highlight the relevance of "intangibles" and "signals."

ILLUSTRATION CAPSULE 17   Differentiating Features That Raise the Performance a User Gets

To enhance the performance a buyer gets from using its product/service, a company can incorporate features and attributes that

- Provide buyers greater reliability, durability, convenience, or ease of use.
- Make the company's product/service cleaner, safer, quieter, or more maintenance-free than rival brands.
- Exceed environmental or regulatory standards.

- Meet the buyer's needs and requirements more completely, compared to competitors' offerings.
- Give buyers the option to add on or to upgrade later as new product versions come on the market.
- Give buyers more flexibility to tailor their own products to the needs of their customers.
- Do a better job of meeting the buyer's future growth and expansion requirements.

Source: Adapted from Michael E. Porter, *Competitive Advantage* (New York: Free Press, 1985), pp. 135–38.

---

connotes quality), attractive packaging, extensive ad campaigns (i.e., how well known the product is), ad content and image, the quality of brochures and sales presentations, the seller's facilities, the seller's list of customers, the firm's market share, length of time the firm has been in business, and the professionalism, appearance, and personality of the seller's employees. Such signals of value may be as important as actual value (1) when the nature of differentiation is subjective or hard to quantify, (2) when buyers are making a first-time purchase, (3) when repurchase is infrequent, and (4) when buyers are unsophisticated.

> *A firm whose differentiation strategy delivers only modest extra value but clearly signals that extra value may command a higher price than a firm that actually delivers higher value but signals it poorly.*

Keeping the Cost of Differentiation in Line   Once a company's managers identify what approach to creating buyer value and establishing a differentiation-based competitive advantage makes the most sense, given the company's situation and what rivals are doing, they must develop the capabilities and build in the value-creating attributes at an acceptable cost. Differentiation usually raises costs. The trick to profitable differentiation is either to keep the costs of achieving differentiation below the price premium the differentiating attributes can command in the market-place (thus increasing the profit margin per unit sold) or to offset thinner profit margins with enough added volume to increase total profits (larger volume can make up for smaller margins provided differentiation adds enough extra sales). It usually makes sense to incorporate extra differentiating features that are not costly but add to buyer satisfaction—FedEx installed systems that allowed customers to track packages in transit by connecting to FedEx's World Wide Web site and entering the airbill number; some hotels and motels provide in-room coffeemaking amenities for the convenience of guests or early-morning complimentary coffee-to-go in their lobbies; many McDonald's outlets have play areas for small children.

What Makes a Differentiation Strategy Attractive   Differentiation offers a buffer against the strategies of rivals when it results in enhanced buyer loyalty to a company's brand or model and greater willingness to pay a little (perhaps a lot!) more for it. In addition, successful differentiation (1) erects entry barriers in the form of customer loyalty and uniqueness that newcomers find hard to hurdle, (2) lessens buyers' bargaining power since the products of alternative sellers are less attractive to them, and (3) helps a firm fend off threats from substitutes not having comparable features or attributes. If differentiation allows a company to charge a higher price and have bigger profit margins, it is in a stronger position to withstand the efforts of powerful vendors to get a higher price for the items they supply. Thus, as with cost leadership, successful differentiation creates lines of defense for dealing with the five competitive forces.

For the most part, differentiation strategies work best in markets where (1) there are many ways to differentiate the company's offering from that of rivals and many buyers perceive these differences as having value, (2) buyer needs and uses of the item or service are diverse, (3) few rival firms are following a similar differentiation approach, and (4) technological change is fast-paced and competition revolves around evolving product features.

The Pitfalls of a Differentiation Strategy   There are, of course, no guarantees that differentiation will produce a meaningful competitive advantage. If buyers see little value in the unique attributes or capabilities a company stresses, then its differentiation strategy will get a "ho-hum" reception in the marketplace. In addition, attempts at differentiation are doomed to fail if competitors can quickly copy most or all of the appealing product attributes a company comes up with. Rapid imitation means that a firm never achieves real differentiation, since competing brands keep changing in like ways each time a company makes a new move to set its offering apart from rivals'. Thus, to build competitive advantage through differentiation a firm must search out lasting sources of uniqueness that are burdensome for rivals to overcome. Other common pitfalls and mistakes in pursuing differentiation include:[11]

Any differentiating element that works well tends to draw imitators.

- Trying to differentiate on the basis of something that does not lower a buyer's cost or enhance a buyer's well-being, as perceived by the buyer.
- Overdifferentiating so that price is too high relative to competitors or that the array of differentiating attributes exceeds buyers' needs.
- Trying to charge too high a price premium (the bigger the price differential the harder it is to keep buyers from switching to lower-priced competitors).
- Ignoring the need to signal value and depending only on intrinsic product attributes to achieve differentiation.
- Not understanding or identifying what buyers consider as value.

A low-cost producer strategy can defeat a differentiation strategy when buyers are satisfied with a basic product and don't think "extra" attributes are worth a higher price.

The Strategy of Being a Best-Cost Provider

This strategy aims at giving customers *more value for the money*. It combines a strategic emphasis on low cost with a strategic emphasis on *more than minimally acceptable* quality, service, features, and performance. The idea is to create superior value by meeting or exceeding buyers' expectations on key quality-service-features-performance attributes and by beating their expectations on price. The aim is to become the low-cost provider of a product or service with *good-to-excellent* attributes, then use the cost advantage to underprice brands with comparable attributes. Such a competitive approach is termed a *best-cost provider strategy* because the producer has the best (lowest) cost relative to producers whose brands have comparable quality-service-features-performance attributes.

[11]Porter, *Competitive Advantage*, pp. 160–62.

ILLUSTRATION CAPSULE 18   Toyota's Best-Cost Producer Strategy for Its Lexus Line

Toyota Motor Co. is widely regarded as a low-cost producer among the world's motor vehicle manufacturers. Despite its emphasis on product quality, Toyota has achieved absolute low-cost leadership because of its considerable skills in efficient manufacturing techniques and because its models are positioned in the low-to-medium end of the price spectrum where high production volumes are conducive to low unit costs. But when Toyota decided to introduce its new Lexus models to compete in the luxury-car market, it employed a classic best-cost producer strategy. Toyota's Lexus strategy had three features:

- Transferring its expertise in making high-quality Toyota models at low cost to making premium quality luxury cars at costs below other luxury-car makers, especially Mercedes and BMW. Toyota executives reasoned that Toyota's manufacturing skills should allow it to incorporate high-tech performance features and upscale quality into Lexus models at less cost than other luxury-car manufacturers.

- Using its relatively lower manufacturing costs to underprice Mercedes and BMW, both of which had models selling in the $40,000 to $75,000 range (and some even higher). Toyota believed that with its cost advantage it could price

attractively equipped Lexus models in the $38,000 to $42,000 range, drawing price-conscious buyers away from Mercedes and BMW and perhaps inducing quality-conscious Lincoln and Cadillac owners to trade up to a Lexus.

- Establishing a new network of Lexus dealers, separate from Toyota dealers, dedicated to providing a level of personalized, attentive customer service unmatched in the industry.

The Lexus 400 series models were priced in the $48,000 to $55,000 range and competed against Mercedes's 300/400E series, BMW's 535i/740 series, Nissan's Infiniti Q45, Cadillac Seville, Jaguar, and Lincoln Continental. The lower-priced Lexus 300 series, priced in the $30,000 to $38,000 range, competed against Cadillac Eldorado, Acura Legend, Infiniti J30, Buick Park Avenue, Mercedes's C-Class series, BMW's 315 series, and Oldsmobile's Aurora line.

Lexus's best-cost producer strategy was so successful that Mercedes introduced a new C-Class series, priced in the $30,000 to $35,000 range, to become more competitive. The Lexus LS 400 models and the Lexus SC 300/400 models ranked first and second, respectively, in the widely watched J. D. Power & Associates quality survey for 1993 cars; the entry-level Lexus ES 300 model ranked eighth.

The competitive advantage of a best-cost provider comes from matching close rivals on quality-service-features-performance and beating them on cost. To become a best-cost provider, a company must match quality at a lower cost than rivals, match features at a lower cost than rivals, match product performance at a lower cost than rivals, and so on. What distinguishes a successful best-cost provider is having the resources, know-how, and capabilities to incorporate upscale product or service attributes at a low cost. The most successful best-cost producers have competencies and capabilities to simultaneously drive unit costs down and product caliber up—see Illustration Capsule 18.

A best-cost provider strategy has great appeal from the standpoint of competitive positioning. It produces superior customer value by balancing a strategic emphasis on low cost against a strategic emphasis on differentiation. In effect, it is a *hybrid* strategy that allows a company to combine the competitive advantage of both low cost and differentiation to deliver superior buyer value. In markets where buyer diversity makes product differentiation the norm and many buyers are price and value sensitive, a best-cost producer strategy can be more advantageous than either a pure low-cost producer strategy or a pure differentiation strategy keyed to product superiority. This is because a best-cost provider can position itself near the middle of the market with either a medium-quality product at a below-average price or a very good product at a medium price. Often the

> *The most powerful competitive approach a company can pursue is to strive relentlessly to become a lower-and-lower-cost producer of a higher-and-higher-caliber product, aiming at eventually becoming the industry's absolute lowest-cost producer and, simultaneously, the producer of the industry's overall best product.*

majority of buyers prefer a midrange product rather than the cheap, basic product of a low-cost producer or the expensive product of a top-of-the-line differentiator.

Focused or Market Niche Strategies

What sets focused strategies apart from low-cost or differentiation strategies is concentrated attention on a narrow piece of the total market. The target segment or niche can be defined by geographic uniqueness, by specialized requirements in using the product, or by special product attributes that appeal only to niche members. The aim of a focus strategy is to do a better job of serving buyers in the target market niche than rival competitors. *A focuser's basis for competitive advantage is either (1) lower costs than competitors in serving the market niche or (2) an ability to offer niche members something they perceive is better.* A focused strategy based on low cost depends on there being a buyer segment whose requirements are less costly to satisfy compared to the rest of the market. A focused strategy based on differentiation depends on there being a buyer segment that wants or needs special product attributes or company capabilities.

Examples of firms employing some version of a focused strategy include Netscape (a specialist in software for browsing the World Wide Web), Porsche (in sports cars), Cannondale (in top-of-the-line mountain bikes), commuter airlines like Horizon, Comair, and Atlantic Southeast (specializing in low-traffic, short-haul flights linking major airports with smaller cities 100 to 250 miles away), Jiffy Lube International (a specialist in quick oil changes, lubrication, and simple maintenance for motor vehicles), and Bandag (a specialist in truck tire recapping that promotes its recaps aggressively at over 1,000 truck stops). Microbreweries, local bakeries, bed-and-breakfast inns, and local owner-managed retail boutiques are all good examples of enterprises that have scaled their operations to serve narrow or local customer segments. Illustration Capsule 19 describes Motel 6's focused low-cost strategy and Ritz-Carlton's focused differentiation strategy.

Focused low-cost strategies are fairly common. Producers of private-label goods are able to lower product development, marketing, distribution, and advertising costs by concentrating on making generic items imitative of name-brand merchandise and selling directly to retail chains wanting a basic house brand to sell at a discount to price-sensitive shoppers. Discount stock brokerage houses have lowered costs by focusing on customers who are willing to forgo the investment research, advice, and financial services offered by full-service firms like Merrill Lynch in return for 30 percent or more commission savings on their buy-sell transactions. Pursuing a cost advantage via focusing works well when a firm can lower costs significantly by concentrating its energies and resources on a well-defined market segment.

At the other end of the market spectrum, focusers like Godiva Chocolates, Chanel, Rolls-Royce, Häagen-Dazs, and W. L. Gore (the maker of Gore-Tex) employ successful differentiation strategies targeted at upscale buyers. Indeed, most markets contain a buyer segment willing to pay a big price premium for the very finest items available, thus opening the window for some competitors to pursue differentiation-based focus strategies aimed at the very top of the market. Another successful focused differentiator is a "fashion food retailer" called Trader Joe's, a 74-store chain that is a combination gourmet deli and food warehouse.[12] Customers shop Trader Joe's as much for entertainment as for conventional grocery items—the store stocks all kinds of out-of-the-ordinary culinary treats like raspberry salsa, salmon burgers, and jasmine fried rice, as well as the standard goods normally found in

---

[12]Gary Hamel, "Strategy as Revolution," *Harvard Business Review* 74, no. 4 (July–August 1996), p. 72.

**ILLUSTRATION CAPSULE 19   Focused Strategies in the Lodging Industry: Motel 6
and Ritz-Carlton**

Motel 6 and Ritz-Carlton compete at opposite ends of the lodging industry. Motel 6 employs a focused strategy keyed to low cost; Ritz-Carlton employs a focused strategy based on differentiation.

Motel 6 caters to price-conscious travelers who want a clean, no-frills place to spend the night. To be a low-cost provider of overnight lodging, Motel 6 (1) selects relatively inexpensive sites on which to construct its units—usually near interstate exits and high traffic locations but far enough away to avoid paying prime site prices; (2) builds only basic facilities—no restaurant or bar and only rarely a swimming pool; (3) relies on standard architectural designs that incorporate inexpensive materials and low-cost construction techniques; and (4) has simple room furnishings and decorations. These approaches lower both investment costs and operating costs. Without restaurants, bars, and all kinds of guest services, a Motel 6 unit can be operated with just front desk personnel, room cleanup crews, and skeleton building-and-grounds maintenance. To promote the Motel 6 concept with travelers who have simple overnight requirements, the chain uses unique, recognizable radio ads done by nationally syndicated radio personality Tom Bodett; the ads describe Motel 6's clean rooms, no-frills facilities, friendly atmosphere, and dependably low rates (usually under $30 per night).

In contrast, the Ritz-Carlton caters to discriminating travelers and vacationers willing and able to pay for top-of-the-line accommodations and world-class personal service. Ritz-Carlton hotels feature (1) prime locations and scenic views from many rooms, (2) custom architectural designs, (3) fine dining restaurants with gourmet menus prepared by accomplished chefs, (4) elegantly appointed lobbies and bar lounges, (5) swimming pools, exercise facilities, and leisure-time options, (6) upscale room accommodations, (7) an array of guest services and recreation opportunities appropriate to the location, and (8) large, well-trained professional staffs who do their utmost to make each guest's stay an enjoyable experience.

Both companies concentrate their attention on a narrow piece of the total market. Motel 6's basis for competitive advantage is lower costs than competitors in providing basic, economical overnight accommodations to price-constrained travelers. Ritz-Carlton's advantage is its capability to provide superior accommodations and unmatched personal service for a well-to-do clientele. Each is able to succeed, despite polar opposite strategies, because the market for lodging consists of diverse buyer segments with diverse preferences and abilities to pay.

supermarkets. What sets Trader Joe's apart is not just its unique combination of food novelties and competitively priced grocery items but the opportunity it provides to turn an otherwise mundane shopping trip into a whimsical treasure hunt.

When Focusing Is Attractive   A focused strategy based either on low cost or differentiation becomes increasingly attractive as more of the following conditions are met:

- The target market niche is big enough to be profitable.
- The niche has good growth potential.
- The niche is not crucial to the success of major competitors.
- The focusing firm has the capabilities and resources to serve the targeted niche effectively.
- The focuser can defend itself against challengers based on the customer goodwill it has built up and its superior ability to serve buyers comprising the niche.

A focuser's specialized competencies and capabilities in serving the target market niche provide a basis for defending against the five competitive forces. Multisegment rivals may not have the capability to truly meet the expectations of the focused firm's target clientele. Entry into a focuser's target segment is made harder by the focused firm's unique capabilities in serving the market niche—the barrier of trying to match the focuser's capabilities deters potential newcomers. A focuser's capabilities in serving the niche also present a hurdle that makers of substitute products must overcome. The bargaining leverage of powerful customers is blunted somewhat by their own unwillingness to shift their business to rival companies less capable of meeting their expectations.

Focusing works best (1) when it is costly or difficult for multisegment competitors to meet the specialized needs of the target market niche, (2) when no other rival is attempting to specialize in the same target segment, (3) when a firm doesn't have the resources or capabilities to go after a bigger piece of the total market, and (4) when the industry has many different niches and segments, allowing a focuser to pick an attractive niche suited to its resource strengths and capabilities.

The Risks of a Focused Strategy   Focusing carries several risks. One is the chance that competitors will find effective ways to match the focused firm in serving the target niche. A second is that the niche buyer's preferences and needs might shift toward the product attributes desired by the majority of buyers. An erosion of the differences across buyer segments lowers entry barriers into a focuser's market niche and provides an open invitation for rivals to compete for the focuser's customers. A third risk is that the segment becomes so attractive it is soon inundated with competitors, splintering segment profits.

VERTICAL INTEGRATION STRATEGIES AND COMPETITIVE ADVANTAGE

Vertical integration extends a firm's competitive scope within the same industry. It involves expanding the firm's range of activities backward into sources of supply and/or forward toward end users of the final product. Thus, if a manufacturer invests in facilities to produce certain component parts rather than purchase them from outside suppliers, it remains in essentially the same industry as before. The only change is that it has business units in two production stages in the industry's value chain system. Similarly, if a paint manufacturer elects to integrate forward by opening 100 retail stores to market its products directly to consumers, it remains in the paint business even though its competitive scope extends further forward in the industry chain.

Vertical integration strategies can aim at *full integration* (participating in all stages of the industry value chain) or *partial integration* (building positions in just some stages of the industry's total value chain). A firm can accomplish vertical integration by starting its own operations in other stages in the industry's activity chain or by acquiring a company already performing the activities it wants to bring in-house.

The Strategic Advantages of Vertical Integration

The only good reason for investing company resources in vertical integration is to strengthen the firm's competitive position.[13] Unless vertical integration produces sufficient cost savings to justify the extra investment or yields a differentiation-based competitive advantage, it has no real payoff profitwise or strategywise.

---

[13]See Kathryn R. Harrigan, "Matching Vertical Integration Strategies to Competitive Conditions," *Strategic Management Journal* 7, no. 6 (November–December 1986), pp. 535–56; for a discussion of the advan-

Backward Integration Integrating backward generates cost savings only when the volume needed is big enough to capture the same scale economies suppliers have and when suppliers' production efficiency can be matched or exceeded with no drop-off in quality. The best potential for being able to reduce costs via backward integration exists when suppliers have sizable profit margins, when the item being supplied is a major cost component, and when the needed technological skills are easily mastered. Backward vertical integration can produce a differentiation-based competitive advantage when a company, by performing activities in-house that were previously outsourced, ends up with a better-quality product/service offering, improves the caliber of its customer service, or in other ways enhances the performance of its final product. On occasion, integrating into more stages along the value chain can add to a company's differentiation capabilities by allowing it to build or strengthen its core competencies, better master key skills or strategy-critical technologies, or add features that deliver greater customer value.

A vertical integration strategy has appeal only if it significantly strengthens a firm's competitive position.

Backward integration can also spare a company the uncertainty of depending on suppliers of crucial components or support services, and it can lessen a company's vulnerability to powerful suppliers that raise prices at every opportunity. Stockpiling, fixed-price contracts, multiple-sourcing, long-term cooperative partnerships, or the use of substitute inputs are not always attractive ways for dealing with uncertain supply conditions or with economically powerful suppliers. Companies that are low on a key supplier's priority list can find themselves waiting on shipments every time supplies get tight. If this occurs often and wreaks havoc in a company's own production and customer relations activities, backward integration may be an advantageous strategic solution.

Forward Integration The strategic impetus for forward integration has much the same roots. In many industries, independent sales agents, wholesalers, and retailers handle competing brands of the same product; they have no allegiance to any one company's brand and tend to push "what sells" or earns them the biggest profits. Undependable sales and distribution channels can give rise to costly inventory pile-ups and frequent underutilization of capacity, undermining the economies of a steady, near-capacity production operation. In such cases, a manufacturer may find it competitively advantageous to integrate forward into wholesaling and/or retailing in order to have outlets fully committed to representing its products. A manufacturer can sometimes profit from investing in company-owned distributorships, franchised dealer networks, and/or a chain of retail stores if it is able to realize higher rates of capacity utilization or build a stronger brand image. There are also occasions when integrating forward into the activity of selling directly to end users can produce important cost savings and permit lower selling prices by eliminating many of the costs of using wholesale-retail channels.

For a raw materials producer, integrating forward into manufacturing may permit greater product differentiation and provide an avenue of escape from the price-oriented competition of a commodity business. Often, in the early phases of an industry's value chain, intermediate goods are commodities in the sense that they have essentially identical technical specifications irrespective of producer (as is the case with crude oil, poultry, sheet steel, cement, and textile fibers). Competition in

tages and disadvantages of vertical integration, see John Stuckey and David White, "When and When *Not* to Vertically Integrate," *Sloan Management Review* (Spring 1993), pp. 71–83.

the markets for commodity products is usually fiercely price competitive, with the shifting balance between supply and demand giving rise to volatile profits. However, the closer the activities in the chain get to the ultimate consumer, the greater the opportunities for a firm to break out of a commodity-like competitive environment and differentiate its end product through design, service, quality features, packaging, promotion, and so on. Product differentiation often reduces the importance of price compared to other value-creating activities and improves profit margins.

The Strategic Disadvantages of Vertical Integration

The big disadvantage of vertical integration is that it locks a firm deeper into the industry; unless operating across more stages in the industry's value chain builds competitive advantage, it is a questionable strategic move.

Vertical integration has some substantial drawbacks, however. It boosts a firm's capital investment in the industry, increasing business risk (what if the industry goes sour?) and perhaps denying financial resources to more worthwhile pursuits. A vertically integrated firm has vested interests in protecting its present investments in technology and production facilities. Because of the high costs of abandoning such investments before they are worn out, fully integrated firms tend to adopt new technologies slower than partially integrated or nonintegrated firms. Second, integrating forward or backward locks a firm into relying on its own in-house activities and sources of supply (that later may prove more costly than outsourcing) and may result in less flexibility in accommodating buyer demand for greater product variety.

Third, vertical integration can pose problems of balancing capacity at each stage in the value chain. The most efficient scale of operation at each activity link in the value chain can vary substantially. Exact self-sufficiency at each interface is the exception not the rule. Where internal capacity is insufficient to supply the next stage, the difference has to be bought externally. Where internal capacity is excessive, customers need to be found for the surplus. And if by-products are generated, they have to be disposed of.

Fourth, integration forward or backward often calls for radically different skills and business capabilities. Parts and components manufacturing, assembly operations, wholesale distribution, and retailing are different businesses with different key success factors. Managers of a manufacturing company should consider carefully whether it makes good business sense to invest time and money in developing the expertise and merchandising skills to integrate forward into wholesaling or retailing. Many manufacturers learn the hard way that owning and operating wholesale-retail networks present many headaches, fit poorly with what they do best, and don't always add the kind of value to their core business they thought they would. Integrating backward into parts and components manufacture isn't as simple or profitable as it sometimes sounds either. Personal computer makers, for example, frequently have trouble getting timely deliveries of the latest semiconductor chips at favorable prices. Most, though, don't come close to having the resources or capabilities to integrate backward into chip manufacture; the semiconductor business is technologically sophisticated and entails heavy capital requirements and ongoing R&D effort, and mastering the manufacturing process takes a long time.

Fifth, backward vertical integration into the production of parts and components can reduce a company's manufacturing flexibility, lengthening the time it takes to make design and model changes and to bring new products to market. Companies that alter designs and models frequently in response to shifting buyer preferences often find vertical integration into parts and components burdensome because of constant retooling and redesign costs and the time it takes to implement coordinated changes. Outsourcing parts and components is often cheaper and less complicated than making them in-house, allowing a company to be more nimble in adapting its product offering to buyer preferences. Most of the world's automakers, despite their expertise in automotive technology and manufacturing, have concluded that they are better off from the standpoints of quality, cost, and design flexibility purchasing many of their parts and components from manufacturing specialists rather than trying to supply their own needs.

Unbundling and Outsourcing Strategies In recent years, some vertically integrated companies have found operating in many stages of the industry value chain to be so competitively burdensome that they have adopted *vertical deintegration* (or unbundling) strategies. Deintegration involves withdrawing from certain stages/activities in the value chain system and relying on outside vendors to supply the needed products, support services, or functional activities. Outsourcing pieces of the value chain formerly performed in-house makes strategic sense whenever:

- An activity can be performed better or more cheaply by outside specialists.
- The activity is not crucial to the firm's ability to achieve sustainable competitive advantage and won't hollow out its core competencies, capabilities, or technical know-how. (Outsourcing of maintenance services, data processing, accounting, and other administrative support activities to companies specializing in these services has become commonplace.)
- It reduces the company's risk exposure to changing technology and/or changing buyer preferences.
- It streamlines company operations in ways that improve organizational flexibility, cut cycle time, speed decision making, and reduce coordination costs.
- It allows a company to concentrate on its core business.

Often, many of the advantages of vertical integration can be captured and many of the disadvantages avoided by forging close, long-term cooperative partnerships with key suppliers and tapping into the capabilities that able suppliers have developed. In years past, many companies' relationships with suppliers were of an arms-length nature where the nature of the items supplied were specified in detailed, short-term contracts.[14] Although a company might engage the same supplier repeatedly, there was no expectation that this would be the case; price was usually the determining factor for awarding contracts to suppliers, and companies maneuvered for leverage over suppliers to get the lowest possible prices. The threat of switching suppliers was the primary weapon. To make this threat credible, short-term contracts with multiple suppliers were preferred to long-term ones with single suppliers in order to promote lively competition among suppliers. Today, such approaches are being abandoned in favor of dealing with fewer, highly capable suppliers that are treated as long-term *strategic partners*. Cooperative relationships and alliances with key suppliers are replacing contractual, purely price-oriented relationships. There's more of a concerted effort to coordinate related value chain activities and to build important capabilities by working closely with suppliers.

---

[14]Robert H. Hayes, Gary P. Pisano, and David M. Upton, *Strategic Operations: Competing Through Capabilities* (New York: Free Press, 1996), pp. 419–22.

Weighing the Pros and Cons of Vertical Integration

All in all, then, a strategy of vertical integration can have both important strengths and weaknesses. Which direction the scales tip on vertical integration depends on (1) whether it can enhance the performance of strategy-critical activities in ways that lower cost or increase differentiation, (2) its impact on investment costs, flexibility and response times, and administrative overheads associated with coordinating operations across more stages, and (3) whether it creates competitive advantage. The issue of vertical integration hinges on which capabilities and value-chain activities need to be performed in-house in order for a company to be successful and which can be safely delegated to outside suppliers. Absent solid benefits, vertical integration is not likely to be an attractive competitive strategy option.

COOPERATIVE STRATEGIES AND COMPETITIVE ADVANTAGE

Many companies have begun forming strategic alliances and cooperative relationships with other companies to complement their own strategic initiatives and strengthen their competitiveness in domestic and international markets. Strategic alliances are cooperative agreements between firms that go beyond normal company-to-company dealings but that fall short of merger or full partnership and ownership ties.[15] Alliances and/or cooperative agreements can involve joint research efforts, technology sharing, joint use of production facilities, marketing one another's products, or joining forces to manufacture components or assemble finished products.

Companies enter into alliances or establish cooperative agreements for several strategically beneficial reasons.[16] The five most important are to collaborate on technology or the development of promising new products, to improve supply chain efficiency, to gain economies of scale in production and/or marketing, to fill gaps in their technical and manufacturing expertise, and to acquire or improve market access. Allies learn much from one another in performing joint research, sharing technological know-how, and collaborating on complementary new technologies and products. Manufacturers pursue alliances with parts and components suppliers to gain the efficiencies of better supply chain management and to speed new products to market. By joining forces in producing components, assembling models, or marketing their products, companies can realize cost savings not achievable with their own small volumes; they can also learn how to improve their quality control and production procedures by studying one another's manufacturing methods. Often alliances are formed to share distribution facilities and dealer networks or to jointly promote complementary products, thereby mutually strengthening their access to buyers.

While a few firms can pursue their strategies alone, it is becoming increasingly common for companies to pursue their strategies in collaboration with suppliers, distributors, makers of complementary products, and sometimes even select competitors.

Not only can alliances offset competitive disadvantages but they also can result in the allied companies' directing their competitive energies more toward mutual rivals and less toward one another. Who partners with whom affects the pattern of industry rivalry. Many runner-up companies, wanting to preserve their independence, resort to

---

[15]A number of strategic alliances do involve minority ownership by one, occasionally both, alliance members however. See C. A. Bartlett and S. Ghoshal, *Managing Across Borders: The Transnational Solution* (Boston: Harvard Business School Press, 1989), p. 65 and Kenichi Ohmae, "The Global Logic of Strategic Alliances," *Harvard Business Review* 89, no. 2 (March–April 1989), pp. 143–54.

[16]Porter, *The Competitive Advantage of Nations*, p. 66; see also Jeremy Main, "Making Global Alliances Work," *Fortune*, December 17, 1990, pp. 121–26.

alliances rather than merger to try to close the competitive gap on leading companies—*they rely on collaboration with others to enhance their own capabilities, develop valuable new strategic resources, and compete effectively.* Industry leaders pursue cooperative alliances in order to better fend off ambitious rivals and to open up new opportunities.

Strategic cooperation is a much-favored, indeed necessary, approach in industries like electronics, semiconductors, computer hardware and software, and telecommunications where technological developments are occurring at a furious pace along many different paths and advances in one technology spill over to affect others (often blurring industry boundaries). Whenever industries are experiencing high-velocity technological change in many areas simultaneously, firms find it essential to have cooperative relationships with other enterprises to stay on the leading edge of technology and product performance even in their own area of specialization. They cooperate in technology development, in sharing R&D information of mutual interest, in developing new products that complement each other, and in building networks of dealers and distributors to handle their products. Competitive advantage emerges when a company acquires valuable resources and capabilities through alliances and cooperative agreements that it could not otherwise obtain on its own—this requires real in-the-trenches collaboration between the partners to create new value together, not merely an arm's-length exchange of ideas and information. Unless partners value the skills, resources, and contributions each brings to the alliance and the cooperative arrangement results in win-win outcomes, it is doomed.

Alliances and cooperative agreements between companies can lead to competitive advantage in ways that otherwise are beyond a company's reach.

Cooperative strategies and alliances to penetrate international markets are also common between domestic and foreign firms. Such partnerships are useful in putting together the resources and capabilities to do business over more country markets. For example, U.S., European, and Japanese companies wanting to build market footholds in the fast-growing China market have all pursued partnership arrangements with Chinese companies to help in dealing with governmental regulations, to supply knowledge of local markets, to provide guidance on adapting their products to Chinese consumers, to set up local manufacturing capabilities, and to assist in distribution, marketing, and promotional activities.

General Electric has formed over 100 cooperative partnerships in a wide range of areas; IBM has joined in over 400 strategic alliances.[17] Alliances are so central to Corning's strategy that the company describes itself as a "network of organizations." Microsoft and Netscape have both been aggressive users of cooperative strategies, forming scores of alliances with the providers of complementary technologies and products to build and strengthen their competitive positions. In the PC industry cooperative alliances are pervasive because the different components of PCs and the software to run them is supplied by so many different companies—one set of companies provide the microprocessors, another group makes the motherboards, another the monitors, another the keyboards, another the printers, and so on. Moreover, their facilities are scattered across the United States, Japan, Taiwan, Singapore, and Malaysia. Close collaboration on product development, logistics, production, and the timing of new product releases works to the advantage of nearly all PC industry members.

Alliances and cooperative arrangements, whether they bring together companies from different parts of the industry value chain or different parts of the world, are a fact of life in business today.

---

[17]Michael A. Hitt, Beverly B. Tyler, Camilla Hardee, and Daewoo Park, "Understanding Strategic Intent in the Global Marketplace," *Academy of Management Executive*, 9, no. 2 (May 1995), p. 13.

The Achilles' heel of alliances and cooperative strategies is the danger of becoming dependent on other companies for *essential* expertise and capabilities over the long term. To be a market leader (and perhaps even a serious market contender), a company must develop its own capabilities in areas where internal strategic control is pivotal to protecting its competitiveness and building competitive advantage. Moreover, acquiring essential know-how and capabilities from one's allies sometimes holds only limited potential (because one's partners guard their most valuable skills and expertise); in such instances, acquiring or merging with a company possessing the desired know-how and resources is a better solution.

USING OFFENSIVE STRATEGIES TO SECURE COMPETITIVE ADVANTAGE

Competitive advantage is nearly always achieved by successful offensive strategic moves—moves calculated to yield a cost advantage, a differentiation advantage, or a resource or capabilities advantage. Defensive strategies can protect competitive advantage but rarely are the basis for creating the advantage. How long it takes for a successful offensive to create an edge varies with the competitive circumstances.[18] The *buildup period*, shown in Figure 5–2, can be short, if the requisite resources and capabilities are already in place or if the offensive produces immediate buyer response (as can occur with a dramatic price cut, an imaginative ad campaign, or a new product that proves to be a smash hit). Or the buildup can take much longer, if winning consumer acceptance of an innovative product will take some time or if the firm may need several years to debug a new technology and bring new capacity on-line. Ideally, an offensive move builds competitive advantage quickly; the longer it takes, the more likely rivals will spot the move, see its potential, and begin a counterresponse. The size of the advantage (indicated on the vertical scale in Figure 5–2) can be large (as in pharmaceuticals where patents on an important new drug produce a substantial advantage) or small (as in apparel where popular new designs can be imitated quickly).

Competitive advantage is usually acquired by employing a creative offensive strategy that isn't easily thwarted by rivals.

Following a successful competitive offensive is a *benefit period* during which the fruits of competitive advantage can be enjoyed. The length of the benefit period depends on how much time it takes rivals to launch counteroffensives and begin closing the gap. A lengthy benefit period gives a firm valuable time to earn above-average profits and recoup the investment made in creating the advantage. The best strategic offensives produce big competitive advantages and long benefit periods.

As rivals respond with counteroffensives to close the competitive gap, the *erosion period* begins. Competent, resourceful competitors can be counted on to counterattack with initiatives to overcome any market disadvantage they face—they are not going to stand idly by and passively accept being outcompeted without a fight.[19] Thus, to sustain an initially won competitive advantage, a firm must come up with follow-on offensive and defensive moves. Preparations for the next round of strategic moves ought to be made during the benefit period so that the needed resources are in place when competitors mount efforts to cut into the leader's advantage. Unless the firm stays a step ahead of rivals by initiating one series of offensive and defensive

---

[18]Ian C. MacMillan, "How Long Can You Sustain a Competitive Advantage?" reprinted in Liam Fahey, *The Strategic Planning Management Reader* (Englewood Cliffs, N.J.: Prentice-Hall, 1989), pp. 23–24.

[19]Ian C. MacMillan, "Controlling Competitive Dynamics by Taking Strategic Initiative," *The Academy of Management Executive* 2, no. 2 (May 1988), p. 111.

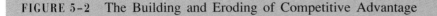

FIGURE 5-2 The Building and Eroding of Competitive Advantage

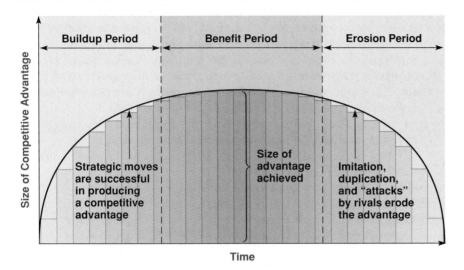

moves after another to protect its market position and retain customer favor, its market advantage will erode.

There are six basic types of strategic offensives:[20]

- Initiatives to match or exceed competitor strengths.
- Initiatives to capitalize on competitor weaknesses.
- Simultaneous initiatives on many fronts.
- End-run offensives.
- Guerrilla offensives.
- Preemptive strikes.

Initiatives to Match or Exceed Competitor Strengths

There are two instances in which it makes sense to mount offensives aimed at neutralizing or overcoming the strengths and capabilities of rival companies. The first is when a company has no choice but to try to whittle away at a strong rival's competitive advantage. The second is when it is possible to gain profitable market share at the expense of rivals despite whatever resource strengths and capabilities they have. Attacking the strengths of rivals is most likely to meet with success when a firm has either a *superior* product offering or *superior* organizational resources and capabilities. The merit of challenging a rival's strengths head-on depends on the trade-off between the costs of the offensive and its competitive benefits. Absent good prospects for added profitability and a more solidified competitive position, such an offensive is ill advised.

One of the most powerful offensive strategies is to challenge rivals with an equally good or better product at a lower price.

---

[20]Philip Kotler and Ravi Singh, "Marketing Warfare in the 1980s," *The Journal of Business Strategy* 1, no. 3 (Winter 1981), pp. 30–41; Philip Kotler, *Marketing Management*, 5th ed. (Englewood Cliffs, N.J.: Prentice-Hall, 1984), pp. 401–6; and Ian MacMillan, "Preemptive Strategies," *Journal of Business Strategy* 14, no. 2 (Fall 1983), pp. 16–26.

The classic avenue for attacking a strong rival is with an equally good offering at a lower price.[21] This can produce market share gains if the targeted competitor has strong reasons for not resorting to price cuts of its own and if the challenger convinces buyers that its product is just as good. However, such a strategy increases total profits only if the gains in unit sales are enough to offset the impact of lower prices and thinner margins per unit sold. A more potent and sustainable basis for mounting a price-aggressive challenge is to *first* achieve a cost advantage and then hit competitors with a lower price.[22] Price-cutting supported by a cost advantage can be continued indefinitely. Without a cost advantage, price-cutting works only if the aggressor has more financial resources and can outlast its rivals in a war of attrition.

Challenging larger, entrenched competitors with aggressive price-cutting is foolhardy unless the aggressor has either a cost advantage or greater financial strength.

Other strategic options for attacking a competitor's strengths include leapfrogging into next-generation technologies to make the rival's products and/or production processes obsolete, adding new features that appeal to the rival's customers, running comparison ads, constructing major new plant capacity in the rival's backyard, expanding the product line to match the rival model for model, and developing customer service capabilities that the rival doesn't have. As a rule, challenging a rival on competitive factors where it is strong is an uphill struggle. Success can be long in coming and usually hinges on developing a cost advantage, a service advantage, a product with attractive differentiating features, or unique competitive capabilities (fast design-to-market times, greater technical know-how, or agility in responding to shifting customer requirements).

Initiatives to Capitalize on Competitor Weaknesses

In this offensive approach, a company tries to gain market inroads by directing its competitive attention to the weaknesses of rivals. There are a number of ways to achieve competitive gains at the expense of rivals' weaknesses:

- Concentrate on geographic regions where a rival has a weak market share or is exerting less competitive effort.
- Pay special attention to buyer segments that a rival is neglecting or is weakly equipped to serve.
- Go after the customers of rivals whose products lag on quality, features, or product performance; in such cases, a challenger with a better product can often convince the most performance-conscious customers to switch to its brand.
- Make special sales pitches to the customers of rivals who provide subpar customer service—it may be relatively easy for a service-oriented challenger to win a rival's disenchanted customers.
- Try to move in on rivals that have weak advertising and weak brand recognition—a challenger with strong marketing skills and a recognized brand name can often win customers away from lesser-known rivals.
- Introduce new models or product versions that exploit gaps in the product lines of key rivals; sometimes "gap fillers" turn out to be a market hit and develop into new growth segments—witness Chrysler's success in minivans. This initiative works well when new product versions satisfy neglected buyer needs.

---

[21]Kotler, *Marketing Management*, p. 402.
[22]Ibid., p. 403.

As a rule, initiatives that exploit competitor weaknesses stand a better chance of succeeding than do those that challenge competitor strengths, especially if the weaknesses represent important vulnerabilities and the rival is caught by surprise with no ready defense.[23]

Simultaneous Initiatives on Many Fronts

On occasion a company may see merit in launching a grand competitive offensive involving multiple initiatives (price cuts, increased advertising, new product introductions, free samples, coupons, in-store promotions, rebates) across a wide geographic front. Such all-out campaigns can throw a rival off-balance, diverting its attention in many directions and forcing it to protect many pieces of its customer base simultaneously. Microsoft is employing a grand offensive to outmaneuver rivals in securing a prominent role on the Internet for its software products.[24] It allocated $160 million and 500 of its most talented programmers to the task of rapidly introducing upgraded versions of Internet Explorer (to overtake Netscape's Navigator Web browser), incorporated Explorer in the Windows 95 package and allowed Internet users to download Explorer free, negotiated deals with America Online and CompuServe to utilize Internet Explorer, put several thousand programmers to work on a variety of Internet-related projects (with R&D budgets of over $500 million), assigned another large group of programmers the task of retrofitting Microsoft's product line to better mesh with the Internet, entered into a joint venture with NBC to form a new cable channel called MSNBC, invested $1 billion in the common stock of Comcast (the second largest U.S. cable provider) to give it leverage in pushing for faster advances in Internet-related cable technologies to speed data transfer, and formed alliances with NBC, ESPN, Disney, Dreamworks, and others to provide content for Microsoft Network and MSNBC. Multifaceted offensives have their best chance of success when a challenger not only comes up with an especially attractive product or service but also has a brand name and reputation to secure broad distribution and retail exposure. Then it can blitz the market with advertising and promotional offers and perhaps entice significant numbers of buyers to switch their brand allegiance.

End-Run Offensives

End-run offensives seek to avoid head-on challenges tied to aggressive price-cutting, escalated advertising, or costly efforts to outdifferentiate rivals. Instead the idea is to maneuver *around* competitors, capture unoccupied or less contested market territory, and change the rules of the competitive game in the aggressor's favor. Examples of end-run offensives include launching initiatives to build strong positions in geographic areas where close rivals have little or no market presence, trying to create new segments by introducing products with different attributes and performance features to better meet the needs of selected buyers, and leapfrogging into next-generation technologies. A successful end-run offensive allows a company to gain a significant first-mover advantage in a new arena and force competitors to play catch-up.

---

[23]For a discussion of the use of surprise, see William E. Rothschild, "Surprise and the Competitive Advantage," *Journal of Business Strategy* 4, no. 3 (Winter 1984), pp. 10–18.

[24]A more detailed account of Microsoft's grand offensive is presented in Brent Schendler, "Software Hardball," *Fortune*, September 30, 1996, pp.106–16.

Guerrilla Offensives

Guerrilla offensives are particularly well-suited to small challengers who have neither the resources nor the market visibility to mount a full-fledged attack on industry leaders.[25] A guerrilla offensive uses the hit-and-run principle, selectively trying to grab sales and market share wherever and whenever an underdog catches rivals napping or spots an opening to lure their customers away. There are several ways to wage a guerrilla offensive:[26]

1. Go after buyer groups that are not important to major rivals.

2. Go after buyers whose loyalty to rival brands is weakest.

3. Focus on areas where rivals are overextended and have spread their resources most thinly (possibilities include going after selected customers located in isolated geographic areas, enhancing delivery schedules at times when competitors' deliveries are running behind, adding to quality when rivals have quality control problems, and boosting technical services when buyers are confused by competitors' proliferation of models and optional features).

4. Make small, scattered, random raids on the leaders' customers with such tactics as occasional lowballing on price (to win a big order or steal a key account).

5. Surprise key rivals with sporadic but intense bursts of promotional activity to pick off buyers who might otherwise have selected rival brands.

6. If rivals employ unfair or unethical competitive tactics and the situation merits it, file legal actions charging antitrust violations, patent infringement, or unfair advertising.

Preemptive Strikes

Preemptive strategies involve moving first to secure an advantageous position that rivals are foreclosed or discouraged from duplicating. What makes a move "preemptive" is its one-of-a-kind nature—whoever strikes first stands to acquire competitive assets that rivals can't readily match. A firm can bolster its competitive capabilities with several preemptive moves:[27]

- Expand production capacity well ahead of market demand in hopes of discouraging rivals from following with expansions of their own. When rivals are "bluffed" out of adding capacity for fear of creating long-term excess supply and having to struggle with the bad economics of underutilized plants, the preemptor stands to win a bigger market share as market demand grows and it has the production capacity to take on new orders.

---

[25]For an interesting study of how small firms can successfully employ guerrilla-style tactics, see Ming-Jer Chen and Donald C. Hambrick, "Speed, Stealth, and Selective Attack: How Small Firms Differ from Large Firms in Competitive Behavior," *Academy of Management Journal* 38, no. 2 (April 1995), pp. 453–82.

[26]For more details, see Ian MacMillan "How Business Strategists Can Use Guerrilla Warfare Tactics," *Journal of Business Strategy* 1, no. 2 (Fall 1980), pp. 63–65; Kathryn R. Harrigan, *Strategic Flexibility* (Lexington, Mass.: Lexington Books, 1985), pp. 30–45; and Liam Fahey, "Guerrilla Strategy: The Hit-and-Run Attack," in Fahey, *The Strategic Management Planning Reader,* pp. 194–97.

[27]The use of preemptive moves is treated comprehensively in Ian MacMillan, "Preemptive Strategies," *Journal of Business Strategy* 14, no. 2 (Fall 1983), pp. 16–26. What follows in this section is based on MacMillan's article.

- Tie up the best (or the most) raw material sources and/or the most reliable, high-quality suppliers with long-term contracts or backward vertical integration. This move can relegate rivals to struggling for second-best supply positions.
- Secure the best geographic locations. An attractive first-mover advantage can often be locked up by moving to obtain the most favorable site along a heavily traveled thoroughfare, at a new interchange or intersection, in a new shopping mall, in a natural beauty spot, close to cheap transportation or raw material supplies or market outlets, and so on.
- Obtain the business of prestigious customers.
- Build a "psychological" image in the minds of consumers that is unique and hard to copy and that establishes a compelling appeal and rallying cry. Examples include Nike's "Just do it" tag line, Avis's well-known "We try harder" theme; Frito-Lay's guarantee to retailers of "99.5% service"; and Prudential's "piece of the rock" image of safety and permanence.
- Secure exclusive or dominant access to the best distributors in an area.

To be successful, a preemptive move doesn't have to totally block rivals from following or copying; it merely needs to give a firm a "prime" position that is not easily circumvented. Fox's stunning four-year, $6.2 billion contract to televise NFL football (a preemptive strike that ousted CBS) represented a bold strategic move to transform Fox into a major TV network alongside ABC, CBS, and NBC. DeBeers became the dominant world distributor of diamonds by buying up the production of most of the important diamond mines. Du Pont's aggressive capacity expansions in titanium dioxide, while not blocking all competitors from expanding, did discourage enough to give it a leadership position in the industry.

Choosing Whom to Attack

Aggressor firms need to analyze which of their rivals to challenge as well as how to outcompete them. Any of four types of firms can make good targets:[28]

1. *Market leaders.* Offensive attacks on a market leader make the best sense when the leader in terms of size and market share is not a "true leader" in serving the market well. Signs of leader vulnerability include unhappy buyers, a product line that is inferior to what several rivals have, a competitive strategy that lacks real strength based on low-cost leadership or differentiation, strong emotional commitment to an aging technology the leader has pioneered, outdated plants and equipment, a preoccupation with diversification into other industries, and mediocre or declining profitability. Offensives to erode the positions of market leaders have real promise when the challenger is able to revamp its value chain or innovate to gain a fresh cost-based or differentiation-based advantage.[29] Attacks on leaders don't have to result in making the aggressor the new leader to be judged successful; a challenger may "win" by simply wresting enough sales from the leader to become a stronger runner-up. Caution is well advised in challenging strong market leaders—there's a significant risk of squandering valuable resources in

---

[28]Kotler, *Marketing Management*, p. 400.
[29]Porter, *Competitive Advantage*, p. 518.

a futile effort or starting a fierce and profitless industrywide battle for market share.

2. *Runner-up firms.* Runner-up firms are an especially attractive target when a challenger's resource strengths and competitive capabilities are well suited to exploiting their weaknesses.

3. *Struggling enterprises that are on the verge of going under.* Challenging a hard-pressed rival in ways that further sap its financial strength and competitive position can weaken its resolve and hasten its exit from the market.

4. *Small local and regional firms.* Because these firms typically have limited expertise and resources, a challenger with broader capabilities is well positioned to raid their biggest and best customers—particularly those who are growing rapidly, have increasingly sophisticated requirements, and may already be thinking about switching to a full-service supplier.

Choosing the Basis for Attack   A firm's strategic offensive should, at a minimum, be tied to its most potent competitive assets—its core competencies, resource strengths, and competitive capabilities. Otherwise the prospects for success are indeed dim. The centerpiece of the offensive can be a new-generation technology, a newly developed competitive capability, an innovative new product, introduction of attractive new performance features, a cost advantage in manufacturing or distribution, or some kind of differentiation advantage. If the challenger's resources and competitive strengths amount to a competitive advantage over the targeted rivals, so much the better.

> *At the very least, an offensive must be tied to a firm's resource strengths; more optimally, it is grounded in competitive advantage.*

USING DEFENSIVE STRATEGIES TO PROTECT COMPETITIVE ADVANTAGE

In a competitive market, all firms are subject to challenges from rivals. Market offensives can come both from new entrants in the industry and from established firms seeking to improve their market positions. The purpose of defensive strategy is to lower the risk of being attacked, weaken the impact of any attack that occurs, and influence challengers to aim their efforts at other rivals. While defensive strategy usually doesn't enhance a firm's competitive advantage, it helps fortify a firm's competitive position, protect its most valuable resources and capabilities from imitation, and sustain whatever competitive advantage it does have.

> *The foremost purpose of defensive strategy is to protect competitive advantage and fortify the firm's competitive position.*

A company can protect its competitive position in several ways. One is trying to block the avenues challengers can take in mounting an offensive. The options include:[30]

- Hiring additional employees to broaden or deepen the company's core competencies or capabilities in key areas (so as to be able to overpower rivals who attempt to imitate its skills and resources).

- Enhancing the flexibility of resource assets and competencies (so that they can be quickly redeployed or adapted to meet changing market conditions),

---

[30]Porter, *Competitive Advantage*, pp. 489–94.

thereby being in a greater state of readiness for new developments than rivals.

- Broadening the firm's product line to close off vacant niches and gaps to would-be challengers.
- Introducing models or brands that match the characteristics challengers' models already have or might have.
- Keeping prices low on models that most closely match competitors' offerings.
- Signing exclusive agreements with dealers and distributors to keep competitors from using the same ones.
- Granting dealers and distributors volume discounts to discourage them from experimenting with other suppliers.
- Offering free or low-cost training to product users.
- Endeavoring to discourage buyers from trying competitors' brands by (1) providing coupons and sample giveaways to buyers most prone to experiment and (2) making early announcements about impending new products or price changes to induce potential buyers to postpone switching.
- Raising the amount of financing provided to dealers and buyers.
- Reducing delivery times for spare parts.
- Lengthening warranty coverages.
- Participating in alternative technologies.
- Protecting proprietary know-how in product design, production technologies, and other value chain activities.
- Contracting for all or most of the output of the best suppliers to make it harder for rivals to obtain parts and components of equal quality.
- Avoiding suppliers that also serve competitors.
- Purchasing natural resource reserves ahead of present needs to keep them from competitors.
- Challenging rivals' products or practices in regulatory proceedings.

Moves such as these not only buttress a firm's present position, they also present competitors with a moving target. Protecting the status quo isn't enough. A good defense entails adjusting quickly to changing industry conditions and, on occasion, being a first-mover to block or preempt moves by would-be aggressors. A mobile defense is preferable to a stationary defense.

A second approach to defensive strategy entails signaling challengers that there is a real threat of strong retaliation if a challenger attacks. The goal is to dissuade challengers from attacking at all or at least divert them to options that are less threatening to the defender. Would-be challengers can be signaled by:[31]

- Publicly announcing management's commitment to maintain the firm's present market share.
- Publicly announcing plans to construct adequate production capacity to meet and possibly surpass the forecasted growth in industry volume.

---

[31]Ibid., pp. 495–97. The listing here is selective; Porter offers a greater number of options.

- Giving out advance information about a new product, technology breakthrough, or the planned introduction of important new brands or models in hopes that challengers will delay moves of their own until they see if the announced actions actually happen.

- Publicly committing the company to a policy of matching competitors' terms or prices.

- Maintaining a war chest of cash and marketable securities.

- Making an occasional strong counterresponse to the moves of weak competitors to enhance the firm's image as a tough defender.

Another way to dissuade rivals is to try to lower the profit inducement for challengers to launch an offensive. When a firm's or industry's profitability is enticingly high, challengers are more willing to tackle high defensive barriers and combat strong retaliation. A defender can deflect attacks, especially from new entrants, by deliberately forgoing some short-run profits and using accounting methods that obscure profitability.

FIRST-MOVER ADVANTAGES AND DISADVANTAGES

When to make a strategic move is often as crucial as *what* move to make. Timing is especially important when *first-mover advantages* or *disadvantages* exist.[32] Being first to initiate a strategic move can have a high payoff when (1) pioneering helps build a firm's image and reputation with buyers, (2) early commitments to supplies of raw materials, new technologies, distribution channels, and so on can produce an absolute cost advantage over rivals, (3) first-time customers remain strongly loyal to pioneering firms in making repeat purchases, and (4) moving first constitutes a preemptive strike, making imitation extra hard or unlikely. The bigger the first-mover advantages, the more attractive that making the first move becomes.

Because of first-mover advantages and disadvantages, competitive advantage is often attached to when *a move is made as well as to* what *move is made.*

However, a wait-and-see approach doesn't always carry a competitive penalty. Being a first-mover may entail greater risks than being a late-mover. First-mover disadvantages (or late-mover advantages) arise when (1) pioneering leadership is much more costly than followership and the leader gains negligible experience curve effects, (2) technological change is so rapid that early investments are soon obsolete (thus allowing following firms to gain the advantages of next-generation products and more efficient processes), (3) it is easy for latecomers to crack the market because customer loyalty to pioneering firms is weak, and (4) the hard-earned skills and know-how developed by the market leaders during the early competitive phase are easily copied or even surpassed by late-movers. Good timing, therefore, is important in deciding whether to be a first-mover, a fast-follower, or a cautious late-mover.

KEY POINTS

The challenge of competitive strategy—whether it be overall low-cost, broad differentiation, best-cost, focused low-cost, or focused differentiation—is to create a competitive advantage for the firm. Competitive advantage comes from positioning a

---

[32]Porter, *Competitive Strategy*, pp. 232–33.

firm in the marketplace so it has an edge in coping with competitive forces and in attracting buyers.

A strategy of trying to be the low-cost provider works well in situations where:

- The industry's product is essentially the same from seller to seller (brand differences are minor).
- Many buyers are price-sensitive and shop for the lowest price.
- There are only a few ways to achieve product differentiation that have much value to buyers.
- Most buyers use the product in the same ways and thus have common user requirements.
- Buyers' costs in switching from one seller or brand to another are low (or even zero).
- Buyers are large and have significant power to negotiate pricing terms.

To achieve a low-cost advantage, a company must become more skilled than rivals in managing the cost drivers and/or it must find innovative cost-saving ways to revamp its value chain. Successful low-cost providers usually achieve their cost advantages by imaginatively and persistently ferreting out cost savings throughout the value chain. They are good at finding ways to drive costs out of their businesses.

Differentiation strategies seek to produce a competitive edge by incorporating attributes and features into a company's product/service offering that rivals don't have or by developing competencies and capabilities that buyers value and that rivals don't have. Anything a firm can do to create buyer value represents a potential basis for differentiation. Successful differentiation is usually keyed to lowering the buyer's cost of using the item, raising the performance the buyer gets, or boosting a buyer's psychological satisfaction. To be sustainable, differentiation usually has to be linked to unique internal expertise, core competencies, and resources that give a company capabilities its rivals can't easily match. Differentiation tied just to unique physical features seldom is lasting because resourceful competitors are adept at cloning, improving on, or finding substitutes for almost any feature or trait that appeals to buyers.

Best-cost provider strategies combine a strategic emphasis on low cost with a strategic emphasis on more than minimal quality, service, features, or performance. The aim is to create competitive advantage by giving buyers more value for the money; this is done by matching close rivals on key quality-service-features-performance attributes and beating them on the costs of incorporating such attributes into the product or service. To be successful with a best-cost provider strategy, a company must have unique expertise in incorporating upscale product or service attributes at a lower cost than rivals; it must have the capability to manage unit costs down and product/service caliber up simultaneously.

The competitive advantage of focusing is earned either by achieving lower costs in serving the target market niche or by developing an ability to offer niche buyers something appealingly different from rival competitors—in other words, it is either *cost-based* or *differentiation-based*. Focusing works best when:

- Buyer needs or uses of the item are diverse.
- No other rival is attempting to specialize in the same target segment.
- A firm lacks the capability to go after a wider part of the total market.

- Buyer segments differ widely in size, growth rate, profitability, and intensity in the five competitive forces, making some segments more attractive than others.

Vertically integrating forward or backward makes strategic sense only if it strengthens a company's position via either cost reduction or creation of a differentiation-based advantage. Otherwise, the drawbacks of vertical integration (increased investment, greater business risk, increased vulnerability to technological changes, and less flexibility in making product changes) outweigh the advantages (better coordination of production flows and technological know-how from stage to stage, more specialized use of technology, greater internal control over operations, greater scale economies, and matching production with sales and marketing). There are ways to achieve the advantages of vertical integration without encountering the drawbacks.

A variety of offensive strategic moves can be used to secure a competitive advantage. Strategic offensives can be aimed either at competitors' strengths or at their weaknesses; they can involve end-runs or simultaneously launched initiatives on many fronts; they can be designed as guerrilla actions or as preemptive strikes; and the target of the offensive can be a market leader, a runner-up firm, or the smallest and/or weakest firms in the industry.

The strategic approaches to defending a company's position usually include (1) making moves that fortify the company's present position, (2) presenting competitors with a moving target to avoid "out of date" vulnerability, and (3) dissuading rivals from even trying to attack.

The timing of strategic moves is important. First-movers sometimes gain strategic advantage; at other times, such as when technology is developing fast, it is cheaper and easier to be a follower than a leader.

SUGGESTED READINGS

Aaker, David A. "Managing Assets and Skills: The Key to a Sustainable Competitive Advantage." *California Management Review* 31, no. 2 (Winter 1989), pp. 91–106.

Barney, Jay B. *Gaining and Sustaining Competitive Advantage.* Reading, Mass.: Addison-Wesley, 1997, especially chapters 6, 7, 9, 10, and 14.

Cohen, William A. "War in the Marketplace." *Business Horizons* 29, no. 2 (March–April 1986), pp. 10–20.

Coyne, Kevin P. "Sustainable Competitive Advantage—What It Is, What It Isn't." *Business Horizons* 29, no. 1 (January–February 1986), pp. 54–61.

D'Aveni, Richard A. *Hypercompetition: The Dynamics of Strategic Maneuvering* (New York: Free Press, 1994), chaps. 1, 2, 3, and 4.

Hamel, Gary, "Strategy as Revolution." *Harvard Business Review* 74, no. 4 (July–August 1996), pp. 69–82.

Harrigan, Kathryn R. "Guerrilla Strategies of Underdog Competitors." *Planning Review* 14, no. 16 (November 1986), pp. 4–11.

———. "Formulating Vertical Integration Strategies." *Academy of Management Review* 9, no. 4 (October 1984), pp. 638–52.

———. "Matching Vertical Integration Strategies to Competitive Conditions." *Strategic Management Journal* 7, no. 6 (November–December 1986), pp. 535–56.

Hout, Thomas, Michael E. Porter, and Eileen Rudden. "How Global Companies Win Out." *Harvard Business Review* 60, no. 5 (September–October 1982), pp. 98–108.

MacMillan, Ian C. "Preemptive Strategies." *Journal of Business Strategy* 14, no. 2 (Fall 1983), pp. 16–26.

_____. "Controlling Competitive Dynamics by Taking Strategic Initiative." *The Academy of Management Executive* 2, no. 2 (May 1988), pp. 111–18.

Porter, Michael E. *Competitive Advantage* (New York: Free Press, 1985), chaps. 3, 4, 5, 7, 14, and 15.

_____. "What Is Strategy." *Harvard Business Review* 74, no. 6 (November–December 1996), pp. 61–78.

Rothschild, William E. "Surprise and the Competitive Advantage." *Journal of Business Strategy* 4, no. 3 (Winter 1984), pp. 10–18.

Schnarrs, Steven P. *Managing Imitation Strategies: How Later Entrants Seize Markets from Pioneers.* New York: Free Press, 1994.

Stuckey, John and David White, "When and When *Not* to Vertically Integrate." *Sloan Management Review* (Spring 1993), pp. 71–83.

Venkatesan, Ravi. "Strategic Outsourcing: To Make or Not to Make." *Harvard Business Review* 70, no. 6 (November–December 1992), pp. 98–107.

6 MATCHING STRATEGY TO A COMPANY'S SITUATION

The task of matching strategy to a company's situation is complicated because of the many external and internal factors managers have to weigh. However, while the number and variety of considerations is necessarily lengthy, the most important drivers shaping a company's best strategic options fall into two broad categories:

- The nature of industry and competitive conditions.
- The firm's own resources and competitive capabilities, market position, and best opportunities.

The dominant *strategy-shaping industry and competitive conditions* revolve around what stage in the life cycle the industry is in (emerging, rapid growth, mature, declining), the industry's structure (fragmented versus concentrated), the relative strength of the five competitive forces, the impact of industry driving forces, and the scope of competitive rivalry (particularly whether the company's market is globally competitive). The pivotal *company-specific considerations* are (1) whether the company is an industry leader, an up-and-coming challenger, a content runner-up, or an also-ran struggling to survive, and (2) the company's set of resource strengths and weaknesses, competitive capabilities, and market opportunities and threats. But even these few categories occur in too many combinations to cover here. However, we can demonstrate what the task of matching strategy to the situation involves by considering the strategy-making challenges that exist in six classic types of industry environments:

1. Competing in emerging and rapidly growing industries.
2. Competing in high-velocity markets.
3. Competing in maturing industries.
4. Competing in stagnant or declining industries.
5. Competing in fragmented industries.
6. Competing in international markets.

and in three classic types of company situations:

1. Firms in industry leadership positions.
2. Firms in runner-up positions.
3. Firms that are competitively weak or crisis-ridden.

> The best strategy for a given firm is ultimately a unique construction reflecting its particular circumstances.
>
> **Michael E. Porter**

> Competing in the marketplace is like war. You have injuries and casualties, and the best strategy wins.
>
> **John Collins**

> You do not choose to become global. The market chooses for you; it forces your hand.
>
> **Alain Gomez**
> *CEO, Thomson, S.A.*

> . . . there's no purely domestic industry anymore.
>
> **Robert Pelosky**
> *Morgan Stanley*

> It is much better to make your own products obsolete than allow a competitor to do it.
>
> **Michael A. Cusamano and Richard W. Selby**

STRATEGIES FOR COMPETING IN EMERGING INDUSTRIES

An emerging industry is one in the early, formative stage. Most companies in an emerging industry are in a start-up mode, adding people, acquiring or constructing facilities, gearing up production, trying to broaden distribution and gain buyer acceptance. Often, there are important product design and technological problems to be worked out as well. Emerging industries present managers with some unique strategy-making challenges:[1]

- Because the market is new and unproven, there are many uncertainties about how it will function, how fast it will grow, and how big it will get. Firms have to scramble to get hard information about competitors, how fast products are gaining buyer acceptance, and users' experiences with the product; because of the industry's newness, there are no organizations or trade associations gathering and distributing information to industry members. The little historical data available is virtually useless in making sales and profit projections because the past is an unreliable guide to the future.

- Much of the technological know-how tends to be proprietary and closely guarded, having been developed in-house by pioneering firms; some firms may file patents to secure competitive advantage.

- Often, there are conflicting judgments about which of several competing technologies will win out or which product attributes will gain the most buyer favor. Until market forces sort these things out, wide differences in product quality and performance are typical and rivalry centers around each firm's efforts to get the market to ratify its own strategic approach to technology, product design, marketing, and distribution.

- Entry barriers tend to be relatively low, even for entrepreneurial start-up companies; well-financed, opportunity-seeking outsiders are likely to enter if the industry has promise for explosive growth.

- Strong experience curve effects often result in significant cost reductions as volume builds.

- Since all buyers are first-time users, the marketing task is to induce initial purchase and to overcome customer concerns about product features, performance reliability, and conflicting claims of rival firms.

- Many potential buyers expect first-generation products to be rapidly improved, so they delay purchase until technology and product design mature.

- Sometimes, firms have trouble securing ample supplies of raw materials and components (until suppliers gear up to meet the industry's needs).

- Many companies, finding themselves short of funds to support needed R&D and get through several lean years until the product catches on, end up merging with competitors or being acquired by financially strong outsiders looking to invest in a growth market.

The two critical strategic issues confronting firms in an emerging industry are (1) how to finance start-up and initial operations until sales take off and (2) what

---

[1]Michael E. Porter, *Competitive Strategy* (New York: Free Press, 1980), pp. 216–23.

Strategic success in an emerging industry calls for bold entrepreneurship, a willingness to pioneer and take risks, an intuitive feel for what buyers will like, quick response to new developments, and opportunistic strategy making.

market segments and competitive advantages to go after in trying to secure a leading position.[2] Competitive strategies keyed either to low cost or differentiation are usually viable. Focusing should be considered when financial resources are limited and the industry has too many technological frontiers to pursue at once. Because an emerging industry has no established "rules of the game" and industry participants employ widely varying strategic approaches, a well-financed firm with a powerful strategy can shape the rules and become the recognized industry leader.

Dealing with all the risks and opportunities of an emerging industry is one of the most challenging business strategy problems. To be successful, companies usually have to pursue one or more of the following avenues:[3]

1. Try to win the early race for industry leadership with bold entrepreneurship and a creative strategy. Broad or focused differentiation strategies keyed to product superiority typically offer the best chance for early competitive advantage.

2. Push to perfect the technology, to improve product quality, and to develop attractive performance features.

3. As technological uncertainty clears and a dominant technology emerges, adopt it quickly. (However, while there's merit in trying to be the industry standard bearer on technology and to pioneer the "dominant product design," firms have to beware of betting too heavily on their own preferred technological approach or product design—especially when there are many competing technologies, R&D is costly, and technological developments can quickly move in surprising new directions.)

4. Form strategic alliances with key suppliers to gain access to specialized skills, technological capabilities, and critical materials or components.

5. Try to capture any first-mover advantages by commiting early to promising technologies, allying with the most capable suppliers, expanding product selection, improving styling, capturing experience curve effects, and getting well-positioned in new distribution channels.

6. Pursue new customer groups, new user applications, and entry into new geographical areas (perhaps utilizing joint ventures if financial resources are constrained).

7. Make it easier and cheaper for first-time buyers to try the industry's first-generation product. Then as the product becomes familiar to a wide portion of the market, begin to shift the advertising emphasis from creating product awareness to increasing frequency of use and building brand loyalty.

8. Use price cuts to attract the next layer of price-sensitive buyers.

9. Expect well-financed outsiders to move in with aggressive strategies as industry sales start to take off and the perceived risk of investing in the industry lessens. Try to prepare for the entry of powerful competitors by forecasting *(a)* who the probable entrants will be (based on present and future entry barriers) and *(b)* the types of strategies they are likely to employ.

---

[2]Charles W. Hofer and Dan Schendel, *Strategy Formulation: Analytical Concepts* (St. Paul, Minn.: West Publishing, 1978), pp. 164–65.

[3]Phillip Kotler, *Marketing Management*, 5th ed. (Englewood Cliffs, N.J.: Prentice-Hall, 1984), p. 366, and Porter, *Competitive Strategy*, chapter 10.

The short-term value of winning the early race for growth and market share leadership has to be balanced against the longer-range need to build a durable competitive edge and a defendable market position.[4] New entrants, attracted by the growth and profit potential, may crowd the market. Aggressive newcomers, aspiring to industry leadership, can quickly become major players by acquiring and merging the operations of weaker competitors. Young companies in fast-growing markets face three strategic hurdles: (1) managing their own rapid expansion, (2) defending against competitors trying to horn in on their success, and (3) building a competitive position extending beyond their initial product or market. Up-and-coming companies can help their cause by selecting knowledgeable members for their boards of directors, by hiring entrepreneurial managers with experience in guiding young businesses through the start-up and takeoff stages, by concentrating on outinnovating the competition, and perhaps by merging with or acquiring another firm to gain added expertise and a stronger resource base.

STRATEGIES FOR COMPETING IN HIGH VELOCITY MARKETS

Some companies find themselves in markets characterized by rapid-fire technological change, short product life cycles (because of the pace with which next-generation products are being introduced) entry of important new rivals, frequent launches of new competitive moves by rivals (including mergers and acquisitions to build a stronger, if not dominant, market position), and rapidly evolving customer requirements and expectations—all occurring at once. High-velocity change is the prevailing condition in microelectronics, in personal computer hardware and software, in telecommunications, in the whole cyberspace arena of the Internet and company intranets, and in health care.

High-velocity market environments pose a big strategy-making challenge.[5] Since news of this or that important competitive development is a daily happening, it is an imposing task just to monitor, assess, and react to unfolding events. Competitive success in fast-changing markets tends to hinge on building the following elements into company strategies:

1. *Invest aggressively in R&D to stay on the leading edge of technological know-how.* Having the expertise and capability to advance the state of technological know-how and translate the advances into innovative new products (and to remain close on the heels of whatever advances and features are pioneered by rivals) is a necessity in high-tech markets. But it is often important to focus the R&D effort in a few critical areas not only to avoid stretching the company's resources too thinly but also to deepen the firm's expertise, master the technology, fully capture experience curve effects, and become the dominant leader in a particular technology or product category.[6]

---

[4]Hofer and Schendel, *Strategy Formulation*, pp. 164–65.

[5]The strategic issues companies must address in fast-changing market environments are thoroughly explored in Richard A. D'Aveni, *Hyper-Competition: Managing the Dynamics of Strategic Manuevering* (New York: Free Press, 1994). See, also, Richard A. D'Aveni, "Coping with Hypercompetition: Utilizing the New 7S's Framework," *Academy of Management Executive,* 9, no. 3 (August 1995), pp. 45–56 and Bala Chakravarthy, "A New Strategy Framework for Coping with Turbulence," *Sloan Management Review* (Winter 1997), pp. 69–82.

[6]For insight into building competitive advantage through R&D and technological innovation, see Shaker A. Zahra, Sarah Nash, and Deborah J. Bickford, "Transforming Technological Pioneering into Competitive Advantage," *Academy of Management Executive,* 9, no. 1 (February 1995), pp. 32–41.

2. *Develop the organizational capability to respond quickly to important new events.* Quick reaction times are essential because it is impossible to predict or foresee all of the changes that will occur. Moreover, a competitor has to alertly and swiftly shift resources to respond to the actions of rivals or new technological developments or evolving customer needs or opportunities to move against slower competitiors. Resource flexibility tends to be a key success factor, as does the ability to *adapt* existing competencies and capabilities, to *create new competencies and capabilities*, and to *match rivals* on whatever technological approaches and product features they are able to pioneer successfully. Absent such organizational capabilities as speed, agility, flexibility, and innovativeness in finding new and better ways to please customers, a company soon loses its competitiveness. Being a fast follower, if not the first mover, is critical.

3. *Rely on strategic partnerships with outside suppliers and with companies making tie-in products to perform those activities in the total industry value chain where they have specialized expertise and capabilities.* In many high-velocity industries, technology is branching off to create so many new paths and product categories that no company has the resources and competencies to pursue them all. Specialization (to promote the necessary technical depth) and focus strategies (to preserve organizational agility and leverage the firm's expertise) are essential. Companies build their competitive position not just by strengthening their own resource base but also by partnering with suppliers making state-of-the-art parts and components and by collaborating with the leading makers of tie-in products. For example, the makers of personal computers rely heavily on the makers of faster chips, the makers of monitors and screens, the makers of hard disks and disk drives, and software developers to be the source of most of the innovative advances in PCs. The makers of PCs concentrate on *assembly*— none have integrated backward into parts and components, because the most effective way to provide a state-of-the-art product is to outsource the latest, most advanced components from technologically sophisticated suppliers. An outsourcing strategy also allows a company the flexibility to replace suppliers that fall behind on technology or product features or that cease to be competitive on price. Moreover, computer software developers collaborate with the various hardware manufacturers to have cutting-edge software products ready for the market when next-generation hardware products are introduced.

> *In fast-paced markets, in-depth expertise, speed, agility, innovativeness, opportunism, and resource flexibility are critical organizational capabilities.*

When a fast-evolving market environment entails many technological areas and product categories, competitors have little choice but to employ some type of focus strategy and concentrate on being the leader in a particular category. Cutting-edge know-how and first-to-market capabilities are very valuable competitive assets. Moreover, the pace of competition demands that a company have quick reaction times and flexible, adaptable resources—organizational agility is a huge asset. So is the ability to collaborate with suppliers, effectively combining and meshing their resources with the firm's own resources. The challenge is to strike a good balance between building a rich internal resource base that, on the one hand, keeps the firm from being at the mercy of its suppliers and allies and, on the other hand, maintains organizational agility by relying on the resources and expertise of outsiders.

STRATEGIES FOR COMPETING IN MATURING INDUSTRIES

Rapid growth or fast-paced market change doesn't go on forever. However, the transition to a slower-growth, maturing industry environment does not begin on an easily predicted schedule, and the transition can be forestalled by further technological advances, product innovations, or other driving forces that keep rejuvenating market demand. Nonetheless, when growth rates do slacken, the transition to market maturity usually produces fundamental changes in the industry's competitive environment:[7]

1. *Slowing growth in buyer demand generates more head-to-head competition for market share.* Firms that want to continue on a rapid-growth track start looking for ways to take customers away from competitors. Outbreaks of price-cutting, increased advertising, and other aggressive tactics to gain market share are common.

2. *Buyers become more sophisticated, often driving a harder bargain on repeat purchases.* Since buyers have experience with the product and are familiar with competing brands, they are better able to evaluate different brands and can use their knowledge to negotiate a better deal with sellers.

3. *Competition often produces a greater emphasis on cost and service.* As sellers all begin to offer the product attributes buyers prefer, buyer choices increasingly depend on which seller offers the best combination of price and service.

4. *Firms have a "topping out" problem in adding production capacity.* Slower rates of industry growth mean slowdowns in capacity expansion. Each firm has to monitor rivals' expansion plans and time its own capacity additions to minimize industry oversupply. With slower industry growth, the mistake of adding too much capacity too soon can adversely affect company profits well into the future.

5. *Product innovation and new end-use applications are harder to come by.* Producers find it increasingly difficult to create appealing new performance features, find further uses for the product, and sustain buyer excitement.

6. *International competition increases.* Growth-minded domestic firms start to seek out sales opportunities in foreign markets. Some companies, looking for ways to cut costs, relocate plants to countries with lower wage rates. Greater product standardization and diffusion of technology reduce entry barriers and make it possible for enterprising foreign companies to become serious market contenders in more countries. Industry leadership passes to companies that build strong competitive positions in most of the world's major geographic markets and win the biggest global market shares.

7. *Industry profitability falls temporarily or permanently.* Slower growth, increased competition, more sophisticated buyers, and occasional periods of overcapacity put pressure on industry profit margins. Weaker, less-efficient firms are usually the hardest hit.

8. *Stiffening competition leads to mergers and acquisitions among former competitors, drives the weakest firms out of the industry, and, in general, produces industry consolidation.* Inefficient firms and firms with weak competitive strategies can achieve respectable results in a fast-growing industry with booming sales. But the intensifying competition that accompanies industry maturity exposes competitive weakness and throws second- and third-tier competitors into a survival-of-the-fittest contest.

---

[7]Porter, *Competitive Strategy*, pp. 238–40.

As the new competitive character of industry maturity begins to hit full force, there are several strategic moves that firms can initiate to strengthen their positions.[8]

Pruning the Product Line   A wide selection of models, features, and product options has competitive value during the growth stage when buyers' needs are still evolving. But such variety can become too costly as price competition stiffens and profit margins are squeezed. Maintaining too many product versions prevents firms from achieving the economies of long production runs. In addition, the prices of slow-selling versions may not cover their true costs. Pruning marginal products from the line lowers costs and permits more concentration on items whose margins are highest and/or where the firm has a competitive advantage.

In a maturing industry, strategic emphasis needs to be on efficiency-increasing, profit-preserving measures: pruning the product line, improving production methods, reducing costs, accelerating sales promotion efforts, expanding internationally, and acquiring distressed competitors.

More Emphasis on Process Innovations   Efforts to "reinvent" the manufacturing process can have a fourfold payoff: lower costs, better production quality, greater capability to turn out multiple or customized product versions, and shorter design-to-market cycles. Process innovation can involve mechanizing high-cost activities, revamping production lines to improve labor efficiency, building flexibility into the assembly process so that customized product versions can be easily produced, creating self-directed work teams, reengineering the manufacturing portion of the value chain, and increasing use of advanced technology (robotics, computerized controls, and automatic guided vehicles). Japanese firms have become remarkably adept at using manufacturing process innovation to become lower-cost producers of higher-quality products.

A Stronger Focus on Cost Reduction   Stiffening price competition gives firms extra incentive to reduce unit costs. Such efforts can cover a broad front: Companies can push suppliers for better prices, switch to lower-priced components, develop more economical product designs, cut low-value activities out of the value chain, streamline distribution channels, and reengineer internal processes.

Increasing Sales to Present Customers   In a mature market, growing by taking customers away from rivals may not be as appealing as expanding sales to existing customers. Strategies to increase purchases by existing customers can involve providing complementary items and ancillary services, and finding more ways for customers to use the product. Convenience food stores, for example, have boosted average sales per customer by adding video rentals, automatic bank tellers, and deli counters.

Purchasing Rival Firms at Bargain Prices   Sometimes the facilities and assets of distressed rivals can be acquired cheaply. Bargain-priced acquisitions can help create a low-cost position if they also present opportunities for greater operating efficiency. In addition, an acquired firm's customer base can provide expanded market coverage. The most desirable acquisitions are those that enhance the acquiring firm's competitive strength.

Expanding Internationally   As its domestic market matures, a firm may seek to enter foreign markets where attractive growth potential exists and where competitive

---

[8]The following discussion draws on Porter, *Competitive Strategy* pp. 241–46.

pressures are not especially strong. Several manufacturers in highly industrialized nations found international expansion attractive because equipment no longer suitable for domestic operations could be used in plants in less-developed foreign markets (a condition that lowered entry costs). Such possibilities arise when (1) foreign buyers have less sophisticated needs and have simpler, old-fashioned, end-use applications, and (2) foreign competitors are smaller, less formidable, and do not employ the latest production technology. Strategies to expand internationally also make sense when a domestic firm's skills, reputation, and product are readily transferable to foreign markets. Even though the U.S. market for soft drinks is mature, Coca-Cola has remained a growth company by upping its efforts to penetrate foreign markets where soft-drink sales are expanding rapidly.

Building New or More Flexible Capabilities   The stiffening pressures of competition in a maturing or already mature market can often be combatted by strengthening the company's resource base and competitive capabilities. This can mean adding new competencies or capabilities, deepening existing competencies to make them harder to imitate, or striving to make core competencies more flexible and adaptable to changing customer requirements and expectations. Microsoft has responded to competitors' challenges by expanding its already large cadre of talented programmers. Chevron has developed a best-practices discovery team and a best-practices resource map to enhance its speed and effectiveness in transferring efficiency improvements in one oil refinery to its other refineries.

Strategic Pitfalls

Perhaps the greatest strategic mistake a company can make as an industry matures is steering a middle course between low cost, differentiation, and focusing—blending efforts to achieve low cost with efforts to incorporate differentiating features and efforts to focus on a limited target market. Such strategic compromises typically result in a firm ending up "stuck in the middle" with a fuzzy strategy, too little commitment to winning a competitive advantage based on either low cost or differentiation, an average image with buyers, and little chance of springing into the ranks of the industry leaders. Other strategic pitfalls include being slow to adapt existing competencies and capabilities to changing customer expectations, concentrating more on short-term profitability than on building or maintaining long-term competitive position, waiting too long to respond to price-cutting, getting caught with too much capacity as growth slows, overspending on marketing efforts to boost sales growth, and failing to pursue cost reduction soon enough and aggressively enough.

One of the biggest mistakes a firm can make in a maturing industry is pursuing a compromise between low-cost, differentiation, and focusing such that it ends up with a fuzzy strategy, an ill-defined market identity, no competitive advantage, and little prospect of becoming an industry leader.

STRATEGIES FOR FIRMS IN STAGNANT OR DECLINING INDUSTRIES

Many firms operate in industries where demand is barely growing, flat, or even declining. Although harvesting the business to obtain the greatest cash flow, selling out, or preparing for close-down are obvious end-game strategies for uncommitted competitors with dim long-term prospects, strong competitors may be able to achieve good performance in a stagnant market environment.[9] Stagnant demand by itself is not enough to make an industry unattractive. Selling out may or may not be practical, and closing operations is always a last resort. Businesses competing in slow-growth/declining industries have to accept the difficult realities of a stagnating market environment and resign themselves to performance targets consistent with available market opportunities. Cash flow and return-on-investment criteria are more appropriate than growth-oriented performance measures, but sales and market share growth are by no means ruled out. Strong competitors may be able to take sales from weaker rivals, and the acquisition or exit of weaker firms creates opportunities for the remaining companies to capture greater market share.

Achieving competitive advantage in stagnant or declining industries usually requires pursuing one of three competitive approaches: focusing on growing market segments within the industry, differentiating on the basis of better quality and frequent product innovation, or becoming a lower cost producer.

In general, companies that succeed in stagnant industries employ one of three strategic themes:[10]

1. *Pursue a focused strategy by identifying, creating, and exploiting the growth segments within the industry.* Stagnant or declining markets, like other markets, are composed of numerous segments or niches. Frequently, one or more of these segments is growing rapidly, despite stagnation in the industry as a whole. An astute competitor who is first to concentrate on the attractive growth segments can escape stagnating sales and profits and possibly achieve competitive advantage in the target segments.

2. *Stress differentiation based on quality improvement and product innovation.* Either enhanced quality or innovation can rejuvenate demand by creating important new growth segments or inducing buyers to trade up. Successful product innovation opens up an avenue for competing besides meeting or beating rivals' prices. Such differentiation can have the additional advantage of being difficult and expensive for rival firms to imitate.

3. *Work diligently and persistently to drive costs down.* When increases in sales cannot be counted on to increase earnings, companies can improve profit margins and return on investment by stressing continuous productivity improvement and cost reduction year after year. Potential cost-saving actions include (a) outsourcing functions and activities that can be performed more cheaply by outsiders, (b) completely redesigning internal business processes, (c) consolidating underutilized production facilities, (d) adding more distribution channels to ensure the unit volume needed for low-cost production, (e) closing low-volume, high-cost distribution outlets, and (f) cutting marginally beneficial activities out of the value chain.

These three strategic themes are not mutually exclusive.[11] Introducing new, innovative versions of a product can *create* a fast-growing market segment. Similarly, relentless pursuit of greater operating efficiencies permits price reductions that can bring price-conscious buyers back into the market. Note that all three themes are spin-offs of the generic competitive strategies, adjusted to fit the circumstances of a tough industry environment.

The most attractive declining industries are those in which sales are eroding only slowly, there is large built-in demand, and some profitable niches remain. The most

---

[9]R. G. Hamermesh and S. B. Silk, "How to Compete in Stagnant Industries," *Harvard Business Review* 57, no. 5 (September–October 1979), p. 161.

[10]Ibid., p. 162.

[11]Ibid., p. 165.

ILLUSTRATION CAPSULE 20   Yamaha's Strategy in the Piano Industry

For some years now, worldwide demand for pianos has been declining—in the mid-1980s the decline was 10 percent annually. Modern-day parents have not put the same stress on music lessons for their children as prior generations of parents did. In an effort to see if it could revitalize its piano business, Yamaha conducted a market research survey to learn what use was being made of pianos in households that owned one. The survey revealed that the overwhelming majority of the 40 million pianos in American, European, and Japanese households were seldom used. In most cases, the reasons the piano had been purchased no longer applied. Children had either stopped taking piano lessons or were grown and had left the household; adult household members played their pianos sparingly, if at all—only a small percentage were accomplished piano players. Most pianos were serving as a piece of fine furniture and were in good condition despite not being tuned regularly. The survey

also confirmed that the income levels of piano owners were well above average.

Yamaha's piano strategists saw the idle pianos in these upscale households as a potential market opportunity. The strategy that emerged entailed marketing an attachment that would convert the piano into an old-fashioned automatic player piano capable of playing a wide number of selections recorded on 3.5-inch floppy disks (the same kind used to store computer data). The player piano conversion attachment carried a $2,500 price tag. Concurrently, Yamaha introduced Disklavier, an upright acoustic player piano model that could play *and record* performances up to 90 minutes long; the Disklavier retailed for $8,000. At year-end 1988 Yamaha offered 30 prerecorded disks for $29.95 each and since then has released a continuing stream of new selections. Yamaha believed that these new high-tech products held potential to reverse the downtrend in piano sales.

---

common strategic mistakes companies make in stagnating or declining markets are (1) getting trapped in a profitless war of attrition, (2) diverting too much cash out of the business too quickly (thus further eroding performance), and (3) being overly optimistic about the industry's future and spending too much on improvements in anticipation that things will get better.

Illustration Capsule 20 describes the creative approach taken by Yamaha to reverse declining market demand for pianos.

STRATEGIES FOR COMPETING IN FRAGMENTED INDUSTRIES

A number of industries are populated by hundreds, even thousands, of small and medium-sized companies, many privately held and none with a substantial share of total industry sales.[12] The standout competitive feature of a fragmented industry is the absence of market leaders with king-sized market shares or widespread buyer recognition. Examples of fragmented industries include book publishing, landscaping and plant nurseries, real estate development, banking, mail-order catalog sales, computer software development, custom printing, kitchen cabinets, trucking, auto repair, restaurants and fast food, public accounting, apparel manufacture and apparel retailing, paperboard boxes, log homes, hotels and motels, and furniture.

Any of several reasons can account for why the supply side of an industry is fragmented:

- Low entry barriers allow small firms to enter quickly and cheaply.
- The technologies embodied in the industry's value chain are exploding into so many new areas and along so many different paths that specialization is essential just to keep abreast in any one area of expertise.

---

[12]This section is summarized from Porter, *Competitive Strategy*, chapter 9.

- An absence of large-scale production economies permits small companies to compete on an equal cost footing with larger firms.
- Buyers require relatively small quantities of customized products (as in business forms, interior design, and advertising); because demand for any particular product version is small, sales volumes are not adequate to support producing, distributing, or marketing on a scale that yields advantages to a large firm.
- The market for the industry's product/service is becoming more global, allowing competitors in more and more countries to be drawn into the same competitive market arena (as in apparel manufacture).
- Market demand is so large and so diverse that it takes very large numbers of firms to accommodate buyer requirements (restaurants, energy, apparel, computer products and computer software).
- The industry is so new that no firms have yet developed their resource base and competitive capabilities to command a significant market share.

Some fragmented industries consolidate naturally as they mature. The stiffer competition that accompanies slower growth shakes out weak, inefficient firms leading to a greater concentration of larger, more visible sellers. Others remain atomistically competitive because it is inherent in the nature of their businesses. And still others remain stuck in a fragmented state because existing firms lack the resources or ingenuity to employ a strategy powerful enough to drive industry consolidation.

Competitive rivalry in fragmented industries can vary from moderately strong to fierce. Low barriers make entry of new competitors an ongoing threat. Competition from substitutes may or may not be a major factor. The relatively small size of companies in fragmented industries puts them in a weak position to bargain with powerful suppliers and buyers, although sometimes they can become members of a cooperative, using their combined leverage to negotiate better sales and purchase terms. In such an environment, the best a firm can expect is to cultivate a loyal customer base and grow a bit faster than the industry average. Competitive strategies based either on low cost or product differentiation are viable unless the industry's product is highly standardized or a commodity (like sand, concrete blocks, paperboard boxes). Focusing on a well-defined market niche or buyer segment usually offers more competitive advantage potential than striving for broad market appeal. Suitable options in a fragmented industry include

- *Constructing and operating "formula" facilities*—This strategic approach is frequently employed in restaurant and retailing businesses operating at multiple locations. It involves constructing standardized outlets in favorable locations at minimum cost and then polishing to a science how to operate all outlets in a superefficient manner. McDonald's, Home Depot, and 7-Eleven have pursued this strategy to perfection, earning excellent profits in their respective industries.
- *Becoming a low-cost operator*—When price competition is intense and profit margins are under constant pressure, companies can stress no-frills operations featuring low overhead, high-productivity/low-cost labor, lean capital budgets, and dedicated pursuit of total operating efficiency. Successful low-cost producers in a fragmented industry can play the price-cutting game and still earn profits above the industry average.
- *Increasing customer value through integration*—Backward or forward integration into additional value chain activities may contain opportunities

to lower costs or enhance the value provided to customers. One example is a supplier taking on the manufacture of several related parts, assembling them into a modular component system, and providing the ultimate manufacturer with something that is readily inserted or attached to the final product. Another example is a manufacturer opening a series of regional distribution centers to provide overnight delivery to area retailers.

- *Specializing by product type*—When a fragmented industry's products include a range of styles or services, a strategy to focus on one product/service category can be very effective. Some firms in the furniture industry specialize in only one furniture type such as brass beds, rattan and wicker, lawn and garden, or early American. In auto repair, companies specialize in transmission repair, body work, or speedy oil changes.

> *In fragmented industries competitors usually have wide enough strategic latitude to (1) compete broadly or focus and (2) pursue either a low-cost or a differentiation-based competitive advantage.*

- *Specialization by customer type*—A firm can stake out a market niche in a fragmented industry by catering to those customers (1) who are interested in unique product attributes, customized features, carefree service, or other "extras," (2) who are the least price sensitive, or (3) who have the least bargaining leverage (because they are small in size or purchase small amounts).

- *Focusing on a limited geographic area*—Even though a firm in a fragmented industry can't win a big share of total industrywide sales, it can still try to dominate a local/regional area. Concentrating company efforts on a limited territory can produce greater operating efficiency, speed delivery and customer services, promote strong brand awareness, and permit saturation advertising, while avoiding the diseconomies of stretching operations out over a much wider area. Supermarkets, banks, and sporting goods retailers successfully operate multiple locations within a limited geographic area.

In fragmented industries, firms generally have the strategic freedom to pursue broad or narrow market targets and low-cost or differentiation-based competitive advantages. Many different strategic approaches can exist side by side.

STRATEGIES FOR COMPETING IN INTERNATIONAL MARKETS

Companies are motivated to expand into international markets for any of several reasons:

- *To seek new customers for their products or services*—Selling in additional country markets can propel higher revenues and profits and provide an avenue for sustaining attractively high rates of growth over the long-term.

- *A competitive need to achieve lower costs*—Many companies are driven to sell in more than one country because the sales volume in their own domestic markets is not large enough to fully capture manufacturing economies of scale; moreover, locating plants or other operations in countries where labor, materials, or technology costs are lower can often substantially improve a firm's cost competitiveness.

- *To capitalize on its competencies and resource strengths*—A company with valuable competencies and capabilities may be able to leverage them into a position of advantage in foreign markets as well as in its own domestic market.

- *To obtain valuable natural resource deposits in other countries*—In natural resource-based industries (like oil and gas, minerals, rubber, and lumber), companies often find it necessary to pursue access to attractive raw material supplies in foreign countries.

- *To spread its business risk across a wider market base*—A company spreads business risk by operating in a number of different foreign countries rather than depending entirely on operations in its own domestic market.

Whatever the motivation for foreign country operations, strategies for competing internationally have to be situation-driven. Special attention has to be paid to how national markets differ in buyer needs and habits, distribution channels, long-run growth potential, driving forces, and competitive pressures. Aside from the basic market differences from country to country, four other situational considerations are unique to international operations: cost variations among countries, fluctuating exchange rates, host government trade policies, and the pattern of international competition.

Competing in international markets poses a bigger strategy-making challenge than competing in only the company's home market.

Country-to-Country Cost Variations   Differences in wage rates, worker productivity, inflation rates, energy costs, tax rates, government regulations, and the like create sizable variations in manufacturing costs from country to country. Plants in some countries have major manufacturing cost advantages because of lower input costs (especially labor), relaxed government regulations, or unique natural resources. In such cases, the low-cost countries become principal production sites, with most of the output being exported to markets in other parts of the world. Companies with facilities in these locations (or that source their products from contract manufacturers in these countries) have a competitive advantage. The competitive role of low manufacturing costs is most evident in low-wage countries like Taiwan, South Korea, China, Singapore, Malaysia, Vietnam, Mexico, and Brazil, which have become production havens for goods with high labor content.

Another important manufacturing cost consideration in international competition is the concept of *manufacturing share* as distinct from brand share or market share. For example, although less than 40 percent of all the video recorders sold in the United States carry a Japanese brand, Japanese companies do 100 percent of the manufacturing—all sellers source their video recorders from Japanese manufacturers.[13] In microwave ovens, Japanese brands have less than a 50 percent share of the U.S. market, but the manufacturing share of Japanese companies is over 85 percent. *Manufacturing share is significant because it is a better indicator than market share of the industry's low-cost producer.* In a globally competitive industry where some competitors are intent on global dominance, being the worldwide low-cost producer is a powerful competitive advantage. Achieving low-cost producer status often requires a company to have the largest worldwide manufacturing share, with production centralized in one or a few superefficient plants. However, important marketing and distribution economies associated with multinational operations can also yield low-cost leadership.

---

[13]C. K. Prahalad and Yves L. Doz, *The Multinational Mission* (New York: Free Press, 1987), p. 60.

Fluctuating Exchange Rates   The volatility of exchange rates greatly complicates the issue of geographic cost advantages. Currency exchange rates often fluctuate as much as 20 to 40 percent annually. Changes of this magnitude can totally wipe out a country's low-cost advantage or transform a former high-cost location into a competitive-cost location. A strong U.S. dollar makes it more attractive for U.S. companies to manufacture in foreign countries. A falling dollar can eliminate much of the cost advantage that foreign manufacturers have over U.S. manufacturers and can even prompt foreign companies to establish production plants in the United States.

Host Government Trade Policies   National governments enact all kinds of measures affecting international trade and the operation of foreign companies in their markets. Host governments may impose import tariffs and quotas, set local content requirements on goods made inside their borders by foreign-based companies, and regulate the prices of imported goods. In addition, outsiders may face a web of regulations regarding technical standards, product certification, prior approval of capital spending projects, withdrawal of funds from the country, and minority (sometimes majority) ownership by local citizens. Some governments also provide subsidies and low-interest loans to domestic companies to help them compete against foreign-based companies. Other governments, anxious to obtain new plants and jobs, offer foreign companies a helping hand in the form of subsidies, privileged market access, and technical assistance.

Multicountry Competition versus Global Competition

There are important differences in the patterns of international competition from industry to industry.[14] At one extreme is *multicountry* or *multidomestic competition* where each country market is self-contained—buyers in different countries have different expectations and like different styling and features, competition in each national market is independent of competition in other national markets, and the set of rivals competing in each country differ from place to place. For example, there is a banking industry in France, one in Brazil, and one in Japan, but market conditions and buyer expectations in banking differ markedly among the three countries, the lead banking competitors in France differ from those in Brazil or in Japan, and the competitive battle going on among the leading banks in France is unrelated to the rivalry taking place in Brazil or Japan. Because each country market is self-contained in multicountry competition, a company's reputation, customer base, and competitive position in one nation have little or no bearing on its ability to compete successfully in another. As a consequence, the power of a company's strategy in any one nation and any competitive advantage it yields are largely confined to that nation and do not spill over to other countries where it operates. *With multicountry competition there is no "international market," just a collection of self-contained country markets*. Industries characterized by multicountry competition include beer, life insurance, apparel, metals fabrication, many types of food products (coffee, cereals, canned goods, frozen foods), and many types of retailing.

At the other extreme is *global competition* where prices and competitive conditions across country markets are strongly linked together and the term international

> **Multicountry** *(or multidomestic) competition exists when competition in one national market is independent of competition in another national market—there is no "international market," just a collection of self-contained country markets.*

[14]Michael E. Porter, *The Competitive Advantage of Nations* (New York: Free Press, 1990), pp. 53–54.

or global market has true meaning. In a global industry, a company's competitive position in one country both affects and is affected by its position in other countries. Rival companies compete against each other in many different countries, but especially so in countries where sales volumes are large and where having a competitive presence is strategically important to building a strong global position in the industry. In global competition, a firm's overall advantage grows out of its entire worldwide operations; the competitive advantage it enjoys at its home base are linked to advantages growing out of its operations in other countries (having plants in low-wage countries, a capability to serve corporate customers with multinational operations of their own, and a brand reputation that is transferable from country to country). *A global competitor's market strength is directly proportional to its portfolio of country-based competitive advantages.* Global competition exists in automobiles, television sets, tires, telecommunications equipment, copiers, watches, and commercial aircraft.

> **Global competition** *exists when competitive conditions across national markets are linked strongly enough to form a true international market and when leading competitors compete head-to-head in many different countries.*
>
> *In multicountry competition, rival firms vie for national market leadership. In globally competitive industries, rival firms vie for worldwide leadership.*

An industry can have segments that are globally competitive and segments where competition is country by country.[15] In the hotel-motel industry, for example, the low- and medium-priced segments are characterized by multicountry competition because competitors mainly serve travelers within the same country. In the business and luxury segments, however, competition is more globalized. Companies like Nikki, Marriott, Sheraton, and Hilton have hotels at many international locations and use worldwide reservation systems and common quality and service standards to gain marketing advantages with frequent travelers.

In lubricants, the marine engine segment is globally competitive because ships move from port to port and require the same oil everywhere they stop. Brand reputations have a global scope, and successful marine engine lubricant producers (Exxon, British Petroleum, and Shell) operate globally. In automotive motor oil, however, multicountry competition dominates. Countries have different weather conditions and driving patterns, production is subject to limited scale economies, shipping costs are high, and retail distribution channels differ markedly from country to country. Thus domestic firms, like Quaker State and Pennzoil in the United States and Castrol in Great Britain, can be leaders in their home markets without competing globally.

All these considerations, along with the obvious cultural and political differences between countries, shape a company's strategic approach in international markets.

Types of International Strategies

A company participating in international markets has seven strategic options:

1. *License foreign firms to use the company's technology or produce and distribute the company's products* (in which case international revenues will equal the royalty income from the licensing agreement).

2. *Maintain a national (one-country) production base and export goods to foreign markets* using either company-owned or foreign-controlled forward distribution channels.

---

[15]Ibid., p. 61.

3. *Follow a multicountry strategy,* varying the company's strategic approach (perhaps a little, perhaps a lot) from country to country in accordance with differing buyer needs and competitive conditions. While the company may use the same basic competitive theme (low cost, differentiation, best cost) in most or all country markets, product attributes are customized to fit local buyers' preferences and expectations and the target customer base may vary from broad in some countries to narrowly focused in others. Furthermore, strategic moves in one country are made independent of those in another country; cross-country strategy coordination is a lower priority than matching company strategy to host-country market and competitive conditions.

4. *Follow a global low-cost strategy* and strive to be a low-cost supplier to buyers in most or all strategically important markets of the world. The company's strategic efforts are coordinated worldwide to achieve a low-cost position relative to all competitors.

5. *Follow a global differentiation strategy* whereby the company's product is differentiated on the same attributes in all countries to create a globally consistent image and a consistent competitive theme. The firm's strategic moves are coordinated across countries to achieve consistent differentiation worldwide.

6. *Follow a global focus strategy,* serving the same identifiable niche in each of many strategically important country markets. Strategic actions are coordinated globally to achieve a consistent low-cost or differentiation-based competitive approach in the target niche worldwide.

7. *Follow a global best-cost provider strategy* and strive to match rivals on the same product attributes and beat them on cost and price *worldwide*. The firm's strategic moves in each country market are coordinated to achieve a consistent best-cost position worldwide.

Licensing makes sense when a firm with valuable technical know-how or a unique patented product has neither the internal capability nor the resources to compete effectively in foreign markets. By licensing the technology or the production rights to foreign-based firms, the firm at least realizes income from royalties.

Using domestic plants as a production base for exporting goods to foreign markets is an excellent initial strategy for pursuing international sales. It minimizes both risk and capital requirements, and it is a conservative way to test the international waters. With an export strategy, a manufacturer can limit its involvement in foreign markets by contracting with foreign wholesalers experienced in importing to handle the entire distribution and marketing function in their countries or regions. If it is better to maintain control over these functions, a manufacturer can establish its own distribution and sales organizations in some or all of the target foreign markets. Either way, a firm minimizes its direct investments in foreign countries because of its home-based production and export strategy. Such strategies are commonly favored by Korean and Italian companies—products are designed and manufactured at home and only marketing activities are performed abroad. Whether such a strategy can be pursued successfully over the long run hinges on the relative cost competitiveness of a home-country production base. In some industries, firms gain additional scale economies and experience curve benefits from centralizing production in one or several giant plants whose output capability exceeds demand in any one country market; obviously, to capture such economies a company must export to markets in other countries. However, this strategy is vulnerable when manufacturing costs in the home country are much higher than in foreign countries where rivals have plants. The pros and cons of a multicountry strategy versus a global strategy are a bit more complex.

A Multicountry Strategy or a Global Strategy?

The need for a multicountry strategy derives from the sometimes vast differences in cultural, economic, political, and competitive conditions in different countries. The more diverse national market conditions are, the stronger the case for a *multicountry strategy* where the company tailors its strategic approach to fit each host country's market situation. Usually, but not always, companies employing a multicountry strategy use the same basic competitive theme (low-cost, differentiation, or best-cost) in each country, making whatever country-specific variations are needed to best satisfy customers and to position itself against local rivals. They may aim at broad market targets in some countries and focus more narrowly on a particular niche in others. The bigger the country-to-country variations, the more that a company's overall international strategy becomes a collection of its individual country strategies.[16]

> *A multicountry strategy is appropriate for industries where multicountry competition dominates, but a global strategy works best in markets that are globally competitive or beginning to globalize.*

While multicountry strategies are best suited for industries where multicountry competition dominates, global strategies are best suited for globally competitive industries. A *global strategy* is one where a company's approach to competing is mostly the same in all countries. Although *minor* country-to-country differences in strategy do exist to accommodate specific conditions in host countries, the company's fundamental approach (low-cost, differentiation, best-cost or focused) remains the same worldwide. Moreover, a global strategy involves (1) integrating and coordinating the company's strategic moves worldwide and (2) selling in many if not all nations where there is significant buyer demand. Table 6–1 provides a point-by-point comparison of multicountry versus global strategies. The question of which of these two strategies to pursue is the foremost strategic issue firms face when they compete in international markets.

The strength of a multicountry strategy is that it matches the company's competitive approach to host country circumstances. A multicountry strategy is essential when there are significant country-to-country differences in customers' needs and buying habits (see Illustration Capsule 21), when buyers in a country insist on special-order or highly customized products, when regulations require that products sold locally meet strict manufacturing specifications or performance standards, and when trade restrictions are so diverse and complicated they preclude a uniform, coordinated worldwide market approach. However, a multicountry strategy has two big drawbacks: It is very difficult to transfer and exploit a company's competencies and resources across country boundaries, and it does not promote building a single, unified competitive advantage. The primary orientation of a multicountry strategy is responsiveness to local country conditions, not building well-defined competencies and competitive capabilities that can ultimately produce a competitive advantage over other international competitors and the domestic companies of host countries.

A global strategy, because it is more uniform from country to country, can concentrate on building the resource strengths to secure a sustainable low-cost or

---

[16]It is, however, possible to connect the strategies in different countries by making an effort to transfer ideas, technologies, competencies, and capabilities that work successfully in one country market to another country market whenever such transfers appear advantageous. Operations in each country can be thought of as "experiments" that result in learning and in capabilities that merit transfer to other country markets. For more details on the usefulness of such a "transnational" strategy, see C. A. Bartlett and S. Ghoshal, *Managing Across Borders: The Transnational Solution* (Boston: Harvard Business School Press, 1989).

TABLE 6-1   Differences between Multicountry and Global Stategies

	Multicountry Strategy	Global Strategy
Strategic Arena	• Selected target countries and trading areas.	• Most countries which constitute critical markets for the product, at least North America, the European Community, and the Pacific Rim (Australia, Japan, South Korea, and Southeast Asia).
Business Strategy	• Custom strategies to fit the circumstances of each host country situation; little or no strategy coordination across countries.	• Same basic strategy worldwide; minor country-by-country variations where essential.
Product-line Strategy	• Adapted to local needs.	• Mostly the same attributes and variety of models/styles worldwide.
Production Strategy	• Plants scattered across many host countries.	• Plants located on the basis of maximum competitive advantage (in low-cost countries, close to major markets, geographically scattered to minimize shipping costs, or use of a few world-scale plants to maximize economies of scale—as most appropriate).
Source of Supply for Raw Materials and Components	• Suppliers in host country preferred (local facilities meeting local buyer needs; some local sourcing may be required by host government).	• Attractive suppliers located anywhere in the world.
Marketing and Distribution	• Adapted to practices and culture of each host country.	• Much more worldwide coordination; minor adaptation to host country situations if required.
Company Organization	• Form subsidiary companies to handle operations in each host country; each subsidiary operates more or less autonomously to fit host country conditions.	• All major strategic decisions are closely coordinated at global headquarters; a global organizational structure is used to unify the operations in each country.

differentiation-based advantage over both international and domestic rivals. Whenever country-to-country differences are small enough to be accommodated within the framework of a global strategy, a global strategy is preferable to a multicountry strategy because of the value of uniting a company's efforts worldwide to create strong, competitively valuable competencies and capabilities not readily matched by rivals.

Global Strategy and Competitive Advantage

A firm can gain competitive advantage (or offset domestic disadvantages) with a global strategy in two ways.[17] One way exploits a global competitor's ability to deploy R&D, parts manufacture, assembly, distribution centers, sales and marketing, customer service centers and other activities among nations in a manner that

---

[17]Ibid., p. 54.

ILLUSTRATION CAPSULE 21   Multicountry Strategies: Microsoft in PC Software and Nestlé in Instant Coffee

In order to best serve the needs of users in foreign countries, Microsoft localizes many of its software products to reflect local languages. In France, for example, all user messages and documentation are in French and all monetary references are in French francs. In the United Kingdom, monetary references are in British pounds and user messages and documentation reflect certain British conventions. Various Microsoft products have been localized into more than 30 languages.

Nestlé is the world's largest food company with over $50 billion in revenues, market penetration on all major continents, and plants in over 70 countries. A star performer in Nestlé's food products lineup is coffee, accounting for sales of over $5 billion and operating profits of $600 million. Nestlé is the world's largest producer of coffee. Nestlé produces 200 types of instant coffee, from lighter blends for the U.S. market to dark espressos for Latin America. To keep its instant coffees matched to consumer tastes in different countries (and

areas within some countries), Nestlé operates four coffee research labs to experiment with new blends in aroma, flavor, and color. The strategy is to match the blends marketed in each country to the tastes and preferences of coffee drinkers in that country, introducing new blends to develop new segments when opportunities appear, and altering blends as needed to respond to changing tastes and buyer habits.

In Britain, Nescafé was promoted extensively to build a wider base of instant coffee drinkers. In Japan, where Nescafé was considered a luxury item, the company made its Japanese blends available in fancy containers suitable for gift-giving. In 1993 Nestlé began introducing Nescafé instant coffee and Coffee-Mate creamer in several large cities in China. As of 1992 the company's Nescafé brand was the leader in the instant coffee segment in virtually every national market but the U.S., where it ranked number two behind Maxwell House.

Sources: Company annual reports and Shawn Tully, "Nestlé Shows How to Gobble Markets," *Fortune*, January 16, 1989, pp. 74–78 and "Nestlé: A Giant in a Hurry," *Business Week*, March 22, 1993, pp. 50–54.

---

lowers costs or achieves greater product differentiation. A second way draws on a global competitor's ability to deepen or broaden its resource strengths and capabilities and to coordinate its dispersed activities in ways that a domestic-only competitor cannot.

Locating Activities   To use location to build competitive advantage, a global firm must consider two issues: (1) whether to concentrate each activity it performs in one or two countries or to spread it across many nations and (2) in which countries to locate particular activities. Activities tend to be concentrated in one or two locations when there are significant economies of scale in performing them, when there are advantages in locating related activities in the same area to better coordinate them, and when a steep learning or experience curve is associated with performing an activity in a single location. Thus in some industries scale economies in parts manufacture or assembly are so great that a company establishes one large plant from which it serves the world market. Where just-in-time inventory practices yield big cost savings and/or where the assembly firm has long-term partnering arrangements with its key suppliers, parts manufacturing plants may be clustered around final assembly plants.

A global strategy enables a firm to pursue sustainable competitive advantage by locating activities in the most advantageous nations and coordinating its strategic actions worldwide; a domestic-only competitor forfeits such opportunities.

On the other hand, dispersing activities is more advantageous than concentrating them in several instances. Buyer-related activities—such as distribution to dealers, sales and advertising, and after-sale service—usually must take place close to buyers. This means physically locating the ability to perform such activities in every country market where a global firm has major customers (unless buyers in several adjoining countries can be served quickly from a nearby central location). For example, firms that make mining and oil-drilling equipment maintain operations in many international locations to support customers' needs for speedy equipment repair and technical assistance. Large public accounting firms have numerous international offices to service the foreign operations of their multinational corporate clients. A global competitor that effectively disperses its buyer-related activities can gain a service-based competitive edge in world markets over rivals whose buyer-related activities are more concentrated—this is one reason the Big Six public accounting firms have been so successful relative to second-tier firms. Dispersing activities to many locations is also advantageous when high transportation costs, diseconomies of large size, and trade barriers make it too expensive to operate from a central location. Many companies distribute their products from multiple locations to shorten delivery times to customers. In addition, dispersing activities to hedge against the risks of fluctuating exchange rates, supply interruptions (due to strikes, mechanical failures, and transportation delays), and adverse political developments has advantages. Such risks are greater when activities are concentrated in a single location.

The classic reason for locating an activity in a particular country is lower costs.[18] Even though a global firm has strong reason to disperse buyer-related activities to many locations, such activities as materials procurement, parts manufacture, finished goods assembly, technology research, and new-product development can frequently be performed wherever advantage lies. Components can be made in Mexico, technology research done in Frankfurt, new products developed and tested in Phoenix, and assembly plants located in Spain, Brazil, Taiwan, and South Carolina. Capital can be raised in whatever country it is available on the best terms.

Low cost is not the only locational consideration, however. A research unit may be situated in a particular nation because of its pool of technically trained personnel. A customer service center or sales office may be opened in a particular country to help develop strong relationships with pivotal customers. An assembly plant may be located in a country in return for the host government's allowing freer import of components from large-scale, centralized parts plants located elsewhere.

Strengthening the Resource Base and Coordinating Cross Border Activities   A global strategy allows a firm to leverage its core competencies and resource strengths to compete successfully in additional country markets. Relying upon use of the same types of competencies, capabilities, and resource strengths in country after country contributes to the development of broader/deeper competencies and capabilities—ideally helping a company achieve *dominating depth* in some valuable area (whether it be competent performance of certain value chain activities, superior technical expertise, marketing know-how, or some other competitive asset). Dominating depth in a valuable capability or resource or value chain activity is a strong basis for sustainable competitive advantage. A company may not be able to achieve dominating depth with a domestic-only strategy because a one-country customer base may simply be too small to support such a resource buildup.

Aligning and coordinating company activities located in different countries contributes to sustainable competitive advantage in several different ways. If a firm learns how to assemble its product more efficiently at its Brazilian plant, the accumulated knowledge and expertise can be transferred to its assembly plant in Spain. Knowledge gained in marketing a company's product in Great Britain can be used to

---

[18]Ibid., p. 57.

introduce the product in New Zealand and Australia. A company can shift production from one country to another to take advantage of exchange rate fluctuations, to enhance its leverage with host country governments, and to respond to changing wage rates, energy costs, or trade restrictions. A company can enhance its brand reputation by consistently incorporating the same differentiating attributes in its products in all worldwide markets where it competes. The reputation for quality that Honda established worldwide first in motorcycles and then in automobiles gave it competitive advantage in positioning its lawnmowers at the upper end of the market—the Honda name gave the company instant credibility with buyers.

A global competitor can choose where and how to challenge rivals. It may decide to retaliate against aggressive rivals in the country market where the rival has its biggest sales volume or its best profit margins in order to reduce the rival's financial resources for competing in other country markets. It may decide to wage a price-cutting offensive against weak rivals in their home markets, capturing greater market share and subsidizing any short-term losses with profits earned in other country markets.

A company operating only in its home country can't pursue the competitive advantage opportunities of locating activites in the lowest-cost countries, using the added sales in foreign markets to broaden/deepen company competencies and capabilities, and coordinating cross-border activities. When a domestic company finds itself at a competitive disadvantage against global companies, one option is shifting from a domestic strategy to a global strategy.

The Use of Strategic Alliances to Enhance Global Competitiveness

Strategic alliances and cooperative agreements are a potentially fruitful means for firms in the same industry to compete on a more global scale while still preserving their independence. Typically such arrangements involve joint research efforts, technology sharing, joint use of production facilities, marketing one another's products, or joining forces to manufacture components or assemble finished products. Historically, export-minded firms in industrialized nations sought alliances with firms in less-developed countries to import and market their products locally—such arrangements were often necessary to win local government approval to enter a less-developed country's market or to comply with governmental requirements for local ownership. More recently, companies from different parts of the world have formed strategic alliances and partnership arrangements to strengthen their mutual ability to serve whole continents and move toward more global market participation. Both Japanese and American companies are actively forming alliances with European companies to strengthen their ability to compete in the 12-nation European Community and to capitalize on the opening up of Eastern European markets. Many U.S. and European companies are allying with Asian companies in their efforts to enter markets in China, India, and other Asian countries. Illustration Capsule 22 describes Toshiba's successful use of strategic alliances and joint ventures to pursue related technologies and product markets.

Strategic alliances can help companies in globally competitive industries strengthen their competitive positions while still preserving their independence.

Cooperative arrangements between domestic and foreign companies have strategic appeal for reasons besides market access.[19] One is to capture economies of scale in production and/or marketing—the cost reductions can be the difference that allows a

---

[19]Porter, *The Competitive Advantage of Nations*, p. 66; see also Jeremy Main, "Making Global Alliances Work," *Fortune*, December 17, 1990, pp. 121–26.

ILLUSTRATION CAPSULE 22 Toshiba's Use of Strategic Alliances and Joint Ventures

Toshiba, Japan's oldest and third largest electronics company (after Hitachi and Matsushita), over the years has made technology licensing agreements, joint ventures, and strategic alliances cornerstones of its corporate strategy. Using such partnerships to complement its own manufacturing and product innovation capabilities, it has become a $37 billion maker of electrical and electronics products—from home appliances to computer memory chips to telecommunications equipment to electric power generation equipment.

Fumio Sato, Toshiba's CEO, contends that joint ventures and strategic alliances are a necessary component of strategy for a high-tech electronics company with global ambitions:

It is no longer an era in which a single company can dominate any technology or business by itself. The technology has become so advanced, and the markets so complex, that you simply can't expect to be the best at the whole process any longer.

Among Toshiba's two dozen major joint ventures and strategic alliances are

- A five-year-old joint venture with Motorola to design and make dynamic random access memory chips (DRAMs) for Toshiba and microprocessors for Motorola. Initially the two partners invested $125 million apiece in the venture and have since invested another $480 million each.
- A joint venture with IBM to make flat-panel liquid crystal displays in color for portable computers.
- Two other joint ventures with IBM to develop computer memory chips (one a "flash" memory chip that remembers data even after the power is turned off).
- An alliance with Sweden-based Ericsson, one of the world's biggest telecommunications manufacturers, to develop new mobile telecommunications equipment.
- A partnership with Sun Microsystems, the leading maker of microprocessor-based

workstations, to provide portable versions of the workstations to Sun and to incorporate Sun's equipment in Toshiba products to control power plants, route highway traffic, and monitor automated manufacturing processes.
- A $1 billion strategic alliance with IBM and Siemens to develop and produce the next-generation DRAM—a single chip capable of holding 256 million bits of information (approximately 8,000 typewritten pages).
- An alliance with Apple Computer to develop CD-ROM-based multimedia players that plug into a TV set.
- A joint project with the entertainment division of Time Warner to design advanced interactive cable television technology.

Other alliances and joint ventures with General Electric, United Technologies, National Semiconductor, Samsung (Korea), LSI Logic (Canada), and European companies like Olivetti, SCS-Thomson, Rhone-Poulenc, Thomson Consumer Electronics, and GEC Alstholm are turning out such products as fax machines, copiers, medical equipment, computers, rechargeable batteries, home appliances, and nuclear and steam power generating equipment.

So far, none of Toshiba's relationships with partners have gone sour despite potential conflicts among related projects with competitors (Toshiba has partnerships with nine other chip makers to develop or produce semiconductors). Toshiba attributes this to its approach to alliances: choosing partners carefully, being open about Toshiba's connections with other companies, carefully defining the role and rights of each partner in the original pact (including who gets what if the alliance doesn't work out), and cultivating easy relations and good friendships with each partner. Toshiba's management believes that strategic alliances and joint ventures are an effective way for the company to move into new businesses quickly, share the design and development costs of ambitious new products with competent partners, and achieve greater access to important geographic markets outside Japan.

Source: Based on Brenton R. Schlender, "How Toshiba Makes Alliances Work," *Fortune*, October 4, 1993, pp. 116–20.

company to be cost competitive. By joining forces in producing components, assembling models, and marketing their products, companies can realize cost savings not achievable with their own small volumes. A second reason is to fill gaps in technical expertise and/or knowledge of local markets (buying habits and product preferences of consumers, local customs, and so on). Allies learn much from one another in performing joint research, sharing technological know-how, and studying one another's manufacturing methods. A third reason is to share distribution facilities and dealer networks, thus mutually strengthening their access to buyers. And finally, allied companies can direct their competitive energies more toward mutual rivals and less toward one another; by teaming up, both may end up stronger and better able to close the gap on leading companies.

Alliances between domestic and foreign companies have their pitfalls, however. Collaboration between independent companies, each with different motives and perhaps conflicting objectives, is not easy.[20] It requires many meetings of many people working in good faith over a period of time to iron out what is to be shared, what is to remain proprietary, and how the cooperative arrangements will work. Cross-border allies typically have to overcome language and cultural barriers; the communication, trust-building, and coordination costs are high in terms of management time. Often, once the bloom is off the rose, partners discover they have deep differences of opinion about how to proceed and conflicting objectives and strategies. Tensions build up, working relationships cool, and the hoped-for benefits never materialize.[21] Many times, allies find it difficult to collaborate effectively in competitively sensitive areas, thus raising questions about mutual trust and forthright exchanges of information and expertise. There can also be clashes of egos and company cultures. The key people on whom success or failure depends may have little personal chemistry, be unable to work closely together or form a partnership, or be unable to come to consensus. For example, the alliance between Northwest Airlines and KLM Royal Dutch Airlines linking their hubs in Detroit and Amsterdam resulted in a bitter feud among the top officials of both companies (who, according to some reports, refuse to speak to each other) and precipitated a battle for control of Northwest Airlines engineered by KLM; the dispute was rooted in a clash of philosophies about how to run an airline business (the American way versus the European way), basic cultural differences between the two companies, and an executive power struggle over who should call the shots.[22]

Strategic alliances are more effective in combating competitive disadvantage than in gaining competitive advantage.

Most important, though, is the danger of depending on another company for essential expertise and capabilities over the long term. To be a serious market contender, a company must ultimately develop internal capabilities in most all areas instrumental in strengthening its competitive position and building a competitive advantage. When learning essential know-how and capabilities from one's allies holds only limited potential (because one's partners guard their most valuable skills and expertise), acquiring or merging with a company possessing the desired know-how and resources is a better solution. Strategic alliances are best used as a transitional way to combat competitive disadvantage in international markets; rarely can they be relied on as ways to create competitive

---

[20]For an excellent discussion of company experiences with alliances and partnerships, see Rosabeth Moss Kanter, "Collaborative Advantage: The Art of the Alliance," *Harvard Business Review* 72, no. 4 (July–August 1994), pp. 96–108.

[21]Jeremy Main, "Making Global Alliances Work," p. 125.

[22]Details of the disagreements are reported in Shawn Tully, "The Alliance from Hell," *Fortune*, June 24, 1996, pp. 64–72.

ILLUSTRATION CAPSULE 23   Company Experiences With Cross-Border Strategic Alliances

As the chairman of British Aerospace recently observed, a strategic alliance with a foreign company is "one of the quickest and cheapest ways to develop a global strategy." AT&T formed joint ventures with many of the world's largest telephone and electronics companies. Boeing, the world's premier manufacturer of commercial aircraft, partnered with Kawasaki, Mitsubishi, and Fuji to produce a long-range, wide-body jet for delivery in 1995. General Electric and Snecma, a French maker of jet engines, have a 50-50 partnership to make jet engines to power aircraft made by Boeing, McDonnell-Douglas, and Airbus Industrie (Airbus, the leading European maker of commercial aircraft, was formed by an alliance of aerospace companies from Britain, Spain, Germany, and France). The GE/Snecma alliance is regarded as a model because it existed for 17 years and it produced orders for 10,300 engines, totaling $38 billion.

Since the early 1980s, hundreds of strategic alliances have been formed in the motor vehicle industry as car and truck manufacturers and automotive parts suppliers moved aggressively to get in stronger position to compete globally. Not only have there been alliances between automakers strong in one region of the world and automakers strong in another region but there have also been strategic alliances between vehicle makers and key parts suppliers (especially those with high-quality parts and strong technological capabilities). General Motors and Toyota in 1984 formed a 50-50 partnership called New United Motor Manufacturing Inc. (NUMMI) to produce cars for both companies at an old GM plant in Fremont, California. The strategic value of the GM-Toyota alliance was that Toyota would learn how to deal with suppliers and workers in the United States (as a prelude to building its own plants in the United States) while GM would learn about Toyota's approaches to

manufacturing and management. Each company sent managers to the NUMMI plant to work for two or three years to learn and absorb all they could, then transferred their NUMMI "graduates" to jobs where they could be instrumental in helping their companies apply what they learned. Toyota moved quickly to capitalize on its experiences at NUMMI. By 1991 Toyota had opened two plants on its own in North America, was constructing a third plant, and was producing 50 percent of the vehicles it sold in North America in its North American plants. While General Motors incorporated much of its NUMMI learning into the management practices and manufacturing methods it was using at its newly opened Saturn plant in Tennessee, it proceeded more slowly than Toyota. American and European companies are generally regarded as less skilled than the Japanese in transferring the learning from strategic alliances into their own operations.

Many alliances fail or are terminated when one partner ends up acquiring the other. A 1990 survey of 150 companies involved in terminated alliances found that three-fourths of the alliances had been taken over by Japanese partners. A nine-year alliance between Fujitsu and International Computers, Ltd., a British manufacturer, ended when Fujitsu acquired 80 percent of ICL. According to one observer, Fujitsu deliberately maneuvered ICL into a position of having no better choice than to sell out to its partner. Fujitsu began as a supplier of components for ICL's mainframe computers, then expanded its role over the next nine years to the point where it was ICL's only source of new technology. When ICL's parent, a large British electronics firm, saw the mainframe computer business starting to decline and decided to sell, Fujitsu was the only buyer it could find.

Source: Jeremy Main, "Making Global Alliances Work," *Fortune*, December 17, 1990, pp. 121–26.

advantage. Illustration Capsule 23 relates the experiences of companies with cross-border strategic alliances.

Companies can realize the most from a strategic alliance by observing five guidelines:[23]

1. Pick a compatible partner; take the time to build strong bridges of communication and trust, and don't expect immediate payoffs.

2. Choose an ally whose products and market strongholds *complement* rather than compete directly with the company's own products and customer base.

---

[23]Ibid.

3. Learn thoroughly and rapidly about a partner's technology and management; transfer valuable ideas and practices into one's own operations promptly.

4. Don't share competitively sensitive information with a partner.

5. View the alliance as temporary (5 to 10 years); continue longer if it's beneficial but don't hesitate to terminate the alliance and go it alone when the payoffs run out.

Strategic Intent, Profit Sanctuaries, and Cross-Subsidization

Competitors in international markets can be distinguished not only by their strategies but also by their long-term strategic objectives and strategic intent. Four types of competitors stand out:[24]

- Firms whose strategic intent is *global dominance* or, at least, a high ranking among the global market leaders (such firms typically have operations in most or all of the world's biggest and most important country markets and are pursuing global low-cost, best-cost or differentiation strategies).

- Firms whose primary strategic objective is *achieving or maintaining domestic dominance* in their home market, but who pursue international sales in several or many foreign markets as a "sideline" to bolster corporate growth; the international sales of such firms is usually under 20 percent of total corporate sales.

- *Multinational firms employing multicountry strategies* to build their international sales revenues; the strategic intent of such firms is usually to expand sales in foreign markets at a fast enough pace to produce respectable revenue and profit growth.

- *Domestic-only firms* whose strategic intent does not extend beyond building a strong competitive position in their home country market; such firms base their competitive strategies on domestic market conditions and watch events in the international market only for their impact on the domestic situation.

When all four types of firms find themseves competing head-on in the same market arena, the playing field is not necessarily level for all the players. Consider the case of a purely domestic U.S. company in competition with a Japanese company operating in many country markets and aspiring to global dominance. Because of its multicountry sales and profit base, the Japanese company has the option of lowballing its prices in the U.S. market to gain market share at the expense of the U.S. company, subsidizing any losses with profits earned in Japan and its other foreign markets. If the U.S. company, with all of its business being in the U.S. market, retaliates with matching price cuts, it exposes its entire revenue and profit base to erosion. Its profits can be squeezed and its competitive strength gradually sapped even if it is the U.S. market leader. However, if the U.S. company is a multinational competitor and operates in Japan as well as elsewhere, it can counter Japanese pricing in the United States with retaliatory price cuts in Japan (its competitor's main profit sanctuary) and in other countries where it competes against the same Japanese company.

The point here is that a domestic-only company can have a hard time competing on an equal footing with either multinational or global rivals that can rely on profits earned in other country markets to support a price-cutting offensive. When aggressive

---

[24]Prahalad and Doz, *The Multinational Mission*, p. 52.

global or multinational competitors enter a domestic-only company's market, one of the domestic-only competitor's best defenses is to switch to a multinational or global strategy to give it the same cross-subsidizing capabilities the aggressors have.

Profit Sanctuaries and Critical Markets   *Profit sanctuaries* are country markets where a company derives substantial profits because of its strong or protected market position. Japan, for example, is a profit sanctuary for most Japanese companies because trade barriers erected around Japanese industries by the Japanese government effectively block foreign companies from competing for a large share of Japanese sales. Protected from the threat of foreign competition in their home market, Japanese companies can safely charge higher prices to their Japanese customers and thus earn attractively large profits on sales made in Japan. In most cases, a company's biggest and most strategically crucial profit sanctuary is its home market, but multinational companies also have profit sanctuaries in those country markets where they enjoy strong competitive positions, big sales volumes, and attractive profit margins.

Profit sanctuaries are valuable competitive assets in global industries. Companies with large, protected profit sanctuaries have competitive advantage over companies that don't have a dependable sanctuary. Companies with multiple profit sanctuaries have a competitive advantage over companies with a single sanctuary—not only do they have a broader and more diverse market base, but their multiple profit sanctuaries give them multiple financial pockets and the flexibility to redeploy profits and cash flows generated in their market strongholds to support new strategic offensives to gain market share in additional country markets. The resource advantage of multiple profit sanctuaries gives a global or multinational competitor the ability to wage a market offensive against a domestic competitor whose only profit sanctuary is its home market.

A particular nation is a company's **profit sanctuary** *when the company, either because of its strong competitive position or protective governmental trade policies, derives a substantial part of its total profits from sales in that nation.*

To defend against competitive strength of global competitors with multiple profit sanctuaries, companies don't have to compete in all or even most foreign markets, but they do have to compete in all critical markets. *Critical markets* are markets in countries

- That are the profit sanctuaries of key competitors.
- That have big sales volumes.
- That contain prestigious customers whose business it is strategically important to have.
- That offer exceptionally good profit margins due to weak competitive pressures.[25]

The more critical markets a company participates in, the greater its ability to draw upon its resources and competitive strength in these markets to cross-subsidize its efforts to defend against offensives waged by competitors intent on global dominance.

The Competitive Power of Cross-Subsidization   Cross-subsidization—supporting competitive efforts in one market with resources and profits diverted from operations in other markets—is a powerful competitive weapon. Take the case of an aggressive

---

[25]Ibid., p. 61.

global firm with multiple profit sanctuaries that is intent on achieving global market dominance over the long-term and that seeks to improve its market share at the expense of a domestic-only competitor and a multicountry competitor. The global competitor can charge a low enough price to draw customers away from a domestic-only competitor, all the while gaining market share, building name recognition, and *covering any losses with profits earned in its other critical markets.* It can adjust the depth of its price-cutting to move in and capture market share quickly, or it can shave prices slightly to make gradual market inroads over a decade or more so as not to threaten domestic firms precipitously and perhaps trigger protectionist government actions. When attacked in this manner, a domestic company's best short-term hope is to pursue immediate and perhaps dramatic cost reduction and, if the situation warrants, to seek government protection in the form of tariff barriers, import quotas, and antidumping penalties. In the long term, the domestic company has to find ways to compete on a more equal footing—a difficult task when it must charge a price to cover full unit costs plus a margin for profit while the global competitor can charge a price only high enough to cover the incremental costs of selling in the domestic company's profit sanctuary. The best long-term defenses for a domestic company are to enter into strategic alliances with foreign firms or to compete on an international scale, although sometimes it is possible to drive enough costs out of the business over the long term to survive with a domestic-only strategy. As a rule, however, competing only domestically is a perilous strategy in an industry populated with global competitors who engage in cross-subsidization tactics.

A competent global competitor with multiple profit sanctuaries can wage and generally win a competitive offensive against a domestic competitor whose only profit sanctuary is its home market.

To defend against aggressive international competitors intent on global dominance, a domestic-only competitor usually has to abandon its domestic focus, become a multinational competitor, and craft a multinational competitive strategy.

While a company with a multicountry strategy has some cross-subsidy defense against a company with a global strategy, its vulnerability comes from a probable cost disadvantage and more limited competitive advantage opportunities. A global competitor with a big manufacturing share and world-scale state-of-the-art plants is almost certain to be a lower-cost producer than a multicountry strategist with many small plants and short production runs turning out specialized products country by country. Companies pursuing a multicountry strategy thus need differentiation and focus-based advantages keyed to local responsiveness in order to defend against a global competitor. Such a defense is adequate in industries with significant enough national differences to impede use of a global strategy. But if an international rival can accommodate necessary local needs within a global strategy and still retain a cost edge, then a global strategy can defeat a multicountry strategy.[26]

STRATEGIES FOR INDUSTRY LEADERS

The competitive positions of industry leaders normally range from stronger-than-average to powerful. Leaders typically are well-known, and strongly entrenched leaders have proven strategies (keyed either to low-cost leadership or to differentiation). Some of the best-known industry leaders are Anheuser-Busch (beer), Intel (microprocessors), McDonald's (fast food), Gillette (razor blades), Campbell Soup

---

[26]One way a global competitor can attack a multicountry competitor is by developing the capability to manufacture products customized for each country market at its world-scale plants; many manufacturers have become expert at designing assembly lines with the flexibility to turn out customized versions of a mass-produced product—so-called flexible mass production techniques. The advantage of flexible mass production is that it permits product customization and low-cost mass production *at the same time.*

(canned soups), Gerber (baby food), AT&T (long-distance telephone service), East-man Kodak (camera film), and Levi Strauss (jeans). The main strategic concern for a leader revolves around how to sustain a leadership position, perhaps becoming the *dominant* leader as opposed to *a* leader. However, the pursuit of industry leadership and large market share per se is primarily important because of the competitive advantage and profitability that accrue to being the industry's biggest company.

Three contrasting strategic postures are open to industry leaders and dominant firms:[27]

1.   Stay-on-the-offensive strategy—This strategy rests on the principle that the best defense is a good offense. Offensive-minded leaders stress being first-movers to sustain their competitive advantage (lower cost or differentiation) and to reinforce their reputation as *the* leader. A low-cost provider aggressively pursues cost reduc-tion, and a differentiator constantly tries new ways to set its product apart from rivals' brands and become the standard against which rivals' products are judged. The theme of a stay-on-the-offensive strategy is relentless pursuit of continuous improvement and innovation. Striving to be first with new products, better performance features, quality enhancements, improved customer services, or ways to cut production costs not only helps a leader avoid complacency but it also keeps rivals on the defensive scrambling to keep up. Offensive options can also include initiatives to expand overall industry demand—discovering new uses for the product, attracting new users of the product, and promoting more frequent use. In addition, a clever offensive leader stays alert for ways to make it easier and less costly for potential customers to switch their purchases from runner-up firms to its own prod-ucts. Unless a leader's market share is already so dominant that it presents a threat of antitrust action (a market share under 60 percent is usually "safe"), a stay-on-the-offensive strategy means trying to grow *faster* than the industry as a whole and wrest market share from rivals. A leader whose growth does not equal or outpace the industry average is losing ground to competitors.

Industry leaders can strengthen their long-term competitive positions with strategies keyed to aggressive offense, aggressive defense, or muscling smaller rivals into a follow-the-leader role.

2.   Fortify-and-defend strategy—The essence of "fortify and defend" is to make it harder for new firms to enter and for challengers to gain ground. The goals of a strong defense are to hold on to the present market share, strengthen current market position, and protect whatever competitive advantage the firm has. Specific defensive actions can include:

- Attempting to raise the competitive ante for challengers and new entrants by increased spending for advertising, higher levels of customer service, and bigger R&D outlays.

- Introducing more product versions or brands to match the product attributes of challengers' brands or to fill vacant niches that competitors could slip into.

- Adding personalized services and other "extras" that boost customer loyalty and make it harder or more costly for customers to switch to rival products.

- Keeping prices reasonable and quality attractive.

- Building new capacity ahead of market demand to discourage smaller competitors from adding capacity of their own.

[27]Kotler, *Marketing Management*, chapter 23; Michael E. Porter, *Competitive Advantage* (New York: Free Press, 1985), chapter 14; and Ian C. MacMillan, "Seizing Competitive Initiative," *The Journal of Business Strategy* 2, no. 4 (Spring 1982), pp. 43–57.

- Investing enough to remain cost competitive and technologically progressive.
- Patenting the feasible alternative technologies.
- Signing exclusive contracts with the best suppliers, distributors, and dealers.

A fortify-and-defend strategy best suits firms that have already achieved industry dominance and don't wish to risk antitrust action. It also works when a firm wishes to milk its present position for profits and cash flow because the industry's prospects for growth are low or because further gains in market share do not appear profitable enough to go after. But a fortify-and-defend strategy always entails trying to grow as fast as the market as a whole (to stave off market share slippage) and requires reinvesting enough capital in the business to protect the leader's ability to compete.

3. Follow-the-leader strategy—With this strategy the leader uses its competitive muscle (ethically and fairly!) to encourage runner-up firms to be content followers rather than aggressive challengers. The leader plays competitive hardball when smaller rivals rock the boat with price cuts or mount new market offensives that threaten its position. Specific responses can include quickly matching and perhaps exceeding challengers' price cuts, using large promotional campaigns to counter challengers' moves to gain market share, and offering better deals to the major customers of maverick firms. Leaders can also court distributors to dissuade them from carrying rivals' products, provide salespersons with documented information about the weaknesses of an aggressor's products, or try to fill any vacant positions in their own firms by making attractive offers to the better executives of rivals that "get out of line." When a leader consistently meets any moves to cut into its business with strong retaliatory tactics, it sends clear signals that offensive attacks on the leader's position will be met head-on and probably won't pay off. However, leaders pursuing this strategic approach should choose their battles. For instance, it makes sense to assume a hands-off posture and not respond in hardball fashion when smaller rivals attack each other's customer base in ways that don't affect the leader.

STRATEGIES FOR RUNNER-UP FIRMS

Runner-up firms have smaller market shares than the industry leader(s). Some runner-up firms are up-and-coming *market challengers*, using offensive strategies to gain market share and build a stronger market position. Others behave as *content followers*, willing to coast along in their current positions because profits are adequate. Follower firms have no urgent strategic issue to confront beyond "What kinds of strategic changes are the leaders initiating and what do we need to do to follow along?"

Rarely can a runner-up firm successfully challenge an industry leader with a copycat strategy.

A challenger firm interested in improving its market standing needs a strategy aimed at building a competitive advantage of its own. *Rarely can a runner-up firm improve its competitive position by imitating the strategies of leading firms. A cardinal rule in offensive strategy is to avoid attacking a leader head-on with an imitative strategy, regardless of the resources and staying power an underdog may have.*[28] Moreover, if a challenger has a 5 percent market share and needs a 20 percent share to earn attractive returns, it needs a more creative approach to competing than just "try harder."

---

[28]Porter, *Competitive Advantage*, p. 514.

In industries where large size yields *significantly* lower unit costs and gives large-share competitors an *important* cost advantage, small-share firms have only two viable strategic options: initiate offensive moves to gain sales and market share (so as to build the production volumes needed to approach the scale economies enjoyed by larger rivals) or withdraw from the business (gradually or quickly). The competitive strategies most underdogs use to build market share are based on (1) a combination of actions to drive down costs and to lower prices to win customers from weak, higher-cost rivals and (2) using differentiation strategies based on quality, technological superiority, better customer service, best cost, or innovation. Achieving low-cost leadership is usually open to an underdog only when one of the market leaders is not already solidly positioned as the industry's low-cost producer. But a small-share firm may still be able to narrow any cost disadvantage by eliminating marginal activities from the value chain, finding ways to better manage cost drivers and improve operating efficiency, or merging with or acquiring rival firms (the combined production volumes may provide the scale needed to achieve size-related economies).

When scale economies or experience curve effects are small and a large market share produces no cost advantage, runner-up companies have more strategic flexibility and can consider any of the following six approaches:[29]

1. **Vacant-niche strategy**—This version of a focused strategy involves concentrating on customer or end-use applications that market leaders have bypassed or neglected. An ideal vacant niche is of sufficient size and scope to be profitable, has some growth potential, is well-suited to a firm's own capabilities and resources, and is not interesting to leading firms. Two examples where vacant-niche strategies worked successfully are regional commuter airlines serving cities with too few passengers to attract the interest of major airlines and health foods producers (like Health Valley, Hain, and Tree of Life) that cater to local health food stores—a market segment traditionally ignored by Pillsbury, Kraft General Foods, Heinz, Nabisco, Campbell Soup, and other leading food products firms.

2. **Specialist strategy**—A specialist firm trains its competitive effort on one market segment: a single product, a particular end use, or buyers with special needs. The aim is to build competitive advantage through product uniqueness, expertise in special-purpose products, or specialized customer services. Smaller companies that successfully use a specialist focused strategy include Formby's (a specialist in stains and finishes for wood furniture, especially refinishing), Liquid Paper Co. (a leader in correction fluid for writers and typists), Canada Dry (known for its ginger ale, tonic water, and carbonated soda water), and American Tobacco (a leader in chewing tobacco and snuff).

3. **Ours-is-better-than-theirs strategy**—The approach here is to use a differentiation-based focus strategy keyed to superior product quality or unique attributes. Sales and marketing efforts are aimed directly at quality-conscious and performance-oriented buyers. Fine craftsmanship, prestige quality, frequent product innovations, and/or close contact with customers to solicit their input in developing a better product usually undergird this "superior product" approach. Some examples include Beefeater and Tanqueray in gin, Tiffany in diamonds and jewelry, Chicago

---

[29]For more details, see Kotler, *Marketing Management*, pp. 397–412; R. G. Hamermesh, M. J. Anderson, Jr., and J. E. Harris, "Strategies for Low Market Share Businesses," *Harvard Business Review* 56, no. 3 (May–June 1978), pp. 95–102; and Porter, *Competitive Advantage*, chapter 15.

Cutlery in premium-quality kitchen knives, Baccarat in fine crystal, Cannondale in mountain bikes, Bally in shoes, and Patagonia in apparel for outdoor recreation enthusiasts.

4. Content-follower strategy—Follower firms deliberately refrain from initiating trendsetting strategic moves and from aggressive attempts to steal customers away from the leaders. Followers prefer approaches that will not provoke competitive retaliation, often opting for focus and differentiation strategies that keep them out of the leaders' paths. They react and respond rather than initiate and challenge. They prefer defense to offense. And they rarely get out of line with the leaders on price. Union Camp (in paper products) has been a successful market follower by consciously concentrating on selected product uses and applications for specific customer groups, focused R&D, profits rather than market share, and cautious but efficient management.

5. Growth-via-acquisition strategy—One way to strengthen a company's position is to merge with or acquire weaker rivals to form an enterprise that has more competitive strength and a larger share of the market. Commercial airline companies such as Northwest, US Airways, and Delta owe their market share growth during the past decade to acquisition of smaller, regional airlines. Likewise, the Big Six public accounting firms extended their national and international coverage by merging or forming alliances with smaller CPA firms at home and abroad.

6. Distinctive-image strategy—Some runner-up companies build their strategies around ways to make themselves stand out from competitors. A variety of strategic approaches can be used: creating a reputation for charging the lowest prices, providing prestige quality at a good price, going all-out to give superior customer service, designing unique product attributes, being a leader in new product introduction, or devising unusually creative advertising. Examples include Dr Pepper's strategy in calling attention to its distinctive taste and Mary Kay Cosmetics' distinctive use of the color pink.

In industries where big size is definitely a key success factor, firms with low market shares have some obstacles to overcome: (1) less access to economies of scale in manufacturing, distribution, or sales promotion; (2) difficulty in gaining customer recognition; (3) an inability to afford mass media advertising on a grand scale; and (4) difficulty in funding capital requirements.[30] But *it is erroneous to view runner-up firms as inherently less profitable or unable to hold their own against the biggest firms.* Many firms with small market shares earn healthy profits and enjoy good reputations with customers. Often, the handicaps of smaller size can be surmounted and a profitable competitive position established by (1) focusing on a few market segments where the company's resource strengths and capabilities can yield a competitive edge; (2) developing technical expertise that will be highly valued by customers; (3) getting new or better products into the market ahead of rivals and building a reputation for product leadership; and (4) being more agile and innovative in adapting to evolving market conditions and customer expectations than stodgy, slow-to-change market leaders. Runner-up companies have a golden opportunity to make big market share gains if they pioneer a leapfrog technological breakthrough, if they are first to market with a new or dramatically improved product, or if the leaders stumble or become complacent.

---

[30]Hamermesh, Anderson, and Harris, "Strategies for Low Market Share Businesses," p. 102.

Otherwise, runner-up companies have to patiently nibble away at the leaders and build sales at a more moderate pace over time.

STRATEGIES FOR WEAK BUSINESSES

A firm in an also-ran or declining competitive position has four basic strategic options. If it can come up with the financial resources, it can launch an *offensive* turnaround strategy keyed either to low-cost or "new" differentiation themes, pouring enough money and talent into the effort to move up a notch or two in the industry rankings and become a respectable market contender within five years or so. It can employ a *fortify-and-defend* strategy, using variations of its present strategy and fighting hard to keep sales, market share, profitability, and competitive position at current levels. It can opt for an *immediate abandonment strategy* and get out of the business, either by selling out to another firm or by closing down operations if a buyer cannot be found. Or it can employ a *harvest strategy*, keeping reinvestment to a bare-bones minimum and taking actions to maximize short-term cash flows in preparation for an orderly market exit. The gist of the first three options is self-explanatory. The fourth merits more discussion.

The strategic options for a competitively weak company include waging a modest offensive to improve its position, defending its present position, being acquired by another company, or employing a harvest strategy.

A *harvest strategy* steers a middle course between preserving the status quo and exiting as soon as possible. Harvesting is a phasing down or endgame strategy that involves sacrificing market position in return for bigger near-term cash flows or profits. The overriding financial objective is to reap the greatest possible harvest of cash to use in other business endeavors. The operating budget is chopped to a rock-bottom level; reinvestment in the business is held to a bare minimum. Capital expenditures for new equipment are put on hold or given low priority (unless replacement needs are unusually urgent); instead, efforts are made to stretch the life of existing equipment and make do with present facilities as long as possible. Price may be raised gradually, promotional expenses slowly cut, quality reduced in not-so-visible ways, nonessential customer services curtailed, and the like. Although such actions may result in shrinking sales and market share, if cash expenses can be cut even faster, then after-tax profits and cash flows are bigger (at least temporarily). The business gradually declines, but not before a sizable cash harvest is realized.

Harvesting is a reasonable strategic option for a weak business in the following circumstances:[31]

1. When the industry's long-term prospects are unattractive.

2. When rejuvenating the business would be too costly or at best marginally profitable.

3. When the firm's market share is becoming more costly to maintain or defend.

4. When reduced competitive effort will not trigger an immediate or rapid fall-off in sales.

5. When the enterprise can redeploy the freed resources in higher opportunity areas.

---

[31]Phillip Kotler, "Harvesting Strategies for Weak Products," *Business Horizons* 21, no. 5 (August 1978), pp. 17–18.

6. When the business is *not* a crucial or core component of a diversified company's overall lineup of businesses (harvesting a sideline business is strategically preferable to harvesting a mainline or core business).

7. When the business does not contribute other desired features (sales stability, prestige, a product that complements others in the company's lineup of offerings) to a diversified company's overall business portfolio.

The more of these seven conditions present, the more ideal the business is for harvesting.

Turnaround Strategies for Businesses in Crisis

Turnaround strategies are needed when a business worth rescuing goes into crisis; the objective is to arrest and reverse the sources of competitive and financial weakness as quickly as possible. Management's first task is to diagnose what lies at the root of poor performance. Is it an unexpected downturn in sales brought on by a weak economy? An ill-chosen competitive strategy? Poor execution of an otherwise workable strategy? High operating costs? Important resource deficiencies? An overload of debt? Can the business be saved, or is the situation hopeless? Understanding what is wrong with the business and how serious its problems are is essential because different diagnoses lead to different turnaround strategies.

Some of the most common causes of business trouble include: taking on too much debt, overestimating the potential for sales growth, ignoring the profit-depressing effects of an overly aggressive effort to "buy" market share with deep price cuts, being burdened with heavy fixed costs because of an inability to utilize plant capacity, betting on R&D efforts to boost competitive position and profitability and failing to come up with effective innovations, betting on technological long shots, being too optimistic about the ability to penetrate new markets, making frequent changes in strategy (because the previous strategy didn't work out), and being overpowered by the competitive advantages enjoyed by more successful rivals. Curing these kinds of problems and turning the firm around can involve any of the following actions:

- Selling off assets to raise cash to save the remaining part of the business.
- Revising the existing strategy.
- Launching efforts to boost revenues.
- Pursuing cost reduction.
- Using a combination of these efforts.

Selling Off Assets   Assets reduction/retrenchment strategies are essential when cash flow is critical and when the most practical ways to generate cash are (1) through sale of some of the firm's assets and (2) through retrenchment (pruning of marginal products from the product line, closing or selling older plants, reducing the workforce, withdrawing from outlying markets, cutting back customer service, and the like). Sometimes crisis-ridden companies sell off assets not so much to unload losing operations and to stem cash drains as to raise funds to save and strengthen the remaining business activities.

Strategy Revision   When weak performance is caused by bad strategy, the task of strategy overhaul can proceed along any of several paths: (1) shifting to a new competitive approach to rebuild the firm's market position; (2) overhauling internal operations, resource capabilities, and functional strategies to better support the same overall business strategy; (3) merging with another firm in the industry and forging a new strategy keyed to the newly merged firm's strengths; and (4) retrenching into a reduced core of products and customers more closely matched to the firm's resource capabilities. The most appealing path depends on prevailing industry conditions, the firm's resource strengths and weaknesses, its competitive capabilities, and the severity of the crisis. Situation analysis of the industry, major competitors, and the firm's own competitive position and its competencies and resources are prerequisites for action. As a rule, successful strategy revision must be tied to the ailing firm's strengths and near-term competitive capabilities and directed at its best market opportunities.

Boosting Revenues Revenue-increasing turnaround efforts aim at generating increased sales volume. There are a number of options: price cuts, increased promotion, a bigger sales force, added customer services, and quickly achieved product improvements. Attempts to increase revenues and sales volumes are necessary (1) when there is little or no room in the operating budget to cut expenses and still break even and (2) when the key to restoring profitability is increased use of existing capacity. If buyer demand is not especially price sensitive because of differentiating features, the quickest way to boost short-term revenues may be to raise prices rather than opt for volume-building price cuts.

Cutting Costs Cost-reducing turnaround strategies work best when an ailing firm's value chain and cost structure are flexible enough to permit radical surgery, when it can identify and correct operating inefficiencies, when the firm's costs are obviously bloated and there are many places where savings can be quickly achieved, and when the firm is relatively close to its break-even point. Accompanying a general belt-tightening can be an increased emphasis on paring administrative overheads, elimination of nonessential and low-value-added activities, modernization of existing plant and equipment to gain greater productivity, delay of nonessential capital expenditures, and debt restructuring to reduce interest costs and stretch out repayments.

Combination Efforts Combination turnaround strategies are usually essential in grim situations that require fast action on a broad front. Likewise, combination actions frequently come into play when new managers are brought in and given a free hand to make whatever changes they see fit. The tougher the problems, the more likely the solutions will involve multiple strategic initiatives.

Turnaround efforts tend to be high-risk undertakings, and they often fail. A landmark study of 64 companies found no successful turnarounds among the most troubled companies in eight basic industries.[32] Many of the troubled businesses waited too long to begin a turnaround. Others found themselves short of both the cash and entrepreneurial talent needed to compete in a slow-growth industry. Better-positioned rivals simply proved too strong to defeat in a long, head-to-head contest. Even when successful, many troubled companies go through a series of turnaround

---

[32]William K. Hall, "Survival Strategies in a Hostile Environment," *Harvard Business Review* 58, no. 5 (September–October 1980), pp. 75–85. See also Frederick M. Zimmerman, *The Turnaround Experience: Real-World Lessons in Revitalizing Corporations* (New York: McGraw-Hill, 1991), and Gary J. Castrogiovanni, B. R. Baliga, and Roland E. Kidwell, "Curing Sick Businesses: Changing CEOs in Turnaround Efforts," *Academy of Management Executive* 6, no. 3 (August 1992), pp. 26–41.

attempts and management changes before long-term competitive viability and profitability are finally restored.

THIRTEEN COMMANDMENTS FOR CRAFTING SUCCESSFUL BUSINESS STRATEGIES

Business experiences over the years prove again and again that disastrous courses of action can be avoided by adhering to good strategy-making principles. The wisdom gained from these past experiences can be distilled into 13 commandments that, if faithfully observed, can help strategists craft better strategic action plans.

1. *Place top priority on crafting and executing strategic moves that enhance the company's competitive position for the long term.* An ever-stronger competitive position pays off year after year, but the glory of meeting one quarter's and one year's financial performance targets quickly fades. Shareholders are never well served by managers who let short-term financial performance rule out strategic initiatives that will bolster the company's long-term position and strength. The best way to protect a company's long-term profitability is to strengthen the company's long-term competitiveness.

2. *Understand that a clear, consistent competitive strategy, when well crafted and well executed, builds reputation and recognizable industry position; a frequently changed strategy aimed at capturing momentary market opportunities yields fleeting benefits.* Short-run financial opportunism, absent any long-term strategic consistency, tends to produce the worst kind of profits: one-shot rewards that are unrepeatable. Over the long haul, a company that has a well-conceived, consistent competitive strategy aimed at securing an ever-stronger market position will outperform and defeat a rival whose strategic decisions are driven by a desire to meet Wall Street's short-term expectations. In an ongoing enterprise, the game of competition ought to be played for the long term, not the short term.

3. *Avoid "stuck in the middle" strategies that represent compromises between lower costs and greater differentiation and between broad and narrow market appeal.* Middle-of-the-road strategies rarely produce sustainable competitive advantage or a distinctive competitive position—well-executed best-cost producer strategies are the only exception where a compromise between low cost and differentiation succeeds. Usually, companies with compromise or middle-of-the-road strategies end up with average costs, average features, average quality, average appeal, an average image and reputation, a middle-of-the-pack industry ranking, and little prospect of climbing into the ranks of the industry leaders.

4. *Invest in creating a sustainable competitive advantage.* It is the single most dependable contributor to above-average profitability.

5. *Play aggressive offense to build competitive advantage and aggressive defense to protect it.*

6. *Avoid strategies capable of succeeding only in the most optimistic circumstances.* Expect competitors to employ countermeasures and expect times of unfavorable market conditions.

7. *Be cautious in pursuing a rigid or inflexible strategy that locks the company in for the long term with little room to maneuver—inflexible strategies can*

be made obsolete by changing market conditions. While long-term strategic consistency is usually a virtue, some adapting of the strategy to changing circumstances is normal and necessary. Moreover, strategies to achieve top quality or lowest cost should be interpreted as *relative to competitors'* and/ or *in line with customers' needs and expectations* rather than based on single-mindedly striving to make the absolute highest quality or lowest cost product possible no matter what.

8. *Don't underestimate the reactions and the commitment of rival firms.* Rivals are most dangerous when they are pushed into a corner and their well-being is threatened.

9. *Avoid attacking capable, resourceful rivals without solid competitive advantage and ample financial strength.*

10. *Consider that attacking competitive weakness is usually more profitable and less risky than attacking competitive strength.*

11. *Be judicious in cutting prices without an established cost advantage.* Only a low-cost producer can win at price-cutting over the long term.

12. *Be aware that aggressive moves to wrest market share away from rivals often provoke retaliation in the form of a marketing "arms race" and/or price wars*—to the detriment of everyone's profits. Aggressive moves to capture a bigger market share invite cutthroat competition, particularly in markets with high inventories and excess production capacity.

13. *Strive to open up very meaningful gaps in quality or service or performance features when pursuing a differentiation strategy.* Tiny differences between rivals' product offerings may not be visible or important to buyers.

KEY POINTS

It is not enough to understand that a company's basic competitive strategy options are overall low-cost leadership, broad differentiation, best cost, focused low cost, and focused differentiation and that there are a variety of offensive, defensive, first-mover, and late-mover initiatives and actions to choose from. Managers must also understand that the array of strategic options is narrowed and shaped by (1) the nature of industry and competitive conditions and (2) a firm's own competitive capabilities, market position, and best opportunities. Some strategic options are better suited to certain specific industry and competitive environments than others. Some strategic options are better suited to certain specific company situations than others. This chapter describes the multifaceted task of matching strategy to a firm's external and internal situations by considering six classic types of industry environments and three classic types of company situations.

Rather than try to summarize the main points we made about choosing strategies for these eight sets of circumstances (the relevant principles can't really be encapsulated in three or four sentences each), we think it more useful to conclude by outlining a broader framework for matching strategy to *any* industry and company situation. Table 6–2 provides a summary checklist of the most important situational considerations and strategic options. Matching strategy to the situation starts with an overview of the industry environment and the firm's competitive standing in the industry (columns 1 and 2 in Table 6–2):

1. What basic type of industry environment does the company operate in (emerging, rapid growth, high velocity, mature, fragmented, global,

TABLE 6–2   Matching Strategy to the Situation (A Checklist of Optional Strategies and Generic Situations)

Industry Environments	Company Positions/ Situations	Situational Considerations	Market Share and Investment Options	Strategy Options

• Young, emerging industry
• Rapid growth
• High velocity/rapid change
• Consolidating to a smaller group of competitors
• Mature/slow growth
• Aging/declining
• Fragmented
• International/global
• Commodity product orientation
	• Dominant leader
	  –Global/ multinational
	  –National
	  –Regional
	  –Local
	• Leader
	• Aggressive challenger
	• Content follower
	• Weak/distressed candidate for turnaround or exit
	• "Stuck in the middle"/no clear strategy or market image
		• External
		  –Driving forces
		  –Competitive pressures
		  –Anticipated moves of key rivals
		  –Key success factors
		  –Industry attractiveness
		• Internal
		  –Current company performance
		  –Strengths and weaknesses
		  –Opportunities and threats
		  –Cost position
		  –Competitive strength
		  –Strategic issues and problems
			• Grow and build
			  –Capture a bigger market share by growing faster than industry as a whole
			  –Invest heavily to capture growth potential
			• Fortify and defend
			  –Protect market share; grow at least as fast as whole industry
			  –Invest enough resources to maintain competitive strength and market position
			• Retrench and retreat
			  –Surrender weakly held positions when forced to, but fight hard to defend core markets/customer base
			  –Maximize short-term cash flow
			  –Minimize reinvestment of capital in the business
			• Overhaul and reposition
			  –Pursue a turnaround
			• Abandon/liquidate
			  –Sell out
			  –Close down
				• Competitive approach
				  –Overall low-cost
				  –Differentiation
				  –Best-cost
				  –Focused low-cost
				  –Focused differentiation
				• Offensive initiatives
				  –Competitor strengths
				  –Competitor weaknesses
				  –End run
				  –Guerrilla warfare
				  –Preemptive strikes
				• Defensive initiatives
				  –Fortify/protect
				  –Retaliatory
				  –Harvest
				• International initiatives
				  –Licensing
				  –Export
				  –Multicountry
				  –Global
				• Vertical integration initiatives
				  –Forward
				  –Backward

commodity-product)? What strategic options and strategic postures are usually best suited to this generic type of environment?

2. What position does the firm have in the industry (strong vs. weak vs. crisis-ridden; leader vs. runner-up vs. also-ran)? How does the firm's standing influence its strategic options given the stage of the industry's development—in particular, which courses of action have to be ruled out?

Next, strategists need to factor in the primary external and internal situational considerations (column 3) and decide how all the factors add up. This should narrow the firm's basic market share and investment options (column 4) and strategic options (column 5).

The final step is to custom-tailor the chosen generic strategic approaches (columns 4 and 5) to fit *both* the industry environment and the firm's standing vis-à-vis competitors. Here, it is important to be sure that (1) the customized aspects of the proposed strategy are well-matched to the firm's competencies and competitive capabilities and (2) the strategy addresses all strategic issues the firm confronts.

In weeding out weak strategies and weighing the pros and cons of the most attractive ones, the answers to the following questions often point to the "best" course of action, all things considered:

- What kind of competitive edge can the company *realistically* achieve and whether the company can execute the strategic moves/approaches to secure this edge?
- Does the company have the capabilities and resources to succeed in these moves and approaches? If not, can they be acquired?
- Once built, how can the competitive advantage be protected? What defensive strategies need to be employed? Will rivals counterattack? What will it take to blunt their efforts?
- Are any rivals particularly vulnerable? Should the firm mount an offensive to capitalize on these vulnerabilities? What offensive moves need to be employed?
- What additional strategic moves are needed to deal with driving forces in the industry, specific threats and weaknesses, and any other issues/problems unique to the firm?

As the choice of strategic initiatives is developed, there are several pitfalls to avoid:

- Designing an overly ambitious strategic plan—one that overtaxes the company's resources and capabilities.
- Selecting a strategy that represents a radical departure from or abandonment of the cornerstones of the company's prior success—a radical strategy change need not be rejected automatically, but it should be pursued only after careful risk assessment.
- Choosing a strategy that goes against the grain of the organization's culture or that conflicts with the values and philosophies of the most senior executives.
- Being unwilling to *commit wholeheartedly* to one of the five competitive strategies—picking and choosing features of the different strategies usually produces so many compromises between low cost, best cost, differentiation, and focusing that the company fails to achieve any kind of advantage and ends up stuck in the middle.

Table 6–3 provides a generic format for outlining a strategic action plan for a single-business enterprise.

Bleeke, Joel A. "Strategic Choices for Newly Opened Markets." *Harvard Business Review* 68, no. 5 (September–October 1990), pp. 158–65.

Bolt, James F. "Global Competitors: Some Criteria for Success." *Business Horizons* 31, no. 1 (January–February 1988), pp. 34–41.

SUGGESTED READINGS

TABLE 6-3   Sample Format for a Strategic Action Plan

1. Strategic Vision and Mission	**5. Supporting Functional Strategies** • Production
2. Strategic Objectives • Short term • Long term	• Marketing/sales • Finance
3. Financial Objectives • Short term • Long term	• Personnel/human resources • Other
4. Overall Business Strategy	**6. Recommended Actions** • Immediate • Longer-range

Cooper, Arnold C., and Clayton G. Smith. "How Established Firms Respond to Threatening Technologies." *Academy of Management Executive* 6, no. 2 (May 1992), pp. 55–57.

D'Aveni, Richard A. *Hypercompetition: Managing the Dynamics of Strategic Maneuvering.* New York: Free Press, 1994, chaps. 3 and 4.

Gordon, Geoffrey L., Roger J. Calantrone, and C. Anthony di Benedetto. "Mature Markets and Revitalization Strategies: An American Fable." *Business Horizons* (May–June 1991), pp. 39–50.

Lei, David. "Strategies for Global Competition." *Long Range Planning* 22, no. 1 (February 1989), pp. 102–9.

Mayer, Robert J. "Winning Strategies for Manufacturers in Mature Industries." *Journal of Business Strategy* 8, no. 2 (Fall 1987), pp. 23–31.

Ohmae, Kenichi. "The Global Logic of Strategic Alliances." *Harvard Business Review* 67, no. 2 (March–April 1989), pp. 143–54.

Porter, Michael E. *Competitive Strategy: Techniques for Analyzing Industries and Competitors.* New York: Free Press, 1980, chaps. 9–13.

Porter, Michael E. *The Competitive Advantage of Nations.* New York: Free Press, 1990, chap. 2.

Rackham, Neil, Lawrence Friedman, and Richard Ruff. *Getting Partnering Right: How Market Leaders Are Creating Long-Term Competitive Advantage.* New York: McGraw-Hill, 1996.

Sugiura, Hideo, "How Honda Localizes Its Global Strategy." *Sloan Management Review* 33 (Fall 1990), pp. 77–82.

Yip, George S. *Total Global Strategy.* Englewood Cliffs, N.J.: Prentice-Hall, 1992, chaps. 1, 2, 3, 5, and 7.

Zimmerman, Frederick M. *The Turnaround Experience: Real-World Lessons in Revitalizing Corporations.* New York: McGraw-Hill, 1991.

STRATEGY AND COMPETITIVE ADVANTAGE IN DIVERSIFIED COMPANIES

7

In this chapter and the next, we move up one level in the strategy-making hierarchy, from strategic analysis of a single-business enterprise to strategic analysis of a diversified enterprise. Because a diversified company is a collection of individual businesses, corporate strategy making is a bigger-picture exercise than crafting line-of-business strategy. In a single-business enterprise, management has to contend with how to compete successfully in only one industry environment. But in a diversified company managers must come up with a strategic action plan for several different business divisions competing in diverse industry environments—their challenge is to craft a multi-industry, multibusiness strategy.

Crafting corporate strategy for a diversified company has four elements:

1. *Making the moves to enter new businesses.* The first concern in diversifying is what new industries to get into and whether to enter by starting a new business from the ground up or acquiring a company already in the target industry. Picking what industries to diversify into establishes whether the company's diversification effort is based narrowly in a few industries or broadly in many industries. The choice of how to enter each target industry (by launching a new start-up operation or by acquisition of an established leader, an up-and-coming company, or a troubled company with turn-around potential) shapes what position the company will initially stake out for itself going into each of the chosen industries.

2. *Initiating actions to boost the combined performance of the businesses the firm has diversified into.* As positions are created in the chosen industries, corporate strategy making concentrates on ways to strengthen the long-term competitive positions and profits of the businesses the firm has invested in. Corporate parents can help their business subsidiaries be more successful by providing financial resources, by supplying missing skills or technological know-how or managerial expertise to better perform key value chain activities, by providing new avenues

> . . . to acquire or not to acquire: that is the question.
>
> **Robert J. Terry**
>
> Strategy is a deliberate search for a plan of action that will develop a business's competitive advantage and compound it.
>
> **Bruce D. Henderson**
>
> Fit between a parent and its businesses is a two-edged sword: a good fit can create value: a bad one can destroy it.
>
> **Andrew Campbell, Michael Goold, and Marcus Alexander**

for cost reduction, by acquiring another company in the same industry and merging the two operations into a stronger business, and/or by acquiring new businesses that complement existing businesses. Typically, rapid-growth strategies are pursued in a diversified company's most promising businesses, turnaround efforts are initiated in weak-performing businesses with potential, and businesses that are no longer attractive or that don't fit into management's strategic vision long-range plans for the company are divested.

3. *Finding ways to capture the synergy among related business units and turn it into competitive advantage.* When a company diversifies into businesses with related technologies, similar value chain activities, the same distribution channels, common customers, or some other synergistic relationship, it gains competitive advantage potential not open to a company that diversifies into unrelated businesses. Related diversification presents opportunities to transfer skills, share expertise, or share facilities, thereby reducing overall costs, strengthening the competitiveness of some of the company's products, or enhancing the capabilities of business units—any of which can represent a source of competitive advantage.

4. *Establishing investment priorities and steering corporate resources into the most attractive business units.* A diversified company's different businesses are usually not equally attractive from the standpoint of investing additional funds. Management has to (1) decide on the priorities for investing capital in the company's different businesses, (2) channel resources into areas where earnings potentials are higher and away from areas where they are lower, and (3) divest business units that are chronically poor performers or are in increasingly unattractive industries. Divesting poor performers and businesses in unattractive industries frees up unproductive investments for redeployment to promising business units or for financing attractive new acquisitions.

These four tasks are so demanding and time-consuming that corporate-level decision makers generally do not become immersed in the details of crafting and implementing business-level strategies, preferring instead to delegate responsibility for business strategy to the heads of each business unit.

In this chapter we describe the various approaches a company can take in becoming diversified, explain how a company can use diversification to create or compound competitive advantage for its business units, and survey the strategic options an already-diversified company has to improve the overall performance of its business units. In Chapter 8 we will examine the techniques and procedures for assessing the attractiveness of a diversified company's business portfolio.

WHEN TO DIVERSIFY

Most companies begin as small single-business enterprises serving a local or regional market. During a company's early years, its product line tends to be limited, its resource base thin, and its competitive position vulnerable. Usually, a young company's strategic emphasis is on growing the business—increasing sales, boosting market share, and cultivating a loyal clientele. Profits are reinvested and new debt is taken on to expand facilities, add resources, and build competitive capabilities as fast as conditions permit. Price, quality, service, and promotion are tailored more precisely to customer needs. As soon as practical, the product line is broadened to meet variations in customer wants and to capture sales opportunities in related end-use applications.

Opportunities for geographic expansion are normally pursued next. The natural sequence of expansion proceeds from local to regional to national to international markets, though the degree of penetration may be uneven from area to area because of varying profit potentials. Geographic expansion may, of course, stop well short of global or even national proportions because of intense competition, lack of resources, or the unattractiveness of further extending a firm's market coverage.

Somewhere along the way, the potential of vertical integration, either backward to sources of supply or forward to the ultimate consumer, may become a strategic consideration. Generally, integrating forward or backward into more activities along the industry value chain makes strategic sense only if it significantly enhances a company's profitability and competitive strength.

The Conditions That Make Diversification Attractive

Companies with diminishing growth prospects in their present business, with competencies and capabilities that are readily transferable to other businesses, and with the resources and managerial depth to expand into other industry arenas are prime candidates for diversifying. So long as a company has its hands full trying to capitalize on profitable growth opportunities in its present industry, there is no urgency to diversify. But when growth opportunities in the company's mainstay business begin to peter out, diversification is the most viable option for reviving the firm's prospects. Diversification also has to be considered when a firm possesses core competencies, competitive capabilities, and resource strengths that are well suited for competing successfully in other industries.

When to diversify depends partly on a company's growth opportunities in its present industry and partly on the available opportunities to utilize its resources, expertise, and capabilities in other market arenas.

A decision to diversify into new businesses raises the question "What kind and how much diversification?" The strategic possibilities are wide open. A company can diversify into closely related businesses or into totally unrelated businesses. It can expand into businesses where existing competencies and capabilities are key success factors and valuable competitive assets. It can pursue opportunities to get into other product markets where its present technological know-how can be applied and possibly yield competitive advantage. It can diversify to a small extent (less than 10 percent of total revenues and profits) or to a large extent (up to 50 percent). It can move into one or two large new businesses or a greater number of small ones. Joint ventures with other organizations into new fields of endeavor are another possibility.

Why Rushing to Diversify Isn't Necessarily a Good Strategy   Companies that continue to concentrate on a single business can achieve success over many decades without relying upon diversification. McDonald's, Delta Airlines, Coca-Cola, Domino's Pizza, Apple Computer, Wal-Mart, Federal Express, Timex, Campbell Soup, Anheuser-Busch, Xerox, Gerber, and Polaroid all won their reputations in a single business. In the nonprofit sector, continued emphasis on a single activity has proved successful for the Red Cross, Salvation Army, Christian Children's Fund, Girl Scouts, Phi Beta Kappa, and American Civil Liberties Union. Coca-Cola, wanting to escape market maturity for soft drinks in the United States, abandoned most of its early efforts to diversify (into wine and into entertainment) when it realized that the opportunities to sell Coca-Cola products in foreign markets (especially in China, India, and other parts of Asia) would allow it to grow its sales and profits at rates of 15–20 percent for decades to come.

Diversification doesn't need to become a strategic priority until a company begins to run out of attractive growth opportunities in its main business.

There are important organizational, managerial, and strategic advantages to concentrating on just one business.

Concentrating on a single line of business (totally or with a small dose of diversification) has important advantages. It makes clearer "who we are and what we do." The energies of the *total* organization are directed down *one* business path, creating less chance that senior management's time will be diluted or resources will be stretched thinly by the demands of several different businesses. The company can devote the full force of its resources to expanding into geographic markets it doesn't serve and to becoming better at what it does. Important competencies and competitive skills are more likely to emerge. Entrepreneurial efforts can be trained exclusively on keeping the firm's business strategy and competitive approach responsive to industry change and fine-tuned to customer needs. With management's attention focused exclusively on one business, the probability is higher that good ideas will emerge on how to improve production technology, better meet customer needs with new product features, and enhance efficiencies or differentiation capabilities along the value chain. All the firm's managers, especially top executives, can have hands-on contact with the core business and in-depth knowledge of operations. Most senior officers will usually have risen through the ranks and have firsthand experience in field operations. (In broadly diversified enterprises, corporate managers seldom have had the opportunity to work in more than one or two of the company's businesses.) The more successful a single-business enterprise is, the more able it is to parlay its accumulated experience, distinctive competence, and brand-name reputation into a sustainable competitive advantage and an industry leadership position.

The Risks of Concentrating on a Single Business   The big risk of single-business concentration, of course, is putting all of a firm's eggs in one industry basket. If the market becomes saturated or becomes competitively unattractive or can be made obsolete bynew technologies or new products or fast-shifting buyer preferences, then a company's prospects can quickly dim. It is not unusual for changing customer needs, technological innovation, or new substitute products to undermine or wipe out a single-business firm—consider, for example, what the word-processing capabilities of personal computers have done to the electric typewriter business, what compact disk technology is doing to the market for cassette tapes and 3.5-inch disks, and what companies coming out with good-tasting low-fat and nonfat food products are doing to the sales of companies dependent on items with high fat content.

Factors That Signal When It's Time to Diversify   Judgments about when to diversify have to be made case-by-case on the basis of a company's own situation—the growth potential remaining in its present business, the attractiveness of opportunities to tranfer its competencies and capabilities to new business arenas, any cost-saving opportunites that can be exploited by being in closely related businesses, whether it has the resources to support a diversification effort, and whether it has the managerial breadth and depth to operate a multibusiness enterprise. Indeed, because companies in the same industry occupy different market positions and have different resource strengths and weaknesses, it is entirely rational for them to choose different diversification approaches and launch them at different times.

BUILDING SHAREHOLDER VALUE: THE ULTIMATE JUSTIFICATION FOR DIVERSIFYING

Diversifying into new businesses is justifiable only if it builds shareholder value. To enhance shareholder value, more must be accomplished than simply spreading the company's business risk across more than one industry. Shareholders can easily diversify risk on their own by purchasing stock in companies in different industries. Strictly speaking, *diversification does not create shareholder value unless a diversified group of businesses perform better under a single corporate umbrella than they would operating as independent, stand-alone businesses.* For example, if company A diversifies by purchasing company B and if A and B's consolidated profits in the years to come prove no greater than what each would have earned on its own, then A's diversification into business B won't provide its shareholders with added value. Company A's shareholders could have achieved the same 2 + 2 = 4 result by merely purchasing stock in company B. Shareholder value is not *created* by diversification unless it produces a 2 + 2 = 5 effect where sister businesses perform better together as part of the same firm than they could have performed as independent companies.

To create shareholder value, a diversifying company must get into businesses that can perform better under common management than they could perform as standalone enterprises.

Three Tests for Judging a Diversification Move

The problem with such a strict benchmark of whether diversification has enhanced shareholder value is that it requires speculation about how well a diversified company's businesses would have performed on their own. Comparisons of actual performance against the hypothetical of what performance might have been under other circumstances are never very satisfactory and, besides, they represent after-the-fact assessments. Strategists have to base diversification decisions on *future* expectations. Attempts to gauge the impact of particular diversification moves on shareholder value do not have to be abandoned, however. Corporate strategists can make before-the-fact assessments of whether a particular diversification move can increase shareholder value by using three tests:[1]

1. **The attractiveness test:** The industry chosen for diversification must be attractive enough to yield consistently good returns on investment. Whether an industry is attractive depends chiefly on the presence of favorable competitive conditions and a market environment conducive to long-term profitability. Such indicators as rapid growth or a sexy product are unreliable proxies of attractiveness.

2. **The cost-of-entry test:** The cost to enter the target industry must not be so high as to erode the potential for good profitability. A catch-22 can prevail here, however. The more attractive the industry, the more expensive it can be to get into. Entry barriers for start-up companies are nearly always high— were barriers low, a rush of new entrants would soon erode the potential for high profits. And buying a company already in the business often entails a high acquisition cost because of the industry's strong appeal.

3. **The better-off test:** The diversifying company must bring some potential for competitive advantage to the new business it enters, or the new business

---

[1]Michael E. Porter, "From Competitive Advantage to Corporate Strategy," *Harvard Business Review* 45, no. 3 (May–June 1987), pp. 46–49.

must offer added competitive advantage potential to the company's present businesses. The opportunity to create sustainable competitive advantage where none existed before means there is also opportunity for added profitability and shareholder value. The better-off test entails examining potential new businesses to determine if they have competitively valuable value chain matchups with the company's existing businesses—matchups that offer opportunities to reduce costs, to transfer skills or technology from one business to another, to create valuable new capabilities, or to leverage existing resources. Without such matchups, one has to be skeptical about the potential for the businesses to perform better together than apart.

Diversification moves that satisfy all three tests have the greatest potential to build shareholder value over the long term. Diversification moves that can pass only one or two tests are suspect.

DIVERSIFICATION STRATEGIES

Once the decision is made to diversify, a choice must be made whether to diversify into *related* businesses or *unrelated* businesses or some mix of both. Businesses are related when there are competitively valuable relationships among their value chains activities. Businesses are unrelated when there are no common similarities or match-ups in their respective value chains. Figure 7–1 shows the paths a company can take in moving from a single-business enterprise to a diversified enterprise. Vertical integration strategies may or may not enter the picture depending on whether forward or backward integration strengthens a firm's competitive position. Once diversification is accomplished, management's task is to figure out how to manage the collection of businesses the company has invested in—the six fundamental strategic options are shown in the last box of Figure 7–1.

We can better understand the strategic issues corporate managers face in creating and managing a diversified group of businesses by looking at six diversification-related strategies:

1. Strategies for entering new industries—acquisition, start-up, and joint ventures.
2. Related diversification strategies.
3. Unrelated diversification strategies.
4. Divestiture and liquidation strategies.
5. Corporate turnaround, retrenchment, and restructuring strategies.
6. Multinational diversification strategies.

The first three are ways to diversify; the last three are strategies to strengthen the positions and performance of companies that have already diversified.

Strategies for Entering New Businesses

Entry into new businesses can take any of three forms: acquisition, internal start-up, and joint ventures.

Acquisition of an Existing Business   Acquisition is the most popular way to diversify into another industry. Not only is it a quicker way to enter the target market than trying to launch a brand-new operation from the ground up but it offers an effective way to hurdle such entry barriers as acquiring technological experience, establishing

FIGURE 7-1   Corporate Strategy Alternatives

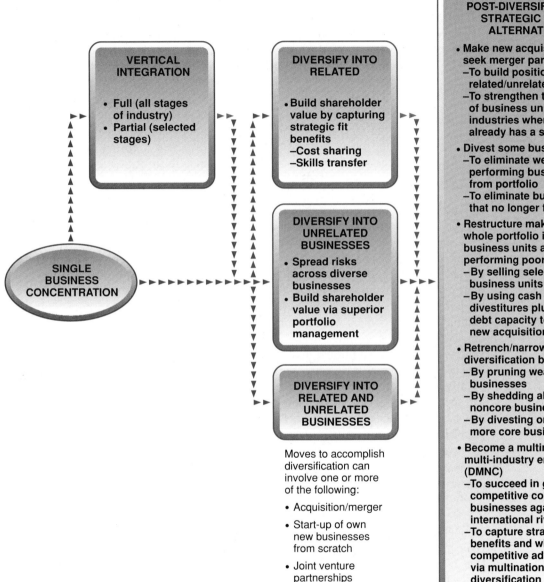

supplier relationships, becoming big enough to match rivals' efficiency and unit costs, having to spend large sums on introductory advertising and promotions to gain market visibility and brand recognition, and securing adequate distribution.[2] In many industries, going the internal start-up route and trying to develop the knowledge, resources, scale of operation, and market reputation necessary to become an effective competitor can take years. Acquiring an already established concern allows the entrant to move directly to the task of building a strong market position in the target industry.

However, finding the right kind of company to acquire sometimes presents a challenge.[3] The big dilemma an acquisition-minded firm faces is whether to pay a premium price for a successful company or to buy a struggling company at a bargain price. If the buying firm has little knowledge of the industry but ample capital, it is often better off purchasing a capable, strongly positioned firm—unless the price of such an acquisition is prohibitive and flunks the cost-of-entry test. On the other hand, when the acquirer sees promising ways to transform a weak firm into a strong one and has the resources, the know-how, and the patience to do it, a struggling company can be the better long-term investment.

One of the big stumbling blocks to entering attractive industries by acquisition is the difficulty of finding a suitable company at a price that satisfies the cost-of-entry test.

The cost-of-entry test requires that the expected profit stream of an acquired business provide an attractive return on the total acquisition cost and on any new capital investment needed to sustain or expand its operations. A high acquisition price can make meeting that test improbable or difficult. For instance, suppose that the price to purchase a company is $3 million and that the business is earning after-tax profits of $200,000 on an equity investment of $1 million (a 20 percent annual return). Simple arithmetic requires that the acquired business's profits be tripled for the purchaser to earn the same 20 percent return on the $3 million acquisition price that the previous owners were getting on their $1 million equity investment. Building the acquired firm's earnings from $200,000 to $600,000 annually could take several years—and require additional investment on which the purchaser would also have to earn a 20 percent return. Since the owners of a successful and growing company usually demand a price that reflects their business's future profit prospects, it's easy for such an acquisition to fail the cost-of-entry test. A would-be diversifier can't count on being able to acquire a desirable company in an appealing industry at a price that still permits attractive returns on investment.

Internal Start-Up   Achieving diversification through *internal start-up* involves creating a new company under the corporate umbrella to compete in the desired industry. A newly formed organization not only has to overcome entry barriers, it also has to invest in new production capacity, develop sources of supply, hire and train employees, build channels of distribution, grow a customer base, and so on. Generally, forming a start-up company to enter a new industry is more attractive when (1) there is ample time to launch the business from the ground up, (2) incumbent firms are likely to be slow or ineffective in responding to a new entrant's efforts to crack the market, (3) internal entry has lower costs than entry via acquisition, (4) the company already has in-house most or

---

[2]In recent years, hostile takeovers have become a hotly debated and sometimes abused approach to acquisition. The term *takeover* refers to the attempt (often sprung as a surprise) of one firm to acquire ownership or control over another firm against the wishes of the latter's management (and perhaps some of its stockholders).

[3]Michael E. Porter, *Competitive Strategy: Techniques for Analyzing Industries and Competitors* (New York: Free Press, 1980), p. 354–55.

all of the skills it needs to compete effectively, (5) adding new production capacity will not adversely impact the supply-demand balance in the industry, and (6) the targeted industry is populated with many relatively small firms so the new start-up does not have to compete head-to-head against larger, more powerful rivals.[4]

Joint Ventures   Joint ventures are a useful way to gain access to a new business in at least three types of situations.[5] First, a joint venture is a good way to do something that is uneconomical or risky for an organization to do alone. Second, joint ventures make sense when pooling the resources and competencies of two or more organizations produces an organization with more resources and competitive assets to be a strong market contender. In such cases, each partner brings special talents or resources that the other doesn't have and that are important for success. Third, joint ventures with foreign partners are sometimes the only or best way to surmount import quotas, tariffs, nationalistic political interests, and cultural roadblocks. The economic, competitive, and political realities of nationalism often require a foreign company to team up with a domestic partner to gain access to the national market in which the domestic partner is located. Domestic partners offer outside companies the benefits of local knowledge, managerial and marketing personnel, and access to distribution channels. However, such joint ventures often pose complicated questions about how to divide efforts among the partners and about who has effective control.[6] Conflicts between foreign and domestic partners can arise over whether to use local sourcing of components, how much production to export, whether operating procedures should conform to the foreign company's standards or to local preferences, who has control of cash flows, and how to distribute profits.

> *The biggest drawbacks to entering an industry by forming a start-up company internally are the costs of overcoming entry barriers and the extra time it takes to build a strong and profitable competitive position.*

RELATED DIVERSIFICATION STRATEGIES

A related diversification strategy involves diversifying into businesses whose value chains possess competitively valuable "strategic fits" with those of the company's present business(es). *Strategic fit* exists between different businesses whenever their value chains are similiar enough to present opportunities for technology sharing, for exercising more bargaining leverage with common suppliers, for joint manufacture of parts and components, for sharing a common sales force, for using the same distribution facilities, for using the same wholesale distributors or retail dealers, for combining after-sale service activities, for exploiting common use of a well-known brand name, for transferring competitively valuable know-how or capabilities from one business to another, or for combining similar value chain activites to achieve lower costs. Strategic fits can exist anywhere along the businesses' respective value chains—in the relationships with suppliers, in R&D and technology activiities, in manufacturing, in sales and marketing, or in distribution activities.

> *Related diversification involves diversifying into businesses with competitively valuable strategic fits and matchups in their value chains.*

What makes related diversification an attractive strategy is the opportunity to convert the strategic fit relationships between the value chains of different businesses

---

[4]Ibid., pp. 344–45.

[5]Peter Drucker, *Management: Tasks, Responsibilities, Practices* (New York: Harper & Row, 1974), pp. 720–24. Strategic alliances offer much the same benefits as joint ventures, but represent a weaker commitment to entering a new business.

[6]Porter, *Competitive Strategy*, p. 340.

ILLUSTRATION CAPSULE 24   Koch Industries' Efforts to Link Its Diversification Strategy to Core Competencies and Capabilities

At Koch Industries, one of the five largest privately held companies in America, development of a company vision and strategy involved an analysis of the company's competencies and capabilities and deciding how to match these competencies and capabilities with perceived market opportunities. One executive observed, "We thought we were in the oil business, but we found out our real expertise is in the gathering, transportation, processing, and trading business." While the company developed these competencies in gathering, refining, transporting, and trading crude oil, management realiza-

tion of what the company's capabilities were led to expansion into gas liquids, and then into gas gathering, transportation, processing, and trading. Involvement in gas operations led Koch into ammonia transportation and trading, operations more closely related to Koch's oil business than service station operations.More recent acquisitions have involved transferring Koch's core capabilities to grain gathering and cattle feedlots, business activities which draw on the company's expertise in gathering, transportation, processing, and trading.

Source: Tyler Cowen and Jerry Ellig, "Market-Based Management at Koch Industries: Discovery, Dissemination, and Integration of Knowledge," *Competitive Intelligence Review* 6, no. 4 (Winter 1995), p. 7.

What makes related diversification attractive is the opportunity to turn strategic fits into competitive advantage.

into competitive advantage. When a company diversifies into businesses that present opportunities to (1) transfer expertise or capabilities or technology from one business to another, (2) combine the related activities of separate businesses into a single operation and reduce costs, (3) leverage a company's brand-name reputation in new businesses, and/or (4) conduct the related value chain activities in such collaborative fashion as to create valuable competitive capabilities, it gains competitive advantage over rivals that have not diversified or that have diversified in ways that don't give them access to such strategic-fit benefits.[7] The greater the relatedness among the businesses of a diversified company, the greater the opportunities for skills transfer and/or combining value chain activities to lower costs and/or collaborating to create new resource strengths and capabilities and/or using a common brand name and the bigger the window for creating competitive advantage.[8]

Moreover, *a diversified firm that exploits these value-chain matchups and captures the benefits of strategic fit can achieve a consolidated performance greater than the sum of what the businesses can earn pursuing independent strategies.* Competitively valuable strategic fits (assuming corporate management is able to effectively capture the benefits of the value chain matchups) make related diversification a 2 + 2 = 5 phenomenon. The competitive edge flowing from strategic fits along the value chains of related businesses provides a basis for them performing better together than as stand-alone enterprises. The bigger the strategic-fit benefits, the more that related diversification is capable of 2 + 2 = 5 performance—thereby satisfying the better-off test for building shareholder value.

---

[7]Michael E. Porter, *Competitive Advantage* (New York: Free Press, 1985), pp. 318–19 and pp. 337–53; Kenichi Ohmae, *The Mind of the Strategist* (New York: Penguin Books, 1983), pp. 121–24; and Porter, "From Competitive Advantage to Corporate Strategy," pp. 53–57. For an empirical study confirming that strategic fits are capable of enhancing performance (provided the resulting resource strengths are competitively valuable and difficult to duplicate by rivals), see Constantinos C. Markides and Peter J. Williamson, "Corporate Diversification and Organization Structure: A Resource-Based View," *Academy of Management Journal*, 39, no. 2 (April 1996), pp. 340–67.

[8]For a discussion of the strategic significance of cross-business coordination and insight into how it works, see Jeanne M. Liedtka, "Collaboration across Lines of Business for Competitive Advantage," *Academy of Management Executive* 10, no. 2 (May 1996), pp. 20–34.

Related Diversification in Actual Practice Some of the most commonly used approaches to related diversification are

- Entering businesses where sales force, advertising, brand name, and distribution facilities can be shared (a maker of cookies and crackers diversifying into salty snack foods).

- Exploiting closely related technologies and technical expertise (a creator of software for mainframe computers diversifying into software for networking of PCs, for company intranets, and for stand-alone PCs).

- Transferring know-how and expertise from one business to another (a successful operator of Italian restaurants acquiring a chain specializing in Mexican food).

- Transferring the organization's brand name and reputation with consumers to a new product/service (a tire manufacturer acquiring a chain of car care centers specializing in brake repair and muffler and shock-absorber replacement).

- Acquiring new businesses that will uniquely help the firm's position in its existing businesses (a cable TV broadcaster purchasing a sports team or a movie production company to provide original programming).

Examples of related diversification abound. BIC Pen, which pioneered inexpensive disposable ballpoint pens, used its core competencies in low-cost manufacturing and mass merchandising as its basis for diversifying into disposable cigarette lighters and disposable razors—both of which required low-cost production know-how and skilled consumer marketing for success. Sony, a leading consumer electronics company, employed a technology-related and marketing-related diversification strategy when it decided to enter the videogame industry and to transfer its competencies and capabilities in electronics technology, its marketing know-how, and its brand name credibility to the manufacture and sale of videogame players and the marketing of videogames. Procter & Gamble's lineup of products includes Jif peanut butter, Duncan Hines cake mixes, Folger's coffee, Tide laundry detergent, Crisco vegetable oil, Crest toothpaste, Ivory soap, Charmin toilet tissue, and Head and Shoulders shampoo—all different businesses with different competitors and different production requirements. But P&G's products still represent related diversification because they all move through the same wholesale distribution systems, are sold in common retail settings to the same shoppers, are advertised and promoted in the same ways, and use the same marketing and merchandising skills. Illustration Capsule 25 shows the business portfolios of several companies that have pursued a strategy of related diversification.

Strategic Fit, Economies of Scope, and Competitive Advantage

A related diversification strategy is appealing from several angles. It allows a firm to preserve a degree of unity in its business activities, reap the benefits of skills transfer and/or lower costs and/or common brand-name usage and/or stronger competitive capabilities, and still spread investor risks over a broader business base.

Diversifying into businesses where technology, facilities, functional activities, or distribution channels can be shared can lead to lower costs because of economies of scope. *Economies of scope* exist whenever it is less costly for two or more businesses to be operated under centralized management than to function as independent businesses. These economies can arise from

Strategic fits among related businesses offer the competitive advantage potential of (a) lower costs, (b) efficient transfer of key skills, technological expertise, or managerial know-how from one business to another, (c) ability to share a common brand name, and/or (d) enhanced resource strengths and competitive capabilities.

ILLUSTRATION CAPSULE 25   Examples of Companies with Related Business Portfolios

Presented below are the business portfolios of three companies that have pursued some form of related diversification. Can you identify the strategic fits and value chain relationships that exist among their businesses?

Gillette

- Blades and razors
- Toiletries (Right Guard, Foamy, Dry Idea, Soft & Dry, White Rain)
- Jafra skin care products
- Oral-B toothbrushes and dental care products
- Writing instruments and stationery products (Paper Mate pens, Parker pens, Waterman pens, Liquid Paper correction fluids)
- Braun shavers, coffeemakers, alarm clocks, mixers, hair dryers, and electric toothbrushes

Philip Morris Companies

- Cigarettes (Marlboro, Virginia Slims, Benson & Hedges, Merit, and numerous other brands)

- Miller Brewing Company (Miller Genuine Draft, Miller Lite, Icehouse, Red Dog)
- Kraft General Foods (Maxwell House, Sanka, Oscar Mayer, Kool-Aid, Jell-O, Post cereals, Birds-Eye frozen foods, Kraft cheeses, Crystal Light, Tombstone pizza)
- Mission Viejo Realty

Johnson & Johnson

- Baby products (powder, shampoo, oil, lotion)
- Band-Aids and wound care products
- Stayfree, Carefree, and Sure & Natural, feminine hygiene products
- Nonprescription drugs (Tylenol, Pepcid AC, Mylanta, Motrin, Monistat-7)
- Prescription drugs
- Surgical and hospital products
- Reach dental products
- Accuvue contact lenses
- Skin care products

Source: Company annual reports

Economies of scope *arise from the ability to eliminate costs by operating two or more businesses under the same corporate umbrella; the cost-saving opportunities can stem from interrelationships anywhere along the businesses' value chains.*

cost-saving opportunities to share resources or combine activities anywhere along the respective value chains of the businesses and from shared use of an established brand name. The greater the economies of scope, the greater the potential for creating a competitive advantage based on lower costs.

Both skills transfer and combining the performance of closely related value chain activies enable the diversifier to earn greater profits from joint operation of different businesses than the businesses could earn as independent, stand-alone enterprises. The key to skills transfer opportunities and to cost saving economies of scope is diversification into businesses with strategic fit. While strategic-fit relationships can occur throughout the value chain, most fall into one of four categories.

Technology Fits   Different businesses have *technology fit* when there is potential for sharing common technology, exploiting the full range of business opportunities associated with a particular technology, or transferring technological know-how from one business to another. Businesses with technology-sharing benefits can perform better together than apart because of potential cost-savings in technology development and new product R&D, because of shorter times in getting new products to market, important complementarity or interdependence between the resulting products that leads to increased sales of both, and/or the technology transfer potential between businesses allows more effective or efficient performance of technology-related activities.

Operating Fits   Different businesses have *operating fit* when there are opportunities to combine activities or transfer skills/capabilities in procuring materials, conducting

R&D, improving production processes, manufacturing components, assembling finished goods, or performing administrative support functions. Sharing-related operating fits usually present cost-saving opportunities; some derive from the economies of combining activities into a larger-scale operation *(economies of scale)*, and some derive from the ability to eliminate costs by performing activities together rather than independently *(economies of scope)*. The bigger the proportion of cost that a shared activity represents, the more significant the shared cost savings become and the bigger the cost advantage that can result. With operating fit, the most important skills transfer opportunities usually relate to situations where supply chain management or manufacturing expertise in one business has beneficial applications in another.

Distribution and Customer-Related Fits When the value chains of different businesses overlap such that the products are used by the same customers, distributed through common dealers and retailers, or marketed and promoted in similar ways, then the businesses enjoy *market-related strategic fit.* A variety of cost-saving opportunities (or economies of scope) spring from market-related strategic fit: using a single sales force for all related products rather than having separate sales forces for each business, advertising the related products in the same ads and brochures, using a common brand name, coordinating delivery and shipping, combining after-sale service and repair organizations, coordinating order processing and billing, using common promotional tie-ins (cents-off couponing, free samples and trial offers, seasonal specials, and the like), and combining dealer networks. Such value-chain matchups usually allow a firm to economize on its marketing, selling, and distribution costs.

In addition to economies of scope, market-related fit can involve opportunities to transfer selling skills, promotional skills, advertising skills, or product differentiation skills from one business to another. Moreover, a company's brand name and reputation in one product can often be transferred to other products. Honda's name in motorcycles and automobiles gave it instant credibility and recognition in entering the lawnmower business without spending large sums on advertising. Canon's reputation in photographic equipment was a competitive asset that aided the company's diversification into copying equipment. Panasonic's name in consumer electronics (radios, TVs) was readily transferred to microwave ovens, making it easier and cheaper for Panasonic to diversify into the microwave oven market.

Managerial Fits This type of fit emerges when different business units have comparable types of entrepreneurial, administrative, or operating problems, thereby allowing managerial know-how in one line of business to be transferred to another. Transfers of managerial expertise can occur anywhere in the value chain. Ford transferred its automobile financing and credit management know-how to the savings and loan industry when it acquired some failing savings and loan associations during the 1989 bailout of the crisis-ridden S&L industry. Wal-Mart transferred its managerial know-how in discount merchandising to its newly created Sam's Wholesale Club division and thereby successfully entered the wholesale discounting business.

Capturing Strategic-Fit Benefits

It is one thing to diversify into industries with strategic fit and another to actually realize the benefits of doing so. To capture economies of scope, related activities must be merged into a single operating unit and coordinated; then the cost savings must be squeezed out. Merged functions and coordination can entail reorganization costs, and management must determine that the benefit of *some* centralized strategic control is great enough to warrant sacrifice of business-unit autonomy. Likewise, where skills or technology transfer is the cornerstone of strategic fit, managers must find a way to make the transfer effective without stripping too many skilled personnel from the business with the expertise. The more a company's diversification strategy is tied to skills or technology transfer, the more it has to develop a big enough and talented enough pool of specialized personnel not only to supply new businesses with the skill or technology but also to master the skill/technology enough to create competitive advantage.

A company with the know-how to expand its stock of strategic assets faster and at lower cost than rivals obtains sustainable competitive advantage.

One additional benefit flows from companies becoming adept at capturing strategic fits across businesses: the potential for the firm to expand its pool of resources and strategic assets and to create new ones *faster and more cheaply* than rivals who are not diversified across related businesses.[9] One reason some firms pursuing related diversification perform better over the long-term than others is that they are better at exploiting the linkages between their related businesses; such know-how over the long term translates into an ability to *accelerate* the creation of valuable new core competencies and competitive capabilities. In a competitively dynamic world, the ability to accumulate strategic assets faster than rivals is a potent and dependable way for a diversified company to earn superior returns over the long term.

UNRELATED DIVERSIFICATION STRATEGIES

Despite the strategic-fit benefits associated with related diversification, a number of companies opt for unrelated diversification strategies—diversifying into *any industry* with a good profit opportunity. *In unrelated diversification there is no deliberate effort to seek out businesses having strategic fit with the firm's other businesses.* While companies pursuing unrelated diversification may try to make certain their diversification targets meet the industry-attractiveness and cost-of-entry tests, the conditions needed for the better-off test are either disregarded or relegated to secondary status. Decisions to diversify into one industry versus another are the product of a search for "good" companies to acquire—*the basic premise of unrelated diversification is that any company that can be acquired on good financial terms and that has satisfactory profit prospects represents a good business to diversify into.* Much time and effort goes into finding and screening acquisition candidates using such criteria as:

A strategy of unrelated diversification involves diversifying into whatever industries and businesses hold promise for attractive financial gain; exploiting strategic-fit relationships is secondary.

- Whether the business can meet corporate targets for profitability and return on investment.
- Whether the new business will require infusions of capital to replace fixed assets, fund expansion, and provide working capital.
- Whether the business is in an industry with significant growth potential.
- Whether the business is big enough to contribute significantly to the parent firm's bottom line.

---

[9]Constantinos C. Markides and Peter J. Williamson, "Related Diversification, Core Competences and Corporate Performance," *Strategic Management Journal* 15 (Summer 1994), pp. 149–65.

- Whether there is a potential for union difficulties or adverse government regulations concerning product safety or the environment.

- Whether the industry is unusually vulnerable to recession, inflation, high interest rates, or shifts in government policy.

Sometimes, companies with unrelated diversification strategies concentrate on identifying acquisition candidates that offer quick opportunities for financial gain because of their "special situation." Three types of businesses may hold such attraction:

- *Companies whose assets are undervalued*—opportunities may exist to acquire such companies for less than full market value and make substantial capital gains by reselling their assets and businesses for more than the purchase price.

- *Companies that are financially distressed*—such businesses can often be purchased at a bargain price, their operations turned around with the aid of the parent companies' financial resources and managerial know-how, and then either held as long-term investments (because of their strong earnings or cash flow potential) or sold at a profit, whichever is more attractive.

- *Companies that have bright growth prospects but are short on investment capital*—capital poor, opportunity-rich companies are usually coveted diversification candidates for a financially strong, opportunity-seeking firm.

Companies that pursue unrelated diversification nearly always enter new businesses by acquiring an established company rather than by forming a start-up subsidiary within their own corporate structures. Their premise is that growth by acquisition translates into enhanced shareholder value. Suspending application of the better-off test is seen as justifiable so long as unrelated diversification results in sustained growth in corporate revenues and earnings and so long as none of the acquired businesses end up performing badly.

Illustration Capsule 26 shows the business portfolios of several companies that have pursued unrelated diversification. Such companies are frequently labeled *conglomerates* because there is no strategic theme in their diversification makeup and because their business interests range broadly across diverse industries.

The Pros and Cons of Unrelated Diversification

Unrelated or conglomerate diversification has appeal from several financial angles:

1. Business risk is scattered over a set of *diverse* industries—a superior way to diversify financial risk as compared to related diversification because the company's investments can be spread over businesses with totally different technologies, competitive forces, market features, and customer bases.[10]

2. The company's financial resources can be employed to maximum advantage by investing in *whatever industries* offer the best profit prospects (as opposed

---

[10]While such arguments have logical appeal, there is research showing that related diversification is less risky from a financial perspective than is unrelated diversification; see, Michael Lubatkin and Sayan Chatterjee, "Extending Modern Portfolio Theory into the Domain of Corporate Diversification: Does It Apply?" *Academy of Management Journal* 37, no. 1 (February 1994), pp. 109–36.

ILLUSTRATION CAPSULE 26   Diversified Companies with Unrelated Business Portfolios

Union Pacific Corporation
- Railroad operations (Union Pacific Railroad Company)
- Oil and gas exploration
- Mining
- Microwave and fiber optic transportation information and control systems
- Hazardous waste management disposal
- Trucking (Overnite Transportation Company)
- Oil refining
- Real estate

Rockwell International
- Industrial automation products (Reliance electric, Allen-Bradley, Sprecher & Schuh, Datamyte, Rockwell, Dodge, Electro Craft)
- Commercial aviation electronics systems
- Semiconductors
- PC modems
- Defense electronics systems
- Aerospace (Rocketdyne reusable Space Shuttle Main Engines, codeveloper of the X-33 and X-34 reusable launcher for satellites and heavy payloads)
- Heavy-duty automotive systems (axles, brakes, clutches, transmissions)
- Light automobile systems (sunroofs, doors, access controls, seat adjustment controls, suspension systems, electric motors, wheels)
- Newspaper printing press systems

Cooper Industries
- Crescent wrenches and Nicholson files
- Champion spark plugs
- Gardner-Denver mining equipment

United Technologies, Inc.
- Pratt & Whitney aircraft engines
- Carrier heating and air-conditioning equipment
- Otis elevators
- Norden defense systems
- Hamilton Standard controls
- Automotive components

Textron, Inc.
- Bell helicopters
- Paul Revere Insurance
- Cessna Aircraft
- E-Z-Go golf carts
- Missile reentry systems
- Textron automotive interior and exterior parts
- Specialty fasteners
- Avco Financial Services
- Jacobsen turf care equipment
- Tanks and armored vehicles,

The Walt Disney Company
- Theme parks
- Movie production (for both children and adults)
- Videos
- Children's apparel
- Toys and stuffed animals
- Television broadcasting (ABC network and The Disney Channel)

American Standard
- Air-conditioning products (Trane, American Standard)
- Plumbing products (American Standard, Ideal Standard, Standard, Porcher)
- Automotive Products (commercial and utility vehicle braking and control systems)

Source: Company annual reports.

to considering only opportunities in related industries). Specifically, cash flows from company businesses with lower growth and profit prospects can be diverted to acquiring and expanding businesses with higher growth and profit potentials.

3. Company profitability may prove somewhat more stable because hard times in one industry may be partially offset by good times in another—ideally, cyclical downswings in some of the company's businesses are counterbalanced by cyclical upswings in other businesses the company has diversified into.

4. To the extent that corporate-level managers are exceptionally astute at spotting bargain-priced companies with big upside profit potential, shareholder wealth can be enhanced.

While entry into an unrelated business can often pass the attractiveness and the cost-of-entry tests (and sometimes even the better-off test), a strategy of unrelated diversification has drawbacks. One Achilles' heel of conglomerate diversification is the big demand it places on corporate-level management to make sound decisions regarding fundamentally different businesses operating in fundamentally different industry and competitive environments. The greater the number of businesses a company is in and the more diverse they are, the harder it is for corporate-level executives to oversee each subsidiary and spot problems early, to have real expertise in evaluating the attractiveness of each business's industry and competitive environment, and to judge the caliber of strategic actions and plans proposed by business-level managers. As one president of a diversified firm expressed it:

> *The two biggest drawbacks to unrelated diversification are the difficulties of competently managing many different businesses and being without the added source of competitive advantage that strategic fit provides.*

> . . . we've got to make sure that our core businesses are properly managed for solid, long-term earnings. We can't just sit back and watch the numbers. We've got to know what the real issues are out there in the profit centers. Otherwise, we're not even in a position to check out our managers on the big decisions.[11]

With broad diversification, corporate managers have to be shrewd and talented enough to (1) tell a good acquisition from a bad acquisition, (2) select capable managers to run each of many different businesses, (3) discern when the major strategic proposals of business-unit managers are sound, and (4) know what to do if a business unit stumbles.[12] Because every business tends to encounter rough sledding, a good way to gauge the risk of diversifying into new unrelated areas is to ask, "If the new business got into trouble, would we know how to bail it out?" When the answer is no, unrelated diversification can pose significant financial risk and the business's profit prospects are more chancy.[13] As the former chairman of a *Fortune* 500 company advised, "Never acquire a business you don't know how to run." It takes only one or two big strategic mistakes (misjudging industry attractiveness, encountering unexpected problems in a newly acquired business, or being too optimistic about how hard it will be to turn a struggling subsidiary around) to cause corporate earnings to plunge and crash the parent company's stock price.

Second, without the competitive advantage potential of strategic fit, consolidated performance of an unrelated multibusiness portfolio tends to be no better than the sum of what the individual business units could achieve if they were independent, and it may be worse to the extent that corporate managers meddle unwisely in business-unit operations or hamstring them with corporate policies. Except, perhaps, for the added financial backing that a cash-rich corporate parent can provide, a strategy of unrelated diversification does nothing for the competitive strength of the individual business units. Each business is on its own in trying to build a competitive edge—the unrelated nature of sister businesses offers no common ground for cost reduction, skills transfer, or technology sharing. In a widely diversified firm, the value added by corporate managers depends primarily on how good they are at deciding what new businesses to add, which ones to get rid of, how best to deploy available financial resources to build

---

[11]Carter F. Bales, "Strategic Control: The President's Paradox," *Business Horizons* 20, no. 4 (August 1977), p. 17.

[12]For a review of the experiences of companies that have pursued unrelated diversification successfully, see Patricia L. Anslinger and Thomas E. Copeland, "Growth through Acquisitions: A Fresh Look," *Harvard Business Review* 74, no. 1 (January–February 1996), pp. 126–35.

[13]Of course, management may be willing to assume the risk that trouble will not strike before it has had time to learn the business well enough to bail it out of almost any difficulty. But there is research that shows this is very risky from a financial perspective; see, for example, Lubatkin and Chatterjee, "Extending Modern Portfolio Theory into the Domain of Corporate Diversification: Does It Apply?" pp. 132–33.

a higher-performing collection of businesses, and the quality of the guidance they give to the managers of their business subsidiaries.

Third, although in theory unrelated diversification offers the potential for greater sales-profit stability over the course of the business cycle, in practice attempts at countercyclical diversification fall short of the mark. Few attractive businesses have opposite up-and-down cycles; the great majority of businesses are similarly affected by economic good times and hard times. There's no convincing evidence that the consolidated profits of broadly diversified firms are more stable or less subject to reversal in periods of recession and economic stress than the profits of less diversified firms.

Despite these drawbacks, unrelated diversification can sometimes be a desirable corporate strategy. It certainly merits consideration when a firm needs to diversify away from an endangered or unattractive industry and has no distinctive competencies or capabilities it can transfer to an adjacent industry. There's also a rationale for pure diversification to the extent owners have a strong preference for investing in several unrelated businesses instead of a family of related ones. Otherwise, the argument for unrelated diversification hinges on the case-by-case prospects for financial gain.

A key issue in unrelated diversification is how wide a net to cast in building the business portfolio. In other words, should a company invest in few or many unrelated businesses? How much business diversity can corporate executives successfully manage? A reasonable way to resolve the issue of how much diversification is to ask "What is the least diversification it will take to achieve acceptable growth and profitability?" and "What is the most diversification that can be managed given the complexity it adds?"[14] The optimal amount of diversification usually lies between these two extremes.

Unrelated Diversification and Shareholder Value

Unrelated diversification is fundamentally a finance-driven approach to creating shareholder value whereas related diversification is fundamentally strategy-driven.

Unrelated diversification is a financial approach to creating shareholder value; related diversification, in contrast, represents a strategic approach.

Related diversification represents a strategic approach to building shareholder value because it is predicated on exploiting the linkages between the value chains of different businesses to lower costs, transfer skills and technological expertise across businesses, and gain other strategic-fit benefits. The objective is to convert the strategic fits among the firm's businesses into an extra measure of competitive advantage that goes beyond what business subsidiaries are able to achieve on their own. The added competitive advantage a firm achieves through related diversification is the driver for building greater shareholder value.

In contrast, *unrelated diversification is principally a financial approach to creating shareholder value* because it is predicated on astute deployment of corporate financial resources and executive skill in spotting financially attractive business opportunities. Since unrelated diversification produces no strategic-fit opportunities of consequence, corporate strategists can't build shareholder value by acquiring companies that create or compound competitive advantage for its business subsidiaries—in a conglomerate, competitive advantage doesn't go beyond what each business subsidiary can achieve independently through its own competitive strategy. Consequently, for unrelated diversification to result in enhanced shareholder

---

[14]Drucker, *Management: Tasks, Responsibilities, Practices,* pp. 692–93.

value (above the 2 + 2 = 4 effect that the subsidiary businesses could produce operating independently), corporate strategists must exhibit *superior skills* in creating and managing a portfolio of diversified business interests. This specifically means:

For corporate strategists to build shareholder value in some way other than through strategic fits and competitive advantage, they must be smart enough to produce financial results from a group of businesses that exceed what business-level managers can produce.

- Doing a superior job of diversifying into new businesses that can produce consistently good returns on investment (satisfying the attractiveness test).
- Doing a superior job of negotiating favorable acquisition prices (satisfying the cost-of-entry test).
- Being shrewd enough to sell previously acquired business subsidiaries at their peak and getting premium prices (this requires skills in discerning when a business subsidiary is on the verge of confronting adverse industry and competitive conditions and probable declines in long-term profitability).
- Wisely and aggressively shifting corporate financial resources out of businesses where profit opportunities are dim and into businesses where rapid earnings growth and high returns on investment are occurring.
- Doing such a good job overseeing the firm's business subsidiaries and contributing to how they are managed (by providing expert problem-solving skills, creative strategy suggestions, and decision-making guidance to business-level managers) that the businesses perform at a higher level than they would otherwise be able to do (a possible way to satisfy the better-off test).

To the extent that corporate executives are able to craft and execute a strategy of unrelated diversification that produces enough of the above outcomes for an enterprise to consistently outperform other firms in generating dividends and capital gains for stockholders, then a case can be made that shareholder value has truly been enhanced. Achieving such results consistently requires supertalented corporate executives, however. Without them, unrelated diversification is a very dubious and unreliable way to try to build shareholder value—there are far more who have tried and failed than who have tried and succeeded.

DIVESTITURE AND LIQUIDATION STRATEGIES

Even a shrewd corporate diversification strategy can result in the acquisition of business units that, down the road, just do not work out. Misfits cannot be completely avoided because it is difficult to foresee how getting into a new line of business will actually work out. In addition, long-term industry attractiveness changes with the times; what was once a good diversification move into an attractive industry may later turn sour. Subpar performance by some business units is bound to occur, thereby raising questions of whether to keep them or divest them. Other business units, despite adequate financial performance, may not mesh as well with the rest of the firm as was originally thought.

A business needs to be considered for divestiture when corporate strategists conclude it no longer fits or is an attractive investment.

Sometimes, a diversification move that seems sensible from a strategic-fit standpoint turns out to lack *cultural fit*.[15] Several pharmaceutical companies had just this experience. When they diversified into cosmetics and perfume, they discov-

---

[15]Ibid., p. 709.

ered their personnel had little respect for the "frivolous" nature of such products compared to the far nobler task of developing miracle drugs to cure the ill. The absence of shared values and cultural compatibility between the medical research and chemical-compounding expertise of the pharmaceutical companies and the fashion-marketing orientation of the cosmetics business was the undoing of what otherwise was diversification into businesses with technology-sharing potential, product-development fit, and some overlap in distribution channels.

When a particular line of business loses its appeal, the most attractive solution usually is to sell it. Normally such businesses should be divested as fast as is practical. To drag things out serves no purpose unless time is needed to get it into better shape to sell. The more business units in a diversified firm's portfolio, the more likely that it will have occasion to divest poor performers, "dogs," and misfits. A useful guide to determine if and when to divest a business subsidiary is to ask the question, "If we were not in this business today, would we want to get into it now?"[16] When the answer is no or probably not, divestiture should be considered.

Divestiture can take either of two forms. The parent can spin off a business as a financially and managerially independent company in which the parent company may or may not retain partial ownership. Or the parent may sell the unit outright, in which case a buyer needs to be found. As a rule, divestiture should not be approached from the angle of "Who can we pawn this business off on and what is the most we can get for it?"[17] Instead, it is wiser to ask "For what sort of organization would this business be a good fit, and under what conditions would it be viewed as a good deal?" Organizations for which the business is a good fit are likely to pay the highest price.

Of all the strategic alternatives, liquidation is the most unpleasant and painful, especially for a single-business enterprise where it means the organization ceases to exist. For a multi-industry, multibusiness firm to liquidate one of its lines of business is less traumatic. The hardships of job eliminations, plant closings, and so on, while not to be minimized, still leave an ongoing organization, perhaps one that is healthier after its pruning. In hopeless situations, an early liquidation effort usually serves owner-stockholder interests better than an inevitable bankruptcy. Prolonging the pursuit of a lost cause exhausts an organization's resources and leaves less to liquidate; it can also mar reputations and ruin management careers. The problem, of course, is differentiating between when a turnaround is achievable and when it isn't. It is easy for managers to let their emotions and pride overcome sound judgment when a business gets in such deep trouble that a successful turnaround is remote.

CORPORATE TURNAROUND, RETRENCHMENT, AND PORTFOLIO RESTRUCTURING STRATEGIES

Turnaround, retrenchment, and portfolio restructuring strategies come into play when a diversified company's management has to restore an ailing business portfolio to good health. Poor performance can be caused by large losses in one or more business units that pull the corporation's overall financial performance down, a disproportion-

---

[16]Ibid., p. 94.
[17]Ibid., p. 719.

ate number of businesses in unattractive industries, a bad economy adversely impacting many of the firm's business units, an excessive debt burden, or ill-chosen acquisitions that haven't lived up to expectations.

Corporate turnaround strategies focus on efforts to restore a diversified company's money-losing businesses to profitability instead of divesting them. The intent is to get the whole company back in the black by curing the problems of those businesses that are most responsible for pulling overall performance down. Turnaround strategies are most appropriate when the reasons for poor performance are short-term, the ailing businesses are in attractive industries, and divesting the money losers does not make long-term strategic sense.

Corporate retrenchment strategies involve reducing the scope of diversification to a smaller number of businesses. Retrenchment is usually undertaken when corporate management concludes that the company is in too many businesses and needs to narrow its business base. Sometimes diversified firms retrench because they can't make certain businesses profitable after several frustrating years of trying or because they lack funds to support the investment needs of all of their business subsidiaries. More commonly, however, corporate executives conclude that the firm's diversification efforts have ranged too far afield and that the key to improved long-term performance lies in concentrating on building strong positions in a smaller number of businesses. Retrenchment is usually accomplished by divesting businesses that are too small to make a sizable contribution to earnings or that have little or no strategic fit with the businesses that management wants to concentrate on. Divesting such businesses frees resources that can be used to reduce debt, to support expansion of the remaining businesses, or to make acquisitions that strengthen the company's competitive position in one or more of the remaining businesses.

Portfolio restructuring strategies involve radical surgery on the mix and percentage makeup of the types of businesses in the portfolio. For instance, one company over a two-year period divested 4 business units, closed down the operations of 4 others, and added 25 new lines of business to its portfolio, 16 through acquisition and 9 through internal start-up. Other companies have elected to demerge their businesses and split into two or more independent companies—AT&T, for instance, has divided into three companies (one for long distance and other telecommunications services that will retain the AT&T name, one for manufacturing telephone equipment callent Lucent Technologies, and one for computer systems, called NCR, that essentially represents the divestiture of AT&T's earlier acquisition of NCR). Restructuring can be prompted by any of several conditions:

1. When a strategy review reveals that the firm's long-term performance prospects have become unattractive because the portfolio contains too many slow-growth, declining, or competitively weak business units.

2. When one or more of the firm's principal businesses fall prey to hard times.

3. When a new CEO takes over and decides to redirect where the company is headed.

4. When "wave of the future" technologies or products emerge and a major shakeup of the portfolio is needed to build a position in a potentially big new industry.

5. When the firm has a unique opportunity to make an acquisition so big that it has to sell several existing business units to finance the new acquisition.

6. When major businesses in the portfolio have become more and more unattractive, forcing a shakeup in the portfolio in order to produce satisfactory long-term corporate performance.

Portfolio restructuring involves revamping a diversified company's business makeup through a series of divestitures and new acquisitions.

7. When changes in markets and technologies of certain businesses proceed in such different directions that it is better to split the company into separate pieces rather than remain together under the same corporate umbrella.

Candidates for divestiture typically include not only weak or up-and-down performers or those in unattractive industries, but also those that no longer fit (even though they may be profitable and in attractive-enough industries).

Many broadly diversified companies, disenchanted with the performance of some acquisitions and having only mixed success in overseeing so many unrelated business units, restructure to enable concentration on a smaller core of at least partially related businesses. Business units incompatible with newly established related diversification criteria are divested, the remaining units regrouped and aligned to capture more strategic fit benefits, and new acquisitions made to strengthen the parent company's position in the industries it has chosen to emphasize.[18]

Most recently, portfolio restructuring has centered on demerging—splitting a broadly diversified company into several independent companies. Notable examples of companies pursuing demerger include ITT, Westinghouse, and Britian's Imperial Chemical and Hanson, plc. Before beginning to divest and demerge in 1995, Hanson owned companies with more than $20 billion in revenues in businesses as diverse as beer, exercise equipment, tools, construction cranes, tobacco, cement, chemicals, coal mining, electricity, hot tubs and whirlpools, cookware, rock and gravel, bricks, and asphalt; understandably, investors and analysts had a hard time understanding the company and its strategies. By early 1997, Hanson had demerged into a $3.8 billion enterprise focused more narrowly on gravel, crushed rock, cement, asphalt, bricks, and construction cranes; the remaining businesses were divided into four groups and divested. Another example of portfolio restructuring is presented in Illustration Capsule 26 (see p. 226).

The strategies of broadly diversified companies to demerge and deconglomerate have been driven by a growing preference among company executives and investors for building diversification around the creation of strong competitive positions in a few, well-selected industries. Indeed, investor disenchantment with the conglomerate approach to diversification has been so pronounced (evident in the fact that conglomerates often have *lower* price-earnings ratios than companies with related diversification strategies) that some broadly diversified companies have restructured their portfolios and retrenched to escape being regarded as a conglomerate.

MULTINATIONAL DIVERSIFICATION STRATEGIES

The distinguishing characteristics of a multinational diversification strategy are a *diversity of businesses* and a *diversity of national markets*.[19] Not only do the managers of a diversified multinational corporation (DMNC) have to conceive and execute

---

[18]Evidence that corporate restructuring and pruning down to a narrower business base produces improved corporate performance is contained in Constantinos C. Markides, "Diversification, Restructuring and Economic Performance," *Strategic Management Journal* 16 (February 1995), pp. 101–18.

[19]C. K. Prahalad and Yves L. Doz, *The Multinational Mission* (New York: Free Press, 1987), p. 2.

a substantial number of strategies—at least one for each industry, with as many multinational variations as conditions in each country market dictate—but they also have the added challenge of conceiving good ways to coordinate the firm's strategic actions across industries and countries. This effort can do more than just bring the full force of corporate resources and capabilities to the task of building a strong competitive position in each business and national market. *Capitalizing on opportunities for strategic coordination across businesses and countries provides an avenue for sustainable competitive advantage not open to a company that competes in only one country or one business.*[20]

The Emergence of Multinational Diversification

Until the 1960s, multinational companies (MNCs) operated fairly autonomous subsidiaries in each host country, each catering to the special requirements of its own national market.[21] Management tasks at company headquarters primarily involved finance functions, technology transfer, and export coordination. Even though their products and competitive strategies were tailored to market conditions in each country, a multinational company could still realize competitive advantage by learning to transfer technology, manufacturing know-how, brand-name identification, and marketing and management skills from country to country quite efficiently, giving them an edge over smaller host country competitors. Standardized administrative procedures helped minimize overhead costs, and once an initial organization for managing foreign subsidiaries was put in place, entry into additional national markets could be accomplished at low incremental costs.

During the 1970s, however, buyer preferences for some products converged enough that it became feasible to market common product versions across different country markets. No longer was it essential or even desirable to have strategies and products custom-tailored to customer preferences and competitive conditions prevailing in specific country markets. Moreover, as Japanese, European, and U.S. companies pursued international expansion in the wake of trade liberalization and the opening up of market opportunities in both industrialized and less-developed countries, they found themselves in head-to-head competition in country after country.[22] *Global competition*—where the leading companies in an industry competed head to head in most of the world's major country markets—began to emerge.

As the relevant market arena in more and more industries shifted from national to international to global, traditional MNCs were driven to integrate their operations across national borders in a quest for better efficiencies and lower manufacturing costs. Instead of separately manufacturing a complete product range in each country, plants became more specialized in their production operations to gain the economies of longer production runs, to permit use of faster automated equipment, and to capture experience curve effects. Country subsidiaries obtained the rest of the product range they needed from sister plants in other countries. Gains in manufacturing efficiencies from converting to state-of-the-art, world-scale manufacturing plants more than offset increased international shipping costs, especially in light of the other advantages globalized strategies offered. With a global strategy, an MNC could

[20]Ibid., p. 15.

[21]Yves L. Doz, *Strategic Management in Multinational Companies* (New York: Pergamon Press, 1985), p. 1.

[22]Ibid., pp. 2–3.

locate plants in countries with low labor costs—a key consideration in industries whose products have high labor content. With a global strategy, an MNC could also exploit differences in tax rates, setting transfer prices in its integrated operations to produce higher profits in low-tax countries and lower profits in high-tax countries. Global strategic coordination also increased MNC's ability to take advantage of country-to-country differences in interest rates, exchange rates, credit terms, government subsidies, and export guarantees. These advantages made it increasingly difficult for a company that produced and sold its product in only one country to succeed in an industry populated with multinational competitors intent on achieving global dominance.

During the 1980s another source of competitive advantage began to emerge: using the strategic fit advantages of related diversification to build stronger competitive positions in several related global industries simultaneously. Being a diversified MNC (DMNC) became competitively superior to being a single-business MNC in cases where strategic fits existed across globally competitive industries. Related diversification proved most capable of producing competitive advantage when a multinational company's expertise in a core technology could be applied in different industries (at least one of which was global) and where there were important economies of scope and brand name advantages to being in a family of related businesses.[23] Illustration Capsule 27 describes how Honda has exploited gasoline engine technology and its well-known name by diversifying into a variety of products powered by gasoline engines.

A multinational corporation can gain competitive advantage by diversifying into global industries having related technologies or possessing value chain relationships that yield economies of scope.

Sources of Competitive Advantage for a DMNC

A strategy of related diversification into industries where global competition prevails opens several avenues of competitive advantage not available to a domestic-only competitor or a single-business competitor:

1. A diversified multinational company can realize competitive advantage by transferring its expertise in a core technology to other lines of business able to benefit from its technical know-how and capabilities.

2. A diversified multinational company with expertise in a core technology and a family of businesses using this technology can capture competitive advantage through a collaborative and strategically coordinated R&D effort on behalf of all the related businesses as a group.

3. A diversified multinational company with businesses that use the same distributors and retail dealers worldwide can (a) diversify into new businesses using the same worldwide distribution capabilities at relatively little expense and use the distribution-related economies of scope as a source of cost advantage over less diversified rivals, (b) can exploit its worldwide distribution capability by diversifying into businesses having attractive sales growth opportunites in the very country markets where its distribution capability is already established, and (c) can gain added bargaining leverage with retailers in securing attractive shelf space for any new products and businesses as its family of businesses grows in number and sales importance to the retailer. Sony, for example, has attractive competitive advantage potential in diversifying into the videogame industry to take on giants like

---

[23]Pralahad and Doz, *The Multinational Mission*, pp. 62–63.

ILLUSTRATION CAPSULE 27   Honda's Competitive Advantage

Expertise in the Technology of Gasoline Engines

At first blush anyone looking at Honda's lineup of products—cars, motorcycles, lawn mowers, power generators, outboard motors, snowmobiles, snowblowers, and garden tillers—might conclude that Honda has pursued unrelated diversification. But underlying the obvious product diversity is a common core: the technology of gasoline engines.

Honda's strategy involves transferring the company's expertise in gasoline engine technology to additional products, exploiting its capabilities in low-cost/high-quality manufacturing, using the widely known and respected Honda brand name on all the products, and promoting several products in the same ad (one Honda ad teased consumers with the question, "How do you put six Hondas in a two-car garage?" and then showed a garage containing a Honda car, a Honda motorcycle, a Honda snowmobile, a Honda lawnmower, a Honda power generator, and a Honda outboard motor). The relatedness in the value chains for the products in Honda's business lineup produces competitive advantage for Honda in the form of economies of scope, beneficial opportunities to transfer technology and capabilities from one business to another, and economical use of a common brand name.

Honda's Competitive Advantage

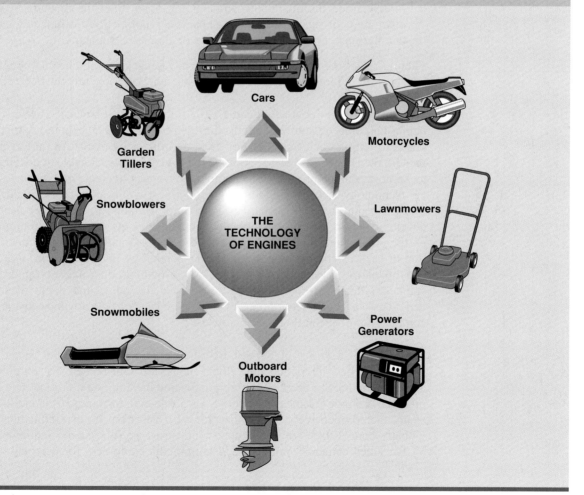

Source: Adapted from C. K. Prahalad and Yves L. Doz, *The Multinational Mission* (New York: Free Press, 1987), p. 62.

Nintendo and SEGA because (a) it has well-established distribution capabilities in consumer electronics worldwide that can be used for videogame game products, (b) it has the capability to go after videogame sales in all country markets where it presently does business, and (c) it has the marketing clout to persuade retailers to give Sony videogame products good visibility in retail stores.

4. A diversified multinational company can leverage its brand name by diversifying into additional businesses able to use its already established brand, thereby capturing economies of scope and marketing benefits. Sony, for example, doesn't have to spend nearly as much advertising and promoting its new videogame products against the offerings of Nintendo and Sega because the Sony brand name already has a strong reputation in consumer electronics worldwide.

5. A diversified multinational company can use the financial and organizational resources it has from operations in other countries to cross-subsidize a competitive assault on the market position of a one-country competitor.

6. A diversified multinational company can draw upon the financial resources in other lines of business to cross-subsidize a competitive offensive against a one-business multinational company or domestic company.

There's a growing evidence that all these advantages are significant enough to result in DMNCs' achieving high returns and having lower overall business risk.[24]

The Competitive Power of a Collaborative R&D Effort and Technology Transfer   By channeling corporate resources directly into a *combined* R&D/technology effort, as opposed to letting each business unit fund and direct its own R&D effort however it sees fit, the DMNC can merge its expertise and efforts *worldwide* to advance the core technology, pursue promising technological avenues to create new businesses, generate technology-based manufacturing economies within and across product/business lines, expedite across-the-board product improvements in existing businesses, and develop new products that complement and enhance the sales of existing products. If, on the other hand, R&D activities are decentralized and put totally under the direction of each existing business unit, R&D/technology investments are more prone to end up narrowly aimed at each business's own product-market opportunities. A splintered R&D effort is unlikely to produce the range and depth of strategic fit benefits as a broad, coordinated companywide effort to advance and exploit the company's full technological expertise.[25]

The Competitive Power of Related Distribution and Common Brand Name Usage   A DMNC that has diversified into global industries with related distribution channels and opportunities to use a common brand name has important competitive advantage potential a single-business competitor or a one-country competitor lacks. Consider, again, the competitive strength that Sony derives from its diversification into such globally competitive consumer goods industries as TVs, stereo equipment, radios, VCRs, video cameras, monitors and multimedia equipment for personal computers,

---

[24]See, for example, W. Chan Kim, Peter Hwang, and Willem P. Burgers, "Multinational's Diversification and the Risk-Return Tradeoff," *Strategic Management Journal* 14 (May 1993) pp. 275–86.

[25]Ibid.

CDs, and videogames—all distributed and marketed through the same types of distributors and retail dealers worldwide and all able to capitalize on use of the Sony brand name. Sony's approach to diversification has allowed it to build worldwide distribution capabilities in consumer electronics products, capture logistical and distribution-related economies of scope, and establish high levels of brand awareness for its products in countries all across the world.[26] A single-business competitor is disadvantaged in competing against Sony because it lacks access to distribution-related economies of scope, it doesn't have Sony's ability to transfer its brand reputation in one line of business to another and achieve advertising economies, and it can't match Sony's clout in bargaining for favorable shelf space in retail stores. A domestic-only competitor is at a disadvantage on costs if its national sales volume is too small to achieve the scale economies afforded by Sony's global-sized sales volume. Moreover, Sony's already-established *global* distribution capabilities and *global* brand-name recognition give it an important cost advantage over a one-country competitor looking at the costs of trying to expand into foreign country markets for the first time and better position itself as a global competitor against Sony. Similarly, Sony's economies of scope (both distribution-related and brand name-related) give it a cost advantage over a one-business competitor (with no existing economies of scope) that might be looking to diversify into a business that Sony is already in.

> *A multinational corporation can also gain competitive advantage by diversifying into global industries with* **related** *distribution channels and opportunities for common use of a well-known brand.*

The Competitive Power of Using Cross-Subsidization to Outcompete a One-Business Company Both a one-business domestic company and a one-business multinational company are weakly positioned to defend their market positions against a DMNC determined to establish a solid long-term competitive position in their market and willing to accept lower short-term profits in order to do so. A one-business domestic company has only one profit sanctuary—its home market. A one-business multinational company may have profit sanctuaries in several country markets but all are in the same business. Each is vulnerable to a DMNC that launches a major strategic offensive in their profit sanctuaries and lowballs its prices and/or spends extravagantly on advertising to win market share at their expense. A DMNC's ability to keep hammering away at competitors with lowball prices year after year may reflect either a cost advantage growing out of its related diversification strategy or a willingness to cross-subsidize low profits or even losses with earnings from its profit sanctuaries in other country markets and/or its earnings from other businesses. Sony, for example, by pursuing related diversification keyed to product-distribution-technology strategic fit and managing its product families on a global scale, has the ability to put strong competitive pressure on domestic companies like Zenith (which manufactures TVs and small computer systems) and Magnavox (which manufactures TVs, VCRs, stereo equipment, and monitors for personal computers). Sony can lowball its prices on TVs or fund special promotions for its TVs, using earnings from its other country markets and lines of business to help support its assault. If Sony chooses, it can keep its prices low or spend lavishly on advertising for several years, persistently pecking away at Zenith's and Magnavox's market shares in TVs over time. At the same time, it can draw upon its considerable resources in R&D, its ability to transfer technology from one product

> *A well-diversified family of businesses and a multinational market base give a DMNC the power and resource strength to subsidize a long-term market offensive against one-market or one-business competitors with earnings from one or more of its country market profit sanctuaries and/or earnings in other businesses.*

---

[26]Ibid., p. 64.

ILLUSTRATION CAPSULE 28   Mitsubishi: The Competitive Power of a Japanese Keiretsu

Mitsubishi is Japan's largest *keiretsu*—a family of affiliated companies. With combined 1995 sales of $184 billion, the Mitsubishi keiretsu consists of 28 core companies: Mitsubishi Corp. (the trading company), Mitsubishi Heavy Industries (the group's biggest manufacturer—shipbuilding, air conditioners, forklifts, robots, gas turbines), Mitsubishi Motors, Mitsubishi Steel, Mitsubishi Aluminum, Mitsubishi Oil, Mitsubishi Petrochemical, Mitsubishi Gas Chemical, Mitsubishi Plastics, Mitsubishi Cable, Mitsubishi Electric, Mitsubishi Construction, Mitsubishi Paper Mills, Mitsubishi Mining and Cement, Mitsubishi Rayon, Nikon, Asahi Glass, Kirin Brewery, Mitsubishi Bank (the world's fifth largest bank and the lead bank for family companies), Tokio Marine and Fire Insurance (one of the world's largest insurance companies), and eight others. Beyond this core group are hundreds of other Mitsubishi-related subsidiaries and affiliates.

The 28 core companies of the Mitsubishi *keiretsu* are bound together by cross-ownership of each other's stock (the percentage of shares of each core company owned by other members ranges from 17 percent to 100 percent, with an average of 27 percent), by interlocking directorships (it is standard for officers of one company to sit on the boards of other *keiretsu* members), joint ventures, and long-term business relationships. They use each other's products and services in many instances—among the suppliers to Mitsubishi Motor's Diamond

Star plant in Bloomington, Illinois, are 25 Mitsubishi and Mitsubishi-related suppliers. It is common for them to join forces to make acquisitions—five Mitsubishi companies teamed to buy a cement plant in California; Mitsubishi Corp. bought an $880 million chemical company in Pittsburgh with financial assistance from Mitsubishi Bank and Mitsubishi Trust, then sold pieces to Mitsubishi Gas Chemical, Mitsubishi Rayon, Mitsubishi Petrochemical, and Mitsubishi Kasei. Mitsubishi Bank and occasionally other Mitsubishi financial enterprises serve as a primary financing source for new ventures and as a financial safety net if *keiretsu* members encounter tough market conditions or have financial problems.

Despite these links, there's no grand Mitsubishi strategy. Each company operates independently, pursuing its own strategy and markets. On occasion, group members find themselves going after the same markets competing with each other. Nor do member companies usually get sweetheart deals from other members; for example, Mitsubishi Heavy Industries lost out to Siemens in competing to supply gas turbines to a new power plant that Mitsubishi Corp.'s wholly owned Diamond Energy subsidiary constructed in Virginia. But operating independence does not prevent them from recognizing their mutual interests, cooperating voluntarily without formal controls, or turning inward to *keiretsu* members for business partnerships on ventures perceived as strategically important.

---

family to another, and its expertise in product innovation to introduce appealing new features and better picture quality. Such competitive actions not only enhance Sony's own brand image but they make it very tough for Zenith and Magnavox to match its prices, advertising, and product development efforts and still earn acceptable profits.

Although cross-subsidization is a potent competitive weapon, it can only be used sparingly because of its adverse impact on overall corporate profitability.

Sony can turn its attention to becoming attractively profitable once the battle for market share and competitive position is won.[27] Some additional aspects of the competitive power of broadly diversified enterprises is described in Illustration Capsule 28.

The Combined Effects of These Advantages Is Potent   Companies with a strategy of (1) diversifying into *related* industries and (2) competing *globally* in each of these industries thus can draw upon any of several competitive advantage opportunities to overcome a domestic-only rival or a single business rival. A DMNC's biggest competitive advantage potential comes from concentrating its diversification efforts in industries where there are technology-sharing and technology-transfer opportunities and where there are important economies of scope and brand-name benefits. The more a company's diversification

---

[27]Ibid.

A President's Council, consisting of 49 chairmen and presidents, meets monthly, usually the second Friday of the month. While the formal agenda typically includes a discussion of joint philanthropical and public relations projects and a lecture by an expert on some current topic, participants report instances where strategic problems or opportunities affecting several group members are discussed and major decisions made. It is common for a Mitsubishi company involved in a major undertaking (initiating its first foray into the U.S. or European markets or developing a new technology) to ask for support from other members. In such cases, group members who can take business actions that contribute to solutions are expected to do so. The President's Council meetings also serve to cement personal ties, exchange information, identify mutual interests, and set up follow-on actions by subordinates. Other ways that Mitsubishi uses to foster an active informal network of contacts, information sharing, cooperation, and business relationships among member companies include regular get-togethers of Mitsubishi-America and Mitsubishi-Europe executives and even a matchmaking club where member company employees can meet prospective spouses.

In recent years, Mitsubishi companies introduced a number of consumer products in the United States and elsewhere, all branded with a three-diamond logo derived from the crest of the founding samurai family—cars and trucks made by Mitsubishi Motors, big-screen TVs and mobile phones made by Mitsubishi Electric, and air conditioners produced by Mitsubishi Heavy Industries. Mitsubishi executives believe common logo usage has produced added brand awareness; for example, in the United States Mitsubishi Motors' efforts to advertise and market its cars and trucks helped boost brand awareness of Mitsubishi TVs. In several product categories one or more Mitsubishi companies operate in stages all along the industry value chain—from components production to assembly to shipping, warehousing, and distribution.

Similar practices exist in the other five of the six largest Japanese *keiretsu*: Dai-Ichi Kangin with 47 core companies, Mitsui Group with 24 core companies (including Toyota and Toshiba), Sanwa with 44 core companies, Sumitomo with 20 core companies (including NEC, a maker of telecommunications equipment and personal computers), and Fuyo with 29 core companies (including Nissan and Canon). Most observers agree that Japan's keiretsu model gives Japanese companies major competitive advantages in international markets. According to a Japanese economics professor at Osaka University, "Using group power, they can engage in cutthroat competition."

Source: Based on information in "Mighty Mitsubishi Is on the Move" and "Hands across America: The Rise of Mitsubishi," *Business Week*, September 24, 1990, pp. 98–107.

strategy yields these kinds of strategic fit benefits, the more powerful a competitor it becomes and the better its profit and growth performance is likely to be. Relying on strategic fit advantages to outcompete rivals is inherently more attractive than resorting to cross-subsidization.

While a DMNC can employ cross-subsidization tactics to muscle its way into attractive new markets or outcompete a particular rival, its ability to use cross-subsidization is limited by the need to maintain respectable levels of overall profitability. It is one thing to *occasionally* use a *portion* of the profits and cash flows from existing businesses to cover *reasonable* short-term losses to gain entry to a new business or a new country market or wage a competitive offensive against certain rivals. It is quite another thing to *regularly* use cross-subsidization tactics to fund competitive inroads in new areas and *weaken overall company performance* on an *ongoing* basis. A DMNC is under the same pressures as any other company to earn consistently acceptable profits across its whole business portfolio. At some juncture, every business and every market entered needs to make a profit contribution or become a candidate for abandonment. As a general rule, *cross-subsidization is justified only if there is a good prospect that the short-term impairment to corporate profitability will be offset by stronger competitiveness and better overall profitability over the long term.*

COMBINATION RELATED-UNRELATED DIVERSIFICATION STRATEGIES

Nothing prevents a company from diversifying into both related and unrelated businesses. Indeed, in actual practice the business makeup of diversified companies varies considerably. Some diversified companies are really *dominant-business enterprises*—one major "core" business accounts for 50 to 80 percent of total revenues and a collection of small related or unrelated businesses account for the remainder. Some diversified companies are *narrowly diversified* around a few (two to five) *related* or *unrelated* businesses. Some diversified companies are *broadly diversified* and have a wide ranging collection of either *related* businesses or *unrelated* businesses. And a few multibusiness enterprises have diversified into unrelated areas but have a collection of related businesses within each area—thus giving them a business portfolio consisting of *several unrelated groups of related businesses*. Companies have ample room to customize their diversification strategies to suit their own risk preferences and to fit most any strategic vision.

Moreover, the geographic markets of individual businesses within a diversified company can range from local to regional to national to multinational to global. Thus, a diversified company can be competing locally in some businesses, nationally in others, and globally in still others.

KEY POINTS

Most companies have their business roots in a single industry. Even though they may have since diversified into other industries, a substantial part of their revenues and profits still usually comes from the original or "core" business. Diversification becomes an attractive strategy when a company runs out of profitable growth opportunities in its core business (including any opportunities to integrate backward or forward to strengthen its competitive position). The purpose of diversification is to build shareholder value. Diversification builds shareholder value when a diversified group of businesses can perform better under the auspices of a single corporate parent than they would as independent, stand-alone businesses. Whether a particular diversification move is capable of increasing shareholder value hinges on the attractiveness test, the cost-of-entry test, and the better-off test.

There are two fundamental approaches to diversification—into related businesses and into unrelated businesses. The rationale for related diversification is *strategic:* diversify into businesses with strategic fit, capitalize on strategic-fit relationships to gain competitive advantage, then use competitive advantage to achieve the desired 2 + 2 = 5 impact on shareholder value. Businesses have strategic fit when their value chains offer potential (1) for realizing economies of scope or cost-saving efficiencies associated with sharing technology, facilities, distribution outlets, or combining related value chain activities; (2) for efficient transfer of key skills, technological expertise, or managerial know-how, (3) for using a common brand name, and/or (4) for strengthening a firm's resources and competitive capabilities.

The basic premise of unrelated diversification is that any business that has good profit prospects and can be acquired on good financial terms is a good business to diversify into. Unrelated diversification is basically a *financial* approach to diversification; strategic fit is a secondary consideration compared to the expectation of financial gain. Unrelated diversification surrenders the competitive advantage potential of strategic fit in return for such advantages as (1) spreading business risk over a variety of industries and (2) gaining opportunities for quick financial gain (if candidate acquisitions have undervalued assets, are bargain-priced and have good upside potential given the right management, or need the backing of a financially strong parent to capitalize on attractive opportunities). In theory, unrelated diversification also offers greater earnings stability over the business cycle, a third advantage. However, achieving these three outcomes consistently requires corporate executives who are smart enough to avoid the considerable disadvantages of unrelated diversification. The greater the number of businesses a conglomerate company is in and the more diverse these businesses are, the more that corporate executives are stretched to know enough about each business to distinguish a good acquisition from a risky one, select capable managers to run each business, know when the major strategic proposals of business units are sound, or wisely decide what to do when a business unit stumbles. Unless corporate managers are exceptionally shrewd and talented, unrelated diversification is a dubious and unreliable approach to building shareholder value when compared to related diversification.

Once diversification is accomplished, corporate management's task is to manage the firm's business portfolio for maximum long-term performance. Six options for improving a diversified company's performance include: (1) make new acquisitions, (2) divest weak-performing business units or those that no longer fit, (3) restructure the makeup of the portfolio when overall performance is poor and future prospects are bleak, (4) retrench to a narrower diversification base, (5) pursue multinational diversification, and (6) liquidate money-losing businesses with poor turnaround potential.

The most popular option for getting out of a business that is unattractive or doesn't fit is to sell it—ideally to a buyer for whom the business has attractive fit. Sometimes a business can be divested by spinning it off as a financially and managerially independent enterprise in which the parent company may or may not retain an ownership interest.

Corporate turnaround, retrenchment, and restructuring strategies are used when corporate management has to restore an ailing business portfolio to good health. Poor performance can be caused by large losses in one or more businesses that pull overall corporate performance down, by too many business units in unattractive industries, by an excessive debt burden, or by ill-chosen acquisitions that haven't lived up to expectations. Corporate turnaround strategies aim at restoring money-losing businesses to profitability instead of divesting them. Retrenchment involves reducing the scope of diversification to a smaller number of businesses by divesting those that are too small to make a sizable contribution to corporate earnings or those that don't fit with the narrower business base on which corporate management wants to concentrate company resources and energies. Restructuring strategies involve radical portfolio shakeups, divestiture of some businesses and acquisition of others to create a group of businesses with much improved performance potential.

Multinational diversification strategies feature a diversity of businesses and a diversity of national markets. Despite the complexity of having to devise and manage so many strategies (at least one for each industry, with as many variations for country markets as may be needed), multinational diversification can be a competitively advantageous strategy. DMNCs can use the strategic-fit advantages of related diversification (economies of scope, technology and skills transfer, and shared brand names) to build competitively strong positions in several related global industries simultaneously. Such advantages, if competently exploited, can allow a DMNC to outcompete a one-business domestic rival or a one-business multinational rival over time. A one-business domestic company has only one profit sanctuary—its home market. A single-business multinational company may have profit sanctuaries in several countries, but all are in the same business. Both are vulnerable to a DMNC that launches offensive campaigns in their profit sanctuaries. A DMNC can use a lower-cost advantage growing out of its economies of scope to underprice rivals and gain market share at their expense. Even without a cost advantage, the DMNC can decide to underprice such rivals and subsidize its lower profit margins (or even losses) with the profits earned in its other businesses. A well-financed and competently managed DMNC can sap the financial and competitive strength of one-business domestic-only and multinational rivals. A DMNC gains the biggest competitive advantage potential by diversifying into *related* industries where it can capture significant economies of scope, share technology and expertise, and leverage use of a well-known brand name.

SUGGESTED READINGS

Barney, Jay B. *Gaining and Sustaining Competitive Advantage*. Reading, Mass.: Addison-Wesley, 1997, chaps. 11 and 13.

Campbell, Andrew, Michael Goold, and Marcus Alexander. "Corporate Strategy: The Quest for Parenting Advantage." *Harvard Business Review* 73, no. 2 (March–April 1995), pp. 120–32.

———. "The Value of the Parent Company." *California Management Review* 38, no. 1 (Fall 1995), pp. 79–97.

Goold, Michael, and Kathleen Luchs. "Why Diversify? Four Decades of Management Thinking." *Academy of Management Executive* 7, no. 3 (August 1993), pp. 7–25.

Hoffman, Richard C. "Strategies for Corporate Turnarounds: What Do We Know about Them?" *Journal of General Management* 14, no. 3 (Spring 1989), pp. 46–66.

Liedtka, Jeanne M. "Collaboration across Lines of Business for Competitive Advantage." *Academy of Management Executive* 10, no.2 (May 1996), pp. 20–34.

Prahalad, C. K., and Yves L. Doz. *The Multinational Mission*. New York: Free Press, 1987, chaps. 1 and 2.

EVALUATING THE STRATEGIES OF DIVERSIFIED COMPANIES

8

Once a company diversifies and has operations in a number of different industries, three issues dominate the agenda of the company's top strategy makers:

- How attractive is the group of businesses the company is in?
- Assuming the company sticks with its present lineup of businesses, how good is its performance outlook in the years ahead?
- If the previous two answers are not satisfactory: (*a*) should the company divest itself of low-performing or unattractive businesses, (*b*) what actions should the company take to strengthen the growth and profit potential of the businesses it intends to remain in, and (*c*) should the company move into additional businesses to boost its long-term performance prospects?

Crafting and implementing action plans to improve the overall attractiveness and competitive strength of a company's business lineup is the central strategic task of corporate-level managers.

Strategic analysis of diversified companies builds on the concepts and methods used for single-business companies. But there are also new aspects to consider and additional analytical approaches to master. The procedure for critiquing a diversified company's strategy, evaluating the attractiveness of the industries it diversified into, assessing the competitive strength and performance potential of its businesses, and deciding on what strategic actions to take next involves the following steps:

> If we can know where we are and something about how we got there, we might see where we are trending—and if the outcomes which lie naturally in our course are unacceptable, to make timely change.
>
> **Abraham Lincoln**
>
> The corporate strategies of most companies have dissipated instead of created shareholder value.
>
> **Michael Porter**
>
> Achieving superior performance through diversification is largely based on relatedness.
>
> **Philippe Very**

1. *Identifying the present corporate strategy*—whether the company is pursuing related or unrelated diversification (or a mixture of both), the nature and purpose of any recent acquisitions and divestitures, and the kind of diversified company that corporate management is trying to create.

2. *Applying the industry attractiveness test*—evaluating the long-term attractiveness of each industry the company is in.

3. *Applying the competitive strength test*—evaluating the competitive strength of the company's business units to see which ones are strong contenders in their respective industries.

4. *Applying the strategic fit test*—determining the competitive advantage potential of any value chain relationships and strategic fits among existing business units.

5. *Applying the resource fit test*—determining whether the firm's resource strengths match the resource requirements of its present business lineup.

6. *Ranking the businesses from highest to lowest on the basis of both historical performance and future prospects.*

7. *Ranking the business units in terms of priority for resource allocation* and deciding whether the strategic posture for each business unit should be aggressive expansion, fortify and defend, overhaul and reposition, or harvest/divest. (The task of initiating *specific* business-unit strategies to improve the business unit's competitive position is usually delegated to business-level managers, with corporate-level managers offering suggestions and having authority for final approval.)

8. *Crafting new strategic moves to improve overall corporate performance*—changing the makeup of the portfolio via acquisitions and divestitures, improving coordination among the activities of related business units to achieve greater cost-sharing and skills-transfer benefits, and steering corporate resources into the areas of greatest opportunity.

The rest of this chapter describes this eight-step process and introduces analytical techniques needed to arrive at sound corporate strategy appraisals.

IDENTIFYING THE PRESENT CORPORATE STRATEGY

Analysis of a diversified company's situation and prospects needs to begin with an understanding of its present strategy and business makeup. Recall from Figure 2–2 in Chapter 2 that one can get a good handle on a diversified company's corporate strategy by looking at:

Evaluating a diversified firm's business portfolio needs to begin with a clear identification of the firm's diversification strategy.

- The extent to which the firm is diversified (as measured by the proportion of total sales and operating profits contributed by each business unit and by whether the diversification base is broad or narrow).

- Whether the firm is pursuing related or unrelated diversification, or a mixture of both.

- Whether the scope of company operations is mostly domestic, increasingly multinational, or global.

- Any moves to add new businesses to the portfolio and build positions in new industries.

- Any moves to divest weak or unattractive business units.

- Recent moves to boost performance of key business units and/or strengthen existing business positions.

- Management efforts to capture strategic-fit benefits and use value-chain relationships among its businesses to create competitive advantage.

- The percentage of total capital expenditures allocated to each business unit in prior years (a strong indicator of the company's resource allocation priorities).

Getting a clear fix on the current corporate strategy and its rationale sets the stage for probing the strengths and weaknesses in its business portfolio and drawing conclusions about whatever refinements or major alterations in strategy are appropriate.

EVALUATING INDUSTRY ATTRACTIVENESS: THREE TESTS

A principal consideration in evaluating a diversified company's business makeup and the caliber of its strategy is the attractiveness of the industries it has diversified into. The more attractive these industries, the better the company's long-term profit prospects. Industry attractiveness needs to be evaluated from three angles:

The more attractive the industries that a company has diversified into, the better its performance prospects.

1. *The attractiveness of each industry represented in the business portfolio.* Management must examine each industry the firm has diversified into to determine whether it represents a good business for the company to be in. What are the industry's prospects for long-term growth? Do competitive conditions and emerging market opportunities offer good prospects for long-term profitability? Are the industry's capital, technology, and other resource requirements well-matched to company capabilities?

2. *Each industry's attractiveness relative to the others.* The issue here is "Which industries in the portfolio are the most attractive and which are the least attractive?" Comparing the attractiveness of the industries and ranking them from most attractive to least attractive is a prerequisite for deciding how best to allocate corporate resources.

3. *The attractiveness of all the industries as a group.* The question here is "How appealing is the mix of industries?" A company whose revenues and profits come chiefly from businesses in unattractive industries probably needs to consider restructuring its portfolio.

Evaluating the Attractiveness of Each Industry the Company Has Diversified Into

All the industry attractiveness considerations discussed in Chapter 3 come into play in assessing the long-term appeal of the industries a company has diversified into:

- *Market size and projected growth rate*—big industries are more attractive than small industries, and fast-growing industries tend to be more attractive than slow-growing industries, other things being equal.

- *The intensity of competition*—industries where competitive pressures are relatively weak are more attractive than industries where competitive pressures are strong.

- *Emerging opportunities and threats*—industries with promising opportunities and minimal threats on the near horizon are more attractive than industries with modest opportunities and imposing threats.

- *Seasonal and cyclical factors*—industries where demand is relatively steady year-round and not unduly vulnerable to economic ups and downs are more attractive than industries where there are wide swings in buyer demand within or across years.

- *Capital requirements and other special resource requirements*—industries with low capital requirements (or amounts within the company's reach) are relatively more attractive than industries where investment requirements could strain corporate financial resources. Likewise, industries which do *not* require specialized technology, hard-to-develop competencies, or unique capabilities (unless such requirements match well with a diversifier's own capabilities) are more attractive than industries where the resource requirements outstrip a firm's resources and capabilities.
- *Strategic fits and resource fits with the firm's present businesses*—an industry is more attractive to a particular firm if its value chain and resource requirements match up well with the value chain activities of other industries the company has diversified into and with the company's resource capabilities.
- *Industry profitability*—industries with healthy profit margins and high rates of return on investment are generally more attractive than industries where profits have historically been low or where the business risks are high.
- *Social, political, regulatory, and environmental factors*—industries with significant problems in such areas as consumer health, safety, or environmental pollution or that are subject to intense regulation are less attractive than industries where such problems are no worse than most businesses encounter.
- *Degree of risk and uncertainty*—industries with less uncertainty and business risk are more attractive than industries where the future is uncertain and business failure is common.

How well each industry stacks up on these factors determines how many are able to satisfy the *attractiveness test*. The ideal situation is for all of the industries represented in the company's portfolio to be attractive.

Measuring Each Industry's Attractiveness Relative to the Others

It is not enough, however, that an industry be attractive. Corporate resources need to be allocated to those industries of *greatest* long-term opportunity. Shrewd resource allocation is aided by ranking the industries in the company's business portfolio from most attractive to least attractive—a process that calls for quantitative measures of industry attractiveness.

The first step in developing a quantitative measure of long-term industry attractiveness is to select a set of industry attractiveness measures (such as those listed above). Next, weights are assigned to each attractiveness measure—it is weak methodology to assume that the various measures are equally important. While judgment is obviously involved in deciding how much weight to put on each attractiveness measure, it makes sense to place the highest weights on those important to achieving the company's vision or objective and that match up well with the company's needs and capabilities. The sum of the weights must add up to 1.0. Each industry is then rated on each of the chosen industry attractivenesss measures, using a 1 to 5 or 1 to 10 rating scale (where *a high rating signifies high attractiveness and a low rating signifies low attractiveness or unattractiveness*). Weighted attractiveness ratings are calculated by multiplying the industry's rating on each factor by the factor's weight. For example, a rating score of 8 times a weight of .30 gives a weighted rating of 2.40. The sum of weighted ratings for all the attractiveness factors provides a quantitative measure of the industry's long-term attractiveness. The procedure is shown below:

Industry Attractiveness Factor	Weight	Rating	Weighted Industry Attractiveness Rating
Market size and projected growth	.15	5	0.75
Intensity of competition	.30	8	2.40
Emerging industry opportunities and threats	.05	2	0.10
Resource requirements	.10	6	0.60
Strategic fit with other company businesses	.15	4	0.60
Social, political, regulatory, and environmental factors	.05	7	0.35
Industry profitability	.10	4	0.40
Degree of risk	.10	5	0.50
Sum of the assigned weights	1.00		
Industry Attractiveness Rating			5.70

Once industry attractiveness ratings are calculated for each industry in the corporate portfolio, it is a simple task to rank the industries from most to least attractive.

Calculating industry attractiveness scores presents two difficulties. One is deciding on appropriate weights for the industry attractiveness measures. The other is getting reliable data on which to assign accurate and objective ratings. Without good information, the ratings necessarily become subjective, and their validity hinges on whether management has probed industry conditions sufficiently to make dependable judgments. Generally, a company can come up with the statistical data needed to compare its industries on such factors as market size, growth rate, seasonal and cyclical influences, and industry profitability. The attractiveness measure where judgment weighs most heavily is in comparing the industries on intensity of competition, resource requirements, strategic fits, degree of risk, and social, regulatory, and environmental considerations. It is not always easy to conclude whether competition in one industry is stronger or weaker than in another industry because of the different types of competitive influences and the differences in their relative importance. Nonetheless, industry attractiveness ratings are a reasonably reliable method for ranking a diversified company's industries from most attractive to least attractive—they tell a valuable story about just how and why some of the industries a company has diversified into are more attractive than others.

The Attractiveness of the Mix of Industries as a Whole

For a diversified company to be a strong performer, a substantial portion of its revenues and profits must come from business units judged to be in attractive industries—those with relatively high attractiveness scores. It is particularly important that the company's principal businesses be in industries with a good outlook for growth and above-average profitability. Having a big fraction of the company's revenues and profits come from industries that are growing slowly or have low returns on investment tends to drag overall company performance down. Business units in the least attractive industries are potential candidates for divestiture, unless they are positioned strongly enough to overcome the unattractive aspects of their industry environments or they are a strategically important component of the portfolio.

EVALUATING THE COMPETITIVE STRENGTH OF EACH OF THE COMPANY'S BUSINESS UNITS

The task here is to evaluate whether each business unit in the corporate portfolio is well-positioned in its industry and whether it already is or can become a strong market contender. Appraising each business unit's strength and competitive position in its industry not only reveals its chances for success but also provides a basis for comparing the relative competitive strength of the different business units to determine which ones are strongest and which are weakest. Quantitative measures of each business unit's competitive strength and market position can be calculated using a procedure similar to that for measuring industry attractiveness.[1] Assessing the competitive strength of a diversified company's business subsidiaries should be based on such factors as;

- *Relative market share*—business units with higher *relative* market shares normally have greater competitive strength than those with lower shares. A business unit's *relative market share* is defined as the ratio of its market share to the market share of the largest rival firm in the industry, with market share measured in unit volume, not dollars. For instance, if business A has a 15 percent share of its industry's total volume and A's largest rival has 30 percent, A's relative market share is 0.5. If business B has a market-leading share of 40 percent and its largest rival has 30 percent, B's relative market share is 1.33.[2] Using *relative* market share instead of *actual* or *absolute* market share to measure competitive strength is analytically superior because a 10 percent market share is much stronger if the leader's share is 12 percent than if it is 50 percent; the use of relative market share captures this difference.[3]

- *Ability to compete on cost*—business units that are very cost competitive tend to be more strongly positioned in their industries than business units struggling to achieve cost parity with major rivals.

- *Ability to match industry rivals on quality and/or service*—a company's competitiveness depends in part on being able to satisfy buyer expectations with regard to features, product performance, reliability, service, and other important attributes.

- *Ability to exercise bargaining leverage with key suppliers or customers*—having bargaining leverage is a source of competitive advantage.

---

[1]The procedure also parallels the methodology for doing competitive strength assessments presented in Chapter 4 (see Table 4-4).

[2]Given this definition, only business units that are market share leaders in their respective industries will have relative market shares greater than 1.0. Business units that trail rivals in market share will have ratios below 1.0. The further below 1.0 a business unit's relative market share, the weaker is its competitive strengh and market position relative to the industry's market share leader.

[3]Equally important, relative market share is likely to reflect relative cost based on experience in producing the product and economies of large-scale production. Businesses with large reative market shares may be able to operate at lower unit costs than low-share firms because of technological and efficiency gains that attach to larger production and sales volume. As was discussed in Chapter 3, the phenomenon of lower unit costs can go beyond just the effects of scale economies; as the cumulative volume of production increases, the knowledge gained from the firm's growing production experience can lead to the discovery of additional efficiencies and ways to reduce costs even further. For more details on how the relationship between experience and cumulative production volume results in lower unit costs, see Figure 3–1 in Chapter 3. A sizable experience curve effect in an industry's value chain places a strategic premium on market share: the competitor that gains the largest market share tends to realize important cost advantages which, in turn, can be used to lower prices and gain still additional customers, sales, market share, and profit. Such conditions are an important contributor to the competitive strength that a company has in that business.

- *Technology and innovation capabilities*—business units recognized for their technological leadership and track record in innovation are usually strong competitors in their industry.
- *How well the business unit's competitive assets and competencies match industry key success factors*—the more a business unit's strengths match the industry's key success factors, the stronger its competitive position tends to be.
- *Brand-name recognition and reputation*—a strong brand name is nearly always a valuable competitive asset.
- *Profitability relative to competitors*—business units that consistently earn above-average returns on investment and have bigger profit margins than their rivals usually have stronger competitive positions than those with below-average profitability for their industry.

Other competitive strength indicators include knowledge of customers and markets, production capabilities, skills in supply chain management, marketing skills, ample financial resources, and proven know-how in managing the business. Analysts have a choice between rating each business unit on the same generic factors or rating each business unit's strength on those strength measures most pertinent to its industry. Either approach can be defended, although using strength measures specific to each industry is conceptually stronger because the relevant measures of competitive strength, along with their relative importance, vary from industry to industry.

As was done in evaluating industry attractiveness, weights need to be assigned to each of the strength measures to indicate their relative importance (using different weights for different business units is conceptually stronger when the importance of the strength measures differs significantly from business to business). As before, the sum of the weights must add up to 1.0. Each business unit is then rated on each of the chosen strength measures, using a 1 to 5 or 1 to 10 rating scale (where *a high rating signifies high competitive strength and a low rating signifies low strength*). Weighted strength ratings are calculated by multiplying the business unit's rating on each strength measure by the assigned weight. For example, a strength score of 6 times a weight of .25 gives a weighted strength rating of 1.50. The sum of weighted ratings across all the strength measures provides a quantitative measure of a business unit's overall competitive strength. The procedure is shown below:

Competitive Strength Measure	Weight	Strength Rating	Weighted Strength Rating
Relative market share	.20	5	1.00
Costs relative to competitors	.25	8	2.00
Ability to match or beat rivals on key product attributes	.10	2	0.20
Bargaining leverage with buyers/ suppliers	.10	6	0.60
Technology and innovation capabilities	.05	4	0.20
How well resources are matched to industry key success factors	.15	7	1.05
Brand name reputation/image	.05	4	0.20
Profitability relative to competitors	.10	5	0.50
Sum of the assigned weights	1.00		
Competitive Strength Rating			5.75

Business units with relatively high overall competitive strength ratings (above 6.7 on a rating scale of 1 to 10) are strong market contenders in their industries. Businesses with relatively low overall ratings (below 3.3 on a 1 to 10 rating scale) are in competitively weak market positions.[4] Managerial evaluations of which businesses in the portfolio are strong and weak market contenders are a valuable consideration in deciding where to steer resources. *Shareholder interests are generally best served by concentrating corporate resources on businesses that can contend for market leadership in their industries.*

Using a Nine-Cell Matrix to Simultaneously Portray Industry Attractiveness and Competitive Strength

In the attractiveness-strength matrix, each business's location is plotted using quantitative measures of long-term industry attractiveness and business strength/competitive position.

The industry attractiveness and business strength scores can be used to graphically portray the strategic positions of each business a diversified company is in. Long-term industry attractiveness is plotted on the vertical axis and competititive strength on the horizontal axis. A nine-cell grid emerges from dividing the vertical axis into three regions (high, medium, and low attractiveness) and the horizontal axis into three regions (strong, average, and weak competitive strength). High attractiveness is associated with scores of 6.7 or greater on a rating scale of 1 to 10, medium attractiveness is assigned to scores of 3.3 to 6.7, and so on; likewise, strong competitive strength is defined as a strength score greater than 6.7, average strength entails scores of 3.3 to 6.7, and so on—as shown in Figure 8-1. Each business unit in the corporate portfolio is plotted on the resulting nine-cell grid based on its overall attractiveness score and strength score and then shown as a "bubble," with the size of each bubble or circle scaled to what percent of revenues it generates relative to total corporate revenues.

The attractiveness-strength matrix helps assign investment priorities to each of the company's business units. Businesses in the three cells at the upper left, where long-term industry attractiveness and business strength/competitive position are favorable, have top investment priority. The strategic prescription for businesses falling in these three cells is "grow and build," with businesses in the high-strong cell having the highest claim on investment funds. Next in priority come businesses positioned in the three diagonal cells stretching from the lower left to the upper right. These businesses are usually given medium priority. They merit steady reinvestment to maintain and protect their industry positions; however, if such a business has an unusually attractive opportunity, it can win a higher investment priority and be given the go-ahead to employ a more aggressive strategic approach. The strategy prescription for businesses in the three cells in the lower right corner of the matrix is typically harvest or divest (in exceptional cases where good turnaround potential exists, it can be "overhaul and reposition" using some type of turnaround approach).[5]

---

[4]If analysts lack sufficient data to do detailed strength ratings, they can rely on their knowledge of each business unit's competitive situation to classify it as being in a "strong," "average," or "weak" competitive position. If trustworthy, such subjective assessments of business-unit strength can substitute for quantitative measures.

[5]At General Electric, each business actually ended up in one of five types of categories: (1) *high-growth potential* businesses deserving top investment priority, (2) *stable base* businesses deserving steady reinvestment to maintain position, (3) *support* businesses deserving periodic investment funding, (4) *selective pruning or rejuvenation* businesses deserving reduced investment funding, and (5) *venture* businesses deserving heavy R&D investment.

FIGURE 8-1   A Representative Nine-Cell Industry Attractiveness-Competitive Strength Matrix

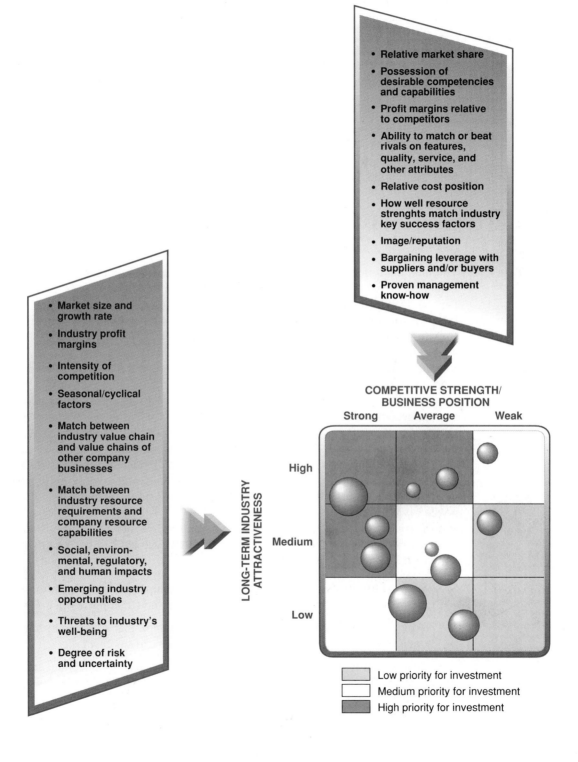

The nine-cell attractiveness-strength grid provides strong logic for concentrating resources in those businesses that enjoy a higher degree of attractiveness and competitive strength, being very selective in making investments in businesses with intermediate positions, and with drawing resources from businesses that are lower in attractiveness and strength unless they offer exceptional turnaround potential. This is why a diversified company needs to consider *both* industry attractiveness and business strength in allocating resources and investment capital to its different businesses.

A company may earn larger profits over the long term by investing in a business with a competitively strong position in a moderately attractive industry than by investing in a weak business in a glamour industry.

More and more diversified companies are concentrating their resources on industries where they can be strong market contenders and divesting businesses that are not good candidates for becoming market leaders. At General Electric, the whole thrust of corporate strategy and corporate resource allocation is to put GE's businesses into a number one or two position in both the United States and globally—see Illustration Capsule 29.

STRATEGIC-FIT ANALYSIS: CHECKING FOR COMPETITIVE ADVANTAGE POTENTIAL

The next analytical step is to determine the competitive advantage potential of any value chain relationships and strategic fits among the company's existing businesses. Fit needs to be looked at from two angles: (1) whether one or more business units have valuable strategic fit with other businesses the firm has diversified into and (2) whether each business unit meshes well with the firm's long-term strategic direction.

When a company's business portfolio includes subsidiaries with related technologies, similar value chain activities, overlapping distribution channels, common customers, or some other competitively valuable relationship, it gains competitive advantage potential not open to a company that diversifies into totally unrelated businesses. The more businesses it has with competitively valuable strategic fits, the greater a diversified company's potential for realizing economies of scope, enhancing the competitive capabilities of particular business units, strengthening the competitiveness of its product and business lineup, and leveraging its resources into a combined performance greater than the units could achieve operating independently.

Consequently, one essential part of evaluating a diversified company's strategy is to check its business portfolio for competitively valuable value chain matchups among the company's existing businesses:

- Which business units have value chain matchups that offer opportunities to combine the performance of related activities and thereby reduce costs?

- Which business units have value chain matchups that offer opportunities to transfer skills or technology from one business to another?

- Which business units offer opportunities to use a common brand name? to gain greater leverage with distributors/dealers in winning more favorable shelf space for the company's products?

- Which business units have value chain matchups that offer opportunities to create valuable new competitive capabilities or to leverage existing resources?

ILLUSTRATION CAPSULE 29   General Electric's Approach to Managing Diversification

When Jack Welch became CEO of General Electric in 1981, he launched a corporate strategy effort to reshape the company's diversified business portfolio. Early on he issued a challenge to GE's business-unit managers to become number one or number two in their industry; failing that, the business units either had to capture a decided technological advantage translatable into a competitive edge or face possible divestiture.

By 1990, GE was a different company. Under Welch's prodding, GE divested operations worth $9 billion—TV operations, small appliances, a mining business, and computer chips. It spent a total of $24 billion acquiring new businesses, most notably RCA, Roper (a maker of major appliances whose biggest customer was Sears), and Kidder Peabody (a Wall Street investment banking firm). Internally, many of the company's smaller business operations were put under the direction of larger "strategic business units." But, most significantly, in 1989, 12 of GE's 14 strategic business units were market leaders in the United States and globally (the company's financial services and communications units served markets too fragmented to rank).

During the 1990s, having divested most of the weak businesses and having built existing businesses into leading contenders, Welch launched initiatives to dramatically boost productivity and reduce the size of GE's bureaucracy. Welch argued that for GE to continue to be successful in a global marketplace, the company had to press hard for continuous cost reduction in each of its businesses, cut through bureaucratic procedures to shorten response times to changing market conditions, and dramatically improve its profit margins. In 1997, GE had the highest market capitalization of any company in the world.

GE Strategic Business Units	Market Standing in the United States	Market Standing in the World
Aircraft engines	First	First
Broadcasting (NBC)	First	Not applicable
Circuit breakers	Tied for first with two others	Tied for first with three others
Defense electronics	Second	Second
Electric motors	First	First
Engineering plastics	First	First
Factory automation	Second	Third
Industrial and power systems	First	First
Lighting	First	Second
Locomotives	First	Tied for first
Major home apliances	First	Tied for second
Medical diagnostic imaging	First	First

Source: Developed from information in Stratford P. Sherman, "Inside the Mind of Jack Welch," *Fortune,* March 27, 1989, pp. 39–50.

Figure 8-2 illustrates the process of identifying the value chains of each of the businesses, then searching for competitively valuable value chain matchups. Without a number of such matchups, one has to be skeptical about the potential for the company's businesses to perform better together than apart and whether its diversification approach is truly capable of enhancing shareholder value.

A second aspect of strategic fit that bears checking out is whether any businesses in the portfolio do not fit in well with the company's overall long-term direction and strategic vision. Sometimes a business, despite having certain value chain matchups, doesn't mesh well with the strategic markets or customer groups or product categories that corporate mangement is concentrating on—in other words, it doesn't fit strategically into the company's overall business picture. In such instances, the business probably needs to be considered for divestiture even though it may be making a positive contribution to company profits and cash flows. Businesses with no real

FIGURE 8-2 Comparing Value Chains to Identify Strategic Fits Among a Diversified Company's Business Units

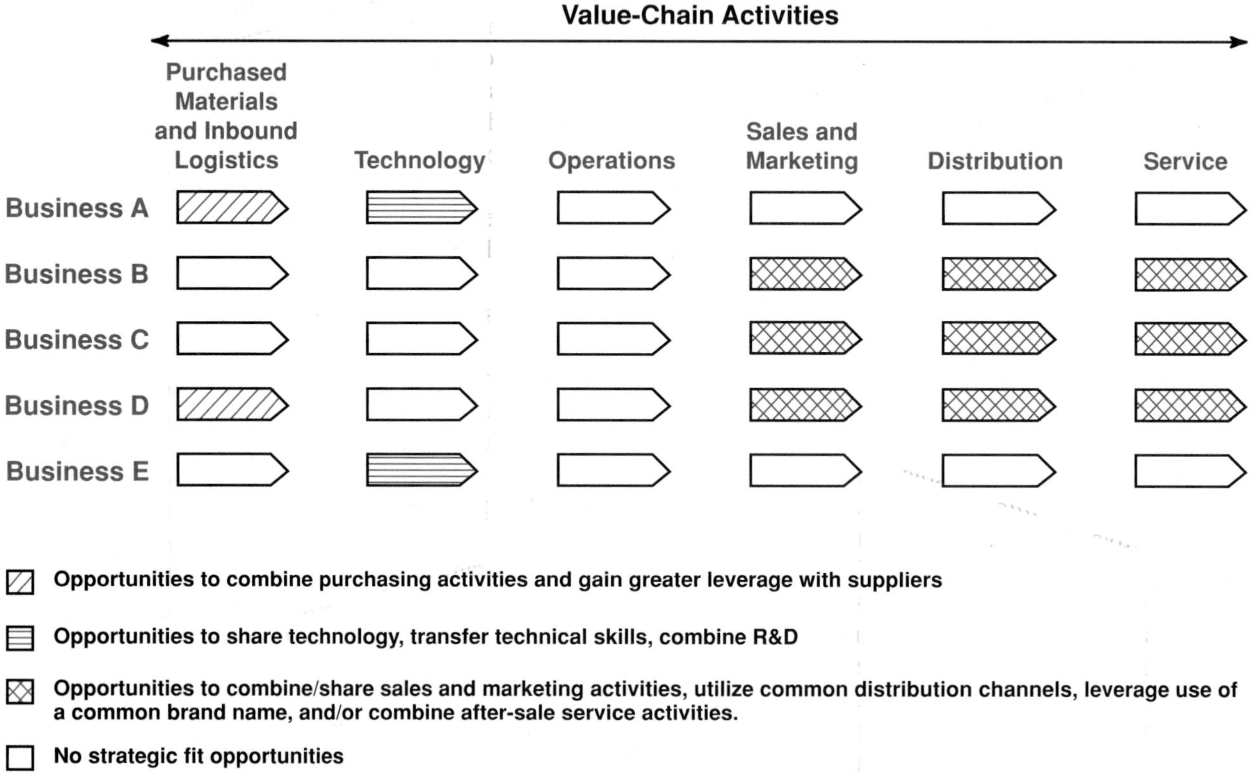

Value-Chain Activities

	Purchased Materials and Inbound Logistics	Technology	Operations	Sales and Marketing	Distribution	Service
Business A	▨	☰	▭	▭	▭	▭
Business B	▭	▭	▭	▩	▩	▩
Business C	▭	▭	▭	▩	▩	▩
Business D	▨	▭	▭	▩	▩	▩
Business E	▭	☰	▭	▭	▭	▭

▨ **Opportunities to combine purchasing activities and gain greater leverage with suppliers**

☰ **Opportunities to share technology, transfer technical skills, combine R&D**

▩ **Opportunities to combine/share sales and marketing activities, utilize common distribution channels, leverage use of a common brand name, and/or combine after-sale service activities.**

▭ **No strategic fit opportunities**

strategic value often end up being treated like an unwanted stepchild and are a distraction to top management. The only reasons to retain such businesses are if they are unusually good financial performers or offer superior growth opportunities—that is to say, if they are valuable *financially* even though they are not valuable strategically.

RESOURCE FIT ANALYSIS: DETERMINING HOW WELL THE FIRM'S RESOURCES MATCH BUSINESS UNIT REQUIREMENTS

The businesses in a diversified company's lineup need to exhibit good *resource fit* as well as good strategic fit. Resource fit exists when (1) businesses add to a company's resource strengths, either financially or strategically and (2) a company has the resources to adequately support the resource requirements of its businesses as a group without spreading itself too thinly. One important dimension of resource fit concerns whether the company's business lineup is well-matched to its financial resources.

Checking Financial Resource Fit: Cash Hog and Cash Cow Businesses

Different businesses have different cash flow and investment characteristics. For example, business units in rapidly growing industries are often "cash hogs"—so labeled because their annual cash flows aren't big enough to cover their annual capital requirements. To keep pace with rising demand, rapid-growth businesses frequently are looking at sizable annual capital investments for some years to come—for new facilities and equipment, for new product development or technology improvements, and for additional working capital to support inventory expansion and a larger base of operations. A business in a fast-growing industry becomes an even bigger cash hog when it has a relatively low market share and is pursuing a strategy to outgrow the market and gain enough market share to become an industry leader. When a rapid-growth business cannot generate a big enough cash flow from operations to finance its capital requirements internally, the needed financial resources must be provided by the corporate parent. Corporate management has to decide whether it is strategically and financially worthwhile to fund the perhaps considerable investment requirements of a cash hog business.

A "cash hog" business is one whose internal cash flows are inadequate to fully fund its needs for working capital and new capital investment.

Business units with leadership positions in slow-growing industries with modest capital requirements may, however, be "cash cows," in the sense that they generate substantial cash surpluses over what is needed for capital reinvestment and other initiatives to sustain their leadership position. It is not unusual for businesses that are market leaders in industries where capital requirements are modest to generate sizable positive cash flows *over and above what is needed for reinvestment in operations*. Cash cow businesses, though often less attractive from a growth standpoint, are valuable businesses from a financial resources perspectives. The surplus cash flows they generate can be used to pay corporate dividends, finance acquisitions, and provide funds for investing in the company's promising cash hog businesses. It makes good financial and strategic sense for diversified companies to keep cash cow businesses in healthy condition, fortifying and defending their market position to preserve their cash-generating capability over the long term and thereby maintain an ongoing source of positive cash flows to redeploy elsewhere.

A "cash cow" business is a valuable part of a diversified company's business portfolio because it generates cash for financing new acquisitions, funding the capital requirements of cash hog businesses, and paying dividends.

Viewing a diversified group of businesses as a collection of cash flows and cash requirements (present and future) is a major step forward in understanding the financial aspects of corporate strategy. Assessing the cash requirements of different businesses in a company's portfolio and determining which are cash hogs and which are cash cows highlights opportunities for shifting corporate financial resources between business subsidiaries to optimize the performance of the whole corporate portfolio, explains why priorities for corporate resource allocation can differ from business to business, and provides good rationalizations for both invest-and-expand strategies and divestiture. For instance, a diversified company can use the excess cash generated by cash cow business units to fund the investment requirements of *promising* cash hog businesses, eventually growing the hogs into self-supporting "stars" having strong competitive positions in attractive, high-growth markets.[6] Star businesses are the cash cows of the future—when the markets of star businesses begin to mature and their growth slows, their competitive strength should produce self-

---

[6]A star business, as the name implies, is one with a leading market share, a widely respected reputation, a solid track record of profitability, and excellent future growth and profit opportunities. Star businesses vary as to their cash hog status. Some can cover their investment needs with self-generated cash flows; others require capital infusions from their corporate parents to stay abreast of rapid industry growth. Normally, strongly positioned star businesses in industries where growth is beginning to slow tend to be self-sustaining in terms of cash flow and make little claim on the corporate parent's treasury. Young stars, however, may require substantial investment capital *beyond what they can generate on their own* and still be cash hogs.

generated cash flows more than sufficient to cover their investment needs. The "success sequence" is thus cash hog to young star (but perhaps still a cash hog) to self-supporting star to cash cow.

On the other hand, if a cash hog business has questionable promise (either because of low industry attractiveness or a weak competitive position), then it becomes a logical candidate for divestiture. Pursuing an aggressive invest-and-expand strategy for a competitively weak cash hog business seldom makes sense if the company has other attractive opportunities and if it will strain the corporate parent's financial resources to keep pumping more capital into the business to keep abreast of fast-paced market growth *and* to build an attractively strong competitive position. Such businesses are a financial drain and lack good financial resource fit. Divesting a less attractive cash hog business is usually the best alternative *unless* (1) it has valuable strategic fits with other business units or (2) the capital infusions needed from the corporate parent are modest relative to the funds available and there's a decent chance of growing the business into a solid bottom-line contributor.

Aside from cash flow considerations, a business has good financial fit when it contributes to the achievement of corporate performance objectives (profit growth, above-average return on investment, recognition as an industry leader, and so on) and

Business subsidiaries that don't exhibit good strategic fit and good resource fit should be considered for divestiture unless their financial performance is outstanding.

when it enhances shareholder value. A business exhibits poor financial fit if it soaks up a disproportionate share of the company's financial resources, if it is a subpar or inconsistent bottom-line contributor, if it is unduly risky and failure would jeopardize the entire enterprise, or if it is too small to make a material earnings contribution even though it performs well. In addition, a diversified company's business portfolio lacks financial fit if its financial resources are stretched thinly across too many businesses. Severe financial strain can occur if a company borrows so heavily to finance new acquisitions that it has to trim way back on new capital expenditures for existing businesses and use the big majority of its financial resources to meet interest obligations and to pay down debt. Some diversified companies have found themselves in such an overextended or overleveraged financial situation that they have had to sell off some businesses to raise the money to meet existing debt obligations and fund essential capital expenditures for the remaining businesses.

Checking Competitive and Managerial Resource Fits

A diversified company's strategy must aim at producing a good fit between its resource capability and the competitive and managerial requirements of its businesses.[7] Diversification is most likely to result in added shareholder value when the company has or can develop the competitive and managerial capabilities to be successful in each of the businesses/industries it has diversified into. The absence of good resource fit with one or more business units is serious enough to make such businesses prime divestiture candidates. Likewise, when a company's resources and capabilities are well suited to competing in new industries, it makes sense to take a hard look at acquiring companies in these industries and expanding the company's business lineup.

---

[7]For an excellent discussion of how to assess these fits, see Andrew Campbell, Michael Goold, and Marcus Alexander, "Corporate Strategy: The Quest for Parenting Advantage," *Harvard Business Review* 73, no. 2 (March–April 1995), pp. 120–32.

Checking a diversified company's business portfolio for competitive and managerial resource fits involves the following:

- Determining whether the company's resource strengths (skills, technological expertise, competitive capabilities) are well matched to the key success factors of the businesses it has diversified into.

- Determining whether the company has adequate managerial depth and expertise to cope with the assortment of managerial and operating problems posed by its present lineup of businesses (plus those it may be contemplating getting into).

- Determining whether competitive capabilities in one or more businesses can be transferred them to other businesses (capabilities that are often good candidates for transfer include short development times in bringing new products to market, strong partnerships with key suppliers, an R&D organization capable of generating technological and product opportunites in several different industry arenas simultaneously, a high degree of organizational agility in responding to shifting market conditions and emerging opportunities, or state-of-the-art systems for doing business via the Internet).

- Determining whether the company needs to invest in upgrading its resources or capabilities to stay ahead of (or at least abreast of) the efforts of rivals to upgrade their resource base. In a world of fast-paced change and competition, managers have to be alert to the need to continually invest in and upgrade the company's resources, however potent its current resources are. All resources depreciate in value as competitors mimic them or retaliate with a different (and perhaps more attractive) resource combination.[8] Upgrading resources and competencies often means going beyond just strengthening what the company already is capable of doing— it may involve adding new resource capabilities (like the ability to manage a group of diverse international manufacturing plants or developing technological expertise in related or complementary disciplines or a state-of-the-art-company intranet or an innovative Web page that draws many visits and gives all of its business units greater market exposure), building competencies that allow the company to enter another attractive industry, or widening the company's range of capabilities to match certain competitively valuable capabilities of rivals.

The complement of resources and capabilities at a firm's command determine its competitive strengths. The more a company's diversification strategy is tied to leveraging its resources and capabilities in new businesses, the more it has to develop a big enough and deep enough resource pool to supply these businesses with enough capability to create competitive advantage. Otherwise its strengths end up being stretched too thinly across too many businesses and the opportunity for competitive advantage lost.

Some Notes of Caution   Many diversification strategies built around transferring resource capabilities to new businesses never live up to their promise because the transfer process is not as easy as it might seem. Developing a resource capability in

---

[8]David J. Collis and Cynthia A. Montgomery, "Competing on Resources: Strategy in the 90s," *Harvard Business Review* 73, no. 4 (July–August 1995), p. 124.

one business nearly always involves much trial and error and much organizational learning, and is usually the product of close collaboration of many people working together over a period of time. The first step in transferring a resource capability developed in this manner to another business involves moving people with much of the know-how to the new business. Then these people not only have to learn the ins and outs of the new business well enough to see how best to integrate the capability into the operation of the receiving business but they also have to be adept in implanting all the needed organizational learning from the donor business. As a practical matter, transferring a resource capability in one business to another business can't be done without the receiving business undergoing significant organizational learning and team-building on its own to get up to speed in executing the transferred capability. It takes time, money, and patience for the transferred capability to be implanted and made fully operational. Sometimes unforeseen problems occur, resulting in debilitating delays or prohibitive expenses or inability on the part of the receiving business to execute the capability proficiently. As a consequence, the new business never performs up to expectations.

A second reason for the failure of a diversification move into a new business with seemingly good resource fit is that the causes of a firm's success in one business are sometimes quite entangled and the means of re-creating them hard to

Diversifying into businesses with seemingly good resource fit is, by itself, not sufficient to produce success.

replicate.[9] It is easy to be overly optimistic about the ease with which a company that has hit a home run in one business can enter a new business with similar resource requirements and hit a second home run. Noted British retailer Marks & Spencer, despite its impressive resource capabilities (ability to choose excellent store locations, having a supplier chain that gives it both low costs and high merchandise quality, loyal employees, an excellent reputation with consumers, and strong management expertise) that have made it one of Britain's premier retailers for 100 years, has failed repeatedly in its efforts to diversify into department store retailing in the United States.

A third reason for diversification failure, despite apparent resource fit, is misjudging the difficulty of overcoming the resource strengths and capabilities of the rivals it will have to face in a new business. For example, Philip Morris, even though it had built powerful consumer marketing capabilities in its cigarette and beer businesses, floundered in soft drinks and ended up divesting its acquisition of 7UP after several frustrating years because of difficulties in competing against strongly entrenched and resource-capable rivals like Coca-Cola and PepsiCo.

RANKING THE BUSINESS UNITS ON THE BASIS OF PAST PERFORMANCE AND FUTURE PROSPECTS

Once a diversified company's businesses have been rated on the basis of industry attractiveness, competitive strength, strategic fit, and resource fit, the next step is to evaluate which businesses have the best performance prospects and which the worst. The most important considerations are sales growth, profit growth, contribution to company earnings, and the return on capital invested in the business (more and more companies are evaluating business performance on the basis of economic value added—the return on invested capital over and above the firm's cost of capital). Sometimes, cash flow generation is a big consideration, especially for cash cow businesses and businesses with potential for harvesting.

---

[9]Collis and Montgomery, "Competing on Resources: Strategy in the 90s," pp.121–22.

Information on each business's past performance can be gleaned from financial records.[10] While past performance is not necessarily a good predictor of future performance, it does signal which businesses have been strong performers and which have been weak performers. The industry attractiveness–competitive strength evaluations should provide a solid basis for judging future prospects. Normally, strong business units in attractive industries have better prospects than weak businesses in unattractive industries.

The growth and profit outlooks for a diversified company's principal or core businesses generally determine whether its portfolio as a whole is capable of strong, mediocre, or weak performance. Noncore businesses with subpar track records and long-term prospects are logical candidates for divestiture. Business subsidiaries with the brightest profit and growth prospects generally should head the list for corporate resource support.

DECIDING ON RESOURCE ALLOCATION PRIORITIES AND A GENERAL STRATEGIC DIRECTION FOR EACH BUSINESS UNIT

Using the information and results of the preceding evaluation steps, corporate strategists can decide what the priorities should be for allocating resources to the various business units and settle on a general strategic direction for each business unit. The task here is to draw some conclusions about which business units should have top priority for corporate resource support and new capital investment and which should carry the lowest priority. In doing the ranking, special attention needs to be given to whether and how *corporate* resources and capabilities can be used to enhance the competitiveness of particular business units.[11] Opportunities for capabilities/technology transfer or for combining activities to reduce costs or for infusions of new financial capital become especially important when a diversified firm has business units in less than desirable competitive positions, when improvement in some key success area could make a big difference to a particular business unit's performance, and when a cash hog business needs financial support to grow into a star performer.

Ranking the businesses from highest to lowest priority process should also clarify management thinking about what the basic strategic approach for each business unit should be—*invest-and-grow* (aggressive expansion), *fortify-and-defend* (protect current position by strengthening and adding resource capabilities in needed areas), *overhaul-and-reposition* (make major competitive strategy changes to move the business into a different and ultimately stronger industry position), or *harvest-divest*. In deciding whether to divest a business unit, corporate managers should rely on a number of evaluating criteria: industry attractiveness, competitive strength, strategic fit with other businesses, resource fit, performance potential (profit, return on capital employed, economic value added, contribution to cash flow), compatibility with the

Improving a diversified company's long-term financial performance entails concentrating company resources on businesses with good to excellent prospects and allocating only minimal resources to businesses with subpar prospects.

---

[10]Financial performance by line of business is typically contained in a company's annual report, usually in the notes to corporate financial statements. Line of business performance can also be found in a publicly owned firm's 10-K report filed annually with the Securities and Exchange Commission.

[11]Collis and Montgomery, "Competing on Resources: Strategy in the 90s," pp.126–28; Hofer and Schendel, *Strategy Formulation: Analytical Concepts*, p. 80; and Michael E. Porter, *Competitive Advantage* (New York: Free Press, 1985), chapter 9.

companies strategic vision and long-term direction, and ability to contribute to enhanced shareholder value.

To get ever-higher levels of performance out of a diversified company's business portfolio, corporate managers have to do an effective job of steering resources out of low-opportunity areas into high-opportunity areas. Divesting marginal businesses is one of the best ways of freeing unproductive assets for redeployment. Surplus funds from cash cow businesses and businesses being harvested also add to the corporate treasury. Options for allocating a diversified company's financial resources include (1) investing in ways to strengthen or expand existing businesses, (2) making acquisitions to establish positions in new industries, (3) funding long-range R&D ventures, (4) paying off existing long-term debt, (5) increasing dividends, and (6) repurchasing the company's stock. The first three are *strategic* actions to add shareholder value; the last three are *financial* moves to enhance shareholder value. Ideally, a company will have enough funds to do what is needed, both strategically and financially. If not, strategic uses of corporate resources should usually take precedence unless there is a compelling reason to strengthen the firm's balance sheet or divert financial resources to pacify shareholders.

CRAFTING A CORPORATE STRATEGY

The preceding analytical steps set the stage for crafting strategic moves to improve a diversified company's overall performance. The basic issue of "what to do" hinges on the conclusions drawn about the strategic and financial attractiveness of the group of businesses the company has diversified into.[12] Key considerations here are:

- Does the company have enough businesses in very attractive industries?
- Is the proportion of mature or declining businesses so great that corporate growth will be sluggish?
- Are the company's businesses overly vulnerable to seasonal or recessionary influences?
- Is the firm burdened with too many businesses in average to weak competitive positions?
- Is there ample strategic fit among the company's different businesses?
- Does the portfolio contain businesses that the company really doesn't need to be in?
- Is there ample resource fit among the company's business units?
- Does the firm have enough cash cows to finance the cash hog businesses with potential to be star performers?
- Can the company's principal or core businesses be counted on to generate dependable profits and/or cash flow?
- Does the makeup of the business portfolio put the company in good position for the future?

Answers to these questions indicate whether corporate strategists should consider divesting certain businesses, making new acquisitions, restructuring the makeup of the portfolio, altering the pattern of corporate resource allocation, or sticking with the existing business lineup and pursuing the opportunities they present.

---

[12]Barry Hedley, "Strategy and the Business Portfolio," *Long Range Planning* 10, no. 1 (February 1977), p. 13; and Hofer and Schendel, *Strategy Formulation*, pp. 82–86.

The Performance Test

A good test of the strategic and financial attractiveness of a diversified firm's business portfolio is whether the company can attain its performance objectives with its current lineup of businesses and resource capabilities. If so, no major corporate strategy changes are indicated. However, if a performance shortfall is probable, corporate strategists can take any of several actions to close the gap:[13]

1. *Alter the strategic plans for some (or all) of the businesses in the portfolio.* This option involves renewed corporate efforts to get better performance out of its present business units. Corporate managers can push business-level managers for strategy changes that yield better business-unit performance and, perhaps, provide higher-than-planned corporate resource support for these efforts. However, pursuing better short-term performance by zealously trimming resource initiatives aimed at bolstering a business's long-term competitive position has dubious value—it merely trades off better long-term performance for better short-term financial performance. In any case there are limits on how much extra near-term performance can be squeezed out.

2. *Add new business units to the corporate portfolio.* Boosting overall performance by making new acquisitions and/or starting new businesses internally raises some new strategy issues. Expanding the corporate portfolio means taking a close look at (*a*) whether to acquire related or unrelated businesses, (*b*) what size acquisition(s) to make, (*c*) how the new unit(s) will fit into the present corporate structure, (*d*) what specific features to look for in an acquisition candidate, and (*e*) whether acquisitions can be financed without shortchanging present business units on their new investment requirements. Nonetheless, adding new businesses is a major strategic option, one frequently used by diversified companies to escape sluggish earnings performance.

3. *Divest weak-performing or money-losing businesses.* The most likely candidates for divestiture are businesses in a weak competitive position, in a relatively unattractive industry, or in an industry that does not "fit." Funds from divestitures can, of course, be used to finance new acquisitions, pay down corporate debt, or fund new strategic thrusts in the remaining businesses.

4. *Form strategic alliances and collaborative partnerships to try to alter conditions responsible for subpar performance potentials.* In some situations, cooperative alliances with domestic or foreign firms, suppliers, customers, or special interest groups may help ameliorate adverse performance prospects.[14] Instituting resource sharing agreements with suppliers, select competitors, or firms with complementary products and collaborating closely on mutually advantageous initiatives are becoming increasingly used avenues for improving the competitiveness and performance potential of a company's businesses. Forming or supporting a political action group may be an

---

[13]Hofer and Schendel, *Strategy Formulation: Analytical Concepts*, pp. 93–100.

[14]For an excellent discussion of the benefits of alliances among competitors in global industries, see Kenichi Ohmae, "The Global Logic of Strategic Alliances," *Harvard Business Review* 67, no. 2 (March–April 1989), pp. 143–54.

effective way of lobbying for solutions to import-export problems, tax disincentives, and onerous regulatory requirements.

5. *Upgrade the company's resource base.* Achieving better performance may well hinge on corporate efforts to develop new resource strengths that will help select business units match the competitively valuable capabilities of their rivals or, better still, allow them to secure competitive advantage. One of the biggest ways that corporate-level managers of diversified companies can contribute to added shareholder value is to lead the development of cutting-edge capabilities and to marshal new kinds of corporate resources for deployment in a number of the company's businesses.

6. *Lower corporate performance objectives.* Adverse market circumstances or declining fortunes in one or more core business units can render companywide performance targets unreachable. So can overly ambitious objective setting. Closing the gap between actual and desired performance may then require downward revision of corporate objectives to bring them more in line with reality. Lowering performance objectives is usually a "last resort" option.

Identifying Additional Diversification Opportunities

One of the major corporate strategy-making concerns in a diversified company is whether to diversify further and, if so, how to identify the "right" kinds of industries and businesses to get into. For firms pursuing unrelated diversification, the issue of where to diversify next is based more on spotting a good financial opportunity and having the financial resources to pursue it than on industry or strategic criteria. Decisions to diversify into additional unrelated businesses are usually based on such considerations as whether the firm has the financial ability to make another acquisition, whether new acquisitions are badly needed to boost overall corporate performance, whether one or more acquisition opportunities have to be acted on before they are purchased by other firms, whether the timing is right for another acquisition (corporate management may have its hands full dealing with the current portfolio of businesses), and whether corporate management believes it possesses the range and depth of expertise to supervise an additional business.

Firms with unrelated diversification strategies hunt for businesses that offer attractive financial returns—regardless of what industry they're in.

Further diversification in firms with related diversification strategies involves identifying attractive industries having good strategic or resource fit with one or more existing businesses.

With a related diversification strategy, however, the search for new industries to diversify into is aimed at identifying other businesses (1) whose value chains have fits with the value chains of one or more businesses in the company's business portfolio and (2) whose resource requirements are well-matched to the firm's corporate resource capabilities.[15] Once strategic-fit and resource-fit opportunities in *attractive* new industries are identified, corporate strategists have to distinguish between opportunities where important competitive advantage potential exists (through cost savings, technology or capabilities transfer, leveraging a well-known brand name, and so on) and those where the strategic-fit and resource-fit benefits are marginally valuable. The size of the competitive advantage potential depends on whether the fits are competitively significant and on the costs and difficulties of merging or coordinating the business unit interrelationships to capture the fits.[16] Often, careful analysis reveals

[15]Porter, *Competitive Advantage*, pp. 370–71.
[16]Ibid., pp. 371–72.

that while there are many actual and potential business unit interrelationships and linkages, only a few have enough strategic importance to generate meaningful competitive advantage.

GUIDELINES FOR MANAGING THE PROCESS OF CRAFTING CORPORATE STRATEGY

Although formal analysis and entrepreneurial brainstorming normally undergird the corporate strategy-making process, there is more to where corporate strategy comes from and how it evolves. Rarely is there an all-inclusive grand formulation of the total corporate strategy. Instead, corporate strategy in major enterprises emerges incrementally from the unfolding of many different internal and external events, the result of probing the future, experimenting, gathering more information, sensing problems, building awareness of the various options, spotting new opportunities, developing responses to unexpected crises, communicating consensus as it emerges, and acquiring a feel for all the strategically relevant factors, their importance, and their interrelationships.[17]

Strategic analysis is not something that the executives of diversified companies do all at once. Such big reviews are sometimes scheduled, but research indicates that major strategic decisions emerge gradually rather than from periodic, full-scale analysis followed by prompt decision. Typically, top executives approach major strategic decisions a step at a time, often starting from broad, intuitive conceptions and then embellishing, fine-tuning, and modifying their original thinking as more information is gathered, as formal analysis confirms or modifies their judgments about the situation, and as confidence and consensus build for what strategic moves need to be made. Often attention and resources are concentrated on a few critical strategic thrusts that illuminate and integrate corporate direction, objectives, and strategies.

Strategic analysis in diversified companies is an eight-step process:

KEY POINTS

Step 1: *Get a clear fix on the present strategy.* Determine whether the company's strategic emphasis is on related or unrelated diversification; whether the scope of company operations is mostly domestic or increasingly multinational, what moves have been made recently to add new businesses and build positions in new industries, the rationale underlying recent divestitures, the nature of any efforts to capture strategic fits and create competitive advantage based on economies of scope and/or resource transfer, and the pattern of resource allocation to the various business units. This step sets the stage for thorough evaluation of the need for strategy changes.

Step 2: *Evaluate the long-term attractiveness of each industry the company is in.* Industry attractiveness needs to be evaluated from three angles: the attractiveness of each industry on its own, the attractiveness of each industry relative to the others, and the attractiveness of all the industries as a group. Quantitative measures of industry attractiveness, using the methodology presented, are a reasonably reliable method for ranking a diversified company's industries from most attractive to least attractive—they tell a

---

[17]Ibid., pp. 58 and 196.

valuable story about just how and why some of the industries a company has diversified into are more attractive than others. The two hardest parts of calculating industry attractiveness scores are deciding on appropriate weights for the industry attractiveness measures and knowing enough about each industry to assign accurate and objective ratings.

Step 3: *Evaluate the relative competitive positions and business strength of each of the company's business units.* Again, quantitative ratings of competitive strength are preferable to subjective judgments. The purpose of rating the competitive strength of each business is to gain clear understanding of which businesses are strong contenders in their industries, which are weak contenders, and the underlying reasons for their strength or weakness. One of the most effective ways to join the conclusions about industry attractiveness with the conclusions about competitive strength is to draw an industry attractiveness/competitive strength matrix displaying the positions of each business on a nine-cell grid.

Step 4: *Determine the competitive advantage potential of any value chain relationships and strategic fits among existing business units.* A business is more attractive *strategically* when it has value chain relationships with other business units that present opportunities to transfer skills or technology, reduce overall costs, share facilities, or share a common brand name—any of which can represent a significant avenue for producing competitive advantage beyond what any one business can achieve on its own. The more businesses with competitively valuable strategic fits, the greater a diversified company's potential for achieving economies of scope, enhancing the competitive capabilities of particular business units, and/or strengthening the competitiveness of its product and business lineup, thereby leveraging its resources into a combined performance greater than the units could achieve operating independently.

Step 5: *Determine whether the firm's resource strengths match the resource requirements of its present business lineup.* The businesses in a diversified company's lineup need to exhibit good *resource fit* as well as good strategic fit. Resource fit exists when (1) businesses add to a company's resource strengths, either financially or strategically and (2) a company has the resources to adequately support the resource requirements of its businesses as a group without spreading itself too thinly. One important dimension of resource fit concerns whether the company's business lineup is well-matched to its financial resources. Assessing the cash requirements of different businesses in a diversified company's portfolio and determining which are cash hogs and which are cash cows highlights opportunities for shifting corporate financial resources between business subsidiaries to optimize the performance of the whole corporate portfolio, explains why priorities for corporate resource allocation can differ from business to business, and provides good rationalizations for both invest-and-expand strategies and divestiture.

Step 6: *Rank the past performance of different business units from best to worst and rank their future performance prospects from best to worst.* The most important considerations in judging business-unit performance are sales growth, profit growth, contribution to company earnings, and the return on capital invested in the business. Sometimes, cash flow generation is a big consideration. Normally, strong business units in attractive industries have significantly better performance prospects than weak businesses or businesses in unattractive industries.

Step 7: *Rank the business units in terms of priority for resource allocation and decide whether the strategic posture for each business unit should be aggressive expansion, fortify and defend, overhaul and reposition, or harvest/ divest.* In doing the ranking, special attention needs to be given to whether and how *corporate* resources and capabilities can be used to enhance the competitiveness of particular business units. Options for allocating a diversified company's financial resources include (1) investing in ways to strengthen or expand existing businesses, (2) making acquisitions to establish positions in new industries, (3) funding long-range R&D ventures, (4) paying off existing long-term debt, (5) increasing dividends, and (6) repurchasing the company's stock. Ideally, a company will have the financial strength to accomplish what is needed strategically and financially; if not, strategic uses of corporate resources should usually take precedence.

Step 8: *Use the preceding analysis to craft a series of moves to improve overall corporate performance.* Typical actions include (1) making acquisitions, starting new businesses from within, and divesting marginal businesses or businesses that no longer match the company's long-term direction and strategy, (2) devising moves to strengthen the long-term competitive positions of the company's businesses, (3) capitalizing on strategic-fit and resource-fit opportunities and turning them into long-term competitive advantage, and (4) steering corporate resources out of low-opportunity areas into high-opportunity areas.

SUGGESTED READINGS

Campbell, Andrew, Michael Goold, and Marcus Alexander. "Corporate Strategy: The Quest for Parenting Advantage." *Harvard Business Review* 73, no. 2 (March–April 1995), pp. 120–32.

Haspeslagh, Phillippe C., and David B. Jamison. *Managing Acquisitions: Creating Value through Corporate Renewal.* New York: Free Press, 1991.

Naugle, David G., and Garret A. Davies. "Strategic-Skill Pools and Competitive Advantage." *Business Horizons* 30, no. 6 (November–December 1987), pp. 35–42.

Porter, Michael E. "From Competitive Advantage to Corporate Strategy." *Harvard Business Review* 65, no. 3 (May–June 1987), pp. 43–59.

9 IMPLEMENTING STRATEGY: BUILDING RESOURCE CAPABILITIES AND STRUCTURING THE ORGANIZATION

We strategize beautifully, we implement pathetically.

An auto-parts firm executive

Strategies are intellectually simple; their execution is not.

Lawrence A. Bossidy
CEO, Allied-Signal

Just being able to conceive bold new strategies is not enough. The general manager must also be able to translate his or her strategic vision into concrete steps that "get things done."

Richard G. Hamermesh

Once managers have decided on a strategy, the emphasis turns to converting it into actions and good results. Putting a strategy into place and getting the organization to execute it well call for a different set of managerial tasks and skills. While crafting strategy is largely a market-driven entrepreneurial activity, implementing strategy is primarily an operations-driven activity revolving around the management of people and business processes. While successful strategy making depends on business vision, shrewd industry and competitive analysis, and good resource fit, successful strategy implementation depends on doing a good job of leading, working with and through others, allocating resources, building and strengthening competitive capabilities, installing strategy-supportive policies, and matching how the organization performs its core business activities to the requirements for good strategy execution. Implementing strategy is an action-oriented, make-things-happen task that tests a manager's ability to direct organizational change, motivate people, develop core competencies, build valuable organizational capabilities, achieve continuous improvement in business processes, create a strategy-supportive corporate culture, and meet or beat performance targets.

Experienced managers are emphatic in declaring that it is a whole lot easier to develop a sound strategic plan than it is to make it happen. According to one executive, "It's been rather easy for us to decide where we wanted to go. The hard part is to get the organization to act on the new priorities."[1] What makes strategy

---

[1]As quoted in Steven W. Floyd and Bill Wooldridge, "Managing Strategic Consensus: The Foundation of Effective Implementation," *Academy of Management Executive* 6, no. 4 (November 1992), p. 27.

implementation a tougher, more time-consuming management challenge than crafting strategy is the wide array of managerial activities that have to be attended to, the many ways managers can proceed, the demanding people-management skills required, the perseverance it takes to get a variety of initiatives launched and moving, the number of bedeviling issues that must be worked out, the resistance to change that must be overcome, and the difficulties of integrating the efforts of many different work groups into a smoothly functioning whole. *Just because managers announce a new strategy doesn't mean that subordinates will agree with it or cooperate in implementing it.* Some may be skeptical about the merits of the strategy, seeing it as contrary to the organization's best interests, unlikely to succeed, or threatening to their own careers. Moreover, company personnel may interpret the new strategy differently, be uncertain about how their departments will fare, and have different ideas about what internal changes are needed to execute the new strategy. Long-standing attitudes, vested interests, inertia, and ingrained organizational practices don't melt away when managers decide on a new strategy and start to implement it—especially when only a handful of people have been involved in crafting the strategy and the rationale for strategic change has to be sold to enough organization members to root out the status quo. It takes adept managerial leadership to overcome pockets of doubt and disagreement, build consensus for how to proceed, secure commitment and cooperation, and get all the implementation pieces into place and integrated. Depending on how much consensus building and organizational change is involved, the implementation process can take several months to several years.

The strategy-implementer's task is to convert the strategic plan into action and get on with what needs to be done to achieve the vision and targeted objectives.

Companies don't implement strategies, people do.

A FRAMEWORK FOR IMPLEMENTING STRATEGY

Implementing strategy entails converting the organization's strategic plan into action and then into results. Like crafting strategy, it's a job for the whole management team, not a few senior managers. While an organization's chief executive officer and the heads of business divisions, departments, and key operating units are ultimately responsible for seeing that strategy is implemented successfully, the implementation process typically impacts every part of the organizational structure, from the biggest organizational unit to the smallest frontline work group. Every manager has to think through the answer to "What has to be done in my area to implement our part of the strategic plan, and what should I do to get these things accomplished?" In this sense, *all managers become strategy implementers in their areas of authority and responsibility, and all employees are participants.*

Every manager has an active role in the process of implementing and executing the firm's strategic plan.

One of the keys to successful implementation is for management to communicate the case for organizational change so clearly and persuasively that there is determined commitment throughout the ranks to carry out the strategy and meet performance targets. The ideal condition is for managers to arouse enough enthusiasm for the strategy to turn the implementation process into a companywide crusade. Management's handling of strategy implementation is successful when the company achieves the targeted strategic and financial performance and shows good progress in realizing its long-range strategic vision.

Unfortunately, there are no 10-step checklists, no proven paths, and few concrete guidelines for tackling the job—strategy implementation is the least charted, most open-ended part of strategic management. The best evidence on dos and don'ts

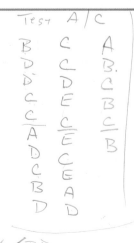

comes from the reported experiences and "lessons learned" of managers and companies—and the wisdom they yield is inconsistent. What's worked well for some managers has been tried by others and found lacking. The reasons are understandable. Not only are some managers more effective than others in employing this or that recommended approach to organizational change, but each instance of strategy implementation takes place in a different organizational context. Different business practices and competitive circumstances, work environments and cultures, policies, compensation incentives, and mixes of personalities and organizational histories require a customized approach to strategy implementation—one based on individual company situations and circumstances and on the strategy implementer's best judgment and ability to use particular change techniques adeptly.

Implementing strategy is more art than science.

THE PRINCIPAL STRATEGY-IMPLEMENTING TASKS

While managers' approaches should be tailor-made for the situation, certain bases have to be covered no matter what the organization's circumstances; these include

- Building an organization with the competencies, capabilities, and resource strengths to carry out the strategy successfully.
- Developing budgets to steer ample resources into those value chain activities critical to strategic success.
- Establishing strategy-supportive policies and procedures.
- Instituting best practices and pushing for continuous improvement in how value chain activities are performed.
- Installing information, communication, and operating systems that enable company personnel to carry out their strategic roles successfully day in and day out.
- Tying rewards and incentives to the achievement of performance objectives and good strategy execution.
- Creating a strategy-supportive work environment and corporate culture.
- Exerting the internal leadership needed to drive implementation forward and to keep improving on how the strategy is being executed.

These managerial tasks, depicted in Figure 9–1, crop up repeatedly in the strategy implementation process, no matter what the specifics of the situation. One or two of these tasks usually end up being more crucial or time-consuming than others, depending on how radically different the strategy changes are that have to be implemented, the organization's financial condition and competitive capabilities, whether there are important resource weaknesses to correct or new competencies to develop, the extent to which the company is already able to meet the resource requirements for creating sustainable competitive advantage, the strength of ingrained behavior patterns that have to be changed, the personal and organizational relationships in the firm's history, any pressures for quick results and near-term financial improvements, and perhaps other important factors.

In devising an action agenda, *strategy implementers should begin with a probing assessment of what the organization must do differently and better to carry out the strategy successfully*, then consider how to make the necessary internal changes as rapidly as practical. The strategy implementer's actions should center on fitting how the organization performs its value chain activities and conducts its internal business to what it takes for first-rate strategy execution. A series of "fits" are needed. Organiza-

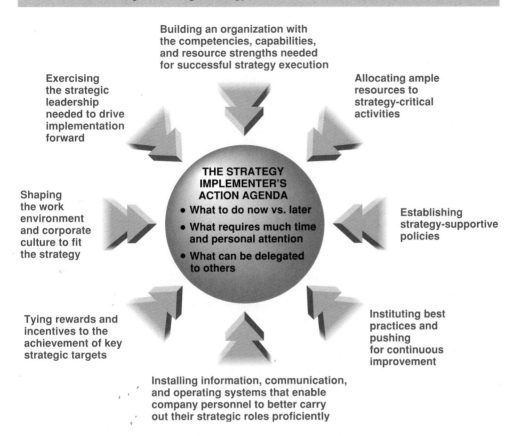

FIGURE 9-1 The Eight Big Managerial Components of Implementing Strategy

Building an organization with the competencies, capabilities, and resource strengths needed for successful strategy execution

Allocating ample resources to strategy-critical activities

Exercising the strategic leadership needed to drive implementation forward

THE STRATEGY IMPLEMENTER'S ACTION AGENDA
• What to do now vs. later
• What requires much time and personal attention
• What can be delegated to others

Establishing strategy-supportive policies

Shaping the work environment and corporate culture to fit the strategy

Tying rewards and incentives to the achievement of key strategic targets

Instituting best practices and pushing for continuous improvement

Installing information, communication, and operating systems that enable company personnel to better carry out their strategic roles proficiently

tional capabilities and resources must be carefully matched to the requirements of strategy—especially if the chosen strategy is based on a competence-based or resource-based competitive advantage. Financial resources must be allocated to provide departments with the people and operating budgets needed to execute their strategic roles effectively. The company's reward structure, policies, information systems, and operating practices need to push for strategy execution, rather than playing a merely passive role or, even worse, acting as obstacles. Equally important is the need for managers to do things in a manner and style that create and nurture a strategy-supportive work environment and corporate culture. The stronger such fits, the better the chances for successful strategy implementation. Systematic management efforts to match how the organization goes about its business with the needs of good strategy execution help unite the organization and produce a team effort to meet or beat performance targets. Successful strategy implementers have a knack for diagnosing what their organizations need to do to execute the chosen strategy well, and they are creative in finding ways to perform key value chain activities effectively.

LEADING THE IMPLEMENTATION PROCESS

One make-or-break determinant of successful strategy implementation is how well management leads the process. Managers can employ any of several leadership styles in pushing the implementation process along. They can play an active, visible, take-charge role or a quiet, low-key, behind-the-scenes one. They can make decisions authoritatively or on the basis of consensus; delegate much or little; be personally involved in the details of implementation or stand on the sidelines and coach others; proceed swiftly (launching implementation initiatives on many fronts) or deliberately (remaining content with gradual progress over a long time frame). How managers lead the implementation task tends to be a function of (1) their experience and knowledge about the business; (2) whether they are new to the job or veterans; (3) their network of personal relationships with others in the organization; (4) their own diagnostic, administrative, interpersonal, and problem-solving skills; (5) the authority they've been given; (6) the leadership style they're comfortable with; and (7) their view of the role they need to play to get things done.

Although major initiatives usually have to be led by the CEO and other senior officers, top-level managers still have to rely on the active support and cooperation of

It is the job of middle and lower-level managers to push needed implementation actions on the front lines and to see that the strategy is well-executed on a daily basis.

middle and lower managers to push strategy changes and see that key activities are performed well on a daily basis. Middle- and lower-level managers not only are responsible for initiating and supervising the implementation process in their areas of authority but they also are instrumental in getting subordinates to continuously improve on how strategy-critical value chain activities are performed and produce the frontline results that allow company performance targets to be met. How successful middle and lower managers are determines how proficiently the company executes its strategy on a daily basis—their role on the company's strategy implementation team is by no means minimal.

The action agenda of senior-level strategy implementers, especially in big organizations with geographically scattered operating units, mostly involves communicating the case for change to others, building consensus for how to proceed, installing strong allies in positions where they can push implementation along in key organizational units, urging and empowering subordinates to get the process moving, establishing measures of progress and deadlines, recognizing and rewarding those who reach implementation milestones, reallocating resources, and personally

The real strategy-implementing skill is being good at figuring out what it will take to execute the strategy proficiently.

presiding over the strategic change process. Thus, the bigger the organization, the more the success of the chief strategy implementer depends on the cooperation and implementing skills of operating managers who can push needed changes at the lowest organizational levels. In small organizations, the chief strategy implementer doesn't have to work through middle managers and can deal directly with frontline managers and employees. They

can personally orchestrate the action steps and implementation sequence, observe firsthand how implementation is progressing, and decide how hard and how fast to push the process along. Either way, *the most important leadership trait is a strong, confident sense of "what to do" to achieve the desired results.* Knowing "what to do" comes from a savvy understanding of the business and the organization's circumstances.

In the remainder of this chapter and the next two chapters, we survey the ins and outs of the manager's role as chief strategy implementer. The discussion is framed around the eight managerial components of the strategy-implementation process. This chapter explores the management tasks of building a capable organization. Chapter 10 looks at budget allocations, policies, best practices, internal support systems, and strategically appropriate reward structures. Chapter 11 deals with creating a strategy-supportive corporate culture and exercising strategic leadership.

BUILDING A CAPABLE ORGANIZATION

Proficient strategy execution depends heavily on competent personnel, better-than-adequate competencies and competitive capabilities, and effective organization. Building a capable organization is thus always a top strategy-implementing priority. Three types of organization-building actions are paramount:

- Selecting able people for key positions.
- Making certain that the organization has the skills, core competencies, managerial talents, technical know-how, competitive capabilities, and resource strengths it needs.
- Organizing business processes, value chain activities, and decision making in a manner that is conducive to successful strategy execution.

Selecting People for Key Positions

Assembling a capable management team is one of the first cornerstones of the organization-building task. Strategy implementers must determine the kind of core management team they need to execute the strategy and then find the right people to fill each slot. Sometimes the existing management team is suitable; sometimes it needs to be strengthened or expanded by promoting qualified people from within or by bringing in outsiders whose experience, skills, and leadership styles suit the situation. In turnaround and rapid-growth situations, and in instances when a company doesn't have insiders with the needed experience and management know-how, filling key management slots from the outside is a fairly standard approach.

Putting together a strong management team with the right personal chemistry and mix of skills is one of the first strategy-implementing steps.

Putting together a core executive group starts with deciding what mix of backgrounds, experiences, know-how, values, beliefs, management styles, and personalities are needed to reinforce and contribute to successful strategy execution. As with any kind of team-building exercise, it is important to put together a compatible group of managers who possess the full set of skills to get things done. The personal chemistry needs to be right, and the talent base needs to be appropriate for the chosen strategy. Picking a solid management team is an essential organization-building function—often the first strategy implementation step to take.[2] Until key slots are filled with able people, it is hard for strategy implementation to proceed at full speed.

But a good management team is not enough. The task of staffing the organization with talented people must go much deeper into the organizational ranks. Companies like Electronic Data Systems (EDS), Microsoft, and McKinsey & Co. (one of the world's premier management consulting companies) make a concerted effort to recruit and retain the best and brightest talent they can find—having a cadre of people with strong technical skills is essential to their business. EDS requires college graduates to have at least a 3.5 grade-point average (on a 4.0 scale) just to qualify for an interview; Microsoft seeks out the world's most talented programmers to write code for its programs; McKinsey recruits MBAs only at the top ten business schools. The Big Six accounting firms screen candidates not only on the basis of their accounting expertise but also on whether they possess the people skills to relate well

---

[2]For an analytical framework in top-management team analysis, see Donald C. Hambrick, "The Top Management Team: Key to Strategic Success," *California Management Review* 30, no. 1 (Fall 1987), pp. 88–108.

with clients and colleagues. Southwest Airlines goes to considerable lengths to hire people who can have fun and be fun on the job; Southwest uses specially developed methods, including interviews with customers, to determine whether applicants for customer-contact jobs have outgoing personality traits that match its strategy of creating a high-spirited, fun-loving, in-flight atmosphere for passengers and going all-out to make flying Southwest a pleasant experience. The company is so selective that only about 3 percent of the candidates interviewed are offered jobs.

Building Core Competencies and Competitive Capabilities

Two of the most important organization-building concerns are that of (1) staffing operating units with the specialized talents, skills, and technical expertise needed to give the firm a competitive edge over rivals in performing one or more critical value chain activities and (2) building competitively valuable organizational capabilities. When ease of imitation makes it difficult or impossible to beat rivals on the basis of a superior strategy, the other main avenue to industry leadership is to outexecute them (beat them with superior strategy implementation—more resources, superior talent, stronger or better capabilities, more attention to detail). Superior strategy execution is essential in situations where rival firms have very similar strategies and can readily duplicate one another's strategic maneuvers. Building core competencies, resource strengths, and organizational capabilities that rivals can't match is one of the best ways to outexecute them. This is why one of management's most important strategy-implementing tasks is to build competitively advantageous competencies and organizational capabilities.

Developing and Strengthening Core Competencies   Core competencies can relate to any strategically relevant factor. Honda's core competence is its depth of expertise in gasoline engine technology and small engine design. Intel's is in the design of complex chips for personal computers. Procter & Gamble's core competencies reside in its superb marketing-distribution skills and its R&D capabilities in five core technologies—fats, oils, skin chemistry, surfactants, and emulsifiers.[3] Sony's core competencies are its expertise in electronic technology and its ability to translate that expertise into innovative products (miniaturized radios and video cameras, TVs and VCRs with unique features, attractively designed PCs). Most often, a company's core competencies emerge incrementally as it moves either to bolster skills that contributed to earlier successes or to respond to customer problems, new technological and market opportunities, and the moves of rivals.[4] Wise company managers try to foresee coming changes in customer-market requirements and proactively build new competencies and capabilities that offer a competitive edge.

Four traits concerning core competencies and competitive capabilities are important to a strategy implementer's organization-building task:[5]

- Core competencies rarely consist of narrow skills or the work efforts of a single department. Rather, they are composites of skills and activities

---

[3]James Brian Quinn, *Intelligent Enterprise* (New York: Free Press, 1992), p. 76.
[4]Ibid.
[5]Quinn, *Intelligent Enterprise*, pp. 52–53, 55, 73, and 76.

performed at different locations in the firm's value chain that, when linked, create unique organizational capability.

- Because core competencies typically reside in the combined efforts of different work groups and departments, individual supervisors and department heads can't be expected to see building the overall corporation's core competencies as their responsibility.

- The key to leveraging a company's core competencies into long-term competitive advantage is concentrating more effort and more talent than rivals on deepening and strengthening these competencies.

- Because customers' needs change in often unpredictable ways and the know-how and capabilities needed for competitive success cannot always be accurately forecasted, a company's selected bases of competence need to be broad enough and flexible enough to respond to an unknown future.

The multiskill, multiactivity character of core competencies makes building and strengthening them an exercise in (1) managing human skills, knowledge bases, and intellect and (2) coordinating and networking the efforts of different work groups and departments at every related place in the value chain. It's an exercise best orchestrated by senior managers who appreciate the strategy-implementing significance of creating valuable competencies/capabilities and who have the clout to enforce the necessary cooperation among individuals, groups, departments, and external allies. Moreover, organization builders have to concentrate enough resources and management attention on core competence-related activities to achieve the *dominating depth* needed for competitive advantage.[6] This does not necessarily mean spending more money on competence-related activities than present or potential competitors. It does mean consciously focusing more talent on them and making appropriate internal and external benchmarking comparisons to move toward best-in-industry, if not best-in-world, status. To achieve dominance on lean financial resources, companies like Cray in large computers, Lotus in software, and Honda in small engines leveraged the expertise of their talent pool by frequently re-forming high-intensity teams and reusing key people on special projects.[7] In leveraging internal knowledge and skills rather than physical assets or market position, it is superior selection, training, powerful cultural influences, cooperative networking, motivation, empowerment, attractive incentives, organizational flexibility, short deadlines, and good databases—not big operating budgets—that are the usual keys to success.[8] One of Microsoft's keys to success in computer software is hiring the very brightest and most talented programmers it can find and motivating them with both good monetary incentives and the challenge of working on cutting-edge software design projects (although Microsoft also assigns small armies of these programmers to work on projects with high-priority or short deadlines).

Core competencies don't come into being or reach strategic fruition without conscious management attention.

Strategy implementers can't afford to become complacent once core competencies are in place and functioning. It's a constant organization-building challenge to broaden, deepen, or modify them in response to ongoing customer-market changes. But it's a task worth pursuing. Core competencies that are

[6]Ibid., p. 73.
[7]Ibid.
[8]Ibid., pp. 73–74.

finely honed and kept current with shifting circumstances can provide a big executional advantage. Distinctive core competencies and organizational capabilities are not easily duplicated by rival firms; thus any competitive advantage that results from them is likely to be durable. Dedicated management attention to the task of building strategically relevant internal skills and capabilities is always one of the keys to effective strategy implementation.

Developing and Strengthening Organizational Capabilities   Whereas the essence of astute strategy-making is *selecting* the competencies and capabilities to underpin the strategy, the essence of good strategy implementation is *building and strengthening* the competencies and capabilities to execute the chosen strategy proficiently. Sometimes a company already has the needed competencies and capabilities in place, in which case the strategy implementation task only involves efforts to strengthen and nurture them so as to promote better execution. Sometimes, however, management has be be proactive in developing *new* competencies and capabilities to complement the company's existing resource base and promote more proficient strategy execution. It is useful here to think of companies as a bundle of evolving competencies and capabilities, with the challenge being one of developing new capabilities and strengthening existing ones to achieve competitive advantage through superior strategy execution.

Organization-building that succeeds in developing valuable new competitive capabilities and strengthening existing ones can enable an enterprise to outcompete rivals on the basis of superior resources.

One issue is whether to develop the desired competencies and capabilities internally or whether it makes more sense to outsource them by partnering with key suppliers or forming strategic alliances. Decisions about whether to outsource or develop in-house capability often turn on the issue of what can be safely delegated to outside suppliers versus what internal capabilities are key to the company's long-term success. Either way, though, implementation actions are called for. Outsourcing involves identifying the most attractive providers and establishing collaborative relationships. Developing the capabilities in-house means hiring new personnel with skills and experience relevant to the desired capability, linking the individual skills/know-how to form organizational capability (a group's capabilities are partly a function of the working relationships among its members), building the desired levels of proficiency through repetition ("practice makes perfect"), and linking all the capability-related value chain activities.[9] Strong linkages with related activities are important. The capability to do something really complex (like design and manufacture a sports utility vehicle or create software that allows secure credit card transactions over the Internet) usually involves a number of skills, technological disciplines, competencies, and capabilities—some performed in-house and some provided by suppliers/allies. An important part of organization building is to think about which skills and activities need to be linked and made mutually reinforcing and then to forge the necessary collaboration and cooperation both internally and with outside resource providers.

Managers create organizational capabilities by integrating the skills and know-how of different people and groups in competitively valuable ways, and continuously tuning and recalibrating the components to match new strategic requirements over time.

All this should reemphasize that capability building is a time-consuming, hard-to-replicate exercise. Capabilities are difficult to purchase (except through outsiders who already have them and will agree to supply them) and difficult to imitate just by

---

[9]Robert H. Hayes, Gary P. Pisano, and David M. Upton, *Strategic Operations: Competing through Capabilities* (New York: Free Press, 1996), pp. 503–07.

watching others (just as one cannot become a good golfer by watching Tiger Woods play golf, a company cannot put a new capability in place by creating a new department and assigning it the task of emulating a capability rivals have). Capability building requires a series of organizational steps:

- First, the organization must develop the *ability* to do something, however imperfectly or inefficiently. This means selecting people with the needed skills and experience, upgrading or expanding individual abilities as needed, and then molding the efforts and work products of individuals into a cooperative group effort to create organizational *ability*.

- Then as experience builds, such that the organization can accomplish the activity consistently well and at an acceptable cost, the ability begins to translate into a *competence* and/or a *capability*.

- Should the organization get so good (by continuing to polish and refine and deepen its skills and know-how) that it is better than rivals at the activity, the capability becomes a *distinctive competence* with potential for competitive advantage.

Building capabilities either internally or in collaboration with others takes time and considerable organizing skill.

Sometimes these steps can be short-circuited by acquiring the desired capability through collaborative efforts with external allies or by buying a company that has the needed capability. Indeed, a pressing need to acquire certain capabilities quickly is one reason to acquire another company—an acquisition aimed at building greater capability can be every bit as competitively valuable as an acquisition aimed at adding the acquired company's products/services to the acquirer's business lineup. Capabilities-motivated acquisitions are essential (1) when an opportunity can disappear faster than a needed capability can be created internally and (2) when industry conditions, technology, or competitors are moving at such a rapid clip that time is of the essence.

Organizational competencies and capabilities emerge from establishing and nurturing collaborative working relationships between individuals and groups in different departments and between a company and its external allies.

The Strategic Role of Employee Training   Training and retraining are important parts of the strategy implementation process when a company shifts to a strategy requiring different skills, managerial approaches, and operating methods. Training is also strategically important in organizational efforts to build skills-based competencies. And it is a key activity in businesses where technical know-how is changing so rapidly that a company loses its ability to compete unless its skilled people have cutting-edge knowledge and expertise. Successful strategy implementers see that the training function is adequately funded and that effective training programs are in place. If the chosen strategy calls for new skills, deeper technological capability, or building and using new capabilities, training should be placed near the top of the action agenda because it needs to be done early in the strategy implementation process.

Matching Organization Structure to Strategy

There are few hard-and-fast rules for organizing the work effort in a strategy-supportive fashion. Every firm's organization chart is idiosyncratic, reflecting prior organizational patterns, executive judgments about how best to arrange reporting relationships, the politics of who to give which assignments, and varying internal circumstances. Moreover, every strategy is grounded in its own set of key success factors and value chain activities. So a customized organization structure is appropriate. The following are helpful guidelines in fitting structure to strategy:

- Pinpoint the primary value chain activities, competencies, and competitive capabilities that are important in successfully executing the strategy.
- Determine whether some value chain activities (especially noncritical support activities, but perhaps selected primary activities) can be outsourced more efficiently or effectively than they can be performed internally.
- Determine which of the strategy-critical activities/capabilities require close collaboration with suppliers, forward channel allies (distributors or dealers or franchisees), makers of complementary products, or even competitors.
- Make those primary value chain activities and capabilities to be performed/ developed internally and strategy-critical organizational units the main building blocks in the organization structure.
- Determine the degrees of authority needed to manage each organizational unit, striking a balance between centralizing decision making under the coordinating authority of a single manager and pushing decision making down to the lowest organizational level capable of making timely, informed, competent decisions.
- If all facets of an internal strategy-critical activity/capability cannot be placed under the authority of a single manager, establish ways to bridge departmental lines and achieve the necessary coordination.
- Determine how the relationships with outsiders are to be managed and assign responsibility for building the necessary organizational bridges.

Pinpointing Strategy-Critical Activities and Competitive Capabilities   In any business, some activities in the value chain are always more critical to success than others. From a strategy perspective, a certain portion of an organization's work involves routine administrative housekeeping (doing the payroll, administering employee benefit programs, handling grievances, providing corporate security, maintaining fleet vehicles). Others are support functions (data processing, accounting, training, public relations, market research, purchasing). Among the primary value chain activities are certain crucial business processes that have to be performed either exceedingly well or in closely coordinated fashion for the organization to develop the capabilities needed for strategic success. For instance, hotel/motel enterprises have to be good at fast check-in/check-out, room maintenance, food service, and creating a pleasant ambiance. A manufacturer of chocolate bars must be skilled in purchasing quality cocoa beans at low prices, efficient production (a fraction of a cent in cost savings per bar can mean seven-figure improvement in the bottom line), merchandising, and promotional activities. In discount stock brokerage, the strategy-critical activities are fast access to information, accurate order execution, efficient record-keeping and transactions processing, and good customer service. In specialty chemicals, the critical activities are R&D, product innovation, getting new products onto the market quickly, effective marketing, and expertise in assisting customers. In the electronics industry, where technology is racing along, a company's cycle time in getting new, cutting-edge products to market is the critical organizational capability. Strategy-critical activities and capabilities vary according to the particulars of a firm's strategy, value chain makeup, and competitive requirements.

Two questions help identify what an organization's strategy-critical activities are: "What functions have to be performed extra well or in timely fashion to achieve sustainable competitive advantage?" and "In what value chain activities would malperformance seriously endanger strategic success?"[10] The answers generally point to the crucial activities and organizational capabilities where organization-building efforts must be concentrated.

Reasons to Consider Outsourcing Certain Value Chain Activities   Managers too often spend inordinate amounts of time, psychic energy, and resources wrestling with functional support groups and other internal bureaucracies, diverting attention from the company's strategy-critical activities. One way to detour such distractions is to cut the number of internal staff support activities and, instead, source more of what is needed from outside vendors.

Each supporting activity in a firm's value chain and within its traditional staff groups can be considered a "service."[11] Indeed, most overheads are just services the company chooses to produce internally. However, many such services can typically be purchased from outside vendors. What makes outsourcing attractive is that an outsider, by concentrating specialists and technology in its area of expertise, can frequently perform these services *as well or better and usually more cheaply* than a company that performs the activities only for itself. But there are other reasons to consider outsourcing. From a strategic point of view, outsourcing non-crucial support activities (and maybe selected primary activities in the value chain) can decrease internal bureaucracies, flatten the organization structure, heighten the company's strategic focus, and increase competitive responsiveness.[12] The experiences of companies that obtain many support services from outside vendors indicate that *outsourcing activities not crucial to building those organizational capabilities needed for long-term competitive success allows a company to concentrate its own energies and resources on those value chain activities where it can create unique value, where it can be best in the industry (or, better still, best in the world), and where it needs strategic control to build core competencies, achieve competitive advantage, and manage key customer-supplier-distributor relationships.*

Outsourcing noncritical value chain activities and even select primary activities has many advantages.

Critics contend that extensive outsourcing can hollow out a company, leaving it at the mercy of outside suppliers and barren of the competencies and organizational capabilities needed to be master of its own destiny.[13] However, a number of companies have successfully relied on outside components suppliers, product designers, distribution channels, advertising agencies, and financial services firms to perform significant value chain activities. For years Polaroid Corporation bought its film medium from Eastman Kodak, its electronics from Texas Instruments, and its cameras from Timex and others, while it concentrated on producing its unique self-developing film packets and designing its next generation of cameras and films. Nike concentrates on design, marketing, and distribution to retailers, while outsourcing virtually all production of its shoes and sporting apparel. Many mining companies outsource geological work, assaying, and drilling. Ernest and Julio Gallo Winery outsources 95 percent of its grape production, letting farmers take on the weather and

---

[10]Peter F. Drucker, *Management: Tasks, Responsibilities, Practices* (New York: Harper & Row, 1974), pp. 530, 535.

[11]Quinn, *Intelligent Enterprise*, p. 32.

[12]Ibid., pp. 33 and 89. See, also, James Brian Quinn and Frederick G. Hilmer, "Strategic Outsourcing," *Sloan Management Review* (Summer 1994), pp. 43–55.

[13]Ibid., pp. 39–40.

other grape-growing risks while it concentrates on wine production and the marketing-sales function.[14] The major airlines outsource their in-flight meals even though food quality is important to travelers' perception of overall service quality. Eastman Kodak, Ford, Exxon, Merrill Lynch, and Chevron have outsourced their data-processing activities to computer service firms, believing that outside specialists can perform the needed services at lower costs and equal or better quality. Chrysler has transformed itself from a high-cost producer into a low-cost producer by abandoning internal production of many parts and components and instead outsourcing them from more efficient suppliers; greater reliance on outsourcing has also enabled Chrysler to shorten the time it takes to bring new models to market. *Outsourcing certain value chain activities makes strategic sense whenever outsiders can perform them at lower cost and/or with higher value-added than the buyer company can perform them internally.*[15]

Reasons to Consider Partnering with Others to Gain Competitively Valuable Capabilities

But there is another equally important reason to look outside for help. *Strategic partnerships, alliances, and close collaboration with select suppliers, distributors, the makers of complementary products and services, and even competitors can add to a company's arsenal of capabilities and contribute to better strategy execution.* Partnering with outsiders can result in bringing new technology on-line quicker, in quicker delivery and/or lower inventories of parts and components, in providing better or faster technical assistance to customers, in geographically wider distribution capability, in the development of multiple distribution outlets, in deeper technological know-how, in economical custom manufacture, in more extensive after-sale support services, and so on. By building, continually improving, and then leveraging these kinds of organizational capabilities, a company develops the resource strengths needed for competitive success—it puts in place enhanced ability to do things for its customers that deliver value to customers and that rivals can't quite match.

Microsoft's Bill Gates and Intel's Andrew Grove meet periodically to explore how their organizations can share information, work in parallel, and team together to sustain the "Wintel" standard that pervades the PC industry. The automobile manufacturers work closely with their suppliers to advance the design and functioning of parts and components, to incorporate new technology, to better integrate individual parts and components to form engine cooling systems, transmission systems, electrical systems, and so on—all of which helps shorten the cycle time for new models, improve the quality and performance of their vehicles, and boost overall production efficiency. The soft-drink producers (Coca-Cola and PepsiCo) and the beer producers (Anheuser-Busch and Miller Brewing) all cultivate their relationships with their bottlers/distributors to strengthen access to local markets and build the loyalty, support, and commitment for corporate marketing programs, without which their own sales and growth are weakened. Similarly, the fast-food enterprises like McDonald's and Taco Bell find it essential to work hand-in-hand with franchisees on outlet cleanliness, consistency of product quality, in-store ambience, courtesy and friendliness of store personnel, and other aspects of store operations—unless franchisees

---

[14]Ibid., p. 43.

[15]Ibid., p. 47. The growing tendency of companies to outsource important activities and the many reasons for building cooperative, collaborative alliances and partnerships with other companies is detailed in James F. Moore, *The Death of Competition* (New York: HarperBusiness, 1996), especially Chapter 3.

deliver sufficient customer satisfaction to attract repeat business on an ongoing basis, a fast-food chain's sales and competitive standing suffer quickly. *Strategic partnerships, alliances, and close collaboration with suppliers, distributors, the makers of complementary products/services and competitors make good strategic sense whenever the result is to enhance organizational resources and capabilities.*

Making Strategy-Critical Activities/Capabilities the Main Building Blocks of the Internal Organization The rationale for making strategy-critical activities and capabilities the main building blocks in structuring a business is compelling: If activities/ capabilities crucial to strategic success are to have the resources, decision-making influence, and organizational impact needed, they have to be centerpieces in the organizational scheme. Plainly, a new or changed strategy is likely to lead to new or different key activities, competencies, or capabilities and, therefore, require new or different organizational arrangements; without them, the resulting mismatch between strategy and structure can open the door to implementation and performance problems.[16]

> **Strategic Management Principle**
>
> *Attempting to carry out a new strategy with an old organizational structure is usually unwise.*

Senior executives seldom send a stronger signal about what is strategically important than by making key business units and critical activities prominent organizational building blocks and, further, giving the managers of these units a visible, influential position in the organizational pecking order. When key business units are put down on a level with or, worse, superseded by less important divisions or departments, they usually end up with fewer resources and less clout than they deserve in the organization's power structure. When top management fails to devote attention to organizing in a way that produces effective performance of strategy-critical activities and processes and develops needed capabilities, the whole strategy implementation effort is weakened. It is thus essential that the primary value-creating, success-causing activities and business processes be prominent in the company's organization structure and deeply ingrained in how the organization does its work. Anything else risks a serious mismatch between structure and strategy.

> **Strategic Management Principle**
>
> *Matching structure to strategy requires making strategy-critical activities and strategy-critical organizational units the main building blocks in the organization structure.*

---

[16]The importance of matching organization design and structure to the particular needs of strategy was first brought to the forefront in a landmark study of 70 large corporations conducted by Professor Alfred Chandler of Harvard University. Chandler's research revealed that changes in an organization's strategy bring about new administrative problems which, in turn, require a new or refashioned structure for the new strategy to be successfully implemented. He found that structure tends to follow the growth strategy of the firm—but often not until inefficiency and internal operating problems provoke a structural adjustment. The experiences of these firms followed a consistent sequential pattern: new strategy creation, emergence of new administrative problems, a decline in profitability and performance, a shift to a more appropriate organizational structure, and then recovery to more profitable levels and improved strategy execution. That managers should reassess their company's internal organization whenever strategy changes is pretty much common sense. A new or different strategy is likely to entail new or different key activities, competencies, or capabilities and, therefore, require new or different internal organizational arrangements; if workable organizational adjustments are not forthcoming, the resulting mismatch between strategy and structure can open the door to implementation and performance problems. For more details, see Alfred Chandler, *Strategy and Structure* (Cambridge, Mass.: MIT Press, 1962).

Although the stress here is on designing the organization structure around the needs of effective strategy execution, it is worth noting that structure can and does influence the choice of strategy. A good strategy must be doable. When an organization's present structure is so far out of line with the requirements of a particular strategy that the organization would have to be turned upside down to implement it, the strategy may not be doable and should not be given further consideration. In such cases, structure shapes the choice of strategy. The point here, however, is that once strategy is chosen, structure must be modified to fit the strategy if, in fact, an approximate fit does not already exist. Any influences of structure on strategy should, logically, come before the point of strategy selection rather than after it.

In grafting routine and staff support activities onto the basic structure, company managers should be guided by the strategic relationships among the primary and support functions comprising the value chain. Activities can be related by the flow of work along the value chain, the type of customer served, the distribution channels used, the technical skills and know-how needed to perform them, their contribution to building a core competence or competitive capability, their role in a work process that spans traditional departmental lines, their role in how customer value is created, their sequence in the value chain, the skills or technology transfer opportunities they present, and the potential for combining or coordinating them in a manner that will reduce total costs, to mention some of the most obvious. If the needs of successful strategy execution are to drive organization design, then the relationships to look for are those that (1) link one work unit's performance to another and (2) can be melded into a competitively valuable competence or capability.

Managers need to be particularly alert to the fact that *in traditional functionally organized structures, pieces of strategically relevant activities and capabilities often end up scattered across many departments.* The process of filling customer orders accurately and promptly is a case in point. The order fulfillment process begins when a customer places an order, ends when the goods are delivered, and typically includes a dozen or so steps performed by different people in different departments.[17] Someone in customer service receives the order, logs it in, and checks it for accuracy and completeness. It may then go to the finance department, where someone runs a credit check on the customer. Another person may be needed to approve credit terms or special financing. Someone in sales calculates or verifies the correct pricing. When the order gets to inventory control, someone has to determine if the goods are in stock. If not, a back order may be issued or the order routed to production planning so that it can be factored into the production schedule. When the goods are ready, warehouse operations prepares a shipment schedule. Personnel in the traffic department determine the shipment method (rail, truck, air, water) and choose the route and carrier. Product handling picks the product from the warehouse, verifies the picking against the order, and packages the goods for shipment. Traffic releases the goods to the carrier, which takes responsibility for delivery to the customer. Each handoff from one department to the next entails queues and wait times. Although such organization incorporates Adam Smith's division of labor principle (every person involved has specific responsibility for performing one simple task) and allows for tight management control (everyone in the process is accountable to a manager for efficiency and adherence to procedures), *no one oversees the whole process and its result.*[18] Accurate, timely order fulfillment, despite its relevance to effective strategy execution, ends up being neither a single person's job nor the job of any one functional department—it is a capability that grows out of the combined pieces of many people's jobs in different units.[19] Other strategy-critical activities that are often fragmented include obtaining feedback from customers and making product modifications to meet their needs, speeding new products to market (a task that is often fragmented among R&D, engineering, purchasing, manufacturing, and market-

Functional specialization can result in the pieces of strategically relevant activities and capabilities being scattered across many different departments.

---

[17]Michael Hammer and James Champy, *Reengineering the Corporation* (New York: HarperBusiness, 1993), pp. 26–27.
[18]Ibid.
[19]Ibid., pp. 27–28.

ILLUSTRATION CAPSULE 30   Process Organization at Lee Memorial Hospital and St. Vincent's Hospital

At acute care hospitals such as Lee Memorial in Fort Myers, Florida, and St. Vincent's in Melbourne, Australia, medical care is delivered by interdisciplinary teams of doctors, nurses, laboratory technicians, and so on that are organized around the needs of the patients and their families rather than around functional departments within the hospital; these hospitals have created focused care or treatment-specific wards within the hospital to treat most of a patient's needs, from admission to discharge. Patients are no longer wheeled from department to department for procedures and tests; instead, teams have the equipment and resources within each focused care unit to provide total care for the patient. While the hospitals had some concern about functional inefficiency in the use of some facilities, process organization has resulted in substantially lower operating cost, faster patient recovery, and greater satisfaction on the part of patients and caregivers.

Source: Iain Somerville and John Edward Mroz, "New Competencies for a New World," in *The Organization of the Future*, edited by Frances Hesselbein, Marshall Goldsmith, and Richard Beckard, (San Francisco: Jossey-Bass, 1997), p.71.

ing), improving product quality, managing relationships with key suppliers, and building the capability to conduct business via the Internet.

Managers have to guard against organization designs that unduly fragment strategically relevant activities. Parceling strategy-critical work efforts across many specialized departments contributes to an obsession with activity (performing the assigned tasks in the prescribed manner) rather than result (lower costs, short product development times, higher product quality, customer satisfaction, competitive advantage). So many handoffs lengthen completion time and frequently drive up overhead costs since coordinating the fragmented pieces can soak up hours of effort on the parts of many people. *One obvious solution is to pull the pieces of strategy-critical processes out of the functional silos and create process-complete departments able to perform all the cross-functional steps needed to produce a strategy-critical result*— see Illustration Capsule 30 for an example of process organization. In recent years, many companies have reengineered their work flows, moving from functional structures to process structures pursued this solution where it was feasible to do so.[20] Nonetheless, some fragmentation is necessary, even desirable. Traditional functional centralization works to good advantage in support activities like finance and accounting, human resource management, and engineering, and in such primary activities as R&D, manufacturing, and marketing.

Thus the primary organizational building blocks within a business are usually a combination of traditional functional departments and process-complete departments. In enterprises with operations in various countries around the world, the basic building blocks may also include geographic organizational units, each of which has profit-loss responsibility for its area. In vertically integrated firms, the major building blocks are divisional units, each of which performs one (or more) of the major processing steps along the value chain (raw materials production, components manufacture, assembly, wholesale distribution, retail store operations); each division in the value chain sequence may operate as a profit center for performance measurement purposes. The typical building blocks of a diversified company are its individual

---

[20]For a detailed review of one company's experiences with reengineering, see Donna B. Stoddard, Sirkka L. Jarvenpaa, and Michael Littlejohn, "The Reality of Business Reengineering: Pacific Bell's Centrex Provisioning Process," *California Management Review* 38, no. 3 (Spring 1996), pp. 57–76.

businesses, with each business unit usually operating as an independent profit center and with corporate headquarters performing support functions for all the businesses.

Determining the Degree of Authority and Independence to Give Each Unit and Each Employee

Companies must decide how much authority to give managers of each organization unit (especially the heads of business subsidiaries, functional departments, and process departments) and how much decision-making latitude to give individual employees in performing their jobs. In a highly centralized organization, top executives retain authority for most strategic and operating decisions and keep a tight rein on business-unit heads and department heads; comparatively little discretionary authority is granted to subordinate managers and individual employees. One weakness of centralized organization is that its vertical, hierarchical character tends to stall decision making until the review-approval process runs its course through the layers of the management bureaucracy. Furthermore, to work well, centralized decision making requires top-level managers to gather and process whatever knowledge is relevant to the decision. When the relevant knowledge resides at lower organizational levels or is technical or detailed or hard to express in words, it is difficult and time-consuming to get all of the facts and nuances in front of the decision maker—knowledge cannot be "copied" from one mind to another. In many cases, it is better to put decision-making authority in the hands of the people most familiar with the situation and train them to exercise good judgment, rather than trying to convey the knowledge and information up the line to the person with the decision-making authority.

There are serious disadvantages to having a small number of all-knowing, top-level managers micromanage the business.

In a highly decentralized organization, managers (and, increasingly, many nonmanagerial employees) are empowered to act on their own in their areas of responsibility—plant managers are empowered to order new equipment as needed and make arrangements with suppliers for parts and components; process managers (or teams) are empowered to manage and improve their assigned process; and employees with customer contact are empowered to do what it takes to please customers. At Starbucks, for example, employees are empowered to exercise initiative in promoting customer satisfaction—there's the story of a store employee, who when the computerized cash register system went off-line, enthusiastically told waiting customers "free coffee."[21] In a diversified company operating on the principle of decentralized decision making, business unit heads have broad authority to run the subsidiary with comparatively little interference from corporate headquarters; moreover, the business head gives functional and process department heads considerable decision-making latitude.

The purpose of decentralization is not to push decisions down to lower levels but to lodge decision-making authority in those persons or teams closest to and most knowledgeable about the situation.

Delegating greater authority to subordinate managers and employees creates a more horizontal organization structure with fewer layers. Whereas in a centralized vertical structure managers and workers have to go up the ladder of authority for an answer, in a decentralized horizontal structure they develop their own answers and action plans—making decisions and being accountable for results is part of their job. Decentralized decision making usually shortens organizational response times, plus it spurs new ideas, creative thinking, innovation, and greater involvement on the part of subordinate managers and employees.

---

[21]Iain Somerville and John Edward Mroz, "New Competencies for a New World," in *The Organization of the Future*, ed. Frances Hesselbein, Marshall Goldsmith, and Richard Beckard, (San Francisco: Jossey-Bass, 1997), p.70.

In recent years, there's been a decided shift from authoritarian, hierarchical structures to flatter, more decentralized structures that stress employee empowerment. The new preference for leaner management structures and empowered employees is grounded in three tenets.

1. *With the world economy moving swiftly from the Industrial Age to the Knowledge/Information/Systems Age, traditional hierarchical structures built around functional specialization have to undergo radical surgery to accommodate greater emphasis on building competitively valuable cross-functional capabilities*; the best companies have to be able to act and react quickly and to create, package, and rapidly move information to the point of need—in short, companies have to reinvent their organizational arrangements.

2. *Decision-making authority should be pushed down to the lowest organizational level capable of making timely, informed, competent decisions*—to those people (managers or nonmanagers) nearest the scene who are knowledgeable about the issues and trained to weigh all the factors. Insofar as strategic management is concerned, decentralization means that the managers of each organizational unit should not only lead the crafting of their unit's strategy but also lead the decision making on how to implement it. Decentralization thus requires selecting strong managers to head each organizational unit and holding them accountable for crafting and executing appropriate strategies for their units. Managers who consistently produce unsatisfactory results and have poor track records in strategy making and strategy implementing have to be weeded out.

3. *Employees below the management ranks should be empowered to exercise judgment on matters pertaining to their jobs.* The case for empowering employees to make decisions and be accountable for their performance is based on the belief that a company that draws on the combined brainpower of all its employees can outperform a company where people management means transferring executives' decisions about what to do and how to do it into the actions of workers-doers. To ensure that the decisions of empowered people are as well-informed as possible, great pains have to be taken to put accurate, timely data into everyone's hands and make sure they understand the links between their performance and company performance. Delayered corporate hierarchies coupled with today's electronic communication systems make greater empowerment feasible. It's possible now to create "a wired company" where people at all organizational levels have direct electronic access to data, other employees, managers, suppliers, and customers; they can access information quickly (via the Internet or company intranet), check with superiors or whoever else as needed, and take responsible action. Typically, there are genuine morale gains when people are well-informed and allowed to operate in a self-directed way. But there is an organizing challenge as well: how to exercise adequate control over the actions of empowered employes so that the business is not put at risk at the same time that the benefits of empowerment are realized.[22]

> *Successful strategy implementation involves empowering others to act on doing all the things needed to put the strategy into place and execute it proficiently.*

---

[22]Exercising adequate control in businesses that demand short response times, innovation, and creativity is a serious requirement. For example, Kidder, Peabody & Co. lost $350 million when a trader allegedly booked fictitious profits; Sears took a $60 million write-off after admitting that employees in its automobile service departments recommended unnecessary repairs to customers. For a discussion of the problems

One of the biggest exceptions to decentralizing strategy-related decisions and giving lower-level managers more operating rein arises in diversified companies with related businesses. In such cases, strategic-fit benefits are often best captured by either centralizing decision-making authority or enforcing close cooperation and shared decision making.[23] For example, if businesses with overlapping process and product technologies have their own independent R&D departments, each pursuing their own priorities, projects, and strategic agendas, it's hard for the corporate parent to prevent duplication of effort, capture either economies of scale or economies of scope, or broaden the vision of the company's R&D efforts to embrace new technological paths, product families, end-use applications, and customer groups. Likewise, centralizing control over the related activities of separate businesses makes sense when there are opportunities to share a common sales force, use common distribution channels, rely upon a common field service organization to handle customer requests for technical assistance or provide maintenance and repair services, and so on. And for reasons previously discussed, limits also have to be placed on the independence of functional managers when pieces of strategy-critical processes are located in different organizational units and require close coordination for maximum effectiveness.

> *Centralizing strategy-implementing authority at the corporate level has merit when the related activities of related businesses need to be tightly coordinated.*

Reporting Relationships and Cross-Unit Coordination The classic way to coordinate the activities of organizational units is to position them so that those most closely related report to a single person (a functional department head, a process manager, a geographic area head). Managers higher up in the pecking order generally have authority over more organizational units and thus the clout to coordinate and unify the activities of units under their supervision. In such structures, the chief executive officer, chief operating officer, and business-level managers end up as central points of coordination. When a firm is pursuing a related diversification strategy, coordinating the related activities of independent business units often requires the centralizing authority of a single corporate-level officer. Also, companies with either related or unrelated diversification strategies commonly centralize such staff support functions as public relations, finance and accounting, employee benefits, and information systems at the corporate level.

But, as the customer order fulfillment example illustrates, it isn't always feasible to position all the pieces of a strategy-critical process and/or all interrelated organizational units vertically under the coordinating authority of a single executive. Formal reporting relationships have to be supplemented. Options for unifying the strategic efforts of interrelated organizational units include the use of coordinating teams, cross-functional task forces, dual reporting relationships, informal organizational networking, voluntary cooperation, incentive compensation tied to group performance measures, and strong executive-level insistence on teamwork and interdepartmental cooperation (including removal of recalcitrant managers who stonewall collaborative efforts).[24] See Illustration

---

and possible solutions, see Robert Simons, "Control in an Age of Empowerment," *Harvard Business Review* 73 (March–April 1995), pp. 80–88.

[23]For a discussion of the importance of cross-business coordination, see Jeanne M. Liedtka, "Collaboration across Lines of Business for Competitive Advantage," *Academy of Management Executive* 10, no. 2 (May 1996), pp. 20–34.

[24]At ABB, a $30 billion European-based company that makes power generation and electrical equipment and offers a wide range of engineering services, a top executive promptly replaced the managers of several plants who were not fully committed to collaborating closely on eliminating duplication in product development and production efforts among plants in several different countries. Earlier, the executive, noting that negotiations among the managers had stalled on which labs and plants to close, had met with all

ILLUSTRATION CAPSULE 31   Cross-Unit Coordination on Technology at 3M Corp.

At 3M, technology experts in more than 100 3M labs around the world have come to work openly and cooperatively without resorting to turf protection tactics or not-invented-here mind-sets. 3M management has been successful in creating a collegial working environment that results in the scientists calling upon one another for assistance and advice and in rapid technology transfer.

Mangement formed a Technical Council, composed of the heads of the major labs; the Council meets monthly and has a three-day annual retreat to discuss ways to improve cross-unit transfer of technology and other issues of common interest. In addition, management created a broader-based Technical Forum, composed of scientists and technical experts chosen as representatives, to facilitate grassroots communication among employees in all the labs. One of the Forum's responsibilities is to organize employees with similar technical interests from all the labs into chapters; chapter members attend regular seminars with experts from outside the company. There's also an annual three-day technology fair at which 3M scientists showcase their latest findings for colleagues and expand their network of acquaintances.

As a result of these collaborative efforts, 3M has developed a portfolio of more than 100 technologies and it has created the capability to routinely utilize these technologies in product applications in three different divisions that each serve multiple markets.

Source: Adapted from Sumantra Ghoshal and Christopher A. Bartlett, "Changing the Role of Top Management: Beyond Structure to Process," *Harvard Business Review* 73, no. 1 (January–February 1995), pp. 93–94.

Capsule 31 for a more detailed example of putting the necessary organizational arrangements into place and creating the desired results.

The key in weaving support activities into the organization design is to establish reporting and coordinating arrangements that:

- Maximize how support activities contribute to enhanced performance of the primary activities in the firm's value chain.
- Contain the costs of support activities and minimize the time and energy internal units have to spend doing business with each other.

Without such arrangements, the cost of transacting business internally becomes excessive, and the managers of individual organizational units, forever diligent in guarding their turf, can weaken the strategy execution effort and become part of the strategy-implementing problem rather than part of the solution.

Assigning Responsibility for Collaboration with Outsiders   Someone or some group must be given authority and responsibility for collaborating with each major outside constituency involved in strategy execution. This means having managers with responsibility for making particular strategic partnerships or alliances generate the intended benefits. If close working relationships with suppliers are crucial, then authority and responsibility for supply chain management must be given formal status on the company's organization chart and a significant position in the pecking order. If distributor/dealer/franchisee relationships are important, someone must be assigned the task of building the bridges of cooperation and nurturing the relationships. If working in parallel with providers of complementary products and services contributes to enhanced organizational capability, then cooperative organizational arrangements of some kind have to be put in place and managed to good effect. Just appointing and empowering relationship managers is not enough; there have to be

the managers, asked them to cooperate to find a solution, discussed with them which options were unacceptable, and given them a deadline to find a solution. When the asked-for teamwork wasn't forthcoming from several managers attending the meeting, they were replaced.

multiple ties at multiple levels to ensure proper communication, coordination, and control.[25]

The key to cooperative alliances and partnerships is effectively managing the relationship and capturing the potential gain in resource capability, not in doing the deal.

The organizing challenge is to find ways to span the boundaries of independent organizations and produce the collaborative efforts needed to enhance a company's own competitive capabilites and resource strengths.[26] *Forming alliances and cooperative relationships presents immediate opportunities and opens the door to future possibilities, but nothing valuable is realized until the relationship grows, develops, and blossoms.* Unless top management sees that such bridge building occurs and that ample effort goes into creating productive working relationships, the company's power to execute its strategy is weakened.

The Strategic Advantages And Disadvantages Of Different Organizational Structures

There are five basic building block schemes for matching structure to strategy: (1) functional and/or process specialization, (2) geographic organization, (3) decentralized business divisions, (4) strategic business units, and (5) matrix structures featuring dual lines of authority and strategic priority. Each has strategic advantages and disadvantages, and each has to be supplemented with formal and informal organizational arrangements to fully coordinate the work effort, develop core competencies, and build competitive capabilities.

Functional and Process Organization Structures   Organizational structures anchored around functionally specialized departments and strategy-critical processes are far and away the most popular way to match structure to strategy in single-business enterprises. However, just what form the functional and process specialization takes varies according to the nature of the value chain. For instance, a technical instruments manufacturer may be organized around research and development, engineering, production, technical services, quality control, marketing, personnel, and finance and accounting. A hotel may have an organization based on front-desk operations, housekeeping, building maintenance, food service, convention services and special events, guest services, personnel and training, and accounting. A discount retailer may divide its organizational units into purchasing, warehousing and distribution, store operations, advertising, merchandising and promotion, customer service, and corporate administrative services. Functional and process organizational approaches are diagrammed in Figure 9–2.

Making specialized functions or processes the main organizational building blocks works well so long as strategy-critical activities closely match functional specialties and/or business processes, there's minimal need for interdepartmental coordination, and top-level management is able to short-circuit departmental rivalries and create a spirit of teamwork, trust, and internal cooperation. Departmental units having expertise in performing every facet of the activity is an attractive way (1) to exploit any learning/experience curve benefits or economy-of-scale opportunities of division of

---

[25]Rosabeth Moss Kanter, "Collaborative Advantage: The Art of the Alliance," *Harvard Business Review* 72, no. 4 (July–August 1994), pp. 105–06.

[26]For an excellent review of ways to effectively manage the relationship between alliance partners, see Kanter, *op. cit.*, pp. 96–108.

FIGURE 9–2   Functional and Process Organizational Structures

A. The Building Blocks of a "Typical" Functional Organizational Structure

B. The Building Blocks of a Process-Oriented Structure

STRATEGIC ADVANTAGES	STRATEGIC DISADVANTAGES
• Centralized control of strategic results.	• Functional specialization is conducive to fragmentation of strategy-critical processes.
• Best suited for structuring a single business.	• Emphasis on functional specialization poses organizational barriers to creating cross-functional core competencies and to close collaboration across departmental lines.
• Well-suited to businesses where the strategy-critical value chain components consist of discipline-specific or process-oriented activities.	
• Promotes in-depth functional expertise.	• Can lead to interfunctional rivalry and conflict, rather than team-play and cooperation.
• Well suited to developing functional and/or process related skills and competencies.	• Multilayered management bureaucracies and centralized decision-making slow response times.
• Conducive to exploiting learning/experience curve effects associated with functional specialization or process specialization.	• Organizing around functional departments development of managers with cross-functional experience because the ladder of advancement is up the ranks within the same functional area.
• Enhances operating efficiency where tasks are routine and repetitive.	• Forces profit responsibility to the top.
• Can be a basis for competitive advantage when dominating depth in a function or process is a key success factor.	• Functional specialists often attach more importance to what's best for the functional area than to what's best for the whole business.
• Process organization provides a way to avoid fragmentation of strategy-critical activities across functional departments.	• Functional myopia often works against creative entrepreneurship and rapid adaptation to changing market circumstances.
	• Functional specialization poses barriers to creating cross-functional competencies and close departmental collaboration.

labor and the use of specialized technology and equipment and (2) to develop deep expertise in an important business function or process. When dominating depth in one or more functional specialties or business processes enhances operating efficiency and/or creates a competitively valuable competence, it becomes a basis for competitive advantage (lower cost or greater organizational capability).

The traditional functional structures that used to dominate single-business enterprises have three big shortcomings: excessive functional myopia, the potential for fragmentation of strategy-critical business processes across functional lines, and the difficulty of building cross-functional competencies and capabilities. Functional specialists are prone to focus inward on departmental matters and upward at their boss's priorities but not outward on the business, the customer, or the industry.[27] Members of functional departments usually have strong departmental loyalties and are protective of departmental interests. There's a natural tendency for each functional department to push for solutions and decisions that advance its well-being and influence. All this creates an organizational environment where functional departments operate as vertical silos or stovepipes and become a breeding ground for bureaucracies, empire building, authoritarian decision making, and narrow perspectives. In addition, the preoccupation of functional departments with developing deeper expertise and improving functional performance works against devising creative responses to major customer-market-technological changes; functional heads are often quick to oppose ideas or alternatives that aren't compatible with functional interests. Classical functional structures also worsen the problems of process fragmentation whenever a firm's value chain includes strategy-critical activities that, by their very nature, are cross-functional rather than discipline specific. Likewise, it's tough to develop cross-functional core competencies and capabilities in an environment dominated by strongly entrenched functional empires that don't "talk the same language" and that prefer to do their own thing without outside interference.

A big weakness of functional departments is that they are prone to develop strong functional mind-sets and approach strategic issues more from a functional than a business perspective.

Interdepartmental politics, functional empire building, functional myopia, process fragmentation, and a need to build cross-functional competencies and capabilities can impose a time-consuming administrative burden on the general manager, who is the only person on a functionally dominated organization chart with authority to contain rivalries and to enforce interdepartmental cooperation. In a functionally dominated structure, much of a GM's time and energy is spent keeping lines of communication open across departments, tempering departmental rivalries, convincing stovepipe thinkers of the merits of broader solutions, devising ways to secure cooperation, and working to mold desirable cross-functional core competencies and capabilities. To achieve the cross-functional coordination necessary for strategic success, a GM either has to (1) supplement the functional organization structure by creating process-complete departments to handle strategy-critical activities that cross functional lines or (2) be tough and uncompromising in insisting that functional department heads be team players and that functional specialists collaborate and cooperate.

Increasingly during the last decade, companies have found that rather than continuing to scatter related pieces of a business process across several functional departments and scrambling to integrate their efforts, it is better to reengineer the work effort and create process departments by pulling the people who performed the pieces in functional departments into a group that works together to perform the whole

---

[27]Hammer and Champy, *Reengineering the Corporation*, p. 28.

process.[28] This is what Bell Atlantic did in cutting through its bureaucratic procedures for connecting a telephone customer to its long-distance carrier.[29] In Bell
Atlantic's functional structure, when a business customer requested a connection
between its telephone system and a long-distance carrier for data services, the request
traveled from department to department, taking two to four weeks to complete all the
internal processing steps. In reengineering that process, Bell Atlantic pulled workers
doing the pieces of the process from the many functional departments and put them
on teams that, working together, could handle most customer requests in a matter of
days and sometimes hours. Because the work was recurring—similar customer
requests had to be processed daily—the teams were permanently grouped into a
process department. In the electronics industry where product life cycles are often
less than a year, companies have formed process departments charged with cutting
the time it takes to develop new technologies and get new products to market. Some
companies, however, have stopped short of creating process departments and, instead, either appointed process managers or interdisciplinary teams to oversee coordination of fragmented processes and strategy-critical activities. While the means of
unifying the performance of strategy-critical processes and activities has varied,
many companies have now incorporated some form of process organization to
counteract the weaknesses of a purely functional structure. The methods of reengineering fragmented processes and creating more process-complete work flows, as well
as the results that reengineering can produce, are presented in Illustration Capsule 32.

Geographic Forms of Organization   Organizing on the basis of geographic areas or
territories is a common structural form for enterprises operating in diverse geographic markets or serving an expansive geographic area. As Figure 9–3 indicates,
geographic organization has advantages and disadvantages, but the chief reason for
its popularity is that it promotes improved performance.

   In the private sector, a territorial structure is typically used by discount retailers,
power companies, cement firms, restaurant chains, and dairy products enterprises. In
the public sector, such organizations as the Internal Revenue Service, the
Social Security Administration, the federal courts, the U.S. Postal Service,   *A geographic organization*
state troopers, and the Red Cross have adopted territorial structures in order   *structure is well-suited to firms*
to be directly accessible to geographically dispersed clienteles. Multina-   *pursuing different strategies in*
tional enterprises use geographic structures to manage the diversity they   *different geographic regions.*
encounter operating across national boundaries, often dividing into a do-
mestic division and an international division or, when international operations are quite large, dividing into divisions for each continent or major country.

   Raymond Corey and Steven Star cite Pfizer International as a good example of a
company whose strategic requirements made geographic decentralization advantageous:

   Pfizer International operated plants in 27 countries and marketed in more than 100 countries. Its product lines included pharmaceuticals (antibiotics and other ethical prescription
   drugs), agricultural and veterinary products (such as animal feed supplements and vaccines
   and pesticides), chemicals (fine chemicals, bulk pharmaceuticals, petrochemicals, and
   plastics), and consumer products (cosmetics and toiletries).

---

[28]Ibid., p. 66.
[29]Ibid., pp. 66–67.

ILLUSTRATION CAPSULE 32   Reengineering: How Companies Do It and the Results They Have Gotten

Reengineering strategy-critical business processes to reduce fragmentation across traditional departmental lines and cut bureaucratic overheads has proven to be a legitimate organization design tool. It's not a passing fad or another management program of the month. Process organization is every bit as valid an organizing principle as functional specialization. Strategy execution is improved when the pieces of strategy-critical activities and core business processes performed by different departments are properly integrated and coordinated.

Companies that have reengineered some of their business processes have ended up compressing formerly separate steps and tasks into jobs performed by a single person and integrating jobs into team activities. Reorganization then follows, a natural consequence of task synthesis and job redesign. The experiences of companies that have successfully reengineered and restructured their operations in strategy-supportive ways suggest attacking process fragmentation and overhead reduction in the following fashion:

- Develop a flow chart of the total business process, including its interfaces with other value-chain activities.

- Try to simplify the process first, eliminating tasks and steps where possible and analyzing how to streamline the performance of what remains.

- Determine which parts of the process can be automated (usually those that are repetitive, time-consuming, and require little thought or decision); consider introducing advanced technologies that can be upgraded to achieve next-generation capability and provide a basis for further productivity gains down the road.

- Reengineer, then reorganize.

- Evaluate each activity in the process to determine whether it is strategy-critical or not. Strategy-critical activities are candidates for benchmarking to achieve best-in-industry or best-in-world performance status.

- Weigh the pros and cons of outsourcing activities that are noncritical or that contribute little to organizational capabilities and core competencies.

- Design a structure for performing the activities that remain; reorganize the personnel and groups who perform these activities into the new structure.

Reengineering can produce dramatic gains in productivity and organizational capability when done properly. In the order-processing section of General Electric's circuit breaker division, elapsed time from order receipt to delivery was cut from three weeks to three days by consolidating six production units into one, reducing a variety of former inventory and handling steps, automating the design system to replace a human custom-design process, and cutting the organizational layers between managers and workers from three to one. Productivity rose 20 percent in one year, and unit manufacturing costs dropped 30 percent.

Northwest Water, a British utility, used reengineering to eliminate 45 work depots that served as home base to crews who installed and repaired water and sewage lines and equipment. Now crews work directly from their vehicles, receiving assignments and reporting work completion from computer terminals in their trucks. Crew members are no longer employees but contractors to Northwest Water. These reengineering efforts not only eliminated the need for the work depots but also allowed Northwest Water to eliminate a big percentage of the bureaucratic personnel and supervisory organization that managed the crews.

There's no escaping the conclusion that reengineering, in concert with electronic communication systems, empowerment, and the use of self-directed work teams, provides company managers with important new organization design options. Organizational hierarchies can be flattened and middle-management layers removed. Responsibility and decision-making authority can be pushed downward and outward to those places in the organization where customer contacts are made. Strategy-critical processes can be unified, performed more quickly and at lower cost, and made more responsive to changing customer preferences and expectations. Used properly, these new design approaches can trigger big gains in organizational creativity and employee productivity.

Sources: Based on information in James Brian Quinn, *Intelligent Enterprise* (New York: Free Press, 1992), p. 162; T. Stuart, "GE Keeps Those Ideas Coming," *Fortune*, August 12, 1991; Gene Hall, Jim Rosenthal, and Judy Wade, "How to Make Reengineering Really Work," *Harvard Business Review* 71, no. 6 (November–December 1993), pp. 119–31; and Ann Majchrzak and Qianwei Wang, "Breaking the Functional Mind-Set in Process Organizations," *Harvard Business Review* 74, no. 5 (September–October 1996), pp. 93–99.

FIGURE 9–3   A Representative Geographic Organizational Structure

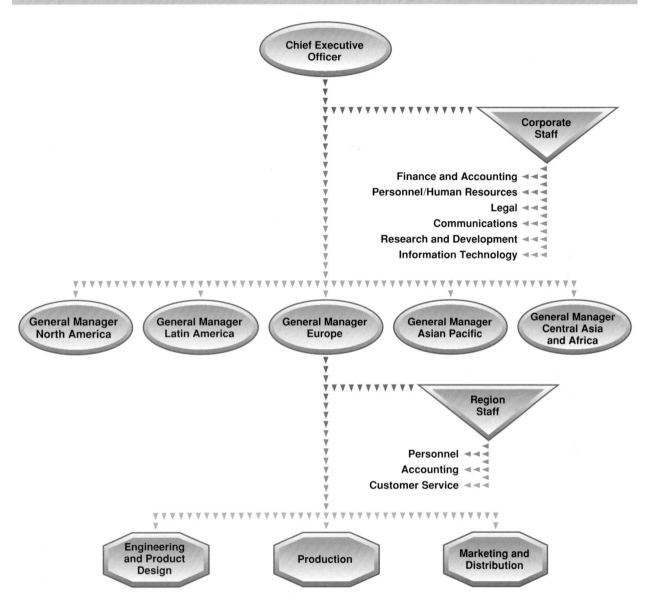

STRATEGIC ADVANTAGES

- Allows tailoring of strategy to needs of each geographical market.
- Delegates profit/loss responsibility to lowest strategic level.
- Improves functional coordination within the target market.
- Takes advantage of economies of local operations.
- Regional units make an excellent training ground for higher-level general managers.

STRATEGIC DISADVANTAGES

- Poses a problem of how much geographic uniformity headquarters should impose versus how much geographic diversity should be allowed.
- Greater difficulty in maintaining consistent company image/reputation from area to area when geographic managers exercise much strategic freedom.
- Adds another layer of management to run the geographic units.
- Can result in duplication of staff services at headquarters and geographic levels, creating a cost disadvantage.

Ten geographic Area Managers reported directly to the President of Pfizer International and exercised line supervision over Country Managers. According to a company position description, it was "the responsibility of each Area Manager to plan, develop, and carry out Pfizer International's business in the assigned foreign area in keeping with company policies and goals."

Country Managers had profit responsibility. In most cases a single Country Manager managed all Pfizer activities in his country. In some of the larger, well-developed countries of Europe there were separate Country Managers for pharmaceutical and agricultural products and for consumer lines.

Except for the fact that New York headquarters exercised control over the to-the-market prices of certain products, especially prices of widely used pharmaceuticals, Area and Country Managers had considerable autonomy in planning and managing the Pfizer International business in their respective geographic areas. This was appropriate because each area, and some countries within areas, provided unique market and regulatory environments. In the case of pharmaceuticals and agricultural and veterinary products (Pfizer International's most important lines), national laws affected formulations, dosages, labeling, distribution, and often price. Trade restrictions affected the flow of bulk pharmaceuticals and chemicals and packaged products, and might in effect require the establishment of manufacturing plants to supply local markets. Competition, too, varied significantly from area to area.[30]

At Andersen Consulting, the basic organizational building blocks are the individual practice groups making up the geographic offices scattered across the world.

Decentralized Business Units   Grouping activities along business and product lines has been a favored organizing device among diversified enterprises for the past 75 years, beginning with the pioneering efforts of Du Pont and General Motors in the 1920s. Separate business/product divisions emerged because diversification made a functionally specialized manager's job incredibly complex. Imagine the problems a manufacturing executive and his/her staff would have if put in charge of, say, 50 different plants using 20 different technologies to produce 30 different products in eight different businesses/industries. In a multibusiness enterprise, the practical organizational sequence is corporate to business to functional area within a business rather than corporate to functional area (aggregated for all businesses).

Thus while functional departments, process departments, and geographic divisions are the standard organizational building blocks in a single-business enterprise, in a

> *In a diversified firm, the basic organizational building blocks are its business units; each business is operated as a stand-alone profit center.*

multibusiness corporation the basic building blocks are the individual businesses.[31] Authority over each business unit is typically delegated to a business-level manager. The approach is to put entrepreneurial general managers in charge of each business unit, give them authority to formulate and implement a business strategy, motivate them with performance-based incentives, and hold them accountable for results. Each business unit then operates as a stand-alone profit center and is organized around whatever functional/process departments and geographic units suit the business's strategy, key activities, and operating requirements.

Fully independent business units, however, pose an obstacle to companies pursuing related diversification: *There is no mechanism for coordinating related activities across business units or for sharing/tranferring/developing mutually beneficial resource*

---

[30]Raymond Corey and Steven H. Star, *Organization Strategy: A Marketing Approach* (Boston: Harvard Business School, 1971), pp. 23–24.

[31]Over 90 percent of the *Fortune* 500 firms employ a business unit or divisional organizational structure.

strengths. As the label implies, divisions divide, creating potentially insulated units with barriers that inhibit sharing or building mutually beneficial resource strengths. It can be tough to get independent business units and autonomy-conscious business-unit managers to coordinate related activities and collaborate in ways that leverage resource strengths and enhance organizational capabilities. They are prone to argue about turf and resist being held accountable for activities outside their control.

To capture strategic-fit and resource-fit benefits in a diversified company, corporate headquarters must superimpose some internal organizational means of cutting across boundaries and coordinating related business-unit activities. One option is to centralize related functions at the corporate level—for example, set up a corporate R&D department (if there are technology and product development fits), create a special corporate sales force to call on customers who purchase from several of the company's business units, combine the dealer networks and sales force organizations of closely related businesses, merge the order processing and shipping functions of businesses with common customers, or consolidate the production of related components and products into fewer, more efficient plants. In addition, corporate officers can develop bonus arrangements that give business-unit managers strong incentives to work together. If the strategic-fit relationships involve skills or technology transfers across businesses, corporate headquarters can mandate the transfer of people with the requisite experience and know-how from one business to another or form interbusiness teams to open the flow of proprietary technology, managerial know-how, and related skills between businesses.

A typical line-of-business organization structure is shown in Figure 9–4, along with the strategy-related pros and cons of this organizational form.

Strategic Business Units   In broadly diversified companies, the number of decentralized business units can be so great that the span of control is too much for a single chief executive. Then it may be useful to group related businesses and to delegate authority over them to a senior executive who reports directly to the chief executive officer. While this imposes a layer of management between business-level managers and the chief executive, it may nonetheless improve strategic planning and top-management coordination of diverse business interests. This explains both the popularity of the group vice president concept among multibusiness companies and the creation of strategic business units.

A *strategic business unit* (SBU) is a grouping of business subsidiaries based on important strategic elements common to all. The elements can be an overlapping set of competitors, closely related value chain activities, a common need to compete globally, emphasis on the same kind of competitive advantage (low cost or differentiation), common key success factors, or technologically related growth opportunities. At General Electric, a pioneer in the concept of SBUs, 190 businesses were grouped into 43 SBUs and then aggregated further into six "sectors."[32] At Union Carbide, 15 groups and divisions were decomposed into 150 "strategic planning units" and then regrouped and combined into 9 new "aggregate planning units." At General Foods, SBUs were

Strategic Management Principle

A decentralized business-unit structure can block success of a related diversification strategy unless specific organizational arrangements are devised to coordinate the related activities of related businesses.

Basic Concept

A strategic business unit (SBU) is a grouping of related businesses under the supervision of a senior executive.

---

[32]William K. Hall, "SBUs: Hot, New Topic in the Management of Diversification," *Business Horizons* 21, no. 1 (February 1978), p. 19. For an excellent discussion of the problems of implementing the SBU concept at 13 companies, see Richard A. Bettis and William K. Hall, "The Business Portfolio Approach—Where It Falls Down in Practice," *Long Range Planning* 16, no. 2 (April 1983), pp. 95–104.

FIGURE 9-4   A Decentralized Line-of-Business Organization Structure

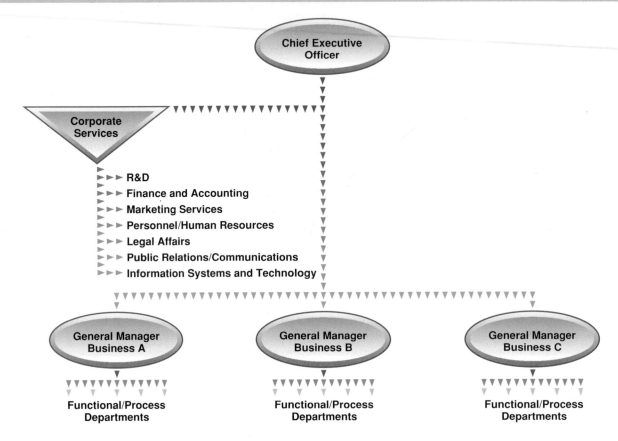

STRATEGIC ADVANTAGES

- Offers a logical and workable means of decentralizing responsibility and delegating authority in diversified organizations.
- Puts responsibility for crafting and implementing business strategy in closer proximity to each business's unique environment.
- Allows each business unit to organize around its own key value chain activities, business processes, and functional requirements.
- Frees CEO to handle corporate strategy issues.
- Puts clear profit/loss accountability on shoulders of business-unit managers.

STRATEGIC DISADVANTAGES

- May lead to costly duplication of staff functions at corporate and business-unit levels, thus raising administrative overhead costs.
- Poses a problem of what decisions to centralize and what decisions to decentralize (business managers need enough authority to get the job done, but not so much that corporate management loses control of key business-level decisions).
- May lead to excessive division rivalry for corporate resources and attention.
- Business/division autonomy works against achieving coordination of related activities in different business units, thus blocking to some extent the capture of strategic-fit and resource-fit benefits.
- Corporate management becomes heavily dependent on business-unit managers.
- Corporate managers can lose touch with business-unit situations, end up surprised when problems arise, and not know much about how to fix such problems.

originally defined on a product-line basis but were later redefined according to menu segments (breakfast foods, beverages, main meal products, desserts, and pet foods). SBUs make headquarters' reviews of the strategies of lower-level units less imposing (there is no practical way for a CEO to conduct in-depth reviews of a hundred or more different businesses). A CEO can, however, effectively review the strategic plans of a lesser number of SBUs, leaving detailed business strategy reviews and direct supervision of individual businesses to the SBU heads. Figure 9–5 illustrates the SBU form of organization, along with its strategy-related pros and cons.

The SBU concept provides broadly diversified companies with a way to rationalize the organization of many different businesses and a management arrangement for capturing strategic-fit benefits and streamlining strategic planning and budgeting processes. The strategic function of the group vice president is to provide the SBU with some cohesive direction, enforce coordination across related businesses, and keep an eye out for trouble at the business-unit level, providing counsel and support as needed. The group vice president, as coordinator for all businesses in the SBU, can promote resource sharing and skills/technology transfers where appropriate and unify the decisions and actions of businesses in the SBU. The SBU, in effect, becomes a strategy-making, strategy-implementing unit with a wider field of vision and operations than a single business unit. It serves as a broadly diversified company's mechanism for capturing strategic-fit benefits across businesses and adding to the competitive advantage that each business in the SBU is able to build on its own. Moreover, it affords opportunity to "cross-pollinate" the activities of separate businesses, ideally creating enough new capability to stretch a company's strategic reach into adjacent products, technologies, and markets.

SBU structures are a means for managing broad diversification and enforcing strategic coordination across related businesses.

Matrix Forms of Organization   A matrix organization is a structure with two (or more) channels of command, two lines of budget authority, and two sources of performance and reward. The key feature of the matrix is that authority for a business/product/project/venture and authority for a function or business process are overlaid (to form a matrix or grid), and decision-making responsibility in each unit/cell of the matrix is shared between the business/project/venture team manager and the functional/process manager—as shown in Figure 9–6. In a matrix structure, subordinates have a *continuing dual assignment*: to the product line/project/business/venture and to their home-base function/process. The resulting structure is a compromise between organizing solely around functional/process specialization or around product line, project, line-of-business, or special venture divisions.

Matrix structures, although complex to manage and sometimes unwieldy, allow a firm to be organized in two different strategy-supportive ways at the same time.

A matrix-type organization is a genuinely different structural form and represents a "new way of life." It breaks the unity-of-command principle; two reporting channels, two bosses, and shared authority create a new kind of climate. In essence, the matrix is a conflict-resolution system through which strategic and operating priorities are negotiated, power is shared, and resources are allocated on the basis of "strongest case" for what is best overall for the unit.[33]

---

[33]For two excellent critiques of matrix organizations, see Stanley M. Davis and Paul R. Lawrence, "Problems of Matrix Organizations," *Harvard Business Review* 56, no. 3 (May–June 1978), pp. 131–42, and Erik W. Larson and David H. Gobeli, "Matrix Management: Contradictions and Insights," *California Management Review* 29, no. 4 (Summer 1987), pp. 126–38.

FIGURE 9–5   An SBU Organization Structure

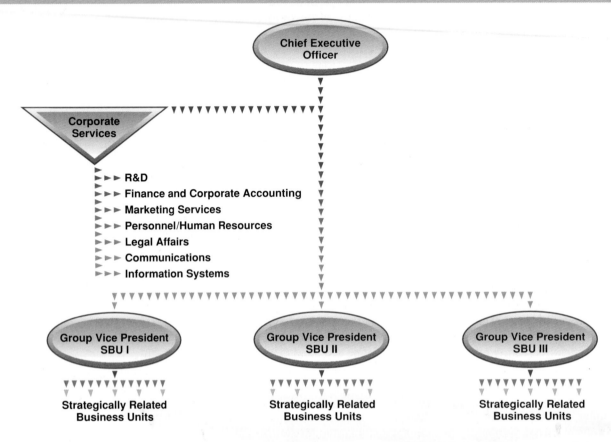

STRATEGIC ADVANTAGES

- Provides a strategically relevant way to organize the business-unit portfolio of a broadly diversified company.
- Facilitates the coordination of related activities within an SBU, thus helping to capture the benefits of strategic fits and resource fits among related businesses.
- Promotes more cohesiveness and collaboration among separate but related businesses.
- Allows strategic planning to be done at the most relevant level within the total enterprise.
- Makes the task of strategic review by top executives more objective and more effective.
- Helps allocate corporate resources to areas with greatest growth and profit opportunities.
- Group VP position is a good training ground for future CEOs.

STRATEGIC DISADVANTAGES

- It is easy for the definition and grouping of businesses into SBUs to be so arbitrary that the SBU serves no other purpose than administrative convenience. If the criteria for defining SBUs are rationalizations and have little to do with the nitty-gritty of strategy coordination, then the groupings lose real strategic significance.
- The SBUs can still be myopic in charting their future direction.
- Adds another layer to top management.
- The roles and authority of the CEO, the group vice president, and the business-unit manager have to be carefully worked out or the group vice president gets trapped in the middle with ill-defined authority.
- Unless the SBU head is strong willed, very little strategy coordination or collaboration is likely to occur across business units in the SBU.
- Performance recognition gets blurred; credit for successful business units tends to go to corporate CEO, then to business-unit head, last to group vice president.

FIGURE 9-6   A Matrix Organization Structure

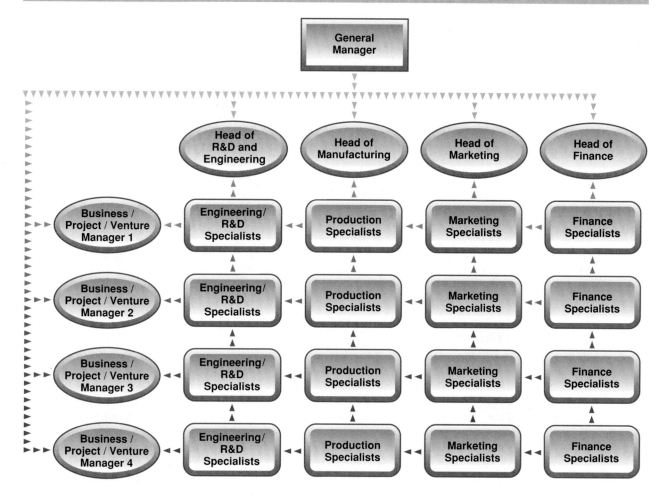

STRATEGIC ADVANTAGES

- Gives formal attention to each dimension of strategic priority.
- Creates checks and balances among competing viewpoints.
- Facilitates capture of functionally based strategic fits in diversified companies.
- Promotes making trade-off decisions on the basis of "what's best for the organization as a whole."
- Encourages cooperation, consensus-building, conflict resolution, and coordination of related activities.

STRATEGIC DISADVANTAGES

- Very complex to manage.
- Hard to maintain "balance" between the two lines of authority.
- So much shared authority can result in a transactions logjam and disproportionate amounts of time being spent on communications, consensus building, and collaboration.
- It is hard to move quickly and decisively without checking with or getting clearance from many other people.
- Promotes organizational bureaucracy and hamstrings creative entrepreneurship and initiative.
- Works at cross purposes with efforts to empower down-the-line managers and employees.

The impetus for matrix organizations stems from growing use of strategies that create a simultaneous need for process teams, special project managers, product managers, functional managers, geographic area managers, new-venture managers, and business-level managers—all of whom have important responsibilities. When at least two of several variables (product, customer, technology, geography, functional area, business process, and market segment) have roughly equal priorities, a matrix organization can be an effective structural form. A matrix structure promotes internal checks and balances among competing viewpoints and perspectives, with separate managers for different dimensions of strategic initiative. A matrix arrangement thus allows each of several strategic considerations to be managed directly and to be formally represented in the organization structure. In this sense, it helps middle managers make trade-off decisions from an organizationwide perspective.[34] The other big advantage of matrix organization is that it can help capture strategic fit. When the strategic fits in a diversified company are related to a specific functional area (R&D, technology, marketing), or cross traditional functional lines, matrix organization can be a reasonable structural arrangement for coordinating activity sharing and skills transfer. Companies using matrix structures include General Electric, Texas Instruments, Citibank, Shell Oil, TRW, Bechtel, Boeing, and Dow Chemical. Illustration Capsule 33 describes how one broadly diversified company with global strategies in each of its businesses developed a matrix structure to manage its operations worldwide. However, in most companies, use of matrix organization is confined to a *portion* of what the firm does rather than its whole organizing scheme.

Many companies and managers shun matrix organization because of its chief weaknesses.[35] It is a complex structure to manage; people end up confused or frustrated over who to report to for what. Working relationships among different organizational units become more complicated. Moreover, because the matrix signals a need for communication and consensus, a "transactions logjam" can result. People in one area are pushed into transacting business with people in another area and networking their way through bureaucracies. Action turns into paralysis since, with shared authority, it is hard to move decisively without first checking with other people and getting clearance. Much time and psychic energy get eaten up in meetings and communicating back and forth. Sizable transactions costs and longer decision times can result with little value-added work accomplished. Even so, in some situations the benefits of conflict resolution, consensus building, and coordination outweigh these weaknesses, as the ABB example in Illustration Capsule 33 indicates.

Supplementing the Basic Organization Structure   None of the basic structural designs is wholly adequate for organizing the total work effort in strategy-supportive ways. Some weaknesses can be corrected by using two or more of the structural designs simultaneously—many companies are large enough and diverse enough to have SBUs, business units with functional and/or process departments, geographic organizational structures in one or more businesses, and units employing matrix principles. But in many companies strategy-supportive organization requires supplementing the formal structure with special coordinating mechanisms and efforts to build

---

[34]Davis and Lawrence, "Problems of Matrix Organizations," p. 132.

[35]Thomas J. Peters and Robert H. Waterman, Jr., *In Search of Excellence* (New York: Harper & Row, 1982), pp. 306–7.

ILLUSTRATION CAPSULE 33   Matrix Organization in a Diversified Global Company: The Case of Asea Brown Boveri

Asea Brown Boveri (ABB) is a diversified multinational corporation headquartered in Zurich, Switzerland. ABB was formed in 1987 through the merger of Asea, one of Sweden's largest industrial enterprises, and Brown Boveri, a major Swiss company. Both companies manufactured electrical products and equipment. Following the merger, ABB acquired or took minority positions in 60 companies, mostly outside Europe. In 1996 ABB had annual revenues of $34 billion and employed 210,000 people around the world, including 130,000 in Western Europe, 30,000 in North America, 10,000 in South America, and 10,000 in India. The company was a world leader in the global markets for electrical products, electrical installations and service, and power-generation equipment and was the dominant European producer. European sales accounted for 60 percent of revenues, while North America accounted for 30 percent and Asia 15 percent.

To manage its global operations, ABB had devised a matrix organization that leveraged its core competencies in electrical-power technologies and its ability to achieve global economies of scale while, at the same time, maximizing its national market visibility and responsiveness. At the top of ABB's corporate organization structure was an executive committee composed of the CEO and 12 colleagues; the committee consisted of Swedes, Swiss, Germans, and Americans, several of whom were based outside Switzerland. The group, which met every three weeks at various locations around the world, was responsible for ABB's corporate strategy and performance.

Along one dimension of ABB's global matrix were 50 or so business areas (BAs), each representing a closely related set of products and services. The BAs were grouped into eight "business segments"; each segment was supervised by a different member of the executive committee. Each BA had a leader charged with responsibility for (1) devising and championing a global strategy, (2) setting quality and cost standards for the BA's factories worldwide, (3) deciding which factories would export to which country markets, (4) rotating people across borders to share technical expertise, create mixed-nationality teams to solve BA problems, and build a culture of trust and communication, and (5) pooling expertise and research funds for the benefit of the BA worldwide. BA leaders worked out of whatever world location made the most sense for their BA.

Along the other dimension of the matrix was a group of national enterprises with presidents, boards of directors, financial statements, and career ladders. The presidents of ABB's national enterprises had responsibility for maximizing the performance and effectiveness of all ABB activities within their country's borders. Country presidents worked closely with the BA leaders to evaluate and improve what was happening in ABB's business areas in their countries.

Inside the matrix were 1,300 "local" ABB companies with an average of 200 employees, each headed by a president. The local company president reported both to the national president in whose country the local company operated and to the leader of the BA to which its products/services were assigned. Each local company was a subsidiary of the ABB national enterprise where it was located. Thus, all of ABB's local companies in Norway were subsidiaries of ABB Norway, the national company for Norway; all ABB operations in Portugal were subsidiaries of ABB Portugal, and so on. The 1,300 presidents of ABB's local companies were expected to be excellent profit center managers, able to answer to two bosses effectively. The local president's global boss was the BA manager who established the local company's role in ABB's global strategy and, also, the rules a local company had to observe in supporting this strategy. The local president's country boss was the national CEO, with whom it was necessary to cooperate on local issues.

ABB believed that its matrix structure allowed it to optimize its pursuit of global business strategies and, at the same time, maximize its performance in every country market where it operated. The matrix was a way of being global and big strategically, yet small and local operationally. Decision making was decentralized (to BA leaders, country presidents, and local company presidents), but reporting and control was centralized (through the BA leaders, the country presidents, and the executive committee). ABB saw itself as a federation of national companies with a global coordination center.

Only about 100 professionals were located in ABB's corporate headquarters in Zurich. A management information system collected data on all profit centers monthly, comparing actual performance against budgets and forecasts. Data was collected in local currencies but translated into U.S. dollars to allow for cross-border analysis. ABB's corporate financial statements were reported in U.S. dollars, and English was ABB's official language. All high-level meetings were conducted in English.

Source: Compiled from information in William Taylor, "The Logic of Global Business: An Interview with ABB's Percy Barnevik," *Harvard Business Review* 69, no. 2 (March–April 1991), pp. 90–105 and company annual reports.

organizational capabilities. Seven of the most frequently used devices for supplementing the basic building block structure are:

- *Special project teams*—creating a separate, largely self-sufficient work group to oversee the completion of a special activity (setting up a new technological process, bringing out a new product, starting up a new venture, merging with another company, seeing through the completion of a government contract, supervising the construction and opening of a new plant). Project teams are especially suitable for short-term, one-of-a-kind situations when the normal organization is not equipped to achieve the same results in addition to regular duties. (At 3M Corp. project teams are the basic organizational building blocks for the company's 3,900 profit centers.)

- *Cross-functional task forces*—bringing a number of top-level executives and/or specialists together to solve problems requiring specialized expertise from several parts of the organization, coordinating strategy-related activities that span departmental boundaries, or exploring ways to leverage the skills of different functional specialists into broader core competencies. Task forces seem to be most effective when they have fewer than 10 members, membership is voluntary, the seniority of the members is proportional to the importance of the problem, the task force moves swiftly to deal with its assignment, they are used sparingly, no staff is assigned, and documentation is scant.[36] Companies that have used task forces successfully form them to solve pressing problems, produce some solutions efficiently, and then disband them.

- *Venture teams*—forming a group of individuals to manage the launch of a new product, entry into a new geographic market, or creation of a specific new business. Dow, General Mills, Westinghouse, General Electric, and Monsanto used the venture-team approach to renew an entrepreneurial spirit. The difficulties with venture teams include deciding who the venture manager should report to; whether funding for ventures should come from corporate, business, or departmental budgets; how to keep the venture clear of bureaucratic and vested interests; and how to coordinate large numbers of different ventures.

- *Self-contained work teams*—forming a group of people drawn from different disciplines who work together on a semipermanent basis to continuously improve organizational performance in such strategy-related areas as shortening the lab-to-market cycle time, boosting product quality, improving customer service, cutting delivery times, eliminating stockouts, reducing the costs of purchased materials and components, increasing assembly-line productivity, trimming equipment downtime and maintenance expenses, or designing new models. American Express cut out three layers of hierarchy when it developed self-managed teams to handle all types of customer inquiries in a single-call, quick-resolution manner.[37]

- *Process teams*—putting functional specialists who perform pieces of a business process together on a team instead of assigning them to their home-base functional department. Such teams can be empowered to reengineer the process, held accountable for results, and rewarded on the

---

[36]Ibid., pp. 127–32.
[37]Quinn, *Intelligent Enterprise*, p. 163.

basis of how well the process is performed. Much of Chrysler's revitalization is due to dramatically revamping its new-model development process using "platform teams."[38] Each platform team consists of members from engineering, design, finance, purchasing, and marketing. The team is responsible for the car's design from beginning to end, has broad decision-making power, and is held accountable for the success or failure of their design. Teams coordinate their designs with manufacturing so that the models will be easier to build and consult regularly with purchasing agents about parts quality. In one case Chrysler purchasing agents elected to pay 30 percent more for a better part because the engineer on the platform team believed the added cost would be offset by the time saved during assembly.

- *Contact managers*—appointing someone to serve as a single point of contact for customers when customer-related activities are so multi-faceted that integrating them for a single person or team to perform is impractical.[39] Acting as a buffer between internal processes and the customer, the contact person answers customer questions and coordinates the solutions to customer problems as if he or she were responsible for performing the called-for activities. To perform this role, contact persons need access to all the information that the persons actually performing the activities use and the ability to contact those people with questions and requests for further assistance when necessary. The best results are achieved when contact persons are empowered to use their own judgment to get things done in a manner that will please customers. Duke Power, a Charlotte-based electric utility, uses empowered customer service representatives to resolve the problems of residential customers while shielding them from whatever goes on "behind the scenes" to produce solutions.

- *Relationship managers*—appointing people who have responsibility for orchestrating and integrating company efforts to build strong working relationships with allies and strategic partners. Relationship managers have many roles and functions: getting the right people together, promoting good rapport, seeing that plans for specific activities are developed and carried out, helping adjust procedures to link the partners better and iron out operating dissimilarities, and nurturing interpersonal ties. Lines of communication have to be established and kept open, with enough information sharing to make the relationship work and frank discussion of conflicts, trouble spots, and changing situations.

Organizational capabilities emerge from effectively coordinating and networking the efforts of different work groups, departments, and external allies, not from how the boxes on the organization chart are arranged.

The ways of developing stronger core competencies and organizational capabilities (or creating altogether new ones) are much more idiosyncratic. Not only do different companies and executives tackle the challenge in different ways but different capabilities require different organizing techniques. Thus generalizing about *how* to build capabilities is misleading. Suffice it to say here that it entails *a process of consciously knitting the efforts of individuals and groups together* and that it is a task senior management must lead and be deeply involved in. Effectively managing both internal processes and external bridge-building with partners to create and develop valuable

[38]"Can Jack Smith Fix GM?" *Business Week*, November 1, 1993, pp. 130–31.
[39]Hammer and Champy, *Reengineering the Corporation*, pp. 62–63.

competencies and capabilities ranks very high on the "things to do" list of senior executives in today's companies.

Perspectives on Organizing the Work Effort and Building Capabilities   All the basic building block designs have their strengths and weaknesses. To do a good job of matching structure to strategy, strategy implementers have to pick a basic design, modify it as needed to fit the company's business makeup, and then supplement it with coordinating mechanisms and communication arrangements to support execution of the firm's strategy. Building core competencies and competitive capabilities is a *process* that nearly always involves close collaboration between individuals and groups in different departments and between a company and its external allies—they emerge from establishing and nurturing cooperative working relationships among people and groups to perform activities in a more customer-satisfying fashion, not from rearranging boxes on an organization chart. While companies may not set up "ideal" organizational arrangements in order to avoid disturbing certain existing reporting relationships or to accommodate the personalities of certain individuals involved, internal politics, and other idiosyncrasies, the goal of building a competitively capable organization usually is predominant in considering how to set up the organization chart.

There's no perfect or ideal organization structure.

ORGANIZATIONAL STRUCTURES OF THE FUTURE

Many of today's companies are winding up the task of remodeling their traditional hierarchical structures once built around functional specialization and centralized authority. Such structures still make good strategic and organizational sense so long as (1) activities can be divided into simple, repeatable tasks that can be mastered quickly and then efficiently performed in mass quantity, (2) there are important benefits to deep functional expertise in each managerial discipline, and (3) customer needs are sufficiently standardized that it is easy to prescribe procedures for satisfying them. But traditional hierarchies are a liability in businesses where customer preferences are shifting from standardized products to custom orders and special features, product life cycles are growing shorter, custom mass-production methods are replacing standardized mass production techniques, customers want to be treated as individuals, the pace of technological change is accelerating, and market conditions are fluid. Multilayered management hierarchies and functionalized bureaucracies that require people to look upward in the organizational structure for answers tend to bog down in such environments. They can't deliver responsive customer service or adapt fast enough to changing conditions. Functional silos, task-oriented work, process fragmentation, layered management hierarchies, centralized decision making, big functional and middle-management bureaucracies, lots of checks and controls, and long response times undermine competitive success in fluid or volatile environments. Success in fast-changing markets depends on strategies built around such valuable competencies and organizational capabilities as quick response to shifting customer preferences, short design-to-market cycles, make-it-right-the-first-time quality, custom-order and multiversion production, expedited delivery, personalized customer service, accurate order filling, rapid assimilation of new technologies, creativity and innovativeness, and speedy reactions to external competitive developments.

During the past decade, new strategic priorities and rapidly shifting competitive conditions have triggered revolutionary changes in how companies are organizing the work effort.

These new components of business strategy have been driving a revolution in corporate organization for the past decade.[40] Much of the corporate downsizing movement was and is aimed at busting up functional and middle-management bureaucracies and recasting authoritarian pyramidal organizational structures into flatter, decentralized structures. The latest organizational designs for matching structure to strategy feature fewer layers of management authority, small-scale business units, reengineered work processes to cut back on fragmentation across functional department lines,[41] the development of stronger competencies and organizational capabilities and the creation of new ones as needed, collaborative partnerships with outsiders, empowerment of firstline supervisors and nonmanagement employees, lean staffing of corporate support functions, open communications vertically and laterally (via e-mail), computers and telecommunications technologies to provide fast access to and dissemination of information, and accountability for results rather than emphasis on activity. The new organizational themes are lean, flat, agile, responsive, and innovative. The new tools of organizational design are managers and workers empowered to act on their own judgments, reengineered work processes, self-directed work teams, and networking with outsiders to improve existing organizational capabilities and create new ones. The new organization-building challenge is to outcompete rivals on the basis of superior organizational capabilities and resource strengths.

The command-and-control paradigm of vertically layered structures assumes that the people actually performing work have neither the time nor the inclination to monitor and control it and that they lack the knowledge to make informed decisions about how best to do it; hence, the need for prescribed procedures, close supervision, and managerial control of decision making. In flat, decentralized structures, the assumptions are that people closest to the scene are capable of making timely, responsible decisions when properly trained and when provided with access to the needed information. There is a strong belief that decentralized decision making shortens response times and spurs new ideas, creative thinking, innovation, and greater involvement on the part of subordinate managers and employees. Hence, jobs are defined more broadly; several tasks are integrated into a single job where possible. People operate in a more self-directed fashion. Decision-making authority is pushed down to the lowest level capable of taking competent, responsible action in a timely fashion. Fewer managers are needed because deciding how to do things becomes part of each person's or team's job and because electronic technology makes information readily available and communications instantaneous.

The organizations of the future will have several new characteristics:

- Fewer boundaries between different vertical ranks, between functions and disciplines, between units in different geographic locations, and between the company and its suppliers, distributors/dealers, strategic allies, and customers.

---

[40]Evidence to this effect is contained in the scores of examples reported in Tom Peters, *Liberation Management* (New York: Alfred A. Knopf, 1992); Quinn, *Intelligent Enterprise;* and Hammer and Champy, *Reengineering the Corporation.*

[41]However, it sometimes takes more than reengineering and process organization structures to eliminate the old functional mind-sets of employees; in particular, managers also have to work at instilling a collaborative culture and fostering a collective sense of responsibility among the members of the process team. Collective responsibility can be ingrained by basing rewards on group performance, rotating assignments among the process team members, holding periodic unitwide meetings to discuss process improvements, and designing process procedures that promote a high degree of collaboration among employees doing different pieces of the process. See Ann Majchrzak and Qianwei Wang, "Breaking the Functional Mind-set in Process Organizations," *Harvard Business Review* 74, no. 5 (September–October 1996), pp. 93–99.

ILLUSTRATION CAPSULE 34   Organizational Approaches for International and Global Markets

A 1993 study of 43 large U.S.-based consumer products companies conducted by McKinsey & Co., a leading management consulting firm, identified internal organizational actions with the strongest and weakest links to rapidly growing sales and profits in international and global markets.

Organizational Actions Strongly Linked to International Success

- Centralizing international decision making in every area except new product development.

- Having a worldwide management development program and more foreigners in senior management posts.

- Requiring international experience for advancement into top management.

- Linking global managers with videoconferencing and electronic mail.

- Having product managers of foreign subsidiaries report to a country general manager.

- Using local executives to head operations in foreign countries (however, this is rapidly ceasing to distinguish successful companies because nearly everyone has implemented such a practice).

Organizational Actions Weakly Linked to International Success

- Creating global divisions.
- Forming international strategic business units.
- Establishing centers of excellence (where a single company facility takes global responsibility for a key product or emerging technology (too new to evaluate pro or con).
- Using cross-border task forces to resolve problems and issues.
- Creating globally-integrated management information systems.

However, the lists of organizational dos and don'ts are far from decisive. In general, the study found that internal organizational structure "doesn't matter that much" as compared to having products with attractive prices and features. It is wrong to expect good results just because of good organization. Moreover, certain organizational arrangements, such as centers of excellence, are too new to determine whether they positively affect sales and profit growth.

Source: Based on information reported by Joann S. Lublin, "Study Sees U.S. Businesses Stumbling on the Road to Globalization," *The Wall Street Journal*, March 22, 1993, p. B4B.

- A capacity for change and rapid learning.
- Collaborative efforts among people in different functional specialities and geographic locations—essential to create organization competencies and capabilities.
- Extensive use of digital technology—personal computers, wireless telephones, videoconferencing, and other state-of-the-art electronic products.

Illustration Capsule 34 reports the results of a study of trends in organizational arrangements in multinational and global companies.

KEY POINTS

The job of strategy implementation is to convert strategic plans into actions and good results. The test of successful strategy implementation is whether actual organization performance matches or exceeds the targets spelled out in the strategic plan. Shortfalls in performance signal weak strategy, weak implementation, or both.

In deciding how to implement strategy, managers have to determine what internal conditions are needed to execute the strategic plan successfully. Then they must create these conditions as rapidly as practical. The process of implementing and executing strategy involves

- Building an organization with the competencies, capabilities, and resource strengths to carry out the strategy successfully.

- Developing budgets to steer ample resources into those value chain activities critical to strategic success.
- Establishing strategy-supportive policies and procedures.
- Instituting best practices and pushing for continuous improvement in how value chain activities are performed.
- Installing information, communication, and operating systems that enable company personnel to carry out their strategic roles successfully day in and day out.
- Tying rewards and incentives to the achievement of performance objectives and good strategy execution.
- Creating a strategy-supportive work environment and corporate culture.
- Exerting the internal leadership needed to drive implementation forward and to keep improving on how the strategy is being executed.

The strategy-implementing challenge is to create a series of tight fits (1) between strategy and the organization's competencies, capabilities, and structure, (2) between strategy and budgetary allocations, (3) between strategy and policy, (4) between strategy and internal support systems, (5) between strategy and the reward structure, and (6) between strategy and the corporate culture. The tighter the fits, the more powerful strategy execution becomes and the more likely targeted performance can actually be achieved.

Implementing strategy is not just a top-management function; it is a job for the whole management team. *All managers function as strategy implementers* in their respective areas of authority and responsibility. *All managers* have to consider what actions to take in their areas to achieve the intended results—they each need an action agenda.

The three major organization-building actions are (1) filling key positions with able people, (2) building the core competencies, resource strengths, and organizational capabilities needed to perform its value chain activities proficiently, and (3) structuring the internal work effort and melding it with the collaborative efforts of strategic allies. Selecting able people for key positions tends to be one of the earliest strategy implementation steps because it takes a full complement of capable managers to get changes in place and functioning smoothly.

Building strategy-critical core competencies and competitive capabilities not easily imitated by rivals is one of the best ways to outexecute rivals with similar strategies and gain a competitive advantage. Core competencies emerge from skills and activities performed at different points in the value chain that, when linked, create unique organizational capability. The key to leveraging a company's core competencies into long-term competitive advantage is to concentrate more effort and more talent than rivals do on strengthening and deepening organizational competencies and capabilities. The multiskill, multiactivity character of core competencies and capabilities makes achieving dominating depth an exercise in (1) managing human skills, knowledge bases, and intellect and (2) coordinating and networking the efforts of different work groups, departments, and collaborative allies. It is a task that senior management must lead and be deeply involved in chiefly because it is senior managers who are in the best position to guide and enforce the necessary networking and cooperation among individuals, groups, departments, and external allies.

Building organizational capabilities is more than just an effort to strengthen what a company already does, however. There are times when management has to be *proactive* in developing *new* competencies and capabilities to complement the company's existing resource base and promote more proficient strategy execution. It is useful here to think of companies as a bundle of evolving competencies and capabilities, with the organization-building challenge being one of developing new capabilities and strengthening existing ones in a fashion calculated to achieve competitive advantage through superior strategy execution.

One capability-building issue is whether to develop the desired competencies and capabilities internally or whether it makes more sense to outsource them by partnering with key suppliers or forming strategic alliances. Decisions about whether to outsource or develop in-house capability often turn on the issues of (1) what can be safely delegated to outside suppliers versus what internal capabilities are key to the company's long-term success and (2) whether noncritical activities can be outsourced more effectively or efficiently than they can be performed internally. Either way, though, implementation actions are called for. Outsourcing means launching initiatives to identify the most attractive providers and to establish collaborative relationships. Developing the capabilities in-house means hiring new personnel with skills and experience relevant to the desired organizational competence/capability, then linking the individual skills/know-how to form organizational capability.

Matching structure to strategy centers around making strategy-critical activities the main organizational building blocks, finding effective ways to bridge organizational lines of authority and coordinate the related efforts of separate internal units and individuals, and effectively networking the efforts of internal units and external collaborative partners. Other big considerations include what decisions to centralize and what decisions to decentralize.

All organization structures have strategic advantages and disadvantages; *there is no one best way to organize*. Functionally specialized organization structures have *traditionally* been the most popular way to organize single-business companies. Functional organization works well where strategy-critical activities closely match discipline-specific activities and minimal interdepartmental cooperation is needed. But it has significant drawbacks: functional myopia and empire building, interdepartmental rivalries, excessive process fragmentation, and vertically layered management hierarchies. In recent years, process organization has been used to circumvent many of the disadvantages of functional organization.

Geographic organization structures are favored by enterprises operating in diverse geographic markets or across expansive geographic areas. SBU structures are well-suited to companies pursuing related diversification. Decentralized business-unit structures are well-suited to companies pursuing unrelated diversification. Matrix structures work well for companies that need separate lines of authority and managers for each of several strategic dimensions (products, buyer segments, functional departments, projects or ventures, technologies, core business processes, geographic areas) yet also need close cooperation between these managers to coordinate related value chain activities, share or transfer skills, and perform certain related activities jointly.

Whatever formal organization structure is chosen, it usually has to be supplemented with interdisciplinary task forces, incentive compensation schemes tied to measures of joint performance, empowerment of cross-functional teams to perform and unify fragmented processes and strategy-critical activities, special project and venture teams, self-contained work teams, contact managers, relationship managers, and special efforts to knit the work of different individuals and groups into valuable competitive capabilities. Building core competencies and competitive capabilities emerge from establishing and nurturing collaborative working relationships between individuals and groups in different departments and between a company and its external allies, not from how the boxes are arranged on an organization chart.

New strategic priorities like short design-to-market cycles, multiversion production, and personalized customer service are promoting a revolution in organization building featuring lean, flat, horizontal structures that are responsive and innovative. Such designs for matching structure to strategy involve fewer layers of management authority, small-scale business units, reengineering work processes to reduce fragmentation across departmental lines, the creation of process departments and cross-functional work groups, managers and workers empowered to act on their own judgments, collaborative partnerships with outsiders (suppliers, distributors/dealers, companies with complementary products/services, and even select competitors), increased outsourcing of noncritical activities, lean staffing of internal support functions, and use of computers and telecommunications technologies to provide fast access to information.

SUGGESTED READINGS

Aaker, David A. "Managing Assets and Skills: The Key to a Sustainable Competitive Advantage." *California Management Review* 31 (Winter 1989), pp. 91–106.

Bartlett, Christopher A., and Sumantra Ghoshal. "Matrix Management: Not a Structure, a Frame of Mind." *Harvard Business Review* 68, no. 4 (July–August 1990), pp. 138–45.

Hall, Gene, Jim Rosenthal, and Judy Wade. "How to Make Reengineering Really Work." *Harvard Business Review* 71, no. 6 (November–December 1993), pp. 119–31.

Hambrick, Donald C. "The Top Management Team: Key to Strategic Success." *California Management Review* 30, no. 1 (Fall 1987), pp. 88–108.

Hammer, Michael, and James Champy. *Reengineering the Corporation.* New York: HarperBusiness, 1993, chaps. 2 and 3.

Howard, Robert. "The CEO as Organizational Architect: An Interview with Xerox's Paul Allaire." *Harvard Business Review* 70, no. 5 (September–October 1992), pp. 107–19.

Kanter, Rosabeth Moss. "Collaborative Advantage: The Art of the Alliance." *Harvard Business Review* 72, no. 4 (July–August 1994), pp. 96–108.

Katzenbach, Jon R., and Douglas K. Smith. "The Discipline of Teams." *Harvard Business Review* 71, no. 2 (March–April 1993), pp. 111–24.

Larson, Erik W., and David H. Gobeli. "Matrix Management: Contradictions and Insights." *California Management Review* 29, no. 4 (Summer 1987), pp. 126–27.

Markides, Constantinos C. and Peter J. Williamson. "Corporate Diversification and Organizational Structure: A Resource-Based View." *Academy of Management Journal* 39, no. 2 (April 1996), pp. 340–67.

Pfeffer, Jeffrey. "Producing Sustainable Competitive Advantage through the Effective Management of People." *Academy of Management Executive* 9, no. 1 (February 1995), pp. 55–69.

Powell, Walter W. "Hybrid Organizational Arrangements: New Form or Transitional Development?" *California Management Review* 30, no. 1 (Fall 1987), pp. 67–87.

Prahalad, C. K., and Gary Hamel. "The Core Competence of the Corporation." *Harvard Business Review* 68 (May–June 1990), pp. 79–93.

Rackham, Neil, Lawrence Friedman, and Richard Ruff. *Getting Partnering Right: How Market Leaders Are Creating Long-Term Competitive Advantage.* New York: McGraw-Hill, 1996.

Quinn, James Brian. *Intelligent Enterprise.* New York: Free Press, 1992, chaps. 2 and 3.

Stalk, George, Philip Evans, and Lawrence E. Shulman. "Competing on Capabilities: The New Rules of Corporate Strategy." *Harvard Business Review* 70, no. 2 (March–April 1992), pp. 57–69.

Yip, George S. *Total Global Strategy: Managing for Worldwide Competitive Advantage.* Englewood Cliffs, N.J.: Prentice-Hall, 1992, chap. 8.

10

IMPLEMENTING STRATEGY: BUDGETS, POLICIES, BEST PRACTICES, SUPPORT SYSTEMS, AND REWARDS

I n the previous chapter we emphasized the importance of building organization capabilities and structuring the work effort so as to perform strategy-critical activities in a coordinated and competent manner. In this chapter we discuss five additional strategy-implementing tasks:

1. Reallocating resources to match the budgetary and staffing requirements of the new strategy.
2. Establishing strategy-supportive policies and procedures.
3. Instituting best practices and mechanisms for continuous improvement.
4. Installing support systems that enable company personnel to carry out their strategic roles day in and day out.
5. Employing motivational practices and incentive compensation methods that enhance commitment to good strategy execution.

LINKING BUDGETS TO STRATEGY

Implementing strategy forces a manager into the budget-making process. Organizational units need big enough budgets to carry out their parts of the strategic plan. There has to be ample funding of efforts to strengthen existing competencies and capabilities and/or to develop new ones. Organizational units, especially those charged with performing strategy-critical activities, have to be staffed with enough of the right kinds of people, be given enough operating funds to do their work proficiently, and have the funds to invest in needed operating systems, equipment, and facilities. Strategy implementers must screen subordinates' requests for new capital projects and bigger operating budgets, distinguishing between what would be nice and what can make a cost-effective contribution to strategy execution and enhanced competitive capabilities. Moreover, implementers have to make a persuasive, documented case to superiors on what additional resources and competitive assets, if any, it will take to execute their assigned pieces of company strategy.

How well a strategy implementer links budget allocations to the needs of strategy can either promote or impede the implementation process. Too little funding slows progress and impedes the ability of organizational units to execute their pieces of the strategic plan. Too much funding wastes organizational resources and reduces financial performance. Both outcomes argue for the strategy implementer to be deeply involved in the budgeting process, closely reviewing the programs and budget proposals of strategy-critical organization units.

> **Strategic Management Principle**
>
> *Depriving strategy-critical groups of the funds needed to execute their pieces of the strategy can undermine the implementation process.*
>
> *New strategies usually call for significant budget reallocations.*

Implementers must also be willing to shift resources from one area to another to support new strategic initiatives and priorities. A change in strategy nearly always calls for budget reallocations. Units important in the old strategy may now be oversized and overfunded. Units that now have a bigger and more critical role may need more people, different support systems, new equipment, additional facilities, and above-average increases in their operating budgets. Strategy implementers need to be active and forceful in shifting resources, downsizing some areas, upsizing others, and amply funding activities with a critical role in the new strategy. They have to exercise their power to allocate resources to make things happen and make the tough decisions to kill projects and activities that are no longer justified. The funding requirements of the new strategy *must* drive how capital allocations are made and the size of each unit's operating budgets. Underfunding units and activities pivotal to strategic success can defeat the whole implementation process.

Aggressive resource reallocation can have a positive strategic payoff. For example, at Harris Corporation, where the strategy was to quickly transfer new research results to organizational units that could turn them into areas commercially viable products, top management regularly shifted groups of engineers out of research projects and moved them (as a group) into new commercial venture divisions. Boeing used a similar approach to reallocating ideas and talent; according to one Boeing officer, "We can do it (create a big new unit) in two weeks. We couldn't do it in two years at International Harvester."[1] Forceful actions to reallocate funds and move people into new units signal a strong commitment to implementing strategic change and are frequently needed to catalyze the implementation process and give it credibility.

Fine-tuning the implementation of a company's existing strategy seldom requires big movements of people and money. The needed adjustments can usually be accomplished through above-average budget increases to units where new initiatives are contemplated and below-average increases (or even small cuts) for the remaining units. The chief exception occurs where a prime ingredient of corporate/business strategy is to create altogether new competencies/capabilities or to generate fresh, new products and business opportunities within the existing budget. Then, as propos-

---

[1]Thomas J. Peters and Robert H. Waterman, Jr., *In Search of Excellence* (New York: Harper & Row, 1980), p. 125.

als and business plans worth pursuing bubble up from below, decisions have to be made about where the needed capital expenditures, operating budgets, and personnel will come from. Companies like 3M, GE, and Boeing shift resources and people from area to area on an as-needed basis to support the launch of new products and new business ventures. They empower "product champions" and small bands of would-be entrepreneurs by giving them financial and technical support and by setting up organizational units and programs to help new ventures blossom more quickly. Microsoft is quick to disband some project teams and create others to pursue fresh software projects or new ventures like MSN.

CREATING STRATEGY-SUPPORTIVE POLICIES AND PROCEDURES

Changes in strategy generally call for some changes in work practices and how operations are conducted. Asking people to alter established procedures and behavior always upsets the internal order of things. It is normal for pockets of resistance to develop and for people to exhibit some degree of stress and anxiety about how the changes will affect them, especially when the changes may eliminate jobs. Questions are also likely to arise over what activities need to be done in rigidly prescribed fashion and where there ought to be leeway for independent action.

Prescribing policies and operating procedures aids the task of implementing strategy in several ways:

1. New or freshly revised policies and procedures provide top-down guidance to operating managers, supervisory personnel, and employees about how certain things now need to be done and what behavior is expected, thus establishing some degree of regularity, stability, and dependability in how management has decided to try to execute the strategy and operate the business on a daily basis.

2. Policies and procedures help align actions and behavior with strategy throughout the organization, placing limits on independent action and channeling individual and group efforts along the intended path. Policies and procedures counteract tendencies for some people to resist or reject common approaches—most people refrain from violating company policy or ignoring established practices without first gaining clearance or having strong justification.

3. Policies and standardized operating procedures help enforce needed consistency in how particular strategy-critical activities are performed in geographically scattered operating units. Eliminating significant differences in the operating practices and procedures of units performing common functions is necessary to avoid sending mixed messages to internal personnel and to customers who do business with the company at multiple locations.

4. Because dismantling old policies and procedures and instituting new ones alter the character of the internal work climate, strategy implementers can use the policy-changing process as a powerful lever for changing the corporate culture in ways that produce a stronger fit with the new strategy.

Company managers, therefore, need to be inventive in devising policies and practices that can provide vital support to effective strategy implementation. McDonald's policy manual, in an attempt to steer "crew members" into stronger quality and service behavior patterns, spells out such detailed procedures as "Cooks must turn, never flip, hamburgers. If they haven't been purchased, Big Macs must be discarded

---

ILLUSTRATION CAPSULE 35   Nike's Manufacturing Policies and Procedures

When Nike decided on a strategy of outsourcing 100 percent of its athletic footwear from independent manufacturers (that, for reasons of low cost, all turned out to be located in Taiwan, South Korea, Thailand, Indonesia, and China), it developed a series of policies and production practices to govern its working relationships with its "production partners" (a term Nike carefully nurtured because it implied joint responsibilities):

- Nike personnel were stationed on-site at all key manufacturing facilities; each Nike representative tended to stay at the same factory site for several years to get to know the partner's people and processes in detail. They functioned as liaisons with Nike headquarters, working to match Nike's R&D and new product design efforts with factory capabilities and to keep monthly orders for new production in line with the latest sales forecasts.
- Nike instituted a quality assurance program at each factory site to enforce up-to-date and effective quality management practices.

- Nike endeavored to minimize ups and downs in monthly production orders at factory sites making Nike's premium-priced top-of-the-line models (volumes typically ran 20,000 to 25,000 pairs daily); the policy was to keep month-to-month variations in order quantity under 20 percent. These factories made Nike footwear exclusively and were expected to co-develop new models and to co-invest in new technologies.
- Factory sites that made mid-to-low-end Nike products in large quantities (usually 70,000 to 85,000 pairs per day), known as "volume producers," were expected to handle most ups and downs in monthly orders themselves; these factories usually produced shoes for five to eight other buyers, giving them the flexibility to juggle orders and stabilize their production.
- It was strict Nike policy to pay its bills from production partners on time, providing them with predictable cash flows.

Source: Based on information in James Brian Quinn, *Intelligent Enterprise* (New York: Free Press, 1992), pp. 60–64.

---

in 10 minutes after being cooked and french fries in 7 minutes. Cashiers must make eye contact with and smile at every customer." Caterpillar Tractor has a policy of guaranteeing its customers 24-hour parts delivery anywhere in the world; if it fails to fulfill the promise, it supplies the part free. Hewlett-Packard requires R&D people to make regular visits to customers to learn about their problems, talk about new product applications, and, in general, keep the company's R&D programs customer-oriented. Mrs. Fields' Cookies has a policy of establishing *hourly* sales quotas for each store outlet; furthermore, it is company policy for cookies not sold within two hours after being baked to be removed from the case and given to charitable organizations. Illustration Capsule 35 describes Nike's manufacturing policies in some detail.

Well-conceived policies and procedures aid implementation; out-of-sync policies are barriers.

Thus there is a definite role for new and revised policies and procedures in the strategy implementation process. Wisely constructed policies and procedures help enforce strategy implementation by channeling actions, behavior, decisions, and practices in directions that improve strategy execution. When policies and procedures aren't strategy-supportive, they become a barrier to the kinds of changes in attitude and behavior strategy implementers are trying to promote. Often, people opposed to certain elements of the strategy or certain implementation approaches will hide behind or vigorously defend long-standing policies and operating procedures in an effort to stall implementation or divert the approach to implementation along a different route. Anytime a company alters its strategy, managers should review existing policies and operating procedures, revise or discard those that are out of sync, and formulate new ones.

None of this implies that companies need thick policy manuals to guide strategy implementation and daily operations. Too much policy can be as stifling as wrong policy or as chaotic as no policy. There is wisdom in a middle approach: prescribe enough policies to give organizational members clear direction and to place desirable boundaries on their actions, then empower them to do act within these boundaries however they think makes sense. Such latitude is especially appropriate when individual creativity and initiative are more essential to good strategy execution than standardization and strict conformity.[2] Creating a strong, supportive fit between strategy and policy can therefore mean more policies, fewer policies, or different policies. It can mean policies that require things to be done a certain way or policies that give employees leeway to do activities the way they think best.

INSTITUTING BEST PRACTICES AND A COMMITMENT TO CONTINUOUS IMPROVEMENT

Identifying and implementing best practices is a journey, not a destination.

If value-chain activities are to be performed as effectively and efficiently as possible, each department and unit needs to benchmark how it performs specific tasks and activities against best-in-industry or best-in-world performers. A strong commitment to searching out and adopting best practices is integral to effective strategy implementation—especially for strategy-critical and big-dollar activities where better quality or lower costs impact bottom-line performance.[3]

The benchmarking movement to search out, study, and implement best practices has stimulated greater management awareness of the strategy-implementing importance of reengineering (the redesign of business processes), total quality management (TQM), and other continuous improvement programs. TQM is a philosophy of managing and set of business practices that emphasizes continuous improvement in all phases of operations, 100 percent accuracy in performing activities, involvement and empowerment of employees at all levels, team-based work design, benchmarking, and fully satisfying customer expectations. A 1991 survey by The Conference Board showed 93 percent of manufacturing companies and 69 percent of service companies had implemented some form of quality improvement program.[4] Another survey found that 55 percent of American executives and 70 percent of Japanese executives used quality improvement information at least monthly as part of their assessment of overall performance.[5] An Arthur D. Little study reported that 93 percent of the 500 largest U.S. firms had adopted TQM in some form as of 1992. Analysts have attributed the quality of many Japanese products to dedicated application of TQM principles. Indeed, *quality improvement processes have now become a globally pervasive part of the fabric of implementing strategies keyed to defect-free manufacture, superior product quality, superior customer service, and total customer satisfaction.*

Management interest in quality improvement programs typically originates in a company's production areas—fabrication and assembly in manufacturing enterprises, teller transactions in banks, order picking and shipping at catalog firms, or customer-contact interfaces in service organizations. Other times, interest begins with executives who hear TQM presentations, read about TQM, or talk to people in other companies that have benefited from total quality programs. Usually, interested man-

---

[2]Ibid., p. 65.

[3]For a discussion of the value of benchmarking in implementing strategy, see Yoshinobu Ohinata, "Benchmarking: The Japanese Experience," *Long Range Planning* 27, no. 4 (August 1994), pp. 48–53.

[4]Judy D. Olian and Sara L. Rynes, "Making Total Quality Work: Aligning Organizational Processes, Performance Measures, and Stakeholders," *Human Resource Management* 30, no. 3 (Fall 1991), p. 303.

[5]Ibid.

TABLE 10-1   Components of Popular TQM Approaches and 1992 Baldridge Award Criteria

DEMING'S 14 POINTS

1. Constancy of purpose
2. Adopt the philosophy
3. Don't rely on mass inspection
4. Don't award business on price
5. Constant improvement
6. Training
7. Leadership
8. Drive out fear
9. Break down barriers
10. Eliminate slogans and exhortations
11. Eliminate quotas
12. Pride of workmanship
13. Education and retraining
14. Plan of action

THE JURAN TRILOGY

1. *Quality Planning*
   • Set goals
   • Identify customers and their needs
   • Develop products and processes
2. *Quality control*
   • Evaluate performance
   • Compare to goals and adapt
3. *Quality improvement*
   • Establish infrastructure
   • Identify projects and teams
   • Provide resources and training
   • Establish controls

CROSBY'S 14 QUALITY STEPS

1. Management commitment
2. Quality improvement teams
3. Quality measurement
4. Cost of quality evaluation
5. Quality awareness
6. Corrective action
7. Zero-defects committee
8. Supervisor training
9. Zero-defects day
10. Goal-setting
11. Error cause removal
12. Recognition
13. Quality councils
14. Do it over again

THE 1992 BALDRIDGE AWARD CRITERIA (1000 points total)

1. *Leadership* (90 points)
   • Senior executive
   • Management for quality
   • Public responsibility
2. *Information and analysis* (80 points)
   • Scope and management of quality and performance data
   • Competitive comparisons and benchmarks
3. *Strategic quality planning* (60 points)
   • Strategic quality and planning process
   • Quality and performance plans
4. *Human resource development and management* (150 points)
   • Human resource management
   • Employee involvement
   • Employee education and training
   • Employee performance and recognition
   • Employee well-being and morale

5. *Management of process quality* (140 points)
   • Design and introduction of products and services
   • Process management—production and delivery
   • Process management—business and support
   • Supplier quality
   • Quality assessment
6. *Quality and operational results* (180 points)
   • Product and service quality
   • Company operations
   • Business process and support services
   • Supplier quality
7. *Customer focus and satisfaction* (300 points)
   • Customer relationships
   • Commitment to customers
   • Customer satisfaction determination
   • Customer satisfaction results
   • Customer satisfaction comparisons
   • Future requirements and expectations

Source: As presented in Thomas C. Powell, "Total Quality Management as Competitive Advantage," *Strategic Management Journal* 16, no. 1 (January 1995) p. 18 and based on M. Walton, *The Deming Management Method* (New York: Pedigree, 1986); J. Juran, *Juran on Quality by Design* (New York: Free Press, 1992); Philip Crosby, *Quality Is Free: The Act of Making Quality Certain* (New York: McGraw-Hill, 1979); and S. George, *The Baldridge Quality System* (New York: Wiley, 1992).

agers have quality and customer-satisfaction problems they are struggling to solve. See Table 10-1 for the different kinds of features emphasized by the leading proponents of TQM and for the criteria employed in selected winners of the Malcolm Baldridge Award for Quality.

While TQM concentrates on the production of quality goods and the delivery of excellent customer service, to succeed it must extend organizationwide to employee efforts in all departments—HR, billing, R&D, engineering, accounting and records, and information systems—that may lack less-pressing customer-driven incentives to

TABLE 10–2 Twelve Aspects Common to TQM and Continuous Improvement Programs

1. **Committed leadership:** a near-evangelical, unwavering, long-term commitment by top managers to the philosophy, usually under a name something like Total Quality Management, Continuous Improvement (CI), or Quality Improvement (QI).

2. **Adoption and communication of TQM:** using tools like the mission statement, and themes or slogans.

3. **Closer customer relationships:** determining customers' (both inside and outside the firm) requirements, then meeting those requirements no matter what it takes.

4. **Closer supplier relationships:** working closely and cooperatively with suppliers (often sole-sourcing key components), ensuring they provide inputs that conform to customers' end-use requirements.

5. **Benchmarking:** researching and observing operating competitive practices.

6. **Increased training:** usually includes TQM principles, team skills, and problem-solving.

7. **Open organization:** lean staff, empowered work teams, open horizontal communications, and a relaxation of traditional hierarchy.

8. **Employee empowerment:** increased employee involvement in design and planning, and greater autonomy in decision-making.

9. **Zero-defects mentality:** a system in place to spot defects as they occur, rather than through inspection and rework.

10. **Flexible manufacturing:** (applicable only to manufacturers) can include just-in-time inventory, cellular manufacturing, design for manufacturability (DFM), statistical process control (SPC), and design of experiments (DOE).

11. **Process improvement:** reduced waste and cycle times in all areas through cross-departmental process analysis.

12. **Measurement:** goal-orientation and zeal for data, with constant performance measurement, often using statistical methods.

Source: Thomas C. Powell, "Total Quality Management as Competitive Advantage," *Strategic Management Journal* 16, no. 1 (January 1995) p. 19.

improve. This is because the institution of best practices and continuous improvement programs involves reforming the corporate culture and shifting to a total quality/continuous improvement philosophy that permeates the organization—see Table 10-2 for the features common to most TQM programs.[6] TQM aims at instilling enthusiasm and commitment to doing things right from top to bottom of the organization. It entails a restless search for continuing improvement, the little steps forward each day that the Japanese call *kaizen*. TQM is a race without a finish. The managerial objective is to kindle a burning desire in people to use their ingenuity and initiative to progressively improve on how tasks are performed. TQM preaches that there's no such thing as good enough and that everyone has a responsibility to

TQM entails creating a total quality culture bent on continuously improving the performance of every task and value-chain activity.

---

[6]For a discussion of the shift in work environment and culture that TQM entails, see Robert T. Amsden, Thomas W. Ferratt, and Davida M. Amsden, "TQM: Core Paradigm Changes," *Business Horizons* 39, no. 6 (November–December 1996), pp. 6–14.

ILLUSTRATION CAPSULE 36   Motorola's Approach to TQM and Teamwork

Motorola is rated as one of the best companies in measuring performance against its strategic targets and in promoting total quality practices that lead to continuous improvement. Motorola was selected in 1988 as one of the first winners of the Malcolm Baldrige Quality Award and has since improved on its own award-winning efforts. In 1993, the company estimated it was saving about $2.2 billion annually from its team-oriented approach to TQM and continuous improvement.

A central feature of Motorola's approach is a year-long contest highlighting the successes of employee teams from around the world in improving internal company practices, making better products, saving money, pleasing customers, and sharing best practices with other Motorola groups. The contest, known as the Total Customer Satisfaction Team Competition, in 1992 attracted entries from nearly 4,000 teams involving nearly 40,000 of Motorola's 107,000 employees. Preliminary judging eventually reduced the 1992 finalists to 24 teams from around the world, all of which were invited to Chicago in January 1993 to make a 12–minute presentation to a panel of 15 senior executives, including the CEO. Twelve teams were awarded gold medals and 12 silver medals. The gold medalists are listed below.

Motorola does not track the costs of the contest because "the benefits are so overwhelming." It has sent hundreds of videos about the contests to other companies wanting details. However, TQM consultants are skeptical whether other companies have progressed far enough in establishing a team-based quality culture to benefit from a companywide contest. The downsides to such elaborate contests, they say, are the added costs (preparation, travel, presentation, and judging) and the risks to the morale of those who don't win.

Gold Medal Teams	Work Location	Achievement
B.E.A.P. Goes On	Florida	Removed bottleneck in testing pagers by using robots.
The Expedition	Malaysia	Designed and delivered a new chip for Apple Computer in six months.
Operation Paging Storm	Singapore	
ET/EV=1	Illinois	Eliminated component alignment defect in papers.
The Mission	Arizona	Streamlined order process for auto electronics.
Class Act	Illinois	Developed quality system for design of iridium satellites.
Dyna-Attackers	Dublin	Cut training program from five years to two with better results.
Orient Express	Malaysia	Cut production time and defect rate on new battery part.
The Dandles	Japan	Cut response time on tooling orders from 23 days to 4.
Cool Blue Racers	Arizona	Improved efficiency of boiler operations.
IO Plastics Misload	Manila	Cut product development time in half to win IBM contract. Eliminated resin seepage in modulator assembly.

Source: Based on information reported in Barnaby J. Feder, "At Motorola, Quality Is a Team Sport," *New York Times*, January 21, 1993, pp. C1 and C6.

participate in continuous improvement—see Illustration Capsule 36 describing Motorola's approach to involving employees in the TQM effort.

Effective use of TQM/continuous improvement techniques is a valuable competitive asset—one that can produce important competitive capabilities (in product design, cost reduction, product quality, and customer service) and be a source of competitive advantage.[7] Not only do ongoing incremental improvements add up over time and strengthen organizational capabilities but TQM/continuous improvement

---

[7]Thomas C. Powell, "Total Quality Management as Competitive Advantage," *Strategic Management Journal* 16 (1995), pp. 15–37. See, also, Richard M. Hodgetts, "Quality Lessons from America's Baldrige Winners," *Business Horizons* 37, no. 4 (July–August 1994), pp. 74–79 and Richard Reed, David J. Lemak, and Joseph C. Montgomery, "Beyond Process: TQM Content and Firm Performance," *Academy of Management Review* 21, no. 1 (January 1996), pp. 173–202.

programs have hard-to-imitate aspects. While it is relatively easy for rivals to undertake benchmarking, process improvement, and quality training, it is much more difficult for them to implant a total quality culture, empower employees, and generate deep and genuine management commitment to TQM philosophy and practices. TQM requires a substantial investment of management time and effort; some managers and employees resist TQM, viewing it as ideological or faddish. It is expensive (in terms of training and meetings) and it seldom produces short-term results. The longer term payoff depends heavily on management's success in instilling a culture within which TQM philosophies and practices can thrive.

Having the capability to generate continuous improvements in important value-chain activities is a valuable competitive asset.

The Difference between TQM and Process Reengineering   Best practices, process reengineering, and continuous improvement efforts like TQM all aim at improved efficiency and reduced costs, better product quality, and greater customer satisfaction. *The essential difference between process reengineering and TQM is that reengineering aims at quantum gains on the order of 30 to 50 percent or more, whereas total quality programs stress incremental progress, striving for inch-by-inch gains again and again.* The two approaches to improved performance of value-chain activities are not mutually exclusive; it makes sense to use them in tandem. Reengineering can be used first to produce a good basic design that dramatically improves a business process. Total quality programs can then be used to work out bugs, perfect the process, and gradually improve both efficiency and effectiveness. Such a two-pronged approach to implementing organizational and strategic change is like a marathon race where you run the first four laps as fast as you can, then gradually pick up speed the remainder of the way.

Reengineering seeks one-time quantum improvement; TQM seeks ongoing incremental improvement.

Capturing the Potential Benefits   Research indicates that some companies benefit from reengineering and TQM and some do not.[8] Usually, the biggest beneficiaries are companies that view such programs not as ends in themselves but as tools for implementing and executing company strategy more effectively. The skimpiest payoffs from best practices, TQM, and reengineering occur when company managers seize them as something worth trying, novel ideas that could improve things; in most such instances, they result in strategy-blind efforts to simply manage better. There's an important lesson here. Best practices, TQM, and reengineering all need to be seen and used as part of a bigger-picture effort to execute strategy proficiently. Only strategy can point to which activities matter and what performance targets make the most sense. Absent a strategic framework, managers lack the context in which to fix things that really matter to business-unit performance and competitive success.

When best practices, reengineering, and TQM are not part of a wider-scale effort to improve strategy execution and business performance, they deteriorate into strategy-blind efforts to manage better.

To get the most from benchmarking, best practices, reengineering, TQM, and related tools for enhancing organizational competence in executing strategy, managers have to start with a clear fix on the indicators of successful strategy execution—defect-free manufacture, on-time delivery, low overall costs, exceeding customers' expectations, faster cycle time, increased product innovation, or some other specific performance measure. Benchmarking most or all value-chain activities against best-

---

[8]See, for example, Gene Hall, Jim Rosenthal, and Judy Wade, "How to Make Reengineering Really Work," *Harvard Business Review* 71, no. 6 (November–December 1993), pp. 119–31.

in-industry and best-in-world performance provides a basis for setting internal performance milestones and longer-range targets.

Then comes the managerial task of building a total quality culture and instilling the necessary commitment to achieving the targets and performance measures that the strategy requires. The action steps managers can take include:[9]

1. Visible, unequivocal, and unyielding commitment to total quality and continuous improvement, including a quality vision and specific, measurable quality goals.

2. Nudging people toward TQ-supportive behaviors by initiating such organizational programs as
   - Screening job applicants rigorously and hiring only those with attitudes and aptitudes right for quality-based performance.
   - Quality training for most employees.
   - Using teams and team-building exercises to reinforce and nurture individual effort (expansion of a TQ culture is facilitated when teams become more cross-functional, multitask, and increasingly self-managed).
   - Recognizing and rewarding individual and team efforts regularly and systematically.
   - Stressing prevention (doing it right the first time) not inspection (instituting ways to correct mistakes).

3. Empowering employees so that authority for delivering great service or improving products is in the hands of the doers rather than the overseers.

4. Using on-line information systems to provide all parties with the latest best practices and actual experiences with them, thereby speeding the diffusion and adoption of best practices throughout the organization and also allowing them to exchange data and opinions about how to improve/upgrade the best practices.

5. Preaching that performance can, and must, be improved because competitors are not resting on past laurels and customers are always looking for something better.

If the targeted performance measures are appropriate to the strategy and if top executives, middle managers, professional staff, and line employees buy into the process of continuous improvement, then the work climate will promote proficient strategy execution and good bottom-line business performance.

INSTALLING SUPPORT SYSTEMS

Company strategies can't be implemented or executed well without a number of support systems for business operations. American, United, Delta, and other major airlines cannot hope to provide world-class service without a computerized reservation system, an accurate and fast baggage handling system, and a strong aircraft maintenance program. FedEx has a computerized parcel-tracking system that can instantly report the location of any given package in its transit-delivery process; it

---

[9]Olian and Rynes, "Making Total Quality Work," pp. 305–6 and 310–11 and Paul S. Goodman and Eric D. Darr, "Exchanging Best Practices Information through Computer-Aided Systems," *Academy of Management Executive* 10, no. 2 (May 1996), p. 7.

has communication systems that allow it to coordinate its 21,000 vans nationwide to make an average of 720,000 stops per day to pick up customer packages; and it has leading-edge flight operations systems that allow a single controller to direct as many as 200 FedEx aircraft simultaneously, overriding their flight plans should weather or special emergencies arise—all these operations essential to FedEx's strategy of next-day delivery of a package that "absolutely, positively has to be there."[10]

Otis Elevator has a sophisticated support system called OtisLine to coordinate maintenance nationwide.[11] Trained operators take all trouble calls, input critical information on a computer screen, and dispatch people directly via a beeper system to the local trouble spot. From the trouble-call inputs, problem patterns can be identified nationally and the information communicated to design and manufacturing personnel, allowing them to quickly alter design specifications or manufacturing procedures to correct recurring problems. Also, much of the information needed for repairs is provided directly from faulty elevators through internally installed microcomputer monitors, further lowering outage time.

Strategic Management Principle

Innovative, state-of-the-art support systems can be a basis for competitive advantage if they give a firm capabilities that rivals can't match.

Procter & Gamble codes the more than 900,000 call-in inquiries it receives annually on its toll-free 800 number to obtain early warning signals of product problems and changing tastes.[12] Arthur Andersen Worldwide has an electronic system linking more than 82,000 people in 360 offices in 76 countries; the system has data, voice, and video capabilities and includes an electronic bulletin board for posting customer problems, for organizing around a customer's problem using people from all over the world, as well as the capability to collect, index, and distribute files containing information on particular subjects, customers, solutions, and company resources.[13] Andersen's Knowledge Xchange system captures the lessons learned in the company's daily work and research and makes it available to Andersen personnel 24 hours a day. Wal-Mart's computers transmit daily sales data to Wrangler, a supplier of blue jeans; using a model that interprets the data and software applications that act on these interpretations, specific quantities of specific sizes and colors are then shipped to specific stores from specific warehouses—the system lowers logistics and inventory costs and leads to fewer stockouts.[14] Domino's Pizza has computerized systems at each outlet to help with ordering, inventory, payroll, cash flow, and work control functions, freeing managers to spend more time on supervision, customer service, and business development.[15] Most telephone companies, electric utilities, and TV broadcasting systems have on-line monitoring systems to spot transmission problems within seconds and increase the reliability of their services. Software companies need systems that allow them to distribute their products on the Internet. At Mrs. Fields' Cookies, computer systems monitor hourly sales and suggest product mix changes, promotional tactics, or operating adjustments to improve customer response—see Illustration Capsule 37. Many companies have installed software systems on their company intranets to catalog best practices

---

[10]James Brian Quinn, *Intelligent Enterprise* (New York: Free Press, 1992) pp. 114–15.

[11]Ibid., p. 186.

[12]Ibid., p. 111.

[13]James Brian Quinn, Philip Anderson, and Sydney Finkelstein, "Leveraging Intellect," *Academy of Management Executive* 10, no. 3 (November 1996), p. 9.

[14]Stephan H. Haeckel and Richard L. Nolan. "Managing by Wire," *Harvard Business Review* 75, no. 5 (September–October 1993), p. 129.

[15]Quinn, *Intelligent Enterprise,* p. 181.

ILLUSTRATION CAPSULE 37   Management Information and Control Systems at Mrs. Fields' Cookies, Inc.

Mrs. Fields' Cookies is one of the best known specialty foods companies with over 800 outlets in operation in malls, airports, and other high pedestrian-traffic locations around the world. The business concept for Mrs. Fields' Cookies, as articulated by Debbi Fields, the company's founder and CEO, is "to serve absolutely fresh, warm cookies as though you'd stopped by my house and caught me just taking a batch from the oven." The company promotes its products mainly by sampling; store employees walk around giving away cookie samples. Another is for Fields to make unannounced visits to her stores, where she masquerades as a casual shopper to test the enthusiasm and sales techniques of store crews, sample the quality of the cookies they are baking, and observe customer reactions.

In 1978 when Debbi Fields opened her second store in San Francisco, 45 miles away from the first store in Palo Alto, she confronted the logistical problems of maintaining hands-on management and control at remote locations. Debbi's husband Randy developed a software program to issue instructions and advice to store managers and to provide a way of exercising control over store operations. Each morning local managers enter information on their store PCs—the day of the week, the month (to pick up seasonal shopping patterns), special mall activities or local events expected to influence traffic patterns, and the weather forecast. Randy's software program analyzes this information, together with the store's recent performance history, and prints out a daily sales goal (broken down by the hour). With the hourly sales quotas also comes an hourly schedule of how many batches of cookies to mix and bake and when to offer free samples.

As the day progresses, store managers type in actual hourly sales figures and customer counts. If customer counts are up but sales are lagging, the computerized software system recommends more aggressive sampling or more suggestive selling. If it becomes obvious the day is going to be a bust for the store, the computer automatically revises the sales projections for the day, reducing hourly quotas and instructing how much to cut back cookie baking. To facilitate crew scheduling by the store manager, sales projections are also provided for two weeks in advance. If a store manager has a specific problem, it can be entered on the system and routed to the appropriate person. The system gives store managers more time to work with their crews and achieve sales quotas, as opposed to handling administrative chores.

When Mrs. Fields' Cookies began to expand into Europe and Asia, the company's information technology department modified the software to take into account the different shopping patterns, buyer preferences, labor laws, languages, and supplier arrangements being encountered in foreign countries. A second generation of software, called the Retail Operations Intelligence system, was also developed; ROI has modules for inventory control, interviewing and hiring, repair and maintenance, lease management, and e-mail. All job applicants must sit at the store's terminal and answer a computerized set of questions as part of the interview process; the questions help store managers identify candidates with aptitudes for warmth, friendliness, and the ability to have a good time giving away samples, baking fresh batches, and talking to customers during the course of a sale.

Because the day-to-day variations in the cookie business are fairly easy to model and employee turnover in retail outlets like Mrs. Fields' is high, having the capability to "manage-by-wire" and run basic store operations on autopilot much of the time is a valuable strategy-implementing, strategy-executing assist. Debbi Fields also uses the electronic system as a means of projecting her influence and enthusiasm into stores far more frequently than she can reach through personal visits.

Source: Developed from information in Mike Korologos, "Debbi Fields," *Sky Magazine*, July 1988, pp. 42–50 and Stephan H. Haeckel and Richard L. Nolan, "Managing by Wire," *Harvard Business Review* 75, no. 5 (September–October 1993), pp. 123–24.

---

information and promote faster best practices transfer and implementation organizationwide.[16] Companies everywhere are rushing to create on-line data systems, connect more employees to the Internet and company intranets, use electronic mail as a

---

[16]Such systems speed organizational learning by providing fast, efficient communication, creating an organizational memory for collecting and retaining best practice information, and permitting people all across the organization to exchange information and updated solutions. See Goodman and Darr, "Exchanging Best Practices Information through Computer-Aided Systems," pp. 7–17.

major means of internal and external communication, and build Web pages to participate in the rapidly expanding world of electronic commerce.

Well-conceived, state-of-the art support systems not only facilitate better strategy execution, they also can strengthen organizational capabilities enough to provide a competitive edge over rivals. For example, a company with a differentiation strategy based on superior quality has added capability if it has systems for training personnel in quality techniques, tracking product quality at each production step, and ensuring that all goods shipped meet quality standards. A company striving to be a low-cost provider is competitively stronger if it has a benchmarking system that identifies opportunities to drive costs out of the business. Fast-growing companies get an important assist from recruiting systems that help attract and hire qualified employees in large numbers. In businesses such as public accounting and management consulting where large numbers of professional staffers need cutting-edge technical know-how, companies can gain a competitive edge if they have superior systems for training and retraining employees regularly and keeping them supplied with up-to-date information. Companies that rely on empowered customer service employees to act promptly and creatively in pleasing customers have to have state-of-the-art information systems that put essential data at employees' fingertips and give them instantaneous communications capabilities. Young companies wanting to build a business spanning a wide geographic area, grow rapidly, go public, and achieve a prominent industry standing have to invest more in organizational systems and infrastructure than small companies content to build a single-location business at a cautious pace. In today's business environment, competitive advantage goes to those firms most able to mobilize information and create systems to use knowledge effectively.

Companies that have learned how to use e-mail and word-processing systems proficiently and pervasively are much less hierarchical and tend to respond much faster to developing events than companies relying on traditional communication methods. Avid users of e-mail become available to anybody and everybody, resulting in a more open and democratic way of operating; moreover, information doesn't get screened and filtered. Because information is quickly broadcast and many people in different geographical areas can communicate readily, companies can conduct debates and develop solutions more rapidly. Microsoft makes exceptionally strong use of e-mail to distribute information, debate issues, mobilize its responses to developing events, speedily put people to work on emerging issues, and redeploy its resources. Intel is another company that uses e-mail to boost its agility. Price Waterhouse utilizes an on-line word-processing system to create client proposals that can be enriched by contributions from personnel in any of its offices around the world.

Installing Adequate Information Systems, Performance Tracking, and Controls

Accurate information is an essential guide to action. Every organization needs systems for gathering and storing data, tracking key performance indicators, identifying and diagnosing problems, and reporting strategy-critical information. Telephone companies have elaborate information systems to measure signal quality, connection times, interrupts, wrong connections, billing errors, and other measures of reliability. To track and manage the quality of passenger service, airlines have information systems to monitor gate delays, on-time departures and arrivals, baggage-handling times, lost baggage complaints, stockouts on meals and drinks, overbookings, and maintenance delays and failures. Many companies have provided customer-contact personnel with instant electronic access to customer databases so that they can respond effectively to customer inquiries and personalize customer services. Companies that rely on empowered employees need measurement and feedback systems to monitor the performance of workers and guide them to act within specified limits so that unwelcome surprises are avoided.[17]

Accurate, timely information allows organizational members to monitor progress and take corrective action promptly.

Electronic information systems allow managers to monitor implementation initiatives and daily operations, steering them to a successful conclusion in case early steps don't produce the expected progress or things seem to be drifting off course. Information systems need to cover five broad areas: (1) customer data, (2) operations data, (3) employee data, (4) supplier/partner/collaborative ally data, and (5) financial performance data. All key strategic performance indicators have to be measured as often as practical. Many retail companies generate daily sales reports for each store and maintain up-to-the-minute inventory and sales records on each item. Manufacturing plants typically generate daily production reports and track labor productivity on every shift. Many retailers and manufacturers have on-line data systems connecting them with their suppliers that monitor inventories, process orders and invoices, and track shipments. Monthly profit-and-loss statements and statistical summaries, long the norm, are fast being replaced by daily statistical updates and even up-to-the-minute performance monitoring that electronic technology makes possible. Such diagnostic control systems allow managers to detect problems early, intervene when needed, and adjust either the strategy or how it is being implemented. Early experiences are sometimes difficult to assess, but they yield the first hard data and should be closely scrutinized as a basis for corrective action. Ideally, statistical reports should flag big or unusual variances from preset performance standards.

Effective companies use computer-aided electronic systems to share data and information at lightning speed.

Statistical information gives the strategy implementer a feel for the numbers; reports and meetings provide a feel for new developments and problems; and personal contacts add a feel for the people dimension. All are good barometers of overall performance and good indicators of which things are on and off track.

Exercising Adequate Controls over Empowered Employees   A major problem facing today's managers is how to ensure that the actions of empowered subordinates stay within acceptable bounds and don't expose the organization to excessive risk.[18] There are dangers to leaving employees to their own devices in meeting performance standards. The media is full of reports of employees whose decisions or behavior went awry, either costing the company huge sums in losses or causing embarrassing lawsuits. Managers can't spend all their time making sure that everyone's decisions and behavior are between the white lines, yet they have a clear responsibility to institute adequate checks and balances and protect against unwelcome surprises. One of the main purposes of diagnostic control systems to track performance is to relieve managers of the burden of constant monitoring and give them time for other issues. But diagnostic controls are only part of the answer. Another valuable lever of control

---

[17]For a discussion of the need for putting appropriate boundaries on the actions of empowered employees and possible control and monitoring systems that can be used, see Robert Simons, "Control in an Age of Empowerment," *Harvard Business Review* 73 (March–April 1995), pp. 80–88.

[18]Ibid. See, also, David C. Band and Gerald Scanlan, "Strategic Control through Core Competencies," *Long Range Planning* 28, no. 2 (April 1995), pp. 102–14.

is establishing clear boundaries on behavior without telling employees what to do. Strictly prescribed rules and procedures discourage initiative and creativity. It is better to set forth what *not* to do, allowing freedom of action within specified limits. Another control device is face-to-face meetings to review information, assess progress and performance, reiterate expectations, and discuss the next action steps.

DESIGNING STRATEGY-SUPPORTIVE REWARD SYSTEMS

Strategies can't be implemented and executed with real proficiency unless organizational units and individuals are committed to the task. Company managers typically try to enlist organizationwide commitment to carrying out the strategic plan by motivating people and rewarding them for good performance. A manager has to do more than just talk to everyone about how important new strategic practices and performance targets are to the organization's future well-being. No matter how inspiring, talk seldom commands people's best efforts for long. *To get employees' sustained, energetic commitment, management has to be resourceful in designing and using motivational incentives—both monetary and nonmonetary.* The more a manager understands what motivates subordinates and the more he or she relies on motivational incentives as a tool for implementing strategy, the greater will be employees' commitment to good day in, day out execution of their roles in the company's strategic plan.

The role of the reward system is to make it personally satisfying and economically beneficial for organizational members to help the company execute its strategy competently, please customers, and realize the company's vision.

While financial incentives (salary increases, performance bonuses, stock options, and retirement packages) are the core component of most companies' reward systems, managers normally make extensive use of such nonmonetary incentives as frequent words of praise (or constructive criticism), special recognition at company gatherings or in the company newsletter, more (or less) job security, interesting assignments, opportunities to transfer to attractive locations, increased (or decreased) job control and decision-making autonomy, and the carrot of promotion and the stick of being "sidelined" in a routine or dead-end job. Effective managers are further alert to the motivating power of giving people a chance to be part of something exciting, giving them an opportunity for greater personal satisfaction, challenging them with ambitious performance targets, and the intangible bonds of group acceptance. But the motivation and reward structure has to be used *creatively* and tied directly to achieving the performance outcomes necessary for good strategy execution.

One of the biggest strategy-implementing challenges is to employ motivational techniques that build wholehearted commitment and winning attitudes among employees.

Strategy-Supportive Motivational Practices

Successful strategy implementers inspire and challenge employees to do their best. They get employees to buy into the strategy and commit to making it work. They structure individual efforts into teams and work groups in order to facilitate an exchange of ideas and a climate of support. They allow employees to participate in making decisions about how to perform their jobs, and they try to make jobs interesting and satisfying. They devise strategy-supportive motivational approaches and use them effectively. Consider some actual examples:

- At Mars Inc. (best known for its candy bars), every employee, including the president, gets a weekly 10 percent bonus by coming to work on time each day that week. This on-time incentive is designed to minimize absenteeism and tardiness and maximize the amount of labor time available for operating high-speed candy-making equipment (utilizing each available minute of machine time to produce the greatest number of candy bars reduces costs significantly).[19]

- In a number of Japanese companies, employees meet regularly to hear inspirational speeches, sing company songs, and chant the corporate litany. In the United States, Tupperware conducts a weekly Monday night rally to honor, applaud, and fire up its salespeople who conduct Tupperware parties. Amway and Mary Kay Cosmetics hold similar inspirational get-togethers for their sales forces.[20]

- Nordstrom typically pays its retail salespeople an hourly wage higher than the prevailing rates paid by other department store chains, plus it pays them a commission on each sale. Spurred by a culture that encourages salespeople to go all out to satisfy customers, to exercise their own best judgment, and to seek out and promote new fashion ideas, Nordstrom salespeople often earn twice the average incomes of sales employees at competing stores.[21] Nordstrom's rules for employees are simple: "Rule #1: Use your good judgment in all situations. There will be no additional rules."

- Microsoft, realizing that software creation is a highly individualistic effort, interviews hundreds of propective programmers to find the few most suited to write code for its programs. It places new recruits onto three-to seven-person teams under experienced mentors to work on the next generation of software programs. While project team members can expect to put in 60-to 80-hour workweeks to meet deadlines for getting new programs to market, the best programmers seek out and stay with Microsoft largely because they believe that Microsoft will determine where the industry moves in the future and working for Microsoft will allow them to share in the excitement, challenge, and rewards of working on this frontier (and only partly because of Microsoft's very attractive pay scales and lucrative stock option program).[22]

- Lincoln Electric, a company deservedly famous for its piecework pay scheme and incentive bonus plan, rewards individual productivity by paying workers for each nondefective piece produced (workers have to correct quality problems on their own time—defects can be traced to the worker who caused them). The piecework plan motivates workers to pay attention to both quality and volume produced. In addition, the company sets aside a substantial portion of its profits above a specified base for worker bonuses. To determine the size of each worker's bonus Lincoln Electric rates each worker on four equally important performance measures: dependability, quality, output, and ideas and cooperation. The higher a worker's merit rating, the higher the incentive bonus earned; the highest rated workers in good profit years receive bonuses of as much as 110 percent of their piecework compensation.[23]

---

[19]Peters and Waterman, *In Search of Excellence*, p. 269.

[20]Ibid., p. xx.

[21]Jeffrey Pheffer, "Producing Sustainable Competitive Advantage through the Effective Management of People," *Academy of Management Executive* 9, no. 1 (February 1995), pp. 59–60.

[22]Quinn, Anderson, and Finkelstein, "Leveraging Intellect," p. 8.

[23]Pheffer, "Producing Sustainable Competitive Advantage through the Effective Management of People," p. 59.

- A California automobile assembly plant run by Toyota emphasizes symbolic egalitarianism. All employees (managers and workers alike) wear blue smocks, there are no reserved spaces in the employee parking lot, there's no executive dining room—everyone eats in the same plant cafeteria, and there are only two job classifications for skilled trades and only one job classification for all other workers.[24]

- Monsanto, FedEx, AT&T, Advanced Micro Devices, and many other companies have tapped into the motivational power of self-managed teams and achieved very good results. Teams work because of the peer monitoring and expectations of coworkers that are brought to bear on each team member.

- Several Japanese automobile producers, believing that providing employment security is a valuable contributor to worker productivity and company loyalty, elect not to lay off factory workers but instead put them out in the field to sell vehicles when business slacks off for a period. Mazda, for example, during a sales downturn in Japan in the 1980s, shifted factory workers to selling its models door-to-door, a common practice in Japan. At the end of the year, when awards were given out to the best salespeople, Mazda found its top ten salespeople were all factory workers, partly because they were able to explain the product effectively. When business picked up and the factory workers returned to the plant, their experiences in talking to customers yielded useful ideas in improving the features and styling of Mazda's product line.[25]

- At GE Medical Systems, a program called Quick Thanks! allows an employee to nominate any colleague to receive a $25 gift certificate redeemable at certain stores and restaurants in appreciation of a job well done. Employees often hand out the award personally to deserving coworkers (in a recent 12-month period over 10,000 Quick Thanks! awards were presented). Peers prove to be tougher than executives in praising colleagues; for the recipient, the approving acknowledgment of coworkers matters more than the $25.[26]

These motivational approaches accentuate the positive; others blend positive and negative features. Consider the way Harold Geneen, former president and chief executive officer of ITT, allegedly combined the use of money, tension, and fear:

> Geneen provides his managers with enough incentives to make them tolerate the system. Salaries all the way through ITT are higher than average—Geneen reckons 10 percent higher—so that few people can leave without taking a drop. As one employee put it: "We're all paid just a bit more than we think we're worth." At the very top, where the demands are greatest, the salaries and stock options are sufficient to compensate for the rigors. As someone said, "He's got them by their limousines."
>
> Having bound his [managers] to him with chains of gold, Geneen can induce the tension that drives the machine. "The key to the system," one of his [managers] explains, "is the profit forecast. Once the forecast has been gone over, revised, and agreed on, the managing director has a personal commitment to Geneen to carry it out. That's how he produces the tension on which the success depends." The tension goes through the company, inducing ambition, perhaps exhilaration, but always with some sense of fear: what happens if the target is missed?[27]

---

[24]Ibid., p. 63.

[25]Ibid., p. 62.

[26]Steven Kerr, "Risky Business: The New Pay Game," *Fortune*, July 22, 1996, p. 95.

[27]Anthony Sampson, *The Sovereign State of ITT* (New York: Stein and Day, 1973), p. 132.

Balancing Positive and Negative Motivational Considerations If a strategy implementer's motivational approach and reward structure induces too much stress, internal competitiveness, and job insecurity, the results can be counterproductive. The prevailing view is that a manager's push for strategy implementation should be more positive than negative because when cooperation is positively enlisted and rewarded, rather than strong-armed by a boss's orders, people tend to respond with more enthusiasm, effort, creativity, and initiative. Yet it is unwise to completely eliminate pressure for performance and the anxiety it evokes. There is no evidence that a no-pressure work environment leads to superior strategy execution or sustained high performance. As the CEO of a major bank put it, "There's a deliberate policy here to create a level of anxiety. Winners usually play like they're one touchdown behind."[28] High-performing organizations need ambitious people who relish the opportunity to climb the ladder of success, love a challenge, thrive in a performance-oriented environment, and find some competition and pressure useful to satisfy their own drives for personal recognition, accomplishment, and self-satisfaction. Unless compensation, career, and job satisfaction consequences are tied to successfully implementing strategic initiatives and hitting strategic performance targets, few people will attach much significance to the company's vision, objectives, and strategy.

Positive motivational approaches generally work better than negative ones.

Linking the Reward System to Strategically Relevant Performance Outcomes

The most dependable way to keep people focused on competent strategy execution and achieving company performance targets is to *generously* reward individuals and groups who achieve their assigned performance targets and deny rewards to those who don't. *The use of incentives and rewards is the single most powerful tool management has to win strong employee commitment to diligent, competent strategy execution.* Failure to use this tool wisely and powerfully weakens the entire implementation/execution process. Decisions on salary increases, incentive compensation, promotions, who gets which key assignments, and the ways and means of awarding praise and recognition are the strategy implementer's foremost devices to get attention and build commitment. Such decisions seldom escape the closest employee scrutiny, saying more about what is expected and who is considered to be doing a good job than any other factor. A company's system of incentives and rewards thus ends up being the way its strategy is emotionally ratified in the form of real commitment. Performance-based incentives make it in employees' self-interest to exert their best efforts to achieve performance targets and to execute the strategy competently[29]

Strategic Management Principle

A properly designed reward structure is management's most powerful strategy-implementing tool.

The key to creating a reward system that promotes good strategy execution is to make strategically relevant measures of performance *the dominating basis* for designing incentives, evaluating individual and group efforts, and handing out rewards. Performance targets have to be established for every unit, every manager, every team or work group, and perhaps every employee—targets that measure whether implementation is on track. If the company's strategy is to be a low-cost provider, the incentive system must reward actions and achievements that result in

---

[28]As quoted in John P. Kotter and James L. Heskett, *Corporate Culture and Performance* (New York: Free Press, 1992), p. 91.

[29]For a countervailing view on the merits of incentives, see Alfie Kohn, "Why Incentive Plans Cannot Work," *Harvard Business Review* 71, no. 6 (November–December 1993), pp. 54–63.

lower costs. If the company has a differentiation strategy predicated on superior quality and service, the incentive system must reward such outcomes as zero defects, infrequent need for product repair, low numbers of customer complaints, and speedy order processing and delivery. If a company's growth requires new product innovation, incentives should be tied to factors such as the percentages of revenues and profits coming from newly introduced products.

Strategic Management Principle

The strategy implementer's standard for judging whether individuals, teams, and organizational units have done a good job must be whether they achieve performance targets consistent with effective strategy execution.

Some of the best performing companies—Banc One, Nucor Steel, Lincoln Electric, Electronic Data Systems, Wal-Mart, Remington Products, and Mary Kay Cosmetics—owe much of their success to incentives and rewards that induce people to do the things critical to good strategy execution and competing effectively. At Banc One (one of the 10 largest U.S. banks and also one of the most profitable banks in the world based on return on assets), producing consistently high levels of customer satisfaction makes a big difference in how well it fares against rivals; customer satisfaction ranks high on Banc One's list of strategic priorities. To enhance employee commitment to the task of pleasing customers, Banc One ties the pay scales in each branch office to that branch's customer satisfaction rating—the higher the branch's ratings, the higher that branch's pay scales. By shifting from a theme of equal pay for equal work to one of equal pay for equal performance, Banc One has focused the attention of branch employees on the task of pleasing, even delighting, their customers.

Nucor's strategy was (and is) to be *the* low-cost producer of steel products. Because labor costs are a significant fraction of total cost in the steel business, Nucor's low-cost strategy entails achieving lower labor costs per ton of steel than competitors'. Nucor management designed an incentive system to promote high worker productivity and drive labor costs per ton below rivals'. Management has organized each plant's workforce into production teams (each assigned to perform particular functions) and, working with the teams, has established weekly production targets for each team. Base pay scales are set at levels comparable to wages for similar manufacturing jobs in the areas where Nucor has plants, but workers can earn a 1 percent bonus for each 1 percent that their output exceeds target levels. If a production team exceeds its weekly production target by 10 percent, team members receive a 10 percent bonus in their next paycheck; if a team exceeds its quota by 20 percent, team members earn a 20 percent bonus. Bonuses are paid every two weeks based on the prior two weeks' actual production levels. The results of Nucor's piece-rate incentive plan are impressive. Nucor's labor productivity (in tons produced per worker) runs over 20 percent above the average of the unionized workforces of the industry's large, integrated steel producers like U.S. Steel and Bethlehem Steel. Nucor enjoys about a $30 to $60 per ton cost advantage (a substantial part of which comes from its lower labor costs), and Nucor workers are the highest-paid workers in the steel industry.

As the example in Illustration Capsule 38 demonstrates, compensating and rewarding organization members on criteria not directly related to successful strategy execution undermines organization performance and condones the diversion of time and energy in less strategically relevant directions.

The Importance of Basing Incentives on Achieving Results, Not on Performing Assigned Functions   To create a system of rewards and incentives that support strategy, emphasis has to be put on rewarding people for accomplishing results, not for dutifully performing assigned functions. Focusing jobholders' attention and energy on "what to achieve" as opposed to "what to do" makes the work environment *results-oriented*. It is flawed management to tie incentives and rewards to satisfactory performance of duties and

---

ILLUSTRATION CAPSULE 38   The Folly of the Reward System in the Claims Division of a Large Insurance Company

The past reward practices of the health care claims division of a large insurance company demonstrate the folly of hoping for one behavior but rewarding another behavior. Seeking to encourage employees to be accurate in paying surgical claims, the company tracked the number of returned checks and letters of complaint filed by policyholders. However, employees in the claims department frequently found it hard to tell from physician filings which of two surgical procedures, with different allowable benefits, was performed, and writing for clarification greatly reduced the number of claims paid within two days of receipt (a performance standard the company stressed). Consequently, the workers' norm quickly became "when in doubt, pay it out."

This practice was made worse by the firm's reward system which called for merit increases of 5 percent for "outstanding" employees, 4 percent for "above average" employees (most employees not rated as outstanding were designated as above average), and 3 percent for all other employees. Many employees were indifferent to the potential of an extra 1 percent reward for avoiding

overpayment errors and working hard enough to be rated as outstanding.

However, employees were not indifferent to a rule which stated that employees forfeited their entire merit raise at the next six-month merit review if they were absent or late for work three or more times in any six-month period. The company, while hoping for performance, was rewarding attendance. But the absent-lateness rule was not as stringent as it might seem because the company counted the number of "times" rather than the number of "days"—a one-week absence counted the same as a one-day absence. A worker in danger of getting a third absence within a six-month period could sometimes stay away from work during the second absence until the first absence was over six months old; the limiting factor was that after a certain number of days the worker was paid sickness benefits instead of his or her regular pay (for workers with 20 or more years of service, the company provided sickness benefits of 90 percent of normal salary tax-free!!!).

Source: Steven Kerr, "On the Folly of Rewarding A, While Hoping for B," *Academy of Management Executive* 9, no. 1 February 1995), p. 11.

---

activities in hopes that the by-products will be the desired business outcomes and achievements.[30] In any job, performing assigned tasks is not equivalent to achieving intended outcomes. Working hard, staying busy, and diligently attending to assigned duties do not guarantee results. (As any student knows, just because an instructor teaches doesn't mean students are learning. Teaching and learning are different things—the first is an activity and the second is a result. The enterprise of education would no doubt take on a different character if teachers were rewarded for the result of what is learned instead of the activity of teaching.)

Incentive compensation for top executives is typically tied to company profitability (earnings growth, return on equity investment, return on total assets, economic value added), the company's stock price performance, and perhaps such measures as market share, product quality, or customer satisfaction that indicate the company's market position, overall competitiveness, and future prospects have improved. However, incentives for department heads, teams, and individual workers are often tied to outcomes more closely related to their area of responsibility. In manufacturing, incentive compensation may be tied to unit manufacturing costs, on-time production and shipping, defect rates, the number and extent of work stoppages due to labor disagreements and equipment breakdowns, and so on. In marketing, there may be

> *It is folly to reward one outcome in hopes of getting another outcome.*

> *The whats to accomplish—the performance measures on which rewards and incentives are based—must be tightly connected to the requirements of successful strategy execution and good company performance.*

---

[30]See Steven Kerr, "On the Folly of Rewarding A While Hoping for B," *Academy of Management Executive* 9 no. 1 (February 1995), pp. 7–14; Kerr, "Risky Business: The New Pay Game," pp. 93–96; and Doran Twer, "Linking Pay to Business Objectives," *Journal of Business Strategy* 15, no. 4 (July–August 1994), pp. 15–18.

incentives for achieving dollar sales or unit volume targets, market share, sales penetration of each target customer group, the fate of newly introduced products, the frequency of customer complaints, the number of new accounts acquired, and customer satisfaction. Which performance measures to base incentive compensation on depends on the situation—the priority placed on various financial and strategic objectives, the requirements for strategic and competitive success, and what specific results are needed in different facets of the business to keep strategy execution on track.

Guidelines for Designing Incentive Compensation Systems The concepts and company experiences discussed above yield the following guidelines for creating an incentive compensation system to help drive successful strategy execution:

1. *The performance payoff must be a major, not minor, piece of the total compensation package*—at least 10 to 12 percent of base salary. Incentives that amount to 20 percent or more of total compensation are big attention getters, likely to really drive individual effort; incentives amounting to less than 5 percent of total compensation have comparatively weak motivational impact. Moreover, the payoff for high performers must be substantially greater than the payoff for average performers and the payoff for average performers substantially bigger than for below average performers.

2. *The incentive plan should extend to all managers and all workers*, not just be restricted to top management. It is a gross miscalculation to expect that lower-level managers and employees will work their tails off to hit performance targets just so a few senior executives can get lucrative bonuses!

3. *The reward system must be administered with scrupulous care and fairness.* If performance standards are set too high or if individual/group performance evaluations are not accurate and well documented, dissatisfaction and disgruntlement with the system will overcome any positive benefits.

4. *The incentives must be tightly linked to achieving only those performance targets spelled out in the strategic plan* and not to any other factors that get thrown in because they are thought to be nice. Performance evaluation based on factors not tightly related to the strategy signal that either the strategic plan is incomplete (because important performance targets were left out) or management's real agenda is something other than what was stated in the strategic plan.

5. *The performance targets each individual is expected to achieve should involve outcomes that the individual can personally affect.* The role of incentives is to enhance individual commitment and channel behavior in beneficial directions. That won't happen when the performance measures an individual is judged by are outside his/her arena of influence.

6. *Keep the time between the performance review and payment of the reward short.* A lengthy interval between review and payment breeds discontent and works against reinforcing cause and effect.

7. *Make liberal use of nonmonetary rewards; don't rely solely on monetary rewards.* Money, when used properly, is a great motivator, but praise, special recognition, handing out plum assignments, and so on can be potent motivators as well.

8. *Skirting the system to find ways to reward nonperformers must be absolutely avoided.* It is debatable whether exceptions should be made for people who've tried hard, gone the extra mile, yet still come up short because of circumstances beyond their control—arguments can be made either way. The problem with making exceptions for unknowable, uncontrollable, or unforeseeable circumstances is that once "good" excuses start to creep into justifying rewards for nonperformers, the door is open for all kinds of "legitimate" reasons why actual performance failed to match targeted performance. In short, people at all levels have to be held accountable for carrying out their assigned parts of the strategic plan, and they have to know their rewards are based on their accomplishments.

Once the incentives are designed, they have to be communicated and explained. Everybody needs to understand how incentives are calculated and how individual/group performance targets contribute to organizationwide performance targets. Moreover, the reasons for anyone's failure or deviations from targets have to be explored fully to determine whether the causes are poor individual/group performance or circumstances beyond the control of those responsible. The pressure to achieve the targeted strategic and financial performance and continuously improve on strategy execution should be unrelenting. A "no excuses" standard has to prevail.[31] But with the pressure to perform must come deserving and meaningful rewards. Without an ample payoff, the system breaks down, and the strategy implementer is left with the unworkable option of barking orders and pleading for compliance.

A Few Cautions about Performance-Based Incentive Pay In some foreign countries, incentive pay runs counter to local customs and cultural norms. Professor Steven Kerr cites the time he lectured an executive education class on the need for more performance-based pay and a Japanese manager protested, "You shouldn't bribe your children to do their homework, you shouldn't bribe your wife to prepare dinner, and you shouldn't bribe your employees to work for the company."[32] Singling out individuals and commending them for unusually good effort can also be a problem; Japanese culture considers public praise of an individual an affront to the harmony of the group. In some countries, employees have a preference for nonmonetary rewards—more leisure time, important titles, access to vacation villages, and nontaxable perks.

A change in strategy nearly always calls for budget reallocations. Reworking the budget to make it more strategy-supportive is a crucial part of the implementation process because every organization unit needs to have the people, equipment, facilities, and other resources to carry out its part of the strategic plan (but no more than what it really needs!). Implementing a new strategy often entails shifting resources from one area to another—downsizing units that are overstaffed and overfunded, upsizing those more critical to strategic success, and killing projects and activities that are no longer justified.

KEY POINTS

---

[31]Tom Peters and Nancy Austin, *A Passion for Excellence* (New York: Random House, 1985), p. xix.

[32]Kerr, "Risky Business: The New Pay Game," p. 96. For a more general criticism of why performance incentives are a bad idea, see Kohn, "Why Incentive Plans Cannot Work," pp. 54–63.

Anytime a company alters its strategy, managers are well advised to review existing policies and operating procedures, deleting or revising those that are out of sync and deciding if additional ones are needed. Prescribing new or freshly revised policies and operating procedures aids the task of implementation (1) by providing top-down guidance to operating managers, supervisory personnel, and employees regarding how certain things need to be done; (2) by putting boundaries on independent actions and decisions; (3) by promoting consistency in how particular strategy-critical activities are performed in geographically scattered operating units; and (4) by helping to create a strategy-supportive work climate and corporate culture. Thick policy manuals are usually unnecessary. Indeed, when individual creativity and initiative are more essential to good execution than standardization and conformity, it is better to give people the freedom to do things however they see fit and hold them accountable for good results rather than try to control their behavior with policies and guidelines for every situation. Hence, creating a supportive fit between strategy and policy can mean many policies, few policies, or different policies.

Competent strategy execution entails visible, firm managerial commitment to best practices and continuous improvement. Benchmarking, instituting best practices, reengineering core business processes, and total quality management programs all aim at improved efficiency, lower costs, better product quality, and greater customer satisfaction. *All these techniques are important tools for learning how to execute a strategy more proficiently.* Benchmarking provides a realistic basis for setting performance targets. Instituting "best-in-industry" or "best-in-world" operating practices in most or all value-chain activities is essential to create a quality-oriented, high-performance work environment. Reengineering is a way to make quantum progress in being world class while TQM instills a commitment to continuous improvement. Effective use of TQM/continuous improvement techniques is a valuable competitive asset in a company's resource portfolio—one that can produce important competitive capabilities (in reducing costs, speeding new products to market, or improving product quality, service, or customer satisfaction) and be a source of competitive advantage.

Company strategies can't be implemented or executed well without a number of support systems to carry on business operations. Well-conceived, state-of-the-art support systems not only facilitate better strategy execution, they can also strengthen organizational capabilities enough to provide a competitive edge over rivals. In an age of computers, computerized monitoring and control systems, E-mail, the Internet, company intranets, and wireless communications capabilities, companies can't hope to outexecute their competitors without cutting-edge information systems and technologically sophisticated operating capabilities that enable fast, efficient, and effective organization action.

Strategy-supportive motivational practices and reward systems are powerful management tools for gaining employee buy-in and commitment. The key to creating a reward system that promotes good strategy execution is to make strategically relevant measures of performance *the dominating basis* for designing incentives, evaluating individual and group efforts, and handing out rewards. Positive motivational practices generally work better than negative ones, but there is a place for both. There's also a place for both monetary and nonmonetary incentives.

For an incentive compensation system to work well (1) the monetary payoff should be a major percentage of the compensation package, (2) the use of incentives should extend to all managers and workers, (3) the system should be administered with care and fairness, (4) the incentives should be linked to performance targets spelled out in the strategic plan, (5) each individual's performance targets should involve outcomes the person can personally affect, (6) rewards should promptly follow the determination of good performance, (7) monetary rewards should be supplemented with liberal use of nonmonetary rewards, and (8) skirting the system to reward nonperformers should be scrupulously avoided.

SUGGESTED READINGS

Denton, Keith D. "Creating a System for Continuous Improvement." *Business Horizons* 38, no. 1 (January–February 1995), pp. 16–21.

Grant, Robert M., Rami Shani, and R. Krishnan, "TQM's Challenge to Management Theory and Practice." *Sloan Management Review* (Winter 1994), pp. 25–35.

Haeckel, Stephan H. and Richard L. Nolan. "Managing by Wire." *Harvard Business Review* 75, no. 5 (September–October 1993), pp. 122–32.

Herzberg, Frederick. "One More Time: How Do You Motivate Employees?" *Harvard Business Review* 65, no. 4 (September–October 1987), pp. 109–20.

Kerr, Steven. "On the Folly of Rewarding A While Hoping for B." *Academy of Management Executive* 9 no. 1 (February 1995), pp. 7–14.

Kiernan, Matthew J. "The New Strategic Architecture: Learning to Compete in the Twenty-First Century." *Academy of Management Executive* 7, no. 1 (February 1993), pp. 7–21.

Kohn, Alfie. "Why Incentive Plans Cannot Work." *Harvard Business Review* 71, no. 5 (September–October 1993), pp. 54–63.

Olian, Judy D. and Sara L. Rynes, "Making Total Quality Work: Aligning Organizational Processes, Performance Measures, and Stakeholders," *Human Resource Management* 30, no. 3 (Fall 1991), pp. 303–33.

Ohinata, Yoshinobu. "Benchmarking: The Japanese Experience." *Long Range Planning* 27, no. 4 (August 1994), pp. 48–53.

Pfeffer, Jeffrey. "Producing Sustainable Competitive Advantage through the Effective Management of People." *Academy of Management Executive* 9, no. 1 (February 1995), pp. 55–69.

Quinn, James Brian. *Intelligent Enterprise*. New York: Free Press, 1992, chap. 4.

Shetty, Y. K. "Aiming High: Competitive Benchmarking for Superior Performance." *Long-Range Planning* 26, no. 1 (February 1993), pp. 39–44.

Simons, Robert. "Control in an Age of Empowerment." *Harvard Business Review* 73 (March–April 1995), pp. 80–88.

Wiley, Carolyn. "Incentive Plan Pushes Production." *Personnel Journal* (August 1993), pp. 86–91.

11

IMPLEMENTING STRATEGY: CULTURE AND LEADERSHIP

I n the previous two chapters we examined six of the strategy implementer's tasks—building a capable organization, steering ample resources into strategy-critical activities and operating units, establishing strategy-supportive policies, instituting best practices and programs for continuous improvement, creating internal support systems to enable better execution, and employing appropriate motivational practices and compensation incentives. In this chapter we explore the two remaining implementation tasks: creating a strategy-supportive corporate culture and exerting the internal leadership needed to drive implementation forward.

Weak leadership can wreck the soundest strategy; forceful execution of even a poor plan can often bring victory.

Sun Zi

An organization's capacity to execute its strategy depends on its "hard" infrastructure—its organizational structure and systems—and on its "soft" infrastructure—its culture and norms.

Amar Bhide

Ethics is the moral courage to do what we know is right, and not to do what we know is wrong.

C. J. Silas
CEO, Philips Petroleum

. . . A leader lives in the field with his troops.

H. Ross Perot

BUILDING A STRATEGY-SUPPORTIVE CORPORATE CULTURE

Every company has its own unique culture—one made distinctive by its own business philosophy and principles, its own ways of approaching problems and making decisions, its own embedded patterns of "how we do things around here," its own lore (stories told over and over to illustrate company values and what they mean to employees), its own taboos and political don'ts, its own organizational personality. The bedrock of Wal-Mart's culture is dedication to customer satisfaction, zealous pursuit of low costs, a strong work ethic, Sam Walton's legendary frugality, the ritualistic Saturday morning headquarters meetings to exchange ideas and review problems, and company executives' commitment to visiting stores, talking to customers, and soliciting suggestions from employees. At McDonald's the constant message from management is the overriding importance of quality, service, cleanliness, and value; employees are drilled over and over on the need for attention to detail and perfection in every fundamental of the business. At Microsoft, there are stories of the long hours programmers put in, the emotional peaks and valleys in encountering and overcoming coding problems, the exhilaration of completing a complex program on schedule, the satisfaction of working on cutting-edge projects, and the rewards of being part of a

---

ILLUSTRATION CAPSULE 39   The Culture at Nordstrom

The culture at Nordstrom, a department store retailer noted for exceptional commitment to its customers, revolves around the company's motto: "Respond to Unreasonable Customer Requests." Living up to the company's motto is so strongly ingrained in behavior that employees learn to relish the challenges that some customer requests pose. Usually, meeting customer demands in pleasing fashion entails little more than gracious compliance and a little extra personal attention. But occasionally it means paying a customer's parking ticket when in-store gift wrapping takes longer than normal or hand-delivering items purchased by phone to the airport for a customer with an emergency need.

At Nordstrom, each out-of-the-ordinary customer request is seen as an opportunity for a "heroic" act by an employee and a way to build the company's reputation for great service. Nordstrom encourages these acts by pro-

moting employees noted for outstanding service, keeping scrapbooks of "heroic" acts, and basing the compensation of salespeople mainly on commission (it is not unusual for good salespeople at Nordstrom to earn double what they would at other department store retailers).

For go-getters who truly enjoy retail selling and pleasing customers, Nordstrom is a great company to work for. But the culture weeds out those who can't meet Nordstrom's demanding standards and rewards those who are prepared to be what Nordstrom stands for.

Nordstrom starts new employees, even those with advanced degrees, out on the sales floor. Promotion is strictly from within, and when a new store is opened, its key people are recruited from other stores around the country to help perpetuate Nordstrom's culture and values and to make sure the new store is run the Nordstrom way.

Source: Based on information in Tracy Goss, Richard Pascale, and Anthony Athos, "Risking the Present for a Powerful Future," *Harvard Business Review* 71, no. 6 (November–December 1993), pp. 101–2 and Jeffrey Pheffer, "Producing Sustainable Competitive Advantage through the Effective Management of People," *Academy of Management Executive* 9, no. 1 (February 1995), pp. 59–60 and 65.

team responsible for developing trailblazing software. Illustration Capsule 39 describes the culture at Nordstrom's.

Where Does Corporate Culture Come From?

The taproot of corporate culture is the organization's beliefs and philosophy about how its affairs ought to be conducted—the reasons why it does things the way it does. A company's culture is manifested in the values and principles that management preaches and practices, in its ethical standards and official policies, in its stakeholder relationships (especially its dealings with employees, unions, stockholders, vendors, and the communities in which it operates), in its traditions, in its supervisory practices, in employees' attitudes and behavior, in the legends people repeat about happenings in the organization, in the peer pressures that exist, in the organization's politics, and in the "chemistry" and "vibrations" that permeate its work environment. All these forces, some of which operate quite subtly, combine to define an organization's culture.

Corporate culture refers to a company's values, beliefs, traditions, operating style, and internal work environment.

Beliefs and practices that become embedded in a company's culture can originate anywhere: from one influential individual, work group, department, or division, from the bottom of the organizational hierarchy or the top.[1] Very often, many components of the culture are associated with a founder or other early leaders who articulated them as a company philosophy or as a set of principles the organization should rigidly adhere to or as company policies. Sometimes, elements of the culture spring from the company's vision, its strategic intent, and core components of its strategy (like obsessive emphasis on low cost or technological leadership or first-rate quality). Over time, these cultural underpinnings take root, become embedded in how the

---

[1]John P. Kotter and James L. Heskett, *Corporate Culture and Performance* (New York: Free Press, 1992), p. 7.

company conducts its business, come to be shared by company managers and employees, and then persist as new employees are encouraged to embrace them. Fast-growing companies risk creating a culture by chance rather than by design if they rush to hire employees mainly for their technical skills and credentials and neglect to screen out candidates whose values, philosophies, and personalities aren't compatible with the organizational character, vision, and strategy that management is trying to cultivate.

A company's culture is a product of internal social forces; it is manifested in the values, behavioral norms, and ways of operating that prevail across the organization.

Once established, company cultures can be perpetuated in many ways: continuity of leadership, screening and selecting new group members according to how well their values and personalities fit in (as well as on the basis of talents and credentials), systematic indoctrination of new members in the culture's fundamentals, the efforts of senior group members to reiterate core values in daily conversations and pronouncements, the telling and retelling of company legends, regular ceremonies honoring members who display cultural ideals, and visibly rewarding those who follow cultural norms and penalizing those who don't.[2] However, even stable cultures aren't static. Crises and new challenges evolve into new ways of doing things. Arrival of new leaders and turnover of key members often spawn new or different values and practices that alter the culture. Diversification into new businesses, expansion into different geographical areas, rapid growth that adds new employees, and the exploding use of the Internet, company intranets, and electronic mail can all cause a culture to evolve. Indeed, one of the most important business phenomena of the late 1990s is the historic impact that widespread use of PCs and information technology is having on corporate cultures and on how a company's internal and external business is conducted.

Although it is common to speak about corporate culture in the singular, companies typically have multiple cultures (or subcultures).[3] Values, beliefs, and practices can vary by department, geographic location, division, or business unit. Global companies are highly multicultural. A company's subcultures can clash, or at least not mesh well, if recently acquired business units have not yet been assimilated or if different units operate in different countries or have varying managerial styles, business philosophies, and operating approaches. The human resources manager of a global pharmaceutical company who took on an assignment in the Far East discovered, to his surprise, that one of his biggest challenges was to persuade his company's managers in China, Korea, Malaysia, and Taiwan to accept promotions—their cultural values were such that they did not believe in competing with their peers for career rewards or personal gain, nor did they relish breaking ties to their local communities to assume cross-national responsibilities.[4] Many companies that have merged with or acquired foreign companies have to deal with language and custom-based cultural differences.

The Power of Culture

The beliefs, vision, objectives, and business approaches and practices underpinning a company's strategy may be compatible with its culture or they may not. When they are, the culture becomes a valuable ally in strategy implementation and execution.

---

[2]Ibid., pp. 7–8.

[3]Ibid., p. 5.

[4]John Alexander and Meena S. Wilson, "Leading across Cultures: Five Vital Capabilities," in *The Organization of the Future*, Frances Hesselbein, Marshall Goldsmith, and Richard Beckard, (San Francisco: Jossey-Bass, 1997), pp. 291–92.

When they are not, a company usually finds it difficult to implement the strategy successfully.[5]

A culture grounded in values, practices, and behavioral norms that match what is needed for good strategy execution helps energize people to do their jobs in a strategy-supportive manner. For example, a culture where frugality and thrift are values widely shared by organizational members is very conducive to successful execution of a low-cost leadership strategy. A culture where creativity, embracing change, and challenging the status quo are pervasive themes is conducive to successful execution of a product innovation and technological leadership strategy. A culture built around such principles as listening to customers, encouraging employees to take pride in their work, and giving employees a high degree of decision-making responsibility is conducive to successful execution of a strategy of delivering superior customer service. When a company's culture is out of sync with what is needed for strategic success, the culture has to be changed as rapidly as can be managed; the more entrenched the culture, the greater the difficulty of implementing new or different strategies. A sizable and prolonged strategy-culture conflict weakens and may even defeat managerial efforts to make the strategy work.

An organization's culture is an important contributor (or obstacle) to successful strategy execution.

Strong cultures promote good strategy execution when there's fit with the strategy and hurt execution when there's little fit.

A tight culture-strategy alignment acts in two ways to channel behavior and influence employees do their jobs in a strategy-supportive fashion:[6]

1. *A work environment where the culture matches well with the conditions for good strategy execution provides a system of informal rules and peer pressures regarding how to conduct business and how to go about doing one's job.* Strategy-supportive cultures shape the mood, temperament, and motivation of the workforce, positively affecting organizational energy, work habits and operating practices, the degree to which organizational units cooperate, and how customers are treated. Culturally approved behavior thrives, while culturally disapproved behavior gets squashed and often penalized. In a company where strategy and culture are misaligned, ingrained values and operating philosophies don't cultivate strategy-supportive ways of operating; often, the very kinds of behavior needed to execute strategy successfully run afoul of the culture and attract criticism rather than praise and reward.

A deeply rooted culture well matched to strategy is a powerful lever for successful strategy execution.

2. *A strong strategy-supportive culture nurtures and motivates people to do their jobs in ways conducive to effective strategy execution; it provides structure, standards, and a value system in which to operate; and it promotes strong employee identification with the company's vision, performance targets, and strategy.* All this makes employees feel genuinely better about their jobs and work environment and the merits of what the company is trying to accomplish. Employees are stimulated to take on the challenge of realizing the company's vision, do their jobs competently and with enthusiasm, and collaborate with others to execute the strategy.

This says something important about the task of leading strategy implementation: *Anything so fundamental as implementing a strategic plan involves moving the organization's culture into close alignment with the requirements for proficient strategy execution.* The optimal condition is a work environment that energizes the organization in a strategy-supportive fashion, promoting "can-do" attitudes and

---

[5]Ibid.
[6]Ibid., pp. 15–16.

acceptance of change where needed, enlisting and encouraging people to perform strategy-critical activities in superior fashion, and breeding needed organizational competencies and capabilities. As one observer noted:

> It has not been just strategy that led to big Japanese wins in the American auto market. It is a culture that enspirits workers to excel at fits and finishes, to produce moldings that match and doors that don't sag. It is a culture in which Toyota can use that most sophisticated of management tools, the suggestion box, and in two years increase the number of worker suggestions from under 10,000 to over 1 million with resultant savings of $250 million.[7]

Strong versus Weak Cultures

Company cultures vary widely in the degree to which they are embedded in company practices and behavioral norms. A company's culture can be weak and fragmented in the sense that many subcultures exist, few values and behavioral norms are widely shared, and there are few traditions. In weak or fragmented culture companies, there's little cohesion and glue across units from a business principles and work climate perspective—top executives don't espouse any business philosophy or extol use of particular operating practices. Because of a lack of common values and ingrained business approaches, organizational members typically have no deeply felt sense of identity with the company's vision and strategy; instead, many employees view the company as a place to work and their job as a way to make a living. While they may have some bonds with and loyalty toward their department, their colleagues, their union, or their boss, the weak company culture breeds no strong employee allegiance to what the company stands for and no sense of urgency about pushing strategy execution along. As a consequence, weak cultures provide no strategy-implementing assistance.

Strong Culture Companies   On the other hand, a company's culture can be strong and cohesive in the sense that the company conducts its business according to a clear and explicit set of principles and values, that management devotes considerable time to communicating these principles and values and explaining how they relate to its business environment, and that the values are shared widely across the company—by senior executives and rank-and-file employees alike.[8] Strong culture companies typically have creeds or values statements, and executives regularly stress the importance of using these values and principles as the basis for decisions and actions taken throughout the organization. In strong culture companies values and behavioral norms are so deeply rooted that they don't change much when a new CEO takes over—although they can erode over time if the CEO ceases to nurture them.

In a strong culture company, values and behavioral norms are like crabgrass: deeply rooted and difficult to weed out.

Three factors contribute to the development of strong cultures: (1) a founder or strong leader who establishes values, principles, and practices that are consistent and sensible in light of customer needs, competitive conditions, and strategic requirements; (2) a sincere, long-standing company commitment to operating the business according to these established traditions; and (3) a genuine concern for the well-being of the organization's three biggest constituencies—customers, employees, and shareholders. Continuity of leadership, small group size, stable group membership,

---

[7]Robert H. Waterman, Jr., "The Seven Elements of Strategic Fit," *Journal of Business Strategy* 2, no. 3 (Winter 1982), p. 70.

[8]Terrence E. Deal and Allen A. Kennedy, *Corporate Cultures* (Reading, Mass.: Addison-Wesley, 1982), p. 22.

geographic concentration, and considerable organizational success all contribute to the emergence of a strong culture.[9]

During the time a strong culture is being implanted, there's nearly always a good strategy-culture fit (which partially accounts for the organization's success). Mismatches between strategy and culture in a strong culture company tend to occur when a company's environment undergoes rapid-fire change, prompting a drastic strategy revision that clashes with the entrenched culture. In such cases, a major culture-changing effort has to be launched. Both IBM and Apple Computer have been going through wrenching culture changes to adapt to the new computer industry environment now driven by the so-called Wintel standard—Microsoft (with its Windows operating systems for PCs and its Windows-based PC software programs) and Intel (with its successive generations of faster microprocessors for PCs). IBM's bureaucracy and mainframe culture clashed with the shift to a PC-dominated world. Apple's culture clash stemmed from strong company sentiment to continue on with internally developed Macintosh technology (incompatible with all other brands of computers) despite growing preferences for Wintel-compatible equipment and software.

> *A strong culture is a valuable asset when it matches the requirements for good strategy execution and a dreaded liability when it doesn't.*

Low-Performance or Unhealthy Cultures

A number of unhealthy cultural characteristics can undermine a company's business performance.[10] One is a politicized internal environment that allows influential managers to operate their fiefdoms autonomously and resist needed change. In politically dominated cultures, many issues get resolved on the basis of turf, vocal support or opposition by powerful executives, personal lobbying by a key executive, and coalitions among individuals or departments with vested interests in a particular outcome. What's best for the company plays second fiddle to personal aggrandizement.

A second unhealthy cultural trait, one that can plague companies suddenly confronted with fast-changing business conditions, is hostility to change and to people who champion new ways of doing things. Executives who don't value managers or employees with initiative or new ideas dampen experimentation and efforts to improve the status quo. Avoiding risks and not screwing up become more important to a person's career advancement than entrepreneurial successes and innovative accomplishments. This trait is most often found in companies with multilayered management bureaucracies that have enjoyed considerable market success in years past but whose business environments have been hit with accelerating change. General Motors, IBM, Sears, and Eastman Kodak are classic examples; all four gradually became burdened by a stifling bureaucracy that rejected innovation. Now, they are struggling to reinvent the cultural approaches that caused them to succeed in the first place.

A third unhealthy characteristic is promoting managers who understand complex organization structures, problem solving, budgets, controls, and how to handle administrative detail better than they understand vision, strategies, competitive capabilities, inspiration, and culture building. While the former are adept at organizational maneuvering, if they ascend to senior executive positions, the company can find itself short of the entrepreneurial skills and leadership needed to introduce new strategies, reallocate resources, build new competitive capabilities, and fashion a new culture—a condition that ultimately erodes long-term performance.

---

[9]Vijay Sathe, *Culture and Related Corporate Realities* (Homewood, Ill.: Richard D. Irwin, 1985).
[10]Kotter and Heskett, *Corporate Culture and Performance*, chapter 6.

A fourth characteristic of low-performance cultures is an aversion to looking outside the company for superior practices and approaches. Sometimes a company enjoys such great market success and reigns as an industry leader for so long that its management becomes inbred and arrogant. It believes it has all the answers or can develop them on its own. Insular thinking, inward-looking solutions, and a must-be-invented-here syndrome often precede a decline in company performance. Kotter and Heskett cite Avon, BankAmerica, Citicorp, Coors, Ford, General Motors, Kmart, Kroger, Sears, Texaco, and Xerox as examples of companies that had low-performance cultures during the late 1970s and early 1980s.[11]

Changing problem cultures is very difficult because of the heavy anchor of deeply held values, habits, and the emotional clinging of people to the old and familiar. Sometimes executives succeed in changing the values and behaviors of small groups of managers and even whole departments or divisions, only to find the changes eroded over time by the actions of the rest of the organization. What is communicated, praised, supported, and penalized by the entrenched majority undermines the new emergent culture and halts its progress. Executives can revamp formal organization charts, announce new strategies, bring in managers from the outside, introduce new technologies, and open new plants, yet fail to change embedded cultural traits and behaviors because of skepticism about the new directions and covert resistance to them.

Once a culture is established, it is difficult to change.

Adaptive Cultures

In fast-changing business environments, the capacity to introduce new strategies and organizational practices is a necessity if a company is to perform well over long periods of time.[12] Strategic agility and fast organizational response to new conditions require a culture that quickly accepts and supports company efforts to adapt to environmental change rather than a culture that has to be coaxed and cajoled to change.

In adaptive cultures, members share a feeling of confidence that the organization can deal with whatever threats and opportunities come down the pike; they are receptive to risk-taking, experimentation, innovation, and changing strategies and practices whenever necessary to satisfy the legitimate interests of stakeholders—customers, employees, shareowners, suppliers, and the communities where the company operates. Hence, members willingly embrace a proactive approach to identifying issues, evaluating the implications and options, and implementing workable solutions—there's a spirit of doing what's necessary to ensure long-term organizational success *provided core values and business principles are upheld in the process.* Entrepreneurship is encouraged and rewarded. Managers habitually fund product development, evaluate new ideas openly, and take prudent risks to create new business positions. Strategies and traditional operating practices are modified as needed to adjust to or take advantage of changes in the business environment. The leaders of adaptive cultures are adept at changing the right things in the right ways, not changing for the sake of change and not compromising core values or business principles. Adaptive cultures are supportive of managers and employees at all ranks who propose or help initiate useful change; indeed, executives consciously seek, train, and promote individuals who display these leadership traits.

Adaptive cultures are a strategy implementer's best ally.

One outstanding trait of adaptive cultures is that top management, while orchestrating responses to changing conditions, demonstrates genuine care for the well-being of

---

[11]Ibid., p. 68.

[12]This section draws heavily from Kotter and Heskett, *Corporate Culture and Performance*, chapter 4.

all key constituencies—customers, employees, stockholders, major suppliers, and the communities where the company operates—and tries to satisfy all their legitimate interests simultaneously. No group is ignored, and fairness to all constituencies is a decision-making principle—a commitment often described as "doing the right thing."[13] Pleasing customers and protecting, if not enhancing, the company's long-term well-being is seen as the best way of looking out for the interests of employees, stockholders, suppliers, and communities where the company operates. Management concern for the well-being of employees is a big factor in gaining employee support for change—employees understand that changes in their job assignments are part of the process of adapting to new conditions and that their job security will not be threatened in the process of adapting to change, unless the company's business unexpectedly reverses direction. In cases where workforce downsizing becomes necessary, management concern for employees dictates that separation be handled in a humane fashion. Management efforts to make the process of adapting to change fair, keeping adverse impacts to a minimum, breeds acceptance of and support for change among all stakeholders.

In less-adaptive cultures where resistance to change is the norm, managers avoid risk-taking and prefer following to leading when it comes to technological change and new product innovation.[14] They believe in moving cautiously and conservatively, endeavoring not to make "mistakes" and making sure they protect or advance their own careers, the interests of their immediate work groups, or their pet projects.

Creating the Fit between Strategy and Culture

It is the *strategy maker's* responsibility to select a strategy compatible with the "sacred" or unchangeable parts of prevailing corporate culture. It is the *strategy implementer's* task, once strategy is chosen, to change whatever facets of the corporate culture hinder effective execution.

Changing a company's culture and aligning it with strategy are among the toughest management tasks—easier to talk about than do. The first step is to diagnose which facets of the present culture are strategy-supportive and which are not. Then, managers have to talk openly and forthrightly to all concerned about those aspects of the culture that have to be changed. The talk has to be followed swiftly by visible actions to modify the culture—actions that everyone will understand are intended to establish a new culture more in tune with the strategy.

Symbolic Actions and Substantive Actions   Managerial actions to tighten the culture-strategy fit need to be both symbolic and substantive. Symbolic actions are valuable for the signals they send about the kinds of behavior and performance strategy implementers wish to encourage. The most important symbolic actions are those that top executives take to serve as role models—leading cost reduction efforts by curtailing executive perks; emphasizing the importance of responding to customers' needs by requiring all officers and executives to spend a significant portion of each week talking with customers and understanding their requirements; and assuming a high profile in altering policies and practices that hinder the new strategy. Another category of symbolic actions includes the events to designate and honor people whose actions and performance exemplify what is called for in the new culture. Many universities give outstanding teacher awards each year to symbolize their esteem for instructors with exceptional classroom talents. Numerous businesses have

[13]Ibid., p. 52.
[14]Ibid., p. 50.

employee-of-the-month awards. The military has a long-standing custom of awarding ribbons and medals for exemplary actions. Mary Kay Cosmetics awards an array of prizes—from ribbons to pink automobiles—to its beauty consultants for reaching various sales plateaus.

The best companies and the best executives expertly use symbols, role models, ceremonial occasions, and group gatherings to tighten the strategy-culture fit. Low-cost leaders like Wal-Mart and Nucor are renowned for their spartan facilities, executive frugality, intolerance of waste, and zealous control of costs.

Awards ceremonies, role models, and symbols are a fundamental part of a strategy implementer's culture-shaping effort.

Executives sensitive to their role in promoting strategy-culture fits make a habit of appearing at ceremonial functions to praise individuals and groups that "get with the program." They honor individuals who exhibit cultural norms and reward those who achieve strategic milestones. They participate in employee training programs to stress strategic priorities, values, ethical principles, and cultural norms. Every group gathering is seen as an opportunity to implant values, praise good deeds, reinforce cultural norms, and promote changes that assist strategy implementation. Sensitive executives make sure that organizational members will construe current decisions and policy changes as consistent with and supportive of the company's new strategic direction.[15]

In addition to being out front personally and symbolically, leading the push for new behaviors and communicating the reasons for new approaches, strategy-implementers have to convince all those concerned that the effort is more than cosmetic. Talk and plans have to be complemented by substantive actions and real movement. The actions taken have to be credible, highly visible, and indicative of management's commitment to new strategic initiatives and the associated cultural changes. There are several ways to accomplish this. One is to engineer some quick successes that highlight the benefits of strategy-culture changes, thus making enthusiasm for the changes contagious. However, instant results are usually not as important as having the will and patience to create a solid, competent team committed to pursuing the strategy. The strongest signs that management is truly committed to creating a new culture include: replacing old-culture managers with "new breed" managers, changing long-standing policies and operating practices that are dysfunctional or that impede new initiatives, undertaking major reorganizational moves that bring structure into better alignment with strategy, tying compensation incentives directly to the new measures of strategic performance, and shifting substantial resources from old-strategy projects and programs to new-strategy projects and programs.

At the same time, chief strategy-implementers must be careful to *lead by example*. For instance, if the organization's strategy involves a drive to become the industry's

Senior executives must personally lead efforts to align culture with strategy.

low-cost producer, senior managers must display frugality in their own actions and decisions: Inexpensive decorations in the executive suite, conservative expense accounts and entertainment allowances, a lean staff in the corporate office, scrutiny of budget requests, and so on. The CEO of SAS Airlines, Jan Carlzon, symbolically reinforced the primacy of quality service for business customers by flying coach instead of first class and by giving up his seat to waitlisted travelers.[16]

[15]Judy D. Olian and Sara L. Rynes, "Making Total Quality Work: Aligning Organizational Processes, Performance Measures, and Stakeholders," *Human Resource Management* 30, no. 3 (Fall 1991), p. 324.
[16]Ibid.

Implanting the needed culture-building values and behavior depends on a sincere, sustained commitment by the chief executive coupled with persistence in reinforcing the culture at every opportunity through both word and deed. Neither charisma nor personal magnetism are essential. However, personally talking to many groups about the reasons for change *is* essential; cultural changes are seldom accomplished successfully from an office. Moreover, creating and sustaining a strategy-supportive culture is a job for the whole management team. Major cultural change requires many initiatives from many people. Senior officers, department heads, and middle managers have to reiterate values, "walk the talk," and translate the desired cultural norms and behavior into everyday practice. In addition, strategy implementers must enlist the support of firstline supervisors and employee opinion leaders, convincing them of the merits of practicing and enforcing cultural norms at the lowest levels in the organization. Until a big majority of employees joins the new culture and shares a commitment to its basic values and norms, there's considerably more work to be done in both instilling the culture and tightening the culture-strategy fit.

The task of making culture supportive of strategy is not a short-term exercise. It takes time for a new culture to emerge and prevail; it's unrealistic to expect an overnight transformation. The bigger the organization and the greater the cultural shift needed to produce a culture-strategy fit, the longer it takes. In large companies, changing the corporate culture in significant ways can take three to five years at minimum. In fact, it is usually tougher to reshape a deeply ingrained culture that is not strategy-supportive than it is to instill a strategy-supportive culture from scratch in a brand-new organization.

Building Ethical Standards and Values into the Culture

A strong corporate culture founded on ethical business principles and moral values is a vital force behind continued strategic success. Many executives are convinced that a company must care about how it does business; otherwise a company's reputation, and ultimately its performance, is put at risk. Corporate ethics and values programs are not window dressing; they are undertaken to create an environment of strongly held values and convictions and to make ethical conduct a way of life. Morally upstanding values and high ethical standards nurture the corporate culture in a very positive way—they connote integrity, "doing the right thing," and genuine concern for stakeholders.

An ethical corporate culture has a positive impact on a company's long-term strategic success; an unethical culture can undermine it.

Companies establish values and ethical standards in a number of ways.[17] Companies steeped in tradition with a rich folklore to draw on rely on word-of-mouth indoctrination and the power of tradition to instill values and enforce ethical conduct. But many companies today set forth their values and codes of ethics in written documents. Table 11–1 indicates the kinds of topics such statements cover. Written statements have the advantage of explicitly stating what the company intends and expects, and they serve as benchmarks for judging both company policies and actions and individual conduct. They put a stake in the ground and define the company's position. Value statements serve as a cornerstone for culture building; a code of ethics serves as a cornerstone for developing a corporate conscience.[18] Illustration Capsule 40

---

[17]The Business Roundtable, *Corporate Ethics: A Prime Asset*, February 1988, pp. 4–10.

[18]For a discussion of the strategic benefits of formal statements of corporate values, see John Humble, David Jackson, and Alan Thomson, "The Strategic Power of Corporate Values," *Long Range Planning* 27, no. 6 (December 1994), pp. 28–42. For a study of the status of formal codes of ethics in large U. S. corporations,

TABLE 11–1   Topics Generally Covered in Value Statements and Codes of Ethics

Topics Covered in Values Statements	Topics Covered in Codes of Ethics
• Importance of customers and customer service • Commitment to quality • Commitment to innovation • Respect for the individual employee and the duty the company has to employees • Importance of honesty, integrity, and ethical standards • Duty to stockholders • Duty to suppliers • Corporate citizenship • Importance of protecting the environment	• Honesty and observance of the law • Conflicts of interest • Fairness in selling and marketing practices • Using inside information and securities trading • Supplier relationships and purchasing practices • Payments to obtain business/Foreign Corrupt Practices Act • Acquiring and using information about others • Political activities • Use of company assets, resources, and property • Protection of proprietary information • Pricing, contracting, and billing

presents the Johnson & Johnson Credo, the most publicized and celebrated code of ethics and values among U.S. companies. J&J's CEO calls the credo "the unifying force for our corporation." Illustration Capsule 41 presents the pledge that Bristol-Myers Squibb makes to all of its stakeholders.

Values and ethical standards must not only be explicitly stated but they must also be ingrained into the corporate culture.

Once values and ethical standards have been formally set forth, they must be ingrained in the company's policies, practices, and actual conduct. Implementing the values and code of ethics entails several actions:

- Incorporating the statement of values and the code of ethics into employee training and educational programs.
- Explicit attention to values and ethics in recruiting and hiring to screen out applicants who lack compatible character traits.
- Communication of the values and ethics code to all employees and explaining compliance procedures.
- Management involvement and oversight, from the CEO down to firstline supervisors.
- Strong endorsements by the CEO.
- Word-of-mouth indoctrination.

In the case of codes of ethics, special attention must be given to sections of the company that are particularly sensitive and vulnerable—purchasing, sales, and political lobbying.[19] Employees who deal with external parties are in ethically sensitive positions and often are drawn into compromising situations. Procedures for enforcing ethical standards and handling potential violations have to be developed.

---

see Patrick E. Murphy, "Corporate Ethics Statements: Current Status and Future Prospects," *Journal of Business Ethics* 14 (1995), pp. 727–40.

[19]Ibid., p. 7.

ILLUSTRATION CAPSULE 40   The Johnson & Johnson Credo

- We believe our first responsibility is to the doctors, nurses, and patients, to mothers and all others who use our products and services.
- In meeting their needs everything we do must be of high quality.
- We must constantly strive to reduce our costs in order to maintain reasonable prices.
- Customers' orders must be serviced promptly and accurately.
- Our suppliers and distributors must have an opportunity to make a fair profit.
- We are responsible to our employees, the men and women who work with us throughout the world.
- Everyone must be considered as an individual.
- We must respect their dignity and recognize their merit.
- They must have a sense of security in their jobs.
- Compensation must be fair and adequate, and working conditions clean, orderly, and safe.
- Employees must feel free to make suggestions and complaints.
- There must be equal opportunity for employment, development, and advancement for those qualified.

- We must provide competent management, and their actions must be just and ethical.
- We are responsible to the communities in which we live and work and to the world community as well.
- We must be good citizens—support good works and charities and bear our fair share of taxes.
- We must encourage civic improvements and better health and education.
- We must maintain in good order the property we are privileged to use, protecting the environment and natural resources.
- Our final responsibility is to our stockholders.
- Business must make a sound profit.
- We must experiment with new ideas.
- Research must be carried on, innovative programs developed, and mistakes paid for.
- New equipment must be purchased, new facilities provided, and new products launched.
- Reserves must be created to provide for adverse times.
- When we operate according to these principles, the stockholders should realize a fair return.

Source: 1982 Annual Report.

The compliance effort must permeate the company, extending into every organizational unit. The attitudes, character, and work history of prospective employees must be combined. Every employee must receive adequate training. Line managers at all levels must give serious and continuous attention to the task of explaining how the values and ethical code apply in their areas. In addition, they must insist that company values and ethical standards become a way of life. In general, instilling values and insisting on ethical conduct must be looked on as a continuous culture-building, culture-nurturing exercise. Whether the effort succeeds or fails depends largely on how well corporate values and ethical standards are visibly integrated into company policies, managerial practices, and actions at all levels.

Building a Spirit of High Performance into the Culture

A results-oriented culture that inspires people to do their best is conducive to superior strategy execution.

An ability to instill strong individual commitment to strategic success and to create an atmosphere in which there is constructive pressure to perform is one of the most valuable strategy-implementing skills. When an organization performs consistently at or near peak capability, the outcome is not only more success but also a culture permeated with a spirit of high performance. Such a spirit of performance should not be confused with whether employees are "happy" or "satisfied" or whether they "get along well together." An organization with a spirit of high performance emphasizes achievement and excellence. Its culture is results-

---

ILLUSTRATION CAPSULE 41   The Bristol-Myers Squibb Pledge

To those who use our products . . .

We affirm Bristol-Myers Squibb's commitment to the highest standards of excellence, safety, and reliability in everything we make. We pledge to offer products of the highest quality and to work diligently to keep improving them.

To our employees and those who may join us . . .

We pledge personal respect, fair compensation, and equal treatment. We acknowledge our obligation to provide able and humane leadership throughout the organization, within a clean and safe working environment. To all who qualify for advancement, we will make every effort to provide opportunity.

To our suppliers and customers . . .

We pledge an open door, courteous, efficient, and ethical dealing, and appreciation for their right to a fair profit.

To our shareholders . . .

We pledge a companywide dedication to continued profitable growth, sustained by strong finances, a high level of research and development, and facilities second to none.

To the communities where we have plants and offices . . .

We pledge conscientious citizenship, a helping hand for worthwhile causes, and constructive action in support of civic and environmental progress.

To the countries where we do business . . .

We pledge ourselves to be a good citizen and to show full consideration for the rights of others while reserving the right to stand up for our own.

Above all, to the world we live in . . .

We pledge Bristol-Myers Squibb to policies and practices which fully embody the responsibility, integrity, and decency required of free enterprise if it is to merit and maintain the confidence of our society.

Source: 1990 Annual Report.

---

oriented, and its management pursues policies and practices that inspire people to do their best.[20]

Companies with a spirit of high performance typically are intensely people-oriented, and they reinforce their concern for individual employees on every conceivable occasion in every conceivable way. They treat employees with dignity and respect, train each employee thoroughly, encourage employees to use their own initiative and creativity in performing their work, set reasonable and clear performance expectations, use the full range of rewards and punishment to enforce high-performance standards, hold managers at every level responsible for developing the people who report to them, and grant employees enough autonomy to stand out, excel, and contribute. To create a results-oriented culture, a company must make champions out of the people who turn in winning performances:[21]

- At Boeing, General Electric, and 3M Corporation, top executives make a point of honoring individuals who believe so strongly in their ideas that they take it on themselves to hurdle the bureaucracy, maneuver their projects through the system, and turn them into improved services, new products, or even new businesses. In these companies, "product champions" are given high visibility, room to push their ideas, and strong executive support.

---

[20]For a more in-depth discussion of what it takes to create a climate and culture that nurtures success, see Benjamin Schneider, Sarah K. Gunnarson, and Kathryn Niles-Jolly, "Creating the Climate and Culture of Success," *Organizational Dynamics* (Summer 1994), pp. 17–29.

[21]Thomas J. Peters and Robert H. Waterman, Jr., *In Search of Excellence* (New York: Harper & Row, 1982), pp. xviii, 240, and 269, and Thomas J. Peters and Nancy Austin, *A Passion for Excellence* (New York: Random House, 1985), pp. 304–7.

Champions whose ideas prove out are usually handsomely rewarded; those whose ideas don't pan out still have secure jobs and are given chances to try again.

- Some companies upgrade the importance and status of individual employees by referring to them as Cast Members (Disney), crew members (McDonald's), or associates (Wal-Mart and J. C. Penney). Companies like Mary Kay Cosmetics, Tupperware, and McDonald's actively seek out reasons and opportunities to give pins, buttons, badges, and medals for good showings by average performers—the idea being to express appreciation and give a motivational boost to people who stand out doing "ordinary" jobs.

- McDonald's has a contest to determine the best hamburger cooker in its entire chain. It begins with a competition to determine the best hamburger cooker in each store. Store winners go on to compete in regional championships, and regional winners go on to the "All-American" contest. The winners get trophies and an All-American patch to wear on their shirts.

- Milliken & Co. holds Corporate Sharing Rallies once every three months; teams come from all over the company to swap success stories and ideas. A hundred or more teams make five-minute presentations over a two-day period. Each rally has a major theme—quality, cost reduction, and so on. No criticisms and negatives are allowed, and there is no such thing as a big idea or a small one. Quantitative measures of success are used to gauge improvement. All those present vote on the best presentation and several ascending grades of awards are handed out. Everyone, however, receives a framed certificate for participating.

What makes a spirit of high performance come alive is a complex network of practices, words, symbols, styles, values, and policies pulling together that produces extraordinary results with ordinary people. The drivers of the system are a belief in the worth of the individual, strong company commitment to job security and promotion from within, managerial practices that encourage employees to exercise individual initiative and creativity in doing their jobs, and pride in doing the "itty-bitty, teeny-tiny things" right.[22] A company that treats its employees well generally benefits from increased teamwork, higher morale, and greater employee loyalty.

While emphasizing a spirit of high performance nearly always accentuates the positive, there are negative reinforcers too. Managers whose units consistently perform poorly have to be removed. Aside from the organizational benefits, weak-performing managers should be reassigned for their own good—people who find themselves in a job they cannot handle are usually frustrated, anxiety-ridden, harassed, and unhappy.[23] Moreover, subordinates have a right to be managed with competence, dedication, and achievement. Unless their boss performs well, they themselves cannot perform well. In addition, weak-performing workers and people who reject the cultural emphasis on dedication and high performance have to be weeded out. Recruitment practices need to aim at hiring only motivated, ambitious applicants whose attitudes and work habits mesh well with a results-oriented corporate culture.

[22]Jeffrey Pheffer, "Producing Sustainable Competitive Advantage through the Effective Management of People," *Academy of Management Executive* 9, no.1 (February 1995), pp. 55–69.

[23]Peter Drucker, *Management: Tasks, Responsibilities, Practices* (New York: Harper & Row, 1974), p. 457.

EXERTING STRATEGIC LEADERSHIP

The litany of good strategic management is simple enough: formulate a sound strategic plan, implement it, execute it to the fullest, win! But it's easier said than done. Exerting take-charge leadership, being a "spark plug," ramrodding things through, and getting things done by coaching others to do them are difficult tasks.[24] Moreover, a strategy manager has many different leadership roles to play: visionary, chief entrepreneur and strategist, chief administrator and strategy implementer, culture builder, resource acquirer and allocator, capabilities builder, process integrator, coach, crisis solver, taskmaster, spokesperson, negotiator, motivator, arbitrator, consensus builder, policy maker, policy enforcer, mentor, and head cheerleader.[25] Sometimes it is useful to be authoritarian and hard-nosed; sometimes it is best to be a perceptive listener and a compromising decision maker; sometimes a strongly participative, collegial approach works best; and sometimes being a coach and advisor is the proper role. Many occasions call for a highly visible role and extensive time commitments, while others entail a brief ceremonial performance with the details delegated to subordinates.

For the most part, major change efforts have to be vision driven and led from the top. Leading change has to start with diagnosing the situation and then deciding which way to handle it. Six leadership roles dominate the strategy implementer's action agenda:

1. Staying on top of what is happening and how well things are going.
2. Promoting a culture in which the organization is "energized" to accomplish strategy and perform at a high level.
3. Keeping the organization responsive to changing conditions, alert for new opportunities, bubbling with innovative ideas, and ahead of rivals in developing competitively valuable competencies and capabilities.
4. Building consensus, containing "power struggles," and dealing with the politics of crafting and implementing strategy.
5. Enforcing ethical standards.
6. Pushing corrective actions to improve strategy execution and overall organization performance.

Staying on Top of How Well Things Are Going

To stay on top of how well the implementation process is going, a manager needs to develop a broad network of contacts and sources of information, both formal and informal. The regular channels include talking with key subordinates, presentations and meetings, reviews of the latest operating results, talking to customers, watching the competitive reactions of rival firms, tapping into the grapevine, listening to rank-

---

[24]For an excellent survey of the problems and pitfalls in making the transition to a new strategy and to fundamentally new ways of doing business, see John P. Kotter, "Leading Change: Why Transformation Efforts Fail," *Harvard Business Review* 73, no. 2 (March–April 1995), pp. 59–67. See, also, Thomas M. Hout and John C. Carter, "Getting It Done: New Roles for Senior Executives," *Harvard Business Review* 73 no. 6 (November–December 1995), pp. 133–45 and Sumantra Ghoshal and Christopher A. Bartlett, "Changing the Role of Top Management: Beyond Structure to Processes," *Harvard Business Review* 73 no. 1 (January–February 1995), pp. 86–96.

[25]For a very insightful and revealing report on how one CEO leads the organizational change process, see Noel Tichy and Ram Charan, "The CEO as Coach: An Interview with Allied Signal's Lawrence A. Bossidy," *Harvard Business Review* 73, no. 2 (March–April 1995), pp. 68–78.

and-file employees, and observing the situation firsthand. However, some information is more trustworthy than the rest, and the views and perspectives offered by different people can vary widely. Presentations and briefings by subordinates may represent "the truth but not the whole truth." Bad news or problems may be minimized or in some cases not reported at all as subordinates delay conveying failures and problems in hopes that more time will give them room to turn things around. Hence, strategy managers have to make sure that they have accurate information and a "feel" for the existing situation. One way this is done is by regular visits "to the field" and talking with many different people at many different levels. The technique of "managing by walking around" (MBWA) is practiced in a variety of styles:[26]

> *MBWA is one of the techniques effective leaders use to stay informed on how well strategy implementation and execution is proceeding.*

- At Hewlett-Packard, there are weekly beer busts in each division, attended by both executives and employees, to create a regular opportunity to keep in touch. Tidbits of information flow freely between down-the-line employees and executives—facilitated in part because "the HP Way" is for people at all ranks to be addressed by their first names. Bill Hewlett, one of HP's cofounders, had a companywide reputation for getting out of his office and "wandering around" the plant greeting people, listening to what was on their minds, and asking questions. He found this so valuable that he made MBWA a standard practice for all HP managers.

- McDonald's founder Ray Kroc regularly visited store units and did his own personal inspection on Q.S.C.&V. (Quality, Service, Cleanliness, and Value)—the themes he preached regularly. There are stories of his pulling into a unit's parking lot, seeing litter lying on the pavement, getting out of his limousine to pick it up himself, and then lecturing the store staff at length on the subject of cleanliness.

- The CEO of a small manufacturing company spends much of his time riding around the factory in a golf cart, waving to and joking with workers, listening to them, and calling all 2,000 employees by their first names. In addition, he spends a lot of time with union officials, inviting them to meetings and keeping them well informed about what is going on.

- Wal-Mart executives have had a long-standing practice of spending two to three days every week visiting Wal-Mart's stores and talking with store managers and employees. Sam Walton, Wal-Mart's founder, insisted, "The key is to get out into the store and listen to what the associates have to say. Our best ideas come from clerks and stockboys."

- Jack Welch, CEO of General Electric, not only spends several days each month personally visiting GE operations and talking with major customers but also arranges his schedule so that he can spend time talking with virtually every class of GE managers participating in courses at the company's famed leadership development center at GE's Crotonville, New York, headquarters. As Welch put it, "I'm here every day, or out into a factory, smelling it, feeling it, touching it, challenging the people."[27]

---

[26]Peters and Waterman, *In Search of Excellence,* pp. xx, 15, 120–23, 191, 242–43, 246–47, 287–90. For an extensive discussion of the benefits of MBWA, see Peters and Austin, *A Passion for Excellence*, chapters 2, 3, and 19.

[27]As quoted in Ann M. Morrison, "Trying to Bring GE to Life," *Fortune*, January 25, 1982, p. 52.

- Some activist CEOs make a point of holding key meetings out in the field—at the premises of a major customer or at the facility of a business unit with a troublesome problem—to get their managers out of their comfort zones and create enough of a shared framework for constructive dialogue, disagreement and open debate, and collective solution.

Most managers attach great importance to spending time in the field, observing the situation firsthand and talking informally to many different people at different organizational levels. They believe it is essential to have a "feel" for situations, gathering their own firsthand information and not just relying on information gathered or reported by others. Successful executives are aware of the isolation of spending too much time in their offices or in meetings, the dangers of surrounding themselves with people who are not likely to offer criticism and different perspectives, and the risk of getting too much of their information secondhand, screened and filtered, and sometimes dated. As a Hewlett-Packard official expresses it in the company publication *The HP Way*:

> Once a division or department has developed a plan of its own—a set of working objectives—it's important for managers and supervisors to keep it in operating condition. This is where observation, measurement, feedback, and guidance come in. It's our "management by wandering around." That's how you find out whether you're on track and heading at the right speed and in the right direction. If you don't constantly monitor how people are operating, not only will they tend to wander off track but also they will begin to believe you weren't serious about the plan in the first place. It has the extra benefit of getting you off your chair and moving around your area. By wandering around, I literally mean moving around and talking to people. It's all done on a very informal and spontaneous basis, but it's important in the course of time to cover the whole territory. You start out by being accessible and approachable, but the main thing is to realize you're there to listen. The second reason for MBWA is that it is vital to keep people informed about what's going on in the company, especially those things that are important to them. The third reason for doing this is because it is just plain fun.

Such contacts give the manager a feel for how things are progressing, and they provide opportunity to speak with encouragement, lift spirits, shift attention from the old to the new priorities, create some excitement, and project an atmosphere of informality and fun—all of which drive implementation forward in positive fashion and intensify the organizational energy behind strategy execution.

Fostering a Strategy-Supportive Climate and Culture

Strategy-implementers have to be out front in promoting a strategy-supportive organizational climate and culture. When major strategic changes are being implemented, a manager's time is best spent _personally leading the changes_ and promoting needed cultural adjustments. Gradual progress is often not enough. Conservative incrementalism seldom leads to major cultural adaptations; more usually, gradualism is defeated by the stubbornness of entrenched cultures and the ability of vested interests to thwart or minimize the impact of piecemeal change. Only with bold leadership and concerted action on many fronts can a company succeed in tackling so large and difficult a task as major cultural change. When only strategic fine-tuning is being implemented, it takes less time and effort to bring values and culture into alignment with strategy, but there is still a lead role for the manager to play in pushing ahead and prodding for continuous improvements.

Successful culture changes have to be personally led by top management; it's a task that can't be delegated to others.

The single most visible factor that distinguishes successful culture-change efforts from failed attempts is competent leadership at the top. Effective management action to match culture and strategy has several attributes:[28]

- A stakeholders-are-king philosophy that links the need to change to the need to serve the long-term best interests of all key constituencies.

- An openness to new ideas.

- Challenging the status quo with very basic questions: Are we giving customers what they really need and want? How can we be more competitive on cost? Why can't design-to-market cycle time be halved? What new competitive capabilities and resource strengths do we need? How can we grow the company instead of downsizing it? Where will the company be five years from now if it sticks with just its present business?

- Creating events where everyone in management is forced to listen to angry customers, dissatisfied stockholders, and alienated employees to keep management informed and to help them realistically assess the organization's strengths and weaknesses.

- Persuading individuals and groups to commit themselves to the new direction and energizing them to make it happen despite the obstacles.

- Repeating the new messages again and again, explaining the rationale for change, and convincing skeptics that all is not well and that fundamental changes in culture and operating practices are essential to the organization's long term well-being.

- Recognizing and generously rewarding those who exhibit new cultural norms and who lead successful change efforts—this helps expand the coalition for change.

Great power is needed to force major cultural change—to overcome the springback resistance of entrenched cultures—and great power normally resides only at the top. Moreover, the interdependence of values, strategies, practices, and behaviors inside organizations makes it difficult to change anything fundamental without simultaneous wider-scale changes. Usually the people with the power to effect change of that scope are those at the top.

Only top management has the power and organizational influence to bring about major cultural change.

Both words and deeds play a part in leading cultural change. Words inspire people, infuse spirit and drive, define strategy-supportive cultural norms and values, make clear the reasons for strategic and organizational change, legitimize new viewpoints and new priorities, urge and reinforce commitment, and arouse confidence in the new strategy. Deeds add credibility to the words, create strategy-supportive symbols, set examples, give meaning and content to the language, and teach the organization what sort of behavior is needed and expected.

Highly visible symbols and imagery are needed to complement actions. One General Motors manager explained how symbolism and managerial style accounted for the striking difference in performance between two large plants:[29]

> At the poorly performing plant, the plant manager probably ventured out on the floor once a week, always in a suit. His comments were distant and perfunctory. At South Gate, the better plant, the plant manager was on the floor all the time. He wore a baseball cap and a UAW jacket. By the way, whose plant do you think was spotless? Whose looked like a junkyard?

---

[28]Ibid., pp. 84, 144, and 148.

[29]As quoted in Peters and Waterman, *In Search of Excellence*, p. 262.

As a rule, the greater the degree of strategic change being implemented and the greater the shift in cultural norms needed to accommodate a new strategy, the more visible and clear the strategy implementer's words and deeds need to be. Moreover, the actions and images, both substantive and symbolic, have to be hammered out regularly, not just restricted to ceremonial speeches and special occasions. In such instances maintaining a high profile and "managing by walking around" are especially useful.

What the strategy leader says and does plants the seeds of cultural change and has a significant bearing on down-the-line strategy implementation and execution.

In global companies, leaders have to learn how to function effectively with diversity in cultures and behavioral norms and with the expectations of people who sometimes fervently insist on being treated as distinctive individuals or groups—a one-size-fits-all leadership approach won't work. Effective cross-cultural leadership requires sensitivity to cultural differences, discerning when diversity has to be accommodated and when differences can be and should be narrowed.[30]

Keeping the Internal Organization Responsive and Innovative

While formulating and implementing strategy is a manager's responsibility, the task of generating fresh ideas, identifying new opportunities, and responding to changing conditions cannot be accomplished by a single person. It is an organizationwide task, particularly in large corporations. One of the toughest parts of strategic leadership is generating fresh ideas from the rank and file, managers and employees alike, and promoting an entrepreneurial, opportunistic spirit that permits continuous adaptation to changing conditions. A flexible, responsive, innovative internal environment is critical in fast-moving high-technology industries, in businesses where products have short life cycles and growth depends on new product innovation, in companies with widely diversified business portfolios (where opportunities are varied and scattered), in markets where successful product differentiation depends on outinnovating the competition, and in situations where low-cost leadership hinges on continuous improvement and new ways to drive costs out of the business. Managers cannot mandate such an internal work climate by simply exhorting people to "be creative."

The faster a company's business environment changes, the more attention managers must pay to keeping the organization innovative and responsive.

Empowering Champions   One useful leadership approach is to take special pains to foster, nourish, and support people who are willing to champion new technologies, new operating practices, better services, new products, and new product applications and are eager to try carrying out their ideas. One year after taking charge at Siemens-Nixdorf Information Systems, Gerhard Schulmeyer produced the merged company's first profit after losing hundreds of millions of dollars annually since 1991; he credited the turnaround to the creation of 5,000 "change agents," almost 15 percent of the workforce, who volunteered for active roles in the company's change agenda while continuing to perform their regular jobs. As a rule, the best champions are persistent, competitive, tenacious, committed, and fanatic about the idea and seeing it through to success.

Identifying and empowering champions helps promote an environment of innovation and experimentation.

To promote a climate where champion innovators can blossom and thrive, strategy managers need to do several things. First, individuals and groups have to be encouraged to be creative, hold informal brainstorming sessions, let their imaginations fly in all

---

[30]For a discussion of this dimension of leadership, see Alexander and Wilson, "Leading across Cultures: Five Vital Capabilities," pp. 287–94.

directions, and come up with proposals. The culture has to nurture, even celebrate, experimentation and innovation. Everybody must be expected to contribute ideas, show initiative, and pursue continuous improvement. The trick is to keep a sense of urgency alive in the business so that people see change and innovation as a necessity. Second, people with maverick ideas or out-of-the-ordinary proposals have to be tolerated and given room to operate. Above all, would-be champions who advocate radical or different ideas must not be looked on as disruptive or troublesome. Third, managers have to promote lots of "tries" and be willing to tolerate mistakes and failures. Most ideas don't pan out, but the organization learns from a good attempt even when it fails. Fourth, strategy managers should be willing to use all kinds of organizational forms to support ideas and experimentation—venture teams, task forces, "performance shootouts" among different groups working on competing approaches, informal "boot-legged" projects composed of volunteers, and so on. Fifth, strategy managers have to see that the rewards for successful champions are large and visible and that people who champion an unsuccessful idea are encouraged to try again rather than be punished or sidelined. In effect, the leadership task is to create an adaptive, innovative culture that responds to changing conditions rather than fearing the new conditions or seeking to minimize them. Companies with innovative cultures include Sony, 3M, Motorola, and Levi Strauss. All four inspire their employees with strategic visions to excel and be world-class at what they do.

Leading the Process of Developing New Capabilities Often, effectively responding to changing customer preferences and competitive conditions requires top management intervention to establish new capabilities and resource strengths. Senior management usually has to lead the effort because core competencies and competitive capabilities typically come from the combined efforts of different work groups, departments, and collaborative allies. The tasks of managing human skills, knowledge bases, and intellect and then integrating them to forge competitively advantageous competencies and capabilities is best orchestrated by senior managers who appreciate their strategy-implementing significance and who have the clout to enforce the necessary networking and cooperation among individuals, groups, departments, and external allies.

It's a constant organization-building challenge to broaden, deepen, or modify organization capabilities and resource strengths in response to ongoing customer-market changes.

The ideal leadership outcome is for senior management to proactively develop new competencies and capabilities to complement the company's existing resource base and promote more proficient strategy execution.

Effective company managers try to anticipate changes in customer-market requirements and proactively build new competencies and capabilities that offer a competitive edge over rivals. Senior managers are in the best position to see the need and potential of new capabilities and then to play a lead role in building capabilities and strengthening company resources. Building new competencies and capabilities ahead of rivals to gain a competitive edge is strategic leadership of the best kind, but strengthening the company's resource base in reaction to the newly developed capabilities of pioneering rivals is the most frequent occurrence.

Dealing with Company Politics

A manager can't effectively formulate and implement strategy without being perceptive about company politics and being adept at political maneuvering.[31] Politics virtually always comes into play in formulating the strategic plan. Inevitably, key

[31]For further discussion of this point see Abraham Zaleznik, "Power and Politics in Organizational Life," *Harvard Business Review* 48, no. 3 (May–June 1970), pp. 47–60; R. M. Cyert, H. A. Simon, and D. B.

individuals and groups form coalitions, and each group presses the benefits and potential of its own ideas and vested interests. Political considerations enter into decisions about which objectives take precedence and which lines of business have top priority in resource allocation. Internal politics is a factor in building a consensus for one strategic option over another.

As a rule, there is even more politics in implementing strategy than in formulating it. Typically, internal political considerations affect whose areas of responsibility get reorganized, who reports to whom, who has how much authority over subunits, what individuals should fill key positions and head strategy-critical activities, and which units will get the biggest budget increases. As a case in point, Quinn cites a situation where three strong managers who fought each other constantly formed a potent coalition to resist a reorganization scheme that would have coordinated the very things that caused their friction.[32]

Company politics presents strategy leaders with the challenge of building consensus for the strategy and how to implement it.

A strategy manager must therefore understand how an organization's power structure works, who wields influence in the executive ranks, which groups and individuals are "activists" and which are defenders of the status quo, who can be helpful and who may not be in a showdown on key decisions, and which direction the political winds are blowing on a given issue. When major decisions have to be made, strategy managers need to be especially sensitive to the politics of managing coalitions and reaching consensus. As the chairman of a major British corporation expressed it:

> I've never taken a major decision without consulting my colleagues. It would be unimaginable to me, unimaginable. First, they help me make a better decision in most cases. Second, if they know about it and agree with it, they'll back it. Otherwise, they might challenge it, not openly, but subconsciously.[33]

The politics of strategy centers chiefly around stimulating options, nurturing support for strong proposals and killing weak ones, guiding the formation of coalitions on particular issues, and achieving consensus and commitment. Successful executives rely upon the following political tactics:[34]

- Letting weakly supported ideas and proposals die through inaction.
- Establishing additional hurdles or tests for strongly supported ideas that the manager views as unacceptable but that are best not opposed openly.
- Keeping a low political profile on unacceptable proposals by getting subordinate managers to say no.
- Letting most negative decisions come from a group consensus that the manager merely confirms, thereby reserving personal veto for big issues and crucial moments.
- Leading the strategy but not dictating it—giving few orders, announcing few decisions, depending heavily on informal questioning, and seeking to probe and clarify until a consensus emerges.

Trow, "Observation of a Business Decision," *Journal of Business*, October 1956, pp. 237–48; and James Brian Quinn, *Strategies for Change: Logical Incrementalism* (Homewood, Ill.: Richard D. Irwin, 1980).
[32]Quinn, *Strategies for Change*, p. 68.
[33]Ibid., p. 65. This statement was made by Sir Alastair Pilkington, Chairman, Pilkington Brothers, Ltd.
[34]Ibid., pp. 128–45.

- Staying alert to the symbolic impact of one's actions and statements lest a false signal stimulate proposals and movements in unwanted directions.

- Ensuring that all major power bases within the organization have representation in or access to top management.

- Injecting new faces and new views into considerations of major changes to prevent those involved from coming to see the world the same way and then acting as systematic screens against other views.

- Minimizing political exposure on issues that are highly controversial and in circumstances where opposition from major power centers can trigger a "shootout."

The politics of strategy implementation is especially critical when it comes to introducing a new strategy against the resistance of those who support the old one. Except for crisis situations where the old strategy is plainly revealed as out-of-date, it is usually bad politics to push the new strategy by attacks on the old one.[35] Bad-mouthing old strategy can easily be interpreted as an attack on those who formulated it and those who supported it. The old strategy and the judgments behind it may have been well-suited to the organization's earlier circumstances, and the people who made these judgments may still be influential. In addition, the new strategy and/or the plans for implementing it may not have been the first choices of others, and lingering doubts may remain. Good arguments may exist for pursuing other actions. Consequently, in trying to surmount resistance, nothing is gained by knocking the arguments for alternative approaches. Such attacks often produce alienation instead of cooperation.

In short, to bring the full force of an organization behind a strategic plan, the strategy manager must assess and deal with the most important centers of potential support for and opposition to new strategic thrusts.[36] He or she needs to secure the support of key people, co-opt or neutralize serious opposition and resistance when and where necessary, learn where the zones of indifference are, and build as much consensus as possible. Political skills are a definite, maybe even necessary, managerial asset.

Enforcing Ethical Behavior

For an organization to display consistently high ethical standards, the CEO and those around the CEO must be openly and clearly committed to ethical and moral conduct.[37] In companies that strive hard to make high ethical standards a reality, top management communicates its commitment in a code of ethics, in speeches and company publications, in policies on the consequences of unethical behavior, in the deeds of senior executives, and in the actions taken to ensure compliance. Senior management repeatedly tells employees that it is not only their duty to observe ethical codes but also to report ethical violations. While such companies have provisions for disciplining violators, the main purpose of enforcement is to encourage compliance rather than administer punishment. Although the CEO leads the

---

[35]Ibid., pp. 118–19.
[36]Ibid., p. 205.
[37]The Business Roundtable, *Corporate Ethics*, pp. 4–10.

High ethical standards cannot be enforced without the open and unequivocal commitment of the chief executive.

enforcement process, all managers are expected to make a personal contribution by stressing ethical conduct with their subordinates and monitoring compliance with the code of ethics. "Gray areas" must be identified and openly discussed with employees, and procedures created for offering guidance when issues arise, for investigating possible violations, and for resolving individual cases. The lesson from these companies is that it is never enough to assume activities are being conducted ethically, nor can it be assumed that employees understand they are expected to act with integrity.

Managers can do several concrete things to exercise ethics leadership.[38] First and foremost, they must set an excellent ethical example in their own behavior and establish a tradition of integrity. Company decisions have to be seen as ethical—"actions speak louder than words." Second, managers and employees have to be educated about what is ethical and what is not; ethics training programs may have to be established and gray areas pointed out and discussed. Everyone must be encouraged to raise issues with ethical dimensions, and such discussions should be treated as a legitimate topic. Third, top management should regularly restate its clear support of the company's ethical code and take a strong stand on ethical issues. Fourth, top management must be prepared to act as the final arbiter on hard calls; this means removing people from a key position or terminating them when they are guilty of a violation. It also means reprimanding those who have been lax in monitoring and enforcing ethical compliance. Failure to act swiftly and decisively in punishing ethical misconduct is interpreted as a lack of real commitment.

A well-developed program to ensure compliance with ethical standards typically includes (1) an oversight committee of the board of directors, usually made up of outside directors; (2) a committee of senior managers to direct ongoing training, implementation, and compliance; (3) an annual audit of each manager's efforts to uphold ethical standards and formal reports on the actions taken by managers to remedy deficient conduct; and (4) periodically requiring people to sign documents certifying compliance with ethical standards.[39]

Leading the Process of Making Corrective Adjustments

No strategic plan and no scheme for strategy implementation can foresee all the events and problems that will arise. Making adjustments and midcourse corrections, as well as pushing for ever better execution is a normal and necessary part of leading the process of implementing and executing strategy. The *process* of deciding when to make adjustments and what adjustments to make varies according to the situation. In a crisis, the typical leadership approach is to have key subordinates gather information, identify options, and make recommendations, then personally preside over extended discussions of the proposed responses and try to build a quick consensus among members of the executive inner circle. If no consensus emerges and action is required immediately, the burden falls on the strategy manager to choose the response and urge its support.

Corrective adjustments in the company's approach to strategy implementation are normal and have to be made as needed.

When the situation allows managers to proceed more deliberately in deciding when to make changes and what changes to make, strategy managers seem to prefer

---

[38]Ibid.
[39]Ibid.

a process of gradually solidifying commitment to a particular course of action.[40] The process that managers go through in deciding on corrective adjustments is essentially the same for both proactive and reactive changes: They sense needs, gather information, broaden and deepen their understanding of the situation, develop options and explore their pros and cons, put forth action proposals, generate partial (comfort-level) solutions, build consensus, and finally formally adopt an agreed-on course of action.[41] The ultimate managerial prescription may have been given by Rene Mc-Pherson, former CEO at Dana Corporation. Speaking to a class of students at Stanford University, he said, "You just keep pushing. You just keep pushing. I made every mistake that could be made. But I just kept pushing."[42]

All this, once again, highlights the fundamental nature of strategic management: The job of formulating and implementing strategy is not one of steering a clear-cut course while carrying out the original strategy intact according to some preconceived plan. Rather, it is one of creatively (1) adapting and reshaping strategy to unfolding events and (2) drawing upon whatever managerial techniques are needed to align internal activities and behaviors with strategy. The process is interactive, with much looping and recycling to fine-tune and adjust visions, objectives, strategies, resources, capabilities, implementation approaches, and cultures to one another in a continuously evolving process. The best tests of good strategic leadership are improving business performance and a company that is agile, that is capable of adapting to multiple changes, and that is a good place to work.

KEY POINTS

Building a strategy-supportive corporate culture is important to successful implementation because it produces a work climate and organizational esprit de corps that thrive on meeting performance targets and being part of a winning effort. An organization's culture emerges from why and how it does things the way it does, the values and beliefs that senior managers espouse, the ethical standards expected of all, the tone and philosophy underlying key policies, and the traditions the organization maintains. Culture thus concerns the atmosphere and "feeling" a company has and the style in which it gets things done.

Very often, the elements of company culture originate with a founder or other early influential leaders who articulate certain values, beliefs, and principles the company should adhere to, which then get incorporated into company policies, a creed or values statement, strategies, and operating practices. Over time, these values and practices become shared by company employees and managers. Cultures are perpetuated as new leaders act to reinforce them, as new employees are encouraged to adopt and follow them, as legendary stories that exemplify them are told and retold, and as organizational members are honored and rewarded for displaying the cultural norms.

Company cultures vary widely in strength and in makeup. Some cultures are strongly embedded, while others are weak and fragmented in the sense that many subcultures exist, few values and behavioral norms are shared companywide, and there are few strong traditions. Some cultures are unhealthy, dominated by self-serving politics, resistant to change, and too inwardly focused; such cultural traits are

---

[40]Quinn, *Strategies for Change*, pp. 20–22.

[41]Ibid., p. 146.

[42]As quoted in Peters and Waterman, *In Search of Excellence*, p. 319.

often precursors to declining company performance. In fast-changing business environments, adaptive cultures are best because the internal environment is receptive to change, experimentation, innovation, new strategies, and new operating practices needed to respond to changing stakeholder requirements. One significant defining trait of adaptive cultures is that top management genuinely cares about the well-being of all key constituencies—customers, employees, stockholders, major suppliers, and the communities where it operates—and tries to satisfy all their legitimate interests simultaneously.

The philosophy, goals, and practices implicit or explicit in a new strategy may or may not be compatible with a firm's culture. A close strategy-culture alignment promotes implementation and good execution; a mismatch poses real obstacles. Changing a company's culture, especially a strong one with traits that don't fit a new strategy's requirements, is one of the toughest management challenges. Changing a culture requires competent leadership at the top. It requires symbolic actions (leading by example) and substantive actions that unmistakably indicate top management is seriously committed. The stronger the fit between culture and strategy, the less managers have to depend on policies, rules, procedures, and supervision to enforce what people should and should not do; rather, cultural norms are so well observed that they automatically guide behavior.

Healthy corporate cultures are also grounded in ethical business principles and moral values. Such standards connote integrity, "doing the right thing," and genuine concern for stakeholders and for how the company does business. To be effective, corporate ethics and values programs have to become a way of life through training, strict compliance and enforcement procedures, and reiterated management endorsements.

Successful strategy implementers exercise an important leadership role. They stay on top of how well things are going by spending considerable time outside their offices, wandering around the organization, listening, coaching, cheerleading, picking up important information, and keeping their fingers on the organization's pulse. They take pains to reinforce the corporate culture through the things they say and do. They encourage people to be creative and innovative in order to keep the organization responsive to changing conditions, alert to new opportunities, and anxious to pursue fresh initiatives. They support "champions" of new approaches or ideas who are willing to stick their necks out and try something innovative. They work hard at building consensus on how to proceed, on what to change and what not to change. They enforce high ethical standards. And they push corrective action to improve strategy execution and overall strategic performance.

A manager's action agenda for implementing and executing strategy is thus expansive and creative. As we indicated at the beginning of our discussion of strategy implementation (Chapter 9), eight bases need to be covered:

1. Building an organization capable of carrying out the strategy successfully.

2. Developing budgets to steer ample resources into those value-chain activities critical to strategic success.

3. Establishing strategically appropriate policies and procedures.

4. Instituting best practices and mechanisms for continuous improvement.

5. Installing support systems that enable company personnel to carry out their strategic roles successfully day in and day out.

6. Tying rewards and incentives tightly to the achievement of performance objectives and good strategy execution.

7. Creating a strategy-supportive work environment and corporate culture.

8. Leading and monitoring the process of driving implementation forward and improving on how the strategy is being executed.

Making progress on these eight tasks sweeps broadly across virtually every aspect of administrative and managerial work.

Because each instance of strategy implementation occurs under different organizational circumstances, a strategy implementer's action agenda always needs to be situation specific—there's no neat generic procedure to follow. And, as we said at the beginning, implementing strategy is an action-oriented, make-the-right-things-happen task that challenges a manager's ability to lead and direct organizational change, create or reinvent business processes, manage and motivate people, and achieve performance targets. If you now better understand the nature of the challenge, the range of available approaches, and the issues that need to be considered, we will look upon our discussion in these last three chapters as a success.

SUGGESTED READINGS

Badaracco, Joe and Allen P. Webb. "Business Ethics: A View from the Trenches." *California Management Review* 37, no. 2 (Winter 1995), pp. 8–28.

Clement, Ronald W. "Culture, Leadership, and Power: The Keys to Organizational Change." *Business Horizons* 37, no. 1 (January–February 1994), pp. 33–39.

Deal, Terrence E., and Allen A. Kennedy. *Corporate Cultures*. Reading, Mass.: Addison-Wesley, 1982, especially chaps. 1 and 2.

Eccles, Robert G. "The Performance Measurement Manifesto." *Harvard Business Review* 69 (January–February 1991), pp. 131–37.

Farkas, Charles M. and Suzy Wetlaufer, "The Ways Chief Executive Officers Lead," *Harvard Business Review* 74 no. 3 (May–June 1996), pp. 110–122.

Floyd, Steven W., and Bill Wooldridge. "Managing Strategic Consensus: The Foundation of Effective Implementation." *Academy of Management Executive* 6, no. 4 (November 1992), pp. 27–39.

Gabarro, J. J. "When a New Manager Takes Charge." *Harvard Business Review* 64, no. 3 (May–June 1985), pp. 110–23.

Ghoshal, Sumantra and Christopher A. Bartlett. "Changing the Role of Top Management: Beyond Structure to Processes." *Harvard Business Review* 73 no. 1 (January–February 1995), pp. 86–96.

Ginsburg, Lee and Neil Miller, "Value-Driven Management," *Business Horizons* (May–June 1992), pp. 25–27.

Green, Sebastian. "Strategy, Organizational Culture, and Symbolism." *Long Range Planning* 21, no. 4 (August 1988), pp. 121–29.

Heifetz, Ronald A. and Donald L. Laurie. "The Work of Leadership." *Harvard Business Review* 75, no. 1 (January–February 1997), pp. 124–34.

Humble, John, David Jackson, and Alan Thomson. "The Strategic Power of Corporate Values." *Long Range Planning* 27, no. 6 (December 1994), pp. 28–42.

Kirkpatrick, Shelley A., and Edwin A. Locke. "Leadership: Do Traits Matter?" *Academy of Management Executive* 5, no. 2 (May 1991), pp. 48–60.

Kotter, John P. "What Leaders Really Do." *Harvard Business Review* 68 no. 3 (May–June 1990), pp. 103–11.

———."Leading Change: Why Transformation Efforts Fail." *Harvard Business Review* 73, no. 2 (March–April 1995), pp. 59–67.

————, and James L. Heskett. *Corporate Culture and Performance*. New York: Free Press, 1992.

Miles, Robert H. *Corporate Comeback: The Story of Renewal and Transformation at National Semiconductor*. San Francisco: Jossey-Bass, 1997.

Murphy, Patrick E. "Corporate Ethics Statements: Current Status and Future Prospects." *Journal of Business Ethics* 14 (1995), pp. 727–40.

O'Toole, James. "Employee Practices at the Best-Managed Companies." *California Management Review* 28, no. 1 (Fall 1985), pp. 35–66.

Paine, Lynn Sharp. "Managing for Organizational Integrity." *Harvard Business Review* 72, no. 2 (March–April 1994), pp. 106–17.

Reimann, Bernard C., and Yoash Wiener. "Corporate Culture: Avoiding the Elitist Trap." *Business Horizons* 31, no. 2 (March–April 1988), pp. 36–44.

Schneider, Benjamin, Sarah K. Gunnarson, and Kathryn Niles-Jolly. "Creating the Climate and Culture of Success." *Organizational Dynamics* (Summer 1994), pp.17–29.

Scholz, Christian. "Corporate Culture and Strategy—The Problem of Strategic Fit." *Long Range Planning* 20 (August 1987), pp. 78–87.

II

CASES IN STRATEGIC MANAGEMENT

A GUIDE TO CASE ANALYSIS

In most courses in strategic management, students use cases about actual companies to practice strategic analysis and to gain some experience in the tasks of crafting and implementing strategy. A case sets forth, in a factual manner, the events and organizational circumstances surrounding a particular managerial situation. It puts readers at the scene of the action and familiarizes them with all the relevant circumstances. A case on strategic management can concern a whole industry, a single organization, or some part of an organization; the organization involved can be either profit seeking or not-for-profit. The essence of the student's role in case analysis is to *diagnose* and *size up* the situation described in the case and then to *recommend* appropriate action steps.

> I keep six honest serving men
> (They taught me all I knew);
> Their names are What and Why and
> When; And How and Where and Who.
> **Rudyard Kipling**

WHY USE CASES TO PRACTICE STRATEGIC MANAGEMENT?

> A student of business with tact
> Absorbed many answers he lacked.
> But acquiring a job,
> He said with a sob,
> "How does one fit answer to fact?"

The foregoing limerick was used some years ago by Professor Charles Gragg to characterize the plight of business students who had no exposure to cases.[1] The facts are that the mere act of listening to lectures and sound advice about managing does little for anyone's management skills and that the accumulated managerial wisdom cannot effectively be passed on by lectures and assigned readings alone. If anything had been learned about the practice of management, it is that a storehouse of ready-made textbook answers does not exist. Each managerial situation has unique aspects, requiring its own diagnosis, judgment, and tailor-made actions. Cases provide would-be

---

[1]Charles I. Gragg, "Because Wisdom Can't Be Told," in *The Case Method at the Harvard Business School,* ed. M. P. McNair (New York: McGraw-Hill, 1954), p. 11.

managers with a valuable way to practice wrestling with the actual problems of actual managers in actual companies.

The case approach to strategic analysis is, first and foremost, an exercise in learning by doing. Because cases provide you with detailed information about conditions and problems of different industries and companies, your task of analyzing company after company and situation after situation has the twin benefit of boosting your analytical skills and exposing you to the ways companies and managers actually do things. Most college students have limited managerial backgrounds and only fragmented knowledge about companies and real-life strategic situations. Cases help substitute for on-the-job experience by (1) giving you broader exposure to a variety of industries, organizations, and strategic problems; (2) forcing you to assume a managerial role (as opposed to that of just an onlooker); (3) providing a test of how to apply the tools and techniques of strategic management; and (4) asking you to come up with pragmatic managerial action plans to deal with the issues at hand.

OBJECTIVES OF CASE ANALYSIS

Using cases to learn about the practice of strategic management is a powerful way for you to accomplish five things:[2]

1. Increase your understanding of what managers should and should not do in guiding a business to success.
2. Build your skills in sizing up company resource strengths and weaknesses and in conducting strategic analysis in a variety of industries and competitive situations.
3. Get valuable practice in identifying strategic issues that need to be addressed, evaluating strategic alternatives, and formulating workable plans of action.
4. Enhance your sense of business judgment, as opposed to uncritically accepting the authoritative crutch of the professor or "back-of-the-book" answers.
5. Gaining in-depth exposure to different industries and companies, thereby acquiring something close to actual business experience.

If you understand that these are the objectives of case analysis, you are less likely to be consumed with curiosity about "the answer to the case." Students who have grown comfortable with and accustomed to textbook statements of fact and definitive lecture notes are often frustrated when discussions about a case do not produce concrete answers. Usually, case discussions produce good arguments for more than one course of action. Differences of opinion nearly always exist. Thus, should a class discussion conclude without a strong, unambiguous consensus on what do to, don't grumble too much when you are *not* told what the answer is or what the company actually did. Just remember that in the business world answers don't come in conclusive black-and-white terms. There are nearly always several feasible courses of action and approaches, each of which may work out satisfactorily. Moreover, in the business world, when one elects a particular course of action, there is no peeking at the back of a book to see if you have chosen the best thing to do and no one to turn to for a provably correct answer. The only valid test of management action is *results*. If the results of an action turn out to be "good," the decision to take it may be presumed "right." If not, then the action chosen was "wrong" in the sense that it didn't work out.

---

[2]Ibid. pp. 12–14; and D. R. Schoen and Philip A. Sprague, "What Is the Case Method?" in *The Case Method at the Harvard Business School,* ed. M. P. McNair, pp. 78–79.

Hence, the important thing for a student to understand in case analysis is that the managerial exercise of identifying, diagnosing, and recommending builds your skills; discovering the right answer or finding out what actually happened is no more than frosting on the cake. Even if you learn what the company did, you can't conclude that it was necessarily right or best. All that can be said is "here is what they did . . . "

The point is this: *The purpose of giving you a case assignment is not to cause you to run to the library or surf the Internet to discover what the company actually did but, rather, to enhance your skills in sizing up situations and developing your managerial judgment about what needs to be done and how to do it.* The aim of case analysis is for *you* to bear the strains of thinking actively, of offering your analysis, of proposing action plans, and of explaining and defending your assessments—this is how cases provide you with meaningful practice at being a manager.

PREPARING A CASE FOR CLASS DISCUSSION

If this is your first experience with the case method, you may have to reorient your study habits. Unlike lecture courses where you can get by without preparing intensively for each class and where you have latitude to work assigned readings and reviews of lecture notes into your schedule, a case assignment requires conscientious preparation before class. You will not get much out of hearing the class discuss a case you haven't read, and you certainly won't be able to contribute anything yourself to the discussion. What you have got to do to get ready for class discussion of a case is to study the case, reflect carefully on the situation presented, and develop some reasoned thoughts. Your goal in preparing the case should be to end up with what you think is a sound, well-supported analysis of the situation and a sound, defensible set of recommendations about which managerial actions need to be taken. The Strat-Tutor software package that accompanies this edition will assist you in preparing the cases—it contains a set of study questions for each case and step-by-step tutorials to walk you through the process of analyzing and developing reasonable recommendations.

To prepare a case for class discussion, we suggest the following approach:

1. *Read the case through rather quickly for familiarity.* The initial reading should give you the general flavor of the situation and indicate which issue or issues are involved. If your instructor has provided you with study questions for the case, now is the time to read them carefully.

2. *Read the case a second time.* On this reading, try to gain full command of the facts. Begin to develop some tentative answers to the study questions your instructor has provided or that are provided on the Strat-Tutor software package. If your instructor has elected not to give you assignment questions or has elected not to use Strat-Tutor, then start forming your own picture of the overall situation being described.

3. *Study all the exhibits carefully.* Often, there is an important story in the numbers contained in the exhibits. Expect the information in the case exhibits to be crucial enough to materially affect your diagnosis of the situation.

4. *Decide what the strategic issues are.* Until you have identified the strategic issues and problems in the case, you don't know what to analyze, which tools and analytical techniques are called for, or otherwise how to proceed. At times the strategic issues are clear—either being stated in the case or else obvious from reading the case. At other times you will have to dig them out from all the information given; if so, the study questions and the case preparation exercises on Strat-Tutor will guide you.

5. *Start your analysis of the issues with some number crunching.* A big majority of strategy cases call for some kind of number crunching—calculating assorted financial ratios to check out the company's financial condition and recent performance, calculating growth rates of sales or profits or unit volume, checking out profit margins and the makeup of the cost structure, and understanding whatever revenue-cost-profit relationships are present. See Table 1 for a summary of key financial ratios, how they are calculated, and what they show. If you are using Strat-Tutor, much of the number-crunching has been computerized and you'll spend most of your time interpreting the growth rates, financial ratios, and other calculations provided.

6. *Use whichever tools and techniques of strategic analysis are called for.* Strategic analysis is not just a collection of opinions; rather, it entails application of a growing number of powerful tools and techniques that cut beneath the surface and produce important insight and understanding of strategic situations. Every case assigned is strategy related and contains an opportunity to usefully apply the weapons of strategic analysis. Your instructor is looking for you to demonstrate that you know *how* and *when* to use the strategic management concepts presented in the text chapters. The case preparation guides on Strat-Tutor will point you toward the proper analytical tools needed to analyze the case situation.

7. *Check out conflicting opinions and make some judgments about the validity of all the data and information provided.* Many times cases report views and contradictory opinions (after all, people don't always agree on things, and different people see the same things in different ways). Forcing you to evaluate the data and information presented in the case helps you develop your powers of inference and judgment. Asking you to resolve conflicting information "comes with the territory" because a great many managerial situations entail opposing points of view, conflicting trends, and sketchy information.

8. *Support your diagnosis and opinions with reasons and evidence.* The most important things to prepare for are your answers to the question "Why?" For instance, if after studying the case you are of the opinion that the company's managers are doing a poor job, then it is your answer to "Why?" that establishes just how good your analysis of the situation is. If your instructor has provided you with specific study questions for the case or if you are using the case preparation guides on Strat-Tutor, by all means prepare answers that include all the reasons and number-crunching evidence you can muster to support your diagnosis. Work through the case preparation exercises on Strat-Tutor *conscientiously* or, if you are using study questions provided by the instructor, *generate at least two pages of notes!*

9. *Develop an appropriate action plan and set of recommendations.* Diagnosis divorced from corrective action is sterile. The test of a manager is always to convert sound analysis into sound actions—actions that will produce the desired results. Hence, the final and most telling step in preparing a case is to develop an action agenda for management that lays out a set of specific recommendations on what to do. Bear in mind that proposing realistic, workable solutions is far preferable to casually tossing out off-the-top-of-your-head suggestions. Be prepared to argue why your recommendations are more attractive than other courses of action that are open. You'll find Strat-Tutor's case preparation guides helpful in performing this step, too.

TABLE 1   A Summary of Key Financial Ratios, How They Are Calculated, and What They Show

Ratio	How Calculated	What It Shows
Profitability Ratios		
1. Gross profit margin	$\dfrac{\text{Sales} - \text{Cost of goods sold}}{\text{Sales}}$	An indication of the total margin available to cover operating expenses and yield a profit.
2. Operating profit margin (or return on sales)	$\dfrac{\text{Profits before taxes and before interest}}{\text{Sales}}$	An indication of the firm's profitability from current operations without regard to the interest charges accruing from the capital structure.
3. Net profit margin (or net return on sales)	$\dfrac{\text{Profits after taxes}}{\text{Sales}}$	Shows after tax profits per dollar of sales. Subpar profit margins indicate that the firm's sales prices are relatively low or that costs are relatively high, or both.
4. Return on total assets	$\dfrac{\text{Profits after taxes}}{\text{Total assets}}$ or $\dfrac{\text{Profit after taxes} + \text{interest}}{\text{Total assets}}$	A measure of the return on total investment in the enterprise. It is sometimes desirable to add interest to aftertax profits to form the numerator of the ratio since total assets are financed by creditors as well as by stockholders; hence, it is accurate to measure the productivity of assets by the returns provided to both classes of investors.
5. Return on stockholder's equity (or return on net worth)	$\dfrac{\text{Profits after taxes}}{\text{Total stockholders' equity}}$	A measure of the rate of return on stockholders' investment in the enterprise.
6. Return on common equity	$\dfrac{\text{Profits after taxes} - \text{Preferred stock dividends}}{\text{Total stockholders' equity} - \text{Par value of preferred stock}}$	A measure of the rate of return on the investment the owners of the common stock have made in the enterprise.
7. Earnings per share	$\dfrac{\text{Profits after taxes} - \text{Preferred stock dividends}}{\text{Number of shares of common stock outstanding}}$	Shows the earnings available to the owners of each share of common stock.
Liquidity Ratios		
1. Current ratio	$\dfrac{\text{Current assets}}{\text{Current liabilities}}$	Indicates the extent to which the claims of short-term creditors are covered by assets that are expected to be converted to cash in a period roughly corresponding to the maturity of the liabilities.
2. Quick ratio (or acid-test ratio)	$\dfrac{\text{Current assets} - \text{Inventory}}{\text{Current liabilities}}$	A measure of the firm's ability to pay off short-term obligations without relying on the sale of its inventories.
3. Inventory to net working capital	$\dfrac{\text{Inventory}}{\text{Current assets} - \text{Current liabilities}}$	A measure of the extent to which the firm's working capital is tied up in inventory.
Leverage Ratios		
1. Debt-to-assets ratio	$\dfrac{\text{Total debt}}{\text{Total assets}}$	Measures the extent to which borrowed funds have been used to finance the firm's operations.
2. Debt-to-equity ratio	$\dfrac{\text{Total debt}}{\text{Total stockholders' equity}}$	Provides another measure of the funds provided by creditors versus the funds provided by owners.

TABLE 1   Ratios, How They Are Calculated, and What They Show (concluded)

Ratio	How Calculated	What It Shows
Leverage Ratios (*cont.*)		
3. Long-term debt-to-equity ratio	$$\frac{\text{Long-term debt}}{\text{Total stockholders' equity}}$$	A widely used measure of the balance between debt and equity in the firm's long-term capital structure
4. Times-interest-earned (or coverage) ratio	$$\frac{\text{Profits before interest and taxes}}{\text{Total interest charges}}$$	Measures the extent to which earnings can decline without the firm becoming unable to meet its annual interest costs.
5. Fixed-charge coverage	$$\frac{\text{Profits before taxes and interest} + \text{Lease obligations}}{\text{Total interest charges} + \text{Lease obligations}}$$	A more inclusive indication of the firm's ability to meet all of its fixed-charge obligations.
Activity Ratios		
1. Inventory turnover	$$\frac{\text{Sales}}{\text{Inventory of finished goods}}$$	When compared to industry averages, it provides an indication of whether a company has excessive or perhaps inadequate finished goods inventory.
2. Fixed assets turnover	$$\frac{\text{Sales}}{\text{Fixed assets}}$$	A measure of the sales productivity and utilization of plant and equipment.
3. Total assets turnover	$$\frac{\text{Sales}}{\text{Total assets}}$$	A measure of the utilization of all the firm's assets; a ratio below the industry average indicates the company is not generating a sufficient volume of business, given the size of its asset investment.
4. Accounts receivable turnover	$$\frac{\text{Annual credit sales}}{\text{Accounts receivable}}$$	A measure of the average length of time it takes the firm to collect the sales made on credit.
5. Average collection period	$$\frac{\text{Accounts receivable}}{\text{Total sales} \div 365}$$ or $$\frac{\text{Accounts receivable}}{\text{Average daily sales}}$$	Indicates the average length of time the firm must wait after making a sale before it receives payment.
Other Ratios		
1. Dividend yield on common stock	$$\frac{\text{Annual dividends per share}}{\text{Current market price per share}}$$	A measure of the return to owners received in the form of dividends.
2. Price-earnings ratio	$$\frac{\text{Current market price per share}}{\text{After tax earnings per share}}$$	Faster-growing or less-risky firms tend to have higher price-earnings ratios than slower-growing or more-risky firms.
3. Dividend payout ratio	$$\frac{\text{Annual dividends per share}}{\text{After tax earnings per share}}$$	Indicates the percentage of profits paid out as dividends.
4. Cash flow per share	$$\frac{\text{After tax profits} + \text{Depreciation}}{\text{Number of common shares outstanding}}$$	A measure of the discretionary funds over and above expenses that are available for use by the firm.

Note: Industry-average ratios against which a particular company's ratios may be judged are available in *Modern Industry and Dun's Reviews* published by Dun & Bradstreet (14 ratios for 125 lines of business activities), Robert Morris Associates' Annual Statement Studies (11 ratios for 156 lines of business), and the FTC-SEC's *Quarterly Financial Report* for manufacturing corporations.

As long as you are conscientious in preparing your analysis and recommendations, and have ample reasons, evidence, and arguments to support your views, you shouldn't fret unduly about whether what you've prepared is the right answer to the case. In case analysis there is rarely just one right approach or set of recommendations. Managing companies and devising and implementing strategies are not such exact sciences that there exists a single provably correct analysis and action plan for each strategic situation. Of course, some analyses and action plans are better than others; but, in truth, there's nearly always more than one good way to analyze a situation and more than one good plan of action. So, if you have carefully prepared the case using either the Strat-Tutor case preparation guides or your instructor's assignment questions, don't lose confidence in the correctness of your work and judgment.

PARTICIPATING IN CLASS DISCUSSION OF A CASE

Classroom discussions of cases are sharply different from attending a lecture class. In a case class students do most of the talking. The instructor's role is to solicit student participation, keep the discussion on track, ask "Why?" often, offer alternative views, play the devil's advocate (if no students jump in to offer opposing views), and otherwise lead the discussion. The students in the class carry the burden for analyzing the situation and for being prepared to present and defend their diagnoses and recommendations. Expect a classroom environment, therefore, that calls for *your* size-up of the situation, *your* analysis, what actions *you* would take, and why *you* would take them. Do not be dismayed if, as the class discussion unfolds, some insightful things are said by your fellow classmates that you did not think of. It is normal for views and analyses to differ and for the comments of others in the class to expand your own thinking about the case. As the old adage goes, "Two heads are better than one." So it is to be expected that the class as a whole will do a more penetrating and searching job of case analysis than will any one person working alone. This is the power of group effort, and its virtues are that it will help you see more analytical applications, let you test your analyses and judgments against those of your peers, and force you to wrestle with differences of opinion and approaches.

To orient you to the classroom environment on the days a case discussion is scheduled, we compiled the following list of things to expect:

1. Expect students to dominate the discussion and do most of the talking. The case method enlists a maximum of individual participation in class discussion. It is not enough to be present as a silent observer; if every student took this approach, there would be no discussion. (Thus, expect a portion of your grade to be based on your participation in case discussions.)

2. Expect the instructor to assume the role of extensive questioner and listener.

3. Be prepared for the instructor to probe for reasons and supporting analysis.

4. Expect and tolerate challenges to the views expressed. All students have to be willing to submit their conclusions for scrutiny and rebuttal. Each student needs to learn to state his or her views without fear of disapproval and to overcome the hesitation of speaking out. Learning respect for the views and approaches of others is an integral part of case analysis exercises. But there are times when it is OK to swim against the tide of majority opinion. In the practice of management, there is always room for originality and unorthodox approaches. So while discussion of a case is a group process, there is no compulsion for you or anyone else to cave in and conform to group opinions and group consensus.

5. Don't be surprised if you change your mind about some things as the discussion unfolds. Be alert to how these changes affect your analysis and recommendations (in the event you get called on).

6. Expect to learn a lot from each case discussion; use what you learned to be better prepared for the next case discussion.

There are several things you can do on your own to be good and look good as a participant in class discussions:

- Although you should do your own independent work and independent thinking, don't hesitate before (and after) class to discuss the case with other students. In real life, managers often discuss the company's problems and situation with other people to refine their own thinking.

- In participating in the discussion, make a conscious effort to contribute, rather than just talk. There is a big difference between saying something that builds the discussion and offering a long-winded, off-the-cuff remark that leaves the class wondering what the point was.

- Avoid the use of "I think," "I believe," and "I feel"; instead, say, "My analysis shows—" and "The company should do . . . because—" Always give supporting reasons and evidence for your views; then your instructor won't have to ask you "Why?" every time you make a comment.

- In making your points, assume that everyone has read the case and knows what it says; avoid reciting and rehashing information in the case—instead, use the data and information to explain your assessment of the situation and to support your position.

- Bring the printouts of the work you've done on Strat-Tutor or the notes you've prepared (usually two or three pages' worth) to class and rely on them extensively when you speak. There's no way you can remember everything off the top of your head—especially the results of your number crunching. To reel off the numbers or to present all five reasons why, instead of one, you will need good notes. When you have prepared thoughtful answers to the study questions and use them as the basis for your comments, *everybody* in the room will know you are well prepared, and your contribution to the case discussion will stand out.

PREPARING A WRITTEN CASE ANALYSIS

Preparing a written case analysis is much like preparing a case for class discussion, except that your analysis must be more complete and put in report form. Unfortunately, though, there is no ironclad procedure for doing a written case analysis. All we can offer are some general guidelines and words of wisdom—this is because company situations and management problems are so diverse that no one mechanical way to approach a written case assignment always works.

Your instructor may assign you a specific topic around which to prepare your written report. Or, alternatively, you may be asked to do a comprehensive written case analysis, where the expectation is that you will (1) *identify* all the pertinent issues that management needs to address, (2) perform whatever *analysis* and *evaluation* is appropriate, and (3) propose an *action plan* and *set of recommendations* addressing the issues you have identified. In going through the exercise of identify, evaluate, and recommend, keep the following pointers in mind.[3]

Identification   It is essential early on in your paper that you provide a sharply focused diagnosis of strategic issues and key problems and that you demonstrate a good grasp of the company's present situation. Make sure you can identify the firm's strategy (use the concepts and tools in Chapters 1–8 as diagnostic aids) and that you can pinpoint whatever strategy implementation issues may exist (again, consult the material in Chapters 9–11 for diagnostic help). Consult the key points we have provided at the end of each chapter for further diagnostic suggestions. Review the study questions for the case on Strat-Tutor. Consider beginning your paper with an overview of the company's situation, its strategy, and the significant problems and issues that confront management. State problems/issues as clearly and precisely as you can. Unless it is necessary to do so for emphasis, avoid recounting facts and history about the company (assume your professor has read the case and is familiar with the organization).

Analysis and Evaluation   This is usually the hardest part of the report. Analysis is hard work! Check out the firm's financial ratios, its profit margins and rates of return, and its capital structure, and decide how strong the firm is financially. Table 1 contains a summary of various financial ratios and how they are calculated. Use it to assist in your financial diagnosis. Similarly, look at marketing, production, managerial competence, and other factors underlying the organization's strategic successes and failures. Decide whether the firm has valuable resource strengths and competencies and, if so, whether it is capitalizing on them.

   Check to see if the firm's strategy is producing satisfactory results and determine the reasons why or why not. Probe the nature and strength of the competitive forces confronting the company. Decide whether and why the firm's competitive position is getting stronger or weaker. Use the tools and concepts you have learned about to perform whatever analysis and evaluation is appropriate. Work through the case preparation exercise on Strat-Tutor if one is available for the case you've been assigned.

   In writing your analysis and evaluation, bear in mind four things:

1. You are obliged to offer analysis and evidence to back up your conclusions. Do not rely on unsupported opinions, over-generalizations, and platitudes as a substitute for tight, logical argument backed up with facts and figures.

2. f your analysis involves some important quantitative calculations, use tables and charts to present the calculations clearly and efficiently. Don't just tack the exhibits on at the end of your report and let the reader figure out what they mean and why they were included. Instead, in the body of your report cite some of the key numbers, highlight the conclusions to be drawn from the exhibits, and refer the reader to your charts and exhibits for more details.

3. Demonstrate that you have command of the strategic concepts and analytical tools to which you have been exposed. Use them in your report.

---

[3]For some additional ideas and viewpoints, you may wish to consult Thomas J. Raymond, "Written Analysis of Cases," in *The Case Method at the Harvard Business School,* ed. M. P. McNair, pp. 139–63. Raymond's article includes an actual case, a sample analysis of the case, and a sample of a student's written report on the case.

4. Your interpretation of the evidence should be reasonable and objective. Be wary of preparing a one-sided argument that omits all aspects not favorable to your conclusions. Likewise, try not to exaggerate or overdramatize. Endeavor to inject balance into your analysis and to avoid emotional rhetoric. Strike phrases such as "I think," "I feel," and "I believe" when you edit your first draft and write in "My analysis shows," instead.

Recommendations   The final section of the written case analysis should consist of a set of definite recommendations and a plan of action. Your set of recommendations should address all of the problems/issues you identified and analyzed. If the recommendations come as a surprise or do not follow logically from the analysis, the effect is to weaken greatly your suggestions of what to do. Obviously, your recommendations for actions should offer a reasonable prospect of success. High-risk, bet-the-company recommendations should be made with caution. State how your recommendations will solve the problems you identified. Be sure the company is financially able to carry out what you recommend; also check to see if your recommendations are workable in terms of acceptance by the persons involved, the organization's competence to implement them, and prevailing market and environmental constraints. Try not to hedge or weasel on the actions you believe should be taken.

By all means state your recommendations in sufficient detail to be meaningful—get down to some definite nitty-gritty specifics. Avoid such unhelpful statements as "the organization should do more planning" or "the company should be more aggressive in marketing its product." For instance, do not simply say "the firm should improve its market position" but state exactly how you think this should be done. Offer a definite agenda for action, stipulating a timetable and sequence for initiating actions, indicating priorities, and suggesting who should be responsible for doing what.

In proposing an action plan, remember there is a great deal of difference between, on the one hand, being responsible for a decision that may be costly if it proves in error and, on the other hand, casually suggesting courses of action that might be taken when you do not have to bear the responsibility for any of the consequences. A good rule to follow in making your recommendations is: *Avoid recommending anything you would not yourself be willing to do if you were in management's shoes.* The importance of learning to develop good judgment in a managerial situation is indicated by the fact that, even though the same information and operating data may be available to every manager or executive in an organization, the quality of the judgments about what the information means and which actions need to be taken does vary from person to person.[4]

It goes without saying that your report should be well organized and well written. Great ideas amount to little unless others can be convinced of their merit—this takes tight logic, the presentation of convincing evidence, and persuasively written arguments.

RESEARCHING COMPANIES AND INDUSTRIES VIA THE INTERNET AND ON-LINE DATA SERVICES

Very likely, there will be occasions when you need to get additional information about some of the assigned cases, perhaps because your instructor has asked you to do further research on the industry or because you are simply curious about what has

---

[4]Gragg, "Because Wisdom Can't Be Told," p. 10.

happened to the company since the case was written. These days it is relatively easy to run down recent industry developments and to find out whether a company's strategic and financial situation has improved, deteriorated, or changed little since the conclusion of the case. The amount of information about companies and industries available on the Internet and through on-line data services is formidable and expanding rapidly.

On-Line Data Services   On-line subscription services available in many university libraries provide access to a wide array of business reference material. For example, both the Web-based Lexis-Nexis Academic Universe and its dial-up service contain full-text 10-Ks, 10-Qs, annual reports, company profiles for more than 11,000 U.S. and international companies, and a variety of other valuable data files. Other subscription on-line data services include Bloomberg Financial News Services, Standard & Poor's Netadvantage, UMI Proquest, and Dun & Bradstreet's Companies Online. Very likely, your library subscribes to one or more of these services, thus making them available for you to use as needed.

Lexis-Nexis and other on-line services provide you with up-to-date company information by updating their databases every 24 hours or less. You may wish to search the Lexis-Nexis *company* library files listed below for the latest company news and financial data if you have access to the dial-up service. The company information included in these Lexis-Nexis files is also available through the Web-based Lexis-Nexis Academic Universe, but the Web-based product does not require that you specify library names or file names.

Publication/Subject	Lexis/Nexis File Name
Hoover company profiles	HOOVER
Securities and Exchange Commission	SEC
Company annual reports	ARS
Company annual 10-K filings	10-K
Company quarterly 10-Q filings	10-Q
Business wire	BWIRE
Public relations newswire	PRNEWS
S&P Daily News	SPNEWS
Disclosure	DISCLO
Consensus earnings projections	EARN
CNN Financial Network	CNNFN
Dow Jones News/CNBC	CNBC
Business Week	BUSWK
Forbes	FORBES
Fortune	FORTUN

Company Web Pages and Other Web Sites Containing Business Information   Most companies now have Web sites with information about products, financial performance, recent accomplishments, late-breaking company developments, and rundowns on company objectives, strategy, and future plans. Some company Web pages include links to the home pages of industry trade associations where you can find information about industry size, growth, recent industry news, statistical trends, and future outlook. A number of business periodicals like *Business Week, The Wall Street Journal,* and *Fortune* have Internet editions that contain the full text of many of the articles that appear in their paper editions. You can access these sites by typing in the proper Internet address for the company, trade association, or publication. The following Web sites are particularly good locations for company and industry information:

- Securities and Exchange Commission EDGAR database (contains company 10-Ks, 10-Qs, etc.) *www.sec.gov/cgi-bin/srch-edgar/*
- NASDAQ *www.nasdaq.com/*
- CNNfn: The Financial Network *cnnfn.com/*
- Hoover's Online *hoovers.com/*
- American Demographics/Marketing Tools *www.marketingtools.com/*
- Industry Net *www.industry.net/*
- Wall Street Journal—Interactive edition *update.wsj.com/*
- Business Week *www.businessweek.com/*
- Fortune *www.pathfinder.com/fortune/*
- MSNBC Commerce News *www.msnbc.com/news/COM_Front.asp/*
- Los Angeles Times *www.latimes.com/*
- New York Times *www.nytimes.com/*
- News Page *www.newspage.com/*
- Electric Library *www.elibrary.com/*
- International Business Resources on the WWW—a Michigan State University site *ciber.bus.msu.edu/busref.htm/*

Some of these Internet sources require subscriptions in order to access their entire database.

Using a Search Engine   Alternatively, or in addition, you can quickly locate and retrieve information on companies, industries, products, individuals, or other subjects of interest using such Internet search engines as Lycos, Alta Vista, Infoseek, Excite, Yahoo!, and Magellan. Search engines find articles and other information sources that relate to a particular industry, company name, topic, phrase, or "keyword" of interest. Some search engines contain bigger databases of submitted Uniform Resource Locator addresses than others, so it is essential to be alert to the coverage of each search engine— *the database covered by each search engine is usually described on the search engine's Web site.* You may find the following brief descriptions of the most-used search engines helpful in selecting which one to try:

- Alta Vista *(www. altavista.com/)*—Alta Vista searches the full text of all documents in its index of over 140 million submitted Web pages and also crawls the Web looking for links to new pages that match your search criteria. The search results give a higher score to documents where the keywords are in the first few words of the document or title; higher scores are also given to documents containing multiple use of the keywords. For the latest information on what you can find using the Alta Vista search engine, visit the Web site.
- Infoseek *(www.infoseek.com/)*—Infoseek lets you use natural language phrases like "find information on discounted Caribbean cruises" as well as traditional keyword searches. It allows the user to narrow the query by specified names, words, or phrases in the document, URL, or title without the use of Boolean operators. Infoseek also provides company capsules that provide financial and market performance data and a variety of news articles for public companies.

- Yahoo *(www.yahoo.com)*—Yahoo is not actually a search engine, but a catalog created from submissions by authors. Yahoo returns Internet sites to a query based on keywords in the title of the document or the keyword in its description of the document. Yahoo's Business & Economy link provides company profiles that include research reports, stock performance, company news, Web addresses, and a business summary.
- Lycos *(www.lycos. com)*—Lycos allows Boolean queries and contains a Pro Search option that allows the user to customize the search by word order, use of natural language query, title or document search, and language. Lycos also allows the user to specify how search results should be returned.
- Excite *(www. excite.com)*—Excite is a full text search engine that scans Web sites and Usenet news. Like Alta Vista, it gives a higher score to documents that contain the keyword in the title or is repeated frequently in the full text of the document. Excite is unusual in that it understands synonyms. Not only does it return documents that match keywords in a query, but it also returns documents that contain synonyms of keywords listed in a query. Excite also allows the use of Boolean operators.

Each of the search engines provide guidelines for how to formulate your query for information sources. Some tips for making the quickest and most effective use of search engines are listed below:

- Make your search as specific as possible. Search engines are very efficient and may retrieve thousands of matches to a very general request.
- Use Boolean operators like AND, AND NOT, OR, and parentheses to narrow the scope of your search. These operators help zero in on those items of greatest relevance to what you are looking for.
- Each search engine will have specific commands that will further limit the search results. Make sure that you inspect the search engine's advanced search tips to determine how to use those capabilities.
- Some search engines are upper- and lowercase sensitive. As a rule, your query should be entered with the correct uppercase and lowercase letters because of the capitalization-sensitive nature of certain search engines.

Keep in mind that the information retrieved by a search engine is "unfiltered" and may include sources that are not reliable or that contain inaccurate or misleading information. Be wary of information provided by authors who are unaffiliated with reputable organizations or publications, or which doesn't come from the company or a credible trade association. Articles covering a company or issue should be copyrighted or published by a reputable source. If you are turning in a paper containing information gathered from the Internet, you should cite your sources (providing the Internet address and date visited); it is also wise to print Web pages for your research file (some Web pages are updated frequently).

The Learning Curve Is Steep   With a modest investment of time, you will learn how to use Internet sources to run down information on companies and industries quickly and efficiently. And it is a skill that will serve you well into the future. Once you become familiar with the data available at the different Web sites mentioned above and with using a search engine, you will know where to go to look for the particular information that you want. Search engines nearly always turn up too many information sources that match your request rather than too few; the trick is to learn to zero in on those most

---

EXHIBIT 2   The Ten Commandments of Case Analysis

To be observed in written reports and oral presentations, and while participating in class discussions.

1. Read the case twice, once for an overview and once to gain full command of the facts; then take care to explore every one of the exhibits.
2. Make a list of the problems and issues that have to be confronted.
3. Do enough number crunching to discover the story told by the data presented in the case. (To help you comply with this commandment, consult Table 1 to guide your probing of a company's financial condition and financial performance.)
4. Look for opportunities to apply the concepts and analytical tools in the text chapters.
5. Be thorough in your diagnosis of the situation (either make a one- or two-page outline of your assessment or work through the exercises on Strat-Tutor).
6. Support any and all opinions with well-reasoned arguments and numerical evidence; don't stop until you can purge "I think" and "I feel" from your assessment and, instead, are able to rely completely on "My analysis shows."
7. Develop charts, tables, and graphs to expose more clearly the main points of your analysis.
8. Prioritize your recommendations and make sure they can be carried out in an acceptable time frame with the available skills and financial resources.
9. Review your recommended action plan to see if it addresses all of the problems and issues you identified.
10. Avoid recommending any course of action that could have disastrous consequences if it doesn't work out as planned; therefore, be as alert to the downside risks of your recommendations as you are to their upside potential and appeal.

---

relevant to what you are looking for. Like most things, once you get a little experience under your belt on how to do company and industry research on the Internet, you will find that you can readily find the information you need.

THE TEN COMMANDMENTS OF CASE ANALYSIS

As a way of summarizing our suggestions about how to approach the task of case analysis, we have compiled what we like to call "The Ten Commandments of Case Analysis." They are shown in Table 2. If you observe all or even most of these commandments faithfully as you prepare a case either for class discussion or for a written report, your chances of doing a good job on the assigned cases will be much improved. Hang in there, give it your best shot, and have some fun exploring what the real world of strategic management is all about.

STARBUCKS CORPORATION

Arthur A. Thompson, *The University of Alabama*

John E. Gamble, *University of South Alabama*

In 1998 Howard Schultz had ample reason to be proud of what Starbucks had accomplished during his past 11 years as the company's CEO. The company had enjoyed phenomenal growth and become one of the great retailing stories of recent history by making exceptional coffee drinks and selling dark-roasted coffee beans and coffee-making equipment that would allow customers to brew an exceptional cup of coffee at home. The Starbucks brand was regarded as one of the best known and most potent brand names in America and the company had firmly established itself as the dominant retailer, roaster, and brand of specialty coffee in North America. It already had over 1,500 stores in North America and the Pacific Rim and was opening new ones at a rate of more than one per day. Sales in fiscal year 1997 were a record $967 million and profits reached an all-time high of $57.4 million. The company's closest competitor had fewer than 300 retail locations. And since going public in 1992, Starbucks has seen its stock price increase nearly ninefold.

Exhibit 1 contains a summary of Starbucks key performance statistics for the 1992–97 period.

COMPANY BACKGROUND

Starbucks began in 1971 when three academics—English teacher Jerry Baldwin, history teacher Zev Siegel, and writer Gordon Bowker—opened a store called Starbucks Coffee, Tea, and Spice in the touristy Pikes Place Market in Seattle. The three partners shared a love of fine coffees and exotic teas and believed they could build a clientele in Seattle much like that which had already emerged in the San Francisco Bay area. Each invested $1,350 and borrowed another $5,000 from a bank to open the Pikes Place store. Baldwin, Siegel, and Bowker chose the name Starbucks in honor of Starbuck, the coffee-loving first mate in Herman Melville's *Moby Dick* (so company legend has it), and because they thought the name evoked the romance of the high seas and the seafaring tradition of the early coffee traders. The new company's logo, designed by an artist friend, was a two-tailed mermaid encircled by the store's name.

The inspiration for the Starbucks enterprise was a Dutch immigrant, Alfred Peet, who had begun importing fine arabica coffees into the United States during the 1950s. Peet viewed coffee as a fine winemaker views grapes, appraising it in terms of country of origin, estates, and harvests. Peet had opened a small store, Peet's Coffee and Tea, in Berkeley, California, in 1966 and had cultivated a loyal clientele. Peet's store specialized

EXHIBIT 1 Key Performance Statistics for Starbucks Corporation, 1992–97

	As of and for the Fiscal Year Ended:					
	September 28, 1997 (52 Weeks)	September 29, 1996 (52 Weeks)	October 1, 1995 (52 Weeks)	October 2, 1994 (52 Weeks)	October 3, 1993 (53 Weeks)	September 27, 1992 (52 Weeks)
Results of Operations Data						
Net revenues						
Retail	$828,074	$600,067	$402,655	$248,495	$153,610	$ 89,669
Specialty sales	117,635	78,655	48,143	26,543	15,952	10,143
Direct response	21,237	17,759	14,415	9,885	6,979	3,385
Total net revenues	966,946	696,481	465,213	284,923	176,541	103,197
Operating income	88,222	56,993	40,116	23,298	12,618	7,113
Provision for merger costs[1]	—	—	—	3,867	—	—
Gain on sale of investment in Noah's[2]	—	9,218	—	—	—	—
Net earnings	$ 57,412	$ 42,128	$ 26,102	$ 10,206	$ 8,282	$ 4,454
Net earnings per common and common equivalent share—fully diluted[3]	$ 0.70	$ 0.54	$ 0.36	$ 0.17	$ 0.14	$ 0.09
Cash dividends per share	—	—	—	—	—	—
Balance Sheet Data						
Working capital	$177,578	$238,450	$134,304	$ 44,162	$ 42,092	$ 40,142
Total assets	850,672	726,613	468,178	231,421	201,712	91,547
Long-term debt (including current portion)	168,832	167,980	81,773	80,500	82,100	1,359
Redeemable preferred stock	—	—	—	—	4,944	—
Shareholders' equity	$531,830	$451,660	$312,231	$109,898	$ 88,686	$ 76,923
Store Operating Data						
Percentage change in comparable store sales[4]	5%	7%	9%	9%	19%	19%
Stores open at year end—continental North America:						
Company-operated stores	1,270	929	627	399	260	162
Licensed stores[5]	94	75	49	26	12	3
	1,364	1,004	676	425	272	165
Stores open at year end—outside continental North America:						
Licensed stores[5]	17	2	—	—	—	—
Total stores	1,381	1,006	676	425	272	165

[1]Provision for merger costs reflects expenses related to the merger with The Coffee Connection, Inc., in fiscal 1994.
[2]Gain on sale of investment in Noah's results from the sale of Noah's New York Bagel, Inc. ("Noah's"), stock in fiscal 1996.
[3]Earnings per share is based on the weighted-average shares outstanding during the period plus, when their effect is dilutive, common stock equivalents consisting of certain shares subject to stock options. Fully diluted earnings per share assumes conversion of the company's convertible subordinated debentures using the "if converted" method, when such securities are dilutive, with net income adjusted for the after-tax interest expense and amortization applicable to these debentures.
[4]Includes only company-operated stores open 13 months or longer.
[5]Operated by licensees through either licensing agreements or joint ventures. Product sales to and royalties and fees from the company's licensees are included in the company's specialty sales revenues. Joint ventures are accounted for on the equity method, and therefore the operations are not consolidated into the company's operations.
Source: 1996 and 1997 annual reports.

in importing fine coffees and teas, dark-roasting its own beans the European way to bring out their full flavor, and teaching customers how to grind the beans and make freshly brewed coffee at home. Baldwin, Siegel, and Bowker were well acquainted with Peet's expertise, having visited his store on numerous occasions and spent many hours listening to Peet expound on quality coffees and the importance of proper bean-roasting techniques. All three were devoted fans of Peet and his dark-roasted coffees, going so far as to order their personal coffee supplies by mail from Peet's.

The Pikes Place store featured modest, hand-built nautical fixtures. One wall was devoted to whole-bean coffees; another had shelves of coffee products. The store did not offer fresh-brewed coffee by the cup, but samples were sometimes available for tasting. Initially, Siegel was the only paid employee. He wore a grocer's apron, scooped out beans for customers, extolled the virtues of fine, dark-roasted coffees, and functioned as the partnership's retail expert. The other two partners kept their day jobs but came by at lunch or after work to help out. During the start-up period, Baldwin kept the books and developed a growing knowledge of coffee; Bowker served as the "magic, mystery, and romance man."[1] The store was an immediate success, with sales exceeding expectations, partly because of a favorable article in the *Seattle Times*. In the early months, each of the founders traveled to Berkeley to learn more about coffee roasting from their mentor, Alfred Peet, who urged them to keep deepening their knowledge of coffees and teas. For most of the first year, Starbucks ordered its coffee beans from Peet's, but then the partners purchased a used roaster from Holland and set up roasting operations in a nearby ramshackle building. Baldwin and Bowker experimented with Alfred Peet's roasting procedures and came up with their own blends and flavors. A second Starbucks store was opened in 1972.

By the early 1980s, the company had four Starbucks stores in the Seattle area and could boast of having been profitable every year since opening its doors. But the roles and responsibilities of the cofounders underwent change. Zev Siegel experienced burnout and left the company to pursue other interests. Jerry Baldwin took over day-to-day management of the company and functioned as chief executive officer; Gordon Bowker remained involved as an owner but devoted most of his time to his advertising and design firm, a weekly newspaper he had founded, and a microbrewery he was launching (the Redhook Ale Brewery).

Howard Schultz Enters the Picture

In 1981, Howard Schultz, vice president and general manager of U.S. operations for Hammarplast—a Swedish maker of stylish kitchen equipment and housewares—noticed that Starbucks was placing larger orders than Macy's was for a certain type of drip coffeemaker. Curious to learn what was going on, he decided to pay the company a visit. The morning after his arrival in Seattle, Schultz was escorted to the Pikes Place store by Linda Grossman, the retail merchandising manager for Starbucks. A solo violinist was playing Mozart at the door, with his violin case open for donations. Schultz immediately was taken by the powerful and pleasing aroma of the coffees, the wall displaying coffee beans, and the rows of red, yellow, and black Hammarplast coffeemakers on the shelves. As he talked with the clerk behind the counter, the clerk scooped out some Sumatran coffee beans, ground them, put the grounds in a cone filter, poured hot water over the cone, and shortly handed Schultz a porcelain mug filled with the freshly brewed coffee. After three sips, Schultz was hooked. He began asking the clerk and

---

[1]Howard Schultz and Dori Jones Yang, *Pour Your Heart Into It* (New York: Hyperion, 1997), p. 33.

Grossman questions about the company, about coffees from different parts of the world, and about the different ways of roasting coffee.

Next, Schultz met with Jerry Baldwin and Gordon Bowker, whose offices over-looked the company's coffee-roasting operation. The atmosphere was informal. Baldwin, dressed in a sweater and tie, showed Schultz some new beans that had just come in from Java and suggested they try a sample. Baldwin did the brewing himself, using a glass pot called a French press. Bowker, a slender, bearded man with dark hair and intense brown eyes, appeared at the door and the three men sat down to talk about Starbucks. Schultz was struck by their knowledge of coffee, their commitment to pro-viding high-quality products, and their passion for educating customers about the mer-its of dark-roasted coffees. Baldwin told Schultz, "We don't manage the business to maximize anything other than the quality of the coffee."[2] Starbucks purchased only the finest arabica coffees and put them through a meticulous dark-roasting process to bring out their full flavors. Baldwin explained that the cheap robusta coffees used in super-market blends burn when subjected to dark roasting. He also noted that the makers of supermarket blends prefer lighter roasts because they allow higher yields (the longer a coffee is roasted, the more weight it loses).

Schultz was struck by the business philosophy of the two partners. It was clear from their discussions that Starbucks stood not just for good coffee, but rather for the dark-roasted flavor profiles that the founders were passionate about. Top-quality, fresh-roasted, whole-bean coffee was the company's differentiating feature and a bedrock value. It was also clear to Schultz that Starbucks was strongly committed to educating its customers to appreciate the qualities of fine coffees, rather than just kowtowing to mass-market appeal. The company depended mainly on word-of-mouth to get more people into its stores, then relied on the caliber of its product to give patrons a sense of discovery and excitement. It built customer loyalty cup by cup as buyers of its prod-ucts developed their palates.

On his trip back to New York the next day, Howard Schultz could not stop thinking about Starbucks and what it would be like to be a part of the Starbucks enterprise. Schultz recalled, "There was something magic about it, a passion and authenticity I had never experienced in business."[3] Living in the Seattle area also had a strong appeal. By the time Schultz landed at Kennedy Airport, he knew he wanted to go to work for Starbucks. Though there was nothing in his background (see Exhibit 2) that prepared him for the experience, Schultz asked Baldwin at the first opportunity whether there was any way he could fit into Starbucks. The two quickly established an easy, comfortable rapport, but it still took a year of numerous meetings and a lot of convincing to get Baldwin, Bowker, and their silent partner from San Francisco to agree to hire Howard Schultz. Schultz pursued a job at Starbucks far more vigorously than Starbucks pursued him. There was some nervousness at Starbucks about bringing in an outsider, especially a high-powered New Yorker, who had not grown up with the values of the company. Nonetheless, Schultz continued to press his ideas about the tremendous potential of expanding the Starbucks enterprise outside Seattle and expos-ing people all over America to Starbucks coffee—arguing there had to be more than just a few thousand coffee lovers in Seattle who would like the company's products. Schultz believed that Starbucks had such great promise that he offered to take a salary cut in exchange for a small equity stake in the business.

---

[2]Ibid., p. 34.

[3]Ibid., p. 36.

EXHIBIT 2   Howard Schultz's Background

- Parents both came from working-class families residing in Brooklyn, New York, for two generations. Neither parent completed high school.
- Grew up in a government-subsidized housing project in Brooklyn; was the oldest of three children. Played sports with the neighborhood kids and developed a passion for baseball; became a die-hard Yankees fan.
- Father was a blue-collar factory worker and taxicab driver who held many low-wage, no-benefits jobs; mother remained home to take care of the children during their preschool years, then worked as an office receptionist. The family was hard pressed to make ends meet.
- Had a number of jobs as a teenager—a paper route, a counter job at luncheonette, an after-school job in the garment district in Manhattan, a summer job steaming yarn at a knit factory. Always gave part of his earnings to his mother to help with family expenses.
- Saw success in sports as his way to escape life in the projects; played quarterback on the high school football team.
- Accepted a scholarship to play football at Northern Michigan University (the only offer he got). (When his parents drove him to the campus to begin the fall term, it was his first trip outside New York. It turned out that he didn't have enough talent to play football, but he got loans and worked at several jobs to keep himself in school.) Majored in communications, took a few business courses on the side, and graduated in 1975 with a B average—the first person in his family to graduate from college.
- Went to work for for a ski lodge in Michigan, then left to go back to New York, landing a sales job at Xerox Corporation. Left Xerox to work for Hammarplast, U.S.A., becoming vice president and general manager in charge of U.S. operations and managing 20 independent sales representatives.
- Married Sheri Kersch in July 1982; became the father of two children.
- Father contracted lung cancer in 1982 at age 60 and died in 1988, leaving mother with no pension, no life insurance, and no savings.

Source: Compiled by the case researchers from information in Howard Schultz and Dori Jones Yang, *Pour Your Heart Into It* (New York: Hyperion, 1997).

But the owners worried that by offering Schultz a job as head of marketing they would be committing themselves to a new direction for Starbucks. At a spring 1982 meeting with the three owners in San Francisco, Schultz once again presented his vision for opening Starbucks stores across the United States and Canada. He flew back to New York thinking a job offer was in the bag. But the next day Baldwin called Schultz and indicated that the owners had decided against hiring him because geographic expansion was too risky and because they did not share Schultz's vision for Starbucks. Schultz was despondent; still, he believed so deeply in Starbucks' potential that he decided to make a last-ditch appeal. He called Baldwin back the next day and made an impassioned, though reasoned, case for why the decision was a mistake. Baldwin agreed to reconsider. The next morning Baldwin called Schultz and told him the job of heading marketing and overseeing the retail stores was his. In September 1982, Howard Schultz took on his new responsibilities at Starbucks.

Starbucks and Howard Schultz: The 1982–85 Period

In his first few months at Starbucks, Schultz spent most of his waking hours in the four Seattle stores—working behind the counters, tasting different kinds of coffee, talking with customers, getting to know store personnel, and educating himself about the retail aspects of the coffee business. By December, Jerry Baldwin decided that Schultz was ready for the final part of his training—roasting coffee. Schultz spent a week at the roaster examining the color of the beans, listening for the telltale second pop of the beans during the roasting process, learning to taste the subtle differences among Baldwin and Bowker's various roasts, and familiarizing himself with the roasting techniques for different beans.

Meanwhile, he made a point of acclimating himself to the informal dress code, blending in with the culture, and gaining credibility and building trust with colleagues. Making the transition from the high-energy, coat-and-tie style of New York to the more casual ambience of the Pacific Northwest required a conscious effort on Schultz's part. One day during the busy Christmas season that first year, Schultz made real headway in gaining the acceptance and respect of company personnel at the Pikes Place store. The store was packed and Schultz was behind the counter ringing up sales when some-one shouted that a customer had just headed out the door with some stuff—two expensive coffeemakers it turned out, one in each hand. Without thinking, Schultz leaped over the counter and chased the thief up the cobblestone street outside the store, yelling "Drop that stuff! Drop it!" The thief was startled enough to drop both pieces and run away. Schultz picked up the merchandise and returned to the store, holding up the coffeemakers like trophies. Everyone applauded. When Schultz returned to his office later that afternoon, his staff had strung up a banner that read "MAKE MY DAY."[4]

Schultz was overflowing with ideas for the company. Early on, he noticed that first-time customers sometimes felt uneasy in the stores because of their lack of knowledge about fine coffees and because store employees sometimes came across as a little arrogant. Schultz worked with store employees on developing customer-friendly sales skills and produced brochures that made it easy for customers to learn about fine coffees.

Schultz's biggest idea for Starbucks' future came during the spring of 1983 when the company sent him to Milan, Italy, to attend an international housewares show. While walking from his hotel to the convention center, Schultz spotted an espresso bar and went inside to look around. The cashier beside the door nodded and smiled. The *barista* (counter worker) greeted Howard cheerfully, then gracefully pulled a shot of espresso for one customer and handcrafted a foamy cappuccino for another, all the while conversing merrily with those standing at the counter. Schultz judged the barista's performance as "great theater." Just down the way on a side street, he entered an even more crowded espresso bar, where the barista, whom he surmised to be the owner, was greeting customers by name; people were laughing and talking in an atmosphere that plainly was comfortable and familiar. In the next few blocks, he saw two more espresso bars. When the trade show concluded for the day, Schultz walked the streets of Milan exploring espresso bars. Some were stylish and upscale; others attracted a blue-collar clientele. What struck Schultz was how popular and vibrant the Italian coffee bars were. Most had few chairs, and it was common for Italian opera to be playing in the background. Energy levels were typically high, and the bars seemed to function as an integral community gathering place. Each one had its own unique character, but they all had a barista who performed with flair and exhibited a camaraderie with the customers. Schultz was particularly struck by the fact that there were 1,500 coffee bars in Milan, a city about the size of Philadelphia, and a total of 200,000 in all of Italy. His mind started churning.

---

[4]Ibid., p. 48.

Schultz's first few days in Milan produced a revelation: The Starbucks stores in Seattle completely missed the point. Starbucks, he decided, needed to serve fresh-brewed coffee, espresso, and cappuccino in its stores (in addition to beans and coffee equipment). Going to Starbucks should be an experience, a special treat; the stores should be a place to meet friends and visit. Re-creating the Italian coffee-bar culture in the United States could be Starbucks' differentiating factor. Schultz remained in Milan for a week, exploring coffee bars and learning as much as he could about the Italian passion for coffee drinks. In one bar, he heard a customer order a *caffè latte* and decided to try one himself—the barista made a shot of espresso, steamed a frothy pitcher of milk, poured the two together in a cup, and put a dollop of foam on the top. Schultz concluded that it was "the perfect drink," and thought to himself, "No one in America knows about this. I've got to take it back with me."[5]

Schultz's Growing Frustration   On Schultz's return from Italy, he shared his revelation and ideas for modifying the format of Starbucks stores with Baldwin and Bowker. But instead of winning their approval, Schultz encountered strong resistance. Baldwin and Bowker argued that Starbucks was a retailer, not a restaurant or bar. They feared that serving drinks would put them in the beverage business and dilute the integrity of Starbucks' mission as a coffee store. They pointed out that Starbucks was a profitable small, private company and there was no reason to rock the boat. But a more pressing reason for their resistance emerged shortly—Baldwin and Bowker were excited by an opportunity to purchase Peet's Coffee and Tea. The acquisition took place in 1984; to fund it, Starbucks had to take on considerable debt, leaving little in the way of financial flexibility to support Schultz's ideas for entering the beverage part of the coffee business or expanding the number of Starbucks stores. For most of 1984, Starbucks managers were dividing their time between their operations in Seattle and the Peet's enterprise in San Francisco. Schultz found himself in San Francisco every other week supervising the marketing and operations of the five Peet's stores. Starbucks employees began to feel neglected and, in one quarter, did not receive their usual bonus due to tight financial conditions. Employee discontent escalated to the point where a union election was called, and the union won by three votes. Baldwin was shocked at the results, concluding that employees no longer trusted him. In the months that followed, he began to spend more of his energy on the Peet's operation in San Francisco.

It took Howard Schultz nearly a year to convince Jerry Baldwin to let him test an espresso bar. After Baldwin relented, Starbucks' sixth store, which opened in April 1984, became the first one designed to sell beverages and the first one in downtown Seattle. Schultz asked for a 1,500-square-foot space to set up a full-scale Italian-style espresso bar, but Jerry agreed to allocating only 300 square feet in a corner of the new store. There was no pre-opening marketing blitz and no sign announcing NOW SERVING ESPRESSO—the lack of fanfare was part of a deliberate experiment to see what would happen. By closing time on the first day, some 400 customers had been served, well above the 250-customer average of Starbucks' best-performing stores. Within two months the store was serving 800 customers per day. The two baristas could not keep up with orders during the early morning hours, resulting in lines outside the door onto the sidewalk. Most of the business was at the espresso counter; sales at the regular retail counter were only adequate.

---

[5]Ibid., p. 53.

Schultz was elated by the test results; his visits to the store indicated that it was becoming a gathering place and that customers were pleased with the beverages being served. Schultz expected that Baldwin's doubts about entering the beverage side of the business would be dispelled and that he would gain approval to take Starbucks to a new level. Every day he went into Baldwin's office to show him the sales figures and customer counts at the new downtown store. But Baldwin was not comfortable with the success of the new store; he believed that espresso drinks were a distraction from the core business of selling fine arabica coffees at retail and rebelled at the thought that people would see Starbucks as a place to get a quick cup of coffee to go. He adamantly told Schultz, "We're coffee roasters. I don't want to be in the restaurant business . . . Besides, we're too deeply in debt to consider pursuing this idea."[6] While he didn't deny that the experiment was succeeding, he didn't want to go forward with introducing beverages in other Starbucks stores. Schultz's efforts to persuade Baldwin to change his mind continued to meet strong resistance, although to avoid a total impasse Baldwin finally did agree to let Schultz put espresso machines in the back of two other Starbucks stores.

Over the next several months, Schultz—at the age of 33—made up his mind to leave Starbucks and start his own company. His plan was to open espresso bars in high-traffic downtown locations that would emulate the friendly, energetic atmosphere he had encountered in Italian espresso bars. Schultz had become friends with a corporate lawyer, Scott Greenberg, who helped companies raise venture capital and go public. Greenberg told Schultz he believed investors would be interested in providing venture capital for the kind of company Schultz had in mind. Baldwin and Bowker, knowing how frustrated Schultz had become, supported his efforts to go out on his own and agreed to let him stay in his current job and office until definitive plans were in place. Schultz left Starbucks in late 1985.

Schultz's Il Giornale Venture

Ironically, as Schultz was finalizing the documents for his new company, Jerry Baldwin announced he would invest $150,000 of Starbucks' money in Schultz's coffee-bar enterprise, thus becoming Schultz's first investor. Baldwin accepted Schultz's invitation to be a director of the new company, and Gordon Bowker agreed to be a part-time consultant for six months. Bowker urged Schultz to make sure that everything about the new stores—the name, the presentation, the care taken in preparing the coffee—was calculated to lead customers to expect something better than competitors offered. Bowker proposed that the new company be named Il Giornale (pronounced *ill jor-nahl-ee*) Coffee Company, a suggestion that Schultz accepted. In December 1985, Bowker and Schultz made a trip to Italy during which they visited some 500 espresso bars in Milan and Verona, observing local habits, taking notes about decor and menus, snapping photographs, and videotaping baristas in action.

Greenberg and Schultz then drew up plans to raise an initial $400,000 in seed capital and another $1.25 million in equity—enough to launch at least eight espresso bars and prove the concept would work in Seattle and elsewhere. The seed capital was raised by the end of January 1986, primarily from Starbucks and two other investors who believed in Schultz and his ideas, but it took Schultz until the end of the year to raise the remaining $1.25 million. He made presentations to 242 potential investors, 217 of whom said no. Many who heard Schultz's hour-long presentation saw coffee as

---

[6]Ibid., pp. 61–62.

a commodity business and thought that Schultz's espresso-bar concept lacked any basis for sustainable competitive advantage (no patent on dark roast, no advantage in purchasing coffee beans, no way to bar the entry of imitative competitors). Some noted that consumption of coffee had been declining since the mid-1960s, others were skeptical that people would pay $1.50 or more for a cup of coffee, and still others were turned off by the company's hard-to-pronounce name. Being rejected by so many potential investors was disheartening (some who listened to Schultz's presentation didn't even bother to call him back; others refused to take his calls). Nonetheless, Schultz continued to display passion and enthusiasm in making his pitch and never doubted that his plan would work. He ended up raising $1.65 million from about 30 investors; most of this money came from nine people, five of whom became directors of the new company.

One of Howard Schultz's earliest moves during the start-up process was to hire Dave Olsen, who in 1974 had opened a coffee bar, Café Allegro, near the busiest entrance to the University of Washington campus. Olsen was a long-standing Starbucks customer, having discovered the quality of Starbucks' coffee beans, gotten to know the owners, and worked with them to develop a custom espresso roast for use in his café. Olsen's successful Café Allegro had become known for *café au lait,* a concoction equivalent to the Italian *caffè latte.* When Olsen heard of Schultz's plans for Il Giornale, he called Schultz and expressed an interest in being part of the new company—he was intrigued by the Italian coffee-bar concept and was looking for a more expansive career opportunity. Olsen not only had coffee expertise but also had spent 10 years in an apron behind the counter at Café Allegro. Schultz immediately picked up on the synergy between him and Olsen. His own strengths were in forming and communicating a vision, raising money, finding good store locations, building a brand name, and planning for growth. Olsen understood the nuts and bolts of operating a retail café, hiring and training baristas, and making and serving good drinks. Plus, Olsen was fun to work with. Schultz put Olsen in charge of store operations, made him the coffee conscience of the company, and gave him the authority to make sure that Il Giornale served the best coffee and espresso possible.

The first Il Giornale store opened in April 1986. It had a mere 700 square feet and was located near the entrance of Seattle's tallest building. The decor was Italian, the menu contained Italian words, and Italian opera music played in the background. The baristas wore white shirts and bow ties. All service was stand-up—there were no chairs. National and international papers hung from rods on the wall. By closing time on the first day, 300 customers had been served, mostly in the morning hours. Schultz and Olsen worked hard to make sure that all the details were executed perfectly. For the first few weeks, Olsen worked behind the counter during the morning rush.

But while the core idea worked well, it soon became apparent that several aspects of Il Giornale's format weren't appropriate for Seattle. Some customers objected to the incessant opera music, others wanted a place to sit down, and many didn't understand the Italian words on the menu. These "mistakes" were quickly fixed, without compromising the style and elegance of the store. Within six months, Il Giornale was serving more than 1,000 customers a day and regulars had learned how to pronounce the company's name. Because most customers were in a hurry, it became apparent that speedy service was a competitive advantage.

Six months after opening the first store, Il Giornale opened a second store in another downtown building. A third store was opened in Vancouver, British Columbia, in April 1987. Vancouver was chosen to test the transferability of the company's business concept outside Seattle. To reach his goal of opening 50 stores in five years, Schultz needed to dispel his investors' doubts about geographic expansion. By mid-1987 sales at the three stores were equal to $1.5 million annually.

Il Giornale Acquires Starbucks

In March 1987 Jerry Baldwin and Gordon Bowker decided to sell the whole Starbucks operation in Seattle—the stores, the roasting plant, and the Starbucks name. Bowker wanted to cash out his coffee-business investment to concentrate on his other enterprises; Baldwin, who was tired of commuting between Seattle and San Francisco and wrestling with the troubles created by the two parts of the company, elected to concentrate on the Peet's operation. As he recalls, "My wife and I had a 30-second conversation and decided to keep Peet's. It was the original and it was better."[7]

Schultz knew immediately that he had to buy Starbucks; his board of directors agreed. Schultz and his newly hired finance and accounting manager drew up a set of financial projections for the combined operations and a financing package that included a stock offering to Il Giornale's original investors and a line of credit with local banks. While a rival plan to acquire Starbucks was put together by another Il Giornale investor, Schultz's proposal prevailed and within weeks Schultz had raised the $3.8 million needed to buy Starbucks. The acquisition was completed in August 1987. After the papers were signed, Schultz and Scott Greenberg walked across the street to the first Il Giornale store, ordered themselves espresso drinks, and sat at a table near the window. Greenberg placed the hundred-page business plan that had been used to raise the $3.8 million between them and lifted his cup in a toast—"We did it," they said together.[8] The new name of the combined companies was Starbucks Corporation. Howard Schultz, at the age of 34, became Starbucks' president and CEO.

STARBUCKS AS A PRIVATE COMPANY: 1987–92

The following Monday morning, Schultz returned to the Starbucks offices at the roasting plant, greeted all the familiar faces and accepted their congratulations, then called the staff together for a meeting on the roasting-plant floor. He began:

> All my life I have wanted to be part of a company and a group of people who share a common vision . . . I'm here today because I love this company. I love what it represents . . . I know you're concerned . . . I promise you I will not let you down. I promise you I will not leave anyone behind . . . In five years, I want you to look back at this day and say "I was there when it started. I helped build this company into something great."[9]

Schultz told the group that his vision was for Starbucks to become a national company with values and guiding principles that employees could be proud of. He indicated that he wanted to include people in the decision-making process and that he would be open and honest with them.

Schultz said he believed it was essential, not just an intriguing option, for a company to respect its people, to inspire them, and to share the fruits of its success with those who contributed to its long-term value. His aspiration was for Starbucks to become the most respected brand name in coffee and for the company to be admired for its corporate responsibility. In the next few days and weeks, however, Schultz

---

[7]As quoted in Jennifer Reese, "Starbucks: Inside the Coffee Cult," *Fortune*, December 9, 1996, p.193.
[8]Schultz and Yang, *Pour Your Heart Into It*, p. 100.
[9]Ibid., pp. 101–2.

came to see that the unity and morale at Starbucks had deteriorated badly in the 20 months he had been at Il Giornale. Some employees were cynical and felt unappreciated. There was a feeling that prior management had abandoned them and a wariness about what the new regime would bring. Schultz determined that he would have to make it a priority to build a new relationship of mutual respect between employees and management.

The new Starbucks had a total of nine stores. The business plan Schultz had presented investors called for the new company to open 125 stores in the next five years—15 the first year, 20 the second, 25 the third, 30 the fourth, and 35 the fifth. Revenues were projected to reach $60 million in 1992. But the company lacked experienced management. Schultz had never led a growth effort of such magnitude and was just learning what the job of CEO was all about, having been the president of a small company for barely two years. Dave Olsen had run a single café for 11 years and was just learning to manage a multistore operation. Ron Lawrence, the company's controller, had worked as a controller for several organizations. Other Starbucks employees had only the experience of managing or being a part of a six-store organization. When Starbucks' key roaster and coffee buyer resigned, Schultz put Dave Olsen in charge of buying and roasting coffee. Lawrence Maltz, who had 20 years of experience in business and eight years of experience as president of a profitable public beverage company, was hired as executive vice president and charged with heading operations, finance, and human resources.

In the next several months, a number of changes were instituted. To symbolize the merging of the two companies and the two cultures, a new logo was created that melded the Starbucks and Il Giornale logos. The Starbucks stores were equipped with espresso machines and remodeled to look more Italian than Old World nautical. The traditional Starbucks brown was replaced by Il Giornale green. The result was a new type of store—a cross between a retail coffee-bean store and an espresso bar/café—that became Starbucks' signature format in the 1990s.

By December 1987, employees at Starbucks had begun buying into the changes Schultz was making and trust had begun to build between management and employees. New stores were on the verge of opening in Vancouver and Chicago. One Starbucks store employee, Daryl Moore, who had voted against unionization in 1985, began to question his fellow employees about the need for a union. Over the next few weeks, Moore began a move to decertify the union. He carried a decertification letter around to Starbucks stores and secured the signatures of employees who no longer wished to be represented by the union. After getting a majority of store employees to sign the letter, he presented it to the National Labor Relations Board and the union representing store employees was decertified. Later, in 1992, the union representing Starbucks' roasting plant and warehouse employees was also decertified.

Expansion into Markets Outside the Pacific Northwest

Starbucks' entry into Chicago proved far more troublesome than management anticipated. The first Chicago store opened October 27, 1987, the same day the stock market crashed. Three more stores were opened in Chicago over the next six months, but customer counts were substantially below expectations—Chicagoans didn't take to dark-roasted coffee as fast as Schultz had anticipated. At the first downtown store, for example, which opened onto the street rather than into the lobby of the building where it was located, customers were hesitant to go out in the wind and cold to get a cup of coffee in the winter months. Store margins were squeezed for a number of reasons: It was expensive to supply fresh coffee to the Chicago stores out of the Seattle ware-house, and both rents and wage rates were higher in Chicago than in Seattle. Gradually, customer counts improved, but Starbucks lost money on its Chicago stores until 1990, when prices were raised to reflect higher rents and labor costs, more experienced store managers were hired, and a critical mass of customers caught on to the taste of Starbucks products.

Portland, Oregon, was the next market entered, and Portland coffee drinkers took to Starbucks products quickly. By 1991, the Chicago stores had become profitable and the company was ready for its next big market entry. Management decided on California because of its host of neighborhood centers and the receptiveness of Californians to innovative, high-quality food. Los Angeles was chosen as the first California market to enter, principally because of its status as a trendsetter and its cultural ties to the rest of the country. L.A. consumers embraced Starbucks quickly—the *Los Angeles Times* named Starbucks as the best coffee in America before the first L.A. store opened. The entry into San Francisco proved more troublesome because of an ordinance there against converting stores to restaurant-related uses in certain prime urban neighborhoods; Starbucks could sell beverages and pastries to customers at stand-up counters but could not offer seating in stores that had formerly been used for general retailing. However, the city council was soon convinced by café owners and real estate brokers to change the code. Still, Starbucks faced strong competition from Peet's and local espresso bars in the San Francisco market.

When Starbucks' store expansion targets proved easier to meet than Schultz had originally anticipated, he upped the numbers to keep challenging the organization. Starting from a base of 11 stores, Starbucks opened 15 new stores in fiscal 1988, 20 in 1989, 30 in 1990, 32 in 1991, and 53 in 1992—producing a total of 161 stores. The opening of 150 new stores in five years significantly exceeded the 1987 business plan's objective of 125.

From the outset, the strategy was to open only company-owned stores; franchising was avoided so as to keep the company in full control of the quality of its products and the character and location of its stores. But company ownership of all stores required Starbucks to raise new venture capital, principally by selling shares to new or existing investors, to cover the cost of expansion. In 1988 the company raised $3.9 million; in 1990, venture capitalists provided an additional $13.5 million; and in 1991 another round of venture capital financing generated $15 million. Starbucks was able to raise the needed funds despite posting losses of $330,000 in 1987, $764,000 in 1988, and $1.2 million in 1989. While the losses were troubling to Starbucks' board of directors and investors, Schultz's business plan had forecast losses during the early years of expansion. At a particularly tense board meeting where directors sharply questioned him about the lack of profitability, Schultz said:

> Look, we're going to keep losing money until we can do three things. We have to attract a management team well beyond our expansion needs. We have to build a world-class roasting facility. And we need a computer information system sophisticated enough to keep track of sales in hundreds and hundreds of stores.[10]

Schultz argued for patience as the company invested in the infrastructure to support continued growth well into the 1990s. He contended that hiring experienced executives ahead of the growth curve, building facilities far beyond current needs, and installing

---

[10]Ibid., p. 142.

support systems laid a strong foundation for rapid, profitable growth on down the road. His arguments carried the day with the board and with investors, especially since revenues were growing approximately 80 percent annually and customer traffic at the stores was meeting or exceeding expectations. Starbucks became profitable in 1990 and profits had increased every year thereafter.

Getting into the Mail-Order Business   The original Starbucks had begun a small mail order operation in the 1970s to serve travelers who had visited a Seattle store or former store customers who had moved away from Seattle. Sales were solicited by mailing out a simple brochure. In 1988, Starbucks developed its first catalog and began expanding its mail-order base to targeted demographic groups. In 1990 a toll-free telephone number was set up. Sales grew steadily as the company's name and reputation began to build. The company's market research indicated that its average mail-order customer was a well-educated, relatively affluent, well-traveled connoisseur interested in the arts and cultural events, and usually a loyal buyer of the company's products. As time went on, the cities and neighborhoods in which the company's mail-order customers were located became one of the beacons used to decide where to open new stores.

Schultz's Strategy to Make Starbucks a Great Place to Work

Howard Schultz strongly believed that Starbucks' success was heavily dependent on customers having a very positive experience in its stores. This meant having store employees who were knowledgeable about the company's products, who paid attention to detail, who eagerly communicated the company's passion for coffee, and who had the skills and personality to deliver consistently pleasing customer service. Many of the baristas were in their 20s and worked part-time, going to college or pursuing other career activities on the side. The challenge to Starbucks, in Schultz's view, was how to attract, motivate, and reward store employees in a manner that would make Starbucks a company that people would want to work for and that would result in higher levels of performance. Moreover, Schultz wanted to cement the trust that had been building between management and the company's workforce.

One of the requests that employees had made to the prior owners of Starbucks was to extend health care benefits to part-time workers. Their request had been turned down, but Schultz believed that expanding health care coverage to include part-timers was the right thing to do. His father had recently died of cancer, and he knew from having grown up in a family that struggled to make ends meet how difficult it was to cope with rising medical costs. In 1988 Schultz went to the board of directors with his plan to expand the company's health care coverage to include part-timers who worked at least 20 hours per week. He saw the proposal not as a generous gesture but as a core strategy to win employee loyalty and commitment to the company's mission. Board members resisted because the company was unprofitable and the added costs of the extended coverage would only worsen the company's bottom line. But Schultz argued passionately, pointing out that if the new benefit reduced turnover, which he believed was likely, then it would reduce the costs of hiring and training—which equaled about $3,000 per new hire. He further pointed out that it cost $1,500 a year to provide an employee with full benefits. Part-timers, he argued, were vital to Starbucks, constituting two-thirds of the company's workforce. Many were baristas who knew the favorite drinks of regular customers; if the barista left, that connection with the customer was broken. Moreover, many part-time employees were called upon to open the stores early, sometimes at 5:30 or 6 AM; others had to work until closing—9 PM or later. Providing these employees with health care benefits, he argued, would signal that the company honored their value and contribution.

The board came round and approved Schultz's plan. Starting in late 1988, part-timers working 20 or more hours were offered the same health coverage as full-time employees. Starbucks paid 75 percent of an employee's health insurance premium and, over the years, extended its coverage to include preventive care, crisis counseling, dental care, eye care, mental health care, and treatment for chemical dependency. Coverage was also offered for unmarried partners in a committed relationship. Since most Starbucks employees are young and comparatively healthy, the company has been able to provide broader coverage while keeping monthly payments relatively low.

The value of Starbucks' health care program struck home when one of the company's store managers and a former barista walked into Schultz's office and told him he had AIDS. Schultz said later:

> I had known [Jim] was gay but had no idea he was sick. His disease had entered a new phase, he explained, and he wouldn't be able to work any longer. We sat together and cried, for I could not find meaningful words to console him. I couldn't compose myself. I hugged him.
>
> At that point, Starbucks had no provision for employees with AIDS. We had a policy decision. Because of Jim, we decided to offer health-care coverage to all employees who have terminal illnesses, paying medical costs in full from the time they are not able to work until they are covered by government programs, usually twenty-nine months.
>
> After his visit to me, I spoke with Jim often and visited him at the hospice. Within a year he was gone. I received a letter from his family afterward, telling me how much they appreciated our benefit plan.[11]

In 1994 Howard Schultz was invited to the White House for a one-on-one meeting with President Clinton to brief him on the Starbucks health care program.

By 1991 the company's profitability had improved to the point where Schultz could pursue another employee program he believed would have a positive long-term effect on the success of Starbucks—a stock option plan for all employees.[12] Schultz wanted to turn all Starbucks employees into partners, give them a chance to share in the success of the company, and make clear the connection between their contributions and the company's market value. Even though Starbucks was still a private company, the plan that emerged called for granting every employee companywide stock options in proportion to base pay. In May 1991, the plan, dubbed Bean Stock, was presented to the board. Though board members were concerned that increasing the number of shares might unduly dilute the value of the shares of investors who had put up hard cash, the plan received unanimous approval. The first grant was made in October 1991, just after the end of the company's fiscal year in September; each partner was granted stock options worth 12 percent of base pay; the value of these first shares was pegged at $6 per share. Each October since then, Starbucks has granted employees options equal to 14 percent of base pay, awarded at the stock price at the start of the fiscal year (October 1). Employees, if they wish, can cash in one-fifth of the shares granted each succeeding year, paying the initial year's price and receiving the current year's price. It took five years for the shares to fully vest. Each of the shares granted in 1991 was worth $132 in October 1996; thus, an employee making $20,000 in 1991 could have cashed in the options granted in 1991 for more than $50,000 in October 1996. In 1991

---

[11]Ibid., p. 129.
[12]Ibid., pp. 131–36.

when the Bean Stock program was presented to employees, Starbucks dropped the term *employee* and began referring to all its people as *partners* because everyone, including part-timers working at least 20 hours per week, was eligible for stock options after six months. At the end of fiscal year 1997, there were 8.7 million shares in outstanding options at an average exercisable price of $19.72 (which compared very favorably to the current stock price of $43.50).

In 1995, Starbucks implemented an employee stock purchase plan. Eligible employees could contribute up to 10 percent of their base earnings to quarterly purchases of the company's common stock at 85 percent of the going stock price. The total number of shares that could be issued under the plan was 4 million. After the plan's creation, nearly 200,000 shares were issued; just over 2,500 of the 14,600 eligible employees participated. Exhibit 3 shows the performance of Starbucks' stock since 1992.

Starbucks was able to attract motivated people with above-average skills and good work habits not only because of its fringe benefit program but also because of its pay scale. Store employees were paid $6 to $8 per hour, well above the minimum wage.

Starbucks believed that its efforts to make the company an attractive, caring place to work were responsible for its relatively low turnover rates. Whereas most national retailers and fast-food chains had turnover rates for store employees ranging from 150 to 400 percent a year, the turnover rates for Starbucks' baristas ran about 65 percent. Starbucks' turnover for store managers was about 25 percent compared to about 50 percent for other chain retailers. There was evidence that Schultz's approaches, values, and principles were affecting company performance in the intended manner. One Starbucks store manager commented, "Morale is very high in my store among the staff. I've worked for a lot of companies, but I've never seen this level of respect. It's a company that's very true to its workers, and it shows. Our customers always comment that we're happy and having fun. In fact, a lot of people ask if they can work here."[13]

Exhibit 4 contains a summary of Starbucks' fringe benefit program. In 1996, the projected cost of benefits was $2,200 for each of the company's 19,900 employees.

Starbucks' Mission Statement

In early 1990, the senior executive team at Starbucks went to an off-site retreat to debate the company's values and beliefs and draft a mission statement. Schultz wanted the mission statement to convey a strong sense of organizational purpose and to articulate the company's fundamental beliefs and guiding principles. The draft was submitted to all employees for review. Changes were made based on employees' comments. The resulting mission statement appears in Exhibit 5.

To make sure the company lived up to the elements of the mission statement, a "Mission Review" system was formed. Employees were urged to report their concerns to the company's Mission Review team if they thought particular management decisions were not supportive of the company's mission statement. Comment cards were given to each newly hired employee and were kept available in common areas with other employee forms. Employees had the option of signing the comment cards or not. Hundreds of cards were submitted to the Mission Review team each year. The company promised that a relevant manager would respond to all signed cards within two weeks. Howard Schultz reviewed all the comments, signed and unsigned, every month.

---

[13]Ben van Houten, "Employee Perks: Starbucks Coffee's Employee Benefit Plan," *Restaurant Business*, May 15, 1997, p. 85.

EXHIBIT 3   Monthly Trading Range and Price-Earnings Ratio of Starbucks' Common Stock, 1992–February 1998

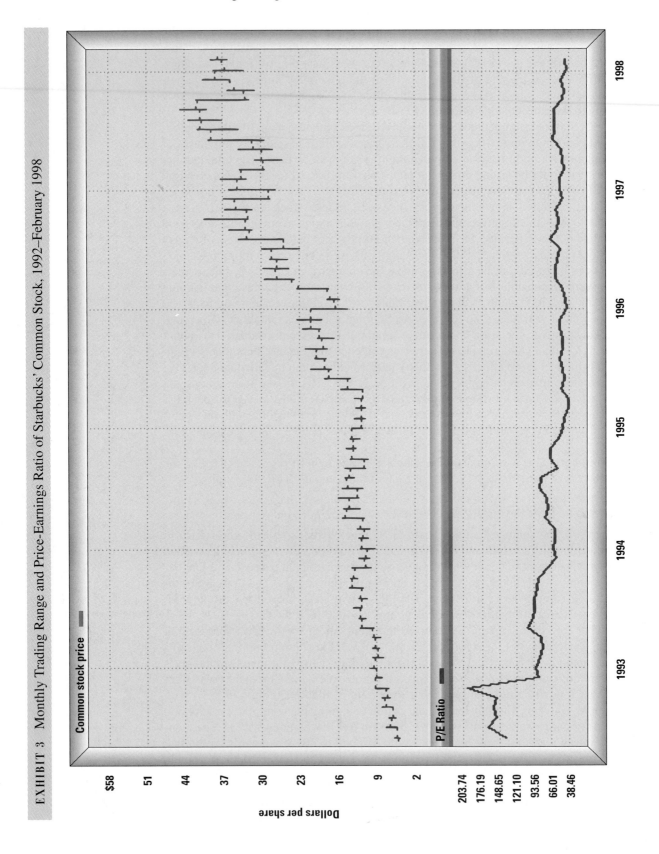

EXHIBIT 4   Components of Starbucks' Fringe Benefit Program

- Medical insurance
- Dental and vision care
- Mental health and chemical dependency coverage
- Short- and long-term disability
- Life insurance
- Benefits extended to committed domestic partners of Starbucks employees
- Stock option plan (Bean Stock)
- Sick time
- Paid vacations (first-year workers get one vacation week and two personal days)
- 401(k) retirement savings plan (the company matched 25 percent of each employee's contributions up to the first 4 percent of compensation
- Stock purchase plan
- Free pound of coffee each week
- Product discounts (30 percent)

Source: Compiled by the case researchers from company documents and other sources.

As the company continued to grow, resulting in a large and geographically scattered workforce, Starbucks assembled a team of people from different regions to go over employee concerns, seek solutions, and provide a report at the company's Open Forums. At these Open Forums, held quarterly in every geographic region where the company did business, senior managers met with all interested employees to present updates on Starbucks' performance, answer questions, and give employees an opportunity to air grievances.

Values and Principles

During these early building years, Howard Schultz and other Starbucks senior executives worked to instill some key values and guiding principles into the Starbucks culture. The keystone value in the effort "to build a company with soul" was that the company would never stop pursuing the perfect cup of coffee. Schultz remained steadfastly opposed to franchising, so that the company could control the quality of its products and build a culture common to all stores. He was adamant about not selling artificially flavored coffee beans—"We will not pollute our high-quality beans with chemicals"; if a customer wanted hazelnut-flavored coffee, Starbucks would provide it by adding hazelnut syrup to the drink rather than by adding hazelnut flavoring to the beans during roasting. Running flavored beans through the grinders would leave chemical residues that would alter the flavor of beans ground afterward; plus, the chemical smell given off by artificially flavored beans would be absorbed by other beans in the store. Furthermore, Schultz didn't want the company to pursue supermarket sales because pouring Starbucks' beans into clear plastic bins, where they could get stale, would compromise the company's distinctive product: fresh, dark-roasted, full-flavored coffee.

Starbucks' management was also emphatic about the importance of pleasing customers. Employees were trained to go out of their way, taking heroic measures if necessary, to make sure customers were fully satisfied—the theme was "just say yes" to customer requests. Employees were also encouraged to speak their minds without fear of retribution from upper management—senior executives wanted employees to be

EXHIBIT 5   The Starbucks Mission Statement

Starbucks Mission Statement

• • •

Establish Starbucks as the premier purveyor of
the finest coffee in the world while maintaining
Our uncompromising principles as we grow. The
Following six guiding principles will help us
measure the appropriateness of our decisions:

• • •

Provide a great work environment and treat
each other with respect and dignity.

• • •

Embrace diversity as an essential component
in the way we do business.

• • •

Apply the highest standards of excellence
to the purchasing, roasting, and fresh
delivery of our coffee.

• • •

Develop enthusiastically satisfied
customers all of the time.

• • •

Contribute positively to our communities
and our environment.

• • •

Recognize that profitability is essential
to our future success.

Source: Howard Schultz and Dori Jones Yang, *Pour Your Heart Into It* (New York: Hyperion, 1997), p. 139.

vocal about what Starbucks was doing right, what it was doing wrong, and what changes were needed. Management wanted employees to contribute to the process of making Starbucks a better company.

A values and principles crisis arose at Starbucks in 1989 when customers started requesting nonfat milk in cappuccinos and lattès. Howard Schultz, who read all customer comment cards, and Dave Olsen, head of coffee quality, conducted taste tests of lattès and cappuccinos made with nonfat and skim milk and concluded they were not as good as those made with whole milk. Howard Behar, recently hired as head of retail store operations, indicated that management's opinions didn't matter; what mattered was giving customers what they wanted. Schultz responded, "We will never offer nonfat milk. It's not who we are." Behar stuck to his guns, maintaining that use of nonfat milk should at least be tested—otherwise, all the statements management had made about the importance of really and truly pleasing customers were a sham. A fierce internal debate ensued. One dogmatic defender of the quality and taste of Starbucks' coffee products buttonholed Behar outside his office and told him that using nonfat milk amounted to "bastardizing" the company's products. Numerous store managers maintained that offering two kinds of milk was operationally impractical. Schultz found himself torn between the company's commitment to quality and its goal of pleasing customers. One day after visiting one of the stores in a residential neighborhood and watching a customer leave and go to a competitor's store because Starbucks did not make lattès with nonfat milk, Schultz authorized Behar to begin testing.[14] Within six months all 30 stores were offering drinks made with nonfat milk. In 1997, about half the lattès and cappuccinos Starbucks sold were made with nonfat milk.

Schultz's approach to offering employees good compensation and a comprehensive benefits package was driven by his belief that sharing the company's success with the people who made it happen helped everyone think and act like an owner, build positive long-term relationships with customers, and do things efficiently. He had a vivid recollection of his father's employment experience—bouncing from one low-paying job to another, working for employers who offered few or no benefits and who conducted their business with no respect for the contributions of the workforce—and he vowed that he would never let Starbucks employees suffer a similar fate, saying:

> My father worked hard all his life and he had little to show for it. He was a beaten man. This is not the American dream. The worker on our plant floor is contributing great value to the company; if he or she has low self-worth, that will have an effect on the company.[15]

The company's employee benefits program was predicated on the belief that better benefits attract good people and keep them longer. Schultz's rationale was that if you treat your employees well, they will treat your customers well.

STARBUCKS BECOMES A PUBLIC COMPANY

Starbucks' initial public offering (IPO) of common stock in June 1992 turned into one of the most successful IPOs of the year (see Exhibit 3 for the performance of the company's stock price since the IPO). With the capital afforded it by being a public company, Starbucks accelerated the expansion of its store network (see Exhibit 1).

---

[14]Schultz and Yang, *Pour Your Heart Into It*, p. 168.

[15]Quoted in Ingrid Abramovitch, "Miracles of Marketing," *Success* 40, no. 3, April 1993, p. 26.

Starbucks' success helped specialty coffee products begin to catch on across the United States. Competitors, some imitating the Starbucks model, began to spring up in many locations. The Specialty Coffee Association of America predicted that the number of coffee cafés in the United States would rise from 500 in 1992 to 10,000 by 1999.

The Store Expansion Strategy

In 1992 and 1993 Starbucks developed a three-year geographic expansion strategy that targeted areas which not only had favorable demographic profiles but which also could be serviced and supported by the company's operations infrastructure. For each targeted region, Starbucks selected a large city to serve as a "hub"; teams of professionals were located in hub cities to support the goal of opening 20 or more stores in the hub in the first two years. Once stores blanketed the hub, then additional stores were opened in smaller, surrounding "spoke" areas in the region. To oversee the expansion process, Starbucks created zone vice presidents to direct the development of each region and to implant the Starbucks culture in the newly opened stores. All of the new zone vice presidents Starbucks recruited came with extensive operating and marketing experience in chain-store retailing.

Starbucks' store launches grew steadily more successful. In 1995, new stores generated an average of $700,000 in revenue in their first year, far more than the average of $427,000 in 1990. This was partly due to the growing reputation of the Starbucks brand. In more and more instances, Starbucks' reputation reached new markets even before stores opened. Moreover, existing stores continued to post year-to-year gains in sales (see Exhibit 1).

Starbucks had notable success in identifying top retailing sites for its stores. The company had the best real estate team in the coffee-bar industry and a sophisticated system that enabled it to identify not only the most attractive individual city blocks but also the exact store location that was best. The company's site location track record was so good that as of 1997 it had closed only 2 of the 1,500 sites it had opened.

Real Estate, Store Design, Store Planning, and Construction

Schultz formed a headquarters group to create a store development process based on a six-month opening schedule. Starting in 1991, the company began to create its own in-house team of architects and designers to ensure that each store would convey the right image and character. Stores had to be custom-designed because the company didn't buy real estate and build its own freestanding structures like McDonald's or Wal-Mart did; rather, each space was leased in an existing structure and thus each store differed in size and shape. Most stores ranged in size from 1,000 to 1,500 square feet and were located in office buildings, downtown and suburban retail centers, airport terminals, university campus areas, or busy neighborhood shopping areas convenient to pedestrian foot traffic. Only a select few were in suburban malls. While similar materials and furnishings were used to keep the look consistent and expenses reasonable, no two stores ended up being exactly alike.

In 1994, Starbucks began to experiment with a broader range of store formats. Special seating areas were added to help make Starbucks a place where customers could meet and chat or simply enjoy a peaceful interlude in their day. Grand Cafés with fireplaces, leather chairs, newspapers, couches, and lots of ambience were created to serve as flagship stores in high-traffic, high-visibility locations. The company also experimented with drive-through windows in locations where speed and convenience were important to customers and with kiosks in supermarkets, building lobbies, and other public places.

To better reduce average store-opening costs, which had reached an undesirably high $350,000 in 1995, the company centralized buying, developed standard contracts and fixed fees for certain items, and consolidated work under those contractors who displayed good cost-control practices. The retail operations group outlined exactly the minimum amount of equipment each core store needed, so that standard items could be ordered in volume from vendors at 20 to 30 percent discounts, then delivered just in time to the store site either from company warehouses or the vendor. Modular designs for display cases were developed. And the whole store layout was developed on a computer, with software that allowed the costs to be estimated as the design evolved. All this cut store-opening costs significantly and reduced store development time from 24 to 18 weeks.

A "stores of the future" project team was formed in 1995 to raise Starbucks' store design to a still higher level and come up with the next generation of Starbucks stores. Schultz and Olsen met with the team early on to present their vision for what a Starbucks store should be like—"an authentic coffee experience that conveyed the artistry of espresso making, a place to think and imagine, a spot where people could gather and talk over a great cup of coffee, a comforting refuge that provided a sense of community, a third place for people to congregate beyond work or the home, a place that welcomed people and rewarded them for coming, and a layout that could accommodate both fast service and quiet moments." The team researched the art and literature of coffee throughout the ages, studied coffee-growing and coffee-making techniques, and looked at how Starbucks stores had already evolved in terms of design, logos, colors, and mood. The team came up with four store designs—one for each of the four stages of coffee making: growing, roasting, brewing, and aroma—each with its own color combinations, lighting scheme, and component materials. Within each of the four basic store templates, Starbucks could vary the materials and details to adapt to different store sizes and settings (downtown buildings, college campuses, neighborhood shopping areas). In late 1996, Starbucks began opening new stores based on one of the four templates. The company also introduced two ministore formats using the same styles and finishes: The *breve bar*, a store-within-a-store for supermarkets or office-building lobbies, and the *doppio*, a self-contained 8-square-foot space that could be moved from spot to spot. Management believed the project accomplished three objectives: better store designs, lower store-opening costs (about $315,000 per store on average), and formats that allowed sales in locations Starbucks could otherwise not consider.

For a number of years, Starbucks avoided debt and financed new stores entirely with equity capital. But as the company's profitability improved and its balance sheet strengthened, Schultz's opposition to debt as a legitimate financing vehicle softened. In 1996 the company completed its second debt offering, netting $161 million from the sale of convertible debentures for use in its capital construction program. Exhibits 6 through 8 present Starbucks' income statement and balance sheet data for recent years.

Product Line

Starbucks stores offered a choice of regular or decaffeinated coffee beverages, a special "coffee of the day," and a broad selection of Italian-style espresso drinks. In addition, customers could choose from a wide selection of fresh-roasted whole-bean coffees (which could be ground on the premises and carried home in distinctive packages), a selection of fresh pastries and other food items, sodas, juices, teas, and

EXHIBIT 6   Starbucks' Income Statement, 1995–97 (In thousands of dollars, except for per share data)

	Fiscal Year Ended		
	September 28, 1997	September 29, 1996	October 1, 1995
Net revenues	$966,946	$696,481	$465,213
Cost of sales and related occupancy costs	432,190	335,800	211,279
Store operating expenses	309,133	210,693	148,757
Other operating expenses	28,116	19,787	13,932
Depreciation and amortization	52,141	35,950	22,486
General and administrative expenses	57,144	37,258	28,643
Operating income	88,222	56,993	40,116
Interest and other income	12,393	11,029	6,792
Interest expense	(7,266)	(8,739)	(3,765)
Gain on sale of investment in Noah's	—	9,218	—
Earnings before income taxes	93,349	68,501	43,143
Income taxes	35,937	26,373	17,041
Net earnings	$ 57,412	$ 42,128	$ 26,102
Net earnings per common and common equivalent share—primary	$ 0.70	$ 0.55	$ 0.37
Net earnings per common and common equivalent share—fully diluted	$ 0.70	$ 0.54	$ 0.36
Weighted-average shares outstanding (000s):			
Primary	81,638	76,964	71,309
Fully diluted	89,231	80,831	71,909

Source: 1997 annual report.

coffee-related hardware and equipment. In 1997, the company introduced its Starbucks Barista home espresso machine featuring a new portafilter system that accommodated both ground coffee and Starbucks' new ready-to-use espresso pods. Power Frappuccino—a version of the company's popular Frappuccino blended beverage, packed with protein, carbohydrates, and vitamins—was tested in several markets during 1997; another promising new product being tested for possible rollout in 1998 was Chai Tea Lattè, a combination of black tea, exotic spices, honey, and milk.

The company's retail sales mix was roughly 61 percent coffee beverages, 15 percent whole-bean coffees, 16 percent food items, and 8 percent coffee-related products and equipment. The product mix in each store varied, depending on the size and location of each outlet. Larger stores carried a greater variety of whole coffee beans, gourmet food items, teas, coffee mugs, coffee grinders, coffee-making equipment, filters, storage containers, and other accessories. Smaller stores and kiosks typically sold a full line of coffee beverages, a limited selection of whole-bean coffees, and a few hardware items.

In recent years, the company began selling special jazz and blues CDs, which in some cases were special compilations that had been put together for Starbucks to use as store background music. The idea for selling the CDs originated with a Starbucks store manager who had worked in the music industry and selected the new "tape of the month" Starbucks played as background in its stores. He had gotten compliments from customers wanting to buy the music they heard and suggested to senior executives that there was a market for the company's music tapes. Research that involved looking through two years of comment cards turned up hundreds asking Starbucks to sell the music it played in its stores. The Starbucks CDs, created from the Capitol Records library, proved a significant addition to the company's product line. Some of the CDs

EXHIBIT 7 Percentage Composition of Starbucks' Income Statement, 1995–97

	Fiscal Year Ended:		
	September 28, 1997 (52 Weeks)	September 29, 1996 (52 Weeks)	October 1, 1995 (52 Weeks)
Statements of Earnings Data			
Net revenues			
Retail	85.6%	86.2%	86.6%
Specialty sales	12.2	11.3	10.3
Direct response	2.2	2.5	3.1
Total net revenues	100.0%	100.0%	100.0%
Cost of sales and related occupancy costs	44.7	48.2	45.4
Store operating expenses[1]	37.3	35.1	36.9
Other operating expenses	2.9	2.8	3.0
Depreciation and amortization	5.4	5.2	4.8
General and administrative expenses	5.9	5.3	6.2
Operating income	9.1	8.2	8.6
Interest and other income	1.3	1.6	1.5
Interest expense	(0.8)	(1.3)	(0.8)
Gain on sale of investment in Noah's	0.0	1.3	0.0
Earnings before income taxes	9.6	9.8	9.3
Income taxes	3.7	3.8	3.7
Net earnings	5.9%	6.0%	5.6%

[1]Shown as a percentage of retail sales.
Source: 1997 annual report.

were specifically collections designed to tie in with new blends of coffee that the company was promoting. Starbucks also sold Oprah's Book Club selections, the profits of which were donated to a literacy fund supported by the Starbucks Foundation.

The company was constantly engaged in efforts to develop new ideas, new products, and new experiences for customers that belonged exclusively to Starbucks. Schultz and other senior executives drummed in the importance of always being open to re-inventing the Starbucks experience.

Store Ambience

Starbucks management looked upon each store as a billboard for the company and as a contributor to building the company's brand and image. Each detail was scrutinized to enhance the mood and ambience of the store, to make sure everything signaled "best of class" and that it reflected the personality of the community and the neighborhood. The thesis was "Everything matters." The company went to great lengths to make sure the store fixtures, the merchandise displays, the colors, the artwork, the banners, the music, and the aromas all blended to create a consistent, inviting, stimulating environment that evoked the romance of coffee, that signaled the company's passion for coffee, and that rewarded customers with ceremony, stories, and surprise. Starbucks was recognized for its sensitivity to neighborhood conservation with the Scenic America's award for excellent design and "sensitive reuse of spaces within cities."

To try to keep the coffee aromas in the stores pure, Starbucks banned smoking and asked employees to refrain from wearing perfumes or colognes. Prepared foods were kept covered so customers would smell coffee only. Colorful banners and posters were used to keep the look of Starbucks stores fresh and in keeping with seasons and holi-

EXHIBIT 8   Starbucks Consolidated Balance Sheets, 1996–97 (In thousands of dollars)

	September 28, 1997	September 29, 1996
Assets		
Current Assets:		
Cash and cash equivalents	$ 70,126	$126,215
Short-term investments	83,504	103,221
Accounts and notes receivable	30,524	17,621
Inventories	119,526	83,370
Prepaid expenses and other current assets	8,763	6,534
Deferred income taxes, net	4,164	2,580
Total current assets	316,607	339,541
Joint ventures and other investments	34,464	4,401
Property, plant, and equipment, net	483,259	369,477
Deposits and other assets	16,342	13,194
Total assets	$850,672	$726,613
Liabilities and Shareholders' Equity		
Current Liabilities:		
Accounts payable	$ 46,324	$ 38,034
Checks drawn in excess of bank balances	25,807	16,241
Accrued compensation and related costs	25,894	15,001
Accrued interest payable	2,927	3,004
Accrued occupancy costs	12,184	7,976
Other accrued expenses	25,893	20,835
Total current liabilities	139,029	101,091
Deferred income taxes, net	12,784	7,114
Capital lease obligations	2,009	1,728
Convertible subordinated debentures	165,020	165,020
Commitments and contingencies (notes 4, 5, 8, and 12)		
Shareholders' Equity:		
Common stock—Authorized, 150,000,000 shares; issued and outstanding, 79,058,754 and 77,583,868 shares	386,877	361,309
Retained earnings, including cumulative translation adjustment of $(1,603) and $(776), respectively, and net unrealized holding gain on investments of $63 and $2,046, respectively	144,953	90,351
Total shareholders' equity	531,830	451,660
Total liabilities and shareholders' equity	$850,672	$726,613

days. Company designers came up with artwork for commuter mugs and T-shirts in different cities that was in keeping with each city's personality (peach-shaped coffee mugs for Atlanta, pictures of Paul Revere for Boston and the Statue of Liberty for New York).

To make sure that Starbucks' stores measured up to standards, the company used "mystery shoppers" who posed as customers and rated each location on a number of criteria.

Building a Top Management Team

Schultz continued to strengthen Starbucks' top management team, hiring people with extensive experience in managing and expanding retail chains. Orin Smith, who had an MBA from Harvard and 13 years' experience at Deloitte and Touche, was brought in as chief financial officer in 1990 and then was promoted to president and chief operating officer in 1994. The four key executives during the company's formative years—Howard Schultz, Dave Olsen, Howard Behar, and Orin Smith—contributed the most to defining and shaping the company's values, principles, and culture. As the company grew, additional executives were added in marketing, store supervision, specialty sales, human resources, finance, and information systems. Schultz also took care to add people to Starbucks' board of directors who had experience growing a retail chain and who could add valuable perspectives.

Employee Training

Accommodating fast growth also meant putting in systems to recruit, hire, and train baristas and store managers. Starbucks' vice president for human resources used some simple guidelines in screening candidates for new positions: "We want passionate people who love coffee . . . We're looking for a diverse workforce, which reflects our community. We want people who enjoy what they're doing and for whom work is an extension of themselves."[16] Some 80 percent of Starbucks employees were white, 85 percent had some education beyond high school, and the average age was 26.

Every partner/barista hired for a retail job in a Starbucks store received at least 24 hours training in the first two to four weeks. The training included classes on coffee history, drink preparation, coffee knowledge (four hours), customer service (four hours), and retail skills, plus a four-hour workshop called "Brewing the Perfect Cup." Baristas were trained in using the cash register, weighing beans, opening the bag properly, capturing the beans without spilling them on the floor, holding the bag in a way that keeps air from being trapped inside, and affixing labels on the package exactly one-half inch over the Starbucks logo. Beverage preparation occupied even more training time, involving such activities as grinding the beans, steaming milk, learning to pull perfect (18- to 23-second) shots of espresso, memorizing the recipes of all the different drinks, practicing making the different drinks, and learning how to make drinks to customer specifications. There were sessions on how to clean the milk wand on the espresso machine, explain the Italian drink names to customers, sell an $875 home espresso machine, make eye contact with customers, and take personal responsibility for the cleanliness of the coffee bins. Everyone was drilled in the Star Skills, three guidelines for on-the-job interpersonal relations: (1) maintain and enhance self-esteem, (2) listen and acknowledge, and (3) ask for help. And there were rules to be memorized: Milk must be steamed to at least 150 degrees Fahrenheit but never more than 170 degrees; every espresso shot not pulled within 23 seconds must be tossed; customers who order one pound of beans must be given exactly that—not .995 pounds or 1.1 pounds; never let coffee sit in the pot more than 20 minutes; always compensate dissatisfied customers with a Starbucks coupon that entitles them to a free drink.

Management trainees attended classes for 8 to 12 weeks. Their training went much deeper, covering not only the information imparted to baristas but also the details of store operations, practices and procedures as set forth in the company's operating manual, information systems, and the basics of managing people. Starbucks' trainers were all store managers and district managers with on-site experience. One of their major objectives was to ingrain the company's values, principles, and culture and to impart their knowledge about coffee and their passion about Starbucks.

---

[16]Kate Rounds, "Starbucks Coffee," *Incentive* 167, no. 7, July 1993, p. 22.

Each time Starbucks opened stores in a new market, it undertook a major recruiting effort. Eight to 10 weeks before opening, the company placed ads to hire baristas and begin their training. It sent a Star team of experienced managers and baristas from existing stores to the area to lead the store-opening effort and to conduct one-on-one training following the company's formal classes and basic orientation sessions at the Starbucks Coffee School in San Francisco.

Product Supply

Dave Olsen, Starbucks' senior vice president for coffee, personally spearheaded Starbucks' efforts to secure top-notch coffee beans to supply the company's growing needs. He traveled regularly to coffee-producing countries—Colombia, Sumatra, Yemen, Antigua, Indonesia, Guatemala, New Guinea, Costa Rica, Sulawesi, Papua New Guinea, Kenya, Ethiopia, Java—building relationships with growers and exporters, checking on agricultural conditions and crop yields, and searching out varieties and sources that would meet Starbucks' exacting standards of quality and flavor. Reporting to Olsen was a group that created and tested new blends of beans from different sources.

Although most coffee was purchased in the commodity market—coffee was the world's second largest traded commodity—coffee of the quality sought by Starbucks was usually purchased on a negotiated basis at a substantial premium above commodity coffees, depending on supply and demand at the time of purchase. Coffee prices were subject to considerable volatility due to weather, economic, and political conditions in the growing countries, as well as agreements establishing export quotas or efforts on the part of the International Coffee Organization and the Association of Coffee Producing Countries to restrict coffee supplies.

Starbucks entered into fixed-price purchase commitments in order to secure an adequate supply of quality green coffee beans and to limit its exposure to fluctuating coffee prices in upcoming periods. When satisfactory fixed-price commitments were not available, the company purchased coffee futures contracts to provide price protection. Nonetheless, there had been occasions in years past when unexpected jumps in coffee prices had put a squeeze on the company's margins and necessitated an increase in the prices of its beverages and beans sold at retail.

Roasting Coffee Beans

Starbucks considered the roasting of its coffee beans to be an art form. Each batch was roasted in a powerful gas oven for 12 to 15 minutes. Highly trained and experienced roasting personnel monitored the process, using both smell and hearing, to judge when the beans were perfectly done—coffee beans make a popping sound when ready. Starbucks' standards were so exacting that roasters tested the color of the beans in a blood-cell analyzer and discarded the entire batch if the reading wasn't on target.

On a daily basis, when he wasn't traveling in search of coffee supplies, Dave Olsen checked coffee samples from the roasting process, sniffing the aromas, tasting sample cups, and recording his observations in a logbook.

In 1998, Starbucks had three roasting plants. The company's smallest plant, built in 1989 and originally thought to be big enough to supply the company's needs for the next 10 years, was dedicated to supplying the company's mail-order business. In 1993, a 305,000-square-foot plant was opened in Kent, Washington, just south of Seattle; its output mainly was being used to supply stores west of the Mississippi. In 1994, the company began construction of an $11 million roasting facility in York, Pennsylvania, that could be expanded to 1 million square feet to supply stores east of the Mississippi.

Bonding with Customers

About 5 million customers per week were patronizing Starbucks stores in early 1998. Stores did about half of their business by 11 AM. Loyal customers patronized a Starbucks store 15 to 20 times a month, spending perhaps $50 monthly. Some customers were Starbucks fanatics, coming in daily. Baristas became familiar with regular customers, learning their names and their favorite drinks. Christine Nagy, a field director for Oracle Corporation in Palo Alto, California, told a *Wall Street Journal* reporter, "For me, it's a daily necessity or I start getting withdrawals."[17] Her standard order was a custom drink: a decaf grande nonfat no-whip no-foam extra-cocoa mocha; when the baristas saw her come through the door, she told the reporter, "They just [said,] 'We need a Christine here.'"

Mail Order Sales

Starbucks published a mail-order catalog that was distributed six times a year and that offered coffee, candies and pastries, and select coffee-making equipment and accessories. A special business gift-giving catalog was mailed to business accounts during the 1997 Christmas holiday season. The company also had an electronic store on the Internet. In 1997, sales of this division were about $21.2 million, roughly 2 percent of total revenues; almost 50,000 mail-order customers were signed up to receive monthly deliveries of Starbucks coffee as of late 1997. Starbucks management believed that its direct-response marketing effort helped pave the way for retail expansion into new markets and reinforced brand recognition in existing markets.

Joint Ventures

In 1994, after months of meetings and experimentation, PepsiCo and Starbucks entered into a joint venture arrangement to create new coffee-related products for mass distribution through Pepsi channels, including cold coffee drinks in a bottle or can. Howard Schultz saw this as a major paradigm shift with the potential to cause Starbucks business to evolve in heretofore unimaginable directions; he thought it was time to look for ways to move Starbucks out into more mainstream markets. Cold coffee products had generally met with very poor market reception, except in Japan, where there was an $8 billion market for ready-to-drink coffee-based beverages. Nonetheless, Schultz was hoping the partners would hit on a new product to exploit a good-tasting coffee extract that had been developed by Starbucks' recently appointed director of research and development. The joint venture's first new product, Mazagran, a lightly flavored carbonated coffee drink, was a failure; when test-marketed in southern California, some consumers liked it and some hated it. While people were willing to try it the first time, partly because the Starbucks name was on the label, repeat sales proved disappointing. Despite the clash of cultures and the different motivations of the two partners, the partnership held together because of the good working relationship that evolved between Howard Schultz and Pepsi's senior executives. Then Schultz, at a meeting to discuss the future of Mazagran, suggested, "Why not develop a bottled version of Frappuccino?"[18] Starbucks had come up with the new cold coffee drink it called Frappuccino in the summer of 1995, and it had

---

[17]David Bank, "Starbucks Faces Growing Competition: Its Own Stores," *The Wall Street Journal*, January 21, 1997, p. B1.

[18]As related in Schultz and Yang, *Pour Your Heart Into It*, p. 224.

proved to be a big hot-weather seller; Pepsi executives were enthusiastic. After months of experimentation, the joint venture product research team came up with a shelf-stable version of Frappuccino that tasted quite good. It was tested in West Coast supermarkets in the summer of 1996; the response was overwhelming, with sales running 10 times over projections and 70 percent repeat business. In September 1996, the partnership invested in three bottling facilities to make Frappuccino, with plans to begin wider distribution. Sales of Frappuccino reached $125 million in 1997 and achieved national supermarket penetration of 80 percent. Sales were projected to reach $500 million in 1998; Starbucks management believed that the market for Frappuccino would ultimately exceed $1 billion.

In October 1995 Starbucks partnered with Dreyer's Grand Ice Cream to supply coffee extract for a new line of coffee ice cream made and distributed by Dreyer's under the Starbucks brand. The new line, featuring such flavors as Dark Roast Espresso Swirl, JavaChip, Vanilla MochaChip, Biscotti Bliss, and Caffe Almond Fudge, hit supermarket shelves in April 1996; by July, Starbucks coffee-flavored ice cream was the top-selling superpremium brand in the coffee segment. In 1997, two new low-fat flavors were added to complement the original six flavors, along with two flavors of ice cream bars; all were well received in the marketplace. Additional new ice cream products were planned for 1998.

Also in 1995, Starbucks worked with Seattle's Redhook Ale Brewery to create Double Black Stout, a stout beer with a shot of Starbucks coffee extract in it.

Licensed Stores and Specialty Sales

In recent years Starbucks had begun entering into a limited number of licensing agreements for store locations in areas where it did not have ability to locate its own outlets. The company had an agreement with Marriott Host International that allowed Host to operate Starbucks retail stores in airport locations, and it had an agreement with Aramark Food and Services to put Starbucks stores on university campuses and other locations operated by Aramark. Starbucks received a license fee and a royalty on sales at these locations and supplied the coffee for resale in the licensed locations. All licensed stores had to follow Starbucks' detailed operating procedures, and all managers and employees who worked in these stores received the same training given to Starbucks managers and store employees.

Starbucks also had a specialty sales group that provided its coffee products to restaurants, airlines, hotels, universities, hospitals, business offices, country clubs, and select retailers. One of the early users of Starbucks coffee was Horizon Airlines, a regional carrier based in Seattle. In 1995, Starbucks entered into negotiations with United Airlines to have Starbucks coffee served on all United flights. There was much internal debate at Starbucks about whether such a move made sense for Starbucks and the possible damage to the integrity of the Starbucks brand if the quality of the coffee served did not measure up. After seven months of negotiation and discussion over coffee-making procedures, United Airlines and Starbucks came up with a way to handle quality control on some 500-plus planes with varying equipment, and Starbucks became the coffee supplier to the 20 million passengers flying United each year.

In addition, Starbucks made arrangements to supply an exclusive coffee blend to Nordstrom's for sale only in Nordstrom stores, to operate coffee bars in Barnes & Noble bookstores, and to offer coffee service at some Wells Fargo Bank locations in California. Most recently, Starbucks began selling its coffees in Chapters, a Toronto book retailer with sites throughout Canada, and in Costco warehouse club stores. A

1997 agreement with U.S. Office Products gave Starbucks the opportunity to provide its coffee to workers in 1.5 million business offices. In fiscal 1997, the specialty sales division generated sales of $117.6 million, equal to 12.2 percent of total revenues.

International Expansion

In markets outside the continental United States (including Hawaii), Starbucks' strategy was to license a reputable and capable local company with retailing know-how in the target host country to develop and operate new Starbucks stores. In some cases, Starbucks was a joint venture partner in the stores outside the continental Untied States. Starbucks created a new subsidiary, Starbucks Coffee International (SCI), to orchestrate overseas expansion and begin to build the Starbucks brand name globally via licensees; Howard Behar was president of SCI.

Going into 1998, SCI had 12 retail stores in Tokyo, 7 in Hawaii, 6 in Singapore, and 1 in the Philippines. Agreements had been signed with licensees to begin opening stores in Taiwan and Korea in 1998. The company and its licensees had plans to open as many as 40 stores in the Pacific Rim by the end of September 1998. The licensee in Taiwan foresaw a potential of 200 stores in that country alone. The potential of locating stores in Europe and Latin America was being explored.

Corporate Responsibility

Howard Schultz's effort to "build a company with soul" included a broad-based program of corporate responsibility, orchestrated mainly through the Starbucks Foundation, set up in 1997. Starbucks was the largest corporate contributor in North America to CARE, a worldwide relief and development organization that sponsored health, education, and humanitarian aid programs in most of the Third World countries where Starbucks purchased its coffee supplies; Starbucks began making annual corporate contributions to CARE when it became profitable in 1991. In addition, CARE samplers of coffee and CARE-related mugs, backpacks, and T-shirts were offered in the company's mail-order catalog; a portion of the price on all sales was donated to CARE. In 1995 Starbucks began a program to improve the conditions of workers in coffee-growing countries, establishing a code of conduct for its growers and providing financial assistance for agricultural improvement projects. In 1997, Starbucks formed an alliance with Appropriate Technology International to help poor, small-scale coffee growers in Guatemala increase their income by improving the quality of their crops and their market access; the company's first-year grant of $75,000 went to fund a new processing facility and set up a loan program for a producer cooperative. Starbucks stores also featured CARE in promotions and had organized concerts with Kenny G and Mary Chapin Carpenter to benefit CARE.

Starbucks had an Environmental Committee that looked for ways to reduce, reuse, and recycle waste, as well as contribute to local community environmental efforts. There was also a Green Team, consisting of store managers from all regions. The company had donated almost $200,000 to literacy improvement efforts, using the profits from store sales of Oprah's Book Club selections. Starbucks stores participated regularly in local charitable projects of one kind or another, donating drinks, books, and proceeds from store-opening benefits. The company's annual report listed nearly 100 community organizations which Starbucks and its employees had supported in 1997 alone. Employees were encouraged to recommend and apply for grants from the Starbucks Foundation to benefit local community literacy organizations.

On the Fourth of July weekend in 1997, three Starbucks employees were murdered in the company's store in the Georgetown area of Washington, D.C. Starbucks offered a $100,000 reward for information leading to the arrest of the murderer(s) and announced it would reopen the store in early 1998 and donate all future net proceeds of that store to a Starbucks Memorial Fund that would make annual grants to local groups working to reduce violence and aid the victims of violent crimes.

Competitors

Going into 1997, there were an estimated 8,000 specialty coffee outlets in the United States. Starbucks' success was prompting a number of ambitious rivals to scale up their expansion plans. Observers believed there was room in the category for two or three national players, maybe more. Starbucks' closest competitor, Second Cup, a Canadian franchisor with stores primarily in Canada, was less than one-third its size; Second Cup owned Gloria Jeans, a franchisor of specialty coffees, with stores located primarily in malls throughout the United States. No other rival had as many as 250 stores, but there were at least 20 small local and regional chains that aspired to grow into rivals of Starbucks, most notably New World Coffee, Coffee People, Coffee Station, Java Centrale, and Caribou Coffee. Observers expected many of the local and regional chains to merge in efforts to get bigger and better position themselves as an alternative to Starbucks. In addition, numerous restaurants were picking up on the growing popularity of specialty coffees and had installed machines to serve espresso, cappuccino, lattè, and other coffee drinks to their customers.

The company also faced competition from nationwide coffee manufacturers such as Kraft General Foods (the parent of Maxwell House), Procter & Gamble (the owner of the Folger's brand), and Nestlé, which distributed their coffees through supermarkets. There were also a number of specialty coffee companies that sold whole-bean coffees in supermarkets. Because many consumers were accustomed to purchasing their coffee supplies at supermarkets, it was easy for them to substitute these products for Starbucks.

Building the Starbucks Brand

So far, Starbucks had spent very little money on advertising, preferring instead to build the brand cup by cup with customers and depend on word-of-mouth and the appeal of its storefronts. The company was, however, engaged in a growing effort to extend the Starbucks brand and penetrate new markets. In addition to expanding internationally, venturing into ice cream with Dreyer's and into Frappuccino with Pepsi, partnering with licensees, and developing specialty and mail-order sales, Starbucks had recently begun selling its coffees in supermarkets.

Supermarket sales were test-marketed in over 500 stores in Chicago in the summer of 1997. Management believed that the tests confirmed the appeal of offering Starbucks coffee to existing customers in convenient supermarket locations while at the same time introducing new customers to its products. Two-thirds of all coffee was sold in supermarkets. In November 1997, Starbucks hired Nestlé veteran, Jim Ailing, as senior vice president of grocery operations to direct Starbucks' supermarket sales effort. The company started rolling out supermarket sales of its coffees in 10 major metropolitan areas in the spring of 1998. Starbucks coffee sold in supermarkets featured distinctive, elegant packaging; prominent positions in grocery aisles; and the same premium quality as that sold in its own stores. Product freshness was guaranteed by Starbucks' FlavorLock packaging, and the price per pound paralleled the prices in Starbucks' retail stores.

The company was also said to be testing "light roast" coffee blends for those customers who found its current offerings too strong. And, in the summer of 1997, Starbucks quietly test-marketed four 20 percent fruit-juice beverages in one market.[19] The single-serve bottled drinks were priced around $2, and at least one contained caffeine. Also on the new-product front was an apple cider made exclusively for Starbucks by Nantucket Nectars. Plus, the company was selling chocolate bars and other candy, and had plans to bring candy production in-house if sales went well enough.

The Future

Industry analysts in 1998 saw Starbucks as being well on its way to becoming the Nike or Coca-Cola of the specialty coffee segment. It was the only company with anything close to national market coverage. The company's most immediate objective was to have 2,000 stores in operation by the year 2000. Its longer range objective was to become the most recognized and respected brand of coffee in the world. The company's efforts to greatly increase its sphere of strategic interest via its joint ventures with Pepsi and Dreyer's, its move to sell coffee in supermarkets, and the possibility of marketing fruit-juice drinks and candy under the Starbucks label represented an ongoing drive on Schultz's part to continually reinvent the way Starbucks did business.

In order to sustain the company's growth and make Starbucks a strong global brand, Schultz believed that the company had to challenge the status quo, be innovative, take risks, and alter its vision of who it was, what it did, and where it was headed. Under his guidance, management was posing a number of fundamental strategic questions: What could Starbucks do to make its stores an even more elegant "third place" that welcomed, rewarded, and surprised customers? What new products and new experiences could the company provide that would uniquely belong to or be associated with Starbucks? What could coffee be—besides being hot or liquid? How could Starbucks reach people who were not coffee drinkers? What strategic paths should Starbucks pursue to achieve its objective of becoming the most recognized and respected brand of coffee in the world?

(A visual-enhanced version of this case can be viewed online at www.mhhe.com/thompson and is hyperlinked to Starbucks Web page—www.starbucks.com.)

---

[19]"Starbucks Eyes More Than Just Java," *Brandweek*, December 10, 1997, p.10.

"CHAINSAW AL" DUNLAP AND SUNBEAM CORPORATION

Arthur A. Thompson, *University of Alabama*

John E. Gamble, *University of South Alabama*

On July 18, 1996, Albert J. Dunlap was named CEO of Sunbeam Corporation, a troubled maker of small appliances and other household products. The company's stock price surged 50 percent over two days after the appointment was announced. Investors expected Dunlap would pursue a slash-and-burn makeover similar to those he had employed at other ailing companies—divest fringe businesses, cut jobs, improve operating efficiency, boost profits, sell the company at a tidy profit for shareholders, cash in his own stock options, and then move on to tackle his next challenge. Only months before, Dunlap had become $100 million richer by turning Scott Paper Company around and then cutting a deal to sell Scott to Kimberly-Clark at a price very favorable to Scott shareholders.

In November 1996, Dunlap announced his plan to restructure Sunbeam. The strategy: cut Sunbeam's workforce in half, to 6,000 workers; sell or close 18 of Sunbeam's 26 factories; reduce the number of warehouses from 61 to 37; divest the divisions that made outdoor furniture, bathroom scales, bedding, clocks, and thermometers; eliminate six regional offices; and cut the number of products offered by 87 percent, to 1,500. Dunlap indicated that he wanted to complete the restructuring effort within 45 days and have Sunbeam begin 1997 as a "new company." The strategic initiatives to transform Sunbeam were expected to produce annual savings of $225 million. To cover the costs of the changes, Dunlap announced, the company would take a pretax restructuring charge of $300 million in the fourth quarter of 1996. Dunlap observed, "We planned this like the invasion of Normandy. We attacked every aspect of the business."[1]

Dunlap's plan for overhauling Sunbeam included some ambitious objectives for the company:

---

[1]As quoted in Robert Frank and Joann S. Lublin, "Albert Dunlap's Ax Falls Again and Again at Sunbeam Corp.," *The Wall Street Journal Interactive Edition*, November 13, 1996.

- Double revenues (after the divestitures) from $1 billion to $2 billion.
- Raise operating profit margins from the current 2.5 percent to 20 percent.
- Realize a 25 percent return on equity.
- Generate at least $600 million of free cash flow.
- Launch at least 30 new products a year.
- Increase international sales from $200 million to $600 million.

All of the targets were to be achieved within three years. In publicly announcing the new objectives and strategy for Sunbeam, Dunlap said, "Our growth mission is to become the dominant and most profitable small household appliance and outdoor cooking company in North America, with a leading share of Latin America and Asia Pacific markets."[2]

COMPANY HISTORY AND BACKGROUND

In 1897 John Stewart and Thomas Clark founded a small company, Chicago Flexible Shaft Company, to make agricultural tools in Dundee, Illinois. In 1910 Stewart and Clark moved into the manufacture of small electrical appliances, successfully introducing a lightweight iron. Shortly afterward, the company created a domestic appliance division and adopted the Sunbeam brand name in advertising its appliances. In 1930 the company launched the Sunbeam Mixmaster, which proved extremely popular. Other new Sunbeam appliances soon followed—an electric shaver, the first automatic coffeemaker, and the first pop-up electric toaster. The company changed its name to Sunbeam Corporation in 1946. Over the next several years Sunbeam introduced a series of new products: hair dryers, humidifiers, knife sharpeners, massage pillows, electric fry pans, electric blankets, cordless electric mixers, a rotisserie, and snowblowers.

In 1960 Sunbeam acquired the John Oster Manufacturing Company, a rival maker of household appliances best known for its Osterizer food blender. Then in 1981 Sunbeam was acquired by Pittsburgh-based Allegheny International Corporation, a broadly diversified manufacturer of industrial and consumer products. Allegheny merged its household air pollution control devices and bathroom scale businesses into the Sunbeam division. A major downturn in sales in Allegheny's other divisions, along with poor executive management and heavy debt associated with the Sunbeam acquisition, forced Allegheny into bankruptcy in 1988. Mutual fund manager Michael Price, hedge fund manager Michael Steinhardt, and financier Paul Kazarian teamed up to buy Allegheny from its creditors in 1989. Kazarian was installed as CEO to get things turned around. He quickly focused all efforts on housewares and outdoor furniture, and the company was renamed Sunbeam-Oster. An international division was established to extend the company's marketing reach. In August 1992, Sunbeam-Oster went public, allowing the original investors to convert a portion of their ownership into cash. However, Kazarian's management style proved controversial and, when six top executives complained to the board about his hard-driving manner and erratic behavior (also reported in a very unflattering article that appeared on the front page of *The Wall Street Journal*), Kazarian was removed as CEO in January 1993. (He later sued over his removal and won a settlement of $160 million.)

The board hired a veteran executive of General Electric's appliance division, Roger Schipke, to replace Kazarian. Schipke promptly reorganized Sunbeam's management and relocated the company's headquarters to Fort Lauderdale, Florida. Two acquisitions

---

[2]As quoted in Gail DeGeorge, "Al Dunlap Revs His Chain Saw," *Business Week*, November 25, 1996, p. 37.

were made—the consumer products unit of DeVilbiss Health Care was purchased in 1993, and Rubbermaid's outdoor furniture business was purchased in 1994. Earnings increased about 20 percent in 1994. The company formally changed its name from Sunbeam-Oster back to Sunbeam in 1995. But in 1995 Sunbeam's performance turned down; the stock price fell from about $26 in October 1994 to around $15 by October 1995. New products, investments made to improve production efficiency, and entry into Asian markets failed to turn things around. Sunbeam's two largest shareholders, Michael Price (whose mutual funds owned 21 percent of Sunbeam's stock at the time) and Michael Steinhard (whose mutual funds also owned 21 percent), tried to find a buyer for the company in late 1995, but no offers materialized.

Four days before Sunbeam reported first-quarter 1996 profit declines of 40 percent and sales declines of 4 percent for North American household appliances and 5 percent for outdoor products, Roger Schipke and two other Sunbeam directors resigned. Earnings had plunged 83 percent since July 1994. Sunbeam had lost market share in major stores in such key product categories as blenders, mixers, can openers, and out-door grills. According to Wall Street analysts, the company's earnings had underper-formed expectations for five consecutive quarters. A Dean Witter analyst observed that Sunbeam was "really suffering from a lack of strong direction."[3] Three months after Schipke resigned, the Sunbeam board—led by Michael Price—convinced Albert Dunlap to become chairman and CEO and take on the challenge of rejuvenating Sunbeam.

Just prior to the announcement of Dunlap's hiring, Sunbeam's stock price was trad-ing in the range of $12 per share. The day of the announcement, it rose to $15 in after-hours trading, the following day it rose to $18, and in November 1996, when the revival plan for Sunbeam was made public, the stock traded in the mid-20s.

Exhibit 1 summarizes Sunbeam's performance since the company went public in 1992. Exhibit 2 shows the performance of the company's stock price during the 1992–98 period.

ALBERT J. DUNLAP

Dunlap was born in 1936 and grew up in Hoboken, New Jersey. His father, who spent his entire working life as a boilermaker at Todd Shipyards in Hoboken and earned a comfortable income, was a passionate union member and served as a union steward. Dunlap's parents taught him the importance of not wasting money; his mother was a strict disciplinarian who set tough goals and objectives and insisted that Dunlap and his sister follow the rules. According to Dunlap, his family offered constant encourage-ment and believed in his future.[4] The family moved from an apartment in Hoboken to a house in nearby Hasbrouck Heights when Al was a teenager. Dunlap liked sports, was named to the Bergen County all-star football team while in high school, and won a title as shot put champion as well. Dunlap graduated from the U.S. Military Academy at West Point in 1960, at which time his parents gave him a new Pontiac Bonneville convertible and a vacation in Europe. He did not enjoy his time as a West Point cadet and hated engineering, but he was determined to graduate because of his competitive-ness and because he believed it was the right, and smart, thing to do. Dunlap earned his paratrooper wings at Fort Benning and completed three years of active duty at a

---

[3]As quoted in Jenni Youssef, "Search On for a CEO: Schipke Resigns at Sunbeam," *HFN: The Weekly Newspaper for the Home Furnishing Network*, April 29, 1996, p. 49.

[4]Albert J. Dunlap, with Bob Andelman, *Mean Business: How I save Bad Companies and Make Good Companies Great* (New York: Fireside Books, 1997), p. 109.

EXHIBIT 1   Selected Financial Data for Sunbeam Corporation, 1992–97 (In millions of dollars, except per share amounts)

	Fiscal Year Ended					
	December 28, 1997	December 29, 1996	December 31, 1995	January 1, 1995	January 2, 1994	January 3, 1993
Statement of Operations Data						
Net sales	$1,168.2	$ 984.2	$1,016.9	$1,044.3	$927.5	$ 839.8
Cost of goods sold	837.7	900.6	809.1	764.4	674.2	615.5
Selling, general, and administrative expense	131.1	214.0	137.5	128.9	119.3	121.5
Restructuring, impairment, and other costs	—	154.8	—	—	—	—
Operating earnings (loss)	$ 199.4	$ (285.2)	$ 70.3	$ 151.0	$134.0	$ 102.8
Earnings (loss) from continuing operations	$ 123.1	$ (196.7)	$ 37.6	$ 85.3	$ 76.9	$ 36.2
Earnings from discontinued operations, net of taxes	—	0.8	12.9	21.7	11.9	12.1
Loss on sale of discontinued operations, net of taxes	(13.7)	(32.4)	—	—	—	—
Net earnings (loss)	$ 109.4	$ (228.3)	$ 50.5	$ 107.0	$ 88.8	$ 48.3
Earnings Per Share Data						
Average common and common equivalent shares outstanding	87.5	82.9	82.8	82.6	87.9	84.8
Diluted earnings (loss) per share from continuing operations	$ 1.41	$ (2.37)	$ 0.45	$ 1.03	$ 0.87	$ 0.43
Diluted earnings (loss) per share	$ 1.25	$ (2.75)	$ 0.61	$ 1.30	$ 1.01	$ 0.57
Cash dividends declared per share	$ 0.04	$ 0.04	$ 0.04	$ 0.04	$ 0.04	$ 0.01
Balance Sheet Data (at period end)						
Working capital	$ 459.9	$ 352.6	$ 411.7	$ 294.8	$261.4	$ 400.2
Total assets	1,120.3	1,072.7	1,158.7	1,008.9	928.8	1,043.8
Long-term debt	194.6	201.1	161.6	124.0	133.4	133.5
Shareholder's equity	531.9	395.3	601.0	454.7	370.0	477.2

Source: 1996 and 1997 annual reports.

nuclear missile installation. He married in 1961 and went through a bitter divorce in 1966. Two years later, he married a bank teller he met while working at Sterling Pulp & Paper in Eau Claire, Wisconsin; they celebrated their 30th anniversary in 1998.

Al Dunlap believed his experiences at West Point and in the military gave him an excellent preparation for a career in business. In his book *Mean Business: How I Save Bad Companies and Make Good Companies Great*, Dunlap writes:

> The end product of West Point is character. It builds men and women who take responsibility. That is why West Point is the best business school in the world . . . West Point teaches you how to lead, how to think, how to deal with adversity, how to take responsibility, how to detail your actions. It teaches you for military purposes, but its lessons can easily be applied to business.[5]

[5]Ibid., pp. 110–11.

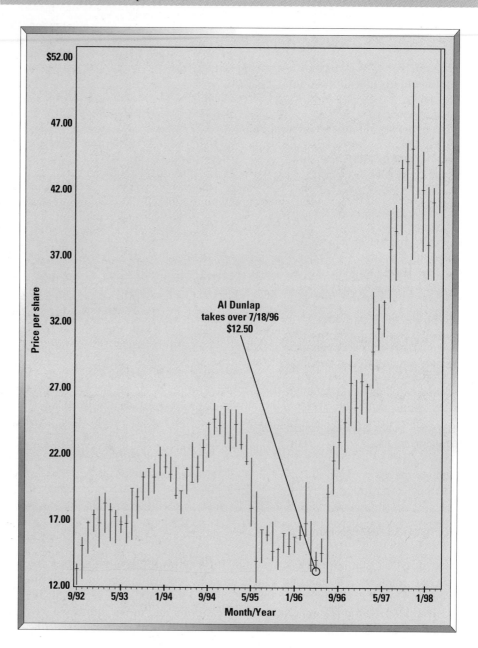

EXHIBIT 2   Monthly Performance of Sunbeam's Stock Price, September 1992–April 1998

Dunlap's Early Business Career

Al Dunlap began his business career as a management trainee at Kimberly-Clark; he worked in a series of jobs at a nonunion mill in Connecticut. He then was transferred to Kimberly-Clark's paper plant in Neenah, Wisconsin, where he became a superintendent. At the Neenah plant, Dunlap reported to the general superintendent, Frank

Nobbe, a stern disciplinarian who was known for setting high standards, demanding the best from employees, and chewing them out when they didn't do things to suit him. Dunlap recalls Nobbe's strong influence in shaping his business career:

> I worked blue-collar shifts for a couple of years in Neenah, learning every position—machine tender, back tender, beaterman, fourth hand, fifth hand, third hand. I learned a lot, and not just about making paper products. I learned about life in a factory on shift . . . I saw the inefficiencies, the management bureaucracy. I learned why products get made right and why they get made wrong. I saw some really good leadership and I saw terrible management. The good came from Nobbe. He would walk through the mills and talk to workers. He knew them by their first names. He was tough, but he knew and respected his people. He'd get his hands dirty. Like me, he was a guy who came up through the ranks. He'd give you hell but he'd stick by you, too.
>
> Bad management stemmed in most cases from "ivory-tower" disease: Layers of managers sending and shuffling memos, never actually answering questions or solving problems, and always making life more difficult for workers on the shop floor . . .
>
> During my four years at the Neenah plant, I rose from superintendent to project leader, first in R&D, then in paper machine start-up and installation. As a result, I received a hands-on education in the entire pulp to tissue to converting to finished product process. When I was in R&D, I learned how to blend my practical knowledge with our scientists' research and innovate better products and processes.
>
> I took my experiences along with me to every higher rung of the ladder. Nothing was unimportant; every bit of data and experience made the next challenge—whether in tissue, cups, timber, oil, land, or media—easier to conquer.[6]

At the age of 29, Dunlap was hired by Ely Meyer, the 75-year-old owner of Sterling Pulp & Paper, to be general superintendent of the company's troubled plant in Eau Claire, Wisconsin. Dunlap's challenge was to fix problems with a new pulp mill and paper machine, as well as resolve an assortment of labor and operating problems. In his first 16 weeks on the job, Dunlap had to deal with a flood at the plant (located on property where two rivers come together), an explosion that blew the roof off a building and shut half the plant down for a week, a fire in a warehouse, and a wildcat strike by the union. Without panicking, Dunlap dealt with the calamities and set in motion efforts to reduce the likelihood of further explosions and fires. The plant had had a long history of labor problems, and Dunlap persuaded the disgruntled union leaders to halt wildcat strikes by agreeing to open lines of communication and to address the union grievances that had validity, provided the union acted responsibly. Over the next 10 years, Dunlap improved the working relationship with the union, cut costs at the plant (partly by laying off workers), changed out managers he considered were performing poorly, and played a major role in helping Sterling develop new products, increase its market share, and become more profitable. Meyer treated Dunlap like a son and was instrumental in introducing Dunlap to Judy Stringer, the bank teller he married less than a year later.

When Meyer died and Sterling sold the Eau Claire plant, Dunlap moved on to a job in strategic planning at American Can Company in Greenwich, Connecticut. As head of special projects, Dunlap coordinated a study that prompted American Can to abandon its matrix management system, which blurred responsibility for bottom-line results, and instead return to a business-unit structure in which the business-unit head had full authority and responsibility for the performance of the division. Dunlap was then named senior vice president and group executive of the Performance Plastics Division, which made plastic wraps for meat, cheese, cream cheese, potato chips, and Kool-Aid. The

---

[6]Ibid., pp. 113–14.

division had historically been one of American Can's poorest performers; Dunlap was given the task of making it a success within a year or else disposing of it.

Dunlap overhauled the division's management team (which he characterized as "brain dead") and targeted areas in which the division had higher costs than competitors to stop the manufacture of money-losing products (like plastic bags for bread). The strategy Dunlap fashioned over the next couple of years was to focus on higher-margin products, improve efficiency, cut costs, and come up with a series of new products. Dunlap stuck to his guns in closing an unprofitable plant in Scranton, Pennsylvania, despite opposition from then Lieutenant Governor William Scranton. Under Dunlap's guidance, the Performance Plastics Division became a profitable leader in several market segments, partly because of such new products as microwavable trays for TV dinners, a polyfoil tube for toothpaste, reheatable packaging for military rations, and plastic ketchup bottles.

Despite being made a member of American Can's management executive committee in 1981, Al Dunlap was not comfortable with what he viewed as a stodgy, out-of-touch management bureaucracy that stifled innovation and tolerated bloated costs.

Al Dunlap's Growing Expertise and Reputation as a Turnaround Expert, 1983–95

Dunlap's Prescriptions for Lily-Tulip, 1983–86   In 1983, Dunlap was recruited by George Roberts of Kohlberg Kravis Roberts & Co. (KKR), a Wall Street investment banking firm, to be the new CEO of Lily-Tulip, the nation's second largest supplier of disposable cups to the food service industry. KKR had purchased Lily-Tulip for $180 million in a leveraged buyout in 1982 and was looking for a person with turnaround skills to get Lily-Tulip out of the red. Twelve months after taking the job, Dunlap had the company in the black and on the road to becoming a very successful investment for KKR. Dunlap's initiatives to turn Lily-Tulip around included the following:

- Firing all but two senior managers his first day on the job.
- Cutting headquarters staff by 50 percent and salaried staff by 20 percent.
- Relocating the headquarters operation from Toledo to Georgia to be closer to plants.
- Disposing of unproductive plants in New Jersey and Maine.
- Cutting waste products by 15 percent, greatly reducing material costs.
- Increasing the R&D budget.
- Investing in new plant equipment to make the manufacturing process less labor-intensive.
- Launching a new foam-and-plastic cup for either hot or cold liquids.

In 1982, the year before Dunlap was hired, Lily-Tulip lost $11 million and had debt of $165 million; in 1984, following Dunlap's first full year on the job, the company earned $23 million and its debt had been paid down to only $43 million. In 1985, Lily-Tulip went public, earning KKR a $120 million stock profit on its original $30 million equity investment. When he left Lily-Tulip in 1986, Dunlap had stock-option gains totaling more than $6.5 million.

Dunlap's Turnaround Strategy at Crown-Zellerbach and Diamond International   In 1986 Sir James Goldsmith, an internationally renowned European billionaire who specialized in hostile takeovers and who had been knighted by British prime minister Harold Wilson, interviewed Dunlap for the head position at Crown-Zellerbach, a timberlands company based in San Francisco that had recently become a part of Goldsmith's far-flung business empire. Goldsmith and Dunlap hit it off, and, after listening to Dunlap's rendition of how he engineered the Lily-Tulip turnaround, Goldsmith hired Dunlap as Crown-Zellerbach's CEO. Goldsmith had a major impact in shaping Dunlap's business philosophy and increasing his financial sophistication, plus he introduced Dunlap to his circle of friends and business acquaintances, many of whom possessed considerable wealth and power. Goldsmith, speaking offhandedly to a reporter, once described Dunlap as a "Rambo in Pinstripes"—a person who went into chaotic situations, cleaned them up, fought the good fight, and won the war.

When Dunlap arrived at Crown-Zellerbach, he saw a top-heavy company that had excessive costs and lacked a strong focus and mission. Goldsmith was interested in the company's 3 million acres of timberland assets and in its oil and gas resources but did not want to retain the pulp and paper divisions. Goldsmith also asked Dunlap to take a crack at turning around Crown-Zellerbach's industrial parts supply business, which had lost $19 million on sales of $56 million during the prior year. Dunlap's program for overhauling Crown-Zellerbach included the following:

- Selling the company's San Francisco headquarters building and moving the headquarters of the timber business to Portland, Oregon (most of the timber operations were in Oregon and Louisiana) and the headquarters of the rest of the company to Hilton Head, South Carolina.

- Cutting 30 percent of the administrative staff in the timber products group and shifting 40 percent of the timberlands hourly workforce from the company's payroll to independent contractors, then tying their earnings potential to individual production (thereby giving high-performing employees the opportunity to make more money).

- Renegotiating the labor contract with the union representing the timber group to save $4.1 million annually.

- Installing a new head to run the timber portion of the business.

- Investing $20 million in new equipment to improve the efficiency of the company's sawmills.

- Replacing Crown-Zellerbach's strategy of cutting more timberlands when timber prices fell (to maintain revenues) with one of cutting more timberlands when prices were high and reducing cutting when prices were low (to enhance profitability).

- Replacing the head of the industrial parts division, reducing the number of distribution centers the division had from 22 to 4, cutting office staff and jobs at the distribution centers by 33 percent, reducing the number of parts stocked from 11,000 to 2,000, and writing off $7 million in obsolete inventory.

In a little over a year, Dunlap had the industrial parts division operating close to breakeven and the timberlands division generating operating profits of $71 million (versus $20 million in its best-ever year under Crown-Zellerbach's management).

Goldsmith then gave Dunlap the assignment of revamping another of his underperforming timber and land companies—Diamond International. Dunlap quickly diagnosed Diamond as "a sleepy little company run by well-intentioned people who had not been exposed to aggressive market practices."[7] In short order, Dunlap fashioned a new direction and strategy for Diamond that featured the following:

---

[7]Ibid., p. 239.

- Restructuring the company by selling some forest-product businesses and keeping others.
- Revamping the strategies of retained operations, including seeking out better uses of landholdings (such as selling 165,000 acres with high potential for commercial and residential development and leasing lands for recreational use) and shifting to a more profitable product mix (growing Christmas trees and blueberries).
- Streamlining administration.
- Updating equipment.
- Designing a new incentive system that was largely responsible for a 10 percent increase in productivity.

In less than a year, Diamond went from losing money to generating a positive cash flow of $2 million.

"Chainsaw" Al Dunlap in Australia, 1989–93   Through his association with Sir James Goldsmith, Dunlap came to know Kerry Packer, a wealthy Australian with a diverse range of business investments. In 1989, when Packer purchased Australian National Industries (ANI), a large engineering enterprise that had run into major financial and strategic difficulty by diversifying into manufacturing and equipment leasing, he asked Dunlap to come to Australia to put the once-strong operation back on sound footing. Dunlap did a quick study of ANI and reported to Packer that the operation lacked focus, had excessive costs, and was poorly managed. Packer gave Dunlap a free hand in restructuring the company. Over the next 11 months, Dunlap orchestrated a series of actions that amounted to radical surgery (see Exhibit 3). In 1991, Packer sold his interest in ANI for a profit of $180 million.

Dunlap returned to London after his 11-month blitz turnaround at ANI, but Packer soon invited him back to Australia to head a restructuring of Packer's main company, Consolidated Press Holdings (CPH), a conglomerate consisting of some 431 different businesses. Dunlap's turnaround at CPH (see Exhibit 3) took a little less than two years; CPH went from losing $25 million to making a profit of $623 million.[8]

While Dunlap was in the process of turning CPH around, the Australian press began to refer to him as "Chainsaw Al," picking up on a characterization of Dunlap by a well-known British personality, John Aspinall, who said, "Al is like a chainsaw. He goes in and cuts away all the fat and leaves a great sculpture."[9]

Dunlap's Turnaround at Scott Paper   Scott Paper began as a producer of bags and wrapping paper and later expanded into making toilet tissue, paper towels, paper napkins, and other consumer products. In 1994 it was the eighth largest paper company in the United States and had the second largest market share of tissue products. After a six-month search, rather than opt for an executive with experience in packaging and consumer goods, Scott Paper's board of directors decided to hire Al Dunlap as chairman and CEO because of his track record in radically restructuring companies. A number of Scott's board members saw Dunlap as a person who would inject new life and energy into a company they viewed as bureaucratic, slow-moving, and lacking a sound strategy for the future. In 1993, Scott Paper's sales declined 7 percent, operating profits were down 19 percent, net income was down 30 percent (before restructuring charges that resulted in a $277 million loss for the year), and the company had $2.5 billion in debt.

---

[8]Ibid., p. 80.
[9]Ibid., p. 132.

EXHIBIT 3 Turnaround Actions Engineered by Al Dunlap at Australian National Industries and Consolidated Press Holdings, 1989–93

Company	Years	Major Components of the Turnaround Effort
Australian National Industries	1989	• Fired virtually all senior managers, closed and sold nine administrative office buildings, pared headquarters staff from 200 to 23, and cut out management perks • Sold all but five core businesses and refocused the company on leveraging its traditional expertise in engineering • Closed two inefficient plants and six warehouses • Cut workforce by 47% (including those employed in divested operations) • Set up a $6 million incentive program for managers to achieve $100 million in cost savings • Reduced debt from $570 million to $240 million
Consolidated Press Holdings (an Australian media conglomerate)	1991–93	• Replaced a number of senior executives and board members; cut out management perks low-interest loans, company cars, country club memberships) • Divested 300 of 431 businesses and refocused the company on its core television and magazine publishing businesses • Pruned the costs of core businesses, including laying off a number of workers • Paid off $2.2 billion in debt and generated a cash surplus of $1 billion (principally through asset sales)

The Scott board gave Dunlap a five-year contract at a salary of $1 million annually as well as a package of stock options tied to Scott's performance. Dunlap purchased $2 million worth of Scott's stock at $38 a share the day he took over the company and another $2 million at $50 per share several months later—all with personal funds.

Dunlap's first day on the job was April 19,1994. At a meeting attended by 1,600 people at the company's Philadelphia headquarters that afternoon, Dunlap placed blame for the company's poor condition on Scott management's underperformance and a massive failure of leadership. Dunlap further announced that over the coming months he would be cutting thousands of jobs and selling billions of dollars of assets. Dunlap believed that Scott was a potentially sound paper products company (even though it had not had a decent marketing program for its consumer products for 10 years). But he saw Scott currently as a poorly managed commodity paper company lumbering behind competitors and saddled with ancillary health care, food-service, electricity generation, and coated-paper businesses. He indicated that the major downsizing and restructuring would be over by December 31 and that the company would then get on with building its core business in toilet/facial tissue and paper towels. By July 1994, a detailed restructuring plan was put together with the aid of a consulting team from Coopers & Lybrand, led by partner C. Don Burnett, who had worked with Dunlap on other turnaround projects. By December 31, the principal initiatives to reshape the company were completed as Dunlap had promised back in July. The primary elements of Dunlap's turnaround strategy for Scott Paper are shown in Exhibit 4.

EXHIBIT 4   The Key Elements of Dunlap's Turnaround Strategy for Scott Paper Company, 1994–95

- Sold Scott's coated-paper manufacturing subsidiary, S. D. Warren, for $1.6 billion. (Warren's principal products were paper used in magazines and specialty papers used for quick printers and corporate in-house publications.)
- Sold the power generation assets at the company's Mobile, Alabama, plant for $350 million.
- Divested the company's food service operation and health care joint venture as well as the adult disposable diaper business.
- Eliminated 6,000 jobs via divestiture of noncore businesses.
- Sold the company's pulp mills and reduced the degree of backward integration into the raw materials needed for making paper products.
- Closed Scott's Philadelphia headquarters, sold the 750,000-square-foot Scott Plaza building for $39 million, cut upper management positions at headquarters by 70%, and relocated Scott's executive offices to 30,000 square feet of leased office space in Boca Raton, Florida (saving $6 million annually).
- Disbanded Scott's 11-member operating committee, composed of the most senior executives, which approved all major decisions and actions. Built an inner circle of five key executives—two holdovers from Scott's executive ranks, two persons brought in by Dunlap who had worked with him previously, and one new recruit from outside.
- Cut the number of middle and lower management positions by nearly 50%.
- Cut out $30 million in consultants' fees.
- Cut $2.9 million in costs for compensation experts.
- Eliminated $3 million in trade association fees and newspaper and magazine subscriptions.
- Eliminated all charitable donations (a total of $5 million).
- Eliminated more than 11,000 jobs, 35% of Scott's payroll without losing a single day of production due to union work stoppages. (About 22% of the unionized workforce was eliminated.)
- Benchmarked the 52 papermaking machines in the Scott manufacturing system against the company's five best-performing machines and then implemented a best practices program to improve paper machine performance at all of Scott's plants.
- Launched construction of two state-of-the-art manufacturing plants (one in Kentucky and one in Arizona) and committed $400 million for capital improvements at Scott operations around the world.
- Focused Scott's business on toilet/facial tissues and paper towels for both the consumer market (sold through supermarkets, convenience stores, and mass merchants like Wal-Mart and Kmart) and the away from home market (such as hotels, restaurants, hospitals, and stadiums).
- Began to transform Scott from a paper products company into a fast-moving packaged products company.
- Eliminated the cultural infighting and policy clashes between Scott's consumer goods group and its away-from-home group.
- Brought in a new head of purchasing to consolidate the number of suppliers, drive harder bargains with suppliers via more competitive bidding, and reduce the costs of purchased materials.
- Brought in a new head of marketing to completely rebuild the marketing department. The new head (a veteran of 20 years with Procter & Gamble) hired 14 new marketing directors (whose experience included years at P&G, Coca-Cola, Colgate-Palmolive, and Kimberly-Clark) and retained three new advertising agencies to promote Scott products and build its brand image.

EXHIBIT 4 *(concluded)*

- Pruned weak-selling products from the product line and relaunched products with weak brand names as products carrying Scott's best-known brand names (like Scott, Scotties, Viva, Scot-Towels, and Cottonelle)—reducing the number of brand names from 27 to less than 10.
- Repackaged every existing Scott product.
- Expanded the product line of the away-from-home group to include cleaning and paper products for workshops, commercial kitchens, and washrooms.
- Greatly expanded the line of wet wipe products.
- Developed a global strategy to coordinate and extend Scott's presence in foreign markets (the company had operations in 21 countries and sold its products in 80 countries when Dunlap took over as CEO)—became the first international tissue company to have a presence in China, and also entered markets in India and Indonesia.
- Launched 107 new-product initiatives in 22 countries during Dunlap's first 12 months, employing the theme of "Scott the World Over."

When he took the Scott job in 1994, Al Dunlap was not widely known in U.S. business circles. But this quickly changed. Dunlap's turnaround efforts at Scott Paper were widely publicized in the business press. Many reporters featured his "Rambo in Pinstripes" and "Chainsaw Al" nicknames in their stories, portraying him as a heartless hatchet man who tore companies apart with his style of shock therapy—selling off assets, dismantling the old guard and the old culture, revamping strategies, laying off workers—all in the name of higher profits and capital gains for shareholders. Many reports of his actions at Scott Paper were unfavorable, largely because of the drastic job cuts and plant closings, and the writers' skepticism about the legitimacy of the rapid-fire changes he was making.

In 1995, Dunlap negotiated a deal to sell Scott Paper to Kimberly-Clark. Scott shareholders got .765 shares of Kimberly-Clark stock for each Scott share. During Dunlap's 603 days as Scott's CEO, the value of the company's stock rose a total of $6.5 billion and the stock price was up each of the 20 months he was CEO. When Dunlap was hired, Scott's stock was selling at $38 per share; the merger with Kimberly-Clark called for Scott shareholders to receive the presplit equivalent of $120 per share. Dunlap left Scott Paper with an $80 million profit on the stock options and other incentives he received while at Scott and on the shares he purchased himself; he got another $20 million from a noncompete agreement signed with Kimberly-Clark when the merger became final. The members of his new management team, who in late 1994 collectively purchased $10 million in Scott's stock with personal funds (at Dunlap's urging—to show support for and commitment to the restructuring effort), profited handsomely as well.

AL DUNLAP AT SUNBEAM CORPORATION

After completing the merger with Kimberly-Clark, Dunlap spent the next several months entertaining prospective offers; he was approached about the CEO positions at such companies as Apple Computer, RJR Nabisco, and Waste Management. Dunlap met with representatives of Michael Price and Michael Steinhard, whose mutual funds owned over 40 percent of Sunbeam's shares, to review the situation at Sunbeam. He later met with Michael Price, who convinced him to take the Sunbeam job despite the company's grim condition and its relatively small size (sales of $1.2 billion compared to Scott Paper's sales of $5 billion). The board offered Dunlap a $1 million annual salary, options to buy 2.5 million shares at $12.25, and a grant of 1 million unrestricted shares. Dunlap purchased $3 million worth of Sunbeam stock (245,000 shares at $12.25) from the company the day he became chairman and CEO; then, in February 1997, he purchased another $2 million on the open market. When the company announced the hiring of Al Dunlap, trading in the company's stock was halted because of an expected imbalance in buy and sell orders. The next morning, when trading was resumed, Sunbeam's stock rose from 12½ to 18⅝ on volume of 7.5 million shares (versus a normal trading volume of 300,000 shares).

As he had done at Scott, Dunlap again brought in Don Burnett and a group of Coopers & Lybrand consultants to help put together the strategic plan for Sunbeam's turnaround. Altogether, 17 teams containing both Coopers & Lybrand consultants and Sunbeam managers were formed to review all aspects of Sunbeam's operations and flesh out the details of an action agenda. Dunlap's turnaround effort had four elements: (1) put together a strong management team of the best insiders and talented new outsiders; (2) eliminate waste, reduce costs, and make Sunbeam more efficient and cost competitive; (3) focus on core businesses and divest everything else; and (4) implement an aggressive strategy for global growth.

In typical Dunlap style, things happened swiftly across a broad front within days of his arrival. All but one senior executive, Sunbeam's general counsel, was dismissed. Russell Kersh, one of Dunlap's five key executives at Scott, was brought in immediately as executive vice president and chief financial officer. Over the next few months Dunlap recruited another 24 people for management positions at Sunbeam from those who had worked for him at Scott Paper, Crown-Zellerbach, and Lily-Tulip. Donald R. Uzzi, who had previously been president of Quaker Oats' beverage division (whose main products at the time were Gatorade and Snapple) and had also worked at Procter & Gamble and PepsiCo, was brought in as executive vice president of marketing and product development. The new top managers at Sunbeam were all encouraged by Dunlap to invest personal funds in Sunbeam stock and were given stock option incentives linked to the company's performance. At the same time, Dunlap announced that senior executives would receive no annual salary increases and no cash bonuses—their performance payoff was to come from the increased value of their stock options if the company's stock price rose. The company's board of directors also agreed to being totally compensated by Sunbeam stock.

A detailed action plan was developed in four and a half months; then the radical surgery was implemented and executed in 45 days. Dunlap's rescue plan for Sunbeam included the following:

- Consolidating six existing Sunbeam headquarters offices into one, and reducing the headquarters staff by 60 percent, from 308 to 123.
- Reducing the staff count in other managerial and clerical positions from 1,529 to 697.
- Defining Sunbeam's core businesses as small electric appliances and appliance-related products (small kitchen appliances, health and home products, outdoor cooking equipment, personal care and comfort products, and professional products).

- Divesting all remaining noncore businesses, accounting for about $250 million in sales—decorative bedding (sold for $2.5 million), outdoor furniture (sold for about $84.5 million), gas logs, a low-end scales business, a plant that made shells for electric blankets, and the time and temperature division that made clocks and thermometers. (Dunlap believed that most of these businesses were acquired by prior management at premium prices and then poorly managed, which in his view explained why his divestiture program resulted in the divested businesses being sold for amounts below their original purchase prices.)
- Reducing the number of factories from 26 to 8 worldwide—some of the 26 plants were operating at 30 to 50 percent of capacity, others were not cost effective, and some made items that were dropped from the product line.
- Reducing the number of warehouses from 61 to 18.
- Cutting the worldwide workforce of 12,000 in half—3,000 through divestitures of various businesses and 3,000 through layoffs.
- Liquidating $100 million in obsolete inventory.
- Cutting the number of variations of items in the product line (stock-keeping units, or SKUs—different models, styles, or colors) from 12,000 to 1,500. While this move cost Sunbeam an estimated $45 million in sales, the cost savings were significant enough to produce an estimated profit increase of $15 million.
- Discontinuing Sunbeam's practice of shipping 110-volt electrical products to foreign markets in Europe and Asia, where the electrical standard was 220 volts. The new management team at Sunbeam decided on a strategy of reengineering a line of 42 products made to run on 220 volts and selling them in 10 regions of Europe and Asia. The new strategy was expected to facilitate the tripling of Sunbeam's foreign sales in three years.[10]

By January 1997, with the major restructuring components either completed or in the final stages, Sunbeam was ready to proceed with efforts to grow its core business. The strategy incorporated the following major initiatives:

- A concerted program to introduce 30 new products domestically annually and cut new-product development time from two and a half years to 6 months.
- Introducing newly designed packaging (with trilingual labeling) to make Sunbeam's product offerings more attractive, distinctive, and appealing.
- Opening 10 new Sunbeam factory outlet stores in early 1997, with plans to have 20 by year-end and to add 20 per year over the next several years.
- Initiating new advertising campaigns to strengthen consumer awareness of the Sunbeam and Oster brands. (Sunbeam's new commercials carried the tags "Sunbeam—Now There's a Bright Idea" and "There's a New Sunbeam Shining.")
- Increasing international sales by more than 25 percent through a program to build a network of foreign distributors and give Sunbeam increased global distribution capability and market coverage—15 new licensing agreements with major international distributors were signed by early 1997, and more were planned during the year.

---

[10]Dunlap and Andelman, *Mean Business*, pp. 281–85.

- Setting up Internet sales of Sunbeam products and selling Sunbeam products on cable-TV-based QVC.
- Starting a mail-order catalog operation for Sunbeam products.
- Putting a program in place to participate in major bridal shows and make Sunbeam and Oster products the first choices of newlyweds in the $35 billion bridal registry market segment.
- Hiring a new vice president of operations to institute benchmarks for quality and production in Sunbeam's plants, shorten the time needed to get new products into the marketplace, and improve purchasing and warehousing.
- Launching an internal initiative to dramatically improve customer service levels and become the housewares industry leader in customer service.

The company's strategy to reach $2 billion in sales included (1) generating new sales of $200 million via the factory outlet stores, mail-order catalog, home-shopping via the Internet and QVC, and stronger relationships with domestic retailers; (2) increasing sales by $300 million through the introduction of new products; (3) increasing international sales from $200 million to $600 million; and (4) growing the sales of existing products by $100 million. These were very ambitious goals, given that the housewares industry was expected to grow only 5 percent annually.

To create a positive outlook on the part of the company's workforce, Al Dunlap got Sunbeam's board to approve making every manager and every domestic employee eligible for stock options. The plan allowed for options of up to 11.3 million shares to be granted. In addition, employees were given the option of buying Sunbeam shares through payroll deductions and could put up to half of their 401(K) plan in company stock, with 100 percent company matching (also in stock).

New-Product Introductions   Sunbeam's efforts to grow its core businesses led to a string of new-product introductions during 1997. Included were the following:

- A new line of heating pads with soft gel interiors.
- A new line of Allergysmart air filters and humidifiers with automatic shutoffs, glow-in-the-dark controls, and state-of-the-art filtering and air-freshening technology.
- A new line of "intelligent" electric blankets and mattress pads that could sense different body temperatures and respond by providing more heat to those areas of the body that need it and less to those that don't.
- New six-spray and eight-spray models of Massage Plus shower heads.
- An automatically inflating blood pressure monitor.
- New Sunbeam and Oster food steamers and a new Sunbeam Carousel rotisserie.
- New Sunbeam and Oster toasters with Toast Logic controls that automatically compensated for common fluctuations in household voltage and featured windows, extra-wide slots, a stop button, cool-touch housing, and a removable dishwasher-safe crumb tray.
- A new Steam Master iron with several innovative features.
- Improved versions of the Sunbeam Mixmaster and the Osterizer blender.
- A 12-piece hair-clipping kit and three new models of mustache and beard trimmers.
- A new line of digital bath scales.

- A soft-serve ice cream machine for home use.
- Two new lines of gas grills with new shapes, new materials, and new features.

The company was also working to develop the next generation of gas grills to deliver improved performance and a wider selection of features. In early 1998, Sunbeam moved (through its Health at Home group) to enter the $350 million water filtration market by introducing Fresh Source—a countertop water filtration product that removed microbiological cysts, chlorine, and lead from household water supplies.

Sunbeam's 1998 product line included mixers, blenders, food processors, juice extractors, steam irons, toasters, crock pots, barbecue grills, dental care products, electric blankets, humidifiers, and barber and beauty care equipment. The company sold its products under the brand names Sunbeam, Grillmaster, Toast Logic, Mixmaster, Oster, and Osterizer. Major customers included mass merchants such as Wal-Mart, Kmart, Target, Home Depot, and Costco; department stores such as Bloomingdale's, Dayton's, Hudson's, Dilliard's, and Macy's; and leading drugstore chains that stocked small appliances. Wal-Mart was Sunbeam's largest customer, accounting for approximately 15 percent of sales.

Sunbeam's principal competitors included Black & Decker, Hamilton Beach/Proctor Silex, Rival, KitchenAid, West Bend, Regal, and HPA/Betty Crocker. Exhibit 5 shows the market shares of the various small-appliance competitors in selected product categories. Overall, Sunbeam had an estimated 9.5 percent share of the electric housewares market in 1996 versus 29.2 percent for Hamilton Beach/Proctor Silex, 17.7 percent for Black & Decker, and 6.1 percent for Rival.

Cost-Control Efforts

Management had put in place a strong cost-control program to ensure that Sunbeam would have a cost structure that allowed it to be competitive in global markets. A key initiative for 1998 was to increase the outsourcing of parts and components, thereby shifting from the current make/buy ratio of approximately 70/30 to one of 50/50.

Exhibits 6 and 7 present the company's financial statements for the period 1995–97.

The AMA Controversy

In 1997, the American Medical Association (AMA) and Sunbeam discussed granting Sunbeam the right to display the AMA seal on the packaging of certain Sunbeam health care products—such as blood pressure monitors, heating pads, thermometers, and bathroom scales. Along with the seal on the package would be a notice informing the consumer that valuable medical information, created or approved by the AMA and a panel of physicians, could be found inside the package.[11] In return, Sunbeam would give the AMA a royalty on the sales of items carrying the AMA seal and information. The idea originated with the AMA's marketing department, which was looking for ways to generate revenues while providing useful medical information to consumers. AMA representatives indicated that Sunbeam was selected from among five other manufacturers because of its broad line of high-quality health-related products.

An agreement was signed in August 1997. A week later, Al Dunlap and John Seward, a physician who served as the AMA's chief executive officer, held a joint press conference to announce the partnership and answer questions. Shortly thereafter, the agreement came under fire from critics within the AMA and from a number of public interest groups

---

[11] Albert J. Dunlap, "Why I'm Taking On the Arrogant AMA," *The Wall Street Journal Interactive Edition*, November 17, 1997.

EXHIBIT 5   Market Shares of Appliance Makers in Selected Product Categories, 1995–96

Product Category/Company	1995	1996
Can Openers	(Based on shipments of 6.9 million units)	(Based on shipments of 6.9 million units)
Hamilton Beach/Proctor Silex	26%	24%
Black & Decker	25	13
Rival	25	26
Sunbeam/Oster	9	13
Presto	5	4
Others	10	20
Blenders	(Based on shipments of 5.8 million units)	(Based on shipments of 6.2 million units)
Hamilton Beach/Proctor Silex	42%	47%
Sunbeam/Oster	29	29
Braun	9	10
HPA/Betty Crocker	9	5
Waring	5	5
Others	6	4
Electric Irons	(Based on shipments of 15.6 million units)	(Based on shipments of 15.6 million units)
Black & Decker	38%	38%
Hamilton Beach/Proctor Silex	30	29
Sunbeam	16	17
N.A.P. (Norelco)	6	5
Rowenta	3	7
Singer	1	n.a.
Others	6	4
Electric Hand Mixers	(Based on shipments of 5.4 million units)	(Based on shipments of 5.3 million units)
Hamilton Beach/Proctor Silex	22%	24%
Black & Decker	19	15
Sunbeam/Oster	17	13
KitchenAid	10	6
West Bend	7	10
HPA/Betty Crocker	6	11
Rival	5	6
Others	7	15
Food Choppers	(Based on shipments of 1.4 million units)	(Based on shipments of 1.6 million units)
Black & Decker	38%	32%
Hamilton Beach/Proctor Silex	22	19
Cuisinart	15	17
HPA/Betty Crocker	11	8
Sunbeam/Oster	10	5
Others	4	19

Source: *Appliance Manufacturer*, April 1996, p.31; *Appliance: A Portrait of the U.S. Appliance Industry,* April 1997, p.3.

EXHIBIT 6   Sunbeam's Consolidated Statements of Operations, 1995–97 (Dollars in thousands, except per share amounts)

	Fiscal Years Ended		
	December 28, 1997	December 29, 1996	December 31, 1995
Net sales	$1,168,182	$ 984,236	$1,016,883
Cost of goods sold	837,683	900,573	809,130
Selling, general, and administrative expense	131,056	214,029	137,508
Restructuring, impairment, and other costs	—	154,869	—
Operating earnings (loss)	199,443	(285,235)	70,245
Interest expense	11,381	13,588	9,437
Other (income) expense, net	(1,218)	3,738	173
Earnings (loss) from continuing operations before income taxes	189,230	(302,561)	60,635
Income taxes (benefit):			
Current	8,369	(28,062)	(2,105)
Deferred	57,783	(77,828)	25,146
	66,152	(105,890)	23,041
Earnings (loss) from continuing operations	123,128	(196,671)	37,594
Earnings from discontinued operations, net of taxes	—	839	12,917
Loss on sale of discontinued operations, net of taxes	(13,713)	(32,430)	—
Net earnings (loss)	$ 109,415	$(228,262)	$ 50,511
Earnings (loss) per share of common stock from continuing operations:			
Basic	$ 1.45	$ (2.37)	$ 0.46
Diluted	1.41	(2.37)	0.45
Net earnings (loss) per share of common stock:			
Basic	$ 1.29	$ (2.75)	$ 0.62
Diluted	1.25	(2.75)	0.61
Weighted-average common shares outstanding:			
Basic	84,945	82,925	81,926
Diluted	87,542	82,925	82,819

Source: 1997 annual report.

and editorial writers. Both sets of critics accused the AMA of poor judgment in pursuing a policy of endorsing commercial products in general and of poor ethics in endorsing Sunbeam's products without testing them in particular. Following two board meetings, the AMA decided to terminate its agreement with Sunbeam. Al Dunlap objected strenuously to the AMA's walking away from its contractual obligations, saying that the AMA was "too political" and "too arrogant." He directed Sunbeam's lawyers to ask the federal court in Chicago to enforce the contractual agreement and award $20 million in damages to Sunbeam. The fallout within the AMA over the Sunbeam deal resulted in the resignation of John Seward and three other top AMA officials.

EXHIBIT 7   Sunbeam's Consolidated Balance Sheets, 1996–97 (Dollars in thousands)

	December 28, 1997	December 29, 1996
Assets		
Current assets:		
Cash and cash equivalents	$ 52,378	$ 11,526
Receivables, net	295,550	213,438
Inventories	256,180	162,252
Net assets of discontinued operations and other assets held for sale	—	102,847
Deferred income taxes	36,706	93,689
Prepaid expenses and other current assets	17,191	40,411
Total current assets	658,005	624,163
Property, plant, and equipment, net	240,897	220,088
Trademarks and trade names, net	194,372	200,262
Other assets	27,010	28,196
Total assets	$1,120,284	$1,072,709
Liabilities and Shareholders' Equity		
Current liabilities:		
Short-term debt and current portion of long-term debt	$ 668	$ 921
Accounts payable	105,580	107,319
Restructuring accrual	10,938	63,834
Other current liabilities	80,913	99,509
Total current liabilities	198,099	271,583
Long-term debt	194,580	201,115
Other long-term liabilities	141,109	152,451
Deferred income taxes	54,559	52,308
Commitments and contingencies		
Shareholders' equity		
Preferred stock (2 million shares authorized, none outstanding)	—	—
Common stock (issued 89,984,425 and 88,441,479 shares)	900	884
Paid-in capital	483,384	447,948
Retained earnings	141,134	35,118
Other	(30,436)	(25,310)
	594,982	458,640
Treasury stock, at cost (4,454,394 and 4,478,814 shares)	(63,045)	(63,388)
Total shareholders' equity	531,937	395,252
Total liabilities and shareholders' equity	$1,120,284	$1,072,709

Source: 1997 annual report.

Al Dunlap's Philosophy on How to Manage Corporate Turnarounds

By 1998, Al Dunlap had built quite a reputation for himself. He was well regarded by Wall Street and the investment community for his track record in dramatically boosting shareholder value at troubled companies. And he was well thought of by a number of business associates who had been a part of one or more of his turnarounds. But the roughshod, ax-wielding manner in which he "Dunlapped a company" generated many unflattering stories in the business press, partly because some reporters viewed him as abrasive, ruthless, dogmatic, intolerant, and/or egotistical. He was frequently criticized for the unfeeling manner in which he had laid off workers in massive numbers and fired executives. His outspokenness about the stupidity of prior managers in the companies he took over was often considered offensive. Mention of his name raised hackles in many quarters.

In interviews with business reporters and in his book *Mean Business* (which many reviewers said was an exercise in self-congratulation because of the manner in which it trumpeted his record), Al Dunlap made known his convictions about how and how not to manage companies:

> By the time I get to a company, the preponderance of damage is done. I come in looking for a pulse . . . Corporations are allowed to get so bad, then they ask me to come in at the eleventh hour and fix it. The only way to fix it then is to take dramatic action.[12]

> I have no desire to protect a culture, the corporate entity, or the in-place management. I don't think any of that is important. What's important is deploying those assets in the best possible fashion. Build where you can build. Shut down operations where they should be shut down. Sell where and when necessary.[13]

> If you do a restructuring—or, more aptly, a rescue—you must do it in one year.[14]

> You either get the pain and suffering accomplished in the first twelve months or you don't do it at all . . . It is far better to make a change and make it quickly. Slow death is terrible.[15]

> If you don't have a vision of the future, you are going nowhere . . . You've got to know where you are going today *and* tomorrow, because the decisions you make today will influence you beyond today . . . Look ahead ten years but don't expect or demand precise adherence to such a long-term vision . . . Review action plans daily, weekly, monthly, yearly, to assess whether conditions have changed and whether it's time for you to shift in a different direction.[16]

> Two questions you should always be asking yourself: "What business are we in, anyhow? What business should we be in?" When you have the answers, sell everything else and focus on the core business. When you are in too many businesses, it is distracting. People don't focus.[17]

> Set major goals that make a difference, goals that are attainable. Don't let people stray from these goals. Hold them accountable with great tenacity. Focus, focus, focus on your handful of goals. If you set too many goals, you will fail.[18]

> Outsource as many functions as possible . . . Outsourcing allows you to be more focused on a few things and not consumed by things that do not really have very much to do with whether the business succeeds . . . You should only do, in-house, what gives you a competitive advantage.[19]

[12]As quoted by James McNair, "New Executive Cut Jobs, Reformed Sunbeam's Image," *Knight-Ridder/Tribune Business News* (originated from *The Miami Herald*), December 2, 1996.

[13]Ibid., pp. 233–34.

[14]Speech given by Albert J. Dunlap at a conference sponsored by the Conference Board and reported in the *Journal of Business Strategy*, March–April 1997, p. 5.

[15]Dunlap and Andelman, *Mean Business*, pp. 11, 168.

[16]Ibid., pp. 91, 100.

[17]Ibid., pp. 69, 81.

[18]Ibid., p. 40.

[19]Ibid., p. 55.

When I fire people, *of course* I feel for them. But what I keep uppermost in my mind is that if I don't release them today, I'm going to have to cut more of them in six months or a year anyway. Doing it piecemeal is a fraud upon everybody—the employees, management, and the shareholders. No one's job, my own included, will be safe until I execute my responsibilities, thoroughly and completely . . . People who get let go should be people who are not performing a necessary function, or have not been effective . . . I cannot keep the people who created the debacle I am expected to fix.[20]

The best bargain is a CEO who has a competitive compensation package with an opportunity for a big stock equity payoff . . . I believe passionately in motivation. I believe corporations should reward successful people . . . executive compensation should be tied to shareholder return.[21]

Directors are responsible for seeing that a company has proper management in place. They should monitor management to ensure it does what it is supposed to do. If not, the directors should take corrective action.[22]

I put a high premium on loyalty. That doesn't mean just keeping people who agree with me. I recognize loyalty in people who speak their minds and tell me when they think I am doing something wrong.[23]

Al Dunlap had no patience for company cultures in which initiative was stifled and employees were not encouraged to be aggressive and innovative in their efforts to wring higher performance from the company's business assets. He believed taking aggressive actions to quickly stamp out a bad culture was one of the first orders of business in launching a successful turnaround:

If you have a great culture, nourish it, sustain it, grow it. If you have a bad culture, don't just put it in remission; kill it . . . A culture reflects the way things are; you have to change it to be the way you want it to be.[24]

Change how you conduct the business. Have people challenge everything you do. Change the product mix . . . sell those businesses that don't fit.[25]

I have moved many corporate headquarters because that is the ultimate way to change their culture. Moving sends a signal that a new headquarters, in a new city, means a new way of doing business.[26]

One senior executive who became part of Dunlap's inner circle at Scott Paper observed that Dunlap's culture-changing approach was "to pee all over the old culture and point out the issues and the reasons it was not successful."[27]

Sunbeam in Early 1998

In the early weeks of 1998, Sunbeam's stock price dropped from the high 40s to the high 30s, partly due to rumors that Dunlap might leave Sunbeam to take the CEO job at ailing Waste Management and partly due to Wall Street concerns that Sunbeam's fourth-quarter 1997 earnings would not meet expectations. In an interview with

---

[20]Ibid., pp. 39, 174, 234.

[21]Ibid., p. 179.

[22]Ibid., p. 216.

[23]Ibid., p. 232.

[24]Dunlap and Andelman, *Mean Business*, pp. 233–34.

[25]Dunlap's speech to management conference sponsored by the Conference Board as reported in *The Journal of Business Strategy*, March–April 1997, p. 6.

[26]Dunlap and Andelman, *Mean Business*, p. 238.

[27]Ibid.

Fortune published in January, Dunlap said, "I'm a shareholder-value creator. I believe in quantum leaps to create additional shareholder value. At this stage of a turnaround, you either have to acquire, merge, or sell."[28] Dunlap had already announced the hiring of two investment banking firms in October 1997 to help explore Sunbeam's quantum leap options. One of the consultants was urging Dunlap to make acquisitions. By February, rumors were circulating that a major deal was imminent.

On March 2, Sunbeam announced plans to acquire Coleman (a maker of camping and leisure products), Signature Brands (the maker of Mr. Coffee machines and Health-o-meter scales), and First Alert (a maker of smoke alarms and fire extinguishers)—all publicly traded companies—for $1.8 billion plus the assumption of $700 million in debt. The deal was a Wall Street first—no company had ever before announced the acquisition of three other publicly traded companies on the same day. Also that day, it was announced that Al Dunlap had signed a three-year contract to remain at Sunbeam. Dunlap said it was his intention to build Sunbeam into the "dominant consolidator" of the durable consumer products industry, indicating that the three acquisitions were only the first in a long-range plan to grow Sunbeam and extend its product reach.[29]

Sunbeam management indicated that it could reap $150 million in cost savings and other synergies by combining the operations of the four companies. The acquired companies had combined 1997 sales of $1.6 billion, 10,120 employees, and 21 plants. Sunbeam's stock rose to a high of $53 following news of the deal. Exhibit 8 provides some details on the three acquisitions and their effect on Sunbeam.

The Coleman Acquisition   Coleman's products were distributed through mass merchandisers, sporting goods chains, and outdoor specialty stores. Coleman was the world's leading manufacturer of lanterns and stoves for outdoor recreational use. Its families of products accounted for $860 million in sales in 1996. Coleman's major customers included Wal-Mart, Kmart, Target, Home Depot, Price/Costco, and Canadian Tire. Sales to Wal-Mart and Sam's accounted for 15 percent of Coleman's 1996 revenues. International sales accounted for about 33 percent of company revenues in 1997; Coleman products were sold in 100 countries, with 80 percent of foreign sales concentrated in Europe and Japan. Coleman's strongest competitors ranged from Rubbermaid and Igloo (a subsidiary of Brunswick Corporation) in coolers and jugs to American Camper (another Brunswick subsidiary) and Dayton Hudson in lanterns and stoves to Honda, Kawasaki, and Yamaha in power generators. Other principal competitors included Kelty, Nike, American Camper, and JanSport in backpacks; Sears in tents and pressure washers; Hot Springs in hot tubs; Eveready and Rayovac in flashlights and other lighting products; and First Alert, Nighthawk, and American Sensor in smoke detectors and other safety and security products. The company had strategic initiatives in place to introduce new products and to expand its presence in foreign markets. Coleman products and the Coleman brand had a good reputation among consumers for quality and superior customer service.

At the end of 1996, Coleman had 4,200 domestic employees and 2,800 foreign employees. The company had no domestic employees represented by unions, but the company's international workforce included 350 union employees in France and Italy and 1,100 union employees in Mexico. Coleman made its products at 16 plants.

---

[28]Patricia Sellers, "Can Chainsaw Al Really Be a Builder?," *Fortune*, January 12, 1998, p.

[29]As quoted in Rick Brooks and Greg Jaffe, "Sunbeam's Not So Odd Couple: Chainsaw Al, Mr. Coffee," *The Wall Street Journal*, March 3, 1998, p. B4.

EXHIBIT 8   Data on Sunbeam's Three Acquisitions

	Coleman	Signature Brands	First Alert
Sales revenues (in millions)			
1997	$1,154.0	$275.5	$187.0
1996	1,220.2	283.0	205.6
1995	933.6	267.9	246.3
Net profits (in millions)			
1997	$ (2.5)	$ (2.2)	$ (7.8)
1996	(41.9)	3.0	(18.7)
1995	39.3	0.7	11.4
Major product lines	Camping equipment (lanterns, stoves, tents, utensils), coolers and jugs, sleeping bags, backpacks, flashlights and handheld spotlights, portable outdoor furniture, smoke alarms, carbon monoxide detectors, hot tubs, thermostats, portable power generators, air compressors, power washers	Mr. Coffee coffeemakers, coffee filters, hot and iced tea makers, Health-o-meter scales for bath and kitchen use, upscale Borg scales for home use, economy Counselor scales for home use, professional-caliber medical and fitness scales, office and restaurant scales, massage pads, water filtration products	Residential smoke detectors, carbon monoxide detectors, radon detectors, fire extinguishers, rechargeable flashlights and lanterns, motion sensors for operating exterior and interior lighting equipment, photoelectric nightlights, fire escape ladders, fire security safes, and other safety-related products
Number of production facilities	16	2	3
Employees	7,000	995	2,125

Source: Company 10K reports.

The Signature Brands Acquisition   Signature Brands' consumer products were sold to mass merchants, warehouse clubs, department store chains, catalog showrooms, hardware chains, supermarket chains, drugstore chains, hotels and restaurants, and mail-order catalog merchants. Wal-Mart and Kmart accounted for 27 percent and 12 percent, respectively, of the company's annual revenues in 1997. In its media advertising, Signature emphasized the Mr. Coffee and Health-o-meter brands, both of which had good recognition among consumers shopping for coffeemakers and scales. The Mr. Coffee brand of automatic coffeemakers competed against Hamilton Beach/Procter Silex, Black & Decker, Braun, Krups, Bunn, Regal, West Bend, and several others. The company's major competitors in teamakers were Cuisinart and T-Fal. Consumer demand for coffeemakers and teamakers was flat, and new products with innovative features were required to generate meaningful revenue increases. In 1997, sales of automatic drip coffeemakers accounted for 43 percent of revenues, sales of teamakers accounted for 8 percent of revenues, and sales of consumer scales accounted for 19 percent of revenues.

The company's lines of professional scales for hospitals, physicians, clinics, nursing homes, and offices were marketed through a combination of direct sales and independent sales representatives to dealers, distributors, office megastores (Staples,

Office Depot, and OfficeMax), mail-order companies, and major buying groups. The company's line of medical scales faced competition domestically from Detecto and Scaletronix and internationally from SECA, a German manufacturer. Signature office scales competed with Sunbeam and Micro General products, and Signature food-service scales competed with those marketed under the Detecto, Taylor, Edlund, and Cooper brands.

Signature operated two major production facilities (one in Ohio and one in Illinois), both unionized. The Ohio plant assembled coffee appliances and produced a substantial portion of the coffee filters. The company relied on foreign and domestic suppliers for a number of the parts and components used in its coffee and tea appliances, and some entire products were made by contractors in Taiwan, Hong Kong, and China. The Illinois plant made scales; a few models of scales were supplied by outside contractors. The plants had made a number of improvements in efficiency and cost in recent years. Signature had nearly 1,000 employees.

The First Alert Acquisition   First Alert was the leading manufacturer and marketer of smoke detectors. It sold its products to mass merchants such as Wal-Mart, Kmart, and Sears; home center and hardware chains such as Home Depot, Lowe's, Builders Square, True Value/Cotter, and Ace Hardware; catalog showrooms such as Service Merchandise; warehouse clubs such as Sam's and Price/Costco; electrical wholesale distributors in the United States; and about 100 independent foreign distributors supplying 500 customers in some 50 countries worldwide. First Alert's principal foreign markets were Canada, Great Britain, Australia, and the Scandinavian countries. Sales to Wal-Mart and Sam's accounted for approximately 15 percent of the company's revenues. First Alert spent about $35 million annually on cooperative, print, radio, and television advertising.

First Alert's competition consisted of an assortment of foreign and domestic companies, with the chief competitors varying from product category to product category. None of First Alert's rivals had a broad enough product line to make it as the company's principal competitor.

All of First Alert's manufacturing took place at its two plants in Juarez, Mexico, except for fire extinguisher manufacturing, which took place at one of the company's facilities in Illinois. The company had 2,125 full-time employees, most of whom were located at either the Juarez plants (1,811 workers) or facilities in Illinois (249 employees).

A Sudden Turn of Events

On March 19, 1998, Sunbeam announced that its first-quarter results might fall below Wall Street expectations because retailers were curtailing their inventories more than anticipated. That day, the company's stock price dropped 9.4 percent, to about $45. Then on Friday, April 3, the company announced that it would report a loss for the first quarter, citing a decline in sales from a year earlier and charges related to its three acquisitions. It also said that sales would be about 5 percent lower than the $253 million recorded in the first quarter of 1997. The price of Sunbeam's shares plunged to $34 ⅜, down $11 ⁷⁄₁₆ on the day's trading. In subsequent days, the stock price dropped further, to around $30 per share.

That same Friday, Al Dunlap announced that he had fired Donald Uzzi, the company's executive vice president for consumer products, who had been brought in as a key member of Dunlap's new turnaround team for Sunbeam. Uzzi was replaced by Lee Griffith, former vice president of sales; Griffith was given the title of president of

Sunbeam's household products division. Dunlap indicated that the company was looking for another executive to serve as president of its outdoor leisure business, which included the new Coleman-brand products. In the meantime, Dunlap said that Russell Kersh, his longtime lieutenant in prior turnarounds and currently Sunbeam's chief financial officer, would become Coleman's acting CEO.

In a conference call to discuss the company's situation with analysts, Al Dunlap said that the plunge in the price of the company's shares was "nonsense." He indicated that the unexpectedly low sales were an anomaly caused by retailers demanding unacceptably low prices on seasonal products. Sunbeam refused to cut prices because, in Dunlap's words, "We are not going to damage our brands."[30] Kersh said that the company did not intend to mislead analysts in its earlier March 19 announcement but that the company had overestimated demand from retailers.

(Sunbeam's Web site address is www.sunbeam.com.)

---

[30]As quoted in "Sunbeam's Shares Dive as Investors Doubt Dunlap," *The Wall Street Journal*, April 6, 1998, p. A5.

CARIBBEAN INTERNET CAFÉ

CASE 3 / IVEY

CASE

3

IVEY

In June 1996, David Grant was visiting his home in Kingston, Jamaica, while on summer vacation from the MBA program at the Richard Ivey School of Business in London, Ontario. He was gathering information on the feasibility of opening an Internet café in Kingston upon his graduation from the MBA program in 1997. David had always wanted to be his own boss, and he felt that the timing was right to pursue this business opportunity in Jamaica.

Prior to entering the MBA program, David had worked as a computer systems engineer at the local telephone company, Jamaica Telecommunications Limited (JTL). JTL, 80 percent owned by a British telecommunications company, was one of seven Internet service providers on the island. If this venture turned out to be feasible, David intended to lease the telephone lines from JTL. He had also worked as a part-time teacher at the University of Technology and as a computer programmer in Jamaica.

Michelle Theobals, *The University of Western Ontario*

Murray Bryant, *The University of Western Ontario*

THE CONCEPT

A typical Internet café offered computer services (including access to the Internet), a small menu of light snack foods, and an assortment of beverages. While he was studying in London, David visited a number of Internet cafés and became intrigued by the concept. A café seemed to be the perfect vehicle for people to use the Internet and other computer services without making an expensive investment in computer hardware. In addition, a cybercafé provided a social outlet: Customers could "surf the Net" together, listen to music, or simply relax and socialize.

Prepared under the supervision of Professor Murray Bryant. The authors may have disguised certain names and other identifying information to protect confidentiality.

Ivey Management Services prohibits any form of reproduction, storage, or transmittal without its written permission. This material is not covered under authorization from CanCopy or any reproduction rights organization. To order copies or request permission to reproduce materials, contact Ivey Publishing, Ivey Management Services, c/o Richard Ivey School of Business, the University of Western Ontario, London, Ontario, Canada, N6A 3K7; phone 519-661-3208; fax 519-661-3882; e-mail *cases@Ivey.uwo.ca.*

Copyright © 1998, Ivey Management Services. One-time permission to reproduce granted by Ivey Management Services on September 18, 1998.

COMPETITIVE ENVIRONMENT

In Jamaica, although there was high awareness of the Internet, there was very low accessibility and usage. Mainly corporations and universities used the Internet. However, even at these institutions, individuals had to reserve time to access the Internet and they were limited to short time periods. Private usage was still low, and David expected that it would remain that way at least for the next three years. The main reasons for the low penetration rates were (a) the high cost of computers as a percentage of average salary, (b) the lack of telephone lines in some areas in Kingston, and (c) the high rates currently being charged by the existing Internet service providers. Most providers charged a flat rate for a fixed number of hours per month, and then hourly rates for any extra usage. This pricing scheme tended to penalize those users who only checked e-mail and used the Internet for a few hours per month. The average hourly rate charged by the service providers was JA$90.[1]

There were a large number of restaurants and cafés in Kingston; however, none of these establishments provided Internet services. Most of the cafés provided outdoor seating, music, games, or other entertainment, and traditional drinks and restaurant fare. Most cafés did not serve coffee as, traditionally, the beverage was not very popular in Jamaica.

CARIBBEAN INTERNET CAFÉ

David planned to introduce the European café concept to Jamaica, offering brewed coffee (e.g., local and imported premium coffee beans, espresso, cappuccino, and caffè latte), imported wines, fresh tropical juices, and baked products such as croissants, bagels, doughnuts, and other pastries. He envisioned three areas in his café: a computer area with booths, a wine lounge with some comfortable sofas, and a general café area with tables and chairs. Initially, he would purchase five Pentium processor computers and connect to the Internet via a 56 kbps[2] telephone line leased from JTL. The café would also provide printing services, a scanner, and the latest office software (spreadsheet, word processing, and presentations). Caribbean Internet Café (CIC) would not have a kitchen. All the baked products would be sourced from local bakeries as needed.

The target market would be computer-literate 18- to 35-year-old university students and professionals with a relatively high disposable income. Most of these persons would have limited access to the Internet at work or school, but might wish additional access for leisure or research. This group would also be busy and trendy, and would appreciate a venue where they could relax and unwind, but where they would also have access to the facilities to work if necessary. David estimated the total size of his target segment in Kingston to be about 20,000. CIC would initially accommodate 50 seats: 15 at the computer terminals (3 per booth), 15 in the wine lounge, and 20 in the general area.

David thought that New Kingston, the city's business district, would be a good location. Most banks, insurance companies, other financial institutions, and corporations had head offices or branches in this area. There were also two major hotels and a shopping center. Most workers in New Kingston were in white-collar jobs such as banking, insurance, programming, and consulting. In addition, New Kingston was close to several affluent suburbs from which CIC could attract patrons.

---

[1]All dollar amounts in the case are in Jamaican currency, unless otherwise stated. The exchange rate was approximately JA$25 = CAN$1 and JA$35 = U.S.$1.

[2]kbps = kilobytes per second

EXHIBIT 1   Equipment Required for the Caribbean Internet Café

Item	Number of Items	Unit Cost (U.S.$)	Total Cost (JA$)*
General Equipment			
Telephone system	1	$ 150	$ 5,250
Counter fixtures	1	10,000	350,000
Espresso machines	2	2,000	140,000
Cash register	1		50,000
Photocopier	1	800	28,000
Hardware			
Pentium systems, colour monitors, CD ROMs and modems	5	$ 2,000	$ 350,000
Colour ink-jet printer	1	400	14,000
Laser printer	1	800	28,000
Software			
Windows 95	1	$ 100	$ 3,500
Microsoft Office	1	350	12,250
Furniture			
Tables or booths	20	$ 150	$ 105,000
Chairs or stools	50	100	175,000
Sofas	2		50,000
Other			
Artwork/sculptures	4		$ 10,000
China, cutlery, glassware			100,000
Flowers/plants			5,000
Total			$1,426,000

*Inclusive of import duties and taxes.

PRELIMINARY INVESTIGATIONS

While visiting Kingston, David began to gather data on the investments and costs that would be necessary to start his venture. He first made a list of the equipment that he would need. He intended to purchase most of these items in the United States and ship them to the island himself. In this manner, he could save the exorbitant markups that many stores charged in Jamaica. The list of equipment and costs is shown in Exhibit 1.

David intended to staff CIC with university students majoring in computer science and hospitality. They would work part-time for about 15 hours per week, and would double as Internet tutors and waiters. Wages for the students would be approximately JA$40 per hour. The café would be open to the public for 84 hours, six days per week, and employees would be needed for around 90 hours per week. An average of two employees on duty would be required. Although he planned to be on hand to manage the finances and to oversee the operation, David intended to hire a manager with experience in the Jamaican restaurant industry. This person would assist with the start-up, staffing, training, menu development, quality control, and customer service. He estimated that the salary for this person would be JA$40,000 per month.

David found a number of suitable sites in New Kingston, and estimated that the lease costs would be JA$30,000 per month. He preferred to lease rather than purchase the property, since mortgage rates were currently very high (25 percent per annum) and he did not want to fund a down payment. He estimated that telephone bills and utilities would cost JA$15,000 per month and that he would need to make an initial deposit with the utility companies of JA$7,000. David spoke to a former co-worker at JTL and determined that he could lease the link to the Internet for JA$10,000 per month. Internet service would be provided by JTL at a cost of $60 per computer per hour. He also obtained a quote from an insurance company to insure the contents of the facility for a premium of JA$10,000 per month.

Advertising, marketing, and promotion would cost JA$10,000 per month. However, he expected to spend an additional JA$20,000 on advertising just prior to opening the café. Other up-front costs such as legal fees, incorporation expenses, licences and permits, and decorating expenses were estimated at a total of JA$120,000. Miscellaneous monthly administrative and maintenance expenses would be JA$50,000.

PRICING

After examining the rates of the local Internet service providers, David decided that he would charge a 30 percent premium on their average hourly rates, for a total of JA$120 per hour. He thought that customers would accept this rate since they would not have to purchase several hours up-front. Time on the computers would be available in one-hour slots. David estimated that 40 percent of his customers would pay for access to a computer. The other clients would probably share a computer with a friend or simply socialize in the café or wine lounge. All customers would spend an average of one hour in the café. He expected that the average customer would spend JA$140 on drinks and JA$60 on food. Average costs per customer for drinks and food would be JA$50 and JA$30, respectively.

AN OFFER FROM JTL

As David looked over his list of expenses, he felt overwhelmed. He wondered how he would finance the venture. He had approximately JA$500,000 in savings that he was willing to invest in the café. He approached friends, relatives, and other potential investors with his idea, but to no avail. Finally, he contacted his former boss at JTL and showed her his business plan. Together, they prepared a proposal for the senior management. JTL expressed some interest in the proposal; management thought that the café would increase usage and awareness of the Internet in general, thereby increasing JTL's sales of Internet service.

After several rounds of meetings and negotiations, JTL made David an offer. JTL proposed to invest JA$500,000 in shares in CIC (50 percent partner) and to provide a further JA$1,250,000 as a long-term loan to the company. CIC would be charged a special concessionary interest rate of 10 percent per annum on the loan. In addition, JTL commissioned a market study conducted by an independent market research firm. The firm agreed with David's estimate of the total segment size, and then made three estimates of potential usage of the café in the first year. The market research firm projected that, optimistically, 50 percent of the segment would visit the café, on average, five times per year. A realistic projection was that 40 percent of the segment would visit the café an average of three times per year. Finally, a pessimistic estimate was that 30 percent of the segment would visit twice per year.

THE DECISION

After an exhausting "vacation," David sat down to review his notes. He wondered if he should proceed with the CIC venture and, if so, if it would be a profitable business for him and JTL.

KUVO RADIO

Joan Winn, *University of Denver*

Christina L. Móntez, *University of Denver*

Florence Hernandez-Ramos, KUVO radio's president and CEO, reflected on the Hispanic-owned jazz radio station with pride. For over 10 years the station had broadcast up to 23½ hours of classic jazz every day of every week. Special weekend programming included blues, Latin jazz, tejano, salsa, Native American rhythms, and a Brazilian fantasy. (See Exhibits 1 and 2 for a terminology list and the programming schedule.) These sounds were peppered with hourly National Public Radio (NPR) news and information, and book reviews by local authors and bookstore owners. Hernandez-Ramos believed that KUVO's unique programming mix justified its tag line "Oasis in the City," a refreshing escape from the rock and country commercial radio stations.

But as the 1996 spring membership drive was coming to a close, Hernandez-Ramos's pride turned to concern over the future of the station. KUVO, a licensed educational broadcasting station, was a 501(c)(3) nonprofit organization and a member of both NPR and Public Radio International (PRI). As such, it relied largely on donations of "members," rather than commercial sales, to cover its operating costs. During the nine-day membership campaign, the first of three during the year, 1,457 members had pledged $79,928, 5 percent less than the $84,247 pledged in the fall membership drive and 8 percent less than the $86,000 spring-drive goal. With the threat of cuts in federal funding for public radio, the station would not have enough funds to sustain its current operations if membership contributions did not increase. (See Exhibit 3 for operating expenses.) KUVO also relied on sponsorship from profit and nonprofit organizations, but legal restrictions regarding advertising on public radio stations deterred many corporate sponsors. Without increased support from listeners, donors, and volunteers, the station's future was uncertain.

THE ORGANIZATION AND ITS HISTORY

The story of KUVO's becoming a player in the Denver metropolitan broadcast area was, in the words of Florence Hernandez-Ramos, one of "[t]rying to find people who would essentially believe in a pipe dream." KUVO's birth was, in large part, the result of efforts by the Hispanic[1] community to increase its presence in the American media, an often difficult task for minorities.

---

[1]This term is used interchangeably with *Latin*. See Exhibit 1 for definitions.

EXHIBIT 1   Terminology Guide to Radio, Jazz, and the KUVO Format

Blues	A 12-bar song form that evolved from black spirituals and work songs; unique elements are blue notes, speechlike inflection, and emotional expression (*Jazz for Beginners,* 1995).
Brazilian fantasy	A programming format that included bossa nova and other Brazilian music with jazz influences.
Chicano	A person of Mexican descent born and raised in the United States (American Heritage Dictionary, 1985).
Classic jazz	The various types (big band, swing, be-bop, cool, modal) of jazz music produced between approximately 1920 and 1970.
Format	Programming broadcast over 20 hours weekly (*Broadcasting and Cable Yearbook, 1995*).
Fusion	Classic jazz themes electrified and rock influenced; produced between 1970 and the present.
Hispanic	Of or pertaining to the language, people, and culture of Spain, Portugal, or Latin America (American Heritage Dictionary, 1985).
Latin jazz	Latin rhythms combined with jazz.
Latino	A native or descendant of Latin America, including the Caribbean (American Heritage Dictionary, 1985).
Native American rhythms	Programming that included music from various Native American tribes from the United States.
Salsa	Literally, "sauce" or "juice" in Spanish; with regard to music, it refers to the encounter of Afro-Cuban and Puerto Rican music with big band jazz in the Latin barrios of New York; one unifying theme in salsa is the reference to the syncretic Afro-Catholic religions (*World Music Rough Guide,* 1994).
Smooth jazz	Classic jazz themes with pop music influences; produced between 1975 and the present.
Special programming	Programming broadcast from 1 to 20 hours weekly (*Broadcasting and Cable Yearbook, 1995*).
Straight-ahead jazz	Synonym for classic jazz.
Tejano	A modern, urban version of conjunto (an accordion-led style of Tex-Mex music), using synthesizers and other electric instruments (*World Music Rough Guide,* 1994).

In 1982, of the 300 public radio stations in the continental United States (including Indian reservations) and Alaska, African Americans controlled 16, Hispanics 12, and Native Americans 9. The Hispanic-controlled stations comprised the National Federation of Community Broadcasting (NFCB), an organization dedicated to increasing Hispanic access to media. In the western United States, Hugo Morales of Fresno, California, managed the Western Community of Bilingual Radio and Radio Bilingue, the regional arms of the NFCB. Only one Spanish-language station operated in Denver (KBNO, an AM station), despite the fact that 13 percent—approximately 378,000 people—of the Denver metropolitan area's population was of Hispanic origin.[2] By 2020,

[2]J. Accola, "'Huge' Hispanic Market Ignored, Consultant Says," *Rocky Mountain News,* September 20, 1996, p. 2B.

EXHIBIT 2   Programming Guide

	Sun.	Mon.	Tues.	Wed.	Thurs.	Fri.	Sat.
2–5 AM	Jazz						Jazz
5–7 AM		KUVO Morning Show Music & Features w/Carlos Lando					
7–8 AM	Alternative Voices						
8–9 AM	La Nueva Voz						
9–1 PM	Cancion Mexicana	Latino USA				Telling it Like it Was w/Lou Rawls	
1–3 PM	Latin Musicians	Jazz					
3–4 PM	Salsa on Sunday						
4–6 PM	Brazilian Fantasy	Marketplace News					
6–7 PM	Jazz	Jazz Smithsonian w/ Lena Horne	Making the Music w/Wynton Marsalis	Piano Jazz w/Marian McPartland	Jazzset	Jazz at the Kennedy Center w/Dr. Billy Taylor	Jazztown
7–10 PM		Jazz					All Blues 7–9 PM
10–1 AM							
1–2 AM		Jazz Smithsonian w/ Lena Horne	Making the Music w/Wynton Marsalis	Piano Jazz w/Marian McPartland	Jazzset	Jazz at the Kennedy Center w/Dr. Billy Taylor	So What? Acid Jazz

Source: KUVO, 1996.

Colorado's Hispanic population is expected to reach 20 percent.[3] See Exhibit 4 for statewide population demographics.

In November 1982, the owners of the 89.3 FM frequency were forced to relinquish their rights to the station, having failed to raise enough money to air their planned "alternative, community-action" broadcast. At that time, National Public Radio had two subscriber stations in Colorado, both through university-owned affiliates, one at

[3]R. Schwab, "Hispanic Chamber Gains New Clout," *The Denver Post,* September 15, 1996, pp. 1G, 20G.

EXHIBIT 3 KUVO/Denver Educational Broadcasting, Inc., Statement of Revenue and Expenses

	For the Years Ended December 31					
	1990	1991	1992	1993	1994	1995
Revenues						
Underwriting	$ 88,689	$178,568	$ 83,813	$ 105,458	$ 128,777	$135,886
Memberships	159,736	180,718	194,326	228,184	232,104	320,790
Grants	129,195	156,826	243,628	262,476	310,033	183,125
Channel charges	44,488	46,712	49,248	51,500	54,296	57,578
Miscellaneous	10,650	11,261	13,271	23,811	36,094	16,316
Total cash	$432,758	$574,085	$ 584,286	$ 671,429	$ 761,304	$713,695
In-kind[1]	$ 71,195	$161,231	$ 84,869	$ 85,941	$ 52,679	$ 31,909
Trade[2]	44,956	44,631	105,451	38,928	35,497	7,418
Volunteer[3]	153,575	191,122	194,892	213,706	217,644	239,969
Total noncash	$269,726	$396,984	$ 385,212	$ 338,575	$ 305,820	$279,296
Total Revenues	$702,484	$971,069	$ 969,498	$1,010,004	$1,067,124	$992,991
Expenses						
Salaries	$185,840	$216,463	$ 227,953	$ 256,953	$ 260,031	$286,625
Professional Services	90,220	155,134	99,444	102,016	90,105	81,122
Programming	183,948	232,450	326,019	287,286	407,676	368,348
Rent/Utilities	59,195	56,384	50,135	46,842	54,150	55,587
Ad & Promotion	88,192	175,893	203,324	197,339	88,899	53,918
General/Administrative	64,640	80,465	74,981	79,286	126,323	101,988
Depreciation	30,799	21,034	31,925	29,279	25,255	25,256
Interest	4,878	9,620	5,770	6,655	0	0
Total Expenses	$707,712	$947,443	$1,019,551	$1,005,656	$1,052,439	$972,844
Loss on Abandonment of Lease	—	—	—	—	$20,555[4]	—
Surplus/deficit	($5,228)	$23,626	($50,053)	$4,348	($5,870)	$20,147

Notes
1. "In-kind" donations are goods and services, recorded at their fair market value.
2. KUVO "trades" air time for goods and services. Revenue is recorded at the fair market value of the related goods and services or the air time given.
3. Volunteer services are valued at hourly rates established by the Corporation for Public Broadcasting.
4. KUVO entered into a 20-year lease for the facilities at the Five Points Media Center Building in July 1994.

the University of Denver (KCFR, which became independent in 1988), and the other at Colorado State University in Fort Collins (KCSU), 60 miles north of Denver.

A group of Denver's concerned Hispanic citizens, led by Hugo Morales and the NFCB, attended the bid meeting of the Federal Communications Commission (FCC) to forestall sale of the station to the highest bidder. NPR was concerned about the low participation of minorities in public radio and supported Morales's group in their request for FCC approval of the transfer of the rights to the station.

After having won the rights to the frequency, the new licensees faced two immediate tasks: To raise money for broadcasting equipment and to name a chief executive officer and board of directors. For the board, Morales, Hernandez-Ramos, and Mark Hand (a

EXHIBIT 4   Demographic Trends

While the KUVO footprint reaches a 60-mile radius from its location atop Lookout Mountain in Golden, Colorado, the majority of the listener membership is found in the Denver metropolitan area. The U.S. Census data shown below refers to the Denver-Boulder Consolidated Metropolitan Statistical Area (CMSA), which includes the following seven counties (within approximately a 30-mile radius from the transmitter): Adams, Arapahoe, Boulder, Denver, Douglas, Gilpin, and Jefferson.

	1980	1990	% Change
Total population Denver-Boulder CMSA	1,620,902	1,848,319	14.0
Persons of Hispanic origin	173,773	223,361	28.5
(% of total population)	(10.7%)	(12.1%)	
By country/region of origin			
Mexico	108,697	150,483	38.4
Puerto Rico	2,067	4,246	105.4
Cuba	1,169	1,609	37.6
All others	61,840	67,023	8.4
By race			
White	89,679	124,212	38.5
Black	1,183	2,902	145.3
All others	82,911	96,247	16.1
Number of households speaking Spanish or Spanish Creole at home	45,965	102,010	121.9
Number of households speaking Portuguese or Portuguese Creole at home	367	352	−4.1

Source: U.S. Bureau of the Census, 1980, 1990.

friend of Morales) decided to draw upon the national pool of Hispanics in radio and then gradually replace those chosen with locals as the station became more well known. A solution to the search for a CEO was not so easy: There were few Hispanic media personalities in Denver. Of those few, all had highly remunerative positions; running a start-up radio station for a noncompetitive salary was not in their plans.

In 1982, Florence Hernandez-Ramos was engaged in a career as a paralegal for the state attorney general's office. A native of Lamar, Colorado, Hernandez-Ramos had graduated from the University of Colorado in Boulder and had moved to Denver in 1968. Morales was impressed with Hernandez-Ramos's professionalism and her involvement in cultural activities in the Denver area. Consequently, Morales encouraged Hernandez-Ramos to apply for the CEO position at the new station. Shortly thereafter, Hernandez-Ramos had a new job and spent her first day in Washington, D.C., learning the ins and outs of public radio.

The capitalization issue remained: The station needed at least $200,000 to acquire the equipment necessary to broadcast. The station eventually obtained a one-year, federally funded operating and technical grant of $326,000, with the stipulation that an additional $117,000 be raised for hiring a staff. Hernandez-Ramos was both elated and overwhelmed—these numbers, pocket change for many companies, appeared astronomically high and unachievable. Nevertheless, she faced the challenge by turning to the very people for whom the station was intended, the Hispanic community. For 22 months, Hernandez-Ramos and Morales sponsored every grassroots fund-raising campaign they could think of, from break-dancing contests to social dances to bake-outs. They enlisted the community to make colorful paper flowers to sell during the annual Cinco de Mayo celebration and Posadas (a mid-December Mexican Christmas tradition). Hernandez-Ramos recalled with humor and pride the Adopt-A-Watt doll campaign: Youth groups from a local recreation center made dolls that were awarded to individuals who donated $10 or more toward obtaining a 25,000-watt transmitter. The fund-raising efforts were not in vain. On August 29, 1985, the station went on the air at 89.3 FM as KUVO.

The Mission

As politically and socially active members of the community, both Hernandez-Ramos and Morales saw the radio station as a vehicle for establishing a voice for the Latino community. From the beginning, the station's programming was intended to serve Denver's Hispanic community. Hence, the station was named KUVO, the shortened version of *¿Qué (hu)vo?* (What's going on?). KPSA (*¿Qué pasa?*) had already been assigned to an AM station in New Mexico. The station owners had envisioned that the station would play Spanish-language music, because it was a common-language heritage that united *la raza bronce,* the bronze-colored race. But through the casual marketing research conducted during the fund-raising efforts, the organizers noticed that the majority of the surveys, completed in English, expressed a preference for jazz programming, which was conspicuously absent from Denver radio at the time. So, KUVO decided to play jazz and Spanish-language music, at first glance a rare mix.

Once jazz selections were on the air, listeners happily welcomed them—but something was amiss: few of those who called in "sounded Hispanic." "What are *they* doing listening to our station?!" thought KUVO's founders. The question was asked not with prejudice, but with perplexity. To confuse everyone more, listeners who called in during Spanish-language programming spoke English and requested tejano and similar musical genres produced along the Mexican-American border and in the southwest United States, rather than traditional Mexican music. This diversity of the listening audience was critical in establishing the station's current mission:

> The mission of Denver Educational Broadcasting, KUVO, is to provide alternative educational, informational, and entertainment opportunities that enrich, maintain, reflect, and institutionalize a multilingual, multicultural perspective and foster appreciation for cultural diversity with an emphasis on the Chicano/Hispanic experience.

RADIO: A NATIONAL OVERVIEW

In spite of the advent of television in 1946, its steady popularity, and the relatively recent explosion of cable and direct-TV satellites, American radio continued to grow. According to the *Broadcasting and Cable Yearbook 1995,* both AM and FM radio authorizations and broadcasts continued to rise.[4] Between 1984 and 1994, adult contemporary, country-and-western, Top 40, and album-oriented rock stations dominated commercial radio.

The national growth in public radio was reflected in the number of contributors. In 1970, when public radio was first established, approximately 33,000 individuals donated. By 1980, the number of contributors had grown to 487,000; by 1990, 1,275,000 people had donated money to support public radio. As the number of contributors to public radio grew, so had the average contribution. In 1990, the mean gift amount was $57.44.

---

[4]*Broadcasting and Cable Yearbook 1995,* vol. 1. New Providence, NJ: A Broadcasting and R. R. Bowker Publication.

Public radio had evolved into a source of in-depth news coverage and programming not found on commercial radio stations. While most public radio stations featured classical music, many ventured into alternative music venues not viewed as commercially viable. Jazz, for example, had experienced significant challenges in spite of its steady growth. According to John Corbett in *Down Beat* magazine, "The road for jazz broadcasting has been rocky since World War II, passing out of network radio in the 50s, moving into a world of increased specialization and fragmentation."[5] In fact, in late 1994, when Alameda, California–based KJAZ went off the air, classic jazz formats ceased to exist on commercial radio.

There was some debate about whether jazz was commercially viable. On the one hand, advertisers looked away from the straight-ahead classic jazz stations because their Arbitron ratings for market share were low. Meanwhile, advertisers turned to the smooth jazz stations, which attracted a larger mainstream audience. For example, Ron Cowan, CEO and chairman of KJAZ, a satellite station that had broadcasted in both northern California and New York, pointed out that advertisers also turned away from jazz stations because "the highly educated jazz listener has different listening habits than the typical 'drive-time' public. Our audience listened to KJAZ at home or in the office . . . Our heaviest listening began at five or six in the evening. We had a little 1,900-watt license, and we got up to a 5.5 share between 6 PM and midnight. Those hours don't mean anything to an advertising buyer who's looking at drive time." According to Cowan, "The mainstream jazz aficionado, by and large, is the best educated and makes the highest income. It's the most desirable demographic for advertisers to reach. That does not hold true for what I would call New Age jazz or yuppie jazz." In 1993, 367 radio stations featured jazz programming as part of their weekly schedule. Of these, 92 percent (337) were FM broadcasts, and 80 percent (295) were on noncommercial, or public radio, stations.

Industry insiders believed that there was little money to be made by record companies in jazz radio. Bob Rusch of North County Distribution, which handled over 800 jazz labels, commented that record companies and distributors did not see financial benefits in sending promo copies to radio stations. Rusch claimed that "labels who spend thousands of dollars sending it out, tracking it, . . . find almost no impact." Local stores often failed to carry specialized jazz labels, reinforcing the perception that radio promotions were ineffective marketing tools.

The Telecommunications Act of 1996 paved the way for radio industry consolidation by allowing companies to own up to eight stations in a single market. In March, 1996, *The Wall Street Journal* reported over $2 billion in radio acquisition deals in one month alone.[6] In Denver, Jacor Communications, one of the largest radio-broadcasting companies in the United States, acquired Noble Broadcasting Group, holder of four Denver radio stations, thereby doubling its Denver-area presence.[7] While some industry insiders believed that consolidation would curtail program diversity, others saw the increase in advertising leverage by these large companies contributing to more program diversity, as stations could experiment with alternative programming without compromising market share.[8]

---

[5] J. Corbett, "The Sorry-assed State of Jazz Radio: Can It Be Fixed?" *Down Beat,* June 1995, pp. 30–35.

[6] J. Millman, "Infinity Is Buying 12 Radio Stations from KKR for Total of $410 Million," *The Wall Street Journal,* March 5, 1996, p. B1.

[7] "Jacor Buys Four Radio Stations in Denver's Biggest Acquisition," *Rocky Mountain News,* July 18, 1996. p. 3B.

[8] J. Lippman, "New Telecom Law Spurs Wave of Radio-Station Deals," *The Wall Street Journal,* March 18, 1996, p. B1.

EXHIBIT 5   Format Distribution of Colorado Radio Stations

Format	Number
Country	53
Adult contemporary	36
Rock/AOR	20
Variety/diverse	14
Religious	14
Oldies	14
News/talk	13
News	13
Talk	9
Classical	8
Progressive	7
Sports	7
Spanish	7
Contemporary hits/Top 40	7
Jazz	5
Middle of the road (MOR)	4
Big band	3
Educational	3
Agricultural and farm	3
Classic rock	3
Children	2
Beautiful music	2
Black	2
Foreign language/ethnic	1
Nostalgia	1
Urban contemporary	1
New Age	1

Note: *The Broadcasting and Cable Yearbook* recognizes 71 different formats.
Source: *Broadcasting and Cable Yearbook 1995.*

DENVER'S RADIO MARKET

In 1995, there were 109 AM stations and 75 FM stations in Colorado. Of these 184 stations, 154 were commercial and 30 were noncommercial.[9] By 1991, the FCC had granted 47 FM licenses to the Denver area "in what many considered to be an already over-radioed area."[10] Industry analysts saw this as the first sign of a rebounding economy and the herald of what would be called a "broadcast boom" by 1993. By 1995, Denver ranked 23rd of 131 radio markets nationwide, with approximately 1,705,800 million listeners. Listeners could tune into one of three AM Spanish-language stations, two public radio stations (not including KUVO), and one station that had special jazz and blues programming. Exhibit 5 provides an overview of Colorado radio programming. Though other stations played occasional jazz selections, none matched KUVO in its jazz focus. KUVO thus assumed a unique position in the Denver radio market.

When KUVO went on the air in 1985, the local radio scene included one FM jazz station, KADX based in Castle Rock, 30 miles south of Denver, and one Spanish-language

---

[9]*Broadcasting and Cable Yearbook 1995.*
[10]P. Wehner, "Over-radioed Denver Gets Another Station," *Colorado Business,* November 1991, p. 10.

station, KBNO, an AM frequency. KDKO, an African American–owned station with a weak AM frequency, played rhythm, blues, and soul. KADX went off the air in 1987. From November 1994 to January 1995, eight stations changed ownership hands, including KHIH (co-owned with KHOW-AM), which eventually began to promote itself as "Smooth Jazz Colorado Style."[11] The new owners set out to make KHIH worth $5 million, the amount for which several other stations had recently been sold or traded.

KHIH was KUVO's main competitor. To music purists, the comparison was weak: KHIH played a bastardization of the classics—jazz themes electrified and "pop influenced." Many dedicated classic jazz aficionados scoffed at KHIH. Yet, for those who didn't know the difference between classic jazz and its newer mutations, KUVO was viewed as the maverick. Predictions on the genre's radio future were divided, but the bottom line was that jazz was hard to sell. However, jazz audiences were loyal listeners and generous supporters.

THE KUVO STUDIO AND STAFF

KUVO's headquarters were located in a predominantly African American area north of downtown Denver in the Five Points Media Center, a newly refurbished building owned by the Piton Foundation. The mayor's office of economic development, TCI, and the Boettcher Foundation had contributed over $2.6 million for renovations. The building was occupied by three public media concerns: KUVO, KBDI Channel 12 television (a Corporation for Public Broadcasting affiliate), and Denver Community Access Television, a cable studio where community members could produce shows for public broadcast. All three organizations provided internship programs to university students. The center's executive director, Jeff Hirota, explained that the center's mission was to use media "as a means of positive social change . . . where we [can] help women and minorities get jobs in the [media] industry . . . Our contribution is to give them hands-on experience in broadcast media."[12]

KUVO's second-floor suite reflected the corporate culture and provided an environment that encouraged quality service delivery. One was welcomed into the media center by the clear sounds of KUVO's live programming. The elevator opened into a comfortable waiting space where a glass facade with a single door handsomely displaying the KUVO logo opened into a reception area. The walls were decorated with framed prints of famous jazz musicians and Chicano art.

The resource room and the offices of the advertising underwriters, volunteer coordinator, and business manager had large windows that faced directly west, offering a sweeping view of downtown Denver and the Rocky Mountains. Hernandez-Ramos's office featured Mexican American folklore items reminiscent of those displayed during Dia de los Muertos (Day of the Dead; the Mexican equivalent of Halloween though a far more meaningful and elaborate holiday). *Gato Guerrero* and other books in the Luis Móntez Mystery Series by Hernandez-Ramos's husband, Manuel Ramos, added to the cultural decor.

The station was overseen by a nine-member board of directors. The KUVO staff was made up of 13 employees, 9 full-time and 4 part-time (see the organization chart in Exhibit 6). Unlike the staff of the early years, KUVO employees in 1996 had extensive experience in radio, public broadcasting, or nonprofit organizations. The

---

[11]S. Steers, "New Rules Prompt Flurry of Radio Sales," *Denver Business Journal,* January 8, 1993, p. 1.

[12]P. Mora, "Live from Five Points Media Center Puts Minorities in Broadcasting: Bilingual Live-wire KUVO Turns 10," *Denver Post,* July 22, 1995, p. E-14.

EXHIBIT 6   KUVO's Organization Chart, 1996

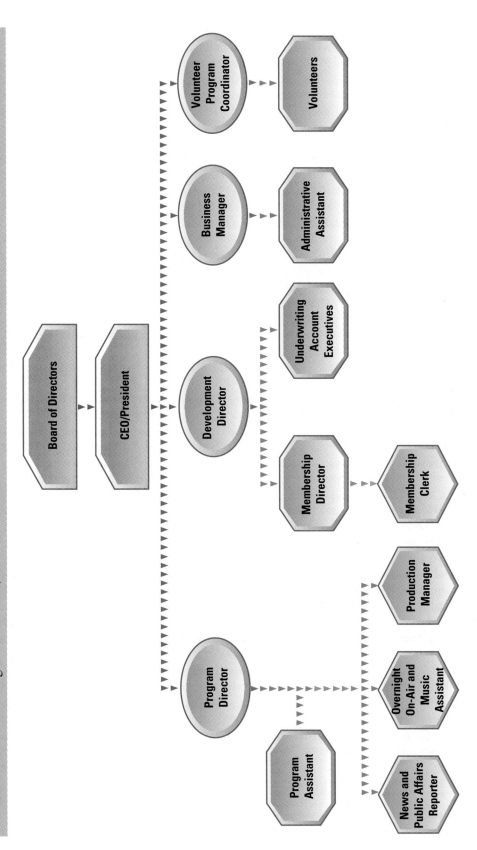

collective experience and enthusiasm for both jazz and the organizational mission made the staff one of KUVO's most valuable assets.

In addition to the paid staff, KUVO also benefited from over 400 volunteers. Approximately two-thirds of this group was involved in programming, with the remaining third in administration. According to Sandra Solimando, volunteer program administrator, the volunteers were a loyal and dedicated group. Forty of the volunteers served as on-air hosts who brought their own style and flavor to programming. Most volunteers offered clerical skills and performed customer (member) service functions such as assisting membership drives, mailing premiums, correcting premium notices, handling phone calls from listeners and members, responding to member letters, and "talking up" the station.

KUVO showed its appreciation for its volunteers in several ways. The *Scat Sheet,* a bimonthly newsletter, highlighted volunteer accomplishments and was sent to all volunteers. Each issue featured a cover story and photograph of two or three volunteers. The *Scat Sheet* also listed upcoming volunteer opportunities and solicited help, printed letters from volunteers temporarily out of the Denver area, and offered general reminders relevant to the group. Volunteers were also recognized at an annual party, replete with food, drink, and music. The resource room was available for use by volunteers and paid staff alike. It contained books, KUVO archives, a computer, and audio-visual equipment. KUVO also rewarded volunteers with pins and other memorabilia.

KUVO LISTENER PROFILE

KUVO's target audience was Denver's Hispanic community, for which the station hoped to serve as a voice. Part of KUVO's mission was to "foster appreciation for cultural diversity with an emphasis on the Chicano/Hispanic experience." Many of the Denver Hispanic community's cultural events were announced on KUVO. The station organized the Milagro Tours, an expedition to New Mexico to explore Native American and southwestern culture. The Hispanic community remained a focal point for KUVO. Paid and volunteer staff included a significant number of Hispanics.

However, the Latino community was not KUVO's primary listening market. KUVO listeners in 1996 composed an audience far different from the one that the station originally set out to serve. A listener profile study completed for KUVO by NPR in 1994 revealed that KUVO's audience fell squarely in the middle class. Specifically, the typical KUVO listener was 42 years old; had an average annual income of $44,000; had completed college; and was a white-collar worker and/or a management employee. Additionally, the listener was likely to have a passport, make investments, and belong to a health club. The study by NPR was the first ever completed for KUVO. The advertising underwriting and membership management staffs used this listener profile information to solicit business contributions.

According to the Arbitron ratings, the most widely used measure of radio listenership, KUVO attracted between 1.4 and 1.5 percent of the Denver radio market (estimated at 1,705,800). KHIH's market share was estimated to be around 5 percent. These numbers indicated the percentage of the listening audience tuned in at a particular time of day. Using a diary method, Arbitron determined the demographics and the number of people listening. These numbers were reported on a weekly basis.

MEMBERSHIP DRIVES AND GOALS

Three times a year, the serene KUVO studio was transformed into a frenzied fund drive with phones ringing, people moving about in every available space, and premiums littering the floor. These membership drives were the major effort to solicit money for KUVO. Listeners were urged to pledge, that is, donate money for the programming that KUVO delivered. By 1996, membership had grown to over 5,300.

The on-air membership drives occurred each year in February, June, and October, the months when most public broadcasting entities conducted fund-raising. Membership drives were held for nine days, from Saturday through the following Sunday. The membership drives sought to attract new members, retain current members, increase the number of pledges made by credit card, upgrade members from one level to another, lower the amount of direct mail, and improve the customer service.

There were seven designated membership levels, each accompanied by premiums, such as coffee mugs and T-shirts, bearing the KUVO logo. Members also received a KUVO membership card, which entitled them to discounts at over 30 retail businesses in the Denver Metropolitan area, and a subscription to the KUVO newsletter, published quarterly.

Prior to the membership drives, KUVO staff and volunteers engaged in extensive business-to-business marketing. The station acquired premiums from retail and restaurant establishments the target audience was likely to patronize. Premiums had been offered by organizations such as the Colorado Latino Dance Festival, the Shrine Circus, and Los Cabos Mexican restaurant. Different premiums were offered for certain hours at different levels as inducements to call in pledges. The most popular premium was the KUVO T-shirt, which bore the logo of various special programming shows. There had been numerous designs over the years, all made by local artists.

An aggressive direct marketing campaign was employed both before and after a membership drive to encourage renewals. Members who had not renewed continued to receive the *Oasis Member Newsletter* as a reminder that they hadn't pledged again. After five notices were mailed, the member was telemarketed.

After a pledge was received, KUVO immediately mailed a pledge form confirming the donation and requesting payment. Members could pay by cash, check, credit card, or through electronic funds transfer (EFT). The KUVO membership director maintained a membership database that contained each member's name, address, phone number, premium, and pledge and renewal dates.

SPONSORS AND ALLIANCES

One-sixth of KUVO's operating budget came from federal funding. Public broadcasting entities referred to the 1995 Republican "Contract with America" as the "Contract on America" as the Republican congress pushed to eliminate federal funding for public broadcasting. Despite an amendment by Representative Dan Miller of Florida to sustain funding until 1998, public radio and public television were increasingly forced to be self-sustaining. KUVO was one of the few all-jazz stations not supported by an academic institution. Because of KUVO's small size and lack of academic sponsorship, it was particularly vulnerable to cuts in funds. Industry analysts believed that "without state assistance, the diversity and depth of public radio will be staring down the long, cold barrel of commercial compromise."[13]

This assessment rang true for Hernandez-Ramos. KUVO had already taken steps to make up for the anticipated loss in federal support. One step was the replacement of "Morning Edition," an expensive NPR broadcast, with a 6 AM–9 AM drive-time music,

---

[13]Corbett, "The Sorry-assed State of Jazz Radio."

news, and information program "á la Lando" created by KUVO program director Carlos Lando, in November 1995.

Another step was a conscientious effort to increase donations from corporate underwriters. Corporate underwriting was public radio's answer to advertising. Underwriting was the solicitation of companies to sponsor, that is, underwrite, certain programming. KUVO promoted underwriting to corporations by pointing out that "[r]ecent surveys indicate that listeners remember your company name, think positively about the fact that your business supports public radio, and are influenced by this association in their decision to purchase your products or services."[14] In 1994 and 1995, KUVO underwriting dollars had fallen short of expectations, and the new underwriting director was concerned about the lack of funds available for promotion material to solicit additional corporate sponsors for 1996.

KUVO targeted corporations that employed KUVO members or were likely to desire an affiliation with an organization such as KUVO. Approximately 30 percent of underwriting came from businesses that called KUVO directly; the remainder were solicited by KUVO staff. There were 40–50 companies that consistently supported the station. Local performing arts organizations, food vendors, bookstores, and automobile dealerships were also notable sponsors, offering discounts to KUVO members. While Denver "[r]adio stations have seen the biggest windfall [in advertising], increasing revenues 39% in the past five years to an estimated $102 million in 1995," most of this money went to commercial stations.[15] Nevertheless, KUVO's business contributions averaged $300–$400 each, considerably more than the base amount KUVO requested from sponsors in solicitations.

As a nonprofit organization, KUVO also maintained alliances with its struggling counterparts. For numerous nonprofit organizations, KUVO provided public service announcements (PSAs). KUVO benefited by being named as a media sponsor. These and the underwriting efforts were critical to KUVO, especially as dollars became harder to bring in.

KUVO maintained significant business-to-business relationships with both profit and nonprofit organizations. In return for sponsoring a KUVO program, an underwriter was entitled to a 20-second spot (in commercial radio, a spot was generally 30 seconds). Legal restrictions regarding advertising on public radio stations severely restricted the potential number of corporate underwriters because these rules were seen as a deterrent to potential sponsors.

The Communications Act required noncommercial licensees to identify sponsors and limited the content and scheduling of those announcements. Some restrictions were as follows:

- acknowledgments may not promote the for-profit underwriter, its services, facility, or product;
- acknowledgments may not contain comparative or qualitative language;
- acknowledgments may not contain "non-identifying verbosity";
- acknowledgments may not contain price information;
- acknowledgments may not contain calls to action; and
- acknowledgments may not contain inducements to buy, sell, or lease.[16]

---

[14]KUVO media kit, 1996.

[15]M. Conklin, "Area Advertising Market Is Glutted and Still Growing," *Rocky Mountain News,* July 20, 1995, p. 52A.

[16]National Federation of Community Broadcasters, "NFCB's Guide to Underwriting for Public Radio" (NFCB: Washington, D.C., October 1994).

KUVO also solicited "partnerships" with local retailers whose stores KUVO members were likely to patronize. These businesses offered discounts to KUVO members. Recently, KUVO teamed up with the Wild Oats natural food store to promote its new location. In the *Oasis Member Newsletter,* the store publicly thanked KUVO for making its grand opening a smash.[17] Such arrangements served as an effective vehicle for exposing KUVO to the public. KUVO also teamed up with local jazz clubs to promote both itself and the club through remote broadcasts.

KUVO CHALLENGES

KUVO believed that it faced a significant challenge in programming to "stay true" to the Hispanic community. The station was founded with this community in mind and in its mission statement reflected the emphasis on the Chicano experience as key to its success. But jazz music was, in many ways, far from the Hispanic culture. Latin jazz, the fusion of Latin rhythms with jazz, continued to make stronger ties with this culture, but this music was not considered "classic" jazz and was greeted with disdain by many of KUVO's listeners "concerned about the possible loss of REAL jazz radio to the salsa and other non-jazz programs that have been showing up on KUVO."[18]

Despite the listener complaints directed at the Sunday Latin jazz focus, membership drive pledges were highest on Sunday. During the February 1996 membership drive, 1,492 new or renewing members pledged. During the first week, 300 pledges were received on Sunday, and 200 on the second Sunday. This indicated that over one-third of all pledges came during programming that accounted for less than 10 percent of the total format hours. In addition to member enthusiasm, KUVO had won a $20,000 grant from the National Endowment for the Humanities to use for "Ritmo Latino," a 13-hour series on African Cuban music.

While member and sponsor donations continued to increase, operating expenses were expected to rise at a faster pace. In the past, the station had provided informal sales training for the on-air hosts for the membership drives, but lack of money had eliminated further training programs. KUVO volunteers were a dedicated and competent crew, but there was no one currently on KUVO's staff responsible for training and supervision. Though few volunteer tasks required hand-holding per se, there was a need for seeing that a job was done correctly and on time.

Increased funding was also needed for maintenance of KUVO's transmission equipment. KUVO's transmitter was located on Lookout Mountain, in the city of Golden to the west of Denver, which was the location of numerous Denver radio station transmitters. The power (wattage) of a transmitter was a critical component in the distance and quality of radio service delivered. KUVO's signal from the studio was amplified to 25,000 watts, guaranteed to deliver KUVO's sounds 60 miles in all directions. Judging from member calls, the KUVO signal reached as far north as Cheyenne, Wyoming. However, as KUVO's transmission equipment aged, there were increasing complaints of weak signaling, static, and erratic program transmission in outlying cities and counties. As cable and satellite companies increased their music and entertainment offerings, radio stations were under increasing pressure to update their transmission technology to match the clear sound from satellite signals.

---

[17]KUVO, "Future is so bright we need shades!," *Oasis Member Newsletter,* October–December 1995.
[18]Letter published in *Oasis Member Newsletter* (KUVO, 1996).

Florence Hernandez-Ramos believed that KUVO's ultimate challenge was marketing. KUVO's 1996 budget allocated $35,000 for marketing, most of which was expected to pay for membership premiums such as mugs and T-shirts. Despite the obvious lack of money to support fund-raising efforts, all of the department heads expressed confidence as they set to work on a marketing plan for the remainder of the year. Florence Hernandez-Ramos looked at the latest returns and wondered if the station would be able to meet its upcoming expenses. She hoped they were headed in the right direction.

(If time permits, we suggest visiting KUVO's Web site at www.kuvo.org.)

THE CRAFT-BREWING INDUSTRY IN 1994

Anurag Sharma, *University of Massachusetts*

Julia Dvorko, *University of Massachusetts*

In 1993, the craft-brewing industry was a minor segment of the U.S. beer industry. Of the nearly 200 million barrels of beer sold during the year, craft brews accounted for sales of less than 1.7 million barrels (see Exhibit 1). The total craft-brewing industry dollar volume, estimated at $900 million (see Exhibit 2), represented just about 1.8 percent of the total $50 billion that consumers spent on beer in 1993. The relative insignificance of craft brews is even more striking when measured against the over 87 million barrels shipped in 1993 by the industry leader Anheuser-Busch—or about 52 times as much as the total sales of craft-brewed beer.

Despite small volume, however, craft beer was the fastest-growing segment of the U.S. beer market. While total U.S. domestic beer sales had remained relatively flat during the previous few years, and although the U.S. per capita domestic beer consumption had even declined from 23.1 gallons per capita in 1984 to 21.5 gallons per capita in 1994, sales of craft-brewed beer had actually grown at an average annual rate of 41 percent since 1987 (see Exhibit 3). Industry observers expected the high growth to continue during the next several years.

Depending on the production capacity and market arrangement, craft brewers were usually classified as one of four broad types of establishments: microbreweries, brewpubs, regional specialty breweries, and contract brewers (see Appendix 1 for discussion of each). As of September 1994, according to the Institute for Brewing Studies, there were 554 such establishments in the United States, and their number was keeping pace with the rate of growth in overall demand for craft beers; 101 brewpubs and 62 microbreweries had sprouted up in the 12 months ending in September 1994 (see Exhibit 4). This explosion in the number of craft brewers was all the more intriguing because it was accompanied by an unusually low rate of mortality. For instance, according to the Institute for Brewing Studies, only seven microbreweries or brewpubs

This case study is based on a report prepared by Laurent Aussat, Rob Detweiler, Julia Dvorko, and Dave Milkey, and it was partially funded by the School of Management, University of Massachusetts. Copyright © 1997 Julia Dvorko and Anurag Sharma.

EXHIBIT 1   U.S. Domestic Market Shares of Leading Beer Brewers, 1993

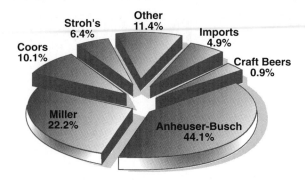

EXHIBIT 2   Annual Dollar Volume of Craft-Brewing Firms (Millions of $)

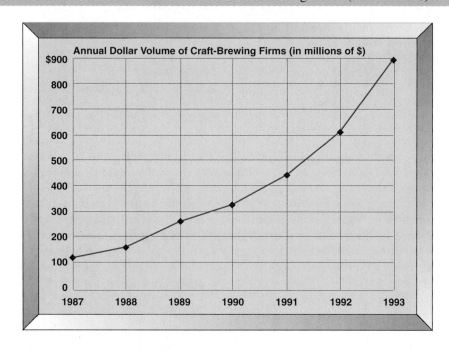

closed operations in the first nine months of 1994. Even so, most breweries remained local throughout their existence, and only a few achieved the status of regional or national prominence.

Given the high rate of growth and the low failure rate in the craft-brew industry segment, it was not surprising that larger producers of mass-market beers, such as Anheuser-Busch, Coors, and Miller, had begun to purchase partial or full interest in several specialty brewers (see Exhibit 5). It seemed in 1994, therefore, that this newest phenomenon in an otherwise staid industry had created some excitement for the old producers and exploitable opportunities for many aspiring entrepreneurs. What is more, the exploding demand indicated that even consumers of beer were thriving on the new wave, as they got to try new-tasting beers more often.

EXHIBIT 3 Craft-Brew Sales Volume, 1988–93 (Thousands of Barrels)

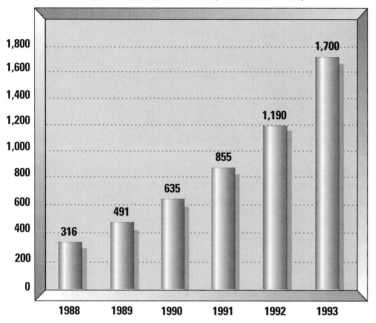

Craft-Brew Sales Volume, 1988–1993 (in 000s of barrels)

EXHIBIT 4 Number of Craft-Brewing Establishments, 1988–94

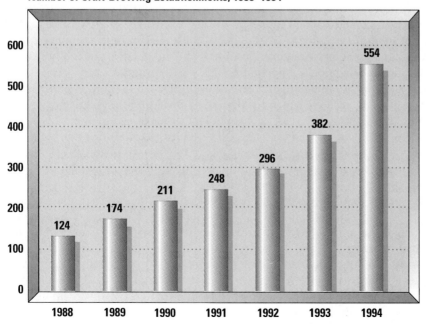

Number of Craft-Brewing Establishments, 1988–1994

EXHIBIT 5	Some Major Brewers' Acquisitions of Microbreweries as of November 1994
Brewer	**Target**
Anheuser-Busch	Redhook Ale Brewery (25%)
Miller	Leinenkugel Brewing Company (100%)
	Molson Breweries, U.S. (100%)
Coors	Stroh Brewing (100%)

Source: *Business Week,* April 24, 1995.

INDUSTRY ECONOMICS

As a small but rapidly growing segment of the beer industry, craft brewing was affected by several economic forces worth noting. We discuss below the nature of direct and indirect competition, impediments (or lack thereof) to new entry, and the role and influence of economic interests upstream and downstream from the micro-brewers.

Competition

In the first half of the 1990s, competition for craft beers came from three primary sources: (1) mainstream premium brands, such as Budweiser and Miller; (2) high-quality imports, such as Heineken, and (3) other microbrands both regional and national.

The mainstream brands of large producers represented only a limited threat to craft beer because competition between these two types of beer was indirect. While Budweiser was a popular beer for everyday consumption, for example, microbrews served somewhat different tastes and they were consumed less frequently than popular beers. In fact, according to an *American Demographics* survey of microbrew drinkers, specialty beers accounted for most of the beer consumption for less than 20 percent of the respondents. Due to their higher prices and exclusive "quality" image, craft beers were not likely to become everyday beers consumed in high volumes. Microbrews were also thought to be attracting consumers who did not drink beer otherwise. In general, the "cannibalization" of popular brands was not significant.

Competition with mainstream beers (those produced in large volumes and backed by extensive advertising) was possible largely because of the "niche" positioning of the craft brews—presented not as just another beer but as a new product possessing distinctive taste and exclusive image. Nevertheless, large breweries seemed to have understood the emerging rules-of-the-game in this new segment and were countering with their own microbrands—either through acquisitions of existing brands or through the introduction of their own microbeers.

While some industry experts had opinionated that the acquired microbrands would be rejected by consumers because they lacked the image of smallness and exclusivity, these brands did indeed become formidable competitors. They shared in the considerable financial resources and the powerful distribution system of the mainstream popular brands. Moreover, capitalizing on the demand for good-quality beer generated by the likes of the Boston Beer Company and Pete's Wicked, the majors were quickly introducing their own products to compete with a series of "mainstream microbrands." It was feared that the majors would eventually leverage their economies in production,

EXHIBIT 6   Market Shares of the Top Five Craft-Brewing Companies, 1993

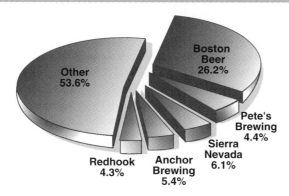

distribution, and advertising to compete on price—a move that the smaller craft brewers would not be able to match.

Imports, sold as specialty beers, were the most direct competition to microbrews—they had the same exclusive image and high prices, and much of the growth of craft beers had come at their expense. Part of the reason for the success of locally crafted beers over imports was that imports did not have the freshness and local flavor provided by the craft beers. In addition, according to some commentators, the "microbrew revolution" of the 1990s went hand in hand with the resurgence of American regional cuisines and pride in local ingredients. The relatively new phenomenon of a brewpub serving local beer as well as local food was a reflection of consumers' craving for something special and unusual. While imports introduced consumers to the taste of good beer, their attraction was somewhat diminished in the face of locally made specialty beer. Hence, although imports had been growing at a good clip in recent years (11.3 percent growth between 1992 and 1993), local and regional specialty brews, as well as those with a national reputation (such as Sam Adams, Pete's Wicked, and Sierra Nevada), were formidable competitors poised to take market share.

Despite the impressive growth in demand, however, craft brewers were increasingly competing among themselves. On the one hand, this young segment was already showing signs of increasing concentration, as the larger players became more prominent (see Exhibit 6). There was an unmistakable emergence of national brands such as Sam Adams and Pete's Wicked, and it was an established fact that everybody in the industry—even regional suppliers serving limited markets—had to compete with them. These large players had upped the ante in the industry by using extensive marketing campaigns to support the visibility and acceptance of their respective brands (see Exhibit 5). On the other hand, competition was becoming more fragmented and severe on the regional level, as more and more brewmasters opened shop in a given geographical area and encroached upon one another's markets—thus diluting the image of exclusivity. The intensity of local competition varied in different regions of the country, however, with the Northwest being a leader in the number of craft brewers and their share in the beer market (5 percent—followed by the Northeast, where craft brewers held a 1.5 percent share of the market.[1] The number of craft breweries was insignificant in the Midwest and the South. The Northwestern market was, in fact, considered near its saturation point, and the bigger craft brewers

---

[1]Institute for Brewing Studies.

(e.g., Red Hook) located there were already moving into the Northeast, which still offered potential for growth.

Substitute Products

Although those who consumed craft beer were thought to have switched mostly from wine, indirect competition for microbrews also came from other alcoholic beverages (such as spirits and champagne) and from nonalcoholic beverages (such as soft drinks, juices, and coffee). It was not clear, however, whether future growth for craft beers would come from displacing some of these substitute products or from creating new markets altogether. If the source of growth was the former, as seemed likely the case, ambitious craft brewers could expect stiff resistance from well-entrenched producers of both alcoholic and nonalcoholic beverages.

In recent years, there had been a trend of consumers' spending less on alcoholic beverages. Between 1985 and 1993, according to the Consumer Expenditure Survey from the Bureau of Labor Statistics, total spending on alcoholic beverages had dropped at an average annual rate of about 10 percent. Only people over 65 were spending more in 1993 than they did in 1985. According to the December 1994 issue of *Number News,* the average household spent $268 on alcoholic beverages in 1993, down 14 percent from the previous year. The decline was not uniform across all kinds of alcoholic drinks, however. While wine consumption had dropped 22 percent and the consumption of spirits was down 20 percent, beer consumption had dropped only about 3 percent during the previous year.

The Bureau of Labor Statistics also revealed that the money spent on alcoholic beverages for at-home consumption represented 58 percent of the total household spending on alcohol, and 56 percent of that amount was spent on beer. Moreover, consumers now often chose beer over champagne as a holiday beverage. This phenomenon may have been at least partly driven by the proliferation of seasonal winter and Christmas beers—dark, rich, flavorful specialty beverages designed to represent a festive atmosphere.

Another substitute for microbeers sold commercially was home-brewed beer. Since 1979, when federal laws were changed to permit production of up to 200 gallons a year, home brewing has flourished all over the United States. In 1995, annual domestic sales of home-brewing equipment and supplies approached $200 million. Although home brewing had a reputation as an amateurish pastime that could not produce good, professionally made beer, one of the most popular microbeer brands, Pete's Wicked, was born out of Pete Slosberg's fascination with home brewing. Slosberg's home-brewed beer was so popular among his friends and relatives, the story goes, that he finally decided to start his own business. Many craft-beer producers started in the same way. It was widely believed that home brewing played the same role that imported brews did in introducing consumers to the taste of good beer. There was a considerable amount of synergy between home-brewed and specialty beers. Hence, home brewing presented not so much competition as complementarity to microbrewing. In fact, people who brewed their own beer were usually big fans of microbeers.

Entry Barriers

Although competition was intensifying in some regions of the country and at the national level, the high growth rate of the segment and the persistent appeal of locally brewed beer provided good opportunities for new entrants. The capital needs for starting a new brewery were not substantial, and beer-making know-how was widely dispersed, as many people did brew their own beer at home relatively inexpensively.

Initial capital needs varied greatly among new microbreweries/brewpubs. The Entrepreneur Business Group estimated the start-up investment at a minimum of $482,000 and an average of $750,000.[2] Brewpubs were less capital-intensive than microbreweries, with basic costs for the restaurant and brewing equipment being around $120,000. Brew equipment for a microbrewery (including very expensive packaging equipment) cost anywhere between $120,000 and $400,000. The estimate of the start-up costs made by the Entrepreneur Business Group assumed an initial high volume of production, as well as additional personnel, a well-equipped office, and intensive marketing. Most of these expenses could be considered superfluous by the starting entrepreneurs, however, and start-up costs could actually be much lower. For most start-ups, these costs would include only basic equipment, various licenses, a lease on a building, and some alteration costs. A well-equipped office and salaried staff would perhaps be the least of concerns for an entrepreneur short on capital. Many start-ups were, in fact, significantly undercapitalized. Where the lack of financial resources did, indeed, become a problem was when, after initial success, rapid expansion of production capacity and more intensive marketing created needs for cash and capital.

Choosing the location for a new microbrewery was another important decision for aspiring craft brewers. With many local markets approaching saturation, particularly in the Northwest and the Northeast, it was critical for a craft brewer to be located in a community that either did not already have a brewer or could support another one without creating destructive price competition. Affluent urban communities and communities with a large number of college graduates were seen as good targets.

Distributors and Consumers

Product in the craft-brewing industry could be distributed in one of three ways: (1) through a three-tier-system involving wholesaler, retailer, and consumer (some states, such as Texas, required this by law); (2) through a two-tier system involving retailer and consumer; and (3) directly to consumer, as done by the brewpubs and some of the microbreweries that sold beer on premises.

Wholesalers were traditional distributors of microbrews. While microbreweries had some clout with them because of the higher margins, wholesalers were usually much larger than most microbrew producers. Because there were usually few big wholesalers in each state that had a license for distribution in a certain part of the state only, and because it was difficult to get a new license (Massachusetts, for instance, was very restrictive in this respect), producers usually did not have a choice. Wholesalers typically managed a large portfolio of products and tended to be dependent on the volume provided by large producers, who had also started promoting their own microbrands. Although there were some microbrands that had national reputation and that rounded out the product portfolios of major wholesalers, it was very difficult for most microbrew producers to break into this traditional channel of distribution. Even if a microbrewer did gain acceptance by a particular wholesaler, it was unlikely that the relationship would be symmetric—the wholesaler would probably have all the power.

Craft-beer producers could and did try to bypass wholesalers altogether by selling direct to retailers. That approach was often a tough sell, since large retailers did most of their business with wholesalers. This began to change somewhat in recent times, however, because of the higher margins typically available from microbrews (about 25 per-

---

[2]Microbrewery, Entrepreneur Business Guide.

cent versus the 18–19 percent industry standard).[3] After 1990, the specialty-beer sections and specialty-beer-related promotions increased steadily in large retail outlets. Small retailers, like package stores, had limited shelf space and carried fewer products with high margin potential. Even so, small retailers were often appropriate targets for start-up microbrewers that did not have the volume to go through larger retailers. Small retailers were likely to gain undue power than large retailers; and since small retailers were often local business, they were also inclined to support local and regional producers.

Restaurants and pubs were usually the initial choice for craft-brewing start-ups that at first used only kegs to avoid the high costs of bottling equipment. Selling in pubs also created consumer awareness and an initial customer base that would become critical in the future, when the beer would, hopefully, be distributed through wholesalers and liquor stores. Lately, however, even these outlets have tended to exercise considerable power over producers because of the increasing proliferation of specialty beers. Brewpubs and some microbreweries did, indeed, sell their product directly to the customer. This mode of distribution had limits, however, and could support only a small volume of sales.

Some data regarding the consumer profile were beginning to become available in recent years. A survey of beer drinkers made by *American Demographics* at the end of 1994 showed that

- Education and income were the two best predictors of who would drink microbrews. The majority of beer drinkers who tried a microbrew had a graduate-school education and a household income of over $75,000.
- Younger people were more likely to have tried a microbrew. Thirty-six percent of beer drinkers between the ages of 25 and 34 had tried a microbrew. In contrast, 27 percent of beer drinkers between the ages of 34 and 45, and 20 percent of those 45 and older, had tried microbrews.
- The appeal of microbrewed beer was strongest among white Americans and in certain regions. White beer drinkers were almost twice as likely as black beer drinkers to try a microbrew. As for the regional variations, 32 percent of beer drinkers on the West Coast had tried microbrews, versus 29 percent in the Northeast, 25 percent in the Midwest, and 18 percent in the South.
- Men were more likely than women to have tried a microbrew (18 percent and 8 percent, respectively), although one should consider that men account for 70 percent of all beer consumed in America. The survey indicated that women beer drinkers were more attracted to microbrews than to the mainstream brands.

Suppliers

The main ingredients that go into the making of microbeers are malt, hops and yeast.[4] Malt, or treated barley (moistened, germinated, and dried), is readily available in standard qualities in the open market. Hops, on the other hand, are like grapes in that they are grown in specific regions of the world and within those regions specific varieties can be chosen for brewing. Hops are considered important because they give the beer its character, its unique flavor. In fact, hops play the same role in brewing beer as

---

[3]Institute for Brewing Studies.

[4]Mass producers (Miller, Coors, Anheuser-Busch, and others) add so called adjuncts, such as corn and rice. However, craft-beer producers do not use these ingredients because, it is widely believed, they dilute the flavor of the beer.

grapes do in making wine. The best varieties are grown in small quantities and can be purchased only from a limited number of suppliers. For instance, the Boston Brewing Company has used Noble hops, recognized for their superior taste and aroma, from specific growing areas. These include East Kent Goldings and Fuggles from England; Hallertau-Hallertauer, Tettrnang-Hallertauer, and Tettnang-Tettnauer from Germany; and Bohemian Saaz from the Czech Republic. It is, in other words, common for micro-brewers to spend considerable time shopping in Europe and elsewhere or developing networks to obtain high-quality hops.

The third important ingredient, yeast, is actually a single-celled eukaryotic organism that, at defined conditions, converts sugar into alcohol and carbon dioxide. Many different groups, or strains, of the yeast *Saccharomyces cerevisiae* are used in the brewing process. Two major types of strains, bottom fermenting and top fermenting, are used for the brewing of two major types of beer—lagers and ales, respectively. Within one class, two types of beer can be produced using the same yeast strain (e.g., a brewery could produce a pale ale and a porter using the same strain); the same type of beer, however, could also be made by using two different yeast strains (e.g., two breweries making porter using two different strains). A large variety of yeast strains could be acquired from the Seibel Institute in Chicago, the best-known supplier of this input in America. Many brewers also developed and used their own proprietary strains with time. This, however, required a capability to do so with consistency and high quality, as well as additional facilities (such as very expensive deep freezers) in which to store the yeast.

SUCCESS FACTORS IN THE CRAFT BEER INDUSTRY

Although in the 1990s the craft-beer phenomenon was a fairly recent one, the experience of many producers was widely advertised in the media—perhaps because of the romance associated with a brewmeister's passionately crafting his own beer just for the sake of doing so. With publicity had come scrutiny, and assessments about what made some craft-brewers more successful than others. Below is a discussion of product attributes and marketing activities considered important in making and selling craft beers.

Product Attributes

A focus on quality, freshness, and distinctiveness was the key to the initial success of microbrew pioneers. Although useful in the marketing of all consumables, these factors had particular significance in the context of craft-brewed beers. Operationally, *quality* meant consistency of the product. It may be a pleasant surprise for consumers to find that their favorite local beer tasted different every time they tried it, but it could also be an annoyance which start-ups could ill afford. *Freshness* was probably the easiest for start-ups to guarantee, but it posed distribution problems, because most of the freshest beers were unpasteurized and required precious cold-storage space in the stores. Still, freshness was a trump for brewpubs and local microbreweries that could sell beer on the premises. It worked against them, however, when the beer was distributed to distant locations. *Distinctiveness* was a trademark of many microbrands, as well as of numerous brewpubs. Still, distinctiveness of a product became more and more of a problem as competition intensified. It was often very difficult to tell the difference between, say, one Scotch ale and another. Microbreweries that were able to continually come out with truly distinctive products (even if this distinctiveness remained unchallenged for only a short time) had an advantage over the competition.

One way in which microbreweries tried to achieve distinctiveness for their products was to offer a variety of flavors and styles. This feature was usually appealing to consumers used to the uniformity of the mainstream "lite" brands. This was perhaps why seasonal beers produced by microbreweries during certain periods of the year remained so popular. Each season had its own brands: spring was the time for strong, rich bock beers; summer was the season for lighter wheat and fruity brands; fall was famous for its numerous Oktoberfests, featuring amber to red German-style lagers; and winter had traditionally been a peak time for strong and spicy Christmas beers like Catamount Christmas Ale. Stouts, porters, and chocolate ales—all dark and full-bodied beers—were also sold during the winter.[5] Seasonal beers were priced higher because of their "exclusive" character, and they usually played a promotional role. Moreover, seasonal beers raised the prestige and popularity of the flagship brands without cannibalizing their sales. Capitalizing on this trend, brewpubs were now coming out not only with their own seasonal brands but also with seasonal menus that complemented them.

Noting the importance of the above attributes of crafted beers, Jim Koch of the Boston Beer Company commented, "I think we were the first to have legible freshness dating. You have to do it as a matter of principle rather than economics . . . It's a matter of a brewer's integrity. If somebody buys Sam Adams, they paid a lot of money for it and they expect to get a great beer."[6] Quality, freshness, distinctiveness, and variety were therefore all important product attributes. Even so, with the increased competition, each attribute became a given for microbrews. Customers expected every microbeer to be good, fresh, and distinctive. They also increasingly expected variety. Hence, success in the market was driven by additional distribution and marketing issues.

Channel Management

The industry analysis presented above shows the power of distributors and the critical need to manage the channels through which crafted beers reached the consumers. From a distributor's perspective, the decision to add a new product to a portfolio was actually a financial decision—typically the product was added only if it provided additional value to the operation. Shortened product life-cycles, an increasing number of product introductions, and a concern about the staying power of the microbrew movement made distributors hesitant to supplement their portfolios with microbrews.

The keys to developing successful strategies were to understand and to cooperate closely with the distributor. A craft-beer producer could take part in a distributor's portfolio management and sales force education, in order to ensure that its brand added value. The producer could learn about the distributor's market (retailers and local customers) and understand the retailers' needs, so as to develop special price and other promotions. Although the relationships with the distributors were important, most small start-ups simply could not afford to develop close relationships. It was, in fact, advisable to approach a wholesaler or a retailer with at least some kind of established brand and a customer base. Hence, large microbrewers had some success in penetrating the distribution channels, while small start-ups trying to establish a presence often found themselves in a catch-22.

---

[5]Consumers' insatiable need for variety was seen by many as a threat to the industry's future. Specialty beer drinkers did not seem to have brand loyalty—their only criterion seemed to be "good" beer. Naturally, this presented problems in building and then sustaining brands.

[6]"A Second Look at Koch," *Beverage World, Periscope Edition,* December 31, 1994, p. 17.

Marketing and Brand Building

As the craft-beer segment became increasingly crowded and producers competed for attention with more and more unusual names and label designs, having a distinctive brand and label became very important. Passion Pale (from the fruit), Four Horsemen Ale, Out of Bounds Stout, and Noah's Dark were only a few examples of exotic labels crowding the store shelves. An unusual name was not, however, the only key to distinctive brand identity. There had to be a concept behind the name, whether it was a local flavor or something more imaginative.

Consider, for example, a very successful brand name used by the Pete's Brewing Company—Pete's Wicked. It is a highly suggestive name, and at first it was a very unusual one. The image of naughtiness, irreverence, and fun was reinforced by the label, with its distinctive "webby" picture designed in "mysterious" dark colors. As Mark Bozzini, the president of Pete's Brewing Company, recalled, "People were initially trying the beer because of its name . . . but then they kept buying it because of the product." Having Pete Slosberg (His Wickedness, as he is called) impersonate the brand helped to round off the concept of "alternative beer."[7]

Heavy advertising was expensive and therefore beyond the means of most craft-beer makers, although traditional tactics designed to build brands and increase volume were seeing much use among the larger producers. Special price promotions for retailers were becoming more common, as was point-of-purchase advertising (posters and car stickers in the stores, table tents and coasters in the bars). It was common for small brewers to create brochures describing the brewery and its brands. Some breweries and brewpubs also created newsletters to disseminate information about new products and promotions. Others advertised in local papers and numerous specialized publications (such as *Yankee Brew News* in the Northeast). Finally, tours of the premises and local beer festivals were also commonly used to create consumer awareness.

While most of the above options were relatively inexpensive, most craft brewers were undercapitalized and therefore relied heavily on word-of-month and public relations to create awareness of their beer. Good products and customer service were considered key to managing word-of-mouth. Brewery tours served well during the initial stage of craft-beer operations, and also later on. During the tours, customers got acquainted not only with the product itself but also with the brewery's image—the processes, people, credos, and beliefs of the brewers about the product and their customer service. Popularity of the small local producers often sprang from such intimate acquaintance with their work, and empathy was born among customers after their meetings with the owners. Brewers hoped that customers who felt enthusiastic about the beer would tell both their friends and local retailers about the new product. Organization of the tours required some initial marketing, but, given the interest in local breweries, tours were usually very inexpensively advertised via, for example, a signboard on a major road close to the brewery.

In addition, speaking engagements with local community organizations (such as the Rotary Club or local chamber of commerce) helped producers promote their cause. While advertising in the press was not very expensive, the cash-strapped producers of craft beers mostly tried to get their word out without paying for it. Maintaining a good relationship with the press (offering tours, returning calls, being polite and responsive) often guaranteed numerous news stories that created a good reputation for free, particularly immediately after a brewery opened its doors to the public.

---

[7]"Thumping the Tub for Microbrews: Pete's Ale Grows at Wicked Rates," *Beverage World, Periscope Edition,* September 30, 1994.

Finally, brewers could also make creative use of packaging to build brand awareness. Packaging equipment was costly, however, for most small operators. They typically started with kegs and aspired to soon move into the industry standard of 12-ounce bottles sold in six-packs.

APPENDIX 1

The craft-brewing industry is represented by four main types of establishments as defined by the Institute for Brewing Studies: microbreweries, brewpubs, regional breweries/regional specialty breweries, and contract brewing companies.

A *microbrewery* is a brewery that produces less than 15,000 barrels of beer per year. The products of microbreweries are distributed either through three-tier (wholesaler–retailer–consumer) systems, through two-tier (retailer–consumer) systems, or direct to the consumer through carryouts, on-site taprooms, or brewery restaurant sales. Mass Bay Brewing Company (6,450 barrels produced in 1993) and Catamount Brewing of Vermont (13,000 barrels produced in 1993) are two examples of microbreweries. As of 1993, microbreweries accounted for 28 percent of the craft-beer market.[8]

A *brewpub* is a restaurant-brewery that sells the majority (more than 50 percent) of its beer on-site. The Northampton Brewery of Northampton, Massachusetts, is a brewpub. As of 1993, brewpubs accounted for 12 percent of the craft-beer market.

A *regional brewery* is a brewery producing between 15,000 and 500,000 barrels per year. The distribution system is usually two-tier or one-tier. Most regional breweries are referred to as regional specialty breweries because they position their flagship (best-selling) brand as a microbrew or specialty beer. Sierra Nevada Brewing Company, Anchor Brewing Company of California, and Full Sail Brewing Company of Oregon are well-known regional specialty breweries. The term *regional* refers not to the distribution system but to the brewery size. As in the above examples, products can be distributed nationally. As of 1993, regional breweries accounted for 26 percent of the craft-beer market.

A *contract brewer*, finally, is a brewery that contracts out the majority of its production to other breweries. The contract brewer is usually responsible for centralized development of new products, marketing, and distribution. Two of the biggest contract brewers in the United States are the Boston Beer Company (450,000 barrels shipped in 1993) and Pete's Brewing Company (75,000 barrels shipped in 1993). In 1993 contract breweries accounted for 34 percent of the total craft-beer market.

The following table shows the number of craft brewers in each category.

Breakdown of U.S. Craft-Brewing Establishments	
Microbreweries	193
Brewpubs	342
Regional specialty breweries	10
Contract breweries	7
Total	552

Source: Institute for Brewing Studies.

---

[8]The source for this and all other market-share figures: *New Brewer,* May–June 1994.

THE BERKSHIRE BREWING COMPANY (A)

On the evening of September 30, 1994, Chris Lalli (29 years old) and Gary Bogoff (41 years old) were putting finishing touches on a building that had once housed a cigar factory in the town of Deerfield, Massachusetts. Along with personal friends who had financially invested in their aspirations to become

Julia Dvorko, *University of Massachusetts*

Anurag Sharma, *University of Massachusetts*

entrepreneurs, the two had done most of the work needed to make the building ready for the brand-new Berkshire Brewing Company (BBC). The brewery was to begin production the following morning, October 1, and, unlikely as it had seemed many times during the preceding three years, the first batch of Extra Pale Steel Rail Ale would be in process within hours.

Chris and Gary had met in 1990 through Chris's father, a selectman for the town of Montgomery, Massachusetts. At the time Gary, a superintendent of highways in Montgomery, reported to Chris's father. The two became friends and began putting to good use the home-brewing setup in the basement of Chris's house. Their friendship grew, and by the end of 1991 Chris and Gary had decided to open a microbrewery. They aspired to build a state-of-the-art brewery for delivering, in Gary's words, "a fresh and wholesome-tasting, quality beer to the beer-drinking public of western Massachusetts."

Although he had held a variety of administrative jobs in the U.S. Air Force and in the manufacturing sector, Chris Lalli had for many years aspired to become a brewmaster. In the year or so before deciding to open a brewery, he had indeed achieved the respect of many in local home-brewing circles and his beers had won several awards in their own right. To hone his skills, Chris had apprenticed at a number of brewpubs and microbreweries. In recent months he had frequently been invited as a judge for home-brew competitions. Chris was to be the master brewer of BBC and, as such, he was to be responsible for all production-related activities.

Gary Bogoff had worked as a carpenter, a contractor, and, as noted above, a superintendent of highways for the town of Montgomery. During the three years prior to

This case is based on a report by Laurent Aussat, Rob Detweiler, Julia Dvorko, and Dave Milkey, and it was partially funded by the School of Management, University of Massachusetts. Copyright © Julia Dvorko and Anurag Sharma.

the opening of the BBC, he brewed his beer with Chris and apprenticed at three breweries. Given that he had a little more experience in actually managing a company than Chris did, Gary was to be responsible for sales, marketing, distribution, customer service, and financial management. (See Appendix 1 for Chris's and Gary's personal statements.)

Starting a company, Chris and Gary quickly realized, took more than knowing how to make beer or even how to hustle. The partners' dreams were bigger than their combined savings, which amounted to a meager $23,000. There was not much in their track records to give potential lenders any confidence in their ability to repay loans; and since the company did not as yet exist, there was nothing they could offer as collateral to cautious bankers. It took them three long, hard years to put together a business plan and to raise the necessary financing. Chris and Gary managed to obtain $50,000 through a private loan, and $100,000 from friends and family members, who were to receive 1 percent of equity for each $5,000 invested (a total of 20 percent). They then leveraged the credibility thus gained from private backing to raise an additional $90,000 from a loan secured by the Small Business Administration.

The starting capital of $263,000 was not enough, however, to give the aspiring entrepreneurs much room to make mistakes or to indulge in the luxury of hiring outside help. With revenues still in the future, the drain on the limited cash was severe. In spite of laudable thriftiness, for example, Chris and Gary spent about $150,000 just on the lease and the renovation of the old cigar factory, and on brewing equipment. As a result, most of the work—including plastering and painting the walls, and adding wiring—had to be done by Chris and Gary themselves. In fact, the owners often successfully solicited the time and labor of the friends and family members who had provided part of the initial capital for the business. One of their shareholder-friends, a designer by profession, had even created the labels for the bottles on his own time.

"The hard work has paid off . . . so far," Gary said as he took a break from polishing the fermentation tank. The brewery was on the verge of starting production. Still, he knew that much uncertainty lay ahead. While the brewing capacity was now in place, BBC's viability as a business would be tested over the next couple of months as he and Chris tried to stabilize the production process and sell the first locally brewed craft beer in the area. Gary walked slowly into the small, disorganized cubicle on the production floor and stared down at the black folder that happened to be sitting on top of a heap of papers on the crowded metal table. After a moment's thought, he picked up the folder, sat down on a chair, put his feet up on a clean corner of the table, and opened the folder to thumb through BBC's business plan.[1]

THE BREWERY

Chris and Gary had put together a brewing system that consisted of two main components—the brew house and the fermentation house. The brew house, where the whole process of brewing beer would begin, had a seven-barrel one-time brewing capacity. Since brewing one batch of beer was expected to take about six hours, Chris estimated that he could brew as much as 35–42 barrels of beer per week on a single-shift basis. The production volume would be greatly restricted, however , by the seven-barrel capacity of the fermentation house (where the beer would be conditioned and carbonated and where it would stay a few days). Hence, within four weeks after the start of

---

[1]Financial projections from the business plan are shown in Exhibits 1 and 2.

operations, Chris planned to expand the fermentation house capacity to 14 barrels—which would, in turn, increase the weekly production capacity to 21 barrels.[2]

As shown in Exhibits 1 and 2, Chris and Gary estimated that they would need to reach a production level of 28 barrels per week to become profitable. To reach that level, it would be necessary to buy another 14-barrel fermentation system in July of 1995. With that system, BBC could reach the weekly production capacity of 42 barrels. The two partners were confident that they would be able to expand up to that level with the money they had. Beyond that, it would be necessary to find additional financing.

The business plan called for a weekly production of 80 barrels by the end of the third year, and 100 barrels by the end of the fifth year. Chris and Gary thought this a very conservative estimate, given the high rate of growth in the industry. After conquering western Massachusetts in the first few years, the partners planned to start distributing in the eastern part of the state—a move they thought could be made with the 42-barrel-a-week production capacity by the fall of 1995. Although Chris and Gary were certainly not considering national distribution, they did not rule out trying to reach the neighboring states of Vermont, Connecticut, and New Hampshire.

The two-story, 12,400 square-foot building, which at the time of opening would be only 30 percent utilized, was secured with a view toward future expansion. The partners had also toyed with the idea of opening a brewpub on the second floor at some point. But that would happen in a very remote future, if at all—definitely not during the five years covered by the initial business plan.

MARKET

The original business plan identified the target market as 274,900 people in the 30-to-65 age bracket living in Hampden, Hampshire, and Franklin counties of western Massachusetts. This age group was of interest because, in Gary's view, only the people who were over 30 would most likely spend the money to buy their beer, which was more expensive than popular beers such as Budweiser. Because of the low start-up capacity of the brewery (seven barrels[3] per week), Gary and Chris had chosen to saturate a particular market rather than to thinly cover a broad geographical area. They wrote in their business plan that "BBC will make a greater impression on the marketplace if it is concentrated and available in a specific location, rather then being dispersed throughout western Massachusetts." They decided to focus their initial efforts on the city of Northampton, which had an attractive demographic profile that comprised a large number of young professionals, and which offered a relatively large on-premises market (bars and restaurants) with about 45 pouring licenses.

The location of the brewery in Deerfield placed the production facility not only close to the initial target market but also to other potential markets. Deerfield, located only 12 miles from Northampton, was also within a short distance from the other towns of the so-called Five-College Area (see Appendix 2). In addition, the proximity of two popular regional landmarks—Historic Deerfield Village and Yankee Candle Store and Museum—placed BBC on a heavily traveled "tourist trail."

At the time of BBC's opening there was only one operating brewery in the target area: The Northampton Brewery, a restaurant that brewed its own beer and served most of it on premises. Chris and Gary did not think that Northampton Brewery would

---

[2]Not counting the supplemental equipment—kegs, taps, and tap handles—that had to be bought as well, a used fermentation system in good state would cost around $13,700.

[3]1 barrel = 31 gallons.

EXHIBIT 1   Income Statement Projections for Year 1 Production of the Berkshire Brewing Company, as of Fall 1994

	1st Quarter	2nd Quarter	6 Months	3rd Quarter	4th Quarter	Full Year
Barrels/week*	7.33	17.67	12.50	31.33	38.00	23.58
Average barrels/month	32	77	54.00	136	165	102.19
Average yearly barrels/month	380	920		1,628	1,976	1,226
Price per barrel						$ 160.00
Sales revenues	$ 15,200	$36,800	$ 52,000	$65,120	$79,040	$196,213
Cost of Sales						
Materials ($155/7 barrel batch)	$ 2,103	$ 5,092	$ 7,196	$ 9,011	$10,937	$ 27,151
Direct labor	0	1,472	1,472	4,969	6,625	13,066
(Direct labor hours/week)		40	40	135	180	43
Manufacturing Costs						
Salaries (principals)	$ 3,000	$ 3,000	$ 6,000	$ 4,500	$ 6,000	$ 16,500
Indirect labor						
Employee benefits	600	981	1,581	1,420	1,894	4,895
Payroll/taxes	700	894	1,494	1,231	1,641	4,367
Federal/state liquor taxes	950	2,300	3,250	4,070	4,940	12,260
Insurance	1,125	1,125	2,250	1,125	1,125	4,500
Utilities	1,256	1,370	2,615	1,425	1,500	5,540
Supplies	1,050	1,350	2,400	1,575	1,650	5,625
Equipment repairs and maintenance	750	900	1,650	900	1,050	3,600
Building rent (3000 sq. ft. @ $4.00/ft.)	3,000	3,000	6,000	3,000	3,000	12,000
Distribution costs (trucking)	525	750	1,275	1,050	1,050	3,375
Depreciation	5,673	6,643	12,315	7,473	7,473	27,261
Total manufacturing costs	$ 18 518	$22,313	$ 40,831	$27,769	$31,323	$ 99,922
Total cost of sales	20,621	28,878	49,499	41,749	48,885	140,132
Gross profit	(5,421)	7,922	2,501	23,371	30,155	56,081
Gross profit margin (%)	(35.66%)	21.53%	4.81%	35.89%	38.15%	28.58%
General and Administration						
Officer salary	6,000	6,000	12,000	6,000	7,500	25,500
Office salaries	0	0	0	0	0	0
Payroll taxes	780	780	1,560	780	975	3,315
Advertising	750	900	1,650	1,350	1,500	4,500
Brewery license	450	0	450	450	0	900
Office supplies	450	450	900	450	450	1,800
Telephone	450	450	900	600	600	2,100
Travel and entertainment	300	450	750	300	450	750
Legal and accounting	450	450	900	450	450	1,800
Total G&A costs	$ 9,630	$ 9,480	$ 19,110	$10,605	$12,275	$ 41,990
Operating profit	(15,051)	(1,558)	(16,609)	12,766	17,880	14,091
Less: Interest expense	1,785	1,827	3,612	1,827	1,827	7,266
Profit before taxes	$(16,836)	$(3,385)	$(20,221)	$10,939	$16,053	$ 6,825

*1 barrel = 2 kegs.

EXHIBIT 2   Income Statement Projections for Year 2 Production of the Berkshire Brewing Company, as of Fall 1994

	1st Quarter	2nd Quarter	6 Months	3rd Quarter	4th Quarter	Full Year
Barrels/week	42.00	42.00	42.00	53.33	60.00	49.33
Average barrels/month	182	182	182	230.93	259.80	213.78
Average yearly barrels/month	2,182	2,182	101,400	2771.20	3117.60	2,565
Price per barrel			160.00			$160.00
Sales:	$87,293	$87,293	$174,586	$110,848	$124,704	$410,138
Cost of Sales:						
Materials ($155/7 barrel batch)	12,079	12,079	24,158	15,339	17,256	56,753
Direct labor	6,625	6,625	13,250	6,625	6,625	26,500
(Direct labor hours/week)	180	180	180	180	180	180
Manufacturing Costs						
Salaries (principals)	$ 7,500	$ 7,500	$ 15,000	$ 7,500	$ 7,500	$ 30,000
Indirect labor						
Employee benefits	1,766	1,766	3,531	1,766	1,766	7,062
Payroll taxes	1,836	1,836	3,672	1,836	1,836	7,345
Federal/state liquor taxes	5,456	5,456	10,912	6,928	7,794	25,634
Insurance	1,125	1,125	2,250	1,125	1,125	4,500
Utilities	1,950	1,950	3,900	2,206	2,206	7,950
Supplies	1,725	1,800	3,525	1,875	1,875	7,275
Equipment repairs and maintenance	1,200	1,500	2,700	1,575	1,575	5,850
Building rent (3000 sq. ft. @ $4,00/ft.)	3,000	3,000	6,000	3,750	3,750	13,500
Distribution costs (trucking)	1,050	1,050	2,100	1,125	1,125	4,350
Depreciation	7,473	7,473	14,945	14,928	14,928	44,801
Total manufacturing costs	$34,080	$34,455	$ 68,536	$ 44,432	$ 45,298	$158,267
Total cost of sales	52,784	53,159	105,944	66,396	69,179	241,519
Gross profit	34,508	34,133	68,642	44,452	55,525	168,619
Gross profit margin (%)	39.53%	39.10%	39.32%	40.10%	44.53%	41.11%
General and Administration						
Officer salary	$ 7,500	$ 7,500	$ 7,500	$ 7,500	$ 7,500	$ 30,000
Salaries	0	0	0	0	0	0
Payroll taxes	1,049	1,049	2,097	1,049	1,049	4,194
Advertising	3,000	3,000	6,000	3,000	3,000	12,000
Brewery license	0	0	0	450	0	900
Office supplies	450	450	900	450	450	1,800
Telephone	600	750	1,350	750	750	2,850
Travel and entertainment	900	900	1,800	900	900	3,600
Legal and accounting	450	450	900	450	450	1,800
Total G&A costs	$13,949	$14,099	$ 20,547	$ 14,099	$ 14,099	$ 56,244
Operating profit	20,560	20,035	48,095	30,354	41,426	112,375
Less: Interest expense	1,827	1,827	3,654	3,727	3,728	11,110
Profit before taxes	$18,733	$18,208	$ 44,441	$ 26,625	$ 37,698	$101,265
Less: Income tax	5,245	5,908	12,443	7,455	10,555	28,354
Net Profit	$13,488	$13,110	$ 31,997	$ 19,170	$ 27,143	$ 72,910

*1 barrel = 2 kegs.

directly compete with BBC since they planned to self-distribute their beer to the area pubs, restaurants, and package stores.

In fact, when Chris and Gary had spoken with bar and restaurant owners in their target area, they had been well-received. The restaurant owners all seemed very excited about the new beer, and some even promised to replace their slowest-selling product with the BBC keg. The enthusiasm for the "first local beer" ran high. Based on their informal survey, Chris and Gary expected that they would be a presence in the majority of the 45 licensed bars and restaurants in the Northampton area.

PRODUCT

Chris and Gary planned to enter the Northampton market with two products: an extra pale ale and an amber pale ale. Steel Rail Extra Pale Ale, the first beer, would be a full-flavored, medium-bodied, light-colored beer designed for the consumers who were used to the lighter mainstream brands but who were more discriminating than others in their taste for beer. The second beer, Berkshire Traditional Pale Ale, would be a copper-colored, full-bodied beer with a strong hop character in both flavor and aroma. Chris and Gary planned to add specialty and seasonal brews to their offerings as the business grew.

The positioning of BBC's craft brew was considered in the business plan as follows: "The product line that BBC will be introducing into its target area is unique because it will be fresh, unpasteurized, and local in origin." While other microbeers available in the target market contained preservatives and shelf-life extenders, Chris and Gary hoped to emphasize freshness as the main selling point of their beers. They felt that the quality of their product would be outstanding, and they firmly believed that the consumers who tried the Berkshire brews would at once see their superiority in terms of quality. Chris and Gary hoped that the local character of their business would be reinforced by the BBC brand name, which referred to the county (Berkshire) and the mountain range (the Berkshires) in the western part of the state. Consumers, they hoped, would know that by patronizing BBC they were supporting a local business run by the "two ordinary guys, the guys like we are."

The two friends had determined product prices by using the *Massachusetts Beverage Price Journal,* an industry publication that listed prices for all specialty beers in the market. At $80 per keg, their prices would be comparable to those of other microbeers sold in the area. A keg contains 15.5 gallons, so their price would translate into a cost of $5.16 per gallon or $.645 per pint for the retailers (who usually sold premium beer for $2.50 to $3.00 per pint).

DISTRIBUTION

At the start of operation Chris and Gary intended to sell their products exclusively in kegs to the establishments that had taps. After some time, then, they would package a portion of their beer production in five-liter mini kegs to be sold in liquor/package stores. Once the BBC brews were established in the retail market, Chris and Gary planned to buy the equipment (at about $45,000) to distribute their beer in 12-ounce bottles in standard six-packs.

Chris and Gary were well aware that, because their beer contained no preservatives, swift distribution was crucial. Typically, in order to maintain freshness, the beer had to be kept refrigerated at all times—in transportation, in storage, and on the shelf. Without refrigeration, the quality would break down rapidly. According to the owners, after two months of unrefrigerated storage the beer could be considered spoiled.

For this reason, Chris and Gary initially planned to self-distribute to the restaurants and pubs. In fact, Gary himself would deliver the ordered amount of product as soon as the beer was ready. Due to the small local market, they felt that it would be possible for Gary to deliver the beer in a regular truck—for the time being at least, they could do without specialized transportation. However, Chris and Gary knew that it would be necessary to invest in a refrigerated truck when their production volume and geographic coverage increased.

Although most microbeers, as well as popular beers, were sold through the three-tier system (wholesaler–retailer–consumer), Chris and Gary did not plan to use a local distributor in western Massachusetts at any time soon. They felt that traditional wholesalers, used to moving a large volume of product, would not pay sufficient attention to a small local brewery such as BBC. Their main concern was that distributors' reps would not rotate the stock properly and that, as a result, the beer would lose its freshness before consumption by unsuspecting customers. It was clear, however, that when they began distributing their beer to the eastern part of the state, Chris and Gary would not be able to avoid using a distributor. They were hoping that in the medium term they would find a wholesaler that specialized in microbeers.

ADVERTISING AND PROMOTION

BBC's owners were of the opinion that advertising and promotion of BBC products should concentrate on educating consumers about the quality and distinctive character of Berkshire brews. As Chris and Gary put it, "Our best advertisement is the product itself." They were steadfast in their view that consumers who tasted BBC beers would become dedicated customers.

The first step in the consumer education process would be to ensure favorable coverage in the local media. With the initial marketing budget set at $500 a month, Chris and Gary clearly could not afford heavy advertising campaigns. Instead, they hoped to attract the attention of the local press and were counting on informed articles about BBC in regional publications. Such publicity would introduce the company's product to the local market at practically no cost. Chris and Gary also planned to run radio ads on one of the local stations and perhaps even to sponsor a radio show.[4] Newspaper ads were another possibility.

As part of their overall promotional strategy, Gary and Chris envisioned Berkshire Brewing Nights—complete with hat, T-shirt, and key-chain giveaways—at the local establishments. One of their shareholder-friends, the same one who designed the labels, created special glasses with the company logo, "steel rail" key-chains, and posters.[5] The company would also produce point-of-sale materials such as coasters and table tents.

Chris and Gary also planned to conduct brewery tours once a week and hoped that such tours would educate consumers about themselves and their beer. During the tours, they felt, the visitors could witness the entire brewing process and taste the Berkshire beers. At the end of each tour visitors could be asked to sign up for the brewery mailing list. Chris and Gary planned to eventually publish a BBC newsletter. The owners also hoped to eventually host an annual beer festival and sponsor sporting events.

---

[4]The sponsorship of radio shows (which would feature a 60-second spot, as well as periodic mention of the sponsors during the show) cost about $100 a month. The radio spots cost $12–$25 per spot depending on the number of runs and the length of the spot.

[5]The recurring "rail" theme in the company's promotional materials, and in the name of their flagship brew, referred to the fact that the brewery was located close to a set of old railroad tracks in Deerfield.

CAUTIOUS OPTIMISM

As Gary and Chris finished cleaning up the brewery on the evening of September 30, 1994, they could not help thinking about the future. Although they were optimistic about their chances, many questions remained unanswered. Would the customers really accept their product? How fast would they turn a profit? How soon would they need additional investment if they had to grow in order to meet demand? What about competition? What if another microbrewery opened in the area? Could it happen soon, and what would they do in this case? Where would they be three or four years from now? Both realized that all these questions could be answered only with time. While they knew that time would also reveal many more questions and problems that they would need to address expediently, Gary and Chris wondered if there were any obvious business fundamentals or important issues they had not considered.

APPENDIX 1
PERSONAL STATEMENTS

Christopher T. Lalli

For the past five years I have been brewing beer and studying the brewing business. During this time, I have become a recognized brew master in the home-brewing industry and a recognized judge for brewing competitions. My beers have won numerous awards, and I have gained recognition for my expertise.

I constructed a stainless-steel brewing system in my basement that has been used to develop brewing recipes and is designed to operate like a commercial brewing system. My brewing experiences have taken me to numerous brewpubs and microbreweries in which I have served apprenticeships and have also spent time working under the direction of Todd Mot, the head brewer at the Mass Bay Brewing Company. My partner, Mr. Gary Bogoff, and I have designed and constructed a complete seven-barrel brewing system for the Berkshire Brewing Company that we intend to use for the initial production of the brewery.

My enthusiasm for the art of brewing has generated a deep desire to fulfill the quest to develop a successful microbrewery that would eventually develop from a local to a regional brewery and that would then become a bottler for national distribution. We have spent countless hours researching the beer industry in relation to its markets. The many additional hours over the past five years developing, designing, and testing beer formulations have been very successful, and we believe we have products that will give BBC a strong and positive future.

Gary A. Bogoff

My personal work experiences to date have required a wide range of skills in planning, budgeting, personnel management, and equipment and facility maintenance, as well as home and plant construction. I am at the very least a hands-on type of person who becomes totally immersed in the task at hand. My work ethic has always been based on quality service to the client or employer as well as the principle of living by your reputation. This has always been very important to me because in my previous experiences, I have been responsible for very large numbers of personnel.

My interest in the brewing process is based on my personal enjoyment as a home brewer for the past five years and having apprenticed in three breweries during this time. Since I met Chris Lalli, my perception of the brewing industry has led both Chris and me to this juncture. Several years of researching the microbrewing industry, along with our collective experiences and the encouragement of many individuals in the industry, have led us to the conclusion that together we have all the right ingredients to run a very successful microbrewery.

I have had many years of organizing and planning experience and am able to sequence, institute, and see to fruition many different systems and projects, whether it be planning a plant relocation; moving a million-dollar printing press; designing, building, and selling a custom home; or running a highway system with a limited budget. In terms of applying these various skills to the running of a brewery, I see no difference in the thought process required or the desire needed to build a successful organization.

APPENDIX 2

PIONEER VALLEY

With a population of about 700,000, the Pioneer Valley is a metropolitan area that encompasses a variety of industrial cities, college towns, and rural communities in western Massachusetts. The boundaries of the region roughly encircle Hampden, Franklin, and Hampshire counties. The three largest cities in the area are Springfield (the state's third largest city, with a population of 156,983), Chicopee, and Holyoke (with populations of 56,632 and 34,704, respectively). There are also three smaller cities in Pioneer Valley: Northampton, Westfield, and Agawam.

While the urban areas in the region are economically distressed and have relatively high poverty rates (20.1 percent for Springfield and 25.7 percent for Holyoke, compared to 8.9 percent for the state as a whole), the population of the college towns and some rural communities is highly educated and fairly affluent. This is particularly true for the so-called Five-College Area centered around Amherst (35,228 residents). Amherst College, Hampshire College, and the University of Massachusetts are located in Amherst, while the other two highly regarded colleges—Smith in Northampton and Mount Holyoke in South Hadley—are both within a 12-mile radius. Amherst was named one of America's most educated places by *American Demographics.* Over 66 percent of the adults residing in Amherst have a bachelor's degree or higher (compared to the national average of 20 percent).

Overall, there are 15 institutions of higher education in the Pioneer Valley (including the University of Massachusetts, 10 four-year colleges, and three community colleges) with over 60,000 students. Massachusetts as a whole has eight of America's most educated places (the same number as New Jersey), occupying third place after California (14) and New York (12).

The Pioneer Valley is considered an attractive place to live and work. Its great natural beauty, with scenic mountain and river roads, quiet rural communities, and 143,000 acres of park land attract both out-of-state and in-state travelers. The small cities and Springfield boast outstanding cultural resources and downtown shopping districts. Among the major tourist attractions in the area are the Basketball Hall of Fame, the Springfield museums, the Historic Old Deerfield Village, and the Yankee Candle Company store and museums in Deerfield.

Sources: (1) "Pioneer Valley Regional Profile" in *Choosing to Compete: A Statewide Strategy for Job Creation and Economic Growth* (1993); (2) *America's Most Educated Places;* and (3) *American Demographics,* October 1995, p. 44.

THE BERKSHIRE BREWING COMPANY (B)

Anurag Sharma, *University of Massachusetts*

Julia Dvorko, *University of Massachusetts*

Ever since the Berkshire Brewing Company's (BBC's) inception, owners Chris Lalli and Gary Bogoff had always maintained the brewery in perfect order, often staying late to wash the equipment and to clean up the work space. Late in the evening on May 11, 1996, however, Gary was working even harder than usual to prepare for the shareholder meeting that was to convene in the brewery the following day. He had started the cleaning project in the small lab that was used for working with beer yeast, then washed out the tanks in the brew house, checked the fermentation area that was divided into two refrigeration units, and, finally, dusted the third refrigeration unit where the brewed beer was stored before distribution. In the small office, located opposite the brew house, he had also swept the floor and arranged the papers on the desk. Gary now looked into a special grain storage area filled with sacks of barley, and decided that it was clean enough. The bottler, which stood just opposite the entrance to the grain room, had been cleaned recently, so he did not need to do anything else there. He took special care to tidy the central area, where the beer was put into kegs before being removed to cold storage at the end of the day. Apart from the huge shiny water tank, all that remained in the center of the shop floor was a table, an old leather couch that he had brought in from home, and a couple of chairs. Chris and Gary called that space "the socializing corner."

There were always visitors at the brewery, friends and acquaintances who dropped in to have a glass of freshly brewed beer and to chat with the owners. Many hours were spent around the small table in discussions about brewing with local connoisseurs. If only tomorrow's meeting could be as casual as those conversations, thought Gary. He had little doubt, however, that the meeting would not be casual and that it would be a crucial one for BBC's future. It was already late and he still had to take out more folding chairs and to arrange them in the center of the brewing area for the shareholder

This case is based on a report prepared by Laurent Aussat, Rob Detweiler, Julia Dvorko, and Dave Milkey, and it was partially funded by the School of Management, University of Massachusetts. Copyright © 1997 Julia Dvorko and Anurag Sharma.

EXHIBIT 1	Berkshire Brewing Company's Income Statement Composition, Year Ended December 31, 1995	
	Sales	100.00%
	Cost of goods sold	29.09
	Gross income	70.91
	Operating expenses	62.06
	Income from operations	8.85
	Other expenses	4.98
	Income before taxes	3.86
	Taxes	0.16
	Net income	3.71%

meeting. Well, he was not one to complain about long hours, as 70- and even 80-hour weeks had become a norm for both Chris and Gary.

UPDATE

Since the beginning of operations in October of 1994, the company has grown so fast that Gary and Chris were unable to fill all the orders on time. In 1995 they sold 1,500 barrels, and they expected to double this amount in 1996. With sales of $300,000 in 1995, they had already turned a profit (see Exhibit 1) and had decided to introduce a new product in 1996. The first batch of Drayman's Porter, a dark, full-bodied beer with a pronounced chocolate flavor and a taste of malted barley was brewed in January 1996. Extra Pale Steel Rail Ale, which accounted for approximately 50 percent of sales, remained BBC's best-selling product. The remaining 50 percent was equally divided between the Amber Ale and Drayman's Porter.

That was the good news, but not everything had gone quite as Gary and Chris had expected. Problems began as soon as the first batch of the product was ready. Remembering the enthusiasm of the local restaurant operators, Gary and Chris contacted them to make the final arrangements for the distribution of BBC brews. They found out that the tune had changed. Some area restaurants already had exclusive contracts with distributors: in return for the additional keg lines installed by a distributor, they agreed to carry only that distributor's products. Other establishments wanted to know what BBC could do for them. Did the company have discounted trial kegs or free promotional items? But Gary and Chris could not afford to give away T-shirts and did not want to discount the beer. Only several restaurants agreed to accept the BBC beer at once. It quickly became obvious that the Berkshire Brewing could not capture the 45 pub and restaurant accounts as planned.

In response, the BBC owners modified their strategy and turned to the package stores. While they still could distribute beer to the restaurants in kegs, they had to change their packaging format for the stores because most of the small retailers did not have enough shelf space to carry minikegs. Gary and Chris did not have the $45,000 needed to buy a six-pack bottling machine, but they managed to find an affordable bottler for 22-ounce bottles. It turned out that distributing beer in 22-ounce bottles had a certain advantage—BBC beers did not have to compete for the precious cold storage space with the other six-packs. However, the new packaging format meant that more time was needed for distribution: Refrigerated bottles did not maintain the quality of the beer as long as minikegs did and the product had to be rotated more often. Chris

EXHIBIT 2	Breakdown of Berkshire Brewing Company's Operating Expenses, Year Ended December 31, 1995

Item	% of Total Operating Expenses
Rent, utilities, and telephone	28.0%
Salaries	23.0
Depreciation	10.0
Vehicle expenses	7.5
Advertising and marketing	7.2
State excise tax	7.0
Insurance	5.4
Shop and office supplies	1.4
Accounting services	1.2
Bank charges	0.4
Other	9.9
	100%

had to dedicate all his time to distribution, while Gary did most of the brewing. To handle the brewing, the owners hired part-time help.

Local package stores were eager to try out the new local product. They often agreed to take the BBC beer sight unseen. By the beginning of 1996, BBC had 45 accounts split between restaurants and package stores in the western part of the state. They also found a distributor to sell their products in eastern Massachusetts.

The grand advertising and promotional plans Chris and Gary had developed were not realized either. Initially, BBC produced small posters and table tents as point-of-sale materials, but the company soon ran out of these items and did not have the money to make more. Media attention did not last for long: Since the end of 1994 not a single article had appeared in the press. Chris and Gary may have failed to realize that newspapers were willing to write about them in hopes that they would follow up with regular ads. The BBC owners did not do that, and the interest disappeared. As for hosting a radio show, organizing a beer festival or Berkshire Brewing Nights at the restaurants, or sponsoring sports events, they simply had neither the time or the money.

BBC occasionally ran some radio ads, which, according to the owners, were rather effective. Chris and Gary also regularly conducted tours of the brewery and participated in the area brewing festivals. But that was all, as far as marketing was concerned. And, to tell the truth, Chris and Gary did not feel that at this point they should do additional advertising. BBC was operating close to capacity, and they were afraid that with too much advertising, they would not have enough beer for everyone who asked.

INTO THE FUTURE

Yes, thought Gary, at this point selling the beer was not a problem. The problem was making enough of it. And if they wanted to make enough, expanding over the present capacity of 42 barrels per week, they had to buy new brewing equipment and a delivery truck; they also had to set aside some money for advertising—an overall investment of $117,000. Maybe the truck could wait, but they definitely needed the remaining $92,000. Where to find the money was the problem they were going to discuss with their shareholders tomorrow.

One of the options was to get another loan from the bank. Since they had made regular payments for more than a year, their bank was quite willing to lend them more money. Still, Gary and Chris were reluctant to go to the bank, though some shareholders thought that this was exactly what they should do. More loans meant heavy dependence on the bank and eventual loss of control over the business. For the same reason, the BBC owners did not want to go to a venture capital firm. Another option was to seek a private investor who could commit about $100,000. This was, however, a particularly thorny issue. The original investors were promised that each $5,000 they invested would represent 1 percent of the company. With the $100,000 coming in from an outside investor, the original investors' position would be significantly diluted. On the other hand, distributing $100,000 from the owners' holdings meant that their position would be diluted to the combined 60 percent of equity. Neither Gary nor Chris was willing to do that. There also was a possibility of financing the expansion internally— at least partially—but at this point the owners were not sure how much money they could raise this way.

"All these issues have to be resolved in the nearest future if we want to remain profitable," said Gary to the case writers. "Although the industry is doing OK, the competition is increasing. Before the year ends, we will have two competitors within 12 miles—one in Greenfield and one in Northampton. The second one, as I heard, is heavily capitalized and is planning to market himself as 'the local brewery of western Mass.' Yes, we have to grow, but too much growth is bad—you can lose quality. Money creates more problems: you need to hire salespeople, buy more trucks, depend on hired help. Instead of making beer, you will suddenly find yourself speaking to the press all the time.

"Some of the shareholders are really nervous about the coming competition. And, of course, we must be understanding. They have their own goals, different from ours. Most of our shareholders are much older than we are and they have taken money for the investment in the BBC from their retirement funds. So, they are looking for a long-term investment here and they want us to be around for the next 10 years. They think that to do that, we have to grow and to advertise aggressively, so they push us to get the money as quickly as possible and to do our own 'your local brewery' piece before it's too late.

"Well, advertising or no advertising, nobody can beat our quality, especially now that we've finally changed our hops[1] supplier. Now we're getting really high quality hops. We had some trouble with the yeast[2] as well: One of our yeast strains had mutated and the taste of Drayman's Porter had changed quite a bit. Now we fixed this too—one of the grad students at the university will keep the yeast for us and maintain its purity. Some of the shareholders say that there is no guarantee that in the future we won't have problems with the other suppliers, but that is the risk we have to take. Anyway, our beer is so fresh and so good that our customers will see it's much better than most of the brews they can find in the local stores and restaurants. And even if more breweries were to open in the area, there are enough tastes out there to satisfy.

---

[1]Hops, one of the ingredients used for beer production, are added at the beginning of the boiling stage to give a brew its bitter flavor and at the end of the boil to give aroma and hop character. There are presently over 100 varieties of hops around the world. Hops are grown in the Czech Republic, Germany, England, Australia, and Yakima Valley, Washington. (Association of Brewers Glossary)

[2]Yeast, used during the fermentation process, is a vegetable organism of the fungus family. Brewing yeasts are classified into three categories, which are further divided into the so-called "strains" used for brewing specific types of beer. (Association of Brewers Glossary)

Everybody is speaking about a coming shakeout in the industry—well, we'll survive the shakeout because of the quality of our beers."

Finally, everything was ready for the meeting the following day. As Gary locked up the brewery, he could not help wondering what the shareholders would say in the meeting. While he and Chris were not too keen on growing the business for the fear of losing control of the operations and the quality of the beer, Gary knew that some shareholders felt the business had to be much bigger in order to remain viable in the medium term. He knew that the shareholders would press for growth. He was not sure, however, whether the proponents of growth had a clear idea of how fast and to what size BBC should grow. Moreover, Gary wanted to be sure to have the shareholders understand that the company did not have the money to finance any major investment. Any growth effort would have to be financed with external capital. He was not sure, however, that all the options available for raising the money were clearly understood by everyone. Each option had advantages and disadvantages, and in Gary's mind it was important that there be agreement among all parties on how to bring in the additional capital.

KENTUCKY FRIED CHICKEN AND THE GLOBAL FAST-FOOD INDUSTRY IN 1998

Jeffrey A. Krug, *University of Illinois at Urbana–Champaign*

In 1998, Kentucky Fried Chicken Corporation (KFC) was the world's largest chicken restaurant chain and third largest fast-food chain. KFC held over 55 percent of the U.S. market and operated over 10,200 restaurants worldwide. It opened 376 new restaurants (more than one restaurant a day) and operated in 79 countries.

One of the first fast-food chains to go international during the late 1960s, KFC developed one of the world's most recognizable brands. Japan, Australia, and the United Kingdom accounted for the greatest share of KFC's international expansion during the 1970s and 1980s. During the 1990s, KFC turned its attention to other international markets that offered significant opportunities for growth: China, with a population of over 1 billion, and Europe, with a population roughly equal to that of the United States. Latin America offered a unique growth opportunity because of the size of its markets, its common language and culture, and its geographical proximity to the United States. Mexico was of particular interest because of the North American Free Trade Agreement (NAFTA), which went into effect in 1994.

Prior to 1990, KFC expanded into Latin America primarily through company-owned restaurants in Mexico and Puerto Rico. By 1995, KFC had also established company-owned restaurants in Venezuela and Brazil, as well as franchised units in numerous Caribbean countries. During the early 1990s, KFC shifted to a two-tiered strategy in Latin America. First, it established 29 franchised restaurants in Mexico following the enactment of Mexico's new franchise law in 1990. This allowed KFC to expand outside of its company restaurant base in Mexico City, Guadalajara, and Monterrey. KFC was one of many U.S. fast-food, retail, and hotel chains to begin franchising in Mexico following the new franchise law. Second, KFC began an aggressive franchise-building program in South America. By 1998, it was operating franchised restaurants in 32 Latin American countries. Much of this growth was in Brazil, Chile, Colombia, Ecuador, and Peru.

COMPANY HISTORY

Fast-food franchising was still in its infancy in 1952 when Harland Sanders began his travels across the United States to speak with prospective franchisees about his Colonel Sanders Recipe Kentucky Fried Chicken. By 1960, "Colonel" Sanders had granted KFC franchises to over 200 take-home retail outlets and restaurants across the United States. He had also succeeded in establishing a number of franchises in Canada. By 1963, the number of KFC franchises had risen to over 300 and revenues had reached $500 million.

By 1964, at the age of 74, the Colonel had grown tired of running the day-to-day operations of his business and was eager to concentrate on public relations issues. Therefore, he sought out potential buyers, eventually deciding to sell the business to two Louisville businessmen—Jack Massey and John Young Brown Jr.—for $2 million. The Colonel stayed on as a public relations representative and goodwill ambassador for the company.

During the next five years, Massey and Brown concentrated on growing KFC's franchise system across the United States. In 1966, after being taken public, KFC was listed on the New York Stock Exchange. By the late 1960s, the company had gained a strong foothold in the United States, and Massey and Brown turned their attention to international markets. In 1969, KFC signed a joint venture with Japan's Mitsuoishi Shoji Kaisha, Ltd., and acquired the rights to operate 14 existing KFC franchises in England. Subsidiaries were also established in Hong Kong, South Africa, Australia, New Zealand, and Mexico. By 1971, KFC had 2,450 franchises and 600 company-owned restaurants worldwide, and was operating in 48 countries.

Heublein, Inc.

In 1971, KFC entered negotiations with Heublein, Inc., to discuss a possible merger. The decision to seek a merger candidate was partially driven by Brown's desire to pursue other interests, including a political career (Brown was elected governor of Kentucky in 1977). Several months later, Heublein acquired KFC. Heublein was in the business of producing vodka, mixed cocktails, dry gin, cordials, beer, and other alcoholic beverages. However, Heublein had little experience in the restaurant business. Conflicts quickly erupted between Colonel Sanders, who continued to act in a public relations capacity, and Heublein management. Sanders became increasingly distraught over quality control issues and restaurant cleanliness. By 1977, new restaurant openings had slowed to about 20 per year; few restaurants were being remodeled, and service quality had declined.

In 1977, Heublein sent in a new management team to redirect KFC's strategy. The team immediately implemented a back-to-the-basics strategy and discontinued new-unit construction until existing restaurants could be upgraded and operating problems eliminated. KFC then refurbished restaurants, placed emphasis on cleanliness and service, cut out marginal products, and reestablished product consistency. By 1982, KFC's strategic focus had proved successful and the company was again aggressively building new units.

R. J. Reynolds Industries, Inc.

In 1982, R. J. Reynolds Industries, Inc. (RJR), merged Heublein into a wholly owned subsidiary. The merger with Heublein represented part of RJR's overall corporate strategy of diversifying into unrelated businesses, including energy, transportation, food, and restaurants. RJR's objective was to reduce its dependence on the tobacco industry, which had driven RJR sales since the company's founding in North Carolina in 1875. Sales of cigarettes and tobacco products, while profitable, were declining because of reduced consumption in the United States. This was mainly the result of an increased awareness among Americans about the negative health consequences of smoking.

RJR had no more experience in the restaurant business than did Heublein. However, it decided to take a hands-off approach to managing KFC. Whereas Heublein had installed its own top management at KFC headquarters, RJR left KFC management largely intact, believing that existing KFC managers were better qualified to operate KFC's businesses than its own managers were. In doing so, RJR avoided many of the operating problems that plagued Heublein. This strategy paid off as KFC continued to expand aggressively and profitably under RJR ownership. In 1985, RJR acquired Nabisco Corporation for $4.9 billion. Nabisco sold a variety of well-known cookies, crackers, cereals, confectioneries, snacks, and other grocery products. The merger with Nabisco represented a decision by RJR to concentrate its diversification efforts on the consumer foods industry. It subsequently divested many of its non-consumer food businesses. RJR sold KFC to PepsiCo, Inc., one year later.

PEPSICO, INC.

Corporate Strategy

In 1965 the merger of the Pepsi-Cola Company and Frito-Lay, Inc., created one of the largest consumer products companies in the United States: PepsiCo, Inc. Pepsi-Cola's traditional business was the sale of soft drink concentrates to licensed independent and company-owned bottlers that manufactured, sold, and distributed Pepsi-Cola soft drinks. Pepsi-Cola's best known trademarks were Pepsi-Cola, Diet Pepsi, Mountain Dew, and Slice. Frito-Lay manufactured and sold a variety of snack foods, including Fritos corn chips, Lay's potato chips, Ruffles potato chips, Doritos, Tostitos tortilla chips, and Chee-tos cheese-flavored snacks. PepsiCo quickly embarked on an aggressive acquisition program similar to that pursued by RJR during the 1980s, buying a number of companies in areas unrelated to its major businesses. Acquisitions included North American Van Lines, Wilson Sporting Goods, and Lee Way Motor Freight. However, these businesses failed to live up to expectations, mainly because the management skills required to operate them lay outside of PepsiCo's area of expertise.

Poor performance in these businesses led then-chairman and chief executive officer Don Kendall to restructure PepsiCo's operations in 1984. First, the company divested itself of businesses that did not support PepsiCo's consumer product orientation, such as North American Van Lines, Wilson Sporting Goods, and Lee Way Motor Freight. Second, PepsiCo sold its foreign bottling operations to local businesspeople who better understood the culture and business environment in their respective countries. Third, Kendall reorganized PepsiCo along three lines: soft drinks, snack foods, and restaurants.

Restaurant Business and Acquisition of Kentucky Fried Chicken

PepsiCo first entered the restaurant business in 1977 when it acquired Pizza Hut's 3,200-unit restaurant system. Taco Bell was merged into a division of PepsiCo in 1978. The restaurant business complemented PepsiCo's consumer product orientation. The marketing of fast-food followed many of the same patterns as the marketing of soft drinks and snack foods. PepsiCo therefore believed that its management skills could be easily transferred among its three business segments. This was compatible with PepsiCo's practice of frequently moving managers among its business units as a way of developing future top executives. PepsiCo's restaurant chains also provided an additional outlet for the sale of Pepsi soft drinks. Pepsi-Cola soft drinks and fast-food products could also be marketed together in the same television and radio segments, thereby providing higher returns for each advertising dollar. To complete its diversification into the restaurant segment, PepsiCo acquired Kentucky Fried Chicken Corporation from RJR-Nabisco for $841 million in 1986. The acquisition of KFC gave PepsiCo the leading market share in chicken (KFC), pizza (Pizza Hut), and Mexican food (Taco Bell), three of the four largest and fastest-growing segments within the U.S. fast-food industry.

Management

Following the acquisition by PepsiCo, KFC's relationship with its parent company underwent dramatic changes. Whereas RJR had operated KFC as a semi-autonomous unit, satisfied that KFC management understood the fast-food business better than its own management did, PepsiCo acquired KFC in order to complement its already strong presence in the fast-food market. Rather than allowing KFC to operate independently, PepsiCo undertook sweeping changes: Negotiating a new franchise contract to give PepsiCo more control over its franchisees, reducing staff in order to cut costs, and replacing KFC managers with its own. In 1987, a rumor spread through KFC's headquarters in Louisville that the new personnel manager, who had just relocated from PepsiCo's headquarters in New York, had said "There will be no more home-grown tomatoes in this organization."

Such rumors indicated a more serious morale problem, created by several restructurings that led to layoffs throughout the KFC organization, the replacement of KFC personnel with PepsiCo managers, and conflicts between KFC and PepsiCo's corporate cultures. KFC's culture was built largely on Colonel Sanders's laid-back approach to management, under which employees enjoyed relatively good job stability and security. Over the years, a strong loyalty had been created among KFC employees and franchisees, mainly because of Colonel Sanders's efforts to meet his employees' benefits, pension, and other non-income needs. In addition, the friendly, relaxed atmosphere at KFC's corporate offices in Louisville had mirrored the company's corporate culture, which had been left essentially unchanged during the Heublein and RJR years.

In stark contrast, PepsiCo's corporate culture was characterized by a strong emphasis on performance. Top performers expected to move up through the ranks quickly. PepsiCo used its KFC, Pizza Hut, Taco Bell, Frito Lay, and Pepsi-Cola divisions as training grounds for its top managers, rotating its best managers through its five divisions on average every two years. This practice created immense pressure on managers to continuously demonstrate their prowess within short periods, in order to maximize their potential for promotion. This practice also left many KFC managers with the feeling that they had few career opportunities with the new company. One PepsiCo manager commented, "You may have performed well last year, but if you don't perform well this year, you're gone, and there are 100 ambitious guys with Ivy League MBAs at PepsiCo who would love to take your position." An unwanted effect of this performance-driven culture was that employee loyalty was often lost and turnover became higher than in other companies.

When asked about KFC's relationship with its corporate parent, Kyle Craig, president of KFC's U.S. operations, commented:

> The KFC culture is an interesting one because I think it was dominated by a lot of KFC folks, many of whom have been around since the days of the Colonel. Many of those people were very intimidated by the PepsiCo culture, which is a very high-performance, high-accountability, highly driven culture. People were concerned about whether they would succeed in the new culture. Like many companies, we have had a couple of downsizings, which further made people nervous. Today, there are fewer old KFC people around and I think to some degree people have seen that the PepsiCo culture can drive some pretty positive results. I also think the PepsiCo people who have worked with KFC have modified their cultural values somewhat and they can see that there were a lot of benefits in the old KFC culture.
>
> PepsiCo pushes its companies to perform strongly, but whenever there is a slip in performance, it increases the culture gap between PepsiCo and KFC. I have been involved in two downsizings over which I have been the chief architect. They have been probably the two most gut-wrenching experiences of my career. Because you know you're dealing with peoples' lives and their families, these changes can be emotional if you care about the people in your organization. However, I do fundamentally believe that your first obligation is to the entire organization.

A second problem for PepsiCo was its poor relationship with KFC franchisees. A month after becoming president and chief executive officer in 1989, John Cranor addressed KFC's franchisees in Louisville, in order to explain the details of the first contract change in 13 years. The new contract gave PepsiCo greater power to take over weak franchises, relocate restaurants, and make changes in existing restaurants. In addition, it no longer protected existing restaurants from competition with new KFC units, and it gave PepsiCo the right to raise royalty fees as contracts came up for renewal. After Cranor finished his address, the attending franchisees jumped to their feet to protest the changes. The franchisees had long been accustomed to relatively little interference from management in their day-to-day operations (a policy begun by Colonel Sanders). Interference, of course, was a strong part of PepsiCo's philosophy of demanding change. KFC's franchise association later sued PepsiCo over the new contract. The dispute remained unresolved until 1996, when the most objectionable parts of the contract were removed by KFC's new president and CEO, David Novak. A new contract was ratified by KFC's franchisees in 1997.

PepsiCo's Divestiture of KFC, Pizza Hut, and Taco Bell

PepsiCo's strategy of diversifying into three distinct but related markets—soft drinks, snack foods, and fast-food restaurants—created not only one of the world's largest consumer products companies but also a portfolio of some of the world's most recognizable brands. Between 1990 and 1996, PepsiCo grew at an annual rate of over 10 percent, surpassing $31 billion in sales in 1996. However, this sales growth masked troubles in PepsiCo's fast-food businesses. Operating margins (profit as a percentage of sales) at Pepsi-Cola and Frito Lay averaged 12 and 17 percent, respectively, between 1990 and 1996. During the same period, margins at KFC, Pizza Hut, and Taco Bell fell from an average of over 8 percent in 1990 to a little more than 4 percent in 1996. Declining margins in the fast-food chains reflected increasing maturity in the U.S. fast-food industry, more intense competition, and the aging of KFC and Pizza Hut's restaurant base. As a result, PepsiCo's restaurant chains absorbed nearly one-half of the company's annual capital spending during the 1990s while generating less than one-third of PepsiCo's cash flows. Therefore, cash was diverted from PepsiCo's soft drink and snack food businesses

EXHIBIT 1   Tricon Global Restaurants, Inc., Organization Chart, 1998

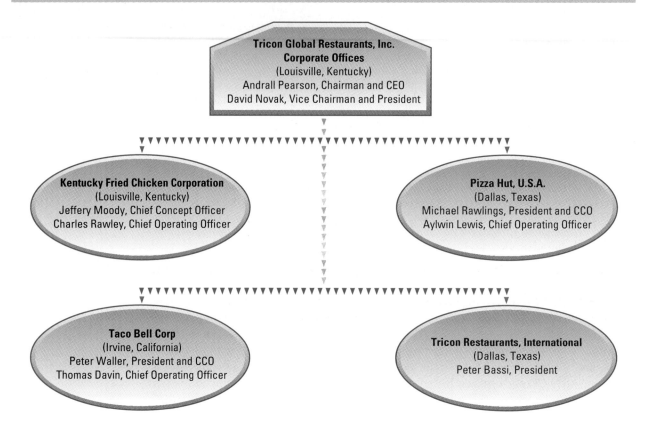

to its restaurant businesses. This reduced PepsiCo's return on assets and its stock price, and made effective competition with Coca-Cola (PepsiCo's leading rival) more difficult. In 1997, PepsiCo spun off its restaurant businesses into a new company called Tricon Global Restaurants, Inc. (see Exhibit 1). The new company was based in KFC's Louisville headquarters. PepsiCo's objectives were to reposition itself as a packaged goods company, to strengthen its balance sheet, and to create more consistent earnings growth. PepsiCo received a one-time distribution from Tricon of $4.7 billion, $3.7 billion of which was used to pay off short-term debt. The balance was earmarked for stock repurchases.

FAST-FOOD INDUSTRY

According to the National Restaurant Association (NRA), food-service sales topped $320 billion for the approximately 500,000 restaurants and other food outlets making up the U.S. restaurant industry in 1997. The NRA estimated that sales in the fast-food segment of the food-service industry grew 5.2 percent, to $104 billion, up from $98 billion in 1996. This marked the fourth consecutive year that fast-food sales either matched or exceeded sales in full-service restaurants, which in 1997 grew 4.1 percent, to $104 billion. The growth in fast-food sales reflected the gradual change in the restaurant industry, in which independently operated sit-down restaurants were becoming dominated by fast-food restaurant chains. The U.S. restaurant industry as a whole grew by approximately 4.2 percent in 1997.

Major Fast-Food Segments

Six major business segments made up the fast-food segment of the food-service industry. Sales data for the leading restaurant chains in each segment are shown in Exhibit 2. Most striking is the dominance of McDonald's, which had sales of over $16 billion in 1996. This represented 16.6 percent of U.S. fast-food sales, or nearly 22 percent of sales among the nation's top 30 fast-food chains. Sales at an average McDonald's restaurant totaled $1.3 million per year, compared to about $820,000 for the average U.S. fast-food restaurant. Tricon Global Restaurants (KFC, Pizza Hut, and Taco Bell) had U.S. sales of $13.4 billion in 1996. This represented 13.6 percent of U.S. fast-food sales and 17.9 percent of the top 30 fast-food chains.

Sandwich chains made up the largest segment of the fast-food market. McDonald's controlled 35 percent of the sandwich segment, while Burger King ran a distant second, with a 15.6 percent market share. Competition had become particularly intense within the sandwich segment as the U.S. fast-food market became more saturated. In order to increase sales, chains turned to new products to win customers away from other sandwich chains, introduced products traditionally offered by other types of chains (such as pizza, fried chicken, and tacos), streamlined their menus, and upgraded product quality. Burger King recently introduced its Big King, a direct clone of the Big Mac. McDonald's quickly retaliated by introducing its Big 'n Tasty, a direct clone of the Whopper. Wendy's introduced chicken pita sandwiches, and Taco Bell introduced sandwiches called wraps, breads stuffed with various fillings. Hardee's successfully introduced fried chicken in most of its restaurants. In addition to offering new products, chains lowered prices, improved customer service, co-branded with other fast-food chains, and established restaurants in nontraditional locations (e.g., McDonald's installed restaurants in Wal-Mart stores across the country).

The second largest fast-food segment was dinner houses, dominated by Red Lobster, Applebee's, Olive Garden, and Chili's. Between 1988 and 1996, dinner houses increased their share of the fast-food market from 8 to over 13 percent. This increase came mainly at the expense of grilled buffet chains, such as Ponderosa, Sizzler, and Western Sizzlin'. The market share of such chains (also known as steak houses) fell from 6 percent in 1988 to under 4 percent in 1996. The rise of dinner houses during the 1990s was partially the result of an aging and wealthier population that increasingly demanded higher quality food and more upscale settings than those of sandwich chains. However, rapid construction of new restaurants, especially among relative newcomers—such as Romano's Macaroni Grill, Lone Star Steakhouse, and Outback Steakhouse—resulted in overcapacity within the dinner house segment. This reduced average restaurant sales and further intensified competition. In 1996, 8 of the 16 largest dinner houses posted growth rates in excess of 10 percent. Romano's Macaroni Grill, Lone Star Steakhouse, Chili's, Outback Steakhouse, Applebee's, Red Robin, Fuddruckers, and Ruby Tuesday grew at rates of 82, 41, 32, 27, 23, 14, 11, and 10 percent, respectively.

The third largest fast-food segment was pizza, long dominated by Pizza Hut. While Pizza Hut controlled over 46 percent of the pizza segment in 1996, its market share slowly eroded thereafter because of intense competition and its aging restaurant base. Domino's Pizza and Papa John's Pizza have been particularly successful. Little Caesars is the only pizza chain to remain predominantly a take-out chain, though it recently began home delivery. However, its policy of charging $1 per delivery damaged its reputation among consumers as a high-value pizza chain. Home delivery, successfully introduced by Domino's and Pizza Hut, was a driving force for success

EXHIBIT 2   Leading U.S. Fast-Food Chains (Ranked by 1996 sales, $ millions)

Sandwich Chains	Sales	Share
McDonald's	$16,370	35.0%
Burger King	7,300	15.6
Taco Bell	4,575	9.8
Wendy's	4,360	9.3
Hardee's	3,055	6.5
Subway	2,700	5.8
Arby's	1,867	4.0
Dairy Queen	1,225	2.6
Jack in the Box	1,207	2.6
Sonic Drive-In	985	2.1
Carl's Jr.	648	1.4
Other chains	2,454	5.2
Total	$46,745	100.0%

Dinner Houses		
Red Lobster	$ 1,810	15.7%
Applebee's	1,523	13.2
Olive Garden	1,280	11.1
Chili's	1,242	10.7
Outback Steakhouse	1,017	8.8
T.G.I. Friday's	935	8.1
Ruby Tuesday	545	4.7
Lone Star Steakhouse	460	4.0
Bennigan's	458	4.0
Romano's Macaroni Grill	344	3.0
Other dinner houses	1,942	16.8
Total	$11,557	100.0%

Grilled Buffet Chains		
Golden Corral	$ 711	22.8%
Ponderosa	680	21.8
Ryan's	604	19.4
Sizzler	540	17.3
Western Sizzlin'	332	10.3
Quincy's	259	8.3
Total	$3,116	100.0%

Family Restaurants		
Denny's	$1,850	21.2%
Shoney's	1,220	14.0
Big Boy	945	10.8
International House of Pancakes	797	9.1
Cracker Barrel	734	8.4
Perkins	678	7.8
Friendly's	597	6.8
Bob Evans	575	6.6
Waffle House	525	6.0
Coco's	278	3.2
Steak 'n Shake	275	3.2
Village Inn	246	2.8
Total	$8,719	100.0%

EXHIBIT 2 Concluded		
Pizza Chains	**Sales**	**Share**
Pizza Hut	$ 4,927	46.4%
Domino's Pizza	2,300	21.7
Little Caesars Pizza	1,425	13.4%
Papa John's Pizza	619	5.8
Sbarro	400	3.8
Round Table Pizza	385	3.6
Chuck E. Cheese's	293	2.8
Godfather's Pizza	266	2.5
Total	$10,614	100.0%
Chicken Chains		
KFC	$ 3,900	57.1%
Boston Market	1,167	17.1
Popeye's Chicken	666	9.7
Chick-fil-A	570	8.3
Church's Chicken	529	7.7
Total	$ 6,832	100.0%

Source: *Nation's Restaurant News.*

among the market leaders during the 1970s and 1980s. However, the success of home delivery drove competitors to look for new methods of increasing their customer bases. Pizza chains diversified into nonpizza items (e.g., chicken wings at Domino's and Italian cheese bread at Little Caesars), developed nontraditional units (e.g., airport kiosks and college campuses), offered special promotions, and offered new pizza variations with an emphasis on high-quality ingredients (e.g., Roma Herb and Garlic Crunch pizza at Domino's and Buffalo Chicken Pizza at Round Table Pizza).

Chicken Segment

KFC continued to dominate the chicken segment, with 1997 sales of $4 billion (see Exhibit 3). However, rather than building new restaurants in the already saturated U.S. market, KFC focused on building restaurants abroad. (In fact, the number of KFC restaurants in the United States declined slightly, from 5,128 in 1993 to 5,120 in 1998.) In the United States, KFC focused on closing unprofitable restaurants, upgrading existing restaurants with new exterior signage, and improving product quality. The strategy paid off. While overall U.S. sales during the 10 years up to 1998 remained flat, annual sales per unit increased steadily in 8 of the 9 years up to 1998.

Despite KFC's continued dominance within the chicken segment, it lost market share to Boston Market, which by 1997 had become KFC's nearest competitor, with $1.2 billion in sales. Emphasizing roasted chicken rather than fried, Boston Market successfully created the image of an upscale deli offering healthy, home-style alternatives to fast foods. It has broadened its menu beyond rotisserie chicken to include ham, turkey, meat loaf, chicken pot pie, and deli sandwiches. In order to minimize its image as a fast-food restaurant, Boston Market had refused to put drive-thrus in its restaurants and had established most of its units in outside shopping malls rather than in the freestanding units at intersections so characteristic of other fast-food restaurants.

EXHIBIT 3 Top U.S. Chicken Chains

U.S. Sales ($ millions)	1992	1993	1994	1995	1996	1997	Annual Growth Rate
KFC	$3,400	$3,400	$3,500	$3,700	$3,900	$4,000	3.3%
Boston Market	43	147	371	754	1,100	1,197	94.5
Popeye's Chicken	545	569	614	660	677	727	5.9
Chick-fil-A	356	396	451	502	570	671	11.9
Church's Chicken	414	440	465	501	526	574	6.8
Total	$4,758	$4,952	$5,401	$6,118	$6,772	$7,170	8.5%
Number of U.S. Restaurants							
KFC	5,089	5,128	5,149	5,142	5,108	5,120	0.1%
Boston Market	83	217	534	829	1,087	1,166	69.6
Popeye's Chicken	769	769	853	889	894	949	4.3
Chick-fil-A	487	545	534	825	717	762	9.0
Church's Chicken	944	932	937	953	989	1,070	2.5
Total	7,372	7,591	8,007	8,638	8,795	9,067	4.2%
Sales per Unit ($ 000s)							
KFC	$ 668	$ 663	$ 680	$ 720	$ 764	$ 781	3.2%
Boston Market	518	677	695	910	1,012	1,027	14.7
Popeye's Chicken	709	740	720	743	757	767	1.6
Chick-fil-A	731	727	845	608	795	881	3.8
Church's Chicken	439	472	496	526	531	537	4.1
Average	$ 645	$ 782	$ 782	$ 782	$ 782	$ 782	3.9%

Source: Tricon Global Restaurants, Inc., 1997 annual report; Boston Chicken, Inc., 1997 annual report; Chick-fil-A, corporate headquarters, Atlanta; AFC Enterprises, Inc., 1997 annual report.

In 1993, KFC introduced its own rotisserie chicken, called Rotisserie Gold, to combat Boston Market. However, it quickly learned that its customer base was considerably different from that of Boston Market's. KFC's customers liked KFC chicken despite the fact that it was fried. In addition, customers did not respond well to the concept of buying whole chickens for take-out. They preferred instead to buy chicken by the piece. KFC withdrew its rotisserie chicken in 1996 and introduced a new line of roasted chicken called Tender Roast, which could be sold by the piece and mixed with its Original Recipe and Extra Crispy Chicken.

Other major competitors within the chicken segment included Popeye's Chicken and Church's Chicken (both subsidiaries of AFC Enterprises in Atlanta), Chick-fil-A, Bojangle's, El Pollo Loco, Grandy's, Kenny Rogers Roasters, Mrs. Winner's, and Pudgie's. Both Church's and Popeye's had similar strategies—to compete head-on with other "fried chicken" chains. Unlike KFC, neither chain offered rotisserie chicken, and both chains limited non-fried-chicken products. Chick-fil-A focused exclusively on pressure-cooked and char-grilled skinless chicken breast sandwiches, which it served to customers in sit-down restaurants located predominantly in shopping malls. As many malls added food courts, often consisting of up to 15 fast-food units competing side-by-side, shopping malls became less enthusiastic about allocating separate store space to food chains. Therefore, in order to complement its existing restaurant base in shopping malls, Chick-fil-A began to open smaller units in shopping mall food courts, hospitals, and colleges. It also opened freestanding units in selected locations.

Demographic Trends

A number of demographic and societal trends in the United States contributed to increased demand for food prepared away from home. Because of the high divorce rate and the fact that people married later in life, single-person households represented about 25 percent of all U.S. households in 1998, up from 17 percent in 1970. This increased the number of individuals choosing to eat out rather than eat at home. The number of married women working outside of the home also increased dramatically during the 25 years up to 1998. About 59 percent of all married women had careers. According to the Conference Board, 64 percent of all married households will be double-income families by 2000. About 80 percent of households headed by individuals between the ages of 25 and 44 (both married and unmarried) will be double-income. Greater numbers of working women increased family incomes. According to *Restaurants & Institutions* magazine, more than one-third of all households had incomes of at least $50,000 in 1996, and about 8 percent of all households had annual incomes over $100,000. The combination of higher numbers of dual-career families and rising incomes meant that fewer families had time to prepare food at home. According to Standard & Poor's *Industry Surveys,* Americans spent 55 percent of their food dollars at restaurants in 1995, up from 34 percent in 1970.

Fast-food restaurant chains responded to these demographic and societal changes by expanding their restaurant bases. However, by the early 1990s, the growth of traditional free-standing restaurants slowed as the U.S. market became saturated. The major exception was dinner houses, which continued to proliferate in response to Americans' passion for beef. Since 1990, the U.S. population has grown at an average annual rate of about 1 percent; the total reached 270 million people in 1997. Rising immigration in the 1990s dramatically altered the ethnic makeup of the U.S. population. According to the Bureau of the Census, Americans born outside of the United States made up 10 percent of the population in 1997. About 40 percent of that number were Hispanic, while 24 percent were Asian. Nearly 30 percent of Americans born outside of the United States arrived since 1990. As a result of these trends, restaurant chains expanded their menus to appeal to the different ethnic tastes of consumers, expanded into nontraditional locations such as department stores and airports, and made food more available through home delivery and take-out service.

Industry Consolidation and Mergers and Acquisitions

The slowdown in growth in the U.S. fast-food market intensified competition for market share among restaurant chains and led to consolidation, primarily through mergers and acquisitions, during the mid-1990s. Many restaurant chains found that market share could be increased quicker and more cheaply by acquiring an existing company rather than building new units. In addition, fixed costs could be spread across a larger number of restaurants. This raised operating margins and gave companies an opportunity to build market share by lowering prices. An expanded restaurant base also gave companies greater purchasing power over suppliers. In 1990, Grand Metropolitan, a British company, purchased Pillsbury for $5.7 billion. Included in the purchase was Pillsbury's Burger King chain. Grand Met (which in 1988 had purchased Wienerwald, a West German chicken chain, and the Spaghetti Factory, a Swiss chain) strengthened the franchise by upgrading existing restaurants and eliminating several levels of management in order to cut costs. This gave Burger King a long-needed boost in improving its position against McDonald's, its largest competitor.

Perhaps most important to KFC was Hardee's acquisition of 600 Roy Rogers restaurants from Marriott Corporation in 1990. Hardee's converted a large number of these restaurants to Hardee's units and introduced Roy Rogers fried chicken to its menu. By 1993, Hardee's had introduced fried chicken into most of its U.S. restaurants. Hardee's was unlikely to destroy the customer loyalty that KFC long enjoyed. However, it did cut into KFC's sales, because it was able to offer consumers a widened menu selection that appealed to a variety of family eating preferences. In 1997, Hardee's parent company, Imasco Ltd., sold Hardee's to CKE Restaurants, Inc. CKE owned Carl's Jr., Rally's Hamburgers, and Checker's Drive-In. Boston Chicken, Inc., acquired Harry's Farmers Market, an Atlanta grocer that sold prepared meals. The acquisition was designed to help Boston Chicken develop distribution beyond its Boston Market restaurants. AFC Enterprises, which operated Popeye's and Church's, acquired Chesapeake Bagel Bakery of McLean, Virginia, in order to diversify away from fried chicken and to strengthen its balance sheet.

The effect of these and other recent mergers and acquisitions on the industry was powerful. The top 10 restaurant companies controlled almost 60 percent of fast-food sales in the United States. The consolidation of a number of fast-food chains within larger, financially more powerful parent companies gave restaurant chains strong financial and managerial resources that could be used to compete against smaller chains in the industry.

International Quick-Service Market

Because of the aggressive pace of new restaurant construction in the United States during the 1970s and 1980s, opportunities to continue such expansion in the 1990s were limited. Restaurant chains that did build new restaurants found that the higher cost of purchasing prime locations resulted in immense pressure to increase annual sales per restaurant. Many restaurants began to expand into international markets as an alternative to continued domestic expansion. In contrast to the U.S. market, international markets offered large customer bases with comparatively little competition. However, only a few U.S. restaurant chains had defined aggressive strategies for penetrating international markets by 1998; key among these were McDonald's, KFC, Pizza Hut, and Taco Bell.

McDonald's operated the largest number of restaurants. In 1998 it operated 23,132 restaurants in 109 countries (10,409 restaurants were located outside the United States). In comparison, KFC, Pizza Hut, and Taco Bell together operated 29,712 restaurants in 79, 88, and 17 countries, respectively (9,126 restaurants were located outside the United States). Of these four chains, KFC operated the greatest percentage of its restaurants (50 percent) outside of the United States. McDonald's, Pizza Hut, and Taco Bell operated 45, 31, and 2 percent of their units outside the United States, respectively. KFC opened its first restaurant outside the United States in the late 1960s. By the time of its acquisition by PepsiCo in 1986, KFC was already operating restaurants in 55 countries. KFC's early expansion abroad, strong brand name, and managerial experience in international markets gave it a strong competitive advantage vis-à-vis other fast-food chains that were investing abroad for the first time.

Exhibit 4 shows *Hotels'* list of the world's 30 largest fast-food restaurant chains at year-end 1993 (*Hotels* discontinued reporting these data after 1994). Seventeen of these chains (ranked by number of units) were headquartered in the United States. There were a number of possible explanations for the relative scarcity of fast-food

EXHIBIT 4   The World's 30 Most Global Fast-Food Chains (Year-end 1993, ranked by number of countries)

Rank	Franchise	Location	Units	Countries
1	Pizza Hut	Dallas, Texas	10,433	80
2	McDonald's	Oakbrook, Illinois	23,132	70
3	KFC	Louisville, Kentucky	9,033	68
4	Burger King	Miami, Florida	7,121	50
5	Baskin-Robbins	Glendale, California	3,557	49
6	Wendy's	Dublin, Ohio	4,168	38
7	Domino's Pizza	Ann Arbor, Michigan	5,238	36
8	TCBY	Little Rock, Arkansas	7,474	22
9	Dairy Queen	Minneapolis, Minnesota	5,471	21
10	Dunkin' Donuts	Randolph, Massachusetts	3,691	21
11	Taco Bell	Irvine, California	4,921	20
12	Arby's	Fort Lauderdale, Florida	2,670	18
13	Subway	Milford, Connecticut	8,477	15
14	Sizzler International	Los Angeles, California	681	14
15	Hardee's	Rocky Mount, North Carolina	4,060	12
16	Little Caesars	Detroit, Michigan	4,600	12
17	Popeye's Chicken	Atlanta, Georgia	813	12
18	Denny's	Spartanburg, South Carolina	1,515	10
19	A&W Restaurants	Livonia, Michigan	707	9
20	T.G.I. Friday's	Minneapolis, Minnesota	273	8
21	Orange Julius	Minneapolis, Minnesota	480	7
22	Church's Chicken	Atlanta, Georgia	1,079	6
23	Long John Silver's	Lexington, Kentucky	1,464	5
24	Carl's Jr.	Anaheim, California	649	4
25	Loterria	Tokyo, Japan	795	4
26	Mos Burger	Tokyo, Japan	1,263	4
27	Skylark	Tokyo, Japan	1,000	4
28	Jack in the Box	San Diego, California	1,172	3
29	Quick Restaurants	Berchem, Belgium	876	3
30	Taco Time	Eugene, Oregon	300	3

Source: *Hotels,* May 1994; 1994 PepsiCo, Inc., annual report.

restaurant chains outside the United States. First, the United States represented the largest consumer market in the world, accounting for over one-fifth of the world's gross domestic product. Therefore, the United States was the strategic focus of the largest restaurant chains. Second, Americans were quick to accept the fast-food concept, whereas many other cultures had strong culinary traditions that were difficult to break down. Europeans, for example, had long preferred to frequent more mid-scale restaurants, where they spent several hours in a formal setting enjoying native dishes and beverages. While KFC was again building restaurants in Germany by the late 1980s, it previously failed to penetrate the German market, because Germans were not accustomed to take-out food or to ordering food over the counter. McDonald's had greater success penetrating the German market, because it made a number of changes in its menu and operating procedures, in order to better appeal to German culture. For

EXHIBIT 5	Market Shares of Top U.S. Chicken Chains, 1988-1997					
	KFC	Boston Market	Popeye's	Chick-fil-A	Church's	Total
1988	72.1%	0.0%	12.0%	5.8%	10.1%	100.0%
1989	70.8	0.0	12.0	6.2	11.0	100.0
1990	71.3	0.0	12.3	6.6	9.8	100.0
1991	72.7	0.0	11.4	7.0	8.9	100.0
1992	71.5	0.9	11.4	7.5	8.7	100.0
1993	68.7	3.0	11.4	8.0	8.9	100.0
1994	64.8	6.9	11.3	8.4	8.6	100.0
1995	60.5	12.3	10.8	8.2	8.2	100.0
1996	57.6	16.2	10.0	8.4	7.8	100.0
1997	55.8	16.7	10.1	9.4	8.0	100.0
Change 1988-1997	(16.3)%	+16.7%	(1.9)%	+3.6%	(2.1)%	

Source: *Nation's Restaurant News.*

example, German beer was served in all of McDonald's German restaurants. KFC had more success in Asia and Latin America, where chicken was a traditional dish.

Aside from cultural factors, international business carried risks not present in the U.S. market. Long distances between headquarters and foreign franchises often made it difficult to control the quality of individual restaurants, as well as to solve servicing and support problems. Transportation and other resource costs were higher than in the domestic market. In addition, time, cultural, and language differences increased communication and operational problems. Therefore, it was reasonable to expect U.S. restaurant chains to expand domestically as long as they achieved corporate profit and growth objectives. As the U.S. market became saturated and companies gained expertise in international markets, however, more companies could be expected to turn to profitable international markets as a means of expanding restaurant bases and increasing sales, profits, and market share.

KENTUCKY FRIED CHICKEN CORPORATION (WWW.KFC.COM)

KFC's worldwide sales, which included totals from both company-owned and franchised restaurants, grew to $8 billion in 1997. U.S. sales grew 2.6 percent over 1996 and accounted for about one-half of KFC's sales worldwide. KFC's U.S. share of the chicken segment fell 1.8 points, to 55.8 percent (see Exhibit 5). This marked the sixth consecutive year that KFC sustained a decline in market share. In 1998, KFC's market share had fallen by 16.3 points since 1988, when it held a 72.1 percent market share. Boston Market, which established its first restaurant in 1992, increased its market share from 0 to 16.7 in the same period. On the surface, it appeared as though Boston Market achieved its market share gain by taking customers away from KFC. However, KFC's sales growth had remained fairly stable and constant over the previous 10 years. Boston Market's success was largely a function of its appeal to consumers who did not regularly patronize KFC or other fried-chicken chains. By appealing to a market niche that was previously unsatisfied, Boston Market was able to expand the existing consumer base within the chicken segment of the fast-food industry.

EXHIBIT 6   KFC Restaurant Count (U.S. restaurants), 1986-1997

	Company-Owned	Percent of Total	Franchised/Licensed	Percent of Total	Total
1986	1,246	26.4%	3,474	73.6%	4,720
1987	1,250	26.0	3,564	74.0	4,814
1988	1,262	25.8	3,637	74.2	4,899
1989	1,364	27.5	3,597	72.5	4,961
1990	1,389	27.7	3,617	72.3	5,006
1991	1,836	36.6	3,186	63.4	5,022
1992	1,960	38.8	3,095	61.2	5,055
1993	2,014	39.5	3,080	60.5	5,094
1994	2,005	39.2	3,110	60.8	5,115
1995	2,026	39.4	3,111	60.6	5,137
1996	1,932	37.8	3,176	62.2	5,108
1997	1,850	36.1	3,270	63.9	5,120
1986–93 Compound Annual Growth Rate					
	7.1%		(1.7%)		1.1%
1993–97 Compounded Annual Growth Rate					
	(2.1%)		1.5%		0.1%

Source: Tricon Global Restaurants, Inc., 1997 annual report; PepsiCo, Inc., annual report, 1994,1995,1996,1997.

Refranchising Strategy

The relatively low growth rate in sales in KFC's domestic restaurants during the 1992–97 period was largely the result of KFC's decision in 1993 to begin selling company-owned restaurants to franchisees. When Colonel Sanders began to expand the Kentucky Fried Chicken system in the late 1950s, he established KFC as a system of independent franchisees. This was done in order to minimize his involvement in the operations of individual restaurants and to concentrate on the things he enjoyed the most—cooking, product development, and public relations. This resulted in a fiercely loyal and independent group of franchisees. As explained earlier, when PepsiCo acquired KFC in 1986, PepsiCo's strategy demanded increased involvement in decisions over franchise operations, menu offerings, restaurant management, finance, and marketing. KFC franchisees were fiercely opposed to increased control by the corporate parent. One method for PepsiCo to deal with this conflict was to expand through company-owned restaurants rather than through franchising. PepsiCo also used its strong cash flows to buy back unprofitable franchised restaurants, which could then be converted into company-owned restaurants. In 1986, company-owned restaurants made up 26 percent of KFC's U.S. restaurant base. By 1993, they made up about 40 percent (see Exhibit 6).

While company-owned restaurants were relatively easier to control compared to franchised outlets, they also required higher levels of investment. This meant that high levels of cash were diverted from PepsiCo's soft drink and snack food businesses into its restaurant businesses. However, the fast-food industry delivered lower returns than the soft drink and snack foods industries. Consequently, increased investment in KFC, Pizza Hut, and Taco Bell had a negative effect on PepsiCo's consolidated return on assets. By 1993, investors became concerned that PepsiCo's return on assets did not match returns delivered by Coca-Cola. In order to shore up its return on assets, PepsiCo decided to reduce the number of company-owned restaurants by selling them back to franchisees. This strategy lowered overall company sales, but it also reduced the amount of cash tied up in fixed assets, provided PepsiCo with one-time cash flow benefits from initial fees charged to franchisees, and generated an annual stream of franchise royalties. Tricon Global continued this strategy after the spinoff in 1997.

Marketing Strategy

During the 1980s, consumers began to demand healthier foods, greater variety, and better service in a variety of nontraditional locations such as grocery stores, restaurants, airports, and outdoor events. This forced fast-food chains to expand menu offerings and to investigate nontraditional distribution channels and restaurant designs. Families also demanded greater value in the food they bought away from home. This increased pressure on fast-food chains to reduce prices and to lower operating costs in order to maintain profit margins.

Many of KFC's problems during the late 1980s surrounded its limited menu and inability to quickly bring new products to market. The popularity of its Original Recipe Chicken had allowed KFC to expand without significant competition from other chicken competitors through the 1980s. As a result, new-product introductions were never an important element of KFC's overall strategy. One of the most serious setbacks came in 1989 as KFC prepared to add a chicken sandwich to its menu. While KFC was still experimenting with its chicken sandwich, McDonald's test-marketed its McChicken sandwich in the Louisville area. Shortly thereafter, it rolled out the McChicken sandwich nationally. By beating KFC to the market, McDonald's was able to develop strong consumer awareness for its sandwich. This significantly increased KFC's cost of developing awareness for its own sandwich, which KFC introduced several months later. KFC eventually withdrew its sandwich because of low sales.

In 1991, KFC changed its logo in the United States from Kentucky Fried Chicken to KFC, in order to reduce its image as a fried chicken chain. (It continued to use the Kentucky Fried Chicken name internationally, however.) It then responded to consumer demands for greater variety by introducing several products that would serve as alternatives to its Original Recipe Chicken. These included Oriental Wings, Popcorn Chicken, and Honey BBQ Chicken. It also introduced a dessert menu that included a variety of pies and cookies. In 1993, it rolled out Rotisserie Chicken and began to promote its lunch and dinner buffet. The buffet, which included 30 items, was introduced into almost 1,600 KFC restaurants in 27 states by year-end. In 1998, KFC sold three types of chicken—Original Recipe and Extra Crispy (fried chicken) and Tender Roast (roasted chicken).

One of KFC's most aggressive strategies was the introduction of its Neighborhood Program. By mid-1993, almost 500 company-owned restaurants in New York, Chicago, Philadelphia, Washington, D.C., St. Louis, Los Angeles, Houston, and Dallas had been outfitted with special menu offerings to appeal exclusively to the black community. Menus were beefed up with side dishes such as greens, macaroni and cheese, peach cobbler, sweet-potato pie, and red beans and rice. In addition, restaurant employees wore African-inspired uniforms. The introduction of the Neighborhood Program increased sales by 5 to 30 percent in restaurants appealing directly to the black community. KFC followed by testing Hispanic-oriented restaurants in the Miami area, offering such side dishes as fried plantains, flan, and tres leches.

One of KFC's most significant problems in the U.S. market was that overcapacity made expansion of freestanding restaurants difficult. Fewer sites were available for new construction and those sites, because of their increased cost, were driving profit margins down. Therefore, KFC initiated a three-pronged distribution strategy. First, it focused on building smaller restaurants in nontraditional outlets such as airports, shopping malls, universities, and hospitals. Second, it experimented with home delivery, beginning in the Nashville and Albuquerque markets in 1994. By 1998, home delivery was offered in 365 of KFC's U.S. restaurants. Other nontraditional distribution outlets being tested included units offering drive-thru and carry-out service only, snack shops in cafeterias, scaled-down outlets for supermarkets, and mobile units that could be transported to outdoor concerts and fairs.

A third focus of KFC's distribution strategy was restaurant co-branding, primarily with its sister chain, Taco Bell. By 1997, 349 KFC restaurants had added Taco Bell items to their menus and displayed both the KFC and Taco Bell logos outside their restaurants Co-branding gave KFC the opportunity to expand its business dayparts. While about two-thirds of KFC's business was dinner, Taco Bell's primary business occurred at lunch. By combining the two concepts in the same unit, sales at individual restaurants could be increased significantly. KFC believed that there were opportunities to sell the Taco Bell concept in over 3,900 of its U.S. restaurants.

Operating Efficiencies

As pressure continued to build from price-conscious consumers, restaurant chains searched for ways to reduce overhead and other operating costs, in order to improve profit margins. In 1989, KFC reorganized its U.S. operations in order to eliminate overhead costs and to increase efficiency. Included in this reorganization was a revision of KFC's crew training programs and operating standards. A renewed emphasis was placed on clean restaurants, fast and friendly service, and product quality. In 1992, KFC reorganized its middle-management ranks, eliminating 250 of the 1,500 management positions at KFC's corporate headquarters. More responsibility was assigned to restaurant franchisees and marketing managers, and pay was more closely aligned with customer service and restaurant performance. In 1997, Tricon Global signed a five-year agreement with PepsiCo Food Systems (which was later sold by PepsiCo to AmeriServe Food Distributors) to distribute food and supplies to Tricon's 29,712 KFC, Pizza Hut, and Taco Bell units. This provided KFC with significant opportunities to benefit from economies of scale in distribution.

INTERNATIONAL OPERATIONS

Much of the early success of the top 10 fast-food chains was the result of aggressive building strategies. Chains were able to discourage competition by building in low-population areas that could only support a single fast-food chain. McDonald's was particularly successful at quickly expanding into small towns across the United States, thereby preempting other fast-food chains. It was equally important to beat a competitor into more densely populated areas where location was of prime importance. KFC's early entry into international markets placed it in a strong position to benefit from international expansion as the U.S. market became saturated. In 1997, 50 percent of KFC's restaurants were located outside of the United States. While 364 new restaurants were opened outside the United States in 1997, only 12 new restaurants were added to the U.S. system. Most of KFC's international expansion was through franchises, though some restaurants were licensed to operators or jointly operated with a local partner. Expansion through franchising was an important strategy for penetrating international markets, because franchises were owned and operated by local entrepreneurs who understood local language, culture, and customs, as well as local law, financial markets, and marketing characteristics. Franchising was particularly important for expansion into smaller countries such as the Dominican Republic, Grenada, Bermuda, and Suriname, which could only support a single restaurant. Costs of operating company-owned restaurants in these smaller markets were prohibitively high. Of the 5,117 KFC restaurants located outside the United States in 1997, 68 percent were franchised, while 22 percent were company-owned and 10 percent were licensed restaurants or joint ventures.

In larger markets such as Japan, China, and Mexico, there was a stronger emphasis on building company-owned restaurants. By coordinating purchasing, recruiting and training, financing, and advertising, KFC could spread fixed costs over a large number of restaurants and negotiate lower prices on products and services. KFC was also better able to control product and service quality. In order to take advantage of economies of scale, Tricon Global Restaurants managed all of the international units of its KFC, Pizza Hut, and Taco Bell chains through its Tricon International division, located in Dallas, Texas. This enabled Tricon Global Restaurants to leverage its strong advertising expertise, international experience, and restaurant management experience across all three chains.

Latin American Strategy

KFC's primary market presence in Latin America during the 1980s was in Mexico, Puerto Rico, and the Caribbean. KFC established subsidiaries in Mexico and Puerto Rico, from which it coordinated the construction and operation of company-owned restaurants. A third subsidiary in Venezuela was closed because of its high fixed costs. Franchises were used to penetrate countries in the Caribbean whose market size prevented KFC from profitably operating company restaurants. In Mexico, KFC, like most other fast-food chains there, relied exclusively on the operation of company-owned restaurants through 1989. While franchising was popular in the United States, it was virtually unknown in Mexico until 1990, mainly because of the absence of a law protecting patents, information, and technology transferred to the Mexican franchise. In addition, royalties were limited.

In 1990, Mexico enacted a new law that provided for the protection of technology transferred into the country. Under the new legislation, the franchisor and franchisee were free to set their own terms and to collect royalties. Royalties were taxed at 15 percent on technology assistance and know-how, and at 35 percent for other royalty categories. The advent of the new franchise law resulted in an explosion of franchises in fast-food, services, hotels, and retail outlets. In 1992, franchises had an estimated $750 million in sales in over 1,200 outlets throughout Mexico. Prior to passage of Mexico's franchise law, KFC limited its Mexican operations primarily to Mexico City, Guadalajara, and Monterrey, in order to better coordinate operations and minimize costs of distribution to individual restaurants. The new franchise law gave KFC and other fast-food chains the opportunity to expand their restaurant bases into rural regions of Mexico, where responsibility for management could be handled by local franchisees.

After 1990, KFC altered its Latin American strategy in a number of ways. First, it opened 29 franchises in Mexico to complement its company-owned restaurant base. It then expanded its company-owned restaurants into the Virgin Islands and reestablished a subsidiary in Venezuela. Third, it expanded its franchise operations into South

EXHIBIT 7 Latin America Restaurant Count—KFC and McDonald's (as of December 31, 1997)

	KFC Company Restaurants	KFC Franchised Restaurants	KFC Total Restaurants	McDonald's
Argentina	—	—	—	131
Bahamas	—	10	10	3
Barbados	—	7	7	—
Brazil	6	2	8	480
Chile	—	29	29	27
Colombia	—	19	19	18
Costa Rica	—	5	5	19
Ecuador	—	18	18	2
Jamaica	—	17	17	7
Mexico	128	29	157	131
Panama	—	21	21	20
Peru	—	17	17	5
Puerto Rico and Virgin Islands	67	—	67	115
Trinidad and Tobago	—	27	27	3
Uruguay	—	—	—	18
Venezuela	6	—	6	53
Other	—	30	30	59
Total	207	231	438	1,091

Source: Tricon Global Restaurants, Inc.; McDonald's, 1997 annual report.

America. In 1990 a franchise was opened in Chile, and in 1993 one was opened in Brazil. Franchises were subsequently established in Colombia, Ecuador, Panama, and Peru, among other South American countries. A fourth subsidiary was established in Brazil, in order to develop company-owned restaurants. Brazil was Latin America's largest economy and McDonald's primary Latin American investment location. By June 1998, KFC operated 438 restaurants in 32 Latin American countries. By comparison, McDonald's operated 1,091 restaurants in 28 countries in Latin America.

Exhibit 7 shows the number of KFC and McDonald's operations in Latin America. KFC's early entry into Latin America during the 1970s gave it a leadership position in Mexico and the Caribbean. It had also gained an edge in Ecuador and Peru, countries where McDonald's had not yet developed a strong presence. McDonald's focused its Latin American investment in Brazil, Argentina, and Uruguay, countries where KFC had little or no presence. McDonald's was also strong in Venezuela. Both KFC and McDonald's were strong in Chile, Colombia, Panama, and Puerto Rico.

Economic Environment and the Mexican Market

Mexico was KFC's strongest market in Latin America. While McDonald's had aggressively established restaurants in Mexico since 1990, KFC retained the leading market share. Because of its proximity to the United States, Mexico was an attractive location for U.S. trade and investment. Mexico's population of 98 million people was approximately one-third that of the United States and represented a large market for U.S. companies. In comparison, Canada's population of 30.3 million people was only

EXHIBIT 8   Mexico's Major Trading Partners, 1992, 1994, and 1996

	1992		1994		1996	
	Exports	Imports	Exports	Imports	Exports	Imports
U.S.A.	81.1%	71.3%	85.3%	71.8%	84.0%	75.6%
Japan	1.7	4.9	1.6	4.8	1.4	4.4
Germany	1.1	4.0	0.6	3.9	0.7	3.5
Canada	2.2	1.7	2.4	2.0	1.2	1.9
Italy	0.3	1.6	0.1	1.3	1.2	1.1
Brazil	0.9	1.8	0.6	1.5	0.9	0.8
Spain	2.7	1.4	1.4	1.7	1.0	0.7
Other	10.0	13.3	8.0	13.0	9.6	12.0
Total	100.0%	100.0%	100.0%	100.0%	100.0%	100.0%
Value (in millions)	$46,196	$62,129	$60,882	$79,346	$95,991	$89,464

Source: International Monetary Fund, *Direction of Trade Statistics Yearbook,* 1997.

one-third as large as Mexico's. Mexico's proximity to the United States meant that transportation costs between the two were significantly lower than those between the United States and Europe or Asia. This increased the competitiveness of U.S. goods in comparison to European and Asian goods, which had to be transported to Mexico across the Atlantic or Pacific Ocean at substantial cost. The United States was, in fact, Mexico's largest trading partner. Over 75 percent of Mexico's imports came from the United States, while 84 percent of its exports went to the United States (see Exhibit 8). Many U.S. firms invested in Mexico in order to take advantage of lower wage rates, which meant that goods produced in Mexico could be shipped back into the United States or to third markets and sold at lower cost.

While the U.S. market was critically important to Mexico, Mexico still represented a small percentage of overall U.S. trade and investment. Since the early 1900s, the portion of U.S. exports to Latin America had declined. Instead, U.S. exports to Canada and Asia, where economic growth outpaced growth in the Mexico, increased more quickly. Canada was the largest importer of U.S. goods. Japan was the largest exporter of goods to the United States, with Canada a close second. U.S. investment in Mexico was also small, mainly because of past government restrictions on foreign investment. Most U.S. foreign investment was in Europe, Canada, and Asia.

The lack of U.S. investment in and trade with Mexico during this century was mainly the result of Mexico's long history of restricting trade and foreign direct investment. The Institutional Revolutionary Party (PRI), which came to power in Mexico during the 1930s, had historically pursued protectionist economic policies in order to shield Mexico's economy from foreign competition. Many industries were government-owned or controlled, and many Mexican companies focused on producing goods for the domestic market without much attention to building export markets. High tariffs and other trade barriers restricted imports into Mexico, and the Mexican government prohibited or heavily restricted foreign ownership of assets in Mexico.

Additionally, a dictatorial and entrenched government bureaucracy, corrupt labor unions, and a long tradition of anti-Americanism among many government officials and intellectuals reduced the motivation of U.S. firms to invest in Mexico. The nationalization of Mexico's banks in 1982 led to higher real interest rates and lower investor confidence.

Afterward, the Mexican government battled high inflation, labor unrest, and lost consumer purchasing power. However, investor confidence in Mexico improved after 1988, when Carlos Salinas de Gortari was elected president. Following his election, Salinas embarked on an ambitious restructuring of the Mexican economy. He initiated policies to strengthen the free-market components of the economy, lowered top marginal tax rates to 36 percent (down from 60 percent in 1986), and eliminated many restrictions on foreign investment. Foreign firms can now buy up to 100 percent of the equity in many Mexican firms, instead of the previous limit of 49 percent.

Privatization

The privatization of government-owned companies came to symbolize the restructuring of Mexico's economy. In 1990, legislation was passed to privatize all government-run banks. By the end of 1992, over 800 of some 1,200 government-owned companies had been sold, including Mexicana and AeroMexico, the two largest airline companies in Mexico, as well as Mexico's 18 major banks. However, more than 350 companies remained under government ownership. These represented a significant portion of the assets owned by the state at the start of 1988. Therefore, the sale of government-owned companies, in terms of asset value, was moderate. A large number of the remaining government-owned assets were controlled by government-run companies in certain strategic industries such as steel, electricity, and petroleum. These industries had long been protected by government ownership. As a result, additional privatization of government-owned enterprises until 1993 was limited. However, in 1993, when President Salinas opened up the electricity sector to independent power producers, Petroleos Mexicanos (Pemex), the state-run petrochemical monopoly, initiated a program to sell off many of its nonstrategic assets to private and foreign buyers.

North American Free Trade Agreement (NAFTA)

Prior to 1989, Mexico levied high tariffs on most imported goods. In addition, many other goods were subjected to quotas, licensing requirements, and other nontariff trade barriers. In 1986, Mexico joined the General Agreement on Tariffs and Trade (GATT), a world trade organization designed to eliminate barriers to trade among member nations. As a member of GATT, Mexico was obligated to apply its system of tariffs to all member nations equally and therefore dropped tariff rates on a variety of imported goods. In addition, import license requirements were dropped for all but 300 imported items. During President Salinas's administration, tariffs were reduced from an average of 100 percent on most items to an average of 11 percent.

On January 1, 1994, the North American Free Trade Agreement (NAFTA) went into effect. The passage of NAFTA, which included Canada, the United States, and Mexico, created a trading bloc with a larger population and gross domestic product than those of the European Union. All tariffs on goods traded among the three countries were scheduled to be phased out. NAFTA was expected to be particularly beneficial for Mexican exporters, because reduced tariffs made their goods more competitive in the United States compared to goods exported to the United States from other countries. In 1995, one year after NAFTA went into effect, Mexico posted its first balance of trade surplus in six years. Part of this surplus was attributed to reduced tariffs resulting from the NAFTA agreement. However, the peso crisis of 1995, which lowered the value of the peso against the dollar, increased the price of goods imported into Mexico and lowered the price of Mexican products exported to the United States. Therefore, it was still too early to assess the full effects of NAFTA.

Foreign Exchange and the Mexican Peso Crisis of 1995

Between 1982 and 1991 in Mexico, a two-tiered exchange rate system was in force that consisted of a controlled rate and a free-market rate. The controlled rate was used for imports, foreign debt payments, and conversion of export proceeds. An estimated 70 percent of all foreign transactions were covered by the controlled rate. The free market rate was used for other transactions. In 1989, President Salinas instituted a policy of allowing the peso to depreciate against the dollar by one peso per day. The result was a grossly overvalued peso. This lowered the price of imports and led to an increase in imports of over 23 percent in 1989. At the same time, Mexican exports became less competitive on world markets.

In 1991, the controlled rate was abolished and replaced with an official free rate. In order to limit the range of fluctuations in the value of the peso, the government fixed the rate at which it would buy or sell pesos. A floor (the maximum price at which pesos could be purchased) was established at Ps 3,056.20 and remained fixed. A ceiling (the maximum price at which the peso could be sold) was established at Ps 3,056.40 and allowed to move upward by Ps 0.20 per day. This was later revised to Ps 0.40 per day. In 1993, a new currency, called the new peso, was issued with three fewer zeros. The new currency was designed to simplify transactions and to reduce the cost of printing currency.

When Ernesto Zedillo became Mexico's president in December 1994, one of his objectives was to continue the stability of prices, wages, and exchange rates achieved by Salinas during his five-year tenure as president. However, Salinas had achieved stability largely on the basis of price, wage, and foreign exchange controls. While giving the appearance of stability, an overvalued peso continued to encourage imports, which exacerbated Mexico's balance of trade deficit. Mexico's government continued to use foreign reserves to finance its balance of trade deficits. According to the Banco de Mexico, foreign currency reserves fell from $24 billion in January 1994 to $5.5 billion in January 1995. Anticipating a devaluation of the peso, investors began to move capital into U.S. dollar investments. In order to relieve pressure on the peso, Zedillo announced on December 19, 1994, that the peso would be allowed to depreciate by an additional 15 percent per year against the dollar compared to the maximum allowable depreciation of 4 percent per year established during the Salinas administration. Within two days, continued pressure on the peso forced Zedillo to allow the peso to float freely against the dollar. By mid-January 1995, the peso had lost 35 percent of its value against the dollar and the Mexican stock market plunged 20 percent. By November 1995, the peso had depreciated from 3.1 pesos per dollar to 7.3 pesos per dollar.

The continued devaluation of the peso resulted in higher import prices, higher inflation, destabilization within the stock market, and higher interest rates. Mexico struggled to pay its dollar-based debts. In order to thwart a possible default by Mexico, the U.S. government, International Monetary Fund, and World Bank pledged $24.9 billion in emergency loans. Zedillo then announced an emergency economic package, called the *pacto*, which reduced government spending, increased sales of government-run businesses, and placed a freeze on wage increases.

Labor Problems

One of KFC's primary concerns in Mexico was the stability of labor markets. Labor was relatively plentiful and wages were low. However, much of the workforce was relatively unskilled. KFC benefited from lower labor costs, but labor unrest, low job retention, high absenteeism, and poor punctuality were significant problems. Absenteeism and poor punctuality were partially cultural. However, problems with worker retention and

EXHIBIT 9	Selected Economic Data for Canada, the United States, and Mexico				
	Annual Percentage Change (%)				
	1993	**1994**	**1995**	**1996**	**1997**
GDP Growth					
Canada	3.3%	4.8%	5.5%	4.1%	n.a.
United States	4.9	5.8	4.8	5.1	5.9%
Mexico	21.4	13.3	29.4	38.2	n.a.
Real GDP Growth					
Canada	2.2%	4.1%	2.3%	1.2%	n.a.
United States	2.2	3.5	2.0	2.8	3.8
Mexico	2.0	4.5	(6.2)	5.1	n.a.
Inflation Rate					
Canada	1.9%	0.2%	2.2%	1.5%	1.6%
United States	3.0	2.5	2.8	2.9	2.4
Mexico	9.7	6.9	35.0	34.4	20.6
Depreciation (appreciation) against U.S. dollar					
Canada (C$)	4.2%	6.0%	(2.7)%	0.3%	4.3%
Mexico (NP)	(0.3)	71.4	43.5	2.7	3.6

Source: International Monetary Fund, *International Financial Statistics,* 1998.

labor unrest were also the result of workers' frustration over the loss of their purchasing power due to inflation and government controls on wage increases. Absenteeism remained high, at approximately 8 to 14 percent of the labor force, though it was declining because of job security fears. Turnover continued to be a problem and ran at between 5 and 12 percent per month. This made employee screening and internal training important issues for firms investing in Mexico.

Higher inflation and the government's freeze on wage increases led to a dramatic decline in disposable income after 1994. Further, a slowdown in business activity, brought about by higher interest rates and lower government spending, led many businesses to lay off workers. By the end of 1995, an estimated 1 million jobs had been lost as a result of the economic crisis sparked by the peso devaluation. Industry groups within Mexico called for new labor laws giving them more freedom to hire and fire employees and increased flexibility to hire part-time rather than full-time workers.

RISKS AND OPPORTUNITIES

The peso crisis of 1995 and resulting recession in Mexico left KFC managers with a great deal of uncertainty regarding Mexico's economic and political future. KFC had benefited from economic stability between 1988 and 1994. Inflation was brought down, the peso was relatively stable, labor relations were relatively calm, and Mexico's new franchise law had enabled KFC to expand into rural areas using franchises rather than company-owned restaurants. By the end of 1995, KFC had built 29 franchises in Mexico. The foreign exchange crisis of 1995 had severe implications for U.S. firms operating in Mexico. The devaluation of the peso resulted in higher inflation and capital flight out of Mexico. Capital flight reduced the supply of investment funds and led to higher interest rates. In order to reduce inflation, Mexico's government instituted an austerity program that resulted in lower disposable income, higher unemployment, and lower demand for products and services.

Another problem was Mexico's failure to reduce restrictions on U.S. and Canadian investment in a timely fashion. Many U.S. firms had trouble getting approvals for new ventures from the Mexican government. A good example was United Parcel Service (UPS), which sought government approval to use large trucks for deliveries in Mexico. Approvals were delayed, forcing UPS to use smaller trucks and putting the company at a competitive disadvantage vis-à-vis Mexican companies. In many cases, UPS was forced to subcontract delivery work to Mexican companies that were allowed to use larger, more cost-efficient trucks. Other U.S. companies, such as Bell Atlantic and TRW, faced similar problems. TRW, which signed a joint venture agreement with a Mexican partner, had to wait 15 months longer than anticipated before the Mexican government released rules on how it could receive credit data from banks. TRW claimed that the Mexican government slowed the approval process in order to placate several large Mexican banks.

A final area of concern for KFC was increased political turmoil in Mexico during the last several years. On January 1, 1994, the day NAFTA went into effect, rebels (descendants of the Mayans) rioted in the southern Mexican province of Chiapas on the Guatemalan border. After four days of fighting, Mexican troops had driven the rebels out of several occupied towns. Around 150 people—mostly rebels—were killed. The uprising symbolized many of the fears of the poor in Mexico. While President Salinas's economic programs had increased economic growth and wealth in Mexico, many of Mexico's poorest felt that they had not benefited. Many of Mexico's farmers, faced with lower tariffs on imported agricultural goods from the United States, felt that they might be driven out of business because of lower priced imports. Social unrest among Mexico's Indians, farmers, and the poor could potentially unravel much of the economic success achieved in Mexico during the last five years.

Further, President Salinas's hand-picked successor for president was assassinated in early 1994 while campaigning in Tijuana. The assassin was a 23-year-old mechanic and migrant worker believed to be affiliated with a dissident group upset with the PRI's economic reforms. The possible existence of a dissident group raised fears of political violence in the future. The PRI quickly named Ernesto Zedillo, a 42-year-old economist with little political experience, as their new presidential candidate. Zedillo was elected president in December 1994. Political unrest was not limited to Mexican officials and companies. In October 1994, between 30 and 40 masked men attacked a McDonald's restaurant in the tourist section of Mexico City to show their opposition to California's Proposition 187, which would have curtailed benefits to illegal aliens (primarily from Mexico). The men threw cash registers to the floor, cracked them open, smashed windows, overturned tables, and spray-painted the walls with slogans such as "No to Fascism" and "Yankee Go Home."

KFC thus faced a variety of issues in Mexico and Latin America in 1998. KFC halted openings of franchised restaurants in Mexico; all restaurants opened there since 1995 were company-owned. KFC began aggressively building restaurants in South America, which had remained largely unpenetrated by KFC through 1995. Of greatest importance was Brazil, where McDonald's had already established a strong position. Brazil was Latin America's largest economy and a mostly untapped market for KFC. The danger in KFC's ignoring Mexico was that a conservative investment strategy could jeopardize its lead over McDonald's in a large market where KFC had long enjoyed enormous popularity.

OFFICEMAX AND THE OFFICE SUPPLY INDUSTRY

Margaret J. Naumes, *University of New Hampshire*

William Naumes, *University of New Hampshire*

The good news, in September 1996, was that OfficeMax was poised to become the number two firm in the highly competitive office supply industry. The bad news was that this promotion from third place in the industry would occur due to the planned merger of firm number two, Staples, and firm number one, Office Depot. If allowed by the Federal Trade Commission (FTC), the merger would result in a firm with about 1,100 stores and annual sales of more than $10 billion. OfficeMax, by contrast, had just under 500 stores and sales in 1995 of $2.54 billion. Its CEO, Michael Feuer, put a positive spin on the situation: "I view this situation as good news ... Fewer is always better. This will position us with a unique opportunity in the marketplace."[1]

Nine months later, the situation was still unclear. In February 1997, the FTC had asked for additional information. It appeared to be concerned about the impact on customers if the merger was allowed to proceed, in particular about prices in markets where Staples and Office Depot competed directly. In March, the FTC voted to ask for a court order to block the merger. To allay the FTC's concerns about competition, Staples then put together a plan to sell 63 of its stores (in areas where it currently competed only with Office Depot) to OfficeMax in order to preserve competition in those markets. This proposal was sufficient to cause the FTC to reconsider. On the eve of the rescheduled vote, news services quoted "a source familiar with the situation" who predicted that the merger would be approved.[2] However, on Friday, April 4, the FTC voted 4 to 1 to challenge the merger on the grounds that it would violate federal antitrust laws. Staples' CEO, Thomas Stemberg, reacted with astonishment, and replied, "If I were a betting man, I would say this matter is likely to wind up in litigation."[3]

For OfficeMax, the on-again, off-again merger created some uncertainty. One issue was whether the company would be able to acquire the 63 stores Staples offered it. The

This case was developed from published sources. Copyright © 1997. All rights reserved to the authors and to the North American Case Research Association.

[1]"Staples/Office Depot Merger: The Timing Is Right," *Discount Store News,* September 16, 1996, p. 131.

[2]Chris Reidy, "FTC Seen Endorsing Staples Buy," *Boston Globe,* April 3, 1997, p. D1.

[3]Aaron Zitner and Chris Reidy, "Staples' $4 Billion Merger Rejected," *Boston Globe,* April 5, 1997, p. A4.

major issue, however, was the nature of future competition in the office supply industry. Whether or not its merger with Office Depot was allowed to occur, Staples had made it clear that it would no longer settle for the number two spot in the industry. How would this even more aggressive competitor affect OfficeMax's ability to continue its rapid, and finally profitable, growth?

THE COMPETITIVE STRUCTURE OF THE OFFICE SUPPLY INDUSTRY

One of the key points of debate between Staples and the FTC concerned the size of the office supply industry. If the industry's annual sales were $185 billion, as Staples argued, the combined Staples/Office Depot's $10 billion would represent only 5 percent of the market.[4] The FTC, on the other hand, argued that superstores such as Office Depot, Staples, and OfficeMax constituted a market of their own, with annual sales of $23 billion. In this more narrowly defined market, the Staples/Office Depot combination would have 44 percent of the market. Superstores were much more focused than traditional discount retail chains. A superstore carried a wide variety of merchandise in one category such as toys (Toys "R" Us), books (Barnes & Noble), sports (Sports Authority), or office supplies. Due to purchasing power, the superstore chain could set prices equal to or lower than those of stores with diverse product/merchandise lines. The superstores' strategy of wide selection and low price was alleged to make it difficult for retailers with broad product lines and less selection within each line to compete, hence the superstores' nickname *category killers.*

"Office supplies" was not a clear-cut category. Products such as paper for printers and copiers, envelopes, notebooks, paper clips, and file folders are used in offices of all sizes. File cabinets, desks, lamps, computer tables, and other office furniture represented another product line. Computer software and accessories, and potentially computers themselves, were also used in modern offices. In addition, services such as custom printing (stationery, order forms, business cards, etc.) could be included as part of the office supply industry. Thus, the superstores were in competition not only with the mom-and-pop office supply stores serving a local community but also with any store selling office supplies, including Wal-Mart and warehouse stores such as Price/Costco or Sam's Warehouse Clubs. Furniture stores sold desks, sofas, and cabinets appropriate for office use. Entire chains, such as ComputerTown, were devoted to computers, accessories, and software. Kinko's and Sir Speedy advertised themselves as solving office problems by providing comprehensive photocopying services. All three superstore companies carried a full line of office supplies, business machines, computer accessories, and office furniture, and offered some type of business services. See Exhibit 1 for a breakdown of U.S. manufacturers' shipments of office supplies to different resellers, from the annual survey for the Business Products Industry Association.[5]

Changes in the Office Supply Industry

Prior to the 1980s, most small businesses bought their typing paper, adding machine tape, and file folders from small, local office supply stores. Customers walking into such stores would see greeting cards, small gift items, and even toys or collectibles

---

[4]"Deal Places Staples Back at Top of Industry," *The Patriot Ledger* (Quincy, MA), September 5, 1996.
[5]"Superstores Swallow a Bigger Piece of the Pie," *Purchasing,* April 25, 1996, p. 86S7.

EXHIBIT 1	Percentage Breakdown of U.S. Domestic Manufacturers' Shipments of Office Supplies to Different Resellers, 1989-1994					
	1994	**1993**	**1992**	**1991**	**1990**	**1989**
Mass market	10.1%	10.9%	12.4%	7.6%	10.2%	10.4%
Warehouse clubs	4.3	4.1	4.0	4.0	4.0	3.5
Superstores	18.7	15.0	11.4	10.2	7.3	4.3
National wholesalers	15.6	18.4	18.2	19.2	17.3	18.3
Regional wholesalers	4.0	4.5	5.0	5.0	5.1	6.5
Total wholesalers	19.6	22.9	23.2	24.2	22.4	24.8
Mail order	3.4	4.5	4.7	4.3	4.6	4.4
Largest dealers	17.3	14.5	14.9	14.8	13.1	12.7
Large dealers	6.1	7.9	8.1	8.1	10.6	9.2
Total large dealers	23.4	22.4	23.0	22.9	23.7	21.9
Small/medium dealers	10.2	9.3	9.3	11.1	12.5	14.0
Direct and government	3.5	3.2	4.1	6.2	6.6	5.7
Other	6.8	7.7	7.9	9.5	8.7	11.0

Source: Business Products Industry Association.

(Smurfs or china figurines). On the shelves farther back would be posterboard, three-ring notebooks, and lined paper, as well as products aimed primarily at businesses. The store might also have a desk or window for ordering custom photocopying and printing, anything from a company's letterhead to engraved wedding invitations. The store might deliver orders to its larger customers, for whom it might also offer direct billing. Anyone wanting a desk or a file cabinet would need to go to a store specializing in office furniture, or place an order through a catalog. Business machines consisted of typewriters (by the 1970s, electric had replaced manual typewriters in the typical office) and adding machines; copiers were leased; and only a few companies and individuals had seen the possibilities in desktop computers.

By the 1990s, the industry had changed. Superstores purchased less than 1 percent of U.S. manufacturers' shipments of office supplies in 1986; this figure grew to 4.3 percent in 1989, to 11.4 percent in 1992, and to 18.7 percent in 1994. Office Depot led the industry, with 526 stores and $5.3 billion in sales in fiscal 1995, followed by Staples, with 574 stores and $3.1 billion in sales, and OfficeMax, with 564 stores and $2.5 billion in sales. Warehouse clubs, although accounting for only about 4 percent of sales, also targeted business customers by offering low prices for bulk purchases.[6]

The primary impact of these two new channels—superstores and warehouse clubs—was on small office supply retailers. One source estimated that the number of independent dealers nationwide had decreased from more than 12,000 to about 2,000.[7] Certainly, this trend was evident in many urban areas; in Indianapolis, for example, the number of independent office supply dealers fell from 15–20 in 1979 to 5 in 1996.

---

[6]Ibid.

[7]Dean Boyer, "Independent Office Supply Dealers Perfect Strategies," *Pierce County Business Examiner* (Tacoma, WA), October 28, 1996.

Competitive Strategies in Office Supplies

Both superstores and warehouse clubs offered customers low prices. This had the effect of lowering margins for everyone in the office supply industry, from 40 percent to 15 percent. Some of the independent retailers discovered that they were able to match prices with the superstores on most products. Brian Morford, owner of a small office supply company, explained: "Every discount store has loss leaders to bring in customers . . . We don't offer loss leaders, but we offer pretty much the same discounts otherwise. We feel that we're competitive."[8]

In order to remain competitive, independent stores adopted a variety of strategies. Many joined purchasing clubs or cooperatives, and some looked for close ties with key suppliers. Careful inventory management became important. This could take the form of just-in-time deliveries from suppliers or, more commonly, of eliminating items that turned over slowly. Some independent stores concentrated on products that the superstores did not carry, such as specialized paper-handling equipment or computer peripherals. Some focused on service to their customers, particularly small businesses, providing small lots and delivery services. Another approach was to increase, or add, more profitable lines of business, often greeting cards and gifts. Bob Franzen, co-owner of Coast Office Equipment Company in Olympia, Washington, summarized his strategy for survival: "What we have left is a company that does what it does well and stays out of areas we don't."[9]

Disposable supplies and business forms made up less than half of industry sales. The Business Products Industry Association estimated 1994 sales of supplies at $24.4 billion, and of business forms at $6.9 billion.[10] However, a typical office superstore sold not only these products but also computers, software, business machines (such as calculators, copiers and fax machines), and furniture. This also put the superstore in competition with a variety of other specialized retailers, some of them also superstores. Computers and computer accessories, for example, were available from specialized chains as well as electronic superstores such as Circuit City, and from warehouse stores and even Wal-Mart. There were also catalogs devoted to software and peripherals; and Dell and Gateway, among others, offered computers by phone. Estimated sales of microcomputers and peripherals amounted to $42.8 billion in 1994, with an additional $8.0 billion in software. Desks, chairs, file cabinets, and other furniture for the modern office, with annual sales amounting to $8.5 billion, were also available from both furniture and specialty stores, as well as through catalogs. Sales of machines such as typewriters, calculators, copiers, phones, and fax equipment amounted to an additional $12.5 billion; these products were available from a variety of sources, including Service Merchandise and similar discount stores. Even drugstores and supermarkets sold school supplies, an important seasonal sales category.

Some companies specialized in contract sales to large businesses, operating without any retail operations. This was the strategy followed by U.S. Office Products Company, which had grown by acquisition from its first company in 1994 to more than 100 acquired contract stationers and total annual sales of $2.1 billion.[11] Some office products manufacturers, such as Boise Cascade, had their own office products divisions.

---

[8]Ibid.

[9]Ibid.

[10]All sales estimates in this paragraph are from "Superstores Swallow," p. 86S8.

[11]Peter Spiegel, "Supplies Surprise," *Forbes,* November 4, 1996, pp. 98, 100.

Most office supply stores contracted out orders for custom printing, but did offer copying services, putting them in competition with chains such as Kinko's and Sir Speedy.

New Developments in the Office Supply Industry

Two trends gaining in importance in the office supply industry were catalog sales and on-line shopping. Catalogs enabled shoppers to compare prices without leaving work. Michael Feuer, CEO of OfficeMax, pointed out, "Shoppers are much less patient than they were just a couple of years ago. They want a wide selection. Price is the ticket for admission."[12] OfficeMax and Staples both offered catalogs, as did a number of smaller companies. For example, the stores of W. B. Mason, a Boston regional supplier dating back to 1898, contained only office furniture, while the company's full line of supplies was available through its catalog. To compete, W. B. Mason promised overnight delivery within the region via its own fleet of trucks, and "the absolute lowest prices" on all its products. This combination of price and service helped W. B. Mason's sales grow from $30 million in 1993, the first year of the catalog, to $70 million in 1996.[13]

Electronic retail, although still relatively small, was seen as the next major growth area. Dan Sweeney, of IBM's Consulting Group, argued, "Who would have ever thought that you could sell jewelry on television? Or fashion apparel through the mail? I think electronic shopping is inevitable and will represent a significant share of retail activity."[14] Predictions on the number of Americans who would be connected to the Internet in the year 2000 ranged from 32.9 million to 50 million. On-line retail sales were estimated to be $6.9 billion or more.[15] OfficeMax was one of many retailers already developing Web sites and other sales tools, including on-line catalogs. While there were still concerns about security and payment, new technology would continue to make shopping on-line more common and convenient.

OFFICEMAX

Background

OfficeMax, founded in Cleveland, Ohio, in 1988, originally targeted small businesses. Initially it was financed by individuals and private venture capitalists. Within two years, it had attracted the attention of Kmart, which purchased 90 percent of the new company's stock during 1990 and 1991. Co-founder and CEO Michael Feuer described the acquisition as extremely valuable for OfficeMax: "Kmart was one of the best financial partners I ever had in my business career. They never interfered with our business strategy. We had a unique opportunity to build a new paradigm of doing business."[16] He felt that the freedom from reporting publicly to shareholders every quarter had enabled the company to invest and grow rapidly.[17] Sales grew at a compound annual rate of 141 percent in fiscal years 1990 through 1993. This was the result of both new-store openings and acquisitions such as that of the 96 BizMart superstores, purchased in March 1993. By late 1994, OfficeMax had 345 stores and sales of over $1.4 billion.

---

[12]Michael Feuer, "Bullish on the Internet," *Discount Merchandiser,* December 1996, p. 42.

[13]Chris Reidy, "A Question of Competition," *The Boston Globe,* May 23, 1997, pp. E1–2.

[14]Jennifer Pellet, "The Future of Electronic Retail," *Discount Merchandiser,* January 1996, p. 36.

[15]Ibid.

[16]Jay L. Johnson, "OfficeMax: Maximizing the Office Products Superstore," *Discount Merchandiser,* November 1995, p. 38.

[17]Ibid., p. 40.

EXHIBIT 2   OfficeMax Balance Sheet, 1993-1996 (in thousands of $)

	Fiscal Year Ending			
	1/27/96	1/21/95	1/22/94	1/23/93
Assets				
Cash	$ 365,863	$ 174,250	$ 31,744	$ 14,100
Receivables	27,039	28,021	25,211	11,000
Inventories	636,211	468,177	409,028	178,200
Other current assets	20,009	20,898	20,310	3,800
Total current assets	1,049,122	691,346	486,293	207,100
Property, plant, and equipment	256,171	178,884	138,696	52,400
Accumulated depreciation	75,795	46,674	22,897	6,000
Net property and equipment	180,376	132,210	115,799	46,400
Intangibles	343,134	352,548	361,976	193,900
Deposits and other assets	15,236	11,367	22,154	1,200
Total assets	$1,587,868	$1,257,467	$1,009,712	$448,600
Liabilities				
Accounts payable	$ 348,605	$ 331,161	$ 239,048	$119,300
Accrued expenses	156,306	120,105	133,668	57,200
Other current liabilities	44,802	27,197	NA	NA
Total current liabilities	549,713	479,463	372,716	176,500
Other long-term liabilities	47,266	29,428	28,486	13,900
Total liabilities	596,979	508,891	401,202	190,400
Common stock net	850,557	736,551	187,198	187,200
Capital surplus	NA	NA	410,307	70,900
Retained earnings	141,814	16,051	11,005	100
Other equities	(1,482)	(4,026)	NA	NA
Shareholder equity	990,889	748,576	608,510	258,200
Total liabilities and net worth	$1,587,868	$1,257,467	$1,009,712	$448,600

The company also had a history of losses, not earning its first profit until fiscal year 1994. In November 1994, as part of a program to refocus on its core discount store business, Kmart sold 75 percent of its OfficeMax stock, spinning off the office supply chain as an independent company. As part of the arrangement, Kmart freed OfficeMax from all its debt, and provided a pool of cash. The following July, Kmart sold the rest of its OfficeMax stock; OfficeMax received an additional $110 million from this sale, which was used to fund further expansion.

During the 1995 fiscal year, which ended in January 1996, OfficeMax reached $2.54 billion in net sales and $125 million in net income, achieving its goals despite bad weather over much of the United States and a federal government shutdown in January, affecting in particular sales to small businesses.[18] (See Exhibits 2 and 3 for financial statements.) Sales from ongoing operations earned a profit of $56.6 million, with the remainder coming from the sale of the company's stock in Corporate Express, a contract stationery supplier. OfficeMax also opened 80 new superstores, a variety of

---

[18]"President's Letter," OfficeMax annual report, 1996.

EXHIBIT 3 OfficeMax Income Statement, 1993-1996 (in thousands of $)

	Fiscal Year Ending			
	1/27/96	1/21/95	1/22/94	1/23/93
Net sales	$2,542,513	$1,841,212	$1,421,794	$528,205
Cost of goods	1,970,536	1,422,400	1,108,992	411,429
Gross profit	571,977	418,812	312,802	116,776
Selling, general, and administrative expenses	476,310	353,755	284,146	111,742
Income before depreciation and amortization	$ 95,667	$ 65,057	$ 28,656	$ 5,034
Nonoperating income	117,976	(8,725)	(8,734)	(3,874)
Income before taxes	213,643	56,332	19,922	1,160
Provision for income taxes	87,880	25,975	9,073	1,881
Net income before extraordinary items	125,763	30,357	10,849	(721)
Outstanding shares	82,331	76,418	50,945	23,381

stores with more specialized formats, and launched its first national advertising campaign. Some store sales increased 16.7 percent during the year. The company had also focused on internal issues, including increased efficiency at existing stores and improved productivity of new stores, as well as improved inventory turnover.

Aggressive growth continued during 1996 and into 1997. By September 1996, when the Staples/Office Depot merger was announced, OfficeMax had 425 stores and projected revenues for the 1996 fiscal year of $3.3 billion. The company planned to open a total of 160 superstores in 1996 and 1997, in addition to expanding the number of catalog/delivery centers, CopyMax and mini-CopyMax stores, and FurnitureMax office furniture outlets. Two stores were scheduled to open in Mexico City, and the company planned to expand into Asia. OfficeMax continued to experiment with new formats, including BatteryMax, and new technologies, including offering its full product line via an on-line catalog.

Management

"A lot has changed over the past eight years, but the basis on which we operate has not—customer service, great values, exciting store formats. These are the simple secrets to our success and our success lies with effective execution at every level of the business, every day of the week," reported Feuer in his 1996 "President's Letter" to OfficeMax shareholders.[19] Feuer described the company's objective as "to layer-in growth initiatives well into the turn of the century, creating business vehicles that will contribute significant comparable store sales gains year after year . . . The winners during the balance of this century will be the low-cost providers with the strongest balance sheets."[20]

One important thrust of OfficeMax's activities was to improve operating efficiencies and, consequently, profitability. While still owned by Kmart, the company had invested heavily in computer systems. All district and regional managers, as well as top management, had access to a large pool of information, including data for specific

[19]Ibid.
[20]Ibid.

stores and product lines. As a result, the company was able to reduce costs "because [it had] fewer people using better technologies to perform fewer manual chores."[21] Management believed that the company's general and administrative expenses were the lowest in the industry, estimating OfficeMax's at 1.86 percent, compared with competitors' 3 percent.

In order to further reduce inventory costs, the company had developed its own logistics system. This was based on the five ThruMax cross-docking facilities, opened in 1995. These took in bulk shipments from suppliers and broke them down into quantities usable by individual stores or distribution centers (hence the term *cross-docking,* as the merchandise was transferred from one loading dock to another).

Top executives met first thing every morning, and there were regular Saturday-morning executive meetings where everyone present talked about what he or she had done during the week. This was part of the culture, which Feuer described as one that continually found a way to solve problems: "Our philosophy is very simple. Get exceedingly bright, capable people. Hold them accountable. Give them the authority to do their job. Then keep careful track of them, so no one stumbles."[22] Between the rapid growth and top management's high expectations, managers could easily work 11 or 12 hours a day, six or more days a week.

Retail Operations

By 1997, the company had developed five basic formats and was experimenting with several more. The mainstay was the OfficeMax superstore, now found nationwide. The appearance and floor plans of OfficeMax stores had changed several times over the company's eight-year history. Currently, the older stores were being remodeled, many for the second or third time, to have wider aisles and a better sight line, making it easier for customers to find merchandise on their own, or to find employees for assistance. The company continued to open stores in new markets, entering locations such as central California with multiple stores and other, smaller markets with only one.

In addition to carrying a limited amount of office furniture in its superstores, and a more extensive line in its catalog, OfficeMax opened its first 22 FurnitureMax stores in 1995, and added another 65 in 1996. These stores targeted customers ranging from home offices to larger companies. They allowed customers to browse among and compare a variety of chairs, desks, conference tables, filing systems, and other furniture.

Another new concept launched in 1995 was CopyMax, a center within the superstore offering digital printing. Begun with only eight units, CopyMax appeared so successful that the company had begun adding mini-CopyMax units to its superstores during remodeling. This combination was known as a BiMax store. The company also had begun building TriMax stores, incorporating both a CopyMax or mini-CopyMax and a FurnitureMax under the same 40,000-square-foot roof within OfficeMax superstore. Many of the company's new stores were being constructed in the TriMax format.

OfficeMax's product line was also available through a catalog. Customers could place an order at the store for items that were not in stock, or could order direct from one of the three catalog call centers. Items were then delivered from one of 15 delivery centers nationwide.

---

[21]Johnson, "OfficeMax," p. 38.

[22]Ibid., p. 40.

Areas for Expansion

Although not yet profitable, the CopyMax stores within the superstores had proven interesting enough that the company planned to experiment with freestanding CopyMax stores, starting with three in Cleveland, its headquarters city. This could lead to further expansion into other settings, such as banks and office buildings. Another store-within-a-superstore experiment was BatteryMax, which was first opened in mid-1996.

Late in 1996, the company opened its first two stores in Mexico City. These were the first results of a joint venture with Grupo Oprimax, a Mexican company. In December, OfficeMax announced that it had formed a joint venture with Jusco Co. Ltd., a prominent retail company headquartered in Tokyo, to open 200 OfficeMax stores in Japan. This agreement was structured so that OfficeMax would initially own only 19.9 percent of the joint venture, with the possibility of increasing its stake to 50 percent whenever it wanted.[23] This kept OfficeMax below the 20 percent threshold at which generally accepted accounting procedures would require the company to include the venture, including its start-up costs and losses, as part of OfficeMax's consolidated financial statements, essentially allowing the company to treat the venture as an investment during its early stages.[24] The OfficeMax/Jusco partnership enabled the companies to also explore other locations throughout Asia. Competitor Staples' international operations were concentrated in Europe, where it was expanding its holdings of companies in the United Kingdom and in Germany.

A major area for growth was provided by OfficeMax's on-line connections. The company was the only one of the office supply superstores to have sites on all major computer service providers, including America Online and the Microsoft network. Several of these deals were written to prohibit competitors from being part of the service's on-line shopping. OfficeMax was also accessible via the Internet. These sites included information about the company, a service to help customers locate the nearest store, information about customer service, and even a complete catalog. Customers could order electronically, with the order being routed to the nearest delivery center for overnight delivery. This enabled OfficeMax to reach customers in areas where there was not yet an OfficeMax store, and ultimately to locate potential new retail store locations.[25] Other potential applications for the on-line site included assistance with editorial and office problems, including tips on how to do a presentation—with a "by the way, we have all these items, click here if you'd like to buy them from us now," at the end of the help session.[26]

One future idea, code-named CyberMax, was an electronic OfficeMax kiosk, to be located in the lobbies of banks, office buildings, even post offices and airports. These kiosks could provide CopyMax services and could also potentially allow a customer to plug in her laptop computer and print, or even go on-line to order products from the catalog.[27]

OfficeMax was continuing to experiment with its merchandise mix. The company expected sales of computers to continue to grow as a percentage of sales; unfortunately, computers carried a lower margin than many of the company's other products.

---

[23]Laura Liebeck, "Staples, OfficeMax Look Abroad," *Discount Store News,* January 6, 1997, p. 88.

[24]Johnson, "OfficeMax," p. 37.

[25]Jennifer Pellet, " 'OfficeMax Is Everywhere!,' " *Discount Merchandiser,* January 1996, p. 40.

[26]Pellet, "The Future of Electronic Retail," p. 37.

[27]Johnson, "OfficeMax," pp. 37–38.

One evolving product line was known as TechMax.[28] This would boost the stores' range of copiers, fax machines, cellular phones, electronic organizers, and other such "productivity tools" increasingly being demanded by individuals as well as businesses of all sizes.

The company was also beginning to move into the business contract stationery market. OfficeMax had first entered this market in 1993, when it purchased 19 percent of the stock in Corporate Express and Feuer took a seat on Corporate Express's board. Although OfficeMax increased its investment to 20 percent in 1994, the company quickly realized that the contract stationer business was similar to its own delivery business: "Not only does our catalog and delivery center business perform the same functions as a contract stationer, OfficeMax was, in reality, already providing merchandise to larger corporate customers that were being served by contract stationers."[29] In September 1995, the company sold its shares of Corporate Express for an estimated $200 million, although the two companies continued to participate in joint buying and marketing programs. OfficeMax then developed its own version of a contract stationer, OfficeMax Corporate Direct, targeting medium-sized firms with 100–200 employees.

OFFICEMAX AND THE MERGER

Looking to the future, OfficeMax saw both threats and opportunities. "We can go into new markets in a pre-emptive strike," said Feuer.[30] Office Depot and Staples had reduced their expansion plans in order to allow time to digest the merger and to rationalize the combined network of stores. The uncertainties provided by the long FTC investigation process had allowed OfficeMax additional time to carry out its 1996 and 1997 plans, relatively unopposed. However, the threat of a combined Staples/Office Depot was formidable, in penetration and number of stores, in marketing, and in buying power. Even if the merger was not allowed to take place, Staples had effectively announced that it was intent on future aggressive growth. For OfficeMax, the future appeared to be even more competitive than the past.

(OfficeMax's Web address is www.officemax.com.)

---

[28]Feuer, "Bullish on the Internet," p. 42.

[29]"President's Letter."

[30]Paulette Thomas, "OfficeMax Sees Opportunity in Plight," *The Wall Street Journal,* September 1996.

COMPETITION IN THE VIDEO GAME INDUSTRY

Romuald A. Stone, *Keller Graduate School of Management*

Sean McGowan, *Gerard Klauer Mattison & Co., Inc.*

Video and computer games emerged as a great, unforeseen by-product of the electronic age. Advancing chip technology made it possible to put players in the midst of all kinds of action-filled situations. Spurred by increasing processing speeds and graphics and audio capabilities, video game developers created ever more sophisticated, multi-featured games during the 1990s that allowed players to pilot an advanced star fighter to defend against all manner of strange enemies, command a high-tech police helicopter on a series of missions in a futuristic city landscape, fly an exotic jet fighter in combat against enemy aircraft, enter mystical worlds to untangle ancient webs of treachery and deceit, and race against well-known International Grand Prix drivers under realistic track conditions.

The video game industry was a feast-or-famine business. After several years of buoyant growth and profitability, retail sales of video games plummeted to less than $100 million in 1985, only to rebound to record levels in the 1990s. In 1998, video games sales reached $6 billion in the United States alone and totaled well over $10 billion worldwide.

From 1985 to 1994, Nintendo and Sega dominated the industry worldwide, with combined market shares of around 90 percent. The two rivals sparred periodically in an escalating battle for market leadership characterized by industry observers as the "video game wars." Competitive rivalry took on a new dimension in 1995 as "next-generation" game players were released worldwide by Nintendo, Sega, and other competitors, particularly Sony. The early entries included Philips Electronics' CD-I player, 3DO's Interactive Multiplayer, Atari's Jaguar, and Sega's Saturn. Sony followed with its PlayStation, and Nintendo with its Ultra 64 game console. New competitors were challenged to secure adequate retail shelf space for their players and games, and to line up software developers to create games for their particular hardware configuration—games

> *Once upon a time (1988, to be exact), Nintendo sat alone atop the mountain, master of its domain. Then came Sega, scraping and clawing up the slope. The two stood precariously together— plumber versus hedgehog—each trying to elbow the other off the peak (that was 1995). New video game challengers began approaching on all sides, each promising a higher level of technology. Suddenly, the game was wide open again. Surprisingly Nintendo and Sega both lost their grip and got crushed by Sony. Today Sony surveys the competitive landscape from its perch atop the video game industry, taking on all comers. The video game wars continue.*

created for one maker's game player could not be played on a rival's game player because of technical incompatibility. Thus, a buyer of a Nintendo system could play only Nintendo games and a buyer of a Sony PlayStation could play only Sony games. The incompatibility of the different game players, coupled with limited retail shelf space, created a fierce battle for market share among the video game rivals. Most retailers opted to stock only two or three brands of video games—usually those brands whose games proved to be most popular among consumers and thereby generated the greatest sales.

The rapidly growing base of home computers equipped with high-tech entertainment options and CD-ROMs further added fuel to the competitive fire during the mid-1990s. Nintendo and Sega, the longtime industry leaders, found themselves in a fierce battle with Sony, and small-share competitors scrambled to generate enough sales to survive. The changes in technology resulted in a huge industry shakeout. Going into 1998, Sony emerged as the undisputed leader, with 70 percent of the U.S. market; Nintendo held 26 percent and Sega only 4 percent. No other makers were a factor in the U.S. market.

INDUSTRY BACKGROUND[1]

The world's first home video game system was the Odyssey, released by Magnavox in 1972. The Odyssey required that plastic overlays be attached to the consumer's television set. Despite an extensive marketing campaign by Magnavox, the Odyssey sold poorly and died after a year on the market. It took a successful arcade game to build demand for the first home video game systems. In 1972, Nolan Bushnell created the first electronic arcade video game, Pong, and, with $500, he and a friend formed Atari. A simple coin-operated table-tennis game, Pong caught on in bars and arcades. The success of Pong brought numerous imitators into the newly emerging industry. By 1973, 90 percent of all video game machines in arcades were Pong clones, manufactured by 25 competitors of Atari. Home versions of arcade machines quickly followed.

In 1976, Fairfield Camera & Instrument released Channel F, the first home video game system to accept interchangeable cartridges. Previously, home video game systems had consisted of only a limited number of preprogrammed games; once a player tired of those games, the systems were relegated to a closet. With interchangeable cartridges the software became separated from the hardware. By buying a new cartridge, a video game enthusiast could make ongoing use of the game system and build an entertaining video game library.

Atari's Nolan Bushnell believed that interchangeable cartridges were the wave of the future. Two months after the release of Channel F, he sold Atari to Warner Communications for $27 million in order to gain access to the investment capital to release a new game system. Warner's chairman and CEO, Steven Ross, believed in the revolutionary potential of video games and was willing to invest in Warner's newly acquired video game subsidiary. In 1977, Warner's Atari division released its video computer system (VCS), or 2600 home system. Over the next few years, Atari established the 2600 as the market's dominant video game system. Industry growth got a booster shot with the introduction in arcades of Atari's Space Invaders in 1979 and Pac-Man in 1981. Atari was the first company to license an arcade game for a home

---

[1]Based on information in Standard & Poor's *Industry Surveys* (Toys), 1991, pp. L46–47, and DFC Intelligence Research, *The U.S. Market for Video Games and Interactive Electronic Entertainment* (San Diego, 1995).

system when it licensed Space Invaders for the 2600. The 1980s release of Space Invaders on the 2600 was such a hit that sales doubled and Atari became the fastest-growing company in the history of American business. Atari followed with the equally successful home version of Pac-Man in 1982. As the undisputed industry leader through 1982, Atari consistently maintained a 70 to 80 percent share of the home video game market.

Video Games in the 1980s

Competitive rivalry in video games intensified in 1982; 350 new game titles were released that year as the number of competitors grew rapidly. Mattel had entered the industry with its Intellivision system in late 1979, and Coleco made a splash in early 1983 by introducing ColecoVision (both second-generation systems with improved graphics). Other entrants included Milton Bradley (its Vectrex system flopped) and a host of unlikely competitors, including subsidiaries of cereal makers Quaker Oats and General Mills.[2] In December 1981 there was only one manufacturer of Atari-compatible cartridges; a year later there were more than 20. The market quickly became oversupplied, forcing software manufacturers with slow-selling game titles to liquidate their inventories at closeout prices throughout 1983 and into 1984. To compound the difficulties, consumer interest in video games fell off sharply. Sales were so bad that Atari ultimately buried truckloads of unsold video game cartridges in the Arizona desert, forcing parent Warner Communications to report a $539 million loss on its consumer electronics business in 1983.

In 1984 Warner Communications and Mattel were driven to the brink of bankruptcy by the losses of their video game subsidiaries. Warner sold its Atari division that year, and in 1985 both Mattel and Coleco announced they were exiting the video game business. Industry sales of video games collapsed to $100 million in 1985, down from a high of $3 billion in 1982.

Analysts predicted the end of the video game industry, but Nintendo proved observers wrong when it introduced its Nintendo Entertainment System (NES) in New York in the fall of 1985. Encouraged by the earlier success of its Famicom game system in Japan, Nintendo ignored analysts who felt that the video game business was a fad whose time had passed. In 1986, the company sold 1.1 million NES units, largely on the popularity of Super Mario Brothers, a game that eventually sold 40 million copies. Sales of game systems and game cartridges once again took off. By 1988, Nintendo had an 80 percent market share of the $2.3 billion U.S. video game industry.

However, Nintendo learned a valuable lesson from Atari's failure: It was important to control the supply of game cartridges to ensure quality and prevent fierce price competition. To this end, Nintendo required its game developers to follow strict rules regarding the creation and release of new games for its NES game players. Prior to release, Nintendo had to approve the content of a game. In addition, the agreement required licensees to order games from Nintendo. The licensee would develop a game and then place an order with Nintendo, which became the sole manufacturer of cartridges. The minimum order was for 10,000 cartridges, paid in advance. Licensees were charged about twice the cost of manufacturing. This included a royalty to Nintendo but did not include distribution and marketing costs. Nintendo made money whether or not the game sold. Licensees were also limited to developing five NES

---

[2]S. P. Schnaars, *Managing Imitation Strategies* (New York: Simon & Schuster, 1994).

games a year and could not release an NES game on a competing system for a period of two years.[3]

But Nintendo did more than just manage cartridge supplies and new games for its systems. Its strategy involved establishing the strongest brand name in the industry. The Official Nintendo Seal of Quality was prominently displayed on all its products and became familiar to children throughout America. Nintendo also provided "game counselors"—video game experts available to players by phone—which helped maintain customer loyalty. In 1993, Nintendo's game counselors handled 8 million phone calls and letters, with cumulative contacts surpassing the 30-million mark.[4]

Sega's Emergence as an Industry Leader. Sega, which got its start in video games in Japan, entered the U.S. video game market in 1986 with its 8-bit Master System. Although the system was generally considered to have better graphics than Nintendo's, it achieved only a 15 percent market share—stymied largely by Nintendo's high level of brand awareness and more extensive library of games. In addition, Nintendo's sales volume gave the company the margins to fund an aggressive program of game introductions and advertising that Sega, with its limited sales, couldn't match. Sega, however, remained committed to the U.S. market and, in late 1989, introduced its 16-bit Genesis system. While sales of Genesis were respectable, Nintendo remained the dominant player, with a market share of approximately 85 percent, despite the fact that it was competing with the older technology contained in its 8-bit system.[5]

Video Games in the 1990s

In the early 1990s, Nintendo lost its lock on the video game market due to complacency and slowness in reacting to Sega's competitive moves. Nintendo waited 18 months to introduce a 16-bit system to compete with Sega's new Genesis player, believing that a new, more advanced system would undercut the still healthy sales of its 8-bit NES system.[6] By the time Nintendo did release its 16-bit Super NES player, Sega had released even more Genesis games, including the popular Sonic the Hedgehog. In addition, Nintendo's high licensing fees alienated retailers and software developers; Sega's licensing fees were lower. Finally, Nintendo's effort to maintain enthusiasm for its games by limiting supply backfired when retailers lost sales and began looking for other suppliers. Sega also targeted a broader market than Nintendo, focusing on adults as well as teenagers. Its marketing included a take-no-prisoners advertising campaign with TV ads that disparaged Nintendo as a system for ninnies.[7]

By the early 1990s, Sega's Genesis had captured a competitive, if not commanding, market share for 16-bit systems, a small but growing segment of the overall market. Sega's mid-1992 decision to offer its lightning-fast Sonic the Hedgehog game for free with the customer's purchase of the company's 16-bit Genesis system challenged Nintendo's position. When Sega introduced a CD-ROM attachment for its Genesis machine in November 1992, the company gained further momentum. Sega's strength

---

[3]DFC Intelligence Research, *The U.S. Market for Video Games.*

[4]Standard & Poor's *Industry Surveys* (Toys), 1993, p. L.

[5]Ibid.

[6]J. Carlton, "Video Games Sell in Record Numbers This Christmas," *The Wall Street Journal,* December 20, 1993, p. B3.

[7]Ibid.

in the 16-bit market continued to build throughout 1993, giving it a 51 percent share and 16-bit segment leadership by year-end. By the end of fiscal year 1994, Sega had sold over 17 million Genesis players, compared to Nintendo's over 18 million Super NES system players. Despite Genesis's two-year head start over Super NES, the two systems split the U.S. market fairly evenly during 1992–1996 period. Nintendo, however, held a commanding market position over Sega in the Japanese video game market (roughly 90 percent to 10 percent). Nintendo was also the market leader in Europe, but Sega systems sold well in many European countries, giving Sega a solid second-place standing in that geographic market. Poor inventory management worldwide and delays in launching a new product, Saturn, left Sega vulnerable to Sony's entry into the market in 1994.

Sony's Rapid Climb to Market Leadership in the Mid-1990s.   Sony entered the video game business in the fall of 1994 with the launch of its PlayStation in Japan. Sony had been developing PlayStation for several years; indeed, at one point, Sony and Nintendo had decided to jointly introduce a CD-ROM-based game system, but could not agree on several important terms. Sega launched its Saturn in Japan at the same time, and both Saturn and PlayStation debuted in the United States in 1995. Saturn was launched in May, but supplies were limited and prices were high ($400 at retail). PlayStation's launch was in September; its technology was better, and the launch was supported with a number of high-quality game titles that Sony had developed in-house and in conjunction with third-party game developers. Nintendo's N-64 was launched in Japan in May 1996, and in the United States in September 1996; a 64-bit processor powered its system.

Both Sony's PlayStation and Sega's Saturn used a 32-bit processor as the heart of the machine and played games stored on CD-ROMs. Despite Sega's solid reputation among video game consumers and its well-known brands (Sega stopped marketing the Saturn in the United States in the spring of 1997), Sony had won the battle for market leadership in most countries. Sony had the leading market share in Japan, the United States, and Europe, resulting from the strength of its brand name, its superior technology and its willingness to compete on price. In addition, Sony was successful at convincing third-party developers of video games to create games for the PlayStation system, often offering financial incentives to developers for exclusively developing games for Sony's system.

Overall, combined sales of PlayStation and Nintendo's N-64 more than doubled in 1997, rising to about $4.2 billion and driving industry growth of over 50 percent to $5.3 billion (see Exhibit 1). The projected installed bases of 9.1 million PlayStation units and 6.6 million N-64 units were expected to generate $3.6 billion in software sales in 1998 (see Exhibit 2). Industry sales were projected to exceed $6 billion in 1998.

Video game hardware and software systems were selling strongly in Japan and Europe in early 1998. As shown in Exhibit 3, sales of 32- and 64-bit systems had been growing rapidly, creating a large installed base and increasing software demand. The total installed base in Japan rose over 60 percent, to 18 million units, in 1997, while the relatively smaller European base grew to an estimated 6.9 million units.

In Europe, Sony, Nintendo, and Sega all launched their new 64-bit systems about the same time in the spring of 1997. So far, Sony's sales had far exceeded those of the other two systems, especially in the United Kingdom, where PlayStation was trouncing N-64. N-64 sales were expected to accelerate as more N-64 games were introduced during 1998.

EXHIBIT 1　Dedicated Consoles Hardware and Software Retail Sales Estimates, 1990–2000 (millions)

By Company	1990	1991	1992	1993	1994	1995	1996	1997	1998	1999	2000
Nintendo											
NES	$2,904	$1,833	$ 720	$ 370	$ 102	$ 34	$ 15	—	—	—	—
SNES	—	560	1,733	1,890	1,471	823	514	$ 243	$ 137	$ 20	$ 20
Game Boy	491	735	770	513	375	270	193	256	195	175	110
Virtual Boy	—	—	—	—	—	24	8	27	0	0	0
N64	—	—	—	—	—	—	498	1,690	2,550	3,105	2,100
Sega											
Genesis	280	586	1,090	1,706	1,490	719	294	180	0	0	0
Game Gear	—	91	162	219	318	135	77	34	13	0	0
Sega CD	—	—	61	232	215	30	0	—	—	—	—
32-X	—	—	—	—	107	63	0	—	—	—	—
Saturn	—	—	—	—	—	140	368	311	148	0	0
Nomad	—	—	—	—	—	9	9	0	0	0	0
Atari											
Lynx	32	40	32	13	3	—	—	—	—	—	—
Jaguar	—	—	—	7	64	52	0	0	0	0	0
Jaguar CD	—	—	—	—	—	0	0	0	0	0	0
3DO-based	—	—	—	29	238	252	24	0	50	50	42
Sony PlayStation	—	—	—	—	—	375	1,254	2,525	2,950	2,730	1,925
Phillips CD-I	—	—	49	78	64	54	138	21	0	0	0
Total hardware and software	$3,707	$3,845	$4,616	$5,057	$4,444	$2,978	$3,391	$5,287	$6,042	$6,080	$4,197
By Platform											
8-bit	$2,904	$1,833	$ 720	$ 370	$ 102	$ 34	$ 15	—	—	—	—
Portable	523	866	964	745	695	414	279	290	208	175	110
16-bit	280	1,146	2,884	3,828	3,175	1,571	808	423	137	20	20
32/64-bit	—	—	49	115	472	959	2,290	4,574	5,698	5,885	4,067
Total hardware and software sales	$3,707	$3,845	$4,616	$5,057	$4,444	$2,978	$3,391	$5,287	$6,042	$6,080	$4,197
Growth											
8-bit	—	(37%)	(61%)	(49%)	(72%)	(67%)	(56%)	(100%)	N.M.	N.M.	N.M.
Portable	—	66	11	(23)	(7)	(41)	(33)	4	(28%)	(16%)	(37%)
16-bit	—	309	152	33	(17)	(51)	(49)	(48)	(68%)	(85%)	0)
32/64-bit	—	—	—	134	312	103	139	100	25	3	(31)
Total	—	4%	20%	10%	(12%)	(33%)	14%	56%	14%	1 %	(31%)
Total hardware	$1,150	$1,441	$1,854	$1,891	$1,529	$1,027	$1,458	$2,297	$2,173	$1,355	$ 770
Total software	2,557	2,404	2,763	3,166	2,915	1,951	1,933	2,989	3,870	4,725	3,427
Total hardware and software	$3,707	$3,845	$4,616	$5,057	$4,444	$2,978	$3,391	$5,287	$6,042	$6,080	$4,197
Growth											
Total hardware	n.a.	25%	29%	2%	(19%)	(33%)	42%	58%	(5%)	(38%)	(43%)
Total software	n.a.	(6%)	15%	15%	(8%)	(33%)	(1%)	55%	29%	22%	(27%)
Total hardware and software	n.a.	4%	20%	10%	(12%)	(33%)	14%	56%	14%	1 %	(31%)
Sales Composition											
Hardware	31%	37%	40%	37%	34%	34%	43%	43%	36%	22%	18%
Software	69	63	60	63	66	66	57	57	64	78	82
Total	100%	100%	100%	100%	100%	100%	100%	100%	100%	100%	100%

EXHIBIT 2 Actual and Projected U.S. Sales of Hardware and Software for Sony's PlayStation and Nintendo's N-64 Video Game Systems, 1995–2000 (In millions of dollars)

	1995	1996	1997	1998	1999	2000
PlayStation						
Hardware	$210	$ 504	$1,020	$1,050	$ 630	$ 350
Hardware growth rate	—	140%	102%	3%	(40%)	(44%)
Software	$165	$ 750	$1,505	$1,900	$2,100	$1,575
Software growth rate	—	355%	101%	26%	11%	(25%)
Total PlayStation sales	$375	$1,254	$2,525	$2,950	$2,730	$1,925
Total PlayStation growth rate	—	234%	101%	17%	(7%)	(29%)
N-64						
Hardware	—	$ 330	$ 850	$ 900	$ 630	$ 350
Hardware growth rate	—	—	157%	6%	(30%)	(44%)
Software	—	$ 168	$ 840	$1,650	$2,475	$1,750
Software growth rate	—	—	400%	96%	50%	(29%)
Total N-64 sales	—	$ 498	$1,690	$2,660	$3,106	$2,100
Total N-64 growth rate	—	—	239%	51%	22%	(32%)
Total PlayStation/N-64						
Hardware	$210	$ 834	$1,870	$1,950	$1,260	$ 700
Hardware growth rate	—	297.3%	124.1%	4.3%	(35.4%)	(44.4%)
Software	$165	$ 918	$2,345	$3,550	$4,575	$3,325
Software growth rate	—	456.4%	155.4%	51.4%	28.9%	(27.3%)
Total PlayStation/N-64 sales	$375	$1,752	$4,215	$5,500	$5,835	$4,025
Total PlayStation/ N-64 growth rate	—	367.3%	140.5%	30.5%	6.1%	(31.0%)

Source: Gerard Klauer Mattison & Co., Inc., estimates and corporate reports.

EXHIBIT 3 Actual and Estimated Worldwide Sales of 32- and 64-Bit Hardware Systems, 1994–2000 (In millions of units)

	1994	1995	1996	1997	1998	1999	2000
United States	—	1.0	4.8	11.8	13.5	9.0	5.0
Europe	—	0.6	1.9	4.4	6.4	6.4	5.0
Japan	0.8	3.6	6.6	7.0	6.9	6.6	5.0
Rest of world	0.0	0.3	0.8	1.5	1.9	2.0	2.0
Total	0.8	5.4	14.1	24.7	28.7	23.9	17.0
Cumulative Installed Base							
United States	—	1.0	5.8	17.6	31.1	40.1	45.1
Europe	—	0.6	2.4	6.9	13.2	19.6	24.6
Japan	0.8	4.4	11.0	18.0	24.9	31.4	36.4
Rest of world	0.0	0.3	1.1	2.6	4.6	6.6	8.6
Total	0.8	6.2	20.3	45.0	73.7	97.6	114.6

Source: International Development Group supplied data for regions except United States. Estimates for U.S. market and all estimates for the year 2000 are from Gerard Klauer Mattison & Co., Inc.

Beyond 2000: Anticipated Moves of the Three Industry Leaders

Industry analysts expected the current generation of video game systems to be replaced periodically by more advanced hardware. Although software developers had probably not yet fully exploited all the power of the 32-bit and 64-bit chips in the PlayStation and N-64, respectively, Sony and Nintendo were working on the next generation. So was Sega, whose future as a video game hardware maker depended on its ability to sell a successful new system against Sony and Nintendo.

Sony's Plans. Sony management was quiet about plans for introducing its next hardware system, referred to as PlayStation II among publishers. Sony did not want to shift to the next generation too quickly, preferring to fully exploit the PlayStation I's potential first. It was a delicate balancing act, however; Sony did not want to repeat the mistake that the small company 3DO had made in announcing its 64-bit system (the M-2) too soon after its 32-bit Multiplayer launch, which prompted retailers and consumers to delay hardware purchases. Nor did Sony want to repeat Nintendo's mistake of waiting too long to launch the Super NES, which gave Sega the opportunity to launch Genesis 18 months sooner and thereby "steal" 50 percent of the market.

Sony's strategy for PlayStation was governed partly by its broader consumer electronics position. Sony was not just a video game maker. Although the PlayStation had become an important Sony brand, its sales accounted for only 10 percent of Sony's total revenues of over $55 billion. Some analysts speculated that Sony intended to use the PlayStation game technology as an integral part of a more versatile home entertainment machine, one that would play digital video disk (DVD) movies and music CDs and, perhaps, provide Internet access via the television. Launch of such a product (at a mass market price) did not appear imminent. Sony's president hinted at his company's strategic focus in the company's 1997 annual report:

> The Digital Dream Kids concept defines the future direction of our product development activities. We aim to fulfill the dreams of customers worldwide who are captivated by the potential of digital technology. To do so, we must strive to supply products that are unique and fun to use. This is why we at Sony have to become digital dream kids mesmerized by new technologies. All our hardware and software must be based on the premise of providing enjoyment.

Nintendo's Options. Nintendo's next piece of hardware was expected to be a magnetic storage device, alternately called an optical disk drive (ODD) and a bulky drive. This unit would connect to the N-64, allowing consumers to store certain games on writable disks, which would be useful for complex strategy games that were popular on PCs, but that required substantial memory storage. The prospects for this product were considered dubious by industry watchers. Only existing N-64 owners could use the unit, and add-ons and peripherals in the video game business did not have an encouraging history of selling well. Sega's Sega CD failed, as did its 32-X. The only peripherals that had sold well in the past were those that meaningfully improved the game experience, such as additional controllers for multi-player games (both the N-64 and PlayStation came with only one controller). Moreover, the retail price of the bulky drive was expected to be at least $100; thus, an N-64 with a bulky drive would cost about $250 (assuming no N-64 price cuts), an unattractive price relative to the competition. Also, it was not clear how big the demand was for games requiring memory storage well in excess of the regular memory cards accompanying standard N-64 and PlayStation systems.

Sega's Options.   Sega's low market share gave the company every reason to talk about its next-generation machine (code-named Dreamcast), even though it was not expected to be launched until 1999 at the earliest. Sega had stated that Dreamcast would debut in Japan for the 1998 holiday season; developers and publishers believed it would not be launched until 1999 and did not expect a sizable installed base before 2000. It was to Sega's advantage to persuade consumers not to buy a PlayStation or N-64 and wait until Dreamcast was out.

By all accounts, Dreamcast was expected to surpass Sony and Nintendo in technical capability because it would utilize the newest graphics, memory, and microprocessor chips. It was expected to include a speedy Hitachi microprocessor that operated at 360 million instructions per second—about equal to the fastest of Intel Corporation's Pentium II processors. It would also come with equipped with a 3-D graphics chip based on NEC's Power VR 3-D chips for PCs. Sega's Dreamcast player was expected to have four game controllers for as many as four players, with a small video screen on each controller so a player could, for example, pick a play in a sports game without revealing it to opposing players. Dreamcast was also expected to employ a high-speed CD-ROM drive.

Sega was expected to add multiplayer gaming over the Internet to its new system. Another plus in Sega's favor was its decision to use Microsoft's CE operating system for its game development to make it easier to attract game developers. The thinking was that developers who wrote PC games based on Windows 95/98 operating systems would have a much easier time adapting their games to Windows CE.[8] Some analysts predicted that it would cost Sega as much as $450 million to develop and launch its new system.

In addition to launching Dreamcast, Sega had to address the question of how to implement its video game strategy. Sega operated in several business segments— arcade game manufacturing, arcade operations, a joint venture with Dreamworks, and PC software. The company's consumer products division had posted operating losses of about $65 million over the 1995–1997 period, and the losses had spilled over into fiscal 1998 as well. The parent company had a solid hoard of cash and liquid investments of about $745 million (as of March 31, 1997), but this was down from nearly $1.5 billion a year earlier. Funding hardware launches was very expensive and could entail cash investments in new hardware development and marketing before generating sufficient revenues to realize a profit.

Combating the Industry's Cyclical Characteristics.   Sega's competitors were not expected to sit idly by and wait for Dreamcast to be launched. Nintendo had over $4 billion in cash and was completely focused on the video game business. Sony was seeking to create the next must-have consumer electronics device for the living room. There was another complicating factor—if industry rivals delayed launch of a new-generation game player past 2000, there was a risk that the industry would likely face sharp revenue declines in 2000–2002 from the market saturation of existing hardware and software. It typically took several years for new-generation systems to reach an installed base large enough to generate new interest and sales sufficient to combat the cyclical decline expected to begin in late 1999 or early 2000.

When the Interactive Digital Software Association surveyed gaming CEOs, asking them for their prediction on what the next-generation "dream machine" would look

---

[8]D. Takahashi, "Game Plan," *The Wall Street Journal*, June 15, 1998, p. R10.

like, three predicted the most popular next-generation game player would be an Internet machine based on the PC, six believed it would be a dedicated console, two said it would be an Internet machine attached to the TV, and nine said it would be a "black box" combining all of the functions related to entertainment in the living room.[9] One predicted that in the next 10 years video games would have a level of realism identical to that of film.

THE VIDEO GAME INDUSTRY CYCLE

The Atari 2600, launched in 1979, sold several hundred thousand units in its first year. Sales peaked in 1982, the product's fourth year on the market, after cumulative sales had reached about 15 million units. Software sales peaked the following year, and total retail sales plunged from over $2.2 billion in 1983 to about $120 million in 1985. Since then, the video game industry had seen the introduction of four new generations of technology: 8-bit systems (NES), 16-bit systems (Genesis and SNES), portables (Game Boy and Game Gear), and 32/64 bit systems (PlayStation, Saturn and N-64). The 8-bit and 16-bit generations followed Atari's pattern: Hardware sales peaked in the fourth full year of distribution, software sales peaked the following year, and total retail sales plunged in the sixth year. (This pattern excluded systems that never built any meaningful retail sales momentum, such as NEC's Turbo Grafx, 3DO's Multiplayer and Atari's Jaguar.) In each case, the installed base over the life cycle was higher than that of the previous generation: Atari 2600's installed based was 23 million homes; the Nintendo's NES shipped a total of 35 million units; and combined sales of Sega's Genesis and Nintendo's SNES reached 38 million homes.

The portable generation (Game Boy, launched in 1989, and Game Gear in 1991) followed a different pattern. Hardware sales peaked in the fourth year but did not drop sharply after that. More surprisingly, Game Boy was still selling and was expected to increase over 40 percent to 2.4 million units, in 1997, its ninth year on the market (see Exhibit 4). Analysts expected the current generation of 32/64-bit hardware systems to adhere to the historical pattern. Hardware sales were expected to peak in the fourth full year of distribution (1998), with software sales peaking in the fifth year (1999). Like previous generations, cumulative sales were expected to exceed that of previous generations (see Exhibit 5).

The penetration of video games into U.S. homes rose with each generation for several reasons. First, as players aged, they continued to play. For example, in 1980, a 12-year-old child may have owned an Atari system, but a 30-year-old most likely did not have one. Six years later, the 12-year-old (now 18) would be likely to have (or want) an NES system, as would his younger siblings. Six years after that, the now-24-year-old might have bought the SNES, and in 1998, the 30-year-old might have bought a PlayStation.

Second, each generation of technological improvement increased the types of appealing games that could be created so that over the years the game offerings became more diverse. Sports games on the Atari 2600, for example, were not realistic enough to compel a 25-year-old to play, and few offerings appealed to females. The 300-plus titles available for Sony's PlayStation included a much richer variety of games, with selections that appealed to young and old, male and female.

---

[9]Ibid.

EXHIBIT 4   Video Game Hardware Assumptions and Sales Cycles (In millions)

8-bit	1986	1987	1988	1989	1990	1991	1992	1993	1994
NES	1.1	3.0	7.0	9.0	7.2	4.0	2.0	1.5	0.6
Cumulative 8-bit	1.1	4.1	11.1	20.1	27.3	31.3	33.3	34.8	35.4
Portables	**1989**	**1990**	**1991**	**1992**	**1993**	**1994**	**1995**	**1996**	**1997**
Game Boy	1.00	3.20	4.00	4.00	3.50	3.00	2.00	1.70	2.40
Game Gear	—	—	0.50	0.65	1.00	1.50	0.50	0.30	0.10
Total Portables	1.00	3.20	4.50	4.65	4.50	4.50	2.50	2.00	2.50
Cumulative Portables	1.00	4.20	8.70	13.35	17.85	22.35	24.85	26.85	29.35
16-bit	**1990**	**1991**	**1992**	**1993**	**1994**	**1995**	**1996**	**1997**	**1998**
Genesis	1.3	1.6	4.0	5.0	4.0	1.5	1.1	0.8	0.0
SNES	—	1.8	5.5	5.0	3.7	1.5	1.2	0.7	0.5
Total 16-bit	1.3	3.4	9.5	10.0	7.7	3.0	2.3	1.5	0.5
Cumulative 16-bit	1.3	4.7	14.2	24.2	31.9	34.9	37.2	38.7	39.1
32/64 bit	**1995**	**1996**	**1997**	**1998**	**1999**	**2000**	**2001**	**2002**	**2003**
Saturn	0.3	0.8	0.8	0.5	0.0	0.0	0.0	0.0	0.0
PlayStation	0.7	2.4	6.0	7.0	4.5	2.5	1.3	0.7	0.0
N64	—	1.6	5.0	6.0	4.5	2.5	1.3	0.7	0.0
Total 32/64-bit	1.0	4.8	11.8	13.5	9.0	5.0	2.5	1.4	0.0
Cumulative 32/64-bit	1.0	5.8	17.6	31.1	40.1	45.1	47.6	49.0	49.0

Notes: For some platforms, year 1 and year 2 sales have been combined because year 1 launch was late in the year and/or sales were minimal. Game Gear was launched two years after Game Boy, but its sales are tracked for the same years. Tracked separately, Game Gear sales show a peak in year 4.
Source: Gerard Klauer Mattison & Co., Inc., estimates and corporate reports.

Finally, the emergence of the CD-ROM as a storage medium had lowered the average price of video games, making it possible for more consumers to afford to build a library. A family was more likely to invest in a PlayStation if there were dozens of titles that retailed for under $30 than they would be if all the titles retailed for over $50.

PLAYSTATION VERSUS N-64

From a consumer standpoint, the Sony PlayStation's most attractive features (compared to those of Nintendo's N-64) were its lower software costs and greater library of titles. The average PlayStation title retailed for less than $45, whereas N-64 titles averaged close to $60. Hardware prices were comparable at $150, with some industry participants expecting a possible PlayStation price cut to below $100 sometime in 1998.

From a software developer's point of view, the PlayStation system had both advantages and disadvantages. On the positive side, the manufacturing cost of PlayStation CD-ROMs was far lower than that of N-64 cartridges, and CD-ROMs containing a PlayStation video game could be pressed and shipped to retailers in much less time than Nintendo cartridges (which were made in Japan). Furthermore, N-64 cartridges had to be paid for at the time the order was placed. The longer lead times for getting N-64 cartridges on retailer shelves also meant greater inventory and sales risks for Nintendo game developers. It was very hard to judge how fast a title would sell, particularly in the case of newly introduced games. To keep from losing out on sales and disgruntling both retailers and consumers, publishers of Nintendo games were motivated to order larger quantities to avoid retailer stock-outs of what might prove to be a popular-selling title. In

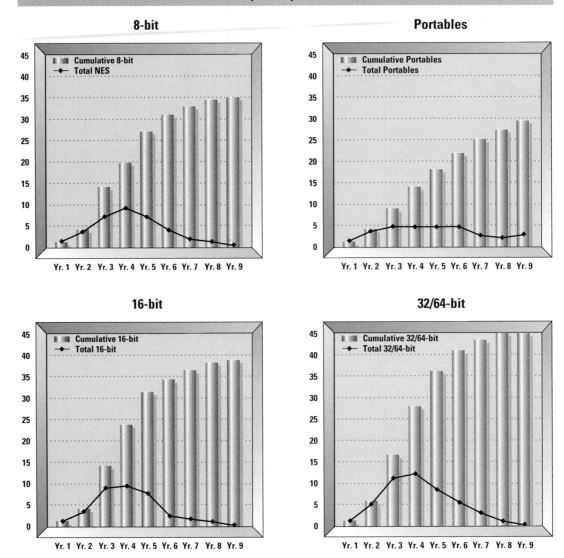

EXHIBIT 5   Video Game Hardware Cycles by Platform (sales in millions of units)

Source: Gerard Klauer Mattison & Co., Inc. estimates and corporate reports.

contrast, retailers could normally be resupplied with additional copies of hot-selling PlayStation titles within a matter of days (the packaging and booklets take longer to complete than the pressing). If a PlayStation's title didn't sell well, no additional discs had to be pressed, and the costs associated with slow-selling inventories were minimized.

Most software publishers liked developing PlayStation games because of their lower prices and short production lead times, features which gave them a lower break-even point for recovering development costs. Exhibit 6 shows the estimated number of units a publisher of game software would have to sell in order to recoup development and marketing costs—the estimated break-even point for the N-64 was 190,000 units, versus 172,000 units for PlayStation titles.

In addition, the ratio of software titles sold per game-playing unit (called the *tie ratio*) for PlayStation had remained remarkably strong from a game developer's per-

EXHIBIT 6	Comparative Costs and Break-Even Volumes for PlayStation Game Titles versus N-64 Game Titles		
Fixed Costs ($ thousands)		**PlayStation**	**N-64**
Development costs		$1,500	$1,500
G&A allocation		500	500
Advertising		600	600
Fixed sales and marketing (excluding advertising)		1,100	1,100
Total fixed costs		$3,700	$3,700
Variable Costs Per Unit			
Cost of sales		$ 8	$ 21
Content royalty		2	2
Co-op advertising		2	2
Total variable costs		$ 12	$ 25
Revenue (wholesale price) per unit		33	44
Variable costs		12	25
Contribution per unit		$ 22	$ 19
Contribution as percentage of wholesale		65.2%	44.3%
Breakeven (thousands of units)		172	190
Breakeven sales as percentage of installed hardware base		1.9%	3.1%
Retail price per unit		$42.00	$60.00
Retail margin		21.4%	26.7%

Notes:
1. Development costs can be higher or lower than the average shown. Titles that are sequels or ports generally cost much less to develop than original or platform-specific titles.
2. Advertising expenditures are essentially fixed at the time of shipping, but are a function of expected sales levels. If a title is not expected to ship a large amount, the publisher could spend much less on advertising than is shown here. Spending levels that would accompany the launch of an expected hit was estimated.
3. Content royalties include royalties paid to external developers and/or licensors (sports, entertainment, etc.). If a title is produced entirely in-house and is not licensed, the publisher would not have a royalty expense. Royalty expense was estimated at approximating 4%–5% of the wholesale cost.

Source: Gerard Klauer Mattison & Co., Inc. estimates.

spective. The tie ratio for PlayStation games was estimated to be 5.82:1 in 1997 and was projected to grow to 6.40:1 in 1998. This compared to tie ratios of less than 5:1 for older systems during their prime and a 2.55:1 ratio for N-64 titles.

In June 1997, Nintendo began cutting the prices it charged third-party licensees for N-64 cartridges from over $30 to as low as $21 in an effort to combat the cost disadvantage of Nintendo cartridges. But even so, the manufacturing cost of an N-64 game cartridge was more than double that of a PlayStation title.

On the other hand, the PlayStation software market was crowded, with over 300 titles vying for shelf space. The competitive disadvantages Nintendo faced from higher cartridge costs and longer lead times to supply retailers had to be balanced against the advantages afforded by Nintendo's strategy of restricting the number of its game titles—which meant that N-64 publishers faced less competition against other N-64 publishers. It was estimated that the average N-64 title sold over 400,000 units in 1997 whereas the average PlayStation title had sales of just 69,000 copies. Because there were fewer N-64 titles, Nintendo software developers stood to make more money if they came up with a game that was popular among owners of N-64 systems. Nintendo management believed that N-64's rapidly growing installed base and recently reduced software prices would attract more game developers and publishers. Some of Nintendo's own titles slated for release in 1997 were delayed until 1998, helping lessen the competition among titles in the under-supplied N-64 market.

VIDEO GAME HARDWARE[10]

The market for interactive multimedia products was characterized by rapidly changing technology and user preferences, evolving formats for compression of audio and video data, and frequent new-product introductions. Even if a competitor's technology and related software titles gained broad market acceptance, success depended upon, among other things, the ability of the firm and its licensees to achieve and maintain technological leadership and to remain competitive in terms of price and product performance.

Recent advances in digital processing, data storage, graphics, data compression, and communications technologies had made possible a new range of interactive software products and services. A number of companies were developing technologies to permit the broadcast of interactive entertainment services directly via satellite, fiber-optic cables, and telephone and cable television lines. Many companies were also developing on-line interactive games and interactive networks for playing video games.[11]

CD-Based Systems[12]

With the introduction in recent years of computer disk drives that read optical laser disks, or compact discs (CDs), the ability to deliver complex entertainment software had made significant technological advances. A CD had over 600 times more memory capacity than an 8-bit standard cartridge, enabling CD systems to incorporate large amounts of data, full-motion video, and high-quality sound, allowing for rich multimedia experiences. As the installed base of CD-ROM drives for personal computers increased and as the video game industry moved toward CD-based delivery systems, analysts believed that the traditional differentiation between the video game market and the personal computer market would become less distinct.

The CD-based market presented particular challenges for software developers and publishers. Entertainment software was expected to incorporate increasingly sophisticated graphics (video and animation), data, and interactive capabilities. The resulting higher development costs would be even further increased because successful software developers would have to incorporate talent from a variety of disciplines in the development process.

CD-based delivery systems did, however, present advantages to software publishers. CDs were less expensive to manufacture than either video game cartridges or floppy disks and, unlike floppy disks, could not be readily copied. Publishers could therefore expect to achieve higher profit margins from the sale of CDs than were currently the norm in the cartridge-based video game or floppy disk–based computer soft-

---

[10]Extracted from The 3DO Company's Form 10-K, 1997.
[11]Extracted from Midway Games' Form 10-K, 1997.
[12]Extracted from Activision's Form 10-K, 1994, p. 8.

EXHIBIT 7   Estimated U.S. Shipments of PC Hardware and Entertainment Software, 1995–2001

	1995	1996	1997	1998	1999	2000	2001
Hardware							
Unit shipments (000)	9,082	10,437	12,169	13,743	15,252	16,929	18,716
% growth	—	14.9%	16.6%	12.9%	11.0%	11.0%	10.6%
Games/Entertainment Software							
Unit shipments (000)	40,361	48,290	63,045	79,221	93,623	109,271	126,681
% growth	—	19.6%	30.6%	25.7%	18.2%	16.7%	15.9%

Source: IDC/LINK, August 1997.

ware market. In addition, once a master copy was made, extra copies could be produced in small batch lots as needed.

Despite all the advantages, CD-ROM technology was far from perfect. The biggest problem related to playing video games was speed. Compared to a cartridge, a compact disk required more time to access data. Access times were important, as most video games required fast-paced action. Any slowdown in the access and processing of data could hurt game play. However, this problem was not insurmountable. As the technology advanced and game developers became more experienced with CD-ROMs speed was expected to become less of a concern.

Portable Game Systems[13]

Nintendo's release in 1989 of the Game Boy, a battery-operated, handheld interactive entertainment system incorporating an 8-bit microprocessor, revolutionized the handheld game machine market. Previously, the only handheld systems available were dedicated to a single game. Sega's color Game Gear handheld system, released in 1991, competed directly with the Nintendo Game Boy. The market for video games on these platforms had declined in recent years and in 1998 did not comprise a sizable component of the video game business.

Personal Computers

Approximately 50 percent of U.S. households had home computers in mid-1998. As prices continued to fall below $1,000, unit sales were expected to steadily increase from the current 12.5 million a year to 17.5 million by 2002 and push the penetration of PCs into U.S. homes to the 60 percent range. The estimated growth rates for U.S. shipments of PC hardware and software through the year 2001 are shown in Exhibit 7.

The growing installed base, coupled with PCs' increasing ease of use as game devices, was expected to allow for robust growth in sales of PC games in the future. PC game publishers might not benefit immediately from the sudden rise in penetration of sub-$1,000 PCs. Most low-end computers were not powerful enough to run the video game industry's top sellers, some of which required special 3-D graphics acceleration cards, fast processors, and extra memory. However, an increase in the number of homes with PCs could increase demand for PC-based video games over time. Even

---

[13]Extracted from Midway Games' Form 10-K, 1997.

minimally equipped new PCs could run simple games. Moreover, today's high-end PCs were tomorrow's low-end models; $999 computers in 1999 would probably be able to run games that required a high-end model in 1989. Finally, higher home penetration of PCs could lead to greater consumer demand for video games; consumers new to PC gaming might trade up to more powerful hardware in order to experience richer game play.

The number of computers that could support the kinds of games played on Sony's PlayStation or Nintendo's N-64 was still fairly small. International Development Group estimated that the installed base of multimedia PCs was about 25 million by year-end 1997. This was consistent with the Homefront survey by Odyssey, which showed that 26 percent of all households had a PC with a CD-ROM drive.

PCs versus Video Game Consoles

Despite the PC's rising importance as a game platform and the emergence of on-line gaming, some analysts felt that dedicated video game consoles would continue to dominate the interactive entertainment market for the following reasons:

- *Ease of use.* Compared to even the most user-friendly PC, a dedicated console was easier to use, required less setup time, and was simpler to move from room to room. There were no compatibility issues, and no risk of accidentally damaging other computer files.
- *Low cost of entry.* For less than $200, a consumer could have a PlayStation or N-64 and at least one title, without a monthly fee or high phone bills.
- *Importance of software.* Manufacturers' software and licensing profits helped fund the pricing and promotion of their hardware systems. Although profits could be substantial on PC titles, it was not in the interest of software companies to promote the purchase of hardware.
- *Console price cuts.* The rapid price cuts of both hardware and software on 32-bit and 64-bit set-top players had served to greatly stimulate consumer demand for hardware. It was believed that hardware prices of 32/64 bit systems might still be headed lower and could fall below $100 before the 1998 holiday season.
- *Engineering.* Dedicated game machines could be more easily engineered than the PC to deliver fast-action graphics to a TV screen.

However, other analysts projected a different picture. Some expected to see superfast Pentium II desktop PCs with advanced graphics cards in 1999 priced at about $700 that could deliver better graphics than Sony or Nintendo players. The strategic decision for Sony and the other game manufacturers was whether to stick with a dedicated $150 machine that was good at doing one thing only, or to develop a system that performed more functions in the living room and brought more value to the consumer. Howard Lincoln, president of Nintendo of America, expressed Nintendo's perspective on this issue as follows:

> "We as an industry are really competing against the VCR, television and the computer. At the same time, I don't know if people want a system that turns on the house lights and plays games. We have the ability to deliver a targeted entertainment experience."[14]

[14]Takahasi, "Game Plan," p. R10.

EXHIBIT 8 Consoles versus PCs: Estimated Entertainment Software Market Share, 1995–2000

	1995	1996	1997	1998	1999	2000
Consoles	$1,951	$1,933	$2,989	$3,870	$4,725	$3,427
PC	1,413	1,642	2,017	2,377	2,715	3,060
Total software	$3,364	$3,575	$5,006	$6,247	$7,440	$6,487
% change	—	6.3%	40.0%	24.8%	19.1%	(12.8%)
Console share	58%	54%	60%	62%	64%	53%
PC share	42	46	40	38	36	47
Total	100%	100%	100%	100%	100%	100%

Note: Excludes sales of consoles not yet announced.
Source: Gerard Klauer Mattison & Co., Inc., and IDC/LINK.

Even with the PC's strong appeal as a game device, PC entertainment software sales were expected to grow less rapidly than those of console video game software (see Exhibit 8). The ratio of entertainment software units to hardware units was much lower for PCs than for video game consoles. The typical buyer of a video game console purchased two to three software titles in the first year, one to two in the second year, and one or two per year thereafter. The cumulative tie ratio was about 4.5–6.6 (see Exhibit 9). PlayStation was tracking far ahead of this rate—it already exceeded five units of software for each unit of hardware sold. Analysts projected this ratio would increase to nine software titles per hardware unit in 2000. N-64 was below this average, due to its relatively small library, but its tie ratio was expected to approach 7:1 in 2000.

PC buyers, however, don't appear to purchase as much software. The tie ratio of cumulative PC entertainment software units to hardware units was much lower, although IDC/LINK forecasted that it would rise (see Exhibit 10).

COIN-OPERATED VIDEO GAMES[15]

Americans were spending approximately $7 billion a year on arcade games as of 1998. With the $6 billion spent on home versions of video game hardware and software, the combined market was two times the size of the $6 billion movie box office. Arcades had experienced a resurgence in interest in recent years, partly because they had begun projecting a "family-friendly" image. Although many arcades were still dark, smoky, scary dens located in shopping malls, a newer breed of family entertainment centers offered batting cages, bumper cars, and fast food to draw the whole family rather than just teen-aged boys.[16] The video arcade had traditionally been the launching ground for games designed for home use and it was becoming clear that video game buyers also liked to try out arcade versions of a game before buying the home version.

---

[15]Extracted from Midway Games' Form 10-K, 1997.

[16]Gerard Klauer Mattison, & Co., Inc., *Interactive Electronic Industry Entertainment: Industry Overview* (New York: Author, 1993), p. 9.

EXHIBIT 9   Video Game Consoles: Estimated Software to Hardware Tie Ratios, 1990–2000 (In millions, except for tie ratios)

	1990	1991	1992	1993	1994	1995	1996	1997	1998	1999	2000
NES											
Cumulative hardware sales	27.30	31.30	33.30	34.80	35.35	35.50	35.60	35.60	35.60	35.60	35.60
Cumulative software sales	162.20	200.20	218.20	228.20	233.20	235.10	236.10	236.10	236.10	236.10	236.10
Tie ratio	5.94	6.40	6.55	6.56	6.60	6.62	6.63	6.63	6.63	6.63	6.63
Genesis											
Cumulative hardware sales	1.25	2.85	6.85	11.85	15.85	17.35	18.45	19.20	19.20	19.20	19.20
Cumulative software sales	3.50	9.50	22.50	45.62	66.62	79.62	84.62	87.62	87.62	87.62	87.62
Tie ratio	2.80	3.33	3.28	3.85	4.20	4.59	4.59	4.56	4.56	4.56	4.56
SNES											
Cumulative hardware sales	—	1.80	7.30	12.30	16.00	17.50	18.70	19.40	19.90	19.90	19.90
Cumulative software sales	—	4.00	22.00	45.00	64.00	77.00	87.00	94.50	98.50	99.50	100.50
Tie ratio	—	2.22	3.01	3.66	4.00	4.40	4.65	4.87	4.95	5.00	5.05
Saturn											
Cumulative hardware sales	—	—	—	—	—	0.30	1.10	1.85	2.35	2.35	2.35
Cumulative software sales	—	—	—	—	—	0.90	4.90	8.28	9.78	9.78	9.78
Tie ratio	—	—	—	—	—	3.00	4.45	4.47	4.16	4.16	4.16
PSX											
Cumulative hardware sales	—	—	—	—	—	0.70	3.10	9.10	16.10	20.60	23.10
Cumulative software sales	—	—	—	—	—	3.00	18.00	53.00	103.00	163.00	208.00
Tie ratio	—	—	—	—	—	4.29	5.81	5.82	6.40	7.91	9.00
Nintendo 6											
Cumulative hardware sales	—	—	—	—	—	—	1.60	6.60	12.60	17.10	19.60
Cumulative software sales	—	—	—	—	—	—	2.80	16.80	46.80	91.80	126.80
Tie ratio	—	—	—	—	—	—	1.75	2.55	3.71	5.37	6.47

Source: Gerard Klauer Mattison & Co., Inc., estimates.

EXHIBIT 10 Estimated PC Tie Ratios, 1995–2000 (Millions, except tie ratios)

	1995	1996	1997	1998	1999	2000
Cumulative hardware sales	40.40	45.00	50.10	55.10	60.20	65.50
Cumulative entertainment software sales	79.35	125.55	181.86	244.95	306.83	365.88
Tie ratio	1.96	2.79	3.63	4.45	5.10	5.59

Source: IDC/LINK, August 1997.

Coin-operated video games were manufactured in self-contained cabinetry containing large video displays. Games were generally designed to permit multiple players to compete against each other, in addition to being able to play against the game itself. Most coin-operated video games cost 50 cents and lasted two minutes. New technologies employed in the manufacture of coin-operated video games utilized advanced video platforms in which digital signals were mapped to computer-generated polygons that allowed for the creation of three-dimensional images.

Coin-operated games were sold through distributors to two primary customers—arcades and route operators. Prices ranged from $3,000 to $15,000. A typical arcade was located in a shopping mall and contained video, pinball, novelty, and redemption games. An arcade would often purchase multiple units of the most popular games. Route operators purchased coin-operated video games and provided the games on a revenue-sharing basis to various establishments, such as restaurants, taverns, convenience stores, and movie theaters, which typically installed only a few games and only rarely leased multiple units of the same game for a particular location. It was estimated that sales to route operators generally comprised between 45 and 50 percent of the coin-operated video game market.

A coin-operated video game would generally have a product life cycle of one to two years, although sales were generally concentrated in the first six to eight months after introduction by the manufacturer. The market for coin-operated video games, particularly in the United States, was mature and stable and was unlikely to experience significant growth in the near term. Growth in international markets might occur, if at all, in emerging markets rather than in developed countries where the coin-operated video game market was also mature.

Development of a new coin-operated video game generally took 18 months or longer, and typically involved the expenditure of substantial funds, including development, testing, and sampling costs. The basic development costs of a coin-operated game could exceed $1 million and, depending on the specific hardware and software requirements, reach $3.5 million per game. Because of changes in technology during the past few years, both the time and the cost required to develop games had increased during the same period. Conversion of a coin-operated game to a home game usually took 6 to 12 months, some of which overlapped with the development period of the coin-operated version of the game.[17]

---

[17]Extracted from Midway Games, Form 10-K, 1997.

VIDEO GAME SOFTWARE

The video game software business had undergone significant consolidation in recent years. Significant barriers existed that made it difficult for new entrants to succeed. Game makers required people who had specialized creative talent and who could use sophisticated technological tools. The cost of developing video games was high, and was likely to increase as technology continued to evolve. In the home video game business, distribution channels were dominated by a select group of companies, and access to retail shelf space was a significant competitive factor.

Competitors varied from very small companies with limited resources to very large corporations with greater financial, marketing and product development resources. Key third parties developing PC entertainment and video game entertainment software included Electronic Arts, Activision, Midway, MicroProse, CUC International, Lucas Arts, Interplay, GT Interactive, Acclaim Entertainment, Maxis, and Brøderbund Software. Nintendo, Sega, and Sony also had their own in-house software development resources. As competition increased, it was expected that significant price competition would reduce developers' profit margins.

The software side of the video game industry focused on several competitive weapons: product quality and features, compatibility of products with popular platforms, brand-name recognition, access to distribution channels, marketing effectiveness, reliability and ease of use, price, and technical support. Given the substantial cost of product development and of the marketing required to support best-selling titles, significant financial resources were increasingly a major competitive asset.

Competitive forces in the entertainment software and video game marketplace had increased the need for higher quality, distinctive entertainment software concepts. Competition for titles, themes, and characters from television, movies, and other media as the basis for "hits" resulted in higher development costs for software producers. Substantial nonrefundable advance licensing fees and significant advertising expenses also increased the financial risk involved. Moreover, the ability to incorporate compelling story lines or game experiences with full-motion video, digital sound, other lifelike technology, and ease of use presented artistic as well as technical challenges that added to the cost equation.[18]

A video game console manufacturer spent millions of dollars developing, designing, and advertising its format around the world. It could seldom recoup its investment through hardware sales alone. Manufacturers sold their machines for the lowest price possible, leaving virtually no room for profit margins for either themselves or retailers. The hardware was marketed much like a loss leader, tempting consumers to try the latest and greatest video games and, hopefully, become addicted to video game entertainment. Establishing a healthy installed base was thus a key success factor for hardware manufacturers. Once a company had its machine in enough homes, the marketing focus shifted to expanding the number of attractive game titles. Sony, Sega, and Nintendo insisted that all software for their respective systems was manufactured by them (or by "approved" third parties). These companies then charged the software publishers a fixed price for making the game cartridges or CDs and earned a royalty rate on unit sales. Every time a publisher sold a game for PlayStation, for example, Sony made money whether it had developed the game or not.[19]

---

[18]Ibid.

[19]"Is Your Favorite Game Company Ripping You Off?," *Next Generation,* June 1997, p. 38.

Software Development and Production

The big three video game console makers (or platform providers) each licensed third parties to develop software for use with their respective game-playing systems. Typically the software developer submitted a prototype for evaluation and approval that included all art work to be used in connection with packaging and marketing of the product. Many third-party developers used contract manufacturing sources in Mexico. The platform providers usually retained the right to limit the number of games and approve timing of release under manufacturing and licensing arrangements. Home video game production was based on estimated demand for each specific title, with on-hand inventories depending on seasonal variations in demand during the market life of a specific game title. At the time a newly developed game was approved for manufacturing, the developer had to provide the platform manufacturer with a purchase order for that product and an irrevocable letter of credit for 100 percent of the purchase price. Initial orders generally required 30 to 75 days to produce depending on the platform. Reorders of cartridge-based products generally required approximately 50 days to produce, while reorders of CD-ROM-based platforms took only 14 days. Shipping of orders required an additional 3 to 10 days, depending on the mode of transport and location of the software producer.[20]

Increasing demand for multifeatured, action-packed game titles had driven up the cost to develop new game titles in the last five years. In the early 1990s, publishers customarily spent around $300,000 to develop a game for PC, Super NES, or Genesis systems. In 1998, the average budget was around $1 million per game, and many complex games, with all kinds of multimedia features, entailed even higher development costs. The development costs for some games had exceeded $10 million (Origin's *Wing Commander IV* was a high-profile example).[21]

The cost of manufacturing an interactive CD that sold for $40 was approximately $1 to $2. A software publisher could produce a video game cartridge (including royalties) for between $15 to $25 per unit.[22] Game developers were dependent on megahits to make up for losses on games that did not achieve break-even sales volumes.[23] In 1996, the top-selling 1 percent of PC video games accounted for 29 percent of industry sales; the bottom 90 percent accounted for 25 percent of sales. Sales were concentrated even more among the most popular titles during the holiday season.

Software Distribution

Retailers of video game software typically devoted a limited amount of shelf space and promotional resources to video game products. Strong competition for shelf space among rival brands of video game products put retailers and distributors in increasingly better position to negotiate favorable terms of sale, including promotional discounts and product return policies. Retailers often required software publishers to pay fees in exchange for preferred shelf space.[24]

The growing penetration of multimedia PCs in households was producing changes in the distribution channels for entertainment software. To reach a broader market,

[20]Extracted from Midway Games' Form 10-K, 1997.

[21] "Is your favorite game company ripping you off?," p. 38.

[22]3 DO Company 10-K, 1993, p. 6.

[23]N. Hutheesing, "Platform Battle," *Forbes,* May 9, 1994, pp. 168–170.

[24]Spectrum Holobyte's Form 10-K, p. 10.

software producers increasingly depended on such new distribution outlets as mass merchandisers, on-line services, and the Internet. These new channels of video game distribution generally carried only top-selling titles.[25]

To be successful in this competitive distribution environment, software producers were pursuing ways to demonstrate to retailers that their products had broad appeal and could become best-sellers. This increasingly meant developing more sophisticated games that utilized the enhanced game-playing capabilities of multimedia PCs and next-generation systems to create products with appealing game play and high-volume sales potential. Software companies were instituting disciplined development processes to lower cost overruns and were creating innovative marketing campaigns to increase customer awareness of their games in order to generate a better return on product investments.[26]

Strategies

The business strategies of most software developers generally incorporated several elements:

- *Creating a portfolio of exciting games.* One obvious key success factor in the industry was to produce games that players found fun and exciting.
- *Exploiting the coin-operated proving ground.* Some game developers, like Midway Games, initially released their video games in the coin-operated video arcade market as a way to gauge player response and gain insight into possible improvements and changes for their home version. If a game was popular in video arcades, it almost always was a success in the home market. Midway considered coin-operated games that sold at least 5,000 units and home games that sold at least 100,000 units per dedicated platform to be successful games.
- *Maintaining platform independence.* By producing games for multiple platforms, a game developer was not dependent on any particular game platform.
- *Exploiting franchise and library value.* Midway, for example, released four different coin-operated games under the Mortal Kombat title and published or licensed home versions of each of those games. Midway also licensed two film adaptations of Mortal Kombat and granted merchandising licenses in the toy, clothing, comic book, strategy guide, and other product lines. In fiscal 1997, Midway released two additional Mortal Kombat home games, Ultimate Mortal Kombat 3 and Mortal Kombat Trilogy. An animated television series based on Mortal Kombat began airing in the fall of 1996, and a sequel to the movie version of Mortal Kombat was released in the fall of 1997. Midway also sought to utilize its large library of video games to release "arcade classics" and updated versions of such classics. For the home market in fiscal 1997, Midway released two collections of arcade classic games and Robotron X, a new version of a classic arcade game.
- *Developing multi-site game-playing capabilities.* Several arcade developers were testing multi-player interactive technology that allowed a player at one arcade to take on players at other arcades. Likewise, some developers were exploring multi-player and interactive formats over the Internet.

---

[25]Ibid.
[26]Ibid.

- *Investing in advanced technology.* Since the video game software business was intensely competitive and characterized by the continuous introduction of new titles and the development of new technologies, developers believed it was imperative that their game design teams have access to the latest design technology. Game developers were continuously upgrading the equipment used to program games so as to give their design teams cutting-edge capability to incorporate three-dimensional graphics, advanced audio effects, and other sophisticated multimedia effects made possible by the ongoing advances in electronic technology.

Games for Girls

One of the most significant developments in the PC software industry had been the phenomenal success of Mattel's Barbie titles, led by Barbie Fashion Designer. The title had sold over 1 million units worldwide, making it not only one of the most successful PC titles ever, but also the fastest to reach that level.

Historically, PC games had appealed much more to males than to females. Developers tended to design games they themselves would like to play, and since most game developers were male, most video games on the market reflected this bias. Some titles had strong crossover appeal for both sexes (Myst, Sim City Tetris, and most "edutainment" titles), but most of the top-selling PC entertainment titles had a decidedly male bent. Many of the best-selling titles of 1997 (Diablo, Duke it Out, Command and Conquer, X-Wing vs. Tie Fighter) had violent combat as the central theme, with varying degrees of gore.

Several developers were actively seeking to address the female market with titles specifically developed for, and marketed to, a female audience. Besides Mattel, other developers of games appealing to females included Purple Moon, Girl Tech, The Learning Company, Creative Wonders, Girl Games, and Segasoft (which was marketing Cosmopolitan Virtual Makeover to women and girls). Industry analysts felt the overall video game market would continue to be dominated by titles with traditional themes (fighting, sports, and strategy), but there was strong consensus that growing PC ownership would stimulate market demand for female-oriented titles.

VIDEO GAME DEVELOPMENT

The development of video games required a blend of technology and creative talent. The development process included game development and design, prototyping, programming, art, computer graphic design, animation, sound engineering, technical writing, editorial review, and quality assurance. It took 12 to 24 months (occasionally longer) to complete a new title with a new engine and 6 to 14 months to make existing titles compatible for play on a different platform. Many games were based on characters and themes that were either owned by the game developer or licensed from third parties.[27] There were four key considerations that firms had to deal with in developing a video game: (1) what development and distribution agreements to arrange, (2) whether to acquire content from outsiders or create original content with an in-house group, (3) which game-playing platform(s) to develop for, and (4) how to attract and retain a skilled workforce.[28]

---

[27]Extracted from Spectrum Halobyte's Form 10-K, 1997, p. 7.

[28]This section extracted from DFC Intelligence Research, *The U.S. Market for Video Games.*

Development and Distribution Agreements

The most common strategy in creating a new title was for a software publisher to hire a developer. The developer was responsible for creating and programming the game and assuring the quality of the product. The publisher handled manufacturing, packaging, marketing, and distribution issues. The publisher bore the risk of unsold inventory if the title was a failure in the marketplace. Generally, game developers were paid a royalty based on wholesale revenues. Royalty payments varied greatly, but typically ranged from 5 to 15 percent.

Many developers were attempting to publish their own titles. Affiliated label and co-publishing programs had become a popular means for small companies to publish their own titles and maintain their independence. Under an affiliated label program, a developer handled marketing and publishing, while a co-publisher dealt with distribution. In return, the developer received a royalty of up to 75 percent of wholesale revenue. A variation on the affiliated label program was expected to become the distribution method of choice.

Acquiring Content

In years past, companies that owned popular intellectual property would license that property for use in video games in return for a modest royalty. By 1998, however, companies with attractive intellectual property were reluctant to license their properties and acquiring content was difficult, time consuming, and costly. In 1998, securing the license to produce a game based on a big movie ran in the $1 million range. In the sports market, a license was reported to cost $500,000 up front, plus a royalty of 5 to 15 percent of the wholesale price for each unit sold.[29] Many large entertainment conglomerates were setting up interactive divisions to create titles based on their own property. In the future, it was expected that many publishers would be forced to base their games on original content or works in the public domain.

Platform Considerations

Historically, no platform or system had achieved long-term dominance in the marketplace. Consequently, many software firms were developing products for all the key hardware platforms—Sony's PlayStation, Sega's Saturn, Nintendo's 64, PCs, on-line networks—as well as titles for some of the earlier generation systems. Because the existing platforms were incompatible with one another, each required a different set of development tools. Publishers had to carefully consider which platforms to develop games for, studying development costs, installed base figures, licensing fees, and player demographics. As of 1998, no CD-ROM platform had a large enough installed base to make it feasible to publish a title for just one platform. Creating titles for several dedicated systems was more time consuming and difficult. As a general rule it took 12 to 18 months to develop a software title for the first CD platform, and 3 to 6 months for each additional platform.

The platform providers controlled who could develop for their system. A license from the platform provider was required to develop for a dedicated system. Licensees paid the platform provider royalty fees based on sales volume. Platform providers nearly always regulated content and limited the number of titles that could be released.

---

[29] "The Licensing Game," *Next Generation*, July 1998, p. 42.

Nintendo and Sega had high licensing fees and were strict about what titles could be released for their systems.

Attracting and Retaining Adequate Talent

Competition for highly skilled employees with technical, management, marketing, sales, product development, and other specialized training was intense. Some software producers had found it necessary to improve their compensation packages in order to attract and retain capable employees.

THE DEMOGRAPHICS OF VIDEO GAME PLAYERS

There were an estimated 7 to 12 million hard-core game console players in the United States. Ninety percent were males, 12 to 30 years old. They represented all income and education levels, and typically bought about six games a year. Many read game magazines like *EGM, GamePro,* and *Next Generation.* The hard-core segment was considered to be growing slowly.

The size of the casual video game player segment was estimated at 30 million U.S. consumers. Eighty percent were male and ranged in age from 5 to 30 years old. They too represented all income and education levels, but bought only one to two games per year. Occasionally they bought a video game magazine at a newsstand. The growth potential for this segment was considered to be high.[30]

Studies had indicated that many children who grew up playing video games continued to do so as adults. There were several key differences between adult and younger players. Adolescents were more concerned with what was "in" and "hot." The adult market was composed of numerous niches, each with an interest in a different type of game. Adults liked titles that fit in with their lifestyle and interests. It was difficult to find one title that appealed to the entire adult market. In addition, the biggest complaint among adults was that most games took too much time to play. Adults liked to play games in short bursts during free moments.[31] As mentioned earlier, video games had not been popular with women, due in large part to their male-oriented content. According to the Software Publishers Association, about 28 percent of computer game players and 21 percent of video game players were female.

MARKETING[32]

In earlier times, the marketing of video games had been unsophisticated. Nintendo and Sega had been able to stimulate demand for their games merely by initiating well-financed advertising campaigns. Demand for popular-selling titles was often so strong that publishers merely had to get their product into the store and it would sell. Advertising was an attempt to gain word-of-mouth publicity and might have consisted of a few pages in the leading video game consumer magazines and a booth at the Consumer Electronics Show.

By the mid-1990s video game marketing had become a sophisticated exercise. The major video game releases were being marketed much like a new release from a major

[30]DFC Intelligence Research, *The U.S. Market for Video Games.*

[31]Ibid.

[32]Ibid.

movie studio. Television advertising, promotional tie-ins, merchandising, direct mail, and special launch parties became commonplace. A well-planned, well-executed marketing campaign was a must to gain buyer attention and generate sufficient sales to create a genuine hit in the marketplace.

Many industry observers believed the video game industry was becoming a "hit-driven" business as competition for shelf space escalated and rivals spent more on marketing. For instance, one title accounted for approximately 49 percent and 23 percent, respectively, of Activision Inc.'s 1996 and 1997 fiscal year revenues. Small game publishers without the resources of the big players in the industry found themselves faced with a catch-22: Growing numbers of video game retailers were reluctant to stock the products of lesser-known game publishers because of their skimpy advertising budgets and shelf space limitations. Instead, most preferred to allocate their limited shelf space to large, proven game developers with good brand recognition and the financial muscle to back new releases with sizable advertising campaigns. Yet without good shelf exposure for their games, small and lesser-known game publishers were hard pressed to generate the revenue necessary to fund large-scale marketing campaigns and build a strong brand image. Their chances of ending up with a hit game were much slimmer than were the chances of publishers having ample marketing resources, good brand recognition, or one or more best-selling games.

Distribution

Toy stores and computer software stores had long been the traditional retailers of video games. However, as the video game business grew in the 1990s, other retailers began carrying video game products, chiefly because of the high margins on video game software. In 1998, over 20,000 stores in the United States stocked video games. Mass merchants (e.g., Wal-Mart, Kmart, and Target.), toy stores, and consumer electronics retailers (notably Best Buy) were gaining in the percentage share of video games sold at retail, while software specialty stores (e.g., Babbages, Software ETC and Egghead) were losing share. Industry analysts believed that future sales of video game products would favor mass merchants and toy stores even further, since growing familiarity of video game buyers with game-playing technology required less expertise and product knowledge on the part of salesclerks.

During the late 1980s, consumer demand for video games was so high that a retailer could sell whatever was put on the shelf. The major complaint of retailers was not having enough products. Nintendo went so far as to ration games in 1988 and 1989. Even the bad games sold. All this had changed by the mid-1990s, as numerous new game titles were released and Nintendo began to face increased competition from Sega and, later, Sony. In 1994, retailers found many of the 16-bit cartridges sitting unsold on the shelf; software sales were concentrated in a handful of hit titles. Most video games had a shelf life of 30 to 60 days at full list price; after 60 days, slow-selling titles were offered at a discount. It was common for retailers holding substantial excess inventories to discount games originally listing for $60 to the $15 to $20 range. The net effect of market overcrowding was a substantial decline in profit margins on software. DFC Intelligence Research noted that video game retailers were most concerned about the difficulty of deciding what to buy, the lack of a return policy, and heavy discounting from increased competition. DFC's research indicated that retailers were increasingly cautious and selective in deciding what and how much to stock, basing their orders on the quality of the game, the amount of advertising the

EXHIBIT 11   Average Software Price Changes, August 1996 versus August 1997

Rank	PC Entertainment Titles			PC Educational Titles			PlayStation Titles		
	8/31/96	8/31/97	% Change	8/31/96	8/31/97	% Change	8/31/96	8/31/97	% Change
Top 10	$40.99	$35.33	(13.8%)	$32.07	$28.54	(11.0%)	$52.92	$45.93	(13.2%)
11–20	40.35	32.63	(19.1)	32.35	28.94	(10.5)	51.93	45.07	(13.2)
21–30	37.65	40.11	6.5	32.39	28.74	(11.3)	50.62	46.15	(8.8)
31–40	38.83	23.54	(39.4)	36.63	25.58	(30.2)	51.81	41.56	(19.8)
41–50	34.40	29.19	(15.1)	29.20	25.07	(14.2)	48.23	41.53	(13.9)

Source: NPD Group's *SofTrends.*

publisher planned to do, and the reputation of the publisher. To combat declining profit margins in traditional channels, several video game companies were experimenting with selling their in different distribution channels, including direct marketing, electronic distribution at retail, on-demand via cable television, and on-line via the Internet. Increased bandwidth of phone and cable systems was expected to make multiplayer networked gaming possible.

Pricing

In 1998, a big percentage of the top-selling PC games had either been on the market for over a year or were sequels to previously released best-sellers. Some of games on the market were actually "minigames" in that they offered just a few additional levels of difficulty. These games had experienced a more pronounced drop in average selling prices, an industry trend for some time. For example, the best-selling title in August 1997 (according to NPD Group's *SofTrends*) was Brøderbund's Myst, which had been on the market for over three years. Its average price was under $20. The number four title, Duke it Out, the latest installment in the Duke Nukem series, was selling for about $10. Galaxy of Games, number eight in August 1997, was a collection of older titles and retailed for under $10. There had been an erosion in average selling prices even among PlayStation video game titles, despite strong sales of Sony's game-playing hardware.

The top 10 PC entertainment titles during January–August 1997 had an average retail price of about $35, down 14 percent from $41 in the comparable period in 1996 (see Exhibit 11). Price discounting of second- and third-tier titles had been even sharper. Falling retail prices had also hit the educational software category, where the average price for the top 10 PC educational titles for the first eight months of 1997 was down 11 percent compared to 1996, and lesser titles were generally down even more sharply.

A portion of the falloff in video game prices was attributable to the length of time many of the best-selling games had been on the market. Among the top 25 entertainment titles during January–August 1997 (ranked by unit sales), 12 had been released more than 12 months prior to August 1997; in August 1996, only 7 had been on the market longer than 12 months. As the data in Exhibit 12 indicate, the older titles were responsible for the average decline in retail prices.

EXHIBIT 12	Average Retail Prices of New Hits vs. Old Hits, August 1996 versus August 1997		
Titles in Top 25	**8/31/96**	**8/31/97**	**% Change**
Launched within 12 months ending August 31	$41.13	$44.29	7.7%
Launched prior to 12 months ending August 31	$37.74	$22.77	(39.7%)

Source: NPD Group's *Softrends*.

SEASONALITY OF VIDEO GAME SALES[33]

Retail sales for video games declined significantly between May and August. Analysts attributed the sales slowdown to several factors. First, children and teenagers spent much more time outside in these months and were not indoors playing video games. They also watched less TV in warmer months, thus making them less reachable via advertising. In addition, because they were out of school, there was less "I got to level 10, how far did you get?" to spur sales. Finally, sales were slower because the publishers released fewer new games during slow-selling months. Two-thirds of video game sales were made in the year-end holiday season.

ON-LINE ENTERTAINMENT

IDC/LINK estimated the number of on-line gaming households in the United States to increase to 4.5 million and 8 million in 1997 and 1998, respectively, from 500,000 in 1995 (see Exhibit 13). On-line gaming revenues were projected to rise to $250 million in 1997 from $100 million in 1995; with a tremendous surge beginning in 1999 (see Exhibit 14).

Consumers could play video games on-line in one of several ways (see Exhibit 15). Whereas in the mid-1990s, there were only a handful of game networks, there were over 15 different on-line gaming networks in 1997.

Most publishers maintained high-quality Web sites where consumers could often download portions of a game to sample. Some publishers were collecting e-mail addresses of consumers that registered their purchases electronically and then marketed directly to these consumers, often guiding them to a particular retailer. Many games sold at retail in 1998 had an on-line component that allowed the player either to access the publisher's Web site or to communicate with other players.

Game TV channels, just as with Web site samples, were being used to promote retail sales. The Sega Channel, for example, gave players access to certain levels of a new game for a limited period of time, hoping to entice the consumer to buy the title at retail.

The multiplayer game was the newest on-line gaming experience and was expected to become the dominant form of on-line gaming. Ultima (from Electronic Arts' Origin team in Austin, Texas) and Netstorm (from Activision) were examples of games that

---

[33]This section extracted from Gerard Klauer Mattison, Interactive Electronic Industry Entertainment: Industry Overview.

EXHIBIT 13   Estimated Number of U.S. On-line Gaming Households, 1995–2001

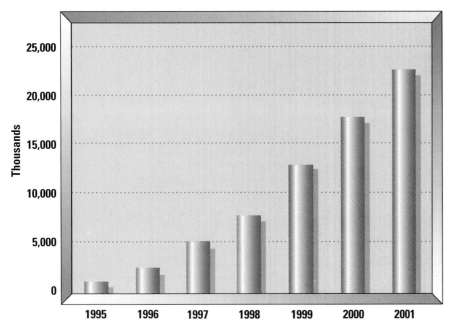

Source: IDC/LINK, July 1997.

EXHIBIT 14   Estimated U.S. On-line Gaming Revenues, 1995–2001

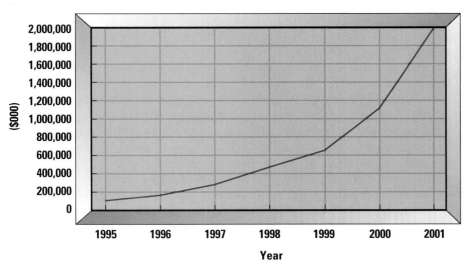

Source: IDC/LINK, July 1997.

EXHIBIT 15   U.S. Sources for Playing Video Games On-line, 1997

Prior to 1997	As of July 1997
America Online	America Online
Catapult	Berkley
DWANGO	Blizzard
Genie	Catapult
I-Magic	Disney
Kesmai	DWANGO
Simutronics	Electronic Arts
	Engage
	Genie
	Hasbro
	I-Magic
	Kesmai
	Microsoft
	Mpath
	Sega
	Simutronics
	3DO
	Sony
	TEN

Note: Represents only a portion of the market players.
Source: IDC/LINK, July 1997.

players could access via the Internet using software that was purchased at retail. Electronic Arts had stated that while it intended to charge consumers about $10 per month to play its games on-line, it expected its main source of revenue to be the retail sales of CDs.

All on-line gaming approaches shared several problems. First, it had not yet been clearly established how content providers would be fairly compensated, thus posing problems to providers in assessing whether on-line distribution would be as profitable as other channels. Additionally, latency (the period between when a signal was sent and a response was registered) was a concern—in a shooting game, for instance, latency caused a delay between when the player pulled the trigger and when the shot was fired. Latency problems arose from the narrow bandwidth in most consumers' modems and the long and (more important) inconsistent route over which data packets traveled during game play. Even a direct route from the East Coast to the West Coast over conventional phone lines could produce a level of latency that was intolerable to most game players.

Greater bandwidth solved some latency problems but unless all players in a multi-player game had high bandwidth connections, the game could still be slowed down. Other solutions included "smart" software that altered the game play to obscure latency (for example, keeping a player from opening a door if the image behind it wasn't ready). Latency was expected to remain a problem and hamper the growth of on-line gaming for several years.

Content providers could pursue any of several approaches to generate revenues from on-line gaming. The most common in 1998 was to sell CDs at retail that allowed users access to on-line servers; once users connected with a server, game publishers could charge hourly or monthly fees to communicate with or compete against other players. Second, they could establish their own interactive Web site, charging by the month or hour, or license their title to one of several on-line networks (M-path, TEN, Dwango, etc.). In both cases, supplemental revenues could be generated by selling advertising space on the screen.

VIDEO GAME CONTENT AND RATINGS

Starting in the late 1980s and continuing on into the 1990s, the content of many video games had become increasingly violent, a condition that troubled and even alarmed growing numbers of parents and other concerned citizens. Violence was especially high in games like Carmageddon and Resident Evil 2, whose animated dismembered corpses, splashes of gore, and horrific themes would have rated a solid R on movie and TV screens for the blood-and-guts content alone.[34] Interstate '76, Activision's popular PC driving adventure, contained substantial profanity, as did Interplay's Redneck Rampage. Shortly releasing Redneck Rampage, Interplay released a "cusspack" over the Internet, significantly expanding the crude vocabulary of the characters in the game. Even characters in Final Fantasy VII, the blockbuster PlayStation RPG from Square, though lacking vocals, belted out one four-letter word in living color with amazing regularity. Observers noted that profanity had not only become accepted but also a sales-enhancing feature in some games.[35]

Game developers were also exploiting the concept that "sex sells." According to Interplay's Kim Motika,

> I think it's an inevitable trend. Violence and sex sell. The bottom line is that it draws attention and revenue. Given that, I believe the industry will continue to develop content of this nature, some will tone down the content and others will not. However, having said this, I believe that the publishing community has an obligation to provide products and content that are of interest to the market and to continue to support the ratings system which allows the consumer to choose whether they are accepting the content.[36]

As parents and concerned citizens became aware of the content of video games, they lobbied for a comprehensive, industrywide video game rating system that would give consumers the information to make informed choices. To address these concerns, Senators Lieberman and Kohl sponsored legislation in 1993 to establish the National Independent Council for Entertainment in Video Devices as an independent agency of the federal government to oversee the development of "voluntary" standards to alert parents to the content of video games. In his testimony before the hearing, Robert Chase, vice president of the National Education Association, expressed a collective concern of many educators, children's advocates, and parents:

> America's children are faced with a bewildering set of messages from television, movies, music, electronic games, and print media. Too often, the almost unrelenting assault on the senses encouraging aggression and irresponsibility are in direct opposition to the values families hope to instill and the morals our society struggles to preserve. Parents, social scientists, and the community at large share deep trepidation about the fruits of this ever-widening dispersal of negative images. The explosion of media in the latter half of this century has

---

[34]J. High, "Gaming 2000;" http://www.gameweek.com/feature/november/4.htm (November 1997).

[35]Ibid.

[36]Ibid.

made the problem all the more pervasive and the challenges for parents and community leaders all the more difficult.[37]

At the same hearing, the Software Publishers Association (SPA) provided a counter argument:

> In our attempt to protect our children from those relatively few video games which contain unacceptable violence, however, we must not lose sight of the fact that the vast majority of video games are appropriate for children, and have the potential for developing many important and socially desirable skills. As stated so eloquently by Bob Keeshan, otherwise known as Captain Kangaroo, Video games . . . provide the potential for heretofore unknown opportunities for information, education and delightful entertainment . . . The technology is to be encouraged because, used appropriately, such games can be a tool for education as well as entertainment.[38]

The SPA indicated in its testimony that the software entertainment industry was committed to moving quickly and decisively on this issue. The SPA was working with a coalition of concerned parties to establish a rating system that would be easy for consumers to understand for the industry to implement.

In July 1994, the U.S. Senate subcommittee endorsed rating guidelines issued by an industry trade group, the Interactive Digital Software Association (IDSA).[39] The IDSA ratings provided age guidance with five categories similar to those used by the Motion Picture Association of America. Some mass merchants (e.g., Sears, Wal-Mart, and Toys "R" Us) had vowed to carry only rated video games.

As of 1998, there had been no agreement on an industry-wide rating system. Some observers believed that the existence of several systems might confuse consumers. There also appeared to be a debate emerging as to whether widespread dissemination of rated products would ultimately hurt or help sales. The industry was pressing for self-regulation rather than letting the government become intrusive. However, the fight for regulation escalated in early 1998 when two politicians in Florida promoted two bills that would "prohibit the public display of . . . video games displaying graphic violence."[40]

In November 1997, the arcade industry got its annual "report card" from Senator Lieberman on providing video game content ratings. The industry did not receive a passing grade, but it had improved slightly over the previous year. The senator praised the industry for what it had accomplished to date. Arcade owners and game manufacturers were continuing to work on refining a content rating system and to implement it in arcade video games.[41]

PROFILES OF THE BIG THREE VIDEO GAME CONSOLE COMPETITORS

The competitive landscape in the video game industry was expected to continue to evolve and change as market shares shifted, old competitors dropped out, and new entrants emerged. The industry's early years were dominated by Atari; then Nintendo

---

[37]U.S. Senate; *Violence in Video Games: Joint Hearing of the Judiciary Subcommittee on Juvenile Justice and Government Affairs Subcommittee on Regulation and Government Information* (testimony of Robert Chase), 103rd Cong., 1993.

[38]Ibid. (testimony of Ilene Rosenthal).

[39]M. Moran, "Retailers See Video Game Ratings as a Helpful Guide," *Video Business 14,* no. 32 (1994), pp. 12, 16.

[40]"News: Outlawed in Orlando?," *Next Generation,* May 1998, p. 16.

[41]"Arcadia," *Next Generation,* March 1988, p. 30.

reigned as the market leader in 1985–89, although Sega also sold several million game players in the United States, Europe, and Japan during this period. The 16-bit era began with Sega's launch of Genesis in Japan in 1988 and in the United States in 1989. Nintendo's Super NES was launched in Japan in 1990 and in the United States the following year. Each of these moves resulted in sharply shifting market shares.

In the early 1990s, several old and new competitors entered the industry. Commodore reentered the video game industry with a CDTV system in 1991, but its Amiga CD32 did not generate significant demand. 3DO's interactive Multiplayer was introduced in the United States in 1993. Although initial reviews were favorable, intense competition, a high introductory price ($699), chronic shortages of players in many stores, and lack of great software kept the 3DO product from winning a significant market share. Once Sony launched its PlayStation, 3DO's sales suffered significantly. 3DO dropped out of the video game business in 1997 and refocused its energies on becoming an interactive entertainment software developer. During the 1993 Christmas season, Atari introduced its Jaguar game player, named the industry's "Best New Game System." Although Atari beat Saturn and the PlayStation to market, the game system never succeeded because of a lack of titles and funding to support development. Similarly, Philips Electronics NV's CD-I system—an interactive compact-disk system used for education, music and games—failed due to high prices, poor performance, and a lack of developer support.

In 1998, the emerging new player in the video game wars was VM Labs. Richard Miller, the former vice president for technology at Atari, founded VM Labs. VM Labs was creating a multifunction gaming console (dubbed Project X) that would feature video games, DVD playback of films, and videophone communications. Its market debut was projected for early 1999.

Nintendo Company, Ltd.[42]

Nintendo began as a playing card manufacturer in 1889 in Kyoto, Japan. In 1998, the company was headed by the great grandson of Nintendo's founder, Hiroshi Yamauchi. Yamauchi had become the company's president in 1922 at the age of 22. Under Yamauchi's leadership Nintendo began to expand into the toy business. Nintendo became NCL, Nintendo Company, Ltd., and went public in the early 1960s. In 1975, Nintendo made its first venture into video games when it got a license to sell Magnavox's video game system in Japan. Nintendo released its own home video game system in 1977 and soon began to develop arcade games.

Nintendo eventually designed a game system that could use interchangeable cartridges. The machine, called the Famicom (short for Family Computer), was released in Japan in 1983. The 8-bit Famicom sold for about $100, considerably less than the $250 to $300 most game systems cost at that time. Nintendo sold 500,000 units in the Famicom's first two months. Nintendo's 14 rivals soon exited the market, leaving Nintendo to become the home video game leader in Japan.

In 1980, Nintendo decided to enter the U.S. market and Nintendo of America (NOA) was established as an independent subsidiary. The first president of NOA was Minoru Arakawa, Hiroshi Yamauchi's son-in-law. The original goal of NOA was to break into the $8-billion-a-year arcade business. Arcade games from Japan were shipped to the United States and distributed by NOA.

---

[42]Nintendo's company background provided by DFC Intelligence Research, *The U.S. Market for Video Games.*

NOA got off to a slow start, mainly because Nintendo lacked a hit game. That changed in 1981 with the release of Donkey Kong, created by legendary Nintendo game developer, Sigeru Miyamota. Donkey Kong was such a success in the United States that NOA ended its second year in business with over $100 million in sales.

In 1984, Nintendo began to think about bringing the Famicom to the United States. But, because the U.S. home video game market had crashed in 1983, manufacturers, distributors, and retailers exhibited little interest in video games. Nintendo decided to proceed cautiously and began to test the Famicom in New York in 1985. For the U.S. release, the Famicom was renamed the Nintendo Entertainment System (NES). By the end of its first year, more than 1 million units had been sold in the United States. Three million units had been sold by the end of 1987, and the Legend of Zelda became the first game to sell over a million copies. Nintendo mania had begun.

As the NES gained momentum, sales increased from $1 billion in 1987 to over $5 billion in 1992. Game Boy, a portable video game system released in 1989, sold 40,000 units the first day it was available in the United States. The Super Nintendo Entertainment System (SNES) was released in the United States in 1991. Sales of the SNES took off in 1992 fueled by Nintendo's marketing expertise and the release of Capcoms's popular Street Fighter II and became Nintendo's top-selling system.

As the competitive rivalry with Sega and other new entrants into the industry began to heat up, Nintendo was forced to undergo some significant changes. Nintendo received a wake-up call in 1993 when Sega passed Nintendo in sales of 16-bit systems. Nintendo suddenly realized it no longer had the monopoly it once enjoyed. Unhappy with the performance of Nintendo's U.S. subsidiary, Yamauchi replaced his son-in-law as the leader of NOA and installed Howard Lincoln, a senior vice president, as chairman.

Nintendo launched its N-64 system in Japan in May 1996 and in the United States in September 1996. The system was powered by a 64-bit processor, but the games are stored on cartridges. The use of cartridges as a storage medium gave Nintendo close control over manufacturing and generated an important source of manufacturing profit on third-party titles. However, cartridges had much higher production costs and retail prices compared to CDs, which have prevented many publishers from developing titles for the N-64.

Financial Performance.   Exhibit 16 presents summary financial data on Nintendo. During fiscal year 1997, Nintendo launched its N-64 game player. Demand for the new player exceeded expectations and supply, which in turn fueled an 18 percent increase in net sales to ¥ 417.5 billion ($3,367 million). Net income increased by 9 percent to ¥ 65.4 billion ($528 million). The company's financial position was considered to be strong. At the end of fiscal 1997, Nintendo had cash and cash equivalents of ¥ 541.5 billion ($4.3 billion), no debt, and total liabilities of ¥ 171.9 billion ($1.3 billion). Its liabilities-to-equity ratio was 0.30. Inventory turnover was down to 24 days, compared with 38 days in 1996.

Sega Enterprises, Ltd.[43]

Sega Enterprises, Ltd. (Sega), was one of the few Japanese companies started by Americans. In 1951, two Americans in Tokyo, Raymond Lemaire and Richard Stewart, began importing jukeboxes to supply American military bases in Japan. Their company eventually expanded into amusement game imports and adopted the

[43]Portions of Sega's company history extracted from Ibid.

EXHIBIT 16   Summary of Selected Financial Data, Nintendo Ltd., 1994–97

	Yen in Millions Except per Share Amounts				Dollars in Millions
	1994	**1995**	**1996**	**1997**	**1997**
Total revenue	¥496,979	¥429,427	¥400,707	¥462,922	$3,733
Operating income	104,411	85,704	133,282	115,490	931
Income taxes	59,379	50,398	73,503	50,012	403
Net income	52,653	41,660	59,870	65,481	528
Per share					
Net income	¥371	¥294	¥423	¥462	$ 3.73
Cash dividends	70	70	100	100	0.81
Cash and cash equivalents	¥343,472	¥396,678	¥483,196	¥541,578	$4,368
Total current assets	518,854	498,445	571,105	660,276	5,325
Total assets	591,227	578,662	649,840	735,620	5,932
Total current liabilities	139,609	107,854	135,568	169,552	1,367
Total liabilities	147,034	109,795	137,315	171,900	1,386
Total shareholder equity	444,193	464,784	512,524	563,718	4,546

Source: Company annual reports.
Notes: U.S. dollar amounts have been translated from yen at the rate of 124 yen = U.S. $1, the approximate foreign exchange rate as of March 31, 1997.

slogan "service and games."[44] The modern Sega began to take shape in 1956 when a Brooklyn-born entrepreneur named David Rosen, who had been stationed in Japan with the Air Force, returned to Japan and began importing mechanical coin-operated amusement machines as Rosen Enterprises. In 1965, the "service and games" company merged with Rosen Enterprises. Not happy with the game machines available from U.S. manufacturers, Rosen decided to make his own. He acquired a Japanese factory that made jukeboxes and slot machines. The company's products were stamped with SEGA—short for *service games*—and Rosen adopted the brand name that has been used ever since.[45] The next year it began its transformation from importer to manufacturer, producing a submarine warfare arcade game called Periscope, which became a worldwide hit.

Sega was acquired by Gulf & Western (G&W) in 1969 and went public in 1974. Hayao Nakayama, a Japanese entrepreneur and former Sega distributor, was recruited to head Sega's Japanese operation; Rosen headed the U.S. operation. Through the 1970s and early 1980s, the video game industry went through a boom period. Sega's revenues reached $214 million in 1982. The overall game industry hit $3 billion in 1982, but collapsed three years later with sales of $100 million. G&W became anxious to get rid of Sega. Nakayama and Rosen organized a buyout of Sega's assets for $38 million in 1984, and thus Sega Enterprises Ltd. was formed. The deal was backed by CSK, a large Japanese software company that in 1998 owned 20 percent of Sega. Nakayama became the chief executive, and Rosen headed the U.S. subsidiary. Sega went public in 1986. Rosen had since become a director of Sega and co-chairman of its American subsidiary.

---

[44]"Sega's American Roots," *The New York Times,* July 4, 1993, p. 6.

[45]R. Brandt, R. D. Hof, and P. Coy, "Sega!" *Business Week,* February 21, 1994, pp. 66–74.

Sega of America was formed in 1986. Its first task was to market Sega's first home video game system, the 8-bit Master System. Sega had been beaten to the punch in Japan by Nintendo, which got a jump on the market with its 1983 release of the 8-bit Famicom. Unfortunately for Sega, Nintendo also won the 8-bit war in the United States and the Master System slowly died out. Meanwhile, Nintendo essentially grabbed the entire home video game market share in the United States and Japan.

Europe was a different story. Sega systems had achieved good market penetration in Europe, while Nintendo sales had been slow. Sega of Europe accounted for a large share of Sega's revenues. Some of Sega's recent sales declines were the result of the slumping European video game market.

Sega did not begin to see large-scale success until the release of its 16-bit Genesis system in 1989. The Genesis system was not an immediate hit; only after the release of Sonic the Hedgehog in 1991 did sales take off. By 1994 Sega overtook Nintendo in the crucial U.S. market. But what Sega did to Nintendo, Sony did to Sega a few years later with the introduction of the PlayStation. Sony's machine attracted such a huge following that Sega could not recover. To try to bolster the declining market share of its Saturn player, Sega instituted rebate and incentive programs.[46]

Sega's Saturn languished at retail throughout most of 1997, especially in the United States. At year-end 1997, Saturn had an estimated total installed base of less than 2 million units. Almost no third-party licensees published titles exclusively on the Saturn, and very few planned to publish any new titles for the Saturn system. Saturn's market failure was attributed to its comparatively high launch price, its lack of blockbuster exclusive titles, and a development system that many developers felt was inferior to that of the PlayStation. As details of Sega's next hardware release emerged, industry observers predicted that Sega was committed to correcting the mistakes it made with Saturn.

Sega's strategy with its next generation system was reportedly based on five elements.[47] First, Sega planned to make it easy for game developers by using PC accelerator-based technology. Third-party developers praised Sega's move to bring the game-playing technology for the PC and the video game console closer together. Second, Sega pledged to improve the attractiveness and quality of its games. Sony had been criticized for the poor quality of many of the games for its PlayStation, and Nintendo also was short on high-quality games. Sega management was confident it could develop good games. Third, Sega hired a new ad agency, vowing to make up for the poor ad campaign that had launched Saturn in 1995. Fourth, Sega planned a much bigger presence in the PC and online market. Fifth, Sega strongly believed its Dreamcast system would be more advanced than what Sony or Nintendo were rumored to be developing.

Financial Performance. Exhibit 17 presents a six-year financial summary for Sega. In fiscal 1997, Sega reported a net sales increase of 4 percent from the previous year to ¥359.9 billion ($2.9 billion), and a 5.1 percent gain in net income, to ¥5.6 billion ($44.9 million). This was largely attributed to a strong performance by its amusement center operations, as well as surging amusement machine sales, both of which offset a drop in consumer product sales (down 3 percent from the prior year).

---

[46]D. P. Hamilton, "Sega Will Take Write-off, Report Loss on Game Player's Weak Sales," *The Wall Street Journal Interactive Edition,* March 16, 1998.

[47]C. Campbell, "Movers and Shakers: Sega on the Threshold," *Next Generation,* September 1997, p. 28.

EXHIBIT 17   Financial Summary, SEGA Enterprises, Ltd., 1992–97 (Years ending March 31)

| | Millions of Yen | | | | | | Thousands of U.S. Dollars |
	1992	1993	1994	1995	1996	1997	1997
Net sales:							
Consumer products	¥135,124	¥229,270	¥235,880	¥188,486	¥169,524	¥164,395	$1,324,698
Amusement center operations	41,410	58,914	61,734	74,204	82,136	88,191	710,644
Amusement machine sales	36,427	57,558	52,144	61,400	84,976	98,241	791,628
Royalties on game software	356	1,195	4,274	9,233	9,546	9,103	73,352
Total	213,317	346,937	354,032	333,323	346,182	359,930	2,900,322
Cost of sales	150,873	251,834	270,305	257,371	270,968	285,146	2,297,711
Gross profit	62,444	95,103	83,727	75,952	75,214	74,784	602,611
Selling, general and administrative expenses	23,153	32,563	37,132	44,744	45,578	43,555	350,967
Operating income	39,291	62,540	46,595	31,208	29,636	31,229	251,644
Net income	14,014	28,017	23,223	14,085	5,304	5,572	44,899
Depreciation and amortization	9,067	15,591	20,049	22,164	23,142	22,914	184,641
Total assets	226,065	295,153	300,968	426,457	441,106	387,279	3,120,701
Total shareholders' equity	90,318	116,511	165,469	175,641	177,644	179,293	1,444,746
Financial ratios							
Return on average assets	8.2%	10.8%	7.8%	3.9%	1.2%	1.3%	—
Return on average equity	16.7	27.1	16.5	8.3	3.0	3.1	—
Payout ratio	8.9	8.7	16.4	27.1	72.0	68.6	—
	Yen						U.S. dollars
Net income per share—primary	¥144.4	¥288.7	¥232.8	¥140.2	¥52.8	¥55.4	$0.45
Net income per share—fully diluted	—	—	—	—	47.3	48.5	0.39
Cash dividends per share (adjusted)	12.8	25.0	38.0	38.0	38.0	38.0	0.31
Number of employees	2,324	3,034	3,492	3,758	3,764	3,872	

Sega initiated a major shakeup in January 1998. After two years of running Sega's home game division, Hayao Nakayama was replaced by Shoichiro Irimajiri as president of Sega Enterprises. Mr. Nakayama was appointed Sega's vice chairman and given responsibility for Sega's arcade business. In addition, Sega cut more than 100 jobs in divisions like SegaSoft, Sega of America, and GameWorks. Japanese news services reported that a division or two would also be liquidated.[48]

[48]M. Webb, "Arcadia: The Latest Arcade and Coin-op News," *Next Generation,* May 1998, p. 33.

In March 1998, Saturn's epitaph seemed assured when Sega announced it would take a large write-off, report a huge loss, and likely scale back sales of its flagship video game system.[49] As a result of the special charge, Sega revised its projections for fiscal year 1998. The company expected to report a pretax loss of ¥9.2 billion on sales of ¥343 billion, compared with its earlier forecast of a pretax profit of ¥21 billion on sales of ¥390 billion. Moody's Investors Service indicated it might downgrade Sega's Baa2 credit rating as a result of its dismal performance.

Sony Corporation[50]

Sony Corporation was established in Japan in May 1946 as Tokyo Tsushin Kogyo Kabushiki Kaisha. In January 1958, it changed its name to Sony Kabushiki Kaisha (*Sony Corporation* in English). Sony Corporation of America was formed in 1960. In 1998, Sony's business consisted of the development, manufacture, and sale of various kinds of electronic equipment. Sony was also engaged worldwide in the development, production, manufacture, and distribution of recorded music, in all commercial formats and musical genres, and image-based software, including film, video, television, and new entertainment technologies.

Sony's electronic products were sold throughout the world, and the Sony trademark had been registered in 193 countries and territories. In most cases, sales of Sony's electronic products were made to subsidiaries located in diverse geographical areas; the subsidiaries in turn sold to local distributors and dealers. For example, Sony Electronics, Inc. was Sony's subsidiary in North America, which had 21 sales and distribution branches and offices throughout the United States.

Eager to claim a stake in the fast-growing video game business, Sony set up a new division in May 1994, Sony Computer Entertainment of America, to develop and market a next generation home video game, called the Sony PlayStation. The PlayStation had been under development for more than four years and represented an important element in Sony's strategy to dominate the entertainment markets for hardware and software. The system was released in Japan in December 1994, in the United States in 1995, and in Europe in the spring of 1997.

Despite Sony's lack of history in video game hardware, and of any particular success in software, the company was considered a formidable competitor because of its global distribution capability of both video game hardware and software, its well-known brand name and image with U.S. consumers, and the content potential contained in the movie libraries of Columbia Pictures and Tri-Star Entertainment (both Sony subsidiaries). Sony made few mistakes in launching its PlayStation and winning the attention of buyers, outcompeting other video game companies in the process. In early 1998, Sony's game division had sold more than 33 million PlayStation game players worldwide, along with 236 million game CDs.[51]

Financial Performance.   Exhibit 18 presents a five-year summary of selected financial data for Sony. For revenue reporting purposes, Sony classified its business into three segments: electronics, entertainment, and insurance and financing. The PlayStation game console and software fell under the "other-products" category (26.5 percent of total revenue) in the electronics business segment (77.5 percent of total revenue). The

---

[49]Ibid.

[50]Extracted largely from Sony Corporation's 1993 annual report.

[51]I. Kunii et al., "The Games Sony Plays," *Business Week,* June 15, 1998, pp. 128–130.

EXHIBIT 18   Financial Summary, Sony Corporation, 1993–97 (Years ending March 31)

	Yen in Millions Except per Share Amounts					Dollars in Thousands Except per Share Amounts
	1993	**1994**	**1995**	**1996**	**1997**	**1997**
Sales and operating revenue	¥4,001,270	¥3,744,285	¥3,990,583	¥4,592,565	¥5,663,134	$45,670,435
Operating income (loss)	130,640	106,962	(166,640)	235,324	370,330	2,986,532
Income (loss) before income taxes	92,561	102,162	(220,948)	138,159	312,429	2,519,589
Income taxes	49,794	78,612	65,173	77,158	163,570	1,319,113
Net income (loss)	36,260	15,298	(293,356)	54,252	139,460	1,124,677
Per share						
Net income (loss)	¥ 92.2	¥ 42.1	¥ (696.9)	¥ 134.0	¥ 309.2	$ 2.49
Cash dividends	50.0	50.0	50.0	50.0	55.0	0.44
Depreciation and amortization*	¥ 275,671	¥ 242,458	¥226,984†	¥ 227,316	¥ 266,532	$ 2,149,452
Capital expenditures (additions to fixed assets)	251,117	195,937	250,678	251,197	298,078	2,403,855
R&D expenses	232,150	229,877	239,164	257,326	282,569	2,278,782
At Year End						
Net working capital	¥ 367,009	¥ 616,089	¥ 537,739	¥ 816,387	¥ 843,596	$ 6,803,194
Stockholders' equity	1,428,219	1,329,565	1,007,808	1,169,173	1,459,428	11,769,581
Stockholders' equity per share	¥ 3,827.39	¥ 3,557.57	¥ 2,695.31	¥ 3,125.57	¥ 3,798.76	$ 30.64
Total assets	¥4,529,830	¥4,269,885	¥4,223,920	¥5,045,725	¥5,680,342	$45,809,210
Average number of shares outstanding during the year (thousands of shares)	417,687	417,454	417,665	421,973	458,992	—
Number of shares issued at year-end (thousands of shares)	373,158	373,728	373,911	374,068	384,185	—

*Including amortization of deferred insurance acquisition costs.
†Excluding write-off of goodwill
Notes:
1. U.S. dollar amounts have been translated from yen, for convenience only, at the rate of ¥124 = $1, the approximate Tokyo foreign exchange market rate as of March 31, 1997.
2. Net income (loss) per share is computed based on the average number of common shares outstanding during each period after consideration of the dilutive effect of common stock equivalents.
3. During the fiscal year ended March 31, 1996, the company changed its method of accounting for assessing the carrying values of intercompany foreign currency commitments to comply with the Emerging Issues Task Force Issue No. 95-2. This did not have a material impact on results of operations for the years ended March 31, 1996 and 1997.
4. The consolidated results for the fiscal year ended March 31, 1995, reflect the write-off of goodwill of ¥265 billion in the Pictures Group and losses in the Pictures Group of approximately ¥50 billion arising from a combination of unusual items, such as abandoning a large number of projects in development and providing for settlement of outstanding lawsuits and contract claims.

other-products division registered a 36.5 percent rise in 1997 sales to ¥1,500 billion ($12,100 million) over 1996, largely due to the solid market performance of Sony's new video game hardware and software products.

During fiscal 1997, the yen depreciated approximately 15 percent against the U.S. dollar, 7 percent against the German mark, and 16 percent against the British pound compared to the previous year. The U.S. dollar, German mark, and British pound represented approximately 67 percent, 5 percent, and 5 percent, respectively, of Sony's overseas sales. It was estimated that sales would have been approximately ¥520 billion lower if the value of the yen had remained the same as in 1996.

In its 1997 letter to shareholders, Sony emphasized its commitment to information technology as a key element in the company's future growth. To this end, Sony was directing its strategic efforts at creating new markets and providing new lifestyle concepts to consumers. Video games seemed poised to remain a significant component of Sony's portfolio and a threat to all industry players. In video games, Sony's challenge was how to manage the transition to a new platform—The PlayStation II.

Sony ended fiscal 1998 with record profits. Consolidated pretax profit rose 45 percent, to ¥453.7 billion ($3.4 billion). Sales rose 19 percent, to ¥6.7 trillion yen. Computer game and player sales boomed, rising 72 percent amid strong demand for PlayStation consoles and software. Operating income in the business line doubled.[52] Sony's PlayStation business accounted for $5.5 billion, or 10 percent of Sony's worldwide revenue, and contributed $886 million, or 22.5 percent of Sony's operating income. According to Sony's chairman, Norio Ohga, "We've never had a business like this."[53]

(You may wish to visit the Web sites for Sony—www.sony.com; Nintendo—www.nintendo.com; and Sega—www.sega.com for additional information.)

---

[52]B. Spindle, "Sony Profit for Year Climbs 45 % to Record," *The Wall Street Journal,* May 8, 1998, p. A12.
[53]Kunii, "The Games Sony Plays."

BRØDERBUND SOFTWARE, INC.

Armand Gilinsky, Jr., *Sonoma State University*

On Thursday, March 23, 1995, William M. (Bill) McDonagh, president and chief operating officer (COO) of Brøderbund Software, Inc., opened his morning newspaper to the business pages. McDonagh saw the following headlines in *The New York Times:*

"The Surging Sales of CD-ROM's Sharply Raise Brøderbund Profit"
"Market Triples for CD-ROM's"
"DreamWorks and Microsoft in Multimedia Venture"

> *Our business is becoming more mainstream.*
> *The opportunities are tremendous.*
> *The competition will be fierce.*
> *There will be more than one winner.*
> **Bill McDonagh**
>
> *Catch me if you can!*
> **Carmen Sandiego**

McDonagh had just completed his first year as president and COO. He realized that Brøderbund had achieved recognition as a major player in what had become an intensely competitive, dynamic consumer software industry. Increasing sales of multimedia personal computers and continued demand for interactive CD-ROM titles had pushed the company's fiscal 1995 second-quarter earnings far in excess of Wall Street analysts' expectations. Brøderbund's stock had closed the previous day at $53.25, rising to an all-time high of $56.00 per share in after-hours trading. Yet McDonagh knew that many observers and analysts disagreed to what extent Brøderbund could sustain its early leadership in the industry; whether it could continue to attract the "critical mass" of managerial, financial, technical, and marketing capabilities necessary to compete; and how he, as president and COO, would be able to address and overcome any barriers to growth.

Now entering its 15th year of existence, Brøderbund had developed, published, marketed, and sold over 25 million units of consumer software. In fiscal year 1994, Brøderbund posted record annual sales of $112 million and profits after tax of $11 million. International sales were static, accounting for less than 10 percent of net revenues. Brøderbund still paid no dividends.

The case writer benefited from the assistance of student researchers Tulara McCauley, Gary Doyle, and Kari Young and Professor Brenda J. Ponsford at Sonoma State University, as well as from the suggestions and support of several reviewers.

Brøderbund's executive team wondered how the growing company would manage the transition to a larger organization. McDonagh remarked,

> It's like pulling at both ends of a rope; the most creative people in the world also tend to be the least efficient. Should we follow where our creative people take us and pursue a broad path to future product development in many market segments, or take a more narrow path, concentrating our resources on a specific market niche, such as education?

To fill out its product line, Brøderbund was looking at several acquisitions and joint venture deals. Rumors that Brøderbund itself was a takeover target surfaced from time to time. Brøderbund's executive team needed to formulate a strategy that would take into consideration this apparent tug-of-war between the need to promote creativity to develop a portfolio of new products and investors' demands for greater operating efficiency to assure a continuously growing earnings stream and stock price appreciation.

COMPANY BACKGROUND

The company was founded in 1980 by its current chairman and chief executive officer (CEO), Doug Carlston, and his brother, Gary, when the personal computer software industry was still in its infancy. The brothers chose the name *Brøderbund* from *Brøder,* a blend of the Swedish and Danish words for brother, and *bund,* German for alliance. The name originated from Gary Carlston's travels to and employment in Sweden. Today, you can find the words *Brøder* and *Søster* on the doors to the restrooms in the corporate lobby.

In his 1986 book, *Software People,* Doug Carlston described Brøderbund's early history as follows:

> When my brother and I started Brøderbund Software in 1980, we had no idea that it would become one of the largest home computer software companies in the world. In fact, we originally entered the software business by accident. We had no business plan, no scheme to make our fortunes. We were just trying to come up with a way to pay our next month's rent.
>
> In most ways, we were unlikely candidates for the roles we assumed. Neither of us knew very much about computers, and neither of us lived anywhere near those centers of innovation where so many high-technology firms were springing up. Before we started our company, I was a lawyer, practicing my trade in rural Maine. My brother Gary had just returned from Sweden, where he had spent five years working as a coach for a women's basketball team. He was now living in Oregon, where, after a stint as field director for the March of Dimes, he became involved in an importing business that proved to be unsuccessful.
>
> What we had was computer fever—a malady we shared with all the other entrepreneurs who were forming similar companies. Of the two of us, I was the one who was more heavily stricken. Programming can be an addiction—those who get drawn into it often forget jobs, family, and friends in their absorption with these fascinating machines. My own addiction began in 1978 when I took the fateful step of entering a Radio Shack store in Waterville, Maine, in order to take a closer look at the computer that was displayed in the window. I ended up walking out with a TRS-80 Model 1 tucked underneath my arm. My life has not been the same since.
>
> Finally, in October 1979, I dissolved my law practice. I was having a lot more fun writing computer games than I was drawing up wills. The fact that I was also making a modest but steadily increasing income from my programming efforts had something to do with my decision, but at the time it wasn't at all clear that this was a prudent career move. I had no idea whether the freelance programming business was going to continue to be financially viable, but I abandoned my law career anyway because the microcomputer software world drew me in a way that I found irresistible.

It immediately struck me—when I realized just how possible it was to make a living at my kind of programming—that I had an opportunity to lead an altogether different way of life. It took me a while to accept that I had stumbled upon such a beautiful loophole in the rules of life, but once I did I knew that my job for the immediate future was to create fantasies and translate them into computer programs. If you think that sounds a lot more like play than work, you know how I reacted to the prospect of this new career. The kind of fascinating sci-fi sagas that had occupied my spare hours—flying interstellar craft to a thousand strange planets—was now my profession as well as my avocation.

It didn't take long for my new career to change the way I lived my life. Something very different from everything I had previously planned for myself suddenly became possible, and I was still young enough to be tempted by the prospect of a romantic journey into an uncertain future. So I went along with the opportunity to become an electronic-age vagabond.

Before long, the Carlston brothers established Brøderbund in order to market Galactic Empire and Galactic Trader, computer game programs Doug had peddled at computer shows during a cross-country car trip with his dog, Benthi. By the summer of 1980, after forming an alliance with a Japanese software house, StarCraft, the company was able to market a substantial line of home entertainment products. Before the end of its third year, Brøderbund had moved from Eugene, Oregon, to California's Marin County; had grown to more than 40 employees; and was selling millions of dollars' worth of software annually. In October 1991, the company moved to headquarters in Novato, California, about an hour's drive north of San Francisco. (A list of milestones in Brøderbund's history is shown in Exhibit 1.)

Cathy Carlston, Doug and Gary's sister, joined the company in 1981. Until her departure in 1989, she served as vice president of educational market planning and was instrumental in formulating Brøderbund's marketing efforts to schools. Gary Carlston, the firm's first CEO, also left in 1989. At the time of their departure, the Carlstons felt that they had achieved financial independence and had taken the business to the point where professional managers were needed.

In 1987, Ed Auer joined the company as senior vice president, COO, and director after a 23-year tenure at CBS, Inc., where he had most recently run that company's software division. Auer was appointed Brøderbund's president in 1989 and retired in 1994, remaining a member of the company's board of directors. Bill McDonagh, an accountant who had been the company's first controller and later chief financial officer, was appointed to his current position in March 1994. (Profiles of the members of the current executive team are shown in Exhibit 2.)

When asked to consider what he saw as the company's most significant early challenges, McDonagh said:

. . . acquiring new products, growing an organization, and building a professional management team. It's not like prospecting for gold anymore or waiting for new products to arrive over the transom; developers now come to us. All of the people who are running this company now grew up with the business. We made up the rules, learning how to manage people as we went along. Hiring Ed Auer in 1987 fostered our transition to a professionally run company.

Carlston and McDonagh nevertheless strove to retain a corporate culture that allowed plenty of room for individuality and creativity at any level. In recent years, Carlston had become more and more distant from day-to-day operations, preferring to concentrate instead on the company's long-range Internet strategy. McDonagh, on the other hand, was involved in every operational decision. McDonagh was known informally to employees as "Bill the Thrill" for his exploits on the company's softball team. New

---

EXHIBIT 1   Milestones in Brøderbund's Evolution

1980–81	Company founded by Doug and Gary Carlston Galactic Empire and Galactic Trader introduced Cathy Carlston joins as executive vice president of educational market planning
1982	Bank Street Writer Plus, an entry-level word processing program Company moves from Oregon to San Rafael, California Bill McDonagh hired as controller Company passes $1 million revenues, 40 employees
1984	The New Print Shop (developed by Pixellite Software)
1985	Where in the World Is Carmen Sandiego? and The New Print Shop Companion Company passes $10 million in revenues
1986	Where in the USA Is Carmen Sandiego?
1987	The New Print Shop Graphics Library Sampler Edition Ed Auer hired as senior vice president and chief operating officer Focus shifts to internal product development; creation of education sales and marketing organization; and expansion of production facilities Proposed initial public offering delayed by unfavorable stock market conditions Revenues—$27.0 million; earnings—$3.0 million; R&D expenses—$2.4 million
1988	The New Print Shop Graphics Library Party Edition and Where in Europe Is Carmen Sandiego? Revenues—$36.6 million: earnings—$5.6 million; R&D expenses—$4.4 million
1989	SimCity (affiliated label product); Where in Time Is Carmen Sandiego?; The Playroom; The New Print Shop Graphics Library School and Business Edition; and TypeStyler (Mac only) Cathy and Gary Carlston leave company to pursue other interests; Ed Auer appointed president Outside consultant hired to standardize staff grade levels and job descriptions Revenues—$36.8 million; earnings—$3.4 million; R&D expenses—$5.5 million; 150 employees
1990	SimEarth (affiliated label product); Where in the World Is Carmen Sandiego? (Deluxe) Sale of Nintendo products division for a loss of $1.6 million Revenues—$50.4 million; earnings—$3.2 million; R&D expenses—$5.9 million
1991	Kid Pix; Where in America's Past Is Carmen Sandiego?; The Treehouse Carmen Sandiego quiz show on PBS; licensing agreement with Western Publishing, Inc. Company moves to new facilities in Novato, California Initial public offering of 3,257,184 shares completed, raising $33 million Revenues—$55.8 million; earnings—$7.0 million; R&D expenses—$6.8 million; 271 employees
1992	28 new products released Acquisition of PC Globe, Inc., a publisher of electronic atlases, for $1.5 million in cash Revenues—$75.0 million; earnings—$9.6 million; R&D expenses—$10.6 million
1993	44 new products released Maxis ends distribution deal with Brøderbund; decides to handle distribution on its own Revenues—$95.6 million; earnings—$13.6 million; R&D expenses—$13.6 million
1994	68 new products released; CD-ROM sales account for over 40% of revenues (over 60% in Q4) Living Books joint venture partnership with Random House announced Fox network broadcasts animated cartoon series based on Carmen Sandiego Ed Auer retires; Bill McDonagh appointed president and COO Agreement to merge with Electronic Arts terminated Sale of common stock investment for $1.6 million in cash; two-for-one stock split announced Revenues—$111.8 million; earnings—$11.0 million; R&D expenses—$16.0 million; 438 employees

Sources: Interviews with company officials; initial public offering prospectus; and 1994 annual report.

employees were introduced at monthly assemblies in a ritual known as "walking around the buoy," in which the inductee walked in a 360-degree circle to show his or her face to the veterans. Executives could still be found eating lunch with groups every day in the cafeteria. Each Friday concluded with a companywide "happy hour" that facilitated sharing ideas and socialization. Dress remained informal.

EXHIBIT 2   Brøderbund's Management Team in 1995

	Age

Douglas G. Carlston, Chairman of the Board and Chief Executive Officer   47

Carlston co-founded the company with his brother Gary in 1980 and served as the president and director until 1989, when he assumed his present title. His first exposure to computers came in the 1960s, when he was working as a programmer at Harvard's Aiken Computation laboratory. He graduated magna cum laude from Harvard and went on to study economics at Johns Hopkins School of Advanced International Studies before entering Harvard Law School, where he received his J.D. Following the commercial success of his first two games, Galactic Empire and Galactic Trader, Carlston quit the practice of law to devote his energies to programming. In addition to the inherent responsibilities of his office, he continues to devote his attention to fostering the creative process behind Brøderbund's product development.

William M. McDonagh, Director, President and Chief Operating Officer   38

McDonagh was appointed president and COO of the company in March of 1994 and elected a member of the board of directors in February of 1995. Now responsible for Brøderbund's day-to-day operations, overseeing development, manufacturing, sales, marketing, customer service and finance, he joined the company in 1982 as Brøderbund's first controller. He was promoted to chief financial officer in 1987 and named senior vice president in 1992. Prior to joining Brøderbund, McDonagh was an auditor with Arthur Andersen & Co. in Chicago. He graduated with a B.A. in accounting from the University of Notre Dame, holds an MBA in finance from Golden Gate University, and is a CPA.

Harry Wilker, Senior VP, Brøderbund Studios   48

Managing all aspects of Brøderbund's product development activities, Wilker is responsible for definition, design, development and publishing of all software products. He started working at Brøderbund in 1987 as manager of technical services, becoming the Productivity Group's executive publisher six months later. From 1990 through 1993, he was vice president of publishing and was promoted to senior vice president of the newly formed Brøderbund Studios in 1994. Prior to joining Brøderbund, Wilker headed Sentient Software in Aspen, Colorado, which he co-founded in 1981. He received a B.S. in political science from George Washington University and a M.A. in political science from State University of New York at Buffalo.

Jan Gullett, Senior VP, Sales and Marketing   41

Gullett leads all of the sales, customer service, marketing and brand management activities at Brøderbund. Gullett joined Brøderbund in 1995, following 18 years at PepsiCo, Sara Lee, and Procter & Gamble, where he progressed through marketing, sales, and general management roles. Most recently, Gullett was vice president, marketing, and vice president and general manager at PepsiCo's KFC division. He has a B.S. from Miami University and an MBA from Harvard.

Mason Woodbury, VP, Customer Services   42

Woodbury manages the direct marketing, customer service, and technical support divisions of the company. He is directly responsible for the evolution of the customer service department, which has grown from a staff of 20 to more than 100 employees. Woodbury joined Brøderbund in 1991 as the director of direct marketing and created relationships with on-line services, such as America Online, Compuserve, Ziff-Davis Interchange and the Microsoft Network. Prior to joining Brøderbund, he was the director of product management at Businessland in San Jose, California. He has a B.S. in business administration and an MBA from Babson College.

Rodney D. Haden, VP, Sales   43

Haden is responsible for directing the company's sales efforts in the United States and Canada. The sales department includes internal sales coordinators, dealer-support staff, training and a national field sales force. Haden joined Brøderbund in 1985 and was promoted to vice president in 1987. Prior to joining Brøderbund, Haden was the vice president of sales for Concentric Data Systems, Inc. Haden holds a B.A. in political science from American University in Washington, D.C.

EXHIBIT 2 Brøderbund's Management Team (Continued)

	Age

Marylyn Rosenblum, VP, Education Sales and Marketing   48

Rosenblum oversees the sales and marketing of Brøderbund products into the education channel. Since joining the company in 1992, she has instituted a number of effective new programs for the education marketplace. Prior to joining Brøderbund, Rosenblum was president of interactive learning materials. Before that, she was vice president, optical publishing, for Grolier Electronic Publishing, where she managed all aspects of the successful introduction of the New Electronic Encyclopedia on CD-ROM. Rosenblum is a graduate of the CBS School of Management and a co-chair of the Education Section Board of the Software Publishers' Association (SPA).

David Kessler, VP and Creative Director   42

As the head of Brøderbund's in-house design department, Kessler is responsible for overseeing the graphic design of the company's packaging, advertising, catalogs and a host of other printed materials. Several thousand projects a year flow through his department. Kessler has been with Brøderbund since 1984. Prior to joining Brøderbund, he was an account supervisor for Ketchum Communications, Inc., in San Francisco. Kessler holds a B.A. in graphic communications and advertising from San Diego State University.

M. W. Mantle, VP, Engineering, Chief Technical Officer   45

Responsible for overseeing the internal technical development of all Brøderbund products, M. W. (Mickey) Mantle's areas of responsibility include computer art and graphics, music and sound, quality assurance and software development. Mantle joined Brøderbund in 1991. As chief technical officer, he oversees Brøderbund's engineering staff and continues to focus on improving the product development process by standardizing development practices and adopting new technologies. Prior to joining Brøderbund, Mantle was general manager of graphics development for Pixar, which he joined shortly after it spun off from Lucasfilm in 1986. He holds a B.S. in computer science from the University of Utah and is widely known in the computer graphics community for his work.

Thomas L. Marcus, VP, Business Development, General Counsel and Secretary   41

In addition to overall corporate legal issues, Marcus is responsible for all of Brøderbund's contract negotiations with outside software developers, affiliated labels and licensees. He became Brøderbund's general counsel when he joined the company in 1986 and was appointed vice president in 1987. In June 1994, he was named vice president of business development to head a newly formed department created to pursue strategic partnerships. Marcus also focuses on the development of Brøderbund's international business. He holds an A.B. degree from Yale University, and received his JD. from the University of California, Berkeley, Boalt Hall.

Steven Dunphy, VP, Business Development   39

Dunphy joined Brøderbund in December 1985 and has held six different positions at the company including international sales manager, director of sales development, and director of business development. In his current role, he is responsible for Brøderbund's international operations, affiliated labels program, OEM and licensing functions. He has a B.A. in English from the University of California at Berkeley.

Albert Sonntag, VP, Operations   35

Sonntag is responsible for Brøderbund's manufacturing, distribution and warehousing, purchasing, facility management, duplication and special projects, such as the company's 1991 consolidation into new headquarters in Novato. He was hired as a production supervisor in 1983. As the company has grown, Sonntag has been charged with ever increasing responsibility, including production manager, manufacturing division manager, and director of operation. He was appointed vice president in 1990. Sonntag earned a B.A. in marketing and production operations at Sonoma State University.

John Baker, VP, Product Development, Education and Entertainment   46

Now guiding the definition, design, development and publishing of all the products within the entertainment and education product group, Baker joined Brøderbund in 1988 as chief technical officer and spent three years building up technical services. Prior to joining Brøderbund, Baker was a senior software engineer for Western Digital Corp. He holds a B.S. in physics and math from the University of New Orleans.

EXHIBIT 2   Brøderbund's Management Team (Concluded)

	Age
Richard Whittaker, VP, Executive Publisher	48

Employed at Brøderbund since 1982, Whittaker has been instrumental to the success of the company's most popular software titles. His most distinguished accomplishment has been his involvement with the evolution of Brøderbund's most successful product line, The Print Shop, where he has managed design and development for the past 10 years. Whittaker has held eight different positions during his tenure, including marketing writer, software editor, product manager, senior product manager, senior editor, software designer, publisher and executive publisher. He graduated from the University of California, Berkeley, where he received a B.A. in psychology. He later attended UCLA taking courses in the Master of Fine Arts, Motion Pictures & Television Program.

Source: Brøderbund Software, Inc., internal company records.

The company described its strategy in its 1994 annual report:

> Brøderbund Software, Inc. offers products in multiple product categories; personal productivity, education, and entertainment. Titles are produced to run on major personal computer platforms, including Windows, Macintosh and multimedia CD-ROM machines.
>
> The company's product strategy is to identify and develop emerging market segments and create new genres of software that achieve sustained consumer appeal and brand name recognition.
>
> Brøderbund's distribution strength is backed by one of the largest sales forces in consumer software. The company seeks out new distribution channels such as super stores and warehouse clubs and as a result, is now selling products in over 16,000 outlets nationwide.
>
> In the often turbulent consumer software industry, Brøderbund has succeeded because of its commitment to technology and its ability to anticipate industry trends, such as the emerging CD-ROM market. The company's products have a long-standing reputation for innovation and quality. Brøderbund has furthered its leadership role by investing in a sophisticated set of studio skills necessary to create high quality CD-ROM products.
>
> The company has also created a new business development department to pursue strategic partnerships and corporate alliances, and to increase Brøderbund's international presence.

PRODUCT DEVELOPMENT

Brøderbund referred to its product development process as a "studio development approach," including design, prototyping, programming, computer graphic design, animation, sound, archival and video recordings, and quality assurance. Doug Carlston described this process in a March 1996 interview in *Upside* magazine:

> It's an approach where you take the requisite combination of skills: product management, graphic skills, all the programming skills, and put it together in a single small team, often no more than five or six people, and they focus on a single project together. Studios . . . [allow] people to make the thousands of decisions that go into the creative process with a relatively tight feedback group. And frankly, we're just copying the best of what we see in other software companies. It's an approach that we adopted only a couple of years ago, at the impetus of the staff themselves.

Although the company focused on internally developed technology, it also acquired certain products and technologies from third parties. Regardless of the source of a program's original design, all programs published by Brøderbund underwent extensive editing and testing prior to release. The full production cycle for a new product typically took 12 to 14 months.

Most elements of the development process were provided by a combination of in-house and third-party resources with the exception of quality assurance activity, which was completed solely at Brøderbund facilities. The company believed that the use of both in-house and third-party designers, artists, and programmers expanded its ability to introduce creative and innovative products. McDonagh explained:

> Our mission is to be a broad developer and publisher of software for home computers. In choosing which products to develop, we use two criteria: market potential and the ability to create an advantage over someone else. We are one of the few software publishers that do both internal and external development. To develop new titles internally, there is increasing industrywide competition for the human resources to develop new products, including programmers, animators, artists, 3-D renderers, computer musicians, and so on. It is very much a creative process. Also, we have to develop "play-makers" who can bring these creative teams together. It's tough to find people with experience at this, so we generally groom people from the inside.
>
> As far as working with third parties is concerned, we have evolved more along the lines of a book publisher, looking for complementary titles rather than those that compete head-to-head with our existing offerings. For the third party developer choosing us, it's like the Beatles deciding on a record company. Third party developers look for a software publisher who has clout in the marketplace, lets them loose to be creative, offers support and technical resources, and delivers good royalties in return. Our most important strategic assets are our reputation and our critical "eye" that enables us to envision products that are destined to become hit titles.

ORGANIZATION

"Being a small company, we don't have any formal training programs," said Patsy Murphy, the company's director of human resources. The average age of Brøderbund's employees had risen to approximately 35 years from 28 years in 1988. The company had a 14 percent employee turnover rate. "Quality of life is the reward here," said Murphy. "We may be in an aggressive, competitive industry, but we do not have a competitive atmosphere."

Brøderbund's future success depended in large part upon the continued service of its key technical and senior management personnel and upon its ability to continue to attract, motivate, and retain highly qualified employees. As of August 31, 1994, the company had 438 employees, including 154 in product development; 127 in sales, marketing, and customer service; 118 in manufacturing and shipping; and 39 in administration and finance. The company had an employee and consultant stock option plan and a profit-sharing and retirement plan. Competition for trained programmers, artists, and writers was intense, and the loss of the services of key personnel could have a material adverse effect on the company's future operations and on new-product development efforts. None of the company's employees was represented by a labor union or was subject to a collective bargaining agreement. The company had never experienced a work stoppage and believed that its employee relations were good.

In early 1995, the market for consumer software was changing rapidly, requiring industry players to be nimble to respond to changing market conditions. In order to increase the agility of its rapidly growing organization, Brøderbund completed the transition from an organization structured along functional lines to a matrix of companywide resources.

Each of the company's publishing areas contained a software engineering group to develop products internally and to convert existing programs to various hardware formats. The engineering department worked on creating more effective development systems to permit development of software programs for several hardware platforms at once. This would enable the internal development staff to speed up the development of new products and to reduce the time to convert a product to a different hardware platform. In addition, Brøderbund engineers developed a proprietary digitized graphics system to deliver richer, more realistic images and animations.

These resources, in turn, supported small product teams, "little production houses," each representing one of the various product families: entertainment, early learning, later learning, and productivity. The company actively encouraged lateral movement of personnel among its product teams.

Jan Gullett, Brøderbund's senior vice president of sales and marketing, echoed this view: "We are a values-driven company. People come here because they want to do good things, not necessarily make a lot of money."

SOCIAL RESPONSIBILITY

Brøderbund demonstrated its commitment to being a responsible corporate citizen in a variety of ways. In 1988, the company created the Brøderbund Foundation, a nonprofit corporation. Douglas Carlston and Bill McDonagh serve on the three-member board of directors of this foundation. Each year, Brøderbund donated approximately 2 percent of its adjusted pretax profits to the foundation, which in turn made grants to qualified nonprofit organizations.

In 1994, Brøderbund became one of a growing number of software developers discovering the importance of building solutions to help parents and people with disabilities find alternatives for better living through technology. According to Karen Boylan, a member of Brøderbund's Education Marketing Group, "By learning how people with special needs use our software, we hope to find ways of building features into a product's design to enhance accessibility."

PRODUCTS AND OTHER VENTURES

By 1995 Brøderbund's best known "evergreen" products were The Print Shop® family of personal productivity products, the Carmen Sandiego™ family of educational products, and Myst® in the entertainment category. Its products won over 250 awards. In March 1995, Brøderbund won 4 of 25 annual Codie Awards, the software equivalent of the motion picture industry's Oscars, handed out by the Software Publisher's Association (SPA). Brøderbund's other products included reference products, education products, and a variety of printing, graphics, and other personal productivity products. (See Exhibit 3 for a listing of Brøderbund's products by product family and Exhibit 4 for a breakdown of revenues by product type.)

Product tie-ins included a weekday children's quiz show on PBS television based on the Carmen Sandiego theme. The company also had an agreement with Western Publishing Company, Inc., to market a variety of printed materials, including children's story and activity books, puzzles, and book covers all based on the adventures of Carmen Sandiego. In February 1994, the Fox TV network began airing a new cartoon series created by DIC Animation City, Inc., based on the Carmen Sandiego software program. Although Brøderbund did not receive significant revenues from these product tie-ins, management believed that these TV series would increase the

EXHIBIT 3 Brøderbund's Product Line

Product Family	List Price	Age Group	Platform	Description
Print Shop				
The Print Shop Deluxe Print Shop Deluxe CD Ensemble	$49.95 79.95	all	DOS/Win/Mac CD-ROM	Create greeting cards, signs, banners, and other personal documents *1995 SPA Codie Award, Best Personal Creativity Program*
Carmen Sandiego				
Where in the World Is Carmen Sandiego?	39.95 49.95	9 and up	DOS/Mac CD-ROM	Games designed to teach geography, history, and astronomy *1995 SPA Codie Award, Best Secondary Education Program*
Entertainment				
Myst Prince of Persia I and II	29.95 to 54.95	14 and up	DOS/Mac CD-ROM	Surrealistic multimedia adventure game Action-like arcade games featuring lifelike animation
Early Learning				
Kid Pix; Math Workshop; The Playroom; The Backyard; The Treehouse	39.95 to 49.95	3 to 12	DOS/Win/Mac CD-ROM	Paint and activity programs combining sounds, graphics, and special effects; *1995 SPA Codie Award*
Edutainment				
The Amazing Writing Machine Spelunx and the Caves of Mr. Seudo Alien Tales	24.95 to 39.95	6 to 12	Mac CD-ROM	Creative writing, illustration, and idea-generation program Ecology, astronomy, biology, reading, music, art, and fantasy Intergalactic game show teaches reading
Other Products				
3D Home Architect PC Globe Maps 'n' Facts TypeStyler	59.95 to 129.95	Adult	Windows CD-ROM Mac	Easy home design, complete with realistic 3D views Electronic atlas Shape and style text to create special effects
Living Books				
Assorted titles	39.95 ea	3 to 10	Win CD-ROM Mac CD-ROM	Stories and poems brought to life with sound effects, original music, humor, and animation.

exposure of the Carmen Sandiego software and enhance brand recognition for the product family. Since its introduction to the market in April 1985, the game had sold more than 4 million units. With the release of new Carmen Sandiego software products on CD-ROM and also for a younger age group, management believed that it had addressed the factors which had caused the decline in revenues from this product family.

On January 1, 1994, Brøderbund and Random House, Inc., became equal partners in a joint venture called Living Books to publish the Living Books line of products. Both Brøderbund and Random House distributed Living Books through their respective distribution channels under an affiliated label agreement. In November 1994, John Girton, an analyst with Van Kasper & Co., noted, "With Living Books, Brøderbund

EXHIBIT 4   Brøderbund Software, Inc. Fiscal 1994 Revenue Breakdown,
             by Product

	1994	Change from FY 1993
Print Shop	32%	+22%
Entertainment	15	+200
Carmen Sandiego	14	(24)
Living Books	13	+200
Early Learning	10	n/a
Affiliated products	9	(45)
Other	7	n/a
Total	100%	+17%
Of which:		
CD-ROM	40%	+400%
Macintosh	30	+150

Source: Brøderbund Software, Inc. internal company records.

was the first company of any size to enter the CD-ROM market, so they were pioneers. That was a significant move for them, because the CD-ROM market is going to get bigger and bigger." In the first quarter of fiscal year 1995, the Living Books venture made its initial contribution to Brøderbund's earnings in the amount of $1.7 million. Brøderbund made plans to move its Living Books division from Novato to a separate facility in San Francisco in late summer of 1995.

In addition, Brøderbund distributed and sold products written and produced by several affiliated software companies: Amtex, Books that Work, Cyan, I-Motion, Inroads Interactive, The Logic Factory, Quadrangle, Starwave, and Vicarious. Affiliated label products were generally marketed under the name of the affiliated label company, and the affiliate remained responsible for product development, marketing, and technical support. This enabled Brøderbund to leverage its investment in its sales force and add a new source of product without incurring the risks inherent in new product development. The company's agreements with its affiliated label producers provided for a specific period of time, after which these rights were subject to negotiated renewal. In the first quarter of fiscal 1995, one of the Company's affiliated labels, Automap, announced it was being purchased by another company. Brøderbund's affiliated label relationship with Automap was terminated at the end of February 1995. During fiscal 1994 revenues from sales of Automap products accounted for less than three percent of net revenues. In fiscal 1995, Brøderbund signed distribution agreements with Starwave, begun by Microsoft co-founder Paul Allen, to create interactive on-line services and CD-ROM software featuring entertainers such as Clint Eastwood (The Logic Factory), the Muppets (I-Motion), and a series of pet titles, including "Multimedia Dogs" and "Multimedia Cats" (Inroads Interactive).

Management felt that new-product introductions were critical to the company's future success. Doug Carlston said:

> Software has phenomenal gross margins compared to most businesses. Properly run, a software company should be kind of a cash cow. And it's enormously tolerant of mistakes. The creative process itself has a lot of built-in opportunities for mistakes. It's relatively difficult to combine the creative personalities with the numerically oriented bean counters who often

run companies when they get to a certain size. And that's a rare chemistry. Creative process also tends to suffer from just size. It's at its best when people are working with a small group of compatriots who are all very much focused on a single goal and don't have to spend an enormous amount of time justifying what they are doing up or down a corporate ladder. The best way to do it is to keep your creative units as small and cohesive as possible.

McDonagh added:

However, blockbusters are not created every day, and there is no way of knowing whether we have or have not created a blockbuster until it takes off in the marketplace. Therefore, new product introductions are only part of a greater challenge: To create software that people want—based on market trends—a program that can command a significant percentage of sales in the market and sustain its presence long enough to recapture its R&D costs. This is critical to any software company's success, including ours.

"Our strategic weakness is predicting what's going to be a hit, making sure that we'll have hit titles on a regular basis," said Gullett. There was also evidence of slackening growth in the consumer software market as well as evidence of emerging price competition. Competitors had begun to enter with new products priced at $19.95 in order to take market share away from an existing Brøderbund product, such as Print Shop, priced at $79.95.

PLATFORM SHIFTS

Brøderbund identified and proactively targeted upcoming market needs, beginning with the shift of its product line from the DOS to Windows platforms and from floppy disk to CD-ROM formats. While the MS-DOS operating system had achieved by 1994 a large worldwide installed base, the number of newly shipped MS-DOS titles dropped by 10 percent during calendar 1994. Half of all those MS-DOS sales were games, with another quarter educational or personal productivity titles. With Windows integrating the business market and CD-ROM taking over the market for games, DOS was clearly at the end of its product life cycle. Replacing MS-DOS was strong consumer demand for "new" products, that is, re-introductions of older products on the newer Windows platform that could also take full advantage of CD-ROM capabilities (see the following table).

	Estimated 1994 Market Shares, by Platform	
Platform	By Sales ($ Revenues)	By Shipments (# of units sold)
Windows	70.8%	66.8%
MS-DOS	14.3	18.9
Macintosh	13.6	11.7
Other	1.3	2.6
Total	100.0%	100.0%

Source: International Data Corp., Framingham, MA.

Brøderbund estimated that future demand for titles that ran on Windows and CD-ROM would continue to expand, but demand for DOS-compatible and floppy-based products would continue to decline.

As hardware platforms consolidated worldwide, Brøderbund expected to publish fewer versions of its products. In the past, Brøderbund might publish DOS, Windows, Macintosh, floppy, and CD-ROM versions of a product. However, by 1995 most of the company's new products were being released only on the Macintosh or Windows CD-ROM platforms. As a result of these platform shifts and in anticipation of potential returns of products on declining platforms, the company increased its inventory reserves for returns to $10.3 million in fiscal 1994 from $6.4 million in fiscal 1993. Future platform shifts and product returns in excess of the company's expectations could have a material adverse effect on operating results and the financial condition.

SALES, DISTRIBUTION, AND OPERATIONS

Brøderbund sold its products to distributors and directly to software specialty retail chains, electronics chains, computer superstores, mass merchandisers, discount warehouse stores, educational dealers, schools, and end users. Brøderbund commonly participated in and provided financial assistance for its retailers' promotional efforts, such as in-store displays, catalogue advertisements, demonstration disks, and other collateral marketing materials. The company spent an estimated 0.4 percent of sales on advertising. Its largest distributor in fiscal 1994 was Ingram/MicroD, which accounted for approximately 21 percent of the company's net revenues. (See Exhibit 5 for a breakdown of Brøderbund's fiscal 1994 revenues by retail channel.)

Although the company's sales policies placed limits on product returns and although product returns had not had a significant effect on Brøderbund's operating results to date, the company could be forced to accept substantial product returns to maintain its relationships with retailers and access to distribution channels.

Sales Force

Brøderbund's 33-person national sales staff operated out of eight offices situated in California (2), Georgia, Illinois, Massachusetts, Pennsylvania, Ohio, and Texas. In addition, the company had distribution arrangements in Europe, Japan, and Australia. The company opened an office in London in 1994 to serve as a hub for its sales and marketing efforts in Europe. International distribution agreements granted the exclusive right to distribute Brøderbund's products in specific geographic territories. In some cases, the distributor purchased finished goods directly from the company for resale. In other cases, the distributor developed a foreign-language version and paid the company a royalty on sales of such products.

EXHIBIT 5   Brøderbund Software, Inc. Fiscal 1994 Revenue Breakdown, by Retail Channel

Software specialty stores	21%
Electronic stores	16
Superstores	16
Warehouse stores	15
Mass merchants	10
Office stores	7
Other	15
Total	100%

Source: Brøderbund Software, Inc. internal company records.

A separate 11-person education marketing and sales group focused on sales to schools. This group also produced material for teachers to tie Brøderbund learning products to current curriculum, provided suggested classroom activities for both on and off the computer, and sponsored a preview center and lending library. The company believed that sales to this market segment were an important element in its overall success because children were often introduced to Brøderbund's products through their schooling.

Direct Sales

Brøderbund promoted its products directly to end-users through direct mailings, catalogues, brochures, in-store demonstrations and presentations to computer user groups, advertising in computer publications, and the circulation of newsletters to specific audiences. The company maintained a substantial mailing list, comprising over 1.6 million users of Brøderbund's products. Direct sales to end users, free product demos, technical support, and press releases were all available from Brøderbund Software-Direct or on-line via Brøderlink, America Online, and Compuserve.

Production

Brøderbund prepared its own master software diskettes and CD-ROM discs, user manuals, and packaging. Almost all of the company's diskette duplication was performed at the company's own facilities, using diskettes acquired in quantity from outside sources. The company used outside sources to procure and duplicate CD-ROM discs, print user manuals, and manufacture packaging and related materials. The assembly and shipment of final products, as well as the majority of floppy disk duplication that was not CD-ROM, was performed by the company at its own 93,000-square-foot facility located in Petaluma, California. Brøderbund also supplemented the use of its own production facilities through reliance on third-party manufacturers.

As of early 1995, the company had not yet experienced any material difficulties or delays in the manufacture and assembly of its products and had experienced very low returns due to product defects. Brøderbund typically shipped product within one to two days after receipt of an order, which was customary in the computer software business. Accordingly, backlog as of any particular date was not representative of actual sales for any succeeding period. Nevertheless, management faced uncertainties in securing a supply of paper and, over the longer term, planning for increased warehouse and production line capacity.

Seasonality

Brøderbund's business was highly seasonal. Typically, net revenues, gross margins, and operating income were highest during the first fiscal quarter, ending November 30 each year; declined in the second fiscal quarter; and were lowest in the third and fourth fiscal quarters. (See Exhibit 6 for quarterly financial information.) This seasonal pattern was due primarily to increased demand for the company's products during the calendar year-end holiday selling season. However, the company's operating results in any given quarter could be increased due to new-product introductions or be adversely affected by delays in new-product introductions, lack of market acceptance of new products, the introduction of competitive products, as well as a variety of other factors including changes in product mix, timing of orders placed by distributors and dealers, and the timing and extent of marketing expenditures.

EXHIBIT 6   Brøderbund Software, Inc. Quarterly Financial Information (unaudited) (in thousands, except per share data)

| | Quarter ended | | | | |
	30–Nov	28–Feb	31–May	31–Aug	Year
Fiscal year 1995:					
Net revenues	$53,089	$45,208			
Gross margin	29,561	30,702			
Net income (loss)	11,593	10,367			
Net income (loss) per share	$0.57	$0.50			
Fiscal year 1994:					
Net revenues	$32,795	$25,350	$25,722	$27,907	$111,774
Gross margin	21,280	17,111	15,433	17,361	71,185
Net income (loss)*	6,243	4,458	(4,112)	4,472	11,061
Net income (loss) per share	$0.31	$0.22	($0.20)	$0.22	$0.55
Fiscal year 1993:					
Net revenues	$32,564	$24,353	$16,443	$22,223	$ 95,583
Gross margin	17,391	14,306	11,053	13,714	56,464
Net income (loss)	4,883	3,696	2,105	2,944	13,628
Net income (loss) per share	$0.25	$0.18	$0.10	$0.15	$0.68

*Includes one-time pre-tax charge of $11 million ($.38 per share) to terminate merger agreement with Electronic Arts (May 1994).
Sources: Brøderbund Software, Inc. 1994 Annual Report and 10-K statements.

INDUSTRY ANALYSIS

As of early 1995, the software market continued to be one of the fastest growing segments of the computer industry. According to the International Data Corporation, revenues for the packaged-software market totaled nearly $78 billion in calendar 1994, $72 billion in 1993, and $64 billion in 1992. The strongest software category sales dollar gains in the first half of 1994 were from home education/reference (+144 percent) and home creativity (+103 percent). Indications were that the majority of these sales were to the home market, and that sales to this segment were expected to continue to grow exponentially. By early 1995, home "edutainment" software had become, by some estimates, a market worth nearly $1 billion, with reported growth rates as much as 128 percent.

Emerging Market Segment

Dataquest, a research firm, classified multimedia products and services into five general categories: content development tools, interactive products, simulation products, video on demand, and enhanced productivity tools. Multimedia software products were designed to combine video, animation, still pictures, voice, music, graphics, and text into a single system. Multimedia products blurred the lines between several formerly distinct products and industries: computers, software, consumer electronics, communications, publishing, and entertainment. Although industry observers predicted that the market for multimedia products (such as interactive TVs and personal communicators) was not expected to take off until the late 1990s, some products were already available by 1995. Most current multimedia products were targeted at the consumer entertainment sector, rather than at the business market. The rationale for such targeting was that consumer multimedia software applications generally ran on computers, TVs, or other entertainment devices, while business software applications typically ran only on computers, from personal computer workstations to mainframes.

Sales of multimedia titles increased significantly in calendar 1994. According to Dataquest, multimedia CD-ROM shipments grew from 16.5 million units in 1993 to 53.9 million units in 1994. Ninety percent of CD-ROM titles were in the game, education, and personal segments. Approximately three-quarters of the reported CD-ROM sales were for the DOS/Windows/MPC formats.

CD-ROM–based multimedia products with voice, animation, video, and sound were expected to continue to gain popularity in the entertainment and education software segment. With a continuing decline in hardware prices, more PCs were expected to turn up in homes and small businesses. Strong sales and marketing operations thus became critical to develop, maintain, and strengthen CD-ROM distribution channels. With smaller margins available to software retailers, dealers and resellers could no longer afford to advertise or to train customers in the use of products. Marketing tactics, to generate enthusiasm and end-user demand for a product, were falling to the PC software companies, who in turn were operating with smaller sales and marketing staffs and reduced budgets. With the advent of the mail-order and mass-market retail channels, distribution channels appeared to be changing. To gain shelf space, smaller software publishers began to look for partners with greater financial and marketing resources. To gain rapid entry into the high-growth consumer software marketplace, large firms sought interindustry collaborations.

Strategic Alliances

Alliances, particularly among large firms, came to dominate the multimedia industry for several reasons: They reduced risks, spread costs, and allowed firms to acquire expertise in the different elements of multimedia quickly. In 1994, several computer, communications, and entertainment companies joined efforts to form a consortium, called First Cities, to develop interactive multimedia for home use. Participating companies were Apple, Bellcore, Bieber-Taki Associates, Corning, Eastman Kodak, Kaleida, North American Philips, Southwestern Bell Corp, Sutter Bay Associates, Tandem, and US West.

DreamWorks SKG, another alliance, was formed in 1995 under the joint leadership of Stephen Spielberg, Jeffrey Katzenberg (formerly head of Walt Disney pictures), and David Geffen (head of Geffen Records). In March 1995, DreamWorks announced that Paul Allen, a co-founder of Microsoft, had invested $500 million in the venture. This was soon followed by an announcement that Microsoft had signed a development agreement with DreamWorks, accompanied by an investment of an undisclosed sum.

These alliances cut across industry lines. This diversity suggested that member companies would perform different roles within the alliances. Jack McPhee, director of the Office of Computers and Business Equipment for the U.S. Department of Commerce, said, "Teaming and strategic alliances have become the order of the day; companies seek to combine their technologies and talents to address anticipated opportunities." For example, entertainment firms could provide the content of the digital media; telephone or cable companies, the ability to deliver the information; and computer hardware and software firms, the ways to use the data. Second, many alliances were international, signaling that the production of multimedia products would be global from the start.

Brøderbund's management believed that new competitors, including large software companies and other large media companies, were bound to increase their focus on the consumer software market, resulting in a proliferation of products, and increasingly fewer opportunities for small software companies to enter. "Currently, there is a proliferation of products competing for shelf space in many of our channels. In the future we expect there to be more industry consolidation as growth slows: People will start to look for partners when they feel the pinch," said McDonagh.

To remain successful, smaller vendors needed to find and exploit niche markets that were untapped by major vendors. To sell these products, smaller vendors needed to develop and maintain relationships with consumer-oriented distribution channels.

The Internet

As of early 1995, the effect of the development of the Internet on publishers, distributors, and retailers remained a major question mark. Still, many observers agreed that the potential market for publishing on the Internet, using multimedia billboards on the World Wide Web, was enormous. An estimated 6 million computers were linked directly to the Internet, a threefold rise from 1994, according to the Internet Society. An estimated 10,000 companies had already erected their own electronic billboards on the Web. The total number of people who could tap into the Internet from computer keyboards on any given day was estimated at 30 million worldwide. According to Forrester Research the total market for Internet business—including services, software, and shopping—had reached an estimated $500 million. By the year 2000, Forrester Research estimated that business on the Internet could reach $10 billion or more. This growth was expected to mirror the exponential growth of commercial online services: America Online had 2.5 million customers, followed by Compuserve (a division of H&R Block) with 1.9 million, Prodigy (a joint venture of IBM and Sears) with 1.6 million, and Dephi (a subsidiary of the News Corporation) a distant fourth with 160,000 subscribers.

According to Gullett, "The World Wide Web is a substitution threat, so we have to make products that are more powerful to take advantage of new Web technology. Over 70% of our user base is on line, 90% have modems. Yet in the long term, we're less positive about the Internet as a distribution vehicle for software applications than the rest of the industry."

Direct Competitors

Among Brøderbund's major direct competitors in the consumer software segment were Microsoft, Davidson & Associates, Sierra-Online, Learning Company, Maxis, MECC, and Edmark. (Exhibits 7, 8, and 9 present recent marketing and financial data on these direct competitors.) Despite the proliferation of these direct competitors, Brøderbund believed that its products competed most favorably with respect to product features and quality, reliability and ease of use, brand-name recognition and strength in distribution channels, and, to a lesser extent, quality of support services and price.

Intellectual Property Issues

Brøderbund regarded the software that it owned or licensed as proprietary. The company relied primarily on a combination of copyrights and trademarks, trade secret laws, and employee and third-party nondisclosure agreements to protect its products. Despite these precautions, the company was mindful of the possibility that

EXHIBIT 7   Brøderbund's Direct Competitors

Company	Date Est.	Location	Industry Rank, 1994	% Sales Increase 1993–94	Best-Selling Titles
Microsoft	1975	Redmond, WA	1	28	MS-DOS, Windows, Office, Word, Excel, Home
Davidson & Associates	1982	Torrance, CA	18	50	Math Blaster, Reading Blaster, Kid Works
Sierra On-Line	n/a	Bellevue, WA	20	21	King's Quest, Leisure Suit Larry, Red Baron, Outpost
Learning Company	1980	Fremont, CA	27	36	Reader Rabbit, Interactive Reading Journey, Treasure Mathstorm
Maxis	1987	Orinda, CA	32	102	Sim City, Sim Earth, Sim Ant
MECC	n/a	Minneapolis, MN	41	18	Oregon Trail, Yukon Trail, Amazon Trail
Edmark	1970	Minneapolis, MN	n/a	66	Bailey's Book House, Millie's Math House, Sammy's Science House, Thinkin' Things Collection

Source: Software Publishers' Association Annual Financial Survey of Members, April 1995.

unauthorized parties might attempt to copy aspects of its products or obtain and use information that is regarded as proprietary. Such software piracy could be expected to be a persistent problem, although it was a systematic risk of trading in the software industry.

Brøderbund was a founding member of the Software Publishers' Association and supported the SPA's antipiracy efforts to police the unauthorized use of computer software. The company had, from time to time, received communications from third parties asserting that features or content of certain of its products may infringe on the intellectual property rights of such parties and in some instances litigation was commenced. As of early 1995, no such claims had had an adverse effect on the company's ability to develop, market, or sell its products.

TERMINATED MERGER AGREEMENTS

In late 1990, Sierra On-Line announced a planned merger with Brøderbund in a stock swap valued at $88 million, but the deal kept running into problems. Uncertainty about the economy and then the Persian Gulf War put Sierra's plans on hold. In March 1991, the two companies renewed talks and signed a letter of intent to merge. The merged entity would have been called Sierra-Brøderbund, and Brøderbund would have become a unit of Sierra. But the deal fell through again. *The Wall Street Journal* quoted Ken Williams, president of Sierra On-Line, as saying:

> There was disagreement regarding the management structure of the combined company. This was unfortunate given the underlying strength of the two companies and the dynamic company which would have evolved. Only strong companies can succeed; you need a critical mass to compete in our industry. Maturity matters in our industry, and merging with other companies is the price of being in business.

EXHIBIT 8   Sales by Top-Selling Software Publishers—Calendar Year 1994

Games

	Dollars	Units
Sierra On-Line	$ 28,032	722,071
LucasArts	17,086	398,308
Microprose	15,459	368,136
Brøderbund	15,171	318,395
Maxis	15,130	462,997
Total Market, Games	$276,772	8,742,741

Education

	Dollars	Units
Learning Company	$ 18,248	410,332
Microsoft	16,621	238,987
Brøderbund	11,758	299,016
Mindscape	9,048	193,100
Davidson	8,886	264,540
Total Market, Education	$135,854	3,690,037

Personal Productivity

	Dollars	Units
Brøderbund	$ 15,947	311,507
Softkey	13,763	512,248
Expert Software	6,437	500,047
DeLorme	4,050	46,935
Microsoft	2,978	70,354
Total Market, Productivity	$ 90,962	3,086,022

Top Selling CD Publishers

	Dollars	Units
Brøderbund	$ 22,748	416,275
Microsoft	21,930	337,330
Sierra On-Line	13,936	338,039
Virgin	8,884	187,068
LucasArts	8,577	177,002
Mindscape	7,524	190,759
Learning Company	6,950	107,620
GT Interactive	6,312	138,527
Electronic Arts	6,128	159,867
Grolier	6,042	68,097
Total Market, CD-ROM	$243,632	5,570,949

Source: Software Publishers' Association Annual Financial Survey of Members, April 1995.

The deal finally was scrapped in April 1991. The Sierra On-Line merger would have allowed early Brøderbund investors to cash out since, at the time, Sierra stock was publicly traded while Brøderbund's was not. Brøderbund then proceeded with an initial public offering in October of that year.

In May 1994, Brøderbund and Electronic Arts terminated an agreement to merge due to financial considerations. Brøderbund recognized a onetime pretax charge of $11

EXHIBIT 9 Leading Consumer Software Companies—Historical Data (Sales in $000)

| | 1994 | | 1993 | 1992 |
	# Employees	Sales	Sales	Sales
Microsoft	16,379	$5,266,000	$4,109,000	$3,252,000
Brøderbund	450	132,068	95,814	86,126
Davidson & Associates	531	87,914	58,569	39,608
Sierra On-Line	650	76,500	63,354	43,269
Learning Company	206	44,761	32,873	23,852
Maxis	136	37,357	18,251	15,209
MECC	190	34,633	20,795	17,960
Edmark	115	16,807	10,118	7,368

Source: Software Publishers' Association Annual Financial Survey of Members, April 1995.

million which consisted of a $10 million payment to Electronic Arts to terminate the merger and $1 million in associated costs.

THE FUTURE

As McDonagh pondered his company's strategic direction in early April 1995, reports in the press offered seemingly contradictory futures for Brøderbund. *Business Week* published its 1995 annual roster of America's largest publicly traded companies, ranked by market value. Brøderbund made this list for the first time, ranked at number 788, with a market value of $1 billion. A sidebar article on Brøderbund went on to note: "'This little software company has a huge following because it has a very consistent track record of developing superb games,' said David T. Farina, an analyst at William Blair & Co. Farina predicted earnings would rise 95 percent, to $36.5 million by the end of fiscal 1996, on sales growth of 76 percent, to $195 million."

That same week, Jeffrey Tarter, publisher of an influential industry newsletter called *Soft•Letter,* noted that although the consumer and entertainment category was the fastest growing category in the personal computer software industry, smaller companies should be prepared for the coming shakeout as the marketplace became increasingly dominated by a handful of powerful companies.

McDonagh responded to these analyses by saying that the challenges for the future would be how to manage changes in technology and a market that was growing faster than the company's ability to deliver new products:

> The good news is that the consumer software industry is on the threshold of becoming a true consumer business. The drivers of this opportunity include the change from a hobbyist-oriented to a mainstream marketplace, one that will be more niche-oriented. Computer uses are changing, too, from playing back software to recording and communicating with software. The bad news is that we are not the only competitor who sees these changes. As for our future, one thing we have that the new entrants—telecommunications companies, media companies, film and video companies—do not have is our expertise to forecast and manage shifts in technology.
>
> Luck had a lot to do with our early success, but we now believe that success comes from having the right people, picking the right titles, and looking at platform shifts opportunistically

EXHIBIT 10   Brøderbund Software, Inc. Consolidated Statements of Income for 1990–1994, Years Ended
August 31 (in thousands, except per share amounts)

	1994	1993	1992	1991	1990
Net revenues	$111,774	$95,583	$75,085	$55,779	$50,387
Cost of revenues	40,589	39,119	32,838	24,358	21,077
Gross margin	71,185	56,464	42,247	31,421	29,310
Operating expenses:					
Sales and marketing	18,621	15,051	11,102	8,565	9,147
Research and development	16,016	13,671	10,624	6,774	5,890
General and administrative	7,500	7,112	6,375	5,919	5,337
Total operating expenses	42,137	35,834	28,101	21,258	20,374
Income from operations	29,048	20,630	14,146	10,163	8,936
Interest and dividend income, net	1,791	1,295	1,318	1,446	1,241
Terminated merger costs	(11,000)				
Income from continuing operations before income taxes	19,839	21,925	15,464	11,609	10,177
Provision for income taxes	8,778	8,297	5,805	4,547	3,959
Income from continuing operations	11,061	13,628	9,659	7,062	6,218
Income (loss) from discontinued operations, net of income taxes					(3,061)
Net income	$ 11,061	$13,628	$ 9,659	$ 7,062	$ 3,157
Per share data:					
Income from continuing operations	$.96	$.68	$.49	$.38	$.33
Net income per share	$.55	$.68	$.49	$.38	$.17
Shares used in computing per-share data	20,145	20,006	19,582	18,767	18,738

Sources: Brøderbund Software, Inc. Annual Reports and Forms 8-K.

instead of as threats. The beauty of being in a technology-driven business is that platform shifts or discontinuities take place every 3–4 years, so there's plenty of opportunity out there for us to develop new products that can take advantage of new platforms.

The real question is the pace of change and what obstacles we can hurdle. Whereas today we are primarily in packaged software, we may expand our reach into communications, leveraging our distinctive competencies in ease-of-use and brand name recognition. We expect that our product portfolio will change dramatically over the next 2–3 years and as a result, the company could double in size. It will be a higher stakes game: Deep pockets will be important for prospective as well as defensive purposes.

Clearly, the increased technical sophistication required in new consumer software products was expected to continue to make the availability of significant financial resources a very important competitive factor. In the event that price competition were to increase substantially, competitive pressures could cause the company to reduce the prices of its products and reduced profit margins could result. Prolonged price competition would, in turn, have a material adverse effect on the company's operating results and long-term competitive position. (See Exhibits 10–12 for Brøderbund's financial statements and recent operating history.)

EXHIBIT 11   Brøderbund Software, Inc. Consolidated Balance Sheets at August 31, 1990–1994 (in thousands, except per share amounts)

	1994	1993	1992	1991	1990
Assets					
Current assets:					
Cash and cash equivalents	$75,000	$54,316	$31,409	$29,621	$18,265
Accounts receivable, net	2,298	5,256	7,781	5,043	5,123
Income tax prepayments	1,156				
Inventories	2,361	3,211	4,127	2,327	1,913
Deferred income taxes	8,759	5,815	3,941	2,223	1,782
Other	757	378	655	360	3,854
Total current assets	90,331	68,976	47,913	39,574	30,937
Equipment and improvements, net	4,335	5,722	4,840	2,665	1,444
Other assets	2,985	2,531	3,473	509	470
Total assets	$97,651	$77,229	$56,226	$42,748	$32,851
Liabilities and stockholders' equity					
Current liabilities:					
Borrowings under bank line of credit	$ —	$ —	$ —	$ 1,462	$ 1,536
Accounts payable	5,656	4,237	2,956	1,948	1,957
Accrued compensation	5,353	4,266	2,572	1,552	1,199
Royalties payable	2,963	2,333	2,234	1,551	1,475
Accrued income taxes		1,238	461	1,551	—
Other	3,354	2,132	2,228	2,256	1,400
Total current liabilities	$17,326	$14,206	$10,451	$10,320	$ 7,567
Deferred income taxes	—	726	1,109	—	—
Other liabilities	146	287	496	—	—
Commitments					
Stockholders' equity:					
Preferred stock, $.01 par value; 1,000,000 shares	—	—	—	3,417	3,236
Common stock $.01 par value					
Authorized shares—40,000,000					
Issued and outstanding shares—19,624,000 in 1994, 18,998,000 in 1993	20,321	13,213	9,001	3,456	3,365
Retained earnings	59,858	48,797	35,169	25,555	18,683
Total stockholders' equity	80,179	62,010	44,170	32,428	25,284
Total liabilities and stockholders' equity	$97,651	$77,229	$56,226	$42,748	$32,851

Sources: Brøderbund Software, Inc. Initial Public Offering Prospectus and Annual Reports.

C-200

RF

EXHIBIT 12 Brøderbund Software, Inc. Consolidated Statements of Cash Flows
Years Ended August 31 (in thousands)

	1994	1993	1992	1	
Operating activities					
Net income	$11,061	$13,628	$ 9,659	$ 7,062	
Adjustments to reconcile net income to net cash provided by (used in) operating activities:					
Depreciation and amortization	3,028	2,760	1,368	892	774
Changes in current assets and liabilities					
Accounts receivable	2,958	2,521	(2,346)	80	1,257
Inventories	850	916	(1,721)	(414)	(989)
Other current assets	(79)	277	(180)	1,421	(664)
Income tax prepayments	(1,156)				
Deferred income taxes	(4,325)	(2,257)	(1,155)	(441)	(132)
Accounts payable	1,419	1,281	191	(9)	(369)
Other current liabilities	2,939	1,697	891	1,285	1,088
Accrued income taxes	(1,238)	777	(958)	1,551	(149)
Net cash provided by operating activities	$15,457	$21,600	$ 5,749	$11,427	$ 3,973
Investing activities					
Acquisition of PC Globe, Inc.			$ (1,500)		
Net additions to equipment and improvements	$ (1,041)	$ (2,436)	(2,918)	$ (1,826)	$ (821)
Proceeds from sale of discontinued operations	—	—	—	2,384	—
Other	(840)	(440)	(211)	(613)	(98)
Net cash used for investing activities	$ (1,881)	$ (2,876)	$ (4,629)	$ (55)	$ (919)
Financing activities					
Reduction of restricted cash deposit	—	—	1,750	—	
Inc. (dec.) in borrowings under bank line of credit	—	—	(1,462)	(74)	123
Exercise of stock options	7,108	4,183	2,130	72	480
Repurchase of common stock				(14)	(651)
Net cash provided by financing activities	$ 7,108	$ 4,183	$ 2,418	$ (16)	$ (48)
Increase in cash and cash equivalents	20,684	22,907	3,538	11,356	3,006
Cash and cash equivalents, beginning of year	54,316	31,409	27,871	16,515	13,509
Cash and cash equivalents, end of year	$75,000	$54,316	$31,409	$27,871	$16,515
Supplemental disclosure of cash flow information					
Income tax payments	$11,591	$ 7,506	$ 6,455	$ 1,783	$ 6,455
Interest payments	$30	$37	$64	$178	$64

Sources: Brøderbund Software, Inc. Initial Public Offering Prospectus and Annual Reports.

(Brøderbund's web address is www.broder.com)

fERENCES

Albemarle, J. "Pushing the PC Limit." *Graduating Engineer,* January 1995.

Bickford, C. "Fun and Games." *MacUser,* October 1994.

Bryant, H. "Myst Opportunities." *Oakland Tribune,* November 20, 1994.

"The Business Week 1000." *Business Week,* March 27, 1995.

Carlston, D. *Software People.* Prentice-Hall: New York, 1986.

Caruso, D., ed. "The Many Arms of Microsoft." *Technology and Media,* 1, no. 2 (July, 1994).

Fisher, L. "Two Companies in Software Drop Merger." *The New York Times,* May 4. 1994.

Gilles, J. "Brøderbund Scores at Software Symposium." *Mann Independent Journal,* March 16, 1995.

Leininger, L. "Disabled—Not!" *MacHome Journal,* January 1995.

Lohr, S. "Investment Is a $2 Billion Bet on the Net." *The New York Times,* May 11, 1995.

The New York Times, national edition, March 23, 1995.

Software Industry Report, April 15, 1991.

Southwick, K. "Doug Carlston Talks Tough." *Upside,* March, 1996.

Tarter, J. *The 1995 Soft•Letter 100,* 11, no. 19 (March 31, 1995).

U.S. Department of Commerce, U.S. Industrial Outlook, 1994.

The Wall Street Journal, November 3, 1991.

GLOSSARY OF PC INDUSTRY TERMS

Compact Disc–Read Only Memory (CD-ROM). Similar to an audio CD or compact disc that one might play on a stereo, these 5-inch shiny plastic disks hold computer instructions that are "played" by the computer. A CD-ROM contains programs or information such as encyclopedia contents coded in digital format on the side opposite the label. "Read only memory" means that users cannot change or add to the information on the disk, as opposed to the dual read-and-write capability of other electronic storage media, such as floppy disks or hard drives.

Edutainment Software. Multimedia software, including games, for educational and home use.

Graphical User Interfaces (GUIs). These special instructions and devices permit users to see vivid illustrations on their computer monitors, rather than just plain numbers and letters on a blank background. Contemporary GUIs allow for very fast and dazzling graphics, including short video clips.

Information Superhighway. A high-speed information network or method of accessing vast amounts of information from remote sites, such as libraries.

Internet. A series of large computers owned by universities, government institutions, and industrial firms connected by a network of telephone and other communication links. Access to the Internet allows users to exchange information such as electronic mail (e-mail) or computer files, and to search for information on various topics from many sources and providers. Some methods of access permit on-line interactions simultaneously with other individuals or groups, and this type of connection is sometimes called chat.

Multimedia. Refers to a software and hardware system that combines graphical capabilities ranging from still pictures to animation and audio capabilities such as voice and music with graphics and text. Typical media may include CD-ROM, laser disk, videotape, audiotape, and computer files such as those created by word processors, specialty graphic, photographic and/or sound programs. Interactive multimedia provides users with an opportunity to issue commands and respond to prompts and queries from the computer, resulting in a multimedia response. An example is an encyclopedia that illustrates a bird, first perhaps by providing a written text or audio explanation, followed by a short video clip showing the bird at rest and then in flight. A game may show characters in action and allow users the choice of various paths and actions.

On-line Service. Computer users often subscribe to commercial network services that provide telephone dial-in access to and software for using the Internet or World Wide Web. Providers include Compuserve, Prodigy, America On-Line, and the Microsoft Network. Subscribers normally pay a monthly access fee and may also pay an hourly rate.

Operating System (OS). A critical piece of software, that, like the grooves in a record album, allows the computer to "play" applications. These complex programs allow other software to operate within the rules of that operating system and the computer on which it is used. Popular operating systems include IBM and Microsoft PC-OS, Microsoft Windows, Apple OS, Macintosh OS, IBM's OS/2 Warp, and UNIX.

Platform Shift. Platform shift refers to computer manufacturers and end users migrating from using one computer operating system or format to a different operating system or format (such as from floppy disk to CD-ROM). This change in vendor or user preference may result in the user's needing to upgrade, expand, or even totally change computer hardware. It also requires software developers to rewrite or modify their programs to work in different operating system environments or on different storage and retrieval formats.

Reduced Instruction Set Computing (RISC). These special integrated circuits or "chips" use advanced designs that require fewer instructions to perform the same tasks, allowing the computer to operate faster.

World Wide Web. The system that connects all the computers together on the Internet, primarily via a graphical user interface.

12

CHURCH'S CHICKEN IN NAVAJOLAND

Jon Ozmun, *Northern Arizona University*

Casey Donoho, *Northern Arizona University*

Mason Gerety, *Northern Arizona University*

Mike Nelson watched from his table as a Navajo family stood at the counter and ordered fried chicken, mashed potatoes, gravy, and biscuits. As they moved away from the order taker, a young couple made their order and a line started to form behind them. It was the beginning of the lunch rush at Church's Chicken Restaurant in Window Rock, Arizona. "Its going to be another good day selling drumsticks in 'Navajoland,'" Mike thought to himself.

Nelson was the owner of the Church's Chicken Restaurant (CCR) in Window Rock. The business had been started in 1991 and had been a success almost from the first day. Fast food was as popular on the Navajo reservation as it was in the rest of the country, and fried chicken seemed to be preferred over hamburgers, tacos, and pizzas by the Native American consumers.

The success of the Window Rock restaurant had prompted Nelson to consider expansion into other population centers of the Navajo reservation (see Exhibit 1). His first choice for the next Church's Chicken Restaurant was Tuba City, Arizona. Nelson preferred Tuba City because it was one of the largest communities on the reservation. In addition, he was already established there with two other retail businesses—a TrueValue hardware store and a V&S variety store.

As Nelson watched the restaurant begin to fill with the lunch crowd, he wondered if Tuba City was the right location choice for his next "drumsticks" business.

NELSON'S BACKGROUND

Michael Nelson, a Navajo, was born in 1941 and raised on the Navajo reservation. He attended Bureau of Indian Affairs (BIA) boarding schools from the 1st through the 12th grades. Nelson attended the BIA high school in Fort Wingate, New Mexico, where he played on the Bears' football and basketball teams. After graduating from

EXHIBIT 1   The Navajo Nation

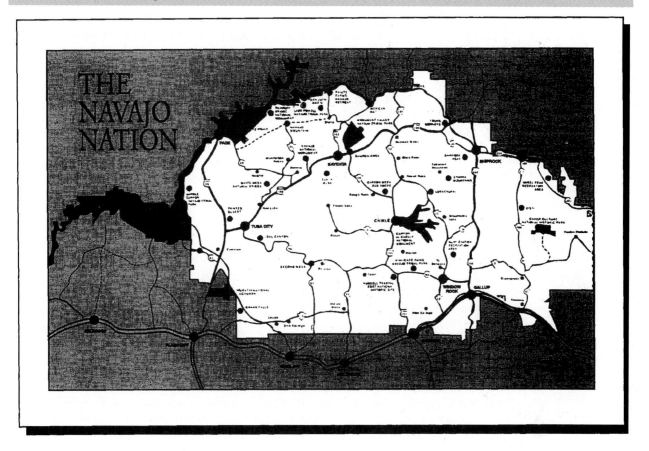

Populations of Major Retail Centers

	Census 1990	Forecast 1995	Forecast 2000
The Navajo Nation	155,276	170,803	187,883
Chinle	7,361	8,208	9,152
Kayenta	5,437	6,062	6,759
Shiprock	8,100	9,032	10,071
Tuba City	7,983	8,901	9,924
Tuba City market area	8,983	10,002	11,141
Window Rock	6,187	6,806	7,487
Window Rock market area	11,718	12,890	14,179

high school, Nelson enrolled at Fort Lewis College in Durango, Colorado, and graduated with a bachelor of science in business administration in 1965.

After graduation, Nelson worked three years (1965–67) for the Farmers Group Insurance Company. For the next six years (1967–72), he worked at the Office of Navajo Economic Opportunity as budget and office manager and business research assistant. He left this position to become a community economic industrial planner for the Phoenix Regional Small Business Administration, working with representatives of manufacturers, distributors, franchisers, banking and investment institutions, and municipal and civic leaders on and off Indian reservations. Nelson held this position until 1975, when he rejoined the Navajo Tribe as an economic planner in the Navajo Economic Planning Office. At the planning office, he developed feasibility studies and business plans for tribal programs.

It was while employed at the Office of Navajo Economic Opportunity that Nelson realized that he wanted to be completely self-employed. He took the first step in this direction in 1971 when he formed Michael Nelson & Associates, Inc. (MNA). During the period 1971–78, Nelson worked for others during the day and for himself at night and on weekends. Then in 1978, he left public employment to devote his time and energies to his own business pursuits.

While employed in the various capacities with the Navajo Tribe, Nelson became completely familiar with the political environment and how it influenced decisions regarding private business development. He also developed lifelong friendships with many of the most influential leaders in the tribal government.

During the next few years, Nelson's contributions to the Navajo business community were acknowledged by several organizations. He received the Small Business Administration's Incentive Award (1980), was named the Outstanding Indian Business Person of the Year (1984 by the U.S. Organization of Indian Businesses), and was named Outstanding Businessman of 1985 (by Minority Business Enterprises in the USA).

MICHAEL NELSON & ASSOCIATES

MNA was incorporated in the state of Arizona in October 1971. Nelson's first business venture was Navajo Westerners, a clothing store in Window Rock. He later added the V&S variety store in Tuba City (1975), convenience stores in Dilkon (1977) and Teesto (1976), and TrueValue hardware stores in Kayenta (1978), Tuba City (1983), and Window Rock (1990). The most recent addition to Nelson's small retailing "empire" was the Church's Chicken Restaurant in Window Rock (1991). All of these businesses were managed by Native Americans (see Exhibit 2).

By 1994, MNA's retail operations had combined assets of over $2 million. For fiscal 1994, MNA earned profits of over $200,000 on $6 million in sales revenues and employed a workforce of 70 Navajos in its operations. In that same year, MNA contributed over $800,000 to the Navajo reservation economy through salaries and wages alone.

EXHIBIT 2 Michael Nelson & Associates Retail Businesses

Location	Business	Product Line(s)	Manager
Dilkon	Convenience store	Gasoline, oil, foods	Pearl Begay
Teesto	Convenience store	Gasoline, oil, foods	Manley Yazzie
Kayenta	TrueValue hardware	Hardware, paint, lumber	Keith Cody
Tuba City	TrueValue hardware	Hardware, paint, lumber	Mason Manygoats
	V&S variety	Gasoline, oil, foods, paper goods	Milford Maloney
Window Rock	TrueValue hardware	Hardware, paint, lumber, Western clothing	Michael Nelson
	CCR	Chicken, other food	Carla Yazzie

CHURCH'S CHICKEN RESTAURANT—WINDOW ROCK

In 1990, Nelson obtained a franchise from Church's Chicken Restaurants, Inc., for the purpose of opening a restaurant in Window Rock, Arizona. In the process, he obtained exclusive rights to Church's Chicken Restaurants in the Arizona portion of the Navajo reservation. The Navajo reservation covers 26,897 square miles (about the size of West Virginia) and has a population of 155,276 (1990 U.S. Census). Window Rock, with a population of 6,187, is the capital of the Navajo Nation. The Window Rock market area population was 11,718 (1990 U.S. Census).

For his CCR location, Nelson leased space in the newly constructed Window Rock Plaza Shopping Center. For an annual payment of $36,000, the Navajo tribe provided Nelson a new 3,000-square-foot facility finished to his specifications. Nelson opened the restaurant at the beginning of 1991, and it made a $23,000 profit the first year. During 1994, CCR realized a net profit of $78,000 on sales of $710,000. This translated into a return on equity of almost 35 percent (see Exhibits 3 and 4).

From the outset in Window Rock, Nelson faced strong competition for the customers' business. There were 10 different restaurant choices available to the customer, including two popular franchises—Kentucky Fried Chicken (KFC) and LottaBurger. Nelson chose to compete directly with KFC for three reasons. First, fried chicken was the "right" product. Nelson's experience convinced him that his target market had a strong preference for fried food. Second, he believed that the Church's franchise offered several distinct advantages over KFC: CCR prices were about 10 percent lower; CCR portions were larger (CCR cut a chicken into six pieces versus KFC's seven pieces); and CCR allowed the flexibility to add items such as Navajo Tacos to the regular franchise menu, which was not possible with KFC. Third, he believed that the Window Rock KFC had a few very good employees but that overall the franchise was poorly managed. In addition, the KFC physical facility was over 20 years old and had not been well maintained.

Nelson's initial analysis of the competitive situation in Window Rock later proved to be correct. The KFC franchise was especially vulnerable to the newer, better-managed CCR. Nelson later learned some specifics from Carla Yazzie, one of the few competent employees at KFC, whom he hired during CCR's third year of operation. Yazzie told Nelson that revenues at the KFC dropped dramatically as soon as the CCR opened for

EXHIBIT 3 Income Statements 1991–94 ($000), Church's Chicken Restaurant—Window Rock, Arizona

	1994	1993	1992	1991
Sales	$712	$664	$594	$457
Cost of sales	250	235	232	174
Gross profit	462	429	362	283
Lease expense	36	36	36	36
Other operating expense	306	286	274	201
Total operating expense	342	322	310	237
Depreciation	11	18	27	16
Interest	11	4	6	3
Before-tax profit	98	85	19	27
Income tax	20	17	3	4
Net profit	$ 78	$ 68	$ 16	$ 23

EXHIBIT 4   Balance Sheets 1991–94, Church's Chicken Restaurant—Window Rock, Arizona

	1994	1993	1992	1991
Assets				
Current assets				
Cash	$ 1,000	$ 1,000	$ 1,000	$ 1,000
Bank accounts	213,483	207,439	111,830	81,591
Inventory	6,476	7,487	3,180	4,285
Total	$220,959	$215,926	$116,010	$ 86,876
Fixed Assets				
Machinery and equipment	$113,690	$107,802	$107,802	$107,802
Accumulated depreciation	(69,046)	(61,442)	(42,855)	(16,293)
Total	$ 44,644	$ 46,360	$ 64,947	$ 91,509
Total assets	$265,603	$262,286	$ 80,957	$178,385
Liabilities and Equity				
Current liabilities	$ 34,239	$ 65,586	$ 38,336	$ 40,467
Long-term debt	6,446	18,542	34,306	49,515
Total	$ 40,685	$ 84,128	$ 72,642	$ 89,982
Total equity	224,918	178,158	108,315	88,403
Total liabilities and equity	$265,603	$262,286	$180,957	$178,385

business. Yazzie indicated that during the first year of direct competition, KFC's revenues were down from about $400,000 in 1990 to about $200,000 in 1991. During the next two years, KFC's revenues increased, back to an annual level of about $400,000.

RESTAURANT INDUSTRY OVERVIEW

The restaurant industry has experienced substantial growth during the past 25 years, and this is expected to continue. U.S. consumers were expected to spend an estimated $215 billion at restaurants and bars in 1995. For every dollar spent at food stores, consumers now spend about half of that at restaurants and bars, up from about one-third for every food dollar in 1970. Industry growth has been driven by two-income families, an increase in the number of restaurant choices, and the availability of take-out and delivery.

The aging baby-boomer generation is a major driving force for the restaurant industry. These older consumers prefer moderately priced restaurants with a casual dining atmosphere, as well as healthier menu items such as grilled chicken sandwiches and salad bars. This segment of the population is expected to grow by 23 percent during this decade. However, the fast-food industry is now quite mature, with sales and new growth expected to fall short of the pace achieved in the 1980s.

Franchise chains now account for about 25 percent of U.S. restaurant outlets and 43 percent of industry sales. Franchising has enabled restaurant companies to rapidly expand. Costs such as those involved in acquiring land, buildings, and equipment are the responsibility of the franchisee, who also pays a royalty (generally 3 to 5 percent of sales) and contributes to advertising (about 4 percent of sales). The franchisee benefits through brand-name recognition, training, and marketing support from the parent company. The franchisee, as entrepreneur, faces less risk than going into business completely on his or

EXHIBIT 5 Chicken Restaurant Distribution by U.S. Census Regions (1993)

Region	Units	% Distribution
Pacific	1,590	13.5
Mountain	509	4.3
West North Central	618	5.2
West South Central	2,104	17.8
East North Central	1,803	15.2
East South Central	945	8.0
Mid Atlantic	1,193	10.1
South Atlantic	2,724	23.1
New England	328	2.8

EXHIBIT 6 Largest U.S. Restaurant Chains, 1993

Rank	Chain	U.S. Sales ($ Millions)	U.S. Units at Year-End
1	McDonald's	14,941	9,744
2	Burger King	6,700	6,064
3	Hardee's	5,486	3,432
4	Pizza Hut	4,803	8,428
5	KFC	3,600	5,128
6	Wendy's	3,500	3,791
7	Taco Bell	2,800	4,809
8	Domino's Pizza	2,500	4,228
9	Little Caesars Pizza	2,290	4,859
10	Dairy Queen	2,213	4,805
11	Subway	2,200	8,302
12	Red Lobster	1,732	620
13	Denny's	1,699	1,452
14	Arby's	1,440	2,536
15	Shoney's	1,318	915
16	Big Boy	1,264	892
17	Dunkin' Donuts	1,188	2,622
18	Jack in the Box	1,126	1,162
19	Olive Garden	1,100	436
20	Long John Silver's	916	1,421

Source: *Industry Surveys,* April 6, 1995.

her own. However, this is somewhat offset by royalty fees and less flexibility in menu selections and operating procedures. About 70 percent of franchise chain outlets are operated by franchisees. The remainder are operated by the parent company.

Chicken restaurants total 11,814 outlets, which represent 3.2 percent of total U.S. restaurants. Exhibit 5 shows the distribution of chicken restaurants by region. While per capita chicken consumption rose more than 50 percent from 1970 to 1990, chicken entrees as a percent of total restaurant orders have remained at 10 percent for several years. Fried chicken still accounts for nearly half of all restaurant chicken sold.

KFC is the giant of the restaurant industry's chicken segment and the fifth largest U.S. restaurant chain overall (see Exhibit 6). A subsidiary of PepsiCo, KFC ended 1993 with 5,128 domestic units and sales of $3.6 billion. Popeye's Famous Fried

EXHIBIT 7   Fastest Growing U.S. Restaurant Chains, 1992–1993

Rank	Chain	Sales ($ Millions) 1992	Sales ($ Millions) 1993	Sales Growth	Units 1992	Units 1993
1	Boston Chicken	$ 42.7	$154.0	261.0%	83	217
2	Lonestar Steakhouse	33.9	80.0	136.3	23	45
3	Italian Oven	22.9	51.9	126.2	35	56
4	Romano's Macaroni Grill	37.2	77.3	107.7	15	28
5	Hooters	109.0	204.0	87.2	94	109
6	Papa John's	92.6	167.0	80.4	220	400
7	Outback Steakhouse	195.3	347.6	77.9	85	146
8	Checker's Drive-in	173.8	292.2	68.1	223	404
9	Taco Cabana	86.0	142.0	65.1	57	107

Source: *Industry Surveys,* April 6, 1995.

Chicken & Biscuits and Church's Chicken, the segment's number two and number three chains, respectively, are operated by America's Favorite Chicken Company. Based in Atlanta, America's Favorite brought in new senior management with a reorganization in 1992 and has recently initiated reimaging campaigns and new menus. There are early indications that the reorganization has generated improvements. While Popeye's added only two new locations in 1993, sales were $600 million, an increase of $20 million over 1992. Similar improvements occurred at Church's, where 1993 sales grew nearly 8 percent to $540 million despite a slight decrease in its locations. The number four chain, Chick-fil-A, also based in Atlanta, posted record sales of $393 million in 1993, 11.3 percent ahead of 1992's record sales. Chick-fil-A occupies a unique niche, with virtually all of its units located in shopping malls.

Bojangle's Famous Chicken 'n Biscuits, the number five chain, had 1993 sales of $190 million in sales with 201 units. This was a $42 million increase over 1992 and is attributed in large part to the introduction of Cajun Roast, a spicy, skinless alternative to traditional fried chicken. Boston Chicken, with 1993 sales of $154 million, is the number six chain. Boston Chicken is also the fastest growing U.S. restaurant franchise (see Exhibit 7). The franchise maintains the core concept of a suburban restaurant serving home-style meals at reasonable prices. More than 130 units were opened in 1993, with 250 scheduled to come on-line in 1994. Boston Chicken's expansion is being aggressively managed by the same management team that brought Blockbuster Video to its leadership position in video rentals. Other major players in the industry segment include Lee's Famous Recipe Chicken (284 units), Golden Fried Chicken ($45 million in sales), and Kenny Rogers Roasters (155 units with 200 more to be added in 1994). Exhibits 8 and 9 show selected operating information for the restaurant industry.

NELSON'S TUBA CITY OPTION

It was Nelson's plan to construct the Tuba City Church's Chicken Restaurant facility on tribal-owned land that he had already leased. The intended site was adjacent to one of his existing businesses, the V&S variety store. Nelson had employed an architect in Flagstaff, Arizona, to develop plans for the building and, following this, had obtained a firm bid for the cost to construct the building. After including the additional costs for fixtures, furniture, and equipment, the total cost for the physical facility was $700,000.

EXHIBIT 8   Restaurant Industry Data: Percentage Breakdowns of Income and Expenses for 1993, Food-only Restaurants, Values Listed Represent Typical Percentage Ranges

Sales		100.0%
Cost of sales		28.7 ↔ 38.0
Gross profit on sales		71.3 ↔ 62.0
Other income		0.0 ↔ 0.6
Controllable expenses		44.1 ↔ 54.0
Occupancy costs		
Rent	2.6 ↔ 8.0%	
Property taxes	0.2 ↔ 1.0%	
Other taxes	0.0 ↔ 1.4%	
Property insurance	0.5 ↔ 1.6%	
Total occupancy costs		3.3 ↔ 12.0%
Income before interest and depreciation		18.4 ↔ 5.2
Interest		0.0 ↔ 1.9
Depreciation		0.8 ↔ 3.1
Restaurant profit		14.9 ↔ 2.2
Corporate overhead		0.0 ↔ 4.0
Other deductions		0.0 ↔ 1.8
Income before taxes		11.8 ↔ 1.3%

Source: The National Restaurant Association Restaurant Industry Operations Report, Deloitte & Touche, 1993.

EXHIBIT 9   Restaurant Chain Performance

	Industry Median	PepsiCo Group*	McDonald's
Sales growth			
5-year average (%)	8.8	14.1	7.7
Latest 12 months (%)	5.7	11.6	3.8
Net profit margin (%)	4.0	5.9	14.3
Return on equity			
5-year average (%)	13.0	24.7	20.1
Latest 12 months (5)	14.0	35.5	17.9

*Includes KFC, Pizza Hut, Taco Bell.
Source: Forbes, January 3, 1994, p. 150.

Tuba City had a larger retail trade sector than Window Rock. There were 11 restaurants, including a seven-year-old, successful KFC (operating out of a clean, attractive, well-maintained facility), plus a McDonald's, a Taco Bell, a Dairy Queen, and a Pancho's Family Restaurant (Mexican). There were no other restaurants within a 30-mile radius of Tuba City. The Church's Chicken Restaurant would be located at the corner of State Highway 264 (Main Street) and Navajo Boulevard, directly across the street from the Navajo police station. This would place the Church's Chicken Restaurant between KFC and McDonald's and on the opposite side of the street from Taco Bell and Dairy Queen. The restaurants were all located within half a mile of each other on Highway 264 (Main Street), as shown in Exhibit 10.

Nelson had already met with Jennifer Simpson, a commercial loan officer at Norwest Bank in Prescott, Arizona, and indicated that he wanted to borrow $650,000.

EXHIBIT 10   Proposed Location of Church's Chicken Restaurant

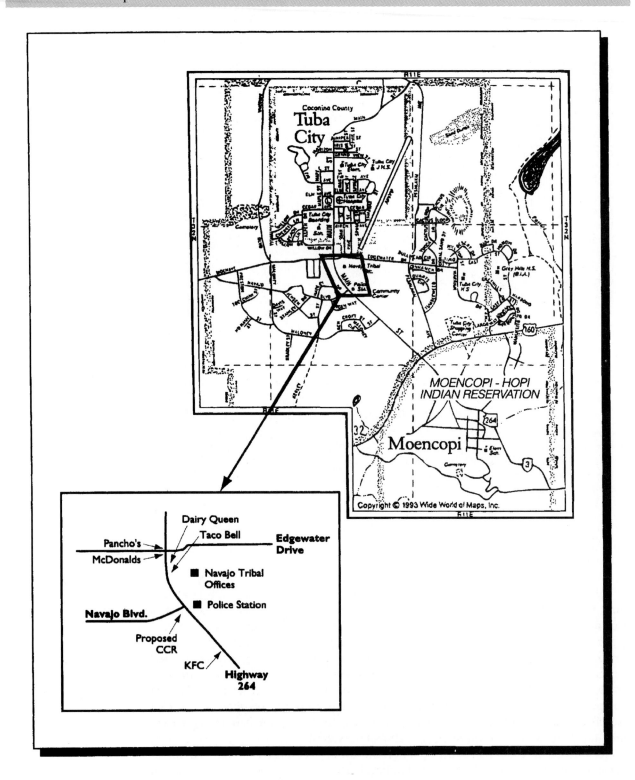

EXHIBIT 11 Capital Requirements and Sources Summary, Church's Chicken Restaurant—Tuba City, Arizona

Requirements	
Design and construct facility	$500,000
Fixtures, furniture, and equipment	200,000
Inventory	10,000
Beginning cash	40,000
Total requirements	$750,000
Sources	
Cash from Michael Nelson	$100,000
Northwest Bank—loan	650,000
Total sources	$750,000

To this he would add $100,000 of his own money to get the new business started (Exhibit 11). Nelson had an excellent record in his business relations with Norwest. They had provided financing for his CCR at Window Rock, and he was current on his loan repayments. Norwest was receptive to providing funding to Nelson provided that the new business venture met their loan application criteria.

Norwest's loan application required that Nelson furnish five years of pro forma income and cash budget statements (Exhibit 12). Based on his recent experience with Norwest Bank in obtaining financing for the CCR in Window Rock, Nelson knew that the loan officer would require detailed substantiation for his projected revenues and costs. The proposed business must also be able to show a positive net income by the third year and a cumulative positive net income for the five-year period. Finally, the proposed business must be able to meet its annual cash requirements without the need for additional cash infusions.

As he watched the customers come and go, Nelson went over in his mind the information required for the loan application. He had estimates of the costs for the physical facilities at Tuba City. Historical income statements were available from the Window Rock CCR to use in estimating the operating costs for the new restaurant. The major tasks remaining were the development of a five-year sales revenue forecast and subsequent pro forma financial statements.

THE SALES FORECAST

Prior to his meeting with Jennifer Simpson at Norwest Bank, Nelson met with a business consultant regarding several financial aspects of the proposed restaurant, including the sales forecast. Nelson had been advised to begin with a base-level (first year) sales forecast and use that to complete revenue projections over the five-year period. The base-level sales forecast would start with first-year operating results from the Window Rock CCR and be adjusted based on traffic count information from Window Rock and Tuba City. Traffic counts would be used to estimate the relative sizes of the customer base in Tuba City and Window Rock. Once the base-level sales forecast was made, it would then be adjusted each year for expected growth market share and/or growth in the Tuba City market area. When this sales forecasting technique had been discussed, Simpson had indicated a receptiveness to its use.

EXHIBIT 12   Letter from Norwest Bank

Mr. Michael Nelson
Church's Chicken Restaurant
Window Rock, Arizona 86887

Dear Mr. Nelson,

It was a pleasure to meet with you last week and discuss the proposal to open a new Church's Chicken Restaurant in Tuba City. Norwest Bank would appreciate the opportunity to provide the financing for this business venture. We invite you to submit a loan application for this proposal at your earliest convenience.

The major categories to be addressed in your loan proposal are:

1. An assessment of the market to be served including demographics, economic factors, and present and anticipated competition.
2. A description of the marketing strategy to be employed.
3. A management plan including the identification of key personnel and their responsibilities.
4. A financial plan including pro forma annual income and cash flow statements for the first five (5) years of operations.

As I noted in our conversation, it is very important that you generate a sales forecast that is based on a reliable methodology and is not overly optimistic. The traffic count model you mentioned, using information from your Window Rock restaurant, together with sales estimates from the Kentucky Fried Chicken restaurant in Tuba City and justifiable growth projections should satisfy our requirements in this area. Our loan review committee will accept cost estimates that are based on your experience with the Window Rock operation.

The loan amortization schedule for your pro forma income and cash flow statements should be based on the following information:

Interest rate: 9.75%
Term of loan: Seven years (84 months)

Principle and interest payments would begin as soon as the restaurant opens for business and would be due monthly.

I hope to receive your loan application in the near future.

Sincerely,

Jennifer Simpson
Commercial Loan Officer

Traffic counts would be taken at two locations—the CCR in Window Rock and the KFC in Tuba City. These counts would be obtained during identical time frames on the same days. Based on his experience in Window Rock and his other retail businesses on the Navajo Reservation, Nelson knew that daily sales during the week (e.g., Tuesday) were stronger than daily sales on the weekend (e.g., Saturday). With this in mind and in an attempt to control the cost of data collection, Nelson decided to collect hourly traffic counts on a Tuesday and Saturday of the same week and adjust these results to estimate weekly counts. In addition, sales revenues would be collected on an hourly basis at the CCR in Window Rock. The traffic count data had two uses: first to compare the size of the markets in Window Rock and Tuba City, and second to estimate the revenues of the KFC in Tuba City. With this information and Nelson's experience in competing directly with KFC in Window Rock, a base-level sales forecast could be made. The traffic counts and revenue data were completed on January 28, 1994, and the results are shown in Exhibit 13.

Once the base-level sales forecast was developed, forecasts for the remaining four years would be made using a "growth model" approach. Using this approach, the second year's revenues would be based on the base year, the third year's based on the second year, and so forth. The adjustment for year-to-year growth would be based on either Nelson's experience at CCR in Window Rock or the expected retail sales growth in the Tuba City market. To facilitate this step, Nelson had gathered information on income and population growth in Arizona, the Navajo Nation, and Tuba City (see Exhibit 14).

THE PRO FORMA FINANCIAL STATEMENTS

Nelson planned to complete the pro forma income statements by using the sales forecasts together with information from the historical income statements at the CCR in Window Rock. To generate the annual cash budget, he intended to use a procedure he had learned while developing an earlier loan proposal for Norwest Bank. During the five-year period of analysis, he did not plan to vary inventory substantially from its beginning level of $10,000. Therefore, net cash generated annually from operations could be estimated by the following calculation:

$$\text{Net cash} = \text{Net income} + \text{Depreciation} - \text{Principal payment}$$

Once net cash from operations was determined, the cash budget for each year could be determined by taking into account the beginning cash and the minimum precautionary cash balance according to the following formula:

$$\text{Excess (needed) cash} = \text{Net cash} + \text{Beginning cash} - \text{Precautionary cash balance}$$

For the first year of operations, beginning cash would be $40,000 with a minimum precautionary cash balance of $5,000.

THE DECISION

Nelson was scheduled to meet with the Norwest Bank commercial loan officer in two weeks. From the bank's point of view, the project would either move ahead or be aborted based on the pro forma income and cash budget statements. But Nelson also wanted to understand just how profitable the Tuba City location might be. He realized that to answer that question he would need to perform a net present value analysis and

EXHIBIT 13   Traffic Counts and Sales Data

Location: Kentucky Fried Chicken—Tuba City, Arizona
Dates: Tuesday, January 24, and Saturday, January 28, 1995

Time Period	Traffic		Walk-in Customers		Drive-in Customers	
	1-24	1-28	1-24	1-28	1-24	1-28
10–11 AM	975	192	13	3	5	2
11–Noon	1,125	789	50	14	11	5
Noon–1 PM	1,386	878	74	36	32	7
1–2 PM	758	803	62	18	12	8
2–3 PM	615	492	38	21	13	8
3–4 PM	819	643	19	21	11	7
4–5 PM	691	511	36	5	8	4
5–6 PM	1,085	728	36	18	14	6
6–7 PM	702	803	13	67	14	10
7–8 PM	706	945	28	40	19	9
8–9 PM	380	783	20	46	9	14
9–Close	—	363	—	24	—	7
Totals	9,242	7,930	389	313	148	87

Location: Church's Chicken Restaurant—Window Rock, Arizona
Dates: Tuesday, January 24, and Saturday, January 28, 1995

Time Period	Traffic		Walk-in Customers		Drive-in Customers		Sales	
	1-24	1-28	1-24	1-28	1-24	1-28	1-24	1-28
10–11 AM	186	320	11	10	8	2	$ 93	$ 40
11–Noon	248	851	18	36	12	9	188	154
Noon–1 PM	1,311	813	62	21	10	2	399	107
1–2 PM	608	404	34	16	9	10	162	123
2–3 PM	1,083	973	79	30	12	12	138	152
3–4 PM	507	762	26	26	14	10	120	156
4–5 PM	668	761	53	20	8	3	201	100
5–6 PM	1,071	836	31	28	16	14	174	182
6–7 PM	801	615	35	30	24	16	248	206
7–8 PM	768	468	34	24	20	14	189	148
8–9 PM	1,405	534	36	33	14	9	301	255
9–Close	523	620	—	6	—	10	—	125
Totals	9,179	7,957	419	280	147	111	$2,213	$1,748

that this required the generation of annual cash flows. Nelson remembered that cash flow was defined as follows:

$$\text{Cash flow} = \text{Net income} + \text{Depreciation} + (\text{Interest expense})/(1 - \text{Tax rate})$$

Nelson refocused his attention to the activity at the restaurant. He noticed that the lunch rush was about over and most of the booths were now empty. Two employees, Navajo youths of high school age, were busy tidying up the facility. Glancing outside, he observed a slow but steady stream of drive-in customers arriving and departing with

EXHIBIT 2 Comparative Commissions Charged by Major Types of Brokerage Firms, Spring 1998

	200 Shares at $20	3,000 Shares at $10
Full-Service Brokers		
Average commission	$116.90	$672.59
Discount Brokers		
Average Commission	66.09	145.05
Electronic Brokers		
Schwab Online	29.95	89.95*
DLJdirect	20.00	60.00†
E*Trade	14.95	74.95
Fidelity	14.95	14.95
Discover Brokerage Direct	14.95	14.95‡
Waterhouse Securities	12.00	12.00
Datek Online	9.99	9.99
Ameritrade	8.00	8.00
Suretrade	7.95	7.95
Web Street Securities	14.95	Free for stocks listed on the NASDAQ

Note: These commission fees are for trades placed at the market price prevailing at the time of execution; orders which specified a limit price customarily entailed an extra fee—equal to $5 at Fidelity and Ameritrade.
*Schwab's fee structure was a flat $29.95 on all trades up to 1,000 shares with a surcharge of 3 cents per share on all shares over 1,000 per trade.
†DLJdirect's fee structure was a flat $20.00 on all trades up to 1,000 shares with a surcharge of 2 cents per share on all shares over 1,000 per trade.
‡Discover's fee structure was a flat $14.95 on all trades up to 5,000 shares; trades in excess of 5,000 shares were charged at a rate of 1 cent per share for the entire order.
Source: Credit Suisse First Boston Company and company annual reports, advertising, and Web sites.

that were only about 30 percent below those of full-service firms—its fees were the highest of the so-called discount brokers. So-called second-tier discount brokers, content to build their business around serving active traders and bargain hunters and offering minimal services beyond trade execution, offered much deeper discounts than Schwab did.

Growing numbers of investors opened accounts with discount brokers during the late 1980s and early 1990s, providing for the first time a competitive alternative to full-service firms. Many banks set up discount brokerage units as an added service to customers, thus putting themselves a step closer to being one-stop financial centers. Banks saw offering brokerage services as a way to make it more convenient for customers to invest in stocks, bonds, and mutual funds and as a vehicle for attracting more self-managed individual retirement accounts (IRAs). Several mutual fund firms, like Fidelity Investments, also started discount brokerage units, chiefly to provide a service for their current investors and to attract new investors. Fidelity already had a number of offices nationwide and toll-free lines, as well as the internal infrastructure to accommodate securities trading; hence, it was simple and inexpensive for Fidelity to enter the discount brokerage business, given its existing resource base.

Discount brokers were able to undercut the commissions of full-service brokers by eliminating expensive investment researchers and professional brokers and utilizing salaried customer service representatives who manned phone lines to provide quotes and handle buy–sell orders but who were not authorized to give investment advice. These representatives were hired for their skills in giving courteous, friendly service over the phone and were paid salaries of $28,000 to $40,000 annually; some firms had modest incentive bonuses for representatives based on the number of phone calls they handled daily and the volume of trades they executed. Discount brokers typically provided customers with little, if any, investment information or news updates on companies. A few, most notably Charles Schwab, Quick & Reilly, and Fidelity, had a network of local offices to serve walk-in customers in large metropolitan areas, but the majority did business primarily by phone and operated mainly out of a central office with perhaps a few branch offices. Banks that had discount brokerage units usually had personnel in their various banking offices and branches who were able to answer questions, open brokerage accounts, and, in some cases, sell mutual funds; however, all stock transactions were normally initiated over the phone, with customers speaking directly to brokerage representatives located in a central office.

Lower cost structures allowed discount brokers to charge commissions substantially lower than those of full-service brokers (see again Exhibit 2). As with full-service brokers, commission fees varied according to the number of shares and the price per share; in some cases there was a commission difference between trades on the New York Stock Exchange (NYSE) and the National Association of Securities Dealers Automated Quotations (NASDAQ). Charles Schwab's fee for a 500-share trade of a $50 stock on the NYSE was $127 and its fee for a 1,000-share trade of a $15 stock of the NASDAQ was $127. In response to growing competition from the new fixed-price strategies of electronic brokerages, a few discount brokers had recently established a fixed fee per trade irrespective of share price and the number of shares.

The cut-rate commissions of discount brokers appealed to knowledgeable investors who took a very active role in managing their portfolios, traded stocks frequently (perhaps making a number of trades each business day), and wanted to minimize the costs of moving in and out of particular stocks. Because commissions were a major cost item to active traders, such traders were quite interested in locating their accounts at a brokerage that would execute their buy–sell orders at a low price. Such investors typically used a wide variety of sources to obtain their investment information and were quite willing to forgo the professional advice and proprietary investment research information that were the trademarks of the full-service brokers. The lower fee structure of discount brokers also appealed to economy-minded investors with modest account balances, since lower transaction costs allowed them to put a bigger fraction of their limited funds into the investments of their choice. Discount brokerages were thought to account for about 25 percent of the retail brokerage market in 1998.

The New Breed of Electronic Brokerage Firms

Electronic brokerage firms began making their appearance in 1995 as use of the Internet exploded and problems of data security were reduced to tolerable levels (both Netscape Navigator and Internet Explorer had implemented sophisticated encryption that allowed data to be transmitted over the Internet without significant risk of security breaches). Many of the new electronic brokerage firms appearing on the scene in 1997 were start-up ventures launched by young Internet entrepreneurs—E*Trade and Web Street Securities were the most visible and successful of these ventures. Several of the new entrants had been established by mutual fund firms and other financial institutions to provide an additional service for their existing customers and bring in new revenues. Most owners and managers of the electronic trading firms were convinced that "the Internet was it" and that the future of retail brokerage was in electronic trading.

Electronic brokers used a value chain to deliver services to customers radically different from that of traditional brokers. They kept overhead low by having few offices and no commission-based professionals. While they had small staffs of salaried financial consultants, registered representatives, and trained customer service personnel answering phones for customers who needed to talk to a "live broker," they relied mainly on the Internet for communicating with customers. Typically, electronic brokers set up a Web site for interested investors to explore—some parts of the Web site were free and open to everyone; other parts were accessible only to those who had an account number and password. Potential investors could open up an account by filling out a form on-line (or request that new-account information and forms be sent through the mail). The Web sites of electronic brokerages consisted of an assortment of Web page features that allowed customers to obtain unlimited delayed stock quotes, get real-time quotes if needed, place buy–sell orders, get order confirmations, check account balances, track portfolio performance, view historical charts, check mutual fund data and ratings, peruse industry and company news, and gain access to research reports from a variety of investment research specialists. Some electronic brokerages had developed their own proprietary software for utilizing the options and features on their Web sites; others obtained software from vendors and paid a royalty per trade.

Internet-savvy investors—intrigued with handling their own trades, tracking their portfolios automatically, and saving on commission fees (which in early 1996 were about $35 for a 100-share trade)—evidenced immediate interest in opening electronic accounts. Close to 400,000 new electronic accounts were opened between April 1995 and April 1996. Customers could use the Internet to access their account information after hours and on weekends, and place orders for execution at the next market opening. As one satisfied electronic investor put it, "My broker was so nice, but boy, they were robbing me. All he ever did was place my trades. I can do that for myself."[4] The CEO of one electronic broker said at the time, "Our mission is to empower the investor. All our information is for free."[5]

Overall, trading stocks on the Internet using on-line brokers was quickly becoming simple, convenient, user-friendly, private, safe, informative, and pleasant—conditions that were expected to result in rapid increases in the percentage of retail trades conducted on-line. Some analysts were projecting that electronic trading would approach 30 percent of daily trading volume by year-end 1998 and 50 percent of all retail trades within five years. Such dramatic growth was consistent with mounting activity on the Internet in general. A 1998 study by the Department of Commerce found that traffic on the Internet was doubling every 100 days; whereas in 1994 only 3 million people were connected to the Internet, by year-end 1997 an estimated 100 million people worldwide, including 62 million Americans, were connected.

The Initial Responses of Traditional Brokerages to the Emergence of Electronic Trading

Full-service and discount brokers initially responded to the growing interest in electronic trading by creating Web sites for their own customers. No electronic trading was offered, but the sites did offer tidbits of current information (daily market commentaries, recent

---

[4]As quoted in "With the World Wide Web, Who Needs Wall Street?," *Business Week,* April 29, 1996, p. 120.
[5]Ibid., p. 121.

market indexes updated daily or weekly, and perhaps a sample research report) and called attention to the brokerage's range of benefits. Smith Barney went a step further; in exchange for registering, browsers at the firm's Web site could get Smith Barney's current top 10 stock picks and click on links to other Web sites with pertinent information. In early 1996, Prudential Securities became the first full-service broker to offer customers Internet access to account balances and to provide delayed stock quotes. Other full-service and discount brokers soon followed Prudential's lead in providing customers an alternative to tracking their stocks from newspaper listings or calling their broker for quotes. But to access their account information on-line, the customers of full-service brokers first had to sign up with the broker to obtain the needed software (sometimes paying a onetime fee of $25) and install the software on their computers, along with a secure browser (either Netscape Navigator or Internet Explorer). In contrast, the software employed by over three-fourths of the electronic brokers allowed customers to use the Internet to access their accounts without having to install proprietary software on their computers. Most brokers offering Internet access of one kind or another were expected to convert by the turn of the century to software that did not have to be installed on a customer's computer.

However, with the exception of Dean Witter—which set up a separate unit, Discover Brokerage, to pursue the electronic brokerage business, none of the leading full-service brokerage firms went so far as to offer Internet trading during 1996 and 1997. On the whole, full-service brokers did not believe that the electronic brokers had the financial strength and credibility to pose a serious competitive challenge; they did not see the Internet as an appealing substitute for a flesh-and-blood broker's advice. As the marketing executive of one full-service brokerage put it in 1996, "It's really not a concern. We find investors want ongoing advice and counsel."[6] The prevailing view was that the vast majority of customers of full-service brokerages would not find trading stocks on the Internet to be appealing. Indeed, one industry expert predicted, "You'll see more people shifting back to a full-service house because they want hand-holding in a crisis."[7]

On the other hand, several prominent discount brokerages—namely, Charles Schwab & Co., Quick & Reilly, and Fidelity Discount Brokerage—moved promptly to take advantage of the opportunities in on-line trading and set up electronic brokerage units. Several of the smaller deep-discount brokerages whose clientele consisted of active traders looking to trade at the lowest possible price also set up electronic units as a way to retain their current customers and attract additional bargain-hunting traders—a prominent example was Ameritrade. But in 1996 and 1997 most discount brokers were reluctant to embrace electronic trading and chose instead to adopt a wait-and-see posture.

The Race among Electronic Brokers to Compete on the Basis of Features, Services, Research Information, and Price

Throughout 1996 and 1997, as Web page technology progressed, data transfers via modems and servers became faster, and the software capabilities of the electronic brokerages were upgraded, the competitors in electronic brokerage made their Web pages livelier and more interesting. Features were added, and investors were provided with more and better information and with greater capability to do their own

---

[6]Ibid., p. 121.
[7]"Schwab Is Fighting on Three Fronts," *Business Week,* March 10, 1997, p. 95.

research. A number of electronic brokerages developed useful account demos and provided tutorials for using their software, made their new account forms easily accessible, and made it easy to navigate among the features available on their Web sites. To make sure they provided good service, most electronic brokerage firms were tracking their Web site availability and disclosing key information and trading rules to their customers. By early 1998, it was common for broker Web sites to deliver some form of investment advice (from either internal sources or outside providers) and to have links to other Web sites containing such relevant investment information as the following:

- The Edgar database, maintained by the Securities and Exchange Commission, which included company 10K and annual reports.
- Mutual fund ratings from Morningstar and others.
- Future earnings estimates generated by First Call or Zack's Research.
- Daily market news summaries from CBS Market Watch, Briefing.com, and others.
- Press releases from companies in an investor's portfolio.
- Business news from sources such as Dow-Jones, CNN, Bloomberg, Reuters, Business Wire, Standard & Poor's, *Fortune,* and *Business Week.*

Exhibit 3 shows the variety of features and services that electronic brokerages were using to attract customers during the first quarter of 1998.

Alliances between Electronic Brokers and Information Providers   The amount and variety of investment information available on the Internet, either free or for a fee, was growing daily, and Internet-savvy investors could, with a modest research effort of their own, arm themselves with a potent volume of data and information about alternative stocks, bonds, mutual funds, and other investments. However, rather than have customers ferret out their own information on the Internet, electronic brokers and those firms in the business of providing investor information via the Internet were actively engaged in forming alliances and strategic partnerships with one another. Brokers needed the content of information providers to make their research and data offerings at their Web sites more appealing to customers and competitive with rival brokerages. Information providers were interested in making their services available to electronic brokers and their customers in order to broaden their user base—information providers made their money either by providing their information for a fee (paid either by the electronic broker or its customers) and/or by selling advertising space on their Web sites where their information products were delivered. Once an electronic broker and an information provider agreed on an alliance or contractual fee arrangement, it was a simple, inexpensive task for broker Webmasters to incorporate direct links on their Web pages to the chosen providers of investor information.

Continuous Upgrading   Competition was forcing electronic brokerages to constantly upgrade and expand their Web sites to provide customers with greater amounts of information, investment research capability, portfolio tracking and account information, and real-time quotes (instead of delayed quotes running 15 to 20 minutes behind the latest trades). Virtually all of the electronic brokerages implemented significant upgrades of their Web sites during 1997 and were engaged in ongoing efforts to improve their software, incorporate better-quality information, and add more and better features, services, and on-line help.

EXHIBIT 3   Features and Services Offered by Electronic Brokerages, 1998

- Ability to open an account on-line or via mail-in forms; account demos; tutorials for using account software.
- Technical support via e-mail or a toll-free line during business hours Monday through Friday. A few firms had tech-support hotlines open 24 hours a day, seven days a week (response times varied from firm to firm, running from under a minute on average to as much as 15 minutes on average).
- Account information—ability to log on to the account and get price updates on each holding in the portfolio. (Most brokerages updated the prices at the close of each trading day; several updated prices and account balances every 15 to 20 minutes; and a few had invested in the capability to provide updates instantly as stock prices changed.)
- Account security.
- Free, unlimited delayed quotes (usually 15 or 20 minutes behind the latest executed trade).
- A limited number of free real-time quotes per transaction (usually 100). A fee was charged for real-time quotes in excess of the specified number—to deliver real-time quotes, the broker had to have software capability to update stock prices directly on the screen each time they changed and then have a source from which to obtain the real-time quotes (often an outside vendor such as Thomson Financial—a primary provider of real-time quotes to many brokerages).
- Full customer control over placing buy–sell orders.
- Confirmations of trades, usually within a few seconds of placing the order.
- A variety of investment products available on-line—stocks, bonds, options, and mutual funds.
- Access to historical information—charts showing price and trading volume histories, 52-week high-low trading range, dividend histories, price–earnings ratios, charts showing how the stock price has performed versus various market indexes such as the S&P 500 and the Dow-Jones Industrial Average.
- A selection of research links available on-line through the brokerage's Web site (10-K reports, annual reports, earnings forecasts, the latest analysis of various technical indicators, company histories and background, analyst recommendations, news summaries, press releases, and editorial content containing advice and recommendations).
- The ability to talk to a financial consultant or registered representative if needed. A few electronic brokerages were affiliated with discount brokers that also had walk-in offices (examples included Schwab Online, Fidelity, and Quick & Reilly).
- Electronic fund transfer services.
- IRAs and 401(k) retirement accounts.
- Checking accounts.
- Electronic bill payment.
- Credit and debit cards.
- Full disclosure of commission schedules and a list of fees for IRAs, bounced checks, margin loans, and other services (posted on the Web site for convenient review by customers).
- Investment tools to screen stocks based on criteria chosen by the customer.
- Financial planning and portfolio optimization tools.
- Alerts issued to customers if outlook for one of their stocks changed suddenly or if the price of a stock in their portfolio swung up or down by a sizable amount in the course of daily trading sessions.

Note: This listing is a representative compilation of features and services offered by one or another of the electronic brokerages. The actual mix of features and services varied significantly from brokerage to brokerage as of early 1998. Broker offerings were in a constant state of flux as brokerages upgraded their Web sites to add new features and improve existing features.

A Battle for Market Share Erupts

In mid-1997, the new electronic brokerage firms started to launch multimillion-dollar advertising campaigns, with TV ads glamorizing low-cost electronic trading and print ads touting easy-to-use services and low commissions (see Exhibit 4 for a sample ad). Nearly all of the campaigns included heavy use of Internet ads in the corners of screens on America Online, PointCast, search engine home pages, and other high traffic sites. The growing numbers of competing electronic brokers made it virtually imperative for indus-

EXHIBIT 4 Sample Ad of Waterhouse Securities

EXHIBIT 5   Commission Schedule for Web Street Securities, April 1998

Trades Executed via the Internet

• Any listed stock trade, any size	$14.95
• NASDAQ stock trade under 1,000 shares	$14.95
• NASDAQ stock trade 1,000 shares or more*	Free
• Equity and index options	$14.95 plus $1.75 per contract
• Mutual funds transaction	$25.00

Trades Executed via a Live Representative

• Any listed stock trade, any size	$24.95
• NASDAQ stock trade under 1,000 shares[†]	$24.95
• NASDAQ stock trade 1,000 shares or more[†]	$24.95
• Equity and index options	$24.95 plus $1.75 per contract
• Mutual funds transaction	$25.00
• Bonds—government, municipals, corporate	Contact a Web Street account executive for pricing.

Margin Rates

• $0–$4,999	2% above broker call[‡]
• $5,000–$9,999	1¾% above broker call
• $10,000–$14,999	1½% above broker call
• $15,000–$19,999	1¼% above broker call
• $20,000–$24,999	1% above broker call
• $25,000+	¾% above broker call

*On stocks trading over $2.00 per share. For stocks trading $2.00 and under per share, $14.95
[†]On stocks trading over $2.00 per share. For stocks trading $2.00 and under per share, $24.95 plus one cent per share.
[‡]Broker call as quoted in *The Wall Street Journal* (7.25% as of April 1998).
Source: www.webstreetsecurities.com, April 17, 1998.

try participants to use the mass media to establish visibility and build a brand name. Moreover, a price war erupted. In June 1997, DLJdirect, a subsidiary of Donaldson, Lufkin & Jenrette, cut its commission rates in half, to $20 per trade. In mid-August, Fidelity, a new unit of Fidelity Brokerage Services and part of the biggest mutual fund group in the United States, began an electronic trading service at a flat $28.95 per trade—about 30 to 40 percent below its standard commission on orders placed through its discount brokerage operation.[8] In October, Ameritrade initiated its electronic brokerage service with a major ad campaign featuring a flat price of $8.00 per trade. Shortly thereafter Fidelity cut its electronic price to $14.95 and Quick & Reilly, another discount broker which had begun an electronic trading unit, cut its fee for on-line trades to $19.95. Then in November, Quick & Reilly initiated a new electronic trading operation under the name Suretrade with a commission of $7.95 per trade. Waterhouse Securities cut its on-line price to $12 per trade on all trades up to 5,000 shares. Web Street Securities executed trades of 1,000 shares or more of stocks listed on the NASDAQ for free. (See Exhibit 5 for a schedule of Web Street Securities' commissions and fees). During the second half of 1997, electronic trading volume doubled, fueled by the extensive ads, the attractive low prices, and the appeal of executing one's own trades.

---

[8]Fidelity Web Express and Fidelity Brokerage Services were units of Fidelity Investments. Fidelity Investments managed $688 billion in assets for its 12 million customers, operated 80 walk-in offices, and had 3,300 mutual funds. The company's discount brokerage operation traded an average of 30 million shares daily.

Growth in electronic trading continued to increase strongly in early 1998, with daily on-line volume reaching 100 million shares on 190,000 trades. Even so, this was still a fraction of the total shares traded daily on the major exchanges—daily trading volume on the NYSE averaged nearly 600 million shares; on the NASDAQ the volume was another 600 million shares, and on the AMEX the volume was about 40 million shares. Electronic brokers were aiming to go beyond appealing just to Internet enthusiasts and appeal to mainstream investors. According to E*Trade's entrepreneurial CEO, Christos Cotsakos, "When the business was just getting started, we went after the early adopters, people who were techno-savvy. Now we're after the mainstream."[9]

To further enhance the attractiveness of electronic trading, more and more brokers were not only significantly upgrading their Web sites but also exploring the merits of offering a more complete array of financial products, including checking, electronic bill payment, credit and debit cards, mortgages, insurance, and consumer loans.

The New Economics of Electronic Trading

Electronic trading was considered by analysts to be a potentially lucrative business. Electronic brokers had essentially four main sources of revenue: the commission income from executing customer trades, the interest earnings on loans to customers who purchased stocks on margin, the interest earned on the cash balances in customer accounts, and the payments for order flow received from the market makers in each NASDAQ-listed stock.

Revenues from Commissions   Electronic brokers derived 50 to 60 percent of their revenues from commission fees as of early 1998. While the commission structure varied somewhat from broker to broker (see again Exhibit 2), most electronic brokers were charging a flat fee per trade, abandoning the practice of basing the commission on the number of shares and the price per share. It was customary, however, to charge a bit more for buying or selling options and for handling mutual funds purchases or sales (see again Exhibit 5).

According to one report, the average commission charged by the 10 largest electronic brokerages had fallen from $52.89 in 1995 to $34.65 at the end of 1996 and to $15.95 at the end of 1997.[10] However, in the first quarter of 1998, the commissions of the top 10 electronic brokerages averaged $15.53, a decline of only 3 percent from the prior quarter.

Commission revenues of all electronic brokers totaled an estimated $268 million in 1996 and about $500 million in 1997, and were expected to reach $2.2 billion in 2001. There was mounting evidence that customers generally doubled or tripled their trading activity once they opened an on-line account. According to the Securities Industry Association, customers with on-line accounts averaged about 32 trades annually in 1997 compared to 12 trades annually by customers with accounts at traditional brokerages.

Revenues from Margin Loans and Account Balances   A number of active traders financed a portion of their stock purchases with funds borrowed from their broker. Such purchases were called margin purchases, and the loans were referred to as margin loans. The interest rate that brokers charged on margin loans depended partly on the going short-term

---

[9]As quoted in Whitford, "Trade Fast, Trade Cheap," p. 112.

[10]Based on estimates by Piper Jaffray, Inc., analyst Bill Burnham and reported in Dow Jones Newswires on February 25, 1998, and in the January issue of *Smart Money*.

prime rate and partly on the size of the loan. The broker's base interest rate (referred to as the broker's call rate) typically was pegged 1 to 1.25 percent below the prime. The loans to customers were then made at the broker's call rate plus as little as 0.5 percent or as much as 2 percent depending on the size of the loan. See Exhibit 5 for an example of one electronic broker's schedule of interest charges on margin loans. Brokers used the cash balances in customers' accounts as a source of funds for making margin loans. Money market conditions in 1998 allowed brokers to earn a spread of 4 to 5 percent on margin loans, paying roughly 3 to 4 percent on customer cash balances and realizing an average of between 8 and 9 percent on margin loans. Margin loans were a major revenue source; according to Ameritrade's CEO, "That's where we really make our money."[11]

Brokers could earn additional interest income by investing any cash balances in customer accounts not used to make margin loans in Treasury bills or other short-term securities. Such short-term investments tended to yield brokers a net margin of 1 to 2 percentage points between the yield on short-term securities and the rate brokers paid customers on account cash balances.

Net interest income from both margin loans and short-term investments was said to average between $8 and $10 per trade.[12] Brokers could also obtain a small amount of revenue from fees earned in lending the shares in customer accounts to traders wishing to sell a stock short.

Order Flow Payments from Market Makers   Payments for order flow originated with firms that specialized in "making a market" for over-the-counter stocks (such as those listed on the NASDAQ). A market maker had responsibility for actually executing trades and posting the price at which a stock traded. Market makers bought stocks at the bid price and sold them at the asking price; they executed trades both for investors and their own accounts. The spread between the bid and asking prices on over-the-counter stocks was typically one-eighth of a point, or $0.125 per share. Market makers made their money on the spread, buying at the bid price and selling at the asking price, and also on trading shares for their own account. The market maker adjusted the bid–ask range up or down in response to the changing balance of incoming orders to buy or sell and in response to changing bid–ask prices.[13] To keep the number of shares being bought or sold in close balance, market makers adjusted the asking price upward when buy orders exceeded sell orders at the prevailing price or when eager buyers were upping their bid prices. Similarly, market makers lowered the asking price when sell orders exceeded buy orders and when bid prices were weakening. Thus, the trades being executed by market makers always reflected demand–supply conditions at any given time. According to NASDAQ rules, market makers had to report all trades within 90 seconds of the trade.

When the stock markets were closed (normal business hours were 9 AM to 4 PM Eastern Time, Monday through Friday), brokers could execute trades for investors on

[11]Whitford, "Trade Fast, Trade Cheap," p. 112.

[12]Suzanne Wooley, "Do I Hear Two Bits a Trade?" *Business Week,* December 8, 1997, p. 113.

[13]Investors wanting to sell shares could either indicate a lower limit price they would accept or they could place an order to sell at the market price. Likewise, buyers could either specify a maximum or limit price they were willing to pay or agree to pay the market price at the time the trade was executed. Most buyers and sellers placed their orders "at the market" since they could get the price at which the last few trades were made and since their order would be executed within less than a minute—the orders of electronic traders, for example, were usually confirmed within 15 seconds.

electronic networks, notably Reuter's Instinet. Also, the NASDAQ allowed firms to execute trades on its electronic system, called SelectNet, during regular business hours.

Because there were several market makers or specialists for each stock listed on the NASDAQ, specialists competed against each other for business in executing the trades for those stocks in which they were market makers. To give brokers an incentive and a reward for sending trades their way, market makers typically paid brokers a piece of the spread between the bid price and the asking price of the shares traded.[14] The "kick-backs" from market makers were said to account for about 20 percent of an electronic broker's overall revenues.[15] Such payments could range from $1 to $2 on a 100-share trade of a $10 stock to perhaps $20 on a 1,000-share trade of a $50 stock or even a $100 on a 5,000-share trade of a $75 stock. It was the payments on order flow from market makers that allowed Web Street Securities to execute large trades on the NASDAQ for "free."

Both margin loans and payments from market makers for order flow were a bigger percentage of overall revenues for electronic brokers than for discount and full-service brokers. One top Ameritrade official said, "I can see a time when, for a customer with a certain size margin account, we won't charge commissions. We might even pay a customer, on a per trade basis, to bring the account to us."

Cost Structure   The current overall cost per trade at an electronic brokerage was said to average about $5. The key cost items were the software and the network of servers to allow customers to log on to the trading system, place and confirm orders, execute trades, and track account balances. Internet technology, being based on software and microprocessor computing power, could easily be scaled to match trading volume—once a firm had the required software package, it could simply add server capacity as trading volumes grew. As a result, costs were somewhat variable and a firm could enter the electronic brokerage industry cost-effectively at far lower trading volumes than traditional full-service and discount brokerages, which used large mainframe computers for data processing and had to spread fixed costs over many trades to achieve low unit costs.

Some electronic brokers had in-house capability to develop and upgrade their own proprietary software and self-clear the transactions of customers; others paid external software developers and related data processing providers fees amounting to $1 to $3 per trade. The reliance on computers and the Internet for interfacing with customers greatly reduced labor costs and the need for walk-in offices. Having customers log on to their accounts and place their own orders also eliminated most order-entry errors, which were often quite expensive for traditional full-service and discount brokerage firms. Customer trades were usually confirmed within 15 seconds of placing the order, while the customer was still on-line; traditional brokers had to print and mail order confirmations. Use of the Internet to provide customers with information further meant much lower costs for telephones, postage, brochures, and other printed materials (research reports, copies of company news releases, and other information of interest).

Whereas discount brokers spent about 4 to 7 percent of revenues on advertising, the advertising budgets of electronic brokers were currently running 15 to 20 percent of

---

[14]The size of the spread between the bid and asking prices had recently come under scrutiny by the National Association of Securities Dealers and federal government officials, and discussions were under way to lower the spread to $\frac{1}{16}$ of a point.

[15]Cited in Whitford, "Trade Fast, Trade Cheap," p. 112.

revenues. Extensive advertising and marketing campaigns were deemed necessary at many electronic brokerages to establish the company's name firmly in the minds of investors contemplating opening an on-line account, to build the size of their account base to more economic levels and spread out fixed costs, and to convey to mainstream investors that electronic trading was simple, economical, convenient, and fun. Ameritrade was expected to spend $40 to $50 million on a year-long media campaign promoting its low $8 fee on most trades. Suretrade was said to be spending $30 million on a campaign advertising its $7.95 commission and trading services. During 1998, electronic brokers were expected to spend over $250 million on marketing and advertising campaigns. However, electronic brokers were starting to do more than just run ads; DLJdirect sent out trial packages of its software to about 300,000 subscribers of *Forbes* in February 1998 in hopes of attracting new customers. Discover Brokerage, whose parent company owned the Discover Card, was marketing its services directly to the 40 million holders of the Discover Card.

In addition to data processing software, Web page construction, and marketing, electronic brokers had to maintain ample capacity to handle trading volume. On October 28, 1997 (the single busiest trading day in the history of the stock exchanges), and again on February 6, 1998 (another very heavy trading day), many customers of electronic brokerages experienced delays in logging on to their accounts to make trades because brokers did not have the server capacity to handle the volume of traffic on their Web sites. For example, Schwab Online, which had 1.1 million on-line accounts in October 1997, had the capacity to handle only 10,000 customers simultaneously on its Web site. On October 28, as the market rebounded swiftly from the previous day's steep decline, some Schwab customers reported costly delays in logging on to their accounts to get quotes and place orders (however, Schwab customers made 92,000 trades that day). Although Schwab moved to increase its capability to 25,000 simultaneous sign-ons, customers again experienced logjams for brief periods on February 6, 1998. However, the strategy at Datek Online was to build capacity ahead of demand—it had the capability to handle 10,000 customers simultaneously and currently had only 50,000 on-line accounts. Electronic brokers with rapidly growing account bases and rising trading volume were moving to increase their capacity to handle more accounts simultaneously. E*Trade, for instance, was increasing its capacity from 10,000 to 25,000, and Fidelity was aiming for a 50 percent increase.

Cost-Sharing Synergies with Sister Businesses   Although industry analysts believed that electronic brokerage firms could realize profit margins of 15 to 20 percent of revenues, the current price and advertising wars and the mounting battle for market position were crimping profitability. *The Wall Street Journal* reported in March 1998 that only 30 percent of the 50 electronic brokerages interviewed were profitable and just 20 percent were breaking even.[16] Analysts estimated that electronic brokerages could make money at commissions as low as $5 a trade if (*a*) they were a subsidiary of a discount or full-service brokerage and already had their own clearing operations and other supporting infrastructure in place or (*b*) they were part of an investment firm affiliated with a stock exchange that also had the "back-office" capability to handle the settlement of securities transactions and take care of other essential customer

---

[16]Daisy Maxey, "Analyst Sees On-Line Brokers Expanding Range of Services," *The Wall Street Journal Interactive Edition,* March 9, 1998.

accounting and data processing operations.[17] The economies of an electronic broker-age being able to share the costs of such back office operations with a sister discount or full-service brokerage (or another investment firm with back-office infrastructure) were said to be substantial. Likewise, an electronic broker could realize cost savings if it could draw upon the offices, customer service personnel, or registered represen-tatives of a sister full-service or discount brokerage to help meet the needs of its on-line customers.

Some industry analysts doubted whether an independent electronic brokerage, with no opportunities for cost-sharing synergies with sister businesses, could earn attractive long-term profits at commission fees under $10 per trade.

Resource Allocation Issues   One of the issues electronic brokerages faced was decid-ing how to make the most prudent use of their limited investment capital in building stronger competitive capabilities. There were pressures to invest in several different directions. Should the firm add enough capability to handle peak-day trading volumes or just enough to comfortably accommodate the projected growth in the average number of daily trades? How much effort should be devoted to software upgrades, added services, and Web page features? How much should be allocated for advertis-ing to attract new customer accounts in sufficient numbers? Electronic brokerages not affiliated with a discount or full-service brokerage or an investment firm having the back-office capability to clear transactions and handle other internal data processing functions had the additional burden of having to allocate resources to these activities. It was unlikely that all of the new entrants could afford to spend aggressively on all fronts.

Furthermore, there was the issue of how to contend with mounting competitive pressures. Additional rivals—including full-service brokers, discount brokers, and other financial services firms—were expected to jump into the industry. Industry ana-lyst Bill Burnham believed full-service brokers were "all scheming how they'll have online offerings without enraging their brokers."[18] Industry observers expected that as many as 6 of the 10 largest U.S. banks and perhaps several large insurance companies would launch electronic brokerage businesses before the end of 1998.

INDUSTRY COMPETITORS

One independent industry authority, Gomez Advisors, made a name for itself by rank-ing the various electronic brokerage services quarterly on a variety of factors to deter-mine which one was best. Gomez created a scorecard that rated each brokerage service on a scale of 1 to 10 on five criteria:

1. Ease of use—such factors as availability of tutorials, well-integrated features, and ability to customize use.
2. Customer confidence—including size of capital base, phone response times, tracking of Web-site availability, disclosure of fees and key information about trading rules.
3. On-site resources—real-time quotes, charts, news updates, editorial content, and screening tools for stocks and mutual funds.

---

[17]Wooley, "Do I Hear Two Bits a Trade?," p. 112.
[18]Ibid.

4. Relationship services—real-time updating of stock holdings and account balances, breadth of product line, security, alerts when there are important developments in a particular security held in a customer's account.

5. Commissions and fees.

There were subcategories for each of the five criteria, upping the total number of factors underlying the ratings to over 50. Gomez arrived at its quarterly ratings by means of an examination of each broker's Web site, a questionnaire, and a telephone interview. Gomez then developed a proprietary process to weigh scores in each category and subcategory to determine which firms were best suited for life goal planners managing their own individual retirement portfolio of mutual funds, hyperactive traders, serious investors, and one-stop shoppers. For example, the "commissions and fees" category was double-weighted in creating an overall suitability score for hyperactive traders. Exhibit 6 shows the five highest rated brokers for each of the four types of investors. (The latest Gomez ratings of electronic brokerages can be seen at www.gomez.com/brokers)

Both *Barron's* and *Smart Money* also published ratings of electronic brokers using their own particular methodology and criteria. *Barron's* studied 19 electronic brokers and rated them (on a scale of 1 to 5) on each of five categories: ease of use, trade execution, reliability, commissions, and research.[19] *Barron's* awarded Discover Brokerage Direct scores of 5 for trade execution and research and scores of 4 on the other three categories, giving it a total of 22 points out of a possible 25 and making it the "best overall online broker." Other electronic brokerages rated high by *Barron's* included Web Street Securities (20 points), Datek Online (20 points), DLJdirect (20 points), E*Trade (19 points), Waterhouse (19 points), Fidelity (17 points), Suretrade (17 points), Schwab Online (17 points), and Ameritrade (16 points). *Barron's* rated Discover Brokerage Direct the "best overall online broker" for 1996 and 1997 as well. The 1998 *Barron's* survey revealed that the entire group of electronic brokers studied had made tremendous strides in upgrading the quality of their Web sites since the previous year's survey, citing the availability of more research information and more on-line help.

Discover Brokerage Direct (a subsidiary of Morgan Stanley Dean Witter) was also *Smart Money*'s top choice. Other electronic brokerages receiving high marks from *Smart Money* included Datek, Waterhouse, Schwab Online, and Fidelity.

Profiles of selected electronic, discount, and full-service brokers are presented below.

Schwab Online and Charles Schwab & Co., Inc. (www.schwab.com)

Schwab Online was the leading electronic brokerage, with 1.5 million on-line accounts as of May 1998, up from 638,000 accounts just 15 months earlier. On-line customer assets reached $103 billion in April 1998, up from $80 billion in December 1997. Schwab had 1.2 million customer log-ons to its Web site on February 5, 1998, a particularly heavy-volume trading day; the previous record was 960,000 log-ons on October 28, 1997 (the busiest trading day in history). Schwab had increased its capacity of 10,000 simultaneous log-ons in October 1997 to 25,000 simultaneous log-ons by February 1998.

Charles Schwab & Co. was one of the nation's largest financial services companies, with 5 million total active accounts, $400 billion in customer assets, 272 branch offices, and 12,700 employees. It had an estimated 35 percent market share in the discount

---

[19]Theresa Carey, "Beyond Cool," *Barron's Online*, March 16, 1998.

EXHIBIT 6 Comparative Ratings of Selected Electronic Brokers as Prepared by Gomez Advisors, First Quarter 1998

Overall Scores	Scores for Life Goal Planners	Scores for Hyperactive Traders	Scores for Serious Investors	Scores for One-Stop Shoppers
1. DLJdirect (7.28)	1. DLJdirect (7.01)	1. DLJdirect (7.77)	1. Web Street Securities (7.87)	1. DLJdirect (6.72)
2. Waterhouse Securities (7.21)	2. Waterhouse Securities (6.93)	2. Waterhouse Securities (7.17)	2. Suretrade (7.27)	1. Lindner Funds (6.72)
3. Lindner Funds (7.05)	3. Wall Street Electronica (6.76)	3. National Discount Brokers (7.06)	3. Waterhouse Securities (7.27)	3. Waterhouse Securities (6.47)
4. National Discount Brokers (6.86)	4. Quick & Reilly (6.72)	4. Schwab Online (6.96)	4. Datek Online (7.10)	4. E*Trade (6.40)
5. Web Street Securities (6.81)	5. Schwab Online (6.71)	5. Suretrade (6.90)	5. AB Watley (6.69)	5. Web Street Securities (6.36)
6. Suretrade (6.75)	6. Lindner Funds (6.51)	6. E*Trade (6.81)	6. DLJdirect (6.64)	6. Quick & Reilly (6.20)
7. Schwab Online (6.68)	8. Web Street Securities (6.40)	8. Web Street Securities (6.71)	8. Quick & Reilly (6.48)	9. Schwab Online (6.15)
9. E*Trade (6.50)	9. E*Trade (6.14)	10. Lindner Funds (6.59)	9. Ameritrade (6.47)	11. Suretrade (6.00)
11. Datek Online (6.32)	11. Fidelity (6.06)	13. Fidelity (6.19)	12. E*Trade (6.27)	13. Ameritrade (5.56)
17. Fidelity (5.97)	17. Datek Online (5.63)	16. Datek Online (6.00)	22. Fidelity (5.88)	14. Datek Online (5.56)
20. Ameritrade (5.71)	24. Ameritrade (5.23)	28. Ameritrade (5.23)	33. Schwab Online (5.18)	18. Fidelity (5.39)
Median score for the 52 firms rated (5.37)	Median score for the 52 firms rated (5.07)	Median score for the 52 firms rated (5.32)	Median score for the 52 firms rated (5.66)	Median score for the 52 firms rated (4.55)
Lowest score for the 52 rated firms (2.39)	Lowest score for the 52 rated firms (2.73)	Lowest score for the 52 rated firms (2.55)	Lowest score for the 52 rated firms (0.07)	Lowest score for the 52 rated firms (2.37)

Source: Web site for Gomez Advisors, www.gomezadvisors.com, April 1, 1998.

brokerage segment and a 32 percent share in electronic brokerage. The company had 1997 revenues of $2.3 billion and net profits of $270 million. Schwab's earnings had grown at a compound rate of nearly 35 percent since 1992, and its stock price had out-performed other major brokerage stocks. Commissions from trading accounted for 49 percent of revenues. According to CEO Charles Schwab, the company's mission was "to coach people on investing."[20] Schwab's strategy was geared to service and product variety, innovation, and value pricing.

---

[20]As quoted in *Business Week,* May 25, 1998, p. 123.

Service and Product Variety   Schwab provided its customers multiple ways to do business—via the Internet, 24-hour access to brokers, and speech-recognition or Touch-Tone telephone trading services. Schwab had been especially successful in catering to small investors. In recent months, about half of Schwab's new accounts were opened by customers who had never invested before. The company had recently retooled its customer service program after studying the practices of such companies as McDonald's and FedEx. A top official explained, "Our current push is to make sure that our customers who need help get it and that our customers who don't, don't get it—and don't have to pay for it."[21]

Innovation   Schwab was regarded as an industry innovator. In 1974, Schwab became the first brokerage firm to discount its commissions, thus triggering the advent of the discount brokerage segment. In 1984, the firm started a new trend in how mutual funds were sold, launching its innovative OneSource and Mutual Fund Marketplace programs that by 1998 provided customers with the ability to purchase 1,400 mutual funds through their Schwab account without having to open an account directly with mutual fund providers. Schwab's supermarket approach that let customers choose among many mutual funds and consolidate their holdings in one account proved extremely popular among small investors building a retirement nest egg and managing their own IRAs and Keogh plans. Schwab's fees from mutual fund sales accounted for 21 percent of revenues.

The company had built a reputation as an aggressive user of new technology to cut costs and pass the savings on to customers. The company spent about 13 percent of its revenues for new technology. When on-line trading first made its appearance in 1995, Schwab quickly set its sights on being a leader in electronic brokerage and became the first major investment firm to conduct trading on the Internet— by year-end 1995 its electronic brokerage unit had 336,000 accounts with $23 billion in assets utilizing the firm's proprietary e.Schwab electronic trading software. Schwab launched trading on the Internet at its Web site in May 1996.

Schwab was making the Internet a centerpiece of its strategy for delivering research, information, and services to account holders. In January 1998, Schwab began offering on-line trading seminars and providing walk-in customers access to the Internet at its branch offices. It also launched an Analyst Center on its Web site that gave all on-line customers access to research information from Dow Jones, Standard & Poor's, First Call, and Big Charts at no cost. Customers could receive security analyst reports and consensus opinions on stocks and industries. Customers with $50,000 or more in their accounts who averaged four trades monthly had access to their own Web pages, a software tool for identifying stock meeting whatever criteria the investor specified, on-line interviews with top executives, a one-page report card on 7,000 mutual funds, and a customized one-page comparison of the investors mutual funds against the performance of major stock indexes.

Value-Pricing   Because of its strong reputation among middle-income and value-conscious investors and its comparatively wide range of products and services, Schwab had been successful in maintaining a higher commission structure than other discount and electronic brokerage firms. Schwab management was opposed to attracting business solely on the basis of low price, believing that the range and quality of its services and products justified a price premium over the fees of deep-discounters. One executive was quoted as saying, "We have no intention of doing $7 trades."[22]

---

[21]"Schwab Is Fighting on Three Fronts," *Business Week,* March 10, 1997, p. 95.
[22]Ibid.

On-line Trading   The company's on-line trading operations grew rapidly. Schwab's director of electronic brokerage marketing said, "The early adopters were the more active traders, but now we're approaching this area where our online customer looks like our average offline customer. Schwab customers aren't as price sensitive as the customers of the deep-discount brokers." Schwab had invested heavily in computer software to make its on-line services user-friendly. In February 1997, Schwab created Market Buzz, a robust gateway on its Web site that offered real-time quotes, calculators for retirement and college planning, and market news, data, and research from 80 different independent financial information providers. During 1997, Schwab Online introduced a number of other Internet-based services, including purchasing mutual funds on-line and a software package that gave investors guidance in allocating their portfolio among stocks, bonds, money market funds, and other investments. *Smart Money* rated Schwab Online as having the best research links in a February 1998 article surveying the service offerings of 12 on-line brokers. Schwab's software updated the prices in customers' accounts every 15 minutes.

Schwab's new Analyst Center at its Web site exemplified the firm's strategic direction for its on-line service—offering retail investors access to "full-service" on-line investing. Top management believed that the firm offered on-line investors a combination of multiple service options, technology, access to information and guidance, and value pricing that was unequaled in the brokerage industry.

Schwab management was committed to building additional on-line capacity (to handle growing on-line trading volumes and to accommodate more simultaneous customer log-ons) and to providing greater reliability and system redundancy in order to enhance customer confidence in its on-line trading operation. Schwab had pledged that if on-line or telephone customers experienced wait times of longer than five minutes during peak trading periods, they could take their orders to a local Schwab branch where the standard commission would be waived (up to a maximum of $500 in commissions per customer per day).

In the late 1970s about 95 percent of Schwab's business was done through branch walk-ins or telephone calls to branch office personnel; in 1998, only 5 percent of the firm's business was done in branch offices. In recent months, 48 percent of all the trades Schwab executed for its 5 million customers were via the firm's on-line trading service versus 28 percent a year earlier; the balance was done by customers telephoning their orders to personnel in the company's central call centers. Schwab handled an average of 60,200 on-line trades a day in the first quarter of 1998 compared with an average of 34,100 in the first three months of 1997. The company expected that on-line trades would eventually account for 75 percent of its trading volume. The head of Schwab's electronic brokerage unit said,

> Online investing is evolving. Phase one was about early adopters getting on the Internet and a fragmented marketplace of firms fighting a price war at the cost of providing service, quality information, and quick access. Phase two is about providing millions more investors with access to an Internet experience where investing smart at a good value is paramount, and where high levels of customer service support and unbiased information, with value pricing, are the competitive differentiators. Phase two is here.

The growth in Schwab's on-line trading volume had already reduced its average commission per trade from $68.50 in 1996 to $49 in early 1998 and resulted in the duties of its salaried customer representatives shifting from taking orders for trades to talking with clients about financial planning, estate planning, mutual fund selection, the pros and cons of variable annuities, retirement planning, fixed-income investing, and insurance.

To combat growing competition and spur its revenue growth, Schwab had plans to boost its 1998 advertising budget by 20 percent, to $100 million, and it had hired a new ad agency to promote its retail brokerage business.

E*Trade Group (www.etrade.com)

The E*Trade Group was formed in 1982 to develop automated trading services for Charles Schwab & Co. and Fidelity Investments. E*Trade began its on-line trading service in 1992, surviving as a fledgling pioneer until the industry began to take off in 1995. The company's trading system consisted of software with 1 million lines of code and a group of fast Internet server computers that cost a reported $12 million.[23] In the first five months of 1996, E*Trade's active accounts grew from 38,000 to 65,000 and its monthly trading volume jumped from 50 million to 170 million shares. Led by 49-year-old Christos Cotsakos, who became CEO in March 1996 after career stints at FedEx and Dun & Bradstreet, E*Trade went public in August 1996 to raise capital for expansion and building a leadership position in the on-line trading industry. The initial public offering raised over $46 million. The company's stock price rose quickly from the initial offering price of $10.50 to $48 per share in 1997 based on the company's growth prospects. Chris Cotsakos was regarded as an energetic evangelist for on-line trading who had innovative ideas for making E*Trade a market leader.

By early 1997, E*Trade was opening 500 accounts and bringing in $8 to $10 million in assets a day; its customers were placing about 6,000 on-line trades daily. On October 27–28, 1997, when trading volumes were particularly heavy, the company's customers placed about 45,000 trades, nearly double the daily average of 24,000 trades. At the time, E*Trade had over 50 servers in operation with the capacity to handle 6,000 simultaneous users. Nonetheless, several irate customers who experienced delays logging on to their accounts to place trades filed a class-action lawsuit against E*Trade accusing the firm of using false and misleading advertising because it did not live up to its claim of providing quotes and completing trades in less than a minute.

In late 1997, E*Trade opened a Mutual Fund Center that allowed customers to select from among 3,500 mutual funds and, with its acquisition of OptionsLink from Hambrecht & Quist, it began providing stock-option management services for 94,000 employees at 79 companies. In the first quarter of 1998, the company handled an average of 23,200 trades a day.[24]

E*Trade earned $4.9 million on revenues of $51 million in the first quarter of the fiscal year ended December 31, 1997. The company had $7.8 billion in customer assets in 325,000 accounts and 600 employees as of January 1998. E*Trade had cut its commission rates seven times in the past four years in arriving at its present $14.95 fee. However, in recent months E*Trade's stock price had dropped from its high of $48 to the low 20s as new rivals with sophisticated investment tools and lower prices appeared on the scene. Moreover, E*Trade's ninth-place ranking in the latest Gomez Advisors survey (Exhibit 6) was down from a third-place ranking three months earlier (partly because Gomez incorporated the "customer confidence" category in its ratings on which E*Trade ranked only 30th).

E*Trade CEO Christos Cotsakos believed the handwriting was on the wall for the army of brokers employed at full-service firms: "The days of the $100,000 broker are

---

[23]*Financial Times,* March 11, 1996.
[24]*Wall Street Journal,* June 2, 1998, p. C20.

coming to an end."[25] In an interview published in *Leaders* in 1997, Cotsakos said, "I believe the brokers will have to migrate to a different type of position, like an advisor or consultant to the individual investor. I believe the days of the huge commissions and huge salaries are numbered . . . Brokerage is not a field I would recommend my daughter go into." He foresaw electronic brokerages outcompeting full-service firms and evolving into one-stop financial services enterprises:

> For years consumers have been paying exorbitantly high prices to get information that is selectively controlled by their brokers. What we've done is to totally eliminate the back office process, automate it and provide institutional-quality information by putting it at their fingertips.
>
> . . . We are going to be adding mutual funds, cash-management accounts and 401(k) plans, and we will be looking at insurance as well as strategic alliances with other financial-service firms.
>
> What we really see ourselves migrating to is a financial services gateway, where people can have access to our proprietary information as well as other content we can aggregate. That way, they can have one-stop shopping with a customized, personalized screen that meets all their financial needs, whether it's banking, buying flowers, viewing their stock portfolio, downloading information to their tax advisors, or doing a transaction.[26]

Ameritrade (www.ameritrade.com)

Ameritrade Holding Corporation was a small Omaha-based firm with four subsidiaries: Ameritrade and Accutrade (both deep-discount brokerages with on-line trading units); AmeriTrade Clearing, which provided securities clearing services for its two sister brokerages, banks, and other brokers and securities dealers; and AmeriVest, which provided discount brokerage services to banks, savings and loan associations, and credit unions. The company successfully completed an initial public offering of common stock in March 1997 and its shares were traded on the NASDAQ. Corporate revenues were $77 million in fiscal 1997, with net income of $13.8 million.

Ameritrade launched its deep-discount brokerage and no-frills on-line service in the fall of 1997. The Ameritrade brokerage subsidiary was formed by consolidating three small company-owned brokerages—Ceres Securities (a deep-discount brokerage the company started in 1994); K. Aufhauser (a New York firm acquired in 1995 that had launched the first Internet trading site in August 1994); and eBroker (a deep-discount electronic brokerage formed in 1996 to target the most price-sensitive on-line traders). The three firms combined had 98,000 core accounts. Ameritrade immediately attracted the attention of on-line investors with its fees of $8 for Internet trades (see Exhibit 7) and a $25 million ad campaign consisting of TV spots, print ads in *USA Today* and *The Wall Street Journal,* radio ads, and direct mail. By year-end 1997, Ameritrade had added 51,000 new accounts, bringing its account total to 147,000. Ameritrade planned to spend another $20 million advertising its on-line service in 1998, prompting analysts to forecast that the company would pick up an additional 100,000 to 125,000 accounts by October 1998. Ameritrade Holding Corporation was expected only to break even in 1998 due to the expenses of the heavy ad campaign.

To help build its customer base and increase brand awareness, Ameritrade had entered into strategic marketing agreements for services and content with America Online, CompuServe, Excite, Intuit, Infoseek, the Microsoft Network, Yahoo!, the Motley Fool, and the *USA Today* Information Network. These agreements gave

---

[25]As quoted in *Institutional Investor,* January 1997, p. 23.
[26]As quoted in "Declaring War on Brokerage Fees," *Leaders,* April, May, June 1997.

EXHIBIT 7   Schedule of Ameritrade's Commissions and Fees, April 1998

Ameritrade Credit Policy

3% interest paid on credit balances over $1,000*

Equities

1+ Shares	Price
On-line trades	$ 8
Touch-Tone trades	$12
Phone trades placed with a broker	$18

Note: $5 additional fee for limit, stop, and stop limit orders.

Options

$25 + $1.75 per contract

10% discount on trades placed electronically
(Internet, Touch-Tone), $29 minimum commission.

Mutual Funds

Fund Type	Buy	Sell	Exchange
No-load	$18.00	$18.00	$18.00
Load funds (front-end)	No fee, load only	$18.00	$18.00
Load funds (back-end)	$18.00	No fee, load only	$18.00

Note: All Fidelity Funds transactions carry the additional $18 fee.

Bonds (Minimum commission = $40; Treasuries = $25 auction)

Units	Price per Unit
1–50 bonds	$5.00 per bond
Over 50 bonds	$2.50 per bond

Margin Rates

Dollar Range	Above/Below Prime
Under $25,000	+0.75%
$25,000–$49,999	+0.25%
$50,000–$99,999	−0.75%
$100,000–$249,999	−1.00%
$250,000–$999,999	−1.25%
Above $999,999	−1.75%

*All prices are in U.S. dollars.
Source: www.ameritrade.com, April 17, 1998.

Ameritrade valuable exposure and gave Ameritrade customers access to a wider range of information and resources and improved trading experiences.

Ameritrade executives expected that its customers would average two trades monthly versus an average of less than one per month for the typical full-service brokerage client. Ameritrade's primary target market was investors who were comfortable with computers, were knowledgeable about how to find investment-related information on the Internet on their own, didn't like going through a broker, and were looking to execute their trades at a very low cost. Ameritrade's technical support hotline was open 10 hours a day Monday through Friday.

Ameritrade programmers were developing a new computer game called Darwin, to be distributed free on CD-ROM, that would teach novice investors who wanted to trade options about the Black/Scholes model, butterfly spreads, and other tricks of options trading through a format with the excitement and features of the popular video game Doom.[27] Ameritrade executives, having spent time in investor chat rooms on the Internet, could tell from the comments and complaints that losses were often the result of the trader's own lack of understanding and know-how. Ameritrade's plan was to use Darwin to provide a valuable tutorial for customers (since it was not good customer relations to tell novice investors that they were ill-equipped to be successful options traders and that losing their money had been their own fault).

The Quick & Reilly Group/Suretrade

The Quick & Reilly Group was a financial services firm that consisted of Quick & Reilly, Inc., the third largest discount brokerage in the United States, with 1 million accounts and 117 branch offices; U.S. Clearing, a clearing and trade execution service for more than 350 brokerage and banking firms; JJC Specialist, which made a market in the stocks and securities for 229 NYSE-listed companies and was the second largest specialist on the floor of the NYSE; Nash Weiss, which made a market in 3,500 over-the-counter stocks; and Suretrade, a deep discount Internet brokerage that began doing business in November 1997. In early 1998, the Quick & Reilly Group was acquired by Boston-based Fleet Financial Group, one of the two largest banks in New England with 1,200 branch offices and 2,400 ATMs throughout its service region. Fleet had assets of $85 billion and net income of $1.3 billion in 1997. Top executives indicated that, while Quick & Reilly would operate as an independent subsidiary within Fleet Financial, the firm would pursue opportunities to market Quick & Reilly products available to Fleet's customers and to market Fleet's products to Quick & Reilly customers. Fleet Financial's CEO said, "In 1998, we will utilize the Quick & Reilly platform to expand the investment products and services available to our customers and to begin cross-selling other Fleet products, such as mortgages and credit cards."

Quick & Reilly (www.quick-reilly.com) was the first NYSE member firm to offer discount commissions to individuals, in 1975. It launched its Internet trading system, called QuickWay Net, in November 1996. QuickWay Net, developed in partnership with a subsidiary of Reuters, gained a reputation as one of the fastest, easiest to use, and most comprehensive trading systems on the Internet and had been continuously enhanced since its introduction. Exhibit 8 shows the features on QuickWay Net.

Suretrade (www.suretrade.com)   Suretrade offered the lowest commission of any electronic brokerage firm (see again Exhibit 2) and its Web site offered customers a good range of features and services (see Exhibit 9). Suretrade had attracted 50,000 accounts in its first three months of operation. At its Web site, Suretrade was frank with customers about what they could expect:

> How can we bring you such an extraordinary value, combining excellent Internet trading functionality, content and security, along with a fantastic low commission structure? Our relationship will be an electronic one. It costs us less to answer e-mails than it costs us to

---

[27]Whitford, "Trade Fast, Trade Cheap," p. 114.

EXHIBIT 8   Features of Quick & Reilly's Quickway Net Trading System, October 1997

- Free, unlimited access to 15-minute-delayed stock, mutual fund, option, and option chain quotes.
- Confirmation of market orders within seconds of execution, with portfolio updated automatically.
- Free, unlimited access to the client's portfolio and the ability to create charts as well as monitor investments in real time.
- 24-hour-a-day, seven-day-a-week, access to brokers for trading assistance.
- Free research, company news, and other information on stocks, bonds, and mutual funds from Reuters.
- Ability to research mutual funds by searching by mutual fund families, individual funds, or investment objectives.
- Free stock screening tools.
- Free portfolio management tools. Automatically receive up to 300 securities quotes of choice, including fund quotes, e-mailed daily.
- Free research, company news, and other information on stocks and mutual funds from Reuters.
- Reuters IncLink, with detailed profiles on more than 12,000 publicly traded companies.
- Investment research and information from more than 25 publications.
- Morningstar on Demand—free highly regarded evaluations of mutual funds, including data on 3-, 5-, and 10-year returns.

Source: Company press release, October 6, 1997.

---

answer phone calls. Remember, our great prices aren't for everyone. They are for brokerage clients ready to conduct their affairs electronically. Our low commissions are the reward for clients who are committed to electronic brokerage.[28]

Discover Brokerage Direct (www.discoverbrokerage.com)

Discover Brokerage Direct got its start in electronic brokerage as Lombard Institutional Brokerage, a small discount firm in San Francisco that began offering on-line trading in September 1995. Lombard was acquired by Dean Witter Discover in January 1997 to serve as its on-line entry and changed Lombard's name to Discover Brokerage Direct to create a stronger association with the 40 million holders of the Discover Card. Dean Witter Discover then acquired the Morgan Stanley Group (a leading Wall Street investment banking firm) in May 1997, creating a company with great financial strength, global scope, and market leadership in a variety of financial service businesses. Dean Witter was the third largest full-service brokerage, with over 400 branch offices, 9,950 brokers, 3 million customer accounts, and $300 billion in customer assets.

Discover's strategy was to compete on value and service. Top management saw price-cutting as "a dangerous strategy."[29] Stephen R. Miller, chairman and chief operating officer of Discover Brokerage Direct, said,

---

[28]Company Web site, April 17, 1998.
[29]"Do I Hear Two Bits a Trade?," *Business Week,* December 8, 1997, p. 96.

EXHIBIT 9   Features of Suretrade's On-line Trading System, April 1998

- $7.95 per trade for up to 5,000 shares, applying to market or limit orders conducted over the Internet or by Touch-Tone telephone.
- No hidden charges. Suretrade does not impose additional charges such as inactivity fees and postage and handling fees.
- Accounts are protected up to $50 million per customer ($500,000 under SIPC, including $100,000 for cash claims) and an additional $49.5 million in protection provided by Aetna Casualty and Surety Company.
- Confirmation of orders within seconds of execution, with portfolio updated automatically.
- Free real-time quotes (up to 100 per day) from Thomson Financial.
- Free, unlimited portfolio access and the ability to create charts as well as monitor investments in real time.
- Free Reuters company news, market news, and other information on stocks, bonds, and mutual funds. Reuters IncLink provides free detailed profiles on 12,000 publicly traded companies.
- Free access to
    The professional version of Briefing.com.
    The premium version of Zack's Company Reports.
    INVESTools, including Morningstar on Demand.
    BASELINE, providing fundamental, technical and earnings estimates on over 7,500 stocks.
    BigCharts, a charting service oriented to technical investors.
    Second Opinion from MarketEdge.
- Ability to trade stocks, options, mutual funds and bonds via SURETRADE.com and stocks and options through a Touch-Tone telephone.

Source: www.suretrade.com, April 17, 1998.

Our goal is to be a leader in the value segment of the marketplace, and we believe that no name is more associated with the value concept than the Discover Card. Millions of people who trust the Discover Card for quality and service will be interested in exploring new financial products carrying the Discover brand. Furthermore, our current securities customers can look forward to an expanded range of financial products and services they can access by phone or online over the Internet.

Discover Brokerage Direct began an extensive marketing campaign in January 1998 to build a bigger customer base; its campaign included a direct-mail appeal to the more than 40 million holders of the Discover Card. The company's ads featured its number one ratings by *Barron's* and *Smart Money*. Discover Brokerage featured commissions as low as $14.95 a trade, 24-hour customer support, and access to over 3,500 mutual funds (many with no loads or transaction fees); customers could also place trades with a registered professional or by Touch-Tone phone. Discover's Web site (with a color scheme of Discover pumpkin and Lombard teal) provided customers with numerous data and research options and featured up-to-the-minute account information—customers could watch the prices change for their holdings as trades were executed. Discover also offered extensive customizing ability so clients could design their own investment-information centers according to their own interests. Discover was planning to add substantially more research information to its site and to improve its real-time bond trading service—both a direct result of being able to draw upon the resources and expertise of Dean Witter and Morgan Stanley.

Web Street Securities (www.webstreetsecurities.com)

Web Street Securities was a newcomer to the field formed by two entrepreneurs, Joe and Avi Fox—both in their 30s, whose prior venture was a failed international investment banking firm. After a month and a half of research into on-line trading during the summer of 1996, the two brothers decided to cast their future with electronic brokerage. Web Street opened its doors for business in August 1997. It launched its major bid for investor attention and market share in early 1998 with a colorful, active Web site, attention-getting TV spots (that intoned "You're a player now" when the head of the household portrayed in the ad opened an account on-line), and full-page ads in *USA Today* and other publications (see Exhibit 10). Web Street reportedly budgeted $20 million for its national ad campaign.

Web Street's site directed customers to the "Trading Pit" to execute orders, provided real-time updates of account information (customers could watch the prices being updated on the screen as trades occurred), and allowed customers to click on news updates and research sources (see Exhibit 10). The average Web Street customer was currently making four trades monthly. The company was rated best for active traders and second best overall by Gomez Advisors. Customers could place trades with a live broker 24 hours a day for $24.95 per trade. They could also purchase bonds (corporate, municipal, state, or federal) and any of 3,800 mutual funds (load and no-load).

Web Street had only $100 million in assets under management in January 1998 and had set a goal of 100,000 accounts by July 1998. There were plans to take the company public in the near future.

DLJdirect (www.dljdirect.com)

DLJdirect was the on-line trading unit of Donaldson Lufkin & Jenrette, a premier investment research house and one of the nation's 10 largest investment banking firms, with over $55 billion in assets. DLJ and its affiliates handled 10 percent of the trading volume of the New York Stock Exchange. DLJ's research operation had been ranked among the five best investment research firms for 24 straight years by *Institutional Investor;* its research covered 1,100 companies in 80 industries. DLJ handled initial public offerings for 30 companies in 1996 and was ranked fourth among investment banking firms in lead-managing new stock issues of companies as of August 1997.

Originally launched as PC Financial Network, DLJdirect pioneered on-line investing in the late 1980s and had executed over $23 billion in on-line transactions by 1998. DLJdirect provided access to its service both through the major on-line services (America Online, Prodigy, and CompuServe) and the Internet; customers could also place trades with brokers or through Touch-Tone phones. Clients could trade stocks, options, bonds, and Treasuries and could select from about 7,000 mutual funds (out of the 9,500 currently available funds). It provided comparatively strong research links (see again Exhibit 6), and on-line clients with account balances of $100,000 or more were provided access to DLJ's proprietary research information on 1,100 companies as well as opportunities to buy initial public offerings of stock in which DLJ was a lead manager or participant. In addition, DLJdirect offered real-time quotes, stock and portfolio alerts, a personal stock ticker, and screening tools. DLJdirect promoted itself as "a serious company for the serious investor."

Datek Online Holdings, Inc. (www.datek.com)

Datek Online was headed by Jeffrey A. Citron, a 27-year-old who had started working at 17 as an office clerk in a small Brooklyn, New York, brokerage called Datek Securities. By age 20, Citron had earned $1 million trading securities and was driving

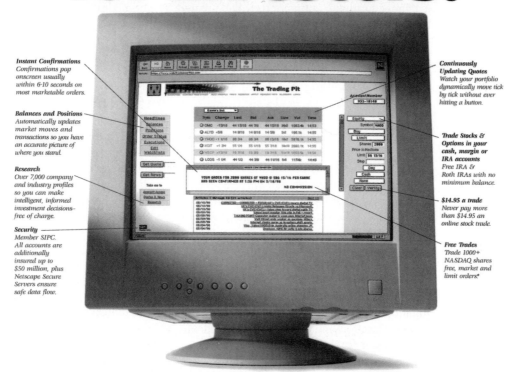

a Mercedes. A few years later, Citron and co-worker Joshua Levine used their computer skills to automate much of Datek's brokerage operations and started to explore ways to computerize stock trades. When in 1988 NASDAQ ordered securities dealers who were market makers in over-the-counter stocks to execute small orders via a computerized electronic system, Citron and Levine came up with a software trading system that allowed Datek Securities to become the biggest brokerage that executed small trades and to make millions of dollars in trading profits—the company had trading profits of about $95 million in 1996, up from $3.8 million in 1992.[30] Citron and Levine became multimillionaires. But during the 1991–96 period, various officials at Datek Securities were fined and suspended on several occasions for violating trading rules in executing small trading orders on the NASDAQ.

In 1992, Citron and Levine founded a company to function as a computerized stock exchange, utilizing software they had created. The company was quite successful and, by 1998, was handling 4 percent of all NASDAQ trading volume.[31] In 1993, Jeffrey Citron formed his own brokerage firm, which he sold a few months later to Joshua Levine. In 1995, Citron established a company to sell electronic trading software, while Levine formed two companies—Big Think (to supply Datek Securities with new computer technology) and Big J Software, a software consulting company whose principal clients were securities firms. In early 1996, Citron, Levine, and Sheldon Maschler, former chief trader at Datek Securities who was the central figure in many of the firm's trading violations and was later suspended from securities trading for one year beginning in February 1997, formed a company to develop and license trading software to Datek Securities and other electronic brokerage operations; the new company achieved revenues of nearly $100 million in 1996. In 1997, Datek Securities established Datek Online as an electronic brokerage and Jeffrey Citron became CEO. In early 1998, Datek Securities and Levine's Big Think were merged as Datek Online Holdings; Citron, Levine, Erik Maschler (son of Sheldon Maschler), and several others emerged as the principal owners.

Jeffrey Citron had been labeled a "technology wizard" by *Forbes* and as "one of the 20 most important players on the financial Web" by *Institutional Investor.* One industry observer estimated that Datek Online executed approximately 11,500 trades daily during the fourth quarter of 1997, the fourth largest in the industry behind Schwab (45,350 daily transactions), E*Trade (21,400 trades), and Waterhouse (12,150 trades).[32] A principal reason for Datek's success was its innovative software programs—it had the fastest execution of electronic stock trades. Datek Online's low commissions appealed to active traders. In early 1997, Datek had 10,000 on-line accounts; in April 1998, it reportedly had 80,000 accounts containing $1.5 billion in assets.

Jeffrey Citron and the other investors in Datek Online had plans to take the company public, but their connections with Datek Securities and its record of trading violations were considered a liability. A lengthy feature article in the *New York Times* in May 1998 detailing the numerous entanglements of Datek Online's owners with Datek Securities and the many sanctions imposed on Datek Securities did nothing to enhance public confidence in Datek Online Holdings. However, the *New York Times* article indicated that Jeffrey Citron had recently tightened management controls at Datek Online Holdings, outlawed certain questionable trading practices, hired a major accounting

[30]*The New York Times,* May 10, 1998, Section 3, p. 4.
[31]Ibid.
[32]Bill Burnham, analyst at Piper Jaffrey, as reported in Ibid.

firm as auditor, and completed the sale of the company's securities trading unit, the center of most of the questioned practices and the target of several ongoing investigations of securities fraud. The purchasers of the securities trading unit, renamed Heartland Securities, were two of the current owners of Datek Online Holdings, Erik Maschler and Aaron Elbogen; in 1970, Elbogen had been one of the original co-founders of Datek Securities.

Merrill Lynch

Merrill Lynch was a diversified financial services firm whose principal businesses were in investment banking, full-service brokerage, and asset management. In investment banking, Merrill Lynch was the top-ranked firm globally in 1997 in managing new debt issues and in managing new stock issues; it was the third-ranking firm globally in advising and handling mergers and acquisitions (it ranked first in the United States in mergers and acquisitions). In full-service brokerage, where it was also the market leader, Merrill Lynch had 800 branch offices worldwide, approximately 15,300 brokers and account executives, 9 million retail customer accounts, and $1.2 trillion in client accounts. The firm had an exceptionally broad range of products and services, and the name Merrill Lynch was known to virtually all investors worldwide. Merrill Lynch consistently ranked among the leading research providers in the industry, covering some 3,900 companies in 55 countries with its staff of analysts. Current information on these companies was available to all retail clients through their brokers by means of a computer retrieval system available in each branch office. On the securities-dealer side of its brokerage business, Merrill Lynch was a market maker for the stocks of 550 U.S. companies and 4,800 foreign companies traded in over-the-counter markets. In 1997, Merrill Lynch had revenues of $31.7 billion and net income of $1.9 billion. The company had a total of 56,600 employees.

Top management's vision was for Merrill Lynch to be a world-class company that delivered global products, services, and intelligence of the highest caliber through trusted local relationships and to build leadership positions in securities markets throughout the world. Management was committed to serving clients through personalized advice and guidance, helping to create customized solutions to client problems.

Because of its strong strategic emphasis on using brokers to deliver personalized client services, Merrill Lynch had held back in pursuing on-line trading. The company had gone so far as to create a proprietary software package for clients to install on their own computers that allowed them to access their accounts and review account balances; customers were charged $25 for the software. Merrill Lynch was said to be planning to let clients in its fee-based asset-management plans engage in on-line trading for their accounts later in 1998. A Merrill Lynch executive indicated the reason the firm wasn't rushing to offer on-line trading was that "this is not one of the highest-rated things that our clients are asking for."[33]

(For some updated information on the Internet brokers, visit www.gomez.com.)

---

[33]As quoted in *The Wall Street Journal*, June 2, 1998, p. C20.

DELL COMPUTER CORPORATION

Arthur A. Thompson, *The University of Alabama*

John E. Gamble, *University of South Alabama*

In 1984, at the age of 21, Michael Dell founded Dell Computer with a simple vision and business concept—that personal computers could be built to order and sold directly to customers. Michael Dell believed his approach to PC manufacturing had two advantages: (1) bypassing distributors and retail dealers eliminated the markups of resellers, and (2) building to order greatly reduced the costs and risks associated with carrying large stocks of parts, components, and finished goods. While Dell Computer sometimes struggled during its early years in trying to refine its strategy, build an adequate infrastructure, and establish market credibility against better-known rivals, its build-to-order and sell-direct approach proved appealing to growing numbers of customers in the mid-1990s as global PC sales rose to record levels. And, just as important, the strategy gave the company a substantial cost and profit-margin advantage over rivals that manufactured PCs in volume and kept their distributors and retailers stocked with ample inventories.

Going into 1998, Dell Computer had a 12 percent share of the PC market in the United States, trailing only Compaq Computer and IBM, which held first and second place in the market, respectively. Worldwide, Dell Computer had nearly a 6 percent market share (see Exhibit 1). And the company was gaining market share quickly in all of the world's markets. The company's fastest growing market for the past several quarters was Europe. Even though Asia's economic woes in the first quarter of 1998 resulted in a slight decline in Asian sales of PCs, Dell's sales in Asia rose 35 percent. Dell's sales at its Internet Web site were averaging $5 million a day and were expected to reach $1.5 billion annually by year-end 1998. Dell Computer had 1997 revenues of $12.3 billion, up from $3.4 billion in 1994—a compound average growth rate of 53 percent. Over the same period, profits were up from $140 million to $944 million—an 89 percent growth rate. Since 1990, the company's stock price had exploded from a split-adjusted price of 23 cents per share to $83 per share in May 1998—a 36,000 percent increase. Dell Computer was the top-performing big company stock so far during the 1990s and seemed poised to become the stock of the decade.

Dell's principal products included desktop PCs, notebook computers, workstations, and servers. The company also marketed a number of products made by other

EXHIBIT 1   World's Top Five PC Vendors, Based on Factory Shipments, 1996 and 1997

1997 Rank	Vendor	1997 Market Shipments of PCs*	1997 Market Share	1996 Market Shipments of PCs*	1996 Market Share	Percent Growth 1996–1997
1	Compaq Computer	10,064,000	12.6%	7,211,000	10.4%	40%
2	IBM	7,239,000	9.1	6,176,000	8.9	17
3	Dell Computer	4,648,000	5.8	2,996,000	4.3	55
4	Hewlett-Packard	4,468,000	5.6	2,984,000	4.3	50
5	Packard Bell NEC	4,150,000	5.2	4,230,000	6.1	(2.0)
	Others	49,369,000	61.8	45,727,000	66.0	8
	All vendors	79,938,000	100.0%	69,324,000	100.0%	15%

*Includes branded shipments only and excludes original equipment manufacturer (OEM) sales for all manufacturers.
Source: International Data Corporation.

manufacturers, including CD-ROM drives, modems, monitors, networking hardware, memory cards, storage devices, speakers, and printers. The company's products and services were sold in more than 140 countries. Sales of desktop PCs accounted for about 65 percent of Dell's total revenues; sales of notebook computers, servers, and workstations accounted for about 33 percent of revenue. In early 1998, the company had 16,000 employees.

COMPANY BACKGROUND

At age 13, Michael Dell was running a mail-order stamp-trading business, complete with a national catalog, and grossing $2,000 per month. At 16, he was selling subscriptions to the *Houston Post,* and at 17 he bought his first BMW with money he had earned. He enrolled at the University of Texas in 1983 as a premed student (his parents wanted him to become a doctor) but soon became immersed in computers and started selling PC components out of his college dormitory room. He bought random-access memory (RAM) chips and disk drives for IBM PCs at cost from IBM dealers, who often had excess supplies on hand because they were required to order large monthly quotas from IBM. Dell resold the components through newspaper ads (and later through ads in national computer magazines) at 10–15 percent below the regular retail price.

By April 1984 sales were running about $80,000 per month. Dell dropped out of college and formed a company, PCs Ltd., to sell both PC components and PCs under the brand name PCs Limited. He obtained his PCs by buying retailers' surplus stocks at cost, then powering them up with graphics cards, hard disks, and memory before reselling them. His strategy was to sell directly to end users; by eliminating the retail markup, Dell's new company was able to sell IBM clones (machines that copied the functioning of IBM PCs using the same or similar components) at about 40 percent below the price of an IBM PC. The price discounting strategy was successful, attracting price-conscious buyers and producing rapid growth. By 1985, the company was assembling its own PC designs with a few people working on six-foot tables. The company had 40 employees, and Michael Dell worked 18-hour days, often sleeping on a cot in his office. By the end of fiscal 1986, sales had reached $33 million.

During the next several years, however, PCs Ltd. was hampered by a lack of money, people, and resources. Michael Dell sought to refine the company's business model, add needed production capacity, and build a bigger, deeper management staff and corporate infrastructure while at the same time keeping costs low. The company was renamed Dell Computer in 1987, and the first international offices were opened that same year. In 1988 Dell added a sales force to serve large customers, began selling to government agencies, and became a public company—raising $34.2 million in its first offering of common stock. Sales to large customers quickly became the dominant part of Dell's business. By 1990 Dell Computer had sales of $388 million, a market share of 2–3 percent, and an R&D staff of over 150 people. Michael Dell's vision was for Dell Computer to become one of the top three PC companies.

Thinking its direct sales business would not grow fast enough, in 1990–93, the company began distributing its computer products through Soft Warehouse Superstores (now CompUSA), Staples (a leading office-products chain), Wal-Mart, Sam's Club, and Price Club (now Price/Costco). Dell also sold PCs through Best Buy stores in 16 states and through Xerox in 19 Latin American countries. But when the company learned how thin its margins were in selling through such distribution channels, it realized it had made a mistake and withdrew from selling to retailers and other intermediaries in 1994 to refocus on direct sales. At the time, sales through retailers accounted for only about 2 percent of Dell's revenues.

Further problems emerged in 1993. Dell reportedly had $38 million in second-quarter losses that year from engaging in a risky foreign-currency hedging strategy. Also, quality difficulties appeared in certain PC lines made by the company's contract manufacturers, profit margins declined, and buyers were turned off by the company's laptop PC models. To get laptop sales back on track, the company took a charge of $40 million to write off its laptop line and suspended sales of laptops until it could get redesigned models into the marketplace. The problems resulted in losses of $36 million for the company's fiscal year ending January 30, 1994.

Because of higher costs and unacceptably low profit margins in selling to individuals and households, Dell did not pursue the consumer market aggressively until sales on the company's Internet site took off in 1996 and 1997. Management noticed that while the industry's average selling price to individuals was going down, Dell's was going up—people who were buying their second and third computers, who wanted powerful computers with multiple features, and who did not need much technical support were choosing Dell. It became clear that PC-savvy individuals liked the convenience of buying direct from Dell, ordering exactly what they wanted, and having it delivered to their door within a matter of days. In early 1997, Dell created an internal sales and marketing group dedicated to serving the individual consumer segment and introduced a product line designed especially for individual users.

By late 1997, Dell had become the industry leader in keeping costs down and wringing efficiency out of its direct sales and build-to-order business model. Industry observers saw Dell as being in strong position to capitalize on several forces shaping the PC industry—sharp declines in component prices, rapid improvements in PC technology, and growing customer interest in having PCs equipped with the power, components, and software they wanted.

Exhibit 2 through Exhibit 5 contain a five-year review of Dell Computer's financial performance and selected financial statements contained in the company's 1998 annual report.

MICHAEL DELL

Michael Dell was widely considered one of the mythic heroes within the PC industry and was labeled "the quintessential American entrepreneur" and "the most innovative

EXHIBIT 2 Financial Performance Summary, Dell Computer, 1994–98 (In millions, except per share data)

	February 1, 1998	February 2, 1997	January 28, 1996	January 29, 1995	January 30, 1994
Results of Operations Data					
Net revenue	$12,327	$7,759	$5,296	$3,475	$2,873
Gross margin	$ 2,722	$1,666	$1,067	$ 738	$ 433
Operating income (loss)	$ 1,316	$ 714	$ 377	$ 249	$ (39)
Income (loss) before extraordinary loss	$ 944	$ 531	$ 272	$ 149	$ (36)
Net income (loss)	$ 944	$ 518	$ 272	$ 149	$ (36)
Income (loss) before extraordinary loss per common share					
Basic	$ 1.44	$ 0.75	$ 0.36	$ 0.23	$ (0.07)
Diluted	$ 1.28	$ 0.68	$ 0.33	$ 0.19	$ (0.07)
Weighted average shares					
Basic	658	710	716	618	597
Diluted	738	782	790	750	597
Balance Sheet Data					
Working capital	$ 1,215	$1,089	$1,018	$ 718	$ 510
Total assets	$ 4,268	$2,993	$2,148	$1,594	$1,140
Long-term debt	$ 17	$ 18	$ 113	$ 113	$ 100
Total stockholders' equity	$ 1,293	$ 806	$ 973	$ 652	$ 471

Source: 1998 annual report.

guy for marketing computers in this decade." He was the youngest CEO ever to guide a company to a Fortune 500 ranking. His prowess was based more on an astute combination of technical knowledge and marketing know-how than on being a techno-wizard. In 1998 Michael Dell owned about 16 percent of Dell Computer's common stock, worth about $10 billion.

Once pudgy and bespectacled, Michael Dell wore expensive suits and contact lenses, ate only health foods, attended executive seminars at Stanford, and was a frequent speaker at industry conferences. He lived in a three-story 33,000-square-foot home on a 60-acre estate. The company's glass-and-steel headquarters building in Round Rock, Texas (an Austin suburb), had unassuming, utilitarian furniture, abstract art, framed accolades to Michael Dell, laudatory magazine covers, industry awards plaques, bronze copies of the company's 11 patents, and a history wall that contained the hand-soldered guts of the company's first personal computer.[1]

In the company's early days Michael Dell hung around mostly with the company's engineers. He was so shy that some employees thought he was stuck up because he never talked to them. But people who worked with him closely described him as a likable young man who was slow to warm up to strangers.[2] He was a terrible public speaker and wasn't good at running meetings. A *Business Week* reporter labeled him

---

[1]As described in *Business Week,* March 22, 1993, p. 82.
[2]"Michael Dell: On Managing Growth," *MIS Week,* September 5, 1988, p. 1.

EXHIBIT 3   Consolidated Statement of Income, Dell Computer, 1996–98 (In millions, except per share data)

	Fiscal Year Ended		
	February 1, 1998	February 2, 1997	January 28, 1996
Net revenue	$12,327	$7,759	$5,296
Cost of revenue	9,605	6,093	4,229
Gross margin	2,722	1,666	1,067
Operating expenses			
Selling, general and administrative	1,202	826	595
Research and development	145	88	62
Engineering	59	38	33
Total operating expenses	1,406	952	690
Operating income	1,316	714	377
Financing and other	52	33	6
Income before income taxes and extraordinary loss	1,368	747	383
Provision for income taxes	424	216	111
Income before extraordinary loss	944	531	272
Extraordinary loss, net of taxes	—	(13)	—
Net income	944	518	272
Preferred stock dividends	—	—	(12)
Net income available to common stockholders	$ 944	$ 518	$ 260
Basic earnings per common share (in whole dollars)			
Income before extraordinary loss	$ 1.44	$ 0.75	$ 0.36
Extraordinary loss, net of taxes	—	(.02)	—
Earnings per common share	$ 1.44	$ 0.73	$ 0.36
Diluted earnings per common share (in whole dollars)			
Income before extraordinary loss	$ 1.28	$ 0.68	$ 0.33
Extraordinary loss, net of taxes	—	(.02)	—
Earnings per common share	$ 1.28	$ 0.66	$ 0.33
Weighted-average shares outstanding			
Basic	658	710	716
Diluted	738	782	790

Source: 1998 annual report.

"the enfant terrible of personal computers" in a June 13, 1988, article and quoted a former executive who said, "Dell's got an ego like God."[3] But Lee Walker, a 51-year-old venture capitalist brought in by Michael Dell to provide much-needed managerial and financial experience during the company's organization-building years, became

[3]Kevin Kelly, "Michael Dell: The Enfant Terrible of Personal Computers," *Business Week,* June 12, 1988, p. 61.

EXHIBIT 4 Consolidated Statement of Financial Position, Dell Computer, 1997–98 (In millions)

Assets	February 1, 1998	February 2, 1997
Current assets		
Cash	$ 320	$ 115
Marketable securities	1,524	1,237
Accounts receivable, gross	1,514	934
Less allowance for doubtful accounts	(28)	(31)
Net accounts receivable	1,486	903
Inventories of production materials	189	223
Work-in-process and finished goods inventories	44	28
Other	349	241
Total current assets	3,912	2,747
Property, plant, and equipment		
Land and buildings	$ 137	$ 133
Computer equipment	135	104
Office furniture and fixtures	45	32
Machinery and other equipment	126	59
Leasehold improvements	66	46
Total property, plant, and equipment	509	374
Less accumulated depreciation and amortization	(167)	(139)
Net property, plant, and equipment	342	235
Other assets	14	11
Total assets	$4,268	$2,993
Liabilities and Stockholders' Equity		
Current liabilities		
Accounts payable	$1,643	$1,040
Accrued and other	1,054	618
Total current liabilities	2,697	1,658
Long-term debt	17	18
Deferred revenue on warranty	225	219
Other	36	13
Commitments and contingent liabilities	—	—
Total liabilities	2,975	1,908
Put options	—	279
Stockholders' Equity		
Preferred stock and capital in excess of $.01 par value; shares issued and outstanding: none	—	—
Common stock and capital in excess of $.01 par value; shares issued and outstanding: 644 and 692, respectively	747	195
Retained earnings	607	647
Other	(61)	(36)
Total stockholders' equity	1,293	806
Total liabilities and equity	$4,268	$2,993

Source: 1998 annual report.

EXHIBIT 5   Geographic Area Information, Dell Computer, 1996–98 (In millions)

	Fiscal Year 1998				
	Americas	**Europe**	**Asia-Pacific and Japan**	**Eliminations**	**Consolidated**
Sales to unaffiliated customers	$8,531	$2,956	$840	$ —	$12,327
Transfers between geographic areas	67	17	—	(84)	—
Total sales	$8,598	$2,973	$840	$ (84)	$12,327
Operating income	$1,152	$ 255	$ 33	$ —	$ 1,440
Corporate expenses					(124)
Total operating income					$ 1,316
Identifiable assets	$1,363	$ 605	$172	$ —	$ 2,140
General corporate assets					2,128
Total assets					$ 4,268

	Fiscal Year 1997				
	Americas	**Europe**	**Asia-Pacific and Japan**	**Eliminations**	**Consolidated**
Sales to unaffiliated customers	$5,279	$2,004	$476	$ —	$ 7,759
Transfers between geographic areas	50	32	—	(82)	—
Total sales	$5,329	$2,036	$476	$ (82)	$ 7,759
Operating income (loss)	$ 609	$ 193	$ (6)	$ —	$ 796
Corporate expenses					(82)
Total operating income					714
Identifiable assets	$ 903	$ 390	$125	$ —	$ 1,418
General corporate assets					1,575
Total assets					$ 2,993

	Fiscal Year 1996				
	Americas	**Europe**	**Asia-Pacific and Japan**	**Eliminations**	**Consolidated**
Sales to unaffiliated customers	$3,474	$1,478	$344	$ —	$ 5,296
Transfers between geographic areas	66	192	—	(258)	—
Total sales	$3,540	$1,670	$344	$(258)	$ 5,296
Operating income (loss)	$ 285	$ 171	$ (21)	$ —	$ 435
Corporate expenses					(58)
Total operating income					377
Identifiable assets	$ 867	$ 409	$123	$ —	$ 1,399
General corporate assets					749
Total assets					$ 2,148

Source: 1998 annual report.

Michael Dell's mentor, built up his confidence, and was instrumental in turning him into a polished executive.[4] Walker served as the company's president and chief operating officer during the 1986–90 period; he had a fatherly image, knew everyone by name, and played a key role in implementing Michael Dell's marketing ideas. Under

---

[4]"The Education of Michael Dell," *Business Week,* March 22, 1993, p. 86.

Walker's tutelage, Michael Dell became intimately familiar with all parts of the business, overcame his shyness, learned to control his ego, and turned into a charismatic leader with an instinct for motivating people and winning their loyalty and respect. When Walker had to leave the company in 1990 because of health reasons, Dell turned to Morton Meyerson, former CEO and president of Electronic Data Systems, for advice on how to transform Dell Computer from a fast-growing medium-sized company into a billion-dollar enterprise.

Though sometimes given to displays of impatience and a strong temper, Michael Dell usually spoke in a quiet, reflective manner and came across as a person with maturity and seasoned judgment far beyond his age. He became an accomplished public speaker. He delegated authority to subordinates, believing that the best results came from "[turning] loose talented people who can be relied upon to do what they're supposed to do." Business associates viewed Michael Dell as an aggressive personality, an extremely competitive risk-taker who had always played close to the edge. Moreover, the people he hired were aggressive and competitive, traits that translated into an aggressive, competitive, intense corporate culture with a strong sense of mission and dedication.

Developments in Early 1998

Dell's sales were up strongly in the first quarter of 1998, even in product areas where the company had previously lagged, pushing its global market share to 7.9 percent and its U.S. share to 11.8 percent. Unit shipments were 1.6 million units, compared to 978,000 in the first quarter of 1997. In laptop PCs, Dell moved into third place in U.S. sales and fifth place worldwide. And it climbed into second place in higher-margin products like servers and Windows NT–based workstations. Dell announced the formation of an alliance with Data General Corporation to enter the market for data storage equipment.

In the first quarter of 1998, about half of the industry's PC sales consisted of computers selling for less than $1,300. Dell's average selling price was $2,500 per unit, down 9 percent from the prior quarter. The company was planning to broaden its product line to include lower-priced PCs equipped with Intel's low-end Celeron chip; Dell's new budget models were priced in the $1,200 range.

COMPETING VALUE CHAIN MODELS IN THE PERSONAL COMPUTER INDUSTRY

When the personal computer industry first began to take shape in the early 1980s, the founding companies manufactured many of the components themselves—disk drives, memory chips, graphics chips, microprocessors, motherboards, and software. Believing that they had to develop key components in-house, companies built expertise in a variety of PC-related technologies and created organizational units to produce components as well as to handle final assembly. While certain "noncritical" items were typically outsourced, if a computer maker was not at least partially vertically integrated and an assembler of some components, then it was not taken seriously as a manufacturer.

But as the industry grew, technology advanced quickly in so many directions on so many parts and components that the early personal computer manufacturers could not keep pace as experts on all fronts. There were too many technological innovations in components to pursue and too many manufacturing intricacies to master for a vertically integrated manufacturer to keep its products on the cutting edge. As a consequence, companies emerged that specialized in making particular components. Specialists could marshal enough R&D capability and resources to either lead the technological developments in their area of specialization or else quickly match the advances made by their competitors. Moreover, specialist firms could mass-produce a component and supply it to several computer manufacturers far cheaper than any one manufacturer could fund the needed component R&D and then make only whatever smaller volume of components it needed for assembling its own brand of PCs.

Thus, in recent years, computer makers had begun to outsource most all components from specialists and to concentrate on efficient assembly and marketing of their brand of computers. Exhibit 6 shows the value chain model that such manufacturers as Compaq, IBM, Hewlett-Packard, and Packard-Bell used in the 1990s. It featured arm's-length transactions between specialist suppliers, manufacturer/assemblers, distributors and retailers, and end-users. However, Dell, Gateway, and Micron Electronics employed a shorter value chain model, selling direct to customers and eliminating the time and costs associated with distributing through independent resellers. Building to order avoided (a) having to keep many differently-equipped models on retailers' shelves to fill buyer requests for one or another configuration of options and components and (b) having to clear out slow-selling models at a discount before introducing new generations of PCs. Selling direct eliminated retailer costs and markups (retail dealer margins were typically in the 4 to 10 percent range). Dell Computer was far and away the world's largest direct seller to large companies and government institutions, while Gateway was the largest direct seller to individuals and small businesses. Micron Electronics was the only other PC maker that relied on the direct sales and build-to-order approach for the big majority of its sales.

DELL COMPUTER'S STRATEGY

Dell Computer's strategy was built around a number of core elements: build-to-order manufacturing, mass customization, partnerships with suppliers, just-in-time components inventories, direct sales, market segmentation, customer service, and extensive data and information sharing with both supply partners and customers. Through this strategy, the company hoped to achieve what Michael Dell called "virtual integration"—a stitching together of Dell's business with its supply partners and customers in real time such that all three appeared to be part of the same organizational team.[5]

Build-to-Order Manufacturing and Mass Customization

Dell built its computers, workstations, and servers to order; none were produced for inventory. Dell customers could order custom-built servers and workstations based on the needs of their applications. Desktop and laptop customers ordered whatever configuration of microprocessor speed, random access memory (RAM), hard-disk capacity, CD-ROM drive, fax/modem, monitor size, speakers, and other accessories they preferred. The orders were directed to the nearest factory. Until recently Dell had operated its assembly lines in traditional fashion, with workers each performing a single operation. An order form accompanied each metal chassis across the production floor;

---

[5]This was the term Michael Dell used in an interview published in the *Harvard Business Review.* See Joan Magretta, "The Power of Virtual Integration: An Interview with Dell Computer's Michael Dell," *Harvard Business Review,* March–April 1998, pp. 73–84.

EXHIBIT 6   Comparative Value Chains of PC Manufacturers

Traditional PC Industry Value Chain (utilized by Compaq Computer, IBM, Hewlett-Packard, most others)

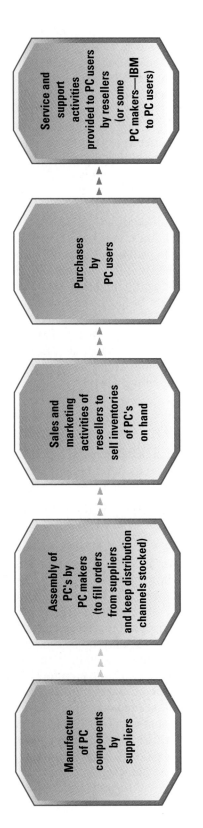

Build-to-Order/Direct Sales Value Chain (employed by Dell Computer, Gateway, and Micron Electronics)

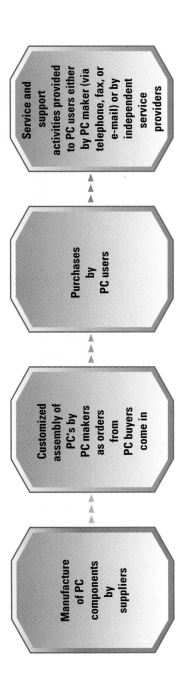

drives, chips, and ancillary items were installed to match customer specifications. As a partly assembled PC arrived at a new workstation, the operator, standing beside a tall steel rack with drawers full of components, was instructed what to do by little red and green lights flashing beside the drawers. When the operator was finished, the components were automatically replenished from the other side of the drawers and the PC chassis glided down the line to the next workstation. However, Dell reorganized its plants in 1997, shifting to "cell manufacturing" techniques whereby a team of workers operating at a group workstation (or cell) assembled an entire PC according to customer specifications. The result had been to reduce assembly times by 75 percent and to double productivity per square foot of assembly space. Assembled computers were tested, then loaded with the desired software, shipped, and typically delivered within five to six business days of the initial order.

This sell-direct strategy meant, of course, that Dell had no in-house stock of finished goods inventories and that, unlike competitors using the traditional value chain model (Exhibit 6), it did not have to wait for resellers to clear out their own inventories before it could push new models into the marketplace. (Resellers typically operated with 60–70 days' inventory.) Equally important was the fact that customers who bought from Dell got the satisfaction of having their computers customized to their particular liking and pocketbook.

Dell had three PC assembly plants—in Austin, Texas; Limerick, Ireland; and Penang, Malaysia. The company was constructing another plant in Ireland to serve the European market as well as a new plant in China (the company expected the market for PCs in China to soon be huge). Both of the new plants were expected to come into use at the end of 1998.

Partnerships with Suppliers

Michael Dell believed it made much better sense for Dell Computer to partner with reputable suppliers of PC parts and components rather than to integrate backward and get into parts and components manufacturing on its own. He explained why:

> If you've got a race with 20 players all vying to make the fastest graphics chip in the world, do you want to be the 21st horse, or do you want to evaluate the field of 20 and pick the best one?[6]

Management believed long-term partnerships with reputable suppliers yielded several advantages. First, using name-brand processors, disk drives, modems, speakers, and multimedia components enhanced the quality and performance of Dell's PCs. Because of the varying performance of different brands of components, the brand of the components was as important or more important to some buyers than the brand of the overall system. Dell's strategy was to partner with as few outside vendors as possible and to stay with those vendors as long as they maintained their leadership in technology, performance, and quality. Second, because Dell committed to purchase a specified percentage of its requirements from each of its long-term suppliers, Dell was assured of getting the volume of components it needed on a timely basis even when overall market demand for a particular component temporarily exceeded the overall market supply. Third, Dell's formal partnerships with key suppliers made it feasible to have some of their engineers assigned to Dell's product design teams and for them to be treated as part of Dell. When new products were launched, suppliers' engineers were stationed in

---

[6]As quoted in Magretta, "The Power of Virtual Integration."

Dell's plant. If early buyers called with a problem related to design, further assembly and shipments were halted while the supplier's engineers and Dell personnel corrected the flaw on the spot.[7] Fourth, Dell's long-run commitment to its suppliers laid the basis for just-in-time delivery of suppliers' products to Dell's assembly plants in Texas, Ireland, and Malaysia. Some of Dell's vendors had plants or distribution centers within a few miles of Dell's Texas assembly plant and could deliver daily or even hourly if needed. To help suppliers meet its just-in-time delivery expectations, Dell openly shared its daily production schedules, sales forecasts, and new-model introduction plans with vendors.

Michael Dell explained one aspect of the information-sharing relationship with suppliers as follows:

> We tell our suppliers exactly what our daily production requirements are. So it's not, "Well, every two weeks deliver 5,000 to this warehouse, and we'll put them on the shelf, and then we'll take them off the shelf." It's, "Tomorrow morning we need 8,562, and deliver them to door number seven by 7 AM."[8]

Dell also did a three-year plan with each of its key suppliers and worked with suppliers to minimize the number of different stock-keeping units of parts and components in designing its products.

Why Dell Was Committed to Just-in-Time Inventory Practices   Dell's just-in-time inventory emphasis yielded major cost advantages and shortened the time it took for Dell to get new generations of its computer models into the marketplace. New advances were coming so fast in certain computer parts and components (particularly microprocessors, disk drives, and modems) that any given item in inventory was obsolete in a matter of months, sometimes quicker. Having a couple of months of component inventories meant getting caught in the transition from one generation of components to the next. Moreover, there were rapid-fire reductions in the prices of components—most recently, component prices had been falling as much as 50 percent annually (an average of 1 percent a week). Intel, for example, regularly cut the prices on its older chips when it introduced newer chips, and it introduced new chip generations about every three months. And the prices of hard-disk drives with greater and greater memory capacity had dropped sharply as disk drive makers incorporated new technology that allowed them to add more gigabytes of hard-disk memory very inexpensively.

The economics of minimal component inventories were dramatic. Michael Dell explained:

> If I've got 11 days of inventory and my competitor has 80 and Intel comes out with a new 450-megahertz chip, that means I'm going to get to market 69 days sooner.
>
>   In the computer industry, inventory can be a pretty massive risk because if the cost of materials is going down 50 percent a year and you have two or three months of inventory versus eleven days, you've got a big cost disadvantage. And you're vulnerable to product transitions, when you can get stuck with obsolete inventory.[9]

Collaboration with suppliers was close enough to allow Dell to operate with only a few days of inventory for some components and a few hours of inventory for others.

---

[7]Ibid., p. 75.

[8]Ibid.

[9]Ibid., p. 76.

Dell supplied data on inventories and replenishment needs to its suppliers at least once a day—hourly in the case of components being delivered several times daily from nearby sources. In a couple of instances, Dell's close partnership with vendors allowed it to operate with no inventories. Dell's supplier of monitors was Sony. Because the monitors Sony supplied with the Dell name already imprinted were of dependably high quality (a defect rate of fewer than 1,000 per million), Dell didn't even open up the monitor boxes to test them.[10] Nor did it bother to have them shipped to Dell's assembly plants to be warehoused for shipment to customers. Instead, utilizing sophisticated data exchange systems, Dell arranged for its shippers (Airborne Express and UPS) to pick up computers at its Austin plant, then pick up the accompanying monitors at the Sony plant in Mexico, match the customer's computer order with the customer's monitor order, and deliver both to the customer simultaneously. The savings in time, energy, and cost were significant.

The company had, over the years, refined and improved its inventory-tracking capabilities and its procedures for operating with small inventories. In 1993, Dell had $2.6 billion in sales and $342 million in inventory. In fiscal year 1998, it had $12.3 billion in sales and $233 million in inventory—an inventory turn ratio of seven days. By comparison, Gateway, which also pursued a build-to-order strategy, had 1997 sales of $6.3 billion and inventories of $249 million—an inventory turn ratio of 14 days. Compaq had inventories of $1.57 billion at year-end 1997, and 1997 sales of $24.6 billion (thus turning its inventories about every 23 days). Dell's goal was to get its inventory turn down to three days before the year 2000.

Direct Sales

Selling direct to customers gave Dell firsthand intelligence about customer preferences and needs, as well as immediate feedback on design problems and quality glitches. With thousands of phone and fax orders daily, $5 million in daily Internet sales, and daily contacts between the field sales force and customers of all types, the company kept its finger on the market pulse, quickly detecting shifts in sales trends and getting prompt feedback on any problems with its products. If the company got more than a few similar complaints, the information was relayed immediately to design engineers. When design flaws or components defects were found, the factory was notified and the problem corrected within a matter of days. Management believed Dell's ability to respond quickly gave it a significant advantage over rivals, particularly over PC makers in Asia, that made large production runs and sold standardized products through retail channels. Dell saw its direct sales approach as a totally customer-driven system that allowed quick transitions to new generations of components and PC models.

Despite Dell's emphasis on direct sales, industry analysts noted that the company sold 10–15 percent of its PCs through a small, select group of resellers.[11] Most of these resellers were systems integrators. It was standard for Dell not to allow returns on orders from resellers or to provide price protection in the event of subsequent declines in market prices. From time to time, Dell offered its resellers incentive promotions at up to a 20 percent discount from its advertised prices on end-of-life models. Dell was said to have no plans to expand its reseller network, which consisted of about 50–60 dealers.

---

[10]Ibid.

[11]"Dell Uses Channel to Move System Inventory," *Computer Reseller News,* January 12, 1998.

EXHIBIT 7   Rapid Expansion of Dell Computer's Target Customer Segments, 1995–1997

Target Customer Segments, 1995	Target Customer Segments, 1996	Target Customer Segments, 1997
• Large customers (both corporate and governmental buyers)	• Large companies • Midsize companies • Government agencies and educational institutions	• Global enterprise accounts • Large companies • Midsize companies • Federal agencies • State and local government agencies • Educational institutions
• Small customers (both small businesses and individuals)	• Small customers (both small businesses and individuals)	• Small companies • Individual consumers

Source: Joan Magretta, "The Power of Virtual Integration: An Interview with Dell Computer's Michael Dell," *Harvard Business Review*, March–April 1998, p. 78.

Market Segmentation

To make sure that each type of customer was well served, Dell had made a special effort to segment the buyers of its computers into relevant groups and to place managers in charge of developing sales and service programs appropriate to the needs and expectations of each market segment. Until the early 1990s, Dell had operated with sales and service programs aimed at just two market segments—(1) corporate and governmental buyers who purchased in large volumes and (2) small buyers (individuals and small businesses). But as sales took off in 1995–97, these segments were subdivided into finer, more homogeneous categories (see Exhibit 7).

In 1998, 90 percent of Dell's sales were to business or government institutions and of those 70 percent were to large corporate customers who bought at least $1 million in PCs annually. Many of these large customers typically ordered thousands of units at a time. Dell had hundreds of sales representatives calling on large corporate and institutional accounts. Its customer list included Shell Oil, Exxon, MCI, Ford Motor, Toyota, Eastman Chemical, Boeing, Goldman Sachs, Oracle, Microsoft, Woolwich (a British bank with $64 billion in assets), Michelin, Unilever, Deutsche Bank, Sony, Wal-Mart, and First Union (one of the 10 largest U.S. banks). However, no one customer represented more than 2 percent of total sales. Because corporate customers tended to buy the most expensive computers, Dell commanded the highest average selling prices in the industry—over $1,600 versus an industry average under $1,400.

Dell's sales to individuals and small businesses were made by telephone, fax, and the Internet. It had a call center in the United States with toll-free lines; customers could talk with a sales representative about specific models, get information faxed or mailed to them, place an order, and pay by credit card. Internationally, Dell had set up six call centers in Europe and Asia that customers could dial toll free.[12] The call centers were equipped with technology that routed calls from a particular country to a particular call center. Thus, for example, a customer calling from Lisbon, Portugal, was automatically directed to the call center in Montpelier, France, and connected to a Portuguese-speaking sales representative. Dell began Internet sales at its Web site (www.dell.com) in 1995, almost overnight achieving sales of $1 million per day. In 1997 Internet sales reached an average of $3 million daily, hitting $6 million some days during the Christmas shopping period. In the first quarter of 1997, Dell's Internet sales averaged nearly $4 million daily; and the company expected that 1998 sales at its Web site would reach $1.5 billion. The fastest growing segment of Dell's international segment was on the Internet in Europe, where sales were running at a weekly volume of $5 million in early 1998. Internet sales were ramping up rapidly from Asian buyers. In early 1998, Dell's Internet sales were about equally divided between sales to individuals and sales to business customers. Nearly 1.5 million people visited Dell's Web site weekly to view information and place orders, about 20 times more than called to talk with sales representatives over the telephone.

In 1997, 31 percent, or $3.8 billion, of Dell's sales came from foreign customers. Europe, where resellers were strongly entrenched and Dell's direct sales approach was novel, was Dell's biggest foreign market. Dell's European sales were growing at 50 percent annually. The market leader in Europe was Compaq, with a 14.8 percent market share, followed by IBM with 8.3 percent, Dell with 7.8 percent, Hewlett-Packard with 7.6 percent, and Siemens Nixdorf (Germany) with 5.6 percent. In Britain, which Dell had entered in the late 1980s, Dell had a 12 percent share, trailing only Compaq. Sales of PCs in Europe were expected to reach 22–24 million in 1998 and 28.5 million in 1999. Total European sales in 1997 were 19.7 million units.

Customer Service

Service became a feature of Dell's strategy in 1986 when the company began providing a guarantee of free on-site service for a year with most of its PCs after users complained about having to ship their PCs back to Austin for repairs. Dell contracted with local service providers to handle customer requests for repairs; on-site service was provided on a next-day basis. Dell also provided its customers with technical support via a toll-free number, fax, and e-mail. Dell received close to 40,000 e-mail messages monthly requesting service and support and had 25 technicians to process the requests. Bundled service policies were a major selling point for winning corporate accounts. If a customer preferred to work with his or her own service provider, Dell gave that provider the training and spare parts needed to service the customer's equipment.

Selling direct allowed Dell to keep close track of the purchases of its large global customers, country by country and department by department—information that customers found valuable. Maintaining its close customer relationships allowed Dell to become quite knowledgeable about its customers' needs and how their PC network functioned. Aside from using this information to help customers plan their PC needs and configure their PC networks, Dell used its knowledge to add to the value it delivered to its customers. For example, Dell recognized that when it delivered a new PC to a corporate customer, the customer's PC personnel had to place asset tags on it and then load the software from an assortment of CD-ROMs and diskettes—a process that could

---

[12]"Michael Dell Rocks," *Fortune,* May 11, 1998, p. 66.

take several hours and cost $200–$300.[13] Dell's solution was to load the customer's software onto one of its own very large Dell servers at the factory and, when a particular version of a customer's PC came off the assembly line, to use its high-speed server network to load that customer's software onto the PC's hard disk in a few seconds. If the customer so desired, Dell would place asset tags on the PC at the factory. Since Dell charged customers only an extra $15 or $20 for the software-loading and asset–tagging services, the savings to customers were considerable. One large customer reported savings of $500,000 annually from having Dell load its software and place asset tags on its PCs at the factory.[14] In 1997, about 2 million of the 7 million PCs Dell sold were shipped with customer-specific software already loaded on the PCs.

Corporate customers paid Dell fees to provide support and service. Dell then contracted with third-party providers to make the necessary service calls. When a customer with PC problems called Dell, the call triggered two electronic dispatches—one to ship the needed parts from Dell's factory to the customer sites and one to notify the contract service providers to prepare to make the needed repairs as soon as the parts arrived.[15] The service providers sent the bad parts back to Dell. Dell then endeavored to diagnose what went wrong and what could be done to see that the problem wouldn't happen again. Problems relating to faulty components or flawed components design were promptly passed along to the relevant supplier, who was expected to improve quality control procedures or redesign the component. Dell's strategy was to manage the flow of information gleaned from customer service activities both to improve product quality and speed execution.

Dell had plans in place to build Application Solutions Centers in both Europe and North America to assist its customers and independent software providers in migrating their systems and applications to Intel's new next-generation, 64-bit computing technology. Dell was partnering with Intel, Microsoft, Computer Associates, and other prominent PC technology providers to help customers make more effective use of the Internet and the latest computing technologies. Dell, which used Intel microprocessors exclusively in its computers, had been a consistent proponent of standardized Intel-based platforms because the company believed those platforms provided customers with the best total value and performance. Dell management considered both Intel and Microsoft as long-term strategic partners in mapping out its future.

In recent months Dell, following Compaq's lead, had created a capital services group to assist customers with financing their PC networks.

Virtual Integration and Information-Sharing

But what was unique about Dell's latest incarnation of its strategy was how the company was using technology and information-sharing with both supply partners and customers to blur the traditional arm's-length boundaries in the supplier–manufacturer–customer value chain that characterized Dell's earlier business model and other direct-sell competitors. Michael Dell referred to this feature of Dell's strategy as "virtual integration."[16] On-line communications technology made it easy for Dell to communicate inventory levels and replenishment needs to vendors daily or even hourly.

---

[13]Magretta, "The Power of Virtual Integration," p. 79.

[14]"Michael Dell Rocks," p. 61.

[15]Kevin Rollins, "Using Information to Speed Execution," *Harvard Business Review,* March–April, 1998, p. 81.

[16]Magretta, "The Power of Virtual Integration," p. 74.

Boeing offers an example of how the lines were becoming blurred between Dell and its customers. Boeing, which had 100,000 Dell PCs, was served by a staff of 30 Dell employees who resided on-site at Boeing facilities and were intimately involved in planning Boeing's PC needs and the configuration of Boeing's network. While Boeing had its own people working on what the company's best answers for using PCs were, Dell and Boeing personnel worked closely together to understand Boeing's needs in depth and to figure out the best ways to meet those needs.

A number of Dell's corporate accounts were large enough to justify dedicated on-site teams of Dell employees. Customers usually welcomed such teams, preferring to focus their time and energy on the core business rather than being distracted by PC purchasing and servicing issues.

In addition to using its sales and support mechanisms to stay close to customers, Dell had set up a number of regional forums to stimulate the flow of information back and forth with customers. The company formed Platinum Councils composed of its largest customers in the United States, Europe, Japan, and the Asia-Pacific region; regional meetings were held every six to nine months.[17] In the larger regions, there were two meetings—one for chief information officers and one for technical personnel. As many as 100 customers and 100 Dell executives and representatives, including Michael Dell himself, attended the three-day meetings, at which Dell's senior technologists shared their views on the direction of the latest technological developments, what the flow of technology really meant for customers, and Dell's plans for introducing new and upgraded products over the next two years. There were also breakout sessions on such topics as managing the transition to Windows NT, managing the use of notebooks by people out in the field, and determining whether leasing was better than buying. Customers were provided opportunities to share information and learn from one another (many had similar problems) as well as exchange ideas with Dell personnel. Dell found that the information gleaned from customers at these meetings assisted in forecasting demand for the company's products.

Dell had developed customized intranet sites (called Premier Pages) for its 3,000 largest global customers; These sites gave customer personnel immediate on-line access to purchasing and technical information about the specific configurations of products that their company had purchased from Dell or that were currently authorized for purchase.[18] The Premier Pages contained all of the elements of Dell's relationship with the customer—who the Dell sales and support contacts were in every country where the customer had operations, detailed product descriptions, what software Dell loaded on each of the various types of PCs the customer purchased, service and warranty records, pricing, and the available technical support.[19] Dell was readying Premier Page software improvements for introduction in the second half of 1998 with even greater functionality. One new feature made it easy for a customer to specify what types of machines and options their personnel should be authorized to purchase. Other features included allowing customer personnel to access detailed information about Dell products on-line, view all the different machines and options the customer had authorized for its personnel, obtain the price of the particular PC they wanted, place an

---

[17]Magretta, "The Power of Virtual Integration," p. 80.

[18]Ibid.

[19]"Dell Turns to Servers—Chairman and CEO Michael Dell Discusses the Vendor's Plans for High-End Servers and Online," *Information Week,* April 27, 1998.

order, and have the order automatically routed to higher-level managers for approval. These features eliminated paper invoices, cut ordering time, and reduced the internal labor needed to staff corporate purchasing functions. Dell was said to have the most comprehensive Web-based PC commerce capability of any PC vendor. The company's goal was to generate 50 percent of its sales on the Internet within the next two or three years by setting up Premier Pages for virtually all of its large customers and adding more features to further improve functionality. So far, customer use of Premier Pages had boosted the productivity of salespeople assigned to these accounts by 50 percent.

The company also gave its large customers access to Dell's own on-line internal technical support tools, allowing them to go to www.dell.com, enter some information about their system, and gain immediate access to the same database and problem-solving information that Dell's support personnel used to assist call-in customers.[20] This tool was particularly useful to the internal help-desk groups at large companies.

Demand Forecasting

Management believed that accurate sales forecasts were key to keeping costs down and minimizing inventories, given the complexity and diversity of the company's product line. Because Dell worked diligently to maintain a close relationship with its large corporate and institutional customers, and because it sold direct to small customers via telephone and the Internet, it was possible for the company to keep a finger on the pulse of demand—what was selling and what was not. Moreover, the company's market segmentation strategy paved the way for in-depth understanding of its customers' evolving requirements and expectations. Having credible real-time information about what customers were actually buying and having first hand knowledge of large customers' buying intentions gave Dell strong capability to forecast demand. Furthermore, Dell passed that knowledge on to suppliers so they could plan their production accordingly. The company worked hard at managing the flow of information it got from the marketplace and seeing that it got to both internal groups and vendors in timely fashion.

Forecasting was viewed as a critical sales skill. Sales-account managers were coached on how to lead large customers through a discussion of their future needs for PCs, workstations, servers, and peripheral equipment. Distinctions were made between purchases that were virtually certain and those that were contingent on some event. Salespeople made note of the contingent events so they could follow up at the appropriate time. With smaller customers, there was real-time information about sales, and direct telephone sales personnel often were able to steer customers toward configurations that were immediately available to help fine-tune the balance between demand and supply.

Research and Development

Company management believed that it was Dell's job to sort out all the new technology coming into the marketplace and help steer customers to options and solutions most relevant to their needs. The company talked to its customers frequently about "relevant technology," listening carefully to customers' needs and problems and endeavoring to identify the most cost-effective solutions. Dell had about 1,600 engineers working on product development and spent about $250 million annually to

---

[20]Interview with Michael Dell, *Internet Week,* April 13, 1998.

improve users' experience with its products—including incorporating the latest and best technologies, making its products easy to use, and devising ways to keep costs down. The company's R&D unit also studied and implemented ways to control quality and to streamline the assembly process. Much time went into tracking all the new developments in components and software to ascertain how they would prove useful to computer users. For instance, it was critical to track vendor progress in making longer-lasting batteries because battery life was important to the buyers of portable computers. Dell was the first company to put lithium ion batteries with a life of 5.5 to 6 hours in all of its laptop models.

Advertising

Michael Dell was a strong believer in the power of advertising and frequently espoused its importance in the company's strategy. Thus, Dell was the first computer company to use comparative ads, throwing barbs at Compaq's higher prices. Although Compaq won a lawsuit against Dell for making false comparisons, Michael Dell was unapologetic, arguing that "[the ads were] very effective. We were able to increase customer awareness about value."[21] Dell insisted that the company's ads be communicative and forceful, not soft and fuzzy.

The company regularly had prominent ads in such leading computer publications as *PC Magazine* and *PC World,* as well as in *USA Today, The Wall Street Journal,* and other business publications. In the spring of 1998, the company debuted a multi-year worldwide TV campaign to strengthen its brand image.

Entry into Servers

Dell entered the market for low-end PC servers (those priced under $25,000) in the second half of 1996. The company had opened a 23,000-square-foot plant dedicated to server production, trained 1,300 telemarketers to sell servers, assigned 160 sales reps with systems know-how to big customer accounts, and recruited a staff of systems experts to help the sales reps. It had contracted with companies such as Electronic Data Systems, which had in-depth systems and networking expertise, to help provide service to large customers with extensive server networks. Dell's server plant used "cell" manufacturing instead of an assembly line to permit faster product updates and keep costs low; there were 30 cells at the plant, each with a self-contained work team that performed the entire assembly process from a kit of components and a customized motherboard.

Dell's entry into servers had several purposes. The use of servers by corporate customers was growing rapidly. The margins on servers were large. Moreover, purchase price was not as significant a factor in selecting which brand of server to buy because servers required far more in the way of service, support, and software. Several of Dell's rivals, most notably Compaq, were using their big margins on server sales to subsidize price cuts on desktops and notebooks in an attempt to win corporate PC accounts away from Dell. According to Michael Dell, "To neutralize that, Dell needs to be in the server market." The company expected that sales of servers would grow to about 50 percent of corporate revenues by 2001.

Dell's build-to-order and sell-direct strategies gave it a significant pricing advantage over rivals. Servers from such competitors as Compaq, IBM, and Hewlett-Packard, all

---

[21]"The Education of Michael Dell," p. 85.

of which relied on networks of resellers, were estimated to cost 15 to 20 percent more than Dell servers. However, analysts were skeptical about whether Dell could provide the same quality of service and support to server customers that resellers could. To counter that perception, Dell had bolstered its field sales and support staff to 600 employees and created an in-house consulting group to assist customers. For customers that required extensive system support and integration, Dell partnered with systems experts that were not resellers, such as Electronic Data Systems and Arthur Andersen.

RECENT DEVELOPMENTS IN THE PC INDUSTRY

There were an estimated 250 million PCs in use in 1997, and sales of PCs were approaching 100 million annually (see Exhibit 8). Michael Dell believed there would be 1.4 billion PCs in use within 10 years. Going into 1998, household penetration of PCs was estimated to be 45 percent. There were over 5 million new PC-owning households in 1997, many lured by the introduction of reasonably equipped sub-$1,000 PCs. The three most influential factors in home ownership of PCs were education, income, and the presence of children in the household. Household penetration was expected to exceed 50 percent by the year 2000.

A number of factors were affecting the competitive structure of the world market for PCs in 1998: declining component prices, the troubled economies of several Asian countries, potential slowdowns in the industry growth rate, the attempts of Dell's rivals to shift to build-to-order manufacturing, continuing advances in PC technology, and the moves of several PC makers to expand into marketing more than just PCs to their customers.

Declining Component Prices

Sharp drops in the prices of a number of PC components (chiefly, disk drives, memory chips, and microprocessors) starting in late 1997 had allowed PC makers to dramatically lower PC prices—sales of PCs priced under $1,500 were booming by early 1998. Compaq, IBM, Hewlett-Packard, and several other PC makers had begun marketing sub-$1,000 PCs in 1997. In December 1997, the average purchase price of a desktop computer fell below $1,300 for the first time. It was estimated that about half of all PC sales in 1998 were of computers carrying price tags under $1,500. Growth in unit volume was being driven largely by sub-$1,000 PCs. The low prices were attracting

EXHIBIT 8	Actual and Projected Worldwide Shipments of PCs

Year	PC Volume
1980	1 million
1985	11 million
1990	24 million
1995	58 million
1996	69 million
1997	80 million
2000	118 million (projected)

Source: International Data Corporation.

first-time buyers into the market and were also causing second- and third-time PC buyers looking to upgrade to more powerful PCs to forgo top-of-the-line machines priced in the traditional $2,000–$3,500 range in favor of lower-priced PCs that were almost as powerful and well-equipped. Powerful, multifeatured notebook computers that had formerly sold for $4,000 to $6,500 in November 1997 were selling for $2,000 to $4,500 in April 1998. The profits of many PC makers slipped in early 1998 because of the need to discount unsold higher-priced machines still in inventory and on retailers' shelves.

Economic Problems in Asia

Economic woes in a number of Asian countries (most notably, Japan, South Korea, Thailand, and Indonesia) were putting a big damper on PC sales in Asia. Asian sales of PCs in 1998 were expected to grow minimally, if at all, and some analysts expected unit volume to fall below 1997 levels. Sharp appreciation of the U.S. dollar against Asian currencies had made U.S.-produced PCs more expensive to Asian buyers. In contrast, sales in the United States and Europe were quite robust, mainly because of lower PC prices.

Disk-drive manufacturers and the makers of printed circuit boards, many of which were in Asia, were feeling the pressures of declining prices and skimpy profit margins. Industry observers were predicting that competitive conditions in the Asian-Pacific PC market favored growing market shares by the top four or five players and the likely exit of PC makers that could not compete profitably.

Slowing Industry Growth

Most industry observers were warning of a global slowdown in the sales of PCs in 1998, partly due to the economic difficulties in several Asian countries and partly due to the potential for market maturity for PCs. Industry growth rates were projected to be close to 15 percent annually for the remainder of the decade, down from the average annual growth rate of 20 percent during the 1990–96 period. However, U.S. shipments of PCs in 1997 had risen 21 percent, to 31 million units, a much higher rate than most industry analysts had expected. Sales of servers were the fastest growing segment of the PC industry; in 1997 revenues jumped 35 percent, to $10.5 billion, on shipments of 1.7 million units.

Attempts to Clone Dell's PC Strategy

Dell's competitors—Compaq, IBM, Packard Bell NEC, and Hewlett-Packard—were shifting their business models to build-to-order manufacturing to reduce their inventories and speed new models to market. Compaq launched its build-to-order initiative in July 1997 and hoped to cut costs by 10 to 12 percent. Compaq's revamped assembly plants could turn out a custom-built PC in three to four hours and could load the desired software in six minutes. Packard Bell NEC's program allowed customers to place orders by phone. But all three were finding that it was hard to duplicate Dell's approach because of how long it took to develop just-in-time delivery schedules with suppliers, to coordinate their mutual production schedules, and to shift smoothly to next-generation parts and components as they appeared on the market. Extensive collaboration was needed to plan smooth technology transitions. Compaq and Hewlett-Packard had spent 18 months planning their build-to-order strategies and expected it would take another 18 or more months to achieve their inventory and cost-reduction goals.

At the same time, such computer retailers as Tandy Corporation's Computer City, CompUSA, OfficeMax, and Wal-Mart had gotten into the build-to-order and sell-direct business. CompUSA was offering customers two lines of desktop computers that could be ordered at any of its 134 stores, by phone, at its Web site, or through its corporate sales force; its goal was to undercut Dell's price by $200 on each configuration. Wal-Mart was offering build-to-order PCs made by a contract manufacturer at its Web site.

Dell was seen as having the right strategy to appeal to customers well versed in PC technology who knew what options and features they wanted and who were aware of the price differentials among brands. According to one industry analyst, "Dell is everybody's target. No matter who you talk to in the industry, Dell is the brand to beat."[22]

The Moves of PC Makers to Broaden Their Business

Several leading players in the PC industry made moves in late 1997 and early 1998 to expand into selling more than just PCs in an effort to improve profitability. The sharp declines in the prices of PCs had crimped gross profit margins and prompted such companies as Compaq, Gateway, Hewlett-Packard, and IBM to view selling PCs as an entrée to providing a bigger lineup of products.

To move beyond simple PC manufacturing, Compaq in late 1997 acquired Digital Equipment Company (DEC), which derived $6 billion in revenues from providing a range of PC services to corporate customers. Gateway announced in May 1998 that it would start bundling into the sale of its PCs to individuals and households a wide range of software, peripheral devices like printers and scanners, maintenance and troubleshooting services, and even its own Internet service. Gateway's CEO Ted Waitt explained, "We're about customer relations a lot more than we are about PCs. If we get a 5 percent margin on a $1,500 PC, we make $75. But if we can make $3 a month on Internet access, that's another $100 over three years. Three years from now, I don't think just selling PC hardware will allow anyone to have a great business."[23] Gateway had begun asking customers ordering a PC to identify their major interests and hobbies; if a customer identified gardening or sports or investing, Gateway offered to include related software packages with the PC. Gateway had also announced a plan to lease PCs to individuals and households and to finance PCs on low monthly payment plans in hopes of getting the customer to trade in the old PC for a new PC later when the lease expired or the last payment was made. Both Hewlett-Packard and IBM had always viewed the PC business as part of a larger portfolio of products and services they offered customers. A substantial portion of Hewlett-Packard's revenues and profits came from sales of servers and printers. IBM derived a big portion of its revenues from mainframe computers, software, and technical and support services.

PROFILES OF SELECTED COMPETITORS IN THE PC INDUSTRY

Dell's principal competitors in the global PC market had varying strategies and resource capabilities.

---

[22]As quoted in *Business Week,* September 29, 1997, p. 38.
[23]David Kirkpatrick, "Old PC Dogs Try New Tricks," *Fortune,* July 6, 1998, pp. 186–88.

Compaq Computer (www.compaq.com)

Compaq was the world's leading PC manufacturer, with a global market share of approximately 13 percent. It had overtaken IBM to become the market leader in PCs in 1994. Compaq had revenues of $24.6 billion and profits of $1.9 billion in 1997. Compaq's strategy was to sell almost exclusively through resellers—distributors and PC retailers, particularly large computer stores like CompUSA. It was starting to build computers to order and operate its factories with smaller inventories of parts and components, but it had to soft-pedal direct sales so as not to alienate its worldwide reseller network. Because Compaq had bigger components inventories than Dell and because its resellers sometimes had sizable inventories of Compaq's models on hand, Compaq was slower than Dell in getting new generations of its PCs into the marketplace.

Compaq offered a full line of desktop PCs, from sub-$1,000 PCs to top-of-the-line models. It was the most aggressive seller of PCs priced under $1,000 and in recent months had averaged over a 60 percent share of the sub-$1,000 segment. It also offered a broad line of laptop PCs, but its 9 percent share of the laptop segment put it in third place behind Toshiba, the global market leader in laptop PCs (with a 20 percent share), and IBM (with an 11 percent share). Compaq shipped a total of 10 million desktop and laptop PCs worldwide in 1997, up from 7.2 million in 1996. Compaq was also the market leader in PC servers priced under $25,000 and was a strong third (behind IBM and Hewlett-Packard) in low-end or entry servers (those priced under $100,000). Compaq executives expected that sales of PCs to individuals and households would continue to account for about 15 percent of revenues, sales of desktop PCs to corporate customers would fall from 48 percent of revenues in 1997 to about 32 percent in 2000, and sales of servers and workstations would grow to 50 percent of revenues from 35 percent in 1997. Compaq's goal was to have $50 billion in revenues in 2000.

Compaq's market strength was greatest among Fortune 1000 companies; it had weaker penetration in the small and medium business segments. To combat the volume discounts that Dell and other direct vendors typically used to help win the accounts of small and medium businesses, Compaq had recently begun working more closely with its resellers on special pricing to make the Compaq brand more competitive in the bidding process. To boost its subpar 3 percent share of the Japanese market for PCs, Compaq had recently signed a deal that gave Canon Sales Company exclusive distribution and sales rights to Compaq's consumer-oriented Presario models.

In early 1998, Compaq acquired floundering Digital Equipment Company (DEC) for $9.6 billion, a move intended to turn Compaq into more of a full-spectrum global supplier of computer hardware and services and put it into better position to challenge IBM as a "global enterprise computing company." DEC had 1997 revenues of $13 billion (versus $14.5 billion in 1996) and net earnings of $141 million (versus a loss of $112 million in 1996). The merged companies would have combined revenues of $37.6 billion, making Compaq the second largest computer company in the world.

DEC considered itself to be a "network solutions company" with strengths in multi-vendor integration, Internet security, continuous computing, high-availability data, and high-performance networked platforms. Its chief products were large servers (those priced over $1 million), entry servers (those priced under $100,000), large computers and workstations, and personal computers (55 percent of revenues). Services accounted for 45 percent of revenues (about $6 billion); DEC had 25,000 engineers and support people in the field working with customers (Compaq had 8,000 sales and support people in the field, many of whom spent much of their time servicing retailers of Compaq PCs). DEC's gross margins on services averaged 34 percent, compared to Compaq's 25 percent margins on PC sales. Compaq's corporate customers had been requesting the company to provide more service for years.

In May 1998, Compaq announced plans to cut about 15,000 jobs at DEC when the acquisition was completed; the layoffs were expected to come mainly in DEC's personal computer division, portions of its sales force, and corporate computer operations—where there were significant overlaps with Compaq's business. DEC had a total of 53,500 employees, down from a peak of 130,000 in the 1980s. Despite recent workforce downsizings, DEC still employed about 65 percent more people than Compaq to produce about half the volume of sales revenues. DEC management indicated that the company's selling, general, and administrative costs of $3.18 billion in 1997 (24 percent of total 1997 revenues) would likely be cut in half following the merger. Compaq had selling, general, and administrative expenses of $2.95 billion on sales of $24.6 billion in 1997 (equal to 12 percent of revenues).

Compaq believed that DEC's expertise in networking and information systems integration, coupled with the combined product lines, would give it an advantage with large corporate customers over companies like Dell that offered mainly PC-related services. Compaq also believed that DEC's worldwide service and support capabilities would help it win corporate business for PCs, workstations, and servers away from IBM. (Prior to the Compaq–DEC merger, Dell had contracted with DEC's service organization to maintain its PowerEdge line of servers at a number of corporate accounts; Dell was expected to sign Unisys or Wang to replace DEC.)

IBM (www.ibm.com)

IBM was considered to be a "computer solutions" company and operated in more segments of the overall computer industry than Dell. PC sales accounted for $15.7 billion of IBM's 1997 revenues of $68 billion. IBM had 1997 sales of $1.3 billion in workstations; $4.3 billion in entry servers (those priced under $100,000), where it was the market leader; and $6.0 billion in midrange servers (those priced between $100,000 and $1 million), where it was also the market leader. The company had for many years been the global leader in mainframe computers, and it derived $19.3 billion in revenues from providing technical service and support to customers—the company had 160,000 technical support personnel in the field to service customers. In 1997 IBM introduced a long-awaited generation of mainframe computers based on PC-type microprocessors that offered the speed of traditional mainframes at lower purchase and operating costs.

During the 1990s IBM had experienced 2 percent annual revenue growth—revenues rose from $69.7 billion in 1990 to $78.5 billion in 1997. Net income of $6.1 billion in 1997 was barely above the 1990 level of $6.0 billion and well below the company's record earnings of $6.6 billion in 1984. The company was struggling to reinvent itself as the growing use of PCs continued to erode corporate dependence on mainframe computers. IBM's sales of computer hardware were flat; its fastest growing businesses were in services and software. To boost its growth potential and add attractive new products to its lineup, the company had purchased spreadsheet software pioneer Lotus Development in 1995 for $3.5 billion and Edmark, a publisher of educational software for children, in 1997. Also in 1997, IBM sold its ownership interest in Prodigy (an on-line service provider that had once enjoyed a dominant position against rival America Online) for $250 million after investing $1.2 billion.

IBM's market share in PCs was eroding—it had lost more market share in the 1990s than any other PC maker. Its main strengths in PCs were in laptop computers and in desktop sales to corporate customers, many of which also had IBM mainframe computers and had been longtime IBM customers. IBM was regarded as a high-cost producer of PCs and, traditionally, had commanded a premium price for its PCs. IBM saw notebook computers as the key to winning corporate accounts due to the need of many corporate personnel for mobile computing capability. The company's laptop PCs, while highly rated for their performance features and quality, were typically higher priced than comparably equipped models of rival sellers. IBM competed against PC rivals by emphasizing confidence in the IBM brand and the company's long-standing strengths in software applications, service, and technical support. IBM had responded to the direct-sales inroads Dell had made in the corporate market by allowing some of its resellers to custom-assemble IBM PCs to buyer specifications; it was hoping this effort would cut costs up to 10 percent. IBM's PC division was believed to be operating at breakeven or a slight loss in the first quarter of 1998.

Hewlett-Packard (www.hp.com)

Dell regarded Hewlett-Packard (H-P) as a strong competitor because of H-P's global leadership in printers (a 52 percent market share), strong reputation with corporate customers in most all parts of the world, and growing strategic emphasis on the PC segment. Since 1995 H-P's share of the PC market had been rising almost as quickly as Dell's. H-P was co-designing the next-generation microprocessor with Intel—code-named the Merced and scheduled for introduction in late 1999 and full-market rollout in 2000. H-P's partnership with Intel on the Merced was expected to put H-P on the cutting edge of PC technology for the next several years and boost its brand image in PCs.

H-P marketed its PC line through resellers that had the capability to deliver orders to major corporate accounts within 12 to 24 hours. Despite rapidly growing sales, H-P's PC division had not yet achieved profitability; the division recorded a small loss in the first quarter of 1998.

H-P was the market leader in revenue, units, and growth in the Windows NT–based workstation market. Compaq was a close second. H-P marketed over 25,000 products that included desktop and notebook PCs, printers, workstations, servers, digital cameras, scanners, calculators, storage devices, networking software and equipment, test and measurement equipment, and medical electronics products.

Gateway (www.gateway.com)

Gateway, formerly called Gateway 2000, was a South Dakota–based company with 1997 revenues of $6.3 billion and profits of $110 million. Founder and chairman Ted Waitt, 34, who wore his hair in a ponytail, owned 46 percent of the company; his brother owned 9 percent. Waitt had dropped out of college in 1985 to go to work for a computer retailer in Des Moines, Iowa; after nine months, he quit to form his own company. The company, operating out of a barn on his father's cattle ranch, sold add-on parts by phone for Texas Instruments PCs. In 1987, the company, using its own PC design, started selling fully-equipped PCs at a price near that of other PC makers. Sales took off and in 1991 Gateway topped *Inc.* magazine's list of the nation's fastest growing private companies. The company went public in 1993, achieving sales of $1.7 billion and earnings of $151 million. The company had differentiated itself from rivals with eye-catching ads; some featured white-and-black-spotted cows while others featured company employees (including one with Waitt dressed as Robin Hood).

Despite growing at a rate of nearly 38 percent annually since 1993, Gateway was struggling to achieve acceptable profitability—the company's profit margin had eroded steadily from a high of 9.6 percent in 1992 to only 1.7 percent in 1997. Gateway, like Dell, built to order and sold direct. But its market strengths were concentrated in the individual, small-business, and school segments, where it outsold Dell. It was the market leader in the education segment. At the beginning of 1997 Gateway's consumer line of desktop PCs was priced on average 12 percent below comparable Dell consumer models; by December 1997, Dell had an average price advantage of 5 percent over Gateway in the consumer segment. One of Gateway's strategies to boost profit margins was to strengthen its appeal to medium-sized and large corporations. The company had recently hired 80 salespeople to court new corporate customers and was strengthening its efforts to sell to corporate customers through dealers as well.

Gateway had entered the server segment in 1997 by purchasing Advanced Logic Research, Inc. (ALR). ALR's server manufacturing facility in California began making servers for Gateway for direct sale to Gateway customers. However, in 1998 ALR was continuing to make ALR servers for sale through its network of resellers.

Toshiba

Toshiba was a $48-billion Japanese electronics and electrical equipment manufacturer with 303 subsidiaries and affiliates worldwide; it ranked as the world's 37th largest corporation in terms of revenues. Its Toshiba America Information Systems division was the leading vendor in the U.S. market for portable computers, with a 20.4 percent share in 1997. The division offered the widest array of portable PCs of any manufacturer, selling both direct and through dealers and having a commanding lead over rivals in both channels. In addition to Toshiba portable PCs in all price ranges, the division also marketed desktop PCs, disk drives, plain-paper copiers, facsimile systems, voice-mail systems, digital key telephones, optical-fiber modems, and digital cameras under the Toshiba brand name. Headquartered in Irvine, California, it had $4 billion in annual sales.

Providers of House-Label Brands

There were about 35,000 resellers of generic, or "white-box," PCs in North America alone. This house-label segment constituted a $7.6-billion market in the United States and Canada, representing shipments of 6.4 million units and 30 percent of sales through resellers. No single no-name brand, however, accounted for more than 0.25 percent market share, and most accounted for far less. Generic PCs assembled in "screwdriver shops" had been a part of the PC business since its inception—Steve Wozniak and Steve Jobs launched Apple from a garage using purchased components. Rising technological savvy about how PCs worked and the widespread availability of individual components made it fairly easy for an enterprising operation to assemble a generic PC. To keep costs and prices low, the makers of generic PCs typically incorporated components from low-end suppliers and their products did not match name-brand PCs in performance and dependability. White-box PCs appealed mainly to very price-conscious buyers; most businesses that had tried generic brands had learned the hard way that the cheapest PC was not always the least expensive in the long run due to problems with quality and reliability.

Roughly two-thirds of the resellers who built their own systems for sale under their own brand also carried name brands. In 1998 resellers expected the sales of generic PCs to rise to about 35 percent of their total PC sales.

ACER IN CANADA

Prescott C. Ensign, *The University of Western Ontario*

In late summer 1996, Anthony Lin, general manager of Acer America's Canadian operation, believed that if the right approach and line of products were introduced and the right market segments focused on, the firm could have a prosperous future. Lin, after having been in Mississauga, Ontario, only a few weeks, knew that he had just two more days before he flew to Acer America headquarters in San Jose, California, to deliver his proposal for the future of the Canadian operation. He had to decide whether the Canadian market was worth pursuing and, if so, in what manner. He was contemplating the various markets to target and the channels by which the firm could reach these markets. Although he had determined that assembly in Canada was a real possibility, such a move would require solid justification.

ANTHONY LIN

Since joining the Acer group—a multinational enterprise in the global personal computer (PC) industry—in 1982, Lin had held a variety of positions. Most recently, he had been in Copenhagen, Denmark, as the managing director of Acer Scandinavia A/S, and as the general manager of Acer North Europe. Lin had turned around the firm to a profitable position with significant sales revenue growth in the Scandinavian countries. From an internal report, Acer Scandinavia had 80 percent growth in sales revenue in 1995. Further, according to Dataquest, Acer moved from the eighth to the fifth position among PC vendor market share in Denmark during early 1996. Lin had also spent two years at Acer America's headquarters, where he had become well acquainted with the executives as well as the firm's logistics and operations. For example, he knew that the flow of materials handled in California would not place the highest priority on processing smaller orders such as those "drop shipments" coming from Canada. Lin knew

Prepared under the supervision of Professor Jaideep Anand. The authors may have disguised certain names and other identifying information to protect confidentiality.

that Acer would permit him to seize opportunities, but he also realized that the firm wouldn't pour money into Canada without justification.

Though Lin had been in Canada only a few weeks, he was looking forward to the task ahead. He had been charged with the responsibility of overseeing all the sales and marketing activities across Canada, as well as customer service and support. If all went well, he would be in Canada for three to five years, at which point the local people he had helped would be entrusted with the business. Although he was fully charged with generating and executing a strategic plan for the Canadian organization, his role was one of assistance. Lin was to ensure that the Acer operation in Canada developed within the local PC industry network. He knew that there were incentives for the entire Acer workforce in Canada and he was excited about an additional employee who would be joining his team of 10. A goal had been set—double revenue by the end of 1996 and, within two years, to be in the top 10 in terms of Canadian PC market share.

Anthony Lin recognized that real and substantial differences existed between Canada and the United States. For example, Acer America did not worry about AST because it was not considered to be a serious competitor in the United States, whereas AST had developed a strong reputation and market position in Canada and was a significant player in the Canadian PC industry. Lin knew that even though government sales appeared to be marginal, in reality, government was a major buyer which purchased through a variety of channels. He was certain that Canadian assembly would improve Acer's profile and might even be necessary to satisfy government and Quebec orders. He also recognized that the "clones" were very strong in Canada. In general, mail order was a viable means of distribution in the United States (e.g., Dell and Gateway focused efforts on this channel), whereas Canadians were more reluctant to make purchases through the mail. Such differences needed to be articulated and considered in whatever action was undertaken.

Lin knew that assembly to order offered a variety of benefits: it would shorten delivery time, materials requirement planning (MRP) would be much smoother, and lower transport costs would make the operation more competitive. The ability to control inventory was high on his list of reasons for Canadian assembly. Local production would also assist in configuration of bilingual PCs, would shorten the reaction time to the ever changing market, and would take into consideration the corporate image of assembly in Canada. However, Lin knew that there were costs and other disadvantages involved with Canadian production.

STAN SHIH AND THE HISTORY OF ACER

Acer was founded in Taiwan in 1976 as Multitech International by Stan Shih, his wife (who still played a major role at Acer), and a handful of friends. Multitech International began with registered capital of U.S. $25,000 and 11 employees. Shih, reflecting on his impetus to start a business said, "Traditional Chinese family companies often mix up company money and family money. Little information is shared with employees. I knew there had to be a better way of running a business." Prior to the 1976 venture, Shih had learned a few difficult lessons while working for others. He had directed the development of Taiwan's first pen-watch and had managed Taiwan's largest manufacturer of calculators.

Multitech International prospered in the late 1970s and early 1980s, and continued to innovate and increase its level of PC technology. During the firm's first 10 years, average sales grew by 100 percentage points per year. The period from 1981 to 1988 was a transition from a domestic to an international firm. Until 1989, Multitech International's

EXHIBIT 1	Acer Corporate Revenue and Net Income (In millions of U.S. dollars)											
	1984	1985	1986	1987	1988	1989	1990	1991	1992	1993	1994	1995
Revenue	$55	$100	$180	$330	$ 530	$680	$970	$1,000	$1,200	$1,900	$3,200	$5,800
Net income	$ 1	$ 5	$4.5	$ 16	$26.5	$ 5.8	$ 2.4	($ 22.7)	$ 2.4	$ 80	$ 205	$ 310

Source: Acer documents.

products were manufactured only in Taiwan. Shih encouraged a corporate culture based on his belief that "human nature is basically good" and that people must be dealt with honestly. Reportedly, Shih's patience with managers included the allowance for mistakes to be written off as a "tuition payment" for educational development.

Shih and his creative engineers continuously strove to develop original products, breaking out of the typically Taiwanese "pattern of copycat manufacturers." Multitech International sought to free itself of the mold where unrecognized production of components and entire computers were produced, only to have the moniker of a famous brand placed on the finished good. In 1982 Multitech International launched a Chinese home computer. (China was expected to become the world's largest PC market by the turn of the century.) In 1983 it introduced its first IBM compatible computer, and in 1986 unveiled a PC based on the Intel 386 microprocessor before IBM did. With revenues of U.S. $530 million in 1988, the business was renamed Acer (Latin for active, sharp, clever, and incisive). Shih took the firm public in 1989, offering shares on the Taiwanese stock exchange. By 1990 Acer was the 13th largest PC maker in the world, with revenues of U.S. $1 billion. The following year, due to a slowdown in the economy and overcapacity, Acer recorded its first loss (U.S. $22.7 million after taxes) and cut 400 jobs in Taiwan. Despite the ensuing upheaval, ISO 9000 certification was obtained in 1992. The following year Acer recorded sales of U.S. $1.7 billion, and by 1994 was the world's seventh-largest PC brand.

In late 1995 Acer reported that it expected to produce 4 million PCs that year, twice the previous year's figure. As well, it anticipated a 60 percent leap in revenues for 1995 to U.S. $5 billion, which would be accompanied by a 50 percent jump in earnings. Actual 1995 revenues for Acer exceeded that estimate, reaching U.S. $5.8 billion by year-end. Such growth, occurring with only a few acquisitions, was considered remarkable by most observers.

By 1996 Acer had become the seventh largest PC manufacturer worldwide, the second largest monitor maker, and the fourth largest keyboard maker. The firm operated 80 offices in 38 countries, had more than 15,000 employees, and supported dealers in over 100 countries. Exhibit 1 provides an overview of Acer's revenue and net income.

ACER ORGANIZATIONAL CHARACTERISTICS

2000 in 2000. In 1994, Acer "Vision 2000" was to have over $2,000 *yi* NT (U.S. $8 billion) in annual revenue by the year 2000. When 1995 revenue reached U.S. $7 billion, Vision 2000 was revised upward to U.S. $10 billion a year in revenue by the turn of the century.

21 in 21. Acer proclaimed that it would have 21 publicly-owned businesses worldwide by the 21st century and be among the top five in the information technology industry by the turn of the century. Lin knew that two more Acer units had gone public in the past two weeks and that two more were scheduled to go public shortly.

Operating Strategy

To remain competitive and take advantage of efficiencies in manufacturing and engineering, as well as make swift marketing decisions locally, Acer decentralized control. In 1990 it reorganized into a "federation of companies" with world headquarters in Taipei, strategic business units organized along product lines, and five regional business units organized along geographic lines (see Appendix A). Each of these units operated as a profit center, and managed itself as if it were a self-owned corporation. Shih indicated that "technology markets change too fast and Acer has too broad a product line to afford the luxury of centralized control." In 1992 Acer made the decision to reengineer "in the face of strong competition" to "reach economies of scale in low-cost manufacturing." Two reengineering programs were introduced: fast food and client server.

Fast Food   This business model was similar to that used by fast-food restaurants. "Components" were prepared in large, centralized mass-manufacturing facilities and then shipped to assembly sites close to local customers. This process made it possible to enjoy production economies of scale and tailor each product to suit the needs of the individual customer. This was reflected in a new corporate mission statement, "fresh technology enjoyed by everyone, everywhere," and also by standardized quality, customized products, and lower inventory costs. Inventory turnover of more than 12 times per year assisted in a return on equity of 70 to 126 percentage points above industry average. At Acer, fresh meant the "best"—proven, high-value, low-risk technology which was affordable and had a long useful life span. The "fresh" concept was not applied only to technology. Shih claimed, "Fresh ideas are very powerful when applied to business strategy. Keeping the company fresh is the only way to compete successfully in this rapidly changing industry."

Client Server   Borrowing from the terminology of computer networks, the client server management model let each business unit act independently but also coordinated each unit's efforts to gain maximum benefit from use of Acer's international resources. At the heart of Acer's client server organization was a closely linked network of mature and experienced managers who committed to the success of their own part of the Acer group as well as to Acer's overall long-term growth.

Lin knew that distributive manufacturing played an important role in global operations. Acer considered itself to be one of the most vertically integrated microcomputer manufacturers in the world, with product assembly separated into three stages:

1. Components whose prices did not fluctuate (housing, power supply, fans, and keyboard) were shipped in bulk via boat.
2. Components that were price or technology sensitive, such as motherboards, were shipped via aircraft.
3. Components such as microprocessors, hard-disk drives, and memory were sourced locally on a just-in-time basis to meet individual tastes.

In response to market turbulence, components with very unstable prices such as DRAMs and CPUs were purchased and installed at the last moment, ideally a few days before delivery to the market.

Final assembly at more than 30 sites around the world was made easy by a modular design in which assembly of various parts took only a few minutes. The housing for both desktops and laptops allowed for various physical configurations. With the interchangeability of subassemblies (components), a number of arrangements were possible. Acer's production operation allowed regional units to receive volume discounts on purchases under the Acer umbrella yet produce the exact quantity and models based on local market demand.

GLOBAL BRAND—LOCAL TOUCH

As part of Shih's plan to avoid Acer's being perceived as a Taiwanese firm, the business units cooperated but were free to buy from sources outside the organization network. In fact, a business unit was able to establish its own business partners—through spinoffs, joint ventures, or some other type of relationship-building strategy. These independent business units were to be owned by local investors and managed by the local workforce. Because he believed in decentralization of control and ownership, Shih hoped that the local distributors, who were permitted to buy shares, would be motivated to promote Acer products. It was Shih's intent to have the majority of ownership held in the local country. In his view, this would prevent claims that Acer was a Taiwanese firm. He believed that corporate control was not gained through ownership but by intangible means—a common interest in brand name and technology.

Freedom at Acer Hong Kong

Acer's operation in Hong Kong serves as a point of reference. In 1986 Michael Mak was a partner in Altos Far East Ltd. In 1990 Acer bought Altos America and gained control of Altos Far East Ltd. As of 1996, Acer Far East Ltd. was under the auspices of Acer Computer International Ltd. (headquartered in Singapore and responsible for Asia, the Middle East, Africa, and Pacifica). Mak was entrepreneurial by nature, and his personality was congruent with the freedom Acer corporate allowed.

Although he did not receive any financial assistance from the Acer group (his operation was self-financing), Mak believed he was given credit for what he had built up in Hong Kong. Top management at Acer was open-minded and trusted him personally; he had the autonomy to run the business as if it were his own.

Developing relationships with the value-added resellers (distributors who supplied the network of PC dealers) was considered challenging. Mak characterized the channel development process as "Talk, talk, and more talk—you must keep communicating." There was an existing independent distributor for Acer in Hong Kong prior to the Acer purchase of Altos Far East Ltd., but Mak continued building more channels. Because the distributors were not dedicated to a single firm, staying in a favorable position with them was important.

In 1995 the Hong Kong channel structure changed in response to new market conditions. Acer Hong Kong moved from supplying the conventional network exclusively and added mass merchandising and department stores as avenues for sales. These channels relied directly on the vendor for support; the customer could not get help from the point of purchase but had to rely on the manufacturer. Acer Hong Kong was well situated to provide such support to the end user. Building on abilities and resources, Mak's group was able to provide help lines necessary for customer support.

Distribution was vital in the Hong Kong business environment. Acer Hong Kong utilized approximately 30 reseller channels. Mak described the situation as follows:

> The channels are not exclusive—they're biased and so are we. We favor those that are devoted, and consequently work more closely with those with whom we have good relationships. The channel is very important—in terms of an ongoing relationship; for things to work it must be win–win. With any change we make, we must not take advantage of the channels.

Local Touch

There were competitors based in Hong Kong that only competed locally. It was estimated that 30 to 40 percent of the overall market was satisfied by generic products. Mak viewed the progress from a starting point of zero in 1991 and subsequent "stealing of market share" as an accomplishment. Working with different types of channels, as the operation grew in scope and scale, and meeting the necessity of support from the vendor required much attention to detail. Channel structure had changed and brand perception was important; this required great local knowledge of the home environment. Mak's assessment was that

> We have to know their lifestyle, we have become part of their daily life. Because the kitchen is so close to the customer, we can react effectively—we can react dynamically. If you have the right person in the right place, that's more important. If the person isn't right, flexibility is lost; that person shouldn't be on the job. Only through know-how and know-who can you make use of ideas from other places.

Opportunities for Learning

The various Acer subsidiaries (Singapore, Indonesia, Malaysia, Hong Kong, etc.) were all linked electronically. Contact was reported on a day-to-day basis and best practices were often exchanged between subsidiaries. The heads of the various geographic operations met every three to four months. Mak indicated that it was the small things that were taken away, many things that could not be easily articulated or even identified. For example, he had personally borrowed from a Mexican video commercial—adopting some of it and adapting some of it.

THE GLOBAL INFORMATION TECHNOLOGY INDUSTRY ———————

A general consensus existed that dramatic changes were occurring in the global information technology industry. Many problems were linked to the supply of components. Margins in this highly segmented industry attracted many new players, resulting in what was generally regarded as fierce competition. Competitors tried to outdo each other by lowering price, or skimming, by being the first to market with the introduction of the newest, most advanced generation of components. With component prices extremely unstable, introductions of new generations of components were more frequent. Oversupply of product or even components could quickly turn to losses passed on through the value chain. In North America, the leading distribution firms were considered to be in a good position because they had price protection as well as return capabilities.

Acer manufactured more PCs, keyboards, and monitors for the 30 largest computer firms than any other original equipment manufacturer (OEM) producer in the world. OEM accounted for 29 to 39 percent of Acer's sales. As of April 1995, Acer held third place in the U.S. retail channel. Shih's understanding of the global information technology industry and its key success factors are provided in Appendix B.

The Global Market for PCs

From a geographic perspective, the Asia-Pacific region, including Japan, was expected to be the fastest growing market. In the more mature areas of North America and western Europe, the home market was forecast to become the largest single segment of the market, larger than the business segment and far ahead of education and government markets. In some markets, the home segment would account for as much as half of all PC demand in units. With the proliferation of multimedia, some expected the home PC to continue evolving as an indispensable educational tool. Others pointed to the Web and Internet as the new domain that might act as a catalyst for PC sales; but with the advent of a U.S. $500 Web/Net browser, the multimedia PC could become obsolete for many.

Dataquest forecast 71.6 million in unit shipments, a 19.1 percent unit growth in the worldwide PC market for 1996 (13.6 percent growth in the U.S. market in 1996). This represents a decline from the previous year's 25.6 percent growth to a U.S. $125 billion market. According to 1996 Dataquest reports, the world market for PCs was expected to grow at a compound annual rate of 15.9 percent in unit shipments and 14.3 percent in revenues until 1999—the year the market was expected to reach 100 million units shipped per year.

Estimated worldwide PC growth was 72.2 million units, up 22 percent from 1995, noting opportunities outside the United States. In 1995, the percentage of the populations owning a PC was 26 percent in the United States, less than 12 percent in Western Europe, less than 8 percent in Japan, and less than 1 percent in Asia-Pacific countries. The percentage growth forecast for 1996 was 18 percent in the United States, 15 percent in Western Europe, 36 percent in Asia-Pacific countries, 38 percent in Japan, and 25 percent in the rest of the world.

Hambrecht & Quist's figures and estimates are shown in Exhibit 2.

PC vendor Compaq, which held the top position worldwide (as well as in the United States) with 1995 sales of 1.2 million more units than in 1994, decided in March 1996 it would lower the pricing grid, changing industry rivalry. Some expected many of the smaller suppliers to exit the market. Nearly 50 percent of the PC industry was supplied by firms that individually maintained less than a 2 percent share of the market. Industry watchers conjectured that Apple and Packard Bell, both in financial difficulty, would be absorbed by even larger suppliers. More secure firms such as AT&T and Digital Equipment exited all or part of the PC industry. In 1995 Packard Bell was the leader in the desktop market in the United States, but its gamble on low price rather than value at the high end left the firm with cash flow problems. Exhibit 3 provides information on worldwide PC shipments by vendor.

EXHIBIT 2   Worldwide PC Unit Shipments, in Millions

	1993	1994	1995	1996*	1997*	1998*
North America corporate	10.9	12.6	14.2	16.0	17.9	19.1
North America consumer	5.2	7.3	9.7	11.8	14.1	16.6
Europe	10.3	11.4	13.9	16.4	19.1	21.2
Japan/rest of world	12.3	16.0	21.4	27.0	33.9	36.3
Total	38.8	47.4	59.2	71.2	85.0	93.2

*Estimated.

EXHIBIT 3	Worldwide PC Unit Shipments in Millions (market share)	
Vendor	**1995**	**1996***
Compaq	5.8 (9.9%)	7.2 (10.0%)
Apple	5.0 (8.5%)	5.7 (7.9%)
IBM	4.5 (7.7%)	5.4 (7.5%)
Packard Bell	3.3 (5.6%)	3.9 (5.4%)
NEC	2.7 (4.6%)	3.4 (4.7%)
Hewlett-Packard	2.5 (4.3%)	3.6 (5.0%)
Dell	2.0 (3.4%)	2.7 (3.8%)
Acer	1.8 (3.1%)	2.3 (3.2%)
Fujitsu	1.8 (3.1%)	1.3 (1.8%)
Toshiba	1.5 (2.6%)	1.9 (2.6%)
Other	27.9 (47.4%)	33.2 (46.3%)
Total market	58.8 (100%)	71.7 (100.0%)

*Estimated.
Source: Dataquest.

THE CANADIAN INFORMATION TECHNOLOGY INDUSTRY

Canadian Distributors

With regard to the information technology industry in Canada, a significant proportion of lower-priced consumer products had moved directly to mass merchandisers and bypassed the distributors. Distributor sales to mass merchandisers continued to rise; ultimately, growth in the mass-merchandising channel would have come at the expense of the traditional retail outlets that were struggling to compete against mass merchandisers' rock-bottom pricing strategies. The home market was acknowledged to be driving growth in microcomputer sales. Home users were not only projected to buy in greater number but were choosing expensive, feature-rich machines. Typical configurations included large hard drives, multimedia components, fax modems, and large software bundles. Aggregate distributor sales for 1993 were CDN $2.6 billion and CDN $3.1 billion for 1994. Total distributor revenues were CDN $3.9 billion for 1995. Projected distributor sales were CDN $4.4 billion for 1996 and CDN $4.7 billion for 1997. Distributors were estimated to receive a markup of 7 to 10 percentage points on sales to dealers and resellers whose margin was approximately 10 to 15 percent on sales to end users. Retailers, who sold directly to end users, could expect a margin of 18 to 20 percent (3 to 5 percent above that in the United States). In the United States, among vendors selling branded PCs, 60 percent of sales were to retailers with the remaining 40 percent sold to distributors. In Europe, among a similar group of firms, 20 percent of sales were to retailers with 80 percent sold to distributors. Exhibit 4 provides distributor revenue by product segment.

Throughout 1995, mass merchandisers (e.g., Future Shop and London Drugs) continued to grow in importance. There was a clear trend away from small local retailers to the national mass merchandise chains. Maximizing sales to the mass merchandise sector was a major priority with most manufacturers and distributors. Both groups had set up special detailing teams that visited stores to arrange displays, organize shelf facings, take stock, and train salespeople. A few distributors performed such a role with smaller retailers. Mass merchandisers received significant "market development

EXHIBIT 4	Distributor Revenues by Product Segment in Canada			
	1994	**1995**	**1996**	**1997***
Peripheral products	30%	26%	24%	23%
Central processing units	18	22	23	25
Software	21	20	19	18
Storage	11	12	13	14
Communication products	10	11	12	12
Other (e.g., supplies and accessories)	10	9	9	8

*Projected.
Columns sum to 100%.
Source: Evans Report.

funds." Manufacturers provided these funds because of high volumes through these mass outlets and because mass merchandisers had formal marketing entities that could maximize effectiveness of such funds. Large system integrators were expanding their marketing departments so that they might be able to take greater advantage of "market development funds" offered by manufacturers. Lacking the resources to implement formal programs, smaller systems integrators and retailers were unlikely to see increases in market development funds opportunities.

In 1995, distributor revenue by customers was 29 percent from value-added resellers and regional systems integrators; 25 percent from national system integrators (e.g., SHL and Hamilton); 21 percent from smaller and local retailers; 18 percent from mass merchandisers; 5 percent from other sources; and 2 percent from original equipment manufacturers. Distributor revenues were expected to decline at least a full percentage point each year through 1997, whereas distributor revenues from mass merchandisers was expected to increase over 1.5 percentage points per year through 1997.

With regard to sales by geographic region, distributors in 1995 made 49 percent of all sales in Ontario. Western Canada, which accounted for 24 percent in 1995, was expected to account for 25 percent by 1997. Quebec, with a 20 percent share in 1995, was expected to have 19 percent by 1997. Eastern Canada had a 6 percent share in 1994 and a 7 percent share in 1995.

Distributor revenue broken down by product segment and customer is reported in Exhibit 5. These figures cover sales by distributors only and do not include sales made by manufacturers which may also sell directly to these channels.

Peripherals   Value-added resellers and regional systems integrators topped the list of distributors' customers purchasing peripherals. These buyers lacked the volume to deal with manufacturers directly. National systems integrators tended to deal directly with laser printer vendors, but usually dealt with distributors for lower volume products such as inkjet printers, scanners, and monitors (the one product Acer produced in this category).

CPUs   Value-added resellers and regional systems integrators were distributors' leading group of customers for CPUs. These firms bought from distributors because they lacked the volume required to buy from "tier-one" CPU manufacturers. National systems integrators bought from distributors in situations where they could not meet the required volume commitments to buy direct or when manufacturers were unable to fulfill orders on a timely basis. For distributors to get mass merchandiser business, they

EXHIBIT 5   Distributor Revenues by Product Segment and Customer in Canada

	Peripherals	CPUs	Software	Storage	Communication
Value-added resellers and regional systems integrators	30%	28%	21%	34%	47%
National system integrators (e.g., SHL and Hamilton)	22	26	32	24	19
Smaller retailers/local retailers	21	25	21	12	17
Mass merchandisers	19	20	26	12	5
Direct	5	0	0	0	8
Original equipment manufacturer	3%	1%	0%	18%	4%
Value of segment (millions of Canadian $)	$1,000	$869	$793	$458	$415

Columns sum to 100%.
Source: Evans Report.

often had to match the manufacturers and allow the chains to negotiate market development funds directly with the manufacturers.

Communication   Most value-added resellers bought from distributors because they lacked the internal technical resources to sell and support the products. Two types of distributors existed to service the networking requirements of customers. There were specialized networking distributors with support groups to assist with network and cabling solutions, and more broadly focused distributors who had set up special support groups for more technical products such as Unix-based systems.

Canadian Distributors and Vendors

Data on revenue by product segment and customer are presented in Exhibit 6. The figures represent the combined revenue of both computer vendors and the previously analyzed distributors.

CPUs   Large manufacturers tended to pursue a "two-pronged" strategy, using distributors to address the needs of retail channels and small value-added retailers and regional systems integrators while employing direct sales to address large corporate accounts. The rationale was that consumers demanded that the product be in the store; corporate accounts would accept lead times of a month or more. Small manufacturers employed a different approach. These firms hardly ever used distributors but instead relied on dealing directly with hundreds of small value-added resellers, regional systems integrators, and retail outlets across Canada.

Canadian Vendors

In 1995, 32 percent of sales by PC manufacturers were made to dealers. This channel was a particular favorite of the Canadian-based PC manufacturers. Distributors accounted for 18 percent of sales; a direct sales force was used for 15 percent of sales. Mass merchandisers were responsible for 13 percent of manufacturers sales in 1994. Mass merchandisers accounted for 14 percent of sales in 1995 and were expected to be 16 percent of sales in 1996 and 17 percent of sales in 1997. Value-added resellers and regional systems integrators accounted for 8 percent of sales; original equipment manufacturers accounted for the remaining 4 percent of sales.

EXHIBIT 6   1995 Distributor and Vendor Revenues by Product Segment and Customer in Canada

	Peripherals	CPUs	Software	Storage	Communication
Value-added resellers and regional systems integrators	17%	13%	24%	19%	45%
National system integrators (e.g., GE Capital, SHL and Hamilton)	26	14	30	18	19
Smaller retailers/local retailers	19	37	18	6	4
Mass merchandisers	20	17	24	6	1
Direct	2	15	4	0	30
Original equipment manufacturer	16%	4%	0%	51%	1%
Value of segment (millions of Canadian $)	$2,300	$3,800	$960	$1,300	$1,600

Columns sum to 100%.
Source: Evans Report.

Although distributors could offer savings in the areas of administration and logistics, the direct relationship between dealer and manufacturer facilitated close collaboration in the areas of sales, marketing, and training. The direct approach provided the greatest control, but dealers could expect discounts if relationships were good. If logistically efficient, the manufacturer could obtain superior rents. Service delivery and support might also give cause to sell directly. Large or otherwise important accounts might merit such attention. The possible danger with such treatment was that relations with other channels could be disrupted.

The Canadian Market for PCs

In 1995 the home and home-office segment represented 28 percent of the PC market in Canada. This segment was expected to account for 31 percent of the market by 1996, and 32 to 33 percent by 1997. In the business market, large firms represented 23 percent of sales in 1995 and were expected to decline to 20 or 21 percent by 1997. Small and mid-size firms represented 18 percent and 14 percent of shipments, respectively, in 1995. Government agencies accounted for 9 percent of shipments, and educational institutions 8 percent. By 1997, these latter four market segments were expected to decline collectively by three percentage points. Vendors were aware that home and commercial markets had developed distinct characteristics. The home market was not only growing rapidly but was particularly lucrative, with consumers choosing expensive, full-featured products. PC vendors anticipated increasing funds on advertising and store-level promotions to increase sales in this particular market.

Analysts had estimated that there were 5.23 million PCs in Canada compared with 74.24 million PCs operating in the United States. This amounted to 0.188 computers per person in Canada and 0.287 computers per person in the United States. Computing power, measured in millions of instructions per second (mips) was 10,533 mips in Canada and 173,676 mips in the United States. This was 379.2 mips per thousand people in Canada and 672.9 mips per thousand people in the United States.

- *Geographic region.* In 1995, Ontario received 51 percent of PC shipments, Quebec received 23 percent, the West received 22 percent, and the East received 4 percent. Manufacturers did not anticipate this pattern changing in the foreseeable future.

- *Price.* In the early 1980s, prices decreased on an annual basis of 15 percent or more. In the latter half of that decade, prices fell 5 to 10 percentage points per

EXHIBIT 7   Canadian PCs by Type: Unit Shipments and Revenue

	1994	1995	1996*	1997*
Portables—units shipped in thousands	192	229	293	331
—(revenue in millions of Canadian $)	$500	$575	$625	$675
Desktops—units shipped in thousands	1,193	1,360	1,469	1,587
—(revenue in millions of Canadian $)	$1,515	$2,030	$2,375	$2,470
Servers—units shipped in thousands	43	58	68	75
—(revenue in millions of Canadian $)	$675	$810	$875	$925

*Projected
Source: Evans Report.

year. In 1993 there was a decline of three percentage points—the last year prices fell. That year the average PC cost CDN $1,750 and the average home model cost CDN $1,900. Prices rose 6 percent in 1994 to an average of CDN $1,849 for a typical PC and CDN $2,040 for a typical home unit. A dramatic 11 percent increase in 1995 brought the average PC price to CDN $2,052 and CDN $2,358 for the average home PC. The average PC was expected to sell for CDN $2,113 in 1996 and CDN $2,000 in 1997. By 1997 the price differential between home and business PCs was expected to be $500. This trend in prices began in 1993; prior to that time, business PCs cost more on average than home PCs. In the mid-1980s, an average business PC typically sold for CDN $1,000 to CDN $2,000 more than a home PC.

- *Sales.* Microcomputer sales approached CDN $2.7 billion in 1994, up 17 percent from the previous year. Sales in 1995 reached CDN $3.395 billion. Revenues for 1996 were expected to be CDN $3.877 billion and CDN $4.001 billion in 1997. Unit shipments for 1995 were 1,654,191—a 15 percent increase over 1994. The number of units shipped in 1996 was expected to be 1,835,296. Shipments in 1997 were anticipated to be 2,000,473 units.

- *Retirement.* In 1995, 18 percent of PCs were retired. The retirement rate was expected to be 20 percent for 1996 and 22 percent for 1997.

Data on unit shipments and revenue in the Canadian PC market are provided in Exhibit 7. The desktop portion of units shipped was expected to decline, although revenue from these sales was expected to increase.

With regard to vendors, Exhibit 8 provides a breakdown of the 12 leaders in the PC market in Canada based on unit shipments. This includes unit shipments for all markets (commercial, home, and nonprofit).

Compared to share of unit shipments, 1995 revenues provide a different picture. Compaq and IBM each accounted for 21 percent of 1995 industry revenue. Apple captured 16 percent and AST 8 percent of industry revenue. NEC received 6 percent of industry revenue, Toshiba had 5 percent and Sidus had 3 percent.

With regard to the home market for PCs, Apple captured 18 percent of this lucrative market in 1995. Compaq was next with an 11 percent share. IBM and AST followed with 10 percent each. Packard-Bell held a 6 percent share of the home market. The industry watched closely as an additional competitor, Hewlett-Packard, entered the home PC market in Canada.

Anthony Lin had kept his eye on what competitors in North America were doing. NEC was phasing out PC manufacturing in the United States. Apple, too, was cutting back manufacturing worldwide, including Canada. Digital Equipment, with Canada's

EXHIBIT 8   Leading Vendors in Canada by Market Share

	Pre-1993 Rank	1993	1994	1995
Compaq	6 in 1990, 4 in 1991, 3 in 1992	7.6%	12.0%	12.7%
IBM	1 in 1992	14.8	14.6	12.6
Apple	1 in 1991, 2 in 1992	11.1	11.0	9.8
AST	18 in 1991, 5 in 1992	5.0	5.7	7.7
Sidus*	11 in 1991, 6 in 1992	4.7	7.3	5.5†
NEC				5.0
3D*	8 in 1991, 4 in 1992	3.7	3.7	
Dell	7 in 1992	2.8	2.7	
Seanix*		2.7	2.5	
Empac*		2.6	2.6	
STD*		2.5	2.5	
Mynix*		2.2	2.5	

*Canadian-based firms.
†Sidus's share drops to 4 percent if OEM shipments are excluded.
Source: Evans Report.

largest computer and manufacturing assembly plant, was holding its course. Sidus was expanding operations and purchasing land for a manufacturing plant to open in Austin, Texas. Likewise, Gateway was planning a U.S. $18 million manufacturing facility in the United States. AT&T was moving out of the PC business, while MCI had just acquired SHL. On August 9, Compaq announced intentions to "build to order," something the generic/clone builders had already been doing. Compaq's impetus was the threat of losing business. IBM already built to order for Canada. With light assembly capabilities, IBM's build to order program pursued its major dealers first and its distributors second. AST supported a Canadian configuration center which focused on direct dealers. Sidus had recently retrenched, freeing up resources, in order to concentrate on its core computer manufacturing business. Distributors such as Merisel and Ingram Micro had even added configuration facilities. Lin contemplated competitors' actions and wondered if assembly in Canada wasn't so much an extra or added feature, but a necessity.

ACER'S OPERATION IN NORTH AMERICA—ACER AMERICA

Ronald Chwang was the president and CEO of Acer America Corporation, the eighth-largest computer manufacturer in the United States. Chwang held a Ph.D. in electrical engineering, was a Canadian citizen, and a graduate of McGill University. According to him, Acer America, headquartered in San Jose, California, had successfully managed key technology transitions to the latest Intel Pentium processors and provided the first consumer PCs pre-loaded with Microsoft Windows 95.

Acer America posted revenues of U.S. $1.44 billion in 1995 and U.S. $858 million in 1994. Prior to that, Acer America had been credited for pushing Acer corporate toward negative earnings from 1990 through 1992. Acer America accounted for about 10 percent of all Acer employees worldwide and was responsible for engineering, manufacturing, and marketing operations in the United States and, now, in Canada. The United States was one of five countries with manufacturing; the others were the Netherlands, Taiwan, Malaysia, and the Philippines.

EXHIBIT 9   Top 10 U.S. PC Vendors, 1995

Vendor	Shipments in Millions (market share)
Compaq	2.198 (11.8%)
Apple	2.153 (11.5%)
Packard Bell	2.125 (11.4%)
IBM	1.640 (8.8%)
Gateway 2000	.934 (5.0%)
Dell	.787 (4.2%)
AST	.721 (3.9%)
Toshiba	.618 (3.3%)
Acer	.464 (2.5%)
Hewlett-Packard	.445 (2.4%)
Other	6.615 (35.4%)
U.S. total	18.700 (100.0%)

Source: International Data Corporation.

Chwang knew that Acer America, with clear financial visibility, was preparing for the next stage of business growth and an eventual initial public offering in the United States. In formal company documents, Chwang stated that "Mr. Lin has demonstrated the ability to consistently generate business opportunities for Acer, as well as to develop strategies for future growth." In 1996 Acer America's sales were 60 percent consumer and 40 percent commercial. Exhibit 9 provides the top PC vendors in the United States in 1995.

Lin knew that there had been a change in channel structure after the North American Free Trade Agreement (NAFTA), and that the North American market was vastly different than it had been. With an open border, product could move easily north or south as long as 50 percent or more of the product value was added in one of the three member countries. As a result, most warehousing of PCs was in the United States. It was primarily national and was centralized, with logistics being the major concern. Lin considered distributors to be very strong in the United States. For a vendor to succeed, developing a direct relationship with distributors was vital. Distributors achieved economies by having more than one vendor. Exhibit 10 provides U.S. PC sales in units and Exhibit 11 provides U.S. PC revenues.

ACER'S CURRENT SITUATION IN CANADA

Acer operations in Canada served as a conduit for Acer America to deliver products to Canadian distributors. The Canadian facility handled only shipment and repair of Acer products for customers in Canada, and at this point was selling no products directly to consumers in Canada, but was providing repair and shipment of all Acer products to Canadian customers. The intent of Anthony Lin, general manager of Acer America's operation in Canada, was to have a full line of products sold via different channels to different target groups—commercial, home and nonprofit (government and education).

Lin was fully aware of Acer's philosophy to utilize local distributors because their past experience, knowledge of the existing environment, and an understanding of the market placed them in the best position to access markets. Lin, with assistance from a veteran of the Canadian computer industry, believed he had a strong understanding of what was and was not possible. He readily recognized many of the usual problems

EXHIBIT 10   U.S. PC Unit Sales by Distributor (In thousands)

Distributor	1991	1992	1993	1994	1995	1996*	1997*
Computer specialty stores	3,726	3,952	4,231	4,385	4,477	4,512	4,540
Computer superstores	330	564	835	1,159	1,505	1,832	2,166
VARs/system integrators	942	1,023	1,067	1,111	1,155	1,200	1,243
Local assemblers	1,033	1,215	1,382	1,560	1,669	1,764	1,844
Office product superstores	134	253	357	473	593	732	878
Consumer electronics stores	722	809	898	990	1,086	1,189	1,296
Consumer electronics superstores	225	378	540	733	944	1,154	1,325
Warehouse clubs	174	233	292	342	410	479	537
Other mass merchants	336	511	632	773	927	1,085	1,244
Direct marketing/mail order	1,220	1,650	1,985	2,185	2,370	2,550	2,720
Direct sales force	772	654	572	514	466	430	410
Other distribution channels	399	420	439	458	477	497	518
Total U.S. PC unit sales	10,014	11,663	13,229	14,681	16,079	17,425	18,721
Yearly growth rate	6.7%	16.5%	13.4%	11.0%	9.5%	8.4%	7.4%

*Estimated.
Source: Evans Report.

EXHIBIT 11   U.S. PC Revenue (In U.S. $ millions)

Distributor	1991	1992	1993	1994	1995	1996*	1997*
Computer specialty stores	$ 9,885	$10,764	$11,527	$12,100	$12,410	$12,733	$12,989
Computer superstores	637	1,209	1,988	2,751	3,499	4,226	4,848
VARs/system integrators	3,917	4,195	4,472	4,741	5,014	5,221	5,426
Local assemblers	2,064	2,544	3,057	3,615	3,900	4,011	4,110
Office product superstores	226	495	815	1,077	1,308	1,583	1,881
Consumer electronics stores	1,166	1,429	1,806	2,042	2,212	2,385	2,571
Consumer electronics superstores	348	694	1,128	1,540	1,907	2,319	2,671
Warehouse clubs	269	415	593	702	817	941	1,061
Other mass merchants	509	899	1,262	1,564	1,823	2,108	2,397
Direct marketing/mail order	2,770	4,129	5,061	5,764	6,193	6,613	7,036
Direct sales force	2,108	1,836	1,632	1,515	1,390	1,310	1,283
Other distribution channels	839	938	1,019	1,102	1,147	1,193	1,214
Total U.S. PC unit sales	$24,738	$29,548	$34,360	$38,514	$41,622	$44,642	$47,488
Yearly growth rate	0.5%	19.4%	16.3%	12.1%	8.1%	7.3%	6.4%

*Estimated.
Source: Evans Report.

associated with taking a product into Canada; for example, bilingual requirements for packaging. Technical support lines would also have to be in English and French.

As a veteran of the Acer organization, Lin knew that decision making had been characterized as informal but following a consistent pattern. The process took into account seniority, rank, and professionalism, as well as recognized expertise and dedication to Acer.

Lin believed that Canadian service, both to resellers, and ultimately, to customers, could be improved by local PC assembly, which would offer "an immense opportunity." Dealers wanted no inventory because PCs depreciated so rapidly; therefore, both they and their customers would appreciate the short cycle times afforded through local assembly. As well, the short lead times for components would give Acer local control over the "on/off switch," thereby increasing the firm's local competitiveness. Lin considered a PC's primary ingredients to be a microprocessor, hard disk, and memory. Acer made memory from scratch but neither of the other two components. With an understanding of Shih's smiling curve, Lin viewed the cost structure for the PC industry from producer to consumer as comprising three parts: raw materials, assembly, and developing and sustaining channels. Raw materials and channel management were high costs, whereas assembly was comparatively lower.

In the era of liberalized trade, some multinational enterprises were consolidating operations and withdrawing from Canada, with the result that the Canadian market was increasingly being served from the United States. Currently, Acer's Canadian operations—an office in Mississauga, Ontario—served as an intermediary between Acer America and the Canadian market. Acer had always gone against the flow, but should its operation in Canada be a satellite sales office or a self-sufficient entity? The latter option would require Lin to devise strategy, structure, and control mechanisms.

APPENDIX A

World Headquarters

Acer Incorporated	Taipei, Taiwan

Regional Headquarters

Acer America Corporation	(North America)	San Jose, California, US
Acer Computer B.V.	(Europe)	The Netherlands
Acer Computer International Ltd.	(Asia, Middle East, Africa, Pacifica)	Singapore
Acer Computec Latin America	(Latin America)	Mexico
Acer Sertek Incorporated	(Taiwan and Greater China)	Taipei, Taiwan

Worldwide Operations

Acer Computer International, CIS	Moscow, Russia
Acer Computer (Far East) Ltd.	Hong Kong
Acer Computer (M.E.) Ltd.	Dubai, United Arab Emirates
Acer Computer Turkey	Istanbul, Turkey
Acer Japan Corporation	Tokyo, Japan
Acer Korea Co. Ltd.	Seoul, South Korea
Acer Market Services Ltd.	Beijing, Peoples Republic of China
Acer Sales & Services Sdn Bhd	Kuala Lumpur, Malaysia
Acer Sertek Incorporated	Taipei, Taiwan

Australia & New Zealand

Acer Computer Australia Pty Ltd.	North Ryde, New South Wales, Australia

Sales offices in South Australia, Western Australia, Australian Capital Territory, Victoria, and Queensland.

Acer Computer New Zealand Ltd.	Auckland, New Zealand

Sales office in Wellington.

Latin America

Acer Latin America	Miami, Florida
Sales offices:	
Acer Argentina	Buenos Aires, Argentina
Acer Chile	Santiago, Chile
Acer Columbia	Bogota, Columbia
Acer de Venezuela	Caracas, Venezuela

Europe

Acer Belgium NV	Antwerpen, Belgium
Acer Computer B.V.	The Netherlands
Acer Computer France	Paris, France
Acer Computer GmbH	Hamburg, Germany
Acer Computer HandelsgmbH	Wien, Austria
Acer Computer Norway A/S	Asker, Norway
Acer Computer Representative Hungary	Budapest, Hungary
Acer Computer Iberica, S.A.	Barcelona, Spain
Acer Italy s.r.l.	Milan, Italy
Acer Scandinavia A/S	Denmark
Acer UK Limited	United Kingdom

North America

Acer America   San Jose, California

Sales offices in: Mississauga, Ontario (Canada); Boston, Massachusetts (Boston); Rolling Meadows, Illinois (North Central West); Farmington Hills, Michigan (Midwest); Dallas, Texas (South Central); Duluth, Georgia (Southeast); Wyckoff, New Jersey (North Mid Atlantic); Bayville, New York (New York Metro); Issaquah, Washington (Northwest); Akron, Ohio (North Central East); Costa Mesa, California (Southwest); Vienna, Virginia (Government Sales).

Africa

Acer Africa (Pty) Ltd   South Africa

APPENDIX B

PC Industry Value-Added Curve

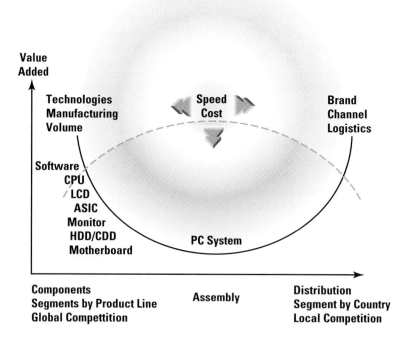

The primary key to success in today's industry is providing value. By doing well in "value-added" business segments, companies can succeed in the current dis-integrated business environment. To explain the dis-integration trend, Stan came up with this chart that looks like a big smile; he calls it his "smiling curve." Value is added in component production on the left side and marketing/distribution on the right.

Today, there is no longer any value added in assembling computers—everyone can make a PC. To succeed in the new information technology (IT) age, you have to gain a top position in component segments, like software, CPUs, DRAM, ASICs, monitors, storage, etc., or else as a distribution leader in a country or region.

The key to success on the components side of the chart is global competitiveness. Universal standards in components mean global competition, so if you're going to pursue a segment along the left side, you need technology and a strong manufacturing capability for economies of scale. On the distribution side, where competition is local, you can succeed through a good image, brand name awareness, well-managed channels, and effective logistics.

Note that in today's dis-integrated industry environment there is one simple rule: If you are not one of a market segment's leaders, you cannot survive. Whether on the right side or the left side of the curve, speed and cost are two main factors for success in such an environment. "Speed" means fast time to market with new products and fast responses to change in the industry. "Cost" includes minimizing overhead, inventory reduction and risk management. Only the leaders of each segment will survive, so whoever understands this curve will end up smiling in the future.

In today's PC industry, a lot of the leading companies are "computerless computer companies." They primarily concentrate on marketing, and have little or no involvement on the components side of the business. Speed is the primary factor that will determine the success or failure of these companies in the future. Cost is also an important long-term factor for success. On the component side, Acer is among the top five worldwide in all the segments we currently pursue. On the distribution side, Acer is currently the seventh largest PC brand in the world, ninth largest in the United States, and number one in the Middle East, Latin America, and Southeast Asia. Already enjoying top-level status in so many developing countries, the company's current target is to achieve a top 10 position in Europe, and top 5 status worldwide.

(Acer's web address is *www.acer.com.*)

OUTBACK STEAKHOUSE GOES INTERNATIONAL*

Marilyn L. Taylor, *University of Missouri at Kansas City*

George M. Puia, *Indiana State University*

Krishnan Ramaya, *University of Kansas*

Madelyn Gengelbach, *University of Missouri at Kansas City*

In early 1995 Outback Steakhouse enjoyed a position as one of the most successful restaurant chains in the United States. Entrepreneurs Chris Sullivan, Bob Basham, and Tim Gannon, each with more than 20 years of experience in the restaurant industry, started Outback Steakhouse with just two stores in 1988. In 1995 the company was the fastest growing U.S. steakhouse chain, with over 200 stores throughout the United States.

Outback achieved its phenomenal success in an industry widely considered one the most competitive in the United States. Fully 75 percent of entrants into the industry failed within the first year. Outback's strategy was driven by a combination of factors unique in food-service industry. As Chairman Chris Sullivan put it, "Outback is all about a lot of different experiences that have been recognized as entrepreneurship." Within six years of commencing operations, Outback was voted the best steakhouse chain in the country. The company also took top honors, along with Olive Garden, as America's favorite restaurant. In December 1994, Outback was awarded *Inc.* magazine's prestigious Entrepreneur of the Year award. In 1994 and early 1995 the business press hailed the company as one of the biggest success stories in corporate America in recent years.

Support for the development of this case was provided by the Center for Entrepreneurial Leadership, Ewing Marion Kauffman Foundation, Kansas City, Missouri. The authors express deep appreciation to the following individuals at the Ewing Marion Kauffman Foundation: Dr. Ray Smilor, vice president, and Dr. Mabel Tinjacha, program specialist, of the Center for Entrepreneurial Leadership. In addition, the authors also wish to express special appreciation to Outback executives Bob Merritt, CFO and treasurer, Nancy Schneid, vice president of marketing, and Hugh Connerty, president (of Outback International), who contributed special time and attention to this particular case. The research team has had sustained commitment from all the senior executives including Chris Sullivan, chairman and CEO; Bob Basham, president and COO; Tim Gannon, senior vice president, and Ava Forney, assistant to the chairman and CEO; as well as other Outback officers, executives and employees. Numerous "Outbackers" have given enthusiastically and generously of time, knowledge, and skills to make this case study possible.

In late 1994 Hugh Connerty was appointed president of Outback International. In early 1995 Connerty, a highly successful franchisee for Outback, explained the international opportunities facing Outback Steakhouse as it considered its strategy for expansion abroad:

> We have had hundreds of franchise requests from all over the world. [So] it took about two seconds for me to make that decision [to become President of Outback International] . . . I've met with and talked to other executives who have international divisions. All of them have the same story. At some point in time the light goes off and they say, "Gee we have a great product. Where do we start?" I have traveled quite a bit on holiday. The world is not as big as you think it is. Most companies who have gone global have not used any set strategy.

Despite his optimism, Connerty knew that the choice of targeted markets would be critical. Connerty wondered what strategic and operational changes the company would have to make to assure success in those markets.

HISTORY OF OUTBACK STEAKHOUSE, INC.

In the early 1970s, recent college graduates Chris Sullivan, Bob Basham, and Tim Gannon met when they joined Steak & Ale, the Pillsbury subsidiary and restaurant chain that had hired the three into their first career positions as management trainees. During the 1980s, Sullivan and Basham became successful franchisees of 17 Chili's restaurants in Florida and Georgia, with franchise headquarters in Tampa, Florida.[1] Meanwhile Tim Gannon played a significant role in several New Orleans restaurant chains. Sullivan and Basham sold their Chili's franchises in 1987 and used the proceeds to fund Outback, their start-from-scratch entrepreneurial venture. They invited Gannon to join them in Tampa in the fall of 1987. The trio opened their first two restaurants in Tampa in 1988.

The three entrepreneurs recognized that Americans' in-home consumption of meat, especially beef, had declined.[2] Nonetheless, upscale and budget steakhouses were extremely popular. The three concluded that people were cutting in-home red meat consumption but were still very interested in going out to a restaurant for a good steak. They saw an untapped opportunity for serving quality steaks at an affordable price, that is, for filling the space between high-priced and budget steakhouses.

Using an Australian theme associated with the outdoors and adventure, Outback positioned itself as a place providing not only excellent food but also a cheerful, fun, and comfortable experience. The company's "Statement of Principles and Beliefs" referred to employees as "Outbackers" and highlighted the importance of hospitality, sharing, quality, fun, and courage.

Catering primarily to the dinner crowd, Outback restaurants offered a menu that featured specially seasoned steaks and prime rib. The menu also included chicken, fish,

---

[1]Casual-dining-chain legend and mentor Norman Brinker played a key role in all of the restaurant chains the two were associated with prior to Outback.

[2]American consumption of meat declined from the mid-1970s to the early 1990s primarily as a result of health concerns about red meat. In 1976 Americans consumed 131.6 pounds of beef and veal, 58.7 pounds of pork, and 12.9 pounds of fish per capita. In 1990 the per capita figures had declined to 64.9 pounds of beef and veal, 46.3 pounds of pork, and 15.5 pounds of fish. The dramatic decrease was attributed to consumer attitudes toward a healthier, low-fat diet. Menu items that gained in popularity were premium baked goods, coffees, vegetarian menu items, fruits, salsa, sauces, chicken dishes, salad bars, and spicy dishes. [George Thomas Kurian, *Datapedia of the United States 1790–10000* (Maryland: Bernan Press, 1994) p. 113.]

and pasta entrees in addition to the company's innovative appetizers.[3] CFO Bob Merritt cited Outback's food as a main reason for the company's success. As he put it:

> One of the important reasons for our success is that we took basic American meat and potatoes and enhanced the flavor profile so that it fit with the aging population . . . Just look at what McDonald's and Burger King did in their market segment. They tried to add things to their menu that were more flavorful; [for example,] McDonald's put the Big Mac on the menu . . . As people age, they want more flavor . . . higher flavor profiles. It's not happenstance. It's a science. There's too much money at risk in this business not to know what's going on with customer taste preferences.

The company viewed suppliers as "partners" and was committed to work with suppliers to develop and maintain long-term relationships. Purchasing was dedicated to obtaining ingredients and supplies of the highest possible quality. Indeed, the company was almost fanatical about quality. At about 40 percent of total costs, Outback's food costs were among the highest in the industry. As Tim Gannon, the company's vice president and chief chef, put it, "We won't tolerate less than the best." One example of the company's quality emphasis was its croutons. Made daily on site, the croutons had 17 different seasonings, including fresh garlic and butter. The croutons were cut into irregular shapes so that customers would recognize they were handmade. The emphasis on quality attracted people. On Friday and Saturday nights customers waited up to two hours for a table. Most felt that Outback provided exceptional value for the average entree price of $15 to $16.

Outback focused not only on the productivity and efficiency of its Outbackers but also their long-term well-being. Executives referred to the company's employee commitment as "tough on results, but kind with people." A typical Outback restaurant staff consisted of a general manager, an assistant manager, and a kitchen manager, plus 50 to 70 mostly part-time hourly employees. The company used aptitude tests, psychological profiles, and interviews as part of the employee selection process. Every applicant interviewed with two managers. The company placed emphasis on creating an entrepreneurial climate where learning and personal growth were strongly emphasized. As Chairman Chris Sullivan explained:

> I was given the opportunity to make a lot of mistakes and learn, and we try to do that today. We try to give our people a lot of opportunity to make some mistakes, learn, and go on.

In order to facilitate ease of operations for employees, the company's restaurant design devoted 45 percent to kitchen area. Wait staff were assigned only three tables at a time. Most Outback restaurants were only open 4:30–11:30 PM daily. Outback's wait staff enjoyed higher income from tips than in restaurants that also served lunch. Restaurant management staff worked 50–55 hours per week, in contrast to the 70 or more hours common in the industry. Company executives felt that the dinner-only concept had led to effective utilization of systems, staff, and management. "Outbackers" reported that they had more fun working at Outback than at other restaurant companies, and that they were less worn out.

Outback executives were proud of their "B-locations [with] A-demographics" location strategy. They deliberately steered clear of high-traffic locations targeted by companies that served a lunch crowd. Until the early 1990s most of the restaurants were leased locations, retrofits of another restaurant location. The emphasis was on choosing

---

[3]Outback's signature trademark was its best-selling Aussie-Tizer, the Bloomin' Onion. The company expected to serve 9 million Bloomin' Onions in 1995.

locations where Outback's target customers would be in the evening. The overall strategy payoff was clear. In an industry where a sales-to-investment ratio of 1.2:1 was considered strong, Outback's restaurants generated $2.10 for every $1 invested in the facility. The average Outback restaurant unit generated $3.4 million in sales.

In 1995 management remained informal. Headquarters were located on the second floor of an unpretentious building near the Tampa airport. There was no middle management—top management selected the joint venture partners and franchisees who reported directly to the president. Franchisees and joint venture partners, in turn, hired the general managers at each restaurant.

Outback provided ownership opportunities at three levels of the organization: the individual restaurant level; through multiple store arrangements (joint venture and franchise opportunities), and through a stock ownership plan for every employee. Health insurance was also available to all employees, a benefit not universally available to restaurant industry workers. Outback's employment and ownership opportunities for restaurant-level general managers were atypical in the industry. A restaurant general manager invested $25,000 for a 10 percent ownership stake in the restaurant, a contract for five years in the same location, a 10 percent share of the cash flow from the restaurant as a yearly bonus, opportunity for stock options, and a 10 percent buyout arrangement at the end of the five years. Outback store managers typically earned an annual salary and bonus of over $100,000, compared to an industry average of about $60,000–$70,000. Outback's management turnover of 5.4 percent was one of the lowest in the industry, in which the average was 30–40 percent.

Community involvement was strongly encouraged throughout the organization. The corporate office was involved in several nonprofit activities in the Tampa area and also sponsored major national events such as the Outback Bowl and charity golf tournaments. Each store was involved in community participation and service. For example, the entire proceeds of an open house held just prior to every restaurant opening went to a charity of the store manager's choice.

Early in its history the company had been unable to afford any advertising. Instead, Outback's founders relied on their strong relationships with local media to generate public relations and promotional efforts. One such relationship was with Nancy Schneid, who had extensive experience in advertising and radio. Schneid later became Outback's vice president of marketing. Under her direction the company developed a full-scale national media program that concentrated on television advertising and local billboards. The company avoided couponing, and its only printed advertising typically came as part of a package offered by a charity or sports event.

Early financing for growth had come from limited partnership investments by family members, close friends, and associates. The three founders' original plan did not call for extensive expansion or franchising. However, in 1990 some friends, disappointed in the performance of several of their Kentucky-based restaurants, asked to franchise the Outback concept. The converted Kentucky stores enjoyed swift success. Additional opportunities with other individuals experienced in the restaurant industry arose in various parts of the country. These multi-store arrangements were in the form of franchises or joint ventures. Later in 1990 the company turned to a venture capital firm for financing for a $2.5 million package. About the same time, Bob Merritt joined the company as CFO.[4] Merritt's previous experience with initial public offerings

---

[4]Merritt had worked as CFO for another company that had come to the financial markets with its initial public offering.

EXHIBIT 1   Outback Steakhouse, Inc., Consolidated Statements of Income, 1990–94

	Years Ended December 31				
	1994	1993	1992	1991	1990
Revenues	$451,916,000	$309,749,000	$189,217,000	$62,211,500	$24,811,400
Costs and Expenses					
Costs of revenues	175,618,000	121,290,000	73,475,000	23,760,600	9,535,300
Labor and other related expenses	95,476,000	65,047,000	37,087,000	26,200,100	9,885,700
Other restaurant operating expenses	93,265,000	64,603,000	43,370,000		
General & administrative expenses	16,744,000	12,225,000	9,176,000	3,617,100	1,551,400
(Income) from oper of unconsol. affl.	(1,269,000)	(333,000)		(914,500)	(278,400)
	379,834,000	262,832,000	163,108,000	52,663,300	20,694,000
Income from operations	72,082,000	46,917,000	26,109,000	9,548,200	4,117,400
Non-operating income (expense)					
Interest income	512,000	1,544,000	1,428,000	414,800	217,600
Interest expense	(424,000)	(369,000)	(360,000)	(145,900)	(117,100)
	88,000	1,175,000	1,068,000	268,900	100,500
Income before elimination Minority partners interest and income taxes	72,170,000	48,092,000	27,177,000	9,817,100	4,217,900
Elimination of minority partners interest	11,276,000	7,378,000	4,094,000	998,700	435,400
Income before provision for income taxes	60,894,000	40,714,000	23,083,000	8,818,400	3,782,500
Provision for income taxes	21,602,000	13,922,000	6,802,000	2,786,500	1,175,000
Net income	$39,292,000	$26,792,000	$16,281,000	$6,031,900	$2,607,500
Earnings per common share	$0.69	$0.61	$0.39	$0.29	$0.15
Weighted-average number of common shares outstanding	43,997,000	43,738,000	41,504,000	20,915,800	17,086,000
Pro forma					
Provision for income taxes	22,286,000	15,472,000	8,245,000	3,350,900	1,429,800
Net income	$38,608,000	$25,242,000	$14,838,000	$5,467,500	$2,352,700
Earnings per common share	$0.88	$0.58	$0.36	$0.26	$0.14

helped the company undertake a quick succession of three highly successful public equity offerings. During 1994 the price of the company's stock ranged from $22.63 to $32.00. The company's income statements, balance sheets, and a summary of the stock price performance appear as Exhibits 1, 2, and 3, respectively.

EXHIBIT 2 Outback Steakhouse, Inc., Consolidated Balance Sheets, 1990–94

	December 31				
	1994	**1993**	**1992**	**1991**	**1990**
Assets					
Current assets					
Cash and cash equivalents	$ 18,758,000	$ 24,996,000	$ 60,538,000	17,000,700	2,983,000
Short-term municipal securities	4,829,000	6,632,000	1,316,600		
Inventories	4,539,000	3,849,000	2,166,500	1,020,800	319,200
Other current assets	11,376,000	4,658,000	2,095,200	794,900	224,100
Total current assets	39,502,000	40,135,000	66,116,700	18,816,400	3,526,300
Long-term municipal securities	1,226,000	8,903,000	7,071,200		
Property, fixtures, and equipment, net	162,323,000	101,010,000	41,764,500	15,479,000	6,553,200
Investments and advances to unconsolidated affiliates	14,244,000	1,000,000			
Other assets	11,236,000	8,151,000	2,691,300	2,380,700	1,539,600
	$228,531,000	$159,199,000	$117,643,700	36,676,100	11,619,100
Liabilities and Stockholders' Equity					
Current liabilities					
Accounts payable	$ 10,184,000	$ 1,053,000	$ 3,560,200	643,800	666,900
Sales taxes payable	3,173,000	2,062,000	1,289,500	516,800	208,600
Accrued expenses	14,961,000	10,435,000	8,092,300	2,832,300	954,800
Unearned revenue	11,862,000	6,174,000	2,761,900	752,800	219,400
Current portion of long-term debt	918,000	1,119,000	326,600	257,000	339,900
Income taxes payable			369,800	1,873,200	390,000
Total current liabilities	41,098,000	20,843,000	16,400,300	6,875,900	2,779,600
Deferred income taxes	568,000	897,000	856,400	300,000	260,000
Long-term debt	12,310,000	5,687,000	1,823,700	823,600	1,060,700
Interest of minority partners in consolidated partnerships	2,255,000	1,347,000	1,737,500	754,200	273,000
Total liabilities	56,231,000	28,774,000	20,817,900	8,753,700	4,373,300
Stockholders' equity					
Common stock, $0.01 par value. 100,000,000 shares authorized for 1994 and 1993; 50,000,000 authorized for 1992 42,931,344 and 42,442,800 shares issues and outstanding as of December 31, 1994 and 1993, respectively. 39,645,995 shares issued and outstanding as of December 31, 1992.	429,000	425,000	396,500	219,000	86,300
Additional paid-in capital	83,756,000	79,429,000	74,024,500	20,296,400	4,461,100
Retained earnings	88,115,000	50,571,000	22,404,800	7,407,000	2,698,400
Total stockholders' equity	172,300,000	130,425,000	96,825,800	27,922,400	7,245,800
	$228,531,000	$159,199,000	$117,643,700	36,676,100	11,619,100

EXHIBIT 3   Outback Steakhouse, Selected Financial and Stock Data, 1988–94

Year	Systemwide Sales*	Company Revenues	Net Income	Earnings per Share	Company-owned Stores	Franchised and Joint Venture	Total
1988	$ 2,731	$ 2,731	$ 47	$0.01	2	0	2
1989	13,238	13,238	920	0.04	9	0	9
1990	34,193	34,193	2,260	0.08	23	0	23
1991	91,000	91,000	6,064	0.17	49	0	49
1992	195,508	189,217	14,838	0.36	81	4	85
1993	347,553	309,749	25,242	0.58	124	24	148
1994	548,945	451,916	38,608	0.88	164	50	214

Performance of Outback Steakhouse's Common Stock, 1991–94

1991	High	Low
Second quarter (from June 18)	$ 4.67	$ 4.27
Third quarter	6.22	4.44
Fourth quarter	10.08	5.50
1992		
First quarter	$13.00	$ 9.17
Second quarter	11.41	8.37
Third quarter	16.25	10.13
Fourth quarter	19.59	14.25
1993		
First quarter	$22.00	$15.50
Second quarter	26.16	16.66
Third quarter	24.59	19.00
Fourth quarter	25.66	21.16
1994		
First quarter	$29.50	$23.33
Second quarter	28.75	22.75
Third quarter	30.88	23.75
Fourth quarter	32.00	22.63

*Systemwide Sales, Company Revenues, and Net Income are in thousands of dollars.

OUTBACK'S INTERNATIONAL ROLLOUT

Outback's management recognized that the U.S. market could accommodate at least 550–600 Outback steakhouse restaurants. At the rate the company was growing (70 stores annually), Outback would near the U.S. market's saturation within 4–5 years. Outback's plans for longer-term growth hinged on a multipronged strategy. The company planned to roll out an additional 300–350 Outback stores, expand into the lucrative Italian dining segment through its joint venture with the Houston-based Carrabbas Italian Grill, and develop new dining themes. By late 1994 Outback's management had also begun to consider the potential of non-U.S. markets for the Outback concept. As Chairman Chris Sullivan put it:

> We can do 500–600 [Outback] restaurants, and possibly more over the next five years . . . [However,] the world is becoming one big market, and we want to be in place so we don't miss that opportunity. There are some problems, some challenges with it, but at this point

there have been some casual restaurant chains that have gone [outside the United States] and their average unit sales are way, way above the sales level they enjoyed in the United States. So the potential is there. Obviously, there are some distribution issues to work out, things like that. But we are real excited about the future internationally. That will give us some potential outside the United States to continue to grow as well.

In late 1994 the company began its international venture by appointing Hugh Connerty as president of Outback International. Connerty, like Outback's three founders, had extensive experience in the restaurant industry. Prior to joining Outback, he developed a chain of successful Hooters restaurants in Georgia. He used the proceeds from the sales of these franchises to fund the development of his franchise of Outback restaurants in northern Florida and southern Georgia. Connerty's success as a franchisee was well recognized. Indeed, in 1993 Outback began to award a large crystal trophy with the designation "Connerty Franchisee of the Year" to the company's outstanding franchisee of the year.

Much of Outback's growth and expansion was generated through joint venture partnerships and franchising agreements. Connerty commented on Outback's franchise system:

> Every one of the franchisees lives in their areas. I lived in the area I franchised. I had relationships that helped with getting permits. That isn't any different than the rest of the world. The loyalties of individuals that live in their respective areas [will be important.] We will do the franchises one by one. The biggest decision we have to make is how we pick that franchise partner . . . That is what we will concentrate on. We are going to select a person who has synergy with us, who thinks like us, who believes in the principles and beliefs.

Outback developed relationships very carefully. As Hugh Connerty explained:

> Trust . . . is foremost and sacred. The trust between [Outback] and the individual franchisees is not to be violated. The company grants franchises one at a time. It takes a lot of trust to invest millions of dollars without any assurance that you will be able to build another one.

However, Connerty recognized that expanding abroad would present challenges. He described how Outback would approach its international expansion:

> We have built Outback one restaurant at a time . . . There are some principles and beliefs we live by. It almost sounds cultish. We want International to be an opportunity for our suppliers. We feel strongly about the relationships with our suppliers. We have never changed suppliers. We have an undying commitment to them and in exchange we want them to have an undying commitment to us. They have to prove they can build plants [abroad].

He explained:

> I think it would be foolish of us to think that we are going to go around the world buying property and understanding the laws in every country, the culture in every single country. So the approach that we are going to take is that we will franchise the international operation with company-owned stores here and franchises there so that will allow us to focus on what I believe is our pure strength, a support operation.

U.S. RESTAURANTS IN THE INTERNATIONAL DINING MARKET

For U.S. restaurant companies in the early 1990s, prospects for international expansion appeared promising. Between 1992 and 1993 alone, international sales for the top 50 restaurant franchisers increased from $15.9 billion to $17.5 billion. Franchising was

EXHIBIT 4   Top 50 U.S. Restaurant Franchises Ranked by Sales (in millions), 1993–94

		Total Sales		International Sales		Total Stores		International Stores	
Rank	Firm	1994	1993	1994	1993	1994	1993	1994	1993
1	McDonald's	$25,986	$23,587	$11,046	$9,401	15,205	13,993	5,461	4,710
2	Burger King	7,500	6,700	1,400	1,240	7,684	6,990	1,357	1,125
3	KFC	7,100	7,100	3,600	3,700	9,407	9,033	4,258	3,905
4	Taco Bell	4,290	3,817	130	100	5,615	4,634	162	112
5	Wendy's	4,277	3,924	390	258	4,411	4,168	413	377
6	Hardee's	3,491	3,425	63	56	3,516	3,435	72	63
7	Dairy Queen	3,170	2,581	300	290	3,516	3,435	628	611
8	Domino's	2,500	2,413	415	275	5,079	5,009	840	550
9	Subway	2,500	2,201	265	179	9,893	8,450	944	637
10	Little Caesars	2,000	2,000	70	70	4,855	4,754	155	145
Average of firms 11–20		1,222	1,223	99	144	2,030	1,915	163	251
Average of firms 21–30		647	594	51	26	717	730	37	36
Average of firms 31–40		382	358	7	9	502	495	26	20
Average of firms 41–50		270	257	17	23	345	363	26	43
Non-Fast-Food Chains in Top 50									
11	Denny's	$ 1,779	$ 1,769	$ 63	$ 70	1,548	1,515	58	63
13	Dunkin' Donuts	1,413	1,285	226	209	3,453	3,047	831	705
14	Shoney's	1,346	1,318	0	0	922	915	0	0
15	Big Boy	1,130	1,202	100	0	940	930	90	78
17	Baskin-Robbins	1,008	910	387	368	3,765	3,562	1,300	1,278
19	T.G.I. Friday's	897	1,068	114	293	314	NA	37	NA
20	Applebee's	889	609	1	0	507	361	2	0
21	Sizzler	858	922	230	218	600	666	119	116
23	Ponderosa	690	743	40	38	380	750	40	38
24	Int'l House of Pancakes	632	560	32	29	657	561	37	35
25	Perkins	626	588	12	10	432	425	8	6
29	Outback Steakhouse	549	348	0	0	NA	NA	NA	NA
30	Golden Corral	548	515	1	0	425	425	2	1
32	TCBY Yogurt	388	337	22	15	2,801	2,474	141	80
37	Showbiz/Chuck E. Cheese	370	373	7	8	332	NA	8	NA
39	Round Table Pizza	357	340	15	12	576	597	29	22
40	Western Sizzlin	337	351	3	6	281	NA	2	NA
41	Ground Round	321	310	0	0	NA	NA	NA	NA
42	Papa John's	297	NA	0	NA	632	NA	0	NA
44	Godfather's Pizza	270	268	0	0	515	531	0	0
45	Bonanza	267	327	32	47	264	NA	30	NA
46	Village Inn	266	264	0	0	NA	NA	NA	NA
47	Red Robin	259	235	27	28	NA	NA	NA	NA
48	Tony Roma's	254	245	41	36	NA	NA	NA	NA
49	Marie Callender	251	248	0	0	NA	NA	NA	NA

NA: Not ranked in the top 50 for that category.
Source: Data taken from "Top 50 Franchises," *Restaurant Business,* November 1, 1995, pp. 35–41.

the most popular means for rapid expansion. Exhibit 4 provides an overview of the top U.S. restaurant franchisers, including their domestic and international revenues and number of units, in 1993 and 1994.

International expansion was an important source of revenues for a significant number of players in the industry. The international growth and expansion in the U.S. restaurant industry over the last two decades was largely driven by major fast-food restaurant chains. Some of these companies—for example, McDonald's, Wendy's, Dairy Queen, and Domino's Pizza—were public and free-standing. Others—such as Subway and Little Caesars—remained private and free-standing. Some of the largest players in international markets were subsidiaries of major consumer products firms such as PepsiCo (Pizza Hut, Kentucky Fried Chicken, and Taco Bell) and Grand Metropolitan PLC (Burger King). In spite of the success enjoyed by fast-food operators in non-U.S. markets, casual dining operators were slower about entering the international markets. (See Appendix A for brief overviews of the publicly available data on the top 10 franchisers and casual dining chains that had ventured abroad as of early 1995.)

One of the major forces driving the expansion of the U.S. food-service industry was changing demographics. In the United States, prepared foods had become the fastest growing category because they relieved the cooking burdens on working parents. By the early 1990s, U.S. consumers were spending almost as much on restaurant fare as on prepared and nonprepared grocery store food.

In 1992 alone, there were more than 3,000 franchisers in the United States, operating about 540,000 franchised outlets—a new outlet of some sort opened about every 16 minutes. In 1992, franchised business sales totaled $757.8 billion, about 35 percent of all retail sales. Franchising was used as a growth vehicle by a variety of businesses including those related to automobiles, petroleum, cosmetics, convenience goods, computers, and financial services. However, food service constituted the franchising industry's largest single group. Franchised restaurants generally performed better than freestanding units. For example, in 1991 franchised restaurants experienced per store sales growth of 6.2 percent versus an overall restaurant industry growth rate of 3.0 percent. However, despite generally favorable sales and profits, franchisor–franchisee relationships were often difficult.

Abroad, franchisers operated an estimated 31,000 restaurant units. The significant increase in restaurant franchising abroad was driven by universal cultural trends, rising incomes, improved international transportation and communication, rising educational levels, increasing number of women entering the workforce, demographic concentrations of people in urban areas, and the willingness of younger generations to try new products.[5] However, there were substantial differences in these changes between the United States and other countries, and from country to country.

U.S. food themes were common throughout Canada as well as Western Europe and East Asia. As a result of the opening of previously inaccessible markets like Eastern Europe, the former Soviet Union, China, India, and Latin America, the potential for growth in U.S. food establishments abroad was enormous.

FACTORS AFFECTING COUNTRY SELECTION

Outback had not yet formed a firm plan for its international rollout. However, Hugh Connerty indicated the preliminary choice of markets targeted for entry:

> The first year will be Canada . . . Then we'll go to Hawaii . . . Then we'll go to South America and then develop our relationships in the Far East, Korea, Japan, . . . the Orient. At the second year we'll begin a relationship in Great Britain and from there a natural progression throughout Europe. But we view it as a very long-term project. I have learned that people [in other countries] think very different than Americans.

---

[5]Ref. AME 76 (KR).

U.S. restaurant chains had to consider numerous factors when determining which non-U.S. markets to enter. Some of these factors are summarized in Exhibit 5. Issues regarding infrastructure and demographics are expanded below. Included are some of the difficulties that U.S. restaurant companies encountered in various countries. Profiles of Canada, South Korea, Japan, Germany, Mexico, and Great Britain appear as Appendix B.

Infrastructure

A supportive infrastructure is essential. Proper means of transportation and communication, basic utilities such as power and water, and locally available supplies are important elements in the decision to introduce a particular restaurant concept. A restaurant must have the ability to get resources to its location. Raw materials for food preparation, equipment for manufacture of food served, employees, and customers must be able to enter and leave the establishment. The network that brings these resources to a firm is commonly called a supply chain.

The level of economic development is closely linked to the development of a supportive infrastructure. For example, the U.S. International Trade Commission said:

> Economic conditions, cultural disparities, and physical limitations can have substantial impact on the viability of foreign markets for a franchise concept. In terms of economics, the level of infrastructure development is a significant factor. A weak infrastructure may cause problems in transportation, communication, or even the provision of basic utilities such as electricity . . . International franchisers frequently encounter problems finding supplies in sufficient quantity, of consistent quality, and at stable prices . . . Physical distance also can adversely affect a franchise concept and arrangement. Long distances create communication and transportation problems, which may complicate the process of sourcing supplies, overseeing operations, or providing quality management services to franchisees.[6]

Some food can be sourced locally, some sourced regionally or nationally, and some imported. A country's transportation and distribution capabilities may become an element in the decision of the country's suitability for a particular restaurant concept.

Sometimes supply-chain issues require firms to make difficult decisions that affect the costs associated with the foreign enterprise. Family Restaurants Inc. encountered problems providing brown gravy for its CoCo's restaurants in South Korea. "If you want brown gravy in South Korea," said Barry Krantz, company president, "you can do one of two things. Bring it over, which is very costly. Or, you can make it yourself. So we figure out the flavor profile, and make it in the kitchen." Krantz concedes that a commissary is "an expensive proposition but the lesser of two evils."[7]

In certain instances a country may be so attractive for long-term growth that a firm dedicates itself to create a supply chain for its restaurants. An excellent illustration is McDonald's expansion into Russia in the late 1980s:

> Supply procurement has proved to be a major hurdle, as it has for all foreign companies operating in Russia. The problem has several causes: the rigid bureaucratic system, supply shortages caused by distribution and production problems, available supplies not meeting McDonald's quality standards . . . To handle these problems, McDonald's scoured the country for supplies, contracting for such items as milk, cheddar cheese, and beef. To help ensure

---

[6]"Industry and Trade Summary: Franchising" (Washington, DC: 1995), U.S. International Trade Commission, pp. 15–16.
[7]"World Hunger," *Restaurant Hospitality,* November 1994, p. 97.

EXHIBIT 5   Factors Affecting Companies' Entry into International Markets

External Factors

Country market factors
  Size of target market, competitive structure—atomistic, oligopolistic to
  monopolistic, local marketing infrastructure (distribution etc.)

Country production factors
  Quality, quantity and cost of raw materials, labor, energy and other productive
  agents in the target country as well as the quality and cost of the economic
  infrastructure (transportation, communications, port facilities, and similar
  considerations)

Country environmental factors
  Political, economic, and sociocultural character of the target country—government
  policies and regulations pertaining to international business

  Geographical distance—impact on transportation costs

  Size of the economy, absolute level of performance (GDP per capita), relative
  importance of economic sectors—closely related to the market size for a
  company's product in the target country

  Dynamics including rate of investment, growth in GDP, personal income, changes
  in employment; dynamic economies may justify entry modes with a high
  break-even point even when the current market size is below the break-even point

  Socio-cultural factors—cultural distance between home country and target country
  societies

  The closer the cultural distance, the quicker the entry into these markets (e.g.,
  Canada)

Home-country factors
  Big domestic market (allows a company to grow to a large size before it turns to
  foreign markets)

  Competitive structure; firms in oligopolistic industries tend to imitate the actions of
  rival domestic firms that threatens to upset competitive equilibrium; hence, when
  one firm invests abroad, rival firms commonly follow the lead

  High production costs in the home country

Internal Factors

Company product factors
  Products that are highly differentiated with distinct advantages over competitive
  products give sellers a significant degree of pricing discretion

  Requiring an array of pre- and post-purchase services makes it difficult for a
  company to market the product at a distance

  Products that require considerable adaptation

Company resource commitment factors
  The more abundant a company's resources in management, capital, technology,
  production skills, and marketing skills, the more numerous its entry mode options.
  Conversely, a company with limited resources is constrained to use entry modes
  that call for only a small resource commitment. Size is therefore a critical factor in
  the choice of an entry mode. Although resources are an influencing factor, it must
  be joined with a willingness to commit them to foreign market development. A high
  degree of commitment means that managers will select the entry mode for a
  target from a wider range of alternative modes than managers with a low
  commitment.

  The degree of a company's commitment to international business is revealed by
  the role accorded to foreign markets in corporate strategy, the status of the
  international organization, and the attitudes of managers.

Source: Franklin Root, *Entry Strategies into International Markets* (1987).

ample supplies of the quality products it needed, it undertook to educate Soviet farmers and cattle ranchers on how to grow and raise those products. In addition, it built a $40 million food-processing center about 45 minutes from its first Moscow restaurant. And because distribution was (and still is) as much a cause of shortages as production was, McDonald's carried supplies on its own trucks.[8]

Changing from one supply chain to another can affect more than the availability of quality provisions—it can affect the equipment that is used to process the food. For example,

> Wendy's nearly had its Korean market debut delayed by the belatedly discovered problem of thrice-frozen hamburger. After being thawed and frozen at each step of Korea's cumbersome three-company distribution channel, ground beef there takes on added water weight that threw off Wendy's patty specifications, forcing a hasty stateside retooling of the standard meat patty die used to mass-product its burgers.[9]

Looking at statistics such as the number of ports, airports, paved roads, and vehicles as a percentage of capital stock per worker can give a bird's-eye view of the level of infrastructure development.

Demographics

Just like the domestic market, restaurants in a foreign market need to know who their customers will be. Different countries will have different strata in age distribution, religion, and cultural heritage. These factors can influence the location, operations, and menus of restaurants in the country.

A popular example is India, where eating beef is contrary to the beliefs of the 80 percent of the population that is Hindu.[10] Considering India's population of nearly 1 billion people, restaurant companies find it hard to ignore this market even if beef is a central component of their traditional menu. "We're looking at serving mutton patties," says Ann Connolly, a McDonald's spokeswoman.[11]

Another area where religion plays a part in affecting the operation of a restaurant is the Middle East. Dairy Queen expanded to the region and found that during the Islamic religious observance of Ramadan no business was conducted; indeed, the windows of shops were boarded up.[12]

Age distribution can affect who should be in the target market. For example, "[McDonald's in Japan] also made modifications [not long after entering the market], such as targeting all advertising to younger people, because the eating habits of older Japanese are very difficult to change."[13] Age distribution can also affect the pool of labor available. In some countries over 30 percent of the population is under 15 years old; in other countries over 15 percent is 65 or older. These varying demographics could create a change in the profile for a potential employee in the new market.

Educational level may be an influence on both the buying public and the employee base. Literacy rates vary, and once again this can change the profile of employees as well as the buying public.

---

[8]*International Business Environments and Operations,* seventh ed., 1995, pp. 117–19.
[9]"U.S. Restaurant Chains Tackle Challenges of Asian Expansion," *Nation's Restaurant News,* February 14, 1994, p. 36.
[10]*CIA World Factbook,* India, 1995.
[11]"Big McMuttons," *Forbes,* July 17, 1995, p. 18.
[12]Interview with Cheryl Babcock, Professor, University of St. Thomas, October 23, 1995.
[13]"Franchise Management in East Asia," *Academy of Management Executive* 4, no. 2 (1990), p. 79.

Restaurant companies can compare countries by using statistical demographic components like literacy rates, total population and age distribution, and religious affiliations.

Income

Buying power is another demographic measure that can provide clues to how a restaurant might fare in the target country, as well as how the marketing program should position the company's products or services. Depending on the country and its economic development, the firm may have to attract a different segment than in the domestic market. For example, in Mexico,

> major U.S. firms have only recently begun targeting the country's sizable and apparently burgeoning middle class. For its part, McDonald's has changed tactics from when it first entered Mexico as a prestige brand aimed almost exclusively at the upper class, which accounts for about 5 percent of Mexico's population of some 93 million. With the development of its own distribution systems and improved economies of scale McDonald's lately has been slashing prices to aid its penetration into working-class population strongholds. "I'd say McDonald's pricing now in Mexico is 30 percent lower, in constant dollar terms, than when we opened in '85," says Moreno [Fernando Moreno, now international director of Peter Piper Pizza], who was part of the chain's inaugural management team there.[14]

There are instances where low disposable income does not translate to a disinterest in dining out in a Western-style restaurant. While Americans dine at a fast-food establishment such as McDonald's one or two times per week, lower incomes in the foreign markets make eating at McDonald's a special, once-a-month occurrence: "These people are not very wealthy, so eating out at a place like McDonald's is a dining experience."[15] China provides another example:

> At one Beijing KFC last summer, [the store] notched the volume equivalent of nine U.S. KFC branches in a single day during a $1.99 promotion of a two-piece meal with a baseball cap. Observers chalk up that blockbuster business largely to China's ubiquitous "spoiled-brat syndrome" and the apparent willingness of indulgent parents to spend one or two months' salaries on splurges for the only child the government allows them to rear.[16]

Statistics outlining the various indexes describing the country's gross domestic product, consumer spending on food, consumption and investment rates, and price levels can assist in evaluating target countries.

Trade Law

Trade policies can be friend or foe to a restaurant chain interested in expanding to other countries. Trade agreements such as the North American Free Trade Agreement (NAFTA) and the General Agreement on Tariffs and Trade (GATT) can help alleviate the ills of international expansion if they achieve their aims of "reducing or eliminating tariffs, reducing non-tariff barriers to trade, liberalizing investment and foreign exchange policies, and improving intellectual property protection . . . The recently signed Uruguay Round Agreements [of GATT] include the General Agreement on Trade in Services (GATS), the first multilateral, legally enforceable agreement covering trade and investment in the

---

[14]"U.S. Operators Flock to Latin America," *Nation's Restaurant News,* October 17, 1994, p. 47.

[15]Interview with Cheryl Babcock.

[16]"U.S. Restaurant Chains Tackle Challenges of Asian Expansion," p. 36.

services sector. The GATS is designed to liberalize trade in services by reducing or eliminating governmental measures that prevent services from being freely provided across national borders or that discriminate against firms with foreign ownership."[17]

Franchising, one of the most popular modes for entering foreign markets, scored a win in the GATS agreement. For the first time franchising was addressed directly in international trade talks. However, most countries have not elected to make their restrictions on franchising publicly known. The U.S. International Trade Commission pointed out:

> Specific commitments that delineate barriers are presented in Schedules of Commitments (Schedules). As of this writing, Schedules from approximately 90 countries are publicly available. Only 30 of these countries specifically include franchising in their Schedules . . . The remaining two-thirds of the countries did not schedule commitments on franchising. This means that existing restrictions are not presented in a transparent manner and additional, more severe restrictions may be imposed at a later date . . . Among the 30 countries that addressed franchising in the Schedules, 25 countries, including the United States, have committed themselves to maintain no limitations on franchising except for restrictions on the presence of foreign nationals within their respective countries.[18]

Despite progress, current international restaurant chains have encountered a myriad of challenges because of restrictive trade policies. Some countries make the import of restaurant equipment into their country difficult and expensive. The Asian region possesses "steep tariffs and [a] patchwork of inconsistent regulations that impede imports of commodities and equipment."[19]

OUTBACK'S GROWTH CHALLENGE

Hugh Connerty was well aware that there was no mention of international opportunities in Outback's 1994 annual report. The company distributed that annual report to shareholders at the April 1995 meeting. More than 300 shareholders packed the meeting to standing room only. During the question-and-answer period a shareholder had closely questioned the company's executives as to why the company did not pay a dividend. The shareholder pointed out that the company made a considerable profit in 1994. Chris Sullivan responded that the company needed to reinvest the cash that might be used as dividends in order to achieve the targeted growth. His response was a public and very visible commitment to continue the company's fast-paced growth. Connerty knew that international expansion had the potential to play a critical role in that growth. His job was to help craft a strategy that would assure Outback's continuing success as it undertook the new and diverse markets abroad.

(Outback's Web address is www.outbacksteakhouse.com.)

APPENDIX A

This appendix provides summaries of the 1995 publicly available data on (1) the two casual dining chains represented among the top 50 franchisers that had operations abroad (Applebee's and T.G.I. Friday's/Carlson Companies, Inc.) and (2) the top 10 franchisers in the restaurant industry, all of which are fast-food chains (Burger King,

---

[17]"Industry and Trade Summary: Franchising," p. 30.
[18]Ibid.
[19]"U.S. Restaurant Chains Tackle Challenges of Asian Expansion," p. 36.

Domino's, Hardee's, International Dairy Queen, Little Caesars, McDonald's, PepsiCo [including KFC, Taco Bell and Pizza Hut], Subway, and Wendy's).

(1) Casual Dining Chains with Operations Abroad

Applebee's

Applebee's was one of the largest casual dining chains in the United States. It ranked 20th in sales and 36th in stores for 1994.[20] Like most other casual dining operators, much of the company's growth had been fueled by domestic expansion. Opening in 1986,[21] the company experienced rapid growth and by 1994 had 507 stores.[22] The mode of growth was franchising, but in 1992 management began a program of opening more company-owned sites and buying restaurants from franchisees.[23] The company positioned itself as a neighborhood bar and grill and offered a moderately priced menu including burgers, chicken, and salads.

In 1995 Applebee's continued a steady program of expansion. Chairman and CEO Abe Gustin set a target of 1,200 U.S. restaurants and had also begun a slow push into international markets. In 1994 the company franchised restaurants in Canada and Curacao and signed an agreement to franchise 20 restaurants in Belgium, Luxembourg, and the Netherlands.[24]

Year	1989	1990	1991	1992	1993	1994†
Sales*	$ 29.9	$38.2	$45.1	$56.5	$ 117.1	$208.5
Net income*	$ 0.0	$ 1.8	$ 3.1	$ 5.1	$ 9.5	$ 16.9
EPS	$(0.10)	$0.13	$0.23	$0.27	$ 0.44	$ 0.62
Stock price close	$ 4.34	$2.42	$4.84	$9.17	$232.34	$13.38
Dividends	$ 0.00	$0.00	$0.01	$0.02	$ 0.03	$ 0.04
Number of employees	1,149	1,956	1,714	2,400	4,600	8,700

*($000)
†1994: ROE: 19.2%; Cash $17.2 million; Current ratio 1.13; Long-term debt $23.7 million

T.G.I. Friday's/Carlson Companies, Inc.

T.G.I. Friday's was owned by Carlson Companies Inc., a large, privately held conglomerate that had interests in travel (65 percent of 1994 sales); hospitality (30 percent); and marketing, employee training and incentives (5 percent). Carlson also owned a total of 345 Radisson Hotels and Country Inns plus 240 units of Country Kitchen International, a chain of family restaurants.

Most of Carlson's revenues came from its travel group. The company experienced an unexpected surprise in 1995 when U.S. airlines announced that it would put a cap on the commissions it would pay to book U.S. flights. Because of this change, Carlson decided to change its service to a fee-based arrangement and expected sales to drop by

[20]"Top 50 Franchisers," *Restaurant Business,* November 1, 1995, pp. 35–41.

[21]"Applebee's International, Inc.," *Hoover's Company Profile Database,* 1996 (Austin, TX: The Reference Press Inc. from America Online Service).

[22]"Top 50 Franchisers."

[23]"Applebee's International, Inc."

[24]Ibid.

$100 million in 1995.[25] To make up for this deficit, Carlson began to focus on building its hospitality group of restaurants and hotels through expansion in the United States and overseas.[26] The company experienced significant senior management turnover in the early 1990s and founder Curtis Carlson, age 80, had announced his intention to retire at the end of 1996. His daughter was announced as next head of the company.

T.G.I. Friday's grew 15.7 percent in revenue and 19.4 percent in stores in 1994. With 37 restaurants overseas, international sales were 12.7 percent of sales and 11.8 percent of stores systemwide.[27] Carlson operated a total of 550 restaurants in 17 countries.[28] About one-third of overall sales came from activities outside the United States.

Year	1986	1987	1988	1989	1990	1991	1992	1993	1994
Sales*	$1.3	$1.5	$1.8	$2.0	$2.2	$2.3	$2.9	$2.3	$2.3

*$ billions; no data available on income; excluding franchisee sales.

(2) The Top 10 Franchisers in the Restaurant Industry

Burger King

In 1994 Burger King was number two in sales and number four in stores among the fast-food competitors.[29] Burger King did not have the same presence in the global market as McDonald's and KFC. For example, McDonald's and KFC had been in Japan since the 1970s. Burger King opened its first Japanese locations in 1993 By that time, McDonald's already had over 1,000 outlets there. In 1994 Burger King had 1,357 non-U.S. stores (17.7 percent of systemwide total)[30] in 50 countries,[31] and overseas sales (18.7%) totaled $1.4 billion.[32]

Burger King was owned by the British food and spirits conglomerate Grand Metropolitan PLC. Among the company's top brands were Pillsbury, Green Giant, and Häagen-Dazs. Grand Met's situation had not been bright during the 1990s, with the loss of major distribution contracts like Absolut vodka and Grand Marnier liqueur, as well as sluggish sales for its spirits in major markets. Burger King was not a stellar performer, either, and undertook a major restructuring in 1993 to turn the tide including reemphasis on the basic menu, cuts in prices, and reduced overhead. After quick success, BK's CEO James Adamson left his post in early 1995 to head competitor Flasgston Corporation.

---

[25]"Carlson Companies, Inc.," *Hoover's Company Profile Database*, 1996.
[26]Ibid.
[27]"Top 50 Franchisers."
[28]"Carlson Companies, Inc."
[29]"Top 50 Franchisers."
[30]Ibid.
[31]"Grand Metropolitan PLC," *Hoover's Company Profile Database, 1996.*
[32]"Top 50 Franchisers."

Year	1986	1987	1988	1989	1990	1991	1992	1993	1994
Sales*	$5,291	$4,706	$6,029	$9,298	$9,394	$8,748	$7,913	$8,120	$7,780
Net income*	$ 261	$ 461	$ 702	$1,068	$1,069	$ 432	$ 616	$ 412	$ 450
EPS	$ 16	$ 19	$ 24	$ 28	$ 32	$ 33	$ 28	$ 30	$ 32
Stock price-close	$ 228	$ 215	$ 314	$ 329	$ 328	$ 441	$ 465	$ 476	$ 407
Dividend/Share	$ 5.1	$ 6.0	$ 7.5	$ 8.9	$ 10.2	$ 11.4	$ 12.3	$ 13.0	$ 14.0
Employees (000s)	131	129	90	137	138	122	102	87	64

*$ million
1994 Segments sales (profit): North America: 62% (69%); U.K. & Ireland 10% (10%); Africa & Middle East 2% (1%); Other Europe: 21% (18%); Other Countries: 5% (2%).
Segment Sales (Profits) by Operating Division: Drinks 43% (51%); Food 42% (26%); Retailing 14% (22%); Other 1% (1%).

Domino's

Domino's Pizza was eighth in sales and seventh in stores in 1994.[33] Sales and store unit growth had leveled off; from 1993 to 1994 sales grew 3.6 percent, and units only 1.4 percent.[34] The privately held company registered poor performance in 1993, with a 0.6 percent sales decline from 1992.[35] Observers suggested that resistance to menu innovations contributed to the share decline. In the early 1990's the company did add deep dish pizza and buffalo wings.

Flat company performances and expensive hobbies were hard on the owner and founder Thomas Monaghan. He attempted to sell the company in 1989 but could not find a buyer. He then replaced top management and retired from business to pursue a growing interest in religious activities. Company performance began to slide, and the founder emerged from retirement to retake the helm in the early 1990s.[36] Through extravagant purchases of the Detroit Tigers, Frank Lloyd Wright pieces, and antique cars, Monaghan put the company on the edge of financial ruin. He sold off many of his holdings (some at a loss), reinvested the funds to stimulate the firm, and once again reorganized management.[37]

Despite all its problems, Domino's had seen consistent growth in the international market. The company opened its first foreign store in 1983 in Canada.[38] Primary overseas expansion areas were Eastern Europe and India. By 1994 Domino's had 5,079 stores with 823 of these in 37 major international markets. International brought in 17 percent of 1994 sales. Over the next 10–15 years the company had contracts for 4,000 additional international units.[39] These units would give Domino's more international than domestic units.[40] International sales were 16.6 percent of total, and international stores were 16.5 percent of total in 1994.[41]

---

[33]"Top 50 Franchisers."
[34]Ibid.
[35]Ibid.
[36]"Domino's," *Hoover's Company Profile Database,* 1996.
[37]Ibid.
[38]Ibid.
[39]"Big News Over There!," *Restaurants and Institutions,* July 1, 1994.
[40]Ibid.
[41]"Top 50 Franchisers."

Years	1986	1987	1988	1989	1990	1991	1992	1993	1994
Sales*	$1,430	$2,000	$2,300	$2,500	$2,600	$2,400	$2,450	$2,200	$2,500
Stores	3,610	4,279	4,858	5,185	5,342	5,571	5,264	5,369	5,079
Employees (000s)	NA	NA	NA	NA	100	NA	NA	NA	115

*$ million

Hardee's

Hardee's was number six in sales and eleven in stores for 1994.[42] In 1981 the large diversified Canadian company, Imasco purchased the chain. Imasco also owned Imperial Tobacco (Player's and du Maurier, Canada's top two sellers), Burger Chef, two drug store chains, the development company Genstar, and CT Financial.

Hardee's had pursued growth primarily in the U.S.[43] Of all the burger chains in the top 10 franchises, Hardee's had the smallest international presence with 72 stores generating $63 million USD (1.8 percent and 2.0 percent of sales and stores, respectively) in 1994.[44]

Hardee's sales grew by about 2 percent annually for 1993 and 1994. A failed attempt by Imasco to merge their Roy Roger's restaurants into the Hardee's chain forced the parent company to maintain both brands. Hardee's attempted to differentiate from the other burger chains by offering an upscale burger menu, which received a lukewarm reception by consumers.[45]

Years	1986	1987	1988	1989	1990	1991	1992	1993	1994
Sales*	$5,522	$6,788	$7,311	$8,480	$9,647	$9,870	$9,957	$9,681	$9,385
Net income*	$ 184	$ 283	$ 314	$ 366	$ 205	$ 332	$ 380	$ 409	$ 506
EPS	$ 0.78	$ 1.12	$ 1.26	$ 1.44	$ 1.13	$ 0.64	$ 0.68	$ 0.74	$ 0.78
Stock price-close	$16.25	$12.94	$14.00	$18.88	$13.81	$18.25	$20.63	$20.06	$19.88
Dividends	$ 0.42	$ 0.48	$ 0.52	$ 0.56	$ 0.64	$ 0.64	$ 0.68	$ 0.74	$ 0.78
Employees (000)	NA	NA	NA	190	190	180	NA	200	200

*$ million—all $ in Canadian
1994 Segment Sales (Operating Income): CT Financial Services 47%; (28%); Hardee's 32% (11 %); Imperial Tobacco 16% (0%); Shoppers Drug Mart 2% (9%); Genstar Development 1% (2%).

International Dairy Queen, Inc.

Dairy Queen was one of the oldest fast-food franchises in the United States: the first store was opened in Joliet, Illinois in 1940.[46] By 1950, there were over 1,100 stores, and by 1960 Dairy Queen had locations in 12 countries.[47] Initial franchise agreements focused on the right to use the DQ freezers, an innovation that kept ice-cream at the constant 23 degrees (F) necessary to maintain the soft consistency. In 1970 a group of investors bought the franchise organization; but, the group has been only partly successful in standardizing the fast-food chain. In 1994 a group of franchisees filed an

---

[42]Ibid.

[43]"Imasco," *Hoover's Company Profile Database,* 1996.

[44]"Top 50 Franchisers."

[45]"Imasco," *Hoover's Company Profile Database,* 1996.

[46]"International Dairy Queen," *Hoover's Company Profile Database,* 1996.

[47]Ibid.

antitrust suit in an attempt to get the company to loosen its control on food supply prices and sources. DQ franchises cost $30,000 initially plus continuing payments of 4 percent of sales.

The company's menu consisted of ice cream, yogurt. and Brazier (hamburgers and other fast food) items. Menu innovations had included Blizzard (candy and other flavors mixed in the ice cream). The company had also acquired several companies including the Golden Skillet (1981), Karmelkorn (1986) and Orange Julius (1987).

In 1994, Dairy Queen ranked number seven in sales and six in stores.[48] By that same year the company had expanded its presence into 19 countries[49] with 628 stores and $300 million USD in international sales.[50] 1994 was an excellent year for DQ: sales were up 22.8 percent over 1993. This dramatic change (1993 scored an anemic 3.0 percent gain[51] was fueled by technology improvements for franchisees and international expansion.[52] In 1992 Dairy Queen opened company-owned outlets in Austria, China, Slovenia, and Spain.[53] DQ announced in 1995 that they had a plan to open 20 stores in Puerto Rico over a four year period.[54]

Years	1986	1987	1988	1989	1990	1991	1992	1993	1994
Sales*	$ 182	$ 210	$ 254	$ 282	$ 287	$ 287	$ 296	$ 311	$ 341
Net income*	$ 12	$ 15	$ 20	$ 23	$ 27	$ 28	$ 29	$ 30	$ 31
EPS	$0.42	$0.51	$ 0.70	$ 0.83	$ 0.97	$ 1.05	$ 1.12	$ 1.79	$ 1.30
Stock price-close	$7.75	$8.00	$11.50	$14.75	$16.58	$21.00	$20.00	$18.00	$16.25
Dividends	$ 0	$ 0	$ 0	$ 0	$ 0	$ 0	$ 0	$ 0	$ 0
Employees (000s)	459	503	520	549	584	592	672	538	564

*$ million.
1994 Restaurants: U.S. 87%; Canada 9%; Other 4%; Restaurants by type: DQ's: franchised by company: 62%; franchised by territorial operators 27%; foreign 3%; Orange Julius: 7%; Karmelkorn 1%, Golden Skillet less than 1%; Sales by Source: Good supplies & equipment to franchises 78%; service fees 16%; franchise sales & other fees 3%; real-estate finance & rental income 3%.

Little Caesars

Little Caesars ranked 10th in sales and 8th in stores for 1994. Sales growth had slowed to a halt: a 1992–93 increase of 12.2 percent evaporated into no increase for 1993–94.

These numbers were achieved without a significant overseas presence. Of the top ten franchises, only Hardee's had a smaller number of stores in foreign lands. Little Caesars received 3.5 percent of sales from foreign stores. Only 3.2 percent of the company's stores were in non-U.S. locations, namely, Canada, Czech and Slovak Republics, Guam, Puerto Rico. and the United Kingdom.

---

[48]"Top 50 Franchisers."

[49]"International Dairy Queen," *Hoover's Company Profile Database, 1996.*

[50]"Top 50 Franchisers."

[51]Ibid.

[52]"International Dairy Queen," *Hoover's Company Profile Database, 1996.*

[53]Ibid.

[54]Ibid.

Years	1986	1987	1988	1989	1990	1991	1992	1993	1994
Sales*	$520	$725	$908	$1,130	$1,400	$1,725	$2,050	$2,150	$2,000
# of stores	1,000	1,820	2,000	2,700	3,173	3,650	4,300	5,609	4,700
Employees	26	36	43	54	63	73	86	92	95

*$ million.

McDonald's

At the top in 1994 international sales and units, McDonald's Inc. was the most profitable retailer in the United States during the 1980s and into the 1990s. The company opened its first store in California in 1948, went public in 1965, and by 1994 had over 20 percent of the U.S. fast-food business. McDonald's opened its first international store in Canada in 1967. Growing domestic competition in the 1980s gave impetus to the company's international expansion. By 1994 there were over 15,000 restaurants under the golden arches in 79 countries. The non-U.S. stores provided about one-third of total revenues and half of the company's profits. McDonald's planned to open 1,200–1,500 new restaurants in 1995—most outside the United States. International markets had grown into an attractive venue for the burger giant because there was "less competition, lighter market saturation, and high name recognition" in international markets.[55]

The company's growth was fueled by aggressive franchising. In the early 1990s two-thirds of the McDonald's locations were franchised units and franchisees remained with the company an average of 20 years. McDonald's used heavy advertising ($1.4B in 1994) and frequent menu changes and other innovations (1963: Filet-O-Fish sandwich and Ronald McDonald; 1968: Big Mac and first TV ads; 1972: Quarter Pounder, Egg McMuffin [breakfast]; 1974: Ronald McDonald House; 1975: drive thru; 1979: Happy Meals; 1983: Chicken McNuggets; 1986: provided customers with list of products' ingredients; 1987: salads; 1980s: Value Menus; 1991: McLean DeLuxe, a low-fat hamburger [not successful] and experimentation with decor and new menu items at local level; 1993: first restaurants inside another store [Wal-Mart]). The company planned to open its first restaurants in India in 1996 with menus featuring chicken, fish sandwiches, and vegetable nuggets. There would be no beef items.

From 1993 to 1994, McDonald's grew 10.2 percent in sales and 8.7 percent in stores.[56] Because of their extensive experience in international markets, international sales had grown to 42.5 percent of their total revenues,[57] and half its profits.[58] Indeed, McDonald's was bigger than the 25 largest full-service chains put together.[59]

---

[55]Ibid.

[56]"Top 50 Franchisers."

[57]Ibid.

[58]"McDonald's," *Hoover's Company Profile Database, 1996.*

[59]Ibid.

Years	1986	1987	1988	1989	1990	1991	1992	1993	1994
Sales*	$4,144	$4,894	$5,566	$6,142	$6,640	$6,695	$7,133	$7,408	$8,321
Net income (in millions)	$ 480	$ 549	$ 656	$ 727	$ 802	$ 860	$ 959	$1,083	$1,224
EPS	$ 0.63	$ 0.73	$ 0.86	$ 0.98	$ 1.10	$ 1.18	$ 1.30	$ 1.46	$ 1.68
Stock price-close	$10.16	$11.00	$12.03	$17.25	$14.56	$19.00	$24.38	$28.50	$29.25
Dividends	$ 0.11	$ 0.12	$ 0.14	$ 0.16	$ 0.17	$ 0.18	$ 0.20	$ 0.21	$ 0.23
Employees (000s)	159	159	169	176	174	168	166	169	183

*$ million; 1994: debt ratio 41.2%; ROE 20.7%; cash $180 million; Current ratio 0.31.

PepsiCo: KFC, Taco Bell, and Pizza Hut (latter is not in the top 50)

PepsiCo owned powerful brand names such as Pepsi-Cola and Frito-Lay and was also the world's number one fast-food chain, with its ownership of KFC, Taco Bell. and Pizza Hut.

KFC was third in sales and stores of the top 50 franchises in 1994.[60] Active in the international arena since the late 1960s, KFC had been a major McDonald's competitor in non-U.S. markets. In 1994, the company had $3.6 billion in sales and 4,258 stores in other countries. McDonald's had been commonly number one in each country it entered, but KFC had been number two in international sales and had the number one sales spot in Indonesia. In 1994, KFC international revenues were 50.7 percent of sales with 45.3 percent of stores in international locations.

Taco Bell was fourth in sales and fifth in stores of the top 50 franchises in 1994.[61] This ranking had been achieved with minimal international business to date. Taco Bell had $130 million in sales and 162 stores internationally. The company attempted to enter the Mexican market in 1992 with a kiosk and cart strategy in Mexico City. The venture did not fare well, and Taco Bell soon pulled out of Mexico.[62] In 1994, international revenues were 3.0 percent of sales and 2.9 percent of stores were international locations. PepsiCo's corporate financial performance is summarized below:

Years	1986	1987	1988	1989	1990	1991	1992	1993	1994
Sales*	$9,291	$11,485	$13,007	$15,242	$17,803	$19,608	$21,970	$25,021	$28,474
Net income (in millions)	$ 458	$ 595	$ 762	$ 901	$ 1,077	$ 1,080	$ 1,302	$ 1,588	$ 1,784
EPS	$ 0.58	$ 0.76	$ 0.97	$ 1.13	$ 1.35	$ 1.35	$ 1.61	$ 1.96	$ 2.22
Stock price-close	$ 8.66	$ 11.11	$ 13.15	$ 21.31	$ 26.00	$ 22.88	$ 30.40	$ 40.88	$ 36.25
Dividend/share	$ 0.21	$ 0.22	$ 0.25	$ 0.31	$ 0.37	$ 0.44	$ 0.50	$ 0.58	$ 0.68
Employees (000s)	214	225	235	266	308	338	372	423	471

*$ million.
1994 segment sales (operating income): restaurants: 37% (22%); beverages 34% (37%); snack foods 29% (41%).

---

[60]"Top 50 Franchiser."

[61]Ibid.

[62]"U.S. Operators Flock to Latin America," *Nation's Restaurant News,* November 17, 1994.

Subway

Founded more than 29 years ago, Subway remained privately held in 1994. The company had experienced explosive growth over the past few years. It ranked ninth in sales and second in stores for 1994.[63] Sales grew 13.6 percent from 1993 to 1994, and 26 percent from 1992 to 1993.[64] Stores grew 17.1 percent from 1993 to 1994, and 15.3 percent from 1992 to 1993.[65] In 1994, Subway overtook KFC as the number two chain in number of stores behind McDonald's.[66] The company attributed its growth at least partially to an exceptionally low-priced and well-structured franchise program. In addition store sizes of 500–1,500 square feet were small. Thus, the investment for a Subway franchise was modest.[67]

The company's growth involved a deliberate strategy. The formula involved no cooking on site, except for the baking of bread. The company promoted the "efficiency and simplicity" of its franchise and advertised its food as "healthy, delicious, (and) fast."[68] The company advertised regularly on TV with a $25 million budget and planned to increase that significantly. All stores contributed 2.5 percent of gross sales to the corporate advertising budget. Subway's goal was to equal or exceed the number of outlets operated by the largest fast-food company in every market that it entered.[69] In most cases the firm's benchmark was burger giant McDonald's.

International markets played an emerging role in Subway's expansion. In 1994, international sales were 10.6 percent of sales, compared to 8.9 percent the previous year.[70] International stores were 9.5 percent of total in 1994, and 7.5 percent in 1993.[71] Subway boasted a total of 9,893 stores in all 50 states and 19 countries.[72]

Wendy's

Wendy's was number five in sales and number nine in stores for 1994.[73] In 1994, after 25 years of operation, Wendy's had grown to 4,411 stores.[74] This growth had been almost exclusively domestic until 1979, when Wendy's ventured out of the U.S. and Canada to open its first outlets in Puerto Rico, Switzerland, and West Germany. Wendy's granted J.C. Penney the franchise rights to France, Belgium, and Holland, and had one store opened in Belgium by 1980.[75]

Wendy's still saw opportunities for growth in the United States. Industry surveys had consistently ranked Wendy's burgers number one in quality but poor in convenience (Wendy's had one store for every 65,000 people while McDonald's, in contrast, had one for every 25,000).[76] Growth was driven primarily by franchising. In 1994, 71 percent of the stores were operated by franchisees and 29 percent by the company.

---

[63]"Top 50 Franchisers."
[64]Ibid.
[65]Ibid.
[66]Ibid.
[67]Subway's site on the Internet, accessed March 24, 1996.
[68]Ibid.
[69]Ibid.
[70]"Top 50 Franchisers."
[71]Ibid.
[72]Subway's site on the Internet, accessed March 24, 1996.
[73]"Top 50 Franchisers."
[74]Ibid.
[75]"Wendy's," *Hoover's Company Profile Database, 1996.*
[76]Ibid.

Company restaurants provided 90 percent of total sales while franchise fees provided 8 percent. The company had made menu and strategic changes at various points in its history. For example in 1977 the company first began TV advertising; 1979, introduced its salad bar; 1985, experimented with breakfast; 1986 and 1987, introduced Big Classic and SuperBar buffet (neither very successful); 1990, grilled chicken sandwich and 99-cent Super Value Menu Items; and 1992, packaged salads.

Wendy's planned to add about 150 restaurants each year in foreign markets.[77] With a presence of 236 stores in 33 countries in 1994, international was 9.1 percent of sales and 9.4 percent of stores in 1994.[78]

Years	1986	1987	1988	1989	1990	1991	1992	1993	1994
Sales*	$1,140	$1,059	$1,063	$1,070	$1,011	$1,060	$1,239	$1,320	$1,398
Net income*	$ (5)	$ 4	$ 29	$ 24	$ 39	$ 52	$ 65	$ 79	$ 97
EPS	$(0.05)	$ 0.04	$ 0.30	$ 0.25	$ 0.40	$ 0.52	$ 0.63	$ 0.76	$ 0.91
Stock price-close	$10.25	$ 5.63	$ 5.75	$ 4.63	$ 6.25	$ 9.88	$12.63	$17.38	$14.38
Dividend/share	$ 0.21	$ 0.24	$ 0.24	$ 0.24	$ 0.24	$ 0.24	$ 0.24	$ 0.24	$ 0.24
Employees (000s)	40	45	42	39	35	39	42	43	44

*$ million.

APPENDIX B

Country Summaries

Canada

In the 1990s Canada was considered an ideal first stop for U.S. business seeking to begin exporting. Per capita output, patterns of production, market economy, and business practices were similar to those in the United States. U.S. goods and services were well received in Canada: 70 percent of all Canadian imports were from the United States. Canada's market conditions were stable, and U.S. companies continued to see Canada as an attractive option for expansion.

Canada had one of the highest real growth rates among the OECD during the 1980s, averaging about 3.2 percent. The Canadian economy has softened during the 1990s, but Canadian imports of U.S. goods and services were expected to increase about 5 percent in fiscal year 1996.

Although Canada sometimes mirrored the United States, there are significant cultural and linguistic differences from the United States and between the regional markets in Canada. These differences highlighted the international marketing and were evident in the mounting friction between the English- and French-speaking areas of Canada. The conflict had potential for splitting of territory between the factions, slicing Canada into two separate countries. The prospect of this outcome left foreign investors tense.

---

[77]Ibid.

[78]"Top 50 Franchisers," Restaurant Business, November 1, 1995, pp. 35–41.

Note: the material in this appendix is adapted from the Department of Commerce Country Commercial Guides and the CIA World Fact Book.

Germany

In the mid-1990s Germany was the largest economy in Europe, and the fifth largest importer of U.S. goods and services. Since reunification in 1990, the eastern part of Germany had continued to receive extensive infusions of aid from western Germany, and these funds were only just beginning to show an impact. The highly urbanized and skilled West German population enjoyed a very high standard of living with abundant leisure time. In 1994, Germany emerged from a recession, and scored a GDP of $2 trillion.

A unique feature of Germany was the unusually even distribution of both industry and population—there was no single business center for the country. This was a challenge for U.S. firms. They had to establish distribution networks that adequately covered all areas of the country. In Germany there was little opportunity for regional concentration around major population centers as in the United States.

The country was a good market for innovative high-tech goods and high-quality food products. Germans expected high-quality goods, and would reject a less expensive product if quality and support were not in abundance. Strongest competition for U.S. firms were the German domestic firms not only because of their home-grown familiarity of the market, but also because of the consumers' widely held perception that German products were "simply the best."

A recurring complaint from Germans was the prevalent "here today, gone tomorrow" business approach of American firms. Germans viewed business as a long-term commitment to support growth in markets, and did not always receive the level and length of attention necessary from U.S. companies to satisfy them.

Conditions in the former area of East Germany were not the doomsday picture often painted, nor were they as rosy as the German government depicts. It would take 10–15 years for the eastern region of the country to catch up to the western region in terms of per capita income and standard of living.

Japan

Japan had the second largest economy in the world. Overall economic growth in Japan over the past 35 years had been incredible: 10 percent average growth during the 1960s, 5 percent in the 1970s and 80s. Growth ground to a halt during the 1990s due to tight fiscal policy. The government tightened fiscal constraints in order to correct the significant devaluation of the real estate markets. The economy posted a 0.6 percent growth in 1994 largely due to consumer demand. The overall economic outlook remained cloudy, but the outlook for exports to Japan remained positive.

Japan was a highly homogeneous society with business practices characterized by long-standing close relationships among individuals and firms. It took time for Japanese businessmen to develop relationships and for non-Japanese business people the task of relationship building in Japan was formidable. It was well known that the Japan's market was not as open as the United States but the U.S. government had mounted multifaceted efforts to help U.S. businesspeople to "open doors." While these efforts were helpful, most of the responsibility in opening the Japanese market to U.S. goods or services remained with the individual firm. Entering Japan was expensive and generally required four things: (1) financial and management capabilities and a Japanese-speaking staff residing within the country, (2) modification of products to suit Japanese consumers, (3) a long-term approach to maximizing market share reasonable profit levels, and (4) careful monitoring of Japanese demand, distribution, competitors, and government. Despite the challenges of market entry, Japan ranked as the second largest importer of U.S. goods and services.

Historically Japanese consumers were conservative and brand conscious, although the recession during the 1990s nurtured opportunities for "value" entrants. Traditional conformist buying patterns were still prominent, but more individualistic habits were developing in the younger Japanese aged 18–21. This age cohort had a population of 8 million people, and boasted a disposable income of more than $35 billion.

Japanese consumers were willing to pay a high price for quality goods. However, they had a well-earned reputation for having unusually high expectations for quality. U.S. firms with high-quality, competitive products had to be able to undertake the high cost of initial market entry. For those that were willing, Japan could provide respectable market share and attractive profit levels.

Mexico

Mexico had experienced a dramatic increase in imports from the United States since the late 1980s. During 1994 the country's experienced 20 percent growth over 1993. In 1994, Mexico's peso experienced a massive devaluation brought on by investor anxiety and capital flight. Although the Mexican government implemented tight fiscal measures to stabilize the peso, their efforts could not stop the country from plunging into a serious recession.

Inflation rose as a result of the austerity policies and it was expected to be between 42 and 54 percent in 1995. Negative economic growth was anticipated in 1995 as well. The U.S. financial assistance package gave Mexico nearly $50 billion and restored stability to the financial markets by mid-1995. The government was taking measures to improve the country's infrastructure. Mexico's problems mask that its government had, on the whole, practiced sound economic fundamentals.

Mexico was still committed to political reform despite the current economic challenges. After ruling the government uninterrupted for 60 years, the PRI party had begun to lose some seats to other political parties. Mexico was slowly evolving into a multiparty democracy.

Despite the economic misfortunes of recent years, Mexico remained the United State's third largest trading partner. Mexico still held opportunities for U.S. firms able to compete in the price-sensitive recessionary market. Mexico had not wavered on NAFTA since its ratification and in the mid-1990s 60 percent of U.S. exports to Mexico entered duty free.

South Korea

South Korea had been identified as one of the U.S. Department of Commerce's 10 "Big Emerging Markets." The country's economy overcame tremendous obstacles after the Korean War in the 1950s left the country in ruins. The driving force behind South Korea's growth was export-led development and energetic emphasis on entrepreneurship. Annual real GDP growth from 1986 to 1991 was over 10 percent. This blistering pace created inflation, tight labor markets, and a rising current account deficit. Fiscal policy in 1992 focused on curbing inflation and reducing the deficit. Annual growth, an enviable 5 percent in 1992, rose to 6.3 percent in 1993. Fueled by exports, 1994's growth was a heady 8.3 percent. South Korea's GDP was larger than that of Russia, Australia, or Mexico.

The American media had highlighted such issues as student demonstrations, construction accidents, and North Korean nuclear problems and trade disputes. Investors needed to closely monitor developments related to North Korea. However, the political landscape in South Korea had been stable enough over the 1980s to fuel tremendous economic expansion. The country was undertaking significant infrastructure improvements. Overall, South Korea was a democratic republic with an open society and a free press. It was a modern, cosmopolitan, fast-paced and dynamic country with abundant business opportunities for savvy American businesses.

There had been staggering development of U.S. exports to South Korea: $21.6 billion in 1994 and over $30 billion expected in 1995. While South Korea was 22 times smaller than China in terms of population, it imported two times more U.S. goods and services than China in 1994.

Although South Korea ranked as the United State's sixth largest export market, obstacles for U.S. firms still remained. Despite participation in the Uruguay Round of GATT and related trade agreements, customs clearance procedures and regulations for labeling, sanitary standards, and quarantine often served as significant non-tariff barriers.

The United Kingdom (or Great Britain)

The United Kingdom (UK) was the United States' fourth largest trading partner and the largest market for U.S. exports in Europe. Common language, legal heritage, and business practices facilitated U.S. entry into the British market.

The UK had made significant changes to its taxation, regulation, and privatization policies that changed the structure of the British economy and increased its overall efficiency. The reward for this disciplined economic approach had been sustained, modest growth during the 1980s and early 1990s. GDP grew 4.2 percent in 1994, the highest level in six years. The UK trimmed its deficit from $75 billion in fiscal 1994 to $50 billion in fiscal 1995.

The UK had no restrictions on foreign ownership and movement of capital. There was a high degree of labor flexibility. Efficiencies had soared in the UK and in the mid-1990s the country boasted the lowest real per unit labor cost of the Group of Seven (G7) industrialized countries.

The shared cultural heritage and warm relationship with the United States translated into the British finding U.S. goods and services as attractive purchases. These reasons, coupled with British policy emphasizing free enterprise and open competition, made the UK the destination of 40 percent of all U.S. investment in the European Union.

The UK market was based on a commitment to the principles of free enterprise and open competition. Demand for U.S. goods and services was growing. The abolition of many internal trade barriers within the European Common Market enabled European-based firms to operate relatively freely. As a result, U.S. companies used the UK as a gateway to the rest of the European Union. Of the top 500 British companies, one in eight was a U.S. affiliate. Excellent physical and communications infrastructure combined with a friendly political and commercial climate were expected to keep the UK as a primary target for U.S. firms for years to come.

ROCKY MOUNTAIN ADVENTURES, INC.

John E. Gamble, *University of South Alabama*

As Bill Peisner's LanChile flight ascended from the Arturo Benitez Airport in Santiago, Chile, Bill looked to the Andes Mountains off the Boeing 767's starboard wing and began to reflect on his most recent trip to South America. During the past six and a half days, he and his six fellow anglers had caught and released over 500 rainbow, brown, and brook trout, most of which ranged from 1 to 3 pounds, but many of which were of trophy size—the largest just over 6 pounds. The fly-fishing was matched by the beauty of the rivers that ran within view of the Tres Monjas peaks, whose snow-capped granite spires soared over 7,000 feet from their base, and was surpassed only by the camaraderie of the group of trout anglers. As Bill assessed the trip, he found it difficult to believe that this lifestyle was actually an important part of his job.

Bill and his partner, Dave Costlow, were the owners of Rocky Mountain Adventures (RMA), an outdoor outfitter in Fort Collins, Colorado. The company sold and rented outdoor recreation equipment, led whitewater rafting excursions on five Colorado rivers, guided fly-fishing excursions in Colorado and Wyoming, and coordinated guided fly-fishing, hiking, and rafting expeditions in Siberia and the Patagonia region of Chile and Argentina. The scope of RMA's operations and its annual revenues had increased substantially since the company had been purchased by Dave and Bill in 1993. Prior to acquisition by its current owners, RMA was a small Fort Collins outfitter with approximately 5,000 rafting customers per year. In 1997, RMA, under the leadership of Peisner and Costlow, generated nearly $1 million in revenues from retail sales of outdoor equipment, apparel, and gear; fees charged for guided rafting and fishing trips; photography sales; paddlesport and fly-fishing instructional fees; and outdoor equipment rentals.

Prior to the spring of 1998, Bill Peisner and Dave Costlow had identified a number of avenues for additional growth. The opportunities they had identified included adding a second-floor restaurant to their Fort Collins store, building a mountain outpost and lodge in northern Colorado or southern Wyoming, attempting to build more customer traffic on some of the rivers where they currently outfitted whitewater trips, and putting together additional fly-fishing and rafting expeditions in exotic international locations.

Bill's 12-hour flight gave him time to think over the success of the company and ponder RMA's future. The company had experienced considerable growth and had allowed the partners to lead exciting lives, but it had yet to provide an exceptional return on their investment. Bill thought by the time he arrived in Denver he might have a better evaluation of some of the growth opportunities that he and Dave had discussed prior to his trip to Patagonia.

COMPANY BACKGROUND

Rocky Mountain Adventures, Inc., was established as Adrift Adventures in the late 1970s in Fort Collins, Colorado, by Pat and Robin Franklin. The Franklins, who had long been interested in outdoor recreation, began the business to add a degree of excitement to their lives and to supplement their Colorado State University salaries. During its first decade, the company was operated out of the Franklins' garage, where they stored their rafts, paddles, life preservers, and other gear. Nearly every Saturday during the summer months, the Franklins would load their rafts onto a trailer and drive to Ted's Place—a small Fort Collins service station—to meet rafters who had called the Franklins' home earlier in the week to schedule a rafting trip. Once all of the rafters had converged on Ted's Place, the excursion party would leave for the Cache La Poudre River outside of town to spend the day negotiating the river's rapids.

Adrift Adventures' volume gradually increased over the years to the point where the Franklins were forced to hire additional guides during the summer rafting season in Colorado and to rent a warehouse to store the company's rafts. By 1993 the company's revenues and net income had grown to approximately $125,000 and $30,000, respectively. The Franklins were quite pleased with Adrift Adventures' performance, but were forced to sell the business when Pat accepted a job as an assistant professor at San Francisco State University.

A Change in Ownership

Dave Costlow's interest in outdoor recreation dated back to his teenage years in Virginia, when he began to enjoy canoeing. As his canoeing proficiency developed during his 20s, Dave became interested in other paddlesports like rafting and kayaking. Dave eventually became a rafting guide with the University of Virginia's (UVA) outdoor recreation outing program while he was enrolled in the university's Ph.D. program in educational psychology during the late 1980s and early 1990s. Bill Peisner's outdoor experiences began when he fished and rafted along Michigan's Red Cedar River as a young adolescent. Bill continued to fish and raft during high school and through his college years at Rollins College and UVA. Like Dave, Bill met other rafters at UVA and eventually began to work with the university's outdoor recreation program.

Bill and Dave worked together on a number of the university rafting excursions, and as they neared the completion of their graduate programs they began to discuss the possibility of jointly operating an outfitting business in Utah, Colorado, or Wyoming. The director of the UVA outdoor recreation outing program knew of Bill and Dave's interest in purchasing a rafting business and told Bill he had heard that Adrift Adventures was for sale. Bill was elated that he had heard so quickly of an outfitting business for sale and called the Franklins to gather some basic information about the business and its sales price. After Bill briefed Dave on his conversation with the Franklins, the two decided to fly to Fort Collins in October 1992 to more closely inspect the business. While Bill and Dave were in Colorado and immediately upon their return, they evaluated the potential acquisition by examining the outdoor recreation opportunities in Colorado and assessing Adrift Adventures' competitive position in the local outfitting industry.

Bill and Dave determined that Adrift Adventures was in pretty good shape from both competitive and financial standpoints, and there appeared to be ample opportunity to grow and build the company into a much more successful business. Dave, Bill, and the Franklins all agreed on a price for the business, and in March 1993 Bill and Dave took over operations. During the first couple of months after the transfer of ownership, the new partners changed the name of the company to Rocky Mountain Adventures and took advantage of the off-season by developing strategies to attract customers and creating a set of operating policies and procedures. The partners also closely evaluated the retail store's inventory of merchandise, rental equipment, and rafting equipment. The company's assets were adequate but very limited, and it was obvious that Bill and Dave would have to make substantial investments into the business beyond the purchase price.

The New Partners' Strategy to Grow the Business   At the beginning of their first year as partners, Bill and Dave agreed not to take salaries so that all excess cash flows could be invested back into the business. Capital expenditures primarily went to improve the Fort Collins retail store; to open rafting outposts in Buena Vista, Colorado, and Estes Park, Colorado; and to purchase additional inventory and equipment. In 1996 Bill and Dave believed that the capital requirements of the business had subsided and that they could begin taking meager annual salaries.

The first strategy implemented by the partners in 1993 was to increase the number of RMA's rafting customers. The company was permitted by the U.S. government to take 100–120 rafters per day down the Cache La Poudre (pronounced *pooder*), but on average RMA sold only 50 guided rafting trips per day. Bill and Dave believed that the company could approach its limit of 100 rafters per day by developing a differentiation strategy keyed to a distinctive image and by utilizing a more effective marketing approach.

For the most part, rafting outfitters had something of a ragtag image. Many river outfitters operated lean organizations, did only essential maintenance on equipment, and often operated on the fly with only minimal attention to detail. Whereas it was common for many of the outfitters to use heavily worn equipment and to transport rafters from their outposts to the river in old school buses with a dilapidated appearance, RMA purchased and maintained quality rafts, and emblazoned its white buses with a big blue surging wave. The company marketed its trips to individual vacationers and to corporations and other organizations that might be interested in large group trips. The company reached its regulated limit of rafters within three years after implementing the new marketing campaign. Over the next year, RMA began offering rafting trips on four other Colorado rivers to continue to increase its annual revenues.

The company expanded its guided outdoor recreation activities to fly-fishing in 1995 when the U.S. Department of Agriculture (USDA) Forest Service issued a prospectus for guided fly-fishing trips on the Cache La Poudre River. During this same time, the company also began to offer kayak instruction courses in the Fort Collins area to both area residents and visitors. International fly-fishing, rafting, and hiking expeditions were added to the company's array of outfitting services in 1994 and 1995 as part of the company's strategy for growth. Exhibit 1 provides RMA's income statements for 1994–97. A balance sheet for year-end 1997 is presented in Exhibit 2.

EXHIBIT 1   Rocky Mountain Adventures, Inc., Income Statements, 1994–97

	1997	1996	1995	1994
Revenues				
Guided rafting trips	$494,104	$456,689	$416,200	$286,246
Guided fishing trips	9,847	7,696	9,394	336
International excursions	109,874	23,222	45,048	10,940
Equipment rentals	66,895	40,207	40,590	15,314
Photography	47,855	41,828	28,807	15,598
Instruction	21,235	12,552	7,537	5,356
Retail sales				
Food	2,341	3,689	3,679	1,860
T-shirts	32,755	30,671	36,102	21,436
Accessories	20,854	21,972	13,278	10,367
Gear	158,958	126,539	50,360	25,444
Books	3,437	2,226	2,212	998
Other	7,203	10,170	10,340	9,189
Total revenues	$975,358	$777,461	$663,547	$403,084
Cost of retail sales	184,590	171,461	85,571	101,222
Gross profit	$790,768	$606,000	$577,976	$301,862
Expenses				
Advertising	48,750	45,374	40,258	40,994
Bank and credit card processing fees	11,058	9,680	8,790	6,005
Instruction expenses	11,761	6,548	3,893	2,280
Bad debt	204	0	38	0
Insurance	34,873	29,622	21,229	21,751
Interest expense	23,226	11,449	15,661	7,688
Legal and accounting	10,133	8,424	2,696	3,358
Licensing and memberships	5,830	6,107	5,959	2,753
Depreciation	32,654	24,391	25,956	34,002
Amortization	2,539	2,539	2,452	2,452
Travel expense	5,695	4,607	1,997	3,512
International trip expenses	91,960	17,252	37,865	0
Office and operating supplies	14,478	12,803	7,028	5,173
Rafting trip expenses	65,947	55,273	52,416	66
Vehicle repair	11,963	17,360	13,241	8,615
Skiing/kayak rental expenses	4,410	132	175	0
Photography expenses	24,144	20,060	10,099	2,135
Fishing trip expenses	2,179	1,244	2,647	0
Rent	31,670	32,252	36,908	36,130
Property maintenance/repair	9,529	14,059	12,857	0
Telephone	12,845	16,168	15,643	14,882
Utilities	8,102	8,393	6,840	4,522
Wages	306,931	257,560	168,910	118,658
Payroll taxes	36,776	30,871	19,663	12,952
Total expenses	$807,657	$632,168	$513,221	$327,928
Net income	($16,889)	($26,168)	$64,755	($26,066)

Source: Rocky Mountain Adventures, Inc.

EXHIBIT 2   Rocky Mountain Adventures, Inc., Balance Sheet, December 31, 1997

Assets

Current assets

Cash	($12,937)
Deposits	6,300
Prepaid expenses	4,543
Receivables	79
Inventory—food & beverage	664
Inventory—T-shirts	4,876
Inventory—accessories	6,090
Inventory—gear	50,037
Inventory—books	1,546
Total current assets	61,198

Property and equipment

Ski and snowshoe equipment	9,164
River equipment	6,227
Fishing equipment	1,099
Rental gear and instruction kayaks	6,118
Inflatable boats	76,142
Computers and office machines	11,340
Photo lab equipment	10,231
Furniture	1,523
Main office remodeling	20,336
Buena Vista remodeling	840
Leasehold improvements	19,032
Retail fixtures	8,231
Signage	8,756
Telephone system	3,250
Tools and equipment	2,290
Vehicles and trailers	34,132
Accumulated depreciation	(114,899)
Total property and equipment	103,812

Other assets

Buena Vista property	84,141
Main office land improvement	3,781
Chile cabin	20,626
Chile assets	7,524
Goodwill	33,000
Other	38,691
Accumulated depreciation	(9,660)
Total other assets	178,103
Total assets	$343,113

EXHIBIT 2   Rocky Mountain Adventures, Inc., Balance Sheet,
            December 31, 1997 (*continued*)

Liabilities and Stockholders' Equity

Current liabilities

Accounts payable	$13,940
Use tax payable	(24)
Gift certificates	3,515
Deferred revenue	9,454
Layaway	756
Line of credit	129,600
Note payable—stockholders	16,273
Note payable—other short term loans	7,200
Total current liabilities	180,714

Long-term liabilities

Note payable—bank	6,624
Note payable—Buena Vista mortgage	64,545
Total long-term liabilities	71,169
Total liabilities	251,883

Stockholders' equity

Common stock	67,200
Additional paid in capital	7,594
Retained earnings	16,436
Total stockholders' equity	91,230
Total liabilities and stockholders' equity	$343,113

Source: Rocky Mountain Adventures, Inc.

OVERVIEW OF THE OUTDOOR RECREATION INDUSTRY

The outdoor recreation industry included the manufacture of equipment and the provision of services for such activities as mountain biking, mountain and rock climbing, camping, fishing, hunting, hiking, backpacking, kayaking, canoeing, rafting, skiing, and golf. Some of these activities required highly specialized equipment and the use of a guide or instructor, while others required virtually no specialized equipment or unique skills. In 1995, almost 67 percent of Americans walked for recreation, 44 percent enjoyed swimming, and 27 percent found bird-watching a pleasurable recreation. Participation rates for outdoor activities declined as the need for specialized equipment and skills increased. About 25 percent of Americans camped and hiked, 14 percent played golf, about 8 percent went downhill skiing, 8 percent participated in river rafting or floating, 4.5 percent enjoyed mountain climbing, 3 percent went fly-fishing, and 0.7 percent kayaked on U.S. lakes, streams, and rivers.

Participation rates varied greatly by income level and age. Only about one-third of low-income families or individuals participated in outdoor activities, and even fewer participated in outdoor recreation that required travel or expensive equipment. Even though middle-income and high-income households accounted for most outdoor recreation that required travel or specialized equipment, members of high-income households were about twice as likely to engage in more costly outdoor recreation than middle-income individuals. Exhibit 3 presents U.S. participation rates for selected outdoor activities in 1987 and 1993–97, and Exhibit 4 presents U.S. participation rates based on income level.

EXHIBIT 3 U.S. Participation Rates for Selected Outdoor Activities, 1987, 1993–97 (U.S. population, 6 years or older, in millions)

Recreational Activity	1987	1993	1994	1995	1996	1997	% Change (1996–97)	% Change (1987–97)
Golf	22.3	24.2	26.6	24.6	23.7	26.3	+11.0	+18.0
Downhill skiing	13.8	13.7	14.0	13.0	13.7	12.4	(9.2)	(9.9)
Hiking/backpacking	19.8	18.9	21.0	21.0	19.9	20.0	+0.4	+0.7
Water skiing	14.2	11.9	11.1	11.0	9.6	8.4	(12.7)	(12.7)
Mountain biking	1.5	7.4	9.2	9.4	9.9	8.4	(14.5)	+458.0
Mountain/rock climbing	—	4.7	6.2	4.8	4.7	4.7	(0.3)	+0.2*
Basketball	35.7	42.1	47.3	46.5	45.6	45.1	(1.0)	+26.2
Softball	31.0	30.1	30.8	26.0	25.3	22.1	(12.6)	(28.6)
Camping	35.2	34.8	39.5	38.6	38.0	41.2	+8.4	+17.0
Fly-fishing	10.4	6.1	6.9	6.2	5.7	6.0	+6.0	(42.1)
Snowboarding	—	2.2	2.4	3.4	3.2	4.2	+32.8	+228.0†

*Seven-year change
†Nine-year change
Source: Sporting Goods Manufacturers Association, *Sports Participation Trends Report, 1997.*

EXHIBIT 4 U.S. Participation Rates for Selected Outdoor Activities by Household Income, 1995

Recreational Activity	Household Income		Percentage Point Difference
	$100,000 or More	$25,000–$49,999	
Golf	30.0%	14.5%	15.5
Downhill skiing	20.7	7.8	12.9
Swimming	59.6	48.1	11.5
Hiking	32.8	26.2	6.6
Canoeing	9.9	4.2	5.7
Water skiing	14.8	9.4	5.4
River rafting, floating	11.7	7.9	3.8
Walking	74.8	71.9	2.9
Kayaking	3.1	1.3	1.8
Mountain climbing	6.1	4.6	1.5
Rock climbing	5.1	3.6	1.5
Snowboarding	0.9	1.0	(0.1)
Basketball	11.8	13.2	(1.4)
Softball	10.4	15.2	(4.8)
Camping	19.6	24.4	(4.8)

Source: USDA Forest Service, *1994–1995 National Survey on Recreation and the Environment.*

Growth or decline in various outdoor activities was explained to some degree by the composition of the U.S. population. The 81 million baby boomers (those born between 1945 and 1964) were the most important consumer group to the outdoor recreation industry because of their discretionary purchasing power, lifestyles that favored recreational activities, and a growing amount of leisure time as they approached retirement.

EXHIBIT 5   U.S. Participation Rates for Selected Outdoor Activities, by Age Group, 1995

Recreational Activity	Age					
	16–24	25–29	30–39	40–49	50–59	60 and Over
Golf	15.3%	19.0%	17.7%	15.4%	12.0%	10.3%
Downhill skiing	15.5	14.3	9.9	8.0	3.9	1.0
Swimming	60.6	54.7	53.0	44.8	34.8	21.8
Hiking	31.5	30.2	29.5	27.0	18.1	9.6
Canoeing	11.7	9.3	8.2	7.4	4.9	1.9
Water skiing	17.7	15.8	10.7	7.1	3.6	0.8
River rafting, floating	15.8	11.9	8.4	6.3	3.3	1.4
Walking	68.2	72.5	74.7	72.0	65.5	51.8
Kayaking	2.7	1.8	1.3	1.4	0.9	0.2
Mountain climbing	8.2	6.3	5.3	3.7	2.3	1.7
Rock climbing	8.3	5.5	3.9	2.9	1.8	0.7
Snowboarding	1.5	1.1	0.9	0.9	0.6	0.1
Basketball	31.0	18.7	14.1	8.7	4.7	1.1
Softball	20.4	22.6	17.7	12.1	6.3	1.9
Camping	27.6	25.5	26.0	22.6	15.6	9.0

Source: USDA Forest Service, *1994–1995 National Survey on Recreation and the Environment.*

As a generation, baby boomers had adopted a "back-to-nature" philosophy, but it was expected that as baby boomers aged, their spending on outdoor activities would become secondary to that for their children's college education and their own retirement and future medical expenses. The demographic composition of the United States would continue to shift, as there were 5 million fewer adults under the age of 35 in 1997 than in 1988. In addition, the number of people aged 30 to 44 was expected to decline by 7 million and the number of people aged 45 to 70 was expected to increase by more than 20 million between 1998 and 2008.

The projected decline in the number of adults aged 30 to 44 was based on the current size of Generation X (Americans born between 1965 and 1979), which was approximately 44 million. Like baby boomers, Generation Xers enjoyed outdoor recreation, but since their generation was about one-half the size of the generation before them, it was expected that boomers would continue to dominate U.S. spending patterns for years to come. Like the original boomers, the 62 million echo boomers or Generation Y (Americans born between 1980 and 1995) were destined to become a dominating consumer group with a projected annual buying power of more than $100 billion. Manufacturers such as Frito-Lay and Nike were already taking actions to build loyalty to their brands among the echo boomers, who would represent 30 million teenage consumers by 2006.

Exhibit 5 presents the U.S. participation rates for selected outdoor recreation activities by age. Most Americans tended to participate less in outdoor activities as they became older—especially strenuous activities like downhill skiing, water skiing, basketball, and mountain or rock climbing. Walking, hiking, swimming, golf, softball, and camping were the most common outdoor activities for those aged 40 and over. Even though print and broadcast media provided vast coverage of strenuous outdoor activities like rock climbing, kayaking, whitewater rafting, and snowboarding, these activities were performed by

EXHIBIT 6 U.S. Participation Rates for Selected Outdoor Activities,
           by Gender, 1995

Recreational Activity	Gender		Percentage Point Difference
	Men	Women	
Golf	22.4%	7.8%	14.6
Downhill skiing	10.5	6.5	4.0
Swimming	45.6	43.1	2.5
Hiking	27.1	20.9	6.2
Canoeing	9.1	5.1	4.0
Water skiing	11.5	6.6	4.9
River rafting, floating	8.7	6.6	2.1
Walking	65.1	68.5	(3.4)
Kayaking	1.8	0.9	0.9
Mountain climbing	5.8	3.3	2.5
Rock climbing	5.1	2.5	2.6
Snowboarding	1.0	0.7	0.3
Basketball	18.5	7.4	11.1
Softball	16.2	10.1	6.1
Camping	22.9	18.7	4.2

Source: USDA Forest Service, *1994–1995 National Survey on Recreation and the Environment.*

relatively few people, regardless of age. Less than 10 percent of those aged 16 to 24 actually participated in kayaking and rock climbing, and fewer than 150,000 people annually engaged in other high-risk outdoor activities like skydiving.

The typical adventure outdoor recreation enthusiast was a 25–34-year-old unmarried male earning between $40,000 and $60,000 per year. However, much of the growth in outdoor recreation participation rates was accounted for by young women. Women's participation in a variety of outdoor activities had grown substantially in the 1990s. Between 1991 and 1996, women's participation in hiking had increased by 10 percent, in canoeing by 17 percent, in backpacking by 21 percent, and in whitewater rafting and kayaking by 116 percent. Overall women's participation in outdoor and physical fitness activities grew by 11.8 percent between 1987 and 1996, while men's participation grew by 2.9 percent over the same time period. Exhibit 6 presents 1995 participation rates for selected outdoor activities by gender.

The Market for Outdoor Recreation Equipment

Almost all outdoor recreation required some type of equipment. Camping required equipment ranging from tents to canteens; snowboarding and downhill skiing required special apparel and ski equipment; water sports like rafting, canoeing, and kayaking required a boat, life vests, and paddles; and rock climbing required ropes, lanyards, harnesses, and specialized footwear. Specialized footwear was even available for serious walkers. In 1997, the total U.S. sporting goods industry (apparel, footwear, and sports equipment) grew by 5.2 percent to reach $44.1 billion at the wholesale level. The wholesale value of specialized outdoor equipment was $1.6 billion in 1997. Sporting goods manufacturers' associations expected the entire sporting goods industry to grow by 5.3 percent in 1998. Rapid growth for the specialized outdoor segment

EXHIBIT 7   Top 10 Products Sold by Outdoor Retailers, 1996–97

Product Category	1997 Rank	1996 Rank
Outerwear/performance apparel	1	1
Canoes/kayaks/paddling accessories	2	3
Hiking boots	3	2
Skis/ski boots/bindings	4	4 (tie)
Sportswear	5	Not a separate category until 1997
Camping and backpacking accessories	6	5
Backpacks	7	6
Fly fishing gear	8	7 (tie)
Climbing gear	9 (tie)	10
Mountain bikes	9 (tie)	4 (tie)
Tents	10 (tie)	7 (tie)
Sleeping bags	10 (tie)	Not in top 10

Source: "1997 State of the Market," *Outdoor Retailer.*

in future years was thought to be linked to manufacturers' abilities to develop techno-logically advanced products and to further appeal to women and Generation Xers.

Outdoor recreational equipment was sold through specialty outdoor retailers, specialty bicycle shops, specialty ski shops, general sporting goods stores, and discount retailers. Combined, these retailers sold approximately $5 billion in specialized outdoor equipment, apparel, and footwear. The top 10 products sold by outdoor retailers in 1996 and 1997 are presented in Exhibit 7. Outdoor equipment and gear accounted for 34 percent of the industry's 1997 retail sales, while apparel accounted for 33 percent, accessories accounted for 20 percent, and footwear accounted for 13 percent.

About 70 percent of outdoor specialty retailers operated stand-alone, single-store operations with annual retail sales of $1 million or less, and about one-half of all specialty outdoor retailers had annual sales volumes of $500,000 or less. Outdoor specialty store annual sales averaged $250 per square foot in 1997, compared to an average sales per square foot of $169 for the entire retailing industry. Small specialty stores were able to achieve high sales volumes relative to store size because of their pricing practices and relatively small locations (66 percent of stand-alone outdoor retail stores were less than 3,000 square feet). The small specialty stores were usually able to charge premium prices for much of the merchandise stocked in their stores since many items were either highly differentiated brands or hard-to-locate products.

Single-store retailers were becoming increasingly concerned about the growing presence of specialty discounters, full-line discounters, and mail-order catalogs that chose to focus on the growing market for outdoor apparel, footwear, and equipment. These national catalog discounters and larger multistore "big box" retailers were putting pressure on specialty retailers' margins by offering consumers discount pricing on many of the brands and categories of merchandise traditionally offered only by smaller specialty shops.

Outdoor Outfitters and Guides

The services of professional outfitters and guides were available to about 13 million adventure travelers during 1997. When selecting an outfitter for a guided trip, most outdoor recreation customers considered the organization's safety record, attention to

EXHIBIT 8 Services Provided by Outfitters and Revenue Contribution by Service Category

Service	Revenue Contribution
Guided trips	26.6%
Nonguided trips	26.4
Retail (soft goods)	10.3
Retail (hard goods)	9.6
Lodging	9.5
Restaurant	7.7
Camping	1.5
Alcohol sales	1.0
Other	7.4
Total	100.0%

Source: Professional Paddlesports Association, 1997.

customer service, quality of gear, reputation for quality outdoor experiences, and ability to keep trips on schedule. Exhibit 8 presents a list of services typically offered by outfitters and the percentage of business accounted for by each service. Outfitters and guides had provided equipment, provisions, and expertise to outdoor adventurers throughout the western United States from the time the pioneers migrated from the East during the 1800s. Modern outfitters focused on guiding adventure travel for those who did not have the skills or equipment to safely outfit and lead their own outdoor excursions.

Outfitters usually found private landowners unwilling to allow public excursions on their property and were required to have Bureau of Land Management (BLM) or USDA Forest Service permits to operate in the wilderness regions owned by the U.S. government. These permits had become increasingly scarce since wilderness purists had begun lobbying the government to make fewer permits available and a number of new entrants to the outfitting industry had emerged during the 1990s. Some colleges and universities had begun to offer outfitting services to their students and faculty and, in some cases, to the general public. Also, outdoor retailers like L. L. Bean offered fly-fishing, rafting, kayaking, and cycling instruction and outfitting services to selected catalog customers. In addition, some large hotel chains and travel agencies offered outdoor recreation packages that included outfitting services to guests and customers. The new entrants' attraction to the industry stemmed from the industry's growth during the 1990s and the growing number of corporations that scheduled adventure travel retreats to build cooperative cultures and to boost the morale of employees who worked 60- to 80-hour weeks.

The Impact of Governmental Policies and Practices on Outfitters   Many outfitters were finding that recent changes in government policies made it increasingly difficult to offer quality outfitting services to its customers while consistently earning profits. Government regulation tended to vary considerably among the various regional offices of the Forest Service and the BLM. Outfitter associations testified at a congressional committee hearing in April 1997 that many individual government resource managers let their ideological beliefs affect how they interpreted and enforced the Wilderness Act of 1964—a situation that had an uneven impact on the balance between preserving the primeval character of wilderness areas and permitting people to enjoy the recreational attractions of such areas.

Outfitters found that while many wilderness resource managers had not changed their approach to outfitter regulation in recent years, other resource managers interpreted the act to require rigorous preservation of the wilderness. Outfitter associations charged that these managers who either felt pressure from or shared beliefs with wilderness purists enforced the act in a manner that allowed fewer recreational permits for outfitters and required outfitters to reduce party size. Outfitters found that new restrictions on the number of guided trips and on the size of guided parties severely limited the viability of offering outfitting services. Outfitters expressed confusion over enforcement of the act to Congress since, in many cases, self-guided users were offered unlimited access to wilderness areas without permits and with no restrictions.

Outfitters had also begun to see their profit margins erode as a result of increases in launch fees, concessions fees, and entrance fees charged by the BLM, the Forest Service, and various state parks agencies. For example, outfitters operating in the Canyonlands National Park were required to pay for a computer system used by the park service to manage self-guided users in addition to negotiated contractual fees paid to the government. Outfitters were also concerned about midseason fee increases that were implemented after their rate schedules had been published and customer reservations had been accepted. The BLM and Forest Service contract award process was also very costly to outfitters. Contract proposals typically took hundreds of hours and approximately $20,000 in professional fees to develop. Successful bidders were typically awarded a contract with a duration of five to seven years. Many outfitters claimed that more time was needed to recapture the cost of preparing the proposal. Outfitters also suggested that it was difficult to develop a long-term business plan and sustain profitability given the short-term nature of agency contracts. During 1998, members of the U.S. Senate sponsored the Craig-Wyden Outfitters Policy Act, which intended to ensure more consistent wilderness resource management, provide longer-term contracts to outfitters, eliminate unnecessary and duplicative paperwork, evaluate government user fees, revise the process of awarding contracts, and eliminate the need for government approval of outfitter rates and charges where competition existed. The bill was strongly opposed by wilderness groups and private boaters, but outfitter associations were hopeful that the bill would become law during 1999.

Outdoor Recreation in Colorado

Colorado offered outdoor recreational opportunities that appealed to a wide variety of tastes and interests. Downhill ski resorts such as Aspen, Vail, Steamboat, and Breckenridge were among the many in the state that were known worldwide. Colorado also boasted 54 of the 68 U.S. mountain peaks measuring over 14,000 feet. Each year hundreds of thousands of tourists visited the Mesa Verde cliff dwellings and the 700-foot-high sand drifts of the Great Sand Dunes National Monument Park. Many others camped and visited the vast plains of eastern Colorado to get a feel for the Old West. Regardless of geographic region, the state offered a scenic backdrop to almost any outdoor recreational activity. Almost unlimited hiking trails and camping sites existed within the state, and numerous mountains, foothills, and rocks were readily available throughout the western section of the state for climbers of varying skill levels. Colorado's lakes, rivers, and streams were easily accessible to rafters, kayakers, and fishers. Big-game hunters from around the United States and other countries came to Colorado to hunt bighorn sheep, elk, and deer.

Colorado's diversity and quality of outdoor recreational activities made it a popular destination for travelers of all types. In 1997 the expenditures of Colorado's 25.1 million adult overnight business and pleasure travelers totaled $7.1 billion, while expenditures in mountain resorts accounted for about 37 percent of total overnight travel spending. Most spending in mountain resorts was made by an estimated 2.5 million tourists on sightseeing trips; 2.1 million downhill ski vacationers; and 1.9 million overnight participants in outdoor recreation like camping, rafting, and fishing.

Outdoor Recreation Activities Near Fort Collins, Colorado

Fort Collins is located in the northeastern section of Colorado about 60 miles north of Denver where the plains meet the Front Range of the Colorado Rocky Mountains. Fort Collins's climate made outdoor recreation possible throughout the year, although water-related activities were practical only during the very late spring and summer since conditions became unbearable in the colder months. Fort Collins averaged 300 days of sunshine annually, with annual rainfall accumulation of only about 8 inches.

The most popular locations in the area for outdoor recreation were the foothill mountains just a few miles west of the city, the Rocky Mountain National Park 35 miles southwest of the city, and the Poudre River Canyon located 10 miles northwest of Fort Collins. Two foothill mountain parks, Horsetooth Mountain Park and Lory State Park, comprised nearly 5,000 acres and were easily accessible to Fort Collins locals and visitors for hiking, mountain biking, horseback riding, and wildlife viewing. Water sports and recreation were available near the parks at the Horsetooth Reservoir—the largest lake in northern Colorado.

The Rocky Mountain National Park covers 410 square miles and includes 18 peaks over 13,000 feet that form the Continental Divide. Many of the park's 3 million–plus annual visitors also enjoyed recreation provided by the park's 150 lakes and traveled the Trail Ridge Road—the nation's highest paved highway, which begins in the town of Estes Park and meanders along the ridges of the Rocky Mountain range. The Poudre River Canyon runs east from the Continental Divide to the foothills and into the plains of eastern Colorado. During the spring and early summer snowmelt the river includes stretches of easy Class I conditions to very challenging Class V expert conditions for whitewater rafters and kayakers. As summers progressed and the river began to recede, the Poudre took on its role as one of the most highly rated trout streams in Colorado. Exhibit 9 provides a map of Colorado and a more detailed map of the Fort Collins area.

ROCKY MOUNTAIN ADVENTURES

Rocky Mountain Adventures was a comprehensive outfitter—offering outdoor recreation equipment and guided whitewater rafting trips, fly-fishing trips, and international river expeditions. The company's guides also instructed beginning and novice kayakers and trout anglers who wanted to improve their outdoor recreation skills. The company's Fort Collins retail store was its primary location, but it also operated outposts in Buena Vista and Estes Park that acted as excursion departure points and allowed its customers in those locations to purchase needed accessories and trip photographs.

The Retail Store

Rocky Mountain Adventures' retail store was located north of Fort Collins on U.S. Highway 287, just minutes from the Cache La Poudre River. The store had been the company's primary gathering place and departure point for guided rafting and kayaking

EXHIBIT 9   Map of Colorado and Inset of Fort Collins and Its Surrounding Area

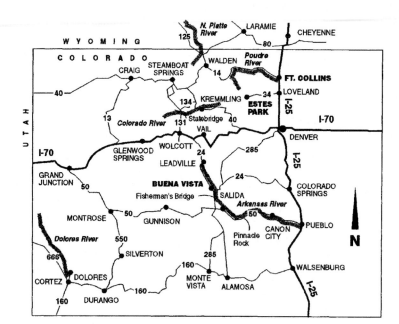

trips on the Poudre since Bill Peisner and Dave Costlow became owners of the company in 1993. RMA's retail store offered a wide variety of merchandise to outfit fly-fishers or paddlers. The 3,000-square-foot store carried such fly-fishing equipment and apparel as rods, reels, fly-making supplies, line, instructional books and videotapes, waders and other outerwear, and T-shirts. The store was also a full-service paddling shop with several lines of kayaks and such paddling gear and accessories as life jackets, dry suits, wet suits, booties, paddles, helmets, dry bags, rescue equipment, and books. Self-guided paddlers could rent kayaks, canoes, rafts, and any and all necessary paddling gear at the Fort Collins store. RMA also rented cross-country ski and snowshoe equipment and carried a considerable variety of outdoor apparel. The store's selection of footwear was restricted to specialty lines targeted to fishers, climbers, and paddlers. The financial statements presented in Exhibit 1 show the contribution of hard-line and soft-line retail sales toward RMA's total revenues.

Pigeon Express™ souvenir photographs were one of the most interesting and best-selling items at RMA's Fort Collins store. Almost all outfitters offered rafting customers souvenir photographs of their whitewater excursion. Outfitters would position photographers along scenic or precarious points along the river to photograph kayakers and rafters as they made their way through the rapids. The photographer would drive back to town and process the photographs, which would then be displayed and ready for purchase when the paddlers returned to the shop. During the peak season it was difficult, if not impossible, to get the photos processed and displayed before the excursion group returned, and as a result many of the photos taken were never purchased.

During Dave and Bill's first year as owners of Rocky Mountain Adventures, they learned quickly that photographs were high-margin items that were easily sold if available and were also quickly perishable since they had no value once the rafters had left the shop. When it became impossible to have photos processed and displayed upon the rafters' return to the Fort Collins store, RMA allowed rafters to purchase photographs sight unseen and receive the photographs by mail at their homes within a few days of their rafting trip. Even though the company offered a money-back guarantee to its customers in the event that they were not pleased with the photographs, the owners found that many customers were hesitant to purchase photos they had not seen. During its first three seasons, RMA's $16.00 trip photos contributed approximately $2.00 in additional sales per rafting customer.

Prior to the company's fourth season on the Poudre River, Dave, Bill, and the company's photographer attempted to identify a new process for making photos available to RMA's rafting customers. The trio discussed the possibility of utilizing a combination of digital cameras, laptops, modems, and cell phones to ensure that the photos were processed and displayed in time, but determined that the cost of the equipment and slow electronic file transmissions would make a high-tech solution impractical.

After a couple of hours of brainstorming, RMA's photographer almost jokingly proposed that the company use homing pigeons to deliver the film to the store for developing. The group didn't produce any other viable alternatives, so Dave decided to give pigeons a try. He began to train a few pigeons over the off-season to return to the Fort Collins store once released from the Poudre River area. Dave also created Lycra backpacks for the pigeons that were just large enough to carry a canister of film. Dave spent hundreds of hours training the pigeons, but the development of the backpacks was as big a challenge as training the birds. Custom-fitted backpacks were needed, since each bird's size and girth were slightly different. Dave's first experimental run worked well, with the pigeon traveling about 20 miles from the Poudre River to the shop within 30 minutes. In 1997 RMA's 25 Pigeon Express™ carriers helped the company average $5.00 per customer in photograph sales. However, Dave noted that successful implementation of the film delivery system did come with some costs:

> The maintenance of the birds requires about two hours per day. We have to clean their lofts, exercise, feed and water them twice a day—year round. You have to inoculate the birds twice a year to combat disease. It is just like having a pet. Training new birds is really not that much of a problem now because they follow the older birds on training flights. Early on it required a lot of time to train birds because I trained them to follow the river canyon to avoid hawks and falcons, rather than take the most direct route to the outpost. I also spent a lot of time trying to get the birds not to sit on power lines and tree limbs on their way back. But right now it only requires about 2–3 hours per week to train young birds. I do usually train more birds than I need since there is a pretty high infant mortality rate and since some birds do not turn out to be good flyers. Also, from time to time, we will lose a bird to hawks.

Guided Whitewater Rafting Trips

Rocky Mountain Adventures operated guided rafting trips on the Cache La Poudre River, the Arkansas River, the Colorado River, the North Platte River, and the Dolores River. The company also offered guided kayaking on Lake Estes in Estes Park. Exhibit 9 highlights the locations of these Colorado rivers and Estes Park. Each river had its own unique characteristics that lured rafters and kayakers to its waters. The Cache La Poudre River was Colorado's only designated National Wild and Scenic River. As a Wild and Scenic River, the Poudre was free-flowing from its headwaters and was protected from development and damming. The 25-mile river included stretches of varying whitewater difficulty levels (Exhibit 10 provides definitions of river difficulty ratings). RMA whitewater rafting trips on the Poudre that consisted primarily of Class II runs were enjoyable for families and beginners, since river conditions were not overly hazardous. The company also led excursions along the Poudre that had more

EXHIBIT 10   International Scale of River Difficulty

Class	Difficulty Rating	Description of Conditions
I	Easy	Fast-moving water with riffles and small waves. Few obstructions, all obvious and easily missed with little training. Risk to swimmers is slight; self-rescue is easy.
II	Novice	Straightforward rapids with wide, clear channels that are evident without scouting. Occasional maneuvering may be required, but rocks and medium-sized waves are both easily missed by trained paddlers. Swimmers are seldom injured and group assistance, while helpful, is seldom needed.
III	Intermediate	Rapids with moderate, irregular waves which may be difficult to avoid and which can swamp an open canoe. Complex maneuvers in fast current and good boat control in tight passages or around ledges are often required; large waves or strainers may be present but are easily avoided. Strong eddies and powerful current effects can be found, particularly on large-volume rivers. Scouting is advisable for inexperienced parties. Injuries while swimming are rare; self-rescue is usually easy but group assistance may be required to avoid long swims.
IV	Advanced	Intense, powerful but predictable rapids requiring precise boat handling in turbulent water. Depending on the character of the river, it may feature large, unavoidable waves and holes or constricted passages demanding fast maneuvers under pressure. A fast reliable eddy turn may be needed to initiate maneuvers, scout rapids, or rest. Rapids may require "must" moves above dangerous hazards. Scouting is necessary the first time down. Risk of injury to swimmers in moderate to high, and water conditions may make self-rescue difficult. Group assistance for rescue is often essential but requires practiced skills. A strong Eskimo roll is highly recommended.
V	Expert	Extremely long, obstructed, or very violent rapids that expose a paddler to above-average endangerment. Drops may contain large, unavoidable waves and holes or steep, congested chutes with complex, demanding routes. Rapids may continue for long distances between pools, demanding a high level of fitness. What eddies exist may be small, turbulent, or difficult to reach. At the high end of the scale, several of these factors may be combined. Scouting is mandatory but often difficult. Swims are dangerous, and rescue is difficult even for experts. A very reliable Eskimo roll, proper equipment, extensive experience, and practical rescue skills are essential for survival.
VI	Extreme	One grade more difficult than Class V. These runs often exemplify the extremes of difficulty, unpredictability and danger. The consequences of errors are very severe and rescue may be impossible. For teams of experts only, at favorable water levels, after close personal inspection and taking all precautions. This class does not represent drops thought to be unrunnable, but may include rapids that are only occasionally run.

Source: American Whitewater Affiliation.

exciting Class III and IV whitewater runs that appealed to more experienced adult rafters. RMA customers who chose a two-day excursion could camp along the river's edge or find more comfortable accommodations at the riverside Rustic Inn.

Whitewater runs on the Arkansas River were challenging, with the Browns Canyon run the least challenging of the river's four popular runs. Rafters could take in the beautiful scenery along all four stretches, but the thrilling rapids were what appealed most to rafters who came to the Arkansas River. The Royal Gorge and Numbers sections of the river were generally thought to be among the most challenging whitewater runs in Colorado. RMA offered half-day and full-day trips along the Browns Canyon section and only full-day trips along the faster sections that required greater technical skills of rafters.

RMA's rafting trips along the North Platte River began at an elevation of 8,000 feet and wound through miles of quiet river valley meadows and pasturelands before entering the 800-foot-deep North Gate Canyon, where rafters experienced Class III and Class IV rapids. Rafters could sign up for either one-day or two-day excursions with Rocky Mountain Adventures and, regardless of trip duration, could expect to view impressive fields of spruce and wildflowers and bald eagles, golden eagles, prairie falcons, elk, and deer while on their trip.

The company also offered full-day trips on the Upper Colorado River. The Upper Colorado was located just over two hours from Estes Park, a destination frequented by visitors interested in a first-time whitewater rafting experience. The waters of the Upper Colorado River were relatively tranquil and ideal for beginners and families with children as young as six. Even though the river was not characterized by intensely turbulent rapids, it did offer beautiful canyon scenery, and RMA guides made a point of beaching at various points to allow rafters to take a dip in natural hot springs and inspect preserved dinosaur tracks in the Dinosaur National Monument park.

RMA's Dolores River trips were targeted toward the hard-core experienced rafter moreso than its other trips. Serious rafters could take guided three-day, 45-mile or six-day, 75-mile journeys through southwestern Colorado. RMA guides and rafters plunged through famous Class IV rapids like "Snaggletooth" during the day and during the evening prepared river-style meals over campfires and slept near their rafts along the bank of the river. Rafters usually chose to stop along the way to scout out Indian cliff dwellings and Anasazi rock carvings.

RMA's guided kayak trips were restricted to half-day and full-day trips on Lake Estes. The trips were oriented toward the beginning or intermediate kayaker who wanted to learn new skills while taking in the scenery of the Rocky Mountain National Park. Exhibit 11 provides a listing of RMA's guided rafting and kayaking trips, and Exhibit 12 presents a sample itinerary for a half-day rafting trip.

Most of RMA's customers were visitors to the Rocky Mountain National Park who scheduled their trips prior to their arrival. Other customers booked rafting trips after seeing an RMA travel brochure displayed in Estes Park hotels, condominiums, or restaurants. Some local guest ranches offered RMA rafting trips among their selection of guest activities. Bill Peisner estimated that only about 10 to 15 percent of RMA's customers were locals. Both Bill and Dave believed that the quality of the company's outfitting and guide services was essential to the company's long-term success. First-time beginning rafters tended to select an outfitter that was publicized in local advertising, but experienced rafters tended to ask about an outfitter's reputation prior to booking rafting services. Word of poor-quality guide services tended to travel quickly around the region and made it difficult to attract full-day and multiday rafting customers who were willing to pay the higher guide fees.

To ensure consistent quality guide services, Dave and Bill jointly screened raft guide applicants for technical expertise, dependability in reporting to work, and ability and willingness to be polite to customers. The business was seasonal, and as a result RMA did not provide year-round employment to most of its rafting guides. The company did provide year-round employment to two guides who helped supervise the Arkansas, Dolores, Upper Colorado, and North Platte rivers during the summer. The company also reemployed a number of guides year after year, but each season it was necessary to find additional guides. Finding qualified guides was not overly difficult since there were quite a few local rafters and a considerable number of college students

EXHIBIT 11   Rocky Mountain Adventures' Guided Rafting Kayaking Trips

Trip Location	Trip Duration	River Conditions	Age Restriction	Price per Person
Cache La Poudre River Whitewater Rafting Trips				
Lower Cache La Poudre River	½ day	Class III	7	Adult: $34 Youth: $28
Mishawaka Falls	½ day	Class III and IV	13	$50
Mishawaka Falls	¾ day	Class III and IV	13	$54–$58
Upper Cache La Poudre	Full day	Class III and IV	13	$74
Upper Cache La Poudre	2 days	Class II, III, and IV	13	$155–$169
Arkansas River Whitewater Rafting Trips				
Browns Canyon	½ day	Class III	8	$32
Browns Canyon	Full day	Class III	8	$63
Texas Creek	Full day	Class III and IV	13	$63
Numbers Section	Full day	Class IV and V	18	$78
Royal Gorge	Full day	Class III, IV, and V	18	$84
North Platte Whitewater Rafting Trips				
North Gate Canyon	Full day	Class III and IV	13	$83
North Gate Canyon	Overnight	Class III and IV	13	$189
Dolores River Whitewater Trips				
Dolores Canyon	3 day	Class III and IV	13	$294
Dolores Canyon	6 day	Class III and IV	13	$570
Upper Colorado River Whitewater Trips				
Upper Colorado River	Full day	Class II and III	6	Adult: $61 Youth: $51
Lake Estes Kayaking Trips				
Lake Estes	½ day	N/A	12	$28
Lake Estes	Full day	N/A	12	$49

Source: Rocky Mountain Adventures, Inc.

from around the country who came to Colorado for summer employment. Once a qualified staff was selected during early May, Bill conducted training sessions for RMA guides in late May that included a review of technical skills and an in-depth discussion of the company's philosophy toward safety and customer service. Other temporary personnel were also trained to become attentive to customer needs and to help alleviate customers' rafting fears while honestly and fully informing customers of the risks associated with whitewater rafting.

RMA was permitted by either the Bureau of Land Management or the Forest Service to guide rafting and kayaking trips along all five rivers where it operated. Government permits allowed outfitters to take up to 120 rafters down a river each weekday and 100 rafters each during the weekend. Bill estimated that there were probably 45 out of 90 rafting days a summer when RMA was forced to turn customers away since it had met its daily limit on the Poudre River. A customer unable to book a rafting trip with Rocky Mountain Adventures could contact one of the four other permitted outfitters on the Poudre River. Rocky Mountain Adventures competed against 50 other outfitters on the Upper Colorado, 15 others on the North Platte, and 12 others on the Dolores River. Competition was strongest on the Arkansas River, where gov-

EXHIBIT 12   Sample Itinerary for a Half-Day Whitewater Rafting Trip

8:15 AM Meeting Time and Check-in
Arrive at Rocky Mountain Adventures building. No need to arrive early unless you want to do so, as there is time built in for you to do everything you need to do before your trip. You check in with the trip leader, read and sign the liability waiver, and if you desire get fitted for a wetsuit, booties, etc. You then change into your rafting clothes, wonder if you look funny in your wetsuit, and ask about that sunglasses strap you forgot before going to the trip talk.

8:30 AM Trip Talk
During this time your entire rafting group assembles and your trip leader gives you the necessary information about how to paddle, have a safe trip, stay in the boat, and have fun.

8:50 AM Life Jacket Fitting
During this time period you pick a life jacket and your guide ensures that it fits properly.

8:55 AM Board Vehicles for River

9:00 AM Leave for River
You are off for your adventure! Once at the put-in you meet your guide (if you have not already done so) and crew. Most crews consist of 6 to 7 rafters plus your guide. Your guide gives you last-minute instructions, reminders, and suggestions. Then you practice turning and paddling as a team so that you feel more comfortable in the raft before the first big rapid.

9:25 AM–11:45 AM River Trip
Splash, excitement, teamwork, waves, laughs.

12:15 PM Approximate Return Time
You return your life jacket on the way to the changing rooms. Next, you get into your travel clothes, see about photos of your trip, hang out with us for a while, and then you are off to your next adventure.

Source: Rocky Mountain Adventures, Inc.

ernment permits were not required until the late 1980s and where a total of 63 outfitters led whitewater rafting excursions. The Forest Service intended to decrease the number of outfitters on the Arkansas River to 45 within the next 5–10 years. Exhibit 13 provides each permitted outfitter's number of rafting customers on the Cache La Poudre River for selected years between 1986 and 1997. Exhibit 14 presents RMA's rafting customer volume on the Upper Colorado, North Platte, Dolores, and Arkansas rivers between 1993 and 1997.

Fly-Fishing

The late summer and early fall were the height of the fly-fishing season in Colorado, and during those periods most of Bill and Dave's time began to shift from supervising guided rafting excursions to supervising guided fly-fishing trips. The company did offer some guided fishing trips in Wyoming as early as June, but the Wyoming trips were guided by RMA employees and required little direct supervision by the two partners. Like its rafting customers, RMA's fly-fishing customers were primarily visitors to the area, but the company did guide a considerable number of local anglers. RMA's

EXHIBIT 13 Annual Rafting Volume by Outfitter, Cache La Poudre River, 1986, 1990–97

Outfitter	1986	1990	1991	1992	1993	1994	1995	1996	1997
Whitewater Adventures	586	453	2,493	4,260	4,519	4,969	6,872	8,182	6,992
Best Rapids	930	3,425	4,523	4,956	6,464	7,169	8,246	8,653	8,401
Colorado Outdoor Center	115	330	338	247	539	418	617	715	771
Blazing Paddles	—	2,626	2,153	4,765	3,793	6,211	6,940	6,984	6,959
Rocky Mountain Adventures	1,408	4,945	4,838	5,116	6,044	6,063	8,067	8,616	8,858
Total	3,039	11,779	14,345	19,344	21,359	24,830	30,742	33,235	31,981

Source: USDA Forest Service.

EXHIBIT 14 Rocky Mountain Adventures' Annual Rafting Volume, Arkansas, North Platte, Delores, and Upper Colorado Rivers, 1993–97

River	1993	1994	1995	1996	1997
Arkansas River	298	467	503	504	539
Dolores River	2	5	35	0*	14
North Platte	59	16	28	60	49
Upper Colorado	0	8	26	50	132
Total	359	496	592	614	734

*The Dolores River had no water suitable for rafting during the 1996 summer season.
Source: Rocky Mountain Adventures, Inc.

fly-fishing customers who were visitors to the area found out about the company in pretty much the same way as its rafting customers. RMA placed ads in Estes Park hotels, condominiums, and restaurants and had agreements with a number of area guest ranches to provide rafting trips and fly-fishing trips to the guest ranch visitors. The company also guided group trips each year that resulted from presentations to fly-fishing associations that Bill and Dave made during the winter months.

RMA's guided fly-fishing trips were individualized to each angler's experience and capabilities. The guides could take the expert trout angler directly to the best fishing spots or could provide instruction and tips to the novice prior to heading to the trout streams. RMA's guides led fly-fishing expeditions on the Cache La Poudre River, the Big Thompson River just below the town of Estes Park, the North Platte River, and private stocked lakes. A list and description of RMA's guided fishing trips are presented in Exhibit 15.

Like whitewater rafting, guided fly-fishing was regulated by the U.S. government through the issuance of permits to a limited number of outfitters. RMA competed against 2 other outfitters on the Poudre River, 4 others on the Big Thompson River, and about 12 others in Wyoming on the North Platte River. As in its approach to competing with its rivals in the rafting business, RMA believed that customer service and the quality of its guided trips were essential to building an advantage. To maintain the company's image and reputation, Bill and Dave were very careful in selecting RMA fishing guides. The partners' approach to hiring and training fly-fishing guides was identical to that for rafting guides. Bill and Dave jointly interviewed applicants and

EXHIBIT 15   Rocky Mountain Adventures' Guided Fly Fishing Trips and Instruction

Trip Location	Type of Fishing	Trip Duration	Number of Anglers	Total Price of Trip
Cache La Poudre River				
	Walk/wade	½ day	1	$80
	Walk/wade	½ day	2	$140
	Walk/wade	Full day	1	$150
	Walk/wade	Full day	2	$240
	Float fishing	Full day	1 or 2 per raft	$260
Big Thompson Lake				
	Walk/wade	½ day	1	$80
	Walk/wade	½ day	2	$140
	Walk/wade	Full day	1	$150
	Walk/wade	Full day	2	$240
North Platte River				
	Float fishing	Full day	1 or 2 per raft	$295
	Float fishing	2 days/overnight	1 or 2 per raft	$440

Source: Rocky Mountain Adventures, Inc.

then agreed on which people would be hired. RMA had one seasonal fishing-guide supervisor who returned each year to work for the company. The supervisor and the two partners conducted training sessions for its guides prior to the beginning of the season. Once the season began, the supervisor and the two partners coordinated the Wyoming and Colorado fishing trips and work schedules.

International Expeditions

In addition to leading excursions in Colorado and Wyoming, Rocky Mountain Adventures had outfitted trips in the Patagonia region of Chile and Argentina and on the Katun River in Siberia. RMA attempted to customize its international expeditions to customers' needs and interests and promoted the junkets in whitewater-rafting and fly-fishing association publications. The company also utilized annual direct-mail campaigns that were targeted to avid fly-fishers and rafters. It was very common for RMA to lead group trips that featured the same core members year after year. Word-of-mouth played a large role in RMA's ability to put together international fishing and rafting trips, as satisfied customers would tell other avid outdoorsmen of their adventures abroad.

Patagonia encompasses the Southern Cone of the South American continent, beginning about 800 miles south of Santiago, Chile and Buenos Aires, Argentina and continuing to Cape Horn. The climate of the Patagonia region is much like that of the Pacific Northwest. Its topography is comprised of temperate rain forests, snow-capped Andean coastal mountains, and numerous rivers winding through the Andes and eventually emptying into the Pacific Ocean. RMA's trips were scheduled during January and February, when weather conditions were most favorable for fishing, hiking, and rafting. The company's Siberian trip was scheduled during late August, when Siberian temperatures ranged between 75 and 45 degrees Fahrenheit at day and between 55 and 35 degrees at night.

RMA promoted its international adventure travel packages as wilderness experiences where accommodations were primitive and the land and water pristine. The company partnered with O'Farrell Safaris for its lodging facilities in Argentina and with Mario Toro in Chile, who owned a small farm near the Rio Futaleufu and the Rio Azul. The lodge owned by Martin and Natalia O'Farrell was rustic in design but was actually quite comfortable. Lodging facilities were much more spartan in Chile and Siberia. The rafters that joined RMA's Siberian expedition spent evenings camping on the banks of the Katun.

Anglers and hikers who chose to visit Patagonia were not overly concerned with RMA's lodging facilities. Hikers came to the region to enjoy the breathtaking scenery of the Andes Mountains, which included great boulder fields, vast alpine meadows, peaks that rose from the ocean to heights of over 9,000 feet, and high dormant volcanoes. Anglers were treated to the same scenery as hikers but were also rewarded with bountiful catches of trophy-size brown, rainbow, and brook trout.

Bill Peisner acted as lead fishing guide on the Patagonia expeditions and was assisted by local guides who were more familiar with the local weather and fishing conditions. Fly-fishing trips typically lasted 11 days and included 6½ days of fishing. Trips were priced at $2,780 per angler. This fee did not include airfare, fishing licenses, or hotel and meal expenses other than what was offered by the local RMA partners. The company's seven-day hiking trips were priced at $1,400. Hiking trips could also be arranged by the day at the rate of $150–$300 per day, depending on the quality of accommodations. RMA did provide lodging within the Chilean National Park to its multiday hiking customers, but hikers were responsible for their air travel to and from the region. The hiking trips were guided by a Chilean naturalist and wildlife artist who contracted with the company to coordinate and lead its Patagonia hiking trips. The company also offered 6-day and 13-day adventure trips that included fly-fishing, whitewater rafting, hiking, and mountain treks by horseback. RMA priced the 6-day trip at $1,500 per person and the company's price for the 13-day adventure travel excursion was $2,500 per person. In 1997, RMA outfitted Patagonia fishing trips for six customers and coordinated Patagonia hiking trips for three customers. The company had 14 hiking customers and 14 fly-fishing customers for its Patagonia trips in 1996. No multiactivity Patagonia adventure travel trips were booked during 1996 or 1997.

In 1994 RMA led a 16-day Siberian rafting expedition that the company offered through an alliance with a Siberian guide that Bill met in Chile. The journey began at the foot of Mount Belukha, the highest point in Siberia, and ended where the Katun joined the Ob River. The journey included seven days of negotiating Class II, III, and IV rapids and daily treks along side canyons to explore abandoned villages and archeological sites. The trip also included nine days that were allocated for travel to and from the Katun and sightseeing in some of Russia's historic cities. The Siberian trip was promoted through the company's ads, but RMA had been unable to put a second expedition team together since the 1994 trip.

Instruction

Rocky Mountain Adventures provided kayak instruction classes for first-time, novice, and intermediate paddlers. The company offered a three-hour kayak instruction class for beginners that was held year-round in a heated Fort Collins city pool. The course focused on such basic kayaking skills as paddling techniques and the Eskimo roll. The company also offered more advanced full-day and two-day courses on the upper Colorado and Lake Estes during the spring and summer that included paddle stroke instruction and river maneuvers like eddy turns, peel outs, and ferrying.

The company also provided courses that focused on swiftwater rescue techniques. RMA's one-day first responder class was intended to prepare the novice rescuer for low-

EXHIBIT 16 Rocky Mountain Adventures' Instructional Courses

Type of Instruction	Course Duration	Pricing	1997 Enrollment
Beginner kayak clinic	3 hours	$45	75
Kayak paddling techniques	Full day	$75	20
Whitewater kayaking skills	2 days	$165	20
Swiftwater first responder	Full day	$99	—
Swiftwater technician I	3 days	$210	25
Introductory raft guide training	3 days	$300	12
Advanced raft guide training	3 days	$300	6

risk and shore-based swiftwater rescues. The three-day swiftwater technician I course was designed for those who were frequently around whitewater and were likely to find themselves in rescue situations. Course participants were drilled in self-rescue techniques and acquired the necessary skills to perform in-water rescue missions under hazardous conditions. RMA also conducted introductory and advanced paddle raft guide training courses for aspiring rafting guides. The three-day courses covered paddle and oar techniques, river hydrology, river navigation, safety techniques, and first aid. The pricing and 1997 enrollment for each RMA instructional program is listed in Exhibit 16.

RMA'S GROWTH OPPORTUNITIES

Bill Peisner and Dave Costlow had discussed a number of possibilities for increasing RMA's revenues and net income. Bill was intrigued by the thought of adding a second floor to the Fort Collins retail store to allow the owners to open a restaurant. Bill had thought that upon their return from the river, many rafters would enjoy being able to select a meal from such menu items as grilled free-range chicken sandwiches, broiled or grilled trout, fresh fruits, or other tasty and healthy fare. With the proper menu, food quality, and service, the restaurant might also become popular with Fort Collins locals during dinner hours. Bill estimated that the cost to construct the second floor and purchase all necessary restaurant equipment and fixtures would be approximately $200,000–$250,000. The two owners had also discussed the purchase of an espresso and sandwich cart that would be located outside of the store to sell food and beverages to the company's rafting customers as an alternative to adding a second-floor restaurant. The company could begin a joint venture with a local restaurant that would take responsibility for preparing food off-site, stocking the cart, and serving customers. Bill and Dave estimated that the cart could be acquired for about $30,000.

Dave and Bill had also discussed purchasing land adjoining the North Platte River in northern Colorado or southern Wyoming to build and operate a mountain outpost and lodge. The lodge would offer its guests multiday guided rafting and fly-fishing trips and extensive instructional courses. There were a number of guest ranches in northern Colorado and southern Wyoming that offered a variety of outdoor recreation activities to their visitors, but there wasn't a lodge dedicated to rafters and fly fishers. RMA could offer multiday all-inclusive fly-fishing packages where the company would provide lodging accommodations and guide anglers on fly-fishing or rafting excursions. The lodge could be targeted to serious trout anglers and rafters, as were its international outings. Bill estimated that the mountain outpost could charge its kayaking guests $200 per day and trout anglers $300 per day. These fees were comparable to the fees charged by most guest ranches in the area. The estimated cost to acquire land and build five cabins and a dining hall was $200,000–250,000.

The two partners were also interested in offering additional international expeditions if they were unique and could be scheduled during the Colorado off-season. The company's Colorado rafting and fly-fishing operations were highly seasonal, with most of its business occurring between late May and early September; the Patagonia trips were usually scheduled during January and February. The company did offer snowshoe and cross-country ski rentals and outings during the winter months, but these guided trips contributed very little to the company's overall profitability. Dave commented, "Our entire winter cross-country ski and snowshoe business doesn't match one day's rafting business during the summer."

Bill and Dave each worked over 70 hours per week during the height of the Colorado summer tourist season and had practically no time alone while on expeditions. During an expedition they were responsible for everything—lodging, meals, fishing, and even fellowship. Having the late-fall and early-spring downtime was beneficial because it allowed the partners to catch up on some rest and to plan for the upcoming Colorado summer tourist season, but it did lead to volatile cash flows throughout the year. Bill and Dave believed that additional international trips would be successful, since the company had developed a good reputation among avid fly-fishers for providing quality international fishing excursions. In fact, many of its international fly-fishing expedition customers returned at least every other year. Bill felt strongly that these customers would enjoy visiting new rivers and new countries if such trips were available at a price comparable to that of the Patagonia trips. However, both partners were certain that their families would not want them away from home an additional two to four months during the year.

The company could potentially use the additional trips to provide year-round employment for an additional RMA guide, but leading an international trip required highly specialized skills that took years to develop. Bill stated that additional international trips could very likely bring in the necessary revenue to justify a permanent employee who could be responsible for river operations during the summer and lead international expeditions during the winter. However, finding the right person would be difficult. Bill explained, "It's a very demanding job. You are completely responsible for your customers while they are with you. You not only have to know how to row a raft and guide a fishing trip, but you have to understand the local language, culture, and customs. You have to make sure that the raft is waiting at the river, the lodging accommodations and food are ready and satisfactory. It's really an 18-hour-a-day job when you're guiding an international trip."

There were also opportunities that required little additional capital or commitment from the two owners. The owners had discussed finding new customers for its Pigeon Express™ photographs. The company had recently purchased a Fuji minilab that had the capability of finishing many more photos than what was currently required by Pigeon Express™. Dave thought that with five additional birds and one additional photographer, the company could provide photography and photo finishing services to other rafting outfitters in the Fort Collins area.

Even though RMA offered rafting excursions on five Colorado rivers, its trips on the Poudre River accounted for most of its rafting-related revenues. The company had not been overly aggressive at building traffic on the Arkansas, Upper Colorado, Dolores, or North Platte rivers because of the distance of these rivers from Fort

Collins. The Poudre was more easily managed since its proximity to Fort Collins allowed Bill and Dave to closely supervise the company's operations and personally take over if unforeseen problems emerged. There were many times each season when either Bill or Dave were forced to guide rafts or drive a busload of rafters from the gathering point to the river when employees were absent from work. It was very difficult for the company to even remotely approach the limit of 100 rafters per day on these outlying rivers since the company lacked supervisors at each river.

The partners had thought about not renewing some permits to provide more time to focus on the rivers that were closest to Fort Collins. It was difficult to make rafting on the Dolores River a central part of the company's operations since the snowmelt made the length of a whitewater season highly unpredictable. Also, the amount of tourism near the North Platte River was much less than that near the Cache La Poudre River and Estes Park, which made it difficult to reach the company's permitted capacity on the river. Bill and Dave believed that the Arkansas offered the greatest promise since it was the most rafted river in the world, with over 300,000 rafters each season. The partners had thought that with the proper strategies, Rocky Mountain Adventures could potentially provide outfitting services to 25 customers per day on the Arkansas River. However, there were 62 other outfitters along the Arkansas River, making competition there stronger than on other rivers. The Upper Colorado River also provided opportunity for growth since it was on the opposite side of Estes Park from the Cache La Poudre River. The partners estimated that in the event that they chose to abandon some river operations, RMA could sell its permits on the Arkansas, Delores, Upper Colorado, and North Platte rivers for about $30,000–$50,000 each.

Aggressive expansion of its operations on outlying rivers would require additional rafts and gear, new staff members, and a manager to coordinate rafting on each river. Fully equipped six-person rafts would cost approximately $3,000 each, experienced guides could be hired at $70–$80 per day, and a permanent full-time manager could be hired for $25,000–$30,000. RMA used 19 rafts and 30 guides to meet whitewater rafting demand on the Cache La Poudre River.

There was also an opportunity that Bill and Dave had begun pursuing just days before Bill's departure for Patagonia. Bill and Dave had contacted the owners of Colorado Outdoor Center to determine if they had an interest in selling their Poudre River whitewater rafting permit. Colorado Outdoor had held its permit for close to 20 years but had never approached the 100-rafter-per-day limit and, as a result, its owners had decided to abandon their rafting business outside the immediate Boulder area. Colorado Outdoor had already obtained Forest Service approval to sell its permit to an existing permit holder. Preliminary conversations between the two sets of owners had revolved around a price of $100,000. Colorado Outdoor's permit was renewable as long as it or its assignee complied with all regulations. Holding two permits would allow RMA to take up to 200 rafters per day down the Poudre. However, Colorado Outdoor's permit only allowed two daily launch windows—a one-hour period when rafts could depart from launch sites within the Rocky Mountain National Park. RMA's existing permit granted six launch windows per day, which allowed the company to offer departure times throughout the day. Colorado Outdoor's owners were negotiating an increase in the number of permitted launch windows with the Forest Service when Bill had left for Patagonia.

Bill's wife, Kathy, would meet his flight in Denver and then drive him home to Fort Collins. He intended to sleep late and go into work around noon the next day. Dave would open the store at 10:00 AM and would want to discuss the partners' plans for the upcoming rafting season and the Colorado Outdoor Center rafting permit purchase as soon as Bill arrived. Bill wanted to have his mind made up by the time he landed in Denver so that he and Dave could have a productive discussion. Bill felt the Colorado Outdoor deal probably needed to be finalized quickly before another competitor stepped in with a better offer.

The company's banking relationships would allow RMA to fund the purchase of the permit or to pursue other options. Both partners wanted to avoid becoming overly leveraged and were concerned about financing multiple projects at the same time.

(You can see a picture-enhanced version of this case at *www.mhhe.com/thompson*. RMA's Web address is *www.omnibus.com/rma.html*.)

NATIONAL MEDIA CORPORATION

Patricia Feltes, *Southwest Missouri State University*

Phillip Hall, *St. Ambrose University*

Turn on your television set and you can watch attractive women in eye-catching costumes performing carefully choreographed routines on exercise cycles, handsome men stretching biceps with body-building equipment, a serious chef whipping up culinary delights, or a panel of celebrities discussing beauty creams or real estate opportunities or communication in marriage or the future according to a well-known psychic. Are you watching a music video, an exercise program, a cooking show, a talk show? Or are you watching a commercial? Where does television entertainment end and advertising begin? Many television viewers in recent years have asked themselves that question. For National Media Corporation and the other members of the transactional television industry, however, entertainment and advertising are not mutually exclusive concepts.

Direct response transactional television programming is the more formal name for what are generally called infomercials. These are television shows, usually 30 minutes long, dedicated to promoting a specific product or set of products in a format mirroring those of other types of programs. Infomercials, which usually invite viewers to order products by calling a toll-free number, are considered a form of direct marketing to retail customers.

In 1997 National Media Corporation was the world's largest publicly held transactional television company, offering infomercial programming to a potential audience of more than 370 million households in more than 70 countries and in 25 languages. In 1996, National Media made a profit of $16.6 million on $292.6 million in sales. By fiscal 1997, however, the company had sustained a loss of $45.7 million on sales of $358.2 million. Its stock price peaked at $17.125 in 1996 and closed at $5.1875 on July 16, 1997.

As *Wall Street Journal* writer Lisa Brownlee put it: "How could a company that brought you the Flying Lure and the Regal Ware Royal Diamond line of nonstick pots and pans wind up hard-pressed in an industry that commonly marks up a product about five times the cost before selling it?"[1] Had National Media acquired other companies beyond its ability to pay for and manage them? Was its history of litigation bogging

---

[1]Lisa Brownlee, "Leading Player in Infomercials Talks to Suitors," *The Wall Street Journal,* July 16, 1997, pp. B1, B8.

down its ability to compete? Had it overcommitted to media time? What strategy and actions would it take to restore National Media Corporation to profitability?

THE COMPANY

Goals, Strategies, and Competitive Advantage

National Media's goal was to be recognized as a worldwide leader in direct marketing. Through direct response transactional television programming and integrated consumer marketing techniques, National Media pursued a business strategy that focused on (1) effectively utilizing and leveraging its global presence, (2) continuing to develop and market innovative consumer products to enhance its library of infomercials, and (3) engineering the most efficient business model possible.

In 1997, National Media planned to expand its competitive advantage by (1) offering its technical capability to other infomercial distributors directly or through alliances, (2) building on the awareness developed through this network to expand into other consumer distribution outlets, and (3) more aggressively using its mailing lists. National Media believed that its international media partnerships; multi-country coverage; and fully integrated program production, product sourcing, and order fulfillment would serve it well in the future.

Products

In fiscal 1997, National Media offered the buying public almost 150 products, 62 of which were first introduced that year. (See Exhibit 1 for examples.) The five most successful products in fiscal 1997, 1996, and 1995 accounted for 41.2 percent, 46.0 percent, and 54.0 percent, respectively, of the company's net revenues. The majority of National Media's products generated their most significant domestic revenues in the first six months following the initial airing of the infomercial in which they were featured. Internationally, the company's products typically generated revenues more evenly over a longer period, due in part to the addition of new markets each year. Of fiscal 1997's revenue, 22 percent came from products introduced during that year, 66 percent came from products introduced during fiscal 1996 and 1995, and approximately 12 percent came from products introduced prior to fiscal 1995.

The company's best-selling product in fiscal 1996 was the Ab-Roller Plus, a type of exercise device. At its peak, the product garnered over $100 million a year in sales. In fiscal 1997, the product encountered patent infringement litigation and thus could no longer be sold by National Media in the United States.

The Great North American Slimdown with Larry North, a weight-loss product, was featured in the company's 1997 product line but could not offset lack of sales in other areas. Consumers did not flock to purchase MicroWise cookware, Auri car wax, the E-Force aerobic rider, the PowerWalk Plus treadmill, or the MiniMax home gym.[2] This points to the challenge faced by any infomercial company: to pick winners again and again and again.

---

[2]Brownlee, "Leading Player in Infomercials."

EXHIBIT 1   A Representative Sample of National Media
             Corporation's Products

Product Category	Product Offerings	Fiscal Year First Aired
Automotive	Motor-Up	1996
	Touchless Car Care	1995
	Autofom Car Polish	1993
	ColorCote 2000 Colored Car Polish	1992
	Auri Car Polish	1990
Beauty and Personal Care	Accents	1996
	Jet Aire Professional Hair Styling System	1993
	Frankie Avalon's Zero Pain Topical Pain Reliever	1993
	Sudden Youth Skin Care System	1992
Crafts	Bedazzler Plus Bead Punch Kit	1993
	Purrfect Punch Embroidery System	1992
Health and Fitness	Ab-Roller Plus	1996
	Top Ten Trainer	1996
	E-Force	1995
	Powerwalk Plus	1994
	Bruce Jenner's Minimax Exercise System	1994
	Bruce Jenner's Stairclimber Plus Stair Climber	1993
	Tony Little's Target Training System Video Tapes	1993
	Bruce Jenner's Super Step Stair Climber	1992
Kitchen and Household	Goo Gone	1995
	Regal Ware Royal Diamond Cookware	1994
	Sterling Spring Water Filter	1993
	American Harvest Jet Stream Oven	1992
	Deni Turbo Sealer Food Packager	1992
	Astonish All-Purpose Cleaner	1991
Music	Dance Party	1996
	Legends	1996
	Shades of Love	1996
	Alltime Classics	1995
	Hits of the 60's	1995
	Hits of the 70's	1995
	Rock and Roll Days	1995
Outdoor	Medicus Golf Club	1993
	Kangaroo Lure Fishing Lure	1993
	Flying Lure Fishing Lure	1992
Self-improvement	Alphanetics Reading Improvement Materials	1992
	The Human Calculator Mathematics Teaching Materials	1991

New-Product Development

National Media's product development and marketing department was responsible for generating product ideas and then researching, developing, and analyzing those products and the resultant sales. In addition, the department continually pursued product opportunities with third parties. In the 1990s the company placed an increased emphasis on the development of products suitable for international distribution. In fiscal

1997, 14 new products for non-U.S. markets were introduced. In addition, National Media used its international network to market 47 new products developed by other, independent domestic infomercial companies that year.

Varying contractual agreements were made between National Media and third parties depending on the degree of time and investment needed to bring the products involved to full development. The company generally sought exclusive worldwide rights in all means of distribution for each product developed or acquired.

Once National Media decided to bring a product to market, it arranged to make a 30-minute infomercial providing in-depth demonstrations and explanations of that product. Each program was planned to be both informative and entertaining. The infomercials were produced in-house or by independent companies. The cost of producing an infomercial ranged from $175,000 to $350,000, plus an additional fee (based on a percentage of product sales) paid to producers, hosts, and spokespersons.

Operations

National Media outsourced manufacturing to various firms in the United States, Europe, and Asia. A technical engineering company in Hong Kong was used to coordinate and direct manufacturing sources in Asia. National Media did not take an inventory position in a product before market testing was completed.

The majority of National Media's U.S. customers paid by credit card over the telephone; a much smaller number paid by check. In Europe and Asia, products were generally paid for by "cash on delivery," the usual method in both market areas.

Media Access

During peak periods, National Media purchased approximately 1,000 hours of cable and broadcast television time per week in the United States and 650 hours per week internationally. In fiscal 1997, approximately 52 percent of the money used to purchase media time went to cable television and approximately 48 percent went to network affiliates and independent television. Internationally, most of the media time was purchased from satellite and terrestrial broadcast access owners. The infomercials were generally aired in the United States between 3:00 AM and 2:00 PM Eastern time, seven days a week.

In the past, approximately one-half of the cable air time in the United States and a majority of the international satellite and terrestrial air time utilized by National Media was purchased under long-term contracts that provided for specific time slots. In late fiscal 1997, however, National Media reduced the number of its long-term contracts in U.S. markets.

Management

A number of changes in management occurred at National Media at the end of fiscal 1997. Leaving the company were Mark Hershhorn, former president and chief executive officer (from April 1995 to April 1997); David Carman, former executive vice president of National Media and chief executive officer of Quantum (a competitor acquired by National Media); and Brian McAdams, former chairman of the board and chairman of the executive committee. Each of these departures involved substantial severance packages.

As of May 30, 1997, National Media's management consisted of the following key people:

Robert N. Verratti, 54, president and chief executive officer and director. Verratti was a special adviser for acquisitions to Warren Musser, chairman and CEO of Safeguard Scientics. Safeguard Scientics and the Safeguard Group owned 26.6 percent of the common shares of National Media. Musser was a member of National Media's board.

John W. Kirby, 37, executive vice president of the company, and chairman and chief executive officer of DirectAmerica.

Paul R. Brazina, 52, vice president and chief financial officer.

Michael D. Levey, 48, executive vice president of the company and chief executive officer of Positive Response Television.

Paul Meier, 41, executive vice president of the company and chief executive officer of Prestige Marketing Limited and Suzanne Paul Holding Pty. Limited.

Brian J. Sisko, 36, senior vice president, chief administrative officer, secretary and general counsel.

A number of agreements with the company provided for employment of family members; loans to company officials; consulting contracts for prior executives; and the purchase of services and/or goods from managers, directors, or their connections.

Joint Ventures and Acquisitions

National Media announced in September 1997 that it would provide infomercial programming to GTE MainStreet. The GTE subsidiary had begun testing the use of infomercials over its interactive television systems to cable subscribers in Florida and southern California and to hotel guests at the Boston Harbor Hotel in Boston, Massachusetts. One of National Media's two infomercials chosen for the GTE test, featuring the company's Zero "G" Strider, starred former Olympic medallist Bruce Jenner. The infomercials were added to GTE MainStreet's other 95 interactive offerings of games, community events, and travel and investment information.

As suggested earlier, National Media Corporation's corporate strategy involved aggressive expansion. In May 1996, the company paid $26 million for stock in Positive Response Television, an infomercial production company. Positive Response Television developed "Amazing Discoveries," a series of infomercials showcasing Spanek vertical roasters cookware and Auri car wax, among other products, and starring founder and CEO Mike Levey. Levey was something of a cult-status star of infomercials, with fans located everywhere from U.S. college campuses to the Netherlands.[3]

International

The international infomercial industry began in Western Europe in the late 1980s and expanded throughout Europe and into non-European countries during the early 1990s. In the United States, infomercials were considered simply an alternative to more traditional retailing distribution systems. In many international markets, however, such alternatives were not readily available and the infomercial approach was considered a unique source of specialty consumer goods.

An early entrant into the international market, Quantum Marketing International began operations in 1990 and was acquired by National Media in 1991. National Media believed Quantum's large library of infomercials would become or remain more valuable as the company distributed those programs around the world and extended the time period during which each product generated revenues.

---

[3]Tim Carvell, "A Star Is Born in the Wee Hours," *Fortune,* May 26, 1997, pp. 36–37, 40.

Although fiscal 1997 proved to be a difficult year for National Media, it did find the company expanding internationally. Revenue increased with National Media's acquisition of Prestige Marketing and Suzanne Paul, direct-marketing companies in New Zealand and Australia. National Media also added approximately 100 million television households worldwide to its potential viewing audience. This number was equivalent to the size of the total television household audience in the United States.

A joint venture with Mitsui & Company, called Quantum Asia, was begun in late 1995 after a successful partnership with Mitsui in Japan. In July of 1997, Quantum Asia began infomercial broadcasting in Thailand, reaching approximately 13 million television households.

Government Regulation

As a result of a prior settlement with the Federal Trade Commission, National Media had agreed to two consent orders. These were the results of an investigation into claims made on two of the company's infomercials. In addition, the 1996 acquisition of Positive Response Television brought in other consent order settlements regarding claims that could not be made about certain products.

National Media collected and remitted sales tax only in the states in which it had a physical presence. Some states were attempting to require direct marketers to collect and remit a tax on sales to customers residing in those states, whether or not the marketer had a presence there.

Litigation

In July 1997, National Media and Precise Exercise Equipment announced a settlement in a dispute over patent infringement charges regarding the Ab-Roller Plus and other related products. Precise Exercise Equipment, a leading designer of innovative fitness products, challenged National Media's rights to worldwide marketing of the product. The technology for the abdominal "rolling" machine was invented by Precise's president, Donald Brown. The negotiated settlement included (1) geographical limitations on National Media's marketing of the product by eliminating sales or presentations within the United States and (2) an agreement for a proposed alliance for future product development and marketing. Precise estimated the value of the total settlement at approximately $20 million.[4]

National Media faced a number of class-action suits from fiscal 1994 to fiscal 1997. In fiscal 1996, a settlement was reached in a suit regarding the company's ongoing relationship with Positive Response Television, which was a supplier of the company at the time. In fiscal 1994, ValueVision terminated their proposed tender offer and merger agreement. This resulted in suits by National Media against ValueVision, with the eventual settlement including joint venture agreements between the two companies, preferential service benefits for National Media, and payment of early termination penalties to certain National Media executives for property leases owned by them. A stockholder class-action suit filed against National Media because of the failed merger was settled with cash payments, the majority of which came from the company's insurer.

Other legal action involving National Media included the following:

- *February 1997.* National Media filed suit against Guthy-Renker in connection with a failed joint venture.

---

[4]Ibid., July 17, 1997.

- *March 1997.* WWOR-TV of New Jersey alleged that the company wrongfully terminated a contract for media time.
- *May 1995/fiscal 1997.* Prior to its acquisition by National Media, Positive Response Television was charged with making false and misleading statements in its public filings, press releases, and other public statements with respect to its business and financial prospects. The company reached an agreement in fiscal 1997 with a charge of $187,000 on its income statement and the remaining $368,000 paid by the insurer.
- *March 1997.* Sintiger, Inc., a distributor of sunglasses, filed suit alleging patent infringement.
- *September 1995/April 1997.* A suit was filed by Blublocker Corporation, a distributor of sunglasses, against Positive Response Television alleging unfair competition and false advertising. In fiscal 1997, Positive Response, now owned by National Media, agreed to pay Blublocker $400,000 and recorded this charge in the fourth quarter.

Financial

As mentioned earlier, fiscal 1997 ended with a net loss for National Media of $45.7 million, or $2.07 per primary share—see Exhibits 2–4 for the company's recent financial statements. This compared badly with fiscal 1996, in which the company netted income

EXHIBIT 2 National Media Corporation's Income Statements, 1994–97 (In thousands of $)

	Year ended March 31			
	1997	**1996**	**1995**	**1994**
Revenues:				
Product sales	$337,508	$285,676	$168,689	$167,920
Retail royalties	16,337	5,597	5,303	3,694
Sales commissions and other revenues	4,334	1,334	2,175	988
Net revenues	358,179	292,607	176,167	172,602
Operating costs and expenses:				
Media purchases	131,136	86,518	51,961	56,215
Direct costs	196,972	151,198	97,605	95,070
Selling, general, and administrative	69,823	33,772	23,634	20,667
Severance expense for former Executive Officers	2,500	—	2,650	—
Interest expense	1,542	1,015	689	300
Total operating costs and expenses	401,973	272,503	176,539	181,301
(Loss) income before income taxes	(43,794)	20,104	(372)	(8,699)
Income taxes	1,897	3,525	300	—
Net (loss) income per common and common equivalent share:	$ 45,691	$ 16,579	$ 672	$ 8,699
Primary	$(2.07)	$.74	$(.05)	$(.72)
Fully diluted	$(2.07)	$.71	$(.05)	(.72)
Weighted average number of common and common equivalent shares outstanding:				
Primary	22,071,700	23,175,900	14,023,800	12,077,900
Fully diluted	22,071,700	23,287,600	14,023,800	12,077,900

Source: Company annual reports.

EXHIBIT 3   National Media Corporation's Balance Sheets, 1995–97 (In thousands of $)

	Fiscal Year Ending		
	March 31 1997	March 31 1996	March 31 1995
Assets			
Current assets:			
Cash and cash equivalents	$ 4,058	$ 18,405	$13,467
Accounts receivable, net	40,179	32,051	14,344
Inventories, net	30,919	22,605	15,387
Prepaid media	3,563	4,271	2,660
Prepaid show production	6,765	5,469	3,463
Deferred costs	3,318	4,102	1,820
Prepaid expenses and other current assets	2,505	2,339	1,228
Deferred income taxes	2,591	3,142	1,782
Total current assets	93,898	92,384	54,151
Property and equipment, net	14,182	6,954	4,413
Excess of cost over net assets of acquired businesses and other intangible assets, less accumulated amortizaiton of $9,472 and $2,548	50,732	15,078	4,659
Other assets	6,820	2,132	920
Total assets	$165,632	$116,548	$64,143
Liabilities and shareholders' equity			
Current liabilities:			
Accounts payable	$ 21,810	$ 20,412	$12,093
Accrued expenses	30,830	26,510	17,786
Deferred revenue	686	1,771	279
Income taxes payable	552	1,344	300
Deferred income taxes	2,351	2,749	1,428
Current portion of long-term debt and captial lease obligations	17,901	876	184
Total current liabilities	74,130	53,662	32,070
Long-term debt and capital lease obligations	959	4,054	3,613
Deferred income taxes	240	393	354
Other liabilities	1,743	1,977	1,481
Shareholders' equity:			
Preferred stock, $.01 par value; authorized 10,000,000 shares; issued and outstanding 95,000 and 136, 375 shares Series B convertible preferred stock (liquidation preference of $3,800)	1	1	3
Common stock, $.01 par value; authorized 75,000,000 shares; issued and outstanding 24,752,792 and 18,177,292 shares	248	182	149
Additional paid-in capital	127,764	48,135	31,877
Retained earnings	(29,122)	16,569	(10)
	98,891	64,887	32,019
Treasury stock, 707,311 and 686,710 common shares, at cost	(4,244)	(3,791)	(3,791)
Notes receivable, directors, officers, employees, consultants, and others	—	(473)	(1,868)
Foreign currency translation adjustment	(6,087)	(4,161)	265
Total shareholders' equity	88,560	56,462	26,625
Total liabilities and shareholders' equity	$165,632	$116,548	$64,143

Source: Company annual reports.

EXHIBIT 4   National Media Corporation Consolidated Statements of Cash
            Flows (In thousands)

	Year ended March 31		
	1997	1996	1995
Cash flows from operating activities			
Net (loss) income	$(45,691)	$ 16,579	$ (672)
Adjustments to reconcile net (loss) income to net cash (used in) provided by operating activities:			
Depreciation and amortization	9,966	2,099	1,650
Amortization of loan discount	484	399	150
Provision for deferred rent expense	328	384	402
Tax benefit from exercise of stock options	(347)	2,051	—
Decrease (increase) in:			
Accounts receivable, net	1,721	(18,242)	1,139
Inventories	(3,057)	(8,591)	(3,987)
Prepaid cable and advertising costs	1,374	(3,936)	(370)
Deferred costs	4,233	(2,282)	402
Other current assets	855	(1,060)	(395)
Increase (decrease) in:			
Accounts payable	(2,358)	8,569	(415)
Accrued expenses	(6,007)	9,505	4,713
Deferred revenue	(1,583)	1,236	(1,456)
Income taxes payable	(3,405)	1,044	300
Notes payable	1,400	—	—
Other	(3,480)	(2,225)	440
Net cash (used in) provided by operating activities	(45,567)	5,530	1,901
Cash flows from investing activities			
Additions to property and equipment	(8,439)	(3,923)	(832)
Investment in common stock	(1,250)	—	—
Cost of companies acquired, net of cash acquired	(1,236)	(897)	—
Net cash used in investing activities	(10,925)	(4,820)	(832)
Cash flows from financing activities			
Proceeds from revolving line of credit	22,400	—	5,000
Principle payments on revolving line of credit, long-term debt, and capital lease obligations	(15,493)	(166)	(4,771)
Net proceeds from issuance of common stock	28,754	—	—
Exercise of stock options and warrants	7,820	5,085	242
Payments received on notes receivable	473	2,483	492
Net proceeds from issuance of investment units	—	—	9,415
Net cash provided by financing activities	$ 43,954	$ 7,402	$10,378

Source: Company annual reports.

of $16.6 million, or $.74 per primary share. Revenues for fiscal 1997 were $358.2 million, which exceeded fiscal 1996's total of $292.6 million by 22 percent.

Revenues from international operations in fiscal 1997 were $169.7 million, compared to $151.0 million for fiscal 1996. Revenues from the domestic market for fiscal

1997 were $188.5 million, compared to $141.6 million for 1996, primarily due to acquisitions.

National Media's fiscal-year loss included a significant loss incurred by subsidiary Positive Response Television; reserves for excess and/or obsolete inventory and accounts receivable; write-downs and amortization of production costs; and severance payments, legal costs, and settlements.

A primary operating cost during fiscal 1997 was the company's media commitment. In fiscal 1996, National Media spent approximately 30 percent of its $292.6 million in revenues on air time. In 1997, the percentage of revenue committed to media costs grew to 36 percent of the company's $358.2 million revenue. Williams Worldwide, an infomercial ad agency in California, stated that the biggest financial drain on industry members was the cost of television time. In 1996, the agency projected that infomercial producers collectively spent $650 million a year for media.[4]

Losses during fiscal 1997 could also be traced to the costs involved in litigation and settlement expenses during the year. The patent infringement regarding the Ab-Roller Plus was a primary concern in legal expenses.

In July 1997, the company announced that—as a result of its financial losses, its weakened cash position, and its technical violation of loan agreements with CoreStates Bank—it received a "going concern" warning from its auditors.

Financial results for the quarter ended June 30, 1997, showed a continuation of the losses of the prior year. National Media reported a net loss of approximately $13.0 million for the quarter, compared to net income of $4.6 million for the quarter ended June 30, 1996. This was equal to a loss of $.54 per share of common stock. Total net revenues were $67.2 million, compared to $109.3 million in 1996. The company's international operations were a bright spot. While North American revenues dropped to $26.7 million from $75.5 million, net revenues from international operations for the quarter were $40.5 million, compared to the previous year's $33.8 million.

Turnaround Strategies

Following the poor financial figures for the year ending March 31, 1997, Robert N. Verratti, National Media's president and chief executive officer, stated his expectations that the company could be turned around:

> The Company continued to progress as far as developing its global audience and continued to produce substantial revenues, clearly demonstrating the growing viability of the transactional television business. We have begun a process aimed at reducing expenses while making the domestic part of our business more nimble and reactive to the vagaries of the infomercial business in the United States.

According to Verratti, actions planned or already being taken by the firm included:

- Curtailment of long-term or unprofitable media contracts, including cost reductions in the company's largest U.S. media contract. These actions were expected to eliminate approximately $4 million in annual costs.
- Restructuring of the Positive Response Television subsidiary. The staff at PRTV was reduced by approximately 90 percent. In addition, the company was negotiating with Mike Levey, the creative force at the subsidiary, to have Levey produce and appear in infomercials for third parties as well as National Media productions.

---

[4]Brownlee, "Leading Player in Infomercials."

- Reduction in the size of the global workforce.
- Development of a plan to reduce costs and increase the efficiency of fulfillment operations.
- Discussions with domestic and international lending institutions, strategic partners, and others regarding operational financing.

In August 1997, Verratti commented on the 1997 first-quarter results (for the three months ending June 30, 1997), "We began initiating our action plan in early July, including the reduction of global expenses. Those reductions are not reflected in our first quarter results and we expect continued losses through the quarter which will end September 30, 1997. We have been concentrating on new shows and product offerings for the fall television season. Our fall line-up will include several shows featuring some of the industry's most proven performers, as well as shows for new fitness equipment and housewares."

INDUSTRY

The direct response transactional television industry was first developed in the United States after the Federal Communications Commission, in 1984, rescinded its limitations on advertising minutes per hour. The deregulation of the cable television industry and the expansion of channels that began in the 1980s increased the supply of media time, important to the growth of the new industry. Producers combined direct response marketing and retailing principles within a television-show format and used purchased media time to air what soon came to be known as infomercials. After an initial growth period, the industry consolidated through the end of the 1980s. Increased attention from the Federal Trade Commission and federal and state consumer protection agencies led to greater regulation or threats of regulation of the industry. In response, the National Infomercial Marketing Association, a self-regulatory organization, was formed.

By the 1990s, infomercials and home-shopping cable channels had become more familiar and acceptable to both regulatory agencies and consumers. As the infomercial industry matured, the variety of its products increased and industry members became more sophisticated in their approach.

Infomercials were attractive to both the product manufacturer and to the owners of the stations that carried them. In an infomercial, a product could be demonstrated under controlled conditions and described more fully than in a brochure or other advertising medium. Parts of the program could be reshot if something went wrong or if the product was not shown to its full advantage. Well-known personalities could be included in the presentation, and could even be shown using or demonstrating the product. The infomercial could be filmed before a studio audience to give viewers a feeling of participation and enthusiasm.

In addition, unlike direct-mail marketing, viewers chose to watch infomercials. If the product was of interest or the presentation was entertaining, a viewer flipping through the channels stopped at that station for at least a little while. If the infomercial producer had been successful, the viewer would find the show of such interest that he or she would continue to view it and be inspired to purchase the product. Viewers generally watched infomercials in a relaxed state, with defenses down, increasing their susceptibility to suggestion. They could at any time call the given phone number and order the product with minimal effort.[5] Interactive television, which allowed viewers

---

[5]Julia Reed, "Hitting Up the Public Where It Lives," *U.S. News and World Report,* 101 (December 8, 1986), pp. 60–61.

C-353

ate directly with the show or the sponsoring company, was becoming
sible. Some observers saw it as an opportunity to generate the ultimate
ing.

sting network owners were faced with an ongoing challenge: how
lable air time at a profit to themselves. Infomercials helped to fill
egular entertainment programming, which had to be purchased and
rough advertising sponsors, infomercials brought in revenue from their
n fact, the producers not only paid for use of the media but also often guar-
etworks a percentage of the sales generated by the infomercials in their market
Rather than having to sell time to advertisers, the advertisers (i.e., the infomercial
ogramming companies) came to the station owners to bid on the air time available.

Market

The market for shopping by television expanded during the 1990s. Customers could no
longer be stereotyped as "middle-aged housewives" with an interest in imitation diamond jewelry but rather encompassed people from a wide variety of backgrounds.
Although computer shopping was often written about as the next wave of retailing, the
reality was that the majority of U.S. consumers still did not have a personal computer
at home in 1997. The international market was even less likely to turn to a computer to
meet buying needs. Television sets, on the other hand, were ubiquitous worldwide.

Some experts viewed infomercials and other forms of shopping shows as dangerous
to a certain segment of the population. Ronald Colman, an expert on compulsive shoppers, said, "TV is a wonderful marketing tool; it offers live impact and the pressure of
the clock running out."[6] Television shopping offered companionship and excitement to
isolated people in particular. "Addiction is a disease of isolation, whether it involves
spending, drugs or alcohol. It thrives when the abuser is separated from others, and TV
shopping is perfect for that," said a spokesperson from Debtors Anonymous.

Competitors

Infomercial producers found that competitors came from a number of sources.
Old-fashioned store retailing was still the primary way consumers found and purchased merchandise. In most U.S. markets, department stores, mass merchandisers,
specialty stores, niche outlets, and so on provided ample opportunities for consumer
buying. U.S. retail sales in 1995 totaled $2,340.8 billion, or approximately $8,909 per
capita. This was a 4.9 percent increase from 1994 figures. Nonstore retailers accounted
for $69.8 billion of the 1995 figures and $64.0 billion in 1994.[7]

The direct response transactional television industry was difficult to assess, since
the only public company of any size was National Media. Other direct infomercial
competitors were privately held. It was also a difficult industry to quantify, since measures of size were mixed. It was, however, an ultracompetitive business that depended
on fad products for short-term success (and survival) while always searching for the
next big hit. In addition, any winning promotion was a magnet for copycat producers.

Guthy-Renker, named for founders Bill Guthy and Greg Renker, was a very active
but privately held infomercial company with estimated revenues in 1996 of $300 mil-
lion. Rupert Murdoch's News Corporation controlled 37.5 percent of the company.

---

[6]Steve McKee, "Splurge Through the Tube," *American Health,* March 1989, p. 60.

[7]U.S. Department of Commerce, *Statistical Abstract of the United States, 1996,* p. 765.

Guthy-Renker called itself the nation's biggest buyer of paid programming because it spent $100 million a year on U.S. airtime. It was founded in 1988 and hit it big with Anthony Robbins's Personal Power motivational tapes and the Perfect Smile teeth whitener.

Other direct competitors included Kent & Spiegel Direct, a privately held infomercial company based in Culver City, California. When interviewed regarding the 1997 profitability of the firm he cofounded, Peter Spiegel remarked, "We're making money. Guthy-Renker's making money."[8]

Related but not fully comparable competitors were the shopping networks and shopping shows. This form of direct retailing also used television as its way to sell directly to consumers, but its approach differed from that of infomercials. Shop-at-home television programs generally acted as "active catalogs" or bazaars showing a variety of separate objects for a few minutes each in the context of a television show. The best known of the television shopping networks was QVC, Inc., which had been subsumed into a major communications firm. The Home Shopping Network, the other major company, continued to maintain an individual identity. (See Exhibits 5 and 6 for the Home Shopping Network's recent financial performance.)

Potential competitors included organizations such as Fidelity Investments, the giant mutual fund and investment company. In September 1997, Fidelity was in talks with CBS to develop a program about investments and personal finance. The company stressed that this would be primarily an educational show but would likely feature Fidelity fund managers among others.[9]

Technology

Some media experts predicted that the television of the future would act as a smart computer. Interactive video, which offered viewers an opportunity to instantly respond to presentations on the screen, was expected to be available at a reasonable cost by the end of the 1990s. Even more futuristic was a concept of combining movies and shopping. As viewers watched a movie on television, they could stop the action in order to ask about or purchase specific clothes, furniture, or other products shown in the movie.[10]

Fiber-optic cable technology was already available in many television markets. The number of channels available to subscribers could increase to 500, requiring a continuing demand for programming. This could lead to growing costs as competitors vied for the available supply.[11]

Regulation

On October 4, 1992, Congress enacted the Cable Television Consumer Protection and Competition Act of 1992 (the Cable Act). As part of the Cable Act (the "must-carry" provision), a certain number and type of programs became eligible for mandatory carriage. This meant that cable systems were required to provide space to programs and services designated "must carry." Must-carry offerings were to meet Federal Communication Commission standards regarding their value to the public

---

[8]Brownlee, "Leading Player in Infomercials."

[9]James S. Hirsch, "Fidelity, CBS Are Considering Finance Show," *The Wall Street Journal*, September 19, 1997, pp. B1, B8.

[10]Laura Zinn, "Retailing Will Never Be the Same," *Business Week*, July 26, 1993, pp. 54–60.

[11]"Warnaco, Clairborne Said to Be Considering QVC," *Women's Wear Daily*, 165, no. 72 (April 15, 1993), p. 9.

EXHIBIT 5 Home Shopping Network, Inc., Balance Sheets, 1993–96 (In thousands of $)

	Year Ending			
	December 31, 1996	December 31, 1995	December 31, 1994	December 31, 1993
Assets				
Cash	$ 16,274	$ 25,164	$ 33,648	$ 35,566
Receivables	33,868	23,634	43,657	27,849
Inventories	100,527	101,564	118,801	110,930
Notes receivable	—	—	—	5,707
Other current assets	33,411	32,633	32,740	37,349
Total current assets	184,080	182,995	228,846	217,401
Property, plant & equipment at cost	226,508	227,484	247,797	247,147
Accumulated depreciation	129,387	118,710	116,697	105,777
Net property & equipment	97,121	108,774	131,100	141,370
Invest. & adv. to subs	24,981	14,000	10,000	10,000
Other non-current assets	113,594	99,161	67,978	132,372
Deferred charges	3,649	23,142	—	—
Deposits and other assets	7,622	8,223	8,575	—
Total assets	$ 431,047	$ 436,295	$ 446,499	$ 501,143
Liabilities and Shareholders' Equity				
Accounts payable	$ 65,266	$ 84,297	$ 75,264	$ 88,858
Current long-term debt	250	1,555	1,690	25,345
Accrued expenses	82,755	84,599	128,819	79,559
Income expenses	8,267	4,973	—	15,586
Other current liabilities	10,000	—	—	—
Total current liabilities	166,538	175,424	205,773	209,348
Deferred charges	NA	NA	6,792	8,314
Long-term debt	97,934	135,810	27,491	86,927
Total liabilities	$ 264,472	$ 311,234	$ 240,056	$ 304,589
Minority interest (liabilities)	1	—	—	—
Common stock net	920	977	976	968
Capital surplus	140,062	169,057	167,463	160,371
Retained earnings	28,297	7,677	69,560	52,783
Treasury stock	—	48,718	27,136	14,027
Other equities	(2,705)	(3,932)	(4,420)	(3,541)
Shareholder equity	166,574	125,061	206,443	196,554
Total liabilities and net worth	$ 431,047	$ 436,295	$ 446,499	$ 501,143

Source: Company annual reports.

interest, convenience, and necessity. A suit was brought questioning the constitutionality of the must-carry provision, but in April 1997, the Supreme Court upheld the provision and required cable operators to carry local broadcast stations. Without that ruling, smaller cable operators could have seen their signals bumped by the major companies. Instead the smaller organizations were assured of some continuing security regarding access to the television-watching public.

Barry Diller of the Home Shopping Network was particularly pleased with the Supreme Court's ruling regarding the must-carry rule. His organization intended to move away from a reliance on home-shopping programs on the twelve broadcast

EXHIBIT 6   Home Shopping Network Inc., Income Statements, 1993–96 (In thousands of $)

	Fiscal Year Ending			
	December 31, 1996	December 31, 1995	December 31, 1994	December 31, 1993
Net sales	$1,014,705	$919,796	$1,126,514	$1,046,580
Cost of goods	625,697	602,849	730,504	704,040
Gross profit	389,008	316,947	396,010	342,540
R & D expenditures	94,598	98,216	98,835	93,686
Selling, general and administrative expenses	217,141	244,150	241,230	231,631
Income before depreciation and amortization	77,269	(25,419)	55,945	17,223
Depreciation & amortization	33,483	38,854	29,066	24,172
Non-operating income	(606)	(20,855)	9,153	(1,755)
Interest expense	9,918	10,077	5,512	10,863
Income before tax	33,262	(95,205)	30,520	(19,567)
Provide for income tax	12,641	(33,322)	12,819	(4,028)
Net income loss before extraordinary items	20,621	(61,883)	17,701	(15,539)
Extraordinary items and disc. ops	(1)	NA	(924)	(7,242)
Net income loss	$ 20,620	$ (61,883)	$ 16,777	$ (22,781)
Outstanding shares	91,989	97,718	93,113	93,627

Source: Company annual report.

stations it owns and instead develop and present shows focusing on local news, personalities and culture.[12]

Where to Now?

A merger or sale of National Media was a possibility. The company acknowledged that it had had talks with several organizations, but no formal discussions were planned. Two possible acquirers were suggested by analysts. King World Productions, which distributed the *Oprah Winfrey* show and game shows *Jeopardy* and *Wheel of Fortune,* was considered to have a mild interest in the company. Guthy-Renker, however, was considered a strong candidate to acquire National Media. Analysts suggested that Guthy-Renker could benefit from National Media's strong international presence. Bill Guthy and Greg Renker admitted that they had dinner with National Media heads in June of 1997 but would not confirm any discussions regarding merger or purchase.[13]

Merger or joint ventures with a shopping channel were also considered a possibility. National Media might be able to find some synergy with shopping companies like the Home Shopping Network.

Although results for 1997 were dismal and the first quarter of the new year did not show any improvement, some analysts believed that National Media would show sub-

[12]Amy Barrett, "The Broadcast Winners Are . . . ," *Business Week,* April 14, 1997, p. 46.
[13]Brownlee, "Leading Player in Infomercials."

stantial gains in the future. One of the reasons for that optimism was the belief that the expansion and investments which the company made in 1996 and 1997 would begin to prove their worth through positive returns. In addition, the company's extensive commitment and connections worldwide made it an early player in the international marketplace.

(You can visit *www.quantumtv.com* for updated information on National Media Corp.)

FOODWORLD SUPERMARKETS IN INDIA

David Wylie, *Babson College*

Madras, India

August 1996

In May, we opened our first FoodWorld Supermarket in Madras. We were convinced that such a modern concept would work in India, but the early results have exceeded our expectations. We will be opening two more this month and have plans for over 100 within the next 10 years. It is a terrific opportunity!

I am confident overall, but unsettled about a number of issues. After all, this will be India's first national chain of supermarkets. Most people still shop at all the small mom-and-pop stores which almost completely dominate Indian food retailing. Do we have the formula right? Should we adjust the merchandise mix or the marketing plan? Is the store really large enough to generate excitement, and if not, will suitable real estate be available? Will we be prepared to manage such a large chain and adapt to the different market conditions in different parts of India? Will our people be qualified to manage and operate all these stores?

I would like to think that we have all of this resolved. You see, we have no direct experience in food retailing and no significant modern retailing expertise exists in India. We are inventing things as we go along. Things have to be different here, we can't just copy what is done in other parts of the world.

Pradipta K. Mohapatra
President, Retail Group, RPG Enterprises

RPG ENTERPRISES AND THE SPENCERS ACQUISITION

RPG Enterprises (RPG) was the fourth largest conglomerate (called business house in India) in India, with sales of over 45 billion rupees (U.S. $1.3 billion) in 1995. RPG business interests spanned a variety of industries including tires, power/transmission, agribusiness, telecommunications, financial services, and, with the acquisition of Spencers & Co. in 1989, retailing. It boasted partnerships with a number of international companies, including 16 of the Fortune 500 companies.

Prepared under the supervision of Professor Nirmalya Kumar, International Institute for Management Development.

Spencers & Co. had been founded in 1865 as a small store in Madras offering imported specialty items to the large British expatriate and military population. By 1897, it had grown to be the largest store in India, a 65,000-square-foot enclosed collection of specialty stores. In 1981, this facility was destroyed by fire. Spencers had been at its peak in 1940, when it had 50 stores in virtually all major cities throughout India. Still it offered only imports, and had virtually no Indian customers. When India gained independence from the British in 1947, Spencers' executives didn't believe that the demand for imports would erode. It plummeted, however, and in the early 1970s, the deteriorating chain was sold to an entrepreneur who continued to offer food, clothing, cosmetics and other high-priced specialty items to the expatriate community.

Spencers' fortunes continued to slide. By 1989, it was only a shell of its former self. Only nine stores remained in operation in several of the larger cities in India, including a 20,000-square-foot store in Madras and a 10,000-square-foot store in Bangalore, which were the largest stores of any kind in each city. (Refer to Exhibit 1, Map of India.) The other stores only had 2,000 to 3,000 square feet, but had excellent central locations. Spencers' profits were fleeting and it was offered for sale.

RPG purchased Spencers that year, and established it as a separate division with Pradipta K. Mohapatra, a seasoned RPG executive, at its helm. The decision to acquire this retail company was largely justified by its undervalued real estate portfolio, a distribution infrastructure (which in fact was non-existent), and a profitable travel agency specializing in the distribution of airline tickets.

A number of Spencers stand-alone divisions were obvious losers and were quickly slated for closing: furniture manufacturing, restaurants, manufacturing of air conditioners and other small electrical appliances, pharmaceutical production, and repair shops. The travel agency was clearly a winner and was kept. RPG executives were, however, initially undecided about whether to close down the retail operations altogether.

The "Spencers" brand name was well known throughout India as synonymous with quality, but unfortunately also with high prices. Indeed, there was a popular expression in India: "You don't have to pay the Spencers' price." In addition, RPG had no experience in retailing. They couldn't rely on existing expertise within Spencers, since its employees were poorly qualified at every level and grossly underpaid, even by Indian standards. The general manager of the large Madras store, for example, was only paid the equivalent of about $70 per month. It appeared that it would be most prudent and profitable to close down the stores and simply rent the space.

Yet Spencers' nine stores still remained the largest chain in India of any kind of retail operation, and it seemed wasteful simply to throw away whatever potential there might be for improvement. The decision was ultimately made to refit one store to test its potential. If the experiment failed, they would close the retail operations.

The store in Bangalore, therefore, was modernized in 1991, retaining its profile as a department store offering hardware, food, kitchen appliances and clothing. When it reopened, sales exploded to four times the previous levels and the store broke even in the first month.

FOODWORLD

The following year, interest in retailing among RPG executives derived from the initial success of Spencers' experiment was piqued when a large international consulting firm was retained to assist with the strategic growth planning for RPG. Retailing had been flagged as one of the target industries to consider as part of the RPG engine for growth, along with telecommunications and financial services. It was apparent that an

EXHIBIT 1   Map of India

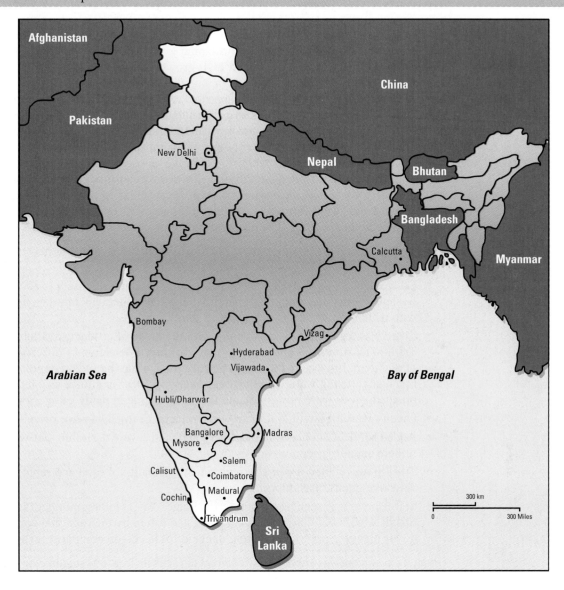

emerging middle class in India might provide a catalyst for bringing modern retailing to India, where retailing had remained virtually unchanged for generations. The consultants, however, stopped short of recommending what kind of retailing to enter, suggesting instead that RPG executives themselves should explore those formats which might be the best match for RPG and mesh with the future growth of India. Several broad objectives were drafted:

- Become a pioneer in an organized, large-scale, world-standard retailing operation in India.
- Become the largest retail chain in India.
- Be willing to make substantial investments to establish a national presence.

Fine-tuning the Spencers format appeared to be the most obvious next step in preparation for expansion, especially since Spencers executives were unfamiliar with alternative formats.

After a careful study of retailing formats in relation to the opportunities in India, RPG executives then narrowed their choice to clothing or supermarkets, wanting to choose the least risky option. While clothing had high growth prospects and margins, it would require, they surmised, expertise in design, branding, and managing independent manufacturers. In addition, a potential threat appeared to loom from current and future competition, making it more difficult to achieve a meaningful scale of operations. Supermarkets, however, offered the same growth prospects and a more moderate investment. While initial margins and entry levels for other pioneering companies might be low, the option of starting a chain of supermarkets seemed to offer the most potential.

A consumer study was then commissioned to assess consumer attitudes toward current retail options and to measure responses in particular to proposed new formats. Nine focus groups were formed in two major cities and 2,110 households were interviewed in depth in six cities. The results were summarized as follows:

- Consumers regarded shopping as a chore, although few consumers were familiar with any alternatives to traditional store formats.
- Convenience was important since daily shopping and sensitivity to food freshness remained an integral part of shopping habits. Few families had cars with which to carry large quantities of purchases.
- There was a growing dissatisfaction with the range of products available. Traditional stores did not have the space to carry a selection of different brands of any item. Increasing television penetration among the Indian population and brand advertising were whetting consumer appetites for choice as international branded goods were now available for the first time in many categories.
- Quality was important, but there was a reluctance to pay a price premium.
- Added services such as home delivery and credit were desirable, but were seldom actually used.
- Trust in the retailer, especially with regard to quality of food and replacement of defective goods, was important.
- Self-service was seen as a distinct advantage. An exploding number of new brands were being introduced and promoted (often by international consumer goods manufacturers), generating demand for hands-on comparison shopping.

Given the results of this survey, they decided to focus their efforts on developing a suitable format for a national supermarket chain. They realized, however, that they would have to face the challenge of a steep learning curve. They would need a partner well versed in food retailing technology because of the importance of using technology to achieve suitable operating efficiencies and low cost logistics. Without any experience in modern food retailing, they were reluctant to proceed without such a partner. For almost a year, they traveled abroad searching for a partner, finally negotiating an agreement with Dairy Farm, a Hong Kong–based retail giant with a great deal of experience in multinational operations, a focus on Asia, and familiarity with the operation of both supermarkets and drugstores. Most important, they felt there was a positive chemistry with Dairy Farm executives, who demonstrated the patience to invest in the long-term opportunity presented in India.

The supermarket they visualized would have about 4,500 square feet of selling space, a self-service format in an air-conditioned and pleasant ambience. It would have extensive assortments of groceries, personal care and cleaning products, kitchenware, and tableware. No meat would be offered, but a fresh produce stand would be leased to an independent vendor. It would also incorporate fast food and bakery sections. They would need to deliver outstanding service with an empowered and well-trained staff. They would have to achieve dominance in tightly focused geographical areas. Finally, they would have to achieve suitable margins by developing a scale to negotiate better prices from suppliers and by achieving the efficiencies of regional distribution centers for at least 15 to 20 stores.

INDIA

India was the second most populous country in the world, with a population approaching a billion people. It was also one of the densest, with over 724 people per square mile. In contrast, the United States, France, and Switzerland had densities of 26, 265, and 434 people per square mile, respectively. India's geographic diversity was only exceeded by the diversity of its people. From the towering Himalayas to the north to the densely populated alluvial plains in the middle to the plateaus of the south, more than 1,500 languages were spoken. Although Hindi and English were the official languages, 14 other languages were recognized by the constitution. The population was overwhelmingly Hindu, but there were significant numbers of Muslims (more than 10 percent of the population), Christians, Buddhists, Sikhs, Jains, and Parsis.

Rural India, comprising 80 percent of the population, was largely supported by primitive agriculture. Most of its hundreds of millions lived below the poverty level. Urban India, however, was heavily industrialized, although vast numbers of people lived in slum conditions, many of them rural refugees. The population was growing at 2 percent per annum while becoming increasingly urban. The inflation adjusted gross domestic product of India had been growing an average of 5.1 percent over the previous 10 years.

Population Distribution	
Population (millions)	**Number of Towns**
More than 10	3
5–10	4
1–5	4
0.5–1.0	26
0.1–0.5	178
Less than 0.1	3,543
Villages	570,000

While a stereotype of malnourished masses dominated the perception of many Western visitors, the economic diversity of the Indian population was much more complex. While reliable statistics are often unavailable, around 40 million Indians lived in relative luxury, enjoying annual household incomes of over 90,000 rupees, or about U.S. $2,500. The buying power of the rupee, however, was considerable. One study estimated that the purchasing power of this level of income was equivalent to about U.S. $600,000. Another 150 million people lived in households with incomes exceeding 30,000 rupees (U.S. $850 or U.S. $20,000 in local purchasing power). This newly emerging middle class was growing at over 5 percent per year and could afford many of the staples of a middle-class existence, including televisions, refrigerators, and motorcycles or mopeds. Automobiles, however, were generally only within reach of the top 1 percent of the population.

Growth of this middle class was, however, a relatively new phenomenon. Since India had gained independence in 1947, the economy had been centrally planned by a large government bureaucracy which controlled investment, production, and competition without regard for market forces. A severe financial crisis in 1991, however, forced a liberalization of economic restrictions. This cleared the way for widespread entrepreneurialism, foreign investment, imports without restrictive tariffs, and unleashed market opportunities. Multinational companies like Coca-Cola rushed in to unleash their brands on the Indian marketplace. Indeed, the number of national brands available had exploded in the previous 10 years. The number of tea brands, for example, had grown from 31 to 148, and washing powders from 26 to 61. Since 1991, this foreign investment in India had created so much demand for office space and professional managers that Bombay had the most expensive real estate in the world. Managers' salaries had often grown tenfold within four years while inflation had fallen from over 16 percent in 1991 to under 7 percent in 1995.

FOOD RETAILING IN INDIA

Retailing in urban India still remained about the same as it had for several generations. While several larger stores and specialty shops in each major city catered to the less price-sensitive appetites of the most wealthy segments of the population with wide selections of imported goods, virtually all other retailers were small independent, owner-managed shops. Most had no employees other than family members who might assist with cleaning or deliveries. As almost every store sold products at the MRP (the maximum allowed retail price printed by the manufacturers on every item and enforced by the government), very little price competition existed between formats, and since the cost of goods was very similar for all of the stores, gross margins were determined mostly by the mix of products offered.

Typical Gross Margins by Product Category	
Product Category	**Gross Margin**
Staples	3%
Other food products	15%
Furniture	25%
General merchandise and hardware	18%

The one main exception to this rule were the 400,000 fair-price shops, a government-sponsored distribution system which sold medium-quality staple products (mostly rice, wheat, cooking oil, and sugar) at prices generally lower than market. Seventy-eight percent of these outlets were in rural areas, constituting an essential and one of the only elements of the government's safety net for the poor. In urban areas, these shops accounted for only 5 percent of total retail food sales.

The number of stores outside the fair-price shops was huge. Estimates varied, but one 1993 survey by Euromonitor suggested that there were over 3.54 million retail outlets in India. This did not, however, include the vast number of vendors and street markets who did not generally report to the government and were not counted in the census. Unofficial estimates indicated that there might be as many as 5 to 8 million such retailers in the informal economy.

Number of Retail Outlets in India	
Grocery stores	1,575,000
General merchandise stores	531,000
Convenience stores/tobacconists	276,000
Chemists	212,000
Confectioners	141,000
Supermarkets	30
Other retail	805,000

Grocery Stores

Dry groceries were usually purchased by the housewife from small neighborhood grocery stores with an average size of about 250 square feet. Her loyalty was strong, based on convenience and added services such as credit and free home delivery. These grocers sold primarily unbranded staples which were individually weighed and packed. Staples such as rice would frequently be purchased on a monthly basis, coinciding with monthly paydays. Typically, these retailers would also carry a small range of branded cleaning and personal care products. These were often offered in "sachets," or single-use packages. Space constraints often limited the selection to no more than one or two brands. Such stores lined the more heavily traveled streets, often simply counters which opened onto the sidewalk behind which the owner/manager would take orders.

The gross margins of these small grocers ranged between only about 7 to 10 percent of sales, but operating costs were similarly low. Property costs only represented 1 to 2 percent of sales, while labor costs were generally provided by the store owner and his family, working 15 hours a day, seven days a week. Profits before tax, therefore, ranged from 4 to 6 percent of sales. Since most of sales were not formally logged, virtually none of these small grocers paid any income tax. Working capital requirements represented only about two weeks of sales.

General Merchants

General merchandise stores (400–600 square feet) were somewhat larger than the small grocery stores and stocked a wider range of cleaning and personal care products, as well as snack foods and confectionery. Groceries were generally prepackaged, but unbranded, and service was still from behind the counter. Services such as home delivery and credit were also available.

Gross margins were several percentage points higher than in the small grocery stores, mainly due to the product mix being skewed toward higher margin items. Since operating costs were somewhat higher as well, however, profits remained about the same.

Convenience Stores

These outlets were found on virtually every street corner and ranged in size from kiosks of 50 to 60 square feet to larger shops of 100 to 150 square feet. Usually run by a single owner from behind a counter, they offered such items as cigarettes, soft drinks, or betel leaf (a popular chewing snack containing tobacco and spices wrapped in a betel leaf). Some might also offer a very restricted range of household cleaning and personal care products as well as biscuits, confectionery, and some over-the-counter medicines.

Convenience stores were generally open every day of the week for 18 hours a day. Their prices were equivalent to those of other stores, and gross margins were a similar 7 to 10 percent of sales. Operating costs, however, were so low that profits were often 5 to 7 percent.

Vendors

Along every sidewalk in the cities were vendors who operated small booths or carts, or simply laid out their products on the ground. They would usually offer only a single product such as fresh coconut milk, bananas, or a very limited selection of clothing, household items, or fruits and vegetables.

Supermarkets

Supermarkets were a more recent phenomenon in India. By 1996, only a handful had appeared in the major cities. These 3,000- to 5,000-square-foot self-service stores stocked a wide range (by Indian standards) of groceries, snacks, processed foods, confectionery, cleaning and personal care products, and cosmetics. They generally stayed open from 9:30 AM to 7:30 PM, six days a week. They stocked most national brands as well as a number of regional and specialty brands, as well as their own brands of prepackaged dry groceries. Many had small bakery sections, and some were experimenting with fresh produce and dairy products. Frozen foods were often available as well, although only a very limited selection was available in India. Most consumers were in the habit of buying fresh products daily from local stores and vendors. In addition, freezer space was expensive and limited in both stores and homes.

A typical supermarket carried about 6,000 stock-keeping units (SKUs). Most, however, had no item-based inventory control, still using a cash register at the point of sale and tracking sales only on a category or departmental basis. Supermarket margins were typically in the range of 14 percent to 16 percent. These higher margins were largely due to the ability to get somewhat better prices from suppliers on bulk purchases, and the ability to generate income from selling advertising space and special in-store promotions to manufacturers.

The cost structure of a supermarket was typically 3 percent for property and 3.5 percent for labor. Air conditioning and lighting rose utilities to 3.5 percent, interest costs were 1.5 percent, leaving 3 to 5 percent of sales as profits before tax.

There were virtually no multiunit supermarket chains. One German company, Nanz, in partnership with Marsh supermarkets of United States and Escorts, an Indian engineering firm, had set up a six-store chain in and near the Indian capital city of Delhi. However, this chain specialized in imported and other higher priced foods for the most well-to-do segment of the population. Most supermarkets, like their smaller counterparts, were owner managed.

Most of the supermarkets tried to cater to that portion of the population which sought a wider selection; could afford, had storage space for, and the means of transport for a larger shopping basket; and were not scared off by the typical perception that large, brightly lit, air-conditioned supermarkets must be more expensive.

DISTRIBUTION OF CONSUMER GOODS

Consumer goods were distributed through a multi-level distribution system. Hindustan Lever (HL), a subsidiary of Unilever, had the most extensive distribution system in India. Its structure, however, was typical of those used by other consumer packaged goods companies.

Forty-seven exclusive HL carrying and forwarding agents (CFAs) transported merchandise from the factory or warehouse to 3,500 redistribution "stockists" or distributors. While the CFAs did not take title to the product, they received a 2 to 2½ percent margin and invoiced the stockists and received payment on behalf of the manufacturer.

The stockists had exclusive geographical territories and a sales force which called on both wholesalers and directly on larger retailers and retailers in urban areas. They offered credit to their customers and received margins in the range of 3 to 9 percent.

The wholesalers provided the final link to those rural and smaller retailers who could not purchase directly from the stockists. Sales to these retailers were cash only. Wholesalers carried a full range of products including brands competing directly with HL. Wholesalers received 2 to 3 percent margins out of that received by the stockists and distributed about 40 percent of the total volume of merchandise handled by the stockists. The remaining 60 percent of merchandise was sold directly to retailers by stockists.

The network was completed by whatever means was required to reach remote villages, including vans, motorized rickshaws, bicycles, bullock carts, and in some areas, boats. It was estimated that through this network, HL reached only about 64 percent of all villages and a total of about 3 million retailers. HL had a 400-person sales force to oversee this distribution network. Each salesperson made about 40 calls a day on distribution channel members.

Gross margins for retailers ranged from to 5 to 15 percent while the total cost of the distribution network represented between 10 and 20 percent of the final retail price. This cost was considerably lower than distribution costs in most Western countries.

CONSUMER BUYING BEHAVIOR

The Wealthy

Those within the more wealthy segment of the population with household incomes greater than 90,000 rupees per year (U.S. $2,500) relied almost entirely on domestic help for their shopping. They would buy staples, vegetables and fresh foods from a number of loyal local small grocers and vendors, and other products from a variety of general merchants. This segment was concentrated in urban areas and comprised only about 4 percent of the population.

The Poor

The poorer segments of the Indian population tended to buy basic staples with the first part of their paychecks which typically were distributed on the first of each month. For most food stores, over 40 percent of total sales came within the first few days of each month. During the month, poor customers would buy whatever fresh foods and consumer goods they could afford daily, often filling in at the end of the month with some additional staples purchased on credit. Many consumer products such as soap, toothpaste, or over-the-counter drugs or cosmetics were bought only in single-use packages (sachets). Indeed, many of the smaller stores were festooned with linked packets of such items. Twenty-five percent of the population lived below the poverty level, while another 56 percent enjoyed only modest household incomes below 30,000 rupees (U.S. $850) per year.

The Middle Class

The middle class was comprised of those who enjoyed household incomes between 30,000 rupees (U.S. $850) and 90,000 rupees (U.S. $2,500) per year (about 15 percent of the population). This segment was divided in its purchasing habits. Many families on the upper end often would emulate the wealthy and use part-time domestic help to do their shopping, often necessitated by a growing pattern of households with two working parents. Many families at the lower end of the middle class, however, would continue to do their own shopping, especially if they had recently emerged from the ranks of the poor and remained extremely cost conscious, frequenting their favorite local shops. They were, however, concerned about quality, often leaving a list with a trusted shopkeeper to pick out and deliver the best quality products. Almost always (92 percent in one survey), it was the wife who did all the shopping for a household.

In a survey conducted by Spencers, upper-middle-class consumers frequented the following outlets for their food needs:

Shopping Patterns	
Outlet Type	**Percent Who Named Outlet as Most Frequently Used**
Big grocery store	30
Supermarket	16
Small grocery store	11
General merchant	11
Wholesale dealer	8
Others/no fixed shop	24

The typical middle-class household spent 1,800 rupees per month for those categories of foods which FoodWorld anticipated offering. This did not include milk or fresh vegetables.

Monthly Household Expenditures		
Food Category	**Rupees per Month**	**Percent of Total Purchases**
Cereals and breads	779	43.2%
Oils and oilseeds	244	13.6
Sugar	191	10.6
Meat, egg, and fish	189	10.5
Pulses (lentils)	106	5.9
Coffee, tea, spices	104	5.8
Tobacco	104	5.8
Beverages (including alcohol)	83	4.6
Total (Rs/month)	1,800	100.0%

THE DECISION TO START FOODWORLD

PK Mohapatra and his staff ultimately made the decision "to offer the Indian house-wife the freedom to choose from a wide range of products at a convenient location in a clean, bright, and functional ambiance without a price penalty." It was determined that households with incomes over 4,000 rupees per month would represent the target customers. Choosing locations; sourcing the right merchandise; developing a promotional plan; designing, building, and fixturing the stores; and attracting the best people to staff the stores and corporate office still, of course, remained a challenge.

The name FoodWorld was chosen after extensive research and deliberation because it reflected the breadth of the offering and because it translated well into every major regional language in India. Government regulations also necessitated posting the name in the local language at every location.

Based on their now expanded experience, Spencers' executives developed a pro forma financial plan for the FoodWorld concept. (Refer to Exhibit 2, Operating Assumptions; Exhibit 3, Stand-alone Store Model Pro Forma; and Exhibit 4, Supermarket Project Pro Forma—Five Year.)

HUMAN RESOURCES

Hiring suitably trained people to manage and staff each store offered perhaps the most formidable obstacle to implementing the FoodWorld concept.

Because most retail stores were owner operated and retailing as a career was considered to be at the bottom end of the social scale, graduates of prestigious universities did not want to work in retailing. Therefore, few qualified candidates for management positions could be found. Some could perhaps be attracted from other service industries to run one or two stores, but not enough to accommodate the planned growth. Recruiting and retaining professionally trained managers was and would continue to be a major challenge facing the firm.

Attracting and training enough front-line staff members would also be a challenge, since FoodWorld would need a cast of thousands to implement the full expansion plan. Spencers therefore created a school for retailing, the National Institute of Retailing (NIR). The curriculum consisted of such courses as store maintenance, working the cash register, serving the customer, and self-grooming and presentation. Students for the NIR were recruited from rural high schools, particularly those who had chosen vocational paths and did not plan on or couldn't afford any further education. They were accepted for either a three-month certificate course or a six-month work/study program based on their aptitude to learn, their self-confidence, and their energy rather than on any particular skills they might have acquired.

Given the wage levels and social status associated with a front-line retail position, albeit at a modern supermarket, most of the candidates came from the lower end of the socioeconomic strata of Indian society. Consequently, attending NIR represented a tremendous opportunity for them and generated a high level of enthusiasm. However, because India was a highly stratified society, these employees perceived themselves, as did the customers, as being considerably lower in social status than their customers. A delicate balance was required to overcome this cultural bias. Instilling the confidence to smile, make eye contact, and help customers while not being perceived as cheeky would be a challenge.

EXHIBIT 2   Operating Assumptions* Monthly Sales per Square Foot and Gross Margins (Sales expressed in rupees per square foot)

Period	Stores Opening in Years 1 and 2	Stores Opening in Years 3 and Onward
Year 1, QI	Rs 500	Rs 750
Year 1, QII	750	900
Year 1, QIII & IV	900	900
Year 2, QI & II	900	900
Year 3	10% increase	10% increase
Year 4	10% increase	10% increase
Year 5 and onwards	5% increase	5% increase
Gross margins—store	12%	12%

Gross margins—back room*	Year 1	2%
	Years 2–5	Growing to 6%

*Back-room margins were comprised of merchandising efficiencies, including volume and cash payment discounts and revenues from suppliers and manufacturers for promotions and displays.

Operating and Opening Costs

Rent	Rs 25 per square foot
	Assumed to grow at 5% above inflation
Salaries	Staffing at 22 full-time equivalents for 7 days of weekly operation
	Salary cost at Rs 72,000 per store per month
	Assumed to grow at 5% above inflation per year
Packing	Rs 1 for every Rs 250 of sales (shopping bags, etc.)
Taxes	1% on 50% of sales (for Bangalore stores only)
Bank charges	2% on credit card sales
	20% of sales assumed to be on credit cards
Depreciation	Computers—five years
	Others—seven years
Advertising	Mailings—Rs 25,000 per month
	Semiweekly fliers—covered by supplier funding
Property	40% owned (purchased at Rs 3,500 per sq. ft.)
	60% leased (Rs 25 per month per sq. ft.)
	Growth at 5% above inflation

Store fittings		
	Computers	Rs 800,000
	Shelving	800,000
	Air conditioning	950,000
	Electrical	300,000
	Furniture	200,000
	Generator	250,000
	Chillers and freezers	250,000
	Construction, signs, bakery	450,000
	Total	Rs 4,000,000

Rent advance	15 months
Working capital	25% of Sales
Paid-up stock (inventory less accounts payable)	Year 1: 4 weeks
	Year 2: 3 weeks
	Year 3: 2 weeks
	Year 4: 2 weeks
	Year 5: 1 week
	(Primarily from improved credit terms and efficiency)
Inventories	2.5 weeks at store, 3.5 weeks at warehouse
Inventory turnover	8 times

*Some of the data may have been disguised.

EXHIBIT 3   FoodWorld Stand-Alone Store Model Pro Forma*, 4,000 square feet (× 100,000 rupees)

	Year 1		Year 2		Year 3		Year 4		Year 5	
	Rs	%	Rs	%	Rs	%	Rs	%	Rs	%
Sales	366.0	100.0%	453.6	100.0%	499.0	100.0%	548.9	100.0%	576.3	100.0%
Sales per sq. ft. (Rs)/month	762.5		945.0		1,039.5		1,143.5		1,200.6	
Gross margin	43.9	12.0%	54.4	12.0%	59.9	12.0%	65.9	12.0%	69.2	12.0%
Store operating expenses										
Salaries	8.6	2.4%	9.7	2.1%	10.2	2.0%	10.7	1.9%	11.2	1.9%
Rent	12.0	3.3%	12.6	2.8%	13.2	2.6%	13.8	2.5%	14.4	2.5%
Utilities	3.0	0.8%	3.0	0.7%	3.0	0.6%	3.0	0.5%	3.0	0.5%
Packing	1.5	0.4%	1.8	0.4%	2.0	0.4%	2.2	0.4%	2.3	0.4%
Taxes	1.8	0.5%	2.3	0.5%	2.5	0.5%	2.7	0.5%	2.8	0.5%
Bank charge	1.5	0.4%	1.8	0.4%	2.0	0.4%	2.2	0.4%	2.3	0.4%
Advertising	6.0	1.6%	3.0	0.7%	3.0	0.6%	3.0	0.5%	3.0	0.5%
Other	3.5	1.0%	4.5	1.0%	4.5	0.9%	4.5	0.8%	4.5	0.8%
Subtotal	37.9	10.3%	38.6	8.5%	40.3	8.1%	42.0	7.7%	43.5	7.6%
Lease	8.5	2.3%	8.5	1.9%	8.5	1.7%	8.5	1.5%	8.5	1.5%
WC interest	2.8	0.8%	3.5	0.8%	3.8	0.8%	4.2	0.8%	4.4	0.8%
Subtotal	11.3	3.1%	11.9	2.6%	12.3	2.5%	12.6	2.3%	12.9	2.2%
Depreciation	2.3	0.6%	2.3	0.5%	2.3	0.5%	2.3	0.4%	2.3	0.4%
Profit	(7.5)	(2.0%)	1.7	0.4%	5.1	1.0%	8.9	1.6%	10.5	1.8%

*Some of the data may have been disguised.

EXPANSION PLAN

There were a number of arguments in favor of an expansion plan based on achieving saturation in several cities first rather than starting with seeding FoodWorlds across the country. Certainly, the former model allowed for distribution efficiencies and simplicity in dealing with suppliers and manufacturers on a regional basis. In addition, each state in the country had its own regulations and tax policies, which made it cumbersome to do business in more than one state. Manufacturers, for example, usually kept title to products as they moved into regional warehouses owned by "stockists," the first level in the national distribution chain, in order to avoid paying rather stiff tax penalties on goods moving across state lines. Often, each metropolitan area had its own language or dialect and particular food preferences. While major differences appeared between neighborhoods, for example, when moving from a strictly vegetarian Hindu neighborhood to a Muslim neighborhood, even more substantive differences existed between regions of India.

The areas surrounding Delhi (the capital) and Bombay (the center of commerce) were ruled out immediately because of the high cost of real estate. Indeed, Bombay's prices for commercial real estate exceeded those of Hong Kong, Tokyo, or New York, and Delhi did not lag far behind. It made most sense to concentrate around those areas where Spencers had a strong remaining presence and where real estate prices and availability were within reason. Madras and Bangalore were therefore chosen to become the first epicenters for FoodWorld based on the size of the target population. (Refer to Exhibit 5, Populations and Income Levels of Households in Key Cities.) Each neighborhood within the city was further broken down to reveal target neighborhoods where there were over 4,000 households within a two-kilometer radius of the store with incomes of over 4,000 rupees per month

EXHIBIT 4   FoodWorld Supermarket Project Pro Forma—Five Year* (× 100,000 rupees)

	Year 1		Year 2		Year 3		Year 4		Year 5	
Number of stores	8		20		30		40		50	
Square feet per store	4,000		4,000		4,000		4,000		4,000	
	Rs	%	Rs	%	Rs	%	Rs	%	Rs	%
Sales	2,557	100.0%	6,585	100.0%	12,259	100.0%	17,494	100.0%	23,243	100.0%
Sales per sq. ft. (Rs)/month	799.1		823.1		1,021.6		1,093.4		1,200.6	
Gross margin	307.0	12.0%	790.0	12.0%	1,471.0	12.0%	2,099.0	12.0%	2,789.0	12.0%
Store operating expenses										
Salaries	55.0	2.2%	150.0	2.3%	269.0	2.2%	389.0	2.2%	521.0	2.2%
Rent	51.0	2.0%	129.0	2.0%	218.0	1.8%	310.0	1.8%	410.0	1.8%
Utilities	23.0	0.9%	47.0	0.7%	80.0	0.7%	110.0	0.6%	140.0	0.6%
Packing	11.0	0.4%	26.0	0.4%	49.0	0.4%	70.0	0.4%	93.0	0.4%
Taxes	25.0	1.0%	33.0	0.5%	61.0	0.5%	87.0	0.5%	116.0	0.5%
Bank charge	13.0	0.5%	26.0	0.4%	49.0	0.4%	70.0	0.4%	93.0	0.4%
Other	31.0	1.2%	71.0	1.1%	119.0	1.0%	163.0	0.9%	207.0	0.9%
Subtotal	209.0	8.2%	482.0	7.3%	845.0	6.9%	1,199.0	6.9%	1,580.0	6.8%
Store contribution	98.0	3.8%	308.0	4.7%	626.0	5.1%	900.0	5.1%	1,209.0	5.2%
Other income	55.0	2.2%	198.0	3.0%	490.0	4.0%	875.0	5.0%	1,395.0	6.0%
Central cost										
Corporate	110.0	4.3%	141.0	2.1%	151.0	1.2%	160.0	0.9%	170.0	0.7%
Advertising	17.0	0.7%	96.0	1.5%	120.0	1.0%	150.0	0.9%	180.0	0.8%
Warehousing	79.0	3.1%	109.0	1.7%	184.0	1.5%	175.0	1.0%	232.0	1.0%
Subtotal	206.0	8.1%	346.0	5.3%	455.0	3.7%	485.0	2.8%	582.0	2.5%
PBDIT	(53.0)	(2.1%)	160.0	2.4%	661.0	5.4%	1,290.0	7.4%	2,022.0	8.7%
Finance Cost										
Lease rent	55.0	2.2%	106.0	1.6%	212.0	1.7%	296.0	1.7%	381.0	1.6%
W.C. interest	42.0	1.6%	50.0	0.8%	62.0	0.5%	89.0	0.5%	59.0	0.3%
Debt	0.0	0.0%	21.0	0.3%	0.0	0.0%	0.0	0.0%	0.0	0.0%
Depreciation	7.0	0.3%	47.0	0.7%	70.0	0.6%	93.0	0.5%	116.0	0.5%
Contingency	50.0	2.0%	75.0	1.1%	100.0	0.8%	100.0	0.6%	0.0	0.0%
Profit before tax	(207.0)	(8.1%)	(139.0)	(2.1%)	217.0	1.8%	712.0	4.1%	1,466.0	6.3%

*Some of the data may have been disguised.

(U.S. $114). On average, there were about five people per household. It was estimated that a store would have to attract 2,000 households for most of their shopping needs in order to break even. In Madras, seven neighborhoods were chosen. Real estate availability then dictated the ultimate choice of sites.

RAMASWAMY ROAD

The first store was opened on May 9, 1996, on Ramaswamy Road in a predominantly upper-middle-income residential area of Madras where over 8,000 target households were within a two-kilometer radius. The street was heavily trafficked, but less cluttered

EXHIBIT 5 Populations and Income Levels of Households in Key Cities within the FoodWorld Market Area

Town	Population	Households* with Monthly Incomes of:			
		Rs 5,500 and above	Rs 3,000 to 5,500	Rs 1,500 to 3,000	Total
Madras	5,600,000	75,000	100,000	150,000	325,000
Hyderabad	4,300,000	30,000	50,000	70,000	150,000
Bangalore	4,100,000	45,000	65,000	90,000	200,000
Cochin	1,100,000	20,000	30,000	50,000	100,000
Coimbatore	1,200,000	20,000	30,000	50,000	100,000
Madurai	1,100,000	20,000	25,000	45,000	90,000
Trichy	700,000	15,000	20,000	35,000	70,000
Salem	600,000	10,000	20,000	30,000	60,000
Warrangal	500,000	2,000	5,000	13,000	20,000
Vizag	1,100,000	20,000	15,000	25,000	60,000
Vijayawada	800,000	10,000	20,000	30,000	60,000
Gunter	500,000	2,000	5,000	13,000	20,000
Mysore	600,000	10,000	15,000	20,000	45,000
Hubli/Dharwar	600,000	10,000	15,000	20,000	45,000
Trivandrum	800,000	10,000	20,000	25,000	55,000
Calicut	800,000	10,000	15,000	20,000	45,000
Total		309,000	450,000	691,000	1,450,000

*There were approximately five people per household, on average, in Indian cities.

with small shops than many of the other larger streets in the area. Still, the store's brightly lit and colorful facade stood in stark contrast to its surroundings. Some thought it might even be seen as imposing or threatening, suggesting the higher prices often associated with more modern environments.

Dedicated parking was unavailable, but most customers were expected to live within walking distance of the store. Several spaces were available, however, on the street in front. The store stood back from the street, providing a small courtyard in which a snack-food and a fresh-fruit vendor leased space.

While Mohapatra and his colleagues had wanted a store with between 3,000 and 6,000 square feet of selling space, they found that such large areas were virtually impossible to find in Madras. They had therefore settled on this 2,400-square-foot store. With no room for any back room or storage area, a 600-square-foot apartment on the third floor had also been rented for an office and employee lunchroom, and some storage had been created above the display racks in the store and on the side on the courtyard in front. It was clear that adapting the store design and layout to each available location was going to be a continuing challenge as FoodWorld expanded in different locations and cities.

Inside the store, the aisles were arranged with clear signage and easily accessible arrays of choices of staples, processed foods, health and beauty aids, and dairy products. The decision had been made to offer a selection of all national brands and a more limited selection of the more popular regional and local brands. Since tastes varied so much by city and even by neighborhood within a city, it was important to have just the right products in stock. In order to assure a complete offering, one of each item from competing stores had been purchased from competing stores and a list compiled and shown to a sample of prospective customers who added or deleted items they considered necessary or irrelevant. A final list of 3,500 SKUs was thus created.

The ends of each aisle were rented to manufacturers as promotional displays. Revenue from the seven available end-aisles averaged about 4,000 rupees per month, or about 190 rupees per square foot.

It would have been too labor intensive to offer rice, lentils, and other basic commodities in bulk, so a FoodWorld private label was created for prepackaged amounts of these items. It was expected that up to 25 percent of total sales would be FoodWorld products, lending both customer convenience and image to the store offering.

Every item in the store was marked individually with both a price and a bar code which could be scanned at any of the four cash registers. Believing that item-by-item inventory control would be critical to the success of a chain of markets, FoodWorld had invested in state-of-the-art cash registers and bar-code scanners. Since there was no established norm for bar coding in India, however, Spencers' staff itself had designed and implemented a complete bar-coding system.

Obtaining shopping carts was also a problem, but they were considered necessary to maximize the amount customers would buy on each visit. Imported carts were far too costly an investment, and no company in India manufactured such unusual items. Raghu Pillai, chief executive of FoodWorld, had therefore designed and worked closely with a local metal fabrication shop to develop a cart of their own. While several small problems remained and required fine-tuning before the carts could go in to production, by late August the first were scheduled to arrive in the stores.

Display racks had presented a similar challenge. Imported racks were too costly, and the desired high racks were not available in India, so all of the racks for the new store had to be custom designed and manufactured.

Since customers were used to paying the maximum retail price (MRP) established by manufacturers and enforced by the government for all foodstuffs and packaged goods, FoodWorld prices were set at the MRP.

There was one deviation from this policy. FoodWorld offered something which had never been tried in India, as far as anyone knew. Certain items in the store were offered at prices below normal (5 to 10 percent), and labeled as special values within the store. Four thousand "Value Shopping Guides" (fliers announcing these special bargains along with a series of weekly contests) were delivered by local youngsters directly to each household which fell within the target demographics and were within a two kilometer radius of the store. The cost for this flier and its distribution was .75 rupees per flier (U.S. $.02), net of the contribution by manufacturers which essentially covered production costs. Another 4,000 monthly fliers were also mailed to target households at an average cost of 5.5 rupees. Customers seemed to respond enthusiastically to these promotional programs.

Each store had one store manager to whom three supervisors reported. Reporting to the supervisors were 10 full-time customer service representatives (CSRs) and 8 part-time CSRs who were attending the work-study program at the NIR. They were all well paid by local standards, ranging from front line CSRs, who were paid 2,000 rupees per month (U.S. $57), to the manager, who was paid 10,000 rupees per month (U.S. $285). A bonus program representing between 10 and 20 percent of total compensation was based on store sales, results of a monthly customer satisfaction survey, and a management service audit. Total payroll was 72,000 rupees per store per month.

At the corporate level, general managers of human resources, operations, and merchandising reported to Raghu Pillai, the chief executive of the retail group. He in turn reported to Pradipta Mohapatra, president of the retail group. A total of 17 professionals

EXHIBIT 6   FoodWorld Supermarket's Results from the First Two Months
             (May 9–June 30, 1996)*

Sales	Rs	3,931,000
Average sales per day	Rs	85,000
Number of customers		68,820
Number of transactions (average per day)		
Cash		475
Credit card		23
Average transaction value		
Cash	Rs	148
Credit card	Rs	652
Sales volume (average per day)		
Number of units		3,968
Number of SKUs		992
Average sale per unit	Rs	21.54

Category Sales

	Sales (in Rupees)	Percent of Total	Gross Margin %
Staples	1,134,000	28.85	13.18
Processed foods	807,000	20.53	12.00
Beverages	450,000	11.45	8.86
Cleaning aids	359,000	9.13	9.86
Health and beauty	658,000	16.74	12.10
General merchandise	90,000	2.29	22.41
Perishables	433,000	11.07	11.09
Total	3,931,000	100.00	12.03

FoodWorld Brand Sales

	Sales	Percent of Total
FoodWorld brand	740,000	19.00
Other brands	3,191,000	81.00

*Some of the data may have been disguised.
The prevailing exchange rate was approximately 35 rupees per U.S. dollar.

as well as an administrative staff supported these executives. It was projected that a total of 110 people would be required in the corporate offices by the time 50 stores were in operation. Corporate overhead was projected to be 1,416,000 rupees per month.

EARLY RETURNS

During the first three weeks of operation, 36,000 customers visited the new store. Sales volume and gross margins by the end of the month exceeded pro forma estimates. (Refer to Exhibit 6, Results from the First Two Months.) Some manufacturers and suppliers were showing a willingness to be creative and innovative, even to the point of discussing the implications of a changed relationship derived from dealing with a large chain of stores.

Bolstered by this response, Spencers' executives were eager to proceed with the continuing rollout of the FoodWorld stores. The basic offering, they realized, was strong as was the broad product offering. Sales and margins were beyond expectations. The results from one store, however, were not enough to validate their initial assumptions and conclusions. Another two stores in Madras were already in the pipeline for August openings, and plans were in place for a fourth. A similar rollout scheduled for late fall and early winter in Bangalore would provide a much more meaningful picture and give more direction in determining what adjustments they would have to make to the formula.

FRASER RIVER PLASTICS LTD.

CASE 20

Christopher K. Bart, *McMaster University*

Marvin G. Ryder, *McMaster University*

It was early 1993. Elinore Wickham-Jones, president of British Columbia–based Fraser River Plastics Ltd., was uneasy about the crosscurrents of opinion that were developing regarding the company's future direction. Although the differences of view had perhaps been held for some time, they had surfaced in recent weeks as the merits of several projects—among them a move toward international expansion and an acquisition—were being reviewed. There was, Wickham-Jones felt, more than normal agitation in the atmosphere. Lines were hardening on the questions of how aggressively and in what direction the company should proceed.

THE CANADIAN PLASTICS PROCESSING INDUSTRY IN 1993

Although the history of plastics and plastics products goes back over 100 years, in 1993 the industry was still generally regarded in North America as young and growing. In fact, it had only been since World War II that plastic had begun to achieve its status as a major primary or substitute manufacturing material.

In 1993, there were over 1,400 firms engaged in plastics processing in Canada, with most of the companies located in Ontario and Quebec. Of these Canadian firms, the majority had sales of less than $2 million. The bulk of company shipments constituted proprietary products. The remainder were either produced on a custom basis or as "captive operations" for a larger manufacturing entity. This breakdown, however, was difficult to confirm precisely due to the variety of business practices in which any one manufacturing concern engaged.

In terms of the future, world shipments in the plastics processing industry were estimated in 1993 to be moderately "favorable" given the tentative signals of economic recovery. The factors contributing to this projection were an anticipated moderate level of economic growth; a continuing substitution of plastics for traditional materials; and the emergent growth in the manufacturing sector. Costs depended largely on the type of process used. For instance, reinforced plastic products (e.g., boats and storage tanks) were relatively labor-intensive, whereas extrusion products (e.g., pipes and films) were relatively capital-intensive.

In comparison with other global industries, the plastics industry was still considered a labor-intensive area. For example, in plastics the capital investment per production-related employee ranged between Cdn$5,000 and $42,000, while in petrochemicals it was about Cdn$200,000.

It was anticipated that Canadian plastics manufacturing capacity would be sufficient to meet Canadian demands. In addition, Canadian resin prices, which at one time exceeded world prices by 10 percent, were seen as becoming more competitive with U.S. and other international prices given the recent Canada–U.S. Free Trade Agreement. The prospect, in 1993, of a potential free trade agreement between Canada, the United States, and Mexico was expected to result in significant downward pressure on world prices and consolidation of the North American industry participants through mergers and bankruptcies.

CORPORATE HISTORY

The Early Years: 1984 to 1988

In the fall of 1984, two Vancouver, British Columbia, businessmen, Herbert Rudd and Oliver Farthingham, visited Portland, Oregon, on a tour sponsored by the Vancouver Board of Trade. Of the several plants they visited, one facility, Damian Plastics Inc., particularly caught their attention. This plant used an injection-molding process to manufacture heavy plastic products such as utility crates, garbage cans, and packing cartons. Damian used advanced techniques to minimize the raw material weight in the large products it produced, while retaining, through unique design, the essential rigidity and toughness. Both men, especially Farthingham, who had experience in plastics, felt there was a ready market for the products in Canada because (1) they would have a competitive edge over comparable but more expensive plastic products and (2) they could be marketed as substitutes for more expensive metal containers. The two men returned home with a tentative licensing agreement for all of Canada that included technical assistance from Damian and access to all mold designs.

The immediate problem facing Rudd and Farthingham was raising the $160,000 equity needed to build a plant and get into operation. By November, they had put together a group of local businesspeople and raised the required funds. Some of the backers, like Elinore Wickham-Jones, were associated with wholesale and industrial supply firms through which a sizable portion of the new plant's output could be marketed. On December 9, 1984, the company was incorporated under the name Fraser River Plastics Ltd. Its three major shareholders were Farthingham (20 percent), Wickham-Jones (18 percent), and Rudd (13 percent). Farthingham became Fraser River's first president. Rudd was made secretary–treasurer, and Wickham-Jones became a vice president.

Rudd located a 2-acre site for the company's manufacturing plant in Chilliwack, British Columbia—a small town near Vancouver. Bids were accepted on the building's construction in February 1985, and manufacturing equipment was ordered. During this early period, the company was being run by the three officers on a part-time basis, since all had their own full-time businesses as well. On April 1, 1985, Gunther Heinzman, a former plant manager of a Victoria plastics firm, was hired as general manager of Fraser River.

Heinzman recalled:

> Elinore took me out to the site in Chilliwack. It was just a ploughed field! A few days later we did the first public showing of our products at a trade fair in Victoria. All that I had available was two plastic garbage cans, three sizes of the packing cartons, and six pieces of Damian's literature.
>
> One week later, the first carload of products arrived from Portland. Most of it had to be stored in a small warehouse owned by one of our shareholders since there were no storage facilities yet.

In August 1985, production began at Chilliwack while finishing touches were made on the plant. There was a ready and substantial demand for the products. FRP's prices, although high, gained customer acceptance, and the products proved to be good substitutes for conventional products. It was not long before the company was operating in the black.

Through 1986, the company's operations expanded dramatically. A temporary office annex was erected at the Chilliwack site, and the plant's capacity was increased to accommodate demand. Substantial orders for the company's products also came in from Alberta. To cut transportation costs and get local exposure, Fraser River purchased an empty plant in Calgary, ordered equipment, and hired a general manager to take charge there. The Calgary plant was in full operation by June 1986.

In time, Fraser River's success became known among those familiar with plastics processing. Not surprisingly, in 1987 another group of entrepreneurs set up a facility to produce similar injection-molding products; their plant was in Prince Rupert, British Columbia. Fraser River had no legal remedy, since the products and processes it licensed from Damian were poorly protected by patents. In addition, the initial barriers to entry—such as the special molds and know-how—started to crumble. Although the new firm marketed its products under its own name, there was little, save some cosmetic design differences, to distinguish the Prince Rupert products from those manufactured by Fraser River. As one company executive put it, "The plant in Prince Rupert was the first time we really experienced direct competition."

Fraser River's response was an offer to purchase the Prince Rupert competitor. This offer was accepted in November 1987, and Fraser River retained the old company's major shareholder as general manager. The purchase was not well received, however, by the Prince Rupert company's minority shareholders. They took their proceeds from the sale and shortly thereafter set up another injection-molding plant in Nanaimo, British Columbia.

By 1988, Wickham-Jones and Farthingham had become concerned about the limitations of the present three-person board in light of the company's growth and changing external circumstances. There were also signs, particularly in relation to the acquisition of the Prince Rupert company, that some of Fraser River's minority shareholders were disturbed and would like to see a broader representation of views at the board level. As a consequence, three new members were added to Fraser River's board: Owen Palmer, head of a local supermarket chain; Joanna Young, a management consultant who ran the local office of a large national firm; and Michelle O'Reilly, Fraser River's legal counsel.

Up to this point, the organization of the company had been loosely structured. Each of the firm's plants—in Chilliwack, Calgary, and Prince Rupert—had its own managers and field sales force reporting to Gunther Heinzman, the company's general manager. Wickham-Jones, Farthingham, and Rudd were considered the overall management committee. They had the primary responsibility for major decisions such as site selection, price, expansion, and capital investments, but they were also involved on an ad hoc basis in many overlapping operating functions.

The First Transition: 1989 to 1992

At the suggestion of Farthingham, Joanna Young reviewed the company's organization in early 1989 to "assess the marketing strengths and weaknesses of the company and to suggest desirable changes." Her principal recommendation was as follows:

> There is a clear need for greater continuity, consistency, and detail in the top supervision of overall operations. The current dispersed nature of responsibilities among the company's executives should be focused in the hands of a single chief executive with time for close day-to-day contact with the organization. As chief executive officer, this person would be responsible for all company operations and for initiating and implementing policy changes with the concurrence of the board.

Prior to submitting her report, Young reviewed its content with Farthingham and discussed the need for a full-time president. Farthingham agreed with the notion but noted that his own commitments in other companies prevented him from assuming this expanded role. It was not, in any case, his cup of tea: "I've always considered myself a front man, an entrepreneur, a hustler." As a consequence, Farthingham suggested that he become chair and Wickham-Jones become president. In taking on the president's role, Wickham-Jones agreed to reduce the time spent on her family business and to run Fraser River on a full-time basis.

At the time of the reorganization, Gunther Heinzman was made manufacturing vice president. Although his title changed, his operating duties with respect to plant operation and supervision remained the same.

Heinzman commented on the reorganization:

> It was an inevitable change. As general manager, I didn't have the time needed to run the sales organization. I didn't like the pressure at the top. Besides, my strength is manufacturing. That's what I know best and that's where I'm most comfortable.

Shortly after the reorganization, Lucas Feck was hired for the position of marketing vice president. Feck recounted his early days:

> I suppose it was the entrepreneurial attitude and capabilities of the people at Fraser River which attracted me to the company. It was like running my own business; there was freedom to run things as I thought they should be.
>
> When I joined, Fraser River had experienced no stiff competition from new entrants yet. The company was begging for more structure and policies in its administration. For instance, at Calgary, the sales manager had no fixed sales price. Hell, there wasn't even a price list, so no one in the marketplace—including our customers—knew what the prices of the products were from one day to the next. There was no fixed collection policy for the company, and there was a high turnover in sales personnel.
>
> During my first 18 months, I restructured the sales organization. I set up the company's first sales forecast and budgets for each territory and established a reporting system so that salespeople knew how they and their region were doing on a monthly basis. I even instituted an advertising budget—another first!

Throughout 1989, the company continued to grow. Demand was strong and prices were reasonable in spite of the advent of significant competition and an emerging economic recession. The year was also marked by two acquisitions: Beaver Plastics in Vancouver, British Columbia, and Simcoe Plastics of Kamloops, British Columbia.

Beaver Plastics was a company owned by Farthingham that manufactured plastic pipe using an extrusion-molding process. In late 1989, Farthingham expressed concern over having to wear two hats in promoting the products of both Fraser River and Beaver. Even customers were associating the two firms as one. Sales representatives from the two companies often called on the same wholesaler/distributor accounts. In fact, some of Fraser River's fittings were made to fit the plastic pipe produced by Beaver. At the same time, Fraser River was looking for opportunities to expand its product lines. With this in mind, in early 1990 Farthingham offered his company for sale to the board of Fraser River. The sale was negotiated for cash and debt, and by year's end Wickham-Jones reported that the sales, profits, and growth resulting from the acquisition were "very encouraging."

Simcoe Plastics was a family-owned operation that manufactured plastic shower curtains and raincoats using a manufacturing process known as calendering. In October 1989, Wickham-Jones heard that the company was for sale. She believed that the purchase of Simcoe would provide Fraser River with instant product diversification as well as give Fraser River the capability of producing other items, such as plastic wall coverings and backing for upholstery fabrics.

Fraser River completed its purchase of Simcoe by November 1989. The most significant operational change involved experimentation with the production of plastic-coated wall coverings. By doing so, the company hoped to take up the apparent slack in Simcoe's manufacturing facilities.

Despite the worsening recession, Fraser River concluded its 1990 fiscal year on a particularly strong note (see Exhibits 1 and 2). The strong profit showing, however, did not completely compensate for a number of developing problems:

1. The plant manager in the Calgary manufacturing facility was fired because of a failure to reduce inefficiencies and waste in the plant.

2. Inefficiency was also a problem at Simcoe, although the waste factor had been reduced substantially since the company's acquisition. Simcoe was experimenting with production of new plastic products. Costs there were mounting rapidly, a matter of increasing concern to Fraser River executives. Some blamed these problems on overreliance on the management that Fraser River had inherited when it bought Simcoe. For example, the plant manager, who had remained when the firm was acquired by Fraser River, did not have the necessary qualifications to successfully oversee the plant's experimental work. As a consequence, he was fired in May 1990, and Heinzman was instructed to supervise more closely the operation of the plant and its product development activities.

3. Two large competitors had entered Fraser River's traditional markets. One, Moldform Ltd., was a subsidiary of a large conglomerate organization. The other, Plastech Ltd., was a division of a company involved in other plastic-processing operations. Both operated in British Columbia and Alberta. Market shares were unknown. But a rough estimate gave Fraser River about 40 percent of the western Canada market and 15 percent each to Moldform and Plastech. The balance of 30 percent was shared by a variety of small companies manufacturing limited product lines and capitalizing on low overheads and local contracts to operate.

EXHIBIT 1   Fraser River Plastics, Consolidated Balance Sheets, 1988–92 (In thousands of Canadian dollars)

	1992	1991	1990	1989	1988
Assets					
Current assets:					
Cash	$ 25	$ 30	$ 5	$ 565	$ 110
Term deposits and marketable securities	—	583	2	—	690
Accounts receivable	2,453	1,155	1,215	423	540
Inventories	3,827	2,625	1,923	2,163	357
Deposits	13	25	140	2	3
Total current assets	6,318	4,428	3,285	3,153	1,700
Property, plant and equipment, at cost less accumulated depreciation	4,453	2,935	2,743	1,940	1,468
Other assets	17	28	7	15	60
Excess of cost of subsidiaries over the net book value of acquired assets, at cost less amortization	105	145	185	105	130
Total assets	$10,893	$7,536	$6,220	$5,213	$3,358
Liabilities and Shareholders' Equity					
Current liabilities:					
Bank overdraft and loan	$ 2,348	$ 863	$ 515		
Accounts payable and accrued charges	892	1,042	338	$1,063	$ 145
Income and other taxes payable	618	738	962	1,065	260
Royalty payable	—	—	70	90	400
Total current liabilities	3,858	2,643	1,885	2,198	805
Deferred revenue	28	33	33		
Long-term debt	3,150	1,120	1,282	715	875
Total liabilities	7,036	3,796	3,200	2,913	1,680
Shareholders' equity:					
Preferred shares	—	—	—	—	253
Common shares	205	205	205	32	32
Contributed surplus	70	70	70	70	70
Retained earnings	3,582	3,465	2,745	2,198	1,323
Total shareholders' equity	3,857	3,740	3,020	2,300	1,678
Total liabilities and shareholders' equity	$10,893	$7,536	$6,220	$5,213	$3,358

In 1991, the demand for Fraser River products in British Columbia softened, due mostly to increased competition and local market saturation.

To expand the company's geographic market, the company built a manufacturing facility in Winnipeg, Manitoba. Sales of Fraser River's products in midwestern Canada had risen during the past several years, but transportation costs had reduced the firm's competitive position and profit margin. The risk of entering the region against established competition was accepted by company executives. The company also had

EXHIBIT 2   Fraser River Plastics Ltd., Statement of Income and Selected Financial Ratios, 1988–92
            (In thousands of Canadian dollars)

	1992	1991	1990	1989	1988
Net sales	$16,445	$15,750	$10,903	$7,835	$5,403
Cost of sales	11,228	10,765	7,178	3,990	3,455
Gross profit	5,217	4,985	3,725	3,845	1,948
Selling, general, and administrative expenses	3,605	2,750	1,898	838	655
Royalty expenses	332	332	332	625	338
Total operating expenses	3,937	3,082	2,230	1,463	993
Operating profit	1,280	1,903	1,495	2,382	955
Interest and other income	128	135	40	163	80
	1,408	2,038	1,535	2,545	1,035
Interest, long-term debt	493	138	92	70	77
Amortization of excess cost of subsidiaries over net book value of acquired assets	40	40	35	27	
	533	178	127	97	77
Earnings before income taxes	875	1,860	1,408	2,448	958
Income taxes	480	825	610	1,208	453
Net earnings	$ 395	$ 1,035	$ 798	$1,240	$ 505
Earnings per common share	$ 0.08	$ 0.20	$ 0.15	$ 0.24	$ 0.10
Dividends paid	278	315	251	365	
Dividends per common share	.05	.06	.05	.07	
Selected Financial Ratios					
Current assets/current liabilities	1.6	1.7	1.7	1.4	2.1
Total assets/total liabilities	1.5	2.0	1.9	1.8	2.0
Long-term debt/equity	0.8	0.3	0.4	0.3	0.5
Gross profit/net sales	0.32	0.32	0.34	0.49	0.36
Inventory turnover	2.9	4.1	3.7	1.8	9.7
SG&A expense/gross profit	0.69	0.55	0.51	0.22	0.34
EBIT/gross profit	0.17	0.37	0.38	0.64	0.49

encouraging internal projections covering the size and future growth of the market in eastern Canada. (Exhibit 3 shows financial results by separate facilities, through 1992.)

At a board meeting, Wickham-Jones later informed the other members that because of the decline in market growth and increasing competition, particularly in British Columbia, she and Marketing Vice President Lucas Feck were investigating numerous potential corporate acquisitions for Fraser River, including a car dealership, a precision tool manufacturing operation, a hotel, and a corrugated steel manufacturing operation. To date, no deal had been consummated.

In September 1992, Wickham-Jones hired Clayton Dunwood as Fraser River's vice president for administration. Dunwood assumed complete responsibility for the accounting and financial affairs of the company. Wickham-Jones felt that Dunwood

EXHIBIT 3   Operating Performance of Fraser River's Plants and Business Segments, 1990–92 (In thousands of Canadian dollars)

	Chilliwack and Prince Rupert			Calgary			Winnipeg and Toronto†			Beaver Plastics		Simcoe Plastics	
	1992	1991	1990	1992	1991	1990	1992	1991	1990	1992	1991	1992	1991
Dollar sales	$6,365	$6,790	$6,115	$6,710	$5,180	$4,365	$ 335	$403	$75	$2,950	$3,660	$1,303	$1,318
Discounts	275	220	310	153	183	175	20	33	5	57	50	28	20
Net sales	6,090	6,570	5,805	6,557	4,997	4,190	315	370	70	2,893	3,610	1,275	1,298
Cost of goods sold	4,148	4,420	4,075	4,412	3,332	2,748	312	280	50	2,265	2,765	930	1,073
Gross margin	1,942	2,150	1,730	2,145	1,665	1,442	3	90	20	628	845	345	225
Operating costs	1,382	1,093	920	1,190	847	657	153	95	48	733	580	278	313
Royalty*	165	192	192	167	140	137							
Pretax profit (loss)	$ 395	$ 865	$ 618	$ 788	$ 678	$ 648	$(150)	$ (5)	$(28)	$ (105)	$ 265	$ 47	$ (88)

*Each of the plants producing injection-molded products pays a royalty fee internally to Fraser River Plastics Ltd. The parent company in turn pays a royalty fee to its licensor (Damian) based on the total company production of such products, but to a limit of $332,000 as of 1991.

†Toronto sales operations have been supplied with production from Manitoba and British Columbia plants.

would be of particular help to her in the area of investigation of future corporate acquisitions. However, Lucas Feck continued to be especially disappointed with Fraser River's efforts in this area. He commented on Fraser River's need for new companies:

> Since 1989 I have been pushing other senior managers to find new areas for investment and growth. Fraser River's bread-and-butter products have become commodity items. The industry is easy to enter. We have to have other businesses to support the overheads which have built up in the company. When I look at our markets here in British Columbia, I don't see anywhere to go . . . and it looks like it's going to be an uphill battle to crack the eastern market. That's why I firmly believe that we should be planning our growth more—with, say, 20 percent coming from new acquisitions.
>
> We haven't had a new company here in some time. It's very frustrating when you consider the number of firms that we've looked at. Of course, you get people like Joanna Young and that lawyer, O'Reilly. Whenever we bring a good acquisition to the board, they're always harping on how there are better deals around. Yet, they can't suggest any themselves.

Through 1992, Wickham-Jones also pursued another venture. Through various publications, she was aware of the need for the type of products produced by Fraser River in other parts of the world, particularly in the less developed countries (LDCs) in Asia. She believed this represented an opportunity for Fraser River, with its accumulated expertise in plastic products. Wickham-Jones concentrated her efforts on finding a partner to provide the international expertise and contacts that Fraser River lacked. Preliminary discussions were held with one such partner—a Canadian manufacturer of logging and sawmill equipment with sales offices in a number of foreign countries and a record of joint venture projects with nationals of those countries (mainly to set up logging and sawmill operations). The proposed agreement was for the two companies to form a joint venture limited partnership supplying capital, equipment, and expertise for new ventures in the manufacture of plastic products. Hopefully, Canadian-based resin suppliers could be brought into the deal. Conscious of the reactions multinationals received when they "invaded the LDCs," the joint venture company was to keep a low profile in its international undertakings.

By December, Wickham-Jones reported that she had identified several countries in Asia as possible sites for a first undertaking. The pursuit of the joint venture's arrangements was, for the most part, being conducted by Wickham-Jones alone. She was, many felt, personally committed to the project and was devoting more and more of her time to it. Wickham-Jones commented:

> Sure, I'm committed. I really believe we can turn Fraser River into a worldwide organization and provide a useful service to other countries at the same time.
>
> And, yes, this project is taking up a lot of my time. But that's because we don't know anything about operating on an international level. Once I know what's involved, I'll probably hire another vice president and put him in charge of our international operations. In addition, the universities are full of young aggressive people who can be brought on board to help "fill the gaps" created in Fraser River . . . We should also be able to buy talent either from the market or other organizations.

Exhibit 4 shows Fraser River's corporate structure as of the end of 1992, and Exhibit 5 is an unofficial organization chart for corporate headquarters.

THE SITUATION IN EARLY 1993

In January 1993, Wickham-Jones received drafts of Fraser River's financial statements for the 1992 fiscal year (see Exhibits 1–3). Overall, growth in company sales was sluggish, as a result of sharper competition—in particular, from smaller local plastic

EXHIBIT 4   Fraser River Plastics Ltd. Corporate Structure (Case writers' summary; no official organization charts existed at the company)

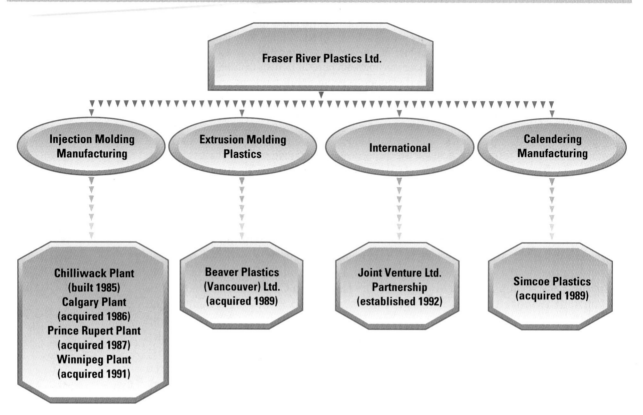

Notes:
All companies 100% owned by Fraser River Ltd. except potential joint venture (50%).
It was a general corporate policy to incorporate a separate company for each plant and business to ensure maximum limited liability.

manufacturing plants. These plants had contributed to the considerable market erosion experienced by Fraser River, especially in British Columbia. The company's share in Alberta, on the other hand, had remained strong. Profits had slipped a bit due to interest payments.

Unfortunately, Simcoe Plastics had not made much progress. To improve the situation, a qualified and experienced plastics engineer had been hired in late 1992 to take over the plant. The board considered making Simcoe more independent, by hiring a general manager, but that action had been deferred for the moment.

Beaver Plastics was also in trouble. The British Columbia market for extruded pipe was saturated and extremely competitive. At present, there were few growth prospects unless the international and eastern projects began to take off. Unfortunately, the eastern market had become a sore spot. Acceptance of Fraser River's products had not been as favorable as initially thought. Despite this, Wickham-Jones forecast that within two years the Winnipeg plant would be self-supporting.

In the meantime, two specific issues had arisen that required action. The first concerned the proposed international joint venture. Fraser River's potential partner in that venture had reported that preliminary inquiries conducted by its office in Indonesia had revealed substantial interest on the part of both government officials and local businesspeople. A request had been made for Fraser River to send an investigative

EXHIBIT 5   Fraser River Plastics Ltd. Corporate Headquarters Organization, 1992 (Case writers' summary; no official organization charts existed at the company)

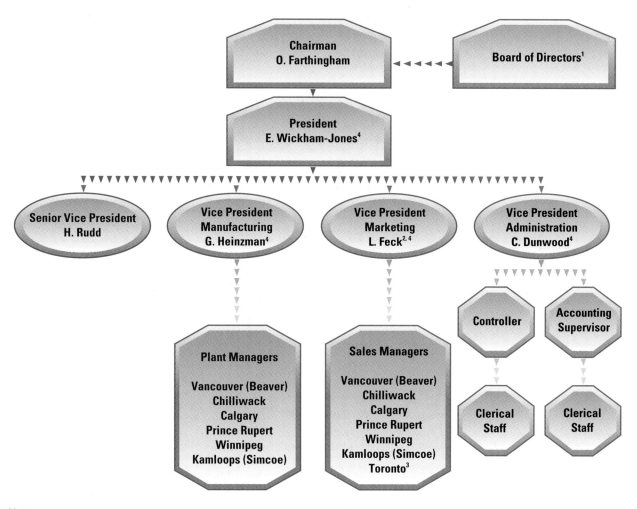

Notes:
1. Board members include O. Farthingham (chairman), E. Wickham-Jones, H. Rudd, J. Young, M. J. O'Reilly, and Grant Ackerfeldt.
2. Feck was also president of Beaver Plastics Ltd.
3. One sales representative only.
4. Wickham-Jones's and Feck's offices are located in one corner of a wholesale warehouse owned by Wickham-Jones in Vancouver. Heinzman and Fraser River's accounting staff, on the other hand, are situated one hour's drive away at the Chilliwack plant. This arrangement suited Feck because he had been made president of Beaver Plastics—which was also located in Vancouver.

team to Indonesia. Wickham-Jones felt that if she delayed a response too long, the "partner" might begin to doubt Fraser River's good faith or abilities to proceed.

In addition, Wickham-Jones had heard of another plastics company that was for sale and that, if acquired, might serve to strengthen and broaden Fraser River's product line. The company involved, Plasti-Weave, was located in Kelowna, British Columbia— approximately 80 kilometers away from the Chilliwack facility. Plasti-Weave was a very small operation with sales of less than $1 million in 1992 (see Exhibit 6). It had developed a significant and potentially patentable process of "weaving" plastic strips into strong sheets that could be used as substitutes for jute in carpet backing, furniture

EXHIBIT 6　Plasti-Weave Financial Statements, 1991 and 1992 (In thousands of Canadian dollars)

Balance Sheet Data	1992	1991
Current assets	$800	$619
Fixed assets (net)	70	57
Other assets	9	7
Total assets	$879	$683
Current liabilities	$183	$114
Deferred taxes	1	—
Long-term shareholder loan	77	64
Capital stock	1	1
Retained earnings	617	504
Total liabilities and equity	$879	$683
Income Statement Data		
Sales	$950	$616
Other income—interest	4	2
Cost of goods sold	556	345
Expenses	192	148
Income taxes	77	28
Net income	$129	$ 97
Dividends paid	$ 16	$ 12
Selected financial ratios:		
Current assets/Current liabilities	4.4	5.4
Total assets/Total liabilities	3.4	3.8
Long-term debt/Equity	0.12	0.13
Gross profit/Net sales	0.41	0.44

manufacture, and so on. In 1992, Plasti-Weave realized that a major expansion would be required to exploit the potential of the new product. A new plant and warehouse would have to be built in Kelowna at an approximate cost of $750,000. The owner of Plasti-Weave, Clifford Bell, who was also the inventor of the manufacturing process, did not want to commit himself to this level of debt at the age of 62, or to be responsible for managing the company. Two recent heart attacks had resulted in his decision to sell, if the price was right. However, one of the conditions of sale was that he be retained as a consultant to the company for at least 10 years.

Wickham-Jones was enthusiastic about acquiring Plasti-Weave, but was unsure what the board's reaction would be in light of the $1 million asking price. She was confident, nevertheless, that the board would approve the deal—if she pushed hard enough for it.

FRASER RIVER'S EXECUTIVES LOOK TO THE FUTURE

As the company considered 1992 results and considered the various paths it might follow in 1993, key executives voiced their own points of view.

Oliver Farthingham—Chairman of the Board

Oliver Farthingham began his own business upon graduation from high school. He had interests in an automotive body repair business and a partnership in a Canadian distributorship for narrow-aisle forklift trucks. As chairman of the board, Farthingham's day-to-day involvement with Fraser River was limited, but this did not stop him from doing what he liked to do best—promote the Fraser River name. In fact, he was regarded as one of the most outspoken people in the company. Farthingham commented on Fraser River and its operations:

> As chairman, I'm a "positive thinker." I'm sure not a worrier . . . I'm a doer and a real strategist. I also think that I have an ability to persuade people and inspire confidence.
>
> Although my job and title around here have changed, I still have the reputation for being a "high price" zealot. Fraser River's prices have generally been the highest in the industry. Sometimes our shareholders question me on this point. I always tell them that we're not in business to make plastic products—but rather to make profits. People respect me for that.
>
> The world is full of pessimists and timid people. That's not my style. I'm quite innovative and have a knack for foresight. Look at our acquisitions. For instance, there's our plant in Prince Rupert. It made us look strong in our clients' and competitors' eyes. Sure it's not as strong today due to the competition, but that's because the guy we having running the show there has lost his aggressiveness.
>
> As for the purchase of Simcoe, I don't buy the stories about our failure in developing new products there. The problem is that we've just been fooling around and haven't devoted our full efforts to these experimental projects.
>
> Plastics, unfortunately, is a cyclical industry where profits are driven by the economy, crude oil supplies, and costs. This means, therefore, that we have to look for new products and new companies. We should especially be considering more exciting ventures like sports bars, cappuccino kiosks, or even roller blade rinks. They're the rage in the U.S. right now. Market demand is phenomenal—200 percent growth annually. Competition is low. We can get in on the ground floor. And we can buy the managerial talent we need to run them for us. They are opportunities that won't wait for us.
>
> The pessimists, however, say that we don't have the resources to handle these deals. Well, Fraser River has been in this position in the past and we've survived. Look at how we originally got started. To be an entrepreneur takes guts! I'm a risk taker and I know when the odds are in our favor. We can't afford to burden ourselves with negative thoughts.
>
> I feel I have a personal obligation to all of our shareholders to keep our reputation and profits the most attractive in the industry. After all, we still have the same number of shareholders we started out with. To keep them, we have to show them that their investment is better left in the company and to reward them with bigger dividends. We also have to provide them with some vehicle for eventually cashing out. So, I guess this means we'll have to consider going public. I think it would enhance our image greatly too.

Elinore Wickham-Jones—President

Elinore Wickham-Jones had accomplished two of the major objectives in her life— she was financially well off and she had built a company from the ground up. Wickham-Jones had used most of her personal savings to invest in the formation of Fraser River. As vice president, she had been known for her analytical brilliance. When she became president, she committed herself to making the company grow into a national plastic manufacturing concern.

> From 1985 to 1991, we managed to grow in spite of ourselves and our mistakes. To our credit, though, we moved quickly, we were flexible, and did not get bogged down in bureaucracy or paperwork.

Today, not all of our operations are as strong as we'd like, but there is still potential in them. Take Beaver Plastics, for instance. It was a natural combination with Fraser River. Sure, things are slow right now, but once we establish ourselves out east or in other new territories, we will be all right.

Simcoe Plastics is another case in point—and there, our plant manager was not as good as we thought he was. We've learned a lot from our R&D work at Simcoe—even though it cost us $200,000.

I'd like to see Fraser River grow on an even-keel basis through acquisitions and internal expansion. Of course, we're only interested in profitable and growing ventures. But we can't afford to be in it just for the money. We need to maintain our profits so that we can fund other projects as opportunities present themselves.

That's why I'm particularly keen on both our Plasti-Weave acquisition proposal and the joint venture. Right now, we're heavily committed to what are essentially simple plastic products in just one market, Canada. Consequently, we have to reduce the associated risk. We haven't begun to exploit the American market opened to us through the Canada–U.S. Free Trade Agreement, and with a North American Free Trade Agreement soon to be completed, markets in Central and South America are becoming available.

Unfortunately, these new programs always seem to bring us back to the issue of financing. So, we need more capital and that probably means an equity issue. The question, however, becomes one of when and how.

Herbert Rudd—Senior Vice President

Herbert Rudd completed the 10th grade but then left school because his parents needed him to work on the family farm. Like most farmers, Rudd became an expert in home repairs. After he left home, he worked for a small home contractor until he decided to start his own construction business.

As senior vice president, Rudd's primary responsibility had been to represent the company at industry and trade fairs and exhibits both in Canada and abroad. He commented:

Oliver and I are the real entrepreneurs in this company. So, we make decisions primarily on gut feel. But I do think I have a good business sense and that's what I use to guide me in my judgments.

Looking back, I feel our biggest mistake has been the operation of large plants such as we have in Chilliwack and Calgary. Right now, small competitors have lower overhead and transportation costs and a more competitive price.

The joint venture project is a fantastic concept with unlimited potential for our company. I can't give any firm projections, but something tells me that this is the right road to go on. Look at Mexico. There are more people earning over $50,000 per year than there are living in Canada. I expect a western hemisphere free trade agreement by the year 2000. Some people are worried about staffing international ventures. Heck, there's a lot of talent in this company that's just not being used. After all, a boy doesn't become a man until he has a man's job to do.

Looking at the products we manufacture, though, I can't honestly say if they're better than everybody else's. I know they do the same job. But, looking at them, there's nothing to distinguish them from your ordinary loaf of bread. I also think that we have a problem communicating to our customers. Our salesmen could do a better job finding out what our customers want and what new products we should be producing.

Another major concern of mine is that we're just a limited product company and there's too much risk in it. That's why I'm in favor of diversification. And I really don't care what sort of companies we acquire. We can always hire someone to run them for us.

Lucas Feck—Vice President (Marketing)

Lucas Feck received his bachelor's degree in commerce from a large American university. Upon graduation he joined a multinational chemical company that operated a subsidiary in Canada. Within four years, he became its general manager. After the subsidiary was purchased by another multinational conglomerate, Feck became disenchanted and resigned to start his own small business. Despite the new company's success, Feck became bored and sold his interest. He went back to school and earned an MBA. After graduating, he contacted several large executive placement firms looking for a position in a small to medium-sized growth business. This led to his being hired as marketing vice president for Fraser River Plastics.

Feck was by far the most avid promoter of expanding the company by means of acquisitions. Because Feck had been actively involved in a number of acquisition investigations that had failed to result in a concrete purchase, he had come to believe that the company's present structure was standing in the way of its ability to make acquisitions.

> Our neck is really in the noose today because of the competition we're up against, especially in British Columbia. So I'm pretty strong on the idea of acquisitions. They're the key to our future. Personally, I believe we could run or manage any type of company—hotels, food processing, even steel corrugation plants. Others don't.
>
> Take this Plasti-Weave acquisition. It's a natural combination with our business—plastics. But, better still, it represents a real chance for Fraser River to latch onto a proprietary item. It involves a new technology. We can get the jump on the industry and at the same time start moving out of "commodity product" lines.
>
> As for the joint venture idea, I think we have some real problems because we've never considered (1) who's going to be moving from Fraser River to staff the project, and (2) who we're going to find to fill the gaps created in Fraser River. I've been pushing Elinore on this point, but she keeps saying, "Not to worry."
>
> I think our biggest problem around here, however, has to be that senior management is perpetually caught up 110 percent with day-to-day tasks. I don't think that we'll ever find any new growth or good acquisitions as long as we don't free up some of our time. Elinore Wickham-Jones has a problem divorcing herself from finance and administration. She's also been spending a lot of her time these days on the joint venture project . . . That's her style though.
>
> Oliver Farthingham's style, however, is to "represent" the company. He shouldn't be doing that as chairman of the company. He should be setting goals. After all, isn't the board responsible for the overall direction of the company? So what if "management" wants to do one thing. The board can just overturn it.
>
> I do know this . . . I only get my kicks from challenges. Day-to-day work is a necessity, of course, but it's not challenging to me. I'm not interested in managing a division. I just want senior management responsibility and exciting work. Otherwise, I get bored.

Gunther Heinzman—Vice President (Production)

Heinzman was in charge of the company's six plants located in Chilliwack, Vancouver (Beaver), Prince Rupert, Calgary, Winnipeg, and Kamloops (Simcoe). Each plant had its own production manager reporting directly to Heinzman.

A native of Germany, Heinzman had emigrated to Canada with his parents. His first job was in a small manufacturing concern, working on the production line. Since then, he had spent most of his life in production.

I learned this business from the ground up. Every free moment I had during the day and at night was spent reading every trade journal I could get my hands on. But, I guess you could say that even today, I'm kept pretty busy just keeping my end under control.

I've never been a frivolous person. I suppose it comes from my German background. That's why I have always run a tight ship. If Elinore ever told me to cut costs, I wouldn't know where to start because I think we're already at maximum efficiency. And I've tried to instill this objective into each one of my plant managers. I've trained every one of them, except the Simcoe manager, and I'm very proud of them. Naturally, I'm a little more liberal today, but I like to do things as cheap as possible. Sometimes Elinore has to say to me: "Don't hold the penny so close to your eye, Gunther, that you can't see the dollar behind it."

When I look at our acquisitions, there are some real lessons to be learned. I don't regret our purchase of the Prince Rupert plant because it has always supported itself. The manager there runs the company as if it was his own. After all, it used to be his own. Simcoe, however, should be a warning to future acquisitions. And, as for this Plasti-Weave deal, I won't say anything about it because I don't know anything about it. And that's because I haven't been involved in the discussions.

I'm not opposed to acquisitions but I'm naturally afraid of things that I don't know too much about. Elinore, of course, is more enthusiastic about acquisitions. Me, I'm a little more nervous about them. We have three different kinds of production processes here already—for injection, extrusion, and calendering—and I'm not sure how much more work I could handle.

As for this joint venture, Elinore is again playing her cards close to the vest and I don't think it's such a good idea. It's a big responsibility for her to be carrying alone. Besides, I'm a nationalist. Canada has been good to me and to this company. I think we could spend our dollars much wiser here.

CAMPBELL SOUP COMPANY

21

John E. Gamble, *University of South Alabama*

Arthur A. Thompson, Jr.,
The University of Alabama

In 1998 Campbell Soup Company was one of the world's leading manufacturers and marketers of branded consumer food products with approximately 24,250 employees, total revenues of $6.7 billion, 36 manufacturing plants in 10 nations, and over 2,000 products on the market. Its major products in the United States were its flagship red-and-white label canned soups, Prego spaghetti sauces, Godiva chocolates, Pepperidge Farm baked goods, V-8 vegetable juices, Swanson broths, Franco-American canned pastas, and Pace Mexican salsas. Devos Lemmens sauces, Arnott's baked goods, and Homepride sauces were the best-selling Campbell brands in various international markets.

COMPANY BACKGROUND

The company was founded in 1869 by Joseph Campbell, a fruit merchant, and Abram Anderson, an icebox maker, and was originally known for its jams and jellies. In 1891 it was incorporated as the Joseph Campbell Preserve Company in Camden, New Jersey. John T. Dorrance, a brilliant 24-year-old chemist with a Ph.D. from the Massachusetts Institute of Technology, was hired by the company in 1894 and three years later developed a process for creating canned soup in condensed form. The new process took water out of the soup during the canning process, thus dramatically reducing production and distribution costs. Soups made with the new production process were awarded a gold medal at the 1900 Paris Exhibition and by 1905 were selling at the rate of 40,000 cases per week. John T. Dorrance purchased the company in 1900, and it was entirely owned by his family until 1954. It was reincorporated as the Campbell Soup Company in 1922.

When Dorrance died in 1930, he left an estate of over $115 million—the nation's third largest at that time. He also left a company devoted to engineering, committed to providing good products (in recessions it would rather shave margins than cut back product quality or raise price), and obsessed with secrecy. His successor, John T. Dorrance, Jr., headed the company for the next 24 years (1930–54) and few, if any, important decisions were made at Campbell without John Dorrance, Jr.'s approval. In

1954, the company went public, with the Dorrance family retaining majority control. In 1998, the Dorrance family still owned about 50 percent of Campbell's stock and, despite having relinquished direct management control, still exerted considerable shareholder influence. Four of Campbell Soup's 16 board members were grandchildren of John T. Dorrance.

Over the years Campbell had diversified into a number of businesses—from frozen dinners to retail garden centers. However, canned soup had always remained its core business—60 percent of Campbell's 1998 revenues from canned soup were accounted for by the sale of just three varieties: tomato, cream of mushroom, and chicken noodle. The company had had three chief executive officers over the last 20 years, and its corporate strategy had evolved with each change in leadership. The company's diversification strategy and new investment priorities had shifted as each new CEO pursued a course to build value for Campbell Soup Company's shareholders.

THE GORDON McGOVERN ERA: 1980–89

Gordon McGovern was in business school when Margaret Rudkin, founder of Pepperidge Farm, spoke to his class. Rudkin told how she had built her bread company from scratch in an industry dominated by giants. McGovern was impressed. He wrote to Rudkin for a job, received it in 1956, and began his climb through Pepperidge Farm's ranks. When Campbell acquired it in 1961, Pepperidge Farm had sales of $40 million and had only reached $60 million when McGovern became its president in 1968. When McGovern was named president of Campbell in 1980, Pepperidge Farm's annual sales had grown to $300 million under his leadership. McGovern implemented several key elements of Pepperidge Farm's strategy when he took over at Campbell: creativity and a willingness to experiment, emphasis on new-product development, and strong competencies in marketing.

McGovern's Corporate Strategy as Campbell's CEO

During the McGovern years, Campbell's strategic focus was on the consumer. The consumer's "hot buttons" were identified as nutrition (including low sodium), convenience, price, quality, and uniqueness—and managers were urged to press those buttons. Business unit managers were expected to be responsive to consumer perceptions, needs, and demands regarding nutrition, safety, flavor, and convenience. Key business unit strategies included (1) improving operating efficiency, (2) developing new products to capitalize on consumer trends, (3) updating advertising for new and established products, and (4) continuing Campbell's long-standing emphasis on high production standards and premium-quality products.

Early in his tenure, McGovern developed a five-year plan that featured four financial performance objectives: a 15 percent annual increase in earnings, a 5 percent increase in volume, a 5 percent increase in sales (plus inflation), and an 18 percent return on equity by 1986. The two cornerstones of McGovern's growth strategy were (1) developing and introducing new products and (2) making acquisitions every two years that would bring in $200 million in annual sales. Campbell's acquisition strategy was to look for small, fast-growing food companies strong in product areas where Campbell had no presence and companies on the fast track that were in rapidly growing product categories or industries. Under McGovern, Campbell made a number of acquisitions:

1982 Acquisitions

- Mrs. Paul's Kitchens, Inc., a processor and marketer of frozen prepared seafood and vegetable products, with annual sales of approximately $125 million (acquired at a cost of $55 million).
- Snow King Frozen Foods, Inc., engaged in the production and marketing of a line of uncooked frozen specialty meat products, with annual sales of $32 million.
- Juice Bowl Products, Inc., a Florida producer of fruit juices.
- Win Schuler Foods, Inc., a Michigan-based producer and distributor of specialty cheese spreads, flavored melba rounds, food-service salad dressings, party dips, and sauces, with annual sales of $6.5 million.
- Costa Apple Products, Inc., a producer of apple juice retailed primarily in the eastern United States, with annual sales of $6 million.

1983 Acquisitions

- Several small domestic operations (at a cost of $26 million), including Annabelle's restaurant chain of 12 units in the southeastern United States and Triangle Manufacturing Corporation, a manufacturer of physical fitness and sports medicine products.

1984 Acquisitions

- Mendelson-Zeller Company, Inc., a California distributor of fresh produce.

1985 Acquisitions

- Continental Foods Company S.A. and affiliated companies that produced sauces, confectioneries, and other food products in Belgium and France; the cost of the acquisition was $17 million.
- A 20% ownership interest in Arnott's Ltd., an Australian producer of cookies and crackers.

1988 Acquisitions

- Freshbake Foods Group, a British producer of baked goods.

Campbell's Business Portfolio under McGovern

During the McGovern era, Campbell Soup Company was organized into six business units: Campbell U.S., Pepperidge Farm, Vlasic Foods, Mrs. Paul's Kitchens, Other United States, and International. Sales and profit performance by division are shown in Exhibit 1.

The Campbell U.S. Business Unit In 1989 the Campbell U.S. division was the company's largest operating unit, accounting for just over 50 percent of corporate revenues. The Campbell U.S. division was divided into eight profit centers: soup, frozen foods, grocery, beverage, food service, poultry, fresh produce, and pet foods. Exhibit 2 shows the brands Campbell had in this division and the major competitors each brand faced during most of the 1980s.

The soup business group alone accounted for more than 25 percent of the company's consolidated sales (as compared to around 50 percent in the 1970s). Campbell's flagship brands of soup accounted for 80 percent of the $1 billion–plus annual canned soup market; in 1989, Campbell offered grocery shoppers over 50 varieties of canned soup. Heinz was the second largest soup producer, with 10 percent of the market. Heinz had earlier withdrawn from producing Heinz-label soups and shifted to producing soups for sale under the private labels of grocery chains; Heinz was the leading private-label producer of canned soup, holding almost an 80 percent share of the private-label segment.

EXHIBIT 1   Performance of Campbell's Divisions under Gordon McGovern, 1980–89 (in millions of dollars)

	1989	1988	1987	1986	1985	1984	1983	1982	1981	1980
Campbell U.S.										
Sales	$2,776	$2,584	$2,445	$2,507	$2,500	$2,282	$1,987	$1,773	$1,678	$1,608
Operating earnings	175	272	284	302	292	278	250	211	190	205
Pepperidge Farm										
Sales	548	495	459	420	426	435	433	392	329	283
Operating earnings	54	58	54	46	39	35	43	41	35	29
Vlasic Foods										
Sales	441	353	283	263	199	193	168	149	137	130
Operating earnings	39	30	22	24	16	14	13	12	10	8
Mrs. Paul's Kitchens										
Sales	140	150	153	141	138	126	108	—	—	—
Operating earnings	0.4	(4)	10	8	11	14	10	—	—	—
Other United States*										
Sales	—	—	59	76	81	84	64	56	27	35
Operating earnings	—	—	(2)	(7)	(3)	(2)	(1)	(1)	(1)	1
International										
Sales	1,527	1,037	898	766	716	624	599	643	694	512
Operating earnings	(81)	58	69	(61)	35	34	33	46	46	33

*Division eliminated in 1988 and replaced with a new division named Campbell Enterprises.
Source: Campbell's annual reports.

EXHIBIT 2   The Campbell U.S. Division: Products, Rival Brands, Competitors as of 1985

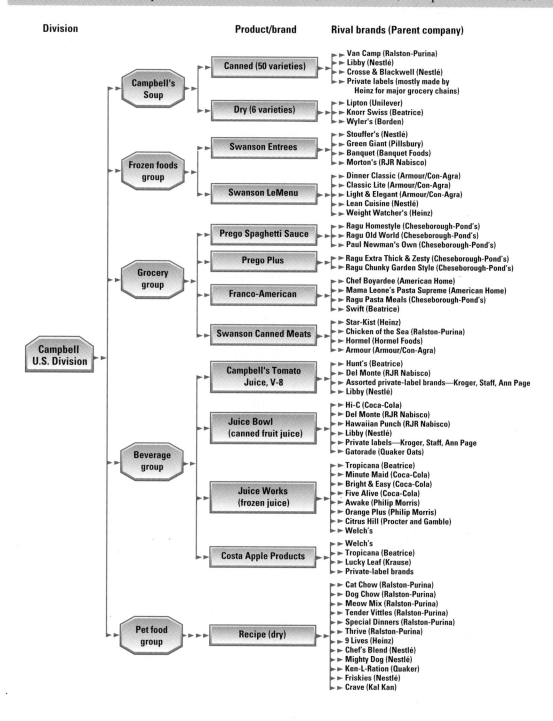

Division	Product/brand	Rival brands (Parent company)

Campbell U.S. Division

Campbell's Soup

- **Canned (50 varieties)**
  - Van Camp (Ralston-Purina)
  - Libby (Nestlé)
  - Crosse & Blackwell (Nestlé)
  - Private labels (mostly made by Heinz for major grocery chains)
- **Dry (6 varieties)**
  - Lipton (Unilever)
  - Knorr Swiss (Beatrice)
  - Wyler's (Borden)

Frozen foods group

- **Swanson Entrees**
  - Stouffer's (Nestlé)
  - Green Giant (Pillsbury)
  - Banquet (Banquet Foods)
  - Morton's (RJR Nabisco)
- **Swanson LeMenu**
  - Dinner Classic (Armour/Con-Agra)
  - Classic Lite (Armour/Con-Agra)
  - Light & Elegant (Armour/Con-Agra)
  - Lean Cuisine (Nestlé)
  - Weight Watcher's (Heinz)

Grocery group

- **Prego Spaghetti Sauce**
  - Ragu Homestyle (Cheseborough-Pond's)
  - Ragu Old World (Cheseborough-Pond's)
  - Paul Newman's Own (Cheseborough-Pond's)
- **Prego Plus**
  - Ragu Extra Thick & Zesty (Cheseborough-Pond's)
  - Ragu Chunky Garden Style (Cheseborough-Pond's)
- **Franco-American**
  - Chef Boyardee (American Home)
  - Mama Leone's Pasta Supreme (American Home)
  - Ragu Pasta Meals (Cheseborough-Pond's)
  - Swift (Beatrice)
- **Swanson Canned Meats**
  - Star-Kist (Heinz)
  - Chicken of the Sea (Ralston-Purina)
  - Hormel (Hormel Foods)
  - Armour (Armour/Con-Agra)

Beverage group

- **Campbell's Tomato Juice, V-8**
  - Hunt's (Beatrice)
  - Del Monte (RJR Nabisco)
  - Assorted private-label brands—Kroger, Staff, Ann Page
  - Libby (Nestlé)
- **Juice Bowl (canned fruit juice)**
  - Hi-C (Coca-Cola)
  - Del Monte (RJR Nabisco)
  - Hawaiian Punch (RJR Nabisco)
  - Libby (Nestlé)
  - Private labels—Kroger, Staff, Ann Page
  - Gatorade (Quaker Oats)
- **Juice Works (frozen juice)**
  - Tropicana (Beatrice)
  - Minute Maid (Coca-Cola)
  - Bright & Easy (Coca-Cola)
  - Five Alive (Coca-Cola)
  - Awake (Philip Morris)
  - Orange Plus (Philip Morris)
  - Citrus Hill (Procter and Gamble)
  - Welch's
- **Costa Apple Products**
  - Welch's
  - Tropicana (Beatrice)
  - Lucky Leaf (Krause)
  - Private-label brands

Pet food group

- **Recipe (dry)**
  - Cat Chow (Ralston-Purina)
  - Dog Chow (Ralston-Purina)
  - Meow Mix (Ralston-Purina)
  - Tender Vittles (Ralston-Purina)
  - Special Dinners (Ralston-Purina)
  - Thrive (Ralston-Purina)
  - 9 Lives (Heinz)
  - Chef's Blend (Nestlé)
  - Mighty Dog (Nestlé)
  - Ken-L-Ration (Quaker)
  - Friskies (Nestlé)
  - Crave (Kal Kan)

Although the soup business was relatively mature (McGovern preferred to call it underworked), Campbell's most ambitious consumer research took place in this unit. McGovern opted to grow Campbell's soup sales by turning out a steady flow of new varieties in convenient packages: "Ethnic, dried, refrigerated, frozen, microwave—you name it, we're going to try it."[1] In 1985, Campbell entered the $290 million dry-soup-mix market dominated by Thomas J. Lipton Inc., a business unit of Unilever. Dry-soup sales in the United States were growing faster than sales of canned soup. Lipton's aggressive response to test marketing of an early Campbell dry-soup product resulted in Campbell's rushing a six-flavor line into national distribution ahead of schedule.

In 1982 McGovern caused a stir when he announced publicly that Campbell's Swanson TV-dinner line was "junk food": "It was great in 1950, but in today's world it didn't go into the microwave; it didn't represent any variety or a good eating experience to my palate."[2] Over the past five years, Swanson's sales volume had slipped 16 percent. McGovern maintained that consumers had discovered better quality alternatives to the TV-dinner concept. Campbell's frozen foods group answered the challenge by creating a new frozen gourmet line, LeMenu. Campbell committed about $50 million to manufacturing, marketing, and trade promotion costs when initial market tests of the LeMenu line proved encouraging.

LeMenu—served on round heatable plates and consisting of such delicacies as chicken cordon bleu, al dente vegetables, and sophisticated wine sauces—produced 21 percent growth in the frozen meal unit, with sales of $150 million during its first year of national distribution (1984), double Campbell's sales projection. In addition, the Swanson line of TV-dinners was overhauled; the resulting products had less salt and more meat stock in gravies, new desserts and sauces, and new packaging with a redesigned logo.

The grocery business unit's star was Prego spaghetti sauce. By 1984 the Prego brand had captured 25 percent of the still-growing spaghetti sauce market, becoming the number two sauce behind Ragu. A Prego Plus spaghetti sauce line was introduced in 1985.

Pepperidge Farm   Pepperidge Farm was Campbell's third largest division in 1989, with 10 percent of the company's consolidated sales. Although the division was one of Campbell's best performers during the late 1970s (with sales rising at an average compound rate of 14 percent), by the mid-1980s growth had slowed and a number of newly introduced products had produced disappointing results (Star Wars cookies, Vegetables in Pastry). To remedy the division's weak performance, a number of steps were taken:

- The Costa Apple Products unit, acquired in 1982, was transferred to the Campbell U.S. beverage group.
- Pepperidge Farm divested itself of operations that no longer fit into its strategic plan, including Lexington Gardens, Inc., a garden center chain.
- Deli's Vegetables in Pastry went back into research and development to improve quality.
- A new management team was put in place and a comprehensive review of each product was initiated.

Exhibit 3 shows Pepperidge Farm's product portfolio during the 1980s.

---

[1] As quoted in *Business Week,* December 24, 1984, p. 67.
[2] Ibid.

EXHIBIT 3   The Pepperidge Farm Division: Products, Rival Brands, and Competitors in 1985

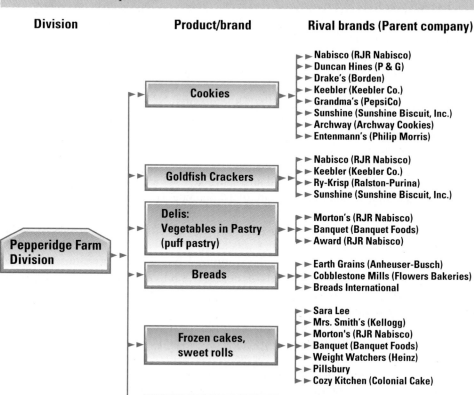

Division	Product/brand	Rival brands (Parent company)
Pepperidge Farm Division	Cookies	Nabisco (RJR Nabisco) Duncan Hines (P & G) Drake's (Borden) Keebler (Keebler Co.) Grandma's (PepsiCo) Sunshine (Sunshine Biscuit, Inc.) Archway (Archway Cookies) Entenmann's (Philip Morris)
	Goldfish Crackers	Nabisco (RJR Nabisco) Keebler (Keebler Co.) Ry-Krisp (Ralston-Purina) Sunshine (Sunshine Biscuit, Inc.)
	Delis: Vegetables in Pastry (puff pastry)	Morton's (RJR Nabisco) Banquet (Banquet Foods) Award (RJR Nabisco)
	Breads	Earth Grains (Anheuser-Busch) Cobblestone Mills (Flowers Bakeries) Breads International
	Frozen cakes, sweet rolls	Sara Lee Mrs. Smith's (Kellogg) Morton's (RJR Nabisco) Banquet (Banquet Foods) Weight Watchers (Heinz) Pillsbury Cozy Kitchen (Colonial Cake)
	Godiva Chocolates	Hershey Nestlé

Vlasic Foods   Vlasic, Campbell's fourth largest division, was the leading producer and marketer of pickles and relishes in the United States, with a 31 percent market share. During the 1982–84 period, Vlasic also had responsibility for the Win Schuler Foods unit, whose products were marketed in several states in the upper Midwest. When sales of the Win Schuler unit flattened in 1984, partly due to a sagging Midwest economy, McGovern transferred the unit to the refrigerated foods group in the Campbell U.S. business division.

In 1985 Vlasic implemented new labels that used color bands and a new flavor scale to help consumers find their favorite tastes quickly on the supermarket shelf. Following up on marketing research indicating consumer desires for new and interesting flavors, Vlasic had introduced Zesty Dills and Bread and Butter Whole Pickle lines in 1985. Heinz was Campbell's leading national competitor in this area, but there were a number of important regional and private-label brands that competed with Heinz and Vlasic for shelf space.

Mrs. Paul's Kitchens   The Mrs. Paul's business unit produced frozen fish entrees, frozen breaded vegetables, and frozen chicken nuggets. When Campbell acquired Mrs. Paul's in 1982, it was rumored that Heinz and Pillsbury, among others, were considering the same acquisition. In 1983, the Mrs. Paul's division responded to consumer preferences for convenience seafood products that were nutritious, low in calories, microwavable, and lightly coated, by introducing Light & Natural Fish Fillets. Quality improvements were also made in existing products, and a promising new product,

Light Seafood Entrees, was introduced in 1984. Market share increased about 25 percent over 1983, and Light Seafood Entrees went national in 1985. This line, which featured seven varieties of low-calorie, microwavable seafood dishes, accounted for 11 percent of 1985's volume. However, sales of the company's established product lines of breaded seafood items eroded in the years following acquisition because they had to be fried in cooking oil prior to serving. Revenues had dropped in both 1988 and 1989, and the division was barely profitable in 1989 (see Exhibit 1).

Other United States   Grouped into the Other United States business division were Triangle Manufacturing Corporation, a manufacturer of health-and-fitness products; Campbell Hospitality, a restaurant unit that operated 59 Pietro's restaurants, 15 Annabelle's restaurants, and 6 H. T. McDoogal's restaurants; and Snow King Frozen Foods, Inc., a manufacturer of frozen specialty meat products. Triangle's best-known product line was The Band wrist and ankle weights, which had the number two position in its category, with a market share of 14 percent. Triangle was trying to build on its strength by entering the exercise equipment market and by selling its products internationally. The Hospitality division struggled through most of the 1980s to sustain sales and earnings growth. Snow King was also a weak performer. In 1988, this division was reorganized and renamed the Campbell Enterprises Division; it included Triangle Manufacturing; Godiva International; V8 and Campbell juices; Campbell Food Services; Snow King Frozen Foods; and Pietro's, Annabelle's, and H. T. McDoogal's restaurant chains. All three restaurant chains were divested in 1989.

International   The International business unit was Campbell's second largest division throughout the 1980s and accounted for about one-fifth of corporate revenues in 1989. Campbell International had subsidiaries in about 12 foreign countries as of 1989 and had plans to expand further. The division was reorganized in 1985 to build a more solid base for sales and earnings growth. McGovern's goal was for the International division to contribute 25 percent of Campbell's corporate sales and earnings. His strategy was to develop and strengthen Campbell's presence in international markets and to make Campbell a premier international company.

A number of acquisitions were completed in 1989 to strengthen Campbell's international competitive position. The Habitant soup and pickle brands, the Laura Secord brand of jams, and a refrigerated distribution company were all acquired by Campbell's Canadian subsidiary. In Europe, Campbell acquired a German specialty food importer and an Italian producer of institutional foods. Also during 1989, the company increased its ownership in Australia's leading cookie company, Arnott's Ltd., to 32 percent, acquired 50 percent ownership in an Australian juice manufacturer, and obtained complete ownership of Melbourne Mushrooms. The International division's three biggest profit contributors in 1989 were Campbell Soup Canada, the European food and confectionery group, and the operations in Australia.

Even though the company had a number of successes internationally, Campbell management had encountered some difficulties. Campbell's Italian business suffered losses during 1989 as a result of excessive costs brought on by an aggressive and poorly controlled attempt to build market share. Campbell was also having difficulty with making its recently acquired Freshbake Foods unit profitable. The British food processing company was struggling to absorb a number of acquisitions it had made prior to its own acquisition by Campbell in 1988. Campbell management found it necessary to institute an extensive restructuring process at Freshbake, including closing a number of plants.

McGovern's Approach to Managing Campbell's Business Portfolio

Every Saturday morning McGovern did his family's grocery shopping, stopping in the store aisles to straighten Campbell's displays and inspect those of competitors, studying packaging and reading labels, and trying to learn all he could about how and what people were eating. He encouraged his managers to do the same. Several board meetings were held in the back rooms of supermarkets so that afterward directors could roam the store interviewing customers about Campbell products.

McGovern decentralized Campbell management to facilitate entrepreneurial risk-taking and new-product development, devising a new compensation program to reward efforts in these areas. He restructured the company into some 50 autonomous units, each with the leeway to develop new products even if the new-product ideas were closely related to another business unit's products. Thus, the Prego spaghetti sauce unit—not the frozen food group—initiated frozen Mexican dinners. And although it wasn't his job, the director of market research created Today's Taste, a line of refrigerated entrees and side dishes. "It's like things are in constant motion," the director said. "We are overloaded but it's fun."[3]

McGovern believed the new structure encouraged managers of business units, who had to compete for corporate funding, to be more creative and venturesome in developing promising products:

> These business divisions allow the company to really get its arms around chunks of the business. The managers are answerable to the bottom line—to their investments, their hiring, their products—and it's a great motivation for performance.[4]

As part of this motivation, Campbell began annually allotting around $30 to $40 million to support the creation of new product families; it often took $10 million to develop and test new products. In addition, it took $10 to $15 million in advertising and couponing to launch a new brand. McGovern believed a special new-product venture fund was needed to encourage managers to think big in terms of new-product development. He emphasized that it was no disgrace to fail if the effort was a good one. High failure rates were common in the industry—only about 20 percent of new products lasted more than one year on the market—but Campbell's failure rate on new-product introductions was running even higher. In fact, during the 1980s, only about one out of eight new Campbell products reaching the market was successful.

Every Friday morning McGovern held meetings to discuss new products. The fact-finding sessions were attended by financial, marketing, engineering, and sales personnel. Typical McGovern questions included: "Would you eat something like that?" "Why not?" "Have you tried the competition's product?" "Is there a consumer niche?[5]

McGovern's New-Product Development and Marketing Strategies

McGovern instituted a number of internal changes to make Campbell's new-product development strategy produce the desired results. Much revolved around efforts to enhance the sophistication of Campbell's corporate marketing strategies and approach to marketing research. Under McGovern, Campbell's market research

---

[3]As quoted in *The Wall Street Journal*, September 17, 1984, p. A10.

[4]*Advertising Age*, January 3, 1983, p. 38.

[5]*The Wall Street Journal*, September 17, 1984, p. A10.

unearthed several findings and projections that drove the company's new-product development effort:

- Women comprised 43 percent of the workforce (with a level of 50 percent projected by 1990).
- Two-income marriages represented 60 percent of all U.S. families and accounted for 60 percent of total family income.
- Upper-income households would grow 3.5 times faster than the total household formations.
- More than half of all households consisted of only one or two members; 23 percent of all households contained only one person.
- More and more consumers were exhibiting a growing preference for refrigerated and fresh produce over canned and frozen products.
- The percentage of meals eaten at home was declining.
- Nearly half of the adult meal planners in the United States were watching their weight.
- Poultry consumption had increased 26 percent since 1973.
- Ethnic food preparation at home was increasing, with 40 percent, 21 percent, and 14 percent of households preparing Italian, Mexican, and Oriental foods, respectively, at home from scratch.
- There was a growing consumer movement toward avoidance of sugar, salt, calories, chemicals, cholesterol, and additives.
- The "I am what I eat" philosophy had tied food into lifestyles that embraced exercise machines, hot tubs, jogging, racquetball, backpacking, cross-country skiing, and aerobic dancing.

In response to growing ethnic food demand, Campbell began marketing ethnic selections in regions where consumer interests for particular food types were strong. For instance, it marketed spicy Ranchero Beans only in the South and Southwest, and its newly acquired Puerto Rican foods in New York City and Florida (which had sizable Puerto Rican populations).

Campbell's product-development guidelines emphasized convenience, taste, flavor, and texture. The strategic themes McGovern stressed were these:

- Concentrate on products that represent superior value to consumers and constantly strive to improve those values.
- Develop products that help build markets.
- Develop products that yield a fair profit to Campbell.

In pursuing these guidelines, Campbell adopted several operating practices:

- Using ongoing consumer research to determine eating habits; this included checking home menus, recipes, and food preparation techniques to learn which food items were served together.
- Studying meal and snack eating occasions to learn which household members participated so that preliminary estimates of volume potential could be made for possible new products and product improvement ideas.
- Testing new or improved products in enough households across the United States to allow reliable national sales projections to be made. Once a product met pretest standards, testing in a sample of supermarkets and sales outlets was conducted.

- Rolling out the new products on a regional or national plan and using test-market data to establish the sequence in which area markets should be entered.

By 1983 McGovern's strategy had turned Campbell into the biggest new-products generator in the combined food-and-health and beauty aids categories, with a total of 42 new products. Prego spaghetti sauce, LeMenu frozen dinners, Great Starts breakfasts, and Chunky New England Clam Chowder were among the leading products introduced by Campbell Soup during the early 1980s. Meanwhile Campbell's marketing budget grew from $275 million in 1982, to $488 million in 1985, and to $552 million in 1989. Ad expenditures jumped from $67 million in 1980 to $197 million in 1989. Prior to McGovern, Campbell often trimmed ad spending at the end of a quarter to boost earnings.

In 1982 McGovern was named *Advertising Age*'s Adman of the Year for his efforts in transforming Campbell into "one of the most aggressive market-driven companies in the food industry today."[6] *Advertising Age* cited the company's emphasis on nutrition and fitness as opposed to the former "mmm, mmm, good" emphasis on taste. Print ads featured government research studies concerning soup's nutritional values and a new slogan, "Soup is good food."

Production, Quality, and Cost Considerations during the McGovern Era

Gordon McGovern also stressed the importance of high production quality; a 1984 article in *Savvy* quoted him as saying, "I want zero defects. If we can't produce quality, we'll get out of the business." That same year, Campbell held its first Worldwide Corporate conference dedicated to quality. Hundreds of Campbell managers from all levels and most company locations spent three days at this conference. Management believed that the ultimate test of quality was consumer satisfaction, and the company's goal was to instill a strong quality-conscious attitude among employees in every single operation throughout the company.

Before McGovern took over, Campbell used to adjust the design of new products so that they could be produced with existing equipment and plant facilities. For example, a square omelet was specified for Swanson's breakfasts because it was what the installed machine would make. After McGovern's appointment, although low-cost production was still a strategic factor, market considerations and consumer trends—not existing machinery and production capabilities—were deciding factors in production, packaging, and labeling. Still, the company spent between $150 million and $300 million annually throughout the 1980s for improved equipment, new plants and plant expansions, better packaging technology, and distribution facilities.

Campbell executives believed the company's key strengths during the 1985–89 period were: (1) a worldwide system for obtaining ingredients; (2) a broad range of food products that could be used as a launching pad for formulating, producing, and marketing new products; and (3) an emphasis on low-cost production.

Campbell's Performance Under Gordon McGovern

McGovern's campaign for renewed growth via new-product introduction and acquisition produced good results early on. By year-end 1984, sales were up 31 percent—to $3.7 billion—and earnings had risen by 47 percent—to $191 million. During McGovern's 10-year reign as CEO, Campbell introduced 922 new items—more than

---

[6]*Advertising Age,* January 3, 1983, p. 38.

any other food-processing company. By the late 1980s, however, there were signs that Campbell's brand managers had become so involved in new-product development that they had not only neglected the old stand-by products but also slighted cost-control and profit margin targets. According to one Campbell executive:

> We became fat cats. We said, "We can't fail." We began to throw things against the market-place that had long paybacks and were in processes, packaging, and distribution that we didn't understand.[7]

Campbell's growth in operating earnings for fiscal years 1985–89 fell short of McGovern's 15 percent target rate (see Exhibit 4), and McGovern in 1989 initiated several internal restructuring moves to eliminate many of the inefficiencies and cost excesses that had crept into the company's operations and new-product development efforts.

McGOVERN'S RESIGNATION AND RECRUITMENT OF A REPLACEMENT

Beginning in the late 1980s, the heirs of John T. Dorrance began to show frustration with Campbell Soup's industry-lagging performance and began to openly criticize McGovern's approach to running the company. Managers at Quaker Oats believed that the Dorrance family might be interested in a merger between the two companies and approached Campbell's chairman of the board, Robert Vlasic, in March 1989 to explore the issue. The Dorrance heirs were split on the prospect of a merger, with one faction publicly announcing its intent to sell its shares and another vying to block a merger at all costs. The heirs supporting Campbell Soup's independence successfully prevented a merger but were unable to bring prompt reconciliation among the Dorrance family.

Disenchanted with the family squabble and stung by outspoken criticism of his performance by family members, Gordon McGovern resigned as CEO and took early retirement in November 1989. Campbell's search for a replacement, spearheaded by Ippy Dorrance and Robert Vlasic, quickly focused on Gerber's CEO, David Johnson, as the best candidate to replace McGovern. A native of Australia, David Johnson had a bachelor's degree in economics from the University of Sydney and an MBA from the University of Chicago. Starting out as a management trainee with the international division of Colgate-Palmolive in Australia, he moved up through the ranks to become managing director of Colgate's South African operations in 1967. In 1973, he moved to Hong Kong as president of Warner-Lambert/Parke Davis Asia; there, exposed to the Orient's fundamentally different customs and approaches, he came to appreciate that if managers were creative enough to look beyond accepted solutions to business problems, it was easy to find innovative answers. Looking back on his Hong Kong experiences, Johnson observed that he gained "an elasticized mind, opened to a greater run of possibilities than I'd ever known before."[8]

Warner-Lambert brought Johnson to the United States in 1976 as president of its personal products division; a year later, he was promoted to president of the company's American Chicle division. When Warner-Lambert acquired Entenmann's in 1979, Johnson took over as head; he then moved to General Foods when GF acquired

---

[7]As quoted in *Financial World,* June 11, 1991, p. 53.
[8]Jeffrey Zygmont, "In Command at Campbell," *Sky Magazine,* March 1993, p. 60.

EXHIBIT 4   Financial Summary, Campbell Soup Company, 1989–98 (in millions, except per share amounts)

	1998	1997	1996	1995	1994	1993	1992	1991	1990	1989
Net sales	$6,696	$7,964	$7,678	$7,250	$6,664	$6,577	$6,263	$6,204	$6,205	$5,672
Earnings before taxes	1,073	1,107	1,179	1,042	963	520	779	667	179	107
Earnings before cumulative effect of accounting change	1,062	713	802	698	630	257	491	402	4	13
Net earnings	660	713	802	698	630	8	491	402	4	13
Taxes on earnings	384	394	395	344	333	263	309	266	175	93
Interest—net	175	165	126	115	64	74	87	90	94	56
Earnings per share	$1.46	$1.51	$1.61	$1.40	$1.26	$0.02	$0.97	$0.79	$0.01	$0.03
Dividends per share	$0.82	$0.75	$0.67	$0.61	$0.55	$0.46	$0.36	$0.28	$0.25	$0.23
Wgt. avg. shares outstanding	460	472	498	498	501	504	504	508	518	518
Capital expenditures	256	331	416	391	421	371	362	371	397	302
Depreciation and amortization	261	328	326	294	255	242	216	209	201	192
Assets	5,633	6,459	6,632	6,315	4,992	4,897	4,353	4,149	4,115	3,932
Stockholders' equity	874	1,420	2,742	2,468	1,989	1,704	2,027	1,793	1,691	1,778

Source: Campbell annual reports.

Entenmann's from Warner-Lambert in 1982. As Entenmann's chief executive from 1979 to 1987, he engineered the company's drive from a regional to a national provider of bakery products, more than quadrupling sales and profits. In 1987, Johnson left Entenmann's to become CEO of Gerber Products, a company whose performance had been lackluster for several years. He proceeded to craft a turnaround strategy for Gerber that involved divesting seven business divisions (toys, furniture, trucking) and refocusing Gerber's attention on its core baby foods business. By 1990, 27 months after Johnson became CEO, Gerber's sales were up 30 percent, profits were up 50 percent, and the stock price had tripled. With the Dorrance family's blessing, Campbell lured Johnson away from Gerber as McGovern's successor.

THE DAVID JOHNSON ERA: 1990–97

When David Johnson became chairman and CEO of Campbell Soup Company in January 1990, he saw his first priority as crafting a strategy for Campbell that would grow earnings and win the confidence of the Dorrance heirs. While at Gerber, Johnson viewed Campbell, a competitor of Gerber's in some product categories, as an underperforming company that was a likely target for corporate raiders, once even commenting, "Boy, that's a troubled company. I could really run that one."[9] In interviewing for the job at Campbell, Johnson determined that the arguments and differences between the Dorrance family and Campbell's prior management were more a function of "poor results" than of activist family members wanting to meddle in company affairs or the desire of some to sell out their stake and invest their inheritance elsewhere. Johnson deemed the challenge worthy for several reasons:

> It was a company that was founded on incredible strength on which you could build. I knew that it had excellent R&D. I knew it had terrific brands. It had lost its direction, lost its focus, was underperforming, and I knew that it could be refocused and reorganized within six months, and that we could really get it going very quickly.[10]

Johnson immediately embarked on a course of boosting Campbell's performance quickly, not only to pacify disgruntled shareholders but also to get the company's stock price high enough to discourage would-be acquirers from launching a takeover attempt:

> Under those circumstances, when you come in, it's not the pretties of "Here is my vision. Let me explain the principles from the book." When you move in, you've got to do it in an exciting fashion, lay down the challenge—Boom! Strike! Crash! It's short term focus. You know that dirty word we're all accused of? "Short term." Isn't it terrible? Under those circumstances, if you don't win the first year, if you don't win in the short term, you're dead.[11]

Johnson's Turnaround Strategy

To spur Campbell's managers and give them something to shoot for in rejuvenating the company's performance, Johnson set financial objectives of 20 percent earnings growth, 20 percent return on equity, and 20 percent cash return on assets: "I used to say, if perfect human vision is 20-20, then perfect business vision is 20-20-20, which was shorthand for earnings, return and cash."[12] This was followed by the establishment

---

[9]As quoted in *Fortune,* September 9, 1991, p. 143.

[10]As quoted in *Sky Magazine,* March 1993, p. 54.

[11]As quoted in *Fortune,* December 14, 1992, p. 112.

[12]Ibid.

of four corporate-level strategic principles to guide the creation of business and functional strategies in each divisional unit:

- The primary purpose of the corporation is to *build shareholder wealth.* It is imperative to provide dividend growth and long-term stock appreciation to reward the stockholders of the corporation.

- Campbell must exploit its *brand power.* Campbell's strong brands have been the basis of the company's strengths over the past 90 years and should be the focal point for the future.

- Campbell's ability to sustain its brand power and build on its powerful brands is only possible through *people power.* The company's employees have to be responsible for maintaining the existing brands, for building on these brands, and for finding new markets for these brands. Campbell should encourage individual risk-bearing and teamwork with rewards linked to results.

- It is important to *preserve the company's independence.* Management needs to preserve the heritage of Campbell Soup Company and resist any outside thrust for control through delivery of superior performance on building long-term shareholder wealth.

Johnson disagreed with McGovern's view that Campbell's growth should come primarily from the acquisition of small, fast-growing food companies and from the introduction of new products that served some niche of the food industry. Instead, Johnson believed that Campbell Soup should concentrate on growing sales of its best-known brands—the red-and-white soup line, Prego, Pepperidge Farm, Vlasic, and Swanson—and to increase its U.S. market share in these product categories. During the 1980s, for example, Campbell's tonnage in canned soups had risen a paltry 1 percent annually and Campbell's market share of the U.S. soup market, according to Wall Street estimates, had slipped from a lofty 80 percent in the 1950s and 1960s to 70 percent in the mid-1980s to around 65 percent in 1990. Johnson also decided to press harder and faster than McGovern had in order to gain increased penetration of foreign markets.

While McGovern had pursued ways to reduce costs and eliminate inefficiencies during his 1989 restructuring, Johnson saw opportunities to achieve further economies and better profit margins, principally by eliminating unprofitable and slow-selling items from Campbell's product lineup and by divesting peripheral lines of businesses that did not complement the company's strengths or bolster the market power of its flagship brands. Consequently, the strategy Johnson crafted to boost Campbell's performance incorporated six major initiatives:

- Divesting poorly performing and nonstrategic business units and reorganizing Campbell's six divisions.
- Eliminating weak items from the company's product lineup.
- Requiring that new-product introductions exploit Campbell Soup's strengths, core competencies, and organizational capabilities as well as have the potential to achieve the three 20-20-20 financial performance targets.
- Focusing on the global marketing of the company's competencies and capabilities.
- Installing and expanding low-cost business systems at the corporate level to support the operations of the business divisions.
- Improving utilization of assets to maximize the return to stockholders.

EXHIBIT 5   Divested Campbell Soup Company Businesses, 1990–96

- Fried chicken plant in Sumpter, South Carolina
- Salmon Farms
- Snow King Frozen Foods—frozen meat products
- Triangle Manufacturing Corporation—a health-and-fitness products manufacturer
- Mushroom farms
- Menderson-Zeller, Inc.
- Recipe pet food
- D. Lazzaroni Cookie Company (Italy)
- Win Schuler Foods, Inc.
- Juice Bowl
- Juice Works
- The fresh produce and frozen vegetable portions of the British company Freshbake Foods—the frozen entree portion of Freshbake was retained.
- Campbell Chilled Foods, Ltd. (United Kingdom)
- Mrs. Paul's frozen seafood
- Poultry processing operations
- Marie's salad dressings
- Beeck-Feinkost G.m.b.H. chilled foods (Germany)
- Beef farms in Argentina
- Durkee and Early California olives
- Groko B.V. frozen vegetable processing (Holland)

Source: Campbell annual reports and 10-Ks.

Exhibit 5 shows the business lines that were divested—Johnson saw all of them as either nonstrategic and unrelated to Campbell's core competencies or as chronic money-losers or low-return businesses. This pruning of Campbell's portfolio resulted in the sale of 8 plants and the shutdown of 12 others worldwide, plus a workforce reduction of 8,000 people during Johnson's first 18 months as CEO. As the remaining plants bid to absorb the production of the closed plants, overall capacity utilization rose from 60 percent to 80 percent; Campbell's Maxton, North Carolina, plant was able to increase its output by 50 percent and become Campbell's first canned-soup plant to drive manufacturing costs below 50 percent of the retail price of its products. Included among the initial plant closings was that of the company's 131-year-old Camden, New Jersey, plant with its distinctive water towers painted to look like giant Campbell Soup cans.

Johnson's restructuring continued throughout his tenure, with major initiatives approved by the board in 1993 and 1996. The 1993 restructuring program identified six plants and 14 businesses that were to be sold. In 1996 the board approved an additional restructuring that eliminated additional plants and businesses, along with 2,100 administrative and operational positions at various Campbell Soup facilities. Both restructuring programs were intended to shift production from underutilized or inefficient production facilities to more cost-effective locations and to eliminate nonstrategic, poor-performing businesses from the portfolio. Under Johnson, Campbell Soup went on to divest a total of 26 businesses that had an average net profit margin of 1 percent. Campbell Soup also closed over 10 older and inefficient plants between 1990 and 1997 to boost capacity utilization.

Once Johnson assessed that the turnaround was well under way, he offset the divestitures with 20 acquisitions of higher-margin businesses with ample growth potential. In 1996 David Johnson commented on the strategy of moving Campbell from a position of "best in class" to "best in show," the contribution of the newly acquired businesses, and the company's prospects for growth:

> We begin this new attack from a position of great strength. Our balance sheet and cash flow are strong. Since 1990, we have divested non-strategic and low-margin businesses with approximately $800 million in sales and acquired strategic, higher-margin businesses with more than $1.2 billion in sales, including Mexican sauce leader Pace Foods. Our management team has transformed Campbell into a place where results count and where the bar is constantly raised . . . We are poised for breaking away from our competitors in the food industry. This strategic growth plan is designed to vault our company into the ranks of the world's renowned consumer goods companies, in terms of financial profile and market multiple.[13]

Exhibit 6 presents a listing and description of business acquisitions initiated by David Johnson. By year-end 1996 the new businesses Johnson had added to Campbell's portfolio achieved an average net profit margin of 12 percent.

Many of Johnson's acquisitions were intended to add brands and infrastructure that were necessary for the growth of Campbell's international business. The acquisition of Pace Foods was one of the few acquisitions not specifically aimed at growing international food sales. Pace Foods, the leading U.S. producer and marketer of Mexican salsa, was Campbell's biggest acquisition ever. The $1.12 billion purchase price represented 5 times Pace's sales and 20 times its earnings. A number of companies, including Heinz and Lea & Perrin, had been attempting to buy Pace for a number of years, but owner Kit Goldsbury was not interested. The chief operating officer of Pace Foods stated that Goldsbury agreed to the sale to Campbell because Goldsbury could identify with and liked Campbell's management team.[14]

Salsa (a spicy blend of jalapeños, tomatoes, onion, and garlic) surpassed ketchup in 1991 as the nation's best-selling condiment. The salsa category grew at just under a 13 percent compound annual rate from 1988 to 1993 as sales increased from $325 million to $700 million. The rapid growth in sales of salsa products was attributed to their spicy flavor and low fat content (a jar of Pace salsa contained no fat and only 70 calories), to the excellent way they complemented such snack foods as tortilla chips, to growing consumer popularity of Mexican dishes, and to a fast-increasing Hispanic population.

Johnson's Revised New-Product Development and Marketing Strategies

David Johnson instituted a more cautious approach to new-product development and challenged Campbell marketers to become more aggressive in marketing the company's products. Johnson was quick to comment, "There's no such thing as mature markets, only tired marketers,"[15] when told that low industry growth rates were obstacles to Campbell's growth. New-product ideas were more heavily researched and tested before they were put on the market. Moreover, new products were expected to provide quicker paybacks on investment; potential products that held little promise for near-term profitability and for meeting the 20-20-20 financial performance standards were tabled.

The search for new-product ideas was limited to areas where Campbell had production and marketing expertise; as one executive put it, "We want to be in areas we

---

[13]As quoted in *PR Newswire,* September 5, 1996.
[14]*The Wall Street Journal,* November 29, 1994, p. A3.
[15]As quoted in *Chief Executive,* November 1996.

EXHIBIT 6   Businesses Acquired by Campbell Soup, 1990–97

1994 (Acquisitions totaled $14 million)
- Dandy mushrooms (Australia)
- Fray Bentos canned meats (Australia)

1995 (Acquisitions totaled $1.26 billion)
- Pace Foods—the leading salsa brand in the United States with annual sales of $700 million. The company was purchased for $1.12 billion.
- Increase in share ownership of Arnott's, Ltd. to 65%.
- Fresh Start Bakeries—maker of buns and English muffins for quick-service restaurants in the United States, Europe, and South America. At the time of the acquisition, the company had approximate annual sales of $75 million, 480 employees, and had been a supplier to McDonald's for more than 30 years. The business was integrated into Campbell's Food Service unit.
- Stratford-upon-Avon Foods—a food-service company operating in the United Kingdom with annual sales of $60 million. The business manufactured, marketed, and distributed canned baked beans, vegetable and fruit products, and branded and private-label pickles.
- Greenfield Healthy Foods—U.S. manufacturer of all-natural, low-fat cakes and cookies. The company provided Pepperidge Farm with new resources to enter the $800 million healthy snack category.
- Homepride sauces—the best-selling cooking sauce in the United Kingdom. The business, purchased for an estimated $93 million, allowed Campbell to build gravy and sauce sales in the United Kingdom.

1996 (Acquisitions totaled $186 million)
- Joint venture began between Arnott's Ltd. and Helios Foods, one of Indonesia's most prominent food companies—thereby providing Arnott's with biscuit manufacturing capability in Asia.
- Joint venture began in Malaysia with Cheong Chan that provided manufacturing facilities for canned soups, ketchup, and soy sauces in Southeast Asia. Campbell Soup also acquired a minority interest in Cheong Chan.
- Joint venture between Godiva and J. Osawa, Ltd., to immediately open 33 retail stores and outlets for Godiva chocolates. An additional 20 stores were planned to open by the year 2000.
- Increase in share ownership of Arnott's Ltd. to 70%.

1997 (Acquisitions totaled $228 million)
- Erasco Group—the leading wet soup brand in Germany with annual sales of $223 million and 900 employees. The business was purchased for approximately $210 million. Campbell management believed that the acquisition would accelerate the company's growth throughout Germany and the European Union.
- Kettle Chip Company—a salty snack company operating in Australia and acquired for $18 million.

---

know we are good at and in processes we are good at."[16] Despite the more conservative approach to new-product development, Campbell introduced nearly 300 new products during Johnson's first three years as the company's chief executive. Johnson committed between $77 and $88 million annually to R&D during his last three years as CEO to improve existing products and to develop new products that would be

---

[16]As quoted in *Financial World*, June 11, 1991, p. 53.

successful in U.S. and international markets. New items included cream of broccoli soup (which became the first new soup since 1935 to rank in the top five best-selling soups), Joseph A. Campbell premium-quality ready-to-serve soups, cheese tortellini soup, Light 'n Tangy V8, Swanson Kids Fun Feast frozen dinners, Vlasic Sandwich Stackers, Prego pizza sauce, and more varieties of Pepperidge Farm products. Johnson suggested that the company's new approach to product development had been successful in developing products that consumers desired and had allowed the company to achieve sales growth in traditionally mature markets. "Innovations and breakthroughs are so simple, but they come only if you're immersed in your field and determined to make the necessary connections. For instance, take our Stackers, which are pickles sliced to lay flat on a sandwich. A simple idea, but it took off: The overall Stackers market grew 55% last year. In addition, we're tapping into growing consumer segments, such as the healthy food category. For example, our new line of cream soups is 98% fat free."[17]

Johnson's Corporate Reorganization

Johnson's reorganization effort was aimed at capturing strategic-fit benefits among related products and product families. Johnson concluded that McGovern's 50 autonomous units had resulted in lack of communication and cooperation within the company. For example, the U.S. soup division once ran a promotion with Nabisco crackers even though Pepperidge Farm produced a competing product. Also, U.S. tomato paste plants did not share technology with Mexican tomato paste plants since the Mexican plants were in a different division. A three-division structure was established during Johnson's first year as Campbell CEO to improve communication and technology sharing between businesses in similar product categories and geographies (see Exhibit 7). This initial structure was modified three times over the next five years. Each shuffling of businesses within the three-division structure was directed at improving the strategic fit within the portfolio of businesses. The series of new alignments also helped Campbell Soup put more emphasis on the company's international businesses.

Johnson's International Push

Johnson was convinced that a sizable fraction of Campbell Soup's growth should come from international expansion because the world market for processed food products was projected to grow over twice as fast as the 1 percent growth rate projected for the $200 billion U.S. food-processing industry. Johnson wanted at least one-third of Campbell's revenues to come from outside the United States by 2000. Johnson saw such companies as Coca-Cola and Gillette, whose international operations contributed 70 to 80 percent of total sales, as prototypes for Campbell Soup's future:

> Clearly, we're not going to be a Coca-Cola or Gillette in two years, but we're inching toward that aim as we go into the next century . . . We're expanding in the U.K., Canada, and Australia, and trying to establish more beachheads in Asia Pacific. Our acquisition of Germany's Erasco increases our total international soup sales to 21% of total soup sales. We bought an operation in Malaysia called Cheong Chan, where we're now making the investments that will enable us to produce soup instead of importing it. We're looking for ventures in China and growing in Taiwan.

---

[17]As quoted in *Chief Executive,* November 1996.

EXHIBIT 7 Comparison of Campbell's Business Unit Structure under Gordon McGovern and David Johnson

Campbell's Structure under Gordon McGovern		Campbell's Structure under David Johnson		Campbell's Structure under Dale Morrison	
Division	**Example Brands/Services**	**Division**	**Example Brands/Services**	**Division**	**Example Brands/Services**
• Campbell U.S.		• U.S.A.		• Soups and Sauces	All worldwide dry and canned soups, Franco American pastas
–Soup Group	Red-and-white, Healthy Request, Chunky	–U.S. Soup Group	Dry and canned soup, Franco-American		V8, Campbell's tomato juice
–Frozen Food Group	Swanson, LeMenu	–Beverage Group	V8, Campbell's tomato juice		Prego spaghetti sauces, Pace salsas, Swanson broths
–Grocery Group	Prego, Franco-American, Swanson, canned meats	–Meal Enhancement Group	Open Pit barbecue sauce, Pace salsas, Vlasic, Prego, food service		Erasco, Cheong Chan, Homepride, Leibig, Stockpot
–Beverage Group	Campbell's Tomato Juice, V8, Juice Bowl, Juice Works	–Frozen Foods Group	Swanson	• Biscuit and Confectionery	Arnott's Ltd., Pepperidge Farm, Godiva Chocolatier, Kettle Chips
–Pet Food Group	Recipe	• Bakery and Confectionery	Arnott's Ltd., Pepperidge Farm, Delacre, Godiva Chocolatier, Lami Lutti confections, Kettle Chips		
• Pepperidge Farm	Pepperidge Farm breads and cookies, Godiva chocolates, Costa apple juice, Deli's frozen entrees			• Food Service	Distribution of Campbell soups and specialty kitchen entrees to food-service markets
• Vlasic Foods	Pickles and relishes	• International Grocery			
• Mrs. Paul's Kitchens	Frozen fish, frozen chicken, frozen vegetables	–International Soup Group	Red-and-white canned soup, Erasco, Cheong Chan, Homepride		
• Other United States	Triangle Manufacturing Corp.—fitness products Campbell Hospitality—restaurants Snow King Frozen Foods—frozen meats	–International Specialty Foods	Stratford-upon-Avon, Fray Bentos, Swift		
• International	Soup—Canada and Mexico Freshbake Foods Group (Britain)—baked goods				

Source: Campbell annual reports.

EXHIBIT 8 Sales and Earnings of Campbell Soup Company by Geographic Region, 1991–98 (Millions of dollars)

	1998	1997	1996	1995	1994	1993	1992	1991
United States								
Net sales	$4,850	$5,495	$5,332	$5,012	$4,639	$4,744	$4,649	$4,496
Earnings before taxes	1,124*	1,155	1,123	957	854	715	809	695
Europe								
Net sales	859	1,201	1,122	1,143	1,041	1,050	1,043	1,149
Earnings before taxes	36*	50	71	74	64	(170)	45	49
Other countries								
Net sales	1,044	1,408	1,347	1,179	1,011	917	652	656
Earnings before taxes	123*	122	172	171	154	99	70	55

*Earnings before interest and taxes.
Source: Campbell annual reports.

Campbell marketed its soups in Mexico, Canada, Argentina, Poland, Hong Kong, and China, and its baked goods in Europe and Asia Pacific. In 1993 Campbell increased its 33 percent share of Australia's Arnott's Ltd. to 58 percent to gain an organizational base for increasing its long-term presence in baked goods in the Pacific Rim and Asia. Johnson increased Campbell's ownership of Arnott's further to 65 percent in 1995 and to 70 percent in 1996. To help familiarize himself with Campbell's international operations and to better gauge the company's potential for foreign expansion, Johnson had all of Campbell's top international executives report directly to him for the first 12 months he was at Campbell.

International marketing of prepared foods was not easy. Taste preferences varied significantly from country to country (and sometimes within countries), prompting international producers to employ multicountry strategies to gear product characteristics to local preferences and eating habits. Britain's Freshbake Foods Group, which Campbell acquired in 1988, never performed up to expectations partly because Campbell management didn't cater adequately to the taste preferences of British consumers. Also, Campbell's penetration of the European soup market had proved more difficult than originally expected because the predominant forms of store-bought soups on the continent were dry and ready-to-serve soups; demand for Campbell's mainstay condensed soups was virtually nonexistent in Europe, and consumers had to be persuaded of the merits of switching to a different preparation technique.

Campbell management opened a Hong Kong taste kitchen as part of the company's effort to ensure that the products it introduced would appeal to Asia's 2 billion consumers, whose per capita soup consumption averaged six bowls per week. The Hong Kong kitchen proved to be a success, having a role in creating such popular sellers as scallop, watercress, duck-gizzard, and ham soups. The kitchen was experimenting with other soup varieties made from pork, dates, figs, and snake.

Campbell had been successful in Mexico with spicy soups such as Creama de Chile Poblano and had captured 10 percent of Argentina's $50 million soup market within one year of introducing nine varieties of its red-and-white canned soup. A summary of Campbell Soup's geographic performance between 1991 and 1998 is displayed in Exhibit 8.

THE DALE MORRISON ERA BEGINS: MID-1997 TO PRESENT

When David Johnson's contract expired and Johnson retired as Campbell Soup Company CEO in July 1997, the company announced that 48-year-old Dale Morrison would become its new chief executive effective July 15, 1997. Morrison joined Campbell Soup in June 1995 as president of Pepperidge Farm, where he was largely responsible for a turnaround of the business that had averaged 2 to 3 percent sales growth between 1990 and 1995. Morrison initiated a number of cost-cutting programs that allowed the company to place a greater emphasis on marketing. Such products as Pepperidge Farm Goldfish crackers and Milano cookies benefited from increased advertising and marketing innovations like milk-carton-style packaging for Goldfish that was easier for children to manage than the previous paper-bag-style packaging. Morrison also made a point of visiting all Pepperidge Farm plants and met with the company's independent distributors, whom Morrison reclassified as sales development associates. Morrison's strategies resulted in a 10 percent sales increase in 1996, a 13 percent sales increase in 1997, and a 20 percent earnings increase in both years.

Dale Morrison was appointed president of International Specialty Foods in November 1996, where he was responsible for international grocery, food-service, frozen and specialty foods, and bakery and confectionery businesses. Prior to joining Campbell Soup management, Morrison spent 14 years with PepsiCo, where he held management positions with both Frito-Lay and Pepsi-Cola. Dale Morrison also coordinated the merger of several British snack foods companies while at Frito-Lay. Morrison held a number of positions with General Foods from 1972 to 1981, marketing such brands as Tang, Post cereals, and Kool-Aid.

Even though David Johnson's five-year contract with Campbell Soup expired in July 1997, he agreed to a continuing role as chairman of the board through July 1999, from which he could aid Morrison in an advisory role. Johnson said, "My priority is to ensure that we continue our relentless commitment to building shareowner wealth. I will assist Dale in exploring the strategies needed to achieve Campbell's vision of becoming the best consumer products company in the world."[18] Exhibit 9 presents a graph tracking Campbell Soup's common stock performance since 1989.

Morrison's strategies were, for the most part, a continuation and refinement of Johnson's initiatives. He agreed with David Johnson that Campbell Soup should become more like Coca-Cola, with fast sales growth in international markets and a tight focus on the core business. Morrison wanted to increase the Campbell Soup Company's annual sales growth to 8–10 percent and believed that the company's greatest opportunity for rapid growth lay in its premium brands that were differentiated from competing brands in terms of taste, perceived quality, and image. Morrison wanted growth to come more from volume increases than from price increases and intended to allocate greater resources to advertising some of the company's more highly differentiated brands like Joseph A. Campbell premium-quality ready-to-serve soups and Pepperidge Farm Goldfish crackers and Milano cookies. Ultimately, Morrison's plan called for advertising to increase from 3.5 percent of sales to 8 percent of sales. Morrison also intended to enhance Campbell products' differentiated image in international markets. The choice to upgrade the quality of soup cans and labels in Japan, for example, was intended to improve the image of Campbell soups in a country where consumers were drawn to products with high-quality packaging.

---

[18]As quoted in *Milling and Baking News,* July 8, 1997, p. 14.

EXHIBIT 9   Campbell Soup Company's Stock Performance, by Quarter, 1989–98

Continued Portfolio Restructuring

In September 1997 Dale Morrison announced the spinoff of seven low-growth businesses with combined sales of $1.4 billion—about 18 percent of Campbell Soup Company's 1997 sales. The spinoff was part of the company's strategic growth plan devised by David Johnson and announced in September 1996. Under the plan, Vlasic Foods International would become a stand-alone company with operations in the United States, Europe, and South America and over 9,000 employees. The new company's shares would be distributed tax free to Campbell shareholders, and upon the completion of the spinoff the new company would be ranked 21st among 32 publicly traded food companies. Campbell's Swanson frozen food business in the United States and Canada and its frozen food lines in the United Kingdom would make up Vlasic Foods International's frozen food division. The grocery division would include Campbell's Vlasic retail and food-service products, Swift Armour meats in Argentina, Open Pit barbecue sauces, Stratford-upon-Avon's retail and food-service pickle and canned vegetable businesses in the United Kingdom, Gourmet Specialty Foods in Germany, and the U.S. fresh mushroom business.

Morrison commented at the time of the announced spinoff that shareholders would benefit greatly by a separation of Campbell Soup businesses:

> This is a watershed day for Campbell Soup Company and its shareowners. Spinning off these businesses allows us to focus on our most profitable businesses with the highest growth potential. Our core businesses have gross margins in excess of 45%. Net sales for these businesses grew 10% and earnings grew 15% in fiscal 1997. This is an outstanding platform to drive significant volume growth while continuing to deliver top-quartile earnings. The creation of this new company gives great brands like Vlasic and Swanson tremendous opportunities for

growth under a dedicated management team. In both cases, shareowners will reap the rewards of highly focused companies.[19]

Some Wall Street analysts were not as optimistic that the new company would become a strong competitor in the processed-food industry. One portfolio manager suggested that the spinoff would allow Campbell to achieve higher growth rates in terms of sales and earnings, but Vlasic Foods International would find growth difficult: "Whenever a company spins off the crummy parts, it's always good for what's left. What they're spinning off didn't have the value or the growth rate of the other divisions."[20] Another analyst commented on the attractiveness of frozen food, where over the last ten years the size of the market had declined and margin points were gained only through price cuts. "There is not going to be a mad rush to own this [new] food company. Swanson has been a stagnant brand at best, though I suppose it's a bit better than Schlitz beer."[21]

Even though frozen foods were a highly competitive food category that had become commoditylike after the 1980s, Vlasic Foods International did include a number of popular brands and products. Swanson was the originator of the TV dinner in 1954 and continued to maintain category leadership with products like Hungry Man dinners, Great Start breakfasts, and Fun Feast kids' meals. Vlasic was the leader in U.S. pickle sales, with a 36 percent market share, and approximately 35 percent of Vlasic's sales came from products introduced within the previous five years. In addition, Swift was Argentina's largest exporter of beef, Open Pit was the best-selling barbecue sauce in the midwestern United States, Gourmet Specialty Foods was Germany's number one specialty foods company, and the company's mushroom business was the largest in the world. The new company's third- and fourth-quarter sales and earnings fell below projections, and sales of pickles and frozen foods were down about 10 percent for the year. The company's stock closed at $22¾ on the first day of trading in March 1998, but was trading in the $13–$15 range in early September 1998. The market performance of Vlasic Foods' common stock price in the months immediately following its spinoff is depicted in Exhibit 10.

Morrison continued to restructure Campbell's portfolio during May and June 1998 to allow the company to focus on core brands and activities directly related to either product quality or image. Continental Sweets was sold to a Dutch venture capital fund. Continental Sweets made and distributed sugar and chocolate confectionery; its facilities were located in France and Belgium. The sale of Fresh Start Bakeries, a supplier of English muffins and buns to quick-service restaurants was announced and the European-based Delacre premium biscuit business was sold to United Biscuits for $125 million. All three divestitures were said to be part of Campbell's plan to divest non-strategic businesses. Morrison also chose to divest the company's can-making assets to Silgan Holdings—a supplier of food cans with annual sales of approximately $1.5 billion. The can-making operations were sold for $123 million and the transaction included a 10-year supply agreement between Campbell Soup and Silgan that called for can purchases by Campbell totaling over $200 million each year. The company also announced plans to close its Pace salsa plant in San Antonio, Texas, and shift production of Pace products to Campbell's Paris, Texas, plant, which produced Prego spaghetti sauce, Franco-American gravies, and an assortment of soups.

The spinoff and divestitures allowed Campbell Soup to implement a $2 billion share buyback plan that would repurchase 8 percent of the company's 451 million outstanding

---

[19]Securities and Exchange Commission, Form 8-K, September 9, 1997.

[20]*Knight-Ridder/Tribune Business News,* September 10, 1997.

[21]As quoted in the *New York Times,* September 10, 1997, p. D1.

EXHIBIT 10   Vlasic Foods International's Stock Performance, by Week, March–September 1998

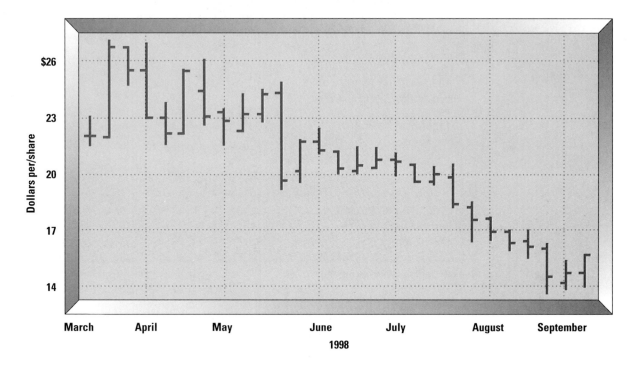

shares between 1999 and 2001. The strategy to boost earnings per share and return on stockholders' equity was a continuation of an ongoing Johnson strategy of repurchasing 2 percent of the company's outstanding shares annually. The company also retained a Johnson strategy of repurchasing shares in addition to the $2 billion buyback plan to offset per share dilution resulting from incentive compensation programs.

Morrison also initiated acquisitions during 1997 and 1998 to aid in Campbell's strategic growth plan. In 1997 the company purchased the remaining 30 percent of Arnott's outstanding shares to increase its ownership of the Australian biscuit company to 100 percent of outstanding shares. The additional shares were purchased for $290 million. The company also acquired Leibig soups in 1997 for $180 million. Leibig was France's leading producer of wet soups, with annual sales of approximately $75 million. In June 1998 Campbell Soup acquired privately held Fortun Foods—the market leader in premium refrigerated soups, with about 50 percent market share of the rapidly growing category and annual sales of $40 million. The company's Stockpot brand of fresh, chilled soup was distributed to restaurants, supermarkets, and convenience stores in over 20 countries. Campbell Soup had tried unsuccessfully a number of times since the 1980s to develop freshly made chilled soup without preservatives. Fortun's manufacturing process transferred hot soup from the kettle to a vacuum-sealed bag that was then immediately refrigerated. The company's proprietary process allowed Stockpot soups to stay fresh for about 120 days.

Morrison's acquisitions and divestitures prompted a realignment of Campbell Soup divisions and business units. Morrison created a soups and sauces division that included all soup and sauce brands marketed globally. The biscuit and confectionery division was reorganized to include all global brands of baked goods, and the makeup of the food service division was adjusted to include all businesses that were dedicated

EXHIBIT 11   Sales and Earnings of Campbell Soup Company by Division, 1995–98 (Millions of dollars)

	1998	1997	1996	1995
Soups and sauces				
Sales	$4,434	$4,156	$3,742	$3,415
Operating earnings	1,110	1,012	978	863
Biscuits and confectionery				
Sales	1,522	1,546	1,459	1,348
Operating earnings	206	154	183	164
Food service				
Sales	455	459	418	345
Operating earnings	53	62	55	40
Other				
Sales	334	1,904	2,149	2,204
Operating earnings	(86)	99	150	135
Interdivision				
Sales	(49)	(101)	(90)	(62)

Source: Campbell annual reports.

to supplying the growing quick-service restaurant industry. A special Campbell's Other division was temporarily formed to handle the details of transferring the divested businesses to the new owners and to report the historical performance of divested businesses.

Morrison believed that skills transfer would become more readily achieved by abandoning Campbell's previous geographically based divisions and placing all businesses sharing common R&D, production, and marketing activities in a common division. Exhibit 7 presents a comparison of business divisions and units under Gordon McGovern, David Johnson, and Dale Morrison. Exhibit 11 provides the sales and operating earnings for Morrison's divisions from 1995 to 1998. The 1995 and 1996 financial data shown in the exhibit have been reorganized to match Campbell Soup Company's divisional structure in 1997 and 1998.

CAMPBELL SOUP IN 1998

Soups and Sauces

In mid-1998, the Soups and Sauces division was Campbell's largest operating unit, accounting for about two-thirds of the company's total consolidated sales. The U.S. and international markets for canned soup were mature and possibly entering a declining stage. During most of the 1990s soup consumption grew at 2–3 percent annually, but in 1998 U.S. wet soup consumption declined about 1 percent. Worldwide soup sales continued to grow at 3 percent during 1998. The decline in the size of the U.S. wet soup category was attributed to the increased popularity of fresh foods, a 40 percent decrease in the usage of cooking soups in recipes, and an overall reduced tendency of consumers to purchase canned products.

Campbell's market share in the condensed soup category had declined from 80 percent in 1993 to 74 percent in 1997. The division forewent its usual 3–7 percent annual price increases in 1998 since much of its lost market share was being captured by lower-priced private-label brands. The Soups and Sauces division had introduced 19 new varieties of soup in 1997 but was unable to grow its soup sales beyond 3 percent. Campbell was able to achieve volume increases from the sale of canned soups by about 1 percent in 1998 as a result of new-product introductions such as more varieties of 98 percent fat-free soups, increased advertising, and the contributions of international acquisitions like Erasco and Leibig.

The division implemented a plan to increase advertising spending by 18 percent in 1998 and intended to eventually increase the advertising budget for Campbell soups and sauces from 3.5 percent of sales to 8 percent of sales in 1998. Dale Morrison believed that increased advertising was necessary to support new products and newly packaged products and to promote soup in appealing ways to children. Campbell's fastest growing soup and sauce products during 1998 were Swanson broths, V8, and Franco-American pastas. Swanson's 20 percent annual growth was in large part a result of new 32-ounce recloseable aseptic packaging and its positioning as a 100 percent fat-free seasoning alternative that could be used in a number of recipes. V8's growth was primarily the result of a recent product introduction—V8 Splash, a beverage combining carrot and tropical fruit juices. The popularity of the new beverage helped V8 grow by 10 percent during 1998. Franco-American had seen very little growth during most of the 1980s and 1990s, but new-product introductions like Superiore Hearty Twists helped create growth of 20 percent for the business in 1998.

Campbell planned additional product introductions in 1998 and 1999 to improve the sales volumes of products like tomato soup and Prego. A new 32-ounce recloseable plastic package was planned for Campbell Tomato Soup that would allow consumers to pour a single serving or use what was called for by a recipe and then store the remaining portion in the refrigerator for later use. Campbell marketers believed that having soup in the refrigerator would lead to higher consumption since most people opened the refrigerator more often than the pantry. Campbell also introduced a new upscale line of pasta sauces, branded Prego Primore, that were expected to generate additional sales volume for Prego in 1998 and 1999. Joseph A. Campbell premium-quality soups had not experienced the sales gains expected by Campbell management and were rebranded Simply Home in 1998.

Even though the company had been largely successful with its new-product introductions in recent years, Campbell management still believed in David Johnson's commitment to thoroughly assessing a product's potential on the market prior to its launch. Robert Bemstock, president of Campbell's U.S. Grocery division, explained, "In the early 1990s we were launching two new, single SKU products with more than $10 million in sales a year. We're now launching more than 20 a year. Tremendous up-front discipline is the key. We spend 12–18 months in rigorous testing."[22]

Other new products that were set for launch in 1998 and 1999 were Campbell's single-serve microwavable Soup to Go; new varieties of Chunky soup; and Rugrats Pasta with Chicken and Broth and Blue's Clues Alphabet Soup, both targeted to children under the age of 10. The company dropped its Intelligent Quisine (IQ) meal program in June 1998 prior to a nationwide launch. The IQ dinners were designed for people with high blood pressure, high cholesterol, and diabetes and were shipped to consumers by United Parcel Service. The company spent $30 million and five years developing and testing the line of prepared foods for those on restricted diets, but concluded that the line would not meet its projected $200 million annual sales volume.

---

[22]As quoted in *Prepared Foods,* September 1997, p. 14.

Biscuits and Confectionery

Campbell's Biscuits and Confectionery business unit had 1998 sales of $1.5 billion and operating earnings of $206 million. The division included Pepperidge Farm in North America; Godiva Chocolates in North America, Europe, and Asia; Arnott's in the Pacific Rim/Asia; and Kettle Chips in Australia. Such products as Goldfish crackers, Swirl bread, and Milano cookies helped the Biscuits and Confectionery division achieve a sales increase of 5 percent in 1998 prior to the impact of exchange rates. Godiva grew its U.S. sales volume by more than 10 percent in 1998 and made some headway in increasing penetration of European and Asian markets. Campbell management expected the business to continue to increase its strength in Asia as more Godiva retail outlets were opened in Japan. The company also planned to open additional free-standing boutiques in shopping malls and Godiva departments in upscale department stores throughout the United States.

Pepperidge Farm continued its transformation, begun by Dale Morrison in 1995, with continued increases in sales volume. The company's increased promotion of Goldfish crackers allowed sales of the product to grow 25 percent in 1996 and 40 percent in 1997. Other market-leading Pepperidge Farm products included Milano cookies, which grew by 35 percent in 1997; Dessert Classics frozen cakes; and Frozen Garlic Bread, which grew more than 40 percent after being moved adjacent to frozen pasta in grocery freezers. Pepperidge Farm management had established a "2 × 2" program with the objective of doubling sales between 1997 and 2000. The program called for Pepperidge Farm to achieve its growth objective by developing several innovative new products and lowering operating costs by eliminating any expenditures that did not provide value to the customer.

Campbell management believed that a controlling interest in Arnott's Ltd. would yield a competitive advantage in the $3 billion Asian cookie and cracker market. The 132-year-old Arnott's was one of Australia's best-known food companies, had access to low-cost ingredients, and had efficient manufacturing processes. Arnott's Australian location also provided a shipping cost advantage for products exported to the entire Asian/Pacific Rim region. Arnott's did experience slight volume increases in 1998, but its contribution to Campbell earnings was substantially hindered by the weak Australian dollar. The Biscuit and Confectionery's 1998 sales increase of 5 percent was reduced to a 2 percent sales decline when currency exchanges from Asia Pacific sales were included in the division's annual sales.

Food Service

Dale Morrison, like David Johnson, realized the importance of Campbell's Food Service unit in growing corporate sales and earnings. In 1997 U.S. consumers ate approximately 45 percent of all meals away from home and spent a projected $226 billion in restaurants. Americans spent an additional $71 billion on meals eaten in business, school, and hospital cafeterias; military bases; and hotels during the year. In 1998 the restaurant industry's total food and beverage purchases were expected to exceed $119 billion. Campbell Soup management intended for the company to make Campbell products readily available to both consumers who purchased food for home preparation and those who chose to dine away from home. Morrison believed that Campbell Soup should position itself to provide soups and other processed foods to consumers in their homes and other locations: "If you look at the U.S. soup business, you could say we have an 80% share of the condensed and ready-to-serve market, and where do we go from there? But if you look at soup consumption in total . . . we really have a 38% share. Under that frame of reference, there's real opportunity."[23]

In 1998 the sales of the Food Service division reached $445 million—a 2 percent increase over 1997. The division provided pot pies to Kentucky Fried Chicken and a wide variety of Prego entrees and Campbell soups to restaurants and cafeterias. V8 Splash beverages and Pace Mexican salsas were also distributed to restaurants, delicatessens, and cafeterias. The company introduced hot soups into convenience stores and college cafeterias and also provided complete meals to supermarket delis and cafeterias that included entrees and side dishes packaged in 5.5- and 2.5-pound aluminum trays. Campbell management was hopeful that the acquisition of Stockpot soups would allow it to capture a greater share of the food-service market for soups because of Stockpot's proprietary manufacturing process that allowed soups to be shipped fresh and without preservatives.

In 1998 Campbell Soup Company was ranked number three on *Fortune*'s list of most admired food companies and had been listed as the second most profitable food company among the Fortune 500. However, Campbell Soup's financial and market performance fell considerably short of being rated "best in show." Dale Morrison was nonetheless pleased with the company's performance in 1998 and believed that the company was positioned to continue to deliver a return to its shareholders that outpaced the market:

> This was an exceptional year at Campbell. We continued to deliver strong results while completing the most far-reaching portfolio reconfiguration in the history of Campbell Soup Company. Our reconfiguration and accelerated productivity programs continued to expand gross margins, which were up 3.3 points to 51.7 percent in fiscal 1998. We are a more focused company and we are excited about our growth plan for the new year. U.S. soup is our highest priority. Across businesses we have new products, new advertising and new marketing initiatives to build on Campbell's strong equity with consumers and to drive volume growth. We remain committed to delivering long-term shareowner wealth through top quartile earnings growth.[24]

---

[23]Ibid.

[24]As quoted in *PR Newswire,* September 3, 1998.

THE BLACK & DECKER CORPORATION

John E. Gamble, *University of South Alabama*

Arthur A. Thompson, Jr., *The University of Alabama*

Going into 1998, the Black & Decker Corporation was a diversified global manufacturer and marketer of household, commercial, and industrial products. The company operated 50 manufacturing plants—25 in the United States and 25 in 13 other countries—and its products were marketed in over 100 countries. Black & Decker (B&D) was the world's largest producer of power tools, power tool accessories, security hardware, and electric lawn and garden products. The company's Price Pfister brand of kitchen and bathroom faucets was among the fastest growing brands in North America and had gained market share for nine consecutive years. Its electric housewares business was the U.S. volume leader, and the company was among the top sellers in the global market for small household appliances. B&D was also the worldwide leader in golf club shafts, glass-container-making equipment, and certain types of mechanical fastening systems.

In January 1998 B&D's chief executive officer, Nolan D. Archibald, announced that the company would divest its small household appliance, glass-container-making equipment, consumer fastening systems, and golf club shaft businesses within the next six months. Archibald also stated that the company would eliminate over 3,000 jobs worldwide and four manufacturing plants in Canada, Latin America, and Australia. The combined sales of the businesses identified for divestiture accounted for 18 percent of B&D's 1997 total revenues. Archibald told analysts that the elimination of the businesses that manufactured and marketed such products as Black & Decker irons and other housewares, True Temper golf club shafts, and Emhart glass-making machinery would allow the company to position itself for greater growth. "This [portfolio restructuring] will allow us to focus on core operations that can deliver dependable and superior operating and financial results."[1]

COMPANY BACKGROUND

Black & Decker was incorporated by Duncan Black and Alonzo Decker in 1910 and initially produced milk cap machines and candy dippers. In 1916 the company introduced its first power tool—a portable half-inch electric drill that was eventually placed

---

[1]As quoted in *Knight-Ridder/Tribune Business News,* January 28, 1998.

on display in the Smithsonian Institution. Over the next 40 years, Duncan Black and Alonzo Decker undertook a number of actions that established their company as the dominant name in power tools and accessories. B&D introduced the first portable screwdriver in 1922, the first electric hammer in 1936, finishing sanders and jigsaws in 1953, and the Dustbuster handheld vacuum in 1978. The company expanded internationally when it began sales operations in Russia, Japan, and Australia in 1919 and opened a production facility in Canada in 1922. The company eventually became known worldwide for its power tools, particularly so in Europe. Black & Decker was managed by the original partners until Black's death in 1951 and Decker's in 1956. As managers, Black and Decker achieved growth by adding to the company's lineup of power tools and accessories and by increasing its penetration of foreign markets. Until the mid-1980s, the company maintained a corporate growth strategy tied exclusively to product-line extensions and international expansion.

Diversification into Small Household Appliances

Black & Decker began to pursue diversification in the 1980s because of the growing maturity of its core power tools business. In 1984 B&D acquired the housewares business of General Electric (GE) for $300 million. GE's brands had about a 25 percent share of the small-appliance market and generated annual revenues of about $500 million. GE sold its small-appliance division, despite its number one market position, because of the division's low profitability. GE's strong suit in appliances was in irons and toaster ovens, where its share of the market was close to 50 percent; sales of GE irons alone totaled about $250 million. Among the 150 other products acquired by B&D were coffeemakers, hair dryers and hair curlers, food mixers and processors, toasters, electric skillets, can openers, waffle irons, and blenders. Also in 1984, B&D purchased three European tool manufacturers to fill in product gaps and strengthen its manufacturing base; the acquisition involved a Swiss manufacturer of portable electric woodworking tools for professional users, the leading European manufacturer of drill bits, and a German producer of hobby and precision power tools.

The acquisition of GE's housewares division launched B&D on a course to transform the company from a power tools manufacturer into a consumer products company. In early 1985, the firm changed its name from Black & Decker Manufacturing Company to Black & Decker Corporation to reflect its new emphasis on selling rather than merely manufacturing products.

Black & Decker's CEO—Nolan D. Archibald

The chief architect of Black & Decker's foray into diversification was Nolan D. Archibald. Black & Decker hired Archibald as president and chief operating officer in 1985, shortly after the acquisition of GE's housewares business. Prior to joining B&D, Archibald was president of the $1.7 billion consumer durables group at Beatrice Companies, where he was responsible for such business units as Samsonite luggage, Culligan water treatment products, Del Mar window coverings, Stiffel lamps, and Aristocraft kitchen cabinets. Archibald, then 42, was chosen from a pool of some 50 candidates for B&D position and turned down offers to be president at two other companies. Archibald had been at Beatrice since 1977 and was successful in engineering turnarounds in three of Beatrice's businesses. Prior to that, he had headed a turnaround of Conroy Inc.'s Sno-Jet Snowmobile business. Archibald spent two years of his youth as a Mormon missionary, was an All-American basketball player at Utah's Dixie College, became a standout player at Weber State College in Utah, earned his MBA degree at Harvard Business School, and tried out (unsuccessfully) for the Chicago Bulls professional basketball team. Corporate headhunters rated Archibald as a good strategic thinker who was personable, versatile, and sensitive to people.

According to one Black & Decker dealer, prior to Archibald's becoming president in September 1985, "Black & Decker had been coasting along for quite a few years like a ship without a captain."[2] Archibald wasted little time in reorganizing B&D's worldwide manufacturing operations. Within three months, Archibald initiated a restructuring plan to close old, inefficient plants and boost factory utilization rates by consolidating production within B&D's newest and biggest plants. Approximately 3,000 jobs were eliminated, including a number of high-level managerial jobs. In 1985, B&D took a $215 million write-off for plant shutdowns and other cost-saving reorganization efforts.

Before 1985, B&D had pursued a decentralized, multi-country strategy. Each geographic area had its own production facilities, its own product-design centers, and its own marketing and sales organizations to better cater to local market conditions. Over the years, this strategy had resulted in short production runs at scattered production sites, reduced overall manufacturing efficiency, and prevented the achievement of scale economies—for example, there were about 100 different motor sizes in B&D's product line. Archibald set the company on a more globalized approach to product design and manufacturing, with much greater communication and coordination between geographic operating units. As production at plants was organized around motor sizes, the number of product variations was reduced and production runs were lengthened. From 1984 to 1989 seven plants were closed and nearly 3,000 jobs were eliminated. Archibald also insisted more emphasis be put on quality control—during the early 1980s, B&D's reputation in power tools had been tarnished by shoddy product quality.

Meanwhile, Archibald put additional resources into new-product development and redesign of the company's power tool and small-appliance lines. Archibald set a goal for the tool division to come up with more than a dozen new products each year—more than B&D had introduced in the five years before his arrival. He also created panels of dealers to suggest new products and features that consumers desired. The company introduced a number of highly successful products, including its Snakelight flashlights; cordless power tools; Macho rotary hammers that could punch holes in stone, brick, and concrete; DeWalt professional power tools; and VersaPak rechargeable batteries, which fit both Black & Decker power tools and household appliances.

One of Archibald's biggest marketing challenges was transferring consumers' brand loyalty for GE small appliances over to Black & Decker. Some observers believed that B&D would have trouble because the company's traditional customers were men, whereas buyers of houseware products were usually women—a headline in *The Wall Street Journal* asked, "Would You Buy a Toaster from a Drillmaker?" B&D executives believed, however, that many women were familiar with the Black & Decker name because they bought power tools as gifts for men and because B&D had pioneered the development of household appliances powered by rechargeable batteries. Black & Decker's handheld Dustbuster vacuum cleaner was the market leader, with a 45 percent share. B&D also had been marketing a cordless rotary scrub brush, a cordless rechargeable shoe shiner, and a rechargeable flashlight. Even before acquiring GE's housewares business, B&D had planned to introduce a line of cordless kitchen appliances, but gaining ample retail shelf space was often a hit-or-miss proposition. The GE acquisition was attractive because being able to offer retailers a full line of housewares would give B&D extra clout in competing for shelf space.

---

[2]As quoted in *Business Week,* July 13,1987, p. 90.

B&D's competitors in small appliances saw the brand-name transition from GE to Black & Decker as an opportunity to gain market share that once was GE's. Sunbeam Appliance quadrupled its 1985 ad budget to $42 million because it wanted to replace GE as the best-known brand in small appliances. Norelco launched a new line of irons and a handheld can opener powered by rechargeable batteries. Hamilton Beach introduced a battery-operated carving knife. Nearly all small-appliance producers were rumored to be trying to develop cordless adaptations of irons, coffeemakers, handheld mixers, and electric carving knives.

Archibald responded to the brand transfer challenge with a series of actions. Since Black & Decker had until 1987 to put its own name on all the GE products it acquired, it led off the transfer process by first putting its name on GE's innovative, expensive, high-margin Spacemaker products that were mounted under kitchen cabinets—a line that was not as strongly identified with the GE name as other lines were. Then B&D introduced a new iron (invented by GE) that shut off automatically when it sat too long or was tipped over; B&D's TV ads for the iron showed an elephant walking away from an iron that had been left on, followed by the tag line "Even elephants forget." The brand transfer was accomplished product by product, in each case accompanied by heavy advertising. Under Archibald, B&D spent approximately $100 million during the 1985–1987 period to promote the brand transition. The company also organized a large team of brand transition assistants to hang paper tags on display models of newly rebranded products in about 10,000 retail stores across the United States—the tags stated that GE previously sold products now made by Black & Decker. Most analysts regarded Archibald's program as successful; a Harvard Business School professor stated, "It is almost a textbook example of how to manage a brand transition."[3]

Archibald was promoted to chairman, president, and chief executive officer in 1986; was also listed that year among *Fortune* magazine's 10 Most Wanted Executives; and was named as one of the Six Best Managers of 1987 by *Business Week*. By year-end 1988, Archibald was widely credited with engineering another impressive turnaround, having boosted Black & Decker's profits to $97.1 million—up sharply from the loss of $158.4 million posted in 1985. Archibald was also the recipient of the American Marketing Association's 1996 Edison Achievement Award for his accomplishments as B&D's chief executive.

Failed Acquisition Attempts

In early 1988 Black & Decker began an unsolicited takeover bid for American Standard Inc., a diversified manufacturer of bathroom fixtures, air-conditioning products, and braking systems for rail and automotive vehicles. American Standard had revenues of $3.4 billion and earnings of $127 million in 1987 (compared to revenues of $1.9 billion and earnings of almost $70 million for Black & Decker). After several months of negotiations, the takeover effort failed and B&D withdrew from the battle.

In January 1989, B&D negotiated a deal with Allegheny International to purchase its Oster/Sunbeam appliance division for about $260 million. Oster/Sunbeam was a leading manufacturer and marketer of small household appliances—blenders, can openers, food mixers, electric skillets, steam irons, and other kitchen items. However, in February, Allegheny International backed out of the sale and merged with another company.

---

[3]Ibid.

The Emhart Acquisition

A month later, in March 1989, Black & Decker agreed to acquire Emhart Corporation for $2.8 billion, rescuing the firm from a hostile takeover bid. Emhart had 1988 sales of $2.8 billion, earnings of $127 million, assets of $2.4 billion, and shareholders' equity of $971 million. Emhart was a diversified manufacturer of industrial products (1988 sales of $1.6 billion), information and electronic systems (1988 sales of $654 million), and consumer products (1988 sales of $547 million). Approximately 40 percent of Emhart's sales and earnings came from foreign operations, the majority of which were concentrated in Europe. Exhibit 1 provides a profile of Emhart's business portfolio. Exhibit 2 provides data on the financial performance of Emhart's business units.

In the days following the announcement of the company's friendly plan to acquire Emhart, B&D's stock price dropped about 15 percent. There was considerable skepticism over the wisdom of the acquisition, both from the standpoint of whether Emhart's businesses had attractive strategic fit with B&D's businesses and from that of whether B&D could handle the financial strain of making such a large acquisition. Emhart was significantly larger than B&D, as the following comparison shows:

1988 Financials	Emhart	Black & Decker
Sales revenues	$2.76 billion	$2.28 billion
Net earnings	$126.6 million	$97.1 million
Assets	$2.43 billion	$1.83 billion
Stockholders' equity	$970.9 million	$724.9 million
Long-term debt	$674.3 million	$277.1 million

The acquisition agreement called for Black & Decker to purchase 59.5 million shares (95 percent) of Emhart Corporation common stock at $40 per share—a price almost three times the book value per share ($14.32). Altogether, B&D had to secure $2.7 billion in financing to acquire Emhart. To come up with the funds, B&D worked with a group of banks to form a credit agreement that consisted of term loans due 1992 through 1997 and an unsecured revolving credit loan of up to $575 million. The loans carried an interest rate of ¼ percent above the prevailing prime rate. Scheduled principal payments on the term loans were as follows:

1992	$201,217,000
1993	274,287,000
1994	275,221,000
1995	743,923,000
1996	401,318,000

The credit agreement included covenants that required Black & Decker to achieve certain minimum levels of cash flow coverage of its interest obligations and not to exceed specified leverage (debt to equity) ratios during the term of the loan:

EXHIBIT 1 Emhart Corporation's Business Portfolio in 1989 (At the time of the company's acquisition by Black & Decker)

Business and Product Categories	Trademarks/Names	Primary Markets/Customers
Industrial Businesses (1988 sales of $1.6 billion)		
Capacitors, audible signal devices	Emhart, Mallory, Sonalert, Arcotronica	Telecommunications, computer, automotive, and electronic components industries
Electromechanical devices, solid-state control systems, hydrocarbon leak detection systems	Emhart, Mallory, Pollulert	Appliance, automotive, and environmental controls manufacturers
Commercial door hardware, electronic locking systems	Emhart, Carbin, Russwin	Commercial, institutional building construction, and original equipment manufacturers
Footwear materials (insoles, toe puffs, shanks, eyelets, tacks, and nails)	Emhart, Texon, Aquiline	Manufacturers of footwear
Fastening systems (rivets, locknuts, screw anchors, adhesive systems, sealants, and grouts)	Emhart, Molly, Warren, Gripco, Bostik, Kelox, Dodge, Heli-Coil, POP	Appliance, construction, electronics, furniture/woodwork, packaging, automotive, and other transportation industries
Glass container machinery	Emhart, Hartford, Powers, Sundsvalls	Producers of glass containers for beverage, food, household, and pharmaceutical products
Printed circuit board assembling machinery	Emhart, Dynapert	Electronics industry
Information and Electronic Systems (1988 sales of $654 million)		
Technology-based systems and services (including computer-based systems), scientific research services, program management	Emhart, PRC, Planning Research Corp., PRC System Services, PRC Environmental Management, PRC Medic Computer Systems, Nova, Stellar	Governmental units and agencies, real estate multiple listing services, group medical practices, and public utilities
Consumer Products Businesses (1988 sales of $547 million)		
Door hardware, including lock sets, high-security locks, and locking devices	Emhart, Kwikset	Residential construction
Nonpowered lawn and garden equipment, landscape lighting	Garden America, True Temper	Do-it-yourself homeowners
Underground sprinkling and watering systems	Lawn Genie, Drip Mist, Irri-trol	Landscape specialists, do-it-yourself consumers
Golf club shafts, bicycle-frame tubing	True Temper, Dynamic Gold, Black Gold	Golf club manufacturers
Bathroom and kitchen faucets	Price Pfister, The Pfabulous Pfaucet with the Pfunny Name	Residential and commercial construction
Adhesive, sealants	Bostik, Thermogrip	Residential and commercial construction, do-it-yourself consumers
Fasteners, staplers, nailers	Blue-Tack, POP, Molly	Residential and commercial construction

EXHIBIT 2   Financial Performance of Emhart's Business Groups, 1986–88
(In millions of dollars)

	1988	1987	1986A*	1986B
Revenues				
Industrial				
Components	$ 641.8	$ 671.9		$ 653.9
Fastening systems	640.5	638.8		576.3
Machinery	279.0	291.1		419.2
	$1,561.3	$1,601.8		$1,649.4
Information and electronic systems	653.7	438.3		39.3
Consumer	547.5	414.4		405.6
Total	$2,762.5	$2,454.5		$2,094.3
Operating Income (Loss)				
Industrial				
Components	$ 63.8	$ 65.7	$ 48.2	$ (5.4)
Fastening systems	74.8	78.7	68.3	24.8
Machinery	42.7	34.1	44.4	3.9
	$ 181.3	$ 178.5	$160.9	$ 23.3
Information and electronic systems	37.2	22.3	2.0	2.0
Consumer	84.8	68.3	60.4	51.7
	$ 303.3	$ 269.1	$223.3	$ 77.0
Corporate expense	(35.0)	(32.9)	(30.3)	(34.0)
Total	$ 268.3	$ 236.2	$193.0	$ 43.0
Identifiable Assets				
Industrial				
Components	$ 457.8	$ 472.0		$ 400.3
Fastening systems	428.4	428.2		409.7
Machinery	167.8	164.8		297.2
	$1,054.0	$1,065.0		$1,107.2
Information and Electronic Systems	546.7	361.3		334.5
Consumer	702.7	225.1		266.1
	$2,303.4	$1,651.4		$1,707.8
Corporate	123.2	378.5		148.9
Total	$2,426.6	$2,029.9	$000.0	$1,856.7

*1986 before provision for restructuring.
Source: Emhart 1988 annual report.

Fiscal Year	Maximum Leverage Ratio	Minimum Cash Flow Coverage Ratio
1992	3.25	1.35
1993	2.75	1.50
1994	2.25	1.55
1995 and thereafter	1.50	1.60

Note: The leverage ratio was calculated by dividing indebtedness, as defined by the credit agreement, by consolidated net stockholders' equity. The cash flow coverage ratio was calculated by dividing earnings before interest, taxes, depreciation, and amortization of goodwill minus capital expenditures by net interest expense plus cash income tax payments and dividends declared.

Other covenants in the credit agreement limited Black & Decker's ability to incur additional indebtedness and to acquire businesses or sell assets.

Black & Decker also entered into factoring agreements in which it sold its receivables at a discounted rate to avoid waiting 30–60 days to collect on its invoices. The company ended its sale-of-receivables program in December 1997 when it became able to meet its liquidity requirements without factoring receivables.

Black & Decker recorded the excess amount of its purchase price for Emhart over the book value of Emhart's net assets as goodwill to be amortized on a straight-line basis over 40 years. This resulted in B&D's having increased depreciation and amortization charges of about $45 million annually.

Initial Divestitures

Senior management at Black & Decker realized early on that as much as $1 billion of Emhart's business assets would have to be sold to reduce B&D's interest expenses and debt obligations and enable the company to meet its covenant agreements. According to accounting rules, these assets had to be sold within a year, or be consolidated with the rest of B&D assets—a move that could cause B&D to fail to meet its maximum leverage covenant. The Emhart businesses identified for sale within one year from the acquisition date included footwear materials, printed circuit board assembly equipment (Dynapert), capacitors, chemical adhesives (Bostik), and the entire information and electronic systems business unit (PRC). During 1989 and early 1990, B&D sold the Bostik chemical adhesives division to a French company for $345 million, the footwear materials business to the United Machinery Group for approximately $125 million, and the Arcotronics capacitors business to Nissei Electric of Tokyo for about $80 million; the net proceeds from these sales were used to reduce debt. In early 1990, when the one-year period expired, B&D was forced to consolidate about $566 million of the unsold assets, boosting the goodwill on its balance sheet by $560 million and raising annual amortization charges by $14 million. To keep from violating the maximum debt/equity ratio allowed under its credit schedule, B&D was forced to issue $150 million in new preferred stock, $47 million of which was purchased from its 401(K) employee thrift plan when no other buyers came forward.

Throughout 1991 Black & Decker continued to struggle to meet its covenant agreements. The company divested Emhart's Garden America business unit and the Mallory Controls operations in North America and Brazil for a combined total of about $140 million. The company also sold its True Temper Hardware unit, its PRC Medic unit, and its U.S. Capacitors business for a combined total of nearly $110 million. The prices B&D got for the Emhart businesses it sold were generally below management's expectations, partly because oncoming recessionary effects reduced what buyers were willing to pay.

Nonetheless, these divestitures (of what were described by B&D management as "nonstrategic assets") and the sale of $150 million in preferred stock allowed B&D to reduce its total debt from a peak of $4 billion following the Emhart acquisition in April 1989 to $2.9 billion at year-end 1991. Even so, B&D was still hard pressed to generate enough cash to meet its debt repayment schedule, a problem compounded by the 1990–91 recession, which hit the company's tool and household goods businesses fairly hard. The company's stock price fell from the mid-20s at the time of the Emhart acquisition to a low of $11–$12 in early 1991. By early 1992, the stock price had recovered to the low 20s, partly because a decline in the prime rate from 10 percent to 6.5 percent had lowered B&D's interest burden substantially.

Subsequent Divestitures: 1993–96

During the next four years, Black & Decker's corporate management sought to find buyers for several nonstrategic businesses acquired as part of the Emhart deal. Three were ultimately sold.

Dynapert   The Dynapert business unit provided automated equipment for assembling printed circuit boards to electronics customers around the world. The equipment was among the most complex computer-controlled machinery being used in industrial applications. Dynapert had two manufacturing plants (one in the United States and one in England) and sales and service facilities throughout the world. The unit had launched a "total quality" program and implemented just-in-time manufacturing techniques.

Sales were made directly to users by an employee sales force and independent sales representatives. Dynapert faced competition from both U.S. and foreign manufacturers. Competition centered on technological and machine performance features, price, delivery terms, and provision of technical services. The Dynapert division, which generated 1991 sales of about $180 million, was put on the market shortly after the Emhart acquisition and was sold two years later to Dover Corporation's Universal Instrument division for an undisclosed amount.

Corbin Russwin   Emhart's Corbin Russwin manufactured locks and door hardware for the European commercial security hardware market. The unit employed 550 people at its Berlin, Germany, plant. Yale and Valour, Inc., the British manufacturer of Yale locks, purchased the Corbin Russwin unit from Black & Decker in 1994 for $80 million. B&D recorded a gain of $18 million on the combined sales of the Corbin Russwin and Dynapert units.

PRC Information Systems and Services   The PRC Information Systems and Services segment consisted of a single business unit known as PRC, Inc., headquartered in McLean, Virginia. PRC and its predecessors had been in business since the mid-1970s. A majority of PRC's business came from contracts with various agencies and units of the federal government. Approximately 40 percent of PRC's 1991 revenues were from contracts with the Department of Defense. In addition, PRC was the leading provider of (1) on-line printed residential real estate multiple listing systems and (2) computer-aided emergency dispatch systems. The types of services PRC provided were highly competitive, and strategic defense expenditures were expected to decline given the improvement of foreign relations. Many of PRC's competitors were large defense contractors with significant financial resources. As the Department of Defense's expenditures for weapons programs continued to decline, these large contractors were expected to bid more aggressively for the types of contract work done by PRC.

In 1991, PRC had sales of $684 million and pretax operating earnings of $32.3 million. In mid-1991 B&D appointed a new person to head PRC; shortly thereafter, PRC launched an initiative to pursue new markets. The objective was to shift PRC's business mix so that half came from U.S. customers and half from overseas customers. However, PRC management had great difficulty developing new nongovernment customers and was only growing at about one-third the rate of its closest competitors under B&D ownership.

Black & Decker put PRC on the market following the Emhart acquisition but had little success in locating interested buyers for the PRC unit until 1995, when PRC Realty Systems and PRC Environmental Management, Inc., were sold for $60 and $35.5 million, respectively. Litton Industries agreed to purchase the remaining PRC operations in 1996 for $425 million. Prior to Litton's purchase of PRC, when it appeared that finding a buyer was becoming increasingly unlikely, Black & Decker management had considered a spinoff of the unit. The spinoff was never finalized because Wall Street showed little interest in a $350 million public offering of PRC stock. PRC's 1995 sales and after-tax earnings were $800 million and $38.4 million, respectively.

Exhibit 3 provides a 10-year summary of Black & Decker's financial and operating performance. Exhibit 4 tracks the company's market performance between 1988 and September 1998.

BLACK & DECKER'S BUSINESS PORTFOLIO IN 1998

In 1998 Black & Decker Corporation was a diversified multinational enterprise with a business lineup that consisted of

- Power tools and power tool accessories for both do-it-yourselfers and professional tradespeople.
- Security hardware for residential markets in the United States and residential and commercial hardware in certain European countries.
- Lawn and garden products.
- Plumbing products.
- Commercial fastening systems.

Exhibit 5 provides a more detailed listing of the goods produced and marketed by each of these businesses (along with the businesses included in the company's portfolio at year-end 1997 that were divested in 1998). Exhibit 6 provides 1995–97 financial performance data by business segment and by geographic area. A brief description of each of B&D's business groups follows.

Power Tools and Accessories

In 1998 Black & Decker was the world's largest manufacturer, marketer, and servicer of power tools and accessories. The company's products were available at almost all retail outlets that sold power tools in the United States, Europe, and other developed countries. In fact, Black & Decker products were so popular in the United Kingdom that many British do-it-yourselfers referred to working on home improvement projects as "Black & Deckering." Black & Decker was named as the top-performing hardware brand by 6 out of 10 U.S. retailers included in a 1997 survey conducted by *Discount Store News*. Other brands highly rated by hardware retailers were Stanley, General Electric, Skil, Rubbermaid, Makita, and Dutch Boy. Black & Decker's products, most of which carried a two-year warranty, were also highly rated by consumers in terms of performance.

Industry Growth and Competition   The market for power tools and accessories was regarded as mature and cyclical. Volume was influenced by residential and commercial construction activity, by consumer expenditures for home improvement, and by the overall level of manufacturing activity (a number of manufacturers used power tools in performing certain production tasks—automotive and aerospace firms, for example, were heavy users of power tools). Worldwide sales of power tools were an estimated

EXHIBIT 3 Summary of Black & Decker's Financial and Operating Performance, 1988–97 (In millions of dollars except per share and employee data)

	1997	1996	1995	1994	1993	1992	1991	1990	1989	1988
Sales	$4,940.5	$4,914.4	$4,766.1	$4,365.2	$4,121.5	$4,045.7	$3,952.6	$4,313.2	$3,172.5	$2,280.9
Operating income	489.3	356.9	426.1	351.9	302.7	177.1	365.2	458.1	259.2	159.1
Operating income excluding restructuring and goodwill amortization	552.6	514.5	494.5	424.9	364.4	391.3	436.0	524.1	284.5	164.7
Income taxes	122.3	43.5	9.0	62.7	60.7	44.3	54.5	72.4	32.9	28.6
Earnings data:										
Earnings (loss) from continuing operations	227.2	159.2	216.5	89.9	64.1	(95.3)	16.1	19.7	30.0	97.1
Discontinued operations	—	70.4	38.4	37.5	31.1	22.0	36.9	31.4	—	—
Extraordinary item	—	—	(30.9)	—	—	(22.7)	—	—	—	—
Cumulative effects of accounting change	—	—	—	—	(29.2)	(237.6)	—	—	—	—
Net earnings (loss)	227.2	229.6	224.0	127.4	66.0	(333.6)	53.0	51.1	30.0	97.1
Total assets	$5,360.7	$5,153.5	$5,545.3	$5,264.3	$5,166.8	$5,295.0	$5,456.8	$5,829.7	$6,258.1	$1,825.1
Long-term debt	1,623.7	1,415.8	1,704.5	1,723.2	2,069.2	2,108.5	2,625.8	2,754.7	2,629.7	277.1
Total debt	1,862.5	1,705.8	2,351.7	2,393.3	2,564.6	2,563.8	2,870.3	3,266.2	4,057.5	492.6
Stockholders' equity	1,791.4	1,632.4	1,423.2	1,169.4	1,048.9	1,074.0	1,027.1	920.7	720.7	724.9
Capital expenditures	203.1	196.3	203.1	181.5	190.3	167.7	94.9	103.1	112.1	98.4
Depreciation and amortization	$ 214.2	$ 214.6	$ 206.7	$ 195.4	$ 182.4	$ 188.3	$ 187.1	$ 197.8	$ 131.0	$ 93.5
Number of employees	28,600	29,200	29,300	29,200	30,500	32,300	31,900	35,900	38,600	20,800
Number of shares outstanding	96.5	96.1	94.4	85.3	84.5	76.3	62.6	61.4	59.6	59.2
Dividends per share	$0.48	$0.48	$0.40	$0.40	$0.40	$0.40	$0.40	$0.40	$0.40	

Source: Black & Decker Corporation annual reports.

EXHIBIT 4 Market Performance of Black & Decker's Common Stock, by Quarter, 1988– September 1998

(*a*) Trend in Black & Decker's Common Stock Price

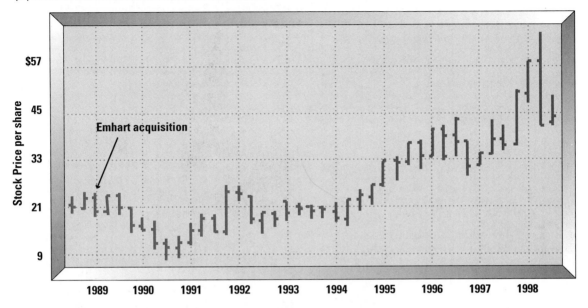

(*b*) Performance of Black & Decker's Stock Price versus the S&P 500 Index

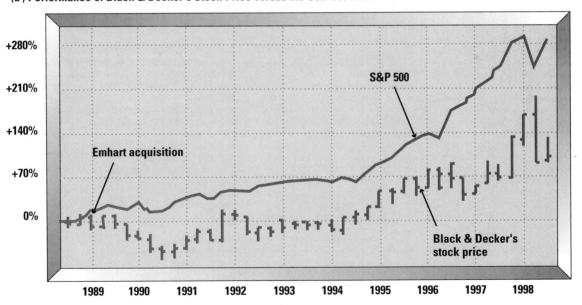

$10 billion in 1997. The North American market for power tools was estimated at $3.5 billion, European sales were estimated at $4.0 billion, Asia/Pacific sales were an estimated $2.0 billion, and Latin American sales of power tools were approximately $500 million. From 1995 to 1997 the power tool industry in the United States grew at an annual rate of 4–6 percent but that rate was expected to slow to 3–4 percent from 1998 to

EXHIBIT 5   Black & Decker's Business Portfolio at year-end 1997

Consumer and Home Improvement Products Group

Power tools (1997 sales: $2.07 billion)
- Drills
- Screwdrivers
- Saws
- Sanders
- Grinders
- Workmate workcenters

Power tool accessories (1997 sales: $342 million)
- Drill bits
- Screwdriver bits
- Saw blades

Consumer-use fastening products (1997 sales: $81 million)
- Blind fasteners
- Wall anchors
- Rivets and rivet guns
- Staple and glue guns

Security hardware (1997 sales: $574 million)
- Lock sets
- Deadbolts
- Door closers
- Exit devices
- High security locks
- Master keying systems

Plumbing products (1997 sales: $242 million)
- Faucets and fixtures
- Valves
- Fittings

Commercial and Industrial Products Groups

Fastening systems (1997 sales: $460 million)
- Rivets and riveting tools
- Threaded inserts
- Stud welding fastening systems
- Lock nuts
- Self-drilling screws
- Construction anchors

Household products (1997 sales: $588 million)
- Cordless vacuum cleaners
- Cordless flashlights
- Cordless scrub brushes
- Irons
- Toasters
- Toaster ovens
- Coffee makers
- Can openers
- Food mixers
- Food processors and choppers
- Blenders

Lawn and garden care products (1997 sales: $262 million)
- Hedge and lawn trimmers
- Edgers
- Electric lawn mowers
- Blowers and vacuums

Outdoor recreational products (1997 sales: $82 million)
- Golf club shafts
- Tubing for bicycle frames
- Kayak paddles

Glass container-making machinery (1997 sales: $239 million)

2000. Demand in Europe was expected to grow even more slowly than in the United States. Worldwide, the biggest percentage growth during the early and mid-1990s occurred in emerging Asian countries where the use of power tools was quickly replacing the use of hand tools. However, the economic uncertainty and currency devaluations that began in late 1997 were expected to substantially decrease demand for power tools there until the region regained financial and economic stability.

Market Segments   There were two distinct groups of buyers for power tools: professional users and do-it-yourselfers. Professional users included construction workers, electricians, plumbers, repair and maintenance workers, auto mechanics, and manu-

EXHIBIT 6 Black & Decker's Financial Performance by Business Segment and Geographic Area, 1995–97

	Business Segments		
	Consumer	Commercial	Corporate and Eliminations*
1997			
Sales to unaffiliated customers	$4,241.6	$ 698.9	$ —
Operating income	400.8	82.2	6.3
Operating income excluding goodwill amortization	448.8	97.5	6.3
Identifiable assets	5,627.3	1,519.3	(1,785.9)
Capital expenditures	181.6	18.9	2.6
Depreciation	130.8	16.5	2.6
1996			
Sales to unaffiliated customers	$4,212.0	$ 702.4	$ —
Operating income	273.0	75.7	8.2
Operating income excluding goodwill amortization	410.6	95.7	8.2
Identifiable assets	5,002.5	1,382.0	(1,231.0)
Capital expenditures	177.5	17.3	1.5
Depreciation	128.6	16.0	2.8
1995			
Sales to unaffiliated customers	$4,075.6	$ 690.5	$ —
Operating income	348.5	74.8	2.8
Operating income excluding goodwill amortization	399.8	91.9	2.8
Identifiable assets	4,929.2	1,382.8	(766.7)
Capital expenditures	184.1	15.7	3.3
Depreciation	115.9	15.4	4.6

facturing workers. Professional users were very conscious of quality and features; they tended to buy only tools that were durable, functional, dependable, and capable of precision. In contrast, do-it-yourselfers were often first-time buyers who used power tools infrequently; they were thus less knowledgeable than professional users.

Because the needs of professional users and do-it-yourself consumers tended to be sharply different, some manufacturers catered to one segment only and others carried two distinct product lines (heavy-duty professional versus consumer). Professional users tended to purchase their tools through jobbers, contractor supply firms, industrial supply houses, building supply centers, and some home improvement centers. Tools for the consumer segment were sold at home improvement centers, building materials centers, mass merchandisers (Sears), discount chains (Wal-Mart, Kmart), and hardware stores.

Until the late 1980s, the consumer tool segment was growing at a faster clip than the professional segment. But narrowing price differentials and a rising interest on the part of gung-ho do-it-yourselfers in professional-quality tools had, in the U.S. market, spurred demand for heavy-duty professional tools. The sales of both consumer-grade

EXHIBIT 6   Black & Decker's Financial Performance by Business Segment and Geographic Area, 1995–97 (*Concluded*)

	Geographic Areas			
	United States	Europe	Other	Corporate and Eliminations*
1997				
Sales to unaffiliated customers	$2,855.7	$1,368.9	$ 715.9	$ —
Sales and transfers between geographic areas	232.8	189.8	367.9	(790.5)
Total sales	3,088.5	1,558.7	1,083.8	(790.5)
Operating income (loss)	337.9	145.5	(.4)	6.3
Identifiable assets	3,771.7	2,461.0	818.4	(1,690.4)
1996				
Sales to unaffiliated customers	$2,726.1	$1,466.8	$ 721.5	$ —
Sales and transfers between geographic areas	246.6	176.4	256.0	(679.0)
Total sales	2,972.7	1,643.2	977.5	(679.0)
Operating income (loss)	282.3	67.5	(1.1)	8.2
Operating income excluding restructuring costs†	317.4	117.2	5.4	8.2
Identifiable assets	3,258.5	2,375.9	783.6	(1,264.5)
1995				
Sales to unaffiliated customers	$2,551.2	$1,503.6	$ 711.3	$ —
Sales and transfers between geographic areas	287.8	165.0	206.0	(658.8)
Total sales	2,839.0	1,668.6	917.3	(658.8)
Operating income (loss)	300.2	96.0	27.1	2.8
Identifiable assets	3,216.6	2,488.4	763.9	(923.6)

*Corporate assets included in corporate and eliminations were $423.9 million at December 31, 1997, $366.0 million at December 31, 1996, and $688.1 million at December 31, 1995, and principally consist of cash and cash equivalents, other current assets, property, other sundry assets, and, for 1995, net assets of the discontinued PRC segment. The remainder of corporate and eliminations includes certain pension credits and amounts to eliminate intercompany items, including accounts receivable and payable and intercompany profit in inventory.
†In 1996 restructuring costs in the amount of $87.7 million and $3.6 million were charged to the Consumer and Commercial segments, respectively.
Source: Black & Decker 1997 annual report.

and professional-grade cordless products were also becoming increasingly popular, with a compound annual growth rate of over 10 percent during the mid-1990s.

Competition   Power tool manufacturers competed on such variables as price, quality, product design, product innovation, brand-name reputation, size and strength of retail dealer networks, and after-sale service. All makers were working to bring out new products that were lightweight, compact, cordless, quiet, less prone to vibration, strong, and easy to manipulate. The major manufacturers had sales forces whose main task was to expand and strengthen the network of retail dealers carrying their line of tools. Salespeople signed on new dealers and called on major accounts—wholesale distributors, discount chains, home improvement centers, and other mass merchandisers—to win better access to shelf space in their retail outlets, help with promotion and display activities, and upgrade dealers' product knowledge and sales skills. Some manufacturers offered training seminars and provided training videos to dealers/distributors. Manufacturers that concentrated on the professional segment engaged in limited advertising and promotion activities, spending their dollars for trade magazine ads, trade shows, and in-store displays. Those that concentrated on the consumer segment, like Black & Decker, spent comparatively more for TV and magazine ads, and for co-op ad programs with dealers.

Black & Decker's Competitive Position   In 1998 Black & Decker was the overall leader in the world power tool industry, followed by Bosch/Skil Power Tools, a division of Robert Bosch Corporation (one of Germany's leading companies), and Japanese brands Makita and Hitachi. Other competitors were Atlas/Copco, Delta/Porter Cable, Hilti, Ryobi, and Electrolux. For most of the company's history, B&D's greatest strength was in the consumer tools segment (see Exhibit 7); it was the market leader in the United States, Europe (where it had had a presence since the 1920s), and many other countries outside Europe. No other manufacturer came close to matching B&D's global distribution capabilities in the do-it-yourself segment. Makita and Ryobi were the leaders in Japan and several other Asian countries. Bosch was strongest in Europe.

In consumer tools Black & Decker's strongest U.S. competitor was Sears, which marketed tools under the Sears Craftsman label. Sears's long-time supplier of tools, Ryobi, produced 75 percent of Sears's tool requirements. Skil's strength was in power saws; its 1992 joint venture with Robert Bosch Power Tools was contrived to give the two brands more clout in gaining shelf space and greater global coverage capabilities. B&D's consumer-grade power tools were also carried by Sears, and its new Quantum power tools were sold exclusively by Wal-Mart. Quantum was an intermediate line that was more durable than typical consumer lines but did not meet the performance of the company's professional power tools. B&D's WoodHawk circular saws, Wizard rotary tools, and products that utilized the VersaPak interchangeable battery were among the company's best-selling consumer tools.

Although surveys showed that consumers associated the Black & Decker name with durable power tools, trade professionals considered Black & Decker products to be for do-it-yourselfers. During the late 1980s, the company's charcoal-gray professional tools line was not seen by professional users as sufficiently differentiated from B&D's traditional black line of consumer tools. Professionals preferred tools made by Makita, Skil, and Milwaukee (a U.S. tool manufacturer with a reputation for high-quality, heavy-duty tools). During the 1970s and 1980s, Makita had steadily increased its share of the professional segment and by 1991 had captured 53 percent of the U.S. professional handheld power tool segment.

In 1991 B&D executives formed a team, headed by the president of B&D's power tools division, to come up with a new strategy for the professional market segment. The team elected to create an entirely new line of industrial-grade tools for professional users under the brand DeWalt, a name borrowed from a 65-year-old maker of high-quality stationary saws acquired by B&D in 1960. The team changed the tools' color from gray to industrial yellow, which was easy to see, signaled safety, and distinguished the B&D brand from other leading brands of professional power tools. Every product in B&D's professional line was redesigned based on input from professionals, dealers, and B&D engineers. The redesigned versions were all tested by professional users; every item had to meet or beat Makita's tools in user tests before going into production. As part of the introduction of the new DeWalt line in March 1992,

EXHIBIT 7 Estimated U.S. Sales and Market Shares of Power Tool Manufacturers, 1979, 1991, and 1997 (Dollar values in millions)

	1979		1991		1997	
	Dollar Sales	Percent Share	Dollar Sales	Percent Share	Dollar Sales	Percent Share
Consumer Tools						
Black & Decker	$169	44.5%	$ 325	39.7%	$460	43.1%
Sears/Ryobi	107	28.2	280	34.0	305	28.5
Milwaukee	6	1.5	4	0.5	6	0.6
Makita	2	0.5	43	5.2	32	3.0
Porter Cable	—	—	—	—	—	—
Delta	—	—	—	—	—	—
Skil	52	13.7	82	10.0	165	15.4
Others	44	11.6	86	10.6	102	9.4
Total	$380	100.0%	$ 820	100.0%	$1,070	100.0%
Professional Tools						
Black & Decker	$205	42.1%	$ 125	17.9%	$ 918	36.7%
Sears/Ryobi	9	1.8	50	7.1	285	11.4
Milwaukee	89	18.2	145	20.7	436	17.4
Makita	22	4.5	160	22.9	304	12.2
Porter Cable	NA	NA	50	7.1	240	9.6
Delta	NA	NA	40	5.7	209	8.4
Skil	54	11.1	40	5.7	32	1.3
Others	109	22.3	90	12.9	76	3.0
Total	$488	100.0%	$700	100.0%	$2,500	100.0%
Total Tools						
Black & Decker	$374	43.1%	$ 450	29.6%	$1,378	38.6%
Sears/Ryobi	116	13.4	330	21.7	590	16.5
Milwaukee	95	10.9	149	9.8	442	12.4
Makita	24	2.8	203	13.4	336	9.4
Porter Cable	NA	NA	50	3.3	240	6.7
Delta	NA	NA	40	2.6	209	5.9
Skil	106	12.2	122	8.0	197	5.5
Others	153	17.6	176	11.6	210	9.4
Total	$868	100.0%	$1,520	100.0%	$3,570	100.0%

NA = not available
Source: Compiled by the case researchers from a variety of sources, including telephone interviews with company personnel; data for 1979 are based on information in Skil Corporation, Harvard Business School, case #9-389-005.

B&D created "swarm teams" of 120 young, high-energy marketers who visited construction sites in bright yellow-and-black Chevy Blazers to demonstrate DeWalt tools. Swarm teams also promoted DeWalt tools at NASCAR events, vocational clubs, union apprenticeship programs, and retail locations. The company intended to double the number of swarm-team members in the United States between 1998 and 1999. In 1996 DeWalt swarm teams, in fleets of yellow-and-black Range Rover Defenders, invaded Europe with the charge of making DeWalt a leading brand on that continent. B&D also instituted a policy of offering professional users the loan of a DeWalt power tool when waiting for their equipment to be fixed at any of the company's 100 U.S. service centers. There were also DeWalt demonstration booths at each of the service centers.

Initial response to the DeWalt line was excellent. As the brand began to gain in popularity with professional users, Black & Decker developed additional DeWalt tools. In 1997, newly introduced DeWalt products were awarded two Industrial Design Excellence Awards from the Industrial Designers Society of America. The success of the new DeWalt line exceeded B&D management's expectations and surpassed its $200 million sales volume objective for 1995 by over $100 million. In 1998 DeWalt power tools had become the power tool brand of choice for professionals and serious do-it-yourselfers, had accounted for nearly $1 billion in sales, and had captured nearly 45 percent of the $1.9 billion U.S. market for handheld power tools. DeWalt held about 20 percent of the $600 million U.S. benchtop power tool market in 1998.

Black & Decker was also the world leader in the $6 billion market for such accessories as drill bits, saw blades, and screwdriver bits. Vermont American, Irwin Hanson/American Tool, Bosch, Freud, and Wolfcraft were B&D's closest competitors in the accessories market, but no other toolmaker had as broad a product line or geographic coverage as Black & Decker. Most of the company's growth in accessory sales was accounted for by accessory lines developed for DeWalt power tools and a line of new premium woodworking saw blades. The company intended to maintain its market leadership by expanding into more woodworking supply and industrial/construction distribution channels and continuing to introduce innovative products.

Lawn and Garden Equipment

Black & Decker's lawn and garden tools like Groom 'N' Edge, Vac 'N' Mulch, and Leafbuster were distributed through the same channels as the company's power tools. In addition, the buyers of B&D's hedge trimmers, string trimmers, lawn mowers, edgers, and blower/vacuums could get the items repaired at B&D's 150 company-owned service centers worldwide and several hundred other authorized service centers operated by independent owners. Where feasible, B&D's lawn and garden products had a global design. The company had recently begun to offer cordless electric string trimmers and hedge trimmers in North America and Europe. The cordless hedge trimmer could run continuously for about 30 minutes and the cordless string trimmer could trim areas in a half-acre lawn that were hard to reach for a lawn mower on single battery charges. As of 1998, Black & Decker marketed its 13-inch cordless lawn mower only in Europe.

Security Hardware

B&D's security hardware business was the world leader in door hardware for homes and businesses. The company had developed good-better-best product lines that covered all major residential price points. The Kwikset brand was positioned as an affordable product for nonprofessionals; B&D had boosted Kwikset's sales by providing retailers with a videotape that took the mystery out of changing locks for do-it-yourselfers. Kwikset Plus was a midrange product, and the company's TITAN products were designed for the fine home market. TITAN NightSight handsets and deadbolts featured lighted keyways, and TITAN Lockminder deadbolts featured a red light to indicate when the deadbolt was locked. The TITAN line also included the Society Brass Collection of solid brass designer hardware for doors. All TITAN products boasted a lifetime finish that was protected against tarnishing, rust, and corrosion.

This business, acquired from Emhart, had achieved significant cost savings by integrating its purchasing, distribution, and marketing activities with B&D's other consumer products businesses. B&D's worldwide distribution network was also providing the hardware group wider geographic sales opportunities. In many instances, door hardware was sold in the same retail channels as B&D's power tools and accessories. Black & Decker had introduced new lines of locksets, garage door locks, fire resistant locks, and high-security locks for European markets, but had found it difficult to develop low-cost operations and achieve significant gains in market share. In 1998 the company intended to develop new products under its Netherlands-based NEMEF brand for distribution to European markets and intended to restructure its German operations to improve its cost position in Europe.

Plumbing Products

B&D's plumbing products business, Price Pfister, had gained market share since the Emhart acquisition to become the third largest manufacturer and marketer of plumbing fixtures in North America by year-end 1997. Price Pfister had benefited from access to B&D's retail distribution network by gaining more shelf space in home improvement centers. Price Pfister's fashionable but affordably priced new products had become popular with plumbing wholesalers and plumbing contractors. Price Pfister had increased its brand recognition through in-store merchandising activities and through TV ads using the theme "The Pfabulous Pfaucet with the Pfunny Name" in the early 1990s and "The Pfabulous Pfaucet. Pforever. No Drips, No Tarnish, No Worries" in 1997 and 1998.

Price Pfister's major competitors in the $1.8 billion North American market for sink, tub, shower, and lavatory plumbing hardware were American Standard, Kohler, Delta, and Moen. The industry had grown at a slow 2–3 percent since 1995 and was expected to grow at a comparable rate over the next few years. Plumbing products with new styles and features were in the highest demand. New decorative faucets like Price Pfister's Georgetown and Roman lines, introduced between 1995 and 1997, accounted for 15 percent of the unit's sales in 1997. Price Pfister intended to introduce three new lines in 1998. The company also produced a less expensive B&D brand of conventional faucets that were offered through mass merchandiser and hardware store channels.

Fastening Systems

Black & Decker was among the global leaders in the $1.8 billion fastening and assembly systems market. This business unit marketed fastening products under 26 different brands and trademarks to automotive, electronics, aerospace, machine tool, and appliance companies in the United States, Europe, and the Far East. The industry's recent growth rate had ranged between 3 percent and 5 percent, and future growth was expected to remain within that range. Some emerging markets did generate higher growth rates as new industries and companies emerged and plant capacity was added.

Products were sold directly to users and also through distributors and manufacturers' representatives. Competition, which came from many manufacturers in several countries, centered on product quality, performance, reliability, price, delivery, and ability to provide customers with technical and engineering services. Major competitors included Textron, TRW, and Eaton, and such regional companies as Raymond, Gesipa, Huck, and Fukui. Black & Decker was the global leader in commercial blind riveting and automotive stud welding systems, and its other fastening system categories held strong positions in various geographic regions. B&D management intended to maintain its leadership in the automotive stud welding category with product innovations. Thirty percent of the unit's 1997 sales were accounted for by products introduced within the past five years.

BLACK & DECKER'S BUSINESS DIVESTITURES IN 1998

Household Products

By 1990 Black & Decker had become a worldwide leader in the manufacture and sale of products used for home cleaning, garment care, cooking, and food and beverage preparation. It had the largest market share of any full-line producer of household appliances in the United States, Canada, Mexico, and Australia and a growing presence in Europe, Southeast Asia, and Latin America. The household products division was using the worldwide distribution network and brand-name recognition that had been established by the tools division to gain greater global penetration in household appliances. However, by 1996, the company had lost substantial market share in almost every housewares product category. Its Toast 'R' Ovens and irons were the only remaining B&D products that held leading shares of their respective markets. (See Exhibit 8 for market shares of the major competitors by product category for 1990, 1993, and 1996.)

Like the market for power tools, the market for small household appliances was both mature and cyclical. Growth opportunities existed mainly in the form of creating innovative new products and increasing market penetration in the countries of Eastern Europe and other developing nations where household appliance saturation rates were low. It was difficult to grow sales in the United States without introducing innovative new products since most small appliances had very high household saturation rates. In 1996 blenders were found in 80 percent of U.S. households, coffeemakers in 74 percent, and toasters in 90 percent. Apparently, many consumers had both a toaster and toaster oven, since toaster ovens had a 42 percent U.S. household saturation rate.

Black & Decker's housewares business unit had been successful at launching new products that might entice a consumer into replacing an existing small appliance for one offering more features or better performance. The company's Snakelight flexible flashlight, introduced in 1994, quickly became one of the most popular small appliances ever developed by the company. In 1996 the company introduced a revamped Quick 'N Easy line of irons with a new Sure Steam system and in 1998 added a proprietary coated soleplate. The company also introduced cordless products such as the ScumBuster, a submersible scourer and scrubber, and the FloorBuster, an upright vacuum cleaner that achieved rapid sales increases. The company introduced a ScumBuster Outdoors in late 1997 to follow up on the success of the ScumBuster.

The company's Kitchentools designer line of small kitchen appliances, launched in late 1997, won five Industrial Design Excellence Awards in 1998. The Kitchentools line carried premium pricing; the stand mixer was listed at a suggested retail price of $289.99, the thermal coffeemaker at $159.99, the blender at $139.99, the food processor at $229.99, the hand mixer at $69.00, and the can opener at $34.99. Even though the Kitchentools line was praised for its quality and innovative styling, it did not sell as well as Black & Decker management had expected. The company also had some difficulty manufacturing the products and getting them to market by the planned launch date.

The small-appliance business was one of the businesses identified for divestiture by Nolan Archibald in January 1998. Black & Decker had lost substantial market share in

EXHIBIT 8 Unit Volume for Selected Small Appliances and Market Shares of Leading Producers, 1990, 1993, and 1996

Product / Leading Brands (% of Total Volume)	1990	1993	1996
Can openers (Total unit volume)	6,200,000 units	6,380,000 units	6,910,000 units
Rival	33%	27%	26%
Hamilton Beach/Proctor Silex	13	15	24
Black & Decker	26	28	13
Oster/Sunbeam	11	13	13
Coffeemakers (Total unit volume)	17,740,000 units	14,390,000 units	15,000,000 units
Mr. Coffee	28%	31%	32%
Hamilton Beach/Proctor Silex	19	18	24
West Bend	—	3	9
Black & Decker	20	17	8
Food processors (Total unit volume)	4,760,000 units	1,916,000 units	1,525,000 units
Hamilton Beach/Proctor Silex	21%	19%	40%
Cuisinart	Unknown	13	18
Black & Decker	25	21	10
Oster/Sunbeam	18	19	8
Hand mixers (Total unit volume)	4,400,000 units	5,060,000 units	5,280,000 units
Hamilton Beach/Proctor Silex	14%	18%	24%
Black & Decker	34	28	15
Oster/Sunbeam	25	18	13
HPA/Betty Crocker	—	—	11
Irons (Total unit volume)	16,950,000 units	17,460,000 units	15,600,000 units
Black & Decker	50%	50%	38%
Hamilton Beach/Proctor Silex	24	30	29
Oster/Sunbeam	17	10	17
Rowenta	—	—	7
Toaster ovens (Total unit volume)	2,800,000 units	3,340,000 units	3,670,000 units
Black & Decker	57%	56%	56%
Toastmaster	13	16	17
Hamilton Beach/Proctor Silex	19	20	11
HPA/Betty Crocker	—	—	6
Toasters (Total unit volume)	8,900,000 units	9,850,000 units	10,760,000 units
Hamilton Beach/Proctor Silex	35%	50%	37%
Toastmaster	27	31	30
Rival	—	—	17
HPA/Betty Crocker	—	—	5
Black & Decker	16	13	4

Source: Compiled by case researchers from data presented in *Appliance,* April 1991 and April 1997.

recent years and had seen its profit margins erode despite its best efforts to maintain efficient operations. Between 1995 and 1997 the company had completely overhauled its supply-chain management to reduce finished goods inventory and improve customer service and production planning. The company had cut logistics costs by $150 million during that time but still only averaged about 2 percent profit margins on its housewares products. The business unit was sold to Windmere-Durable in May 1998 for $315 million. The agreement allowed Black & Decker to retain its Dustbuster, Floor-Buster, ScumBuster, and Snakelight product lines. In June 1998 the company announced the sale of its housewares operations in New Zealand and Australia to Gerard Industries, an Australian electrical products manufacturer.

Recreational Outdoor Products

B&D's True Temper Sports business unit was the leading global designer, manufacturer, and marketer of steel golf club shafts, with over a 60 percent market share in the steel shaft segment, which was three times that of its closest rival. True Temper also manufactured graphite shafts but had a very limited market share in that segment since it focused on the premium end of the market. The division supplied more than 800 golf club manufacturers around the world, including such industry leaders as Callaway Golf, Ping, Titleist, and Taylor Made. The sales of this unit had grown at a compounded annual rate of 12 percent between 1995 and 1997. True Temper Sport's growth rate reflected the overall growth in the golf equipment industry. The unit also manufactured specialty tubing for the bicycle and sporting goods industries. Many of the bicycles and kayak paddles used by U.S. Olympians were manufactured from True Temper precision tubing.

Black & Decker sold the business to Cornerstone Equity Investors in June 1998 for $200 million. The new owners stated that they intended not only to maintain True Temper's leadership in golf club shafts but also to develop new product categories requiring specialty tubing. True Temper's president said that the new company would develop new precision tubing products for such sporting goods industries as downhill ski equipment and archery equipment.

Glass-Container-Forming Machinery

Several U.S. manufacturers and a number of foreign firms competed with B&D's glass-container-making machinery business. However, B&D's Emhart glass-container-forming machinery division was considered the global leader and offered the world's most complete line of glass-container-making equipment. Important competitive factors were price, technological and machine performance features, product reliability, and technical and engineering services.

An increasing worldwide preference for plastic and other non-glass containers had led to a slowing growth rate for glass-container-forming equipment and inspection equipment. There was little seasonal variation in industry demand. Glass-container-making equipment was in 24-hour use in virtually all plants worldwide, creating a predictable need for servicing and rebuilding; nearly two-thirds of the unit's revenues came from rebuilding and repair services and technology upgrades. In January 1998 the business was identified as a non-strategic asset that was to be divested and was sold to Bucher Holding A.G. of Switzerland in September 1998 for $158 million.

BLACK & DECKER'S SLIMMED-DOWN
BUSINESS PORTFOLIO GOING INTO 1999

By year-end 1998 Black & Decker had completed the divestiture of its small-appliance, True Temper recreational products, and Emhart glass-forming machinery businesses. The company had also sold its consumer glue gun and stapler business to Longwood Industries for an undisclosed amount in July 1998. Black & Decker was able to sell the businesses for more than management's expected $500 million, allowing it to reduce future operating expenses by more than $100 million annually (primarily as a result of eliminating 3,000 jobs from its payroll). In addition, the recent divestitures were expected cut the company's amortization of goodwill associated with the Emhart acquisition by about $30 million annually for the next 30 years.

The sale of the small-appliance, True Temper, and glass-forming machinery businesses, along with the sale of other Emhart businesses in earlier years, completed the divestiture of the so-called non-strategic business assets gained in the 1989 acquisition of Emhart. Price Pfister and Kwikset were two Emhart businesses that initially captured the attention of Black & Decker management and were now among the three remaining Emhart businesses still included in Black & Decker's portfolio in 1999.

Nolan Archibald expressed confidence that the company's new focus on power tools and businesses that were closely aligned with power tools would allow the company to begin to provide B&D's shareholders with above-average returns.

(B&D's Web address is *www.blackanddecker.com.*)

BLOUNT INTERNATIONAL, INC.

C A S E

23

Gordon M. Amsler,
Troy State University

Blount International, Inc., originally formed as the Blount Brothers Construction Company, celebrated its 50th anniversary in 1996. Blount had grown from a small lo-cal contracting business into an important heavy-construction firm and then into a diversified international manufacturer of outdoor products (saw chains, industrial cutting products, and home and garden products); industrial and power equipment (timber harvesting and processing equipment); and sporting equipment (small-arms ammunition, reloading equipment, and associated gun care products). The company's recent transition to international manufacturing had produced dramatic increases in revenues, 30 percent of which came from outside the United States in 1997. Blount had grown at an annual rate of 15 percent since 1991, with sales reaching $716.9 million in fiscal 1997 (up 68 percent from 1993). The company's 1997 net income of $59.1 million was equal to $1.56 per share, compared to only $0.56 per share in 1993, when the transformation from heavy construction to diversified manufacturing began. Exhibit 1 presents a summary of the company's financial performance since 1990.

> *"Growth is what we're all about—growth as a people, growth as a company."*
> **Winton "Red" Blount**

To surpass $1 billion in sales over the next five years was the company's stated goal. Blount had rebounded during the 1990s mainly by acquiring companies in unrelated industries and by divesting its original core business—heavy construction—in 1994. Management had emphasized international expansion as a means of entering new businesses and new marketplaces and sustaining the company's growth. In 1996, Blount established a manufacturing facility in Brazil and an outdoor products distributorship in Malaysia, and added international representation to its sporting equipment division.

Following several disappointing experiences with diversification going as far back as 1967, Blount began building its current diversified portfolio of businesses in the 1980s. The company positioned itself to become the world's leading manufacturer of

This case study was generously supported by the efforts of D. Joseph McInnes, Sydney Watson, Shirley Milligan, Red Blount, and John Panettiere. Mr. McInnes was particularly helpful in arranging meetings with Mr. Blount and Mr. Panettiere, who graciously and patiently responded to the questions of the case writer.

EXHIBIT 1   Blount International, Inc., and Subsidiaries, Selected Financial Data (Dollar amounts in millions, except per share data)

	12 Months ended December 31			10 Months ended December 31	12 Months ended the Last Day of February							
	1997	1996*	1995*	1996*	1996	1995	1994	1993	1992	1991	1990
Operating Results											
Sales	$716.9	$649.3	$621.4	$526.7	$644.3	$588.4	$488.0	$426.5	$382.5	$355.1	$335.5
Operating income from segments	117.9	113.1	104.9	91.2	112.8	101.9	73.6	43.4	25.4	28.3	31.3
Income from continuing operations	59.1	53.8	49.4	44.0	53.6	40.7	21.6	10.3	(4.3)	0.6	7.1
Net income	59.1	55.2	49.4	45.4	53.6	40.7	11.3	14.4	0.7	2.2	21.8
Earnings per share											
Basic											
Income from continuing operations	$1.57	$1.40	$1.30	$1.14	$1.41	$1.08	$0.58	$0.56	$(0.35)	$0.06	$0.59
Net income	1.57	1.44	1.30	1.18	1.41	1.08	0.30	0.78	0.06	0.19	1.81
Diluted											
Income from continuing operations	$1.53	$1.38	$1.27	$1.13	$1.38	$1.05	$0.56				
Net income	1.53	1.41	1.27	1.16	1.38	1.05	0.29				
End-of-Period Financial Position											
Total assets	$637.8	$533.8	$522.4	$533.8	$546.5	$520.8	$499.6	$459.4	$479.4	$496.3	$518.0
Working capital	171.1	166.2	122.2	166.2	136.2	123.3	105.1	58.2	70.0	86.9	75.3
Property, plant, and equipment—gross	376.8	301.9	293.8	301.9	295.5	279.9	276.2	270.4	273.1	244.7	225.8
Property, plant, and equipment—net	188.5	131.7	136.7	131.7	135.5	134.4	140.5	149.1	157.1	147.3	140.4
Long-term debt	138.8	84.6	95.9	84.6	95.9	98.3	106.2	82.0	126.1	124.1	100.3
Total debt	$140.3	$ 85.8	$108.7	$ 85.8	$107.6	$106.0	$112.2	$ 94.8	$151.4	$144.4	$102.4
Net debt to total capitalization†	28.8%	5.9%	24.8%	5.9%	23.6%	16.8%	20.5%	26.8%	48.9%	40.7%	9.2%
Stockholders' equity	$316.1	$290.8	$244.6	$290.8	$ 255	$207.7	$ 171	$156.6	$144.9	$155.4	$158.4
Current ratio	2.3 to 1	2.4 to 1	1.9 to 1	2.4 to 1	1.9 to 1	1.7 to 1	1.6 to 1	1.3 to 1	1.4 to 1	1.5 to 1	1.3 to 1

EXHIBIT 1 (Concluded)

	12 Months ended December 31			10 Months ended December 31	12 Months ended the Last Day of February						
	1997	1996*	1995*	1996*	1996	1995	1994	1993	1992	1991	1990
Other Data											
Property, plant, and equipment additions‡	$ 78.5	$ 21.3	$ 19.8	$ 18.7	$ 19.3	$ 14.7	$ 14.7	$ 20.7	$33.3	$ 27.1	$ 19.0
Depreciation and amortization	25.0	23.3	22.3	19.2	22.2	22.9	22.8	23.4	22.3	17.3	15.8
Interest expense, net	7.0	7.5	6.8	5.6	7.4	8.5	9.5	10.4	15.5	11.1	4.5
Stock price											
Class A high	$26.88	$19.44	$17.58	$19.44	$17.58	$16.38	$10.83	$11.30	$ 8.6	$13.75	$13.25
Class A low	18.81	12.69	12.25	14.13	12.25	9.38	4.04	4.70	3.8	6.87	9.25
Class B high	27.00	18.94	17.58	18.94	17.58	16.29	10.83	11.30	9.8	14.67	13.25
Class B low	18.75	14.75	12.58	14.75	12.58	9.67	4.25	4.80	3.8	7	9.25
Per common share dividends											
Class A	$0.261	$0.228	$0.198	$0.228	$0.198	$0.173	$0.154	$0.300	$0.30	$ 0.45	$ 0.45
Class B	0.244	0.212	0.181	0.212	0.181	0.156	0.138	0.267	0.27	0.40	0.40
Shares used in earnings per share computations (in millions)											
Basic	37.6	38.4	37.9	38.4	38.0	37.8	37.3	18.4	17.94	12.0	12
Diluted	38.5	39.1	38.9	39.2	38.9	38.8	38.2				
Employees (approximate)	5,700	4,400	4,400	4,400	4,400	4,600	4,700	4,800	4,700	4,600	5,000

*In April 1996, the Company changed its fiscal year from one ending the last day of February to one ending the last day of December.
†Total debt less cash, cash equivalents and unexpended industrial development revenue bonds.
‡Includes property, plant, and equipment of acquired companies at date of purchase of $59.8 million in the twelve months ending December 31, 1997, and $0.6 million and $5.0 million in the 12 months ended the last day of February, 1996, and 1995.
Source: Annual reports 1997, 1995, 1994, and 1993.
Note: In November 1997, the board of directors approved a two-for-one stock split which was effected on December 8, 1997. Share and per share data for 1994–97 have been restated to reflect the effect of the split. Share and per share data for earlier years have not been restated.

timber harvesting equipment by acquiring Omark Industries in 1985. Omark was a prominent manufacturer of saw chain (for chain saws), hydraulic loaders, and feller buncher and log loader products. Other Omark businesses included two well-known names in hunting equipment: Outers (gun care products) and Weaver (telescopic sights). In 1990–91 Blount acquired Gear Products, Inc., a maker of various types of hydraulic pump drives, and Dixon Industries, Inc., whose main products were zero-turning-radius lawn mowers. In 1994, Blount added CTR Manufacturing, Inc., and Ram-Line, Inc.; CTR's products included portable firewood mills, and Ram-Line's included synthetic stocks for a wide variety of rifles and shotguns. Blount broadened its participation in sporting goods by acquiring the Simmons Outdoors Group in 1995. Blount's January 1997 acquisition of Frederick Manufacturing Company and Orbex, Inc. (suppliers of blades and accessories for lawn mowers) added further strength to its outdoor products group;[1] and in November of that year the acquisition of Federal Cartridge (a leading maker of ammunition) nearly doubled the size of Blount's shooting sports business. Initially, these moves were intended to provide the company with "balanced diversification" in strong-operating market segments and thereby reduce its dependence on construction.[2]

Going into 1998, Blount International's business portfolio consisted of three major business groups:

	1997	
	Sales	**Operating Income**
Outdoor products group	$319.3 million	$67.1 million
Blount Oregon Cutting Systems Division		
Dixon Industries		
Frederick and Orbex		
Industrial and power equipment group	$239.1 million	$32.7 million
Blount Forestry and Industrial Equipment Division (Prentice and Hydro-ax)		
CTR Manufacturing, Inc.		
Gear Products, Inc.		
Sporting equipment group	$158.5 million	$18.1 million
Blount Sporting Equipment Division		
Simmons Outdoor Corporation		
Omark		

BLOUNT'S CORPORATE OBJECTIVES

Blount International's strategic, operating, and financial objectives were stated in the company's 1997 annual report as follows:

---

[1]PR Newswire Association, January 3, 1997.

[2]Remarks by John M. Panettierre, CEO of Blount International, at the June 24, 1996, annual shareholders meeting quoted in the second-quarter company report.

Strategic Objectives
- Maintain balanced diversification among businesses and markets.
- Seek leadership position in a manageable number of niche markets.
- Expand international presence to grow the businesses and protect core markets.
- Search for superior growth opportunities within existing businesses.

Operating Objectives
- Emphasize innovation and quality.
- Focus operating units on customer satisfaction.
- Develop new products to meet or exceed our customers' expectations.
- Strive for continuous improvements through total quality management.
- Empower employees through training and education.

Financial Objectives
- At least 20% return on average shareholder equity.
- 15% average annual growth in revenues and net income.
- 35% debt-to-capital ratio.
- 7–10% return on sales after taxes.
- 40% of sales from international operations.

A major objective of Blount International was to have 20 percent of annual sales coming from new products, up from the 16 percent average for 1995–96. Exhibits 2 and 3 contain the company's financial statements and performance for 1996 and 1997.

COMPANY HISTORY AND BACKGROUND

The business roots of Blount International can be traced to the pre–World War I entrepreneurial activities of the grandfather of founders Winton and Houston Blount.[3] Around the turn of the century, Winton Madison Blount built a railroad from Union Springs, Alabama, to Tallassee, Alabama, a distance of 50 miles. This railroad, known as the Birmingham & South Eastern (B&SE) railroad served as a primary link between the cotton-growing regions near Union Springs and a textile mill at Tallassee. Upon the death of Winton Madison Blount, Winton "Beau" Blount succeeded his father as president of the B&SE railroad. Beau Blount expanded the family's enterprise to include the sand and gravel businesses that became the foundation for the expansion into much larger ventures. Following the death of Beau Blount in 1944, his sons Winton M. "Red" Blount and Houston Blount returned from military service and began to shape a construction company.

With the purchase of four war-surplus D-7 Caterpillar tractors following the end of World War II, the Blount Brothers Construction Company was born. In his account, *Doing It My Way*, Red Blount wrote, "We began literally at the ground level by digging ponds in Bullock County, Alabama."[4] From that beginning, and the residual business from the railroad, the construction company grew to take on everything from roads, dams, bridges, and other infrastructure projects to ballistic missile silos and wind tunnels for the Air Force, launch complexes at Cape Canaveral for NASA, an indoor "ocean" for the U.S. Navy that was large enough to test ship designs, and a 60-story

---

[3]Winton M. Blount, *Doing It My Way* (Greenwich Publishing Group, 1996), p. 15.
[4]Ibid., p.30.

EXHIBIT 2 Blount International, Inc., Consolidated Statements of Income, 1996 and 1997 (In thousands, except share data)

	1997	1996
Sales	$716,942	$649,312
Cost of sales	482,934	426,890
Gross profit	234,008	222,422
Selling, general and administrative expenses	134,632	130,006
Income from operations	99,376	92,416
Interest expense	(9,511)	(9,868)
Interest income	2,501	2,389
Other income, net	1,295	451
Income before income taxes	93,661	85,388
Provision for income taxes	34,536	31,594
Income from continuing operations	59,125	53,794
Discontinued operations, net	—	1,426
Net income	$59,125	$55,220
Basic earnings per share		
Continuing operations	$1.57	$1.40
Discontinued operations	—	0.04
Net income	$1.57	$1.44
Diluted earnings per share		
Continuing operations	$1.53	$1.38
Discontinued operations	—	0.03
Net income	$1.53	$1.41

glass-sheathed office building in Pittsburgh for PPG Industries. Blount also constructed the Louisiana Superdome in New Orleans.

The company's successful expansion prompted Houston Blount to leave Blount Construction and become involved in the construction materials industry through a newly formed company, Vulcan Materials. As chairman and CEO of Vulcan Materials, Houston Blount created a major southern industrial corporation and supplier of construction aggregates. Red Blount stayed on to become the guiding force at Blount Brothers Construction Company. Exhibit 4 summarizes Red Blount's vision for the company and business philosophy.

In the mid-1960s Blount Brothers Construction began a move into private-sector work with the construction of a paper mill for Union Camp Corporation. In 1968 Red Blount was appointed U.S. Postmaster General in the cabinet of President Richard Nixon. Upon his appointment, Blount insisted that the company halt bidding on government projects to avoid any suggestion of a conflict of interest.

Early Diversification Moves

Before his appointment as Postmaster General, and in an era when unrelated diversification was in vogue, Red Blount initiated the company's first diversification efforts. He was enthusiastic about the diversification strategies of other construction companies and thought that Blount Brothers should spread its business risks across several industries. Blount recalled, "We began diversifying in 1967, the year before I left for Washington,

EXHIBIT 3 Condensed Consolidated Balance Sheets, Blount International, 1996–97 (In thousands of dollars)

	December 31, 1997	December 31, 1996
Assets		
Cash and cash equivalents	$ 4,848	$ 58,708
Accounts receivable	135,668	115,875
Inventory	132,852	82,026
Other current assets	27,847	24,419
Property, plant, and equipment, net	188,506	131,678
Other assets	148,090	121,133
Total assets	$637,811	$533,839
Liabilities		
Notes payable and current maturities of long-term debt	$ 1,464	$ 1,250
Other current liabilities	128,670	113,564
Long-term debt	138,837	84,592
Other liabilities	52,752	43,667
Total liabilities	321,723	243,073
Stockholders' equity	316,088	290,766
Total liabilities and stockholders' equity	$637,811	$533,839

Source: Blount International, Inc.

EXHIBIT 4 The Blount Philosophy

We want to create within the Blount organization a place where people can and will want to come and devote their lives to building a more successful organization. To do so, we seek to create a climate where individuals can develop to their maximum potential. It is our belief that if people are set free to express themselves to the fullest, their accomplishments will be far beyond their dreams, and they will not only contribute to the growth of the company, but will be more useful citizens and contribute to the larger community.

We hold a deep and abiding faith in the American enterprise system. We understand and have tolerance for a wide range of individual interpretations of this system, but we brook no adherence to any other way of life. We believe in a person's responsibility and duty as a citizen to look beyond the office, and we encourage participation in civic, cultural, religious, and political affairs in our country. We do not seek conformity; we seek participation.

We believe we have no greater responsibility to the American enterprise system than to ensure that our business operates at a reasonable profit. There is no way to provide opportunity for growth or job security other than to make profits. To accomplish this on a continuing basis, we believe growth is necessary to provide opportunities on an ever increasing scale for our people to make their mark. Therefore, we are dedicated to growth—growth as a company—growth as an organization—and growth as individuals.

This is what we stand for. This is what we are about.

Source: Winton M. Blount, *Doing It my Way,* (Greenwich Publishing Group, 1996), p. 15.

when we acquired the Benjamin F. Shaw Company of Wilmington, Delaware."[5] Shaw manufactured and installed piping systems for power and chemical plants, and had a long history of successful work for the U.S. government and for the power generation industry. The purchase price in 1967 was "only a few hundred thousand dollars," but Shaw recorded revenues of $120 million in 1978 under the chairmanship of Blount's son, Winton M. Blount III. Shaw's operations were eventually merged into Blount. Other acquisitions quickly followed, including a steel fabricating business in Indiana and a mobile home operation that "appeared to be making money."[6] However, the loans that the previous owners of the mobile home business had guaranteed for buyers, and which Blount assumed with the purchase, subsequently led to a $15 million loss as borrowers defaulted in years following the acquisition. According to Red Blount, while he was in Washington, the company bought "a hodgepodge of businesses without any clear plan as to what it was trying to accomplish. There was no rhyme or reason for them."[7] Nearly all of these mostly small operations were losing money and were sold or closed after Blount resumed the presidency of the company in January 1974.

J. P. Burroughs & Sons, a manufacturer of agricultural products acquired by Blount in 1972, proved to be one of the company's few acquired businesses that operated profitably in the 1970s. With the acquisition of Burroughs and its 2,000 shareholders, Blount Brothers went public and the company's stock was listed on the American Stock Exchange. Additional acquisitions in the agribusiness sector included that of Modern Farm Systems (grain bins, metal farm buildings, and storage tanks) in 1976, followed by those of York Foundry and Engine Works (belt conveyors and bucket elevators), Redex Industries (dryers and grain handling equipment), and Mix-Mill Manufacturing Company (feed grinding and mixing equipment). These additions generated nearly half of Blount's operating income by 1979. Further diversification in 1979 led to the acquisition of Washington Steel, adding specialty steels to the mix of construction and agribusiness markets. Purchased for $61 million, Washington Steel pushed Blount's annual revenues to approximately $500 million. "Several years later," Red Blount wrote, "agricultural markets went into a tailspin and we ended up divesting our agribusiness operations."[8] This divestiture, which occurred in the mid-1980s, was followed in 1989 by the sale of Washington Steel to German businessman Dietrich Gross for $280 million, four times its purchase price. The sale of Washington Steel was considered necessary in order to stabilize Blount's balance sheet following several years of losses in the company's domestic construction division.

Management Changes at the Top

With its increasing manufacturing base, Blount Construction sought an experienced executive to manage its diverse operations. Oscar Reak was recruited in 1979 from the presidency of Cutler-Hammer, Inc., which had earlier been acquired by Eaton Corporation. Reak served as president of Blount from 1979 until his retirement in 1987, and returned for an interim period following the sudden and unexpected resignation of president Bill Van Sant in 1991.

Van Sant joined Blount in 1987 as president and chief operating officer, having previously served in those positions at Cessna Aircraft Company. He became CEO in

---

[5]Ibid., p. 125.
[6]Ibid., p. 127.
[7]Ibid.
[8]Ibid., p. 129.

1989 when Red Blount decided to step down from active management and assume the position of chairman of the board. Van Sant opposed the sale of Washington Steel and, following his resignation from Blount, became chairman and CEO of Lukens, Inc., which then bought Washington Steel from Dietrich Gross, the German businessman who had earlier purchased the company from Blount.

In 1992, John Panettiere became CEO of Blount International (as the company had been renamed in 1991). With previous experience at automobile manufacturing companies Ford and American Motors and at heavy-equipment manufacturers Fiat-Allis and Grove Worldwide, Panettiere brought a new style to Blount. Panettiere was a more cost-conscious and bottom-line oriented senior executive than the company had had in the past. His numbers-oriented approach initially clashed with the people-oriented culture that had existed at Blount since its founding. Despite those differences, the management style that evolved under Panettiere's leadership incorporated the best of both approaches.

Blount International in the 1990s

"No single change has affected Blount more in the decade of the 1990s than our decision to get out of the construction business," wrote Red Blount in *Doing It My Way.*[9] The company had been distracted by the relative ease with which it was granted construction projects in the Middle East in the early 1980s. By 1989, President and CEO Bill Van Sant recommended that Blount get out of the construction business because of its cyclical nature and because of the gains that were being realized in the manufacturing sectors. It did not, and therefore met with difficulty over the next four years; the company's 1993 letter to shareholders stated, "The Company has incurred significant domestic construction losses in each of its last three fiscal years . . . the Company continues to be unable to obtain domestic work with satisfactory margins due to market conditions."[10] Commercial construction in the private sector remained essentially flat as manufacturing capacity utilization slowly recovered. The amount of new work did not meet senior management's expectations. As John Panettiere stated in an interview with the case writer: "We had this 'Pac-Man' called construction that was eating away at the resources of the company. "

In March 1994 Caddell Construction Company, Inc., agreed to provide the consulting and construction management services Blount needed to complete and close out the company's domestic and foreign construction projects. John Caddell, president of Caddell Construction, had been president of Blount's construction division and had left the company in 1983 to form his own noncompeting firm. As part of the 1994 agreement, Caddell acquired the right to use the name *Blount* in the construction business for a number of years. The projects included in the agreement had a remaining contract value of $94 million and were expected to be completed within two years, though Blount would remain liable for any losses in excess of current estimates.[11]

Thus began Blount's transition away from heavy construction. Blount International's acquisitions in the 1990s, as described earlier in this case, focused on manufacturing. Exhibit 5 presents the company's organization chart.

---

[9]Ibid., p. 206.

[10]1993 annual report, p. 13.

[11]1994 annual report, p. 18.

EXHIBIT 5   Blount International's Organization Chart, August 1998

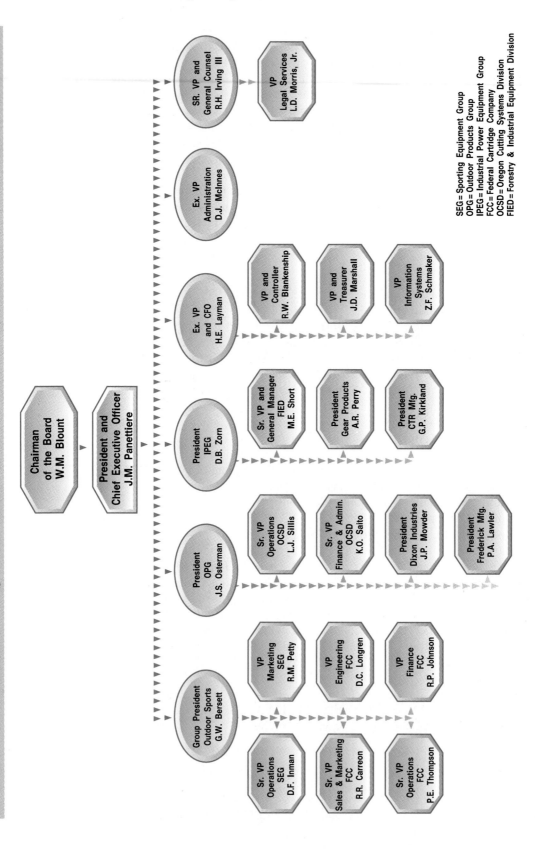

SEG = Sporting Equipment Group
OPG = Outdoor Products Group
IPEG = Industrial Power Equipment Group
FCC = Federal Cartridge Company
OCSD = Oregon Cutting Systems Division
FIED = Forestry & Industrial Equipment Division

Chairman of the Board
W.M. Blount

President and Chief Executive Officer
J.M. Panettiere

SR. VP and General Counsel
R.H. Irving III

VP Legal Services
L.D. Morris, Jr.

Ex. VP Administration
D.J. McInnes

Ex. VP and CFO
H.E. Layman

VP and Controller
R.W. Blankenship

VP and Treasurer
J.D. Marshall

VP Information Systems
Z.F. Schmaker

President IPEG
D.B. Zorn

Sr. VP and General Manager FIED
M.E. Short

President Gear Products
A.R. Perry

President CTR Mfg.
G.P. Kirkland

President OPG
J.S. Osterman

Sr. VP Operations OCSD
L.J. Sillis

Sr. VP Finance & Admin. OCSD
K.O. Saito

President Dixon Industries
J.P. Mowder

President Frederick Mfg.
P.A. Lawler

Group President Outdoor Sports
G.W. Bersett

VP Marketing SEG
R.M. Petty

VP Engineering FCC
D.C. Longren

VP Finance FCC
R.P. Johnson

Sr. VP Operations SEG
D.F. Inman

Sr. VP Sales & Marketing FCC
R.R. Carreon

Sr. VP Operations FCC
P.E. Thompson

BLOUNT INTERNATIONAL'S PRODUCT GROUPS

Outdoor Products

Oregon Cutting Systems Division (Oregon); Dixon Industries, Inc. (Dixon); and Frederick/Orbex comprised Blount International's outdoor products segment. Believed to be the world leader in the production of chain for chain saws, Oregon, based in Portland, Oregon, also produced chain-saw guide bars, saw-chain drive sprockets, and maintenance tools used primarily on portable gasoline and electric chain saws and timber harvesting machinery. Oregon's products were used primarily by professional loggers, construction workers, farmers, and homeowners. In the construction industry, Oregon's diamond-segmented chain-cutting system, known as the Industrial Cutting System (ICS), was used as a fast, flexible way of cutting concrete, including steel-reinforced concrete. Oregon's products were sold to distributors, dealers, mass merchandisers serving the retail replacement market, and original equipment manufacturers (OEMs). As a means of promoting its products, Oregon cooperated with the OEMs in improving the design and specifications of its chain and saws. However, sales of replacement saw chain accounted for approximately 75 percent of the company's saw-chain sales in 1997.

Acquired in 1991, Dixon Industries, Inc., of Coffeyville, Kansas, had produced zero-turning-radius (ZTR) riding lawn mowers since 1973. With its patented "Z" drive, a Dixon ZTR mower had the ability to turn in its own length, a feature that reduced cutting time. Dixon pioneered ZTR development and was the only manufacturer to have produced a line of products for both residential and commercial use with various features for mulching or bagging, including a recently introduced line of walk-behind models. Dixon's unique mechanical transaxle differentiated it from its competitors by allowing the operator to turn the mower in a circle no larger than the machine. It also provided a cost advantage over the more expensive hydrostatic drives used by competitors. In late 1997, Dixon introduced a new line of mowers, the Estate Line, designed for large lawns and available in 42-inch, 50-inch, and 60-inch sizes.

The acquisition of Frederick/Orbex Manufacturing gave Blount an advantage in the lawn mower replacement blade industry. Frederick produced a line of premium mower accessories under the Silver Streak brand, while Orbex manufactured a variety of high-end lawn mower blades. Through Oregon Cutting Systems, Blount was also the world's largest supplier of various other cutting equipment such as trimmer lines for grass trimmers, and lightweight hand and power saws. Toro and Deere were major competitors in the lawn and garden equipment market.

Industrial and Power Equipment Group

The industrial and power equipment group, based in Zebulon, North Carolina, produced equipment for timber harvesting and log loading, industrial loaders and tractors, and bearings and mechanical power transmission components. Blount management believed the division to be the world leader in the production of hydraulic timber harvesting equipment; its products include a variety of self-propelled and truck-mounted loaders and feller bunchers under the Prentice brand name. A line of feller bunchers and related attachments was produced under the Hydro-Ax brand name. CTR Manufacturing, Inc., of Union Grove, North Carolina, produced a line of delimbers, slashers, and firewood processors under the CTR brand name.

A major advantage for Blount was the variety of options available in the timber harvesting segment. In the Prentice/Hydro-Ax lines, Blount offered an array of equipment ranging from truck- and trailer-mounted loaders to tri-wheel and four-wheel feller bunchers and track-mounted boom feller bunchers. CTR produced firewood mills that could be operated by one person. The Gear Products, Inc. (GPI), division located in Tulsa, Oklahoma, had manufactured a wide variety of power transmission products for over 30 years. GPI designed, manufactured, and distributed bearings and power transmission components to manufacturers of other types of equipment such as man-lifts for utility work and for construction, marine, and forestry uses. GPI's products included hydraulic pump drives with up to nine drive assemblies; these drives were used by over 350 OEMs in the construction, forestry, utility, petroleum, marine, mining and agriculture industries. Blount faced competition from a number of domestic and foreign manufacturers in the heavy materials handling business. Regal-Beloit was a competitor of GPI's in the gear-cutting business. In addition to the locations previously mentioned, Blount's industrial and power equipment segment had manufacturing facilities in Owatonna, Minnesota, and Prentice and Spencer, Wisconsin. Domestic manufacturers supplied a majority of the components used in the company's products.

Sporting Equipment Group

Headquartered in Montgomery, Alabama, Blount International's sporting equipment segment produced small-arms ammunition, reloading equipment, primers, gun care products, and accessories and distributed imported sports optical products. This segment included many familiar brand names: CCI (ammunition and primers); Speer (ammunition and bullets); RCBS (handloading equipment); Outers (gun care products); Ramline (synthetic gun stocks, magazines, and accessories); Polar Cap (scope covers and other shooting sports accessories); and Weaver (telescopic sights and spotting scopes). Simmons Outdoor Corporation marketed a wide array of sports optical equipment, with 40 models of telescopic sights and 54 models of binoculars imported from foreign suppliers. These products were distributed from a warehouse in Thomasville, Georgia. Because of the high brand-name recognition of the companies in this segment, Blount management considered its sporting equipment group to be the leader in the domestic gun care and reloading markets. The 1997 acquisition of Federal Cartridge made Blount one of the largest providers of shooting sports equipment in the world. This segment also produced powerloads used in the construction industry to drive fasteners into metal and concrete. Blount's sporting equipment group faced competition from a wide variety of sporting goods manufacturers.

Exhibit 6 shows selected financial data for the company's three business segments for the period 1991–97.

John Panettiere

While John Panettiere held senior management positions at Blount (first as president and COO in 1992, then as president and CEO in 1993), the company's class A stock price increased from a low of $5 3/4 to a recent close of $28 3/16, including a three-for-two split in 1995, and a two-for-one split on December 9, 1997. Under Panettiere, Blount International pursued a strategy that combined focused, balanced diversification; leadership in niche markets; international scope; and acquisition of companies with superior growth opportunities. The company "focused on manufacturing niche-market products holding leading share positions because of superior competitive attributes, distribution skill, and exceptional customer service."[12] Blount described the

---

[12] 1996 annual report, p. 14.

EXHIBIT 6　Business Segment Data, Blount International, Inc., 1991–97 (In millions of dollars)

	12 Months Ended December 31*			10 Months Ended December 31*		12 Months Ended February 29					
	1997	1996†	1995†	1996†	1995†	1996	1995	1994	1993	1992	1991
Sales											
Outdoor products	$319.3	$292.7	$282.0	$239.3	$238.2	$291.6	$268.1	$234.5	$213.2	$196.8	$189.6
Industrial and power equipment	239.1	209.5	232.2	165.7	196.8	240.6	207.6	162.0	128.9	101.4	85.9
Sporting equipment	158.5	147.1	107.2	121.7	86.6	112.1	112.8	91.5	84.4	84.3	79.6
Total	$716.9	$649.3	$621.4	$526.7	$521.6	$644.3	$588.4	$488.0	$426.5	$382.5	$355.1
Operating Income											
Outdoor products	$ 67.1	$ 61.4	$ 53.5	$ 50.7	$ 46.8	$ 57.4	$ 49.6	$ 34.0	$ 20.6	$ 13.4	$ 16.6
Industrial and power equipment	32.7	31.9	39.6	24.0	34.2	42.2	32.9	24.5	12.8	(0.4)	1.0
Sporting equipment	18.1	19.8	11.8	16.5	9.9	13.2	19.3	15.1	10.0	12.4	10.7
Operating income from segments	117.9	113.1	104.9	91.2	90.9	112.8	101.9	73.6	43.4	25.4	28.3
Corporate office expenses	(18.5)	(20.7)	(20.5)	(16.2)	(17.9)	(22.3)	(24.9)	(23.0)	(13.9)	(17.0)	(14.7)
Income from operations	99.4	92.4	84.4	75.0	73.0	90.5	76.9	50.5	29.5	8.4	10.6
Interest expense	(9.5)	(9.9)	(10.6)	(7.9)	(8.9)	(10.8)	(11.2)	(11.0)	(9.7)	(14.4)	(7.5)
Interest income	2.5	2.4	3.8	2.3	3.4	3.4	2.3	1.5			
Other income (expenses), net	1.3	0.5	(0.4)	0.2	0.4	0.6	(2.2)	(4.6)	(1.7)	(0.1)	(1.3)
Income before income taxes	$ 93.7	$ 85.4	$ 77.2	$ 69.6	$ 67.9	$ 83.7	$ 65.9	$ 36.4	$ 18.1	$ (6.0)	$ 1.8
Identifiable Assets											
Outdoor products	$221.9	$196.2	$195.4	$196.2	$195.4	$202.1	$199.5	$202.6	$201.8	$217.3	$214.3
Industrial and power equipment	102.7	102.6	90.5	102.6	90.5	95.9	82.9	69.2	67.8	75.6	63.9
Sporting equipment	236.6	107.7	85.6	107.7	85.6	118.4	71.8	59.2	48.6	58.6	61.7
Corporate office	72.8	121.0	124.7	121.0	124.7	103.5	100.7	88.7	38.9	19.9	23.7
Discontinued operations	3.8	6.3	26.2	6.3	26.2	26.6	62.8	73.2	90.0	94.8	13.8
Total	$637.8	$533.8	$522.4	$533.8	$522.4	$546.5	$517.8	$492.9	$447.1	$466.2	$496.3

*Unaudited.
†In April 1996, the company changed its fiscal year from one ending the last day of February to one ending the last day of December.
Source: Blount International annual reports 1997, 1995, 1994, and 1993.

EXHIBIT 6 Business Segment Data, Blount International, Inc., 1991–97 (In millions of dollars)(Concluded)

	12 Months Ended December 31*			10 Months Ended December 31*		12 Months Ended February 29					
	1997	1996†	1995†	1996†	1995†	1996	1995	1994	1993	1992	1991
Depreciation and Amortization											
Outdoor products	$13.4	$12.8	$12.9	$10.6	$10.6	$12.7	$13.8	$14.5	$14.7	$14.6	$11.7
Industrial and power equipment	4.1	3.9	3.7	3.2	3.0	3.6	3.8	3.6	3.8	3.6	1.9
Sporting equipment	5.7	4.8	4.3	4.0	3.5	4.3	3.8	3.6	3.7	3.4	2.9
Corporate office	1.8	1.8	1.4	1.4	1.1	1.6	1.6	1.1	1.2	0.7	0.7
Total	$25.0	$23.3	$22.3	$19.2	$18.2	$22.2	$22.9	$22.8	$23.4	$22.3	$17.2
Capital Expenditures											
Outdoor products	$13.5	$11.4	$ 7.8	$10.2	$ 5.5	$ 6.8	$ 4.9	$ 5.3	$15.7	$ 8.2	$13.6
Industrial and power equipment	4.2	6.0	2.4	5.6	1.8	2.2	4.9	0.7	2.1	7.6	2.7
Sporting equipment	60.5	3.3	2.9	2.5	2.7	3.5	4.6	1.4	1.4	4.5	4.8
Corporate office	0.3	0.6	6.7	0.4	6.6	6.8	0.3	7.0	0.4	0.1	5.5
Total	$78.5	$21.3	$19.8	$18.7	$16.6	$19.3	$14.7	$14.4	$19.7	$20.4	$26.6

*Unaudited.
†In April 1996, the company changed its fiscal year from one ending the last day of February to one ending the last day of December.
Source: Blount International annual reports 1997, 1995, 1994, and 1993.

key elements of its corporate strategy as follows: "to maintain a balanced diversification among our businesses and markets; to seek leadership positions in a manageable number of niche markets; to expand our international presence; and to search for profitable growth opportunities in all of our businesses."[13]

During an interview with the case researcher, John Panettiere reflected on a wide range of issues. Some of his comments are presented below.

Cash Flow

I came to work the first of May [1992] and we were totally out of the banks by the 23rd day of August, and we have not had to borrow a penny from the banks since then. We currently have cash flow in excess of $100 million per year with a free cash flow of $55 million, after capital expenditures, dividends and taxes.

Acquisitions

While some of the recent acquisitions are small companies, they have internal rates of return that are exceptional: Frederick Manufacturing at over 27 percent, and CTR at 40.1 percent. We gave them delayed payments of three years (for CTR) and paid for it in two and a half. We've owned it for two and a half years, and now it's throwing off about $5 million a year [in cash flow].

Cultural Change

We have had a major change in culture and discipline in this company. When I came in, the management of cash was not an imperative. The managers in the field complained that I was micromanaging, and they were right. I cut their spending authority from $250,000 to $5,000 for capital projects. We initiated a management by objectives approach, which includes a monthly operations guide that measures literally all of the various elements in a given operation: receivables, average day's inventory, cash flow, working capital turnover, capital expenditures, depreciation, number of employees, equivalent overtime, order board, percentage of gross profit, and trend charts that follow each and every major element so that we can quickly see what happened.

Budgeting

We go out and perform quarterly financial reviews, onsite, at every major location. You cannot run 14 site locations within a company via postcards. We have an annual budget process that uses a zero-based budgeting approach. Managers must justify what they are going to have every year by first building a sales plan, then a product plan, followed by a capital plan, and finally an expenses budget. Then we hold them accountable. We build in a 25–30 percent hedge in each one of our businesses. In order to cost-justify new construction and major capital expenditures, we insist that each of our operations achieve optimum levels of utilization by working up to 15 percent of product direct labor hours in overtime before they can justify something; then we recommend that they go up to as much as 15 percent in outsourcing. We can outsource bullets, plating, chain-saw chains and bars, and heat treating, and we can buy axles, engines, and transmissions from the outside.

Process Changes

The first four years that I was here we doubled capacity without building any new facilities. We bought some new equipment and some replacement equipment—one new machine now does the work of seven older machines at Gear Products. And, we've begun to expand our

---

[13]1997 annual report, p. 2.

distribution and service centers. But, after doubling sales, inventories as a company are lower today than five years ago, and our receivables are lower than five years ago. Jim Osterman's division was kicking off about $15 million in operating income. They did $53 million last year, $50 million the year before, and $43 million the year before that. He is the lone survivor of the division presidents who were here when I came in. He has recently been promoted to group vice president; he has proven that he can do the job.

Personnel Changes

Only one out three senior managers in the company in 1992 [Joe McInnes, executive vice president, administration] is still on board. The new people have been identified through networking, executive search firms, and prior contact. I've know Don Zorn [president of the Industrial and Power Equipment group] for 20 years since we worked together at AMC-Jeep and Grove Crane. I tried to hire Hal Layman [executive vice president and CFO] several years ago, but he and his wife decided they wanted to go to Brussels, Belgium, instead of to a town in Pennsylvania with 1,500 people. They were in Belgium for five years, where he was CFO of a $1.4 billion company. I brought him in early on after I got here to draw up the purse strings and find out where the money was going. One of the first priorities was to get out of construction, but we had 15 to 17 projects going on worldwide that we couldn't just walk away from.

We made $7.5 million the first year, $14 million the next ($11 million restated for the effects of the sale of the construction division), $40 million the next, and $55 million last year. I think most of our shareholders are reasonably happy with the progress of the stock.

CORPORATE STRATEGY AT BLOUNT INTERNATIONAL

The following discussion of various strategies is based largely on sections of Blount International's 1995 annual report, which focused heavily on the company's strategy.

Niche Markets

Focusing on large but narrowly defined markets was Blount's key strategy for growth. The company built leading positions around superior manufacturing technology, distribution know-how, product development, and outstanding customer service. Blount's leadership in its defined markets generated high gross margins and returns on invested capital. The high quality of Blount's products reduced the price pressures to which less specialized products were vulnerable. Being active in several niche markets helped Blount reduce the effects of cyclical changes in various market segments.

Targeted Research and Development

The company emphasized developing new products for specific applications that could command a premium price. Blount executives believed that customer satisfaction was, simply, the result of the producing goods that fit customer needs better than the products made by rivals. The company's goal was to have 15 percent of sales coming from products that had been introduced in the past three years. Expenditures for research and development were $8.0 million in 1997, $6.0 million during the 10-month transition to a calendar-year accounting period, and $8.8 million in fiscal 1996.

"Bolt-on" Acquisitions

The company's acquisitions strategy was to find businesses that complemented or added to the existing product portfolio. Management looked for opportunities that would leverage the strengths of existing businesses and add to the profitability of the company. An example of this was the acquisition of Federal Cartridge Company, which management saw as an almost perfect fit with existing product lines and businesses in the sporting equipment group. The company endeavored to maintain a substantial cash balance and a solid financial foundation to support the growth and operations of newly acquired businesses.

International Expansion

In 1997, 31 percent of Blount International's sales came from outside the United States. Sales from global markets were seen as a counterweight to those in the United States, creating a leveling influence and reducing the effect of cyclical individual markets. International operations consisted of a forestry products manufacturing facility in Curitba, Brazil, and an outdoor products office in Malaysia. Oregon Cutting Systems Division manufactured saw chain and related products in Milwaukie, Oregon; Guelph, Ontario, Canada; and Curitiba, Parana, Brazil. The Lewiston, Idaho, operations of the sporting equipment group and the Oregon Cutting Systems Division received ISO-9000 certification to further expand global sales potential. Distribution/sales centers were located in Belgium, France, Germany, Japan, Sweden, and England.

EXECUTIVE COMPENSATION

Blount International's executive compensation program was designed to help the corporation attract, motivate, and retain the executive resources needed in order to maximize its return to shareholders. The program provided the following:

- Levels of compensation that were competitive with those in the various markets in which the corporation competed for executive resources.
- Incentive compensation that varied with the financial performance of the corporation and that effectively rewarded corporate and individual performance.

The objective of Blount's program for senior executive management positions was to provide base salaries that were between the 65th and 80th percentile of the competitive market norms. All base salary increases were calculated according to a philosophy of pay for performance and took into account an individual's long-term value to the corporation.

The Target Incentive Plan

Blount paid cash bonuses to employees upon the achievement of business-segment and individual-performance objectives established for the fiscal year. Target objectives among each of the corporation's operating units were weighted at 50 percent for pretax income, 20 percent for return on capital employed, and 30 percent for attainment of individual performance objectives.

Target bonuses for an incentive plan participant ranged from 5 to 65 percent of the participant's base pay. Participants could earn from 80 percent (minimum threshold) to 200 percent (maximum) of the target bonus.

CORPORATE CIVIC INVOLVEMENT

Blount Foundation

Created in 1970, the Blount Foundation served as the mechanism through which Blount International provided financial assistance to various organizations and activities that served the general welfare. The Blount Foundation gave support to organizations focused on health, education, civic affairs, and cultural activities. The foundation also made various grants to educational institutions. In October 1996, the Blount Foundation gave $7 million to the College of Arts and Sciences of the University of Alabama, the largest gift ever made to the college, and one of the largest in the history of the university.[14] Winton "Red" Blount was a former trustee and head of the board of trustees of the University of Alabama for many years.

Alabama Shakespeare Festival (ASF)

During the dedication ceremonies in 1985 for the opening of the Carolyn Blount Theatre, Dennis Flower, chairman of the Royal Shakespeare Theatre said, "I'm going to be very cautious, because Englishmen always are. But this is the finest theatrical complex and grounds anytime, anywhere, anyplace."[15] Ultimately costing over $22 million, the theatre, which boasted a 750-seat festival stage and a 225-seat octagon, became the home of the Alabama Shakespeare Festival (ASF). While works by playwrights other than Shakespeare were performed there, ASF had become the fifth largest Shakespeare festival in the world and the only one in the southeastern United States with a year-round professional classical repertory company. The new home of the Montgomery Museum of Fine Arts, adjacent to the ASF in the Winton M. Blount Cultural Park, was constructed in an architectural style similar to that of the theater and attracted more than 120,000 visitors a year.

(The company's Web address is *www.blount.com*.)

---

[14]*U of A Developments* 5, no. 2 (February 1997).

[15]Quoted in Blount, *Doing It My Way,* p. 196.

ROBIN HOOD

Joseph Lampel, *New York University*

It was in the spring of the second year of his insurrection against the High Sheriff of Nottingham that Robin Hood took a walk in Sherwood Forest. As he walked he pondered the progress of the campaign, the disposition of his forces, the Sheriff's recent moves, and the options that confronted him.

The revolt against the Sheriff had begun as a personal crusade. It erupted out of Robin's conflict with the Sheriff and his administration. However, alone Robin Hood could do little. He therefore sought allies, men with grievances and a deep sense of justice. Later he welcomed all who came, asking few questions and demanding only a willingness to serve. Strength, he believed, lay in numbers.

He spent the first year forging the group into a disciplined band, united in enmity against the Sheriff and willing to live outside the law. The band's organization was simple. Robin ruled supreme, making all important decisions. He delegated specific tasks to his lieutenants. Will Scarlett was in charge of intelligence and scouting. His main job was to shadow the Sheriff and his men, always alert to their next move. He also collected information on the travel plans of rich merchants and tax collectors. Little John kept discipline among the men and saw to it that their archery was at the high peak that their profession demanded. Scarlock took care of the finances, converting loot to cash, paying shares of the take, and finding suitable hiding places for the surplus. Finally, Much the Miller's son had the difficult task of provisioning the ever-increasing band of Merrymen.

The increasing size of the band was a source of satisfaction for Robin, but also a source of concern. The fame of his Merrymen was spreading, and new recruits were pouring in from every corner of England. As the band grew larger, their small bivouac became a major encampment. Between raids the men milled about, talking and playing games. Vigilance was in decline, and discipline was becoming harder to enforce. "Why," Robin reflected, "I don't know half the men I run into these days."

The growing band was also beginning to exceed the food capacity of the forest. Game was becoming scarce, and supplies had to be obtained from outlying villages. The cost of buying food was beginning to drain the band's financial reserves at the very moment when revenues were in decline. Travelers, especially those with the most to lose, were now giving the forest a wide berth. This was costly and inconvenient to them, but it was preferable to having all their goods confiscated.

Robin believed that the time had come for the Merrymen to change their policy of outright confiscation of goods to one of a fixed transit tax. His lieutenants strongly resisted this idea. They were proud of the Merrymen's famous motto: "Rob the rich and give to the poor." "The farmers and the townspeople," they argued, "are our most important allies." "How can we tax them, and still hope for their help in our fight against the Sheriff?"

Robin wondered how long the Merrymen could keep to the ways and methods of their early days. The Sheriff was growing stronger and becoming better organized. He now had the money and the men and was beginning to harass the band, probing for its weaknesses. The tide of events was beginning to turn against the Merrymen. Robin felt that the campaign must be decisively concluded before the Sheriff had a chance to deliver a mortal blow. "But how," he wondered, "could this be done?"

Robin had often entertained the possibility of killing the Sheriff, but the chances for this seemed increasingly remote. Besides, killing the Sheriff might satisfy his personal thirst for revenge, but it would not improve the situation. Robin had hoped that the perpetual state of unrest, and the Sheriff's failure to collect taxes, would lead to his removal from office. Instead, the Sheriff used his political connections to obtain reinforcement. He had powerful friends at court and was well regarded by the regent, Prince John.

Prince John was vicious and volatile. He was consumed by his unpopularity among the people, who wanted the imprisoned King Richard back. He also lived in constant fear of the barons, who had first given him the regency but were now beginning to dispute his claim to the throne. Several of these barons had set out to collect the ransom that would release King Richard the Lionheart from his jail in Austria. Robin was invited to join the conspiracy in return for future amnesty. It was a dangerous proposition. Provincial banditry was one thing, court intrigue another. Prince John had spies everywhere, and he was known for his vindictiveness. If the conspirators' plan failed, the pursuit would be relentless, and retributions swift.

The sound of the supper horn startled Robin from his thoughts. There was the smell of roasting venison in the air. Nothing was resolved or settled. Robin headed for camp promising himself that he would give these problems his utmost attention after tomorrow's raid.

SEACOAST SCIENCE CENTER: SETTING SAIL

Jill A. Kammermeyer, *University of New Hampshire*

Wendy W. Lull, *Seacoast Science Center, Rye, New Hampshire*

Howard Crunch, a retired U.S. Navy captain, peered through his telescope across the harbor and out to sea. The crisp September day was so clear that he could make out the sailboats near the Isles of Shoals nine miles offshore. He shifted his telescope back along the coast to the undeveloped side of the harbor: Odiorne Point State Park. His gaze followed the curving wooded shoreline to Odiorne Point itself to where the woods ended in a meadow. There, covered with scaffolding, was a low stone building: the new Seacoast Science Center.

Satisfied that, judging from its present state of construction, the building would be completed in time for staff arrivals in January, Crunch left for the Leadership Committee meeting at the University of New Hampshire (UNH). At this meeting the management structure—in fact, the future—of the Seacoast Science Center would be determined. On his way, Crunch remembered the heated discussions at the public meetings convened after UNH announced that it was withdrawing as manager of the Visitor Center. Along with many other people, Crunch had been surprised by the university's announcement. After running the seasonal Visitor Center for years, UNH officials had decided that it would be inappropriate for the university to manage the new year-round facility. Crunch wondered why they hadn't realized that *before* construction had begun, especially given the range of the university's marine research and education.

As Crunch maneuvered for a parking space on campus he recalled how well the involved organizations had cooperatively operated the Visitor Center in the early days. But now that the collective dream of a year-round center was being realized, none of the partners wanted the responsibility of management. Over the last nine months collaborative discussions had turned into contemptuous debates. He wondered how it was that intelligent individuals with a shared vision could disagree so vehemently. The issue was clear: the start-up organization needed to be managed. From his military perspective, it seemed a little late to be making such a strategic decision.

This case is based on field research. All events are real; individuals' names were changed as a courtesy. An earlier version of this case was presented at the October 1996 meeting of the North American Case Research Association. The authors thank Dr. Margaret Naumes. © 1998 Seacoast Science Center. All rights reserved.

EXHIBIT 1   Location of Seacoast Science Center

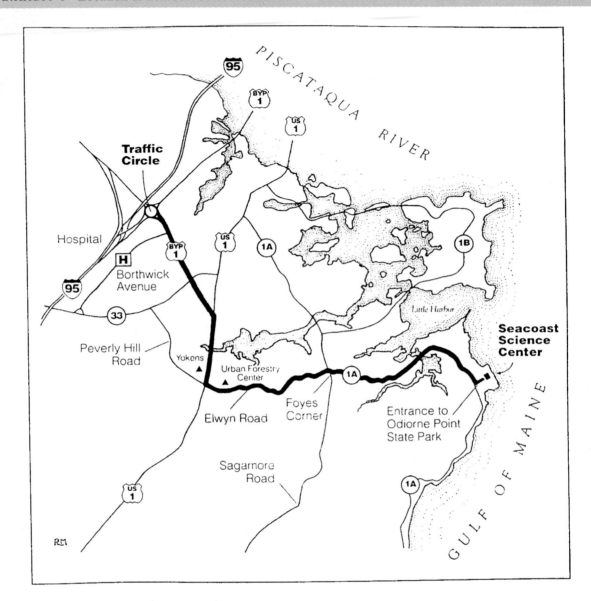

BACKGROUND

Odiorne Point State Park, considered the "birthplace of New Hampshire," was located just south of Portsmouth (see Exhibit 1). The 330-acre park was the site of New Hampshire's first permanent European settlement, established in 1623. Fishermen harvested its bounty and farmers worked its marshes and fields for over 200 years. As the nation grew away from an agrarian society toward industrialization, luxurious summer estates graced its grounds until World War II, when the land was needed for coastal defense and became Fort Dearborn. As military technology improved, Odiorne Point was no longer of strategic military value and in 1961 was designated a New Hampshire State Park. Its seven natural habitats, splendid seascapes, extensive rocky shore, and quiet upland trails could now be enjoyed by all (see Exhibit 2).

Under a cooperative venture cosponsored by the Division of Parks and Recreation (Parks) of the state of New Hampshire and the Audubon Society of New Hampshire (ASNH), interpretive nature programs began in the summer of 1973. Parks provided the land and maintained the grounds; ASNH conducted the programs. These efforts were small but successful. Public concern about the pressures on the coastal environment (development, overuse, population growth) created demand for more programs.

That demand continued to grow. In 1977 ASNH moved its operation out of Fort Dearborn's Fire House (which lacked heat and running water) into the Sugden House, one of the few remaining summer homes on park property. The Sugden House became the Visitor Center for the park, providing a facility for conducting marine field trips for schools in the spring and limited nature exhibits for park visitors in the summer. The following January, the University of New Hampshire (UNH) received designated Sea Grant funding to support a full-time director for the Visitor Center. Thus, UNH became the third organization involved with this environmental educational effort.

With the involvement of these three organizations (Parks, ASNH, UNH) the number of students reached by the center's programs grew from 800 in 1978 to 1,706 in 1985. From 1973 to 1987, the number of people who came to the Visitor Center grew from 500 to 10,000 per year. This significant growth, coupled with the need for increased support, sparked the incorporation of a community advisory group, the Friends of Odiorne Point, Inc. (Friends). This fourth organization helped with park and center cleanup days, and organized community events on site.

In 1987 UNH was awarded a contract from Parks to manage the Visitor Center for $50,000 per season. This prompted the four organizations to formalize their working relationship by creating the Leadership Committee. This was the first formal structure to manage the Visitor Center. Because each partner agreed to provide financial support, all were considered sponsors of the Visitor Center. The four sponsors agreed to follow Leadership Committee recommendations; however, there were no committee by-laws or other specified sponsor responsibilities. The committee was never recognized by the state as the official community advisory group for the Visitor Center or the park.

Demands for programs and exhibits continued to increase throughout the late 1980s. The four sponsors recognized that to preserve the natural feel of the park while keeping pace with visitor demand, they needed to develop a management plan for the park. Funded by a grant from a local foundation, a private consultant was hired to formulate the park plan. The plan recommended expanding the Visitor Center at the park and identified parameters for a year-round facility. Utilizing a $400,000 matching challenge grant awarded by the state legislature in 1987, the Leadership Committee announced a $1.2 million fund-raising campaign for construction. The Leadership Committee assumed that the university would transfer its current oversight from the Visitor Center to the new facility, to be called the Seacoast Science Center (SSC).

SSC construction began in late 1990, with completion and staffing slated for January 1992. The year-round facility would open to the public that spring. In April 1991, UNH announced that, as of the end of the summer season, it would no longer manage Visitor Center operations at Odiorne. UNH considered it neither appropriate nor practical to oversee many of the noneducational issues associated with running a year-round, off-campus facility. The university's official stand was that the increased activity of year-round programming could grow better with a different manager. The heated, lengthy discussions began.

Over the ensuing months the Leadership Committee did not consider specific management responsibilities; only financial matters were discussed. Meeting after meeting,

EXHIBIT 2   Map of Odiorne Point State Park

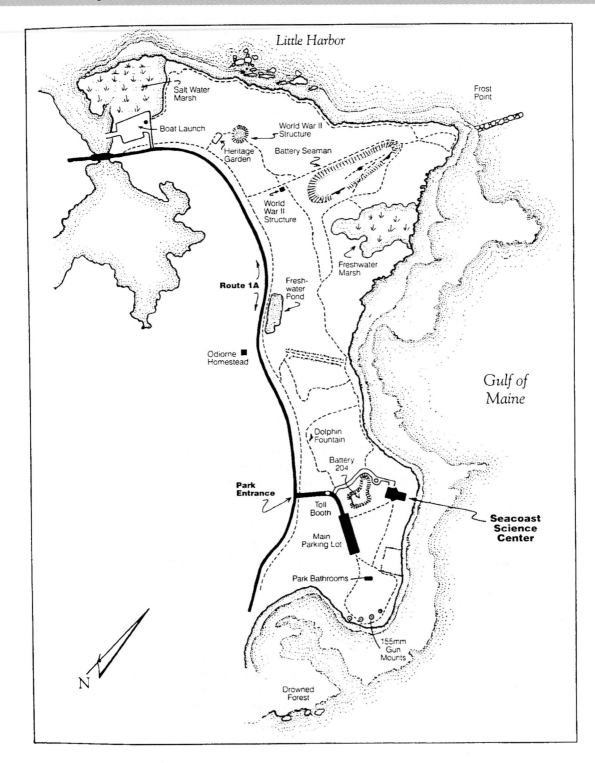

the Visitor Center director presented revised five-year pro-forma operating budgets. Revision after revision, these budgets showed a net operating deficit. Vote after vote, the Leadership Committee members rejected the budgets presented. In the sponsors' internal discussions the lack of sufficient center-generated revenue in the pro forma budgets raised serious concerns. A pivotal assumption of the pro forma budgeting process was that each sponsor would increase its annual contribution to the center over the next five years; this made all the sponsors particularly apprehensive. At this point, the only obvious risk of becoming the SSC manager was a long-term financial obligation.

PROFILES OF THE SPONSORING ORGANIZATIONS

The following are snapshots of each of the four organizations involved with the SSC at the end of its most recently completed fiscal year prior to the decision point. The four sponsors had four different missions, four different management structures, and four different fiscal years. Three sponsors had recently undergone organizational change: Parks recently became self-funded (receiving no state general operating funds); the university had a new president; and the Friends' long-standing, energetic chairperson had just moved to another state.

Division of Parks and Recreation (Parks)

Mission   As Parks Director Winston Willow so often reminded the sponsors,

> The purpose of the Division of Parks and Recreation is to act as the official steward of many of New Hampshire's most valued public parks and historic properties. Maintenance of these assets, as well as all programs, activities, events and facilities shall at all times reflect the highest level of public service consistent with the significance of these "showcases" of the state.

The division's policy had been to encourage the development of working partnerships in all of its activities. Cooperation with other state agencies, private enterprises, federal and local agencies, and nonprofit organizations was essential to the accomplishment of park goals. Promotion of volunteer programs and recognition of one Friends group per park (as a partnership with the public) were encouraged.

Part of Parks' philosophy was that facilities should be available to all citizens of the state, regardless of their ability to pay. The desired visitor experience encouraged interaction with nature and was noncommercial, and promoting parks had been considered inappropriate. Financial management involved cost control rather than revenue generation through increased visitation.

Management   The Division of Parks was administered by Willow, the director of Parks, who reported directly to a commissioner appointed by the governor. Odiorne Point State Park was managed by a seasonal park manager who reported to Pat Poore, the year-round superintendent of the seacoast region of New Hampshire Parks.

Willow saw the center as his ultimate realization of education in parks. He wanted to have the park specifically designated the "education park" of the state park system. It was also the best way he knew to build a strong citizen advocacy for parks in the seacoast region. As the property owner, Parks had the final say in whatever happened at Odiorne Point State Park.

Odiorne was Superintendent Poore's favorite park because it was close to the ideal park experience: nature and family oriented. The other parks in the seacoast region were more commercial, including an R/V park, boat launches, and fishing piers. At Odiorne, the park manager began to open the rest rooms and Visitor Center and clear trails in mid-April. In addition to three hourly seasonal toll booth attendants who collected park entry fees from visitors, an electrician and carpenter came from the state park system to work as needed. On rainy days, the toll collectors were instructed to stop collecting tolls and instead clean park buildings. During prolonged periods of poor weather, toll collectors were asked to stay home to reduce expenses.

Money Odiorne Point State Park's primary source of revenue was the entrance fees collected by an attendant at the toll booth. The fee was $2.50/person; children under 12, New Hampshire residents over 65, park volunteers, and members of the Friends were admitted free. Although the park was open every day from dawn to dusk, tolls were collected only between 8 AM and 4 PM from Memorial Day to Labor Day. The secondary revenue source was rental of the group use area of the park for large picnics, weddings, and special functions. Any adjustment in park fee schedules required state legislative approval.

All state park revenues were deposited in the state park fund and expended only for Parks' use. Parks did not receive funding from the state's general fund. Deficit spending was not permitted by any state agency. In aggregate, the state parks could not deficit budget; thus, the deficits of some individual parks were funded by the surpluses generated at other parks. Willow was credited with this self-funding approach, which he considered to be a feather in his cap. The practical implication of self-funding was to give Parks access to maintenance funds without prior legislative approval. New Hampshire's was one of the first self-funded park systems in the country. Willow had become nationally known for this concept.

Odiorne Point State Park's total operating revenue for the fiscal year beginning August 1, 1989 (ending July 31, 1990), was $41,500. Total expenses for that year were $125,000. Included in the total expenses were the $50,000 paid to Sea Grant Extension Program for conducting educational programs in the Visitor Center (from mid-April to late October) and the $3,000 for center utilities and maintenance.

Audubon Society of New Hampshire (ASNH)

Mission The Audubon Society of New Hampshire was an independent nonprofit 501(c)3 organization, separate from both the National Audubon Society and the New Hampshire state government. Since its founding in 1897, its mission had been to protect and conserve New Hampshire wildlife and wildlife habitat through education, support of environmental legislation, research, and sanctuaries.

Known as a rational voice on environmental issues, ASNH was frequently included when environmental policy was being made, implemented, or enforced in New Hampshire. President Jon Harry felt strongly that reliance on "good science" was critical for making environmental policy recommendations. ASNH maintained a strong interest in protection through land acquisition and stewardship. The quality of its wildlife research and educational programs was well known throughout the state. As an environmental protector, ASNH saw an opportunity to build its influence in the rapidly developing seacoast area of New Hampshire.

Management ASNH was headquartered on the 15-acre Silk Farm Sanctuary in Concord (90 minutes from Odiorne). The 24-member board of trustees, to which President Harry reported, set policy, approved the budget, and authorized new initiatives. President

EXHIBIT 3 Consolidated Budget, ASNH, 1990–91

Classification	Revenue	Expenses
Education	$ 192,500	$ 222,000
Nature Store	255,000	218,000
Membership/development	350,600	187,500
Remote research site	172,000	171,000
Other activities	376,781	547,065
Total	$1,346,881	$1,345,565

Source: ASNH 1991 annual report.

Harry loved new, big ideas and always looked to the future. It was typical of Harry to say, "I am a firm believer in the concept of individual initiative. When individuals embrace an idea, they will succeed."

Nine department heads reported to Harry. These included the Nature Store manager and Kris Black, the director of the education department. ASNH had 16 other employees.

The primary site of ASNH's Nature Store was the store in Concord. ASNH also operated store locations at a seasonal education center and a storefront research center, both in northern New Hampshire. The retail operation participated in town fairs and teacher institutes. The nature-related product mix was relatively upscale. The largest sales categories had been books and optics (binoculars and telescopes).

With a staff of four, the education department conducted teacher training workshops and institutes, school and youth programs, special seasonal events, adult programs, and vacation camps. ASNH programs were conducted on-site in Concord as well as throughout the state at schools and group meetings (e.g. scout troops, Rotary). Approximately 10,000 people participated in these programs yearly. Programs were also conducted at a remote seasonal education center that annually attracted 1,600 visitors vacationing in New Hampshire's popular lakes region.

ASNH had nearly 6,500 members who received program and Nature Store discounts as well as a bimonthly newsletter. Based on where members lived, they automatically belonged to one of 10 ASNH chapters. The Seacoast chapter, which had met in the Visitor Center during the summer for many years, was the second largest, with nearly 1,000 members.

ASNH relied heavily on volunteers in all aspects of its operation. In fiscal 1991, over 300 volunteers donated 11,000 hours at headquarters.

Money Audubon's major revenue and expense categories for 1991 are shown in Exhibit 3. The ASNH consolidated budget for fiscal 1991 covered the period from April 1, 1990, to March 31, 1991.

Friends of Odiorne Point, Inc. (Friends)

Mission The Friends incorporated as a nonprofit corporation in 1986 to take a leadership role in cooperation with the New Hampshire Division of Parks, ASNH, UNH Sea Grant Extension Program, and other appropriate agencies at Odiorne. Its mission was to preserve and protect the natural, historical, and cultural resources of Odiorne Point State Park; maintain the pristine quality of this unique seacoast reserve; support the Visitor Center's marine educational and interpretive programs; promote understanding and appreciation of the current and future educational use of Odiorne Point State Park; and acknowledge the gifts, work, and donations given to the Visitor Center and the park.

Management   The Friends began as a small group of volunteers in 1966. Friends was administered by a 15-member board of directors supported by a paid part-time secretary. Interest in marine education and the park led local residents to serve. The board was active; combined, the directors contributed 3,600 volunteer hours to center, park, and Friends projects in fiscal 1990.

The Friends had 650 members who paid dues at graduated levels beginning at $25. The original members were Visitor Center volunteers, many of whom were also UNH Marine Docents. Volunteering was not a prerequisite of membership. Members received free admission to the park and a quarterly newsletter. The newsletter included the *Tidepool Times,* a marine-related educational insert for teachers.

Howard Crunch had been a director of Friends since its incorporation, and represented the Friends on the Leadership Committee. In addition, Crunch was on the board of ASNH Seacoast Chapter and a UNH Marine Docent. In 1987, Crunch started a bookstore at the Visitor Center. Staffed entirely by volunteers, the bookstore carried primarily marine and nature books. Whenever the center was closed, Crunch sold books out of his van. Thus the store "went" to monthly Audubon Seacoast chapter meetings, weekly Docent training sessions, and other regional environmental events.

Crunch also organized a volunteer group called the Odiorne Guides in 1988. The guides worked at the reception desk and in the bookstore, welcomed and directed school groups, and conducted walking tours. The 35 guides contributed about 1,400 hours each season.

In 1988 Crunch was the impetus in starting an endowment fund for program support for the center. Bookstore profits were designated for this endowment. This effort was significant since the Friends had no prior fund-raising experience. The endowment had been managed by a community charitable foundation since its inception.

Money   Major revenues and expense categories for the Friends in fiscal 1990 are shown in Exhibit 4. The Friends' fiscal 1990 began October 1, 1989, and ended September 30, 1990. Any excess revenue was deposited in bank cash-equivalent accounts.

University of New Hampshire, Cooperative Extension/Sea Grant Program (UNH, CEP, Sea Grant)

Mission   The University of New Hampshire offered its first classes in Durham, New Hampshire, in 1893. By its original land grant, the university combined the professions with liberal arts and sciences and served the public need for educated citizens. This mission, confirmed by the achievement of Sea Grant and Space Grant status, had expanded as the university evolved. Its primary purpose continued to be service to the citizens of New Hampshire.

The Cooperative Extension Program (CEP) met the university's responsibility for public service and the welfare of the state through the Division of Continuing Education. The division's primary mission was to improve people's lives by addressing selected needs and issues with outreach programs. The CEP collaborated with volunteers as well as local and state organizations and agencies to utilize the knowledge and research capabilities of the university in establishing high-quality informal educational programs

EXHIBIT 4	Revenues and Expenses for the Friends of Odiorne Park, Fiscal 1990		
Classification		**Revenue**	**Expenses**
Visitor Center support			$14,500
Membership			
Dues		$22,000	5,500
Newsletter			2,300
Annual appeal		15,200	2,700
Bookstore (net)		6,900	
Fund-raising events		2,200	1,200
Endowment income		5,700	
To endowment			6,900
Administration and staff			6,000
Certificate of deposit			10,000
Interest		1,000	
Total		$53,000	$49,100

Source: 1990 Friends annual report.

for youths and adults. Their approach to this type of programming effort was primarily developmental, introducing new topics for programs to be delivered by others.

Management UNH had a traditional state university structure with seven colleges and schools headed by deans. Offering a broad array of undergraduate, professional, research and graduate programs, the university comprised over 11,000 students, 800 faculty, and 70,000 alumni.

In 1968 (two years after the U.S. Congress formally established its Sea Grant Program) UNH received its first Sea Grant funding. By 1986 the Sea Grant Education Program had become a part of the Cooperative Extension Program, headed by Dean Harold Trumpet. Sea Grant employees comprised 2 percent of the total CEP staff; and a negligible percentage of the university.

Part of the CEP's informal educational effort was the UNH Marine Docent program. Docents were volunteers who made a two-year commitment to teaching marine subjects. Trained by UNH faculty, docents worked at one of three off-campus sites, including the Visitor Center. They also taught outreach programs at schools throughout the state, reaching over 1,200 students. At this time, 40 docents were helping out at the Visitor Center.

Money Sea Grant's total budget represented 3 percent of the CEP's $5 million budget. Sea Grant's budget included the Visitor Center budget since the Visitor Center was managed by Sea Grant. As a state agency, the university could not deficit-budget. The Visitor Center's mission, management, and money are described below.

Visitor Center

Mission As a part of UNH, the seasonal Visitor Center did not have its own institutional identity; however, as a CEP field site it did have a mission: to interpret the natural and social history of the park and New Hampshire's coastal resources by providing a wide variety of programs and experiences.

EXHIBIT 5   Visitor Center Programs and Participants

Program Area	Number of Programs	Number of Participants
General public		
Weekend walks	62	4,300
Family	43	1,000
School		
Teacher workshops	5	225
Field trips	69	2,800
University interns	1	11
Program total	180	8,336

Source: Visitor Center fiscal 1990 annual program report.

Management   The Leadership Committee, comprised entirely of sponsor representatives, provided advice on policies affecting the center and the park. Just as actual park policies could only be set by the commissioner of parks, Visitor Center operating decisions were made by Sea Grant. The Leadership Committee met monthly to discuss park and program activities. Now that the Seacoast Science Center was under construction, the Leadership Committee also reviewed construction and fundraising progress.

Supervision of the Visitor Center, a summer field site of Sea Grant, represented about 5 percent of the Sea Grant program leader's plan of work. The Visitor Center had three full-time and three part-time staff members. Two of the full-time staff were year-round Sea Grant employees. Additional staff consisted of 11 UNH undergraduate interns.

The Visitor Center was open from mid-April to October. During that 110-day season, over 18,600 people visited the center. There were three educational program areas: general, school, and university. General programs included nature walks, tide pool tours, lectures, family programs, special events, and exhibit interpretation for the public. The programs and exhibit interpretation were conducted throughout the season, particularly on weekends. School programs consisted of teacher workshops and teaching school field trips at Odiorne. Each spring semester, the Visitor Center offered an internship course for UNH students. The number of programs and participants for fiscal 1990 is given in Exhibit 5.

Volunteers had been critical to Visitor Center program delivery and exhibit interpretation. Nearly 100 volunteers contributed over 13,000 hours of service in one year. Their activities included teaching, greeting visitors, working in the bookstore, and developing and maintaining the live-animal exhibits. An estimated 90 percent of the teaching, maintenance, and support tasks was done by volunteers.

The volunteers were organized in four groups: UNH Marine Docents, Odiorne Guides, Divers of Odiorne Point, and Teachers in the Park. Docents were recruited and trained by Sea Grant with additional training by the director. The guides were recruited and trained by Friends; Divers of Odiorne Park and Teachers in the Park were newly formed groups.

Money   The Visitor Center's budget for fiscal 1990 is shown in Exhibit 6. The Visitor Center fiscal year was consistent with that of the university, beginning July 1, 1989, and ending June 30, 1990. Although the Visitor Center had a $1,600 loss, the previous year's surplus had carried over and resulted in a break-even fiscal year.

EXHIBIT 6   Visitor Center Revenue and Expenses, Fiscal 1990

Classification	Revenue	Expenses
Sponsor support		
Parks	$50,000	
ASNH	2,700	
Sea Grant/NOAA	6,400	
Friends	9,800	
Program fees	6,900	$18,000
Gifts & grants	3,000	
Salary support		51,800
Administration		10,600
Total	$78,800	$80,400

Source: Visitor Center fiscal 1990 annual program report.

SEACOAST SCIENCE CENTER

The new Seacoast Science Center was being built literally around the old Visitor Center. The construction encapsulated the historic stone Sugden House, not only to reduce costs but because the old walls were no longer weatherproof. When Mr. Sugden sited his home on Odiorne Point in the 1920s, he chose the spot that took best advantage of the point. Enclosing the old building in the new retained its structure and still allowed for breathtaking ocean views.

Harry delighted in giving potential donors tours of the site. As they stood amid the construction activity, his grand gestures matched the grand views: The mouth of the Piscataqua River, three lighthouses, the rocky coast, the Isles of Shoals, and (always last in his description) Crunch's home across the harbor.

After impressing the donors with the site's natural magnificence, he would describe the center's exciting new exhibits. An internationally respected exhibit design firm had been hired from Boston, Massachusetts. The live-animal habitat exhibits they designed would make the SSC a world-class destination. In the new wing, visitors could explore the seven different habitats in the park without ever going outside. In the aquaria and terraria, visitors could watch oceanic fish swim in the 1,000-gallon Gulf of Maine tank, handle sea stars and crabs in the tide pool touch tank, and observe turtles, frogs, and newts in the pond and meadow tanks. In the galleries that wrapped around the former Sugden House, visitors would learn about the social history of Odiorne from post-glacial hunters of the Early Archaic Period to the post–World War II era.

Finally, Harry would remind the donors of the great educational potential and purpose of the center. The goals for Seacoast Science Center were to (1) extend the school program season beyond spring; (2) expand the subjects of programs conducted; and (3) enhance programs for the local community. Like Harry, Crunch enjoyed giving tours of the center-in-progress, although he refused to ask for money. "I'll get them excited, and tell them what things cost, but they'll have to take it from there" was Crunch's rather effective approach to raising money. Because he had played a key role in planning the exhibits, he was able to amaze his guests by describing the complex life-support systems that the living exhibits required. Water chemistry, temperature, and quality were maintained by biological filters and chiggers that had to run 24 hours a day, 365 days a year. Compared to the old "fire hose to the shore" system Crunch had used in the Visitor Center, this was a great leap forward.

Crunch could also discuss program plans in detail because he worked with the Visitor Center director to develop the new center's program plan. Their program planning paradigm was for the existing programs to be offered more frequently to create a year-round schedule.

Volunteers would continue to have an important role throughout all center operations, including the nature store. Crunch envisioned the Seacoast Science Center's permanent store as an expanded version of the Friends' volunteer-run bookstore. He placed great hope in the revenue potential of a year-round nature store.

Because the Leadership Committee members had assumed that UNH would continue as the manager, there had been no strategic planning. Assumptions were simple: The operating budget would increase proportionally from that of the 110-day season to a 362-day year; once the 10,000-square-foot SSC opened, visitation would triple because it would be open three times longer than the seasonal Visitor Center; and any increased staffing needs would be met by volunteers.

As the Seacoast Science Center began to take physical shape, the Visitor Center director began to "build" operating budgets. Too late to alter any construction plans, the pro forma budgets depicted a very different picture from that which ASNH president Jon Harry described to potential donors. Despite the exciting educational potential, the budgets projected operating deficits. Draft after draft, these budgets were rejected by the Leadership Committee; and draft after draft, it became apparent to Dean Harold Trumpet that the university would not be able to continue. The failed budgets brought the financial risk into focus. The risk highlighted how extensive the lack of strategic and operational planning had been. As Parks superintendent Pat Poore noted, "This is where vision collides with reality." The university withdrew as manager.

SETTING SAIL

As Crunch entered the conference room where the Leadership Committee was convened, he sensed weariness and resignation. He tried to lighten the mood with his "Today's the day!" greeting to Trumpet, Willow, and Poore. They each nodded in reply, but without Crunch's enthusiasm.

As he took his seat at the fine old wooden table, Crunch surveyed the group. Questions about each sponsor sailed through his mind. As he looked across the table at Trumpet, he wondered if the university would reconsider its decision to step aside. As an active docent for many years, Crunch had been dismayed that Trumpet had not found a way to keep the new center within the university structure. Although, he had conceded that "if Trumpet couldn't find a way to make it work, maybe it can't be done," he still hoped that the university would retake the helm.

Harry and Nature Store manager Kris Black entered with apologies and scurried to their seats. "Late again," thought Crunch. As usual, Black brought stacks of folders with him while Harry brought a single pad. Crunch was always bemused by the team of Harry and Black. As someone who always claimed that he "never could understand all those numbers," Crunch respected Black's ability to put together budgets. Harry, on the other hand, reminded Crunch of some of his more exhausting fellow officers in the navy who were "all show and no go." One big difference between Harry and his blustering naval colleagues was that Harry was a powerful motivator; had he been able to convince his board that the center's potential was worth a few years of operating deficits?

Willow eased back in his chair as he gave Harry a look of amused disdain. Crunch hoped that this meeting would not dissolve into another table-pounding shouting match between Willow and Harry. Poore attempted to make up for his boss's cool reception with a jocular reference to the university's "ample parking for guests." Over the years, Crunch worked with Willow and Poore on a number of park and Visitor Center projects. Although Crunch preferred Poore's no-nonsense ability to get things done, he knew that Willow's political clout was needed to make things happen.

Grateful for Poore's attempt to set a positive tone, Crunch reminded the committee that construction was on schedule, fund-raising was ahead of projection, and their collective dream was coming true. One big question remained: How should the Seacoast Science Center be managed? He brought the meeting to order with a hearty call: "Let's launch the good ship Seacoast Science Center."

(The organization's Internet address is *www.seacentr.org.*)

INTEGRAL CONSULTING, INC.

P. J. Guinan, *Babson College*

Valerie Mulhern, *Babson College*

David Wylie, *Babson College*

Jeff Elton and Eric Mankin, both principals at Integral, Inc., were pleased with the progress that had been made since they had introduced TeamRoom to the consulting firm almost a year before. They were, however, concerned about the new initiative, Knowledge Management (KM).[1]

Mankin questioned whether the momentum was sustainable: "Is it realistic to assume that our people will just populate our corporate knowledge base? It was one thing to enforce TeamRoom, but KM will take a lot more time if it's to be done right. And right now, we can't bill for this service."

Elton was also concerned: "I realize it's a problem, but we've got to take a chance with this one. If we're able to reward people for using the system initially, they will eventually become hooked on it just as they did with TeamRoom. I think the bigger issue is how to determine if it fits with our current product offerings. Our clients would like this type of product, but where do we get the resources to do this? What will the systems look like—on the Internet and off—and at what cost?"

As the two pondered different alternatives, Alex Costanzo, a senior associate at Integral and one of the leads on KM, reminded them both that the time to make these decisions was yesterday: "Let's face it—we've made a commitment to this thing, let's just do it!"

INTEGRAL, INC.

Integral, Inc., was a rapidly growing management consulting and research firm that specialized in the management of innovation. Headquartered in Cambridge, Massachusetts, Integral was founded in 1988 by Harvard Business School professors Kim

---

[1]Knowledge Management is an initiative that promotes an integrated approach to identifying, capturing, retrieving, sharing, and evaluating business information assets. These assets include databases, documents, policies, and procedures as well as the uncaptured, tacit expertise and experience resident in individual workers. (The Gartner Group)

The author expresses appreciation to Kathleen Curley and to the Lotus Institute for their support of this research. Copyright © by P. J. Guinan and Babson College 1997. Used with permission.

Clark and Steven Wheelwright and by economist Bruce Stangle. Growing at a rate of over 30 percent per year, by 1997 Integral had over 80 employees and branch offices in California, New York, and Cambridge, England.

Integral maintained close relationships with a network of well-respected academic affiliates at leading business schools. Its consultants helped clients apply the latest and best thinking practices to achieve breakthrough solutions in the areas of product development, manufacturing, operations, and strategic planning.

Clients came from a broad range of industries including health care, electronics, automotive, chemical, utility, construction equipment, computer, pharmaceutical, telecommunications, and consumer products. They were based in countries all around the world.

Integral consultants were multidisciplinary, with expertise in a variety of business and technical fields. Senior staff members had advanced degrees from top business schools and possessed an average of nine years of management consulting experience. Newly hired consultants started as associates and, based on skill and experience, rose to become managers and principals. Consultants frequently worked with one to two client engagements at a time, many involving similar issues.

Principals had overall responsibility for each project and for maintaining close client relationships. Case managers coordinated the daily activities of project teams while associates concentrated on the details of each engagement such as fact gathering, analysis, development of recommendations, implementation of solutions, and making client presentations. Project teams were generally comprised of Integral consultants, client representatives, and academic affiliates.

Communications and a smooth flow of information between team members and between different project teams were critical to this collaborative effort. Often geographically dispersed team members had to be able both to coordinate their activities and to leverage the collective knowledge of the firm.

The current communications system was clearly inadequate. E-mail and voice-mail systems had comprised the backbone of the communication system at Integral. The e-mail capabilities (CC Mail), however, had been extremely inflexible. Users could scroll down and see messages, but attaching documents and having conversations was difficult. One consultant commented, "It took hours just to read your mail in this format, let alone respond." Team members could not follow the "flow" of e-mail conversations since there was no easy way to create discussions. Similar problems existed with the voice-mail system; messages, for example, were not always forwarded to the right people. Team members were inadvertently excluded from some of the mailing lists. It was difficult to respond to other team members while on the road because information was not always current.

Meanwhile, access to information was uneven. Along with actually saving time on a particular project, consultants wanted to level the playing field to ensure that everyone had equal access to information that could make their work easier and better. As Kevin Hugh, one of the more senior consultants, stated: "It had gotten to the point of tribal sharing. Depending on who your case team members were, some people would get a lot of good information while others wouldn't. A new system was needed to guarantee better and more equal access to everyone."

The partners at Integral prided themselves on maintaining very low overhead, but they had been forced to allow an administrative infrastructure to grow to support the burgeoning ranks of consultants. This option, however, promised to be expensive and unwieldy. The principals at Integral therefore decided to invest in a technological infrastructure to make the consulting teams more effective and productive and to weave people together.

The senior partners of the firm had tried to quantify the possible impact of the investment in the technology. As Jeff Elton explained, "In a consulting firm, it's not unusual to track work time in order to project possible new revenue streams. We actually started to track the amount of time it took us and the amount of resources required to do certain types of work. We hire new professionals at 30 percent annually. So if we're more productive and have a higher quality of work product, we can charge more, do it faster, make more money." The partners believed that a new system would help in several of these dimensions by enabling communication between teams and promoting the sharing of new ideas. They thought that each team member, especially newly hired consultants, and Integral itself would just naturally be more productive.

TEAMROOM

In the spring of 1996, the principals at Integral decided after considerable research to invest in TeamRoom. TeamRoom was an application created by a team of researchers at the Lotus Institute that operated on a Lotus Notes platform. It was designed to provide team members with electronic space in which to manage objectives and commitments, to collaborate with colleagues, and to store work output. TeamRoom acted as a space for virtual team discussions, facilitated accountability among team members by managing and tracking work flow and performance, and served as a shared repository for all documents (see Exhibits 1 and 2). TeamRoom seemed to be the perfect solution for Integral.

The senior partners remained concerned, however, about Lotus's response to the Internet. It was evident that the Web was going to play an increasingly important role in communications and knowledge accessibility. They knew of Lotus's efforts in developing Dominoe, a program that would allow access to Web applications as well as to internal applications using TeamRoom. While they were unsure how these platforms were going to come together, they had faith in Lotus's commitment to the best possible software and knew that Lotus Notes had one thing that no other technology could offer—replication.[2]

As Eric Mankin stated, "Replication is the thing that really has linked us to Notes—it's just a wonderful thing for people to take their offices with them. It allows us to have the most current information at our fingertips at all times."

Implementation

Senior management was decisive about the pace and character of the introduction of TeamRoom to the firm and how it was to be used on projects. Using TeamRoom simply was made mandatory. Elton described the introduction as follows: "The first thing we did was to unplug CC Mail and require everyone to use Notes mail. No one had a choice about using Notes or TeamRoom. We then launched our first Notes application—expense and professional forecasting."

Along with using brute force, Mankin and Elton also became "cheerleaders" for the technology. Mankin noted, "I find that I have to encourage people to use it regularly. I find myself saying 'You need to use this because I need to see it.'" Such senior management endorsement was critical. Elton agreed: "Eric and I are users. The reason why people are going to use it is because of our endorsement. This is number one and far and away above anything else. Number two is that there's an intuitive quality to using

---

[2]Replication was the process of updating the data in its most current form so that an end user had access to the best possible information.

EXHIBIT 1

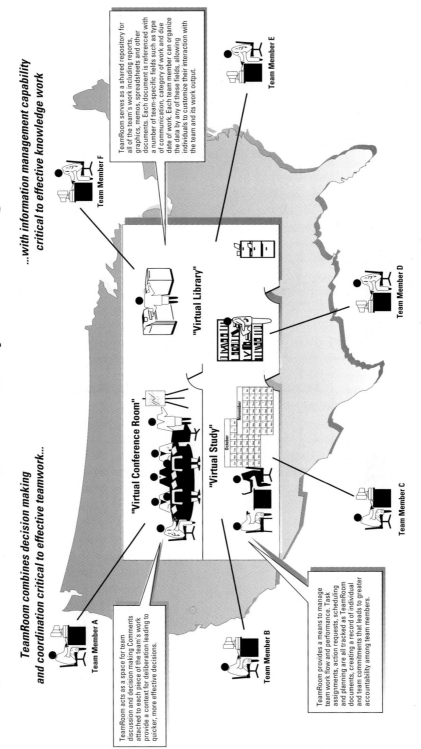

Introduction

TeamRoom provides team members with electronic space in which to manage objectives and commitments, to collaborate with colleagues and to store work output.

"Virtual" TeamRoom Gives Teams Space to Manage Their Work

TeamRoom combines decision making and coordination critical to effective teamwork...

...with information management capability critical to effective knowledge work

TeamRoom serves as a shared repository for all of the team's work including reports, graphics, memos, spreadsheets and other documents. Each document is referenced with a number of team-specific fields such as type of communication, category of work and due date of work. Each team member can organize the data by any of these fields, allowing individuals to customize their interaction with the team and its work output.

Team Member E

Team Member F

"Virtual Library"

Team Member D

"Virtual Conference Room"

"Virtual Study"

November
October

Team Member C

Team Member A

TeamRoom acts as a space for team discussion and decision making Comments attached to each piece of the team's work provide a context for deliberation leading to quicker, more effective decisions.

Team Member B

TeamRoom provides a means to manage team work flow and performance. Task assignments, action requests, scheduling and planning are all tracked as TeamRoom documents, creating a record of individual and team commitments that leads to greater accountability among team members.

EXHIBIT 2

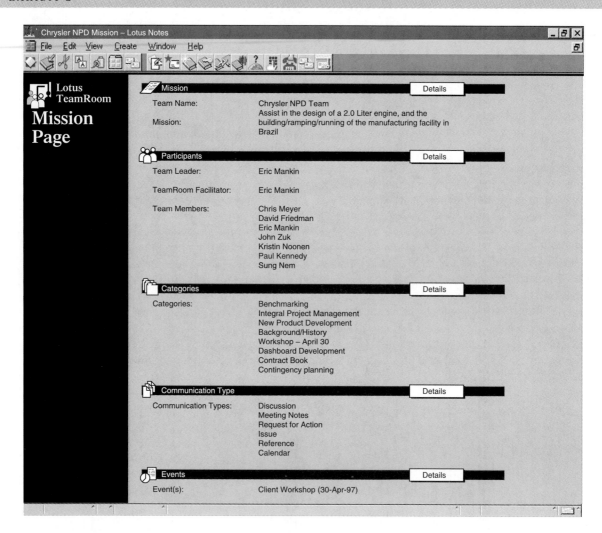

the tool. It's probably one of the first things around here that actually has a probability of working."

It was clear from discussions around Integral that senior support would carry the initiative forward, but there was some concern that "champions" could go only so far in their flag waving and that eventually classic reward systems would have to be employed. Integral rewarded consultants on three dimensions in addition to the more traditional metric of billable hours. The first was how effectively the consultant worked with clients and added value to the engagement. The second was based on the consultant's overall contribution to the firm's knowledge. The third dimension was how well the consultant functioned as part of a collective. Since TeamRoom would help every consultant be more effective on all three levels, using TeamRoom had a natural linkage with existing reward systems.

The Jacobson Group, a professional consulting firm, was hired to train employees in the tools applications of TeamRoom. Richard Weissberg, a principal at Jacobson,

commented on Integral's adoption practices: "Integral has a real shot at making Team-Room work. They have a vision, a real need for the technology. What they can't forget is that it is not always easy to train people to effectively use Groupware. That's where we come in. Integral has to take the time to train their people—otherwise, it simply won't work."

Results

Given the substantial financial and organizational commitment to adopting Team-Room, Integral management had high expectations for its successful implementation and diffusion. Although Integral had no formal ways to evaluate the return on the investment in TeamRoom, Mankin thought that he would recognize success: "I'll know when it is part of the fabric of the ways things get done. We knew CC Mail was successful because it was key to how people communicate. It'll be the same thing with TeamRoom."

Typical of any new technology venture, the adoption of TeamRoom had its growing pains. On one international project, for example, a client had manufacturing centers in Sweden and its corporate headquarters in California. Integral's work teams were made up of consultants from offices in California and England. First, there were significant communication problems between the teams. People were unclear about what should go into the TeamRoom. Consultants in the United Kingdom were not expecting to see so much information about best practices or so many details about the engagement in the TeamRoom. They were reluctant to post detailed or confidential information there, feeling more comfortable communicating about such matters in person. Second, this particular team had little training in the protocols of using the technology. How to find, categorize, and communicate in TeamRoom was not clear to novices. Finally, there was poor communication between teams. For example, there were times when consultants in the United States would meet to discuss an issue and neglect to post the discussion to the TeamRoom for their British counterparts.

Those who used the system did not always think that it was worthwhile spending extra time to put information into the system. One consultant commented, "Right now in the work that we do, you've got a TeamRoom that closes down with a deliverable that's sitting there. That final draft never gets out to the larger knowledge bank. The chance of anybody wanting that particular presentation is small . . . If there's no incentive for me to post it, I'm not going to. You can tell me it's a great thing to do and you can tell me the culture supports this, but I need an incentive."

Despite possible limitations, TeamRoom proved to be especially helpful to new hires. As Integral grew exponentially, there was very little time to bring a new person up to speed. In a culture where time was critical, Integral was extremely hopeful about this capability. Instead of spending hours, days, or weeks with junior people explaining the ropes, the novices were sent to active TeamRooms first to "muck around" in the information before joining a real team. The point was that new employees could learn in hours what otherwise may have taken days or weeks. If the information in the Team-Room was good, the new consultant could benefit from the collective experience of the entire group of individuals working on the project. In this way, the consultant could hit the ground running on an otherwise unfamiliar project. Mankin stated, "The junior people can see the blind alleys that people entered; they can see the presentations and get a feel for the work that we do. From my perspective, that is an incredible advantage. I want to emphasize that they don't have a choice. The new hires must use the TeamRoom."

Elton also pointed out, practically, "When you are growing at 30 percent per year you've got a hundred, two hundred new people. I can't talk to them individually. I don't even know who all of them are. How do you make sure that all these people get access to the same quality and state of knowledge that's out there?"

Although TeamRoom had certainly met with success at Integral, there was a resounding feeling that a good deal of valuable information was lost in the Lotus database black hole. This was particularly evident after a project ended and the related information was archived and became more difficult to find. One of the new consultants stated, "In some ways, I feel as if I'm being mentored through the process. For example, I recently joined a team that had been formed the previous year and TeamRoom provided a lot of relevant information. There were, however, some problems. One of the features in TeamRoom is that it will archive anything after a certain period of nonuse. The archiving system does not have the threading[3] capability, so I have a difficult time sifting through the information. A number of people comment that without threading, the discussion databases are of much less value. There were questions around training in the use of the tool and the general difficulties with finding the "right" information as opposed to wading through lots of unstructured data.

At about this same time, consultants all over the country were talking about the new management buzzword: Knowledge Management. The principals at Integral realized that their adoption of TeamRoom had created a springboard for introducing KM to Integral. This could become one of the most exciting initiatives in years. As Lotus Notes had been the platform for TeamRoom, so would TeamRoom become the foundation for a KM system.

KNOWLEDGE MANAGEMENT

KM was designed to capture information about the best practices from each engagement to form a body of knowledge from which each consultant could draw the best of the best rather than having to wade through the detailed threads of each part of the TeamRoom. The key was to create a system to pull the "nuggets" out of the data; to assign responsibility for defining nuggets, ensuring that they were captured in the system; and to manage their use.

Strategy

The KM initiative began with a small group of senior consultants headed by Elton in the summer of 1996. He envisioned a "knowledge database" that would become "the vessel of our knowledge." His original view of KM ultimately evolved into a company strategy.

With all of the surrounding excitement about KM in the consulting industry, Integral managers thought that KM could both add to the efficiency of the consulting practice and be adopted as an additional product offering. Integral had experience in innovation management and understood some of the major goals and limitations of knowledge transfer. Kevin Hugh made a point of explaining the relationship between KM and Integral's core competency of consulting on innovation management issues: "Innovation management is just an application of KM. We see it as a natural dovetail to innovation products that we sell to their clients. One of our directives is to match

---

[3]Threading was the concept incorporated into TeamRoom that allowed users to follow the progress, or "thread," of each discussion group.

the strategic opportunities of the company with their capabilities. Questions that need to be answered by the client are 'What are you good at?' 'What do you want to be good at in the future?' and 'What are the opportunities in the market with respect to what you are good at and what you want to be good at?' Setting such standards of performance is what, in KM terms, we call establishing the bar. The goal of Integral is to help its clients surpass that bar."

As a leader in the KM initiative, Alex Costanzo articulated Integral's pragmatic approach as follows: "We essentially have three pieces to our approach. First, defining the bar—or the best practice for Integral's key products that we service. Second, the steps that need to be taken to bring everyone up to the bar—to the level of performance where everyone is implementing best-practice approaches. And third, there's an innovation piece—or those value-added creative deliverables which are not predetermined at the beginning of an engagement but which hopefully occur as a team develops certain innovative synergies with the client."

Not surprisingly, developing the technology to enable KM was a difficult process. Consultant Kishore Dhupati described the challenge as follows: "It is not a database. It is not a chat room. It is not an idea exchange in the same vein as a faculty smoke room. It's all of those and a lot more. It is a group of databases that have to systematize knowledge sharing throughout the company." Making these lofty ambitions a reality remained a challenge, similar to implementing any new change that required both process and technology engineering. The management team knew this. After all, they were "innovation experts" and knew firsthand how difficult it was to effect change of any sort in an established organization. A number of individuals had pondered some of these problems and had identified three major issues: reward, culture, and technology.

Reward

At Integral, the consultant reward system was based on both case-project success (noted above) and individual contribution. As in most consulting firms, however, the impact on billable hours was the ultimate measure of success. Nancy Confrey, a senior information technology consultant, explained, "You don't want to do anything that could get in the way of billable time. Anything that you put into this effort is regarded as overhead. People get yanked off this project [working on KM] . . . If we can make KM somehow billable to the client, that's terrific and everyone will be doing it."

The "rub" for KM was how to motivate employees to contribute to the knowledge bank when the client could not yet be billed for these types of activities. One of the questions that had to be addressed was what incentives were needed to motivate contributions to the knowledge bank. Whatever the solution, it would have to overcome the prevailing opinion, which could be stated as follows: "If I'm rewarded based on new knowledge that I create, why should I use someone else's knowledge?"

Culture

The culture at Integral promoted sharing knowledge between case teams. Hugh noted, "Knowledge is valuable for consulting. In consulting by definition, what we sell is knowledge." And yet there was a real concern that teams might not want to endorse wholeheartedly an approach which suggested that standardization be practiced whenever possible. People might begin to question their own value to a case team. Costanzo

commented, "There may be a number of different forces here working against this approach, not the least of which is 'Not Invented Here.'"

Confrey reiterated the problem: "People definitely need to be able to feel that they personally are adding value. In a culture like ours, that's very important. You need to show that you solved the problem your own way as though no one has ever done it before." Indeed, many of the consultants were hesitant to admit that much of their work could be reduced to standardized methods. Confrey was, however, reasonably pragmatic when she said, "When both dollar value and innovativeness in the open market as well as the internal market decrease that's when you find that people are less possessive. When it's not the hottest idea anymore, people are more likely to standardize these initiatives."

On the other hand, too much reliance on standardized and dependable solutions could discourage innovation and creativity. Integral had to walk a fine line between knowing when to be creative and innovative and when to use standard approaches.

Elton highlighted another problem: "To get knowledge into the knowledge base requires you to sit back, think about what you really learned, put it in there in a cogent way, and attach the right things to it. At the same time, thinking takes time away from billable hours too" (see Exhibit 3).

A number of initiatives were under way at Integral to address these problems. The most interesting by far was the notion of developing a "virtual idea trading zone." The notion was to develop a "knowledge currency" where individuals would be rewarded for the value of the contributions made to the knowledge base. In this type of market, an individual would be rewarded for creating and sharing knowledge and discouraged from keeping information a secret from colleagues. This "currency" would concurrently foster an atmosphere of both competition and cooperation. Efforts to implement this plan were under way. No one really knew how the exchange would work or if indeed it would work at all.

Technology

A number of issues had to do with balancing the human requirements and the technical capabilities of the system. Computer-based systems should, for example, formalize knowledge gathering rather than allow the process to remain as "tribal hunting." Technology should enable everyone to hunt more effectively and to get a "kill" every time.

Although creating and managing such automated processes were difficult, a number of consulting firms were using them, including KPMG, Arthur Andersen, and Ernst and Young. They had all made substantial investments in such systems so that Integral was not alone in its efforts to computerize what was usually considered to be an extremely unstructured problem. Technology firms such as Lotus were racing to create systems to fill this important niche. Integral was not, however, interested in buying off-the-shelf software for KM. Instead, it created its own system based on TeamRoom applications and within the Lotus Notes infrastructure. Because of this, Lotus was very interested in seeing the final product to determine if other companies might be interested in using TeamRoom and Lotus Notes in a similar fashion.

Due to the technical nature of creating a homegrown product, limitations of the piloted KM system were becoming clear. Confrey visualized the problems to be in two major areas. The first was quality of information. At this time, there were different perspectives about what types of knowledge should be included and what should not.

Hugh had considered this problem and suggested that a new role of a "knowledge czar" might evolve at Integral: "We've got an inherent problem with how best to filter

EXHIBIT 3   Knowledge Bank Usage Statistics, July 1, 1997

	Uses	Reads	Writes
Last day	6	260	1
Last week	40	825	3
Last month	575	3,389	32
Last 75 days	1,400	9,378	106

Kbank Nugget Contribution, June 13, 1997

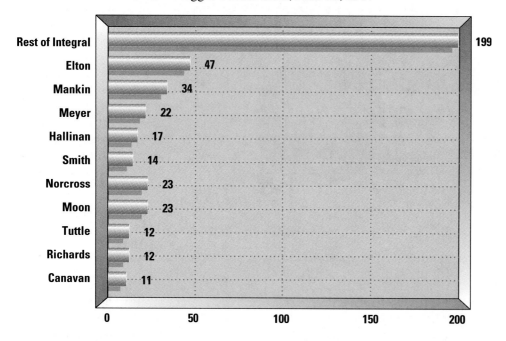

and transfer information from the TeamRooms into the knowledge bank. Each case team could make the decision what to post in the knowledge bank. From that point, the knowledge czar would acknowledge the value of the contribution with a 'little smiley face.'"

Second, there was an issue over quality control once the information got into the database: "What happens is that people just put in what they have and that doesn't require a lot of extra work. There really needs to be more filtering, some more structure around what goes in there, some more instruction about the purpose of the material and the appropriateness to a particular type of client." Interestingly enough, Confrey pointed out, the knowledge that goes into the knowledge bank must have a marketing quality. Realistically, since people have different concepts of what it takes to arouse their interests, tailoring a system to meet everyone's needs might prove to be daunting.

The most critical problem seemed to rest with the absence of an overarching framework, a front interface to the knowledge bank as it existed. Developing a common understanding of that framework and how everyone should use it would take time. Even the most sophisticated search engines couldn't capture what's in an industry-specific PowerPoint presentation that had simply been dropped into the knowledge bank.

EXHIBIT 4

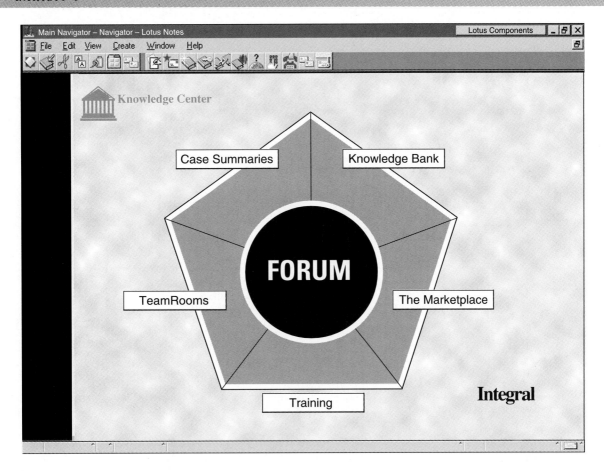

Steps were being taken to create one such framework (see Exhibit 4). It was a graphical depiction of the different segments of Integral's work. This search engine could locate better "nuggets" with subtle industry specific nuances because it offered a filter on the knowledge. Senior management had not yet approved this approach, but various factions within the organization were supportive of this structure. As Confrey stated, "Right now, they are really unable to develop tools on the Internet of the same quality as we have in the client/server world. So all of the tools that they're trying to bring to the Internet world are not truly cross-platform. There's still a long way to go on this. Where information is stored should be transparent to those doing the actual work."

An Opportunity to Redefine the Role of Consulting

As the group at Integral pondered the possible ramifications of throwing themselves into the KM revolution, it became clear that it could transform the entire consulting practice. First, internal processes could drastically improve. As Elton said, "It should take a lot less time to do basic, routine tasks and we should be able to measure the difference." In senior managers' minds, it took a specific amount of time for a junior associate to create what they called a resource analysis. If the associate could structure

the activity of data gathering and compilation in a way that the questions were standardized, then performance gains could be measured by calculating the billing rate of the associate. If the standardized material could be made available quickly to the consultant then he or she could spend more time developing the truly unique and innovative aspects of deliverables.

Integral's role with client offerings could also change because of KM and Team-Room. Specifically, there were examples of active TeamRooms where the client could see and enter material into the TeamRoom along with Integral consultants. Alpha Company was a large organization that ensured fair housing to moderate- and middle-income consumers. It had been working with Integral for some time on how to manage innovation and to improve product development. Steve Morgan, the lead manager from Alpha who had been invited into the TeamRoom by Costanzo, commented, "We're using the TeamRoom to capture all of our documents about this project. It's an interesting way to manage the project. I liked the idea of being able to get my hand on any document that I wanted at any time. I don't think the full potential has been realized yet because Notes is not well understood here. We have an excellent relationship with Integral. We have put a lot of trust in them." TeamRoom was thus another vehicle around which Integral could build trust with its clients.

There was some concern, however, that bringing clients into the knowledge transfer business might cause more significant problems. Developing a complete guide to knowledge transfer might cannibalize future efforts with clients who learned to do some of the work that Integral previously had done for them. To paraphrase one of the consultants, "It's like going to the doctor. If you do your job too well and no one gets sick, no one ever returns."

It was clear that since effectively using a KM system necessitated adopting new habits, the connection between the reward structure at Integral and how consultants were measured would need to be reexamined. To this point, however, there was no consensus. As one of the principals suggested, "We have no accurate way of tracking and enforcing accuracy in the knowledge base." Elton described an example from a recent trip to California. In the knowledge bank for one senior consultant, two managers had created a specific solution that he knew. "When I pulled it up in the knowledge base," he said, "it had just one name on it, with no attribution to the others." Elton observed that it may in fact have been just an oversight but admitted that he did not like the way it made him feel about the entire process: "We're almost setting this tip. It's kind of like a social issue now about who has access to the technology and who doesn't. It's almost like this tyranny of knowledge origination. We are creating a class society of folks who have and haven't contributed to the intellectual capital of the firm."

Emerging Challenges

With TeamRoom behind them and KM just ahead, Elton, Mankin, and Costanzo knew that they needed to move quickly but not how or where. A number of questions needed to be answered. For example, where should they spend their time—on developing in-house capabilities or software capabilities for their clients? If this was a new-product offering, how much effort should go into it? After all, they had seen reengineering come and go—what if KM is just a fad as well? Should they shrink-wrap their own system to sell to other consulting firms, or was it too sensitive to share? And what about the reward system? It was fine to say that people would be rewarded for using the knowledge base but what would really make this happen? Who could evaluate the quality of the "nuggets" adequately and fairly? These were but a few of the challenges that lay ahead for Costanzo as she attempted to implement a pilot version of the KM system. Costanzo was up to the challenge, however, and echoed the Nike motto: "Let's just do it!"

(The company's Web page address is *www.integral-inc.com.*)

W. L. GORE & ASSOCIATES, INC. IN 1998

Frank Shipper, *Salisbury State University*

Charles C. Manz, *University of Massachusetts*

On July 26, 1976, bursting with resolve, Jack Dougherty, a newly minted MBA, from the College of William and Mary, reported for his first day at W. L. Gore & Associates. Jack presented himself to Bill Gore, shook hands firmly, looked Bill in the eye, and said he was ready for anything. Jack was not ready, however, for what happened next. Bill replied, "That's fine, Jack, fine. Why don't you look around and find something you'd like to do?" Three frustrating weeks later Jack found that something: Trading in his dark blue suit for jeans, he loaded material into the mouth of a machine that laminated fabric with the company's patented Gore-Tex® membrane. Later, by 1982, Jack had become responsible for all advertising and marketing in the fabrics group and the story of his experience as a new Associate[1] was part of the folklore at W. L. Gore.

> To make money and have fun.
>
> **W. L. Gore**

In 1998 the process of acclimating Associates was more structured than it was in 1976. Regardless of the job for which they were hired, new Associates took an exploratory journey through the business before settling into an assigned position. A new sales Associate in the fabrics division might spend six weeks rotating through different areas before beginning to concentrate on sales and marketing. Among other things a newcomer learned were how Gore-Tex fabric was made, what it could and could not do, how the company handled customer complaints, and how it made its investment decisions. Anita McBride related her early experience at W. L. Gore & Associates this way:

> Before I came to Gore, I had worked for a structured organization. I came here, and for the first month it was fairly structured because I was going through training—this is what we do

---

Many sources were helpful in providing material for this case, most particularly Associates at W. L. Gore who generously shared their time and viewpoints about the company to help ensure that the case accurately reflected the company's practices and culture. They provided many resources, including internal documents and stories of their personal experiences. Copyright © 1998 by the case authors.

[1]Throughout this case the word *Associate* is used and capitalized because in W. L. Gore & Associates' literature *Associates* is always used instead of *employees*. In fact, the case writers were told that Gore "never had 'employees'—always 'Associates.'"

and this is how Gore is and all of that. I went to Flagstaff for that training. After a month I came down to Phoenix and my sponsor said, "Well, here's your office; it's a wonderful office" and "Here's your desk," and walked away. And I thought, "Now what do I do?" You know, I was waiting for a memo or something, or a job description. Finally after another month I was so frustrated, I felt, "What have I gotten myself into?" So I went to my sponsor and said, "What the heck do you want from me? I need something from you." And he said, "If you don't know what you're supposed to do, examine your commitment and opportunities."

BACKGROUND

W. L. Gore & Associates was formed by Wilbert L. "Bill" Gore and his wife in 1958. The idea for the business sprang from Bill's personal, technical, and organizational experiences at E. I. du Pont de Nemours & Co. and, particularly, his discovery of a chemical compound with unique properties. The compound, now widely known as Gore-Tex, catapulted W. L. Gore & Associates to a high ranking on *Forbes* magazine's 1998 list of the 500 largest private companies in the United States, with estimated 1997 revenues of more than $1.1 billion. The company's avant-garde culture and management practices won it seventh place on *Fortune* magazine's January 1998 list of the best companies to work for in America.

Bill Gore was born in Meridian, Idaho, in 1912. By age six, according to his own account, he was an avid hiker in the Wasatch Mountain Range in Utah. Later, at a church camp in those mountains, he met Genevieve, his future wife in 1935. In their eyes, the marriage was a partnership. He would make breakfast and Vieve, as everyone called her, would make lunch. The partnership lasted a lifetime.

Bill Gore attended the University of Utah, where he earned a bachelor of science in chemical engineering in 1933 and a master of science in physical chemistry in 1935. He began his professional career at American Smelting and Refining in 1936, moved to Remington Arms in 1941, and then to Du Pont in 1945. He held positions as research supervisor and head of operations research. While at Du Pont, he worked on a team to develop applications for polytetrafluoroethylene, referred to as PTFE in the scientific community and known as Teflon by consumers. On this team Bill Gore felt a sense of excited commitment, personal fulfillment, and self-direction.

Having followed the development of computers and transistors, he felt that PTFE had ideal insulating characteristics for use with such equipment. He tried many ways to make a PTFE-coated ribbon cable but with no success until a breakthrough came in his home basement laboratory. One night while Bill was explaining the problem to his 19-year-old son, Bob, the young Gore saw some PTFE sealant tape made by 3M and asked his father, "Why don't you try this tape?" Bill explained that everyone knew that you could not bond PTFE to itself. After Bob went to bed, however, Bill Gore remained in his basement lab and proceeded to try what conventional wisdom said could not be done. At about 4:00 AM he woke up his son, waving a small piece of cable around and saying excitedly, "It works, it works." The following night father and son returned to the basement lab to make ribbon cable coated with PTFE. Because the idea came from Bob, the patent for the cable was issued in his name.

After four months of trying to persuade some of the decision makers at Du Pont to produce his newly discovered PTFE-coated ribbon cable, Bill Gore came to realize that Du Pont wanted to remain a supplier of raw materials for industrial buyers and not a manufacturer of high-tech products for end-use markets. Bill and Vieve began discussing the possibility of starting their own insulated wire and cable business. On January 1, 1958, their wedding anniversary, they founded W. L. Gore & Associates. The basement of their home served as their first facility. After finishing dinner that night, Vieve turned to her husband of 23 years and said, "Well, let's clear up the dishes, go downstairs, and get to work."

When Bill Gore (a 45-year-old with five children to support) left Du Pont, he put aside a career of 17 years and a good, secure salary. To finance the first two years of their new business, he and Vieve mortgaged their house and took $4,000 from savings. All their friends cautioned them against taking on such a big financial risk.

The first few years were rough. Some of the young company's Associates accepted room and board in the Gore home in lieu of salary. At one point 11 Associates were living and working under one roof. One afternoon, while sifting PTFE powder, Vieve received a call from the City of Denver's water department. The caller wanted to ask some technical questions about the ribbon cable and asked for the product manager. Vieve explained that he was not in at the moment. (Bill was out running errands.) The caller asked next for the sales manager and then for the president. Vieve explained that "they" were also not in. The caller finally shouted, "What kind of company is this anyway?" With a little diplomacy the Gores were eventually able to secure an order from Denver's water department for $100,000. This order put the company over the start-up hump and onto a profitable footing. Sales began to take off.

During the next decade, W. L. Gore & Associates developed a number of new products derived from PTFE. Its best-known product became Gore-Tex fabric. In 1986, Bill Gore died while backpacking in the Wind River Mountains of Wyoming. He was then chairman of the board. Bob Gore continued to occupy the position of president and in 1998 functioned as the company's chief executive officer. Vieve Gore, the secretary-treasurer, was the only other officer.

PRODUCTS

In 1998 W. L. Gore had a fairly extensive line of high-tech products that were used in a variety of applications, including electronics, medicine, industrial filtration and seals, and fabric.

Electronic and Wire Products

Gore's electronic wire and cable products enjoyed a reputation for unequalled reliability. The physical properties of the Gore-Tex laminate made the company's electronic products ideal for use in aerospace and defense systems, electronic switching for telephone systems, computers, scientific and industrial instruments, microwave communications, and industrial robotics. For example, Gore wire and cable assemblies were used in space shuttles because they could withstand both the heat of ignition and the cold of space; Gore wire was used to help moon vehicles scoop up rock samples; Gore-manufactured computer wire could transmit signals at up to 93 percent of the speed of light; and Gore cables were used in underground oil-drilling operations and on submarines that required superior microwave signal equipment and no-fail cables that could survive high pressure. According to Sally Gore, leader in human resources and communications at the company, W. L. Gore had become "one of the largest manufacturers of ultrasound cable in the world, since a Gore electronic cable's signal transmission is very, very accurate and it's very thin and extremely flexible and has a very, very long flex life. That makes it ideal for things like ultrasound and many medical electronic applications. The company's electronic products division had a history of developing innovative products for applications requiring high reliability under severe conditions.

Medical Products

The medical division began on the ski slopes of Colorado. Bill Gore was skiing with a friend, Dr. Ben Eiseman of Denver General Hospital. According to Bill, "We were just to start a run when I absentmindedly pulled a small tubular section of Gore-Tex out of my pocket and looked at it. 'What is that stuff?' Ben asked. So I told him about its properties. 'Feels great,' he said. 'What do you use it for?' 'Got no idea,' I said. 'Well give it to me,' he said, 'and I'll try it in a vascular graft on a pig.' Two weeks later, he called me up. Ben was pretty excited. 'Bill,' he said, 'I put it in a pig and it works. What do I do now?' I told him to get together with Pete Cooper in our Flagstaff plant, and let them figure it out."

Gore-Tex-expanded PTFE proved to be an ideal material for combatting cardiovascular disease. When human arteries were seriously damaged or plugged with deposits, the diseased portions could often be replaced with Gore-Tex arteries. Because the patient's own tissues grew into the grafts open porous spaces, the body did not reject the artificial portions. Other Gore medical products included patches that could seal holes in leaking heart valves and sutures that offered surgeons silklike handling coupled with extreme strength.

The company enjoyed a very strong competitive position in the market for artificial arteries and cardiovascular products. Gore-Tex vascular grafts saved limbs from amputation and corrected pulmonary problems in newborn babies. Gore-Tex-expanded PTFE had also been used to help people with kidney disease. In 1985, W. L. Gore & Associates won Britain's Prince Philip Award for Polymers in the Service of Mankind. The award especially recognized the life-saving achievements of the Gore medical products division.

Two products recently developed by the medical division were a new patch material (intended to incorporate more tissue into a graft more quickly than previous materials) and the GORE™ RideOn® Cable System for bicycles (which needed no lubrication and had 70 percent less friction than regular bicycle cable). According to Amy LeGere of the medical division, "All the top pro riders in the world are using it. It was introduced just about a year ago and it has become an industry standard." This product had a positive cash flow very soon after its introduction. Some of Gore's Associates who were also outdoor sports enthusiasts developed the product, realizing that even though they were nominally members of the medical division they could develop a great bicycle cable. Gore Associates maintained that the profitable development, production, and marketing of such specialized niche products was possible because of the company's lack of bureaucracy and confining procedures, the high degree of Associate commitment to innovation, and a culture that encouraged and rewarded product champions.

Industrial Products

W. L. Gore's industrial products division manufactured sealants, filter bags, cartridges, clothes, and coatings. The company's industrial filtration products, such as Gore-Tex filter bags, were being used to reduce air pollution and to recover valuable solids from gases and liquids more completely and economically than alternatives. Associates were working to improve the division's filtration products so that coal-burning power plants would be completely smoke free. Another of Gore's industrial products was a unique joint sealant—a flexible cord of porous PTFE—that could be applied as a gasket to highly complex shapes, sealing them to prevent leakage of corrosive chemicals, even at extreme temperature and pressure. Steam valves packed with this Gore-Tex sealant carried a lifetime guarantee (provided the valve was used properly). The specialized and critical applications of Gore's industrial product line, along with the company's solid reputation for quality, had impressed customers and generated strong revenue growth over the years.

The division had recently introduced Gore's first consumer product—Glide®, a dental floss. Ray Wnenchak of the industrial products division observed:

> [Glide] was a product that people knew about for a while and they went the route of trying to persuade industry leaders to promote the product, but they didn't really pursue it very well. So, almost out of default, Gore decided, "Okay, they're not doing it right. Let's go in ourselves." We had a champion,[2] John Spencer, who took that and pushed it forward through the dentists' offices and it just skyrocketed. There were many more people on the team but it was basically getting that one champion who focused on that product and got it out. They told him, "It couldn't be done, it's never going to work," and I guess that's all he needed. It was done and it worked.

Amy LeGere added, "The champion worked very closely with the medical people to understand the medical market, like claims and labeling, so that when the product came out on the market it would be consistent with our medical products. And that's where, when we cross divisions, we know who to work with . . . so that the end result takes the strengths of all of our different teams." As of 1998, Glide had captured a major portion of the dental floss market and mint-flavored Glide was the largest selling dental floss item in the U.S. market based on dollar volume.

Fabrics Products

W. L. Gore's fabrics division supplied waterproof laminates to manufacturers of foul-weather gear, ski wear, running suits, footwear, gloves, and hunting and fishing garments. Gore-Tex membrane had 9 billion pores randomly dotting each square inch and was extremely lightweight. Each pore was 700 times larger than a water vapor molecule yet thousands of times smaller than a water droplet. Wind and water could not penetrate the pores, but perspiration could escape. As a result, fabrics bonded with Gore-Tex membrane were waterproof, windproof, and breathable. Gore-Tex fibers, like Gore-Tex laminates for fabrics, were impervious to sunlight, chemicals, heat, and cold as well as being strong and uniquely resistant to abrasion; they were therefore used in demanding applications, including the outer protective layer of NASA spacesuits.

Backpackers discovered that a single lightweight Gore-Tex fabric shell was a fine substitute for a poplin jacket and a rain suit, and dramatically outperformed both. Fire-fighters and U.S. Navy pilots had worn Gore-Tex fabric gear, as had some Olympic athletes. Employees in high-tech clean rooms also wore Gore-Tex garments. Mountain climbers, ski enthusiasts, bicyclists, hunters, fishermen, and other outdoor adventurers were particularly attracted to outerwear with a Gore-Tex membrane, and Gore-Tex apparel—wet suits, parkas, pants, headgear, gloves, and boots—had become standard items issued to military personnel.

Gore introduced a new family of fabrics in the 1990s to meet a broad variety of consumer needs (see Exhibit 1). The introduction of these new fabric products posed new challenges for the company in establishing itself as a maker of something other than Gore-Tex. According to Bob Winterling,

---

[2]See page 000 for a definition and description of product champions at W. L. Gore.

EXHIBIT 1   Gore's Family of Fabrics

Brand Name	Activity/Conditions	Breathability	Water Protection	Wind Protection
Gore-Tex®	Rain, snow, cold, windy	Very breathable	Waterproof	Windproof
Immersion™ technology	For fishing and paddle sports	Very breathable	Waterproof	Windproof
Ocean technology	For offshore and coastal sailing	Very breathable	Waterproof	Windproof
Windstopper®	Cool/cold, windy	Very breathable	No water resistance	Windproof
Gore Dryloft™	Cold, windy light precipitation	Extremely breathable	Water resistant	Windproof
Activent™	Cool/cold, windy, light precipitation	Extremely breathable	Water resistant	Windproof

We did such a great job with the brand Gore-Tex that we actually have hurt ourselves in many ways. By that I mean it has been very difficult for us to come up with other new brands, because many people didn't even know Gore. We are the Gore-Tex company. One thing we decided to change about Gore four or five years ago was instead of being the Gore-Tex company we wanted to become the Gore company. Underneath the Gore company we wanted an umbrella of products that resulted from us being the great Gore company. It represented a shift in how we positioned Gore-Tex. Today Gore-Tex is stronger than ever, as it's turned out, but now we've ventured into such things as WindStopper® fabric, which is very big in the golf market. It could be a sweater or a fleece piece or even a knit shirt with the WindStopper behind it or closer to your skin and what it does is it stops the wind. It's not waterproof; it's water resistant. What we've tried to do is position the Gore name and beneath that all of the great products of the company.

ORGANIZATION AND STRUCTURE

W. L. Gore & Associates was a company without titles, hierarchical organization charts, or any other conventional structural arrangement typically employed by enterprises with hundreds of millions of dollars in sales revenues and thousands of employees. Gore had also never formulated a corporate-wide mission or code of ethics statement. Senior executives at Gore neither required nor prohibited the company's business units from developing their own mission and ethics statements. Some business units whose Associates felt a need for formal mission statements and ethics codes had, in fact, proceeded to develop them, but the majority of Gore's business units operated without them. When questioned about the lack of a formal ethics code, one Associate stated, "The company belief is that (1) its four basic operating principles cover ethical practices required of people in business and (2) it will not tolerate illegal practices." Gore's management style had been referred to as *unmanagement*. The company's organization had been guided by Bill Gore's experiences on teams at Du Pont and had evolved on an as-needed basis over the years.

For example, one Monday morning in the summer of 1965, Bill Gore was taking his usual walk through the company's Newark, Delaware, plant when he realized that he

EXHIBIT 2   International Locations of W. L. Gore & Associates

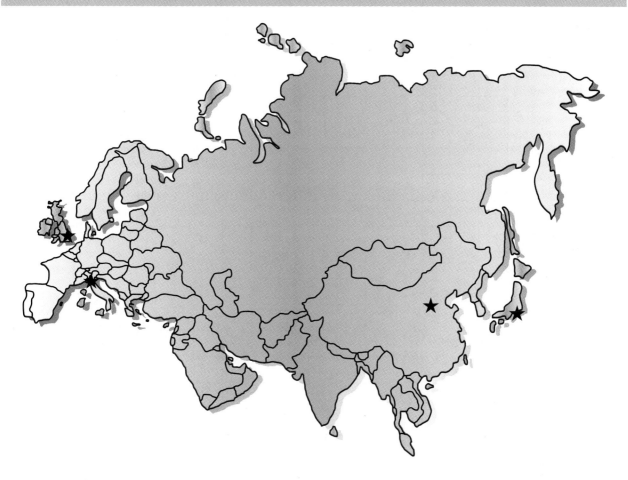

did not know everyone in the plant. In his mind the facility, which had about 200 Associates, had become too big. As a result, he established the practice of limiting plant size to approximately 200 Associates. Thus was born the expansion policy of "Get big by staying small." Gore's objective in insisting on small plants was to accentuate the importance of a close-knit atmosphere to maintaining good communication and personal working relationships.

In 1997, W. L. Gore & Associates had over 44 plants and approximately 6,500 Associates worldwide. In some cases, a number of plants were clustered at a single location (as in Flagstaff, Arizona, which had 10 plants). Overseas, Gore's manufacturing facilities were located in Scotland, Germany, France, India, and China. The company also had two joint ventures in Japan (see Exhibit 2). In addition, the company had sales facilities in 15 countries, including Eastern Europe and Russia.

The Lattice Organization

W. L. Gore & Associates has been described as not only unmanaged but also unstructured. Bill Gore referred to the company's structure as a "lattice organization" (see Exhibit 3). The features of Gore's lattice structure included the following:

EXHIBIT 3   The Lattice Organization

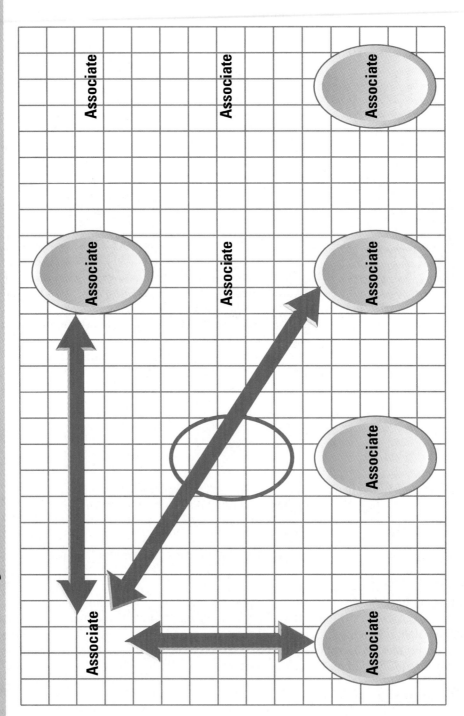

1. Direct lines of communication—person to person—with no intermediary.
2. No fixed or assigned authority.
3. Sponsors, not bosses.
4. Natural leadership as evidenced by the willingness of others to follow.
5. Objectives set by those who must "make them happen."
6. Tasks and functions organized through commitments.

The lattice structure, as described by the people at Gore, was complex and depended on interpersonal interactions, self-commitment to group-known responsibilities, natural leadership, and group-imposed discipline. According to Bill Gore, "Every successful organization has an underground lattice. It's where the news spreads like lightning, where people can go around the organization to get things done." Another feature of the lattice structure was heavy reliance on cross-functional teams. When a puzzled interviewer told Bill that he was having trouble understanding how planning and accountability worked at W. L. Gore & Associates, Bill replied with a grin, "So am I. You ask me how it works? Every which way."

Gore's lattice structure had been criticized for its potential lack of quick response times and decisive action. Bill Gore countered these criticisms by stating, "I'm told from time to time that a lattice organization can't meet a crisis well because it takes too long to reach a consensus when there are no bosses. But this isn't true. Actually, a lattice by its very nature works particularly well in a crisis. A lot of useless effort is avoided because there is no rigid management hierarchy to conquer before you can attack a problem."

The lattice had been put to the test on a number of occasions. For example, in 1975, Dr. Charles Campbell of the University of Pittsburgh reported that a patient's Gore-Tex arterial graft had developed an aneurysm. If the bubblelike protrusion continued to expand, it would explode. Obviously, this life-threatening situation had to be resolved quickly and permanently. Within a few days of his first report, Dr. Campbell flew to Newark to present his findings to Bill and Bob Gore and a few other Associates. During the two-hour meeting, Dan Hubis, a former policeman who had joined Gore to develop new production methods, came up with an idea to correct the problem. He returned to his work area to experiment with some different production techniques. After only three hours and 12 tries, he had developed a permanent solution that saved both the patient and the company's reputation. Hubis's redesigned graft went on to win widespread acceptance in the medical community.

Eric Reynolds, founder of Marmot Mountain Works Ltd. of Grand Junction, Colorado, a major Gore customer, raised another issue: "I don't think Bill realizes how the lattice system affects customers. I mean, after you've established a relationship with someone about product quality, you can call up one day and suddenly find that someone new to you is handling your problem. It's frustrating to find a lack of continuity." Reynolds went on to say, "But I have to admit that I've personally seen at Gore remarkable examples of people coming out of nowhere and excelling."

When Bill Gore was asked if the lattice structure could be used by other companies, he answered, "No. For example, established companies would find it very difficult to use the lattice. Too many hierarchies would be destroyed. When you remove titles and positions and allow people to follow who they want, it may very well be someone other than the person who has been in charge. The lattice works for us, but it's always evolving. You have to expect problems." He maintained that the lattice system worked best when used by progressive, people-oriented entrepreneurs in start-up companies.

Not all Gore Associates functioned well in Gore's unstructured work environment, especially initially. Those who had worked at other companies and become accustomed to a more structured work environment usually encountered adjustment problems. As Bill Gore said, "All our lives most of us have been told what to do, and some people don't know how to respond when asked to do something—and have the very real option of saying no—on their job. It's the new Associate's responsibility to find out what he or she can do for the good of the operation." A few Associates concluded that Gore's flexible, unstructured workplace was not for them and soon left the company. For them, Bill Gore noted, "It's an unhappy situation, both for the Associate and the sponsor. If there is no contribution, there is no paycheck." Anita McBride, an Associate in Phoenix, observed, "It's not for everybody . . . We do have turnover. What you're seeing looks like utopia, but it also looks extreme. If you finally figure the system, it can be real exciting. If you can't handle it, you've got to leave—probably by your own choice, because you're going to be so frustrated."

However, the vast majority of new Associates, after some initial floundering, adapted quickly. Overall W. L. Gore's lattice organization proved to be good for the company's bottom line. The year before he died, Bill Gore estimated that the company's profit per Associate was double Du Pont's profit per employee.

Corporate Culture

Outsiders were often struck by the degree of informality and humor in the Gore organization. Meetings tended to be only as long as necessary. As Trish Hearn, an Associate in Newark, Delaware, said, "No one feels a need to pontificate." Words such as *responsibilities* and *commitments* were commonly heard, whereas words such as *employees, subordinates,* and *managers* were taboo in the Gore culture. The organization took what it did very seriously without its members taking themselves too seriously.

For a company of its size, W. L. Gore had a very flat organizational pyramid. Bill Gore was chief executive officer for over 20 years. No second-in-command or successor had been designated. As of 1995 the executive hierarchy consisted of a president (Bob Gore) and a secretary-treasurer (Vieve Gore) because the two titles were required by the laws of incorporation. All the other members of the Gore organization were, and continued to be, referred to as Associates. Associates had from time to time encountered skepticism and ridicule from outsiders who saw the company's practice of not using job titles as seriously flawed. Sometime in the 1980s, Sarah Clifton, an Associate at one of Gore's Flagstaff plants, was being pressed by outside acquaintances as to what her title at Gore was. She decided to give herself the title of Supreme Commander and had it printed on her business cards (see Exhibit 4). When Bill Gore learned what she did, he expressed approval and frequently recounted the story to others.

Leaders, Not Managers   W. L. Gore & Associates preferred to think of the various people who played key roles in the organization as being leaders, not managers. In an internal memo Bill Gore described the kinds of leaders and their roles:

> 1. *The Associate who is recognized by a team as having a special knowledge, or experience* (for example, this could be a chemist, computer expert, machine operator, salesman, engineer, lawyer). This kind of leader gives the team *guidance in a special area.*

EXHIBIT 4   Sarah Clifton's "Supreme Commander" Business Card

2. *The Associate the team looks to for coordination of individual activities in order to achieve the agreed on objectives of the team.* The role of this leader is to persuade team members to *make the commitments* necessary for success (commitment seeker).

3. *The Associate who proposes necessary objectives and activities and seeks agreement and team consensus on objectives.* This leader is perceived by the team membership as having a good grasp of how the objectives of the team fit in with the broader objectives of the enterprise. This kind of leader is often also a "commitment seeking" leader.

4. *The leader who evaluates the relative contribution of team members (in consultation with other sponsors) and reports these contribution evaluations to a compensation committee.* This leader may also participate in the compensation committee on relative contribution and pay and *reports changes in compensation* to individual Associates. This leader is then also a compensation sponsor.

5. The leader who coordinates the research, manufacturing, and marketing of one product type within a business, interacting with team leaders and individual Associates who have commitments to the product type. These leaders are usually called *product specialists.* They are respected for their knowledge and dedication to their products.

6. *Plant leaders* who help coordinate activities of people within a plant.

7. *Business leaders* who help coordinate activities of people in a business.

8. *Functional leaders* who help coordinate activities of people in a "functional" area.

9. *Corporate leaders* who help coordinate activities of people in different businesses and functions and who try to promote communication and cooperation among all Associates.

10. *Intrapreneuring Associates who organize new teams* for new businesses, new products, new processes, new devices, new marketing efforts, or new or better methods of all kinds. These leaders invite other Associates to "sign up" for their project.

It is clear that leadership is widespread in our lattice organization and that it is continually changing and evolving. The situation that leaders are frequently also sponsors should not confuse that these are different activities and responsibilities.

Leaders are not authoritarians, managers of people, or supervisors who tell us what to do or forbid us doing things; nor are they "parents" to whom we transfer our own self-responsibility. However, they do often advise us of the consequences of actions we have done or propose to do. Our actions result in contributions, or lack of contribution, to the success of our enterprise. Our pay depends on the magnitude of our contributions. This is the basic discipline of our lattice organization.

Egalitarianism and Innovativeness   Several other aspects of the Gore culture were aimed at promoting an egalitarian atmosphere, most notably parking lots with no reserved parking spaces for officials and dining areas—only one in each plant—set up as focal points for Associate interaction. As Dave McCarter of Phoenix explained, "The design is no accident. The lunchroom in Flagstaff has a fireplace in the middle. We want people to like to be here." The location of a plant was also no accident. Sites had been selected on the basis of transportation access, nearby universities, beautiful surroundings, and climate appeal. Land cost had never been a primary consideration. McCarter justified the company's emphasis on selecting attractive plant sites, stating, "Expanding is not costly in the long run. Losses are what you make happen by stymieing people and putting them into a box."

Sally Gore explained the efforts that Bob Gore and other senior leaders made to promote and nurture certain cultural traits:

> We have managed surprisingly to maintain our sense of freedom and our entrepreneurial spirit. I think what we've found is that we had to develop new ways to communicate with Associates because you can't communicate with 6,000 people the way that you can communicate with 500 people. It just can't be done. So we have developed a newsletter that we didn't have before. One of the most important communication media that we developed, and this was Bob Gore's idea, is a digital voice exchange, which we call our Gorecom. Basically everyone has a mailbox and a password. Lots of companies have gone to e-mail, and we use e-mail, but Bob feels very strongly that we're very much an oral culture and there's a big difference between cultures that are predominantly oral and predominantly written. Oral cultures encourage direct communication, which is, of course, something that we encourage.

In those rare cases when an Associate was caught "trying to be unfair" or otherwise take advantage of the freedom given to Gore Associates—such as stealing or being chronically absent—the consequences were swift and severe. "When that happens, all hell breaks loose," said Bill Gore. "We can get damned authoritarian when we have to."

Over the years, W. L. Gore & Associates faced a number of unionization drives. The company neither tried to dissuade Associates from attending an organizational meeting nor retaliated against Associates who passed out union flyers. However, Bill Gore believed that no need existed for third-party representation under the lattice structure. He asked, "Why would Associates join a union when they own the company? It seems rather absurd." As of 1995, none of the Gore plants was organized.

Commitment was spoken of as a two-way street at W. L. Gore & Associates—while Associates were expected to commit to making a contribution to the company's success, the company committed to providing a challenging, opportunity-rich work environment and reasonable job security. The company tried to avoid laying off Associates. If a workforce reduction became necessary, the company used a system of temporary transfers within a plant or cluster of plants and voluntary layoffs.

Exhibit 5 contains excerpts of interviews with two Gore Associates that further indicate the nature of the culture and work environment at W. L. Gore.

The Sponsor Program

Bill Gore believed great products alone did not make a great company. He felt hierarchy stifled creativity and that therefore it was important to avoid smothering the company in thick layers of formal management. Yet he also knew that, as the company grew, he had to find ways to assist new people and to follow their progress. Thus, W. L. Gore & Associates came up with its "sponsor" program.

Job applicants at Gore were initially screened by personnel specialists, who contacted as many as 10 references for each applicant. Each candidate who passed this screening was then interviewed by Associates working in the area of the company where the candidate was being considered for a position. According to those who had gone through them, the interviews were rigorous. Before a candidate was hired, an Associate had to agree to be his or her sponsor. The sponsor's role was to take a personal interest in the new Associate's contributions, problems, and goals, acting as both a coach and an advocate. The sponsor tracked the new Associate's progress, offered help and encouragement, pointed out weaknesses and suggested ways to correct them, and concentrated on how the Associate could better exploit his or her strengths. Sponsoring was not a short-term commitment. All Associates had sponsors, and many had more than one. When individuals were hired initially, they were likely to have a sponsor in their immediate work area. As Associates' commitments changed or grew, it was normal for them to acquire additional sponsors. For instance, if they moved to a new job in another area of the company, they would typically gain a sponsor there.

W. L. Gore often held unconventional views of what made a good Associate. Bill Gore, for example, proudly told the story of "a very young man" of 84, with 30 years of experience in the industry, who walked in, applied, and spent five good years with the company. Other Associates had no problems accepting this man, but the personnel computer did—it insisted that his age was 48. Gore management took pride in having successful Associates with a variety of diverse backgrounds.

An internal memo by Bill Gore described three kinds of sponsorship and how they might work:

1. *Starting sponsor*—a sponsor who helps a new Associate get started on his or her first job at Gore or a present Associate get started on a new job.
2. *Advocate sponsor*—a sponsor who sees to it that the Associate being sponsored gets credit and recognition for contributions and accomplishments.
3. *Compensation sponsor*—a sponsor who sees to it that the Associate being sponsored is fairly paid for contributions to the success of the enterprise.

An Associate could perform any one or all three kinds of sponsorship. Quite frequently, a sponsoring Associate was a good friend, and it was not uncommon for two Associates to sponsor each other as advocates.

Training

Ron Hill, an Associate in Newark, noted that W. L. Gore would "work with Associates who want to advance themselves." Associates were offered a variety of in-house training opportunities, not only in technical and engineering areas but also in leadership development. In addition, the company had established cooperative education programs with universities and other outside providers, picking up most of the costs for the Gore

EXHIBIT 5   Excerpts of Interviews with Two Gore Associates

Excerpt of interview with an Associate that was formerly with IBM and had been with Gore for two years:

Q: What is the difference between being with IBM and Gore?

A: I spent 24 years working for IBM and there's a big difference. I can go 10 times faster here at Gore because of the simplicity of the lattice organization. Let me give you an example. If I wanted to purchase chemicals at IBM (I am an industrial chemist), the first thing I would need to do is get accounting approval, then I would need at least two levels of managers' approval, then a secretary to log in my purchase. The purchase order would go to Purchasing, where it would be assigned a buyer. Some time could be saved if you were willing to "walk" the paperwork through the approval process, but even after computerizing the process, it typically would take one month from the time you initiated the purchase requisition till the time the material actually arrived. Here they have one simple form. Usually, I get the chemicals the next day and a copy of the purchase order will arrive a day or two after that. It happens so fast. I wasn't used to that.

Q: Do you find that a lot more pleasant?

A: Yes, you're unshackled here. There's a lot less bureaucracy that allows you to be a lot more productive. Take lab safety, for example. In my lab at IBM, we were cited for not having my eyewash taped properly. The first time, we were cited for not having a big enough area taped off, so we taped off a bigger area. The next week the same eyewash was cited again, because the area we taped off was 3 inches too short in one direction. We retaped it, and the following week it got cited again for having the wrong color tape. Keep in mind that the violation was viewed as serious as a pail of gasoline next to a lit Bunsen burner. Another time I had the dubious honor of being selected the functional safety representative in charge of getting the function's labs ready for a corporate safety audit. The *function* was a third level in the pyramidal organization: (1) department, (2) project, and (3) function. At the same time I was working on developing a new surface mount package. As it turned out, I had no time to work on development, and the function spent a lot of time and money getting ready for the corporate auditors, who in the end never showed. I'm not belittling the importance of safety, but you really don't need all that bureaucracy to be safe.

Excerpt of interview with an Associate who was a recent engineering graduate:

Q: How did you find the transition coming here?

A: Although I never would have expected it to be, I found my transition coming to Gore to be rather challenging. What attracted me to the company was the opportunity to be my own boss and determine my own commitments. I am very goal oriented, and enjoy taking a project and running with it—all things that you are able to do, and encouraged to do, within the Gore culture. Thus, I thought, a perfect fit!

However, as a new Associate, I really struggled with where to focus my efforts—I was ready to make my own commitments, but to what? I felt a strong need to be sure that I was working on something that had value, something that truly needed to be done. While I didn't expect to have the "hottest" project, I did want to make sure that I was helping the company to make money in some way.

At the time, though, I was working for a plant that was pretty typical of what Gore was like when it was originally founded—after my first project (which was designed to be a "quick win"—a project with meaning, but one that had a definite end point), I was told, "Go find something to work on." While I could have found something, I wanted to find something with at least a small degree of priority! Thus, the whole process of finding a project was very frustrating for me—I didn't feel that I had the perspective to make such a choice, and ended up in many conversations with my sponsor about what would be valuable . . .

In the end, of course, I did find that project—and it did actually turn out to be a good investment for Gore. The process to get there, though, was definitely trying for someone as inexperienced as I was. So much ground would have been gained by suggesting a few projects to me and then letting me choose from that smaller pool. What's really neat about the whole thing, though, is that my experience has truly made a difference. Due in part to my frustrations, my plant now provides college grads with more guidance on their first several projects. (This guidance obviously becomes less and less critical as each Associate grows within Gore.) Associates still are choosing their own commitments, but they're doing so with additional perspective, and the knowledge that they are making a contribution to Gore—which is an important thing within our culture. As I said, though, it was definitely rewarding to see that the company was so responsive, and to feel that I had helped to shape someone else's transition.

Associates. However, it was always left up to the Associate to exercise his or her own initiative in choosing the programs and training to enhance his or her personal development and advancement within the company.

Compensation Practices

Compensation at W. L. Gore & Associates took three forms: salary, profit sharing, and an Associates' stock ownership program (ASOP).[3] Entry-level salaries were average relative to comparable jobs at other companies. Sally Gore said, "We do not feel we need to be the highest paid. We never try to steal people away from other companies with salary. We want them to come here because of the opportunities for growth and the unique work environment." Associates' salaries were reviewed at least once a year and more commonly twice a year. The reviews were conducted by a compensation team at each facility, with sponsors for the Associates acting as their advocates during the review process. Prior to meeting with the compensation committee, the sponsor checked with customers or other Associates to find out what contribution the Associate had made. The compensation team relied heavily on this input. In addition, the compensation team considered the Associate's leadership ability and willingness to help others develop to their fullest.

Profit sharing followed a formula based on economic value added (EVA). Sally Gore explained the company's adoption of a systematic formula for determining profit-sharing awards as follows:

> It's become more formalized and in a way, I think that's unfortunate because it used to be a complete surprise to receive a profit share. The thinking of the people like Bob Gore and other leaders was that maybe we weren't using it in the right way and we could encourage people by helping them know more about it and how we made profit-share decisions. The fun of it before was people didn't know when it was coming and all of a sudden you could do something creative about passing out checks . . . The disadvantage was that Associates then did not focus much on "What am I doing to create another profit share?" By using EVA as a method of evaluation for our profit share, we know at the end of every month how much EVA was created that month. When we've created a certain amount of EVA, we then get another profit share. So everybody knows and everyone says, "We'll do it in January," so it is done. Now Associates feel more part of the happening to make it work. What have you done? Go make some more sales calls, please! There are lots of things we can do to improve our EVA and everybody has a responsibility to do that.

Every month all Associates were informed of the EVA calculations. John Mosko, of Gore's electronic products division, commented, "[EVA] lets us know where we are on the path to getting one [a profit share]. It's very critical—every Associate knows."

Annually, Gore also bought company stock equivalent to a fixed percentage of the Associates' annual income, placing it in the ASOP retirement fund. An Associate became a stockholder after being at Gore for a year. Having an ASOP ensured that Associates participated in the growth and profitability of the company. Bill Gore wanted Associates to feel that they themselves were owners. One Associate stated, "This is much more important than profit sharing." In fact, the ASOP allowed some long-term associates (including a 25-year veteran machinist) to become millionaires.

---

[3]Similar legally to an employee stock ownership plan (ESOP). Again, Gore simply has never allowed the word *employee* in any of its documentation.

W. L. Gore's Guiding Principles and Core Values

In addition to the sponsor program, Gore associates were asked to follow four guiding principles:

1. Try to be fair.
2. Encourage, help, and allow other Associates to grow in knowledge, skill, and scope of activity and responsibility.
3. Make your own commitments, and keep them.
4. Consult with other Associates before taking actions that may be "below the waterline."

The four principles were referred to as *fairness, freedom, commitment,* and *waterline.* The waterline principle was drawn from an analogy to ships. If someone poked a hole in a boat above the waterline, the boat would be in relatively little real danger. If, however, someone poked a hole below the waterline, the boat could be in immediate danger of sinking. The expectation was that "waterline" issues would be discussed across teams and plants before decisions were made.

The operating principles were put to a severe test in 1978. By this time word about the qualities of Gore-Tex fabric was being spread throughout the recreational and outdoor markets. Production and shipment had begun in volume. At first a few complaints were heard. Next, some of the clothing started coming back. Finally, much of the clothing was being returned. The trouble was that the Gore-Tex fabric was leaking.

Peter W. Gilson, who led Gore's fabrics division at the time, recalled, "It was an incredible crisis for us at that point. We were really starting to attract attention; we were taking off—and then this." In the next few months, Gilson and a number of his Associates made some below-the-waterline decisions. First, the researchers determined that oils in human sweat were responsible for clogging the pores in the Gore-Tex fabric and altering the surface tension of the membrane so that water could pass through. They also discovered that a good washing could restore the waterproof property. At first this solution, known as the "Ivory Snow solution," was accepted.

A single letter from Butch, a mountain guide in the Sierras, changed the company's position: "My parka leaked and my life was in danger," Butch wrote. Gilson noted, "That scared the hell out of us. Clearly our solution was no solution at all to someone on a mountain top." All the products were recalled. Gilson remembered: "We bought back, at our own expense, a fortune in pipeline material—anything that was in the stores, at the manufacturers, or anywhere else in the pipeline."

In the meantime, Bob Gore and other Associates set out to develop a permanent fix. One month later, a second-generation Gore-Tex fabric had been developed. Gilson told dealers that if a customer ever returned a leaky parka, they should replace it and bill the company. The replacement program alone cost Gore roughly $4 million.

Sometimes when retail customers were dissatisfied with a garment, they returned it directly to W. L. Gore. Gore stood behind any product made of Gore-Tex fabric even though analysis of returned garments often revealed that the problem was not due to the Gore-Tex laminate. According to Sally Gore, even if garment manufacturers were responsible for design flaws, the Gore-Tex name was still at stake: "So we had to make good on products that we were not manufacturing. We now license the manufacturers of all our Gore-Tex fabric products. They pay a fee to obtain a license to manufacture products with Gore-Tex laminate. In return, we oversee the manufacture and we let them manufacture only designs that we are sure are guaranteed to keep you dry, that really will work. Then it works for them and for us—it's a win–win for them as well as for us."

To further ensure quality, W. L. Gore & Associates had constructed its own product testing facility, including a rain room for garments made with Gore-Tex laminate. Besides a rain/storm test, all garments had to pass abrasion and washing machine tests. Only the garments that passed these tests were licensed to display the Gore-Tex label.

RESEARCH AND DEVELOPMENT

Like everything else at Gore, research and development activities were unstructured. There was no formal R&D department charged with coming up with new products and more efficient manufacturing processes; Associates were expected to be inventive. Empowering Associates to be innovative in developing new products and ferreting out new market opportunities had worked well over the years. The company had been issued many patents but kept most of its inventions under tight wrap as proprietary or trade secrets. For example, few Associates other than those directly involved in the production process were allowed to see Gore-Tex being made. Any Associate could, however, ask for a piece of raw PTFE (known as a silly worm) with which to experiment.

One of the best examples of Gore inventiveness occurred in 1969. At the time, the wire and cable division was facing increased competition. Bill Gore began to look for a way to straighten out the PTFE molecules: "I figured out that if we could ever unfold those molecules, get them to stretch out straight, we'd have a tremendous new kind of material." The new PTFE material would have more volume per pound of raw material with no adverse effect on performance. Thus, fabricating costs would be reduced and profit margins increased. Bob Gore took on the project; he heated rods of PTFE to various temperatures and then slowly stretched them. Regardless of the temperature or how carefully he stretched them, the rods broke.

Working alone late one night after countless failures, Bob in frustration stretched one of the rods violently. To his surprise, it did not break. He tried it again and again with the same results. The next morning, Bill Gore recalled, "Bob wanted to surprise me so he took a rod and stretched it slowly. Naturally, it broke. Then he pretended to get mad. He grabbed another rod and said, 'Oh, the hell with this,' and gave it a pull. It didn't break—he'd done it." The new arrangement of molecules not only changed the wire and cable division, but led to the development of Gore-Tex fabric.

Bill and Vieve did the initial field-testing of Gore-Tex fabric the summer of 1970. They took a tent sewed out of patches of Gore-Tex fabric with them on their annual camping trip to the Wind River Mountains in Wyoming. The very first night in the wilderness, they encountered a hailstorm. The hail tore holes in the top of the tent, and the bottom filled up like a bathtub from the rain. Undaunted, Bill Gore stated, "At least we knew from all the water that the tent was waterproof. We just needed to make it stronger, so it could withstand hail."

All Gore Associates were encouraged to think, experiment, and follow a potentially profitable idea to its conclusion. At the plant in Newark, Delaware, Fred L. Eldreth, an Associate with a third-grade education, designed a machine that could wrap thousands of feet of wire a day. The design was completed over a weekend.

The year before he died, Bill Gore claimed that at his company "the creativity, the number of patent applications and innovative products is triple [that of Du Pont]."

MARKETING APPROACHES AND PRACTICES

W. L. Gore had no formally organized marketing department. Instead, Gore's business philosophy incorporated three beliefs and principles: (1) that the company can and should offer the best-valued products in the markets and market segments where it chose to compete, (2) that buyers in each of Gore's product markets should appreciate the caliber and performance of the items Gore manufactured, and (3) that Gore should become a leader with unique expertise in each of the product categories where it competed. To achieve these outcomes, the company's approach to marketing was based on the following:

1. *Marketing a product requires a leader, or "product champion."* According to Dave McCarter: "You marry your technology with the interests of your champions, since you've got to have champions for all these things no matter what. And that's the key element within our company. Without a product champion you can't do much anyway, so it is individually driven. If you get people interested in a particular market or a particular product for the marketplace, then there is no stopping them." Bob Winterling of the fabrics division elaborated further on the role and importance of the product champion:

> The product champion is probably the most important resource we have at Gore for the introduction of new products. You look at that bicycle cable. That could have come out of many different divisions of Gore, but it really happened because one or two individuals said, "Look, this can work. I believe in it, I'm passionate about it, and I want it to happen." And the same thing happened with Glide floss. I think John Spencer in this case—although there was a team that supported John, let's never forget that—John sought the experts out throughout the organization. But without John making it happen on his own, Glide floss would never have come to fruition. He started with a little chain of drugstores here, Happy Harry's I think, and we put a few cases in and we just tracked the sales . . . Who would have ever believed that you could take what we would have considered a commodity product like that, sell it direct for $3 to $5 apiece? That is so un-Gorelike it's incredible. So it comes down to people and it comes down to the product champion to make things happen.

2. *A product champion is responsible for marketing the product through commitments with sales representatives.* According to Dave McCarter, "We have no quota system. Our marketing and our sales people make their own commitments as to what their forecasts have been. There is no person sitting around telling them that is not high enough, you have to increase it by 10 percent, or whatever somebody feels is necessary. You are expected to meet your commitment, which is your forecast, but nobody is going to tell you to change it . . . There is no order of command, no chain involved. These are groups of independent people who come together to make unified commitments to do something and sometimes when they can't make those agreements . . . you may pass up a marketplace . . . But that's OK, because there's much more advantage when the team decides to do something."

3. *Sales Associates are compensated by salary, not commission.* Sales associates had the same incentives to do a good job as did all other Gore Associates—earning a share of the company's profits and participating in the company's stock option plan. Sales Associates' evaluations were based on achieving their sales forecasts and living up to their other agreed-upon commitments.

Dave McCarter told of another of the company's successes in relying on product champions:

> I interviewed Sam one day. I didn't even know why I was interviewing him actually. Sam was retired from AT&T. After 25 years, he took the golden parachute and went down to Sun Lakes to play golf. He played golf a few months and got tired of that. He was selling life insurance.
> I sat reading the application; his technical background interested me . . . He had managed an engineering department with 600 people. He'd managed manufacturing plants for AT&T and had a great wealth of experience at AT&T. He said, "I'm retired. I like to play golf

but I just can't do it every day so I want to do something else. Do you have something around here I can do?" I was thinking to myself, "This is one of these guys I would sure like to hire but I don't know what I would do with him." The thing that triggered me was the fact that he said he sold insurance . . . He had marketing experience, international marketing experience. So, the bell went off in my head that we were trying to introduce a new product into the marketplace that was a hydrocarbon leak protection cable. You can bury it in the ground and in a matter of seconds it could detect a hydrocarbon like gasoline. I had a couple of other guys working on the product who hadn't been very successful with marketing it. We were having a hard time finding a customer. Well, I thought that kind of product would be like selling insurance. If you think about it, why should you protect your tanks? It's an insurance policy that things are not leaking into the environment. That has implications, big-time monetary. So, actually, I said, "Why don't you come back Monday? I have just the thing for you." He did. We hired him; he went to work, a very energetic guy. Certainly a champion of the product, he picked right up on it, ran with it singlehanded . . . Now it's a growing business. It certainly is a valuable one, too, for the environment.

Cooperative advertising and word-of-mouth advertising by satisfied consumers were the primary vehicles used to promote Gore-Tex fabric products. The company's cooperative advertising program featured high-dollar, glossy campaigns with full-color ads and a sales force dressed in Gore-Tex garments. A recent slogan used in Gore's ad campaigns was, "If it doesn't Gore-Tex, it's not." A number of retailers had praised the effectiveness and caliber of the company's marketing and advertising efforts. Leigh Gallagher, managing editor of *Sporting Goods Business* magazine, described W. L. Gore & Associates' marketing as "unbeatable."

Gore's sales and marketing Associates believed positive buyer experiences with one Gore-Tex product (for instance, a ski parka) carried over to purchases of other Gore-Tex products (gloves, pants, rain suits, and jackets). When the Grandoe Corporation introduced a new line of Gore-Tex ski gloves, its president, Richard Zuckerwar, noted, "Sports activists have long had the benefit of Gore-Tex outerwear to protect them from the elements . . . With this handsome collection of gloves . . . you can now have warm, dry hands without sacrificing style." Clothing manufacturers and distributors who marketed Gore-Tex garments included Apparel Technologies, Lands' End, Austin Reed, Hudson Trail Outfitters, Timberland, Woolrich, North Face, L. L. Bean, and Michelle Jaffe.

W. L. Gore also enjoyed a sterling reputation among its industrial and institutional customers. According to Dave McCarter, "In the technical end of the business, company reputation probably is most important. You have to have a good reputation with your customer." He went on to say that if Gore did not enjoy a solid reputation, many industrial customers would not consider the company's products.

Gore secured a market leadership position in a number of product categories, ranging from waterproof outdoor clothing to vascular grafts. Its market share of waterproof, breathable fabrics was estimated to be close to 90 percent.

Adaptation to Changing Market Circumstances

Several of Gore's divisions had from time to time been confronted with market adversity. The fabric division was hit hard when consumer interest in jogging suits collapsed in the mid-1980s. The fabric division took another hit from the recession of 1989 when people reduced their purchases of high-end athletic apparel. But the division recovered quickly and by 1995 was again the fastest growing division of Gore.

Rival manufacturers—including 3M, Burlington Industries, Akzo Nobel Fibers, and Du Pont—had recently introduced products to compete with Gore-Tex fabrics. Prior to the introduction of their products, W. L. Gore's toughest competition came from firms that violated the patents on Gore-Tex. Gore successfully challenged the patent violators in court, but in 1993 the basic patent on the process for manufacturing Gore-Tex expired. Nevertheless, the company was not without patent protection. As Sally Gore explained,

> What happens is you get an initial process patent and then as you begin to create things with this process you get additional patents. For instance, we have patents protecting our vascular graft, different patents for protecting Gore-Tex patches, and still other patents protecting Gore-Tex industrial sealants and filtration material. One of our patent attorneys did a talk recently, a year or so ago, when the patent expired and a lot of people were saying, "Oh, golly, are we going to be in trouble!" Well, we would be in trouble if we didn't have any patents. Our attorney showed this picture with a great big umbrella, sort of a parachute, with Gore under it. Next, he showed us lots of little umbrellas representing specific Gore products scattered all over the sky. His point was that you can protect certain niche markets and niche areas with specific patents, even though competition indeed increases as your initial patents expire.

Despite the expiration of its initial patent and the introduction of competing laminates for waterproofing fabrics, Gore still had a commanding position in the activewear market in 1998.

The electronics division had suffered a downturn in the sales of its computer cable products when the mainframe computer business gave way to growing use and acceptance of PC technology in the early 1990s. By 1995, the electronics division was seeing a resurgence for its products partially because Associates had developed an assortment of new electronic products for the medical industry.

The aging of America's population had increased the need for health care, and many of Gore's medical products were used to treat the afflictions of the elderly. As a result, Gore invested in the development of additional medical products and the medical division experienced significant growth.

Gore's Financial Performance

As a closely held private corporation, W. L. Gore kept its financial information as closely guarded as its proprietary information on products and processes. It had been estimated that Associates who worked at Gore owned 90 percent of the company's common stock. According to Associate Shanti Mehta, Gore's returns on assets and sales were consistently on a par with the best-performing 10 percent of Fortune 500 companies. According to another source, W. L. Gore & Associates had performed fine by any financial measure. The company was profitable and had enjoyed a positive return on equity for 37 straight years (from 1961 to 1997). By one estimate, the average annual compound growth rate in revenues at W. L. Gore & Associates from 1969 to 1989 was more than 18 percent (discounted for inflation).[4] In 1969, total sales were about $6 million, by 1989, the figure was $600 million. Sales were expected to easily surpass $1.2 billion in 1998. With the increase in the company's size, the percentage increase in sales slowed (see Figure 4). Gore financed its growth without long-term debt unless such debt made sense. For example, "We used to have some industrial revenue bonds where, in essence, to build facilities the government allows banks to lend you money tax free. Up to a couple of years ago we were borrowing money through indus-

---

[4]In comparison, only 11 of the 200 largest companies in the Fortune 500 had positive ROE each year from 1970 to 1988 and only 2 other companies missed a year. The revenue growth rate for these 13 companies was 5.4 percent, compared with 2.5 percent for the entire Fortune 500.

EXHIBIT 6   Growth of W. L. Gore's Sales as Compared to the U.S. Gross Domestic Product, 1989–1997

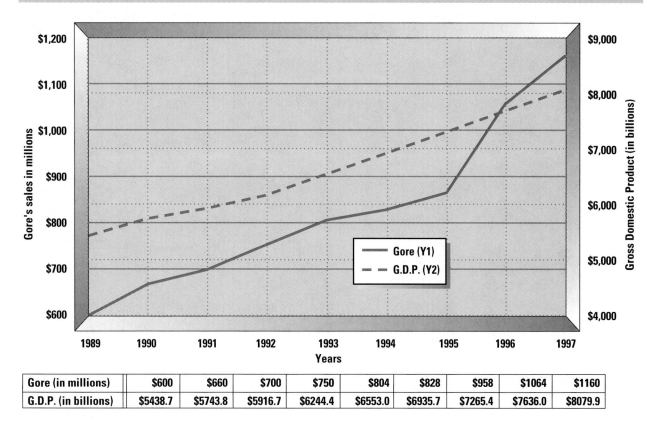

	1989	1990	1991	1992	1993	1994	1995	1996	1997
Gore (in millions)	$600	$660	$700	$750	$804	$828	$958	$1064	$1160
G.D.P. (in billions)	$5438.7	$5743.8	$5916.7	$6244.4	$6553.0	$6935.7	$7265.4	$7636.0	$8079.9

trial revenue bonds. Other than that, we are totally debt free. Our money is generated out of the operations of the business, and frankly we're looking for new things to invest in. I know that's a challenge for all of us today," said Bob Winterling. In 1997, the company's revenues were an estimated $1.16 billion (see Exhibit 6). *Forbes* magazine estimated that W. L. Gore's operating profits were $120 million in 1993, $140 million in 1994, $192 million in 1995, $213 million in 1996, and $230 million in 1997 (see Exhibit 7). Bob Gore predicted that company revenues would reach $2 billion by 2001.

Recently, the company had purchased Optical Concepts Inc., a laser semiconductor technology company, of Lompoc, California. In addition, Gore & Associates was test-marketing a new product, guitar strings.

When asked about cost control, Sally Gore had the following to say:

> You have to pay attention to cost or you're not an effective steward of anyone's money, your own or anyone else's. It's kind of interesting, we started manufacturing medical products in 1974 with the vascular graft and it built from there. The Gore vascular graft is the Cadillac or BMW or the Rolls-Royce of the business. There is absolutely no contest, and our medical products division became very successful. People thought this was Mecca. Nothing had ever been manufactured that was so wonderful. Our business expanded enormously, rapidly out there [in Flagstaff, Arizona] and we had a lot of young, young leadership. They spent some time thinking they could do no wrong and that everything they touched was going to turn to gold. They have had some hard knocks along the way and discovered it wasn't as easy as they initially thought it was. And that's probably good learning for everyone somewhere

EXHIBIT 7   Estimated Operating and Net Profits of W. L. Gore & Associates, 1993–97

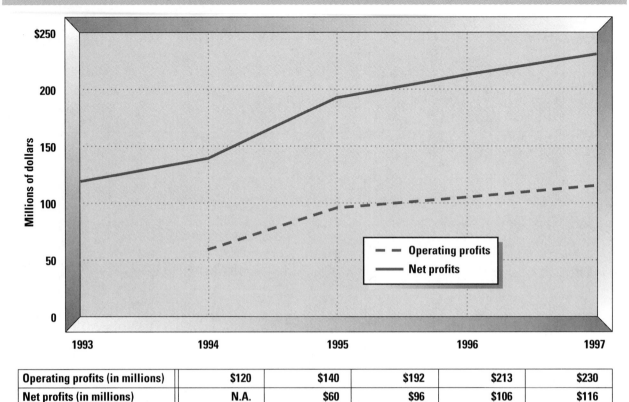

	1993	1994	1995	1996	1997
Operating profits (in millions)	$120	$140	$192	$213	$230
Net profits (in millions)	N.A.	$60	$96	$106	$116

Data from Forbes Magazine's Annual Report on the 500 Largest Private Companies in the U.S.

along the way. That's not how business works. There's a lot of truth in that old saying that you learn more from your failures than you do your successes. One failure goes a long way toward making you say, "Oh, wow!"

(You are encouraged to visit the company's Web site at *www.gorefabrics.com*.)

BIBLIOGRAPHY   Aburdene, Patricia, and John Nasbitt. *Re-inventing the Corporation.* New York: Warner Books, 1985.

Angrist, S. W. "Classless Capitalists." *Forbes,* May 9, 1983, pp. 123–24.

Franlesca, L. "Dry and Cool." *Forbes,* August 27, 1984, p. 126.

"The Future Workplace." *Management Review,* July 1986, pp. 22–23.

Hoerr, J. "A Company Where Everybody Is the Boss." *Business Week,* April 15, 1985, p. 98.

Levering, Robert. *The 100 Best Companies to Work for in America.* New York: Signet, 1985.

McKendrick, Joseph. "The Employees as Entrepreneur." *Management World,* January 1985, pp. 12–13.

Milne, M. J. "The Gorey Details." *Management Review,* March 1985, pp. 16–17.

Price, Debbie M. "Gore-Tex Style." *Baltimore Sun,* April 20, 1997, pp. 1D, 4D.

Price, Kathy. "Firm Thrives without Boss." *AZ Republic,* February 2, 1986.

Posner, B. G. "The First Day on the Job." *Inc.,* June 1986, pp. 73–75.

Rhodes, Lucien. "The Un-manager." *Inc.,* August 1982, p. 34.

Simmons, J. "People Managing Themselves: Un-management at W. L. Gore Inc." *Journal for Quality and Participation,* December 1987, pp. 14–19.

Trachtenberg, J. A. "Give Them Stormy Weather." *Forbes,* March 24, 1986, pp. 172–74.

Ward, Alex. "An All-Weather Idea." *The New York Times Magazine,* November 10, 1985, section 6.

Weber, Joseph. "No Bosses. And Even 'Leaders' Can't Give Orders." *Business Week,* December 10, 1990, pp. 196–97.

"Wilbert L. Gore." *Industry Week,* October 17, 1983, pp. 48–49.

28

HERB KELLEHER AND SOUTHWEST AIRLINES

Isaac Cohen, *San Jose State University*

In 1971, Southwest Airlines began flying between three Texas cities—Dallas, Houston, and San Antonio—using three Boeing 737 aircraft. In 1998, 27 years later, Southwest operated 262 Boeing 737s and provided service to 51 cities throughout the United States. In 1997, Southwest Airlines was the seventh largest domestic carrier (see Exhibit 1), competing successfully with United, American, Delta, U.S. Air, Continental, and Northwest. Born on the eve of deregulation, Southwest initiated the low-cost airline-service revolution, which in turn transformed air transportation into a highly competitive business.

Following the passage of the airline deregulation act in 1978, 120 air carriers went bankrupt; two major carriers (Eastern, Pan American) collapsed; and two others (Continental, TWA) filed bankruptcy under chapter 11 twice.[1] Southwest alone managed to generate profits for 24 consecutive years beginning in 1974. Significantly, no other carrier except Southwest made profits in 1990, 1991, or 1992. In addition, every year from 1992 to 1996 Southwest earned the industry's Triple Crown award, given annually by the Department of Transportation for high customer satisfaction in three areas: baggage handling, on-time performance, and response to passenger complaints. A 1993 book named Southwest as one of the 100 best companies to work for in America, and *Fortune* surveys showed that Southwest was the most admired U.S. airline every year from 1995 to 1998; in the 1998 survey Southwest came out as the sixth most admired American company overall. Southwest had also been recognized as one of the world's safest airlines by *Conde Nast Traveler,* and as one of the country's lowest fare airlines by the July 1997 *Consumer Reports.* Equally impressive, a 1997 survey conducted by researchers from three universities described Southwest Airlines as an "American icon" and placed it among the top 10 "role-model" companies doing business in the United States. In 1998, similarly, a *Fortune* study of the best U.S. companies to work for ranked Southwest Airlines as number one.[2]

---

[1]Kevin Freiberg and Jackie Freiberg, *Nuts: Southwest Airline's Crazy Recipe for Business and Personal Success* (Austin: Bard Press, 1996), p. 5.

[2]"Fact Sheet," Southwest Airlines Company, September 1997, pp. 1–4; January 1998, pp. 1–5; *Fortune,* January 12, 1998, p. 84, March 2, 1998, pp. 71, F-2.

EXHIBIT 1 Total Revenues and Market Share of the Top 10 U.S. Airlines, Domestic Operation, Year-End December 31, 1997

Rank	Airline	Total Revenues	Market Share
1	United	$11.2 billion	17.9%
2	Delta	11.4	18.2
3	American	10.7	17.1
4	U.S. Air	8.0	12.6
5	Northwest	6.5	10.4
6	Continental	5.1	8.1
7	Southwest	3.8	6.1
8	TWA	2.8	4.5
9	America West	1.8	2.9
10	Alaska	1.4	2.2

Note: Federal Express and United Parcel Service are excluded.
Source: *Air Carrier Financial Statistics, Fourth Quarter, December 1996/1997,* Department of Transportation, Bureau of Transportation Statistics, Office of Airline Information (Washington, DC, 1997), pp. 4, 6, 10, 13, 21, 23, 24, 26, 32.

The Airline Industry

The airline industry dates back to the Air Mail Service of 1918–25. Using its own planes and pilots, the U.S. Post Office directly operated mail-shipment flights. With the passage of the Air Mail Act (also known as the Kelly Act) of 1925 the Post Office subcontracted airmail transport to private companies and thereby laid the foundation of a national air transport system. The Post Office paid contractors substantial sums and encouraged them to extend their routes, buy larger planes, and expand their services.

The formative period of the private airline industry came during the Great Depression. The five or six years following Charles Lindbergh's 1927 flight across the Atlantic were years of mergers and acquisitions in which every major carrier came into existence, mostly through the acquisition of smaller lines. American, United, Delta, Northwest, Continental, and Eastern Airlines were all formed during this period. The increase in passenger transport during the 1930s led, in turn, to growing competition, price cutting, bankruptcies, and serious safety problems. It convinced the architects of the New Deal that the entire transport system—not just airmail—required federal regulation. The outcome was the passage of the Civil Aeronautics Act (CAA) of 1938.[3]

The CAA had two major provisions. First, it prohibited price competition among carriers, and, second, it effectively closed the industry to newcomers. The Civil Aeronautics Board (CAB) required that all air carriers flying certain routes charge the same fares for the same class of passengers. The CAB also required all applicants wishing to enter the industry to show that they were "fit, willing and able" to do so and that their service was "required by the public convenience and necessity." Between 1950 and 1975 the board denied all 79 applications it received from carriers asking to enter the domestic scheduled airline industry.[4] The number of scheduled U.S. air carriers was

---

[3]Henry Ladd Smith, *Airways: The History of Commercial Aviation in the United States* (1942; reprinted, New York: Russell and Russell, 1964).

[4]Stephen Breyer, *Regulation and Its Reform* (Cambridge, MA: Harvard University Press, 1982), p. 205.

reduced from 16 in 1938 to just 10 in the 1970s, following mergers, consolidations, and route transfers.[5]

By the mid-1970s, the airline industry was experiencing serious financial troubles. Rising fuel prices, an economic recession, and the introduction of expensive wide-body aircraft (Boeing 747s, Lockheed L-1011s, and McDonald Douglas DC-10s) led to climbing costs, higher fares, reduced traffic, falling revenues, and a growing public demand for opening up the airline industry to competition. As a result, in 1975 a Senate subcommittee chaired by Edward Kennedy held hearings on the airlines. Working closely with Kennedy was a Harvard law professor named Stephen Breyer, who later became a U.S. Supreme Court Justice. A specialist in regulation, the author of *Regulation and Reform,* and the staff director of the Kennedy hearings, Breyer helped Kennedy build up a strong case against airline regulation.

Together, Breyer and Kennedy used the example of Southwest Airlines to bolster their case. They contrasted intrastate air service—which had never been regulated by the CAB—with interstate service—which had been regulated since 1938. The figures were astounding. Air fares charged by an interstate carrier flying the New York–Boston route (191 miles) were almost double those charged by an intrastate carrier (Southwest) flying the Houston–San Antonio route (also 191 miles). Southwest's Texas experience, Breyer and Kennedy insisted, suggested that the demand for air travel was elastic and that lower prices would result in significant increases in demand. They pointed out that when Southwest entered the Houston–Dallas–San Antonio market in the early 1970s with fares 50 percent below those of its competitors, total air travel in the Texas triangle increased by 100–150 percent. And they concluded that the experience of Southwest Airlines in Texas—like that of Pacific Southwest Airlines in California—demonstrated the efficiency of the free market and the urgent need for deregulation.[6] Three years later the airline industry was deregulated by Congress.

Company Background

Southwest's founder and CEO Herb Kelleher graduated from New York University Law School, clerked for a New Jersey Supreme Court justice for two years, and then joined a law firm in Newark. He married a woman from Texas, became increasingly attracted by the wide-open Texas business scene, and eventually moved to San Antonio.

While practicing law in San Antonio in the mid-1960s, Kelleher looked around for start-up business opportunities. Sometime in 1966 a banker client named Rolling King returned from a trip to California and presented Kelleher with an idea: Texas could benefit from a short-haul commuter airline similar to Pacific Southwest Airlines, then an intra-California air carrier. Together, Kelleher and King drew a map of the Texas triangle and a business plan calling for the establishment of a low-cost carrier based in Dallas and serving Houston and San Antonio.[7]

Incorporated in 1967, Air Southwest did not inaugurate service until 1971. Two main competitors serving the state of Texas—Braniff Airways and Texas International—tied up Kelleher's plan in litigation for nearly four years. The fact that Kelleher was a lawyer certainly helped: Southwest won the legal battle first in the Texas

[5]Thomas K. McCraw, *Prophets of Regulation: Charles Francis Adams, Louis D. Brandies, James M. Landis, Alfred E. Kahn* (Cambridge, MA: Harvard University Press, 1984), p. 265.

[6]McCraw, *Prophets of Regulation,* pp. 266–67; Breyer, *Regulation and Its Reform,* pp. 204–5.

[7]Kenneth Labich, "Is Herb Kelleher America's Best CEO?," *Fortune,* May 2, 1994, pp. 46–47.

Supreme Court and then in the U.S. Supreme Court. On June 18, 1971, Southwest finally made its first commercial flight.[8]

Once it began operating, Southwest sought to compete with ground transportation, not air transportation. This was one of the most critical strategic decisions Kelleher made. "We must be able to beat the out-of-pocket costs of driving to provide a viable alternative means of travel," he explained in a 1990 interview, noting that in the mid-1970s Southwest had charged passengers just $15 on the Dallas–San Antonio route while Braniff Airways charged $62. "Obviously we could have raised our fares to $18 or $19 and still had significant advantage over Braniff . . . but we did not." The reason, according to Kelleher, was plain enough: the cost of driving was $18.[9]

Southwest competed with ground transportation on other routes as well. In 1975, Southwest began serving the Rio Grande Valley, and in less than a year traffic between the Valley and Houston–Dallas–San Antonio more than doubled. In 1977 Southwest opened services to Corpus Christie, Lubbock, and El Paso, and in 1978 to Amarillo.[10]

With the coming of airline deregulation in 1978, Southwest was no longer confined to the state of Texas. In 1979 Southwest initiated service to New Orleans; in 1980 to Oklahoma City, Tulsa, and Albuquerque; in 1982 to Kansas City, Las Vegas, Phoenix, San Diego, and Los Angeles; and in 1985 to St. Louis and Chicago.[11] By January 1998 Southwest's top 10 destinations were Phoenix, Houston, Las Vegas, Dallas, Los Angeles, Oakland, Chicago, St. Louis, San Diego, and San Jose.[12] Typically, when Southwest entered a new market, air fares fell, traffic increased, and competition among air carriers—and between air carriers and motor carriers—intensified.

Southwest's Limited Growth Strategy

Any growth strategy that placed market share ahead of profits was unacceptable to Southwest management from the start. Unlike most other major carriers, Southwest Airlines avoided expansion into markets that were likely to increase its costs disproportionately.[13] Southwest's focus on profitability rather than market share was a survival strategy during the early years of deregulation and a winning strategy during the 1990s.

Southwest specialized in high-traffic, short-haul routes on which it could offer frequent service between pairs of cities, thus eschewing the hub-and-spoke system favored by the major carriers. (The hub was analogous to a bicycle wheel, with the routes resembling spokes. Passengers traveled into a central hub airport and transferred to other flights on the same airline to reach their destination.) A 1993 study by the Department of Transportation (DOT) found that in 1992 Southwest's average share in its top 100 city-pair markets was 65 percent. In those 100 markets, the study concluded,

> Southwest is the dominant airline in 93, has a 50 percent or greater share in 80, and a 67 percent or better share in 53. No other airline comes close to these numbers in their respective

---

[8]James Campbell Quick, "Crafting an Organizational Structure: Herb's Hand at Southwest Airlines," *Organizational Dynamics* 21, no. 2 (Autumn 1992), pp. 47–48; *A Tale of Two Men, One Airplane, and a Cocktail Napkin,* Southwest Airlines Company, 1996.

[9]David A. Brown, "Southwest Airlines Gains Major Carrier Status," *Aviation Week and Space Technology,* March 5, 1990, p. 83.

[10]Freiberg and Freiberg, *Nuts,* pp. 29–30; Quick, "Crafting an Organizational Structure," p. 48.

[11]Quick, "Crafting an Organizational Structure," p. 48, Southwest Airlines, *A Tale of Two Men.*

[12]"Fact Sheet," Southwest Airlines, January 1998, p. 2.

[13]"Kristin Dunlap Godsey, "Top Gun: The Crafting Antics of a High Flying Entrepreneur," *Success,* October 1996, p. 24; Freiberg and Freiberg, *Nuts,* pp. 49–50.

top 100 markets. And Southwest's dominance is almost universally pervasive. Compared with a year earlier, its most recent market shares are up in virtually every one of its top 100 markets, often dramatically. In several instances competitors dropped out. All this despite the fact that 82 of Southwest's top 100 markets involve another airline's connecting hub—16 involve two connecting hubs.[14]

A follow-up study by the DOT using 1997 data showed that of the 48 domestic U.S. city-pair markets of 250 miles or less, Southwest served 21 and had a 50 percent or greater share in 16; of the 223 domestic city-pair markets of 251–500 miles, Southwest served 100 and had a 50 percent or greater share in 82.[15]

Southwest's point-to-point service not only consolidated the carrier's position in the markets it served but also contributed to the carrier's efficient mode of operation. The hub-and-spoke system had the disadvantage of causing airplanes to spend time on the ground waiting for passengers from connecting flights; the city-pair system of service facilitated a quick turnaround at gates—planes could leave as soon as the arriving passengers were unloaded and the departing passengers were on board. Short turnaround times at the gates promoted a high level of aircraft utilization, thereby lowering both capital and labor costs.

Southwest's city-pair system was sustained by several innovative elements. First, Southwest used only one type of aircraft—the Boeing 737—and therefore maintenance requirements were standardized. Second, Southwest favored secondary, uncongested airports like Dallas's Love Field, Houston's Hobby, Chicago's Midway, and the Detroit City Airport, thus avoiding excessive delays. Third, Southwest provided no meals, no assigned seats, and no baggage transfers to other carriers (passengers had to recheck their baggage if they were proceeding to further destinations). As a result, food restocking, passenger boarding, and luggage handling were vastly simplified. In 1998, Southwest's average turnaround time at the gate was less than half the industry average—20 minutes versus 45 minutes.[16] Keeping the aircraft in the air an average of 11.3 hours a day[17] (compared to an industry average of 8.6 hours a day), Southwest used its capital assets more efficiently than other carriers did, reducing the number of aircraft needed and lowering fixed investment costs considerably. According to one estimate, in 1995 Southwest used 35 fewer aircraft than it would have had its average turnaround time been the industry average.[18]

Southwest's Aversion to Strategic Planning   Southwest did not embrace formal strategic planning. "Reality is chaotic; planning is ordered and logical. The two don't square with each other," Kelleher said in a 1995–96 interview. "The meticulous nit-picking that goes on in most strategic planning processes creates a mental straitjacket that becomes disabling in an industry where things change radically from one day to next."[19]

Instead of developing long-range strategies, Southwest developed a set of short-term actions and tactical maneuvers to meet a variety of competitive situations. The advanced thinking done in preparing for strategic contingencies enabled the carrier to react

---

[14]Randall D. Bennett and James M. Craun, *The Airline Deregulation Revolution Continues: The Southwest Effect,* Office of Airline Analysis, U.S. Department of Transportation, 1993, p. 2.

[15]Calculated from Domestic Airline Fares, Consumer Report, First Quarter 1997: Passenger and Fare Information, U.S. Department of Transportation, September 1997, pp. 1–5.

[16]*Fortune,* March 2, 1998, p. 82; Roger Hallowell, "Southwest Airlines: A Case Study Linking Employee Needs Satisfaction and Organizational Capabilities to Competitive Advantage," *Human Resource Management* 35, no. 4 (Winter 1996), p. 519; Freiberg and Freiberg, *Nuts,* p. 57.

[17]"Fact Sheet," Southwest Airlines, January 1998, p. 2.

[18]Freiberg and Freiberg, *Nuts,* pp. 51, 60.

[19]Quoted in Freiberg and Freiberg, *Nuts,* pp. 85–86.

EXHIBIT 2 U.S. Major Carriers Unit Cost per Available Seat Mile and Load Factors,* 12 Months Ended Fourth Quarter 1997

Carrier	Unit Cost per Available Seat Mile	Break-even Load Factor*	Actual Load Factor*	Difference between Actual and Breakeven
Alaska	8.6 cents	60.2%	67.3%	7.1%
America West	7.3	62.4	68.8	6.4
American	9.4	62.5	69.5	7.0
Continental	9.2	63.4	71.5	8.1
Delta	9.1	62.7	71.8	9.1
Northwest	9.0	64.0	74.3	10.3
Southwest	7.4	54.6	63.8	9.2
TWA	9.2	69.3	68.6	(0.7)
United	9.5	66.0	71.8	5.8
U.S. Airways	13.5	65.5	71.4	5.9
U.S. Average	9.3 cents	63.4%	70.2%	6.8%

*Load factor is the term used to describe the percent of available seats filled by passengers.

Source: Based on carrier filings at the Department of Transportation, *Aviation Daily,* April 17, 1998, p. 109.

quickly to industry changes, focus on future scenarios, and respond to new initiatives undertaken by other air carriers. United's launching of its United Shuttle service in the Pacific Northwest in 1994 was a case in point.

Southwest Airlines had anticipated United's announcement of the shuttle, and moved quickly to acquire Morris Air—a Salt Lake City–based carrier—in 1993. Acquiring Morris Air was in Southwest's interest because Morris flew only Boeing 737s (the same as Southwest) and because Morris's route structure complemented—not duplicated—Southwest's in the Pacific Northwest. The acquisition also allowed Southwest to add destinations and flights on expected United Shuttle routes, to keep costs down (using only 737s), and thereby to gain an early advantage over United.[20]

Cost Structure

Unquestionably, the key to Southwest's profitability was its relative cost advantage over other carriers. U.S. Department of Transportation statistics showed that in every year between 1987 and 1996 Southwest's cost per available seat mile (ASM) was lower than that of any other major carrier.[21] Exhibit 2 shows that, with the exception of America West, the same trend continued through 1997. SWA's lower costs allowed it to break even by filling only 54.6 percent of its available seats; the industry average breakeven point was 63.4 percent (Exhibit 2). Southwest's cost advantage was rooted in several factors.

Labor   Labor cost is the largest single expense at any airline, typically accounting for about 30 percent of total expenses. As shown in Exhibit 3, in 1997 Southwest's unit labor cost (per ASM) was lower than that of any other major carrier except American West. Southwest's labor cost advantage was not based on lower pay scales or fringe benefits but rather on higher labor productivity. Southwest paid its employees competitive wages and provided good benefits at mean industry levels. But Southwest's employees

[20]Freiberg and Freiberg, *Nuts,* p. 87.

[21]See *Aviation Daily,* March 10, 1997, pp. 409–10.

EXHIBIT 3   Unit Labor, Fuel, Maintenance, and Commission Costs of U.S. Major Airlines, in Cents per Available Seat Mile, 1997

Carrier	Labor	Fuel	Maintenance	Commissions	Total
Alaska	2.84¢	1.25¢	0.76¢	0.65¢	5.50¢
America West	1.78	1.13	0.85	0.64	4.40
American	3.35	1.21	1.22	0.78	6.56
Continental	2.61	1.34	1.08	0.75	5.78
Delta	3.18	1.31	0.80	0.72	6.01
Northwest	3.06	1.43	1.16	0.83	6.48
Southwest	2.55	1.11	0.80	0.40	4.86
TWA	3.30	1.32	1.25	0.66	6.53
United	3.54	1.22	1.24	0.87	6.87
U.S. Air	5.17	1.19	1.61	0.90	8.87

Source: Department of Transportation, T-100 data for 1997.

were far more productive than those of other major airlines; they flew more planes and served more passengers per worker, hence reducing unit labor cost. In the mid-1990s, to cite one example, Southwest used 2.2 station personnel per 1,000 passengers (in contrast to an industry average of 4.2) and 81 employees per aircraft (in contrast to an industry average of 134).[22]

The greater labor productivity of Southwest employees had much to do with the willingness of its flight and ground crews to do everything necessary to turn around an airplane very quickly. Asked by a *Fortune* reporter in March 1998 to distinguish Southwest from other airlines, Kelleher replied, "[W]hen a plane pulls into a gate our people *run* to meet it. . . . It's sheer willpower—no mechanical tricks."[23]

Fuel   Southwest's second largest cost was fuel, amounting to about 15 percent of total expenses. Again, Southwest's unit fuel cost in 1997 was lower than that of any other major carrier (see Exhibit 3). One reason why Southwest benefited from fuel cost advantage was the carrier's exclusive use of the fuel-efficient Boeing 737. Another was the daily efforts made by Southwest pilots to conserve fuel. Trained by management to maximize speed and minimize fuel burn rate, Southwest's pilots routinely requested air traffic controllers for more direct headings in and out of an airport, easier runways to taxi on quickly, and more efficient altitudes to cruise through.[24]

Maintenance   As shown in Exhibit 3, in 1997 Southwest's unit maintenance cost was lower than that of most major carriers. Southwest's use of a single aircraft series (Boeing 737–200, 737–300, 737–500) provided ample opportunities to streamline actual maintenance done by workers, reduce inventory costs for parts, simplify record keeping, and negotiate better deals with part suppliers, all of which were important elements in maintenance cost control.

---

[22]Hallowell, "Southwest Airlines," p. 527.

[23]*Fortune,* March 2, 1998, p. 82.

[24]Freiberg and Freiberg, *Nuts,* pp. 101–2.

EXHIBIT 4   Unit Food, Rentals, and Interest Costs of U.S. Major Airlines, in Cents per Available Seat Mile, 1997

Carrier	Food	Rentals	Interest	Totals
Alaska	0.30¢	1.15¢	0.14¢	1.59¢
America West	0.10	1.32	0.17	1.59
American	0.41	0.69	0.11	1.21
Continental	0.25	1.12	0.18	1.55
Delta	0.26	0.68	0.12	1.06
Northwest	0.26	0.62	0.21	1.09
Southwest	0.03	0.67	0.10	0.80
TWA	0.23	1.02	0.31	1.56
United	0.37	0.87	0.11	1.35
U.S. Air	0.27	1.20	0.43	1.90

Source: Department of Transportation, T-100 data for 1997.

Commissions   Southwest's savings on ticket sales commissions were substantial. Most carriers relied on independent travel agents to sell their tickets, but Southwest had never subscribed to any of the computer reservation systems owned by the major carriers. Instead, travel agents wishing to book passengers on Southwest flights needed to pick up the phone and call the airline's ticket sales representatives. Many independent agents were reluctant to do so and tried to convince customers to switch to another carrier or call Southwest themselves; consequently, close to 50 percent of all Southwest's tickets were sold directly to passengers,[25] cutting the airline commission costs by roughly one half, as shown in Exhibit 3.

Food   Southwest's savings on food were even more impressive. With flights averaging an hour and 15 minutes, Southwest did not serve meals at all, only snacks and beverages. As a result, in 1996, Southwest's unit food cost amounted to less than 1/8 the corresponding cost of Delta, 1/12 that of United, and 1/14 that of American, as indicated by the figures presented in Exhibit 4.

Rentals   Southwest's strong financial position provided the carrier with additional sources of savings. "We do pay cash to Boeing for every delivery, and few airlines can do it," Southwest treasurer John Owen told *Aviation Daily* in May 1997. "We want to own as many aircraft as we can, free and clear—that's our strategy." While other large carriers leased 50 to 60 percent of their fleet, Southwest leased only 48 percent of its aircraft, owning outright the remaining 52 percent.[26] The resulting savings reduced Southwest's rental cost (per ASM) below that of all other major carriers, except Northwest, as shown in Exhibit 4.

Interest   Because not a single aircraft owned by Southwest was encumbered by debt, the carrier's debt to total capitalization rate was relatively low, resulting in unit interest costs much lower than those of airlines whose fleet purchases required the expensive

---

[25]*Fortune,* May 2, 1994, p. 47.
[26]*Aviation Daily,* May 19, 1997, p. 297.

use of debt (see Exhibit 4). Maintaining a conservative amount of debt had been a long-standing strategy of Southwest Airlines from its earliest days. During the 1980s and 1990s, Southwest was the only U.S. airline to have a consistent investment-grade credit rating of A− to A.[27]

Corporate Culture

A strong work ethic was at the core of Southwest's efforts to cut costs, enhance productivity, and increase profits. Hard work was sustained, in turn, by other values and norms that underlay the Southwest culture—most notably, an informal work environment, humor at work, and altruism.

Informal Work Environment   Although Southwest had adopted a formal organizational structure, only four layers of management separated Herb Kelleher at the top from a front-line supervisor at the bottom, making communication across the organization quick and easy, and broadening managers' span of control. Southwest managers, as a result, exercised a large measure of decision-making authority. Station managers, for example, were granted full operational autonomy; they were delegated almost absolute authority over their subordinates, and they ran their stations like independent business units. All Southwest employees were encouraged to take initiative, assume individual responsibility, and operate outside the company's formal structure. "We've tried to create an environment where people are able to . . . bypass the fairly lean structure that we have," Herb Kelleher had recently noted. "Our leanness requires people to be comfortable in making their own decisions and undertaking their own efforts."[28]

Humor at Work   Discussing the role of humor at Southwest Airlines, Kelleher said:

> I crystallized the importance of a sense of humor in a . . . formal way in 1978, when I became chairman. I charged our personnel department . . . with the responsibilities of hiring people with a sense of humor. We look for it in the interactions people have with each other during group interviews."[29]

Southwest executives subscribed to the theory that the use of humor in the workplace relieved the stress of hard work, promoted camaraderie among employees, created a sense of community, nourished adaptability, improved morale, and enhanced customer service.[30] Southwest's devotion to humor and fun was reflected in the ways in which employees entertained, amused, and surprised passengers. Bunny-eared flight attendants sometimes popped out of the overhead luggage bin and yelled "Surprise" just as the passengers started boarding the plane. Flight attendants often turned standard announcements into comedy routines ("Please pass all the plastic cups to the center aisle so we can wash them out and use them for the next group of passengers"). During delays at the gate, ticket agents had been known to conduct contests among passengers (seeking, for instance, the passenger with the largest hole in his or her sock).[31] A flight attendant described her playful interaction with passengers at Southwest as follows:

[27]Ibid.; Freiberg and Freiberg, *Nuts,* p. 5.

[28]Freiberg and Freiberg, *Nuts,* p. 76; see also pp. 83, 87.

[29]Quoted in Quick, "Crafting an Organizational Structure," p. 51.

[30]Brenda Paik Sunoo, "How Fun Flies at Southwest Airlines," *Personnel Journal* 74, no. 6 (June 1995), p. 62; Quick, "Crafting an Organizational Structure," p. 51; Freiberg and Freiberg, *Nuts,* p. 65.

[31]*Fortune,* May 2, 1994, p. 50.

If you see someone being a little ornery, you think, "Oh, he deserves a [rubber] cockroach in his drink." Of course we don't let him drink it, but the assumption is that we're given a lot of flexibility to let our personalities come out and express it to our customers . . . When people ask [me] what we're serving for food, I tear out [magazine] pictures of steak and potatoes and take it up to them . . . And they love it.[32]

Extrovertive, People-Oriented Employees   Kelleher recognized the importance of recruiting employees with extrovertive, people-oriented personalities:

We are interested in people who externalize, who focus on other people, who are motivated to help other people. We are not interested in navel gazers regardless of how lint-free their navels are.[33]

Southwest made every effort to recruit employees who were willing to go beyond the call of duty in serving customers and in working harmoniously with fellow employees. The model employee at Southwest was symbolized by what the company called LUV. LUV, according to Southwest's employee booklet, embodied the carrier's spirit of employees "caring about themselves, each other, and SWA's customers."[34] A core corporate value, Southwest's LUV began in the early 1970s when Southwest offered Love flights aboard the Love Airlines, promoted services within the Love Triangle, and served its passengers Love potions (drinks) and Love Bites (peanuts). It was later sustained by Southwest's choice of LUV as its common stock ticker symbol on the New York Stock Exchange,[35] and "LUV Lines" as the title of its monthly employee newsletter.[36]

To help nurture the desired employee traits, Southwest executives promoted the development of close relationships between the company and its employees' families as well as between the company and its loyal customers. Periodically, managers encouraged employees to bring their children to work and their spouses to company events. They also invited loyal customers to sit on company recruitment panels, to participate in company events, and to attend company parties and celebrations.[37]

The Culture Committee   Formed in 1990, the Culture Committee was dedicated to encouraging "Positively Outrageous Service."[38] Composed of some 100 employees representing a cross section of the organization, the Culture Committee was responsible for devising tributes, contests, and celebrations to keep the "'Southwest spirit" alive. Colleen Barrett, Southwest executive vice president and founder of the Culture Committee, said, "Sometimes we've created a couple of imaginary battles just to keep the blood flowing."[39] Committee members were zealots who exemplified the Southwest culture; they volunteered their time and attended four all-day meetings each year. Sometimes customers served on the Culture Committee.[40] Kelleher believed that the Culture Committee was critical: "We are not big on

---

[32]Sunoo, "How Fun Flies," pp. 70–71.

[33]Quoted in Quick, "Crafting an Organizational Structure," p. 52. The term *altruism* was used by Quick.

[34]Sunoo, "How Fun Flies," p. 72.

[35]Southwest Airlines, *A Tale of Two Men,* Fact Sheet, September 1997, p. 1.

[36]Freiberg and Freiberg, *Nuts,* p. 71.

[37]Freiberg and Freiberg, *Nuts,* p. 148; Donna Henderson, "Southwest Luvs Passengers, Employees, Profits," *Air Transport World* 28, no. 7 (July 1991), p. 37.

[38]Sunoo, "How Fun Flies," p. 72.

[39]Jesse Katz, "Southwest Airlines is the (_) Company on Earth: A) Zaniest B) Savviest; Answer: Both," *Los Angeles Times Magazine,* June 9, 1996.

[40]Sunoo, "How Fun Flies," p. 73.

EXHIBIT 5   Factors Distinguishing Southwest's Corporate Culture from the
Cultures of Other Carriers

What's Hot . . . (Southwest)	What's Not . . . (Other Carriers)
Men in casual attire	Men in suits
Women in comfortable shoes	Women in high heels
CEOs who ride Harleys	CEOs who ride in limos
Sweating on the job	Sweating in the gym
Open seating	Assigned seating
Hugs	Formal handshakes
Leaders	Managers
Flexibility	Strict policy

Source: "What's Hot and What's Not," published in *Southwest Airlines Plane Tails*—an in-house tabloid—in 1995. Quoted in Kevin Freiberg and Jackie Freiberg, *Nuts: Southwest Airlines' Crazy Recipe for Business and Personal Success* (Austin: Bard Press, 1996), p. 207.

---

committees at Southwest but of the committees we have, the Culture Committee is the most important."[41]

Violating the Cultural Norms   So well entrenched and so well guarded were Southwest cultural norms that no attempt to violate them went ignored. For example, a highly decorated military pilot once applied for a pilot's job at Southwest. On paper, he was a top-ranking candidate. But on his way to his Dallas interview he appeared cold, arrogant, and rude to both the customer service agent and the receptionist. Although he was highly qualified, his behavior suggested to the interviewing team (which included pilots) that he simply did not fit the Southwest culture. He was not hired.[42] On her first day of work, a secretary from a temporary agency jostled aggressively for an empty space in the crowded company parking lot. Because she made the mistake of violating one of Southwest's most sacred norms, courtesy, her "un-Southwesternly conduct" was immediately reported by witnesses. She was subsequently terminated.[43]

Quite often, new hires who discovered that they did not fit the mold resigned under heavy peer pressure. A few months after he had been hired, one distraught executive told Southwest EVP Colleen Barrett, "I just made a big mistake. I just don't like this touchy-feely [culture] . . . I feel like an absolute outcast."[44]

Awards and Honors   Award-winning employees were Southwest's cultural heroes and heroines; management regularly called attention to those who preformed heroically. During the 1980s and 1990s, Southwest Airlines granted its most prestigious annual awards—the Founder's and President's awards—to employees who distinguished themselves in customer service, community service, co-worker support, and program innovation. Other awards handed out by Southwest the following titles: Sense of Humor, LUV, Heart and Soul, Creativity and Guts, Training Excellence,

---

[41]Freiberg and Freiberg, *Nuts,* p. 165.
[42]Ibid., p. 68.
[43]*Los Angeles Times Magazine,* June 9, 1996.
[44]Ibid.

EXHIBIT 6   Unit Advertising Costs of U.S. Major Airlines 1994–96

Carrier	Cents per Available Seat Mile		
	1994	1995	1996
Alaska	0.12¢	0.11¢	0.11¢
America West	0.16	0.16	0.18
American	0.13	0.13	0.11
Continental	0.21	0.16	0.13
Delta	0.14	0.11	0.09
Northwest	0.15	0.15	0.16
Southwest	0.27	0.26	0.27
TWA	0.17	0.16	0.17
United	0.11	0.12	0.11
U.S. Air	0.13	0.09	0.10

Source: Based on carrier filings at the Department of Transportation, *Aviation Daily,* March 10, 1997, pp. 409–10.

Hairdresser of the Year, and Positively Outrageous Customer Service. In 1989, Southwest began recognizing its airline mechanics with the Top Wrench Annual Award (also given monthly and quarterly), and in 1992 Southwest's Culture Committee introduced a new recognition program aimed at employees who worked behind the scenes out of the public eye.[45] Recipients of the new Heroes of the Heart Award included Southwest's station administrative coordinators (1993), technical service employees (1994), flight operation employees (1995), and customer service coordinators (1996).[46]

Advertising and Culture   Just as Southwest's employees were the carrier's cultural heroes, Southwest's customers were its cultural fans. Southwest Airlines had spent generously on advertising that promoted its corporate culture, as shown in Exhibit 6. In a rather conservative industry, Southwest had created commercials and promotions that played up it's fun-loving, altruistic, and outrageous culture. One of the most successful promotion projects introduced by Southwest was its "Whale of a Surprise Project," which involved painting three Boeing 737s like killer whales. Undertaken in partnership with Sea World of Texas and Sea World of California, the project received enormous publicity, evoked a great deal of enthusiasm on the part of the traveling public, and appealed particularly to children.[47]

Another example of Southwest's ad campaign was its response to a 1992 Northwest Airlines commercial. Limiting the field of competition to the seven largest domestic carriers and thus excluding Southwest (the eighth), Northwest claimed to have won the Triple Crown for May 1992 and ran print and TV ads to publicize its claim. In a playful ad, Southwest announced:

---

[45]Freiberg and Freiberg, *Nuts,* pp. 192–97.

[46]Southwest Airlines, *A Tale of Two Men;* Sunoo, "How Fun Flies," pp. 72–73.

[47]Southwest Airlines, *A Tale of Two Men;* Godsey, "Top Gun," p. 25.

After lengthy deliberations at the highest executive levels, and extensive consultation with our legal department, we have arrived at an official corporate response to Northwest Airlines' claim to be number one in Customer Satisfaction.

"Liar Liar Pants on Fire."

. . . Northwest simply excluded Southwest Airlines from the competition.[48]

Southwest's ads were designed to reinforce the carrier's corporate culture in two ways: first, by attracting and persuading its customers and, second, by nurturing and energizing its employees. "When we create advertisements for Southwest . . . [w]e understand one fundamental premise," the president of a Southwest media agency observed, "[Southwest] employees watch TV too, . . . [s]o we role-model to [them]."[49] Management believed that running a commercial showing Southwest's employees working hard and fast to keep costs down and fares low was a powerful means of boosting employee morale.

Human Resources

Human resource practices at Southwest Airlines were shaped by the carrier's culture. Southwest Airlines had never laid off an employee,[50] a policy rooted partly in the carrier's familylike culture and partly in its continual growth, and its compensation structure had always rewarded seniority. Southwest Airlines also consistently adhered to the practice of internal promotion; Southwest managers typically rose up through the ranks, earning the respect of their former peers. Internal promotion contributed to cooperative labor–management relations at Southwest Airlines; unlike other major carriers, Southwest had never experienced a major labor dispute. Taken together, Southwest's human resource practices resulted in an exceptionally high level of job satisfaction; the annual employee turnover rate remained between 4 percent and 7 percent, the lowest in the industry.[51] As one Southwest employee said,

> Working here is truly an unbelievable experience. They treat you with respect, pay you well, and empower you. They use your ideas to solve problems. They encourage you to be yourself. I *love* going to work![52]

The People Department   In 1990 Southwest Airlines changed the name of its personnel department to the People Department. "We didn't realize we were setting a trend. We were just doing something that fits into our culture," Elisabeth Saratin, Southwest's vice president of people, explained. Located at the carrier's Dallas headquarters and staffed with 157 employees, the People Department managed recruitment, affirmative action and EEOC plans, learning and development, and compensation and benefits.[53]

Recruitment   Southwest recruited employees by means of newspaper and magazine ads, job fairs, and on-line promotion on the Internet. Typically, one in four applicants received an interview and one in eight applicants interviewed was hired. In 1997

---

[48]Southwest Airlines, *A Tale of Two Men;* Freiberg and Freiberg, *Nuts,* pp. 258–59.

[49]Freiberg and Freiberg, *Nuts,* p. 262.

[50]*Los Angeles Time Magazine,* June 9, 1996.

[51]"Southwest Airlines Charts a High Performance Flight," *Training and Development* 49, no. 6 (June 1995), p. 39; Flynn Gillian, "Southwest Airlines Won't Be Grounded by Strict Compensation Structure," *Personnel Journal* 74, no. 3 (March 1995), pp. 23–24; *Fortune,* January 12, 1998, p. 84.

[52]*Fortune,* January 12, 1998, p. 84.

[53]Sunoo, "How Fun Flies," p. 64; Henderson, "Southwest Luvs Passengers, Employees, Profits," p. 37.

Southwest received over 105,000 applications for just 3,000 positions.[54] Many of the applicants were Southwest customers who fit the carrier's "personality profile." They were other-oriented, extroverted, fun-loving individuals who responded to carefully-designed recruitment ads like the one showing Kelleher impersonating Elvis Presley:

> Work In A Place Where Elvis Has Been Spotted . . . The qualifications? It helps to be outgoing. Maybe even a bit off center. And be prepared to stay for a while . . . If this sounds good to you, just phone our jobline or send your resume. Attention: Elvis.[55]

Another recruitment ad, first used in 1991 and again in 1995, showed a child's picture of a tyrannosaur that was colored outside the lines. It said:

> Brian Shows An Early Aptitude for Working At Southwest Airlines . . . [A]t Southwest Airlines you get check pluses for breaking the mold. For "coloring outside the lines." Guess that's why we've ended up with flight attendants who occasionally break into song. Pilots who do halfway decent impersonations. And a CEO who does—well you never know what he's going to do . . . If Southwest Airlines sounds like a place where you like to work, call our jobline.[56]

Kelleher explained why Southwest's ads focused on attitudes and personalities rather than professional qualifications and skills:

> We can train people to do things where skills are concerned. But there is one capability we do not have and that is to change a person's attitude. So we prefer an unskilled person with a good attitude . . . [to] a highly skilled person with a bad attitude. We take people who come out of highly structured, hierarchical, dictatorial corporate environments if they have the attitude potential.[57]

Screening   Once selected for an interview, candidates were screened. Flight attendants, for instance, first appeared before a panel made up of peers, customers, and representatives of the People Department. The purpose of the interview was twofold: First, to evaluate the candidate's performance before a group—an important element in the flight attendant's job—and, second, to conduct a simple exercise that showed the extent to which the candidate was willing to sacrifice his or her own success for the success of others. Sitting in a large room, and granted adequate time, applicants were asked to prepare a five-minute presentation about themselves. As the presentations were delivered one after the other, the interviewers watched the audience (as well as the speakers) to see who was preoccupied with working on his or her presentation and who was cheering and supporting his or her potential team members. The result: only the applicants who supported the other applicants were likely to be hired, not the ones absorbed in polishing their own presentations.

Following the group interview, successful flight attendant candidates underwent three personal interviews conducted separately by a peer, a recruiter, and a representative of the hiring department. After appraising and ranking the candidates, the three interviewers then convened and reached a consensus on which candidates to hire.

In all job interviews, Southwest utilized the principles of Targeted Selection—an interviewing technique that identified specific dimensions necessary for matching people to jobs. One dimension critical to all job categories at Southwest was teamwork. An

---

[54]Sunoo, "How Fun Flies," pp. 64–65; "Fact Sheet," Southwest Airlines, January 1998, p. 4.

[55]Quoted in Sunoo, "How Fun Flies," p. 66.

[56]The ad is reprinted in Freiberg and Freiberg, *Nuts,* p. 70.

[57]Quoted in Quick, "Crafting an Organizational Structure," p. 51.

interviewer might say, "Tell me about a time in one of your prior jobs where you went above and beyond to assist a co-worker or " "Tell me about a time when you had a conflict with a co-worker."[58]

Training   Just as Southwest's personnel department was renamed the People Department, its training department was renamed the University for People. Located at Dallas's Love Field, the "university" was responsible for running most of Southwest's training programs. Its curriculum included leadership training programs for both new and experienced managers. Significantly, the University for People taught coaching, not policing, as the primary management style. All customer contact employees, including pilots, received customer care training. Employees also attended specialized courses on a variety of topics that included decision making, communication, stress management, safety, career development, employee relations, and performance appraisal. Once a year, Southwest supervisors and executives attended a two-day Frontline Training Program whose main purpose was cultural indoctrination; program coordinators selected a different company theme (teamwork, harmony, trust, diversity) each year and focused the training on creative activities and challenging exercises related to that theme.[59]

Orientation for new employees took place at the carrier's Dallas headquarters and at offices in Phoenix and Chicago. In 1995, for example, the University for People conducted two to five orientations per week, each accommodating between 20 and 100 new recruits.[60] During each orientation, participants were shown three videos. The first featured a group of Southwest employees describing their jobs in song and dance, including the "Southwest Airlines Shuffle":

> We're the Southwest team, that's what we are
> No MVP, we're each a big star
> It's fun to fly and it's fun to serve
> And fun is what our customers deserve.[61]

Kelleher too appeared in the video—clad in leather and rapping:

> My name is Herb
> Big Daddy-O
> You should all know me
> I run this show.[62]

The second video, called "The Graveyard Video," presented an overview of the airline industry, highlighting its volatile nature, competitive challenges, and potential rewards. The final video, "The Spirit Weaver," offered a short documentary of Southwest Airlines' history.[63]

Promotion   Asked once whether Southwest Airlines hired MBAs, Kelleher shot back, "Not if I can help it." "Our culture comes from the heart, not the mind," he said

[58]Sunoo, "How Fun Flies," p. 68; Freiberg and Freiberg, *Nuts,* pp. 67–68.

[59]Hallowell, "Southwest Airlines," p. 523; Sunoo, "How Fun Flies," pp. 71–72; *Training and Development* 49, no. 6 (June 1995), p. 39.

[60]Sunoo, "How Fun Flies," p. 71.

[61]Quoted in Hallowell, "Southwest Airlines," p. 521.

[62]Quoted in *Los Angeles Time Magazine,* June 9, 1996.

[63]Sunoo, "How Fun Flies," p. 71.

on another occasion.[64] In the mid-1990s an estimated 80 percent of all Southwest supervisory positions were filled internally. Employees could either apply for openings or be recommended by their supervisors. All employees applying for supervisory positions were subject to a one-to-one Targeted Selection interview process similar to the one they underwent when they first applied at the company. Not all candidates, however, received the same training. Candidates applying for low-level management positions attended a three-day "Leading with Integrity" class whose chief goal was to further the development of leadership and communication skills. Employees being considered for senior management positions ("Up and Coming Leaders") received training in every department of the company during a six-month period in which they kept their current job. At the end of the training period, representatives of the People Department analyzed the feedback from department heads, peers, and subordinates, and decided on the specific assignment of each candidate.[65]

Profit-Sharing, Benefits, and Compensation In 1973, Southwest introduced a profit-sharing plan, the first in the industry. Although the original plan covered only senior employees, by the mid-1990s all Southwest employees had become participants in the plan (eligibility began on January 1 following the initial appointment). Southwest Airlines allocated 15 percent of its net profits to the plan and invested 25 percent of an employee's profit-sharing account in Southwest stock. Not covered by a traditional pension plan, employees collected their profit sharing when they retired or left the company.[66]

Southwest also matched up to 100 percent of employees' contributions to 401(K) retirement plans, and offered employees the opportunity to purchase company stock at 90 percent of its market value through payroll deductions. Other benefits included a flexible health benefits program, free airline travel for employees and their families, and fully transferable airline passes for employees with distinguished accomplishments such as perfect attendance.[67]

Southwest Airlines paid competitive wages. According to union contracts covering 1997–98, the average monthly pay of Southwest pilots was nearly 10 percent above the industry average. Southwest pilots, however, worked longer hours than the pilots employed by any other major carrier save American West, flying an average of 85 monthly hours compared to the industry average of 80.2. Considering both wages and hours, the average hourly pay of Southwest pilots ($80) was slightly above the industry average, as shown in Exhibit 7.

Labor Relations Labor relations in the airline industry had long been regulated by the Railway Labor Act (RLA). The RLA sanctioned union representation by "class or craft" on a carrierwide basis, encouraged employees to form narrowly defined craft unions, and facilitated a high rate of unionization among employees covered by the act. Not surprisingly, air transportation is one of the nation's most highly unionized industries.

Like the old established carriers, Southwest was a unionized airline; about 84 percent of its employees belonged to a labor organization. Southwest negotiated contracts with a variety of unions, each representing distinct classes of employees: The Teamsters

---

[64]*Los Angeles Times Magazine,* June 9, 1996.

[65]Sunoo, "How Fun Flies," p. 72; Hallowell, "Southwest Airlines," p. 524.

[66]Henderson, "Southwest Luvs Passengers, Employees, Profits," p. 38; Freiberg and Freiberg, *Nuts,* pp. 99–100; *Fortune,* May 2, 1994, p. 47.

[67]Henderson, "Southwest Luvs Passengers, Employees, Profits," p. 38; *Fortune,* May 2, 1994, p. 47.

EXHIBIT 7   Average Monthly Salaries, Average Monthly Flight, Hours, and
            Average Hourly Pay of Pilots Employed by the Major Carriers,
            1997–98

Carrier	Average Monthly Flight Hours	Average Pay (5-Year Seniority, Medium-Size Aircraft)*	Average Hourly Pay
Alaska	80	$5,194	$ 65
America West	90	5,608	63
American	69	5,734	83
Continental	82	4,858	59
Delta	78	8,315	107
Northwest	74	5,237	71
Southwest	85	6,839	80
TWA	71	3,847	54
United	79	7,541	95
U.S. Air	82	7,912	96
Average	80.2	$6,239	$ 78

*Boeing 737, Boeing 757, MD-80
Source: Air Inc., "Pilots Salary Survey, 1997–98," *Aviation Daily,* April 14, 1997, p. 81.

represented airline mechanics, stock clerks, and aircraft cleaners; the International Association of Machinists (IAM) represented customer service and reservation employees; the Transport Workers Union (TWU) represented flight attendants; the Southwest Airline Pilots Association (SWAPA) represented pilots; and the Ramp Operations and Provisioning Association (ROPA) represented baggage handlers.[68]

Southwest Airlines had experienced only one strike since 1971, a six-day machinist walkout in the early 1980s.[69]

Clearly, Southwest had used its corporate culture to facilitate labor–management cooperation. Getting the employees to personally identify with the company, Herb Kelleher persuaded representatives of the Southwest unions to give up restrictive work rules and narrow job classifications, and to accept instead flexible employment practices. As a result, Southwest's union contacts—unlike those of other carriers—stated that any qualified employee may perform any function, hence allowing the Texas carrier to cross-utilize crew members, achieve a record turnaround time, and thereby save both time and money. It was not uncommon, indeed, for Southwest pilots to help at the boarding gates, for ticket agents to load and unload luggage, and for flight attendants to pick up the trash and stock provisions.[70]

Southwest Airlines had distinguished itself in still another way. Its most influential union, SWAPA, was an in-house organization, unaffiliated with outside organizations and totally committed to labor–management cooperation. Representing more than 2,000 pilots, SWAPA negotiated its labor agreements directly with Herb Kelleher. In 1995, following seven months of negotiations, representatives of SWAPA and

[68]Hallowell, "Southwest Airlines," p. 524; Henderson, "Southwest Luvs Passengers, Employees, Profits," p. 38; Freiberg and Freiberg, *Nuts,* pp. 218–19.

[69]*Fortune,* May 2, 1994, p. 47.

[70]Hallowell, "Southwest Airlines," p. 524; *Fortune,* May 2, 1994, p. 50; Freiberg and Freiberg, *Nuts,* p. 57; Patrice Apodaca, "Southwest Readies for United's Shuttle," *Los Angeles Times,* August 23, 1994.

Kelleher signed a 10-year contract that linked Southwest pilots' compensation to the financial success of the airline, effectively freezing wages during the first five years in lieu of stock options and limited bonuses tied to profitability. Beyond the first five years, the contract guaranteed pilots an annual wage hike of 3 percent, in addition to compensation based on profitability.[71] Described by SWAPA president Gary Kerans as "a positive example of good-faith bargaining," called by Kelleher "a bold statement by our pilots,"[72] and cited by Southwest vice president James F. Parker as "a tribute to the farsightedness and . . . visionary attitude of our pilots and their confidence in the company,"[73] the contract reflected Southwest pilots' willingness to gamble on the financial future of the carrier.

Leadership

Over the years, Kelleher's leadership style had crystallized around three key principles, each addressing a different area of management. The first pertained to cost controls. Until 1994, Kelleher had personally approved every expenditure of over $1,000—not because he did not trust his employees but because he knew that if they knew he was watching, they were likely to be "just that much more careful." Kelleher regularly monitored Southwest's costs, and he constantly urged his employees to do the same.[74]

The second principle concerned customer service. Initially, Kelleher read every customer letter, but as Southwest grew he could no longer do so and instead read a weekly sample of customer letters. Experience had taught him a valuable lesson: "The most important, pertinent information about what's wrong in your company comes from your customers. That's why their letters come to my office." Customer complaints identify and localize problems so that they can be addressed and solved, Kelleher explained, adding, "We don't tell [employees] what to do about [customer complaints]. That's up to them. But we let them know that there's a problem that needs fixing."[75]

The third and most important of Kelleher's management principles involved employees. "My parents really instilled in me the idea that everybody should be treated with dignity and respect, and that titles, traditions, ranks, status, and class didn't matter," said Kelleher.[76] He applied this egalitarian notion to his management style and, moreover, led by example. He had been known to come into the cleaners' break room at 3:00 AM on Sunday and pass out donuts or put on a pair of overalls to clean the plane. Every year on Thanksgiving eve—the airline industry's busiest day—he pitched in, helping the Dallas ground crew load luggage and stock provisions. He always insisted that employees come first and customers second, making it clear that the customers were sometimes wrong ("We don't carry those sorts of customers. We write to them . . . 'Fly somebody else. Don't abuse our people.'"). When asked what advice he could offer other CEOs Kelleher said, "Spend more time with your people and less time with other CEOs."[77]

---

[71]Jennifer Laabs, "Southwest Airlines Expected to Reach Ground Breaking Wage Agreement with Pilots," *Personnel Journal* 74, no. 2 (February 1995), p. 12; *Monthly Labor Review* 118, no. 3 (March 1995), p. 64.

[72]*Monthly Labor Review* 118, no. 3 (March 1995), p. 64.

[73]Laabs, "Southwest Airlines," p. 12.

[74]*Fortune,* May 2, 1994, p. 47.

[75]"Southwest Airlines' Herb Kelleher: Unorthodoxy at Work," *Management Review,* January 1995, pp. 11–12.

[76]*Los Angeles Time Magazine,* June 9, 1996.

[77]Freiberg and Freiberg, *Nuts,* pp. 283, 268, 222.

Southwest's Future

Despite Southwest's remarkable success, there were concerns about the carrier's future. One had to do with the effect that Southwest's rapid growth and expansion across the country would have on costs. Southwest's cost advantage over other carriers was rooted in its short-haul service and its rapid turnaround time. Expansion kept stretching Southwest's routes well beyond the company's original service area. During 1996–97, for example, Southwest extended its services to Providence, Baltimore, and three Florida destinations, offering long-haul flights of over 700 miles between Providence and Tampa, Baltimore and Tampa, and Nashville and Fort Lauderdale. In June 1997, Southwest initiated nonstop services between Nashville and two California destinations (Los Angeles and Oakland), spanning a distance of over 1,800 miles.[78] Because longer flights were less labor intensive than shorter ones—there were fewer occasions to load luggage, fuel up, and clean planes—Southwest's labor productivity advantage was expected to decline as its route structure extended. Similarly, because flights lasting five hours often required meals, Southwest's food cost was likely to increase significantly. Finally, winter weather conditions in some of the northern locations could increase turnaround times and/or cause flight delays.

A second concern involved discontent among some of its employees. In June 1997, Southwest flight attendants rejected a new union contract by a margin of 3,123 to 283, or 92 percent.[79] Such a rejection was unexpected by both the union leaders and Southwest management, leading to further negotiations and an improved contract proposal (providing for better compensation and shorter hours for flight attendants) on December 17. Nevertheless, only 58 percent of the unionized flight attendants voted to approve the revised contract.[80]

Last, Kelleher's impending retirement was a source of concern. A heavy drinker (Wild Turkey) and smoker (five packs a day), the 67-year-old executive had periodic health problems. Asked in November 1997 when he planned to retire, Kelleher replied, "In about 2010."[81] According to Wall Street analysts, Kelleher had neither chosen a second in command nor groomed a likely successor. To be sure, he had assembled an impressive team of potential successors, each contending for the top job; yet Kelleher played so many diverse roles at Southwest—astute executive, innovative strategist, motivational leader, prankster, guru, and cheerleader—that it would be hard for a single executive to fill his shoes.

(The company's Web addresses are *www.iflyswa.com* and *www.southwest.com.* In particular, check out Southwest's financial performance during the 1990s as reported in its most recent annual report. Does its performance surprise you?)

---

[78]Scott McCartney, "Turbulence Ahead: Competitors Quake as Southwest Air Is Set to Invade the Northwest," *The Wall Street Journal,* October 23, 1996; "Southwest Airlines Lands Plenty of Florida Passengers," *The Wall Street Journal,* November 11, 1997; "Southwest Airlines Plan Long-Haul Nonstop Service," *Aviation Week & Space Technology,* February 3, 1997.

[79]*Aviation Daily,* June 23, 1997; Allen R. Myerson, "Air Herb," *New York Time Magazine,* November 9, 1997, p. 39.

[80]Telephone interview with Paul Sweetin, president of the flight attendants union, Dallas, February 5, 1998.

[81]*New York Times Magazine,* November 9, 1997, p. 39; *Fortune,* May 2, 1994, p. 52.

GUS PAGONIS AND THE SEARS LOGISTICS GROUP

Stewart W. Husted, *Lynchburg College*

Keith C. Jones, *Lynchburg College*

After years of attempting a turnaround at Sears with only mixed success, CEO Arthur Martinez knew he needed to make some major organizational changes in the huge retail giant. It was his feeling that logistics activities in Sears's value chain represented one of the last great frontiers for cutting costs and improving company profits. Therefore, Martinez hired an executive search firm to find the right person for the job of overhauling Sears's logistical operations. That search led to Heidelberg, Germany, and the office of Lieutenant General William Gus Pagonis, the man who orchestrated the massive buildup of people and military supplies during the Persian Gulf War. At the interview, Pagonis convinced the headhunter that he had plenty of ideas on how Sears could transform its logistics operations and, in so doing, save millions of dollars. Pagonis's confidence was based on a career spent in logistics and on having made the U.S. Army's logistical capabilities one of the Allies' most valuable military assets during Operation Desert Storm. In November of 1993, Pagonis began his new job at Sears.

Pagonis had declared in his 1992 book, *Moving Mountains: Lessons in Leadership from the Gulf War,* that any corporate executive could apply his basic leadership style effectively and achieve organizational success. During his long military career, Pagonis blended traditional military leadership principles and his own personal style to accomplish tremendous results. Pagonis's new position as executive vice president of logistics at Sears provided him with the challenge of adapting his skills to fit the organizational situation and problems of a corporation. Instead of a budget of billions and an army of half a million, Pagonis now controlled a budget of $1.4 billion and a workforce of 10,000 associates and 2,300 third-party warehouse operators.[1]

Before Pagonis came on board at Sears many inside the company had doubts about hiring a 52-year-old retired army general and, moreover, an outsider. Some asked, "Are moving tanks and ammo to soldiers in the desert similar to moving chain saws, stoves, and clothing to consumers?" Others wondered whether a Pentagon veteran could control costs, and whether a military officer's autocratic style would work in an environment

---

[1]William G. Pagonis, interviews on August 25–26, 1995, and October 24, 1996, Lynchburg, Virginia; July 7–9, 1997, Hoffman Estates, Illinois, and Columbus, Ohio.

that required teamwork.[2] But within two weeks, Pagonis had presented a new mission statement and vision to his organization, the Sears Logistics Group (SLG), and had begun educating its members about what he expected of them as leaders and associates.

GUS PAGONIS'S BACKGROUND AND EXPERIENCE

William Gus Pagonis did not intend to make the military a career. Although he enrolled in the Reserve Officers Training Corps at Penn State, he expected to take a job at his cousin's shipping company. Before that could happen, however, the company went out of business and so, in 1964, with a degree in logistics, Pagonis applied for and received a Regular Army commission and entered the military full-time. In 1969, Pagonis returned to Penn State to earn an MBA with a specialization in business logistics and operations research.[3]

During his career in the military, Pagonis rose through the ranks as an infantry and transportation officer. He distinguished himself with two tours in Vietnam and others in Germany and the Pentagon. In Vietnam, he received the Combat Infantryman Badge, the Silver Star, the Bronze Star (with three oak leaf clusters), the Air Medal (three times), and the Army Commendation Medal.[4]

In August 1990, just after Lieutenant General Pagonis arrived at Fort McPherson, Georgia, to assume his responsibilities as Director of Logistics, Forces Command, he received a phone call from the chief of staff to meet immediately with Lieutenant General John Yeosock, commander of Army Central Command. Pagonis jogged down to Yeosock's quarters and met with other army leaders who were having an emergency meeting to develop a logistics plan to support U.S. forces if deployed by the president against the Iraqi invasion of Kuwait. Soon the group flew to McDill Air Force Base in Tampa, Florida, where the assessment was refined. After returning to Fort McPherson the next day and resuming his normal duties, Pagonis was notified that he was to join Yeosock in Saudi Arabia. His temporary assignment was "host nation consultant."

Pagonis and his wife, Cheri, moved 30 times in Pagonis's 29-year military career. This time, Pagonis headed home to say goodbye to Cheri, made a last-minute stop at Dairy Queen (a Pagonis favorite) for a banana split, and started the process of calling the 20 logistics specialists he wanted to serve on his command team in Saudi Arabia. He knew that each of those specialists understood his management style and could hit the ground running.

When his temporary assignment grew, Pagonis stayed on in Saudi Arabia to head up logistics for troop deployment to the Persian Gulf. He remained in command for all three phases of the war, from Desert Shield to Desert Storm and Operation Farewell. In the final phase, the toughest one for a logistician, Pagonis's 22nd Support Command redeployed 365,000 troops, 117,000 wheeled and 12,000 tracked vehicles, 2,000 helicopters, and 41,000 containers of supplies.[5] Never before in military history had a single commander been responsible for all the ships, planes, trucks, and food supplies for the Army. Eighteen months later, in January 1992, Pagonis left Saudi Arabia for Ger-

---

[2]Robert Bernier, "Retired General Speeds Deliveries, Cuts Costs, Helps Sears Rebound," *The Wall Street Journal,* July 16, 1996.

[3]William G. Pagonis with Jeffery L. Cruikshank, *Moving Mountains: Lessons in Leadership from the Gulf War* (Boston: Harvard Business School Press, 1992).

[4]William G. Pagonis, personal biography, 1997.

[5]William G. Pagonis, "The Work of the Leader," *Harvard Business Review,* November 1992.

many, to take the position of Commanding General, 21st Theater Army Area Command, his last military assignment.

Just as Pagonis began thinking about his military retirement, he was approached by the executive headhunting firm that was seeking a logistics leader for Sears and Roebuck. Soon after his interview with Sears CEO Arthur Martinez in the summer of 1993, Pagonis began putting together his plan for logistics at Sears. By November, everyone at Sears knew that Gus Pagonis was in charge of logistics, and that things would never be the same.

BACKGROUND OF SEARS, ROEBUCK AND COMPANY

Sears, Roebuck and Company, once America's top retailer, strayed from its retailing business during the 1980s and became a conglomerate of retailing and financial services companies (Dean Witter brokerage, Allstate insurance, Discover credit card services, and Coldwell Banker real estate). By 1990, the company's net income had tumbled 60 percent. In 1992, Sears lost its place as the biggest general merchandise retailer to Kmart (which was itself later surpassed by Wal-Mart). From 1978 to 1988, Sears's share of general merchandise sales dropped from 18 percent to 13 percent. It was apparent to then CEO Edward Brennan and his management team that Sears's strategy and operations needed drastic changes. Brennan implemented an "everyday low prices" policy; reorganized merchandising around seven unique specialty superstores, such as the Brand Central electronics department; and added such name brands as Nike and General Electric to the Sears merchandise mix. Brennan also divested Sears's nonretailing businesses.

Brennan believed Sears had to revamp its corporate structure as well as revitalize its retailing strategy. Sears was top-heavy. Its selling and administrative expenses were a bloated 30 percent of sales versus 24 percent at J. C. Penney and 14.9 percent at Wal-Mart.[6] Thus, Brennan began by restructuring the headquarters building in Chicago, closing 14 regional offices, and downsizing the organization. In total, more than 50,000 jobs were eventually cut at Sears.

In 1992, Brennan retired and outsider Arthur Martinez from Saks Fifth Avenue was hired as CEO of the Sears Merchandise Group. Martinez said in an interview for *Financial World*, "I came in and said to myself that time is not my ally here, time is my enemy . . . I observed J. C. Penney over a 10-year period and said we need to do it in half the time or less . . . The company didn't know who it wanted to be or who it wanted to compete with . . . Did Sears want to be a discounter, a department store or a specialty store? At the end of the day, what happens to irrelevant stores is that they cease to exist. I think Sears was big enough that it could have gone on for a while, but ultimately it was heading toward an unhappy end."[7]

In his first 18 months, Martinez closed 113 poorly performing stores and shut down the legendary 101-year-old catalog sales unit, which was losing $1.75 billion a year. He then put into place a $4 billion chainwide refurbishing plan and introduced a lineup of 12 concise niche catalogs. The niche catalog operation was farmed out to Hanover Direct, a producer of such successful catalogs as Tweeds and Domestications.[8] In addition, Martinez went to work on improving Sears's image as a retailer.

---

[6]Patricia Sellers, "Why Bigger Is Badder at Sears," *Fortune,* December 5, 1998, p. 79.

[7]Debra Sparks, "Arthur Martinez: *Financial World's* CEO of the Year," *Financial World,* March 25, 1996, p. 48.

[8]Susan Chandler, "Sears Turnaround Is Real—For Now," *Business Week,* p. 102.

He boosted the company's $1 billion marketing budget; expanded the merchandise mix from 40 percent national brands to 50 percent; purchased Orchard Supply Hardware Stores; rescinded the company's policy of honoring only Sears and Discover credit cards; and launched a stylish $40 million ad campaign ("Come See the Softer Side of Sears") by Young & Rubicam that targeted Sears's core female shoppers. Sears thought of itself as a "guys" store for home appliances, auto centers, and Craftsman tools. Marketing research, however, revealed that women were Sears's gatekeeper shoppers.[9] Sears discovered that most of its women shoppers were between 25 and 54, worked, had children, owned a home, and had a median family income of $37,500 (range $25,000 to $60,000). To the company's dismay, women shopped at Sears for their husbands and children, but not for themselves. To change that trend, Sears expanded store space for women's apparel (60 percent of Sears's profits came from apparel sales) and improved the quality of merchandise. It also added a high-volume cosmetics department (Circle of Beauty).

Exhibit 1 presents a five-year summary of Sears' recent financial performance.

THE CHANGES INITIATED BY GUS PAGONIS

It was Arthur Martinez who determined the need to create a position, executive vice president of logistics, and who selected Gus Pagonis to fill it; Martinez believed it was essential that Sears recruit key people with a variety of backgrounds to help shake up the corporation and to rethink the way Sears did things. Pagonis began the shake-up by organizing Sears's logistics chain into four distinct channels: Direct Delivery, Take With, Fashion, and Specialty. Pagonis believed this structure, supported by a Vendor Relations and Transportation unit, was a good fit not only with Sears's own logistical processes and retail channel strategy but also with the company's product families, supplied by more than 4,000 vendors.

Martinez and Pagonis realized that Sears needed to make big reductions in the costs of its logistical activities and in the costs of goods it purchased from suppliers. The search for supply-chain cost savings led Sears to drop its battery supplier of 26 years, Johnson Controls, in favor of A. C. Delco and Exide Corporation. Delco and Exide offered better quality batteries at prices that would ultimately save Sears tens of millions of dollars. In addition, Pagonis and his staff found that using Sears trucks to pick up goods at the plants of certain manufacturers was more economical than having the goods shipped via third-party freight carriers to Sears distribution centers.

Pagonis also instituted better inventory management techniques, improving the inventory turnover rate from 3.4 to 3.7 within 12 months. In 1996, the Sears logistics network moved more than 565 million pieces of merchandise through 22 distribution centers to more than 2,500 Sears stores. Furthermore, the Sears distribution system made more than 4 million deliveries to customers' homes of large products such as appliances, furniture, and home improvement items. The home delivery system consisted of 187 local-market delivery warehouses that off-loaded deliveries of appliances, furniture, and other bulky items from manufacturers. Customers selected items they wanted from the showroom displays in area Sears stores, and the local-market warehouse delivered those items to the customers' homes. Sears's highly automated Fashion Center delivered more than 250 million pieces of floor-ready merchandise to retail shoppers. The entire distribution network was supported by a

---

[9]Sparks, "Arthur Martinez," p. 51.

EXHIBIT 1 Five-Year Summary of Sears's Financial Performance, 1993–97
(In millions of dollars)

	1997	1996	1995	1994	1993
Operating Results					
Revenues	$41,296	$38,064	$34,835	$33,021	$30,427
Costs and expenses	39,302	35,981	33,130	30,288	28,265
Interest	1,409	1,365	1,373	1,279	1,318
Operating income	1,994	2,083	1,705	1,454	844
Other income	106	22	23	17	110
Income before income taxes	2,100	2,105	1,728	1,471	954
Income taxes	912	834	703	614	329
Income from continuing operations	1,188	1,271	1,025	857	625
Income from discontinued operations	—	—	776	402	1,960
Extraordinary gain (loss)	—	—	—	195	(211)
Net income	$ 1,188	$ 1,271	$ 1,801	$ 1,454	$ 2,374
Financial Position					
Retained interest in transferred credit card receivables	$3,316	$2,260	$5,579	$3,543	$2,947
Credit card receivables, net	19,843	19,303	14,527	14,658	12,959
Property and equipment, net	6,414	5,878	5,077	4,253	4,401
Merchandise inventories	5,044	4,646	4,033	4,044	3,518
Net assets of discontinued operations	—	36,167	—	7,231	8,701
Total assets	38,700	3,533	33,130	37,312	37,911
Short-term borrowings	5,208	14,907	5,349	6,190	4,636
Long-term debt	15,632	14,907	11,774	9,985	10,790
Total debt	20,840	18,440	17,123	16,175	15,426
Percent of debt to equity	356%	373%	391%	453%	521%
Shareholders' equity	$5,862	$4,945	$4,385	$10,801	$11,664

Source: 1997 annual report.

strategy team that ferreted out innovative logistics enhancements and a finance section charged with ensuring that any improvements generated a positive bottom-line contribution.[10]

During the mid-1990s, Sears's new executive team made progress in achieving its vision "to make Sears a compelling place to shop, work, and invest." Pagonis fashioned a distribution organization capable of meeting the needs of the company's 66 Orchard Supply Hardware stores, 801 mall stores, 138 NTW tire stores, 121 Tire America stores, 390 company-owned Western Auto stores, 185 Parts America auto supply stores, 900 independently owned Western Auto stores, 322 franchised Sears dealers, 83 Sears Hardware stores, and 125 HomeLife furniture stores. In preparing for

---

[10]James Ireland, interview at Hoffman Estates, July 7, 1997.

an ever faster changing new century, Sears knew that demographics and information technologies would play an increasingly important part in its strategy.[11]

PAGONIS'S APPROACH TO LEADERSHIP AND MANAGING PEOPLE

Gus Pagonis firmly believed that leaders were developed over time through both training and experience. He also recognized that every leader employed his or her own management and leadership style. Pagonis believed that, in order for a corporate leader to be successful, he or she had to develop certain building blocks and techniques (see Exhibit 2). He called this development the "corporate success chain."

All leaders, according to Pagonis, should document and communicate to their subordinates how they operate and what they expect of their people. Pagonis himself did this through written "bulletins." He began using bulletins in 1977 as a battalion commander at Fort Eustis, Virginia, when he found that he could easily brief his staff but that getting word down to his lieutenants and troops was more difficult. At Sears, Pagonis's bulletins were "chopped" by his Sears Log Council, which consisted of the top 30 executives in the Sears Logistics Group (SLG)—*chopping* was the process of agreeing or disagreeing with a bulletin and providing feedback within 60 days. Once the 60-day chopping exercise was completed and received Pagonis's approval, a bulletin became policy.

Under Pagonis, the SLG relied on a "playbook" composed of eight current bulletins, each designed to be a practical guide presented in specific detail. Pagonis and the Log Council revised the bulletins periodically, not merely for the sake of change but as part of a constant effort to define current processes and to improve them. Pagonis also felt that it was essential to standardize the SLG's processes across disciplines.

Communications

Because Pagonis wanted to be kept informed on "all things, regardless of what they were,"[12] he used a wide variety of communications techniques.

Ups/Downs (Negative-free Environment)   Many of the successful management techniques Pagonis implemented at Sears were ones he had perfected in the military. One of his favorites was the "three ups/three downs evaluation system." In an interview for the *McKinsey Quarterly* in 1996, Pagonis stated,

> In my first two weeks here, I was getting no negative information. I kept asking, "Aren't there any problems?" The answer would invariably be, "No, everything is fine." Then I said, "OK, each of you will give me three ups and three downs." We now require that people who come to our meetings tell us three ups and three downs about what they wish to report; they also need to share with us how they plan to fix the downs. Initially people had a problem with the downs. They would put up a chart with their ups, but no downs. But when we told them that they either start providing downs or we would start filling them in for them, we began to see downs listed.
>
>   We also use the "two ups and two downs" approach in our personal evaluation system, and suggest to our associates what they can do to fix their downs. It's of little use to tell someone that they have a problem with their writing, unless we can also tell them, "Penn

[11]Ibid.
[12]G. Pagonis, interview, July 7, 1997.

EXHIBIT 2	Building Blocks to Leadership

1. Loose and tight laboratories.
2. Know yourself.
3. Present yourself.
4. Know the mission.
5. Develop your subordinates.
6. Develop your tools.
7. Apply your tools.
8. Reeducate yourself.
9. Tailor the system.

Source: William G. Pagonis with Jeffery L. Cruikshank, *Moving Mountains: Lessons in Leadership from the Gulf War* (Boston: Harvard Business School Press, 1992), pp. 159–97.

State is offering a course in writing and I am signing you up to take it." We are trying to create a "negative-free" environment. Only then will we get people to open up to others and their managers about problems they face at work. We like to say: "Bad news doesn't get better with age."[13]

Sensing Sessions   Pagonis's "sensing sessions" gave all levels of employees an opportunity to voice their concerns, ask questions, or discuss whatever was on their minds. There was no agenda for these informal meetings. By listening to their employees at these sessions, managers could ascertain the level of morale within the organization. All of Pagonis's "report directs" (individuals he directly supervised) and distribution managers held various types of monthly sensing sessions.

3 × 5 Cards and E-mail[14]   Pagonis introduced SLG employees to the practice of writing notes on 3 × 5 cards to keep him and other senior managers informed of issues as they arose. The notes were meant to be handwritten (unless a subordinate couldn't write legibly), simple, and short. Cards were forwarded through the writer's director to Pagonis unless the information was personal or confidential. In that case, the note was placed in a sealed blue envelope marked "3 × 5 card for Gus." Cards could also be delivered to Pagonis or his staff anywhere in the United States by fax or by using a specially designed e-mail format available on the Sears network.

Green Express   Pagonis received the 3 × 5 cards daily and returned them as quickly as possible. On the back of each, he wrote his directions and comments in green (a color reserved for him). The "green express" cards were delivered directly to the associate via fax, e-mail, or the company's mail system.

Departmental Visits   Pagonis visited every "report direct" several times a month in his or her staff section. Visiting departments gave Pagonis an opportunity to talk informally with associates and discuss or cover anything the report direct chose. Even if the report direct was not around, Pagonis still visited the section. Pagonis believed face-to-face communications gave him an opportunity to learn more about the personal side of individuals, to know what was on their minds, and to stay abreast of their unique situations such as family circumstances. For example, when Pagonis learned one employee had a critically ill child who needed care at odd hours, he allowed the associate

---

[13]Graham Sharman, "Nobody Calls Me General Anymore," *The McKinsley Quarterly,* no. 3, 1996, p. 114.

[14]*Sears Logistics Group Bulletin,* No. 1, p. 3.

EXHIBIT 3   Distribution Center in Columbus, Ohio

to work a flextime schedule. This was done without going through formal Human Resource Department procedures.

Field Visits   Pagonis believed that visiting field operations was critical because it gave him a firsthand grasp of how well SLG directives were being understood and implemented. He also used field visits to determine what could be done to make the jobs of associates easier. Because Pagonis frequently used the corporate helicopter or one of two corporate jets to travel to the various field sites, he made sure that his visits were well planned and productive. A normal Pagonis walk-through of a facility (many of which were as long as four to five football fields—see Exhibit 3) lasted only 20 to 30 minutes. Pagonis knew what or whom he wanted to see and went directly to his destination. Because facility associates were used to seeing him, he did not create a storm effect as he moved through. Many associates joked at how fast he moved and hoped they could keep up with him.

Sit-down Meetings   All SLG meetings were required to begin and end on time. Pagonis scheduled the weekly sit-down meeting for senior staff or their representatives from 7:15 to 9 AM. These meetings were the primary method of distributing guidance or information from the CEO and the Executive Committee. A typical meeting was attended by approximately 25 to 30 staff members and began with a principal or a representative making a five-minute presentation. Each presenter was given three minutes to review three ups and three downs; then a kitchen timer rang and the presenter had two minutes to wrap up before the final bell. At that time, the next presenter stood and took his or her turn. If an issue needed more time, Pagonis allocated the time or asked the presenter to schedule a "Please See Me (PSM)" time, which was available through a sign-up roster. Pagonis strictly adhered to the PSM time allocations to prevent people from waiting in the outer office.

Despite the strict scheduling, lively discussions and disagreements did develop in the sit-down meetings. Pagonis tried to establish the notion of a nonhierarchical workplace in which anyone could challenge Pagonis, any of the vice presidents, or each other. For example, at one meeting, Pagonis said he wanted to turn guard dogs loose in a central returns center in Atlanta where there had been a truck break-in resulting in the theft of merchandise. He felt dogs would be the most effective way to deter theft. However, others said they felt that dogs were not the solution because of liability issues and the relatively high cost of maintaining a dog patrol.

Pagonis said, "People who do not know the logistics group are often surprised that we have such a level of disagreement at our meetings. I do not blame them. How many organizations can you go into where, in a meeting, vice presidents argue with each other in front of their bosses and with their boss? And what is nice about it is that when they leave the meeting, they do not feel frustrated or that they have missed an opportunity to present their case. There are no side meetings that take place before or after our meetings where people say 'I did not get a chance to cover this' or 'I wonder what he meant by that.'"[15]

Another example of the nonhierarchical atmosphere of the sit-down meetings was that section representatives could make decisions on behalf of their bosses, who had only 48 hours to overturn a decision if they chose. A boss who didn't challenge a decision in the allotted time had to live with it.

Stand-up Meetings   Stand-up meetings were scheduled Tuesday through Friday from 8:00 to 8:30 AM and were held even if Pagonis was absent. To a first-time attendee, having a 30-minute meeting with 15 to 20 people crowded into a small conference room (or, often, standing outside the door of the executive suite) was unbelievable—see Exhibit 4. Despite the fact that anyone could attend, not everyone was expected to speak. It was common for stand-up meetings to last less than 15 minutes. Stand-ups were used to cover hot topics and to follow up on previous guidance and directives. Unless Pagonis was notified within 24 hours of a disagreement with any of the comments or directives given at the stand-up meeting, he assumed there was no "disconnect" (lack of communication or disagreement).

The Please See Me (PSM) System   Often 3 × 5 cards and other notes were returned to staff with the Please See Me (PSM) abbreviation written on them by Pagonis. The PSM notation was written in green ink and could be handled at a stand-up meeting or through a direct visit to Pagonis. For example, "PSM—YL" meant "I'll see you at your location. "PSM—SUPER HOT" meant "Get to me *Now!*" Notes (even routine ones) were not allowed to accumulate beyond a five-day work period.

Matrix Information/Decision Papers   Another Pagonis communication vehicle involved digesting information into a concise and easily readable report suitable for background briefing or decision making. These reports, known as "matrix papers", were limited to one sheet of paper. Key points, ups, downs, and a bottom line (outcome or decision required) were presented in a bulleted-list format. A matrix paper contained a "chop block" at the bottom or on the back. It also included a concur/nonconcur from Finance, Information Systems, and Log Cell Strategy departments. Other chops included

---

[15]Sharman, "Nobody Calls Me General Anymore."

EXHIBIT 4   Pagonis and His Staff at a Stand-up Meeting

departments involved in the issue. A comments section was optional. An example of a matrix paper is shown in Exhibit 5. A matrix information paper was designed to prepare the staff for a meeting or to bring associates up to speed on a topic. A matrix decision paper was designed to lay out pertinent information so that a decision could be made.

The Command Climate at Sears and within the SLG

The Sears Executive Committee consisted of the company's 13 top officers. Headed by CEO Arthur C. Martinez, the committee included the presidents of the various segments (Automotive Group, Credit, Merchandising, Full-Line Stores, and Home Stores); the chief financial officer; the senior executive vice president of marketing; the general council and secretary; the chief information officer; the executive vice president of administration; and the executive vice president of logistics (Gus Pagonis). The committee met weekly to develop corporate strategies, goals, and objectives; it also established the command climate for the entire Sears organization.

In the third *Sears Logistics Group (SLG) Bulletin,* Pagonis provided a review of Sears's strategy and how it fit into the game plan for the SLG. Pagonis clearly stated that the SLG game plan must "focus on and integrate with the Sears strategies and goals." The key elements of management's efforts to get Sears back on track were making Sears a compelling place to shop, a market focus, a winning culture, a focus on the core retailing business, and continuous improvement in costs. (See Exhibit 6 for how SLG goals integrated with Sears's overall strategies and goals.)

The bulletin also provided the SLG mission statement and vision as well as directives to field units on how to prepare goals, objectives, and imperatives. This guidance is summarized below.

EXHIBIT 5   Sample Matrix Paper, Sears Logistics Group

MATRIX PAPER

Information Paper: ____X____	September 11, 1995
Decision Paper _____	Bill Kenney, X68378
	Strategy & Analysis

Subject: Penn State Logistics Leaders Forum V

Background

- I attended the Logistics Forum sponsored by Penn State on Sept. 6–8, 1995. The Forum addressed five key themes: (1) Global Supply Chain Issues; (2) Supply Chain Management; (3) Technology for the Supply Chain; (4) Activity-Based Costing for Transportation and Logistics; and (5) Concurrent Session on Performance Measures, Third Party Logistics, Organization Issues and Transportation Issues.
- Session was facilitated by John Coyle, Skip Grenoble, and several faculty members from Penn State Logistics Program.
- In attendance were approximately 40 professionals (22 manufacturing, 8 consulting, 6 logistics firms and 4 others).

Ups	Downs
• Good opportunity to learn ideas presented by participants	• Heavy manufacturing bias to program material made it difficult to obtain relevant competitive benchmarking data. (FIX: Learn from manufacturers)
• Good opportunity to leverage special interests of Sears to Research Agenda of Penn State Business Logistics Faculty.	• I learned that the Federal Highway Administration is evaluating a 300–500% rise in transportation carrier taxes per highway mile in order to offset regulatory programs (e.g., pollution costs, urban congestion costs). (FIX: Factor tax cost increase into contingency plans).
•General quality of agenda and synchronization of discussion topics.	• Manufacturers are ahead of Sears in Logistics Chain Modeling and Systems Optimization. (FIX: Continued emphasis in Strategy Group to integrate Black Box to network-wide simulation models)

Key Points

- Consensus of the group regarding the most compelling logistics issues facing their respective groups are: 1) Sharing of organizational objectives across functions; 2) Organizational structure; 3) System support; 4) Lack of "fit" between the financial reporting system and logistics chain Key Performance Metrics; and 5) Myopic logistics chain focus.

Bottom Line

- Sears should strive for more continuity regarding our representation at the Sponsor's Session.
- We should further leverage resource capabilities and internship potential of the University.

Chop Block	Concur	Non-Concur	Comments (Handwritten)
• Log Cell Strategy			
• Finance			
• IS			
• VR			
• DD			
• Off-Mall			
• HR			
• Outlet Stores			

EXHIBIT 6   Integration of the Sears Logistics Group's Game Plan with Corporate Strategies and Goals

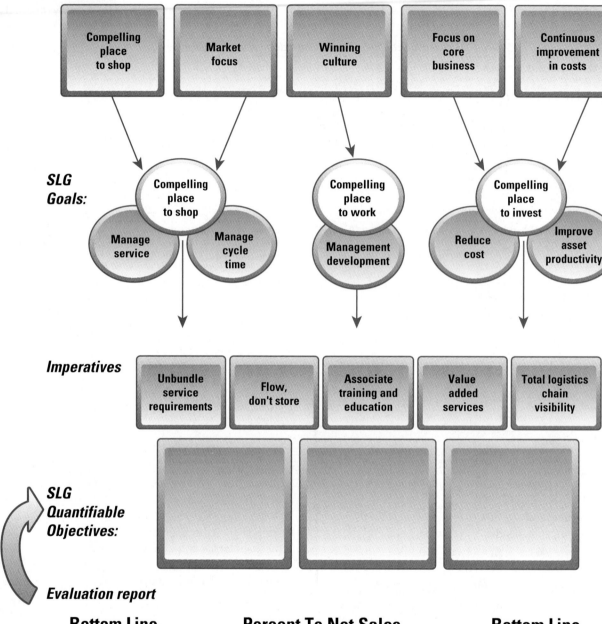

Bottom Line...   Percent To Net Sales...   ...Bottom Line

The SLG's Motto and Charter

Considered an easy way to disseminate the vision, mottoes were printed on everything from T-shirts to stationery. The SLG motto was:

Our Bottom Line
Good Logistics = Sales and Profit

At SLG, the charter was defined as "Single Point of Contact and Control" for all logistics procedures, policies, and decisions within Sears and optimization of the performance of Sears through effective integration of the logistics processes with the company's businesses and stores.

Mission Statement   The SLG mission statement read as follows: "Develop Logistics strategies in conjunction with the businesses and stores to create a competitive advantage for Sears." Each organizational unit within the SLG had its own mission statement that defined the purpose for the unit.

Goals   Goals for the SLG were expressed in nonquantifiable statements. Each direct report updated his or her operation's goals yearly. The SLG's goals were as follows:

- Manage cycle time.
- Manage service.
- Focus on management development.
- Reduce cost.
- Improve asset productivity.

The SLG also set Logistics 2000 Imperatives, which were part of the vision to be met in the year 2000:

- Unbundle service requirements (service requirement should not be dependent on other functions).
- Flow, don't store (keep merchandise moving).
- Associate development, training, and education (associates should receive economic literacy training, cross training, and educational courses).
- Add value and service (add value to goods through the logistics function).
- Create total logistics chain visibility in a perfect environment (awareness of logistics chain value to stakeholders).

Objectives   Objectives were the specific actions the SLG would take to achieve its goals. Unlike goals, objectives were expressed in quantifiable statements. Each objective statement was required to have a date predicting its completion, a list of the benefits to be derived, and a list of resources (costs) needed to support it. Departmental objectives were presented at each Monday-morning staff meeting, and key objectives were provided to the CEO each month.

Activities/Workplace   Each objective had one or more activities. An *activity* was an explanation of how the organization would accomplish each objective. Like objectives, an activity was quantifiable and included benefits, costs (where applicable), and a completion date.

Centralized/Decentralized Command   In *Moving Mountains,* Pagonis quoted sixth-century Chinese poet Lao-tzu as an example summarizing the essence of good leadership:

> A leader is best
> When people barely know he exists,
> Not so good when people obey and acclaim him,
> Worse when they despise him.
> But of a good leader, who talks little,
> When his work is done, his aim fulfilled,
> They will say:
> We did it ourselves.[16]

Pagonis's goal was to build a leadership-supporting environment, one with centralized control and decentralized execution. In this environment, Pagonis controlled the process but not the decisions.

Pagonis believed everyone's utilization of the techniques comprising the "corporate success chain" (see again Exhibit 2) ensured that the leader was given timely information that would allow him or her to provide both a vision and focus for the team (centralized control) and an environment in which subordinates could function freely (decentralized execution). The leader, according to Pagonis, must emphasize the characteristics in his personality that would help him make genuine contact with subordinates. Through this contact, the leader lends authority and empowers people throughout the organization.

Log Council   The SLG Log Council consisted of Pagonis, eight vice presidents, and several other key personnel. The Log Council met as needed to discuss and react to reports from each SLG division or unit.

Training and Education   Pagonis believed strongly that leaders must take personal responsibility for teaching employees and creating a learning organization. In *Moving Mountains,* he quoted Major General Perry M. Smith, a former commandant of the National War College:

> Teaching and leadership go hand-in-glove. The leader must be willing to teach skills, to share insights and experiences, and to work very closely with people to help them mature and be creative . . . By teaching, leaders can inspire, motivate, and influence subordinates at various levels.[17]

Pagonis estimated he spent up to 25 percent of his time training and educating others in the SLG. His definition of training included coaching and counseling when needed. For example, aboard the corporate jet on a flight to the Columbus, Ohio, logistics group, Pagonis took a "ghostbuster" (a special-projects problem solver) and her boss aside for some "training." The subordinate had not asked whether Pagonis would want to visit the Fashion Center at 9 PM after a staff dinner meeting that evening even though others knew he usually did so on such visits. He instructed the subordinate on how to develop a full schedule for one of his field visits and reminded the subordinate's manager that proper training of subordinates was a key management function. The next day, Pagonis once again did some training after he found that the subordinate in charge of the schedule was not ready to leave the hotel when he was (15 minutes ahead of schedule).

---

[16]Pagonis, *Moving Mountains,* p. 228.
[17]Ibid., pp. 223–24.

More formally, two types of training occurred within the SLG. First, all employees were required to dedicate one hour per month to learning about a topic outside their area in order to gain knowledge about Sears as a whole. For example, Pagonis realized when he came to Sears that he needed to brush up on his financial skills, so he met regularly with the SLG's chief financial officer for a year to get himself up to speed. To further educate its employees, Sears created Sears University, which conducted numerous seminars and classes throughout the year on a range of subjects. Special conferences were also held to keep Sears employees up-to-date.

The second type of training with the SLG was cross-functional training, required for all nonsalaried employees in order to broaden their skills and capabilities. All associates in the SLG were expected to understand the retail business in which they operated. In order to learn about the big picture, an employee from finance, for example, was assigned to work in a distribution center for one to three days a year. Classes were held for all associates on basic economic and accounting concepts; everyone was expected to be able to read a financial statement and understand the meaning of such terms as *gross margin, net profit, overhead,* and *costs.*

There were no secrets underlying management decisions. As with all forms of training and education, the goal of creating a more economically literate workforce was to also create a more loyal workforce. The emphasis on cross-functional training facilitated the creation and operation of cross-functional teams. Pagonis relied heavily on such teams to address problems and issues and to coordinate logistical initiatives that involved more than one department.

Since all of the functional areas within the SLG were organized around teams, evaluation of team skills became a part of each employee's review process. Evaluation factors included evidence of the ability to lead and support the team and evidence of taking personal action to provide resources and remove barriers to team success. One of the most prominent teams at SLG was the "ghostbuster" team (named after the popular movie whose title song asked, "When you can't find anyone, who do you call? Ghostbusters!"). Each ghostbuster had specific responsibilities, for which he or she was held accountable, but was also expected support to other members when needed, maintain a cooperative working environment, and be sensitive to the deadlines and constraints of others. When a "hot item" came to the ghostbuster team, all forces were concentrated on solving that problem. If one member of the team was out, the others pulled together to solve the problem, knowing the absent member would do the same in turn.

Physical Fitness

Pagonis's attitude toward keeping physically fit didn't change after his retirement from the military. He strongly encouraged his associates to leave their desk at lunch to help relieve daily stress. He personally set the example by blocking off two hours from 11 AM to 1 PM for a jog, gym workout, or one of his famous basketball games. Pagonis felt so strongly about basketball (point guard was his position, only partly because of his height) that he organized a league and talked the Executive Committee into building a basketball court at the edge of the Sears facility.

Performance Review/Evaluation

At Sears, reviewing the performance of associates was considered an integral management activity. Under Pagonis, the SLG developed a new performance review form to be used for all of its salaried associates. Each associate, in conjunction with a rater, was evaluated according to a list of quantifiable objectives that the associate had set for the evaluation period. Also, the evaluation form allowed for a periodic review of leadership traits and techniques in order to help individuals continually improve their leadership and managerial skills. Salaried employees were evaluated on the following: change leadership, integrity/moral courage, customer satisfaction, empowerment skills, interpersonal skills, team skills, two-way communications, valuing diversity, developing associates and their ideas, business knowledge/literacy, problem solving skills, and initiative/sense of urgency (see Exhibit 7). Most significant in the evaluation process were the three face-to-face meetings each year (initial objective-setting session, 6-month progress review, and 12-month review). The bottom line was that all employees knew where they stood.

Special SLG Rewards System

To help motivate SLG associates, Pagonis established a system of nonmonetary rewards for individual acts judged to be outstanding. The first-level award was a bronze medallion, customized with the SLG logo, which Pagonis personally presented to associates at their place of work. After receiving several medallions, associates were eligible for other rewards such as T-shirts, golf shirts, sweatshirts, or jackets. Employees took great pride in their rewards. In many offices, medallions were framed for viewing, and numerous associates proudly wore the Sears Logistics Group clothing they had won.

THE LOGISTICS ORGANIZATION AT SEARS IN 1992

Prior to Pagonis's arrival, the Sears logistics function was spread throughout the company's various divisions. Each division had its own logistics manager, and in 1990 more than 29,000 people were employed in logistical functions throughout Sears. By 1998 the SLG had been pared down to 10,000 employees. The evolution of a new logistics organization invited an opportunity for changes in management. Early retirement packages created lots of movement within the organization, and 75 percent of the top 49 managers left the company.

Before 1993, no one person was in charge of logistics at Sears. For example, the Sears Logistics Services (SLS) managed distribution for hard-line goods and transportation. Fashion-related goods reported to the vice president of apparel, and vendor relations reported to the chief financial officer. Martinez told Pagonis that he wanted one point of contact for logistics at Sears. This set well with Pagonis, because that was the kind of control he wanted. Being both the coordinator and the allocator made Pagonis an influential executive within the Sears organizational structure.

As the single point of contact for logistics at Sears, Pagonis began by putting into place a well-defined and practical organizational structure. Unlike Sears's previous logistics organization, the new Sears Logistics Group had operating responsibilities at the bottom as well as at the top of the organization. Pagonis segmented the three broad functions of logistics—storage, transportation, and distribution—into nine specific operating units: vendor relations, full-line store logistics, direct-delivery channel, off-mall stores logistics, finance, logistics cell operations and integration, strategy, transportation, and outlet stores.

Some functions included by Pagonis in his nine-group model—for example, vendor relations and outlet stores—were not traditional logistics functions. Pagonis added

EXHIBIT 7   Form Used to Evaluate Leadership Skills of SLG Associates

Each of the 12 Leadership Skills listed below has several components, as shown below. Review the Associate's Self-Assessment. Then consider the extent to which the Associate has consistently demonstrated these behaviors. Write comments and provide ratings. Be sure to include a description of areas needing development.

Rating Scale
5 = Far exceeds expectations; exceptional
4 = Consistently exceeds expectations
3 = Consistently meets expectations
2 = Some expectations met
1 = Expectations not met, unacceptable

Leadership Skill	Comments, Ratings
1. Change Leadership • Takes responsible risks in order to improve customer service, associate morale, and business performance. • Creates an environment where change is viewed as positive and exciting. • Demonstrates personal support for change.	Rating _____
2. Integrity/Moral Courage • Adheres to high standards of personal and business ethics and behaviors. • Demonstrates courage under adversity; willingly expresses even unpopular views.	Rating for Integrity _____ (to be entered into HRMS) Rating for Moral Courage _____ (not entered into HRMS but discussed in feedback session)
3. Customer Service Orientation • Sets and communicates standards for customer service within the unit/department. • Leads by example in serving customers, including handling customer problems through to resolution.	Rating _____
4. Empowerment Skills • Establishes a culture in which associates at all levels willingly and responsibly make decisions to serve customers.	Rating _____
5. Interpersonal Skills • Treats associates and customers with respect and dignity, even when under stress. • Is fair and consistent in dealing with all associates.	Rating _____
6. Team Skills • Leads and supports his/her team; takes personal action to provide resources and remove barriers to team success.	Rating _____

EXHIBIT 7 (concluded)

Leadership Skill	Comments, Ratings
7. **Two-Way Communication Skills** • Seeks out and listens to ideas from all associates; makes a practice of listening to learn. • Fosters open communication.	Rating _____
8. **Valuing Diversity** • Educates staff about the strategic business significance of attracting and retaining a diverse group of associates. • Demonstrates a strong personal commitment to valuing a diverse work group.	Rating _____
9. **Developing Associates and Valuing Their Ideas** • Provides resources and other support for associate development. • Mentors talented associates through coaching, honest feedback, and other means.	Rating _____
10. **Business Knowledge/Literacy** • Serves as a business leader (in unit, district, business) by developing and/or executing of business plans. • Gathers and acts on competitive information. • Demonstrates understanding of how he/she impacts key business performance objectives.	Rating _____
11. **Problem Solving Skills** • Identifies and eliminates persistent or entrenched problems that harm business success. • Seeks out and probes to fully understand information and issues to resolve problems.	Rating _____
12. **Initiative/Sense of Urgency** • Acts quickly and decisively to resolve customer service or business matters.	Rating _____

Part 2: Overall Rating in Leadership Skills

Considering the ratings entered on the Leadership Skills, please circle the single rating which best summarizes Overall Performance in this area.

5 = Far exceeds expectations; exceptional
4 = Consistently exceeds expectations
3 = Consistently meets expectations
2 = Some expectations met
1 = Expectations not met; unacceptable

EXHIBIT 8   Sears Outlet Store in Columbus, Ohio, Strip Mall

vendor relations to the logistics chain in order to hold vendors accountable for shipping goods on time (on-time delivery compliance increased from 35 percent in 1992 to 90 percent in 1996) and undamaged (Sears collected $22 million in damages from vendors in 1996 versus $8 million in 1992). When Sears was responsible for damage, the SLG would assume responsibility for disposing of the damaged goods at outlet stores (see Exhibit 8). One goal of the SLG was to eventually eliminate outlet stores (32 of the original 70 stores had been closed).[18]

Pagonis believed that one important key to the SLG's success was the ability to work with and meet the requirements of Sears businesses (one of three SLG responsibilities, along with stores and customers). To ensure the responsiveness of SLG's operations, SLG associates were located within the full-line, off-mall, and direct delivery channels. These associates were identified as a single point of contact (SPOC). The logistics cell and strategy teams served as the focal point for strategic planning and integration of logistics processes with all businesses and retail stores.

The ghostbusters team (described earlier) addressed problem identification and resolution. Ghostbusters—all of whom were experts in various functional areas of logistics—were empowered to quickly solve problems across functional lines. They shared with each other all information that came to their attention. This team developed an outstanding reputation of being able to solve any problem. Even CEO Martinez used the team to quickly resolve nonlogistical customer complaints addressed to him. This team allowed the SLG to achieve quick responses at the store level, while the strategy team provided long-term planning.

(Sears's Web address is *www.sears.com.*)

---

[18]Charlie Tarver, personal interview, July 7, 1997.

AT&T RESOURCE LINK® (A)

Joel Harmon, *Farleigh Dickinson University*

John Seeger, *Bentley College*

Our people are our competitive advantage.

> **Robert E. Allen,**
> *Chairman and CEO, AT&T*

"We're doing a lot of good for the company and for its people. The challenge now is to fulfill our mission *without* losing money." It was December of 1993 and Jim Meadows, one of AT&T's human resources vice presidents, paced excitedly around his office as he discussed the founding of his organization and its current problems. His energy level was contagious; clearly Meadows was proud of his efforts and the results of Resource Link, an on-payroll temporary employment agency within AT&T.

"Since our start-up in September 1991, we've grown rapidly. We've established our credibility with the AT&T business units that we serve," Meadows said. "But we are not fully recovering our costs, and AT&T has never tolerated units that lose money. We have to figure out a way to become financially self-sufficient by 1995."

AT&T had shed more than 120,000 jobs in the 10 years following its 1984 separation from the telephone operating companies known as the Baby Bells, despite numerous acquisitions and extensive hiring during this period. (See Exhibit 1 for AT&T's annual headcount.) In the process of downsizing, the company—like many other large corporations—frequently released people from one division at the same time another division was hiring similarly qualified staff. Resource Link was a separate organizational unit, set up to hold the best of these people within the company.

In brief, Resource Link (RL) worked as follows: Managerial and technical-professional employees who were "at risk" in a particular AT&T business unit (i.e., had been told that their jobs were being eliminated) or who just wanted a new opportunity could request a transfer to Resource Link. Resource Link was highly selective in recruiting its "associates;" only about 10 percent of applicants were accepted. Associates remained regular full-time AT&T employees, retaining the same salary grade and benefits they had before transferring to RL, but they were no longer in a traditional job or career path. Instead, they moved from project to project as many as three or four times per year. Resource Link marketed and "leased out" its talent pool to the 30 or so business units and support divisions

The authors gratefully acknowledge Suria Malamusa and Marie Rock for their research assistance, the people at AT&T for their generosity, and the reviewers of the Eastern Casewriters Association and the *Case Research Journal* for their helpful suggestions on improving the case. All events and individuals are real. Copyright © 1998 by the case authors and the *Case Research Journal*.

EXHIBIT 1 AT&T Headcount

Year-End	Management/Professional	Occupational	Total
1984	155,278	285,842	441,120
1985	156,148	256,979	413,127
1986	156,619	236,340	392,959
1987	155,970	232,861	373,831
1988	163,072	215,837	378,909
1989	147,534	197,780	345,314
1990	149,750	184,645	334,395
1991	147,761	175,545	323,306
1992	147,514	159,668	317,182
1993	149,515	182,677	312,182

Companies acquired: McCaw, Gretag Data Systems, Datotek, Internet, BarPhone, ETSA, Network of Chase Manhattan, Norfolk Finance, Datald, Teredata, NCR, Germania Electronica, Western Union Global Messaging, U.S. Instrument Rentals, Ecore Int'l, Pacific Corp., Lycom Istel, AIS, Eaton, Parradyne, APT, Fitel.
Companies sold: Solid State Circuit, Thailand Directories, UNIX Systems Labs, Bangkok Manufacturing, Microelectronics Plant Singapore Factory.

within AT&T. (See Exhibit 2 for a simplified representation of AT&T's structure.) Resource Link's charter was to fully recover its costs by billing clients for hours of services rendered by its associates. It operated as a stand-alone, not-for-profit business within AT&T's human resources division.

From the end of 1991 through the end of 1993, the number of associates under contract with Resource Link grew from 31 to almost 400. (Exhibit 3 shows annual employment at RL.) An increasing percentage of RL's associates were volunteers (i.e., they were not at risk when they joined RL). The amount of idle time that associates spent between temporary assignments was, according to Resource Link's analysis, phenomenally low compared to industry averages for temporary agencies and consulting firms. Jim Meadows credited Resource Link with helping the company avoid millions of dollars in severance payments and also fees paid to employment agencies. According to internal surveys, the satisfaction of both Resource Link's customers and associates was quite high. Many within AT&T pointed to RL as evidence that the company still cared about its employees, in spite of its wholesale staff reductions.

Despite these indicators of success, the unit's management was concerned. RL had registered increasingly large financial losses over the first three years of its operation; fiscal 1993 would end with a deficit of over $3 million. The business plan sold to AT&T executives had projected operating in the black by 1995. Continued losses could jeopardize RL's survival. Yet the path to profitability was neither clear nor easy. Associate training and development demanded ever greater investment. Pricing constraints limited revenues. Compensation expenses much higher than anticipated and system inefficiencies exacerbated by rapid growth shrank net income. RL was entering a critical period requiring decisive action.

BACKGROUND

Through the 1980s and early 1990s, American Telephone & Telegraph experienced major upheaval. Prior to its breakup in 1984, AT&T was a centralized, domestic, technology-driven, regulated monopoly. It operated as a single business characterized by a

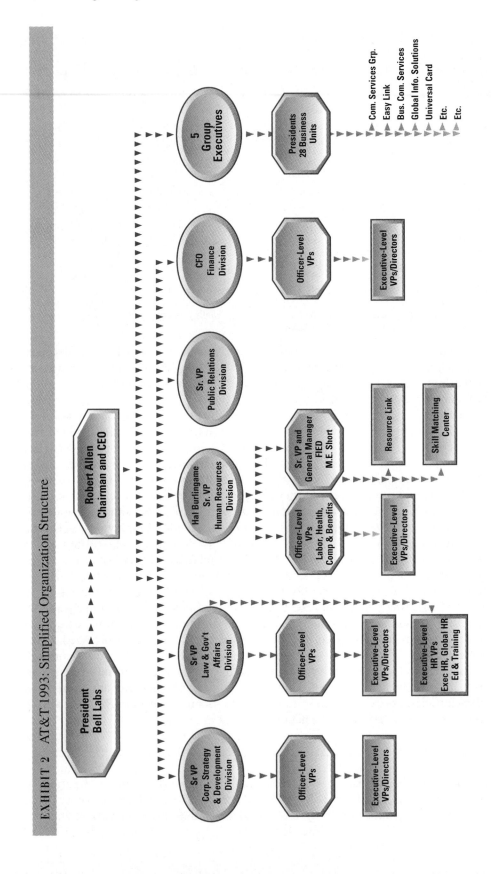

EXHIBIT 2   AT&T 1993: Simplified Organization Structure

EXHIBIT 3	Resource Link Headcount and Source of Associates			
	Year-End	**At-Risk**	**Volunteers**	**Total**
	1991	25	6	31
	1992	171	125	296
	1993	180	217	397

conservative, internally focused culture and employment stability. At $69.4 billion in sales, it was one of the largest corporations in the world, employing over a million people. As the dominant providers of telephone communications in the United States, AT&T people shared a company culture recognized as "Ma Bell's way;" they were intensely conscious of their responsibility and proud of delivering the highest level of telephone service in the world. As part of its monopoly franchise agreement with regulators, however, the telephone company was prohibited from competing in other industries.

In the 1980s, most business analysts believed that AT&T was the only company powerful enough to compete against IBM in the computer industry, and AT&T's leaders were confident they could succeed in an unregulated business environment. AT&T's Bell Laboratories had invented the transistor and wanted to compete in the computer industry. Management willingly cooperated with federal authorities to negotiate an end to the company's telecommunications monopoly. In 1984, AT&T agreed to divest its local telephone service operations and spun off nine independent regional "Baby Bells" to handle the business of providing local telephone service; AT&T became a long-distance telephone service provider and a manufacturer of telephone equipment—thus resolving one of the largest antitrust cases in U.S. history. The surviving AT&T was still a huge corporation, with sales of $30 billion, assets of $16 billion and employment totaling 448,000. And it was free to move into other industry arenas.

By 1991, the company described itself as a global, market-driven multi-business enterprise operating in the highly competitive and turbulent long-distance communications, telephone equipment, and computer industries. It functioned in a much more decentralized fashion than before and was attempting to change the Ma Bell culture to an innovative, risk-taking culture with a focus on customers. About 40 semiautonomous business units and divisions (BU/Ds) competed in such diverse areas as long-distance service, computers, credit cards, and telecommunications systems and equipment. Each was accountable for its own profit and loss, and each had great latitude in the structure it adopted to meet the unique needs of its business environment. Divisions such as finance, information systems, human resources, public relations, and law and government affairs generally were operated as cost centers supporting the business units.

These changes had created a constant staffing challenge. Employees exited from some business units, taking with them talents, skills, and expertise that were still needed in other parts of AT&T. While shrinking businesses paid severance, growing business units paid for recruitment, training, and consultants. Although this drama was now common in corporate America and necessary to transform AT&T into a serious player for the 1990s, it was not a story anyone in AT&T wanted to keep replaying. Loyalty, commitment, and security were casualties of the turmoil, and many employees felt helpless and abandoned. Bouts of labor–management confrontation, service delivery problems, spells of organization gridlock, and a string of negative employee surveys were attributed in large part to crumbling employment stability (which had long been a cornerstone of the "psychological contract" between AT&T

and its employees). AT&T leadership viewed this as a major strategic problem and began exploring ways to increase employment stability and demonstrate commitment to employees. At the same time, the company had to allow its business units the staffing flexibility to meet their fluctuating needs.

The situation became even more acute during 1991 when, reflecting the restructuring of the telecommunications industry that was under way, AT&T acquired NCR, a multinational computer company, and decided to eliminate its own computer systems business. This instantly created an additional 10,000 at-risk AT&T employees. It was in this context that Hal Burlingame, senior vice president of human resources, put together a committee of professional human resource personnel to establish strategies for workforce management that would minimize the impact of organization changes on AT&T business units and on employees.

Idea for an Internal Talent Pool

Among the initiatives that Burlingame's committee considered was the use of at-risk employees as contingent workers to make up a readily available labor pool for the entire organization. The committee proposed using AT&T management and technical employees who might otherwise be laid off to fill jobs elsewhere within the company—jobs that were currently going to new hires or outside contractors. (It was estimated that at least 20,000 contract workers were being used throughout the company during this period, of which about 25 percent were "technical professionals," e.g., project managers, programmers.) The idea of creating an internal talent pool had surfaced earlier, in a 1988 task force recommendation, but had never been seriously considered. The 1991 committee felt the idea was attractive enough to pursue further. Vice President John McMorrow, the committee chair, took the talent pool idea to Burlingame. It was at this point that Jim Meadows was invited into the process.

Jim Meadows

When he entered the planning process, Meadows was 54 and an operations vice president at AT&T. He was married, with three grown children. He had been with AT&T over 30 years, mostly in its traditional businesses. In 1960, just out of college with a business administration degree, he was hired by Western Electric in Oregon. Like that of many other AT&T managers of the era, Meadows's career was to a great extent managed for him by AT&T. With stays averaging about three years, Meadows was moved to central office installation operations in Los Angeles, manufacturing operations in New Jersey, finance in New York, data processing systems in San Francisco (and later materials management there), software development and planning in North Carolina, corporate human resources in North Carolina, production control and customer service in Boston, material logistics and divestiture planning in St. Louis, material logistics for all BU/Ds in Chicago, and (in 1990) computer systems in New Jersey. This rate of movement seemed to suit Meadows, who said of himself, "I love change." He went on:

> I'm more an innovator than a creator. Most of my life has been spent making change. But always other people's changes. I don't think I've ever had a truly original idea in my life. But I've always had the ability to recognize a great idea when I see it and make it happen.
>
> The large-scale changes and downsizing that we [at AT&T] have been experiencing over the last decade have been necessary for the company to compete in a changing world. But it's been costing the company a great deal of money, hurting loyal employees who are being "surplused" or placed "at risk," and tearing apart the corporate culture.

I've been with AT&T since 1960, constantly moving around the company in order to develop my career. In my last assignment, I reengineered myself out of a job. So I can really empathize both with the at-risk folks as well as those looking to enhance their marketability through lateral moves. When I was given a chance to help the company address the workforce management problem, I seized the opportunity.

John McMorrow and I knew one another from Chicago, where we both had worked in the mid-80s, and he knew I was available for reassignment. Because of my background in operations *and* HR, he thought I'd have some credibility with Hal Burlingame and the HR community. He set up a meeting between Hal and me. Hal first asked me to research the feasibility of the Committee's talent pool idea and then he requested a business plan. He wanted RL to be a laboratory to experiment with leading-edge HR technologies and a place where managers can learn to run HR as a business. When he saw the plan, he said, "This is an idea whose time has come," and gave the go-ahead.

I'm very proud of my team and what we have accomplished here, and I feel a deep sense of obligation. Sometimes I think to myself that our staff and associates wouldn't be here except for me. They depend on me and they depend on Resource Link. I want them to do well and I want this thing to grow.

Regarding his management style, Meadows said:

Many of my managers accuse me of "micromanagement" because of my "hands-on" management style. Until recently, that's pretty much been true. In fact, lack of empowerment was a big issue in the upward feedback I got this past spring.

It's a matter of trust. Frankly, as career HR managers, most of my top staff never before had profit and loss responsibility or any real experience in running a business. Here's an example: In October 1992, when we were one year old, I found out at an off-site staff meeting that we had a million dollars' worth of unbilled associate hours; the time tickets had not yet been submitted or logged. Needless to say, I went ballistic! I told my managers that this was a prime example of why I had a lack of confidence.

It's not been easy for me to take a hands-off approach, but I'm trying. I have high standards. This may sound egotistical, but I want us to be the best we can be. I'm fond of saying "You can make me happy, delight me, but you can never satisfy me." I want them to do well for their own sake. Sure, I helped them get to where they are and this is my baby—but I'm not going to be here forever. I want to leave feeling that I made a difference. I want to leave a bit of a legacy.

Planning Phase

In March 1991, Hal Burlingame asked Meadows to research the feasibility of creating an internal talent pool. He instructed Meadows to take a creative entrepreneurial approach, avoid bureaucracy, and keep it simple. Meadows spent the next six weeks studying the issues, reaching out to people in a variety of areas within AT&T. He held meetings with human resource strategic planning groups and with procurement people to examine the volume and cost of contract employees, and he studied workforce trend issues.

It was during this time that Meadows met Doug Merchant, an AT&T strategic human resources planner trained in institutional economics and organization theory and design. Merchant believed a Resource Link type of workforce management structure would translate into significant competitive advantage for AT&T. It could help the company attract the best talent, through a commitment and capacity to enhance their marketability. And it could help the company obtain better economies of scale from its large labor force, through more efficient reallocation of talent. AT&T would thus be more able than competitors to optimally balance organization learning and efficiency on the one hand, and flexibility and innovation on the other.

Meadows felt there was a great fit between Merchant and himself right from the start because of their very complementary knowledge sets and learning styles. "I'm

EXHIBIT 4   THE Resource Link Concept

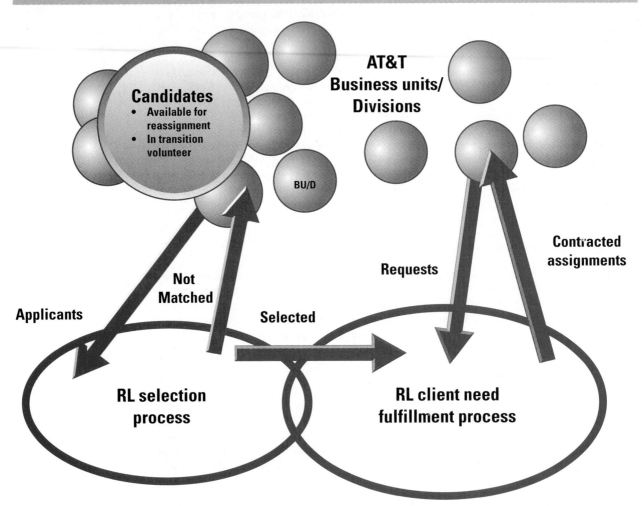

where the 'rubber meets the road,' and he's where the 'rubber meets the sky,' Meadows said. The two had several lengthy and productive brainstorming sessions conceptualizing how to make the talent pool concept work, including, as Meadows put it, "some way-out 'cloud-nine' stuff." Meadows credits these and subsequent sessions with Merchant as being critical to the conceptualization of Resource Link.

On April 11, Meadows made his recommendations. He first presented his conclusions to a council of business-unit human resource leaders to get their reaction. "They asked a lot of hard questions, but were generally enthusiastic," according to Meadows. Later that day, Meadows met with Burlingame alone for one hour to report that he had determined it was not only feasible but *urgent* that the company move toward having both a core and a variable (contingent) workforce. Meadows walked Burlingame through a one-page concept document for Resource Link (similar to Exhibit 4). Meadows recalled that Burlingame was very interested in what the human resource leaders had said. "I think he was impressed that I took the risk of showing it to them before I had shown it to him, which was the effect I hoped for," he said. Meadows believed he had to convey a risk-taking image in order to successfully build the enterprise.

Burlingame gave Meadows the go-ahead to do a full-fledged business plan. Meadows then put together a project team, including representatives from finance, marketing, human resources, and information systems. The team researched workforce issues and trends, benchmarked other companies dealing with the same issues, conducted internal focus groups with potential clients and employees, collected data on usage and demand for nonpayroll workers, identified target markets, and studied in some depth the attributes of the temporary services and consulting industries.

Meadows, at his own request, gave monthly verbal status reports to the HR Leaders Council, using them as a sounding board. Meadows felt that the human resource leaders' reactions continued to be positive, although some remained skeptical. He sensed that some of the more traditional human resource types were threatened by the whole concept of what he and Burlingame were trying to do—setting up a separate, well-run business within human resources. But he felt that it had helped a great deal to have the skeptics as well as the enthusiasts involved in the process every step of the way.

Meadows worked his team hard to prepare for their presentation to senior management. He wanted all members of the team to present their own part of the plan, and, according to several of the members, he drilled them pretty relentlessly until they got it exactly the way he wanted it.

On August 15, the team presented the "talent pool" case to Burlingame. Meadows began by informing him that they already had nine associates under contract and on assignments. He again wanted to demonstrate some risk-taking behavior. Burlingame was impressed and enthusiastically approved the plan, asking only that it be run by the CFO and AT&T's controller. After they had validated the numbers, Burlingame gave the final go-ahead. He thought that Resource Link would not only serve the company well but would also be a good model for learning how to operate human resource functions as a business.

RL STRUCTURE AND SYSTEMS: 1991–93

In September 1991, Resource Link was launched as an independent unit within the human resources division. It was centered in New Jersey, where AT&T is headquartered. Meadows assumed leadership of RL as a human resources vice president reporting directly to Burlingame. The unit's mission was defined as follows:

> To retain and develop strong performing management employees for the business units/divisions, in support of AT&T's variable workforce needs, through cost-effective, flexible staffing alternatives.

Meadows had a high degree of latitude in operating his business. He staffed RL with a blend of disciplines and expertise (e.g., in business start-ups, sales, operations, recruiting, management information systems, finance). All RL staff came from within AT&T. Most were given traditional (i.e., permanent) positions, although a few came aboard as RL associates with one-year staff assignments. Meadows expected his people to exhibit high levels of energy, commitment, and dedication, and he sought to create a culture that was proactive, aggressive, dynamic, and results oriented. Results meant growth, high productivity, and meeting financial commitments. The business plan called for RL to lose no more than $5 million in the first year and to be fully recovering its costs by the end of 1995. Meadows, however, was determined to break even before then and constantly repeated this to his staff.

In 1991, virtually all RL associates had been at risk (available for reassignment) in their former business units. Many had come from the computer division that was

EXHIBIT 5   Top Resource Link Clients: 1993

AT&T Business Unit/Division	Number of Associates
Business communications services	43
Strategy, sales, and customer operations	40
Group technology chief information officer	39
Human resources division (other than RL)	35
NCR	24
Network services division	23
Chief financial officer	21

being eliminated as a result of the NCR acquisition. By the end of 1993, RL's associates came from a wide variety of BU/Ds (see Exhibit 5 for RL's top clients in 1993) and more than half were volunteers (not at risk when they applied). The average associate was 43 years old, with about 18 years of AT&T experience.

Almost 500 associates had worked for RL between 1991 and 1993; more than 100 had left to accept permanent positions elsewhere within AT&T (over 10 percent of these positions were promotions). According to exit interviews, the main reason given for leaving RL was a preference for traditional jobs. Fewer than a dozen associates exited the company, and almost all of those were eligible for a pension. Demand for associates was consistently greater than supply; at the end of 1993, there were over 150 unfilled client requests for RL services.

The growth in associates was accompanied by an elaboration of Resource Link's structure. In late 1991, RL opened its Western District office to serve Chicago and—six months later—California. In mid-1992, the Eastern District office—originally serving only New Jersey, New York, and Pennsylvania—expanded service to Atlanta and Washington, DC. Several associates were placed in AT&T assignments overseas. Also in mid-1992, RL and the new Skills Match Center (SMC) were combined into a new unit within human resources called Career Placement Alternatives (CPA). SMC, formed as an outgrowth of collective bargaining, was a talent pool of "bargained-for" (mostly clerical, union-represented) employees. Although RL and SMC operated in similar fashion, they were independent units serving very different types of employees. Jim Meadows headed both CPA and RL.

Some significant changes in RL's management team occurred during the first part of 1993. The Western and Eastern District managers each left voluntarily to take positions elsewhere in the company. Meadows brought in new leadership with greater experience in operating an ongoing business. The new Western District Manager was John Doran, an experienced operations manager in sales, manufacturing, and management information systems. The new Eastern District Manager was Mary Conrad, an experienced manager with a telemarketing and sales support background. Doran and Conrad were described by other RL managers as "hands on, process oriented, and success minded." In addition, Mike Lowe was brought on board in January 1993 to fill the new position of district manager for associate support. Lowe had been director of human resources for an AT&T subsidiary in Florida. Ironically, Lowe had interviewed Meadows for a leadership position in his unit two years earlier. Each was impressed with the other's credentials. As the year progressed, Lowe's administrative responsibilities were expanded and his title changed to district manager for operations and administrative support. Lowe brought in several people to assist in personnel, reporting, and systems management. By the end of 1993, RL's own staff numbered 40.

Each associate reported to a Resource Link associate support manager. These managers acted as the "matchmakers," selecting and assigning associates according to client needs. They also were responsible for supporting and reviewing the performance of those associates assigned to them. With respect to appraisal and compensation matters, RL viewed itself, not the client, as the supervisor of each associate. RL's account managers, most of whom formerly were line managers highly familiar with the "AT&T way," functioned as salespeople and client liaisons. Details of RL's HR processes are provided below; Exhibit 6 describes RL's 1993 structure.

Recruitment, Selection, and Placement

Jim Meadows strongly believed that recruiting high-performing associates was one of RL's most important tasks; strong performance would ultimately be the best advertisement for RL. He thought that it was absolutely essential to reverse the prevalent perception within AT&T's middle ranks that RL was a dumping ground' for surplus people; having even a few poor performers would dangerously strengthen that kind of perception.

Recruitment was driven by client needs, as shown in Exhibits 4 and 7. A new associate was hired by RL only after he or she was matched to an existing client request. Through 1992, there was no requirement that business units and divisions contact RL before using agency temps or other outside contractors. Beginning in 1993, the company instituted a policy requiring that BU/Ds first give RL an opportunity to satisfy their staffing needs before going outside, although they remained free to reject RL's proposed candidates.

The recruiting process began with a written service request from a BU/D that included a brief description of the assignment and the specific skills for which the client was looking (as well as location and expected length of assignment). A RL account manager then contacted the client to verify the information and to obtain additional details and clarification as necessary. This information was passed to a recruiter, who initiated a search for an employee with skills to match the assignment. The matching process sometimes took days. Recruiters first determined whether any idle or soon-to-be idle associates had the required skills. A computer database (the RL Operations Support System, or R-OSS), containing skills profiles of all RL associates, helped recruiters identify internal candidates, but there was not an automated matching feature in the system. If no suitable internal candidate was identified, recruiters would list the temporary assignment in a companywide electronic job posting system (the Employee Career Opportunity System, or ECOS). Applicants who seemed to match the assignment requirement were contacted by the recruiter. At this point, the recruiter shifted to a marketing perspective to sell the candidate on the benefits of working for RL. Willing candidates then underwent the rigorous screening procedures that were used to select all associates, as described below.

The selection process involved several elements: résumé review, review of the two most recent performance appraisals, a detailed skills inventory, and two tools developed by psychologists from corporate human resources specifically for RL—a structured behavior-description interview by an RL recruiter, and an evaluation of skills conducted by the prospective client. Except for the client interview, each element of the selection process aimed to assess the applicant from two perspectives: (1) a fit for the assignment currently under consideration, and (2) long-term fit given the types of skills frequently sought and the need for associates to remain marketable over time.

Interviews were rigorous, stressing RL's critical need to respond to differing customers, to work in unstructured environments, and to sell oneself. Applicants who had

EXHIBIT 6   Resource Link 1993: Simplified Organization Structure

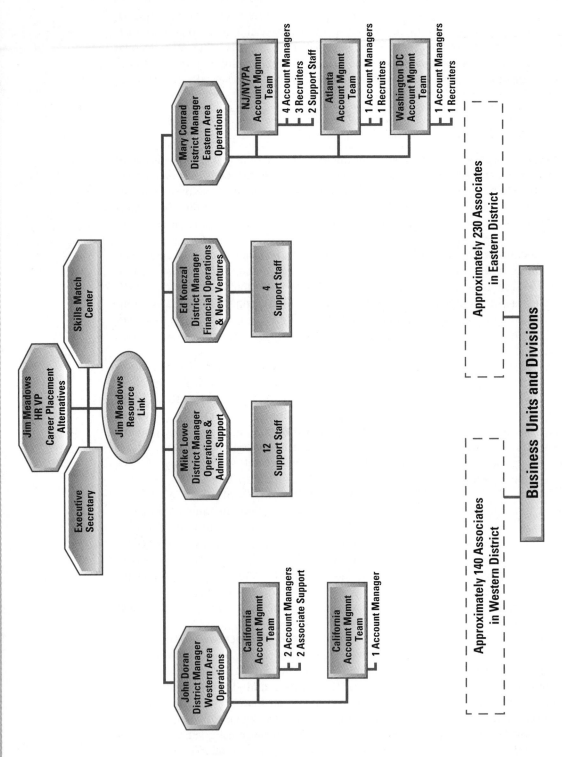

EXHIBIT 7 Resource Link Matching Process

difficulty seeing themselves as self-promoters or as constantly shifting gears tended to drop out at this point. If all parties agreed that the candidate was a good match for the client's assignment, the RL recruiter usually extended a job offer. Applicants who were not already associates were then transferred from their old business unit to RL. Only rarely were new associates hired without an existing client commitment for their services.

According to Pam Mueller, an RL staff manager, less than 10 percent of applicants were selected to join RL. The great majority of those rejected simply lacked the specific skill set for which a RL client was looking. In some cases, however, RL declined to hire a candidate despite his or her fit to a client's current request, out of concern that the candidate lacked skills for success in multiple future assignments and thus would later accrue considerable idle time at a substantial cost to RL. Jim Meadows commented,

> It's not that we never took risks in hiring marginal candidates, perhaps suitable for a current assignment but likely not beyond; we did. But in almost every case we wished we hadn't, because we couldn't resell them.
>
> The demand for skills changes. Our type of work environment requires change. We need change-friendly people who can deal with uncertainty and ambiguity, think strategically, and work in a project-based, teamwork format. It seems that only about 10 percent of AT&T's workforce at this time is built to handle an RL-type structure without a major amount of reorientation and retooling. We began to say to ourselves, "Why are we prolonging the inevitable for them? Let's help them get on with their lives."

Performance Management

The performance appraisal process really began at the start of each assignment when the client established performance objectives for the associate. In fact, the ability to clarify the client's performance expectations was a critical consultative skill.

Customer feedback was the primary factor in an associate's annual performance review, counting for 70 percent of the appraisal. Therefore, associates had at least two face-to-face meetings during the year with RL staff members who provided them with client and developmental feedback. Various staff members participated in the process,

EXHIBIT 8   Example Average Associate Productivity Calculation

Total available hours (40 hours/week × 52 weeks)	2,080
Vacation time	(120)
Personal days	(32)
Holidays	(80)
Training time	(40)
Total available billable hours	1,808
Total hours billed by associate	1,772
Hours idle	36
Idle time: 36 hours idle/1,816 available billable hours	2%
Associate productivity: 1,780 hours billed/1,816 available billable hours	98%

which functioned more like a team-based peer review. The balance of the performance appraisal was divided between productivity and administration.

Productivity was measured by dividing hours worked by available hours. (See Exhibit 8 for a sample average calculation.) The administrative rating concerned such issues as timely reporting of hours worked, bringing in new business for RL, commitment to personal development, and adhering to various administrative procedures.

At the end of each year, each associate received a written performance appraisal. These were all done in one month, in synchronization with the performance review-compensation process undertaken throughout AT&T. However, because of its unique nature, RL had to modify some of the appraisal processes used with other company employees.

Providing annual appraisals to all associates in a one-month period became increasingly problematic as RL grew. Conducting the annual reviews turned into a logistical nightmare. Also, there was concern over the validity of appraisals. Fifty percent of associates were rated by clients as "exceeding objectives," and 20 percent as "far exceeding objectives." RL staff wondered whether clients could make a reliable distinction between an associate who had exceeded objectives and one who had far exceeded them. Further, because clients were not financially responsible for associates' pay increases and performance bonuses, they could afford to be lenient in their ratings. When this appeared to occur, an RL manager discussed it with the client. However, it was very difficult for the RL manager to know when clients were being unreasonably lenient or too severe, given that they could not actually observe the work situation.

Compensation

The annual performance appraisal helped to determine associates' salary increases and bonuses. Associates were paid on the same salary structure as their counterparts in other parts of the company. In addition, if associates met specific performance and productivity criteria, they could earn up to an additional 10 percent above their base pay. Salary increases and bonuses could usually be obtained with satisfactory client ratings and 90 percent productivity. There was also a downside risk, with a maximum of 20 percent of their base pay at risk if they failed to achieve objectives.

Productivity calculations were performed monthly, based on a rolling 12-month average, so pay could be affected each month. The rolling average also prevented pay from being severely affected in a negative way if an associate was without an assignment for only a short time. Resource Link's staff was paid the same way, but the calculation was based on total results for all associates. Meadows believed that this approach helped to drive team behavior. As detailed in a later section, productivity among all the associates was much higher than expected. With superlative appraisals and high productivity, the incentive compensation for the average associate was well above his or her previous salary and therefore the plan was costing RL much more than anticipated.

Reflecting RL's long-term commitment to its associates, associates received salary and benefits even when they were not working. Until late 1993, RL had no policy for letting associates go if assignments could not be found for them for an extended period of time. Toward the end of 1993, RL instituted the following layoff policy: "Associates who are 45 days past their last assignment with no new assignment will receive notice that they will go off payroll in 90 days." Since the layoff process took a total of 135 days, no associates had yet been affected by this policy as of the end of 1993.

Training and Support

RL's goal was to provide an average of five days of training a year for each associate. The purpose was to help associates keep their technical skills current and to strengthen skills critical to being an effective consultant, such as communication, negotiating, and marketing skills, which were not strong among most associates when they joined RL. However, according to several of RL's managers, only sporadic training was actually occurring, driven mostly by the needs of associates' current assignments. There was a consensus that current levels of training and support were inadequate for RL's long-term objectives. But greater expenses in this area would worsen RL's financial position and take staff time away from recruiting and marketing activities. How to prioritize and fund training activities was an ongoing question, but little had been done to address the issue.

Pricing

The price for an associate was based on the average salary and benefits for that associate's salary band within the geographic area where the assignment was located. (At the time, AT&T listed six salary zones, which took into account geographic differences in cost of living.) RL then added estimated overhead and service-delivery expenses, and calculated an hourly rate for that associate. This markup was approximately 15 percent. RL managers acknowledged that their expense estimates were based on limited experience and data. Small (e.g., 3 percent) cost-of-living price increases were effected in 1992 and 1993.

Exhibit 9 illustrates the 1993 range of salary–benefit bases and hourly rates for three levels of associates. The comparability of RL's prices to those of its primary competitors (suppliers of managerial and technical-professional talent such as Management Recruiting International and Brenner Technology) varied by geography. In some locations (e.g., Chicago) the price of associates with certain technical skills was equal to or less than the outside market price for equivalent contracted talent. In other areas (e.g., most of Florida), the marketplace provided equivalent talent at a substantially lower price than did RL—as much as $20–$40 less per hour. In some cases, the price of RL associates was higher than some business units were permitted to pay for contract personnel.

Associates submitted their billable hours on a weekly basis. Manual timesheets were used through January 1993. In February, AT&T's Conversant™ Voice Response System came on-line and associates were able to dial a specific phone number and punch in the time that they worked on a Touch-Tone phone. The automated system then downloaded their hours into RL's billing system in R-OSS.

EXHIBIT 9   Resource Link Pricing Structure (Fully loaded rates)

	Junior/Mid-level (A1–A4) (TA–STA)	Associates at Mid-Level/High (A5–B–C) (MTS1–MTS)	High (C–D)
Annual salary, including benefits	$50,000–$75,000	$75,000–$95,000	$95,000–$145,000
Hourly billed rate	$35–$55	$55–$75	$75–$100

Billing and Receivables

RL billed its clients monthly for the services of its associates at an hourly rate based on the assignment. Clients were billed for services one month in arrears. For example, a client was billed on June 1 for services rendered from May 1 to May 30. Billing and payment were simultaneous transactions; upon mechanical journal entry of RL's bill, funds were instantaneously transferred from the client's books to RL's.

Marketing

Meadows considered aggressive marketing to be another key requirement for RL's success. He still sensed a "tainted goods" perception attached to RL and its associates, stemming from AT&T line managers' recognition that many of his associates had been marked for dismissal by their previous units. That perception had to be overcome, Meadows felt.

Marketing efforts stressed the staffing flexibility that RL could provide its customers as well as the desirable attributes of its associates—for example, their energy, customer focus, and technical competencies; their ability to hit the ground running due to familiarity with AT&T systems and ways; and their status as members of the AT&T community.

The majority of marketing was done through verbal presentations, particularly during 1991–92. Meadows made numerous presentations at meetings and conferences of senior-level directors and officers. RL's account managers held countless meetings with line managers and human resources staff at both the corporate and business-unit levels. Printed marketing materials came more slowly and were at first unsophisticated. A simple fact sheet was prepared and distributed in late 1991, documenting RL's emerging track record of associate usage and performance. This fact sheet was replaced by a two-color folder in mid-1992 and a full-color brochure at the end of that year. The latter materials included testimonials from satisfied AT&T customers. RL also placed articles about itself in internal AT&T publications. "Looking back," said Meadows, "I was being pretty tight with the buck when it came to printed marketing material. I think we should have done more with the print stuff earlier on."

RESOURCE LINK PERFORMANCE: 1991–93

Customer Satisfaction

In 1993, RL conducted a brief survey to assess the satisfaction of its clients in the BU/Ds. On a scale of 1 (very dissatisfied/strongly disagree) to 4 (very satisfied/strongly agree) customers' ratings were as follows:

Overall quality of service	3.45
Ease of doing business with RL	3.40
Pricing of associates	2.90
I would use RL again	3.48

Several of RL's clients in the New Jersey/New York area were interviewed. Clients especially appreciated the convenience and staffing flexibility that RL provided them, and the performance quality and cultural fit of RL associates:

> We started a new data center and needed to hire people skilled in networks and the UNIX operating system. However, some people are opposed to working in New York and others don't care for our 24-hour, seven-day-a-week operation. We wanted to give people a chance to try our environment and see if they wanted to be a part of it. Resource Link did all the screening for exactly the candidates we needed. We didn't have to go through a repeated interview process. All the candidates had what we were looking for. If the operation is unsuccessful, I am not committed to having people staffed to the business unit and I don't have to make people surplus.
> —Emmet Ehlberg, Business Communications Services operations manager in New York

> The main advantage is that you are not spending a lot of money training consultants. Our operation is on the leading edge of technology. If we're going to the trouble of training people, their skills ought to be transferable within AT&T. Another point is that we didn't have to fit people into an organization chart. I didn't have to worry whether a level-six person could report to another level-six. That was a big advantage because I could get the level of expertise I needed to do the job. When the job is completed, I can let these people go off to another assignment. It is so much easier to sign a contract with Resource Link for six months or a year than it is to transfer a permanent employee in and then to try to move them out a year later.
> —Roy Wimmer, Consumer Communications Services district manager in New Jersey

> You can see how associates meet your needs and associates can see how they fit in with your group. So it's a *two-way street.* If you take someone through traditional channels, you're taking them based on a résumé and interview. If a Resource Link associate works for you for a few months it's a better long-term test to see how they'll fit in.
> —Ellen Carp, Global Business Communication Systems staff manager in New Jersey

RL clients also appreciated associates' familiarity with the "AT&T way." External temporary hires needed time to learn about AT&T systems and informal networks; customers felt RL associates were able to work productively from the start. Clients' satisfaction with the price of associates varied greatly by geography. Western-area clients generally were satisfied with the cost of RL associates in relation to the talent available in their marketplace. However, RL managers were aware that clients in some markets could obtain talent at significantly lower cost. Pam Mueller, an RL staff manager, believed that some clients preferred to give the job to an AT&T person because they felt it was the right thing to do. Some clients expressed frustration with the valuable recruiting time they had lost by waiting for RL to conduct fruitless searches for talent scarce within AT&T. One said, "It's like going to a store for something and continually not finding it on the shelf. Sooner or later, you'll stop going to that store."

Employee Attitudes

The results of a 1993 AT&T-wide employee survey showed that the responses of Resource Link associates were more favorable (5 percent higher) in most categories than responses from other employees throughout the company who held more traditional job assignments. The higher ratings applied consistently to categories dealing with management, leadership, respect, teamwork, dedication to the customer, quality process, performance management, operating efficiency, competitive position, and satisfaction with the company. Associates' responses were less favorable than those of traditional employees only on items dealing with employment security.

In a focus group with RL associates, however, one participant said, "I feel much more secure in Resource Link than people in traditional jobs feel." In a separate interview, Tom Bartow, an associate on assignment as a leadership advisor, said,

> After 20 years with AT&T, I would have been out on the street like other people in the company. It makes all the difference in the world being able to rely on Resource Link.

Another associate, Jim Finn, said,

> Resource Link offers me the ability to increase my overall market value by giving me the opportunity to continue to develop myself and my skill set, to work with many new and existing business units, to gain a better understanding of where these BU/Ds are headed and to be a part of the overall growth of AT&T.

In the focus-group discussions, participants also said, "Resource Link has allowed me to grow much more than in traditional roles," "I've added more skills in two years with Resource Link than in the prior four years," and "I came to Resource Link feeling at risk . . . but with many more opportunities to learn and grow, risk goes away." Mike Lowe, an associate support district manager, commented,

> One of the things that we are increasingly fond of saying is you might be more secure working for us than you are in any other business unit.

Another aspect of RL for which associates expressed satisfaction was the freedom from politics and other constraints of traditional jobs. Focus-group participants talked of having more control over their career paths and more exposure to different organizations and bosses. They liked being in a "consultant–customer relationship," and working "adult-to-adult rather than boss-to-subordinate." They especially appreciated being able to "deal with politics in an objective manner" and not having to "play the game." They felt "freer to take risks" and to "communicate more directly without fear of reprisal."

Associates expressed some concerns about working for RL. The greatest dissatiafiers were lack of promotion opportunities and lack of a sense of belonging. Focus-group participants talked about "the lack of a mentor" and about the fact that "upward mobility may be missing." They also talked about "not having a sense of belonging, sharing, learning, and giving" and about "a sense of getting lost in the process." They expressed a need for "coaches to support/monitor developmental needs." They felt that more needed to be done to "invest in us as resources" and to "build skills for development and future employability." As to specific developmental needs, they spoke of consulting, facilitation, human resources, and project management skills. They spoke also of needing to understand more about business trends and issues. And they spoke of needing better skills in job marketing and in personal interviewing and selling.

In mid-1993, RL conducted its own survey of associate satisfaction. In terms of the percentage agreeing or strongly agreeing, typical results were as follows:

88%	"My contract assignment helped advance my career."
97	"My opinions and suggestions are important to Resource Link."
92	"I feel part of the Resource Link team."
99	"I am satisfied working for Resource Link."

Associate Productivity

Over the period 1991–93, associates had worked an average of 99 percent of their available billable hours. The "idle time" of associates was 0 percent in 1991, 0.4 percent in 1992, and 1.9 percent in 1993. RL managers attributed the rise in idle time in 1993 to the large number of associates who were coming off their original assignments and needed to be matched with new clients. They expected idle time to stabilize at around 2 percent. An industry standard of comparison was difficult to obtain given the great variation in types of temporary employment and consulting agencies. The 1991 benchmarking study conducted by RL's business-planning team indicated that the great majority of firms in the industry experienced idle times ranging from 10 percent to 30 percent. Only a very few firms that specialized in high-demand technical disciplines had idle times approaching RL's extremely low level.

Financial Performance

RL's key indicator of financial success was measured operating income (MOI). MOI was determined by subtracting expenses (salaries, benefits, rent, building services, and discretionary costs such as travel and training) from revenues (total associate hourly earnings) before taxes. As with an AT&T business unit, RL was responsible for all of its overhead expenses.

RL's financial results from 1991 to 1993 are shown in Exhibit 10. As can be seen, RL experienced losses of over $3 million in MOI during each of its first two full years of operation (1992 and 1993). Also shown are the estimated yearly cost avoidance/savings that benefited AT&T as the company avoided, for example, making severance payments to surplus employees that RL hired as associates. Resource Link was not financially credited with these cost-avoidance savings in the AT&T accounting system, Jim Meadows said.

Toward the latter half of 1993, the new leadership team brought on earlier in the year began working closely with RL's budget people to closely scrutinize RL's operating systems. According to Mike Lowe:

> This was really the first time that we had "peeled back the onion" and come to understand in gory detail what we were doing.
>
> When RL began, there was a strong sense of "doing God's work"—rescuing people. For HR people, this was a dream come true—a chance to be a "hero" on an individual level, a safety net.
>
> We were just "leaping into the void," making a lot of nonvalidated estimates. We had no idea really of what we'd be facing in terms of expenses other than salary and benefits or in terms of continued market demand. We deeply believed that the key to success was rapid growth, assumed that a sufficient markup was built into our pricing, and had faith that there was a break-even point.

RL's management began to uncover the nature and root causes of several major problems. Perhaps the most fundamental discovery during this period concerned the

EXHIBIT 10   Resource Link's Financial Statement, 1991–93 ($000)

	1991	1992	1993
Revenue	$ 234.6	$15,053.8	$29,937.1
Expenses			
Associate related			
Associate salary and benefits		$11,504.5	$23,356.0
Other expenses		$ 2,881.3	$ 3,603.7
Total associate related expenses		$14,385.8	$26,959.7
Staff related			
Salary and benefits		$ 1,916.7	$ 3,143.9
Other		$ 1,923.3	$ 2,964.4
Total staff related expenses		$ 3,840.0	$ 6,108.3
Total expenses	$1,002.0	$18,225.8	$33,068.0
Net operating results	($ 767.4)	($ 3,172.0)	($ 3,130.9)
Total cost avoidance/savings for AT&T	$ 740.0	$ 4,618.0	$ 2,211.0

In 1991 associate and staff expense was not differentiated. Resource Link was not financially credited with cost-avoidance/savings in the AT&T accounting system.

assumption that fast growth would solve all problems. Lowe described the incident that finally shattered this deep belief:

> At one meeting, Meadows was extremely critical of one of the district managers for blowing (coming in under) projected growth numbers. The manager recalculated the budget to see what the year-end impact would be using the actual (lower) rather than the projected (higher) growth figures. Working with the financial manager, the manager reported that profitability would be *better with slower growth* than with higher growth.
>
> We had been operating under the assumption that each additional associate improved the bottom line. What we actually found was that each additional associate increased expenses faster than they increased revenue for the year in which they were brought into the organization.

Staff manager Pam Mueller elaborated on this discovery:

> Each month that we brought in a large group of new associates we would incur their full salary and benefits and extensive costs in their recruitment and placement. We would not *begin* to recover any of these costs until the subsequent month and not fully recover them until some time later. The faster we grew, the worse the problem became.

With growth exaggerating RL's financial problems, it became even more imperative that RL find ways to capture revenue faster and reduce expenses. It became clear to the team that RL's main information system (R-OSS) needed a major overhaul. It did not provide for automated matching of associate skills to client requests, its billing capabilities were rudimentary, and manual transfers of information were required from one system application to another. Extensive effort was put into developing a more sophisticated version of R-OSS. Although the new release had been expected around October 1993 it was still not on-line at year-end, causing much frustration throughout Resource Link.

MEADOWS'S ASSESSMENT

Right now, I'm concerned about several challenges we are facing. Up to now, Resource Link has not been fully recovering its costs. Our growth forecasts were often off the mark. Our overhead and compensation expenses turned out to be higher than we anticipated . . . The people at the top [of AT&T] understand that losing money at first is part of building a business, yet I've committed to stopping the red ink by 1995. We probably can't do much with pricing—we already charge a bit more per hour than our competitors [e.g., outside temporary employment agencies]. So we somehow need to get better control of our costs.

At the same time, we have not been spending all of our training budget and we need to consider investing more in our associates. For example, many associates need more training to help them with their nontraditional role as a consultant. We also have been very concerned about their current skills becoming obsolete. We make a longer-term commitment to our associates than an outside agency makes to theirs. For this reason, we select our associates with extreme care, based not only on their having skills to meet current client needs but also on their ability to develop and maintain their marketability over time. But who should pay for the investment in their continuous development—Resource Link, our clients, or the corporation?

My staff and I have debated the issue of whether RL is primarily a social intervention or a business. At this point, I believe the business focus needs to come first. These days, there is a relentless pursuit of cost effectiveness throughout AT&T and I feel that has to be the driving mindset within RL as well. In a company like ours, to be credible and show that you're not just another HR passing fancy, you need to have a financial objective and show you are making a contribution. We have made a financial commitment and we intend to fulfill that commitment. Not just because my name is on the line but because RL is much too important, too strategic to the company, to jeopardize.

I wouldn't say there's a crisis just yet. But we're definitely at a major turning point that requires some decisive actions. I think we now have the right kind of management team in place to do the job. But there are a lot of important decisions to be made to get ourselves into the black and to position ourselves for future expansion.

(AT&T's Internet address is *www.att.com.*)

HABITAT FOR HUMANITY INTERNATIONAL

Joel W. Cook, *The George Washington University*

Robert F. Dyer, *The George Washington University*

Habitat for Humanity International (HFHI) was a nonprofit, ecumenical Christian housing ministry whose goals were to eliminate inadequate housing and homelessness from the world, and to make decent shelter a matter of conscience and action. Founded in 1976, HFHI had produced 60,000 homes around the world, thus providing low-income families in more than 2,000 communities with safe, decent, affordable housing. HFHI carried out its mission at the community level through a network of over 1,500 affiliates in all 50 states and operations in 54 nations (see Exhibit 1).[1] Although most individual domestic affiliates constructed relatively few units each year, HFHI's housing production volume in the United States put it in the ranks of the nation's top 20 homebuilders.[2]

Several distinct features of the HFHI program were "sweat equity" (usually around 500 hours of construction work) by the homebuyers themselves (or their families); on-site labor volunteers; support generated by churches; contributions (labor, land, in-kind, and financial) by professionals and corporate sponsors; and individual tax-deductible charitable contributions. Board members and salaried or volunteer staff members of the affiliates set most of the local program goals and objectives and implemented program activities. Some general rules, however, were established by the international organization. According to an "Affiliate Covenant" between each affiliate and HFHI, homes were sold with no profit markup and carried interest-free mortgages. Not a legal document, the Affiliate Covenant also stated religious principles and other key operating policies, including a strict limitation on acceptance of government funds. In practice,

This case originally formed the basis for the 1998 George Washington University/KPMG National MBA Case Competition. The authors gratefully acknowledge the financial support of KPMG, the contributions of HFHI staff members Millard Fuller, David Williams, Mike Willard, Mike Carscaddon, Ted Swisher, and Regina Hopkins, and the research assistance of Jeffrey L. Cummings.

[1]*Habitat for Humanity International Fact Sheet and Map* (Americus, GA: July 1997), p. 1.

[2]*Survey of Habitat for Humanity International (HFHI), Inc. Homeowners and Affiliates: Final Report* (Chicago: Applied Real Estate Analysis, Inc., September 1997), p. I-1.

EXHIBIT 1 Habitat for Humanity International Locations

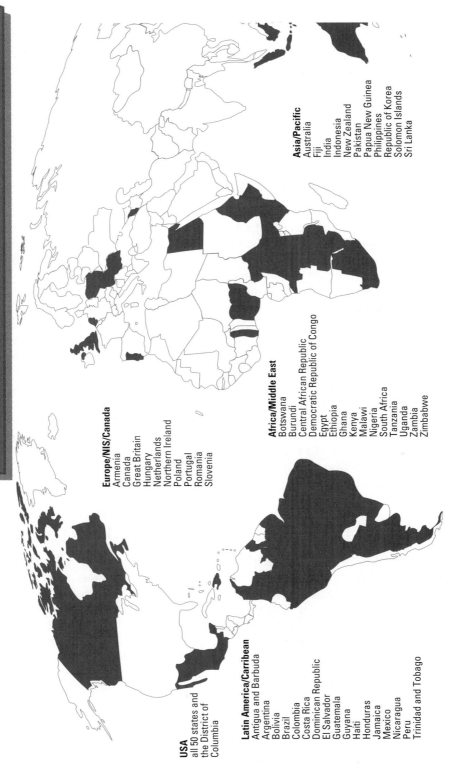

Habitat for Humanity Worldwide

USA
all 50 states and
the District of
Columbia

Latin America/Carribean
Antigua and Barbuda
Argentina
Bolivia
Brazil
Colombia
Costa Rica
Dominican Republic
El Salvador
Guatemala
Guyana
Haiti
Honduras
Jamaica
Mexico
Nicaragua
Peru
Trinidad and Tobago

Europe/NIS/Canada
Armenia
Canada
Great Britain
Hungary
Netherlands
Northern Ireland
Poland
Portugal
Romania
Slovenia

Africa/Middle East
Botswana
Burundi
Central African Republic
Democratic Republic of Congo
Egypt
Ethiopia
Ghana
Kenya
Malawi
Nigeria
South Africa
Tanzania
Uganda
Zambia
Zimbabwe

Asia/Pacific
Australia
Fiji
India
Indonesia
New Zealand
Pakistan
Papua New Guinea
Philippines
Republic of Korea
Solomon Islands
Sri Lanka

affiliates accepted government contributions only for infrastructure improvements or for acquisition of land or homes needing rehabilitation.[3]

Families in need of decent shelter applied to local Habitat affiliates. The affiliate's selection committee chose families from among those applicants based on their level of need, their willingness to become partners in the program, and their ability to repay a no-interest loan. Every affiliate followed a nondiscriminatory policy of family selection; neither race nor religion was a factor in choosing the families who were to receive Habitat houses.[4]

Habitat for Humanity was not a giveaway program. Through partnerships, it worked to empower the poor and involve the rich. Each affiliate strove to foster the local community and build friendships—even across lines of culture and conflict.[5]

THE NEED FOR A SIMPLE, DECENT PLACE TO LIVE

The shortage of affordable housing around the world was an immense problem. An estimated 25 percent of the world's population, 1.4 billion people, lived in substandard housing or were homeless in 1998. In the United States, despite a booming economy since 1993, the wages of low-income families had stagnated and had not kept up with rising rents and mortgage requirements. In 1973, 44.8 percent of U.S. families had enough income to qualify for a median-priced new home; by 1996 only 36.3 percent could afford one. Home-ownership rates for very-low-income families with children dropped by more than 20 percent from 1973 to 1998. Half of all renters below the U.S. poverty level spent more than 50 percent of their income on housing costs. High housing costs thus crowded out expenditures on such necessities as food and clothing. In addition, the shelter that could be afforded by the poor was often substandard. A report titled, "Housing America's Future: Children at Risk," estimated that 9.6 million households with children lived in housing highly likely to contain lead paint. According to the Centers for Disease Control, lead poisoning was the most common and societally most devastating environmental disease of young children. Habitat for Humanity maintained that owning a decent place to live provided not only shelter from the elements and environmental hazards but also family pride and stability. Finally, Habitat for Humanity spoke not only of building houses but also families and neighborhoods.

HISTORY OF HABITAT FOR HUMANITY INTERNATIONAL

Founded in 1976, Habitat for Humanity International became a world leader in addressing the issue of housing for the poor.[6] Using volunteer labor and donations, Habitat built simple houses and sold them at no profit and no interest to people who did not have an adequate place in which to live. The ministry was a growing social and spiritual movement whose purpose was to create tangible results that affected people's lives. By the late 1990s, Habitat for Humanity had grown to reflect many contributions of varied talents and gifts, but initially it was little more than an exciting idea in the minds of two visionary men: Millard Fuller and Clarence Jordan.

---

[3]Ibid.

[4]Fact Sheet, p. 1.

[5]Ibid.

[6]"The History of Habitat for Humanity International," http://www.habitat.org/how/historytext.html (January 27, 1998).

In 1942, Clarence Jordan cofounded Koinonia Farm, a small, interracial Christian farming community outside Americus, Georgia. Jordan was a trained farmer and biblical scholar. The farm served as a springboard for his belief that Christianity requires a social conscience as well as a spiritual dimension. Jordan's stalwart belief that race does not divide people in God's sight made Koinonia such a target for violence that by 1968 the once-thriving community had been reduced to a few families looking for new directions in their community life.[7]

At the same time, Millard Fuller was making his way to a creative rendezvous with Jordan. Raised in rural Alabama, Fuller became active in church organizations and involved in various entrepreneurial ventures. While in college and law school, he continued in his business pursuits and was worth over $1 million before the age of 30.[8] In his book, *A Simple, Decent Place to Live,* Fuller described his ascension to success:

When I was growing up, our family lived in the small east Alabama cotton mill town of Lannett, where my father owned a grocery store and a drive-in, but as early as age six, I had my own little businesses going too . . . Business on the side was part of my life all through Auburn University, although my activities during college were a little more subdued. But then, when I entered law school at the University of Alabama, . . . I met a fellow student who thought big— just like me. We were student tycoons, thinking up any and every idea we could to make money.

We sold pine cones, corn stalks, and Christmas trees. We chopped down chinaberry limbs, painted the berries silver, and sold them as "Oriental berries." We sold advertising for desk blotters and a student telephone directory. We developed a birthday cake service by mailing a letter to students' parents right before the students' birthdays, offering to deliver their dearest college student a cake on the important day. It worked; all the ideas worked. Well, almost all of them. . . .

Still, we were full of ideas.

We sold trash can holders and doormats and holly wreaths by mail through clubs like the YMCA and made so much money, we invested in real estate. We started by renovating an old house . . . By the time we were seniors, we were renting out half a city block to students. As we approached graduation day, we were already making more money than most people would make many years later.

Upon graduation, we opened a law office in the capital city of Montgomery and were lawyers by day and entrepreneurs by night. We sold tractor cushions through Future Farmers of America and gave away tractors as prizes. . . . Our next big project was selling cookbooks to Future Homemakers of America—a logical move from Future Farmers . . . After two years, our businesses were growing by such leaps and bounds, we had to close the law office for lack of time to devote to it.

And with all that income, I bought a choice twenty-acre lot and drew up plans for a bigger house. My partner and I purchased more farm land, and horses to ride on the land, and cars paid for with cash, and boats—all the things I had always thought would make me and my young family happy.

From the very beginning of our partnership, my partner and I shared one overriding purpose: To *make a pile of money.* We were not particular about how we did it; we just wanted to be independently rich. During the eight years we were partners, we never wavered from that resolve, working from breakfast meetings to midnight brainstorming sessions. So when the company treasurer marched into my office one day in 1964 to announce that I was worth a million dollars, I wasn't surprised. I started immediately thinking ahead.[9]

---

[7]*Organizational Development: Affiliate Operations Manual,* vol. 1 (Americus, GA: Habitat for Humanity International, Inc., 1993), p. 15.

[8]Ibid.

[9]Millard Fuller, *A Simple Decent Place to Live: The Building Realization of Habitat for Humanity* (Dallas: Word Publishing, 1995), pp. 14–15.

Then Fuller's life fell apart. His marriage decayed, his health began to fail, and he felt far removed from the religious foundation of his youth. Fuller decided to liquidate his assets and give all the proceeds away. In the summer of 1968, he and his family went to Koinonia Farm to consider the next step in their lives.[10]

In the discipleship setting of Koinonia, Jordan and Fuller developed the concept of "partnership housing"—where those in need of adequate shelter would work side by side with volunteers to build simple, decent houses. The houses would be built with no profit added and no interest charged. Building would be financed by a revolving "Fund for Humanity." The fund's money would come from donations and no-interest loans provided by supporters, the new homeowners' house payments, and fund-raising activities. The Fund for Humanity would then be used to build more houses.[11]

An open letter to the friends of Koinonia Farm told of the new future for Koinonia:

> What the poor need is not charity but capital, not caseworkers but co-workers. And what the rich need is a wise, honorable and just way of divesting themselves of their overabundance. The Fund for Humanity will meet both of these needs. Money for the fund will come from shared gifts by those who feel they have more than they need and from non-interest bearing loans from those who cannot afford to make a gift but who do want to provide working capital for the disinherited . . . The fund will give away no money. It is not a handout.[12]

In 1968, Koinonia laid out 42 half-acre house sites, with four acres in the center reserved as a community park and recreational area. Supporters from around the world donated capital to help start the work. After Jordan's death in late 1969, Fuller continued to provide leadership for the project. The Fund for Humanity built homes and sold them to families for no profit and no interest. As the partner families paid monthly mortgage fees, additional capital was generated to build more homes.[13] Thus, the basic model for Habitat for Humanity was begun.

Fuller often wondered if the Fund for Humanity concept would work in developing countries. In 1973, at the invitation of the Church of Christ in Zaire and under the sponsorship of the Christian Church (Disciples of Christ) in the United States, he and his family moved to Mbandaka, Zaire (now the Democratic Republic of Congo). With the help of the government and the local church, the interest of most of the community, and financial support from the U.S. churches, the Fullers were able to create a Fund for Humanity in the equator region and house 2,000 people within three years. After the Fullers returned to the United States, the Fund for Humanity continued to flourish.[14]

In September 1976, Millard Fuller and his wife, Linda, called together a group of committed Christians to discuss the future of their dream. Habitat for Humanity International was born at this meeting. The following years proved that the vision of a housing ministry was feasible. In 1984, former U.S. president Jimmy Carter and his wife, Rosalynn, took their first Habitat work trip, the Jimmy Carter Work Project, to New York City. Their personal involvement in Habitat's ministry brought the organization national visibility and sparked interest in its work across the nation.[15]

This involvement by Carter was the turning point for HFHI—essentially changing it from a small not-for-profit agency into an internationally known organization with

---

[10]*Organizational Development,* p. 15.
[11]"The History of Habitat for Humanity International."
[12]Ibid.
[13]*Organizational Development,* p. 16.
[14]Ibid.
[15]"The History of Habitat for Humanity International."

enormous fund-raising capability at local and national levels. The first Jimmy Carter Work Project (JCWP) involved dozens of volunteers for a week in starting the renovation of a six-story, 19-unit building in New York City. The Carters worked there in 1984 and returned in July 1985 to aid in the completion of the project. By comparison, the 1997 JCWP in eastern Kentucky and Tennessee (led by the 73-year-old former president) involved more than 2,400 volunteers from around the world in the building of 52 houses in one week (June 15–21). The 1998 JCWP, scheduled for Houston, Texas, held forth a goal of building 100 houses.

Exhibits 2 through 5 shows the rapid growth of HFHI. The organization's U.S. affiliates grew to over 1,400, at a 28 percent compounded annual growth rate from 1987 to 1997 (Exhibit 2); housing production in the United States showed a similar 26 percent growth, to just over 3,400 houses (Exhibit 3); international expansion occurred at an average growth of three countries per year since 1984 (Exhibit 4), while international house-building rates increased at close to 20 percent annually from 1991 to 1996 (Exhibit 5). However, the U.S. affiliate growth rate was expected to slow substantially, since most of the country was now covered by HFHI affiliates.

Habitat had two distinct types of projects: sponsored and affiliated. A sponsored project (usually in a developing country) was one to which Habitat committed funding and provided personnel for at least three years. An affiliate project was one in which a local group entered into a covenant relationship with HFHI and abided by its guidelines. The affiliate was responsible for generating its own funds and recruiting its own personnel through a local board of directors.[16] There were over 20,000 local board members for U.S. affiliates in 1998.

The cost of Habitat houses varied from as little as $500 in some developing countries to an average of $39,700 in the United States. In 1996, U.S. affiliates built three-bedroom houses for an average selling price of $40,057 and four-bedroom houses for $42,883. The no-interest mortgage length ranged from 7 to 30 years.[17] HFHI recently began an accelerated asset recovery program with packages of its U.S. mortgages resold in private placements at a discount in order to provide funding more quickly for the building of future houses.

Volunteers and donors became persuasive spokespersons for Habitat's mission to provide low-income families with new hope in the form of affordable housing. In the late 1990s, the circulation of *Habitat World,* a publication for homeowners, volunteers, and individuals making donations, numbered 1.7 million. Habitat noted that "communities have improved as citizens join together to successfully tackle a significant social problem—decent housing for all."[18]

HABITAT FOR HUMANITY INTERNATIONAL, AMERICUS

The headquarters of HFHI was located in Americus, Georgia, a small town about 120 miles south of Atlanta. Koinonia Farm was located on the outskirts of Americus and Plains; Jimmy Carter's home was about 15 minutes away. HFHI's organization chart (shown in Exhibit 6) illustrates the variety of functions at the Americus headquarters. Millard Fuller, the 62-year-old founder of HFHI, was a hands-on entrepreneurial manager who, despite an extensive national and international travel schedule, maintained

---

[16]*Organizational Development,* p. 17.

[17]Ibid.

[18]"The History of Habitat for Humanity International."

EXHIBIT 2   Cumulative Number of Habitat for Humanity's U.S. Affiliates

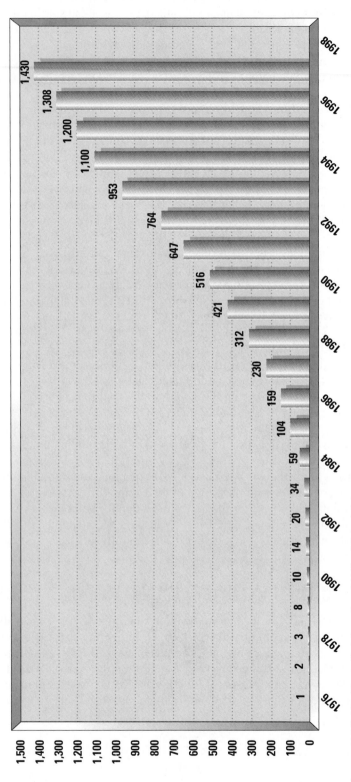

Source: Habitat for Humanity International, U.S. affiliate database.

EXHIBIT 3   Annual Habitat for Humanity U.S. Affiliate Production of New Houses and Repairs

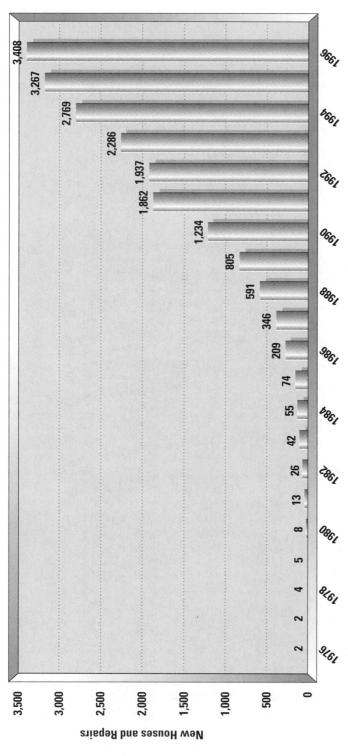

Source: Habitat for Humanity International, house court report; 1993 annual report data; affiliate statistical report.

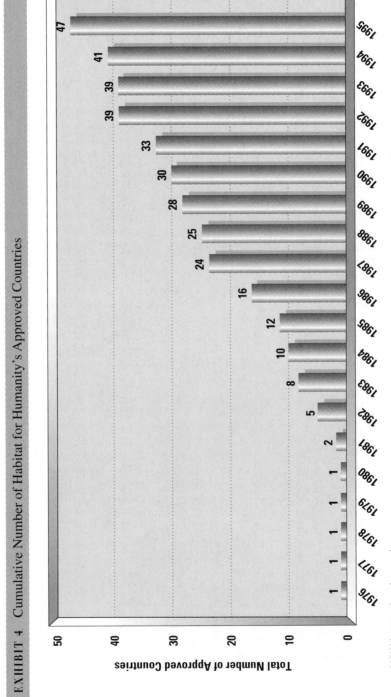

EXHIBIT 4 Cumulative Number of Habitat for Humanity's Approved Countries

Source: HAW international records.

EXHIBIT 5   Annual Production of New Houses, Habitat for Humanity International Affiliates

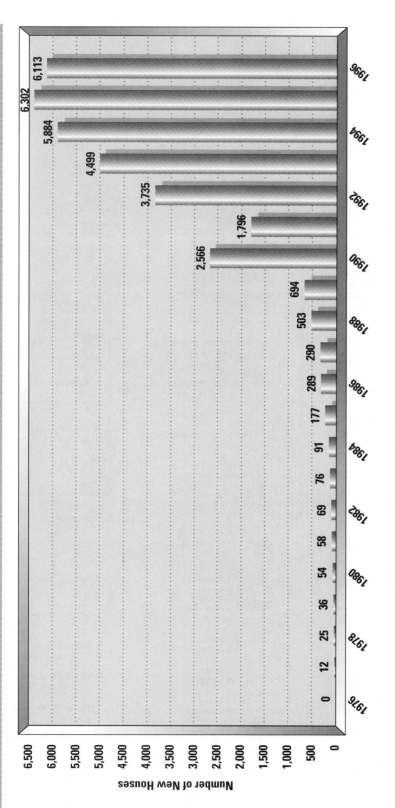

Source: Habitat for Humanity International, 1993 annual report data; operations database.

EXHIBIT 6   HFHI Organizational Structure, 1996

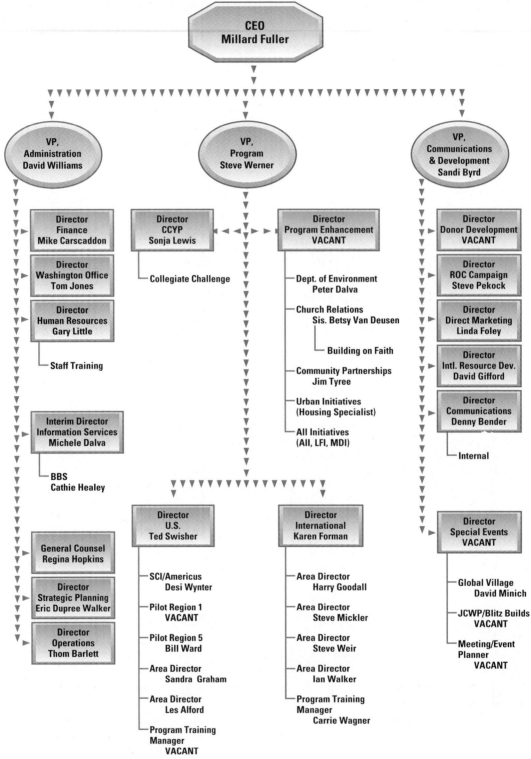

Source: Habitat for Humanity International, internal documents.

EXHIBIT 7   Direct-Mail Income

	Gross Income	Expense	Net Income	Income/Expense
1992	$21,371,188	$ 5,782,525	$15,588,663	3.70
1993	20,174,435	8,777,991	11,396,444	2.30
1994	25,779,335	8,315,102	17,464,233	3.10
1995	28,207,160	13,187,128	15,020,032	2.14
1996	37,698,452	15,968,111	21,730,341	2.36
1997	39,366,011	18,138,760	21,227,251	2.17

Source: Habitat for Humanity International, internal documents.

close contact with Americus staff, from executives to volunteers. During interviews with the case writers, Fuller phoned individuals throughout the organization to get detailed information—from the current circulation figures of *Habitat World* to the current count of students signed up for the Collegiate Challenge (a spring-break home-building blitz). The recipient of many awards, including the *Medal of Freedom* from President Bill Clinton in 1996, Fuller continued to work a 12-hour-day, seven-day-a-week schedule devoted to eliminating poverty housing worldwide.

Ted Swisher supervised the activities of 5 area and 14 U.S. regional affiliate directors who provided support in specific states. Since only about 400 affiliates had full-time staff, the parent organization often provided training, technical support, detailed operations manuals, home-building support, architectural manuals and floor plans, information services, some donated materials, and occasionally some financial support. The affiliates could use HFHI's name, establish an independent 501(c)3 organization, and perform their own local fund-raising. In return, they were asked to "tithe" back to headquarters a percentage of that local fund-raising. (A tithe is normally 10 percent, but actual numbers show that about 3–4 percent of fund-raising was allocated back to Americus.) In a 1996 financial report on the 317 largest U.S. affiliates, $1,266,000 was transferred to the affiliates for various programmatic efforts, while $1,935,000 in tithe money was sent to Americus. Total tithes from U.S. affiliates amounted to $3,961,386 in 1996.

Of great importance to HFHI were the direct media and marketing operations managed from Americus. With the growth in interest in Habitat around the world, and the very positive press from all forms of media, Habitat's direct-mail fund-raising was successful, accounting for over 50 percent of the revenue raised by HFHI Americus. Direct-mail revenues were $37,698,452 in 1996 and budgeted at almost $40 million for 1997 (see Exhibit 7). Exhibits 8, 9, 10, 11, and 12 provide more detailed financial information.

Campus Chapters and Youth Programs

In many interviews, the case writers were informed that part of the long-term future of HFHI was tied to its Campus Chapters and Youth Programs (CCYP). A Campus Chapter was located at a college, university, or high school and designated as an "affiliate" to build houses in partnership with HFHI affiliates; educate students and the local community about HFHI and affordable housing issues; and, to a lesser degree, raise funds for Habitat. The CCYP also included Campus Associates, which performed the same functions as Campus Chapters but were an already-established group (fraternity, sorority, service organization) that agreed to work with HFHI for a defined project or period of time. There were 487 Campus Chapters and over 900 Campus Associates chartered in 47 states and seven countries in 1998.

EXHIBIT 8   Combined Operating Statements of HFHI and Selected Affiliates, 1996 (in thousands of $)

	Habitat for Humanity International, Inc.	Selected Affiliates	Total	Eliminations (See Below)	Combined
Revenues					
Contributions	$70,687	$ 77,932	$148,619	$(3,201)	$145,418
Transfers to homeowners	1,253	58,000	59,253		59,253
Donated assets	6,310	11,551	17,861		17,861
Other income, net	1,947	9,513	11,460		11,460
Interest income		4,482	4,482		4,482
Total revenues	80,197	161,478	241,675	(3,201)	238,474
Expenses					
Program services	48,337	98,647	146,984	(3,344)	143,640
Supporting services					
Fund-raising	15,919	3,146	19,065		19,065
Management and general	2,268	14,732	17,000		17,000
Total supporting services	18,187	17,878	36,065		36,065
Total expenses	66,524	116,525	183,049	(3,344)	179,705
Increase in net assets	$13,673	$ 44,953	$ 58,626	$ 143	$ 58,769

Cash transfers to affiliates: During 1996, HFHI transferred approximately $1,266,000 in cash to the selected affiliates. This amount was recorded as an expense in HFHI's financial statements and revenue in the corresponding affiliates' financial statements. Accordingly, the effects of these transactions have been eliminated from the accompanying combined financial statements.

Affiliate tithes: During 1996, the selected affiliates transferred approximately $1,935,000 in tithes to HFHI. This amount was recorded as revenue in HFHI's financial statements and expense in the corresponding selected affiliates' financial statements. In addition, approximately $143,000 was accrued by the selected affiliates as of December 31, 1996 but was not recognized by HFHI. The effects of these transactions have been eliminated from the accompanying combined financial statements.

In-kind transfers: HFHI routinely transfers in-kind materials to certain of its affiliates. These transactions are recorded as expense in HFHI's financial statements. However, management was unable to determine the aggregate amount of such transfers for the selected affiliates, nor the extent to which these transfers were recorded as revenue in the corresponding selected affiliates' financial statements. Accordingly, the effects of these transactions have not been eliminated from the accompanying combined financial statements.

The biggest single project for CCYP was the Collegiate Challenge, which evolved from a spring-break alternative in the 1980s into a year-round event with seven intensive work weeks scheduled around colleges' spring breaks. The goal of the 1998 Collegiate Challenge, sponsored by Maxwell House Coffee, was to build 100 houses; an estimated 7,300 students were expected to work with 55 HFHI affiliates around the country to meet that goal.

HABITAT FOR HUMANITY AFFILIATES

As mentioned earlier, an Affiliate Covenant was the basic policy statement for HFHI's relationship with a Habitat affiliate. It was signed by the board of directors of the local Habitat affiliate and by a representative of Habitat for Humanity International. Each board agreed to operate by the principles of the document. The covenant described the

EXHIBIT 9　Combined Balance Sheets of HFHI and Selected Affiliates, 1996

	Habitat for Humanity International, Inc.	Selected Affiliates	Total	Eliminations (See Below)	Combined
Assets					
Cash and cash equivalents	$7,679	$27,597	$35,276		$35,276
Investments	3,322	5,550	8,872		8,972
Receivables					
Contributions and accounts, net of allowance for doubtful accounts	8,043	6,614	14,657		14,657
Notes, net of allowance for doubtful accounts	423	2,888	3,311		3,311
Mortgages receivable					
Gross	3,890	220,901	224,791		224,791
Unamortized discount	(1,726)	(62,731)	(64.457)		(64,457)
Net mortgages receivable	2,164	158,170	160,334		160,334
Inventories	1,959	3,431	5,390		5,390
Land, buildings, and equipment, net of accumulated depreciation	7,391	26,915	34,306		34,306
Home construction-in-process		75,519	75,519		75,519
Prepaids and other assets	134	762	896		896
	$31,115	$307,446	$338,561		$338,561
Liabilities and Net Assets					
Accounts payable and accrued expenses	$5,522	$11,776	$17,298	$(143)	$17,155
Home-building grants payable	3,386		3,386		3,386
Notes payable, net of discounts	3,981	27,419	31,400		31,400
Total liabilities	12,889	39,195	52,084	(143)	51,941
Net assets					
Unrestricted	6,497	248,751	255,248	143	255,391
Temporarily restricted	11,729	19,500	31,229		31,229
Total net assets	18,226	268,251	286,477	143	286,620
	$31,115	$307,446	$338,561	$ —	$338,561

Source: 1996 annual report.

purpose of Habitat and the basic assumptions undergirding its work. As a moral and spiritual document rather than a legal one, each covenant is worded in such a way as to permit flexibility in the Habitat family (see Exhibit 13).

Each Habitat affiliate had 501(c)3 status as a nonprofit, tax-exempt corporation. Affiliates were independent entities, responsible for their own fund-raising, family selection, and construction activities. HFHI provided a book titled *How to Start A Habitat for Humanity Affiliate* to each start-up affiliate. The book included information on organizational concepts, by-laws checklists, general personnel policies, business plans, and a long-range plan. It also showed the suggested structure for a local Habitat affiliate with key committees for board nomination, site selection, family selection, family nurturing, building, fund-raising and development.

The Site Selection Committee, ideally staffed by volunteers with previous real estate and construction experience, was to target areas of the community in which the

EXHIBIT 10   Income Summary for Habitat for Humanity International, 1992–97

	1992 Actual	1993 Actual	1994 Actual	1995 Actual	1996 Actual	1997 Budget
Direct mail	$1,371,188	$20,174,435	$25,779,335	$28,207,160	$37,698,452	$39,366,011
Capital campaign	0	0	0	0	2,176,758	3,875,000
Corporate programs	130,474	581,251	1,593,891	2,321,064	2,906,922	3,000,004
Development support						
Employee payroll	0	0	0	0	0	15,000
International fund-raiser	0	0	0	0	0	300,000
Organizations	294,576	192,008	589,714	357,196	360,404	500,000
Miscellaneous	128,937	122,075	209,182	60,933	190,233	50,000
Unclassified	2,746,811	2,283,596	1,788,422	1,247,046	3,892,476	1,499,992
Total development support	$3,170,324	$ 2,597,679	$ 2,587,318	$ 1,665,175	$ 4,443,113	$ 2,364,992
Donor development						
Combined federal campaign	$ 83,513	$ 335,535	$ 344,674	$ 384,429	$ 472,961	$ 300,000
Extraordinary giving	83,399	201,613	323,902	411,186	467,198	500,000
Foundations	1,031,862	810,040	641,247	906,572	804,727	500,000
Habitat World	707,897	568,176	574,380	287,780	0	1,600,000
Matching gifts	89,833	134,728	141,627	213,032	241,348	300,000
Planned giving	282,301	938,437	975,745	1,550,229	2,165,521	2,000,000
Receipt returns	2,216,541	2,502,908	2,626,217	2,573,011	2,874,179	3,000,000
Rylander	0	926,786	1,779,605	787,142	99,849	0
SCI donations	81,069	542,001	248,376	168,692	0	140,000
Top 1,000	732,508	738,590	832,386	1,261,102	1,366,322	1,300,000
Total donor development	$5,308,923	$ 7,698,814	$ 8,488,159	$ 8,543,175	$ 8,492,105	$ 9,640,000
Nondevelopment						
Church relations	$ 493,996	$ 445,390	$ 562,889	$ 449,185	$ 493,539	$ 450,000
GV workcamps	62,930	46,185	940,510	982,920	1,060,750	1,136,496
International tithe	0	0	0	8,171	9,239	15,000
IP fund-raising	118,578	109,716	113,627	147,900	124,374	120,000
Regional centers	42,182	354,091	32,695	321,505	114,725	164,620
Urban initiative	0	0	0	0	0	18,400
La Frontera	0	0	0	0	0	350,000
U.S. affiliate tithe	2,300,242	2,762,642	3,259,037	3,647,774	3,961,470	4,499,640
Total nondevelopment	$3,017,928	$ 3,718,024	$ 4,908,758	$ 5,557,455	$ 5,764,097	$ 6,754,156
Nonheritage						
Amencorps— government	$ 0	$ 0	$ 0	$ 906,792	$ 1,200,358	$ 1,384,670
Amencorps—HFHI	0	0	0	34,681	80,359	0
Educare	0	0	0	254,167	248,936	302,000
GK	2,007,993	2,797,166	4,110,951	6,203,507	6,216,192	4,609,000
JCWP	0	0	0	77,014	57,064	260,000
La Frontera	0	0	0	69,784	142,584	0
Rental income	0	0	0	67,059	72,869	22,700
Sales of merchandise	298,350	817,664	988,760	1,341,079	1,140,476	1,324,692

EXHIBIT 10 (*Concluded*)

	1992 Actual	1993 Actual	1994 Actual	1995 Actual	1996 Actual	1997 Budget
Elderhostel	$ 0	$ 0	$ 0	$ 0	$ 139,703	$ 0
20th Anniversary	0	0	0	0	262,121	0
Americus blitz	0	0	0	0	50,075	75,000
Collegiate challenge	0	0	0	0	71,632	65,000
GV Americus workcamps	0	0	0	0	15,810	0
Planbook	0	0	0	0	2,500	150,000
International transfer reserve	0	0	0	0	0	1,530,000
ROCC cash on hand	0	0	0	0	0	75,000
Mortgage payments	0	0	0	0	0	166,323
Environment—SCI	0	0	0	0	0	50,000
Mortgage sales— SCI	0	0	0	0	0	550,000
SCI corporate sponsorships	0	0	0	0	0	300,000
Federal Home Loan Bank—SCI	0	0	0	0	0	225,000
Pritzker Cousins	0	0	0	0	0	50,000
HOP income (SCI)	0	0	0	0	0	1,200,000
HOP income— loan repayment	0	0	0	0	0	125,000
RV Gypsies	0	0	0	0	7,100	0
Rental income	0	0	0	0	72,869	0
La Frontera	0	0	0	0	142,584	0
Freight reimbursement	0	0	0	0	43,552	120,000
SCI transfers to homeowners	0	0	0	697,300	1,110,234	0
Other income	280,874	573,233	1,395,547	995,588	1,528,217	395,191
Total nonheritage	$ 2,587,217	$ 4,188,063	$ 6,495,256	$10,646,971	$12,605,235	$12,979,576
Grand total	$35,586,054	$38,958,266	$49,852,719	$56,941,000	$74,086,682	$77,979,739

Source: Habitat for Humanity International, documents.

local Habitat affiliate would work. These areas were targeted based on need, willingness of other local community leaders to accept/partner with Habitat, and the availability of low-cost land.

The Family Selection Committee was responsible for drafting the selection criteria and the local affiliate's application document, screening applications, interviewing prospective families, and recommending families to the board for approval for home ownership. General criteria suggested by HFHI included current living conditions of the family (selection of families currently lacking adequate shelter was encouraged),

EXHIBIT 11   Statement of Cash Flows, Habitat for Humanity International, Years Ended December 31, 1996 and 1995

	1996	1995
Operating Activities		
Increase (decrease) in net assets	$13,672,597	$(3,082,183)
Adjustments to reconcile increase (decrease) in net assets to net cash provided by operating activities		
Depreciation expense	782,902	623,060
Net appreciation in fair value of investments	(162,982)	(274,023)
Net loss on sale of equipment	36,859	479,659
(Increase) decrease in unamortized discount on notes payable	(20,759)	26,531
Changes in operating assets and liabilities		
Increase in receivables	(7,403,261)	(979,174)
Increase in inventories	(367,082)	(1,453,526)
Increase in investments acquired by gift	(366,494)	(50,669)
(Increase) decrease in prepaids and other assets	(19,930)	780,021
Increase in accounts payable and accrued expenses	156,549	2,816,869
Increase in home building grants payable	496,760	2,161,978
Net cash provided by operating activities	$ 6,805,159	$ 1,048,543
Investing Activities		
Purchases of investments	$ (937,254)	$ (777,452)
Proceeds from sales and maturities of investments	551,240	217,917
Capital expenditures	(489,316)	(1,812,593)
Proceeds from equipment sales	136,771	329,130
Net cash used in investing activities	$ (738,559)	$(2,042,998)
Financing Activities		
Proceeds from borrowings	$ 4,229,750	$ 1,789,820
Principal repayments	(2,851,769)	(1,118,920)
Net (repayments) borrowings under line of credit	(1,899,990)	343,992
Net cash (used in) provided by financing activities	$ (522,009)	$ 1,014,892
Increase in cash and cash equivalents	$ 5,544,591	$ 20,437
Cash and Cash Equivalents		
Beginning of year	$ 2,134,836	$ 2,114,399
End of year	$ 7,679,427	$ 2,134,836
Supplemental disclosure of cash flow information (cash paid during the year for interest)	$102,248	$48,638

Source: Habitat for Humanity International documents.

family income (high enough to cover Habitat mortgage, insurance, taxes, utility and maintenance expenses but not high enough to qualify for a conventional mortgage), and willingness to participate in "sweat equity" partnership with Habitat. Family selections depended on fair, objective, nondiscriminatory procedures.

The Family Nurturing Committee's basic goal was to help families break the cycle of poverty. The committee sought to welcome the new Habitat family into the affiliate

EXHIBIT 12 Schedule of Functional Expenses, Habitat for Humanity International, Years Ended December 31, 1995 and 1996

	Program Services				Support Services			Total	
	U.S. Affiliates	International Affiliates	Public Awareness and Education	Total	Fund-raising	Management and General	Total	1996	1995
Home building grants	$ 8,130,386	$ 9,919,955		$18,050,341				$18,050,341	$18,003,801
Donated assets distributed	5,733,676	1,097	$ 710	5,735,483	$ 559	$ 7,008	$ 7,567	5,743,050	5,853,517
Home construction costs	1,076,934			1,076,934				1,076,934	527,028
Construction supplies	18,293	297	495	19,085				19,085	(50,267)
Discounts on mortgage notes	544,111			544,111				544,111	346,624
Salaries and benefits	5,354,360	2,607,151	2,680,114	10,641,625	1,828,297	1,266,951	3,095,248	13,736,873	12,468,039
Professional services—direct mail			3,152,690	3,152,690	12,308,187		12,308,187	15,460,977	12,602,060
Professional services—other	261,346	111,276	404,254	776,976	618,717	110,766	729,483	1,506,359	1,727,411
Postage and freight	287,440	44,887	784,184	1,116,511	419,606	126,347	545,953	1,662,464	1,439,035
Travel	502,060	883,774	690,093	2,075,927	193,612	95,021	288,633	2,364,560	1,917,071
Office supplies and materials	214,074	37,122	93,715	334,911	58,853	71,790	130,643	465,554	320,904
Printing	75,456	18,829	1,583,753	1,678,038	110,085	5,288	115,373	1,793,411	1,369,640
Utilities and telephone	383,013	90,403	102,266	575,682	83,658	115,989	199,647	775,329	754,132
Insurance	79,999	39,252	24,150	142,400	23,122	49,016	72,139	214,538	173,218
Interest, service charges, taxes	40,597	58,327	40,233	139,157	54,844	104,836	159,680	298,837	361,475
Repairs and maintenance	54,827	14,635	20,340	89,802	5,848	121,447	127,295	217,097	253,024
Regional and board meetings	65,920	139,429	3,070	208,319	580	(105)	475	208,794	218,362
Office and equipment	168,585	43,151	117,584	329,320	45,222	60,533	105,755	435,075	237,399
Service agreements	61,671	23,755	116,857	202,283	53,247	93,994	147,241	349,524	262,101
Training, recruitment, books	167,594	50,029	39,111	256,734	26,767	24,817	51,584	308,318	295,761
Depreciation	782,903			782,903				782,903	623,060
Other	195,612	108,902	103,660	408,174	88,203	14,766	102,969	511,143	508,853
	$24,197,756	$14,192,271	$ 9,947,279	$48,337,306	$15,919,407	$ 2,268,464	$18,187,871	$66,525,177	$60,212,248

EXHIBIT 13   Affiliate Covenant

Affiliate Covenant (with elaboration)
A Basic Covenant Between Habitat for Humanity International
and an Approved Habitat Affiliate Project

Preface

Habitat for Humanity International and the Habitat for Humanity affiliate work as partners in this ecumenical Christian housing ministry. The affiliate works with donors, volunteers, and homeowners to create decent, affordable housing for those in need, and to make shelter a matter of conscience with people everywhere. Although HFH International will assist with information resources, training, publications, prayer support, and in other ways, the affiliate is primarily and directly responsible for the legal, organizational, fund-raising, family selection, and nurture, financial, and construction aspects of the work.

Mission Statement

Habitat for Humanity works in partnership with God and people everywhere, from all walks of life, to develop communities with God's people in need by building and renovating houses so that there are decent houses in decent communities in which God's people can live and grow into all that God intended.

Method of Operations

Habitat for Humanity sponsors projects in habitat development, by constructing modest but adequate housing. Habitat also seeks to associate with other organizations functioning with purposes consistent with the official purposes of Habitat for Humanity International and the affiliate, as stated in the Articles of Incorporation of both Habitat organizations, namely:

1. To witness to the gospel of Jesus Christ throughout the world by working in cooperation with God's people in need to create a better habitat in which to live and work.
2. To work in cooperation with other agencies and groups which have a kindred purpose.
3. To witness to the gospel of Jesus Christ through loving acts and the spoken and written word.
4. To enable an expanding number of persons from all walks of life to participate in this ministry.

Foundational Principles

1. Habitat for Humanity seeks to demonstrate the love and teachings of Jesus Christ to all people. While Habitat is a Christian organization, it invites and welcomes affiliate board and committee members, volunteers, and donors from other faiths actively committed to Habitat's Mission, Method of Operation, and Principles. The board will reflect the ethnic diversity of the area to be served.
2. Habitat for Humanity is a people-to-people partnership drawing families and communities in need together with volunteers and resources to build decent, affordable housing for needy people. Habitat is committed to the development and uplifting of families and communities, not only to the construction of houses.
3. Habitat for Humanity builds, renovates, and repairs simple, decent and affordable housing with people who are living in inadequate housing and who are unable to secure adequate housing by conventional means.
4. Habitat for Humanity selects homeowner families according to criteria that do not discriminate on the basis of race, creed, or ethnic background. All homeowners contribute "sweat equity"; they work as partners with the affiliate and other volunteers to accomplish Habitat's mission both locally and worldwide.
5. Habitat for Humanity sells houses to selected families with no profit or interest added. House payments will be used for construction or renovation of additional affordable housing.
6. Habitat for Humanity is a global partnership. In recognition of and commitment to the global partnership, each affiliate is expected to contribute at least 10% of its cash contributions to Habitat's international work. Funds specifically designated, by a donor, for local work only may be excluded from the tithe.
7. Habitat for Humanity appeals to the stewardship of Christians and others of good will in the sharing of their resources with the economically poor. Habitat also works in partnership with government to alleviate poverty housing. However, Habitat has chosen to operate under a self-imposed discipline which restricts that partnership. Government funds cannot be accepted for actual construction expenses or administrative expenses, but can be used for acquiring land, acquiring houses to be remodeled, constructing streets or sidewalks, accessing utilities, etc.—setting the stage to build—provided no strings are attached that violate Habitat principles.

EXHIBIT 13   (*Continued*)

Agreement to Covenant

In affirmation of the mission, method of operation, and principles stated in this covenant, we, _____ _____ , a Habitat for Humanity affiliate, covenant with other affiliates and Habitat for Humanity International to accomplish our mission. Each partner commits to enhancing the ability to carry out this mission by: supporting effective communication among affiliates, HFH International, and regional offices; sharing annual reports; participating in regional and national training events; and participating in a biennial review and planning session between each affiliate and the regional office.

This Covenant is valid upon approval by each member of the affiliate board of directors and a designated representative of Habitat for Humanity International.

For Habitat for Humanity International: _____

Date _____

For the Habitat for Humanity affiliate _____ [affiliate name] _____

Date _____

Each member of the board of directors:

_____   _____

_____   _____

_____   _____

_____   _____

_____   _____

Elaboration of the Affiliate Covenant

Ecumenical, Diverse Board

The Board of Directors of the local Habitat affiliate must be ecumenical, reflecting the diversity of denominations in the area. Habitat believes that while Christians may disagree on some points of doctrine, we can agree on service in the name of Christ. Also, while Habitat is avowedly Christian, seeking to exalt Jesus Christ as Lord by demonstrating his love to all people, it welcomes committee and board members of any faith so long as they can accept the loving outreach of the life and teaching of Jesus Christ. The board must also reflect the ethnic diversity of the community and include a wide range of people—clergy and lay persons, professionals and low-income people, men and women. This diversity ensures a broad range of perspectives and wisdom and provides a strong base of operation.

No Profit, No Interest

Building or rehabilitating houses and selling them for no profit and no interest is essential to the vision of Habitat for Humanity. In the Old Testament, God tells his people, "If you lend money to any of my people who are poor, do not act like a moneylender and require him to pay interest" (Exodus 22:25). Habitat does not believe everyone should refuse to charge interest, but believes that Habitat can best serve God's people in need by refusing to charge interest to the poor. In doing this, Habitat seeks to be an alternative to our secular society.

Simple, Decent Houses

The construction of houses at each affiliate should reflect Habitat's philosophy of building simple but adequate houses, for two primary reasons. First, Habitat seeks to be a good steward of its resources by building homes with and for as many families as it can with the money and resources it receives. Second, it is important to build a house which is affordable to the new partner family so that the house will not become a heavier burden than the family can bear.

EXHIBIT 13   (*Concluded*)

Sweat Equity

"Sweat equity" is a key characteristic of Habitat for Humanity. Sweat equity is the unpaid labor invested by each partner family in the Habitat ministry. This physical investment reduces the monetary cost of the house, increases the personal stake of family members in their home, and fosters the development of partnership with other persons. This sweat equity, along with the volunteer labor of other Habitat partners, is important in building partnerships across economic, racial, and national divisions. The amount and type of sweat equity required of each partner family varies from project to project, but most projects require 500 hours of sweat equity. It may be contributed by any member of the family, and often friends, church members, and extended family members can help a homeowner meet the sweat-equity requirements. The work may include helping with the actual construction of the house or performing administrative work in the local Habitat office.

Nondiscrimination

God's love extends to the whole world regardless of race, nationality, or religion. In the same way, Habitat seeks to make decent housing available to all people in a nondiscriminatory manner. The selection criteria used by each affiliate should not discriminate on the basis of race, creed, or ethnic background. HFH International does not set guidelines defining nondiscrimination but trusts that each affiliate understands its local situation and will develop a fair, objective family selection process.

People-to-People Partnership

The focus of Habitat's ministry is not simply the construction of houses, but the development and empowerment of persons and communities. Habitat is interested in the people involved in its ministry, both the owners of Habitat houses and those involved in the construction of the houses. Habitat seeks to break down barriers and form partnerships between people from every walk of life.

Source: Habitat for Humanity International, internal documents.

and to provide them with a support system, educational opportunities, and a forum for discussing issues related to owning a Habitat home. The committee was encouraged to appoint an individual family sponsor or sponsors who would work with the family to help solve many of the long-term problems brought on by years of living in poverty. This committee was the primary liaison with the Habitat homeowner.

The Building Committee was responsible for construction planning and implementation of the construction plan. Members of this committee were expected to have strong experience in residential construction. The committee was involved in site selection as well as the selection of housing amenities, materials, and the architectural designs for the affiliate. The construction implementation had to plan for using a combination of volunteers, homeowners (500 hours of sweat equity), and skilled tradesmen (plumbing, electrical, mechanical, cabinetry, etc.). The committee also had to manage the purchasing of materials, the security of the both purchased and donated materials, and the security of the job site; it also had to build relationships with both material vendors and contractors. Older affiliates generally hired a professional staff to manage most of the role of the building committee.

The Fund-raising and Development Committee was a critical group for any successful affiliate. Habitat had grown such that there were more than enough volunteers to build houses, but the shortage lay in financial resources. Members of this committee had to write proposals to corporations and foundations, research donor sources, telephone or write prospective donors, and speak publicly in many venues on behalf of Habitat. Working with important partners such as churches and requesting in-kind donations from building groups and contractors also were important activities. Exhibit 14 shows the array of support obtained by the Baltimore Sandtown HFHI Affiliate for 1996.

EXHIBIT 14 Fund-raising and Development at HFHI's Sandtown Affiliate

Type of Support	Number of Organizations/Individual Supporters	Representative Organizations
Major grants	8	Local and quasi-governmental organizations
Full house sponsors ($30,000)	1	Foundations, financial institutions, builders
House sponsors ($15,000–$17,500)	3	Foundations, financial institutions, builders
One Church–One Home ($15,000–17,500)	10	Local and regional churches
House partners ($5,000–$10,000)	10	Foundations, financial institutions, builders
Financing	6	Local and quasi-governmental organizations and financial institutions
Program partnerships	3	Youth-work groups
Additional grant support ($500+)	41	Assorted
College and university support	12	Local colleges and universities
Fund-raising events	2	Individuals
In-kind: technical	10	Professionals
In-kind: construction services	13	Assorted
In-kind: support services	19	Assorted
In-kind: building materials	15	Assorted
Leslie Street Project funding and financing	13	Local and quasi-governmental organizations and financial institutions

Source: HFHI Baltimore-Sandtown documents.

In order to support the above local affiliate activities, senior staff at Habitat's international headquarters in Americus, Georgia, focused on the U.S. affiliates' program and coordinated a series of regional centers that provide support services to the local affiliates in each geographic region. The 15 regional centers supported the affiliate programs, hosted regional conferences and training events, and provided guidance and resource materials to existing and prospective affiliates. Exhibit 15 shows the Affiliate Program Structure for Habitat. Based on a 1996 McKinsey Consulting study provided as a pro bono effort to Habitat, headquarters began testing an expanded regional support center concept in the Northeast and Midwest. These Habitat centers were expected to grow from three full-time staff to six to nine staffers, adding new functions and positions in the following areas:

- Development and fund-raising.
- Training.
- Campus chapter relations.
- Church relations.
- Media (Northeastern region only).

The immediate objective was to do a better job in providing needed services, plus assistance with management and financial issues for the affiliates. It was hoped that

EXHIBIT 15   The Affiliate Program Structure

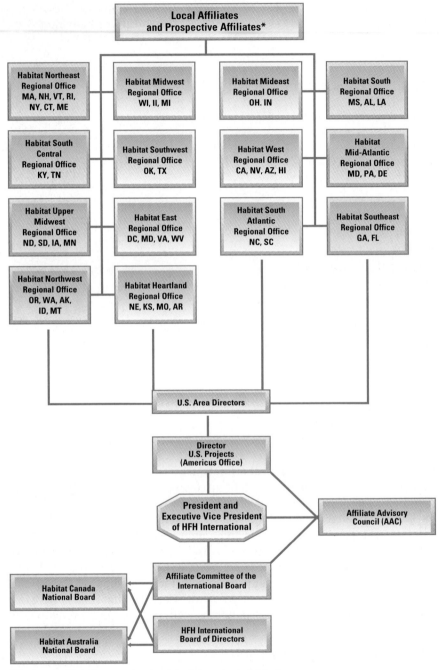

*Each region has its own structures for internal administration.
Source: Habitat for Humanity International, internal documents.

EXHIBIT 16   1996 Affiliate House Building Performance

	Number of Affiliates with Buildings Completed in 1996 New and Major Rehabs	Number of Affiliates with Lifetime Construction New, Major Rehabs, Rehabs
Over 300 houses	—	1
200-299 houses	—	3
100-199 houses	—	21
50-99 houses	1	47
25-49 houses	12	97
15-24 houses	17	129
10-14 houses	22	122
5-9 houses	108	251
3-4 houses	136	212
1-2 houses	613	271
0	380	135
Total	1,289	1,289

Source: 1996 Affiliate Statistical report.

this program would result in a perception that Habitat was doing a better job for its affiliates as well as in an actual increase in the number of houses built.

A network of active state Habitat organizations had also evolved, with state boards of directors made up of representatives from affiliates within the states. Most state organizations had no full-time staff. Active state groups existed in Arizona, Colorado, Kentucky, Michigan, Minnesota, Oregon, and Washington.

Although the Habitat affiliates were given similar recommendations for structure and received similar support from Americus, they were actually extremely diverse, functioning with different objectives, cultures, and modes of operation. The following statistics illustrate the diversity:

- Only 300–400 of the 1,500 affiliates were on-line users of Habitat's electronic bulletin board.
- 380 of 1,289 affiliates did not build a single house in 1996 (see Exhibit 16).
- 300 affiliates produced 70 percent of Habitat's housing output (see Exhibit 16).
- House-building success varied dramatically by region (see Exhibit 17).
- 106 older affiliates (excluding all new 1996 affiliates) recorded no building in 1995 or 1996.
- The average Habitat affiliate built about two houses per year.
- Many affiliates were start-ups with no full-time staff.
- The Lynchburg, Virginia affiliate built 30 houses a year on average, in a community of 30,000 individuals, while New York City built only 5 per year.
- Philadelphia had four affiliates that built 20 total houses per year. Each Philadelphia affiliate identified a specific geographic area in which to build, and each did its own fund-raising, materials buying, and family selection independently, without a coordinated effort on any front (e.g., obtaining quantity discounts, leasing a common warehouse).

EXHIBIT 17   Characteristics of Selected HFHI Affiliates' Programs

State/Affiliate	Year Program Started	Total	New	Rehab	Detached Single-Family	Other	Average Price per Unit ($000)	Average per Square Foot
California								
Fresno	1986	20	18	2	20	0	$40	$28
Sacramento	1985	19	18	1	19	0	$40-50	$41
District of Columbia and Maryland								
Washington	1989	26	23	3	13	duplex-8 row-5	$65	$53
Annapolis	1987	32	23	9	32	0	$73	$25
Florida								
Clay County	1987	16	15	1	16	0	$30	$33
Jacksonville	1988	176	170	6	176	0	$35-40	$35
Mississippi								
Jackson	1988	105	95	10	105	0	$37	$45
Meridian	1989	21	14	7	21	0	$35	$35
New Jersey								
Newark	1986	28	14	14	0	coop-8 condo-6 dup-14	$70	$33
Paterson	1984	60	58	2	2	Du-, 4- or 6-plex-56 condo-2	$57-59	$46
Ohio								
Chagrin Falls	1992	27	11	16	27	0	$45	$41
Cleveland	1987	58	58	0	58	0	$45-50	$41
Oregon								
Bend	1989	23	23	0	20	triplex-3	$40	$36
Eugene	1990	11	11	0	11	0	$35-40	$38
Texas								
Houston	1985	46	2	44	42	duplex-4	$40-42	$40
San Antonio	1975	150	115	35	150	0	$36	$32
Virginia								
New River Valley	1985	17	14	3	17	0	$30	$27
Roanoke	1986	63	63	0	63	0	$33	$43
Wisconsin								
Milwaukee	1984	92	36	56	90	duplex-1, row-1	$34-45	$40
Total		990	781	209	882	108		

Source: Surveys conducted by Applied Real Estate Analysis, Inc.

- Twin Cities Habitat (Minneapolis/St. Paul) had a single board of directors and five full-time management teams to work with six neighborhood affiliates. Each affiliate did site selection, family selection, and building, while the board centrally coordinated fund-raising, bulk buying of materials, and common warehousing.

Each affiliate was expected to complete an annual survey for the HFHI *U.S. Affiliate Statistical Report,* which provided data on basic areas, such as houses built, rehabs completed, fund-raising, revenue generation, homeowner characteristics, and building projections for the next year. Also, an annual affiliate financial statement was submitted to Americus summarizing the financial status of the affiliate.

A good glimpse of the diversity of HFHI's affiliate structure in the United States was provided by a September 1997 study of Habitat affiliates conducted for the U.S. Department of Housing and Urban Development by Applied Real Estate Analysis, Inc. (AREA). The study examined both Habitat affiliates and homeowners' characteristics. AREA worked with HUD and HFHI to select 19 affiliates that would represent a cross section of urban and rural affiliates, staff sizes, and the specific characteristics of individual affiliate building projects. The housing units produced by these affiliates also mirrored the diversity of Habitat housing unit production—detached and attached, new construction and rehabilitation, and scattered-site and cluster homes in different neighborhood settings. See Exhibit 17 for an illustration of the geographic distribution and general program characteristics of selected Habitat affiliates.

Established in 1975, San Antonio was the oldest among the 19 affiliates. Most of the participating affiliates were established in the 1980s; the newest (Eugene) started in 1990. In addition to these 19 affiliates, AREA collected some additional information on two affiliates—one on Chicago's west side and another in Lake County, Illinois—during a pretest of data collection instruments and procedures.

Jacksonville, the largest affiliate, had completed 176 homes at the time of the field study. The number of completed units for the other 18 affiliates ranged from a low of 11 (Eugene) to a high of 150 (San Antonio). The majority of the homes represented were of new construction. However, all but 4 of the 19 affiliates had completed at least one rehabilitated home. Habitat affiliates included in the AREA report primarily built single-family detached homes; three affiliates had experience with duplex and/or townhouse structures, and two had completed condo and/or co-op projects involving rehabilitation.[19]

While all HFHI affiliates strove to provide home ownership opportunities for low- to very-low-income households, specific means of achieving this goal varied from affiliate to affiliate. Within the group of 19 affiliates included in the AREA analysis, housing types ranged from single-family homes to condominiums in multifamily buildings, while construction methods varied from a predominance of rehabilitated units to an overwhelming emphasis on new construction. The average monthly payments for Habitat homeowners in this sample was $269 per month, of which $120 was for taxes and insurance (leaving an average loan repayment amount of $149). Although low purchase prices and zero-interest mortgages remained central to the affordability goals of the program, there were variations in other aspects of financing that did not directly affect the homeowner's monthly housing costs.

Among the more than 1,400 HFHI affiliates, the diversity of program design features was even greater. Not surprisingly, many affiliates changed the characteristics of their programs over time as they worked to serve low-income home purchasers more

---

[19]Survey of Habitat for Humanity International, p. II-8.

efficiently and cost effectively. In the five-volume *Affiliate Operations Manual* prepared in 1993, the international organization offered a myriad of suggestions for program design and implementation. However, since each affiliate was a partner with HFHI and not a legally connected franchised entity, the local organizations ultimately decided their own program structure. The AREA analysis focused on features of the selected affiliates that were illustrative of the HFHI program for low-income homebuyers.[20]

Not all individuals linked to the Habitat network agreed with the laissez-faire approach Habitat international took to the affiliate network. Comments from HFHI staff related to the organization's overall approach to the headquarters/affiliate system included statements such as the following:

- "It would be interesting to look at both profit and nonprofit organizations and the types of standards and criteria evaluation systems they have for their local organizations."
- "What constitutes 'successful' or 'efficient' affiliates in the Habitat network?"
- "Habitat doesn't really do any pruning or disaffiliating of unsuccessful or inactive affiliates. At least, if Habitat International bails out a financially troubled affiliate, it might reexamine issues and perhaps put some controls in place until the affiliate gets back on its feet."
- "Would Habitat be more successful in urban areas if they set up 'company stores' which are run directly by the headquarters in Americus?"
- "Overall, Habitat's image is great but the communications materials used by both headquarters and affiliates lack a coherent, disciplined message. There are too many miscellaneous 'looks' to Habitat's promotional pieces."
- "Habitat International will have to become more analytical and professional in its affiliate network. The future will require them to get greater efficiency out of affiliates because they will hit natural limits to growth with the strategy of signing up more and more affiliates. Professionalism will need to be reflected in:
  –better financial controls used to look at affiliate performance.
  –improved information technology and systems at both headquarters and affiliates.
  –more sophistication in training (who needs what) programs designed by headquarters for the affiliates."
- "It's time that Habitat consider the merging of smaller affiliates in some metropolitan areas. The Twin Cities (Minneapolis/St. Paul) model should be tested elsewhere as an opportunity for enhancing the efficiency and effectiveness of Habitat in an area."
- "Maybe it's time for Habitat International to get more aggressive with its affiliate strategy. This might include 'picking the winners' and investing more resources in the top 300 affiliates that do 70% of the housing output."

Despite such comments, and while the executive directors of several Habitat affiliates in the Baltimore-Washington region agreed that although some signs of tension and discord appeared to exist about the affiliates' view of HFHI and headquarters, most of the comments about HFHI were very positive. There was uniform recognition that Habitat had a very strong, compelling brand name; that Habitat was an incredible fundraising success story; that Millard Fuller and Jimmy Carter continue to be positive,

---

[20]Ibid.

high-profile spokespersons for the organization; and that some very strong programmatic, training, assistance, and support material flowed from HFHI headquarters in Americus, Georgia, and its regional centers to the affiliates.

While the overall interview responses by HFHI affiliate directors were positive, there were concerns expressed in some areas. For example, directors did not feel that Americus had a good grasp of how to make Habitat work in urban areas. Several mentioned that Habitat hadn't gotten away from its rural, Southern roots and noted several "misfires" with urban initiatives at headquarters. Special projects and programs run by Americus required a lot of coordination by the local affiliates—for example, the Oprah Winfrey project or the House that Congress Built—but the affiliates didn't get a share of the funds raised from these efforts.

Some affiliates were concerned about receiving less than timely responses on their questions. Often affiliates went directly to Americus with their issues, bypassing the regional offices. The training provided to affiliates wasn't felt to be particularly well focused or sophisticated. Some felt it was mostly geared to new or start-up affiliates. No "core curriculum" existed tailored to various segments or categories of affiliates. Finally, Americus was felt to be behind with respect to information technology support for affiliates. The absence of standard accounting, volunteer data base, and construction management software for affiliates were mentioned as cases in point. Another telling example was that Americus appeared to be an "Apple/Macintosh shop" while its affiliates predominantly used DOS or Windows 95 platforms.

It is important to note that the topic of affiliate performance measurement was beginning to be mentioned more and more at HFHI. As suggested above, there were no agreed-upon definitions of what constitutes a "successful" affiliate. Habitat did not set performance objectives or utilize formal criteria or measurement of affiliate outputs. Complicating the issue of affiliate performance measurement was the fact that Habitat also had no standardized definitions of types of affiliates in areas, such as

- Geographic area—no common interpretation of what was an urban, rural, or suburban affiliate.
- Size—no groupings or segment definitions for small, medium, or large affiliates in terms of historical building activity, fund-raising, or number of staff in full-time equivalents.

Given all of these issues, there was growing concern within Habitat that overall management systems needed to be evaluated and improved. Interviews with several affiliate executive directors indicated that performance measurement of the HFHI affiliate system also ought to include a discussion of objectives, performance standards, and measurement criteria for the regional offices and Americus headquarters itself as well. Just as Habitat headquarters was interested in improving its U.S. affiliate system, the executive directors felt that performance measurement should be a two-way street. It would be reasonable, they said, to assess how Habitat headquarters does in providing resources, training, and support for the affiliates.

(HFHI's Web address is *www.habitat.org*.)

BLACK DIAMOND EQUIPMENT, LTD.

Steven J. Maranville, *University of St. Thomas*

Madeleine E. Pullman, *Colorado State University*

Jeff Jamison looked above at the glistening ice and snow of the frozen waterfalls. He had waited three weeks for the ice to get to this perfect condition, thick enough to support his weight, and the correct consistency for holding the picks of the two axes in his hands and the tooth-covered crampons on his feet. On this Saturday in early January of 1993, he was trying out a new axe, the Black Prophet, a state-of-the-art climbing tool with a light weight, composite handle, and innovative head design produced by Black Diamond Equipment, Ltd. Everyone in the mountaineering world was talking about the Black Prophet's novel design and waiting for the tool to enter the stores in the coming months. Jeff was lucky enough to have a connection with one of Black Diamond's sales representatives and thus had access to the new Black Prophet before its formal release to the market.

At the top of the last pitch of the climb, he sank the Black Prophet in the ice and suddenly felt a disconcerting snap. Jeff watched with disbelief as pieces of the broken axe plummeted thousands of feet to the canyon floor. As he fought off panic, Jeff realized that he would be forced to descend with only one axe, a doable but challenging feat. During the long, arduous descent, all Jeff could think about was how a tool like that one could have left Black Diamond's factory.

The following Monday, January 4, 1993, Mellie Abrahamsen, Black Diamond's new quality assurance manager, a recent MBA graduate from the University of Utah, entered her office and turned on her computer to scan her e-mail. The news of the axe incident was echoing throughout the plant. Research and Development, Production, Customer Service, Marketing, and the president were all demanding an explanation and a plan. With all the excitement over the new design, preseason orders for the Black Prophet had exceeded expectations. Although the tool was on back order for many customers, the first production run of the axe had already been shipped to mountaineering stores throughout the world. Highlighted at the top of Abrahamsen's e-mail listing was a priority message from Peter Metcalf, president of Black Diamond, calling an emergency meeting with all department heads to develop a plan for handling the crisis.

MONDAY MORNING MEETING

By 9:00 AM Black Diamond's top management team was huddled around the square butcher-block table that filled the center of Metcalf's congested corner office. As Mellie Abrahamsen approached, she could see into Metcalf's office through the two large windows that faced the shop floor. Because she was new to the company, many of the artifacts peculiar to Black Diamond still caught her attention.

Metcalf's office walls were decorated with framed photographs of mountain-climbing and skiing adventures. The management team members sitting around the table were dressed casually; many were wearing Black Diamond sportswear—T-shirts and sweaters with the Black Diamond insignia. Abrahamsen squeezed through the office and found a seat next to Metcalf, from which she had a view out the windows.

Metcalf spoke anxiously to the group: "This incident is a devastating blow. Thank goodness the guy didn't get hurt; but now every one of our axes out there is suspect. If we have to issue a recall on the product, that will kill our axe business. If we have to discontinue our axe program, all the European competitors will step in and copy the technology that we worked so long to perfect. Yet think of the liability implications of an accident from this tool! How could this have happened? I thought this axe had the latest and greatest technology! We've never had problems like this with our regular mountaineering axes."

Maria Cranor, the marketing manager, added to Metcalf's fervent speech: "If customers see this axe as being of poor quality, we'll be forced to cease the axe program. But worse, if customers think Black Diamond is a company that markets unsafe products, our whole business is in jeopardy! Black Diamond must not lose its leadership image."

"My sales representatives are having a fit," Stan Smith, manager of customer service, proclaimed loudly. "They have huge back orders for the axe, and the retail shops have several customers a day asking about the tool. You folks know how this industry is—rumors about tool failures and accidents get around fast."

In a despondent tone, the designer of the Black Prophet, Chuck Brainard, said, "I can't believe this nightmare. Just as we were sitting on top of the world with the most innovative design to enter the market in years—all the competition taken by surprise, and a good ice-climbing season ahead—a major stroke of bad luck hits."

"I can't help but think," said Stan Brown, the production manager, "that the cause of the axe's failure is in its design. It's great to be innovative, but I think the design is so innovative that it just doesn't work."

"Now wait a minute, Stan," Metcalf interjected. "I don't want this to deteriorate into finger pointing."

Brainard spoke up. "No, no, that's all right, Peter. Stan might be right. Maybe we did go too far."

Metcalf went on: "We don't know all the facts. So let's stay focused and not jump to conclusions. This is a companywide problem."

Trying to refocus the group, Cranor said, "We tried to cut the lead time on this project so that we would have at least a year of sales before the French, Swiss, and other U.S. competitors could copy our concept and steal our market share. We have a reputation as a high-quality and innovative design company. This incident is potentially very damaging to our reputation as the market leader for innovation."

"We've got to nip this one in the bud and find a way to reassure our customer base," contended Smith. "I need an answer as soon as possible."

John Bercaw, manager of research and development, said, "Stan, I appreciate the urgent need that you're feeling with regard to handling customer concerns, but we need more than a quick fix. We need to find out why the failure occurred and to put systems in place to prevent this from happening again."

"I agree," Metcalf said. "As I said, this is a companywide problem."

Brainard attempted to clarify the situation. "As I see it, the possible sources of the failure are design, materials, and/or assembly."

"I can speak about the development phase of the project," stated Bercaw. "We worked hard to develop this axe and cut down on the lead time between the conceptualization and production of the final tool. Peter, you know we've been under tremendous pressure to have this new axe into the production phase and on the market in under two years."

Metcalf nodded. "That's been our strategy," he said, "being the 'firstest with the mostest.'"

Bercaw continued. "This project has been a real struggle; we've been working with all sorts of new technologies, like composite construction and modular tool design. The vendors normally don't make tools for these types of applications. They've had a hard time meeting our specifications, and many of the vendors don't want to work on our products because of potential liability implications."

"What about the assembly?" asked Metcalf.

Brown answered, "Well, the shop worked like crazy to get those axes out for the winter season and I put my best people on the rush assembly. The shop has been really taxed, what with the increasing growth rate for all our climbing and mountaineering products. We're always scrambling to meet the back orders. We need more people and new machines to keep up with this demand and improve our quality."

Metcalf persisted. "Do you know of anything in particular that may have been out of the ordinary during assembly?"

Brown replied, "I'd have to talk to Brian, our lead assembler, to see if he has any clues about why that axe could have failed in the field."

Metcalf turned to his left, where Black Diamond's newest management team member was sitting. "I realize that this is all new to you and that you came in after the fact, so I doubt the Quality Assurance Department can do much about this situation now."

Caught somewhat by surprise, Abrahamsen pulled her thoughts together and said, "Since this job is a newly created position, I wasn't here during the design development and testing phase. I would like to see the procedures and testing information on the production lot of axes. Black Diamond wants to be ISO 9000–certified, and we would need to have all those documents for ISO 9000 certification anyway, so this is a good starting place. Meanwhile, I think we should bring all the field axes back for inspection to reinforce customer confidence and prevent what happened on Saturday from happening again."

Looking out of his office's windows, Metcalf pointed to the shop floor and remarked, "Isn't that Brian walking through the shop? Ask him to come in."

Brian Palmer, the lead assembler, entered Metcalf's office. There was no place to sit, so he remained standing. Metcalf explained to Brian the purpose for bringing him into the meeting. Brian indicated that he had heard about the climbing incident involving the Black Prophet.

Metcalf continued. "Brian, we're not on a witch hunt; we're trying to understand the full range of factors that could have contributed to the tool's failure. What can you tell us about the assembly?"

Brian spoke frankly: "I personally put together all of those axes. We didn't have any procedures, because it was the first time we had made a production lot. Normally when we work on a new product, we go through a learning curve trying to figure out the best assembly method. We make so many different types of products in the shop, it's really like a craft shop. And I'm not even sure if I have the most up-to-date prints right now. The vendor had a lot of trouble casting all those parts to the exact dimensions. But I was able to find enough parts that seemed to fit, and with a little extra elbow grease, I hammered the pieces together. I had to work overtime to meet the deadline and get all the preliminary orders out to the customers. But that's what matters—pleasing the customer."

"But is creating a defective axe really pleasing the customer?" questioned Abrahamsen. "What good is it to be first to market if the product fails in the field? Sure, we have to get to market fast; but we also have to make the axe right the first time. The way we deal in the short term with the Black Prophet situation will have some long-term implications for Black Diamond's strategy. I think we should examine the new-product introduction process as well as the ongoing production processes to see how we can prevent this type of thing from happening in the future."

THE MARKET FOR MOUNTAINEERING EQUIPMENT

The established customer for mountaineering products, including mountaineering skis, had traditionally been the serious international mountaineer—professionals as well as expert amateurs. Some dedicated mountaineers worked as professional guides and explorers; nonprofessionals had other jobs, but both professionals and amateurs spent their vacations and weekends climbing in their local areas and traveling throughout the world attempting to conquer remote peaks. This traditional customer base had been primarily in North America, eastern and western Europe, Japan, and Korea, although limited numbers of participants were from other countries.

Mountaineering was as popular in Europe as basketball was in the United States, with mountaineering stars earning high incomes through competitions, product endorsements, and other media exposure. Because of the long history of climbing in Europe, the European market was the biggest segment in the world climbing market, with 10 percent of the market in France alone. Not only did the adult urban European population prefer to spend vacations in mountain villages, but increasingly younger generations of Europeans were forsaking crowded beaches for mountain holidays revolving around mountain sports.

Starting in the 1980s, media exposure had brought mountain sports to previously ignored market segments throughout the world. Rock climbing and mountaineering images had become popular for advertising many types of products and for adding "color" to music videos and movie plots. Because of this exposure, teenage and recreational customers—predominantly in the U.S. market—represented high-growth segments, with the noticeable growth rate in the mid-1980s erupting into an explosive rate of 40 percent in the early 1990s. Customers in this growing market segment had no intention of traveling the world looking for untouched and ever more challenging peaks; instead, they climbed and skied purely for fun in their local and national resort areas.

Customarily, people wishing to learn mountain sports would employ guide services and schools for acquiring the necessary skills. The newer converts, however, were bypassing this conventional route by going to indoor climbing gyms or learning skills from friends. Many industry experts speculated that the breakdown of the conventional training methods would contribute to an increased lack of knowledge regarding mountaineering safety and lead to increased accident rates. In turn, accidents would increase the chances of litigation for all firms involved in the industry. These trends concerned mountain-sports firms worldwide.

COMPETITION IN THE MOUNTAINEERING EQUIPMENT INDUSTRY

Located in Salt Lake City, Utah, Black Diamond Equipment, Ltd., was a major player in the burgeoning international mountaineering industry, on both domestic and global fronts. Black Diamond manufactured and distributed a full range of products for mountain sports, from rock-climbing gear to mountaineering and backcountry skis, and faced few domestic or global competitors whose business was on a similar scale. (Exhibit 1 offers a company/product profile of the mountaineering industry.)

The industry that served the mountaineering market consisted of three groups: retailers, wholesalers, and manufacturers.

Retailers

The retail businesses serving the market's diverse variety of mountaineering customers were one of three types. The first group, the "core" mountaineering shops, were small retail operations specializing in products specific to mountaineering such as ropes, climbing protection, climbing axes, expedition clothing, packs, harnesses, and information guides for local and national sites. Because these shops were usually located in mountain areas such as the Rocky Mountains or the Alps, the shop personnel were experts in the special tools and applications for their regions. In addition, these employees often had personal knowledge of other locations around the world.

Mountaineering shops usually carried products made in their region with specialized products from other countries. The core shops competed on the basis of the expertise of their personnel and their stock of technically appropriate tools. These retailers specialized in high-quality, cutting-edge-technology products. Prices were relatively high. The majority of their customers were highly skilled mountaineers. Black Diamond operated a small retail shop in this category located next to its Salt Lake City manufacturing facility. Black Diamond's full product range sold well in its own shop as well as in other core shops.

Because of their remote locations, many core shops made effective use of catalogs as a direct-marketing tool. Several mail-order companies, including Black Diamond's mail-order division, competed in this core area, selling products both nationally and internationally.

The second group, mom-and-pop stores, were also small retail outlets, but they sold all types of equipment, from camping and backpacking equipment to bikes and skis. The product mix varied depending on the geographical location. Most of these stores carried a limited assortment of climbing products—usually ropes, harnesses, and carabiners (small clips used in all climbing applications to attach the climber to rock or snow). The personnel in mom-and-pop stores usually had limited technical knowledge of the products being sold.

The third group consisted of sporting goods and department store chains, ranging in size from regional chains such as Eastern Mountain Sports (7 stores) to national chains

EXHIBIT 1   Comparative Market Shares of Mountaineering Industry
Competitors, by Product

Product Category	Manufacturers	National Market Share %	International Market Share %
Carabiners	Black Diamond	50	10
	Omega	10	3
	SMC	10	3
	Wild Country	10	20
	DMM	10	20
	Petzl	5	30
	MSR (REI)	5	4
Climbing protections	Black Diamond	50	20
	Metolius	20	10
	Lowe	10	10
	Wild Country	10	25
	DMM	10	25
Harnesses	Black Diamond	45	10
	Petzl	20	50
	REI	20	
	Blue Water	10	10
	Wild Country	5	20
Plastic boots	Scarpa*	40	30
	Merrell	25	5
	Koflach	25	40
	Lowe	15	5
Adjustable ski poles	Black Diamond	60	5
	Life Link	40	5
Mountaineer skis	Rossignol	30	50
	Hagen*	20	10
Climbing accessories	Black Diamond	55	15
	Omega	25	10
	Petzl	20	75
Gloves	Black Diamond	50	5
Axes			
Snow climbing	Charlie Moser	50	10
	Black Diamond	20	5
Ice climbing	Black Diamond	30	10
	Charlie Moser	30	15
	DMM	25	30
	Grivel	15	30
Rock shoes	Scarpa*	25	20
	Sportiva	25	35
	Boreal	25	35
	Five Ten	15	5
Ropes	Mamutt	30	50
	PMI*	20	40
	New England	20	0
	Blue Water	20	10

*European manufacturers producing Black Diamond designs.
Source: Estimates of industry representatives.

such as Recreational Equipment Inc. (REI) (40 stores). These stores, which were located in major cities with access to mass markets, had extensive outdoor clothing departments, tents, stoves, canoes and kayaks, sleeping bags, bikes, skis, and so on. Products in each category were selected for volume sales. Thus, in the climbing department, the product line covered the needs of entry-level or intermediate recreational climbers. The expertise of department store personnel was, however, generally limited.

In the United States, REI was the dominant firm in this group of retailers. REI operated department stores in Seattle, Boston, Los Angeles, and Washington, DC, with limited national competition on this level. Because of its large size and wide scope, REI could buy in volume for all its stores and could offer very competitive prices. The Canadian retailer Mountain Equipment Co-op (MEC) served a similar market in Canada, with a large store in each of Canada's major cities. In France, Au Vieux Campeur owned multiple department stores in major French cities, serving a broad customer base.

Wholesalers

Retail outlets bought their product lines from wholesalers during semiannual outdoor equipment shows held throughout the world. The wholesaler category of firms consisted of (1) companies that either manufactured their own products or subcontracted the manufacturing of their designs and distributed their own product lines, (2) companies licensed to distribute the products of other companies in certain geographic areas, and (3) companies that represented various combinations of the two types. Black Diamond was in this last category. The company distributed equipment designed and manufactured in its Utah plant, equipment manufactured for Black Diamond by other firms, and merchandise designed by Black Diamond and distributed under other manufacturers' names. In all, Black Diamond offered over 250 different items, covering most mountain sports (see Exhibit 2).

REI was Black Diamond's biggest wholesale customer, making up almost 10 percent of Black Diamond's total sales. The next biggest customer, Lost Arrow—Japan, was a Japanese distributor comprising 5 percent of Black Diamond's sales. The other major wholesale customers were North American outdoor sports department store chains, mail-order companies, and Black Diamond's own retail shop and mail-order business. Combined, the top 20 percent of Black Diamond's retail customers—roughly 60 companies—accounted for about 80 percent of total sales.

Domestically, Black Diamond's wholesaling competition came from Omega Pacific, which manufactured and distributed its own metal products, and Blue Water, which wholesaled its own lines of ropes and harnesses. Neither of these companies, however, carried a product line as extensive as Black Diamond's.

The international wholesaling segment included strong competition from two British firms, Denny Morehouse Mountaineering and Wild Country, and a French company, Petzl. These firms wholesaled a full range of mountaineering products manufactured by companies with strong international reputations. Additional competition came from regional firms. Most countries had several smaller manufacturers of specific products such as carabiners or climbing axes that were successful in wholesaling their own products.

Several issues influenced sales in the international marketplace. First, the International Organization for Standardization had mandated that by 1997 "personal protective equipment" would have to meet ISO 9000 quality certification standards in order to be sold in Europe. Companies that had been granted certification stamped their

EXHIBIT 2   Black Diamond's Product Line

Climbing Protection
Camming devices
Nuts
Stoppers
Pitons
Piton hammers
Slings
Runners
Daisy chains
Etriers
Webbing
Belay devices
Carabiners

Harnesses
Sport climbing
Alpine mountaineering
Big wall

Footwear
Mountaineering boots
Ski boots
Rock-climbing shoes

Ropes and Rope Bags

Packs
Hip packs
Backpacks

Tents

Snow and Ice Tools
Axes
Crampons
Ice screws and hooks

Ski Tools
Skis
Bindings
Poles

Climbing Clothing
T-shirts
Sweatshirts
Shorts
Pants
Hats
Belts
Chalk bags

products with a symbol showing that the product's manufacturer had met the relevant ISO 9000 standards. The certification was intended to give consumers more confidence in a product's quality. Most of the European mountaineering manufacturers had initiated the certification process and were well on their way to obtaining certification. In contrast, very few American companies had even begun the certification process. Black Diamond had begun the process but was not yet near completion. (Exhibit 3 provides an overview of the ISO 9000 standards.)

Second, some European countries had a long history of climbing and mountaineering, and certain manufacturers, Grivel, for example, dated back to the late 1800s. Although several European companies had well-established worldwide reputations for quality and innovative products, others relied on home-country support, producing relatively low-quality, low-priced products. All mountainous European countries had small factories for carabiners, skis, axes, or shoes that produced, at relatively low cost, simple products in high volume for domestic consumption.

Third, the European market was predominantly ethnocentric in purchasing behavior. French climbers preferred to buy French products, while German climbers preferred German products. Because of the risks involved in climbing and mountaineering, customers chose equipment they knew the most about and had the most confidence in. Usually, these products were from the buyers' respective countries.

Manufacturers

As a manufacturer, Black Diamond faced both domestic and international competition. Domestic manufacturing firms ran the gamut from small garage operations to large machine shops with 50 or more employees, and most produced either "software" or

EXHIBIT 3   ISO 9000 Standards

The ISO 9000 standards provide the requirements for documenting processes and procedures. The intent of the standards is to ensure that organizations "do what they say and say what they do." The standards offer three quality system models—ISO 9001, ISO 9002, and ISO 9003—with increasing levels of stringency. ISO 9003 covers documentation and procedure requirements for final inspection and testing, ISO 9002 adds production and installation, and ISO 9001 includes design and development. An organization chooses the appropriate standard depending on the strategically important functional areas requiring quality procedures. In most cases, manufacturers use ISO 9001 for covering all areas.

In order to receive ISO 9000 certification, a company will spend several years complying with the requirements in the standards. This compliance usually requires extensive documentation of the company's existing quality program and training for all employees involved in processes related to quality. Individual auditors, who work for the international ISO registration organization, evaluate the company for requirement compliance. The certified companies are reevaluated every two years to ensure continuing compliance.

The following is a brief overview of the ISO 9001 requirements:

- The entire quality system must be defined and documented to ensure that each product meets specifications.
- The contractual requirements for quality between the company and the customer must be defined and documented.
- Procedures are required to ensure that critical processes are under control.
- Procedures are required for inspection at all levels and for identification of nonconforming parts or products.
- Procedures are required to prevent nonconforming parts from getting damaged in storage, delivery, or packing.
- Training is required for all personnel affecting quality.
- The quality system must be audited internally to ensure effectiveness and compliance.

"hardware." The software firms worked with textile products such as ropes and harnesses. The majority of the software firms, including Blue Water, Sterling Rope, and Misty Mountain, were located in the southeastern United States. These more specialized manufacturing firms expanded their market by catering to the needs of nonmountaineering industries, such as construction safety, military applications, and spelunking. The hardware group manufactured or assembled metal products such as carabiners and other climbing tools and protection. This group of manufacturers included Friends, Rock Hardware, and Rock Exotica. These firms had reputations as producers of innovative and high-quality equipment.

REI had recently started up a small manufacturing facility for carabiners. The manager of the facility had many years of engineering experience with Boeing Aircraft and had designed a highly automated manufacturing system capable of both production and quality testing.

Because Black Diamond had begun as a machine shop, the company had strong capabilities in metalworking. Specifically, the Salt Lake City facility manufactured cold-forged metal parts associated with carabiners, axes, and other climbing accessories and protection. Hot-forging and casting were subcontracted by Black Diamond to manufacturers specializing in this area. Black Diamond was beginning to expand into simple soft goods, such as slings and other webbing products, and intended to continue developing its in-house sewing capabilities.

Black Diamond had plans to become vertically integrated. Management believed that in-house performance of operations related to core products would enhance Black Diamond's competitiveness. Consequently, Black Diamond had started reviewing some of its subcontracting practices to determine what functions could be brought in-house. In particular, the company wanted to bring in-house all sewing of climbing gear and some metal treatments such as heat-treating.

Other products, such as skis, ski poles, foot gear, and ropes, required very specific technologies, production skills, and economies of scale for competitive pricing and quality. Black Diamond entered into subcontracting agreements with international manufacturers to design and manufacture such products. The company also subcontracted the production of its harnesses to a technically sophisticated harness manufacturer located next door to the Salt Lake City facility that made the harnesses on a semiautomated assembly line. This process required minimal human involvement, in contrast to a "garment industry" sewing process by which one person sews the complete harness from start to finish.

By the late 1980s, European competition was becoming a more significant factor in the U.S. market. In particular, Petzl, a French company with a full range of products, had taken an aggressive position in the U.S. market. Like several of the European competitors, Petzl had a well-established reputation as a producer of high-quality, innovative products. Petzl had set up a manufacturing facility in the United States within 60 miles of Black Diamond's manufacturing facility and had sponsored several professional U.S. climbers. Black Diamond, of course, was making efforts to sell its own products in Europe, but faced the problem of ISO 9000 certification.

Some international manufacturing activity went on in Korea and Japan. Products produced by these manufacturers were marketed and distributed through other international companies. The majority of these products were low-cost, mass-produced items such as carabiners.

The continuing growth of copyright violations and product piracy—especially prevalent within international markets—added a further dimension to global competition. Several U.S. and European companies had used machine shops in Korea and Japan as subcontractors, supplying dies and other technological know-how. Consequently, unlicensed clones of more expensive items were expected to appear soon in the international market.

BLACK DIAMOND'S OPERATIONS

Black Diamond Equipment, Ltd., opened for business in 1989 after a group of former managers, with employee support, bought the assets of Chouinard Equipment from Lost Arrow Corporation during Chapter 11 bankruptcy proceedings. The bankruptcy resulted from four lawsuits related to climbing equipment accidents during the 1980s. Chouinard Equipment was the first U.S. company to develop and manufacture rock-climbing gear. From its inception and for the following decade, Chouinard Equipment had a reputation for innovation and quality unmatched by any national competitors.

After the purchase, the new owners chose a new name for the company that would reflect its roots yet would project a fresh beginning. Chouinard Equipment's previous logo had been a diamond. The new company decided to keep the diamond image and chose the name Black Diamond because of the different associations the name might evoke: diamond in the rough, rogue, bad boy, unusual. (See Exhibit 4 for the Black Diamond logo.) Furthermore, a black diamond was used to identify the most difficult type of run in ski areas, and the company owners hoped the name would appeal to the "extreme" athlete, their primary targeted customer base. Black Diamond's management believed that "if you target the extremists, the recreational customers will follow."

The mission of Black Diamond was "to design, manufacture, and bring to market, in a profitable and on-time manner, innovative and technical products of high quality, high performance, and exemplary durability that are targeted toward our primary customers—climbers and backcountry skiers." The company was committed to 10 guiding principles:

EXHIBIT 4   Black Diamond Logo

1. Being the market leader, synonymous with the sports we serve and are absolutely passionate about;
2. Having a truly global presence;
3. Supporting the specialty retailer;
4. Creating long-term partnerships with companies we do business with;
5. Being very easy to do business with;
6. Being a fierce competitor with the highest ethical standards;
7. Developing sustainable, competitive advantage;
8. Sharing the company's success with its employees;
9. Creating a safe, personally fulfilling work environment for all employees;
10. Championing the preservation of and access to our mountain environments.

In 1991, the owner-employees relocated the business from Ventura, California, to Salt Lake City, Utah, where they would be closer to the targeted customer. Black Diamond began operations with a staff of roughly 40, covering all functional areas. (See Exhibit 5 for Black Diamond's organizational structure.) Black Diamond was 50 percent owned by employees; the remaining 50 percent of the stock was held by outside investors, predominantly distributors, customers, and friends and family of the main employee stockholders. Of the 50 percent that was employee owned, 75 percent was held by Peter Metcalf, the CEO; Maria Cranor, head of marketing; and Clark Kawakami, the chief financial officer.

In 1993, Black Diamond's annual sales were expected to be approximately $12 million, with a gross profit margin of about 40 percent (around $4.8 million) and a net profit margin of about 10 percent (around $1.2 million). From 1990 through 1993, the climbing industry had experienced tremendous sales growth of 20 to 40 percent per year. The market demanded more innovative products and faster delivery. Black Diamond struggled to keep up with the exploding customer demand by hiring more employees and upgrading shop machinery to increase productivity. Slowly, the original machinery was being replaced by automated machining centers and testing devices. By 1993, the company employed more than 100 people.

Like other metalworking shops, Black Diamond specialized in certain types of metalworking; its areas of specialization consisted of cold-forging metal parts, stamping and forming, computer numerically controlled (CNC) machining, and assembly or fab-

EXHIBIT 5   Black Diamond Organizational Structure

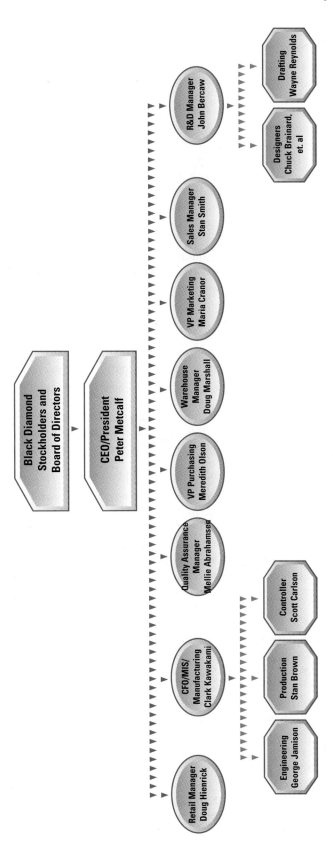

rication. Forging, stamping, and forming, along with the assembly processes, had been done for 20 years by the original Chouinard company, and these processes were considered to be Black Diamond's technical core. These core processes used the same multiton presses that forced metal stock into a die or mold to obtain the desired shape.

Since moving to Salt Lake City, the company had expanded into CNC machines—large programmable machine tools capable of producing small-to-medium-sized batches of intricate parts—in an effort to reduce costs and to move more production processes in-house. These machines were expensive, but they provided the advantages of capacity and product flexibility. Many of Black Diamond's processes, however, required machinery that was too costly to justify purchase for the manufacturing of a limited number of parts. Consequently, Black Diamond subcontracted with other vendors for aluminum hot-forging, investment casting, laser-cutting steel, preshearing metals, anodizing, heat treating, welding, screw machining, wire forming such as springs, and aluminum extrusion. These processes were subcontracted to achieve economies of scale (e.g., aluminum extrusion) or because the specialized equipment and skills required were beyond Black Diamond's capabilities (e.g., hot-forging).

Black Diamond's production facility was divided into several functional areas: the machine shop, which built prototypes and constructed and maintained tool and die apparatus; the punch press room, where parts were pressed out at a rate of one per second by several multiton presses; a room with assorted machines (including CNC machines), each operated by one person doing drilling, milling, or grinding; a tumbling and polishing room, where large batches of parts were polished; the assembly room, where parts were assembled by individuals or teams; and, finally, a room for materials and shipping.

Supported by a material requirements planning (MRP) system, materials were ordered several months in advance for a full batch of products—for example, 5,000 carabiners or 500 axes. When fairly common parts such as springs and aluminum rod stock were involved, the orders arrived on time and met standard quality requirements. The more complex and customized parts, such as investment-cast axe parts, were difficult for vendors to make to specifications and thus often did not meet the assembly deadline.

When the parts arrived in the materials supply area, one person was responsible for spot-checking the order to see if the parts met specifications. For example, when 500 axe heads arrived, the inspector would randomly select 15 parts and would measure 20 key dimensions on each part to determine if the tolerances met specifications. If one dimension was out of tolerance, the quality manager was summoned for an evaluation. Depending on how much impact the flaw would have on other assembly processes, a larger meeting, involving all potentially affected parties, might be necessary to determine a course of action.

Most of Black Diamond's products began as a sheet of steel or aluminum rod. After receiving the metal, the incoming inspector would pull a sample to check hardness and dimensions. When production on an order was ready to begin, the metal was moved from a hallway to the press room. The press operator would receive an order for 5,000 parts and would set up the press to begin cutting and smashing parts to shape. Once the dies were in place, the operator would smash a few sample parts and check with an inspector for approval.

As the dies wore down, the parts might turn out to have excess metal, or the logo engraving might be substandard. Depending on the demand for the parts, the inspector might feel pressure to pass on cosmetically imperfect parts. Once approval was given, the operator would proceed to press out as many parts as possible in the shortest time. Often chips of metal would settle in the die and become imbedded in many parts before being discovered by the operator. When this occurred, thousands of parts needed to be scrapped.

After the smashing process, the parts were usually sent out for heat-treating to harden the metal. The heat-treatment plant was located in California, so this procedure had a turnaround time of several weeks. When the parts returned, they went to the tumbling and drilling rooms for further processing. When color was needed, the parts would be shipped out again for anodizing, an electrolytic process by which metal is covered with a protective and/or decorative oxide film.

Finally, when the main body of a product was finished, the materials department would issue batches of all the other components needed to finish that product. All of these parts would proceed to a group of assemblers, seated around tables, who were responsible for putting together the final product. The assembly room was the epitome of a craft shop environment. Large and expensive products such as axes were assembled in small batches by one individual, while products such as carabiners were assembled in larger batches by teams of people who often rotated jobs. The finished products would go through individual testing and inspection before passing to the shipping area. One inspector might evaluate thousands of parts in a day.

Originally, the company had one employee who was responsible for quality assurance and several shop employees who performed quality control functions. The quality assurance person worked for the R&D department and focused on testing new products, prototypes, and work in production. As the company grew and ISO 9000 certification loomed in the future, several members of the management team decided that quality issues needed more prominent attention. Black Diamond needed not only testing but also a plantwide program to ensure that defects did not occur in the first place.

Black Diamond's original quality assurance officer had left the company to guide climbing expeditions, after which Black Diamond's management created a stand-alone quality assurance department and hired Mellie Abrahamsen as the manager. At the time of Abrahamsen's hiring, the members of R&D and the shop functioned along craft-shop lines. Product designers built prototypes on the shop floor, iterating between field testing and lab testing until they felt the design was ready. When the new design went into production, the shop personnel used trial and error to develop an assembly procedure. Out-of-tolerance parts were often accepted by shop personnel, who invented creative ways of adapting the parts or the procedures for assembling the products.

Implementing a quality-control program would mean introducing formal testing and assembly procedures for both designers and shop workers. As Andrew McLean, a head designer, said, "We are like artists here, and you just can't restrain or rush creativity and get good results." Chuck Brainard complained, "If we have to write procedures for every step of production, we'll be changing those things a million times."

Like most machine-shop workers, Black Diamond's shop employees labored under comparatively unglamorous working conditions, involving, for example, noise, grease, and monotony. Many shop workers lacked a high school education and some could not read or write in English. Although the shop workers were the lowest-paid employees at Black Diamond, the company offered them a generous profit-sharing bonus and tried to involve them in monthly meetings concerning the financial performance of the company. Despite these measures, the shop had a high rate of employee turnover.

Because quality control programs require procedure writing, blueprint reading, and statistical techniques, the shop employees needed elementary math and language training so that they could learn the more complicated subjects. Stan Brown acknowledged that the workers needed training, but said, "I can't let those people miss too much work for training. We really need everyone working nonstop to get products out the door."

Many of the professional employees at Black Diamond were avid climbers and users of the products, taking great pride in trying to make the very best products available. Marketing was concerned about keeping up the company's innovative image with new products every season. Production worried about vendor costs, delivery of parts, and the shop's ability to meet sales forecasts. R&D attempted to simultaneously develop buildable new products, reduce lead time for new-product development, and improve existing products. Customer service tried to keep retailers pacified with partial deliveries and promises.

Finally, the new quality assurance department was charged with implementing quality control procedures, conducting training, testing products, and resolving problems attributed to parts or products not meeting specifications. All functional areas faced the problems inherent in trying to achieve the simultaneous goals of meeting customer demand and ensuring the highest-quality products, and the different areas often clashed on the best means and methods of achieving these goals.

THE BLACK PROPHET

The concept for the Black Prophet axe was originally developed to round out Black Diamond's product line of axes. The product line had two other axes: the Alpamayo, a glacier-walking and snow-climbing axe; and the X-15, a versatile axe for both snow and ice climbing. The Black Prophet was designed specifically for ice climbing and incorporated an innovative ergonomic shape to reduce arm fatigue, a composite,

EXHIBIT 6   The Black Prophet

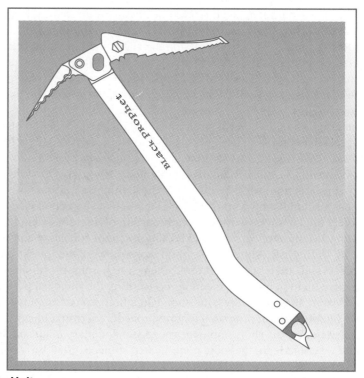

(a) Complete Unit

rubber-bounded shaft construction for gripability and weight reduction, and inter-changeable modular components that allowed the use of different types of tools—a hammer head, picks, or an adze—for miscellaneous ice applications. (Exhibit 6 is a drawing of the Black Prophet and its component parts.)

Designing and producing the axe entailed several years of working with different vendors to develop the appropriate production process for each component. The axe was designed as a prototype and field-tested with different constructions until R&D agreed on a specific configuration. This configuration was then reviewed by sales representatives considered to be mountaineering experts and by other company members at the quarterly meetings. If the tool did not pass the scrutiny of those examiners, R&D would begin a new phase of prototype development and field tests. This development process would continue until a companywide consensus was reached.

The axe required five parts: shaft, head, hammer, pick, and adze. Three parts were cast metal, requiring a casting subcontractor with the ability to meet strict specifications. The composite shaft was produced by a composite and bonding manufacturer, and the pick was manufactured in Black Diamond's plant. Black Diamond received the parts from each vendor, inspected them for conformance to specifications, and assembled the axes.

The Black Prophet, which cost approximately $80 to produce, sold at retail for $200; the wholesale price was $140. The initial shipment of Black Prophets for the winter season of 1993 comprised approximately 200 axes. Management expected the Black Prophet to be one of Black Diamond's top 10 selling winter products, with

EXHIBIT 6   (continued)

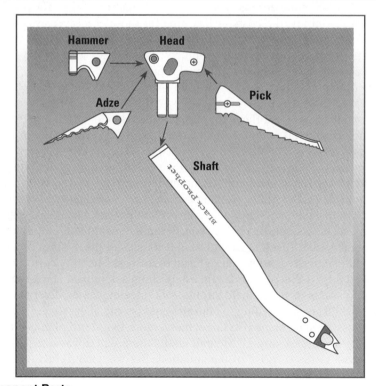

(*b*) **Component Parts**

yearly sales projected to be at least 2,500 units. The entire company regarded it as a very big image item on the world mountaineering scene. Every competitor in the industry had an axe for glacier walking; axes were especially popular in Europe, where Black Diamond foresaw superb potential for its new offering.

The axe had been well received at the previous year's outdoor product show. At that time, no other axe like it was in the wings, and the climbing industry anticipated the Black Prophet's arrival with great excitement. All of the major U.S. and European industry magazines had published articles about the Black Prophet, and famous mountaineers had called Black Diamond requesting Black Prophets for their upcoming expeditions.

THE DILEMMA

As the Monday morning meeting continued, Black Diamond's top management team struggled to find answers to the questions raised by the axe crisis. They knew that the situation required both short- and long-term solutions. In the short term, management needed to address the pressure for immediate delivery confronting customer service. Should management recall all the Black Prophet axes currently on the market? A recall would come with high shipping, testing, and opportunity costs. Or should Black Diamond ignore the incident, assuming the accident was a one-time freak, and continue to sell the axes while refuting any rumors about the product's questionable performance? The possibility of lawsuits had to be considered. For any accident causing injury, legal fees could be expected to run $500,000, and a catastrophic accident could bring a suit for several million dollars. While Black Diamond's insurer would pay legal expenses and any settlement involved, with a cap of $1 million, Black Diamond could expect to pay at least $25,000—the company's insurance deductible—for each legal action. In addition, there would be the costs of lost time for those employees who had to go to court (such costs might involve one or two managers' salaries for a year—at $40,000 to $60,000 per person). Several catastrophic accident cases won by the plaintiffs in a single year could put the company into bankruptcy.

Another option was to continue the sale of Black Prophets—including the axes already released as well as those in production—but to require all units to be sold with a cautionary label. Still another was to just quietly and quickly sell those Black Prophets already in retail outlets and undertake a critical review only of the axes still in production.

Management's response to the short-term issue of customer service would have major implications for Black Diamond's competitive strategy. Would Black Diamond be able to meet the market's rapidly growing demand for all products while improving—or at the very least maintaining—product quality? Would Black Diamond be able to maintain an image as the recognized industry leader in the manufacture of innovative tools and equipment? Would Black Diamond be able to balance the realities of increased risk associated with innovative product design and of increased liability corresponding to the greater potential for accidents, while still establishing a dominant competitive position? Even though various members held strong—and in some cases, divergent—opinions, the management team was willing to consider enterprising alternatives.

Nevertheless, management also knew that a more long-term plan needed to be put into place. "When crises strike," Metcalf said, "there will always be some degree of needing to react to the surprise of the situation. But we need to institute a system of managing crises proactively—that means organizing the business to prevent the preventable crises."

Even though the management team thought the quality assurance department should be a constructive resource in this long-term effort, the department was so new that no one had a clear idea of its role. Abrahamsen also questioned her role: "I was hired to implement a plantwide quality control program and to specifically work on ISO 9000 certification. Representing QA, I'm supposed to improve the efficiency of the company by reducing or eliminating defects in the whole production chain, but I'm not sure that a TQM [total quality management] approach will completely solve Black Diamond's problems. Perhaps the whole process of new-product development and ongoing operations would be more effective if a BPR [business process reengineering] approach were used. Either way, my challenge is to get all these other employees and departments to change the way they do things so they're both more efficient and effective."

(Black Diamond's Web address is www.bdel.com.)

33

SAMSUNG EVERLAND: MANAGING SERVICE QUALITY

IVEY

Charles Dhanaraj, *The University of Western Ontario*

In December 1994, Her Tae-Hak, president of Samsung's Joong-Ang Development Company, South Korea, was concerned with the level of service quality at Yongin Farmland (Farmland). It was clear to Mr. Her that Farmland had to have a coherent service quality management strategy because his goal was to position the company as one of the world's leading theme parks. However, despite the service quality program he had initiated since he assumed his present position in October 1993, preliminary findings indicated that Farmland's service quality levels were much below those at leading theme parks, not only internationally but also within South Korea. He wondered if the moves he had already made were in the right direction, how Farmland could achieve international standards of service quality, whether it would be worth doing, and if it would really provide a sustainable competitive advantage in the world market.

THE GLOBAL THEME PARK INDUSTRY

The early 1990s saw theme parks around the world emerge as major sources of family entertainment. The earliest evidence of a business where people paid money to be terrified was in the early 1600s when several Russians operated a sled ride with a 70-foot vertical drop. In the late 1800s, several theme parks were set up on Coney Island, New York, including the first roller coaster (1884) and an indoor amusement park (Sealion

Prepared under the supervision of Professor John Haywood-Farmer. The author may have disguised certain names and other identifying information to protect confidentiality.

Park). In the 1930s, the amusement industry suffered because of the combined impact of the alternative entertainment offered by movie houses and the economic depression. However, with the opening of Disneyland in 1955 in California, the industry revived. Walt Disney was credited with raising the profile, as well as the profitability, of the industry to new heights.

The Walt Disney Company, with three major theme parks in the United States, one in Japan and one in Europe, was the world's largest theme park chain as measured by revenues. Time Warner's Six Flags Corporation was the second largest, with seven parks in the United States and plans to expand into China and other Far East countries. Paramount and Anheuser-Busch were other conglomerates that owned theme parks. In 1994, total attendance for the world's top 50 theme parks, found in 15 countries, was about 222 million, a growth of 5 percent over 1993. The 23 parks in the top 50 situated in the United States accounted for 47 percent of the total attendance; the six parks in Florida represented 20 percent of total attendance. Exhibit 1 shows some details of the top 10 theme parks.

Asian parks constituted 33 percent of the total worldwide attendance, with Japan's eight parks representing 19 percent. Tokyo Disneyland (TDL), which opened in 1983 as a joint venture with the Oriental Land Company (OLC), was the worldwide leader. Its success set off a wave of theme park development in Asia. OLC and Disney had agreed to open a second Japanese theme park in 2001, Tokyo Disney Sea, which would be comparable to TDL in size. Theme parks were also becoming increasingly popular in other parts of Asia. Asia's largest water park (Ocean Park) was in Hong Kong, and Indonesia was the site of Dreamland, which comprised a theme park (Dunia Fantasi), a waterpark complex, an oceanarium, a golf course, a beach and several hotels. The industry considered China to be a major growth market. Beijing Amusement Park, started in 1981, reported that between 1990 and 1993 its revenues increased by over 2,000 percent and earnings before interest and taxes by 200 percent.

Theme parks required an initial investment, typically ranging from U.S. $50 million to U.S. $3 billion; in addition, many parks periodically added new attractions or renovated existing ones to draw repeat customers. Parks typically reinvested much of their profit in expansion or upgrades. The industry exhibited significant economies of scale and scope. Increasingly, individual parks were becoming larger to generate more operating revenues. Also, companies were expanding to multiple parks to take advantage of their knowledge of theme park management. Admission fees, which ranged from U.S. $5 to U.S. $50 depending on the park's reputation and location, constituted over 60 percent of a theme park's revenues; most of the balance came from food, beverage, and merchandise sales. The Walt Disney Company's financial profile was generally used as a benchmark within the industry. Its theme park revenues were U.S. $2.042 billion in 1988 and U.S. $3.4 billion in 1993. For those two years, respectively, operating income had been U.S. $565 million and U.S. $747 million and return on equity 17 percent and 25 percent. Most of the operating expenses for theme parks (about 75 percent) were for personnel.

Customer satisfaction was a critical issue in theme park management. Successful park managers promoted their properties heavily and used marketing research extensively to gain an understanding of their customers. To reach diverse groups of customers, parks emphasized the beauty of their facilities and the range of entertainment and food services offered. Theme park managers worked with tour operators and government tourist promotion boards to draw tourists to their parks. Theme parks spent about 10 percent of their annual revenues on advertising using such means as television,

EXHIBIT 1   The World's 10 Largest Theme Parks*

Rank	Park Name	Location	Attendance[†]	Size[‡]	Open	Summary
1	Tokyo Disneyland	Tokyo, Japan	15,509	25.0	1983	Concept: "Magic and Dream," 6 subtheme zones, 39 attractions, 37 food and beverage outlets, 39 merchandise outlets
2	Disneyland	Los Angeles, USA	14,100	22.5	1955	World's first family-oriented theme park, 50 attractions, 11 food and beverage outlets, 64 merchandise outlets
3	Magic Kingdom	Orlando, USA	12,900	12.0	1971	Similar to Disneyland, 7 subtheme zones, 36 attractions, 30 food and beverage outlets, merchandise outlets
4	EPCOT Center	Orlando, USA	10,700	28.2	1982	Future world showcase, 30 food and beverage outlets, merchandise outlets
5	EuroDisney	Paris, France	10,700	16.5	1992	Family-oriented theme park, 5 subtheme zones, 29 attractions, 29 food and beverage outlets, merchandise outlets
6	MGM Studios	Orlando, USA	9,500	13.0	1989	Movie and TV program-based theme park, 11 food and beverage outlets, 18 merchandise outlets
7	Universal Studios	Los Angeles, USA	8,000	55.0	1990	Movie and TV program-based theme park, 10 attractions, food and beverage outlets, 6 merchandise outlets
8	Everland (Farmland)	Kyonggi-Do Province, South Korea	7,300	30.0	1976	Family-oriented theme park, 5 subtheme zones, 45 attractions, 27 food and beverage outlets, 29 merchandise outlets
9	Blackpool Pleasure Beach	Blackpool, UK	7,200	5.1	1896	Beachside amusement park, free admission, 80 attractions, food and beverage outlets, merchandise outlets
10	Yokohama Hakkeijima Sea Paradise	Yokohama, Japan	6,000	7.2	1993	Man-made island park, 12 attractions and aquarium, 14 food and beverage outlets, 50 merchandise outlets, lodge and marina

*As of December 1994, as measured by annual attendance.
†Attendance numbers are annual figures given in thousands.
‡Sizes are given in hectares; a hectare comprises 10,000 square meters or about 25 acres. The data refer to the developed area of each site.
Source: *Amusement Business,* International Association of Amusement Parks.

radio, newspaper, yellow page (telephone book), and direct-mail advertisements, and family and group discounts. Because television advertising was an excellent visual medium to capture a park's excitement, some parks expended a major portion of their advertising budget for television promotion.

The seasonal and intermittent nature of the business put a lot of strain on theme park managers. Attendance at theme parks peaked in the spring and summer and during school holidays. Even in the holiday season, bad weather could adversely affect attendance. During peak periods the requirement for employees shot up; quite often management had to find employees beyond the local area and provide housing for them. The sudden surge in demand often choked the service systems such as transportation and building management.

KOREA

The Republic of Korea (South Korea) was a 100,000-square-kilometer, mountainous, democratic republic which occupied the southern portion of the Korean peninsula in eastern Asia and numerous small islands. Russia and, more important, China shared borders with the communist Democratic People's Republic of Korea (North Korea). The southern Japanese island of Kyushu was about 200 kilometers from South Korea across the Korea Strait and the heavily populated east coast of China was about 500 kilometers west across the Yellow Sea. South Korea separated from North Korea in 1948 during the aftermath of World War II. From 1950 to 1953, the two Koreas fought a bitter civil war that ended in a stalemate with the signing of an armistice. The border separating the two Korean states, which roughly followed the 38th parallel just north of the South Korean capital city of Seoul, was a particularly tense region. It was heavily defended because the two countries constantly threatened to resume hostilities. "Incidents" were common; technically, the two countries were still at war because they had never signed a peace treaty.

South Korea consisted of nine provinces (eight mainland and one island) which were further divided into 68 cities (*shi*), 136 counties (*gun*), and six metropolitan cities. Exhibit 2 shows a map. In keeping with the fact that only 22 percent of South Korea was arable, the country had an urbanization rate of 74.4 percent. The populations of the metropolitan cities were Seoul, 10 million; Pusan, 3.8 million; Taegu, 2.2 million; Inchon, 1.8 million; Kwangju, 1.1 million; and Taejon, 1.1 million. South Korea's population of 44 million was growing about 1 percent annually.

Despite its political difficulties, South Korea had seen tremendous economic growth since 1980; indeed, it had often been called a miracle. The per capita gross national product had risen from U.S. $4,210 in 1989 to U.S. $7,513 in 1993 (see Exhibit 3). The growth rate for the second half of the 1990s was expected to be 8 percent. The growth of the South Korean economy had been accompanied by an increasing prominence of large business groups, commonly known as *chaebol*—privately held industrial conglomerates involved in a wide range of businesses. Samsung, Hyundai, Daewoo, LG Group (Lucky-Goldstar), and Ssangyong were some of the better known chaebols.

Located in the transitional zone between continental and subtropical maritime climates, South Korea had a temperate climate similar to that of the mid-Atlantic states of North America. It had four distinct seasons. During the winter (December to mid-March) intense, cold dry spells alternated with periods of milder weather. Temperatures dropped to − 20°C in some places and heavy snow fell in the mountains. The average January temperature in Seoul was about − 3°C. The summers (June to September) were hot and humid, with temperatures rising to 35°C and periods of heavy rain in June and July. The average July temperature in Seoul was about 25°C; 70 percent of the region's 235 centimeters of precipitation fell during the summer. Mid-July to mid-August was the peak of the South Korean vacation season. Many festivals were held in October. The country had been successful in attracting international events, the most prominent being the summer Olympic games in 1988. Tourist growth had been steady, approximately one-third of the tourists in Seoul using a travel package from a travel agency.

EXHIBIT 2   A Map of South Korea and the Surrounding Area

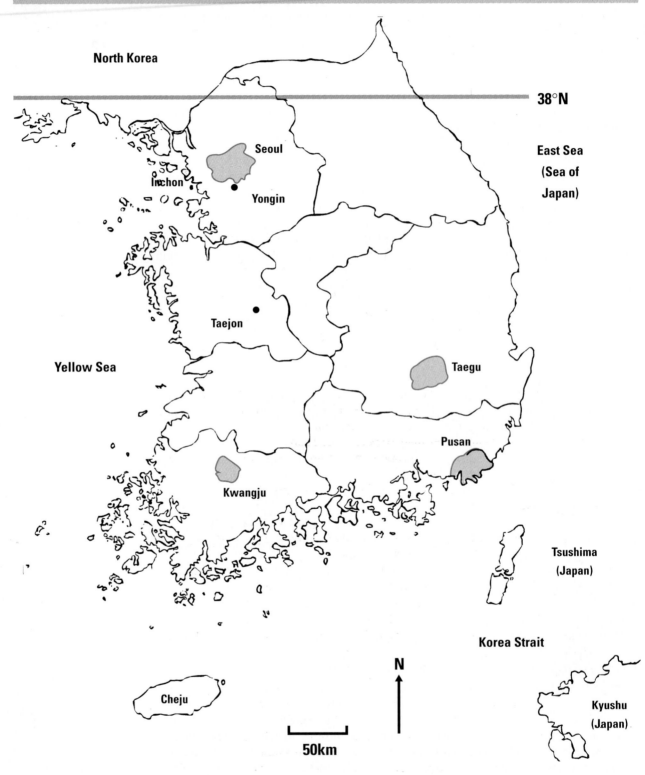

EXHIBIT 3   Major Indicators of the South Korean Economy*

	1989	1990	1991	1992	1993	1994	1995
Gross national product (GNP)†	162.7	178.3	194.5	204.2	216.2	234.3	254.7
Per capita GNP (U.S.$, current)	5,210	5,883	6,757	7,007	7,513	8,508	10,076
Economic growth rate (percent)	6.4	9.5	9.1	5.1	5.8	8.6	9.0
Foreign exchange (won per U.S.$)‡	680	716	761	776	808	790	790

*Figures for 1994 and 1995 are projected.
†Figures are given in billions of U.S.$ at current prices.
‡Values at December 31 in the year stated.
Source: Korea Research Institute documents.

THE HISTORY OF YONGIN FARMLAND

Farmland, which opened in 1976 at Yongin, a small, rural community in Kyonggi-Do Province was the first amusement park in South Korea. Its mission was to provide a better quality of life through healthy open-air leisure activities. The 30-hectare attraction (on a 1,500-hectare site) was managed by Joong-Ang Development Company, a wholly owned subsidiary of the Korean conglomerate Samsung Group. Samsung, with 1994 revenues of about U.S. $64 billion, was active in a number of business areas: electronics, chemicals and petrochemicals, machinery, finance and insurance. In addition to the Farmland management, Joong-Ang was responsible for maintaining all of Samsung's office buildings and two golf courses. The company also invested in several social development activities. One such operation was its Guide Dog Breeding Centre, which bred guide dogs for the blind. Typically, top-quality parents were imported from the United Kingdom. The pups were raised in the breeding center and trained by experts for guiding. The trained dogs were donated to blind people.

Although in the early years fewer than 10 percent of Joong-Ang's employees had worked exclusively for Farmland, the proportion had grown significantly in recent years. Exhibit 4 gives data since 1987.

Although Farmland was nestled in a mountainous region only about 40 kilometers south of Seoul, because of heavy traffic, it could take as much as one to two hours to reach the site by car. Samsung's operations on the site began with an agricultural center to demonstrate how mountainous land could be used productively for growing food products and farm animals. The Wild Safari was opened in 1980, and the Rose Festival, an impressive rose garden filled with 6,000 rose bushes of 160 different varieties arranged according to various themes, opened in 1985. To provide for winter entertainment, the Sled Slope was opened in 1988. A drastic departure from the traditional theme parks was taken when Yongin Farmland opened a motor park in late 1993. Although the motor park operation incurred a loss in the first year of operations, Joong-Ang management hoped that it would show a better performance in the future. Exhibit 5 shows the theme park's financial performance.

THE SOUTH KOREAN LEISURE MARKET

Traditionally, Farmland focused on local customers, most of whom lived within a two-hour drive. South Korea's economic expansion had been a major cause of growth in the leisure industry. Based on the projected population for the year 2000, Farmland

EXHIBIT 4   Employee Growth in Joong-Ang Development*

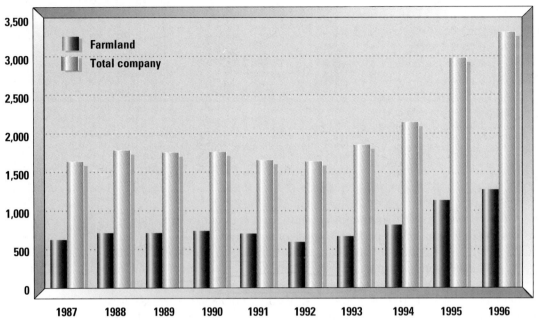

*The employment figures do not include seasonal part-time employees, which typically ranged from 60 to 85 percent of the full-time employment. The figures for 1995 and 1996 are projections.
Source: Company files.

EXHIBIT 5   Income Statements for Yongin Farmland*

	1991	1992	1993	1994†	1995†	1996†
Net sales	38,393	47,173	55,217	85,700	120,000	180,000
Expenses‡						
Park operations	26,209	33,487	40,409	21,300	—	—
Sales and administration	8,524	8,980	10,145	18,200	—	—
Others	1,215	1,350	1,433	31,400	—	—
Total	35,948	43,817	51,987	70,900	100,000	150,000
Operating profit	2,445	3,356	3,230	14,800	20,000	30,000

*Data are given in millions of Korean won for the years ending December 31. In December 1994 the exchange rate was about 790 won per U.S. $.
†Figures for 1994, 1995, and 1996 are projected.
‡Segmented projected expenses for 1995 and 1996 were not available.
Source: Company files.

expected that it would capture 19.3 percent of the population in its primary local market, within about 100 kilometers of the park (see Exhibit 6).

Despite the recent emergence of the South Korean leisure industry, there were already six theme parks in the Seoul area. In addition to Farmland, the most notable among them were Lotte World and Seoul Land. Seoul Land was Farmland's largest competitor. In 1993, it was the 23rd largest (measured by attendance) theme park

EXHIBIT 6   Some Data on Target Domestic Market Segments*

Market	Population†	Estimated Current Capture Rate‡	Portion of Total Attendance§	Projected Population in 2000†
Primary	19.2	19.3%	73%	20.2
Secondary	13.8	7.3	20	14.7
Tertiary	12.5	4.1	8	12.3
Total	43.5	11.3	100	47.2

*Farmland considered its primary market to be those living within a one-hour drive from the site, typically a radius of about 100 kilometers. It considered its secondary market to be those living within a one- or two-hour drive, and its tertiary market to be those living over two hours' drive away but within driving distance. The analysis does not include overseas visitors, who constituted 25 percent of total attendance in 1993, and came primarily from other Asian countries, such as Japan and Singapore.
†Population figures are given in millions.
‡The estimated capture rate is based on statistical projections from the survey respondents.
§The percentage of total attendance is based on three repeat surveys of visitors to Farmland in early 1994.
Source: Company files.

EXHIBIT 7   Attendance at Amusement Parks in the Seoul Area*

	1990	1991	1992	1993
Yongin Farmland	3,786	4,300	4,810	5,113
Lotte World	4,578	4,529	4,605	4,476
Seoul Land	2,198	2,819	2,834	2,648
Dream Land	971	1,319	1,236	1,325
Children's Grand Park	2,107	2,334	2,263	2,159
Seoul Grand Park	1,356	1,431	1,590	1,772

*Attendance numbers are annual figures given in thousands.
Source: Company files.

worldwide; however, by 1994 it was no longer listed in the top 50 because of rapid growth in other parks. Lotte World, started in 1989, prided itself on having the world's largest indoor theme park. The complex included an adjoining hotel, department store, shopping mall, folk village, and sports center. Despite the competition from other parks, Farmland had the highest growth rate within the industry in South Korea (see Exhibit 7).

In 1994, Farmland initiated extensive research to improve its understanding of the leisure pattern of Korean customers. It engaged the Korea Research Institute, which was one of the leading consumer research firms in South Korea, to conduct surveys. Exhibit 8 shows some of the results.

HER TAE HAK

Prior to his assignment to Joong-Ang, Mr. Her had been the CEO of Cheju Shilla, a luxury sea resort hotel on Cheju Island (see Exhibit 2) which Mr. Her had been credited with developing into a world-class property surpassing established hotel chains such as Hotel Hilton in customer service. Since taking over the reins of Joong-Ang,

EXHIBIT 8 Leisure Patterns of South Korean Consumers (1994)

Question: Which is your most favored spot for a one-day holiday trip?

	Total Response	Theme	Nature	Resort/Spa	Fishing	Historic Place	Other
Total	10,043	22.2%	22.0%	9.9%	7.0%	22.6%	16.3%
Sex							
Male	5,354	19.7	22.2	8.4	9.8	22.1	17.8
Female	4,690	25.0	21.8	11.6	3.8	23.3	14.5
Age							
10–20	1,359	41.5	15.1	2.1	3.7	22.1	15.5
21–30	2,634	23.2	26.5	4.3	6.5	22.7	16.8
31–40	2,799	24.8	22.5	7.9	9.4	20.3	15.1
41–50	1,586	12.0	23.0	13.7	8.1	26.5	16.7
Over 50	1,665	10.3	18.7	24.8	5.2	22.9	18.1
Education							
Elementary	719	11.5	22.7	25.5	3.6	18.5	18.2
Middle school	678	46.2	11.0	2.6	3.9	20.2	16.1
Junior high	840	12.2	21.9	18.4	7.1	24.5	15.9
Senior high	491	37.4	19.6	1.6	2.1	26.0	13.3
School graduate	4,286	20.8	23.3	9.9	8.5	21.7	15.8
University	3,030	21.8	22.9	6.7	7.1	24.3	17.2
Occupation							
Professional	264	14.7	19.0	6.9	12.4	28.4	18.6
White collar	1,597	20.4	23.5	6.0	6.9	23.8	19.4
Sales and marketing	1,794	16.5	24.4	10.3	10.0	22.8	16.0
Service industry	772	20.6	21.2	10.6	9.2	21.8	16.6
Farming	281	12.8	31.5	19.3	6.9	15.5	14.0
Manufacturing	577	18.5	25.4	8.4	10.9	21.0	15.8
Housewife	2,582	22.1	21.9	14.8	4.1	22.6	14.5
Student	1,656	38.3	16.3	2.3	4.5	22.2	16.4
Unemployed	520	12.2	21.9	17.4	8.7	23.5	16.3

Question: Normally, when you go to theme parks, how many others accompany you?

0	2–3	4–5	6–10	11–20	Over 21
2%	33%	38%	13%	4%	11%

Question: How many hours do you spend in a theme park?

0–5 hours	6–7	8–9	10–11	12–13	14–15	Over 16
22%	19%	18%	18%	12%	6%	5%

Question: How much do you spend at the park in one day excluding admission (in thousands of won)?

0–5	5–10	10–15	15–20	20–25	25–30	30–35	35–50	Over 50
2%	8%	19%	10%	21%	5%	16%	6%	15%

Question: How do you normally come to the theme park?

Car	Tourbus	Bus	Train/Subway	Other
68%	9%	13%	6%	4%

Source: Korea Research Institute.

Mr. Her had focused on improving Farmland's customer satisfaction level and on developing the plans for Farmland's expansion. Most employees saw Mr. Her as hard-working and kind but aggressively pushing the company toward his new vision for Farmland. As one manager described him:

> Mr. Her is very demanding when it comes to managers. He makes his intentions very explicit and expects his managers to work as hard as he does. However, he also is very kind when it comes to field employees. One day, shortly after he joined the company, he was on his usual daily tour of the park. It happened to be a cold day. He noticed that an employee who was in charge of an attraction was held up in her work spot because of work exigencies and was eating a cold lunch. In Korea, on a cold day, you really need a hot lunch to keep you going. That evening in a manager's meeting Mr. Her related his observation to the group. He was almost in tears as he said that the poor sales girl had to take a cold lunch and was not properly taken care of. He told the managers, "I don't care what you do, but don't let that happen again. I want my employees well taken care of."

To attract more customers, Mr. Her had initiated a move from a combination pricing structure to a single system. When Mr. Her arrived, users had three options. Under the pay-as-you-go option they could pay the admission fees and buy tickets for rides, often in combinations, for example Big 5 for five rides. A second option, known as pay-one-price, was to buy a passport that provided admission as well as an unlimited number of rides for one full day. The third option was to buy unlimited admission for a year by obtaining a membership. In 1993, Farmland estimated that passport users accounted for 17.4 percent of attendance, and membership holders for 25 percent. Farmland wanted to switch gradually to the pay-one-price scheme, the most common pricing scheme in the industry.

THE MASTER PLAN: FARMLAND TO EVERLAND

On the occasion of Samsung Group's 55th anniversary celebrated in March 1993, group chairman Lee Kun-Hee announced that Samsung would shift its focus to quality and globalization to realize its ambitious vision of being one of the world's premiere enterprises. Consequently, the traditional management would undergo sweeping changes in both structure and style to help employees understand Samsung's raison d'être from a broader perspective.

Following the chairman's lead, and with help from several internationally known theme park designers and equipment vendors, such as Duell Corporation (United States), Economic Consulting Services (United States), and WhiteWater West Industries Ltd. (Canada), Mr. Her initiated a master plan within Joong-Ang to revamp Farmland and exploit its full potential. The continuing growth in the number of visitors (see Exhibit 7) dictated an immediate expansion. There were also suggestions that a new name would provide a better image for the new mountain resort; Everland, Green Country, and Nature Land were proposed. A master plan for a phased investment of about U.S. $300 million dollars over the next five years was developed. It included:

- Caribbean Bay, a waterpark with a Caribbean theme to be built adjacent to the existing theme park, at an estimated cost of U.S. $140 million.
- Global Fair, a fun-fair focusing on famous architectural themes from around the world, at an estimated cost of U.S. $85 million.
- Safari Tour, an expansion of the existing zoo, and parks including a nighttime laser show and a fable fantasy parade at an estimated cost of U.S. $50 million.

Funding for this expansion would come mainly from the parent, Samsung Group, and also from corporate sponsorship of the other companies within the Samsung Group. The master plan also indicated that if the first phase were successful, a second phase developing a resort town in Yongin, with luxury hotels, golf courses, and resort accommodations, would be considered. The exact budget for the second phase had not yet been established. A number of managers within the company who were closely involved in developing the master plan believed strongly that the theme park expansion was not only a priority but also would be profitable. They commented:

> What we want to create is a destination resort town and a residential community where people can come, relax, and enjoy themselves in a stress-free environment.

> Samsung employs more than 180,000 people here in Korea. This will give them a place to come and be proud of. There will be plenty here for all members of the family as they grow.

> We feel it is time to change from a farm-oriented name to a name which represents our new mission, which is to create a zeal for long-lasting life that is combined with the harmony of nature.

> If this plan is approved, we will become the prototype destination resort town in the entire world. We have visited them all, and when we're finished, there won't be any better!

Samsung Group approved the master plan in early 1994 and began design and construction activities in mid-1994 to realize the dream concept of the world's best resort town. The company chose the name Everland, representing harmony and peace. Although Joong-Ang would not formally launch the new name until 1996, all in-house documents referred to the theme park as Everland.

THE 1993–94 SERVICE INITIATIVE

One of Mr. Her's first impressions when he joined the Joong-Ang Development Corporation was that the organization had very low quality service. During a management meeting in late 1993, he stated:

> We are supposed to be a service organization. But I find that the concept of service is totally lacking. The most important part of a service organization is the people, and we have not harnessed the people power sufficiently.

Service quality levels were far behind those of local competitors such as Lotte World. Although Joong-Ang had a small group of people responsible for monitoring service quality, there were no systematic efforts in that area. As one manager described the situation:

> We do not take any systematic measurement of whether we are meeting customer satisfaction or not. We did not even make use of the rare measurements we did.

Recruitment was strictly on merit following Samsung Group's standard personnel policy. As a personnel director remarked:

> Often we had the brightest people, but they were extremely poor in human relations. Despite their intelligence, they were just not able to fit into a service industry.

In his inaugural presidential address Mr. Her stressed that although Joong-Ang had a phenomenal opportunity, the company would have to change to take advantage of it. The master plan became a rallying point which made the employees think in new ways. In stressing service quality, Mr. Her emphasized the following five points:

EXHIBIT 9   Mr. Her's Win–Win Philosophy of Service at Everland

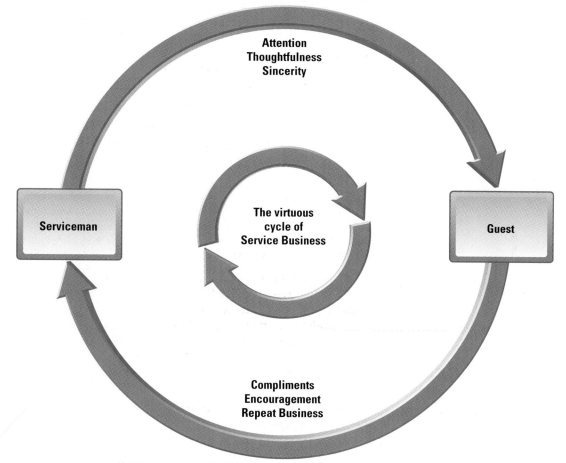

Source: Company files on a speech given by Mr. Her to employees.

- Kindness and courtesy to the customer.
- Clean and hygienic environment.
- Safe and excellent physical facilities.
- Synergy in information.
- A global orientation.

In promoting a win–win approach to service quality, Mr. Her actively promoted the idea that effective service always produced satisfaction and positive behavior in customers. In one of his monthly addresses to the employees, he stated:

> Kindness is a basic thing in human life. I cannot overemphasize this aspect. It is not a one-way kindness, but a two-way process. It is a win–win, which makes both the service provider and the customer happy. I want that to become a mindset for every employee and eventually our company culture. This diagram [see Exhibit 9] explains the concept.

Mr. Her assembled a task force of 30 managers drawn from different departments to study some steps such as greeting customers and telephone etiquette. The group developed specific guidelines which were given to all the employees in early 1994. For example, the group decided that courtesy consisted of the following five key aspects:

- Traditional bow.
- Appearance.
- Walking.
- Telephone etiquette.
- Dress.

Detailed specifications on these five factors were developed, distributed to employees, and emphasized in service training as well as in personnel evaluation.

Mr. Yang, Farmland's managing director, who had been leading the quality movement, commented:

> I find it interesting to look at us the way our customers do. They look at three levels, for which I use the image of three "scopes." First, they use a telescope—looking at us from a distance, either through the way they hear about us from their friends or by watching the impact of our show. Second, they use a microscope—looking at us very closely, trying to discern if we are really meeting their needs, say in times of crisis or emergency. Third, they use a periscope—many times we don't realize our customers are watching our actions, but they are. So I tell my employees now to think of this.
>
> A very useful way we have found to get this notion across to all our employees is to use the same theatrical metaphor Disney uses. All our employees are called "the cast"—which indicates that we are performing all the time and our customers are watching. Even the dormitory which houses our employees is called the cast house. We treat each of our customers as one of our guests. We used to use the term "voice of customers" to document our customers' complaints, compliments, and suggestions. Now we call it "voice of guests" instead. So the message is sent very clearly.

Cleanliness Campaign

The company introduced a cleanliness campaign where every employee was expected to make sure both the offices and the theme park looked clean. Mr. Her's primary goal was to send employees a strong message that if service quality levels were to go up, the park had to be kept clean and neat. He encouraged all managers to set an example. One manager related an incident which was instrumental in influencing his own thinking about leading by example:

> One of our recent quarterly strategic planning meetings of all the senior managers ended with a gala dinner. It was very late by the time we finished the dinner and as soon as the dinner finished, many managers started leaving. A few minutes later, we found Mr. Her gathering and taking the dirty plates and dishes to the dish-washing machine. It was easy to figure out that Mr. Her wanted to help the cleaners since it was already getting late. Soon, the rest of us who were around followed his example. That made a strong impression on me; since then I believe in what Mr. Her stands for.

Management strongly believed that a campaign to pick up trash would induce a sense of cleanliness among employees as well as providing an excellent model of behavior for children visiting the theme park. Management planned to formalize this belief in January 1995 by introducing a practice where tongs and white gloves would be awarded to newly recruited or promoted managers by their immediate boss in the presence of the group with which the manager worked. This plan was intended to symbolize the manager's role as a guardian of cleanliness. Senior managers were often

EXHIBIT 10	Schedule and Outline of the Basic Service Course	
	Day 1	**Day 2**
08:00		Image and appearance
09:00	Introduction	Service communication
10:00	Service philosophy	Telephone etiquette
11:00	Image and appearance (Video shooting for feedback)	Telephone etiquette (continued)
13:00	Lunch	Lunch
14:00	Image and appearance (Feedback and discussion)	Body posture
15:00	Bow etiquette	Guest reception protocol
17:00	Smile and sound power	Review
18:00	End	End

Source: Company files.

seen picking up trash and dropping it off in the garbage bins. Employees had mixed reactions. Some considered it a waste of a manager's precious time to go around picking up trash rather than focusing on other activities, such as planning. However, others saw it as an inspiration to follow. Mr. Yang commented:

> The green service is a very effective way of getting employees into our service campaign. It does three things. First, it gets my managers to the field where the action is. It is a great opportunity for them to see for themselves the vast potential for their company. Second, they get a chance to talk to the customers. They get to hear complaints and compliments firsthand. And, third, they get to see the importance of cleanliness. Clean a place for a day, and you'll never mess it again. And the culture is passed on to future generations.

Service Academy

Establishing a service academy in late 1993 was a key turning point for Joong-Ang. Although there had been personnel in charge of service training, this was the first time a formal group was charged with the responsibility of creating standards and assisting the organization to achieve them through continuous training and assessment. The service academy was also instrumental in developing a training scheme for new employees. The service academy's major directives were set up in a four-point program:

1. To operate as an in-house educational center to train service people.
2. To develop the learning capabilities of the organization.
3. To offer service training for other organizations, including those in the public sector.
4. To present a nationwide campaign for courtesy and kindness.

The service academy offered different types of courses. For example, a basic two-day (17-hour) service course was offered as the first course to all employees, both full-time and part-time. Its objectives were to introduce the important features of service, such as image and appearance, the service philosophy, smiling, bowing and walking, and telephone etiquette to new recruits. Exhibit 10 shows the schedule. Mr. Her personally participated in each training session, during which he delivered his vision of Everland's future, the central role of service quality in the corporate strategy, and the company's service philosophy message. Courses for the new staff were standardized. Management increased training periods: for new full-time recruits from 8 to 16 days; for long-term temporary recruits (who typically worked for one summer or more) from 2 to 9 days; and for short-term temporary recruits (who typically worked for only a few weeks) from two hours to 2 days.

Personnel Policies

The quality efforts were centered around recruitment, education, and retraining. The shopping and restaurants, which had previously been managed by outside vendors, were brought under the management's direct control to ensure the quality of service. Mr. Her often stated to his fellow managers that employee satisfaction was key to customer satisfaction, and stressed the need to create an appropriate organizational climate for the employees. New superior quality, top-of-the-line designer uniforms were introduced in 1994. A Canadian company, Sally Fourmy and Associates, had been hired to offer fashion consulting services for them. The company also planned to build a new dormitory for out-of-town employees within a year.

Part of the service quality campaign was the development of standards and operating procedures. New recruitment guidelines were developed which focused on the individual's ability to fit into the organization, rather than on his or her intellectual prowess. Plans were under way to institutionalize a formal seven-day residential training program for all the new employees. In January 1994, an employee award program was instituted for the best service person based on the individual's record for customer satisfaction on a monthly basis. Managers of each department could forward employees' names to the management innovation group, who consolidated the list to identify the winners. Letters received from customers played a significant role in the choice.

A new scheme to assess employees' service quality performance was also introduced. Each employee was given a letter grade, ranging from A (excellent) to C (unsatisfactory) by his or her immediate boss for their service performance. Those found to be unsatisfactory were required to go through a retraining program. In August 1994, a new program of benchmarking was introduced, under which employees with exemplary service records were sent to tour theme park facilities in the United States, Europe, and Japan to assess the service levels of Joong-Ang's competitors. In 1994, more than 300 employees had participated. Often, returning employees presented a written report to the management on their observations. As one manager noted:

> Over the next five years we plan to send about 1,000 employees abroad to our competitor's facilities. The primary purpose of this trip is to make each of our employees lift their eyes beyond what they see now. We call it "eyes leveling up." We do not attempt to synthesize all their observations and funnel it into our planning. If each employee gets a new drive and motivation to make Everland the world's best, we will have achieved our objectives.

Early Measurements

Korea Research Group, a leading Korean consumer research organization, was engaged to measure customer satisfaction at Farmland in 1993. The formal measurement was done using surveys. In an effort to compare its service quality level with its competitors, arrangements were made also to conduct the survey at Lotte World. The results were not very encouraging; the customer satisfaction index was at 67.2 for Farmland and 70.1 for Lotte World (see Exhibits 11 and 12).

EXHIBIT 11   Service Quality Measurement Results

	Farmland	Lotte World	Comments
Customer satisfaction index	67.2	70.1	Based on two measurements taken by the Korea Research Institute. Scores of 75–80 are considered as internationally comparable levels.
Mystery shopping service quality index	63.0	76.4	As above.
Telephone service quality index	76.4	NA	Internal measurements taken twice yearly.
Employee satisfaction index	69.2	NA	Internal measurements taken twice yearly.

Source: Company files.

Following these measurements, management introduced a mystery shopping procedure, under which an employee went to the different facilities within Farmland and Lotte World posing as a customer and evaluated the services offered. The results corroborated the survey results that indicated that Lotte World was outperforming Farmland. The mystery shopping index for Farmland was 63.0, compared to 76.4 for Lotte World.

The academy developed an employee satisfaction index and used it to assess how satisfied the employees were with the organization. The resulting score of 69.2 was slightly below "just satisfied."

However, not all the indicators had been negative. Mr. Her noted that the number of complimentary letters from the guests had shown a conspicuous increase in 1994. He had yet to receive the formal measures of the customer satisfaction index.

It was clear that Farmland had some way yet to go. As a marketing manager noted:

> Repeat business is very important to our survival. If we don't satisfy our customers, they won't come back and we won't have any business left. But Koreans are very serious people and it is not in our nature to smile at strangers. So it becomes all the more difficult to get the type of service you can see at Disneyland.

Operational Problems in 1993

Although there was some indication that the Samsung Group would consider a proposal to expand Farmland, Mr. Her also had a number of operational issues to contend with.

One major issue was accessibility. One resident who lived near Yongin commented:

> Although it should take me only 15 minutes to drive from my home to Farmland, traffic is so intense that it may take me almost an hour of crawling in the traffic. That's the main reason why I have not visited Farmland yet.

A manager in the marketing group commented on the critical nature of this problem:

> In Korea, we work five and a half days a week and on workdays travel time is long. All house chores have to be done only on weekends. Given this fact, it is only to be expected that Korean customers would not be so keen to travel on a Sunday or on a holiday if the traffic is heavy.

However, many Joong-Ang managers believed that accessibility was only a temporary issue. Mr. Yu, director of personnel, commented:

EXHIBIT 12	Demographic Information of Customer Sample for Customer Service Index Measurements*		
Sex			
Male		80	40.0%
Female		120	60.0
Age			
Child		40	20.0
Youth		40	20.0
Adult		120	60.0
Annual Income†			
<150 million won		58	41.7
151–200 million won		30	21.6
>201 million won		51	36.7
Marital Status			
Married		31	15.5
Single		169	84.5
Place of Residence			
Seoul		54	27.0
Kyonggi-Do Province‡		37	18.5
Nearby provinces		43	21.5
Others		66	33.0

*A total of 200 people were sampled on this day.
†Numbers do not add to 200 because of refusal to answer the question. Percentages were calculated based on those who did respond.
‡Kyonggi-Do was South Korea's northwest province; Seoul and Yongin were located in it.
Source: Korea Research Institute.

Travel difficulties are part of life in Korea, given the small land and the large number of people. The government plans to extend the subway to Yongin. When they do, Farmland will have a subway terminal, which will provide a lot of convenience to people.

A related issue was parking. A manager who had conducted an extensive analysis of parking said:

What we have now is more or less enough for the time being. We have enough space for about 8,000 cars and at four people per car we can accommodate about 32,000 people. If we assume an average stay of six to eight hours, the lot turns over 1.7 times a day. This gives us capacity for a peak daily attendance of 52,000. But the real problem is seasonality. On peak days, we may get more visitors and quite often people may spend more time. If we are going to expand, this will be a major bottleneck.

Part of the expansion plan included augmenting the parking spaces and also providing a park-and-ride scheme for visitors so that they could travel comfortably from the various car parks to the entrance.

Relations with local people could be a problem. Expanding Farmland meant taking over more Yongin valley land. A local farmer expressed his view:

Samsung just wants to expand their business. But they don't realize that cutting down the trees and leveling the ground will cause potential flooding in the surrounding region. This will damage all our crops. How will they compensate us?

It was also a challenge to introduce a dynamic environment within the Farmland organization. In order to succeed in the industry, Farmland had to go through a major reorientation in its organizational style. Mr. Yu, who had pioneered a number of changes within the organization, recalled one event which demonstrated the problems management faced:

> Previously, we had the head office at Seoul and we were managing Farmland by remote control. We faxed information and directives back and forth. But I somehow did not see that this would be the best way to work. I insisted that the head office had to be located where our products are. Only after much persuasion did we decide to move to this place.

Among other things, management was also considering a change in its recruitment process. Traditionally, in line with Samsung's standard practice, Farmland had gone after the academically best graduates and students. However, the managers believed that they needed more people with a strong service orientation and more women. The proportion of women was below 25 percent. Although many managers anticipated problems because most Korean women stopped working after marriage, Mr. Yu had more confidence. In his words:

> I think times are changing. And, even if we have a high turnover, it good for us since fresh blood always brings in fresh ideas and we would be able to preserve some dynamism in our organization.

Mr. Hyun, director of finance, commented on the strategy as he saw it:

> A lot of people say that we are overinvesting in image building and are asking if we can show some reasonable returns. However, Farmland is about a lot more than just making a profit. This is a showcase for both Samsung and Korea. Every year about 25 percent of the Korean population visits us. Our studies show that our customers link the park and the Samsung name. Think of it. We have more than 5 million adolescents visiting us every year, some more than once. Every time they come to our park, they hear the name of Samsung, and they see it in many of our demonstrations, etc. They are our potential customers for the future. And, we want to show them that we stand for excellence. In fact, we are focusing on how to turn our satisfied customers to more-than-satisfied customers. You can imagine what this means to our corporate group.

Mr. Her commented on the current situation:

> I have spent a lot of effort steering the organization towards a new culture—a service culture. We have started on a path that is high risk. We cannot afford to fail. We have started investing a huge amount of time and money in building this park's reputation. Can we really attain global standards of excellence? Although I cannot guarantee success, I am accountable to the corporate group and I am pushing myself and the whole organization towards that goal. What if we do not make a big turnaround? The stakes are high. I am encouraged, though. I have seen visible signs of change. Otherwise, I would have stopped going along this direction.
>
> We are certainly being looked at very closely not only by our Samsung group but by the whole Korean business community, as well as the international community. The whole notion of Samsung building a multibillion-dollar theme resort sounds weird. A billion dollars can easily buy you a semiconductor plant, and when you invest that amount of money in a theme park, you had better have a clear idea of what you are doing. When I set up the service academy at Joong-Ang, some managers suggested that it was an excessive peripheral investment. But to me, the core of the service business is people, and they deserve the best investment we can make. When I introduced the idea of "green service," my own managers were worried that employees might not buy into the idea. We have not had any problem so far, and I think it will be received well. I spend a lot of my own personal time addressing employees, getting involved in the selection process, participating in lunch-box meetings, and

taking time to answer e-mail messages personally. Is it all time well spent? Many think otherwise, but to me it is a strong yes.

I face a number of difficulties. The employees and managers don't have a strong service mentality and they seem reluctant to change their traditional ways of doing things and adopt a new mindset. We also have relatively low-quality facilities that can't really meet guest expectations of a highly service-oriented theme park. This problem is augmented by our difficulty in getting sufficient capital to improve things. Finally, it is difficult to get the importance of training and education properly recognized. I am not the kind of person who gives up easily; because I have a clear, concrete idea where I am leading these people, no matter what, I am going to overcome the obstacles one by one and not give up.

These are times of change for Samsung. Our chairman has made clear in no uncertain terms that we are moving to a new era where quality and not quantity will dictate our survival. The new management philosophy wants to integrate employers, customers, and employees under one big umbrella. We in our corporate group are bringing in a customer focus and we want to become a top name in customer satisfaction. When you look at it in this light, what we are attempting here at Everland is consistent with our corporate theme. The Samsung board's approval of our master plan was a very clear signal to go ahead. And, this is where I come to think that we are indeed headed in the right direction and moving at the right pace. However, I am sure it isn't perfect. What should we add to our program? How can we ensure that our service quality continuously excels against our domestic competitors as well as matching international standards?

(The company's Web address is www.everland.com.)

SARAH NORTON AND WISE RESEARCH

When Jeff Baird knocked on the Dallas motel room door on an early August evening in 1995, he expected to see his bubbling and enthusiastic girlfriend. He expected her to be excited, both because it was her birthday and because she was nearing completion of the first week in a two-week training program for the new job she had recently accepted. Instead, the young woman who answered looked troubled and tired.

Ronald L. Coulter, *Southwest Missouri State University*

D. Michael Fields, *Southwest Missouri State University*

Mary K. Coulter, *Southwest Missouri State University*

Rebecca J. Gordon-Runyan, *WRG Inc.*

"Sarah, you don't look very happy," said Jeff.

"I'm not," explained Sarah. "This week has not gone exactly as I expected, and I am seriously questioning whether or not I should even be here."

Although the tone of the meeting had obviously changed dramatically, Jeff was glad he had made the trip. Sarah was extremely troubled and clearly needed to talk to someone about her concerns. Jeff was happy that he was there to listen as Sarah tried to put in perspective the events of the last four days.

INITIATING THE JOB SEARCH

Sarah Norton was nearing the point where she had just one semester remaining before obtaining her MBA degree from a large state university in Hammonsville, Missouri. She was preparing, with some concern, to begin her job search. Sarah had identified at least three factors that would make finding a job in her field difficult. First, from a general perspective, American industry was still in the process of its most substantial downsizing. Much of the downsizing was at the expense of lower levels of management—which had depressed the hiring environment for MBAs across the nation. Second, Sarah's area of specialization was market research. Although many companies expressed a continued dependence on research in order to be effective in the mature markets that dominated the U.S. marketplace, the research industry was not considered to be a growth industry. This situation was further complicated for MBA students because many undergraduates were in competition for the same jobs and could be employed at lower salaries. Finally, Sarah preferred to remain in Hammonsville. The city of 150,000 was close to her parents, and Jeff was there. The location issue might prove to be particularly limiting because a city of 150,000 would generate a smaller market for researchers. Although the situation was less than encouraging, Sarah still felt that she had some advantages in pursuing and getting a job in her field.

SARAH'S BACKGROUND

Sarah was known to her professors and friends as a mature 32-year-old woman who had grown up in central Missouri in a strong family with loving parents. She had a strong religious background that helped to guide her when she had to make tough personal decisions. She was a very pleasant person to be around, and she was both liked and respected by her colleagues and friends. While her personal philosophy was to respect and treat others as she would like to be treated, she never pushed her moral, ethical, or religious views on others. She was genuine and personable in her relationships and was considered to be a fun person to be around.

Sarah had one younger sister with whom she remained very close. Sarah's first job had been with the state of Missouri in the Professional Registration office of the Board of Healing Arts. She enjoyed working there; the office was operated in a very professional manner, and the employees showed a genuine appreciation for each other. After several years in this job, Sarah realized that she wanted to complete her college degree. At the urging of her sister, Sarah transferred to Hammonsville to work in the local state vocational rehabilitation office. Here Sarah assisted several vocational rehabilitation counselors and took classes at the local state university. Sarah was known for her positive work ethic, strong moral values, and intelligence. She received her undergraduate degree in marketing and management (a double major) and graduated with high honors. During her coursework, Sarah was especially taken with the research classes and decided that she wanted to pursue a career in marketing research.

With this sense of direction, Sarah openly sought opportunities in several research projects with her professors in order to develop her research skills. As a result, she was competent and confident of her ability to do all phases of a research project. She could design questionnaires, input data, analyze and interpret statistical tests, and write reports. She was a proficient statistician. Sarah was also very aware of the importance of collecting and reporting unbiased data. The ethical handling of data had been stressed in her research courses, and such an approach was consistent with her personality and personal values. While no industrywide standards existed for the collection and handling of data, Sarah was aware of the code of ethics developed by the Marketing Research Association, Inc. (see Exhibit 1). This organization consisted of approximately 2,100 members from across the United States. Members used the organization for education and training and for networking opportunities in the field of marketing research.

Sarah knew from her professors' lectures, and from her assigned research readings, that corporations annually spend millions of dollars on research. The results of that research are used to influence multimillion-dollar decisions regarding new product lines, manufacturing employment, and promotional strategies. Sarah was also aware that marketing research conducted by outside research suppliers was a growing industry concern. Articles she had read on the subject reinforced this concern regarding the ethical collection of marketing research data.

EXHIBIT 1   Code of Ethics of the Marketing Research Association

The Code of Professional Ethics and Practices

1. To maintain high standards of competence and integrity in marketing and survey research.
2. To maintain the highest level of business and professional conduct and to comply with federal, state, and local laws, regulations, and ordinances applicable to my business practice and those of my company.
3. To exercise all reasonable care and to observe the best standards of objectivity and accuracy in the development, collection, processing, and reporting of marketing and survey research information.
4. To protect the anonymity of respondents and hold all information concerning an individual respondent privileged, such that this information is used only within the context of the particular study.
5. To thoroughly instruct and supervise all persons for whose work I am responsible in accordance with study specifications and general research techniques.
6. To observe the rights of ownership of all materials received from and/or developed for clients, and to keep in confidence all research techniques, data and other information considered confidential by their owners.
7. To make available to clients such details on the research methods and techniques of an assignment as may be reasonably required for proper interpretation of the data, providing this reporting does not violate the confidence of respondents or clients.
8. To promote the trust of the public for marketing and survey research activities and to avoid any procedure which misrepresents the activities of a respondent, the rewards of cooperation, or the uses of data.
9. To refrain from referring to membership in this organization as proof of competence, since the organization does not so certify any person or organization.
10. To encourage the observance of principles of this code among all people engaged in marketing and survey research.

Source: Used with permission of the Marketing Research Association, Inc., Rocky Hill, CT.

When Sarah completed her undergraduate degree in 1994, the job market was particularly tight. Several of her professors suggested that she consider an MBA degree, so Sarah applied to the graduate school and was accepted into the MBA program. This allowed her to remain in Hammonsville. She also was given a graduate assistantship in the marketing department which paid her tuition and living expenses. While working on her MBA, Sarah continued to develop her marketing research skills. She took 12 hours in her graduate program specifically in research classes and also worked on several special projects for the College of Business for publication and classroom instruction purposes. She also helped acquire secondary data from the library. Sarah had fully expected to return to her assistantship position in the fall of 1995; she had already been offered the head graduate assistant position.

Sarah had agreed to take on the additional responsibilities of head graduate assistant in her final semester of graduate school in the fall—coordinating the schedules and activities of the five graduate assistants who worked in the marketing department. She was confident that the additional time needed would not interfere with either her preparation for classes or what she considered to be her most important activity—finding an entry-level position in the marketing research field. By mid-summer, Sarah had updated her résumé and was ready to begin aggressively pursuing the job market.

REACTING TO THE POSITION ANNOUNCEMENT

Sarah had been casually looking through the employment section of the Hammonsville *News Monitor* on Sunday, July 9, 1995, when she noticed a position announcement for a market research manager. She eagerly read the balance of the ad copy to get more details about the opportunity. The advertisement did not give any specific job requirements, but the copy did provide a catchy reference to details, dilemmas, and deadlines as they related to an entry-level management position. The advertisement gave a post office box number in Hammonsville and asked potential applicants to send a cover letter with their résumés. No company name was provided in the advertisement.

Sarah thought long and hard about applying for the position. If she applied and was offered the position, she thought she might get to stay in Hammonsville. She liked the city, and very few managerial positions ever became available in her specialized area of marketing research. She would likely have to wait to finish the last nine hours on her MBA degree, but she could still finish the degree at the university. She would also have to give up her head graduate assistant position. She especially wanted her professors to know what she was contemplating so they could hire a replacement before the fall semester began. The local university had been good to her, and she did not want to do anything that would appear improper to her professors or to herself. She discussed the situation with her major professor, who encouraged her to look seriously at the position. If it did not appear to be the type of position she wanted, she could simply withdraw from the interview process. Sarah agreed and mailed in her résumé and cover letter.

THE INITIAL RESPONSE AND SARAH'S PREPARATION

Within a week of mailing her application letter, Sarah received a phone call from a woman named Katie. Katie said that Mr. Bill Wise, the company's president, would be arriving in Hammonsville from Dallas to do interviews and that he wanted to interview her. Sarah agreed to meet with Mr. Wise on Thursday, July 27. Sarah inquired as to the name of the organization and was told "Wise Research." A follow-up call was to be made by Katie at a later date to verify the interview time.

Sarah tried to get some background information about the organization so that she could intelligently discuss the company and how she might fit into its plans. She found the company listed in the Hammonsville telephone directory under market research firms. Her professor recommended that she call the number to inquire about the operation prior to the interview, but not to indicate why the call was being made. Sarah called the number and spoke with a young man who said he was the office manager. She asked what type of research they conducted and was informed that the company, located in the Westfield Mall, was strictly involved in fieldwork. The company did not generate any questionnaires, nor did it analyze any of the data it collected. The company simply collected data for other marketing research firms that were providing information to their own clients, such as Procter & Gamble, Ragu, or Campbell's. Sarah, remembering her marketing research text, classified the company as a field service organization (see Exhibit 2); this meant that the firm concentrated on collecting data for research projects. The office manager also indicated that the staff at his facility were not college educated.

The manager, who sounded apprehensive, then asked Sarah why she was interested in this information. Sarah truthfully answered that the president of the company was coming to Hammonsville to interview her for a position, but she did not have any information about the company. The manager seemed upset that the president of the company was coming to Hammonsville and he had not been notified. Sarah specifically indicated that she did not know anything about the position.

EXHIBIT 2 Types of Marketing Research Service Suppliers

Customized research services	Companies that work with individual clients from developing the problem/opportunity through the entire research process. They are also referred to as full-service suppliers.
Field research services	These companies concentrate only on collecting data for research projects. They may specialize in various interviewing methodologies such as mail surveys, telephone surveys, personal surveys, focus groups, or mall intercept surveys.
Data analysis research services	These firms specialize in data coding, data editing, and data analysis. They are sometimes referred to as "tab houses," although some specialize in sophisticated data analysis techniques.
Syndicated research services	Companies that routinely collect information to provide to other firms who subscribe to their services.
Branded products research services	These companies have developed specialized data collection and analysis techniques, which are relevant to address specific types of research problems. Their research is branded and marketed like branded products.
Standardized research services	Firms which do marketing research projects conducted in a standard, prespecified manner; the results are then supplied to several different clients.

THE INTERVIEW PROCESS

The Initial Interview

When Katie called several days later to confirm Sarah's interview, she indicated that the interviews were to be held at a local hotel in Hammonsville. Sarah was somewhat surprised because she had expected to be interviewed at the local office in the mall. When she arrived at the hotel, she dialed the extension number Katie had provided. Karen Wise, Bill Wise's wife, answered the phone. She indicated that she also worked at Wise Research. Karen Wise came to the hotel lobby and gave Sarah an application to complete. This was a standard form with a space for annual salary requirement. Sarah responded $25,000–$35,000, knowing that it was a high request for the local market conditions.

After completing the application, Sarah went upstairs to the Wise's hotel room. The interview with Mr. and Mrs. Wise was informal and was held at a small table set in the center of a large room. Mr. Wise sat on one side, his wife sat on his side of the table but more to the end, and Sarah sat on the other side. Mr. Wise was dressed in a lightweight, short-sleeve shirt without a tie or jacket, and Mrs. Wise wore a dress. Sarah did not get the impression from their appearance or the interview process that either of them had much formal education or training. Both were very pleased with the sample paperwork Sarah had brought.

Sarah brought with her a copy of a marketing plan she had done as a student and three questionnaires she had developed to collect data for various projects. During her interview she discussed her data-entry skills and her knowledge of various statistical packages to analyze data. She also discussed her work on several special projects with professors in the College of Business. She explained that for the past year she had been employed as a graduate assistant in the marketing department. She indicated that she had expected to return to this position in the fall since she had already been offered the head graduate assistant position. She also discussed her undergraduate employment at a popular local restaurant where she had been responsible for operations in the absence of the owner. She had often managed the restaurant when the owner was away for several days.

The Wises discussed the deadlines necessary for different projects and how the manager might sometimes have two projects going one day and eight working the next. They gave Sarah a short history of the company. The organization had been in business for about 25 years and operated five mall research offices. Three of the offices were located in Dallas; one was located in Tulsa; and the Hammonsville office was the newest, having been in existence for about 10 years.

Sarah was then told that the local manager was being let go because he was unable to achieve the required production levels. The person the Wises chose would be trained in Dallas for two weeks and then returned to Hammonsville where he or she would be responsible for the Westfield Mall office. The interview was spent primarily discussing the job requirements. Sarah was given the impression that while there would be some contact between the Dallas office and the Hammonsville office, the manager they hired would have direct contact with the clients and autonomy to work with the employees as he or she saw fit.

Sarah's next question was about validating surveys. Survey validation is a procedure where supervisors, or other objective individuals, recontact a small random sample of respondents to check the accuracy of the fieldwork being done. Validation is particularly needed when the temptation for interviewer cheating may be present. Sarah was told that the clients did the validations and that the supervisor also did some. The context of the interview led Sarah to believe that the Wise's organization was contracting to provide valid survey data. Sarah was then told that callbacks for second interviews would be made that afternoon.

The Second Interview

Karen Wise called and left Sarah a message on her answering machine that Thursday evening. Sarah returned the call later in the evening. Karen told Sarah that the pay was $11 per hour with time and a half paid for any overtime work. Sarah specifically asked if it was 40 hours per week, and Karen replied in the affirmative. Karen Wise said this would come out to be $25,000 per year with benefits that Bill Wise would tell her about the next day. Sarah accepted the second interview and then calculated that it would take about 42.5 hours per week to make $25,000 per year.

The second interview was held in the same hotel and was as casual as the first interview. The Wises told Sarah that they were leaving on vacation as soon as they were done in Hammonsville. Again, no mention was made of touring the local Hammonsville facilities or of meeting the staff. The benefit package presented to Sarah included health insurance premiums paid on a plan of Sarah's choice, up to the amount that the company paid for Dallas employees. This was done because the Wise Research insurance plan did not cover Missouri employees. One week of vacation was offered after one year of employment. A performance review would be scheduled after three months, and then another review would be held nine months later. Mr. Wise stated that it didn't behoove them to give raises in that interim.

In preparation for the second interview, Sarah had compiled a list of 17 questions that she considered to be important. Much of the second interview consisted of Sarah's questions and the corresponding answers (see Exhibit 3), as she sought to gain more information about the research firm.

EXHIBIT 3   The Second Job Interview: Sarah Norton's Questions and Her Notes on Wise Research's Answers

1. How is the staff paid?
   The staff was paid on an hourly basis.

2. Is there a budget for incentives?
   No, but they were considering one on a trial basis and would possibly use the Hammonsville office to try out a new program. They felt there were problems with incentives based just on completions of surveys as some people screen potential respondents while others actually do the interviews. The Wises seemed to be concerned with the fairness of this method.

3. Are paychecks distributed from Dallas?
   The paychecks come from Dallas (verified at a later date).

4. Are the staff paid weekly or monthly?
   Twice a month.

5. What are the benefits? Health insurance? Profit sharing? Bonuses for production?
   Insurance was provided by the company; there was no profit sharing plan; and bonuses for production might include a pizza party on the company for all of the employees, but no specific program was in place.

6. If the Hammonsville office was extremely busy and needed more production, could the manager help do the fieldwork?
   Yes.

7. How do you support your managers?
   Sarah never specifically asked this question but tried to discern information from her conversations. The Wises seemed supportive of their managers. Frequent communication between offices was discussed. They felt that the open lines for assistance from other mall managers would help. Overall, Sarah felt that they would support their managers regarding decisions and actions as long as they were keeping up production.

8. How often are performance reviews done? 3 months? 6 months?
   Reviews were done after the third month and then again at one year.

9. What is the average overtime for a manager?
   No specific time was given, but the Wises did feel that there would be plenty of overtime opportunities. It was mentioned that if the manager frequently had excessive overtime that they would look for either inefficiencies or the need for an additional assistant. Requests for overtime were required prior to actually working. Approval was mandatory.

10. How are the employees trained? Does the manager have latitude in the content of employee training?
    No specific training program had been designed and Sarah would be responsible for how the Hammonsville employees were trained within some guidelines.

11. How does Wise Research get its referrals?
    Companies come to them, and much of their business is repeat. If a mall office does a good job, the client may again specifically ask for that office. The client and mall manager will be able to communicate directly without going through the Dallas office every time. It was mentioned that Hammonsville had a bad reputation and that many clients did not want to use them. The Wises felt this problem could be overcome with time and a new manager.

12. If Sarah increased production in the Hammonsville office, would Wise Research have enough business to keep the office busy?
    Yes, the Wises did not feel that this would be any problem.

13. Would Sarah have autonomy and authority over her office (to setup evaluation system, to tie bonuses to performance, to specify dress, approach, etc.)?
    The Wises would not directly answer this question. Sarah did not feel that the Wises were willing to let the manager operate completely and independently. The manager did have the authority over his or her office to a certain extent, with the final word coming from Dallas.

14. Were any promotion dollars budgeted to raise the image of the Hammonsville office?
    In preparing for the interview Sarah had spoken to a variety of Hammonsville people about being interviewed in the mall. The typical first response she received was always negative toward mall interviewers. They were viewed as interruptive, and most people did not like to talk with them. Sarah felt that some efforts to change people's perceptions about the interviewers' work would enable the Hammonsville office to raise production. The Wises indicated that their organization does not budget for any self-promotion efforts.

EXHIBIT 3   Concluded

15. Where in the mall can interviewers go?
    Interviewers are allowed to go anywhere in the original section of the mall. This is quite a large area, but most interviewers were staying primarily by the research office. Interviewers were typically not going farther into the mall because interviews were typically conducted in the research office and the original section of the mall was so large that it could be a long trip back to the office. The people Sarah talked with often tried to avoid the original mall areas where the interviewers typically stood. The Wises did want to see the interviewers branch out further into the mall.
16. How are focus group participants solicited?
    A file of willing participants was maintained to be used when needed.
17. During the Dallas training what would Sarah be provided with?
    The Wises indicated the company would provide a room close to the mall, and they would provide a rental car if needed. Airfare would be provided from Hammonsville, and Sarah would also receive reimbursement for her expenses.

After completing the interview, the Wises indicated that they would make their decision later that afternoon. They also told Sarah they would call her either that afternoon or the following Monday.

Karen Wise called Sarah from her car phone later that afternoon and offered Sarah the position. Sarah accepted the position and indicated that she could fly out on Monday, August 7,1995, for training in Dallas. The following week Sarah withdrew from her fall graduate program courses, informed the marketing department that she would not be returning for the fall semester, wrapped up her summer work as a research assistant, and prepared her personal calendar to be in Dallas from August 7 to August 21, 1995.

THE DALLAS TRAINING

Sarah arrived at the Dallas Love Field airport around noon on Monday, August 7, and was picked up at the gate by Mark Wise, the son of Mr. and Mrs. Wise. Mark, who was in his early 20s, was very personable and open about the organization. He also spoke very highly of Cindy Brewster, the supervisor with whom Sarah was to train. Mark did bring up the fact that someone had called their Hammonsville office and asked about the position; he was very curious. The first time he discussed it, Sarah let it go without response. He brought the subject up again during the drive and at lunch. He mentioned that they had received a résumé from another employee in the Hammonsville office. They were confused as to how that could have happened because they had just listed a post office box number in the advertisement. Sarah simply commented that Hammonsville was a small town in many respects, even though the population was around 150,000, and that it would not be unusual for word to get around.

Mark also commented that his parents were tired of the Hammonsville situation. They were determined to hire someone who could make the office work, and they wanted to keep that person in Hammonsville no matter what it required. Mark said that the company had received a large number of résumés, and he thought they had interviewed nearly 100 applicants. When Sarah looked at him in disbelief, he quickly added that his statement might not be exactly accurate, but that they had interviewed for two days. He also stated that they felt happy with their decision and excited about her employment.

Sarah and Mark also had a conversation about her educational background. Mark was interested in research and said what he really wanted to know was how to design the questionnaires in order to get the data they wanted. Sarah briefly discussed some of the aspects of questionnaire design and data collection. It seemed very odd to Sarah that Mark had very little understanding of the research process as a whole, but she chalked it up to his being the younger son who did not work full-time at the company.

Mark took Sarah to lunch and then to a car rental agency where the Wises' other son had rented a car for Sarah to use during her two-week training program. Sarah was lodged in a hotel across the parking lot from a shopping mall which housed the research office where she would be training. Mark then took Sarah to the hotel and on to the mall where he gave her an envelope containing $200 in cash and a hand-written note, asking for her signature to indicate that she had received the $200 for expenses.

At the Chesterfield Mall, Sarah was introduced to the office supervisor, Cindy Brewster, and Mark left to return to the main office. Cindy immediately informed Sarah that she had been instructed by the main office not to disclose why Sarah would be in their office for two weeks. Cindy had told the employees that Sarah was an auditor and monitor who would be watching her. Cindy had Sarah complete another standard personnel form, which again requested simple information such as name, address, emergency contact, and salary. Upon completion of the form, Cindy faxed it to the main office.

Cindy then took Sarah on a tour of the facility. It soon struck Sarah that she had seen no evidence of a computer or typewriter. Later she did see a computer sitting on a shelf in the storage room. Sarah asked if they were computerized, and Cindy replied no. Cindy added that only the main office had computers.

In further conversations with Cindy, Sarah discovered that Wise Research considered 37.5 hours as a full-time week. Katie, the office manager at the main office, had sent an envelope for Sarah which Cindy gave to her. Sarah was surprised the front of the envelope was marked For Cindy's Eyes Only and Top Secret. The envelope contained copies of the routine paperwork that supervisors were responsible for completing. Cindy then mentioned that someone had called the Hammonsville office for information about the position. Again, Sarah did not reveal any information, but it seemed very peculiar to Sarah that the organization was so concerned about this incident, particularly if they had interviewed as many people as Mark had indicated.

Sarah and Cindy also discussed the story that Cindy had been ordered to tell her employees concerning Sarah's presence in the office. Cindy said that Wise Research had not yet notified the Hammonsville manager that he was being released, and she asked Sarah if that bothered her. Sarah was vague in her response, and Cindy made it clear that it *did* bother her. Cindy said that if the organization could treat the Hammonsville manager that way, they would also likely do it to her.

Day Two

Work began on Tuesday at 9 AM. Sarah was told to carry her time card in her purse so no one would know that she was clocking in and out. To do this, Sarah arrived before the other employees. Cindy began by showing Sarah the paperwork that was to be completed before 10 AM. At 10 AM Cindy held a briefing where the interviewers were brought up to speed on the outstanding projects and were taken through the steps of preparing for new projects. Cindy introduced Sarah as the auditor and monitor that she had told them about.

As the week progressed, Sarah was shown how to check the completed questionnaires and how to report daily progress to the client. When Wise Research began a project, each interviewer received a sheet that contained (1) an estimate of how many completed questionnaires they should be able to get per hour; (2) what percent of people they would approach (called *net incidence*) who would be eligible to respond based on general criteria, such as age or job; and (3) criteria which were specific (called *category incidence*) to the survey, such as "Do you use body shampoo?" Clients were sent a daily report, and Sarah was told that, in preparing this report, supervisors started with the actual production numbers and worked from them. For example, if interviewers were expected to complete two questionnaires per hour and four were actually completed in one day, the supervisor reported that two hours were worked on the job. This way budgeted hours always matched actual hours. They then took the number four and applied the net incidence and category incidence percentages to come up with a fictional number of people they screened out during the day so the final number showed four completions. This total was then distributed over the categories purely at supervisor discretion. They would just manipulate the data until the numbers totaled those estimated by the client. This report was then faxed to the client. Sarah asked Cindy about this practice, and Cindy said it was the way that everyone did it. She then told Sarah a story about how Karen Wise once was discussing one of the numbers with her and Cindy asked her why it bothered her because the numbers were all fabricated anyway. Karen said she was right, and they both had a good laugh. Cindy indicated that she did feel that it was wrong, though, and Sarah questioned how clients could make good decisions based on potentially biased data.

Sarah learned that the actual jobs each office worked on could vary from a home placement of body shampoo (where the client would use the product and then evaluate it) to a mall taste test of liqueurs. Sarah was concerned by some of these practices, so she asked Cindy what would happen if it appeared that a survey was not going to be completed on time. Cindy replied that first you would call the main office for more time. If that wasn't possible, they were often told to get it done no matter what it takes. This might involve calling uncles, nieces, or anyone demographically acceptable to provide the required data. The main office was also likely to tell the supervisor to write it up. Cindy later told Sarah that some of the other mall offices had interviewers who had been caught so many times with invalidated surveys that they were working under three or four different names so the clients would not recognize them.

Day Three

As training continued, another incident occurred that concerned Sarah. Cindy received a call from another mall supervisor. The other mall supervisor heard Sarah's voice in the background and immediately asked if Karen Wise had brought in the new Hammonsville supervisor for training. Cindy immediately denied that Sarah was the new manager, as she had been instructed to do from the main office. The comment from the other mall supervisor seemed strange to Sarah, since each office has four to six, primarily female, interviewers scheduled per day. She realized there was a high rate of turnover for interviewers, but it seemed suspicious that the other mall supervisor immediately asked if Sarah was a new supervisor instead of an interviewer. Sarah questioned Cindy about this, and they talked about the grapevine that was in place at Wise Research. Sarah asked if the grapevine was used mainly for information or power within the organization. Cindy's reply was "For both."

Day Four

By Thursday of the first week, Sarah was directing the briefings on new projects for the interviewers. Cindy sat back and supervised Sarah's efforts. As they went through the questionnaire, one of the interviewers asked about the coding numbers. This led to a discussion about data entry, and one of the interviewers asked Sarah what would happen if a question was not answered. Sarah indicated they would leave it blank when inputting that response and then continue. Sarah explained that one blank response would not invalidate the entire interview. This seemed very annoying to the interviewers, and again Sarah was surprised at the lack of knowledge the employees had about the whole data collection process.

Throughout the daily training sessions, Cindy and Sarah had discussed the culture of the Wise Research organization and again, on Thursday, they began another conversation. Cindy recounted examples of her experiences. She believed that when she was hired for the supervisor's position, Bill Wise had known that she badly needed the job. She had been out of work for several months and her elderly mother needed care, so an income was imperative. Cindy's background was in psychology, and she had worked for mental health institutions prior to being out of work.

They also discussed many of the things that Cindy's boss had told her to do, such as being dishonest with her employees. Cindy told Sarah that there were things that she had been asked to do that she had refused. Sarah was very concerned about Cindy's comment and asked what those things were. Sarah felt that if Cindy had been asked to do these things then she would probably be asked to do them, too. Sarah was becoming upset at the thought of so much dishonesty in the office. What else could they want? Cindy was not specific in her response to Sarah's direct question and implied other things *were* currently happening, but that she had chosen not to be a part of those activities.

In her supervisory position, which she had held for over eight months, Cindy immediately stood out as a Wise Research leader. She was educated and perceived by the interviewers as a fair supervisor. But Cindy was bothered: although she had received notification of her three-month raise earlier, Wise Research had withheld the monetary rewards until just a few weeks before Sarah's arrival. Cindy had made attempts to gain raises for herself and for her assistant, but her attempts had been ignored. When the main office informed Cindy that she was going to receive a pay increase, she was happy, but she also wondered what the Wises might be wanting from her. When she was told she would be supervising Sarah's training, Cindy felt she understood the timing of her raise.

Cindy was aware of Sarah's training benefits. Sarah had been flown in for two weeks and provided with a car, a nice hotel, and $200 in cash for spending money. When Sarah's personnel records were completed and returned to Cindy, she commented on Sarah's starting pay. Apparently, Sarah's starting pay was more than Cindy was receiving even after having been with the company for more than eight months. Cindy explained that when she was hired, training was provided in Dallas-area malls and that she was responsible for all transportation costs. Every single weekday for what was supposed to be one month and ultimately turned into three, Cindy drove 85 miles round trip for her training. She admitted to feeling slighted by the company when Sarah was being treated so well.

By now Sarah did not have the positive feeling that she had when she first accepted her new position with Wise Research. The final straw came when Sarah and Cindy were discussing pay, and Cindy shared an experience she'd had on the Monday morning of

Sarah's arrival. Apparently Cindy and others had worked the previous Saturday and had been loaned a couple of interviewers from another Dallas-area mall. One of Cindy's interviewers had been befriended by one of these women, and a conversation had ensued about how long each had been with the company and what salary was made per hour. On Monday, the visiting interviewer had gone back to work and complained that Cindy's employee made more money than she did although Cindy's employee had been with the company a shorter time. Cindy had received a phone call from Katie at the main office. Katie told her that she was to fire her interviewer because the interviewer had discussed her salary with another employee. Sarah asked Cindy if the employee had known about this rule or had been shown an employee handbook where this rule was stated. Cindy said that only supervisors and their assistants had employee handbooks and, to her knowledge, her assistant had never seen one. She did say that she felt that discussion of wages was inappropriate, and Sarah stated that she did not feel that way. Sarah said that her salary was hers, it was based on her skills, and that she should be able to discuss it with whomever she wanted.

Cindy had called the employee into the office, told her about the main office's stand, and told the employee that she must be fired. The interviewer began to cry and tried to change Cindy's mind. Cindy explained that it was not her decision and that she had been ordered to do this. The employee asked to talk with someone in the main office; Cindy felt that she should be able to do that, so she placed the call. When she told Katie that the employee wanted to talk with her, Katie responded that she did not know what more could be said but that she would speak to the employee.

The employee was crying and asked to keep her job. Cindy indicated that she literally said, "I beg you for my job." Cindy then heard the employee say that she would talk to Cindy. This surprised Cindy because she'd had no say in the firing. When the employee got off the phone, Cindy told her that she did not have to beg her for her job. She would have to formally write her up, but that she could still work. When Cindy called Katie back to tell her what she had done, she was asked why. Cindy explained that the woman worked several jobs to support a husband who didn't work and three children and that she needed the income. Katie responded that it wasn't their problem. Apparently, however, the interviewer was allowed to remain because she was still working when Sarah was in training.

Sarah had only been in the office for four days, but her winning personality and sincerity had made an impression on other employees. Sarah felt comfortable with Cindy and her staff. Thursday was also Sarah's birthday, and she received a fax from the main office and a card from Cindy. Cindy also said that her brother was making Sarah a handcrafted gift and that it would be done before she left town. One of the interviewers brought Sarah a cupcake, which might not have been so unusual had it not been the employee's day off. However, the kindness shown by the employees of the Chesterfield Mall research office was being overshadowed by concerns that engulfed Sarah.

SARAH'S DILEMMA

Thursday night was Sarah's chance to evaluate the events of the last four days. After another week of training, Sarah would be returning to her hometown. She would return to Hammonsville to take over the research office in the Westfield Mall. She had already sacrificed her graduate assistantship and would now have to complete her MBA degree at a later time. Even though she felt the new company was pleased with her efforts and knowledge, Sarah wondered if she had made a mistake in accepting the position.

This was Sarah's mindset as she anxiously awaited Jeff's arrival. As she waited, she began to consider her options. Should she resign immediately and return to Hammonsville? Would her concerns likely be alleviated in the second week of her training? Should she complete her training, report to the Hammonsville office, attack her work, and simply refuse to do anything that she considered to be unethical? Or, was she simply overreacting to a normal situation in which a company's culture sometimes conflicts with an individual's personal moral philosophies? Sarah was glad that Jeff was coming to Dallas that evening. He could help her sort through her emotions and decide what action would be in her best interest in the long run. The knot in her stomach signaled a sense of urgency in working through her concerns and arriving at a decision sometime before she reported to work the next morning.

STEW LEONARD'S DAIRY

Charles B. Shrader, *Iowa State University*

Steven A. Rallis, *Iowa State University*

Joan L. Twenter, *Iowa State University*

Stewart (Stew) J. Leonard's father, Leo Leonard, owned and operated a small dairy route with four milk trucks. As a young boy, Stew often helped his father with deliveries. By the time Stew was in high school he was operating his own milk route.[1] Stew pursued a college education in hopes that it would prepare him to one day run the dairy. After Stew's graduation from college, his father passed away and Stew took over the business.

In the late 1960s, the state of Connecticut decided to build a highway through Stew Leonard's dairy land. Furthermore, the proliferation of supermarkets and refrigerators had made the cost of running a milk delivery route prohibitive. So Stew decided to move and start a new store. In 1968 the Small Business Administration (SBA) loaned Stew $500,000, the largest SBA loan granted to that date, to start a dairy store in Norwalk, Connecticut. Stew and his wife, Marianne, knew they were risking their net worth of $100,000, but on the basis of Stew's experience selling dairy products since he was a child, he was convinced his ideas would work. He expected to compete with other area stores by stocking mostly his own products in a specialized dairy store.[2]

Stew Leonard and his wife formed a partnership. He refused to form a corporation because he wanted to be liable for any losses.[3] Before opening his own store, Stew Leonard's Dairy, he visited many food stores across the country to gather information on what worked and what did not.[4] During one visit he met a farmer who was bottling

This case was prepared by Charles B. Shrader, Steven A. Rallis, and Joan L. Twenter of Iowa State University and is intended to be used as a basis for classroom discussion rather than to illustrate either effective or ineffective management practices. Partial support for writing the case was provided by the Murray G. Bacon Center for Ethics in Business.

[1]Stew Leonard Jr., "The Customer Is Always Right," *Executive Excellence* 10, no. 8 (1993), pp. 16–17.
[2]Davis K. Fishman, *Stew Leonard's: The Disney World of Supermarkets* (New York: Curtis Brown, 1985).
[3]Ibid.
[4]Les Slater, Interview with Stew Leonard in *Review of Business* 13 (Summer/Fall 1991), pp. 10–12.

and selling milk on the premises.[5] Stew decided his store would do the same. Calculating the cost of the SBA loan and other credit, Stew estimated he needed to gross $20,000 a week to survive. Through long hours and attention to detail, Stew realized $21,850 in his first week in business. By mid-week he was so optimistic about reaching the $20,000 mark that he took his wife on a trip to Grenada in the Caribbean.

The following week, an incident occurred that was to become the foundation of the Stew Leonard management philosophy. When a customer complained that the eggnog she recently purchased was sour, Stew tasted the eggnog and concluded that the customer was wrong. He told her so and added, "We sold over 300 half-gallons of eggnog this week, and you're the only one who's complained." The customer angrily left the store and stated she would never come back.[6] Later that evening Stew could not get the scene out of his mind. Upon reflection, he acknowledged that not only had he failed to empathize with the customer, but he had ignored the potential repercussions of the complaint. His wife, Marianne, said that he had just lost a valuable customer over a 99-cent carton of eggnog. This was a customer who may have later spent thousands of dollars on groceries, money that Stew Leonard's Dairy would now never see. This mistake led Stew to form a mission statement for his business:

Rule 1:   The customer is always right!
Rule 2:   If the customer is ever wrong, reread Rule 1!

These rules, which were engraved on a 6,000-pound boulder and placed at the entrance of the store, became the credo upon which Stew Leonard built his business.[7] By the end of the 1980s, the store had grown from two cash registers, 6,000 square feet, and $20,000 a week in sales to a retail grocery with more than two dozen registers, 37,000 square feet, and annual sales in excess of $100 million.[8] By 1991 a second store had been opened on a 40-acre complex in Danbury, Connecticut. Although the mission statement formed the backbone of the strategy that enabled the organization to expand 27 times in roughly 20 years, Stew implemented additional strategies to achieve his business's remarkable growth.[9]

MARKETING AND CUSTOMER RELATIONS

Initially, Stew Leonard stocked his dairy store with just under a dozen items. Eventually, the store topped out at 800 items (the typical supermarket stocked 15,000). Stew differentiated his store by eliminating middlemen and passing the savings on to his customers.[10]

Stew also sold the idea of freshness. Customers knew they could count on the freshest possible produce, milk, cheese, meats, and baked goods. A glass-enclosed milk-processing plant was located in the center of the store so that customers could see their milk being produced.[11] Beth Leonard, one of Stew's daughters, ran the bakery, which

[5]Fishman, *Stew Leonard's*.

[6]Stew Leonard, "Love That Customer!," *Management Review* 76, no. 10 (October 1987), pp. 36–39.

[7]Leonard, "Love That Customer!"

[8]E. Penzer, "Secrets from the Supermarket," *Incentive* 165, no. 8 (August 1991), pp. 67–69.

[9]M. Raphel, "Confidence Is Number One," *Direct Marketing* 52, no. 5 (September 1989), pp. 30, 32.

[10]E. T. Suters, "Stew Leonard: Soul of a Leader," *Executive Excellence* 8, no. 6 (June 1991), pp. 13–14.

[11]Fishman, *Stew Leonard's*.

filled the store with the aroma of croissants, cookies, and muffins.[12] Free samples and recipes were always made available to customers.

To further distinguish itself from other food stores, Stew Leonard's added entertainment to the marketing mix.[13] A petting zoo with barnyard animals was placed in the parking lot, encouraging parents to bring children. Animated singing animals filled the store, and employees roamed the aisles in cow, chicken, and duck costumes.[14] All of this was part of Stew's emphasis on making grocery shopping an enjoyable experience.[15]

Building on the mission statement "The customer is always right," Stew Leonard's Dairy adopted other customer service systems. A liberal return policy provided internal checks and balances that required employees to constantly monitor quality. Even if a Stew Leonard "team member" knew that a customer was returning an item the store did not sell, the customer got his or her money back.[16] Stew once said:

> Our attitude is that everybody's honest. If we occasionally run into someone who isn't, we just take it on the chin. But the important point is that 999 out of 1,000 customers are honest. We simply refuse to let one dishonest customer determine how we are going to treat the other 999.[17]

Stew Leonard's Dairy exhibited a special commitment to following up on customers' comments. A suggestion box was filled to capacity each day.[18] By 11:00 each morning, all the complaints and suggestions were typed and submitted to the appropriate department. Managers held weekly meetings to report what had been done with the customers' suggestions.

Customer feedback was also gathered through in-store focus groups. Each month 10 specially selected customers were given $20 store gift certificates for meeting with store managers and offering suggestions on what items should be stocked and how items should be displayed.[19]

The dairy store built goodwill in other ways as well. For example, free ice cream cones were given randomly to customers, photographs showing customers with Stew Leonard's shopping bags were posted near the entrance, and elderly customers were given free rides to the dairy in a bus provided by the store.[20] By conducting business in this manner, Stew Leonard's Dairy earned tremendous customer trust and loyalty over the years.[21]

EMPLOYEE RELATIONS

Employees, referred to as team memebers, were well trained in customer relations. Many employees were also Leonard family members.

---

[12]M. Adams, "The Udder Delights of Stew U," *Successful Meetings* 403 (March 1991), pp. 59–61.

[13]T. Englander, "Stew Leonard's: In-store Disneyland," *Incentive* 163, no. 1 (January 1989), pp. 26–30.

[14]Leonard, "The Customer Is Always Right."

[15]Slater, Interview.

[16]Adams, "The Udder Delights of Stew U."

[17]Leonard, "Love That Customer!"

[18]Englander, "Stew Leonard's."

[19]S. Bennett, "What Shoppers Want," *Progressive Grocer* 71, no. 10 (October 1992), pp. 73–78.

[20]Englander, "Stew Leonard's"; D. Feldman, "Companies Aim to Please," *Management Review* 78, no. 5 (May 1989), pp. 8–9.

[21]J. M. Hill, "Supermarkets Can Beat Warehouse Clubs, but Not on Price Alone," *Brandweek* 34, no. 1 (January 1993), p. 25.

The large number of family members working for the company contributed to the company's culture. Of the company's 1,200-plus employees, 25 percent had worked at Stew Leonard's Dairy for at least five years and over half had family as co-workers.[22] Stew believed in nepotism.[23] He was an ardent supporter of employing relatives as team members; he believed they worked much harder than other employees because the presence of a relative was like another boss watching over them.[24]

Team members understood that having a job at Stew Leonard's meant providing superior customer service. The company's two stores were open 364 days a year, and team members were required to work during various times of the day and on holidays. Also, team members were expected to be well groomed and display positive attitudes. As a result of Stew's hiring practices, the store had only a 60 percent turnover rate—much better than the supermarket industry average of 82 percent.[25]

Curiosity about Stew Leonard's training and customer relations methods ran strong among business firms. Inquiries from companies like Kraft, Citibank, and IBM led to the creation of the "Stew Leonard University" by Stew's daughter Jill.[26] "Stew U" was a four-hour seminar intended to give insight into the dairy store's operation. Throughout the seminar, attendees were taught how to handle dissatisfied customers, behave appropriately as team members, and motivate fellow team members.[27]

Stew Leonard's Dairy offered its employees a variety of incentive programs to heighten the level of customer service, such as the following:

1. A monthly "One Idea Club," in which 10 team members and a department manager went to other supermarkets and, on the basis of that experience, made suggestions for improving their own store departments.[28]

2. A "Superstar of the Month" program in which co-workers and department managers nominated a fellow team member for achievement of safety, cleanliness, and attendance. Winners had their photographs posted in the store and were awarded $100.[29]

3. "Ladders of Success" charts placed near checkout lanes demonstrating team members' career progression. Stew Leonard's Dairy fully supported a promotion-from-within policy.[30]

4. Retail gift certificates valued up to $500 if team members' ideas were implemented.[31]

5. Fifty-dollar awards to team members who referred new hires.[32]

6. An ABCD (Above and Beyond the Call of Duty) Award—a polo shirt embroidered with "ABCD Award"—given to employees who performed beyond the duties of their jobs.[33]

---

[22]Leonard, "The Customer Is Always Right."

[23]Slater, Interview.

[24]Fishman, "Stew Leonard's."

[25]S. Weinstein, "How to Hire the Best," *Progressive Grocer* 72, no. 7 (July 1993), pp. 119–22.

[26]Adams, "The Udder Delights of Stew U."

[27]Ibid.

[28]Englander, "Stew Leonard's."

[29]Ibid.; B. Bolger, "Stew Leonard: Unconventional Wisdom," *Incentive* 162, no. 11 (November 1988), pp. 36–40.

[30]Englander, "Stew Leonard's"; Bolger, "Stew Leonard."

[31]Bolger, "Stew Leonard."

[32]Ibid.

[33]Ibid.

7. A "Hall of Fame," which recognized workers who performed admirably during their careers.[34]

8. An Outstanding Performance Award given at the annual Christmas party to three high achievers.[35]

9. A recreation program, supplemented by employee vending-machine funds, providing outings and trips to workers at discount rates.[36]

10. The "Stew's News" company newsletter—called the ultimate company newsletter by *Inc.* magazine—filled with information about bonus plans, contests, and customer comments. Announcements of births, parties, anniversaries, illnesses, and organization successes were included.[37]

11. A "Name Game" reward for cashiers who thanked customers by name. Customers dropped cashiers' names in a box, and at the end of each week the three cashiers who thanked the most customers by name received $30.[38]

These activities were used by Stew Leonard's Dairy to focus team members on the mission statement. Stew knew that everybody was motivated by different things. Occasionally, he would place extra dollars in pay envelopes along with thank-you notes (of which he wrote hundreds every year) for employees who performed exceptionally well. Impromptu inducements were often granted to team members. It was not uncommon for Stew or the other managers to hand out lunch or dinner certificates for special performance such as coming in on a day off.[39]

THE ORGANIZATION

Stew Leonard's overall company goal—customer satisfaction—determined the design of the organization. It was a simple, relatively informal structure. Because the business was a partnership, there was no board of directors or shareholders. There were also no required annual reports or meetings. The partners gained and lost in proportion to the success of the business, and were personally liable for financial obligations. The partnership paid no taxes as an entity; rather, Stew and Marianne were taxed directly for their portion of the business's income.

All four of Stew Leonard's children were actively involved in the business and held corporate titles. Stew Jr., the oldest, was president. He originally planned to work for an accounting firm after earning his MBA at UCLA, but became involved in every detail of his father's company. Tom managed the Danbury store, which opened in the fall of 1991. Beth, after obtaining her master's degree in French and working for a croissant distributor, originated and managed the high-volume in-store bakery.[40] Jill Leonard was the vice president of human resources.[41] And, of course, Marianne continued to provide support as she had from the beginning.

---

[34]Ibid.

[35]Englander, "Stew Leonard's."

[36]Ibid.

[37]Adams, "The Udder Delights of Stew U."

[38]Penzer, "Secrets from the Supermarket."

[39]Ibid.

[40]Fishman, "Stew Leonard's."

[41]Weinstein, "How to Hire the Best."

Marianne's brothers, Frank H. Guthman and Stephen F. Guthman, served as executive vice president and vice president of finance, respectively.[42] Most company decisions were made by the family. However, lower-level employees were allowed a great deal of discretion, especially in the area of customer service.

The company preferred "in-house" control practices. Customers were asked to pay cash for gift certificates and were encouraged to use cash for other purchases.[43] Stew did not make much use of outside consultants in his business. He preferred using the in-house customer focus groups for business advice. As a privately held company, Stew Leonard's Dairy did not publicly reveal its profits.[44] Profits, however, were significant enough to fund the store's numerous expansions as well as a large second home for Stew and his children. The second home, located on Saint Martin in the Caribbean, was named "Carpe Diem" (Latin for "seize the day").[45]

As the business grew from a small dairy to super-retailer to world's largest dairy store, it continued to achieve customer satisfaction, employee development, and tremendous growth. Over the years the store received numerous awards and accolades, for example:

- An award for entrepreneurial excellence from President Ronald Reagan.
- The Connecticut Small Business Advocate of the Year Award.
- A citation from the *Guinness Book of World Records* for doing more business per square foot than any store of any kind in the world.

In addition, a certified in-house Dale Carnegie training school, attended by Fortune 500 firms, was operated in conjunction with Stew Leonard University. In 1991, Stew Leonard's Dairy was nominated for the Malcolm Baldridge National Quality Award in the service category, and it might have become the first retail organization ever to win the award had not the company decided to withdraw from the competition.

In addition to all the other awards, a 1993 issue of *Chief Information Officer (CIO)*, a publication for data processing and computer programming professionals, named Stew Leonard's Dairy as one of the 21 recipients of its customer service award.[46] Criteria for winning this award included a company's successful integration of management information systems and customer service. The store was commended for its ability in tracking sales and using point-of-sale data. The sophisticated system also helped managers anticipate heavy traffic periods so that cash registers could be staffed adequately and product shortages avoided.

TROUBLE LOOMS

On August 25, 1991, Stew Leonard was questioned by a Norwalk, Connecticut, reporter about a visit from the Criminal Investigation Division of the Internal Revenue Service. On August 9, 1991, the IRS had raided the homes of several company officers, seizing boxes of records and cash.[47] Stew said that the raid "came out of the blue" and

---

[42]R. Pastore, "A Virtual Shopping Spree," *CIO,* August 6, 1993, pp. 70–74.

[43]C. J. Levy, "Store Founder Pleads Guilty in Fraud," *The New York Times,* July 23, 1993, pp. B1, B4.

[44]Bolger, "Stew Leonard."

[45]J. Steinberg, "Papers Show Greed Calculation and Betrayal in Stew Leonard Case," *The New York Times,* October 22, 1993.

[46]Pastore, "A Virtual Shopping Spree."

[47]B. Kanner, "Spilled Milk," *New York* 26, no. 42 (October 25, 1993), pp. 68–74.

that he was "as surprised as anyone else."[48] But U.S. customs agents had stopped him back in June that year when, with $80,000 in cash, he boarded a flight to Saint Martin.[49] Stew had not filled out the forms required for taking large sums of money out of the country, and this eventually led the IRS to confiscate store records.[50] Nevertheless, Stew maintained that he did not know what prompted the IRS agents to enter the store with a search warrant on August 9.[51]

Stew and his son Tom told the news reporters and the public that the IRS was simply conducting a routine audit. However, the Criminal Investigation Division did not conduct "audits," which involved possible civil violations; rather, it investigated possible criminal violations of internal revenue laws.[52]

Most people in the community reacted with disbelief to news of the investigation. Many of Stew Leonard's customers, regarding the Leonard family as a pillar of honesty in the community, found it impossible to believe that any wrongdoing had taken place. Ironically, it was Stew Leonard's sophisticated computer system that gave the IRS the primary evidence it needed to charge Stew and other executives with tax evasion.

THE GUILTY PLEA

On July 22, 1993, the U.S. Department of Justice announced that Stewart J. Leonard Sr., Frank H. Guthman, Stephen F. Guthman, and company general manager Tiberio (Barry) Belardinelli had pleaded guilty in federal court to federal tax conspiracy charges. The four defendants admitted that between 1981 and August 9, 1991, they had defrauded the IRS by skimming more than $17 million from Stew Leonard's Dairy in Norwalk, Connecticut. It had taken the IRS almost two years to determine the full extent of the tax evasion scheme. In addition to paper records and large sums of cash, the IRS had found other items indicating the executives' aversion to paying taxes.[53]

According to the IRS, Stew Leonard had avoided $6.7 million in taxes between 1981 and 1991 by not reporting $17 million in sales during that period.[54] The IRS also reported that this case represented the largest computer-driven criminal tax evasion case in U.S. history, calling it a crime of the 21st century.[55]

Stew Leonard Jr., president of the Norwalk store, was cited as having knowledge of the tax conspiracy.[56] A *New York Times* article reported that part of the plea-bargain arrangement was that no charges would be brought against Stew Jr.[57] Observers speculated that the IRS may have given Stew Jr. immunity in order to persuade his father to plead guilty. According to the IRS, Stew Sr. was initially turned in by an employee who had recently been fired.[58]

---

[48]J. Heller, "At Stew Leonard's Business as Usual Despite IRS Audit," *The Fairpress* (Norwalk, weekly edition), August 15, 1991, section CG, p. 54.

[49]Kanner, "Spilled Milk."

[50]Levy, "Store Founder Pleads Guilty in Fraud."

[51]"IRS Crime Unit Probing Records," *The Advocate* (Stamford, CT), August 22, 1991.

[52]Heller, "At Stew Leonard's."

[53]Steinberg, "Papers Show Greed."

[54]C. H. Wamae, "Leonard Checks In at Federal Hospital," *Connecticut Post,* November 30, 1993, p. A7.

[55]Levy, "Store Founder."

[56]Kanner, "Spilled Milk."

[57]Steinberg, "Papers Show Greed."

[58]P. Berman, "Like Father, Like Son," *Forbes,* May 20, 1996, pp. 44–45.

THE "EQUITY PROGRAM"—SKIMMING

In Frank Guthman's basement, in a hollowed-out edition of the 1982 *New England Business Directory,* the IRS's Criminal Investigation Division discovered a computer program that the executives had named "Equity."[59] Apparently, the program had been developed in the latter part of 1981 by Jeffrey Pirhalla, Stew Leonard's computer programmer. Frank Guthman had instructed Jeffrey to create the program in order to reduce sales data stored on Stew Leonard's computer. Frank Guthman had also directed Jeffrey to write the program so that it would reduce Stew Leonard's financial and bank deposit data.

Witnesses in the court proceedings testified that Stew Leonard Sr. and the other executives were informed of the use of this tax evasion tool. In general, the program enabled the defendants to enter a dollar figure that matched a cash receipt withdrawal for the day. Typical cash diversions were $10,000 to $15,000 per day. Furthermore, the program allowed the company to keep dual books that generated accounting spreadsheets disclosing "actual" and "reported" sales. To appease previous IRS auditors, Stew Leonard's Dairy had provided "reported" sales data while the actual sales data were utilized only for store operations.

As part of the scheme, Barry Belardinelli and the Guthmans set up a system that transferred Universal Product Code (UPC) scanner information from the cash registers to two different computer record systems. One set of records systematically understated sales by a predetermined amount. Barry destroyed the tapes with the "real" sales data generated daily from the cash registers. Then he secretly removed cash from bank deposit bags in his office, and the skimmed cash was hidden in "vaults" and "fireplaces" constructed specifically for the execution of this crime. Correspondingly, investigators identified personal and partnership tax forms that were falsely submitted to the IRS.

SHORTWEIGHTING

To make matters worse, on July 23, 1993, a day after Stew Leonard pleaded guilty to tax evasion, the Connecticut State Consumer Products Department charged Stew Leonard's Dairy with violating state labeling laws.[60]) A series of inspections involving a check of 2,658 products in the Norwalk store revealed that 730 of the products checked weighed less than what the label stated—they were "shortweighted"—and 500 items carried no labels or were improperly labeled.[61] The Consumer Products Commissioner reported that this rejection rate, 46.3 percent, was much greater than the statewide average of 5 percent.[62]

Some industry experts believed the shortweighting charges were not fair and were merely the bureaucratic attempt of a vengeful state to embarrass the family. [63] They maintained that store scales were accurate and that the variance noted by investigators was not atypical. Stew Jr. argued that because the company sold so many handpacked and precooked items, product weight could not always be perfectly accurate. [64]

---

[59]B. Ingram, "Stew, We Hardly Knew Ye," *Supermarket Business,* September 1993, pp. 157–58

[60]J. Barron, "Stew Leonard's Is Cited for Shorting Customers," *The New York Times,* July 24, 1993, p. L24.

[61]M. Tash, "Mislabeling Charge May Be More Taxing," *Supermarket News,* August 2, 1993, p. 43.

[62]Ingram, "Stew, We Hardly Knew Ye."

[63]Telephone interview with consultant (H. O'Neill) who worked with Stew Leonard's in making the Baldridge Award application, August 1996.

[64]Kanner, "Spilled Milk"; R. Zemke, "Piling On," *Training* 30, no. 10 (October 1993), p. 10.

Each of the 1,230 violations was subject to a $500 maximum fine.[65] Stew Leonard's had already been assessed fines of $10,500 for similar violations at the Danbury store. The company planned to appeal the Danbury store fines as well as the potentially costly fines on the alleged 1,230 violations. [66]

THE AFTERMATH

Although news of the crime drew harsh criticism from industry professionals and the media, it caused only a minor decline in sales. [67] Some customers condemned the elder Leonard and the store for being hypocritical. The majority of Stew Leonard's clientele was angrier about the shortweighting than the tax evasion. Indeed, many people believed that the tax fraud was a private rather than a business issue. [68] Several shoppers even expressed sympathy for the Leonard family and pledged they would continue to support the company. As had happened early in the investigation, in 1991, some community members thought the IRS was overreacting, even harassing the company. One customer stated that it was okay for the store to cheat the government because everybody else does it. [69] When the *Danbury News Times* polled 5,323 of its readers, 4,556 said they would continue to shop at Stew Leonard's. [70] Employees of Stew Leonard's Dairy, including Stew Leonard Jr., stated that business was good and that they were 100 percent behind the fallen founder. [71]

Stew Leonard was sentenced to 52 months in prison and ordered to pay $15 million in back taxes, penalties, and interest. [72] He was also fined $850,000 for court and probation costs, but this fine was later reduced to $650,000 by a federal appeals court judge. The resulting $650,000 was still much larger than the usual $100,000 fine for tax fraud, because Leonard had profited so greatly from the scheme. [73]

Stew Leonard's brothers-in-law, Frank and Stephen Guthman, were sentenced to 41-month and 18-month prison terms, respectively. Frank Guthman's plea agreement provided that he pay $335,000 in tax, penalties, and interest. Stephen Guthman was not fined. Barry Belardinelli received no prison sentence but was fined $15,000 and put on probation for two years. [74]

Stew Leonard gave no reason for the crime he committed, although he did apologize to customers and employees. At one point, the Leonards insinuated that the tax scheme had been suggested by their lawyer (now deceased) as a way to raise capital for expansion. [75] Later, in 1994, after reflecting on the crisis while in prison, Stew Leonard commented, "Somehow, I just lost sight of my core values." [76] After the incident, the

---

[65]Barron, "Stew Leonard's Is Cited."

[66]Ibid.; E. Zwiebach, "Stew Leonard's Reports Sales Dip," *Supermarket News,* August 2, 1993, pp. 42–43.

[67]Zwiebach, "Stew Leonard's Reports Sales Dip."

[68]Ingram, "Stew, We Hardly Knew Ye."

[69]J. Crispens, "The Reaction from Shoppers: Lukewarm to Mildly Stewed," *Supermarket News,* August 2, 1993, p. 42.

[70]Kanner, "Spilled Milk."

[71]Ingram, "Stew, We Hardly Knew Ye."

[72]Telephone interview with Larry Marini, state investigator, Criminal Investigation Division, Connecticut, March 1995.

[73]S. Silvers, "Judge Reduces Stew's Fine," *Connecticut Post,* October 27, 1994, pp. A1, A13.

[74]Wamae, "Leonard Checks In at Federal Hospital."

[75]Kanner, "Spilled Milk."

[76]Silvers, "Judge Reduces Stew's Fine."

company continued to grow, and was even planning to open a third store. Stew Leonard was scheduled to be released from a Schuylkill, Pennsylvania, prison in December 1997. [77]

DAMAGE CONTROL

Once Stew Sr. was in prison, Stew Jr. had to step up and fill the leadership void. Stew Jr. began running the Norwalk store, which was still in his mother's name. Stew Jr., Tom, and their sisters, Jill and Beth, owned and operated the new Danbury store. [78] They were now faced with monumental decisions regarding damage control. How would they be able to maintain the business? How could they regain goodwill and customer confidence? How could they overcome the stigma associated with skimming and shortweighting? Would they be able to get along without Stew Sr.? What steps could they take to ensure that wrongdoing like this wouldn't happen again? How could they restore the company's reputation?

There were other worries as well. Stew Sr.'s health was in question. Prior to entering prison, he had to have a heart valve and a hip replaced. [79]

To make matters worse, in early 1996, it was reported that Tom was under a grand jury investigation for skimming cash from store vending machines.[80] According to investigators, Tom had been skimming cash from soda machines, hot dog vendors, and other vending locations in the store. Stew Jr. would almost certainly be called to testify before the grand jury.

Stew Jr. had been responsible for withdrawing from the Baldridge award competition in 1991, a move he had made only because of the criminal investigations.[81] Now he wondered if he could put the store back into contention for the prestigious award.

Young Stew Jr. knew he must direct his attention immediately to the challenges facing him. He knew his father would want to return to store management and that it was his mission to pave the way. He pondered how he would be able to regain customers' faith and redeem the Leonard family name.

---

[77]Berman, "Like Father, Like Son"; Telephone interview with E. Suters (author of *The Unnatural Act of Management*), April 1995.

[78]Berman, "Like Father, Like Son."

[79]P. T. Farrelly Jr., "Leonard to Begin Sentence Today at Medical Facility," *The Hour* (Norwalk, CT), November 29, 1993, pp. 1–2.

[80]Berman, "Like Father, Like Son."

[81]Telephone interview with consultant (H. O'Neill).

HOOTERS RESTAURANTS AND THE EEOC

Nancy H. Leonard, *Lewis-Clark State College*

Larry R. Steenberg, *University of Evansville*

Deborah A. Howard, *University of Evansville*

Terry W. Mullins, *Jacksonville University*

In November 1995, postcards and Frisbees preaddressed to Capitol Hill lawmakers and employees of the Equal Employment Opportunity Commission (EEOC) began arriving in Washington, DC. They were sent by bulk mail, paid for by Hooters Restaurants across the United States. According to the *National Journal,* 1,000 disks arrived in Washington daily. Some representative comments on the Frisbees included these:

- Brian Anderson of Pittsburgh: "EEOC, find something else to bitch about. Hooters girls were made for male enjoyment."
- Amy Miller of Oklahoma City: "Hooters has provided good-paying jobs for many single mothers and college students. Why jeopardize putting these people out of work?"
- John and Linda Dearduff of Sloatsburg, New York: "EEOC—you people DEFINE nonessential."
- A man from Columbus, Ohio: "Listen up you equal opportunity Communists— If you pull any of this crap, I'll personally kill every member of Congress. Guaranteed." (The EEOC alerted Federal Protection Services about this one.)

The comments and Frisbees were part of a fight between Hooters and the Equal Employment Opportunity Commission concerning Hooters' refusal to hire male servers in the company's restaurants. Hooters argued that "Hooters Girls" were an intrinsic part of its business strategy. The EEOC felt that Hooters' female-only hiring policy for waitresses might be a violation of the Civil Rights Act of 1964 and began an investigation. The goal of the investigation was to determine if the policy was discriminatory and to make recommendations to Hooters as to how it should deal with this issue.

EXHIBIT 1   Hooters Companies

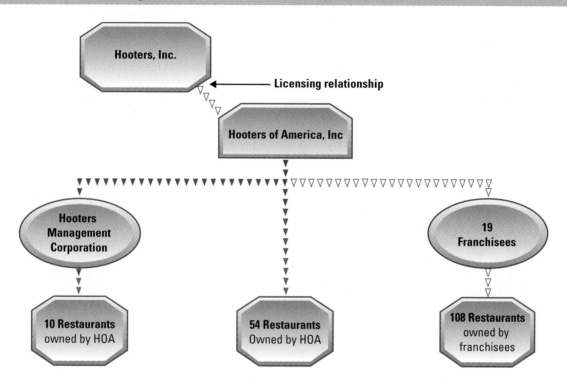

THE HISTORY OF HOOTERS

Hooters was a national restaurant chain that featured the popular Hooters Girls. The first Hooters opened in Clearwater, Florida, in October 1983. In 1995 the company employed more than 13,000 people in 172 restaurants across the country. Hooters expected its revenues to hit $300 million in 1996.

There were three Hooters companies (see Exhibit 1):

1. Hooters, Inc., based in Clearwater, Florida, created the Hooters concept. It licensed the concept to Hooters of America, Inc., which owned and franchised restaurants. Hooters, Inc., did not own any of the restaurants.

2. Hooters Management Corporation was a separate corporation that oversaw the operations of 10 restaurants but did not own any of them.

3. Hooters of America, Inc., based in Atlanta, Georgia, owned 54 restaurants and also had relationships with 19 franchisees, who owned a total of 108 restaurants in 37 states and Puerto Rico.

The Hooters restaurant chain became a big success by employing young, attractive women as waitresses, bartenders, and hostesses (the three "front-of-the-house" positions— that is, positions in which employees meet the public) and dressing them in orange hot pants and cutoff T-shirts fastened in the back to make them tighter. The store hired as Hooters Girls women who projected a certain "Hooters image." Both men and women were hired for all other jobs, including management positions.

Hooters distributed a Hooters Girl calendar; *Hooters Magazine;* and Hooters Girl trading cards, billboards, and television ads—all based on the Hooters Girl concept. Hooters also participated in sports partnerships, such as the Hooters Professional Golf Tour and the Hooters Cup Stock Car Racing Series, at which the Hooters Girls were featured.

Hooters was active in the communities in which its restaurants operated. The Hooters Community Endowment Fund raised money for local and national charities like the Juvenile Diabetes Foundation and the Muscular Dystrophy Association. Since its creation in 1992, the Hooters Community Endowment Fund had contributed more than $5 million to local and national charities. The opening of each new restaurant featured a VIP party to benefit a local charitable organization.

Hooters had experienced resistance to store openings in some communities. Religious and civic groups rallied in opposition to new stores. The tactics often involved opposition to the zoning changes necessary for the construction of the restaurant. Hooters countered this opposition by claiming that its restaurants were family establishments. The company argued that the menu, location, and decor of its restaurants supported this claim, and that the clientele of existing restaurants was not exclusively male. All Hooters restaurants provided a children's menu and offered a beach decor appropriate for all ages. Hooters restaurants were also located in the popular restaurant areas of towns rather than on the outskirts of town.

While this position helped Hooters in zoning hearings, it was no help in the company's dispute with the EEOC. If Hooters restaurants were truly family oriented, having female servers only was not a business necessity. If sex appeal was the basic strategy, however, some of the zoning appeals had merit.

THE CASE

Early in 1993, Savino Latuga, an experienced waiter, learned that jobs were available at the Hooters restaurant that was about to open for business in Orland Park, Illinois. On January 5, 1993, he completed an application for a position as a waiter. He was not offered a job, despite his experience. He also claimed that other men who applied were not hired yet women who applied later were hired.

On February 12, 1993, Latuga, along with David Gonzalez, filed a complaint of gender discrimination with the Equal Employment Opportunity Commission and was granted a right-to-sue letter. This right is guaranteed under Title VII of the Civil Rights Act of 1964, and the EEOC is charged with protecting this right. (See Exhibit 2 for a summary of relevant EEOC legal provisions, guidelines, and complaint processes related to Title VII.)

Latuga claimed that, when it did not hire him, Hooters of Orland Park, Inc. (HOOP), had committed gender discrimination. HOOP was implementing a policy developed and enforced by its parent company, Hooters of America, Inc. (HOA), of hiring only women for the three possible front-of-the-house positions.

Latuga sued both HOOP and HOA, as an individual and as a representative of all men who had been denied employment or had suffered because they could not apply based on Hooters' policy of sex discrimination. On July 8, 1994, the class-action suit against HOA was dismissed because neither HOA nor the class action had been mentioned in the original complaint filed by Latuga with the EEOC. Latuga's individual charges against HOOP stood.

In February 1994, Patrick Salisbury was denied employment at HOOP and John Ginter was denied employment at Hooters of Downers Grove, Illinois (HODG). On April 8, 1994, Ginter and Salisbury filed similar sex discrimination charges with the

---

EXHIBIT 2   The Equal Employment Opportunity Commission

Legal Provision

Title VII of the Civil Rights Act of 1964 prohibits employment discrimination on the basis of race, color, religion, sex and national origin. The statute, however, contains a clause permitting single-sex hiring policies. Section 703(e)(1) says it is lawful for a company to hire employees on the basis of sex "in those certain instances where . . . sex . . . is a bona fide occupational qualification (BFOQ) reasonably necessary to the normal operation of that particular business."

EEOC Guidelines

The EEOC has issued guidelines stating that the BFOQ exception should be narrowly interpreted. Under the guidelines, the exception is applicable only when necessary for authenticity or genuineness, such as a situation requiring an actor or actress. According to an EEOC attorney, other jobs within the BFOQ genuineness factor rule include clothes models, models for cosmetics ads, Playboy bunny, burlesque stripper, go-go dancer and nightclub chorus-line dancer. When authenticity or genuineness is not an issue, an employer may not implement single-sex hiring policies merely because of the preference of the employer, co-worker, client, or customers.

EEOC Complaint Process

Employees who believe they have been discriminated against on the basis of race, color, religion, sex, or national origin concerning their employment must file a claim with the Equal Employment Opportunity Commission (EEOC) if they wish to seek relief for employment discrimination.

The person discriminated against files a *charge* against his employer and is called the *charging party*. The employer is called the *respondent*. The claim must be filed within 180 days of the discriminatory act. After the charge is filed, EEOC must serve notice of the charge on the employer within 10 days. EEOC has 180 days to investigate the claim and is required to investigate every claim filed.

EEOC seeks to conciliate the employee and his/her employer if it finds there is *reasonable cause* to believe discriminatory actions had taken place. If conciliation fails, EEOC may file suit in Federal District Court on behalf of the charging party or may issue a *right-to-sue letter* so the charging party may seek private counsel to file suit.

EEOC may make a finding of *no probable cause* to believe that the complaints made were discriminatory. Even with a no probable cause finding, the charging party will receive a *right-to-sue letter* and may pursue his/her claim in Federal District Court. If the employee chooses to file in Federal District Court after receiving a right-to-sue letter, he/she must file within 90 days of receiving the letter.

EEOC. On July 27, 1995, Latuga joined David Gonzalez, John Ginter, and Patrick Salisbury in a suit which claimed individual and class discrimination. This case added both Hooters Management Corporation (HMC) and HODG to the suit. These four men were granted class certification on July 27, 1995, in order to represent all men who had applied to Hooters and been rejected and all men who had been deterred from applying because of this policy.

In light of previous complaints to the EEOC, the commission had initiated an investigation of Hooters in 1991. The lawsuit initiated in 1995 by the four men in Chicago, Illinois, strengthened the EEOC commitment to this investigation. In late 1995, after a four-year investigation, the EEOC ruled that Hooters' policy of hiring only female waitresses, bartenders, and hostesses violated federal civil rights law and recommended that the company hire men to work alongside its waitresses. (See Exhibit 3 for a summary

EXHIBIT 3   The Courts and EEOC's Bona Fide Occupational Qualification

There have been numerous legal cases concerning bona fide occupational qualification (BFOQ) issues, but the courts have been inconsistent in their rulings. Some of major cases are listed below:

- In *Dothard* v. *Rawinson,* 443 U.S. 321 (1977), the U.S. Supreme Court emphasized that the BFOQ exception is an extremely narrow one suggesting that an employer may not draw distinctions based on sex unless the essence of his or her business otherwise would be undermined.

- In the 5th U.S. Circuit Court of Appeals in *Diaz* v. *Pan American World Airways,* 442 F.2d 385 (E.D. La. 1967), the court held that being female is not a BFOQ for flight attendants. The court stated that the primary function of an airline is to transport passengers safely, and the ability of women flight attendants to provide a more pleasant environment is tangential to the essence of the business.

- This preceding decision was supported in a later case, *Wilson* v. *Southwest Airlines Co.,* 517 F. Supp. 292 (N.D. Texas 1981). The airline claimed its discriminatory hiring policy was justified both because its customers prefer to be served by female employees and because the sex appeal of its employees is necessary for the airline to attract and entertain male passengers. The airline promised "tender loving care" in its ads targeting male business passengers and claimed that the use of attractive females in their high-customer contact positions of ticket agents and flight attendants was an integral part of its corporate image. The court found no evidence that customer preference was so strong that the airline's male passengers would cease doing business with the airline if it hired males, and concluded that sex did not become a BFOQ merely because an employer chose to exploit female sexuality as a marketing tool, or to better ensure profitability.

- In *Levendos* v. *Stern Entertainment, Inc.* 723 F., U.S. App., Supp. 1104 (1990), the court held that male gender is not a BFOQ for waiters employed in high-class restaurants, reasoning that to justify the employer's refusal to hire female servers on the basis of the employer's claim that male waiters presented a better image frustrated the antisex discrimination purpose of Title VII.

- In a New York Human Rights case (*St. Cross* v. *Playboy Club,* Appeal No. 773, Case No. CFS 22618-70, New York Human Rights Appeal Board, 1971), the court found that in jobs where sex or vicarious sexual recreation is the primary service provided (e.g., a social escort or topless dancer), the job automatically calls for one sex exclusively; the employee's sex and the service provided are inseparable. Thus, being female was deemed a BFOQ for the position of a Playboy bunny, female sexuality being reasonably necessary to perform the dominant purpose of the job, which is to titillate and entice male customers.

- BFOQ has also been granted based on privacy: female nurse's aides in a women's nursing home, female nurses in the labor and delivery section of an obstetrics unit, male janitors in a men's bathhouse, male and female washroom attendants, and male security guards whose duties involve searching male employees.

of previous court rulings concerning this issue.) In an 80-page document the EEOC made a settlement offer, asking that Hooters

- Provide $22 million to the EEOC for distribution to male victims of the Hooters Girl hiring policy.
- Establish a scholarship fund to enhance job opportunities or education for men.
- Provide sensitivity training to teach Hooters' employees how to be more sensitive to men's needs.

- Appoint an EEOC-mandated "administrator" to supervise Hooters' business and report to the EEOC.

HOOTERS STATES ITS POSITION

Hooters argued that Hooters Girls were an intrinsic part of its business strategy and that, based on that strategy, it had a legitimate right to hire women who could maintain the Hooters image.

In a press conference held on November 15, 1995, soon after the EEOC settlement offer was made public, Mike McNeil, the vice president for the Atlanta-based Hooters of America, Inc., made the following statement:

I'm here today to tell you about Hooters' recent experiences with the Equal Employment Opportunity Commission and what we consider the Commission's misguided attempt to force us to hire men to work as "Hooters Girls."

If EEOC were to succeed, it could put us out of business. It certainly would cost the jobs of many of the 10,000 women now working as Hooters Girls.

We've met the EEOC officials in conciliation talks to try to find a reasonable middle ground. But frankly their demands are both onerous and silly.

Hooters is fighting back. In addition to our legal defense, we are launching a grassroots campaign to let people know about the EEOC's nonsensical attack on Hooters stores and to encourage the Commission to redirect its energy toward serious and genuine discrimination in hiring. In our case, the issue isn't sex discrimination. It's common sense.

Don't get me wrong. The EEOC's mission is extremely important, and its goals are laudable. But somewhere along the line, the Commission has lost its way. EEOC has a backlog of about 100,000 cases. It's hard to believe that forcing Hooters to change its business concept by hiring "Hooters Guys" should be one of its top priorities.

Hooters Girls have been the basis of our business since the first Hooters store opened in 1983. A lot of places serve good burgers. The Hooters Girls, with their charm and all-American sex appeal, are what our customers come for, and what keeps them coming back.

The EEOC doesn't just want us to hire a male waiter or bartender or two. It wants us to eliminate the Hooters Girl position and make all these jobs available to men. And that's not all. The Commission made several other demands from us, most of which were received in a document which, with appendixes, was 80 pages long!

If not for the disastrous impact of these demands on Hooters and the women who work for us, I might laugh at the thought of men posing as Hooters Girls.

Fact is, the agency's pursuit of political correctness could put us out of business and put many of our loyal, female employees out of work.

In an era when women still make 70 cents for every dollar earned by men, it's hard to believe that the EEOC is spending taxpayers' dollars to take away the jobs of these women.

And, I think you should know that the Civil Rights Act of 1964 explicitly allows businesses to establish hiring rules that take into account factors such as gender or ethnicity when these factors are necessary to maintain the essence of a particular business. For example, a French restaurant has the right to hire only French waiters, and a female exercise club could decide to hire only female locker room attendants. We are convinced that this same standard allows Hooters to hire only women for jobs as Hooters Girls.

There are a lot of unfortunate instances of illegal discrimination in our society today. Frankly, I'm stunned that the EEOC has zeroed in on Hooters.

Our goal today is to let the EEOC know that we think they are wrong. There's a time when government intervention goes too far and this is a perfect illustration of good intentions gone haywire.

The use of the EEOC's limited resources against Hooters is even more tragic because the issues raised by the Commission will be resolved in a private lawsuit brought by four men in

Chicago. Men are going to get their day in court—without intervention by federal bureau-crats.

Hooters Guys? I can only ask, "What next?" An EEOC demand that the Rockettes hire male dancers or that every NFL team sign women to starting positions?

It's time for Washington to get a grip!

Following this press conference, as a protest against the EEOC ruling, Hooters announced a $1 million grassroots advertising campaign in major U.S. cities. It began the campaign with a Washington rally and a full-page newspaper ad in *USA Today* showing Vince, a husky man in a wig, exclaiming, "Come on Washington. Get a grip." Vince also appeared in print ads, radio spots, TV commercials, and billboards across the country. The ads accused the EEOC of "wasting taxpayer dollars, ignoring its mission and setting aside the interests of individuals with real discrimination claims in an effort to force Hooters Restaurants to hire men to be Hooters Girls."

Tad Dixon, public relations manager for Hooters of America, said his office received more than 500 phone calls the day the campaign was announced. Hooters also lobbied representatives in Congress to rip the EEOC for "overregulation" and organized a well-orchestrated mail-in campaign to Congress and the EEOC. Preaddressed postcards and Frisbees poured in to protest the investigation. The postcards were provided by the restaurant and included a picture of Vince—complete with falsies, a blond wig, and Hooters Girl orange garb—along with the message "Hooters Guys? Washington—GET A GRIP!"

DECISION TIME FOR THE EEOC

The EEOC had the option of filing suit against Hooters or dropping the case. In making this decision, the commission had to consider a number of issues:

1. How did Hooters compete in its industry—who was its target market and what did it really "sell"? Was Hooters a restaurant serving hamburgers or an enterprise in which vicarious sex entertainment was the primary service provided?

2. If the restaurants were in fact "hamburger joints," would Hooters' ability to provide food and beverages be jeopardized by hiring male servers?

3. Was Hooters' hiring policy discriminatory?

(Hooters Web address is www.hootersofamerica.com.)

INDEXES

ORGANIZATION INDEX

NAME INDEX

CASE INDEX

SUBJECT INDEX